ITALY

'A long, narrow peninsula,
dense with cities and great
monuments, art works and
ruins, *autostrade* and pizzerias,
sultry sunglassed signorinas
and Vespa-wrangling dudes.'

Contents

About the authors

Dana Facaros and Michael Pauls spent three years in a tiny Italian village, where they suffered massive overdoses of food, art and wine, and enjoyed every minute of it. They reckon they could whip 98 per cent of the world's non-Italian population at Italian Trivial Pursuit (except for sport), and have written over 30 guides for Cadogan.

About the updaters

Various people updated this guide: **Nicky Swallow**, Tuscany, Umbria, Venice; **Mike Usiskin**, Venetia excluding Venice; **Jon Eldan and Carla Lionello**, Lazio, The Marches, Abruzzo and Molise, Piemonte; **Elena Cappuccio**, Lombardy and the Lakes; **Jeremy Roche**, Liguria; **James Alexander and Caroline Mudd**, Campania, Puglia, Calabria and the Basilicata... leaving the authors with only delightful Emilia-Romagna to revisit.

Cadogan Guides
Network House, 1 Ariel Way, London W12 7SL
cadoganguides@morrispub.co.uk
www.cadoganguides.com

The Globe Pequot Press
246 Goose Lane, PO Box 480, Guilford,
Connecticut 06437–0480

Copyright © Dana Facaros and Michael Pauls
    1994, 1998, 2001
    Reprinted 2002
Cover and photo essay design by Kicca Tommasi
Book design by Andrew Barker
Cover photographs by John Ferro-Sims
Maps © Cadogan Guides,
    drawn by Map Creation Ltd
Editorial Director: Vicki Ingle
Series Editor: Linda McQueen
Editor: Georgina Palffy
Layout: Sarah Rianhard-Gardner
Proofreading: Linda McQueen
Indexing: Isobel McLean
Production: Book Production Services

Printed in Italy by Legoprint
A catalogue record for this book is available from
    the British Library
ISBN 1–86011–806–2

The author and publishers have made every effort to ensure the accuracy of the information in this book at the time of going to press. However, they cannot accept any responsibility for any loss, injury or inconvenience resulting from the use of information contained in this guide.

Please help us to keep this guide up to date. We have done our best to ensure that the information in this guide is correct at the time of going to press, but places and facilities are constantly changing, and standards and prices in hotels and restaurants fluctuate. We would be delighted to receive any comments concerning existing entries or omissions. Authors of the best letters will receive a copy of the Cadogan Guide of their choice.

Extract from Petrarch and corresponding English translation on p.79 from *Some Love Songs of Petrarch*, translated and annotated with a biographical introduction by William Dudley Foulke LL.D. (OUP CAT 1920, OUP 1915), included by permission of Oxford University Press.

Italy
a photo essay

by John Ferro Sims

Andagna, Liguria

Menaggio, Lombardy
olive trees, Puglia
chapel, Piemonte
Dolomites, Trentino

Santa Croce, Florence
Venice

Santa Maria Maggiore,
Pianella, Abruzzo
Monster Park, Bomarzo,
Lazio
Paestum, Campania

peppers
Cantuccini and Vin Santo
grapes
alimentari

mosaics, Ravenna,
Emilia-Romagna
Piazza del Popolo, Todi,
Umbria

The Marches

poplars, Emilia-Romagna
Naples

Campidoglio, Rome
the Duomo, Ferrara,
Emilia-Romagna
Passata Festival, Lazio

norcineria, Umbria
designer fashion shop,
Milan
Chianti wine cellar,
Tuscany

the Due Torri, Bologna,
Emilia-Romagna

Capri, Campania

About the photographer
John Ferro Sims was born of Anglo-Italian parents in
Udine, Italy. He worked successfully for five years as an
investment analyst before quitting the world of money
for a career as a professional photographer which has
taken him around the world. He has published 9 books.
all pictures © John Ferro Sims

Introduction

Italy dangles from the centre of western Europe like a Christmas stocking, stuffed to the brim with marvels, some as soaring and grand as a Verdi opera or Brunelleschi's dome over Florence Cathedral, some as weird and unexpected as the pagan tombs buried underneath St Peter's in Rome, or Galileo's erect middle finger, carefully, significantly preserved in a reliquary in Florence's science museum. Even first-time visitors, with eyes and brains spinning, soon become uneasily aware that for every Italian cliché, every Mount Vesuvius, St Mark's Basilica and Leonardo's *Last Supper*, Italy has a hundred other natural wonders and artistic showpieces that any other nation would die for. Someone once tried to count up all the works of art, and concluded that there was at least one per inhabitant, no less.

This national heritage is echoed by even the most ephemeral arts, whether cranked out by the fashion and design workshops or simmered in the kitchen: for every Italian dish or wine you've been craving to try on its home turf, expect a hundred other delights you've never heard of before. Even the common, everyday Italy that co-exists next to the overflow of museums, art cities, ruins and rivieras is an extravagant, daunting place to digest, and as the headlines over the past few years confirm (the Mafia trials, the *tangentopoli* bribery scandals), it is a country that operates on rules entirely unlike those in force back home, full of contradictions and paradoxes, depths and shallows.

As an Umbrian friend of ours told us, you cry twice in Italy: when you first arrive and when you have to leave. In the meantime, pack your intellect, gird your senses and watch out, not only for pickpockets but for a country that might just pick your heart.

A Little Geography

This is not a complex subject: there are tall mountains, and there are not-so-tall mountains. From the Alps down through the Apennines, the Italians are often at a loss to find enough level ground to plant a football field. In all Italy, you'll find only three substantial flatlands: the broad valley of the Po, separating the Alps and Apennines, offering forgettable scenery but Italy's richest farmlands and a score of her most interesting cities; the coastal plain that includes the Maremma of southern Tuscany and northern Lazio; and the thoroughly flat *tavoliere* stretching across Puglia. Most of the really impressive mountains are in the Alps (Mont Blanc, the Matterhorn and the fantastical Dolomites) but the tallest within Italy is the Gran Sasso d'Italia (the 'Big Rock of Italy'), centre of a mighty patch of snow-clad peaks in the Abruzzo.

Not counting the islands, there are about 260,000 square km of Italy, roughly the size of the island of Britain (Americans can think of it as a Colorado). Even with some 55 million Italians, busily tending the world's 5th or 6th most opulent economy, the country rarely seems too crowded. Some large patches of urban sprawl exist – in the Po Valley, for example, or around the Bay of Naples – but the Italians enjoy each other's company, and generally live in tightly packed cities, hill towns and villages, with plenty of good green countryside in between. It is about 1,000 km, as the crow flies, from Mont Blanc to the furthest corner of Puglia, the 'heel' of the Italian boot (1,400 km if you're driving), and the long peninsula is in most places around 150–250 km across.

There are very few easy routes over the Apennines between the Adriatic and the Tyrrhenian; now as in ancient times the main highways parallel the coast or converge on Rome from all points. The long coastline is unevenly blessed; at one extreme there is the delicious Amalfi Coast, the Riviera, the Gargano in Puglia and a few isolated lovely expanses (Calabria's Tyrrhenian Coast, Monte Cónero near Ancona, around Terracina and Gaeta in Lazio, the cliffs by Trieste). Most of the rest is surprisingly dull – much of Tuscany and Lazio, and the greater part of the Adriatic and Ionian coasts.

Some Features of the Landscape

In the north: the beautiful, jagged Dolomites, made of coral of eons past; the 'seven seas', a string of lagoons from Venice to Ravenna along the Adriatic; the caves and underground streams of the karst topography around Trieste and the Friuli; the Italian Lakes, formed by Alpine rivers that can't reach the sea, large enough to form Mediterranean micro-climates on the edge of the Alps; the Ligurian Alps, blocking off the Italian Riviera from the rest of the continent and giving it the mildest winter weather north of Calabria.

In the centre: the Apennines flanked by rolling hills in Tuscany, Umbria and the Marche; in Umbria and Lazio, a string of lakes, mostly of volcanic origin, of which the largest is Lake Trasimeno; the Gran Sasso and Monte Terminillo, the tallest of the Apennines.

In the south: the volcanic playground of coastal Campania, full of extinct volcanoes, dangerous volcanoes, baby volcanoes and bubbling pits; the exotic Gargano Peninsula in Puglia, which geologically has nothing to do with the rest of Italy; and the rough, mountainous toe of Calabria, enclosing a green Alpine plateau called the Sila. Southern Italy is hot and dry, and wanton deforestation in the late 19th century has turned many of its mountain regions into barren wastelands. It is a bit wetter on the coastal plains – enough for most of them to have been malarial wastelands until the Allied occupation forces bathed them in DDT at the end of the Second World War.

As for trees, some very striking ones decorate the landscape, including the beautiful parasol pine, tall erect Lombardy poplars and cypresses, all of which make Italy Italy. Old forests have large numbers of oaks, beeches and evergreens, and palms can be seen around the deep south and in Liguria. Koala bears would thrive in Calabria if anyone wanted to introduce them; a century ago the government planted millions of eucalyptus trees to dry out the wet ground where the malaria mosquitoes lived. However, Italian hunters blast anything that moves, and so wildlife is kept to a minimum. Even in country districts it's rare to hear many birds singing. Up in the mountains there are still plenty of boar, the famous Abruzzo bears still hang on in the Abruzzo National Park, and in the Alps mountain chamois and wolves are still occasionally seen. If you're out in the woods, especially in late spring and summer, watch out for vipers. The late spring is also the best time for wild flowers, of course; they are at their best in the Alps and the mountainous regions in the south.

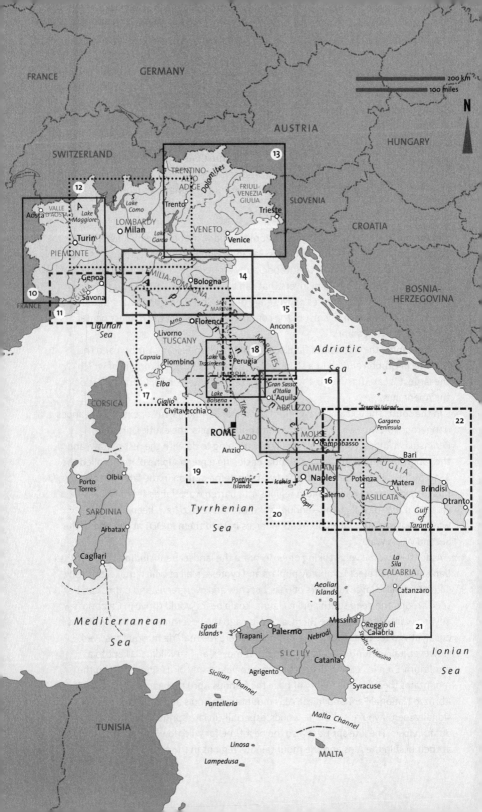

A Guide to the Guide: Italian Regions, Italian Art

To the geographical features mentioned above, add a preposterous amount of history, tradition and language, and you have the political map of Italy, which only acquired its present divisions in the 1960s. There are now 21 amazingly diverse regions with various degrees of political autonomy, two of which are Sicily and Sardinia, while the rest are described in this book from north to south according to regional boundaries, except where from a visitor's viewpoint it made more sense to combine parts of one region with another. This is a brief Guide to the Guide, introducing the regions in the order they are presented in this book.

Northern Italy

This is the wealthiest third of the republic, the most industrial, expensive and dramatically scenic, the land of Alps and lakes. Beginning in the northwestern corner, you have **Piemonte** (Piedmont), the birthplace of modern Italy. At the 'mountains' feet', as the name implies, green Piemonte encompasses both excellent ski slopes in its western Alpine arc and table-flat rice paddies to the east. Car-manufacturing Turin is the region's capital, a rather unexpected and quirky Baroque city that some people love and others hate. Southern Piemonte, around Asti and Alba, produces Barolo, Asti Spumante and other vinous delights. The proximity of France scents the Piemontese kitchen; white truffles are the speciality in the autumn.

The northwest's most spectacular scenery, however, is contained in the small, autonomous, bilingual (French and Italian) region of the **Valle d'Aosta**. The Aosta valleys are one of Italy's great holiday playgrounds, with Courmayeur, Breuil-Cervinia and other stunning resorts on the south slopes of Mont Blanc (Monte Bianco) and the Matterhorn (Cervino), near legendary passes like the Great St Bernard, and in lovely Gran Paradiso National Park. Aosta, the handsome capital, is nicknamed the 'Rome of the Alps' for its extensive ruins.

Over the lush Maritime Alps lies Italy's smallest region, **Liguria**, a rugged rainbow of a coast better known as the Italian Riviera. In the centre lies Genoa, Italy's greatest seaport, while on either side shimmer famous resorts like San Remo, Alassio, Rapallo, Portofino, Portovenere and the magnificent Cinque Terre. The climate is especially mild: palms, olives, flowers and vines grow in profusion. The seafood and the dishes with *pesto* are reason enough to linger.

Chapter Divisions

East of Piemonte lies the large and dynamic region of **Lombardy**. First in its chapter comes a section on Milan, adopted city of Leonardo da Vinci, feverish centre of fashion and finance, home of one of Europe's greatest cathedrals and opera houses, and a vision of the new Italy. This is followed by the three jewels of Lombardy's Po plain: medieval, scholarly Pavia, curley-cue violin-making Cremona, and Renaissance Mantua, product of the exquisite Gonzaga dukes.

Northern Lombardy, and a piece of eastern Piemonte and western Veneto, form the **Italian Lakes**, that fabled district beloved of poets since Roman times. From west to east you'll find charming little Lake Orta; Lake Maggiore with the Borromean Islands and the world-famous resort of Stresa; zig-zagging Lake Lugano, which Italy shares with Switzerland; and romantic Lake Como, forked in the middle with villas at Bellagio, Cernobbio, Tremezzo and Menaggio. North of Como extends the great Alpine valley, the Valtellina, splendid but scarcely known outside Italy. To the south of the Valtellina are more lakes – sweet Iseo and tiny Idro – and two fascinating art cities: Bergamo and Brescia. Westernmost is dramatic Lake Garda, the 'Riviera of the Dolomites', its shores dotted with lovely villages: Sirmione, Gardone, Limone and more, and Italy's biggest theme park, Gardaland.

The next three regions to the east, for centuries influenced or governed by the Most Serene Republic, are collectively known as Venetia. The main attraction of the **Veneto** is of course Venice itself, which only becomes more remarkable the more you learn about it; but there are other lovely cities as well – St Anthony's (and Giotto's) Padua; Palladio's Vicenza; and lovely Verona, of rose-coloured marble, the Scaligers, Valpolicella – and Romeo and Juliet. Magnificent white villas dot the lush landscapes of the Euganean Hills and foothills of the Dolomites; to the south lie the haunting flatlands of the Po Delta.

Rising up in northern Venetia, the strange and fabulous peaks of the Dolomites are the most beautiful mountains in the world. The eastern half, still part of the Veneto, includes Cortina d'Ampezzo, site of the 1956 Winter Olympics, while the western mountains are in the confines of the large autonomous region of **Trentino-Alto Adige**. Trento, the capital of Trentino, is a fine old town associated with the 16th-century Counter-Reformation council; nearby are the rugged Brenta Dolomites, valleys of apple orchards, castles and vineyards. Bilingual Alto Adige, on the Austrian border, prefers to be known as Süd Tirol – an intriguing mix of strudel and pasta, fairy-tale castles and resorts, vineyards and spas. Bolzano is its capital, Merano its most celebrated watering hole. Much of the western portion of Alto Adige is occupied by Stelvio National Park, Italy's largest, where glaciers permit year-round skiing.

East lies the third region of Venetia, **Friuli-Venezia Giulia**, a rich ethnic mix wedged in the corner between Austria and Slovenia, with the neoclassical seaport of Trieste as its capital, a city now regaining some of its lustre of old with the opening of eastern Europe. The region has popular resorts on the coast like Grado and Lignano, intriguing towns like Ùdine and Cividale, more Alps iin the north, and more wine than you can shake a stick at in between.

In between North and Central Italy, **Emilia-Romagna** nearly crosses the entire peninsula, occupying the Po plain and the northern Apennines. Home of Italy's finest cuisine, it also has delicious cities: the arty medieval university town of Bologna; elegant Parma, city of cheese and ham; Modena, of Ferrari, Lambrusco and balsamic vinegar; Busseto, the home of Verdi; Ferrara, fief of the great Renaissance patrons, the Este; Faenza, city of faïence ware; and Ravenna, with its unique and utterly luminous mosaics from the Dark Ages. Here, too, the string of Adriatic resorts begins – with Rimini, biggest and brashest of them all, yet secreting a Renaissance pearl in its heart. Just a short ride from Rimini, up in the mountains you'll find San Marino, the world's smallest and oldest republic, where tourists are more than welcome.

Central Italy

Here, for many, lies the archetypal Italy: those rolling hills, faded ochre farmhouses and villas, the cypresses, the olive groves, the hill towns, the pines of Rome. It was the birthplace of two momentous chapters in Western history – the Roman Empire and the Renaissance.

The first chapter begins where Emilia-Romagna left off, in one of the lesser-known corners of Central Italy, the **Marches** (Le Marche), although landscapes resemble those of Tuscany. Here are two exceptional cities: Urbino, built around Duke Federico's perfect Renaissance palace; and lovely, medieval Ascoli Piceno. In between are a score of pleasant, seldom-visited hill towns, a major pilgrimage target – Loreto – and a string of modest resorts, on either side of the salty old port city of Ancona.

South of the Marches are two even less familiar regions, **Abruzzo and Molise**. Abruzzo, containing the loftiest peaks in the Apennines, is Rome's winter and summer mountain playground; the Abruzzo National Park is the home of the Abruzzo bear and other fauna. The coast is fairly nondescript, lined with family resorts; inland there's a fascinating collection of unspoiled medieval villages and churches. With the highest villages in the Apennines, Molise is a small rather poor region tucked in south of Abruzzo, utterly obscure, quiet and artlessly unprepared for mass tourism.

Back on the western or Tyrrhenian Coast, **Tuscany** probably needs no introduction. There's more to it, however, than just the charmed trio of sublime art cities: Florence, Siena and Pisa. Lucca, Pistoia, Prato and Arezzo have also accumulated more than their share of notable art and architecture, and the rolling, civilized landscape will take you to beautiful hill towns in every direction: San Gimignano, with its medieval 'skyscrapers', brooding Etruscan Volterra, Cortona, Montepulciano and dozens more.

Landlocked, vaguely other-worldly Umbria is in many ways a more rustic version of Tuscany, spangled with historic hill towns like Perugia, the capital and cultural centre; Orvieto with its famous cathedral; Spoleto, synonymous with Italy's most important arts festival; medieval Gubbio; Assisi, the city of St Francis; and a dozen others, set in lovely emerald valleys and hills.

Lazio, ancient *Latium*, includes Rome and a good deal more; despite being right at the centre of things Lazio's attractions are not well known. Northern Lazio was the homeland of the Etruscans, containing fascinating archaeological sites such as those at Tarquinia and Cerveteri. There's plenty to see in Viterbo and Anagni, two places that contributed much to the history of the Popes in the Middle Ages, extraordinary Renaissance villas and gardens (as at Caprarola, Tivoli and Bomarzo), major Roman ruins at Ostia Antica and Tivoli – not to mention Rome itself – and a pretty stretch of coast between Cape Circeo and Formia.

Southern Italy

The four regions of Italy's **Mezzogiorno** often seem an entirely different country from the green and tidy north. Not many visitors ever make it further south than **Campania**, where Naples and its famous bay make up the south's prime attraction – including *Pompeii*, Vesuvius, Capri, Sorrento, the infernal volcanic Phlegraean Fields, dozens of Roman ruins and much more. The wonderful Amalfi Drive between Sorrento and Salerno covers the most spectacular bit of coastline in Italy, passing the truly unique towns of Positano, Amalfi and Ravello. Naples itself, famous for pizza and animated *italianità*, is the best antidote out to the decaffeinated control-freak Europe being forged in Brussels, as well as the south's great art capital. The rest of Campania includes venerable and interesting towns like Salerno, Caserta, Capua and Benevento; the well-preserved Greek temples at Paestum; and the unspoiled Cilento Coast.

Lovers of fine Italian art and cuisine will not find them in **Calabria and the Basilicata**, once the most backward corners of the nation and now struggling gamely to catch up. The west coast from Maratea to Reggio di Calabria, the 'Calabrian Riviera', offers some clean beaches and beautiful scenery (especially around Maratea and Cape Vaticano), and the heavily forested mountain plateau west of Cosenza, the Sila, attracts hikers and nature-lovers. Of the once-mighty Greek cities of the Ionian Coast, there's little left but the great museum at Reggio and some scanty ruins at Metaponto. The bare, eroded hills of the inland Basilicata are not particularly inviting, unless you want to see the famous *sassi* (cave-dwellers' quarters) of Matera.

Puglia (Apulia) for many will be the real find in the south. The flat corn fields of the *tavoliere* cover most of the region, but the rugged limestone Gargano Peninsula offers scenery unique in Italy, along with growing but still enjoyable resorts like Vieste. Puglia did quite well in the Middle Ages, seen in the fine Romanesque cathedrals, including that of Bari, the south's prosperous second city and the burial place of Santa Claus. The *tavoliere* also grows robust wines; on it Emperor Frederick II built his mysterious Castel del Monte. Tàranto, founded by the ancient Greeks, has a museum full of Greek vases, great seafood and a wonderful maritime atmosphere. You won't see anything in Italy like the trulli, the whitewashed houses with conical stone roofs that turn the areas around Alberobello into a fairytale landscape; further south on Italy's 'heel', on the Salentine Peninsula, you can visit Baroque Lecce, the south's most beautiful city.

History

The First Italians

Some 50,000 years ago, when the Alps were covered by an ice cap and the low level of the Mediterranean made Italy a much wider peninsula than it is now, Neanderthal man graced the Ligurian Riviera with his low-browed presence. Even that, however, is not the beginning of the story. Recently, scientists have become excited over the discovery of a new type, *Homo Aeserniensis*, the first known inhabitant of Europe, living in caves around Isernia in Molise a million years ago. Italy makes a convenient bridge from Africa to Europe, and it seems that there was a constant stream of traffic throughout prehistory.

Nevertheless, none of the earliest inhabitants of Italy left much in terms of art or culture, and the peninsula remained a backwater until about the 8th century BC. At that time, most of the population were lumped together as **Italics**, a number of powerful, distinct tribes with related languages. Among them were the Samnites, who dominated much of Campania and the south, the dolmen-building Messapians in Puglia, the Piceni and Umbrii along the northern Adriatic coast, and a boiling kettle of contentious peoples in the centre: Sabines, Aequi, Volscii and Latins. The mighty – 'cyclopean walls' of their cities can still be seen today around southern Lazio.

Two of Italy's most culturally sophisticated peoples lived on the islands: the Siculi of Sicily and the castle-building, bronze-working Sards of the Nuraghe culture. Both kept to themselves and interfered little with affairs on the mainland. Much of the north, the classical Cisalpine Gaul, was the stomping ground of Celtic Ligurians; at the time this area north of the Po was not really thought of as part of Italy.

750–509 BC: Greeks and Etruscans

The most interesting nations of the time, however, were two relative newcomers who contributed much towards bringing Italy out of its primitive state, the **Etruscans** and **Greeks**. With their shadowy past and as yet undeciphered language, the Etruscans are one of the puzzles of ancient history. According to their own traditions, they arrived from somewhere in western Anatolia about 900 BC – Etruscan inscriptions have been found on the Greek island of Lemnos – probably as a sort of warrior aristocracy that imposed itself on the existing populations of Tuscany and Lazio. By the 8th century BC they were the strongest people in Italy, grouped in a loose confederation of 12 city states called the *Dodecapolis*. At the same time the Greeks – whose trading routes had long covered Italy's southern coasts – began to look upon that 'under-developed' country as a New World for exploration and colonization. Cumae, on the Campanian coast, became the first Greek foundation in 750 BC, a convenient base for trading with the Etruscans and their newly discovered iron mines. A score of others soon followed, in Sicily and along the Ionian Sea, and soon they were rivalling the cities of Greece itself in wealth and culture. A third new factor in the Italian equation also appeared at this time, without much fanfare. The year 753 BC, according to the legends, saw the foundation of **Rome**.

Italy was ripe for civilization. In the centuries that followed, the Etruscans spread their rule and their culture over most of the north while the Italic tribes learned from Etruscans and Greeks alike. Some of them, especially the Latins and the Samnites, developed into urbanized, cultured nations in their own right. For the Greek cities, it was a golden age, as Taras (Táranto), Metapontum, Sybaris, Croton, and especially the Sicilian cities like Syracuse and Akragas grew into marble metropolises that dominated central Mediterranean trade and turned much of inland Italy into tribute-paying allies. In the 6th century BC, the Greeks had more wealth than was probably good for them; stories are told of the merchants of Sybaris sending across the Mediterranean, offering fortunes for a cook who could produce the perfect sauce for seafood, and of the sentries of Akragas' army going on strike for softer pillows. From the first, also, these cities dissipated their energies by engaging in constant wars with each other. Some, like Sybaris, were completely destroyed, and by c.400 BC, the failure of the rest to work together sent them into a slow but irreversible economic decline.

The Etruscan story is much the same. By about 600 BC the 12 cities and their allies ruled almost all northern Italy (excluding Cisalpine Gaul), and wealth from their Tuscan mines made them a political force on a Mediterranean scale. Their decline was to be as rapid as that of Magna Graecia. Repeated defeats at the hands of the wild Gauls weakened their confederation, but the economic decline that led to Etruria's virtual evaporation in the 4th century BC is harder to account for. Rome, a border city between the Etruscans and Latins, threw out its Etruscan king and established a **Republic** in 509 BC (*see* Rome's history, p.824). Somehow, probably by the absorption of conquered populations, this relatively new city managed to grow to perhaps 100,000 people, ranking it with Taras and Capua, an Etruscan colony in the growing region of Campania, as the largest on the peninsula. With an economy insufficient to support so many Romans, the city could only live by a career of permanent conquest.

509–268 BC: The Rise of Rome

After the expulsion of the Etruscans, Rome spent a hundred years at war with the various cities of Etruria, while gradually subjugating the rest of the Latins and neigh-bouring tribes. It was successful on all fronts, and a sacking by marauding Gauls in 390 BC proved only a brief interruption in Rome's march to conquest. Southern Etruria and Latium were swallowed up by 358 BC, and Rome next turned its attention to the only power in Italy capable of competing with her on an equal basis: the Samnites.

These rugged highlanders of the southern Apennines, with their capital at Benevento, had begun to seize parts of coastal Campania. The Romans drove them out in 343–41 BC, but in the **Second Samnite War** the Samnites dealt them a severe defeat (Battle of Caudine Forks, 321 BC). In the third war, feeling themselves surrounded by Roman allies, the Samnites formed an alliance with the Northern Etruscans and Celts, leading to a general Italian commotion in which the Romans beat everybody, annexing almost all of Italy by 283 BC.

A strange interlude, delaying Rome's complete domination of Italy, came with the arrival of **Pyrrhus of Epirus**, a Greek adventurer with a large army who was invited in by the cities of Magna Graecia as a protector. From him we get the term 'Pyrrhic victories', for he outmatched the Romans in one battle after another, but was never able to follow up his advantage. After finally losing at Benevento in 275 BC, he quit and returned to Epirus, while the Romans took the deserted Greek cities one by one.

Now the conquest was complete. All along the Romans had been diabolically clever in managing their new demesne, maintaining most of the tribes and cities as nominally independent states, while planting Latin colonies everywhere (re-founded cities like Paestum, Ascoli Piceno, and Benevento were such colonies, together with new ones in the north like Florence). The great network of roads centred on Rome was extended with great speed, and a united Italy seemed close to becoming a reality.

268–91 BC: Empire Abroad, Disarray at Home

After all this, Rome deserved at least a shot at the Mediterranean heavyweight title. The current champ, the powerful merchant thalassocracy of Carthage, was alarmed enough at the successes of its precocious neighbour, and proved happy to oblige. Rome won the first bout, beating Carthage and her ally Syracuse in the **First Punic War** (264–41 BC), and gained Sicily, Sardinia, and Corsica. For the rematch, the **Second Punic War** (219–202 BC), Carthage sent **Hannibal** and his elephants from Spain into Italy over the Alps to bring the war into the Romans' backyard. Undeterred by the brilliant African general's victory at Cannae in 216 BC, where four legions were destroyed, the Romans hung on tenaciously even when Hannibal appeared at the gates of Rome. In Hannibal's absence, they took Spain and much of Africa, and after Scipio Africanus' victory at Zama in 202 BC, Carthage surrendered. The **Third Punic War** was a sorry affair. Rome only waited long enough for Carthage to miss a step in its treaty obligations before razing the city to the ground. The west conquered, Rome looked east. Already by 200 BC she had been interfering in Greek affairs. The disunited Greeks and successor states of Alexander's empire proved easy targets, and by 64 BC the legions were camped on the Cataracts of the Nile, in Jerusalem, and over Asia Minor.

Nothing corrupts a state like easy conquests, and all this time things in Italy were going wrong. Taxation ceased for Roman citizens, as booty provided the state with all the revenues it needed, and tens of thousands of slaves were imported. Italy became a parasite nation. Vast amounts of cheap grain from Africa and Egypt ruined the Italian farmer, who had the choice of selling his freehold and becoming a sharecropper, joining the army, or moving to Rome as part of the burgeoning lumpen proletariat. The men who profited the most from the wars bought up tremendous amounts of land, turning Italy into a country of huge estates (*latifundia*), and becoming an aristocracy powerful enough to stifle any attempts at reform. Only Rome, of course, and a few other cities prospered. In this period many of the Greek and Etruscan towns withered. Many country districts became abandoned, and rural Italy knew constant famine and plagues, while in Rome the new rich were learning the delights of orgies, gladiatorial combats, and being carried around by slaves.

Not that degeneracy and social disintegration had proceeded far enough for Italy to fail to resist. Rome, and indeed all Italy, divided into extremist factions: the reactionary 'Senatorial Party' and the radical 'Popular Party'. (The Senate and the senatorial class were not yet a nobility *per se*. A hefty fortune was all that was needed for entry. Their populist opponents included not only the poor, but most of the businessmen, and the hard-pressed middle class.) In 133 BC a remarkable reformer named **Tiberius Gracchus** was elected Tribune, but his plans for land reforms earned him assassination the following year. His brother **Gaius Gracchus** went even further when he gained the Tribunate in 123 BC, attempting to expand citizenship to most Italians; but he, too, was murdered after the Senate declared martial law that same year. By this time Rome's constitution was reduced to a travesty, and both sides realized that the only real power lay with the legions. The populists staked their hopes on **Gaius Marius**, an illiterate but good-hearted general who saved Italy from the last surprise Celtic raid in 113 BC. Marius' ascent to power proved a disappointment, and a whole new generation of populist statesmen was assassinated one by one.

91–31 BC: Sixty Years of Civil War

Italy had had enough; the year 91 BC saw a coordinated revolt among the southern peoples called the **Social Wars**, which was defeated by the campaigns of Marius and Sulla (the Senate's darling in the army), and by an offer to extend Roman citizenship to all Italians. A military coup by **Sulla** followed, with the backing of the Senate; it was the first time armed Roman soldiers ever actually entered Rome, a religious and constitutional taboo. However, when Sulla's army left for conquest and booty on the Black Sea, a populist counter-movement succeeded in taking power, and ruled Rome for the next three years. Sulla's triumphal return threw them out, and the haughty general unleashed a bloody reign of terror, unlike anything Italy had ever seen. An effective dictatorship was created, and all opponents either murdered or exiled (a redoubtable populist general named Quintus Sertorius still held Spain, and defeated five separate legions sent against him). Italy spiraled into anarchy, with many rural districts reverting to bandit-ridden wastelands, a setting for the remarkable revolt in 73 BC of **Spartacus**, an escaped gladiator who led a motley army of dispossessed farmers and runaway slaves – some 70,000 of them – back and forth across the south until the legions finally defeated him in 71 BC.

All this had exhausted both sides, and finally discredited senatorial rule. After Sulla's death, no-one minded when the consulship and real power passed to **Pompey**, another successful general but one who cared little for politics. Like Sulla before him, Pompey soon set out for the east, where the most glory and booty were to be gained, and his departure left the stage in Rome open to 33-year-old **Julius Caesar**, a tremendously clever soldier-politician, but a good man anyhow. With his two surpassing talents, one for rhetoric and the other for attracting money, he took up the popular cause in better style than anyone had done it before. A taint of connection to the **Catiline conspiracy** of 68 BC, a revolt of adventurers, disaffected nobles, and other loose ends, proved a temporary setback, just as it advanced the fortunes of **Marcus Tullius Cicero**, the great orator, writer, and statesman who dreamed of founding a real republic with a real constitution, opposing both extreme parties and pinning his hopes on the still-surviving Italian middle class. Few people in Rome cared for such principles, however, and after Pompey returned from bashing the Pontic Kingdom and the Cilician pirates, he, Caesar, and a wealthy building contractor named Licinius Crassus sliced up the republic between them, forming the **First Triumvirate** in 59 BC.

What Caesar really wanted, of course, was a military command. Following the accepted practice, he managed to buy himself one in the north, and undertook the conquest of most of Gaul, with well-known results. When Pompey grew jealous and turned against him, Caesar led his army back into Italy, defying the Senate by 'crossing the Rubicon', the river boundary between Italy and Gaul that Roman armies were not allowed to cross without senatorial authorization. Resistance collapsed before him, and he became unchallenged master of Rome while not even holding public office. Pompey and most of the Senate fled to Greece, where Caesar caught up with them three years later. In his four years as ruler of Rome, Caesar surprised everyone, even his enemies; everything received a good dose of reform, even the calendar, and a beginning was made towards sorting out the economic mess and getting Italy back on its feet. His assassination by a clique of republican bitter-enders in 44 BC plunged Italy into civil war again, and left historians to ponder the grand question of whether Caesar had really intended to make himself a king and finally put the now senile republic to sleep. A **Second Triumvirate** was formed, of Caesar's adopted son Octavian, a senatorial figurehead named Lepidus, and Caesar's old friend and right-hand man, a talented, dissipated fellow named **Marcus Antonius** (Mark Anthony), who according to one historian spent the equivalent of $3 billion (of other people's money) in his brief lifetime. While he dallied in the east with Cleopatra, Octavian was consolidating his power in Italy. The inevitable battle came in 31 BC, at Actium in Greece, and it was a complete victory for **Octavian**.

31 BC–AD 251: The Empire

With unchallenged authority through all the Roman lands, Octavian – soon to rename himself **Augustus** – was free to complete the reforms initiated by Caesar. He maintained the forms of the republic while accumulating enough titles and offices for himself to have constitutional justification for his absolute rule. The title he chose for public use was 'first citizen', while behind the scenes the machinery was being perfected for the deification of the Caesars (a practical policy in the eastern half of the empire, where such things were common practice), and for a stable monarchy after his death. It all worked brilliantly: peace was restored, an effective administration created, and Italy was able to recover from its time of troubles with the help of Augustus' huge programmes of public works.

For his career, and those of his successors, you may read the gossipy, shocking, and wonderfully unreliable *Lives of the Caesars* of Suetonius. All Rome tittered at the scandals of the later **Julian Emperors**, but reality was usually much more prosaic. **Tiberius** (AD 14–37) may have been a monster to his girlfriends and boyfriends, but he proved an intelligent and just ruler; his criminally insane successor **Caligula**, or 'Bootkin', lasted only four years (37–41) while the bureaucracy kept things going. **Claudius** (41–54) governed well and conquered southern Britain, while his stepson **Nero** (54–68) generally made a nuisance of himself in Rome but otherwise did little to disturb the system. Nevertheless, a commander in Spain called **Galba** declared him unfit to be emperor and marched on Rome; Nero managed to commit suicide just before they caught him. Now the genie was out of the bottle again, as the soldiers once more realized that the real power lay with them. Another general, **Otto**, commander of the emperor's Praetorian Guard, toppled Galba, and soon lost out in turn to **Vitellius**, commander on the Rhine.

The fourth emperor of the fateful years AD 68–69 was **Vespasian**, leader of the eastern armies. He had the strongest legions and so got to keep the job; his reign (69–79) and those of his sons **Titus** (79–81) and **Domitian** (81–96), the three **Flavian Emperors**, were remembered as a period of prosperity. Vespasian began the Colosseum; whether intentionally or not, this incomparable new charnel house made a perfect symbol for the renewed decadence and militarization of the state.

For the moment, however, things looked rosy. After the assassination of **Domitian**, another bad boy but not an especially calamitous ruler, Rome had the good fortune to be ruled by a series of high-minded and intelligent military men, who carefully chose their successors in advance to avoid civil war. The so-called **Antonine Emperors** presided over the greatest age of prosperity the Mediterranean world ever knew; in Italy they ran a surprisingly modern state (though one still based on slave labour) that would seem familiar to us today: public libraries, water boards to maintain the aqueducts, rent control, agricultural price supports, low-cost loans for starting new businesses and many other such innovations. The first of the Antonines was **Nerva** (96–8), followed by **Trajan** (98–117) and **Hadrian** (117–38), they were both great soldiers and builders on a monumental scale, especially in Rome; after them came **Antoninus Pius** (138–61), little known only because his reign was so peaceful, and **Marcus Aurelius** (161–80), soldier, statesman, and Stoic philosopher. His successor was his useless son **Commodus** (180–93) – whose cowardice was recently immortalized in Hollywood blockbuster *Gladiator* – and the string of good emperors was broken.

The 2nd-century prosperity was not without its darker side. The arts were in serious decline, as if the imagination of the Graeco-Roman Mediterranean was somehow failing. Education was in poor shape, and every sort of fatuous mysticism imported from the East permeated the minds of the people. Economically, this period saw the emergence of the well-known north-south split in Italy. The rural south, impoverished by the Roman Republic, now sank deeper into decline, while even the commerce of wealthy Campania began to fail, ruined by foreign competition. In the north, especially Cisalpine Gaul, a sounder, more stable economy led to the growth of new centres, Milan, Padua, Verona, and Ravenna the most prominent, beginning the economic divide that continues even today. In the balance, though, both politically and economically Italy was becoming an ever less significant part of the empire. Of the 2nd-century emperors, fewer came from Italy than from Spain, Illyria, or Africa.

251–475: Decline and Fall

For all it cost to maintain them, the legions were no longer the formidable military machine of Augustus' day. They were bureaucratic and a little tired, and their tactics and equipment were also falling behind those of the Persians and even some of the more clever German barbarians. The **Goths** were the first to demonstrate this, in 251, when they overran the Balkans, Greece, and Asia Minor. Five years later **Franks** and **Alemanni** invaded Gaul, and in 268 much of the east detached itself from the empire under the leadership of Odenathus of Palmyra. Somehow the empire recovered and prevailed, under dour soldier-emperors like **Aurelian** (270–75), who built Rome's walls, and **Diocletian** (284–305) who completely revamped the structure of the state and economy. His fiscal reforms, such as the fixing of prices and a decree that every son had to follow the trade of his father, ossified the economy and made the creeping decline of Italy and all western Europe harder to arrest. A gigantic bureaucracy was created, taxes reached new heights as people's ability to pay them declined, and society became increasingly militarized in every respect. The biggest change was the division of the empire into halves, each ruled by a co-emperor equally called 'Augustus'; Diocletian, significantly, chose the wealthier east for himself. The new western emperors usually kept their court at army headquarters in Mediolanum (Milan), and later at impregnable **Ravenna** on the Adriatic, and Rome itself became a marble-veneered backwater.

More than ever, the empire had become an outright military dictatorship, in a society whose waning energies were entirely devoted to supporting a bloated, all-devouring army and bureaucracy. Medieval feudalism actually had its origins in this period, as the remaining freehold farmers sold their lands and liberty to the local gentry – for protection's sake, but also to get off the tax rolls. In the cities, the high taxes and uncertain times ruined business and trade; throughout Italy and the West towns both large and small began their fatal declines. Diocletian reduced Italy to the status of a mere province, and the peninsula had little to do with imperial events thereafter. The confused politics of the 4th century are dominated by **Constantine** (306–337), who ruled both halves of the empire, defeated various other contenders (Battle of the Milvian Bridge, outside Rome, in 312), and founded the eastern capital of Constantinople. He adroitly moved to increase his and the empire's political support by favouring **Christianity**. Though still a small minority in most of the empire, the Christians' strong organization and determination made them a good bet for the future. The religious revolution that followed was unexpected and remarkable. Diocletian had been the most ferocious of Christianity's persecutors; by 400, it was the turn of the pagans and Jews to be persecuted. In the next decades, as the empire's cities became Christianized, the **Church** itself became the most powerful and coherent instrument of the Roman élite.

The military disasters began in 406, with Visigoths, Franks, Vandals, Alans and Suevi overrunning Gaul and Spain. Italy's turn came in 408, when the western emperor **Honorius**, ruling from the new capital of Ravenna, had his brilliant general Stilicho (who happened to be a Vandal) murdered. A Visigothic invasion followed, leading to **Alaric's sack of Rome** in 410. St Augustine, probably echoing the thoughts of most Romans, wrote that the end of the world must be near. Rome should have been so lucky; judgement was postponed long enough for **Attila the Hun** to pass through Italy in 451. Then **Gaiseric the Vandal**, who had set up a pirate kingdom in Africa, raided Italy and sacked Rome again in 455. So completely had things changed, it was scarcely possible to tell the Romans from the barbarians. By the 470s, the real ruler in Italy was a Gothic general named **Odoacer**, who led a half-Romanized Germanic army and probably thought of himself as the genuine heir of the Caesars. In 476 he decided to dispense with the lingering charade of the western empire. The last emperor, young, silly Romulus Augustulus, was packed off to premature retirement in Naples, and Odoacer was crowned King of Italy at Pavia.

475–1000: The Dark Ages

At the beginning, the new Gothic-Latin state showed some promise. Certainly the average man was no worse off than he had been under the last emperors; trade and cities even revived a bit. In 493, Odoacer was replaced (and murdered) by a rival Ostrogoth, **Theodoric**, nominally working on behalf of the eastern emperor at Byzantium. Theodoric proved a strong and able, though somewhat paranoid ruler; his court at Ravenna witnessed a minor rebirth of Latin letters with Cassiodorus, Symmachus, and the great Christian philosopher Boethius. Nevertheless, stability was compromised by religious quarrels between the Arian Christian Goths and the orthodox Catholic populations in the cities.

A disaster as serious as those of the 5th century began in 536, with the invasion of Italy by the Eastern Empire, part of the relentlessly expansionist policy of **Justinian**. The historical irony was profound; in the ancient homeland of the Roman Empire, Roman troops now came not as liberators, but foreign, largely Greek-speaking conquerors. His brilliant generals, **Belisarius** and **Narses**, ultimately prevailed over the Goths in a series of terrible wars that lasted until 563, but the damage to an already stricken society and economy was incalculable. Italy's total exhaustion was exposed only five years later, when the **Lombards**, a Germanic tribe that worked hard to earn the title of barbarian, overran northern Italy and parts of the south, establishing a kingdom at Pavia and separate duchies in Benevento and Spoleto. A new pattern of power appeared, with semi-independent Byzantine dukes defending many coastal areas, the **Byzantine Exarchs of Ravenna** controlling considerable territory on the Adriatic and in Calabria, and Lombard chiefs ruling most of the interior. The popes in Rome, occasionally allied with the Lombards against Byzantium, became a force during this period, especially after the papacy of the clever, determined **Gregory the Great** (590–604). Scion of the richest family in Italy, Gregory took political control in Rome during desperate times, and laid the foundations for the papacy's claims to temporal power.

With trade and culture at their lowest ebb, the 7th century marks the rock bottom of Italian history. The 8th showed some improvement; while most of the peninsula lay in feudal darkness, **Venice** was beginning its remarkable career as a trading city, and independent **Amalfi** and **Naples** emulated its success on the Tyrrhenian coast. The popes, along with other bishops who had taken advantage of the confused times to become temporal powers, intrigued everywhere to increase their influence; they finally cashed in with a Frankish alliance in the 750s. At the time the Lombard kings were doing well, finally conquering Ravenna (751) and considerable territories formerly under the dominion of the popes, who invited in **Charlemagne** to protect them. He eliminated the last Lombard king, Desiderius (his father-in-law, incidentally), and tucked all Italy as far south as Rome (with the exception of Venice) into his short-lived patchwork empire, sanctified by a papal coronation as the heir of the Roman Empire. A Lombard Duchy of Benevento survived for centuries up in the mountains, and the Byzantines kept a tenuous hold on the heel and toe; the Greek villages and relics of troglodyte Greek monasticism in Calabria and Puglia date from this period. Arabs from Tunisia were beginning a gradual conquest of Sicily, and their raiders menaced all the peninsula's coasts; they sacked Rome itself in 746.

When Charlemagne's empire disintegrated following his death in 814, Italy reverted to a finely balanced anarchy. Altogether the 9th century was a bad time, with Italy caught between the Arab raiders and the endless wars of petty nobles and battling bishops in the north. The 10th century proved somewhat better – perhaps much better than the scanty chronicles of the time attest. Even in the worst times, Italy's cities never entirely disappeared. Sailing and trading overseas always lead to better technologies, new ideas and economic growth, and Italy's maritime cities had become the most advanced in Europe; even inland cities like Florence and Milan were developing a new economic importance and self-consciousness. Cities do not grow by magic in such unpromising times; even though few of them had managed to attain complete freedom of action, it is clear that even in the 900s many were looking to their own resources, defending their interests against the Church and nobles alike.

A big break for the cities, and for Italy, came in 961 with the invasion of the German **Otto the Great**, heir to the imperial pretensions of the Carolingians. He deposed the last feeble King of Italy, Berengar II of Ivrea, and was crowned Holy Roman Emperor in Rome the following year. Not that any of the Italians were happy to see him, but the strong government of Otto and his successors beat down the great nobles and allowed the growing cities to expand their power and influence. A new pattern was established; Germanic Emperors would be meddling in Italian affairs for centuries, not powerful enough to establish total control, but usually at least able to keep out important rivals.

1000–1154: The Rise of the *Comuni*

On the eve of the new millennium, most Christians were convinced that the turn of the calendar would bring with it the end of the world. If there had been economists and social scientists around, however, they would have had ample evidence to reassure everyone that things were looking up. Especially in the towns, business was very good, and the political prospects even brighter. The first mention of a truly independent *comune* (plural: *comuni*; a term used throughout this book, meaning a free city state; the best translation might be 'commonwealth') was in Milan, where in 1024 a popular assembly is recorded, deciding which side the city would take in the Imperial Wars.

Throughout this period the papacy had declined greatly in power and prestige, a political football kicked between the emperors and the piratical Roman nobles. Beginning in the 1050s, a remarkable Tuscan monk named Hildebrand controlled papal policy, working behind the scenes to reassert the influence of the Church. When he became pope himself, in 1073, **Gregory VII** immediately set himself in conflict with the emperors over the issue of investiture – whether the church or secular powers could name church officials. The various Italian (and European) powers took sides on the issue, and 50 years of intermittent war followed, including the famous penance in the snow of Emperor Henry IV at Canossa in 1077 (*see* p.520). The result was a big revival for the papacy, but more importantly the cities of Lombardy and the rest of the north used the opportunity to increase their influence, and in some cases achieve outright independence, defeating the local barons in war, razing their castles and forcing them to move inside the towns.

Southern Italy knew a different fate. The first **Normans** arrived about 1020, on pilgrimages to Monte Sant'Angelo in the Gargano. They liked the opportunities they saw for conquest, and soon younger sons of Norman feudal families were moving into the south, first as mercenaries but gradually gaining large tracts of land for themselves in exchange for their services. Usually allied to the popes, they soon controlled most of Puglia and Calabria. One of their greatest chiefs, **Roger de Hauteville**, began the conquest of Sicily from the Arabs in 1060, six years before William the Conqueror sailed for England. Roger eventually united all the south into the 'Kingdom of Sicily', and by the 1140s, under **Roger II**, this strange Norman-Arab-Italian state, with its glittering, half-oriental capital of Palermo, had become the cultural centre of the Mediterranean, as well as one of the strongest, best-organized states in Europe.

1154–1300: Guelphs and Ghibellines

While all this was happening, of course, the **First Crusade** (1097–1130) occupied the headlines. It was, in part, a result of the new militancy of the papacy begun by Gregory VII. For Italy, especially Pisa and Venice, the two states with plenty of boats to help ship Crusaders, the affair meant nothing but pure profit. Trade was booming everywhere, and the accumulation of money helped the Italians to create modern Europe's first banking system. It also financed the continued independence of the *comuni*, which flourished everywhere, with a big enough surplus for building-projects like Pisa's cathedral complex, perhaps the biggest undertaking since the time of Trajan and Hadrian. Culture and science were flourishing, too, with a big boost from contact with the Byzantines and the Moslems of Spain and Africa. By the 12th century, far in advance of most of Europe, Italy had attained a prosperity unknown since Roman times. The classical past had never been forgotten – witness the attempt of Arnold of Brescia (1154) to recreate the Roman Republic. Similarly, free *comuni* in the north called their elected leaders 'consuls', and artists and architects turned ancient Roman styles into the Romanesque. Even Italian names were changing, an interesting sign of the beginnings of national consciousness; quite suddenly the public records (such as they were) show a marked shift from Germanic to classical and Biblical surnames: fewer Ugos, Othos, and Astolfos; more Giuseppes, Giovannis and Giulios.

Emperors and popes were still embroiled in the north. **Frederick I, Barbarossa** of the Hohenstaufen – or Swabian – dynasty, was strong enough in Germany, and he made it the cornerstone of his policy to reassert imperial power in Italy. Beginning in 1154, he crossed the Alps five times, molesting free cities that asked nothing more than the right to fight one another continually. He spread terror, utterly destroying Milan in 1161, but a united front of cities called the **Lombard League** defeated him in 1176. Frederick's greatest triumph in Italy came by arranging a marriage with the Normans, leaving his grandson **Frederick II** not only Holy Roman Emperor but also King of Sicily, giving him a strong power base in Italy itself.

The second Frederick's career dominated Italian politics for 30 years (1220–50). With his brilliant court, in which Italian was used for the first time (alongside Arabic and Latin), his half-Moslem army, his incredible processions of dancing girls, eunuchs, and elephants, he provided Europe with a spectacle the like of which it had never seen. Frederick founded universities (as at Naples), gave Sicily a written constitution (perhaps the world's first), and built geometrically arcane castles and towers all over the south. The popes excommunicated him at least twice; the battle of pope and emperor had become serious. All Italy divided into factions: the **Guelphs**, under the leadership of the popes, supported religious orthodoxy, the liberty of the *comuni*, and the interests of their emerging merchant class. The **Ghibellines** stood for the emperor, statist economic control, the interests of the rural nobles, and religious and intellectual tolerance. Frederick's campaigns and diplomacy in the north met with very limited success, and his death in 1250 left the outcome very much in doubt.

His son **Manfred**, not emperor but merely King of Sicily, took up the battle with better luck; Siena's defeat of Florence in 1260 gained that city and most of Tuscany for the Ghibellines. The next year, however, **Pope Urban IV** began an ultimately disastrous precedent by inviting in **Charles of Anjou**, a powerful, ambitious leader and brother of the King of France. As protector of the Guelphs, Charles defeated Manfred (1266) and murdered the last of the Hohenstaufens, **Conradin** (1268). He held unchallenged sway over Italy until 1282, when the famous revolt of the **Sicilian Vespers** started the party wars up again. By now, however, the terms Guelph and Ghibelline had ceased to have much meaning; men and cities changed sides as they found expedient, and the old parties began to seem like the black and white squares on a chessboard. If your neighbour and enemy were Guelph, you became for the moment Ghibelline, and if he changed so would you. (Strangely enough, black and white were respectively the Ghibelline and Guelph colours. They also had distinctive styles of architecture. When you see a castle in Italy with simple rectangular crenellations along the walls, you'll know that Guelphs built it; ornate 'swallow-tail' crenellations are Ghibelline.)

Some real changes did occur out of all this sound and fury. In 1204 Venice hit its all-time biggest jackpot when it diverted the **Fourth Crusade** to the **sack of Constantinople**, winning for itself a small empire of islands in the Adriatic and Levant. Genoa emerged as its greatest rival in 1284, when its fleet put an end to Pisa's prominence at the Battle of Meloria. And elsewhere around the peninsula, some cities were falling under the rule of military *signori* whose descendants would be styling themselves counts and dukes – the **Visconti** of Milan, the **della Scala** of Verona, the **Malatesta** of Rimini. Everywhere the freedom of the *comuni* was in jeopardy; after so much useless strife the temptation to submit to a strong leader often proved overwhelming. During Charles of Anjou's reign the popes extracted the price for their invitation. The **Papal State**, including much of central Italy, was established in 1278. But most importantly, the Italian economy never seemed to mind the trouble. Trade and money flowed as never before; cities built new cathedrals and created themselves incredible skyscraper skylines, with the tall tower-fortresses of the now urbanized nobles. And it was, in spite of everything, a great age for culture – the era of Guelphs and Ghibellines was also the time of Dante (b. 1265) and Giotto (b. 1266).

1300–1494: Renaissance Italy

This paradoxical Italy continued into the 14th century, with a golden age of culture and an opulent economy side by side with almost continuous war and turmoil. With no serious threats from the emperors or any other foreign power, the myriad Italian states were able to menace each other without outside interference. One of the secrets to this state of affairs was that war had become a sort of game, conducted on behalf of cities by bands of paid mercenaries led by a *condottiere*, who were never allowed to enter the cities. The arrangement suited everyone. The soldiers had lovely horses and armour, and no real desire to do each other serious harm. The cities were usually free from grand ambitions; everyone was making too much money to want to wreck the system. Without heavy artillery, walled towns and castles were nearly impossible to take, making the incentives to try hard even less. Best of all, the worst schemers and troublemakers on the Italian stage were fortuitously removed from the scene. Shortly after the election of the French **Pope Clement V** in 1305, the papacy moved to **Avignon**, becoming a puppet of the French king that temporarily had little influence in Italian affairs.

By far the biggest event of the 14th century was the **Black Death** of 1347–48, in which it is estimated Italy lost one-third of its population. The shock brought a rude halt to what had been 400 years of almost continuous growth and prosperity, though its effects did not prove a permanent setback for the economy. In fact, the plague's grim joke was that it actually made life better for most of the Italians who survived; working people in the cities, no longer overcrowded, found their rents lower and their labour worth more, while in the country farmers were able to increase their profits by only tilling the best land.

It is impossible to speak of 'Italian history' in this period, with the peninsula split up into long-established, cohesive states pursuing different ends and warring against one another. Italian statesmen understood the idea of a balance of power long before political theorists invented the term, and, despite all the clatter and noise, most probably believed Italy was enjoying the best of all possible worlds. Four major states, each a European power in its own right, dominated the region's politics: first **Venice**, the oldest and most glorious, with its oligarchic but singularly effective constitution, and its exotic career of trade with the East. The Venetians waged a series of wars against arch-rival Genoa, finally exhausting her after the War of Chioggia in 1379. After that, they felt strong enough to make a major change in policy. Once serenely aloof from Italian politics, Venice now carved out a small land empire for itself, by 1428 including Verona, Padua, Vicenza, Brescia and Bergamo.

Florence, the richest city-state thanks to its banking and wool trade, also enjoyed good fortune, extending its control over most of Tuscany, and gaining a seaport with its conquest of now decadent Pisa in 1406. In 1434, **Cosimo de' Medici**, head of the largest banking house, succeeded in establishing a de facto dictatorship. Even though the forms of the old Republic were maintained, Florence was well on its way to becoming a signorial state like its greatest rival, **Milan**. Under the Visconti, Milan had become rich and powerful, basing its success on the manufactures of the city (arms and textiles) and the bountiful, progressively managed agriculture of southern Lombardy. Its greatest glory came during the reign of **Gian Galeazzo Visconti** (1385–1402), who bought himself a ducal title from the Emperor and nearly conquered all north Italy, before his untimely death caused his plans to unravel.

In the south, the huge **Kingdom of Naples** suffered from the heritage of the Normans, who had made it the only part of Italy where north-European-style feudalism had ever taken root. When times changed, the backward rural barons who dominated the south held back its commerce and its culture. Despite promising periods such as the reign of the King of Aragon, **Alfonso the Magnanimous** (1442–58), a Renaissance prince and patron of the arts who seized Naples and added it to his domains, the south was falling far behind the rest of Italy. The other Italian states included Genoa, a nasty little oligarchy that made money but contributed nothing to the cultural life of the times; the Duchy of Savoy-Piedmont, a quiet backwater still more closely tied to France than Italy; the tiny, stalwart Republics of Lucca and Siena; refined independent courts in Ferrara, Mantua, Modena and Rimini, surviving the rough seas of Italian politics; and finally the Papal States, anarchic while the popes were in France (until 1378), and woefully misgoverned when they came back.

And what of the Renaissance? No word has ever caused more mischief for the understanding of history and culture – as if Italy had been Sleeping Beauty, waiting for some Prince Charming of classical culture to come and awaken it from a 1000-year nap. On the contrary, Italy even in the 1200s was richer, more technologically advanced, and far more artistically creative than it had ever been in the days of the Caesars. The new art and scholarship that began in Florence in the 1400s and spread across the nation grew from a solid foundation of medieval accomplishment. The gilded, opulent Italy of the 15th century felt complacently secure in its long-established cultural and economic pre-eminence. A long spell of freedom from outside interference lulled the nation into believing that its political disunity could continue safely forever; except perhaps for the sanguinely realistic Florentine Niccolò Machiavelli, no-one realized that Italy in fact was a plum waiting to be picked.

1494–1529:The Wars of Italy

The Italians brought the trouble down on themselves, when Duke Lodovico Sforza of Milan invited the French King Charles VIII to cross the Alps and assert his claim to the throne of Milan's enemy, Naples. Charles did just that, and the failure of the combined Italian states to stop him (at the inconclusive Battle of Fornovo, 1494) showed just how helpless Italy was at the hands of emerging monarchies like **France** or **Spain**. When the Spaniards saw how easy it was, they, too, marched in, and restored Naples to its Spanish king the following year (an Aragonese dynasty, cousins to Ferdinand and Isabella, had ruled Naples since 1442). Before long the German emperor and even the Swiss entered this new market for Italian real estate. The popes did as much as anyone to keep the pot boiling. Alexander VI and his son **Cesare Borgia** carried the war across central Italy in an attempt to found a new state for the Borgia family, and

Julius II's madcap policy led him to egg on the Swiss, French and Spaniards in turn, before finally crying 'Out with the barbarians!' when it was already too late.

By 1516, with the French ruling Milan and the Spanish in control of the south, it seemed as if a settlement would be possible. The worst possible luck for Italy, however, came with the accession of the insatiable megalomaniac **Charles V** to the throne of Spain in that year; in 1519 he bought himself the crown of the Holy Roman Empire, making him the most powerful ruler in Europe since Charlemagne. Charles felt he needed Milan as a base for communications between his Spanish, German and Flemish possessions, and as soon as he had emptied Spain's treasury, driven her to revolt, and plunged Germany into civil war, he turned his attentions to Italy. The wars began anew, bloodier than anything Italy had seen for centuries, climaxing with the defeat of the French at Pavia in 1525, and the sack of Rome by an out-of-control imperial army in 1527. The French invaded once more, in 1529, and were defeated this time at Naples by the treachery of their Genoese allies. All Italy, save only Venice, was now at the mercy of Charles and the Spaniards.

1529–1600: Italy in Chains

The final treaties left **Spanish viceroys** in Milan and Naples, and pliant dukes and counts toeing the Spanish line almost everywhere else. Besides Venice and the very careful Republic of Lucca, the last bastions of Italian liberty were **Siena** and **Florence**, where the Medici had been thrown out and the Republic re-established. Charles' army besieged and took the city in 1530, giving it back to the Medici, who gained the title of Grand Dukes of Tuscany. They collaborated with Spain in extinguishing Siena's independence, despite a desperate resistance of seven years (1552–59), and the new Medici state assumed roughly the borders of Tuscany today.

The broader context of these events, of course, was the bitter struggles of the Reformation and **Counter-Reformation**. In Italy, the new religious angle made the Spaniards and the popes natural allies. One had the difficult job of breaking the spirit of a nation that, though conquered, was still wealthy, culturally sophisticated and ready to resist; the other saw an opportunity to recapture by force the hearts and minds it had lost long before. With the majority of the peninsula still nominally controlled by local rulers, and an economy that continued to be sound, both the Spanish and the popes realized that the only real threat would come not from men, but from ideas. Under the banner of combating Protestantism, they commenced a reign of terror across Italy. In the 1550s, the revived **Inquisition** began its manhunt for free-thinkers of every variety; the Index of Prohibited Books followed in 1559 (some works of Dante included), accompanied by public book-burnings in Rome and elsewhere. A long line of Italian intellectuals trudged to the stake, while many more buried their convictions or left for exile in Germany or England. The job of re-educating Italy was put in the hands of the new Jesuit order; their schools and propaganda campaigns bore the popes' message deeply into the Italian mind, while their sumptuous new churches and dramatic sermons helped redefine Catholicism.

Despite the oppression, the average Italian at first had little to complain about. Spanish domination brought peace and order to a country that had long been a madhouse of conflicting ambitions. Renaissance artists attained a virtuosity never seen before, just in time to embellish the scores of new churches, palaces and villas of the mid 16th-century building boom. The combined Christian forces had turned back the Turkish threat at Malta (1566) and Lepanto (1571), and some Italians were bene-fiting to a great extent from Spanish imperialism in the **New World** – especially the Genoese, who rented ships, floated loans and even snatched up a surprising amount of the gold and silver arriving from America.

1600–1796: The Age of Baroque

However, the first signs of decay were already apparent. Palladio's country villas for the Venetian magnates, and Michelozzo's outside Florence, are landmarks in architec-ture but also one of the earliest symptoms. In both cities, the old mercantile economies were failing, and the wealthy began to invest their money unproductively in land instead of risking it in business or finance. **Venice**, between its wars with the Turks and its loss of the spice trade when the Portuguese discovered the route to the Indies, suffered the most. By 1650 she no longer had an important role to play in European affairs, though the Venetians kept their heads and made their inevitable descent into decadence a serene and enjoyable one.

The troubles were not limited to these two cities. After 1600 nearly everything started to go wrong for the Italians. The textiles and banking of the north, long the engines of the economy, both withered in the face of foreign competition, and the old port towns (with the exceptions of Genoa and the new city of Livorno) began to look half empty as the English and Dutch muscled them out of the declining Mediterranean trade. Worst off of all was the south, under direct Spanish or papal rule. Combining incompetence and brutality with outrageously high taxes (the Spaniards' to finance foreign wars, the popes' to build up Rome), they rapidly turned the already poor south into a nightmare of **anarchic depravity**, haunted by legions of bandits and beggars, and controlled more tightly than ever by its violent feudal barons. To everyone's surprise, the south rose up and staged an epic rebellion. Beginning in Naples (**Masaniello's Revolt**, 1647), the disturbances soon spread all over the south and Sicily. For over a year peasant militias ruled some areas, and makeshift revolutionary councils defended the cities. When the Spanish finally defeated them, however, they massacred some 18,000, and tightened the screws more then ever.

Bullied, humiliated and increasingly impoverished, 17th- century Italy at least tried hard to keep up its ancient prominence in the arts and sciences. Galileo Galilei looked through telescopes, Monteverdi wrote the first operas, and hundreds of talented though uninspired artists cranked out pretty pictures to meet the continuing high demand. Bernini and Borromini turned Rome into the capital of Baroque – the florid, expensive *coloratura* style that serves as a perfect symbol for the age itself, an age of political repression and thought control where art became a political tool. Baroque's heavenly grandeur and symmetry helped to impress everyone with the majesty of Church and State. At the same time, Baroque scholars wrote books that went on for hundreds of pages without saying anything, but avoided offending the government and the Inquisition. Baroque impresarios managed the wonderful pageantry of

Church holidays, state occasions and carnivals that kept the ragged crowds amused. Manners and clothing became decorously berserk, and a race for easily bought noble titles occurred that would have made a medieval Italian laugh out loud. Italy was being rocked to sleep in a Baroque cradle.

By the 18th century, there were very few painters, or scholars, or scientists. There were no more heroic revolts either. Italy in this period hardly has any history at all; with Spain's increasing decadence, the great powers decided the futures of Italy's major states, and used the minor ones as a kind of overflow tank to hold surplus princes and those dispossessed by wars elsewhere (Napoleon on Elba was the last and most famous of these). In 1713, after the War of the Spanish Succession, the Habsburgs of **Austria** came into control of Milan and Lombardy, Mantua and the Kingdom of Naples. The **House of Lorraine**, related to the Austrians, won Tuscany upon the extinction of the Medici in 1737.

These new rulers improved conditions somewhat. Especially during the reigns of the **Empress Maria Theresa** (1740–80) and her son Joseph II (1780–92), two of the most likeable Enlightenment despots, Lombardy and the other Austrian possessions underwent serious, intelligent economic reforms – giving them the head-start over the rest of Italy that helped Milan to its industrial prominence today. Naples' hard luck continued when the Austrians transferred it to a branch of the **House of Bourbon** (1731); under them the southern kingdom was independent, but just as poorly governed as before. A new player in Italian affairs, and from the start an important one, was **Piedmont**, which during the War of the Austrian Succession shook loose from the tutelage of France and joined the winning side, earning a royal title in 1720 for **Vittorio Amedeo II**. The infant kingdom, with its brand-new capital of Turin, was poor and a little backward in many ways, but as the only strong and free state in Italy it would be able to play the leading role in the events of the next century, and in Italian unification.

1796–1830: Napoleon, Restoration and Reaction

Napoleon, that greatest of Italian generals, arrived in Italy in 1796 on behalf of the French revolutionary Directorate, sweeping away the Piedmontese and Austrians and setting up republics in Lombardy (the 'Cisalpine Republic'), Liguria, and Naples (the 'Parthenopean Republic'). Italy woke with a start from its Baroque slumbers, and local patriots gaily joined the French cause. In 1799, however, while Napoleon was off in Egypt, the advance through Italy by an Austro-Russian army, aided by Nelson's fleet, restored the status quo. This was often accompanied by bloody reprisals, as peasant mobs led by clerics like the 'Army of the Holy Faith' marched across the south massacring liberals and French sympathizers.

In 1800 Napoleon returned in a campaign that saw the great victory at **Marengo**, giving him the opportunity once more to reorganize Italian affairs. He crowned himself King of Italy; Joseph Bonaparte and later Joachim Murat ruled at Naples. Elisa Bonaparte and her husband got Tuscany. Rome was annexed to France, and the Pope was carted off to Fontainebleau. Napoleonic rule lasted only until 1814, but in that time important public works were begun and laws, education and everything else reformed after the French model; immense Church properties were expropriated, and medieval relics everywhere put to rest – including the Venetian Republic, which Napoleon for some reason took a special delight in liquidating. The French, however, soon wore out their welcome. Besides hauling much of Italy's artistic heritage off to the Louvre, implementing high war taxes and conscription (some 25,000 Italians died in the invasion of Russia), and brutally repressing a number of local revolts, they systematically exploited Italy for the benefit of the Napoleonic élite and the crowds of speculators who came flocking over the Alps. When the Austrians and English came to chase all the little Napoleons out, no-one was sad to see them go.

The experience, though, had given Italians a taste of the opportunities offered by the modern world, as well as a sense of **national feeling** that had been suppressed for centuries. The 1815 Congress of Vienna put the clock back to 1796; indeed the Habsburgs and Bourbons seemed to think they could pretend the Napoleonic upheavals never happened, and the political reaction in their territories was fierce. The only major change from the *ancien régime* was that Venice and its inland empire now belonged to Austria. (Two name changes help to confuse students of this period; Piedmont is often referred to as the 'Kingdom of Sardinia', and Naples acquired the name 'Kingdom of the Two Sicilies'.)

Almost immediately, revolutionary agitators and secret societies like the famous *Carbonari* emerged that would keep Italy convulsed in plots and intrigues. A large-scale revolt in Naples forced the reactionary **King Ferdinand** to grant a constitution (1821), but when Austrian troops came down to crush the rebels he revoked it. The French July Revolution of 1830 also spread to Italy, encouraged by the liberal **King Carlo Alberto** in Piedmont-Savoy, but once more the hated Austrians intervened.

1848–1915: The Risorgimento and United Italy

Conspirators of every colour and shape, including the legendary **Giuseppe Mazzini**, had to wait another 18 years for their next chance. Mazzini, a sincere patriot and democrat, agitated frenetically all through the years 1830–70, beginning by founding the *Young Italy* movement. Generally followed by a small cloud of cops and spies, Mazzini started parties, issued manifestos, plotted dozens of doomed revolts, defined great theories and strategies, checked in and out of exile, and chaired meetings of eternal committees, all with little practical effect. In retrospect, his career as a revolutionary can bear a slight comparison to Marx's – though less Karl than Groucho. It was typical of the times, and the disarray and futility among republicans, radicals, and those who simply wanted a united Italy set the stage for the stumbling, divisive process of the Risorgimento.

The big change came in the revolutionary year of **1848**, when risings in Palermo and Naples (in January) anticipated even those in Paris itself. Soon all Italy was in the streets. Piedmont and Tuscany won constitutions from their rulers, and the people of Milan chased out the Austrians after a month of extremely bloody fighting; at the same time the Venetian Republic was restored. Carlo Alberto, the hope of most Italians for a war of liberation, marched against the Austrians, but his two badly bungled campaigns allowed the enemy to re-establish control over the peninsula. By

June 1849, only Venice, under Austrian blockade, and the recently declared Roman Republic were left. Rome, led by Mazzini, and with a small army under **Giuseppe Garibaldi**, a former sailor who had fought in the wars of independence in Latin America, beat off several attacks from foreign troops invited in by the Pope. The republic finally succumbed to a large force sent by, of all people, the republic of President Louis Napoleon (soon to declare himself Napoleon III) in France. Garibaldi's dramatic escape to safety in San Marino (he was trying to reach Venice, itself soon to surrender) gave the Risorgimento one of its great heroic myths.

Despite failure on a grand scale, at least the Italians knew they would get another chance. Unification was inevitable, but there were two irreconcilable contenders for the honour of accomplishing it. On one side, the democrats and radicals dreamed of a truly reborn, revolutionary Italy, and looked to the popular hero Garibaldi to deliver it; on the other, moderates wanted the Piedmontese to do the job, ensuring a stable future by making **Vittorio Emanuele II** King of Italy. His minister, the polished, clever **Count Camillo Cavour**, spent the 1850s getting Piedmont in shape for the struggle, building its economy and army, participating in the Crimean War to earn diplomatic support, and plotting with the French for an alliance against Austria.

War came in 1859, and French armies did most of the work in conquering Lombardy. Tuscany and Emilia revolted, and Piedmont was able to annex all three. In May 1860, Garibaldi and his red-shirted '**Thousand**' sailed from Genoa (Cavour almost stopped them at the last minute), landed in Sicily, and electrified Europe by repeatedly beating the Bourbon forces in a quick march across the island. The Thousand had become 20,000, and when they crossed the straits bound for Naples it was clear that the affair was reaching its climax. On 7 September, Garibaldi entered Naples, and though he proclaimed himself temporary dictator on behalf of Vittorio Emanuele, the Piedmontese were alarmed enough to occupy Umbria and the Marche. The King met Garibaldi on 27 October, near Teano, and after finding out what little regard the Piedmontese had for him, the greatest and least self-interested leader modern Italy has known went off to retirement on the island of Caprara.

Just as the French made all this possible, some more unexpected help from outside allowed the new Italy to add two missing pieces and complete its unification. When the Prussians defeated Austria in the war of 1866, Italy was able to seize the Veneto. Only Rome was left, defended by a French garrison, and when the Prussians beat France at Sedan in 1870, the Italian army marched into Rome without opposition.

The first decades of the **Italian Kingdom** were just as unimpressive as its wars of independence. A liberal constitutional monarchy was established, but the parliament almost immediately decomposed into cliques and political cartels representing various interests. Finances started in disorder and stayed that way, and corruption became widespread. Peasant revolts occurred in the south, as people felt cheated by inaction after the promises of the Risorgimento, and organized brigandage became a problem, partially instigated by the Vatican as part of an all-out attempt to discredit the new regime. The outlines of foreign policy often seemed to change monthly, though like the other European powers Italy felt it necessary to snatch up some colonies. The attempt revealed the new state's limited capabilities, with highly embarrassing military disasters at the hands of the Ethiopians at Dogali in 1887, and again at Adowa in 1896.

After 1900, with the rise of a strong socialist movement, strikes, riots, and police repression often occupied centre stage in Italian politics. Even so, important signs of progress, such as the big new industries in Turin and Milan, showed that at least the northern half of Italy was becoming a fully integral part of the European economy. The 15 years before the war, prosperous and contented ones for many, came to be known by the slightly derogatory term *Italietta*, the 'little Italy' of modest bourgeois happiness, an age of sweet Puccini operas, the first motorcars, blooming 'Liberty'-style architecture, and Sunday afternoons at the beach.

1915–1945: War, Fascism and War

Italy could have stayed out of the First World War, but let the chance to do so go by for the usual reasons – a hope of gaining some new territory, especially Trieste. Also, a certain segment of the intelligentsia found the *Italietta* boring and disgraceful: irredentists of all stripes, some of the artistic futurists, and the perverse, idolized poet **Gabriele D'Annunzio**. The groups helped Italy leap blindly into the conflict in 1915, with a big promise of boundary adjustments dangled by the beleaguered Allies. Italian armies fought with their accustomed flair, masterminding an utter catastrophe at Caporetto (October 1917) that any other nation but Austria would have parleyed into a total victory. No thanks to their incompetent generals, the poorly armed and equipped Italians somehow held firm for another year, until the total exhaustion of Austria allowed them to prevail (at the battle of Vittorio Veneto you see so many streets named after), capturing some 600,000 prisoners in November 1918.

In return for 650,000 dead, a million casualties, severe privation on the home front, and a war debt higher than anyone could count, Italy received Trieste, Gorizia, the South Tyrol, and scraps. Italians felt cheated, and nationalist sentiment increased, especially when D'Annunzio led a band of freebooters to seize the half-Italian city of Fiume in September 1919, after the peace conferences had promised it to Yugoslavia. The Italian economy was in shambles, and, at least in the north, revolution was in the air; workers in Turin raised the Red Flag over the Fiat plants and organized themselves into soviets. The troubles had encouraged extremists of both right and left, and many Italians became convinced that the liberal state was finished.

Enter **Benito Mussolini**, a professional intriguer in the Mazzini tradition with bad manners and no fixed principles. Before the War he had found his real talent as editor of the Socialist Party paper *Avanti* – the best it ever had, tripling the circulation in a year. When he decided that what Italy really needed was war, he left to found a new paper, and contributed mightily to the jingoist agitation of 1915. In the post-War confusion, he found his opportunity. A little bit at a time, he developed the idea of **Fascism**, at first less a philosophy than an astute use of mass propaganda and a sense for design. (The *fasci*, from which the name comes, were bundles of rods carried before ancient Roman officials, a symbol of authority. *Fascii* also referred to organized bands of rebellious peasants in 19th-century Sicily.) With a little discreet money supplied by frightened industrialists, Mussolini had no trouble in recruiting for his black-shirted gangs, who found their first success beating up Slavs in Trieste and working as a sort of private police for landowners in stoutly socialist Emilia-Romagna.

The basic principle, combining left- and right-wing extremism into something the ruling classes could live with, proved attractive to many, and a series of weak governments stood by while the Fascist *squadre* cast their shadow over more and more of Italy. Mussolini's accession to power came on an improbable gamble. In the particularly anarchic month of October 1922, he announced that his followers would march on Rome. King Vittorio Emanuele III refused to sign a decree of martial law to disperse them, and there was nothing to do but offer Mussolini the post of prime minister. At first, he governed Italy with undeniable competence. Order was restored, and the economy and foreign policy were handled intelligently by non-fascist professionals. In the 1924 elections, despite the flagrant rigging and intimidation, the Fascists only won a slight majority. One politician who was not intimidated was **Giacomo Matteotti**, and when some of Mussolini's close associates murdered him, a major scandal erupted. Mussolini survived it, and during 1925 and 1926 the Fascists used parliamentary methods to convert Italy into a permanent Fascist dictatorship.

Compared to the governments that preceded him, Mussolini looked quite impressive. Industry advanced, great public works were undertaken, with special care towards the backward south, and the Mafia took some heavy blows at the hands of a determined Sicilian prefect named Mori. The most lasting achievement was the **Concordat** of 1929 with the Pope, founding the Vatican State and ending the Church's isolation from Italian affairs. The regime evolved a new economic philosophy, the 'corporate state', where labour and capital were supposed to live in harmony under syndicalist government control. But the longer Fascism lasted, the more unreal it seemed to be, a patchwork government of Mussolini and his ageing cronies, magnified and rendered heroic by cinematic technique – stirring rhetoric before oceanic crowds, colourful pageantry, magnificent, larger-than-life post offices and railway stations built of travertine and marble, dashing aviators and winsome gymnasts from the Fascist youth groups on parade. In a way it was the Baroque all over again, and Italians tried not to think about the consequences. In the words of one of Mussolini's favourite slogans, painted on walls all over Italy, 'Whoever stops is lost'.

Mussolini couldn't stop, and the only possibility for new diversions lay with the chance of conquest and empire. His invasion of Ethiopia and his meddling in the Spanish Civil War, both in 1936, compromised Italy into a close alliance with Nazi Germany. Mussolini's confidence and rhetoric never faltered as he led an entirely unprepared nation into the biggest war ever. Once more, Italian ineptitude at warfare produced embarrassing defeats on all fronts, and only German intervention in Greece and North Africa saved Italy from being knocked out of the War as early as 1941. The Allies invaded Sicily in July 1943, and the Italians began to look for a clever way out. They seized Mussolini during a meeting of the Grand Council, packed him into an ambulance and sent him off first to Ponza, then to a little ski hotel up in the Apennines. The new government under Marshal Badoglio didn't know what to do, and confusion reigned supreme.

While British and American forces slogged northwards, in this ghetto of the European theatre, with the help of the free French, Brazilians, Costa Ricans, Poles, Czechs, New Zealanders and Norwegians, the Germans poured in divisions to defend the peninsula. They rescued Mussolini, and set him up in a puppet state called the Italian Social Republic in the north. In September 1943, the Badoglio government signed an armistice with the Allies, too late to keep the War from dragging on another year and a half, as the Germans made good use of Italy's difficult terrain to slow the Allied advance. Meanwhile Italy finally gave itself something to be proud of, a determined, resourceful Resistance that established free zones in many areas, and harassed the Germans with sabotage and strikes. The *partigiani* caught Mussolini in April 1945, while he was trying to escape to Switzerland; after shooting him and his mistress, they hung him by his feet from the roof of a petrol station in Milan.

1945–the Present

Post-war Italian *cinema verità* – Rossellini's *Rome, Open City*, or de Sica's *Bicycle Thieves* – captures the atmosphere better than words ever could. In a period of serious hardships that older Italians still remember, the nation slowly picked itself up and returned to normal. A referendum in June 1946 made Italy a **Republic**, but only by a narrow margin. The first governments fell to the new Christian Democrat party (DC) under Alcide de Gasperi, which ran the show for decades with a preposterous band of smaller parties. The main opposition was provided by the Communists (PCI), surely one of the most remarkable parties of modern European history. With the heritage of the only important socialist philosopher since Marx, Antonio Gramsci, and the demo-cratic and broadminded leader Enrico Berlinguer, Italian communism is unique, with its stronghold and showcase in the well-run, prosperous cities of Emilia-Romagna.

The fifties was Rome's decade, when Italian style and Italian cinema caught the imagination of the world. Gradually, slowly, a little economic miracle was happening; *Signor Rossi*, the average Italian, started buzzing around in his first classic Fiat *cinque-cento*, northern industries boomed, and life cruised slowly back to normal. The south continued to lag behind, despite the efforts of the government and its special plan-ning fund, the *Cassa per il Mezzogiorno*. Though the extreme poverty and despair of the post-war years gradually disappeared, the region has still not caught up with the rest of Italy. Nationally, the *Democristiani*-controlled government soon evolved a **Byzantine style of politics** that only an Italian could understand. Through the constantly collapsing and reforming cabinets, nothing changed; all deals were made in the back rooms and everyone, from the Pope to the Communists, had a share in the decision-making. One wouldn't call it democracy with a straight face, but for four decades it worked well enough to keep Italy on its wheels.

The dark side of the arrangement was the all-pervasive **corruption** that the system fostered. It is fascinating to read the work of journalists only a few years ago, seeing how almost without exception they would politely sidestep the facts; Italy was run by an unprincipled political machine, whose members were raking in as much for them-selves as they could grab, and everyone knew it, only it couldn't be said openly, for lack of proof. Even more sinister was the extent to which the machine would go to keep on top. The seventies, Italy's 'years of lead', witnessed the worst of the political sleaze, along with a grim reign of extreme left- and right- wing terrorism, culminating in the kidnap and murder in 1978 of an honourable DC prime minister, Aldo Moro, who had attempted to forge a *compromesso storico* between mainstream left and right to balance power. The attacks were attributed to 'leftist groups', though even at the time many suspected that some of the highest circles in the government and army were manipulating them, with the possible collusion of the CIA. They were indeed; only recently has some of the truth of Moro's 'sacrifice' begun to seep out. On another front, Italians woke up one morning in 1992 to find that the government had magically vacuumed 7 per cent of the money out of all their savings accounts, an 'emergency measure' to meet the nation's colossal budget deficit – a deficit caused largely by the thievery of the political class and its allies in organized crime.

Italians are a patient lot but the lid has blown off. It all started in the judiciary, the one independent and relatively uncorrupt part of the government. In the early nineties, heroic prosecutors Giovanni Falcone and Paolo Borsellino went after the Sicilian Mafia with some success, and were spectacularly assassinated for it, causing national outrage. Meanwhile, in Milan, a small group of prosecutors found a minor political kickback scandal that has led them, through years of painstaking work, to the golden string that unravelled the whole rotten tangle of Italian political depravity – what Italians call *tangentopoli*, or 'bribe city'. For a year, the televised hearings of Judge Antonio di Pietro and his Operation *Mani Pulite* ('clean hands') team from Milan were the nation's favourite and most fascinating serial.

All the kingpins fell, notably Socialist leader Bettino Craxi (who died recently after years evading extradition in Tunisia). Others, especially former prime minister Giulio Andreotti, lost their parliamentary immunity. Andreotti was put on trial on two counts – association with the Mafia, and the assassination of a journalist who had come perilously close to uncovering sinister links to Moro's murder. The failure to convict Andreotti on either charge has been a factor in Italians' dwindling faith in their country's ability to make a clean-sweep of its past. The two ruling parties, the DC and the Socialists, may be dead – the 1993 municipal elections, held at the height of the *tangentopoli* hearings, were nearly a sweep for the PDS, the old Communists, beating the neo-fascist MSI and the League, the new northern, racist, party – but many of the same old faces still throng the corridors of power.

Other forces on the scene included, most surprisingly of all, Silvio Berlusconi, a television and publishing magnate (and former protégé of Craxi) whose near-monopolies were threatened by a possible PDS government. Berlusconi thinks big: the only way out was to buy the government for himself. He used his big bankroll and media control (his empire includes half of Italy's TV audience, a third of its magazine readership, books, newspapers – and AC Milan) to create a new, totally synthetic party, called Forza Italia, and sell it to Italians the same way as soap and sex. Meanwhile, Berlusconi managed an improbable three-way alliance with Fini's neo-fascists and Bossi's League. It all worked brilliantly: in the 1994 parliamentary elections, the first of what many Italians called their 'Second Republic', Berlusconi's rightist alliance won an impressive victory, and 'Mr TV' himself became prime minister. It soon became apparent that government under Berlusconi only meant business as usual. The media mogul's refusal to distance himself from his empire while in office, and his heavy-handed attempt to cripple the *Mani Pulite* probes, made many Italians feel the egg on their faces – they had struggled so hard to topple a malodorous old order, only to vote it back into office at the first chance.

It wasn't long before Judge Di Pietro resigned from the *Mani Pulite* investigations, under a cloud of phony political allegations – yet another indication that the probes have not brought the wholesale renewal they seemed to promise. Di Pietro's departure was followed in turn by that of Berlusconi himself, who – surrounded by his own fog of allegations of scandal and bribery – was forced out of office in early 1995 when the Bossi withdrew his support. The political mess that remained was such that President Scalfaro followed the medieval Italian custom of calling in a political outsider to straighten out the country and institute reforms. This was a banker, Lamberto Dini, whose lack of a political past and steady head were virtues enough to keep him in office while the politicians got their house in order.

To many Italians it began to seem as if the only way out of the *imbroglio* created by their own fragmented political system was to anchor their country in Europe. It came as a blow to Italy, a founding parent of the European Union, when German bankers stated that it was improbable Italy would meet the economic requirements to join in the new European currency. Dini, the finance man, started reforms, but it was Romano Prodi and his leftish-centre Olive Tree coalition, with the former communists, the Left Democrats (DS), who brought in the necessary political will. Prodi, like Dini, had the prime virtue of entering the national scene with clean hands, and as one of the country's biggest Europhiles, he rallied the republic to swallow a difficult financial pill: the Italians backed Prodi's stringent economic measures, allowing Italy to squeak into the first round of the Euro in 1999. Prodi had little time to bask in the glory: the same strict measures led to the Communists withdrawing their support of his government in late 1998 and giving it to a new prime minister, leftwing darling Massimo D'Alema of the DS, forming Italy's 60th government since the War. But the D'Alema government proved ineffective, squandering all the gains made in public approval, and was replaced by yet another coalition of the left headed by former Craxian minister Giuseppe Amato.

Meanwhile, Romano Prodi has a new job as EU Commission president after the sorry debacle at Brussels that saw the resignation of all the head honchos when confronted with evidence of gross irresponsibility and patronage. The very idea of an Italian running the big show ten years ago would have been regarded as a joke, and goes to prove how respectable Italy has become in the last few years. At the time of writing new elections are imminent, and the polls favour the return to power of Berlusconi, as leader of a wide-ranging centre-right coalition which includes, for the moment at least, the League. It isn't a sure bet though. The left has found a new champion, the capable and straightforward mayor of Rome Francesco Rutelli, and in recent months he has been closing the gap.

Art and Architecture

04

You'd have to spend your holiday in a baggage compartment to miss Italy's vast piles of architecture and art. The Italians estimate there is at least one work of art per capita in their country, which is more than anyone could see in a lifetime – especially since so much of it is locked away in museums that are in semi-permanent 'restoration'. Although you may occasionally chafe at not being able to see certain frescoes, or at finding a famous palace completely wrapped up in the ubiquitous green netting of the restorers, the Italians on the whole bear very well the burden of keeping their awesome patrimony dusted off and open for visitors. Some Italians find it insupportable living with the stuff all around them; the futurists, for instance, were worried that St Mark's might be blown up by foreign enemies in the First World War – but only as they wanted to do it themselves, their right as Italian citizens.

Pre-Etruscan

To give a chronological account of the first Italian artists is an uncomfortable task. The peninsula's mountainous terrain saw many isolated ancient cultures even during the days of the sophisticated Etruscans and Romans. Most ancient of all, however, is the palaeolithic troglodyte culture on the Riviera, credited with creating some of the first artworks in Europe – chubby images of fertility goddesses. These and other curious trappings may be seen in the Ligurian museums at **Balzi Rossi**, **Pegli** and **Finalborgo**. The most remarkable works from the Neolithic period up until the Iron Age are the thousands of graffiti rock incisions in several isolated Alpine valleys north of Lake Iseo, especially in the **Val Camonica** national park. After 1000 BC Italic peoples all over the peninsula were making geometrically painted pots, weapons, tools and bronze statuettes. The most impressive culture, however, was the tower-building, bronze-working Nuraghe civilization on **Sardinia**, of which echoes are seen on the mainland. Among the most intriguing and beautiful artefacts to have survived are those of the Villanova culture in **Bologna**; the statues and inscriptions of the little-known Middle Adriatic culture at **Chieti** in Abruzzo, and the *steles* of an unknown people at **Pontrémoli**, north of Viareggio; others, of the Luini culture, are in **La Spezia**. Dolmens and strange little temples survive in many corners of central and southern **Puglia**. If you wish to see what was going on across the Mediterranean at the same time, there's also one of the best Egyptian museums in the world in **Turin**.

Etruscan and Greek (8th–2nd centuries BC)

With the refined, art-loving Etruscans we begin to have architecture as well as art. Not much has survived, thanks to the Etruscans' habit of building in wood and decorating with terracotta, but we do have plenty of distinctive rock-cut tombs, the best of which are at **Cerveteri** and **Tarquinia**; many of them contain exceptional frescoes that reflect Aegean Greek styles. The best of their lovely sculptures, jewellery, vases, and much more, are in **Rome** (where there's also a temple façade), **Chiusi**, **Volterra** and **Tarquinia**. There are also fine Etruscan holdings in **Perugia**, **Florence** and **Bologna**.

The Etruscans imported and copied many of their vases from their ancient Greek contemporaries, from Greece proper and the colonies of Magna Graecia in southern Italy. The Doric temple at **Paestum** is the best Greek structure on the peninsula (there are many more in Sicily); **Cumae**, west of Naples, and **Metapontum**, near Tàranto, also merit a visit; of the many excavated Greek cities, usually only foundations remain. **Reggio di Calabria, Tàranto, Naples, Bari** and the **Vatican** are the homes of the most impressive collections of ancient Greek vases, statues, and other types of art.

Roman (3rd century BC–5th century AD)

Italian art during the Roman hegemony is mostly derivative of Etruscan and Greek, with a talent for mosaics, wall paintings, glasswork and portraiture; architecturally, the Romans were brilliant engineers, the inventors of concrete and grand exponents of the arch. Even today their aqueducts, amphitheatres, bridges, baths – and the Pantheon – are impressive. Of course, **Rome** itself has no end of ancient monuments; also nearby is **Ostia Antica**, Rome's ancient port, and the great **Villa Adriana**. Rome also has the stellar museums of Roman antiquities: the Museo Nazionale Romano, the Vatican Museum, the Capitoline Museums and the Museum of Roman Civilization at EUR. **Naples** is the other main destination for Roman art, with the ruins of ancient **Pompeii** and **Herculaneum,** and a spectacular museum of Pompeiian artefacts and of statues from Rome dug up by Renaissance collectors like the Farnese.

Other impressive Roman monuments may be seen in **Benevento** (the best triumphal arch and unusual Roman-Egyptian art); **Capua** (huge amphitheatre and Mithraeum); **Verona** (the arena, gates and theatre complex); **Aosta** (theatre and gates); the excavations of **Aquileia** in Friuli and **Sepino** in Molise; the temples in **Brescia** and **Assisi**; 'the villa of Catullus' in **Sirmione** on Lake Garda; villas, tunnels, canals, markets and other surprises in **Pozzuoli, Baia**, and the western Bay of Naples, and odds and ends in **Fiesole, Bologna, Trieste, Perugia, Cori** (in Lazio), **Spoleto, Rimini, Ancona, Susa, Lecce** and **Alba Fucens** in Abruzzo.

Early Middle Ages (5th–10th centuries)

After the fall of the Roman Empire, civilization's lamp flickered brightly in **Ravenna**, where Byzantine mosaicists adorned the glittering churches of the Eastern Exarchate. Theirs was to be the prominent pictorial and architectural style until the 13th century.

There are fine mosaics and paintings in **Rome** too, in the churches of San Clemente and Santa Prassede. In Rome, Italy's preference for basilican churches and octagonal baptistries began in Constantine's day; the growth of Christian art and architecture through the Dark Ages can best be traced there. The catacombs of Rome and **Naples** are packed with paintings. Ravenna-style mosaics may also be seen in the cathedrals of **Aquileia** and Torcello in **Venice**, where the fashion lingered until St Mark's. In the vicinity of **Tàranto** there are the remains of Greek monasteries and cave paintings, and early-Christian churches at **Nocera** in Campania, and in Benevento. In **Albenga**, on the Riviera, and **Novara**, you'll find unusual 5th-century baptistries with artworks.

'Lombard' art, really the work of natives under Lombard rule, revealed new talent in the 7th–9th centuries, seen in the churches of **Cividale del Friuli**, works in the cathedral of **Monza**, in and around **Spoleto**, and in the Abbey of San Salvatore in **Brescia**. A new style, presaging the Romanesque, may be seen in Sant'Ambrogio in **Milan**.

Romanesque (11th–12th centuries)

At this point an expansive society made new advances in art possible. North and south went separate ways, each contributing distinctive sculptural and architectural styles. We begin to learn the identities of the makers: the great Lombard cathedrals, masterworks of brick art, adorned with blind arcading, reliefs and lofty campaniles, are best exemplified at **Modena** (by master builder-sculptor Wiligelmo), San Michele in **Pavia, Cremona** cathedral, and Santo Stefano in **Bologna**. In **Verona** the cathedral and San Zeno were embellished by Guglielmo's talented student Nicolò; in **Parma** Antelami's baptistry is a milestone in the synthesis of sculpture and architecture.

Pisa's wealth permitted the the largest building programme in Italy in a thousand years –its cathedral. The exotic style owed something to the Muslim world, but the inspiration was completely original – in part a conscious attempt to recapture the grandeur of the ancient world. **Florence** developed its own black and white style, exemplified in buildings like the baptistry and San Miniato. Variations appeared in the other Tuscan cities, each showing some Pisan stripes or Florentine rectangles.

In the south, Byzantine and Muslim influences created a different tendency. **Amalfi** and **Caserta** built a Saracenic cathedral and cloister, Amalfi's adorned with incised bronze doors from Constantinople in a style that was copied all over the south, notably at **Trani** and **Monte Sant'Angelo** in Puglia. The Byzantine painting and mosaics tradition continued, mostly in Sicily, though there is a fine example at Sant'Angelo in Formis near **Capua**. From Muslim geometrical patterns, southern artists acquired a taste for intricate designs using enamel or marble chips in church furnishings and architectural trim – as seen in pulpits and candlesticks in the churches of **Salerno, Ravello**. The outstanding advance of this period is the Pugliese Romanesque, as shown in cathedrals in almost every Pugliese city (**Troia, Sipontum, Monte Sant'Angelo, Ruvo di Puglia, Trani, Altamura** and **Bari**), a style closely related to contemporary Norman and Pisan work – it's difficult to say who should get the credit for being first. Another impressive southern Romanesque cathedral is that of **Anagni** in Lazio; in the same region are the two unusual church façades in **Tuscània**. The Norman influence also appears in churches like the Abbazia della Trinità in **Venosa** (Basilicata) and in the wonderful mosaic pavement of **Ótranto** Cathedral.

This period also saw the erection of urban skyscrapers by the nobility, family fortress-towers built when the *comuni* forced barons into the towns. Larger cities had hundreds of them, before the townspeople demolished them. **San Gimignano** and **Ascoli Piceno** have the most surviving examples. In many cases tall towers were built simply for decoration and prestige. **Bologna**'s Due Torri, along with **Pisa**'s Campanile, are the best examples of medieval Italy's occasional disdain for the horizontal.

Late-Medieval–Early-Renaissance (13th–14th centuries)

In many ways this was the most exciting and vigorous phase in Italian art history, an age of discovery when the artist was like a magician. Great imaginative leaps occurred in architecture, painting and sculpture, especially in Tuscany. From Milan to Assisi a group of masons and sculptors known as the Campionese Masters built magnificent brick cathedrals and basilicas. Some of their buildings reflect the Gothic style of the north (most spectacularly **Milan**), while in **Como** cathedral you can see the transition from Gothic to Renaissance. In **Venice** an ornate, half-oriental style called Venetian-Gothic still sets the city's palaces and public buildings apart, and influenced **Padua**'s exotic Basilica di Sant'Antonio.

This was also an era of transition in sculpture, from stiff Romanesque stylization to the more realistic, classically inspired works of the great Nicola Pisano, his son Giovanni (in the churches of **Pisa, Pistoia** and **Siena**), and his pupil Arnolfo di Cambio (**Florence**). Other outstanding works of the 14th century are Lorenzo Maitani's cathedral in **Orvieto** and the Scaliger tombs of **Verona** by the Campionese Masters.

Painters in Rome and Siena learned from the new spatial sculpture. Most celebrated of the masters of the dawning Renaissance is, of course, the solemn Giotto, whose greatest works are the fresco cycles in **Padua** and **Assisi**. In St Francis' town you can also see excellent works by Giotto's merrier contemporaries from **Siena**. That city's artists, Duccio di Buoninsegna, Simone Martini and Pietro and Ambrogio Lorenzetti, gave Italy brilliant exponents of International Gothic, who were also precursors of the Renaissance. Their brightly coloured scenes, embellished with a thousand details, made Siena into a medieval dream-city; the style carried on into the quattrocento with the courtly frescoes of the northerner Pisanello. In **Florence**, works by Orcagna, Gentile da Fabriano and Lorenzo Monaco laid a unique foundation for the Renaissance. Cathedral and public buildings in the north, especially at **Siena** and **Pistoia**, show a sophisticated understanding of urban design and an original treatment of established forms. Northern European Gothic never made much headway, though French Cistercians did build fine abbey churches like those at **San Galgano** in Tuscany, **Fossanova** in Lazio, and Sant'Andrea in **Vercelli**. The south had little to contribute during this period, but **Naples** developed its own neo-Gothic architecture, and unique geometrically patterned church façades appear at **L'Aquila** and **Brindisi**.

Rome, for once, achieved artistic prominence with home-grown talent. The city's architecture from this period (as seen in the campanile of Santa Maria in Cosmedin) has largely been lost under Baroque remodellings, but the paintings and mosaics of Pietro Cavallini and his school, and the intricate, inlaid stone pavements and architectural trim of the Cosmati and their followers, derived from the Amalfi Coast style, can be seen all over the city; both had an influence that extended far beyond Rome itself.

The Renaissance (15th–16th centuries)

The origins of this high-noon of art are very much the accomplishment of quattrocento **Florence**, where sculpture and painting embarked on a totally new way of educating the eye. The idea of a supposed 'rediscovery of antiquity' has confused the understanding of the time. In general, artists broke new ground when they expanded from the traditions of medieval art; when they sought merely to copy the forms of ancient Greece and Rome, the imagination often faltered. Florentine art soon became recognized as the standard of the age, and examples can be seen everywhere in Tuscany. By 1450 Florentine artists were spreading the new style to the north, especially **Milan**, where Leonardo da Vinci and Bramante spent several years; the collections in the Brera and other galleries, the *Last Supper*, and the nearby **Certosa di**

Pavia are essential works of the Renaissance. Other good museum collections are in **Rome, Parma, Turin** and **Bergamo**; the core of Bergamo is a Renaissance masterpiece. **Mantua** has important works by Alberti and Mantegna, and nearby lies the 'ideal' Renaissance town: **Sabbioneta**. Michelangelo and Bramante, among others, carried the Renaissance to **Rome**, where it thrived under the patronage of enlightened popes. Other Renaissance diversions can be seen in **Rimini**: its remarkable Malatesta Temple; and **Urbino**: the lovely palace and art collection of the archetypal Renaissance prince, Duke Federico da Montefeltro.

The most significant art in the north came out of **Venice**, which had its own distinct school led by Mantegna and Giovanni Bellini; one of the best painters of the school, the fastidious Carlo Crivelli, did much of his work in the Marche (**Ascoli Piceno** and **Ancona**). Under the patronage of the Este family, Renaissance **Ferrara** produced its own school of quattrocento painters (Cosmè Tura, Ercole Roberti). In **Perugia** Perugino was laying the foundations of the Umbrian school, in which Raphael and Pinturicchio earned their stripes. In **Orvieto** Cathedral, the Tuscan painter Signorelli left a *Last Judgement* that inspired Michelangelo. Piero della Francesca was the most important non-Florentine painter before Raphael; his revolutionary works are at **Urbino, Sansepolcro** and **Arezzo**. Southern Italy, trapped in a decline that was even more artistic than economic, hardly participated at all, though examples of the northerners' art can be seen in **Naples** (the Triumphal Arch in the Castel Nuovo).

Despite the brilliant triumphs in painting and sculpture, the story of Renaissance architecture is partially one of confusion and retreat. **Florence**, with Brunelleschi, Alberti and Michelozzo, achieved its own special mode of expression, a dignified austerity that proved difficult to transplant elsewhere. In most of Italy the rediscovery of the works of Vitruvius, representing the authority of antiquity, killed off Italians' appreciation of their own architectural heritage; with surprising speed the dazzling imaginative freedom of medieval architecture was lost forever. Some fine work still appeared, however, notably Codussi's palaces and churches in **Venice**.

High Renaissance and Mannerism (16th century)

At the beginning of the cinquecento Michelangelo, Raphael and Leonardo held court at the summit of European art. But as Italy was losing her self-confidence, and was soon to lose her liberty, artistic currents tended toward the dark and subversive. More than anyone it was Michelangelo who tipped the balance from the cool, classical Renaissance into the turgid, stormy, emotionally fraught movement labelled **Mannerism**. Among the few painters left in exhausted Florence, he had the brilliant Jacopo Pontormo and Rosso Fiorentino to help. Other painters lumped in with the Mannerists, such as Giulio Romano in Mantua and Il Sodoma around Siena, broke new ground while maintaining the discipline and intellectual rigour of the early Renaissance. Elsewhere, and especially among the fashionable Florentine painters and sculptors, art was decaying into mere interior decoration.

For **Venice** it was a golden age, with Titian, Veronese, Tintoretto, Sansovino and Palladio, whose works may be seen throughout Venetia. Another art centre of the age, **Parma**, is embellished with the Mannerist brushes of Correggio and Parmigianino. In

Cremona, Milan, and other lucky galleries, you can see works by Arcimboldo, the cinquecento surrealist. In architecture, attempts to recreate ancient styles and the classical orders won the day. In **Milan,** and later in **Rome**, Bramante was one of the few architects able to do anything interesting with it, while Michelangelo's great dome of St Peter's put a cap on the accomplishments of the Renaissance. Other talented architects found most of their patronage in Rome which after the 1520s became Italy's centre of artistic activity: Ligorio, Peruzzi, Vignola and the Sangallo family among them.

Baroque (17th–18th centuries)

Rome continued its artistic dominance to become the Baroque capital, where the socially irresponsible genius of artists like Bernini and Borromini was approved by the Jesuits and indulged by the tainted ducats of the popes. As an art designed to induce temporal obedience and psychical oblivion, its effects are difficult to describe, but the three great churches along Corso Vittorio Emanuele, Bernini's Piazza Navona fountains and St Peter's colonnades, are fine examples. More honest cities such as Florence and Venice chose to sit out the Baroque, though **Florence** at first approved the works of 16th-century proto-Baroque sculptors like Ammannati, Giambologna and Cellini. Not all artists fit the Baroque mould; genius could survive even in a dangerous, picaresque age, most notably in the person of Michelangelo (works in **Milan** and **Rome**), not to mention other painters such as Mattia Preti, with works in Naples and **Taverna**, in his native Calabria.

The south of Italy, with its long tradition of religious emotionalism, found the Baroque entirely to its tastes, though few towns could afford to build much. **Naples** could, and the Monastery of San Martino by Cosimo Fanzago marks the apotheosis of Neapolitan Baroque. Painting and sculpture even flourished while they were dying in northern Renaissance towns; southern art's eccentricity climaxed in the Sansevero Chapel. A very different sort of Baroque appeared in the deep south, where the studied excess seemed to strike a deep chord in the popular psyche. Much of it is in Sicily, though the Spanish-looking city of **Lecce** developed a Baroque style that lasted from the 16th to the late 18th century, consistent and beautiful enough to make as impressive an architectural ensemble as any medieval or Renaissance city in the north. **Turin**'s town plan, churches, palaces and royal hunting lodges, designed by the priest Guarini and the early 18th-century Sicilian Juvarra, are the most elegant representations of the Baroque spirit in northern Italy. This was a great age of palaces and ornate Italian gardens, most famously in **Tivoli**, Isola Bella in **Lake Maggiore**, Villa Borghese and innumerable other locations in and around **Rome**, as well as around **Padua** and **Vicenza**.

Neoclassicism and Romanticism (late 18th–19th centuries)

Baroque was a hard act to follow, and at this time Italian art and architecture almost cease to exist. Two centuries of stifling oppression had taken their toll on the national imagination, and for the first time Italy not only ceased to be a leader in art, but failed even to make significant contributions. The one bright spot was **Venice**, where Giambattista Tiepolo and son adorned the churches and palaces of the last days of the Serenissima; their works can be seen in many places in the Veneto, and Ùdine in Friuli. Other Venetians, such as Canaletto and Guardi, painted their famous canal scenes for Grand Tourists. In the 19th century the *Macchiaioli*, the Italian Impressionist movement led by Giovanni Fattori, was centred in **Florence**. In sculpture the neoclassical master Canova stands almost alone, a favourite in the days of Napoleon. His best works may be seen in the Villa Carlotta, on **Lake Como**, in **Rome**'s Villa Borghese and at **Possagno**. In architecture it was the age of grand opera houses, many designed by the Bibiena family of Bologna. The Gallerie in **Milan** and **Naples** (late 19th century) and the extravagances of the Piedmontese Alessandro Antonelli (**Turin** and **Novara**) are among the most impressive public buildings, and the neoclassical royal palaces at **Caserta** and **Stra** near Venice the grandest private addresses.

20th Century

The turn-of-the-century Italian Art Nouveau – known as Liberty Style – failed to spread as widely as its counterparts in France and central Europe. There are a few good examples in **Milan**, but the best are linked with the burgeoning tourist industry: the construction of Grand Hotels, casinos and villas, especially in **Venice**, the **Lakes**, the **Riviera, Pésaro, Viareggio** and the great spas at **Merano, Montecatini** and **San Pellegrino**. Two art movements attracted international attention: futurism, a response to Cubism, concerned with relevancy to the present, a movement led by Boccioni, Severini and Balla (best seen in the National Gallery of Modern Art, **Rome**, and in **Milan**); and the mysterious, metaphysical world of De Chirico; while Modigliani, Morandi and Carrà were masters of silences. Their works, among others, are displayed in the museums of **Rome, Venice** and **Milan**. Architecture in this century reached its (admittedly low) summit in the Fascist period (the **EUR** suburb in Rome, and public buildings everywhere in the south). Mussolinian architecture often makes us smile, but, as the only Italian school in the last 200 years to have achieved a consistent sense of design, it presents a challenge to all modern Italian architects – one they have so far been unable to meet.

In **Turin** and **Milan** you can see the works of the most acclaimed Italian architect of this century, Pier Luigi Nervi; good post-War buildings are very difficult to find, and the other arts have never yet risen above the level of dreary, saleable postmodernism. Much of the Italians' artistic urge has been sublimated into the shibboleth of Italian design – clothes, sports cars, suitcases, kitchen utensils, etc. At present, though business is good, Italy is generating little excitement in these fields. Europe expects more from its most artistically talented nation; after the bad centuries of shame and slumber a free and prosperous Italy may well find its own voice and its own style to help interpret the events of the day. If Italy ever does begin to speak with a single voice, whatever it has to say will be worth hearing.

Topics

Bella Figura

The longer you stay in Italy, the more inscrutable it becomes. Nothing is ever quite as it seems: part of the reason why is the obsession with making a good impression – *'fare una bella figura'* – one of the Italian people's most singular traits. You notice it almost immediately. Not only is every Italian an immaculate fashion victim (Italians are by far the biggest consumers of their own fashion industry), but they always seem to be modelling their spiffy threads – posing, gesturing, playing to an audience when they have one, which is nearly always because Italians rarely move about except in small herds. Their cities are their stage, the piazzas and streets like movie sets, with lights suspended over the middle. Long-time observers have even noted that each city's women dress in colours that complement the local brick or stone.

The Italians' natural grace and elegance may be partly instinctive; even back in the 14th century foreigners noted their charming manners and taste for exquisite clothes. Many a painting of the Madonna served not only for piety's sake, but also to advertise Milanese silks or Venetian brocades. In the Renaissance appearance supplanted reality in a thousand ways, especially artificial perspective, which made artistic representations much cleverer than the real thing. Fake, painted marble supplanted real marble, even if it cost more; Palladio built marble palaces out of stucco; *trompe l'œil* frescoes embellished a hundred churches; glorious façades on cathedrals and palaces disguise the fact that the rest is unfinished brick. Even castles were built to impress rather than keep out the enemy, in a day when battles had become brilliant bloodless games, and gorgeous Italian armour deflected few blows.

Castiglione's *The Courtier* advises that it is no use doing a brave and noble deed unless someone is watching; honour, like almost every other virtue, is something bestowed from without. After the French and Spanish burst the Italians' bubble of superiority in the 16th century, Italy's history becomes a saga of trying to do everything to keep up appearances, of nobles mending their socks in the half-light to save up for hiring a servant when visitors were expected.

Bella figura pleases the eye but irritates just about everything else. Fashionable conformity spreads from clothing to opinions, especially in the provinces; the Italians remain the masters of empty flattery, and will say anything to please: 'Yes, straight ahead!' they'll often reply when you need directions, hoping it will make you happy even if they've never heard of your destination. Nor does fashion slavery show any sign of abating; now that more Italians have more money than ever before, they are using it for rarely necessary fur coats, and for designer clothes for the whole family. Even little children go to bed with visions of fashion dancing in their heads; Italy is the last stand of Barbie and Ken dolls, where each little girl owns at least a dozen.

Brick Italy, Marble Italy

'Italy', begins the 1948 Constitution, 'is a Republic based on labour' – an unusual turn of phrase, but one entirely in keeping with a time when a thoroughly humbled Italy was beginning to get back on its feet after the War. The sorrows of the common man

occupied the plots of post-War *cinema verità*, and artists and writers began to celebrate themes of Faith, Bread and Work as if they were in the employ of the Church's
Famiglia Cristiana magazine. To outsiders it seemed that Italy was undergoing a
serious change, but careful observers noted only another oscillation in the grandest,
oldest dichotomy in Italian history. Brick Italy was once more in the driver's seat.

Brick Italy is a nation of hard work, humility and piety that knows it must be diligent
and clever to wrest a comfortable living from the thin soil of this resource-poor, rocky
peninsula. Marble Italy knows its citizens have always done just that, and celebrates
by turning their diligence and cleverness into opulence, excess and foreign conquest.
The two have been contending for Italy's soul ever since Roman quarrymen discovered Carrara marble. Brick Italy's capital was once brilliant, republican Siena; right
now it is hard-working socialist Bologna. Its triumphs came with the Age of the
Comuni , with the modest genius of the Early Renaissance, and with the hard-won
successes of the last 40 years. Marble Italy reached its height in the days of Imperial
Rome; its capital is... Rome, always and forever. After the medieval interlude, marble
made its great comeback with the High Renaissance and Michelangelo, the high
priest of marble. The Age of Baroque belonged to it, as did the brief era of Mussolini.
Confirmed Marble Cities are Naples, Genoa, Turin, Pisa, Parma, Trieste, Perugia and
Verona. Brick partisans include Pavia, Livorno, Lucca, Arezzo, Cremona and Mantua.
Florence and Venice, the two medieval city-republics that became important states
on their own, are the two cities that successfully straddle the fence. Look carefully at
their old churches and palaces, and you will often find marble veneer outside, and
solid brick underneath.

Keep all this in mind when you ponder the infinite subtleties of Italian history. It
isn't always a perfect fit; medieval Guelphs and Ghibellines each had a little brick and
a little marble in them, and the contemporary papacy changes from one to the other
with every shift of the wind. Mussolini would have paved Italy over in marble if he
had been able – but look at the monuments he could afford, and you'll see travertine
and brick more than anything else. For a while in the eighties, with Italy's economic
boom and the glitz of Milanese design, it looked as if Marble Italy was about to make
another comeback. But today, with Italy in the midst of its long and tortuous revolution, the situation is unclear. If and when a new regime emerges, will its monument
to itself be a beautiful symbol of republican aspirations, like Siena's brick Palazzo
Pubblico, or a florid marble pile like Rome's Altar of the Nation, the monument to
Italian unification (and one of the biggest hunks of kitsch on this planet)?

Commedia dell'Arte

The first recorded mention of Arlecchino, or Harlequin, came in 1601 – the year that
saw the debut of *Hamlet* – when the part was played by Tristano Martinelli. Theatre
was blooming all over Europe: Shakespeare and Marlowe in England, Calderón and
Lope de Vega in Spain, the predecessors of Molière in France. All of these had learned
their craft from late-Renaissance Italy, where the *commedia dell'arte* had created a

fashion that spread across the continent. The great companies – the Gelosi, the Confidenti and the Accesi – toured the capitals, while others shared the provinces. Groups of 10 or 12 actors, run as co-operatives, they could do comedies, tragedies or pastorals to their own texts, and provide music, dance and juggling between acts.

The audiences liked the comedies best, with a set of masked stock characters, playing off scenes between the *magnifici* (great lords) and the *zanni* (servants), who provide the slapstick, half-improvised comic relief. These represented every corner of Italy: Arlecchino is a Bergamese; Balanzone, the wise doctor who 'cures with Latin', from Bologna; Pulcinello, white-clad and warbling, a true Neapolitan; Meneghino, the piratical warrior, Milanese; the drunkard Rugantino, a Roman; the nervous rich merchant Pantalone, a Venetian; while the maid Colombina belongs to all. To spring the plot there would be lovers (*innamorati*) – unmasked to remind us that love is life.

Arte doesn't mean art, but a guild; these companies were made up of professional players. The term was invented by Goldoni (*Arlecchino, servitore di due padrone*) in 1745; in the 1500s the companies were often known as the *commedia mercenaria* – they would hit town, set up a stage and start their show within the hour. Cultured Italians deplored the way the 'mercenary' shows were driving out serious drama, written by scholarly amateurs in the princely courts. In the repressive climate, caught between the Inquisition and the Spanish, a culture of ideas survived only in free Venice. Theatre retreated into humorous popular entertainment, but even then the Italians found a way to say what was on their minds. A new stock character appeared, the menacing but slow-witted *Capitano*, who always spoke with a Spanish accent; and the Italians learned from the French, using Arlecchino to satirize the hated Charles V – playing on the pronunciation of the names *harlequin* and *Charles Quint*.

Arlecchino may come from Oneta, a village north of Bergamo, but he carries a proud lineage that goes back to the ancient Greeks and Romans. From his character and appearance, theatre historians trace him back to the antique *planipedes*, comic mimes with shaven heads (everyone knew Arlecchino wore his nightcap to cover his baldness). He's been linked to German and Scandinavian mythological tricksters too, and it's been claimed that his patched costume is that of a Sufi dervish. No doubt he had a brilliant career all through the Middle Ages, but it was only in the 1500s that he took the form of the Arlecchino we know. At that time young rustics from the valleys of Bergamo would go to Venice, Milan and other cities to get work as porters (*facchini*). They all seemed to be named Johnny – *Zanni* in dialect, which became the common term for any of the clownish roles in the plays; hence our word 'zany'.

The name of Arlecchino was a French contribution: at the court of Henri III, an Italian actor who played the role became a protégé of a Monsieur de Harlay, and people started calling him Harlequin. He became a stock role, the most beloved of the *commedia dell'arte* clown masks: simple-minded and easily frightened, an incorrigible prankster, a fellow as unstable as his motley dress. His foil was usually another servant, the Neapolitan Puricinella/Punchinella – Punch – more serious and some-times boastful, but still just as much of a buffoon. Try to imagine them together on stage, and you'll get something rather like Laurel and Hardy. No doubt they have always gone through the world together, and we can hope they always will.

That Etruscan Smile

Everything about the Etruscans is mysterious, and that's the way they liked it: their everyday lives were wrapped in magic and superstition, and we know only superficial details of their religion in the *Fanum Voltumnae* or sacred wood, around Viterbo, where no outsider was allowed. No-one is sure of their origins, though they seem to have come from western Anatolia; their sudden decline and eventual complete disappearance after the 4th century BC was just as shadowy and unaccountable.

What the Etruscans did leave behind are portraits of themselves, some of the most remarkable achievements of ancient art. They weren't the most original of artists, but every style that came from Greece was given an Etruscan twist. Even more than the Greeks, they had a talent for capturing expression and character on every level, from the astute, gentlemanly *Orator* in the Florence museum, to the happy, worldly couples lounging on their stone sarcophagi, the terracotta heads of children in the Villa Giulia and the grinning, rosy-cheeked grotesques that peer out from all Etruscan decoration. Usually they are smiling, a faraway mysterious smile. Battered by dour Romans on one side and crazed Celts on the other, the Etruscans faded away – unless they went right into the ground, like the lost people that became the Irish fairies. But their presence is still felt in central Italy, especially its art: the Romans and the other Italic nations learned much about art from the Greeks, but when you look at their painting – at Pompeii, in Naples, or in Nero's Golden House – it will be clear that something essential, something in the soul, was their heritage from Etruria.

The thread of it has never been lost in all the centuries since. When you get to know Etruscan art, you'll see subtle reflections of it in everything that came after, from Botticelli's paintings to Mussolini's post offices. From the grotesques, revived by Raphael and now gazing out at us from the cornices of old buildings everywhere – one gets the feeling that somehow those mysterious Etruscans are still with us.

Fungus Fever

If you've brought the children, ignore their scoffing. That's not spaghetti with dirt on your plate, but *spaghetti al tartufo*, with truffles, the most prized gourmet delicacy in Italy: earthy, aromatic, aphrodisiac. It's true they're not much to look at, subterranean lumpy *funghi*, bulbous tubers that consent to sprout only in certain corners of France and Italy with the proper calcareous soils, oak trees and exposure. Per ounce these ugly lumps are the most expensive comestibles in the world; luckily, a little truffle goes a long way. Two types of truffles are considered outstanding – the black, found in southwest France and in the Apennines; and the white, found in the Alba and Asti area of Piedmont. The white is the most prized, being rarer, and so more expensive. It's a creamy colour, smooth and irregularly shaped, and can vary in size from that of a walnut to something more like a football. Truffles actually have very little intrinsic taste – it's their power to impart flavour to other foods that makes them so valued. They are usually eaten raw, sliced very finely over meat, fish or pasta – or in stuffing for meat, poultry or game.

Truffles are so expensive because they are so hard to track down. An aura of mystery hangs over their birth; according to legend they are spawned by lightning bolts zapping through oak groves. Prices have led to experiments in cultivation, but most truffles are still brought to market by truffle hunters with keen-nosed truffle hounds; unlike the French, who use pigs, the Italians swear by dogs, suckled on teats rubbed with truffle juice.

The truffle season is short – from October until the snows fall around Christmas. During this time daily auctions take place in Asti and Alba in the wee hours of the morning, when the secretive truffle-hunters arrive to sell the night's harvest (do truffles smell strongest at night, or is it that the best ones are always on someone else's property?). A walnut-sized *tartufo* can easily sell for L100,000. However, if you're given *tartufo* ice-cream, don't despair for the sanity of the Italian kitchen – it's made of cream and chocolate, and like French chocolate *truffes* just looks like its namesake.

Leaning Towers

It isn't always a subject the Italians like to discuss. They'll be happy to sell you as many plastic souvenirs as you like of the most celebrated of the species, in Pisa, but a mention of the dozens of other listing landmarks scattered around Italy makes them uneasy. Italians, of course, think of themselves as the most skilled engineers on this planet. They built the Roman roads and aqueducts, the Pantheon and the dome of St Peter's, the biggest in the world. They invented concrete. Their endless *autostrade* zoom through mile-long tunnels and skim over deep valleys on stilts, remarkable *tours de force* of engineering. They have built more railway tunnels, perhaps, than the rest of Europe put together. Why can't they keep their towers from drooping?

The answer may well be that they built them that way. For centuries there has been a dark undercurrent of thought on the subject that claims Pisa's tower was meant to lean. Goethe thought so, and architects who carefully measured the foundation stones came to the same conclusion. Over a hundred years ago a Professor Goodyear exposed the whole business as 'symmetrophobia' – not fear of the symmetrical, but disdain for it. Italy's medieval master builders, not yet squeezed into the Renaissance straitjacket of monumental symmetry, could still be playful – witness the *parfait* stripes on so many cathedrals, or the floral print that covers Florence's Duomo.

The Italians of today do not like this explanation any better; they brusquely reject any suggestion that their ancestors could have been tempted away from the perpendicular on a whim. You can judge for yourself at Pisa – whose campanile would not look right without the tilt – or at the Garisenda and Asinelli towers of Bologna, a pair of elephantine monstrosities that seem ready to topple any minute. None of Venice's, except for the new St Mark's, are close to being straight; Ravenna has two that are even more precarious, and other examples can be seen at Rovigo and Rome. In Naples they have tilting domes – nothing intentional, but perhaps Providence's reminder that nothing around the Bay of Naples is allowed to stand forever.

Non-Leaning Towers

In most of Italy, when there are no billboards and power lines to block the view, you will see landscapes that have not changed since 1500. Long ago, Italian farmers began the job of making the country into one great formal garden, planting olives and vines in neat rows, and creating avenues of Lombardy poplars or parasol pines. Medieval designers added cities, towns and castles in constantly changing styles, each one complementary to those that came before. The basic feature in many parts of the rugged peninsula is the hill town, orderly and compact, its buildings draped carefully on a peak as if arranged there by a sculptor. By 1500, after 500 years of prosperity, the builders' work was done, and the Italian garden was perfect, cohesive and complete.

Visitors from over the Alps were impressed by the richness and size of Italian towns, and especially by their monumental urge to the vertical. By 1150 Italians were building towers on a scale unmatched until the American cities of the 1900s. Indeed, larger Italian cities had a Manhattanish aspect with hundreds of tall, square defence towers creating incredible skylines – as with skyscrapers, it soon became a matter of prestige among the baronial families to have the tallest; many reached over 200ft (60m). In those rough times the towers weren't just for show; city officials had to take constant complaints from neighbours about siege engines parked on the street, stray showers of boiling oil, and noisy, pitched battles keeping the children up at night. The *comuni* managed to get most of these towers pulled down by about 1350. The great bell-towers of the cathedrals and city halls survive, and they are usually still the tallest buildings in the city. To give some idea of how ambitiously Italy could build, here are the 10 tallest structures completed before the year 1500:

1. **Cremona**, Campanile, 113m (370ft)
2. **Florence**, Cathedral, 110m (364ft)
3. **Milan**, Cathedral, 107m (351ft)
4. **Siena**, Palazzo Pubblico, 103m (338ft)
5. **Venice**, Campanile, 101m (332ft)
6. **Bologna**, Torre Asinelli, 96m (318ft)
7. **Florence**, Palazzo Vecchio, 94m (308ft)
8. **Modena**,Ghirlandina, 84m (276ft)
9. **Verona**, Torre dei Lamberti, 83m (275ft)
10. **Florence**, Giotto's Campanile, 85m (280ft)

Pasta

Croton and Sybaris, among other Greek cities, take the credit for introducing the Italians to their future hearts' delight. *Makaria*, a small, cylindrical form of pasta – perhaps the original *macaroni* – was eaten at funeral banquets; by 600 BC the Sybarites had invented the rolling pin and were making the equivalent of *tagliatelle* and maybe even *lasagne*. Not yet having tomatoes, they were unable to perfect the concept, but in a nation that has trouble baking a decent loaf of bread this delicious and eminently practical new staple found a warm welcome everywhere. Pasta's triumphal march northwards finally slowed to a halt in the rice paddies and treacherous *polenta* morasses of Lombardy; everywhere else it remains in firm control of the country's menus. Pasta does have its cultural ramifications. The artists of the futurist movement declared war on spaghetti, and many of today's Italian *nouveaux riches* wouldn't be caught dead ordering pasta in a restaurant (while their counterparts in northern Europe and America wax ever more enthusiastic about it).

Do you think that pasta is all the same? Well, so do millions of Italians, though an equal number revel in the incredible variety of pasta forms and fashions; in your travels you'll find the same mixture of flour and water turned into broad *pappardelle* and narrow *linguini* ('tiny tongues'), stuffed delights like *ravioli* and *tortellini*, and regional specialities like Puglian *orecchiette* ('little ears'). Other inviting forms, among the 400 or so known shapes, include *vermicelli* ('little worms'), *lumacconi* ('slugs'), *bavette* ('dribbles'), and *strozzapreti* ('priest chokers'). But even these fail to satisfy the nation's culinary whims, and every so often one of the big pasta companies commissions a big-name fashion designer to come up with a new form.

The Pinocchio Complex

The Italians, much as they adore their *bambini*, have produced but one classic of children's literature, the story of a wooden puppet who must pass through trials and tribulations before he can become a real boy – a blessing to his father in his old age.

Since the Risorgimento the Italian government has been a bit of a Pinocchio to the country that painfully carved it out of wood, admittedly half-petrified and half-rotten from the start. Each ring of the thick trunk told a dire tale of defeat and tyranny, corruption, papal misgovernment, foreign rule and betrayal. From this piece of flotsam the Italians created a new creature, a national state that sits in the class of real governments like an exasperating puppet, the bad boy of the EU, with more violations of its trade rules than any other nation. Every day its parliament is in session, its nose grows a little bit longer. With its creaky bureaucracy, unpredictable and not blessed with the soundest of judgements, it is constantly led astray – by the Mafia, power-hungry cabals of 'freemasons', Mussolinis, southern landowners, popes, Jesuits and whale-sized special interests that threaten to gobble it down whole. The parties that make up its *Commedia dell'Arte* coalitions, like flimsy wooden limbs and joints, are liable to trip up or fly off at any moment, making the poor thing collapse (something that since 1946 has occurred on the average of once every 11 months).

Just as Pinocchio is somehow able to walk without strings, so Italy functions with remarkable smoothness, and even prospers. As Europe grows ever closer together, having a wooden-headed political system becomes rather embarrassing. Constitutional reform, with the 1993 referendum that changed the electoral system, may prove the biggest threat to this puppet's career. And, with the revelations of the last few years, Italians are beginning to interest themselves in the all-important question of who, all this time, has been pulling the strings.

Italian Culture

Cinema

After the Second World War, when Italy was at its lowest ebb, when it was financially and culturally bankrupt, when its traditional creativity in painting, architecture and music seemed to have dried up, along came a handful of Italian directors who invented a whole new language of cinema. Neorealism was a response to the fictions propagated by years of Fascism; it was also a response to the lack of movie-making equipment after the Romans, their eyes suddenly opened after a decade of deception and mindless 'White Telephone' comedies, pillaged and sacked Cinecittà in 1943. Stark, unsentimental, often shot in bleak locations and featuring non-professional actors, the genre took shape with directors like Roberto Rossellini (*Rome, Open City*, 1945), Vittorio de Sica (*Bicycle Thieves*, 1948) and Luchino Visconti (*The Earth Trembles*, 1948).

Although neorealism continued to influence Italian cinema (Rossellini's films with Ingrid Bergman, like *Europa 51* and *Stromboli*, Fellini's classic *La Strada* with Giulietta Masina and Anthony Quinn, Antonioni's *The Scream*), Italian directors began to go off in their own directions. The post-War period was the golden age of Italian cinema, when Italy's Hollywood, Cinecittà, produced scores of films every year. Like the artists of the Age of Mannerism, a new generation of individualistic (or egoistic) directors created works that needed no signature, ranging from Sergio Leone's ultra-popular kitsch westerns to the often jarring films of the Marxist poet Pasolini (*Accattone, The Decameron*). This was the period of Visconti's *The Damned*, Antonioni's *Blow Up*, Lina Wertmuller's *Seven Beauties*, De Sica's *Neapolitan Gold*, Bertolucci's *The Conformist*, and the classics of the *maestro* Federico Fellini – *I Vitelloni, La Dolce Vita, Juliet of the Spirits, The Clowns, Satyricon*.

In the seventies the cost of making films soared and the industry went into recession. Increasingly directors went abroad or sought out actors with international appeal to help finance their films (Bertolucci's *Last Tango in Paris* with Marlon Brando and *1900* with Donald Sutherland; the overripe Franco Zeffirelli's *Taming of the Shrew* with Taylor and Burton; Visconti's *Death in Venice*). Fellini was one of the few who managed to stay home (*Roma, Amarcord*, and later *Casanova* – although admittedly with Donald Sutherland in the lead role – *City of Women, The Ship Sails On, Orchestra Rehearsal* and *Intervista*, a film about Cinecittà itself).

Although funds for films became even scarcer in the eighties, new directors appeared to recharge Italian cinema, often with a fresh lyrical realism and sensitivity. Bright stars of the decade included Ermanno Olmi (the singularly beautiful *Tree of the Wooden Clogs* and *Cammina, Cammina*), Giuseppe Tornatore's sentimental and nostalgic *Cinema Paradiso* (1988), Paolo and Vittorio Taviani (*Padre Padrone, Night of the Shooting Stars, Kaos* and *Good Morning Babilonia*), Francesco Rosi (*Christ Stopped at Eboli, Three Brothers, Carmen* and *Cronaca di una Morte Annunciata*), and Nanni Moretti (*La Messa è Finita*), unfortunately rarely seen outside of festivals and film clubs, while Zeffirelli (*La Traviata*) and Bertolucci (*1900, The Last Emperor*) continued to represent Italy in the world's moviehouses. Comedy found new life in Mario Monticelli's hilarious *Speriamo che sia Femmina* and in Bruno Bozzetto, whose animation features (especially *Allegro Non Troppo*, a satire of Disney's *Fantasia*) are a scream.

The nineties served up fairly thin gruel, a recession of inspiration to go with the economy. Worthy exceptions have been *Il Ladro dei Bambini* (1992) by Gianni Amelio, *Mediterraneo* (1991) by Gabriele Salvatores, about Italian soldiers marooned on a Greek island, Nanni Moretti's travelogue to the Ionian islands, *Caro Diario* (1994), Franco Zeffirelli's *Hamlet* (1990), a surprise both for casting Mel Gibson in the leading role and actually setting the film in 12th century Denmark, and *Il Postino* (1995), directed by Michael Radford, a very Italian story about the relationship of a local postman with the poet Pablo Neruda, exiled on an Italian island.

This was also the decade that Fellini spun his final reel. Although critics at home and abroad sometimes complained that he repeated himself in his last films (*Ginger and Fred* and *La Voce della Luna*, 1990), his loyal fans eagerly awaited each new instalment of his personal fantasy, his alternative hyper-Italy that exists on the other side of the looking glass in the gossamer warp of the silver screen. The last director regularly to use Cinecittà ('Cinecittà is not my home; I just live there'), his demise may well bring about the end of Rome's pretensions as Hollywood on the Mediterranean.

In the past few years, Bernardo Bertolucci has returned to the scene with *Stealing Beauty* (1996), a lush Tuscan coming of age drama, and *Besieged* (1998) the story of the romance between an Italian composer and an African political refugee, filmed in Rome. But all in all the most acclaimed recent Italian film has been Roberto Benigni's unlikely comedy on the Holocaust in *La Vita e Bella* (1999).

Italian films are windows of the nation's soul, but if you don't understand Italian you may want to see them at home, where you have the advantage of subtitles. English language films in Italy rarely receive the same courtesy, however – Italians like their movies dubbed. Check listings for films labelled '*versione originale*' – you're bound to find a few in Rome (*see* p.822), Milan (*see* p.230), Bologna (*see* p.533), and often in other big cities as well. There are also Italy's film festivals (where films tend to be subtitled); the most important one is in Venice (last week of August to first week of September); Florence hosts a documentary festival in December.

Literature

Few countries have as grand a literary tradition – even Shakespeare made extensive use of Italian stories for his plots. Besides all the great Latin authors and poets of ancient Rome, the peninsula has produced a small shelf of world classics in the Italian language; try to read a few before you come to Italy, or bring them along to read on the train. (All the books listed below are available in English translations, and may often be found in the English sections of Italian bookstores.) Once you've visited some of the settings of Dante's *Divine Comedy*, and come to know at least historically some of the inhabitants of the *Inferno*, *Purgatorio* and *Paradiso*, the old classic becomes even more fascinating. Dante (1265–1321) was one of the first poets in Europe to write in the vernacular, and in doing so incorporated a good deal of topographical material from his 13th-century world.

His literary successor, Petrarch (1304–74), has been called by many 'the first modern man'; in his poetry the first buds of humanism were born, deeply thought and felt, complex, subtle and fascinating today as ever (his *Canzoniere* is widely available in English). The third literary deity in Italy's late-Medieval/early-Renaissance trinity is Boccaccio (1313–75), whose imagination, humour and realism is most apparent in his 'Human Comedy', the *Decameron*, a hundred stories 'told' by a group of young aristocrats who fled into the countryside from Florence to escape the plague of 1348. Boccaccio's detached point of view had the effect of disenchanting Dante's ordered medieval cosmos, clearing the way for the renaissance of the secular novel.

Dante, Petrarch and Boccaccio exerted a tremendous influence over literary Europe, and in the 15th and 16th centuries a new crop of writers continued in the vanguard – Machiavelli in political thought (*The Prince*), though he also wrote two of the finest plays of the Renaissance (*Mandragola* and *Clizia*); Ariosto in the genre of knightly romance (*Orlando Furioso*, the antecedent of Spenser's *Faerie Queene*, among others); Cellini in autobiography; Vasari in art criticism and history (*The Lives of the Artists*); Castiglione in etiquette, gentlemanly arts and behaviour (*The Courtier*); Alberti in architecture and art theory (*Della Pintura*); Leonardo da Vinci in a hundred different subjects (the *Notebook*, etc.); even Michelangelo had time to write a book of sonnets, now translated into English. Other works include the writings and intriguing play (*The Candlemaker*) of the great philosopher and heretic Giordano Bruno (perhaps the only person to be excommunicated from three different churches); the risqué, scathing writings of Aretino, the 'Scourge of Princes'; the poetry and songs of Lorenzo de' Medici; and the *Commentaries* by Pope Pius II (Enea Silvio), a rare view into the life, opinions and times of one of the most accomplished Renaissance men, not to mention the only autobiography ever written by a pope.

Baroque Italy was a quieter place, dampened by the censorship of the Inquisition. The Venetians kept the flame alight with Casanova's picaresque *Life*, the tales of Carlo Gozzi, and the plays of Goldoni. Modern Italian literature has an official birthdate – the publication in 1827 of Alessandro Manzoni's *I Promessi Sposi* ('The Betrothed'), which not only spoke with sweeping humanity to the concerns of pre-Risorgimento Italy, but spoke in its language – an everyday Italian that nearly everyone could understand, no matter what their regional dialect; the novel went on to become a symbol of the aspiration of national unity. The next writer with the power to capture the turbulent emotions of his time was Gabriele D'Annunzio, whose life of daredevil patriotism and superman cult contrast with the lyricism of his poetry and some of his novels – still widely read in Italy. Meanwhile, and much more influentially, Pirandello, the philosophical Sicilian playwright and novelist obsessed with absurdity, changed the international vocabulary of drama before the Second World War.

The post-War era saw the appearance of neorealism in fiction as well as in cinema, and the classics, though available in English, are among the easiest books to read in Italian – Cesare Pavese's *La Luna e i Falò* (The Moon and the Bonfires), Carlo Levi's tragic *Cristo si è Fermato a Eboli* (Christ Stopped at Eboli), or Vittorini's *Conversazione in Sicilia*. Other acclaimed works of the post-War era include *The Garden of the Finzi-Contini* (about a Jewish family in Fascist Italy) by Giorgio Bassani, and another book

Non è questo 'l terren, ch' i' toccai pria?
Non è questo il mio nido,
Ove nudrito fui sí dolcemente?
Non è questa la patria in ch' io mi fido,
Madre benigna e pia,
Che copre l'un e l'altro mio parente?
Per Dio, questo la mente
Talor vi mova; e con pietà guardate
Le lagrime del popol doloroso,
Che sol da voi riposo,
Dopo Dio, spera: e, pur che voi mostriate
Segno, alcun di pietate,
Vertú contra furore
Prenderà l'arme; e fia 'l combatter corto;
Ché l'antiquo valore
Ne l' italici cor non è ancor morto.

Petrarch (1304–74)

Is not this precious earth my native land?
And is not this the nest
From which my tender wings were taught to fly?
And is not this soil upon whose breast,
Loving and soft, faithful and true and fond,
My father and my gentle mother lie?
'For love of God,' I cry,
Some time take thought of your humanity
And spare your people all their tears and grief!
From you they seek relief
Next after God. If in your eyes they see
Some marks of sympathy,
Against this mad disgrace
They will arise, the combat will be short
For the stern valour of our ancient race
Is not yet dead in the Italian heart.

trans. William Dudley Foulke LL D (1915)

set during the Fascist era, *That Awful Mess on Via Merulana* by Carlo Emilio Gadda; then there's the Sicilian classic that became famous around the world, as well as being made into a classic film – *The Leopard* by Giuseppe di Lampedusa.

The late Italo Calvino, perhaps more than any other Italian writer in the past two decades, enjoyed a large international following – his *If on a Winter's Night a Traveller*, *Italian Folktales*, *Marcovaldo* and *The Baron in the Trees* were all immediately translated into English; perhaps the best of them is *Invisible Cities*, an imaginary dialogue between Marco Polo and Kublai Khan. Much maligned, Sicily continued to produce some of Italy's best literature, from the pens of Leonardo Sciascia and Gesualdo Bufalino. The current celebrity of Italian literature is of course Umberto Eco, professor of semiotics at Bologna University, whose *The Name of the Rose* kept readers all over the world at the edge of their seats over the murders of a handful of 14th-century monks in a remote Italian monastery, while magically evoking, better than many historians, all the political and ecclesiastical turmoil of the period.

Italy has inspired countless of her visitors, appearing as a setting in more novels, poems and plays than tongue can tell. There is also a long list of non-fiction classics, some of which make fascinating reading and are readily available in most bookshops: Goethe's *Italian Journey*, Ruskin's *The Stones of Venice*, D. H. Lawrence's *Etruscan Places* and *Twilight in Italy*, Hilaire Belloc's *The Path to Rome*, Norman Douglas' *Old Calabria*, James/Jan Morris' Venice, Mary McCarthy's *The Stones of Florence* and *Venice Observed*, and many others, including the famously over-the-top travellers' accounts of Edward Hutton and the ever-entertaining H. V. Morton. For the Italian point of view from the outside looking in, read the classic *The Italians* by the late Luigi Barzini, former correspondent for the *Corriere della Sera* in London.

Music and Opera

Italy has contributed as much to Western music as any country – and perhaps a little more. It was an Italian monk, Guido d'Arezzo, who devised the musical scale; it was a Venetian printer, Ottaviano Petrucci, who invented a method of printing music with movable type in 1501 – an industry Italian printers monopolized for years (which is why we play *allegro* and not *schnell*). Italy also gave us the piano, originally the pianoforte because unlike the harpsichord you could play both soft and loud, and the accordion, invented in the Marche, and the violins of the Guarneri and Stradivarius of Cremona, setting a standard for the instrument that has never been equalled. But Italy is most famous as the mother of opera, in many ways the most Italian of arts.

Italian composers first came into their own in the 14th century, led by the blind Florentine Landini, whose *Ecco la Primavera* is one of the first Italian compositions to come down to us. Although following international trends introduced by musicians from France and the Low Countries, musicologists note from the start a special love of melody, even in the earliest Italian works, as well as a preference for vocal music.

Landini was followed by the age of the *frottolas* (secular verses accompanied by lutes), especially prominent in the court of Mantua. The *frottolas* were forerunners of the *madrigal*, the greatest Italian musical invention during the Renaissance. Although sung in three or six parts, the text of the madrigals was given serious consideration, and was sung to be understood; at the same time church music had become so polyphonically rich and sumptuous (most notoriously at St Mark's in Venice) that it drowned out the words of the Mass. Many melodies used were from secular and often bawdy songs, and the bishops at the Council of Trent (1545–63) seriously considered banning music from the liturgy. The day was saved by the Roman composers, led by Palestrina, whose solemn, simple but beautiful melodies set a standard for all subsequent composers.

Two contrasting strains near the end of the 16th century led to the birth of opera: the Baroque love of spectacle and the urge to make everything, at least on the surface, more beautiful, more elaborate, more showy. Musically there were the lavish Florentine *intermedii*, performed on special occasions between the acts of plays; the *intermedii* used elaborate sets and costumes, songs, choruses and dances to set a mythological scene. At the same time, in Florence, a group of humanist intellectuals who called themselves the 'Camerata' came to the conclusion from their classical studies that ancient Greek drama was not spoken, but sung, and took it upon themselves to try to recreate this pure and classical form. One of their chief theorists was Galileo's father Vincenzo, who studied Greek, Turkish and Moorish music and advocated the clear enunciation of the words, as opposed to the Venetian tendency to merge words and music as a single rich unit of sound.

One of the first results of the Camerata's debates was court musician Jacopo Peri's *L'Euridice*, performed in Florence in 1600. Peri used a kind of singing speech (recitative) to tell the story, interspersed with a few melodic songs. No one, it seems, asked for an encore; opera had to wait a few years until the Duchess of Mantua asked her court composer, Claudio Monteverdi (1567–1643), to compose something like what she had heard in Florence. Monteverdi went far beyond Peri, bringing in a large orchestra, designing elegant sets, adding dances and many more melodic songs, or arias. His classic *L'Orfeo* (1607), still heard today, and *L'Arianna* (unfortunately lost but for fragments) were the first operatic 'hits'. He moved on to bigger audiences in Venice, which soon had 11 opera houses. After he died, Naples took over top opera honours, gaining special renown for its clear-toned *castrati*.

Other advances were developing in the more pious atmosphere of Rome, where Corelli was busily perfecting the concerto form and composing his famous *Christmas Concerto*. In Venice, Vivaldi expanded the genre by composing some four hundred concerti for whatever instruments happened to be played in the orchestra of orphaned girls where he was concert-master.

The 18th century saw the sonata form perfected by harpsichord master Domenico Scarlatti. Opera was rid of some of its Baroque excesses and a division was set between serious works and the comic *opera buffa*; Pergolesi (1710–36; his *Il Flaminio* was the basis for Stravinsky's *Pulcinella*) and Cimarosa (1749–1801) were the most sought-after composers, while the now infamous Salieri, antagonist of Mozart, charmed the court of Vienna. Italian composers held sway throughout Europe; with others, like Sammartini, who helped develop the modern symphony, they contributed more than is generally acknowledged today towards the founding of modern music.

Italy innovated less in the 19th century; at this time most of its musical energies were devoted to opera, becoming the reviving nation's clearest and most widely appreciated medium of self-expression. All of the most popular Italian operas were written in the 19th and early 20th century, most of them by the 'Big Five' – Bellini, Donizetti, Rossini, Verdi and Puccini. For Italians, Verdi (1813–1901) is supreme, the national idol even in his lifetime, whose rousing operas were practically the battle hymns of the Risorgimento. Verdi, more than anyone else, re-established Italy on the musical map; his works provided Italy's melodic answer to the ponderous turbulence of Richard Wagner. After Verdi, Puccini held the operatic stage, though not entirely singlehandedly; the later 19th century gave us a number of composers best remembered for only one opera: Leoncavallo's *Pagliacci*, Mascagni's *Cavalleria Rusticana*, Cilea's *Adriana Lecouvreur*, and many others down to obscure composers like Giordano, whose *Fedora*, famous for being the only opera with bicycles on stage, is revived frequently in his hometown of Fóggia.

Of more recent Italian and Italian-American composers, there's Ottorino Respighi (whose works were among the few 20th-century productions that the great Toscanini deigned to direct) and Gian Carlo Menotti, surely the best loved, not only for his operas but for founding the Spoleto Festival. Later there were the innovative post-War composers Luigi Nono and Luciano Berio, two respected names in contemporary academic music.

Next to all of this big-league culture, however, there survive remnants of Italy's traditional music – the pungent tunes of Italian bagpipes (*zampogna*), the ancient instrument of the Apennine shepherds, often heard in the big cities (especially in the South) at Christmas time; the lively *tarantellas* of Puglia; country accordion music, the fare of many a rural festa; and the great song tradition of the country's music capital, Naples, the cradle of everyone's favourite cornball classics, but also of many haunting, passionate melodies of tragedy and romance that are rarely heard abroad – or, to be honest, in Italy itself these days. Naples now prides itself on being the capital of Mediterranean rock 'n' roll, a spurious claim, and not too impressive even if it were true. Listen for yourself; on the *bancarelle* in the street markets of Naples you'll have ample opportunity to audition a wide range of locally produced cassettes and see if anything catches your fancy. Italian pop music climbs to the top of its modest plateau every February at the San Remo song festival, the national run-off for the Eurovision Song Contest and just as hilariously tacky; the likes of *Volare* are nowhere to be seen.

Opera season in Italy runs roughly from November to May. Don't limit your explorations to the prestigious La Scala in Milan. The San Carlo in Naples is equally old and impressive, and La Fenice in Venice hopefully will be impressive once more (when her restoration is complete) – both in cities with a longer and more intense operatic tradition. The Teatro dell'Opera in Rome and the Teatro Comunale in Florence can both put on excellent and innovative productions too. On the next rung down (in size and finances, though not necessarily in quality) are the houses in Parma, Trieste, Genoa, Bergamo, Turin, Modena, Bari and Fóggia. Summer festivals are an excellent place to hear music.

Food and Drink

In Rome people spend most of their time having lunch. And they do it
very well – Rome is unquestionably the lunch capital of the world.

Fran Lebowitz, *Metropolitan Life*, 1978

There are those who eat to live and those who live to eat, and then there are the Italians, for whom food has an almost religious significance, unfathomably linked with love, *la Mamma*, and tradition. In this singular country, where millions of otherwise sane people spend much of their waking hours worrying about their digestion, standards both at home and in the restaurants are understandably high. Few Italians are gluttons, but all are experts on what is what in the kitchen; to serve a meal that is not properly prepared and more than a little complex is tantamount to an insult.

For the visitor this national culinary obsession comes as an extra bonus to the senses – along with Italy's remarkable sights, music, and the warm sun on your back, you can enjoy some of the best tastes and smells the world can offer, prepared daily in Italy's kitchens and fermented in its countless wine cellars. Eating *all'Italiana* is not only delicious and wholesome, but now undeniably trendy. Foreigners flock here to learn the secrets of Italian cuisine and the even more elusive secret of how the Italians can live surrounded by such delights and still fit into their sleek Armani trousers.

Restaurant Generalities

Breakfast (*colazione*) in Italy is no lingering affair, but an early morning wake-up shot to the brain: a *cappuccino* (*espresso* with hot foamy milk, often sprinkled with chocolate – incidentally first thing in the morning is the only time of day at which any self-respecting Italian will touch the stuff), a *caffè latte* (white coffee) or a *caffè lungo* (a generous portion of *espresso*), accompanied by a croissant-type roll, called a *cornetto* or *briosca*, or a fancy pastry. This repast can be consumed in any bar and repeated during the morning as often as necessary. Breakfast in most Italian hotels seldom represents great value.

Lunch (*pranzo*), generally served around 1pm, is the most important meal of the day for the Italians, with a minimum of a first course (*primo piatto* – any kind of pasta dish, broth or soup, or rice dish or pizza), a second course (*secondo piatto* – a meat dish, accompanied by a *contorno* or side dish – a vegetable, salad, or potatoes usually), followed by fruit or dessert and coffee. You can, however, begin with a platter of *antipasti* – the appetizers Italians do so brilliantly, ranging from warm seafood delicacies, to raw ham (*prosciutto crudo*), *salami* in a hundred varieties, lovely vegetables, savoury toasts, olives, pâté and many many more. There are restaurants that specialise in *antipasti*, and they usually don't take it amiss if you decide to forget the pasta and meat and just nibble on these scrumptious hors-d'œuvres (though in the end it may well cost more than a full meal). Most Italians accompany their meal with wine and mineral water – *acqua minerale*, with or without bubbles (*con* or *senza gas*), which supposedly aids digestion – concluding their meals with a *digestivo* liqueur.

Cena, the **evening meal,** is usually eaten around 8pm – earlier in the north and later in the south. This is much the same as *pranzo* although lighter, without the pasta; a *pizza* and beer, eggs or a fish dish. In restaurants, however, they offer all the courses, so if you have only a sandwich for lunch you can have a full meal in the evening.

In Italy the various terms for types of **restaurants** – *ristorante, trattoria* or *osteria* – have been confused. A *trattoria* or *osteria* can be just as elaborate as a restaurant, though rarely is a *ristorante* as informal as a traditional *trattoria*. Unfortunately the old habit of posting menus and prices in the windows has fallen from fashion, so it's often difficult to judge variety or prices. Invariably the least expensive eating place is the *vino e cucina,* a simple establishment serving simple cuisine for simple everyday prices. It is essential to remember that the fancier the fittings, the fancier the **bill,** though neither of these points has anything at all to do with the quality of the food. If you're uncertain, do as you would at home – look for lots of locals.

People who haven't visited Italy for years and have fond memories of eating full meals for under a pound will be amazed at how much **prices** have risen; though in some respects eating out in Italy is still a bargain, especially when you figure out how much all that wine would have cost you at home. In many places you'll often find restaurants offering a *menu turistico* – full, set meals of usually meagre inspiration for a reasonable set price. More imaginative chefs often offer a *menu degustazione* – a set-price gourmet meal that allows you to taste their daily specialities and seasonal dishes. Both of these are cheaper than if you had ordered the same food *à la carte.*

As the pace of modern urban life militates against traditional lengthy homecooked repasts with the family, followed by a siesta, alternatives to sit-down meals have mushroomed. Many office workers now behave much as their counterparts else-where in Europe and consume a rapid snack at lunchtime, returning home after a busy day to throw together some pasta and salad in the evenings.

The original Italian fast food alternative, a buffet known as the 'hot table' (*tavola calda*) is becoming harder to find among the international and made-in-Italy fast food franchises; bars often double as *paninotecas* (which make sandwiches to order, or serve *tramezzini,* little sandwiches on plain, square white bread that are much better than they look); outlets selling *pizza* by the slice (*al taglio*) are common in city centres. At any grocer's (*alimentari*) or market (*mercato*) you can buy the materials for countryside or hotel-room picnics; some will make the sandwiches for you.

Regional Specialities

What comes as a surprise to many visitors is the tremendous regional diversity at the table; often next to nothing on the menu looks familiar, once disguised by a local or dialect name. Expect further mystification, as many Italian chefs have wholeheart-edly embraced the concept of nouvelle cuisine, or rather *nuova cucina,* and are constantly inventing dishes with even more names.

In **Northern Italy,** look for heavier dishes prepared with butter and cream. *Pasta all'uovo* and *risotto* are favourite first courses, while game dishes, liver, *bollito misto* (mixed boiled meats), *fritto misto* (mixed fried meats), sausages and seafood appear as main courses. **Piemonte** is a gourmet region, particularly renowned for its white truffles and cheeses. It also serves up the unique *bagna cauda*, a rich hot dip made with butter, olive oil, garlic, anchovies and cream, eaten with winter salad, *cardi* (a raw artichoke-like thistle), or roasted meats. **Liguria**'s cuisine, on the other hand, matches the criteria of the perfect Mediterranean diet – the *cucina povera* of olive oil, lots of vegetables, a little cheese and wine, and seafood. Liguria also gave the world *pesto*, that tangy, rich, addictive sauce of basil, pine nuts, garlic, olive oil and cheese, usually served with the local *trenette* pasta. The **Lombards** again like their food substantial: *antipasti* include meats (raw *carpaccio*, or *bresaola* – dried salt beef served with lemon, oil and rocket); popular *primi* are saffron-tinted *risotto alla milanese* or pasta stuffed with pumpkin and cheese; meat courses include classics such as *ossobuco alla milanese* (veal knuckle braised with white wine and tomatoes) and the hearty regional pork and cabbage stew, *cazzoela* or *cassuoela* (two of 25 different spellings). If you're really hungry, plump for brick-heavy *polenta*, a cake of yellow maize flour, with various sauces – a Lombard classic is *polenta e osei* (topped with roast birds); another, perhaps fortunately rare, is *stu'a'd'asnin cünt la pulenta* (stewed donkey with polenta).

In the **Veneto**, a typical seashore meal might include oysters from Chioggia or *sarde in saor* (marinated sardines) followed by the classic *risi e bisi* (rice and peas, cooked with Parma ham and Parmesan) or Venice's favourite pasta, *bigoli in salsa* (thick spaghetti, served with a piquant onion, butter and anchovy sauce). *Secondi* range from *fegato alla veneziana* (basically liver and onions) to *seppie alla veneziana* (cuttle-fish in its own ink); in Vicenza try *baccalà alla vicentina*, salt cod cooked with onions, cheese and anchovies. Inland, the rivers yield fish for the famous *brodetto di pesce* (fish soup), and *anguilla* or *bisato in umido* (eel stew). The province is also renowned for its *radicchio*, red chicory, and its white asparagus in springtime. The further north or east you go, the more ethnic the cuisine. Towards the **Trentino-Adige** the cooking displays hearty Austrian influences: goulash and smoked meats with rye bread, and the ubiquitous *speck*, a chewy, dry smoked ham. Desserts in **Friuli** are an epiphany: poppyseed strudel, Hungarian-style *rigojanci* (whipped cream and chocolate) or Slovenian-style *gibanica* (ricotta, honey, poppyseeds and pinenuts).

Emilia-Romagna ranks as Italy's gourmet region *par excellence*, the land of delicious *tortellini* and *lasagne*, Parmesan cheese, Parma ham, balsamic vinegar and a hundred other delicacies. *A panzu pina u s'ragiona mej*, 'You think best with a full belly', they say in the region. A typical *antipasto* would be a selection of *salumi* (cured pork) cuts that might include *mortadella* or *culatello* – tenderest pig's bottom. Pasta is the classic *primo*: *tortelli* (or *anolini*, in Parma, or *cappelletti*) filled with pork, ham, *mortadella* and Parmesan; or *tortellini d'erbetta* filled with herbs and *ricotta*, served with melted butter and freshly grated Parmesan. Alternatively there's *tagliatelle with ragù* (or *alla bolognese*) a smooth sauce of very finely minced pork and veal, prosciutto, onions, carrots, celery, butter and tomato – the lofty origin of the humble British 'spag bol' – or the third great Bolognese pasta dish, *lasagne*. Meat dishes can be heavy: *stracotto*, topside of beef, cooked for hours in wine with herbs and vegetables until it becomes incredibly tender, is one.

Central Italy is the land of beans and chick peas, game, tripe, salt cod (*baccalà*), *porchetta* (whole roast pork with rosemary), Florentine steaks, *saltimbocca alla romana* (veal scallops with ham and sage), and freshwater fish in interesting guises. Pasta seems to come in more interesting shapes than elsewhere, and it might come with rabbit or stewed boar. **Tuscan and Umbrian** cooking uses fresh, simple, high-quality ingredients flavoured with herbs and olive oil, and the local *porcini* mushrooms or truffles. Seafood is more prominent in the **Marches**, along with a fancier version of lasagne called *vincisgrassi*, and stuffed fried olives. Modern **Romans** are as adventurous at the table as their classical ancestors, and their capital is an excellent place to delve into any style of regional cooking, with dozens of restaurants from all over Italy. Lots of cooks in Roman restaurants come from the central Apennines, and you can easily get a taste of the **Abruzzo** there, a region known for its game dishes, sheep cheese, saffron, and the quality of its pasta. The **Molise** is much the same, but the Molisani are especially fond of hot red peppers.

The further south you go, the spicier things get, and the richer the puddings and cakes. **Southern Italy** is the land of homemade pasta, wonderful vegetables and superb seafood, often fried or laced with olive oil. Southern specialities are often seasoned with condiments like capers, anchovies, lemon juice, oregano, olives and fennel. **Campania's** favourites are simple: *pasta e fagioli* (pasta and beans) or *spaghetti alle vongole* (with baby clams); its seafood is exceptional – mussels (*zuppe di cozze*, mussels in a hot pepper sauce) appear frequently, along with oily fish like mackerel and sardines. Aubergines and courgettes make their way into many local dishes, especially *melanzane parmigiana* (aubergine baked with tomato and mozzarella) or *misto di frittura* (deep-fried potato, aubergine and courgette flowers). Naples, of course, invented both *pizza* and *spaghetti*; a genuine Neapolitan pizza cooked in a wood-fired brick oven is the archetypal local eating experience. *Calzoni*, half-moon envelopes of pizza dough, often filled with ham and cheese, and *mozzarella in carrozza*, a fried sandwich of cheese, are excellent street snacks.

Calabria and Basilicata boast the best swordfish anywhere, caught fresh from the Straits of Messina. In more prosperous **Puglia** you'll taste varieties of shellfish seen nowhere else: *fasulare*, small and roundish with tan-coloured shells, and *piedi di porco*, small rugged black shells; you'll even encounter *vongole imperiali*, giants among the clams. A favourite pasta dish is *orecchiette* ('little ears'), often served with greens on top. The local olive oil is dark and strong, close to that of Greece. Also look out for the unusually strongly flavoured *ricotta forte*.

Wine and Spirits

Italy is a country where everyday wine is cheaper than Coca-Cola or milk, and where nearly every family owns some vineyards or has some relatives who supply most of their daily needs – which are not great. Even though they live in one of the world's largest wine-growing countries, Italians imbibe relatively little, usually only at meals. But if Italy has an infinite variety of regional dishes, there is an equally bewildering

Italian Menu Vocabulary

Antipasti (Starters)

These treats can include almost anything; among the most common are:

antipasto misto mixed antipasto
bruschetta garlic toast (with olive oil and sometimes with tomatoes)
carciofi (sott'olio) artichokes (in oil)
frutti di mare seafood
funghi (trifolati) mushrooms (with anchovies, garlic and lemon)
gamberi ai fagioli prawns (shrimps) with white beans
mozzarella (in carrozza) soft cow/buffalo cheese (fried with bread in batter)
prosciutto (con melone) raw ham (with melon)
salsicce sausages

Minestre (Soups) and Pasta

agnolotti ravioli stuffed with meat
cappelletti small *ravioli*, often in broth
crespelle crêpes
frittata omelette
orecchiette ear-shaped pasta
panzerotti ravioli with *mozzarella*, anchovies and egg
pasta e fagioli soup with beans, bacon and tomatoes
pastina in brodo tiny pasta in broth
polenta cake or pudding of corn semolina
ravioli flat stuffed pasta parcels
spaghetti all'Amatriciana with spicy bacon, tomato, onion and chilli sauce
spaghetti alle vongole with clam sauce
stracciatella broth with eggs and cheese
tortellini crescent-shaped pasta parcels

Carne (Meat)

agnello lamb
anatra duck
arrosto misto mixed roast meats
bollito misto mixed boiled meats, or stew
braciola chop
brasato di manzo braised beef with vegetables
bresaola dried raw meat
carpaccio thinly sliced raw beef
cassoeula pork stew with cabbage
cervello brains
cervo venison
coniglio rabbit

costoletta/cotoletta chop
lumache snails
manzo beef
osso buco braised veal knuckle
pancetta bacon
piccione pigeon
pizzaiola beef in tomato and oregano sauce
pollo chicken
polpette meatballs
rognoni kidneys
saltimbocca veal, prosciutto and sage, in wine
scaloppine thin slices of veal sautéed in butter
stufato beef and vegetables braised in wine
tacchino turkey
vitello veal

Pesce (Fish)

acciughe or *alici* anchovies
anguilla eel
aragosta lobster
baccalà dried salt cod
bonito small tuna
calamari squid
cappe sante scallops
cozze mussels
fritto misto mixed fried fish
gamberetti shrimps
gamberi prawns
granchio crab
insalata di mare seafood salad
merluzzo cod
ostriche oysters
pesce spada swordfish
polipi/polpi octopus
sarde sardines
sogliola sole
squadro monkfish
stoccafisso wind-dried cod
tonno tuna
vongole small clams
zuppa di pesce fish in sauce or stew

Contorni (Side Dishes, Vegetables)

aglio garlic
asparagi asparagus
carciofi artichokes
cavolo cabbage
ceci chickpeas
cetriolo cucumber
cipolla onion
fagiolini French (green) beans
fave broad beans

funghi (porcini) mushrooms (boletus)
insalata (mista/verde) salad (mixed/green)
lenticchie lentils
melanzane aubergine
patate (fritte) potatoes (fried)
peperoncini hot chilli peppers
peperoni sweet peppers
peperonata stewed peppers
piselli (al prosciutto) peas (with ham)
pomodoro(i) tomato(es)
porri leeks
rucola rocket
verdure greens
zucca pumpkin
zucchini courgettes

Formaggio (Cheese)
bel paese soft white cow's cheese
cacio/caciocavallo pale yellow, sharp cheese
caprino goat's cheese
parmigiano parmesan cheese
pecorino sharp sheep's cheese
provolone sharp, tangy cheese;
  dolce is less strong
stracchino soft white cheese

Frutta (Fruit, Nuts)
albicocche apricots
ananas pineapple
arance oranges
banane bananas
ciliege cherries
cocomero watermelon
fragole strawberries
frutta di stagione fruit in season
lamponi raspberries
limone lemon
macedonia di frutta fruit salad
mandorle almonds
mele apples
more blackberries
nocciole hazelnuts
noci walnuts
pesca peach
pesca noce nectarine
pompelmo grapefruit
prugna/susina prune/plum
uva grapes

Dolci (Desserts)
amaretti macaroons
crostata fruit flan

gelato (produzione propria) ice cream
  (home-made)
granita flavoured ice, usually lemon or coffee
panettone cake with candied fruit and raisins
semifreddo refrigerated cake
spumone a soft ice cream
torta cake, tart
zabaglione eggs and Marsala wine, served hot
zuppa inglese trifle

Bevande (Beverages)
acqua minerale mineral water
  con/senza gas with/without fizz
aranciata orange soda
birra (alla spina) beer (draught)
latte (intero/scremato) milk (whole/skimmed)
succo di frutta fruit juice
vino (rosso, bianco, rosato) wine (red,
  white, rosé)

Cooking Terms (Miscellaneous)
aceto (balsamico) vinegar (balsamic)
affumicato smoked
bicchiere glass
burro butter
conto bill
coltello knife
cucchiaio spoon
forchetta fork
forno oven
fritto fried
ghiaccio ice
griglia grill
in bianco without tomato
lumache snails
marmellata jam
menta mint
miele honey
olio oil
pane (tostato) bread (toasted)
panini sandwiches (in roll)
panna cream
pepe pepper
ripieno stuffed
rosmarino rosemary
sale salt
salvia sage
tavola table
tovagliolo napkin
tramezzini sandwiches (in sliced bread)
uovo egg
zucchero sugar

array of regional wines, many of which are rarely exported because they are best drunk young. Even wines that are well known and often-derided clichés abroad, like *Chianti* or *Lambrusco*, can be wonderful new experiences when tasted on their home turf. Unless you're dining at a restaurant with an exceptional cellar, do as the Italians do and order the local wine (*vino locale* or *vino della casa*). You won't often be wrong.

Most Italian wines are named after the grape and the district they come from. If the label says DOC (*Denominazione di Origine Controllata*) it means that the wine comes from a specially defined area and was produced according to a certain traditional method. DOCG (*Denominazione di Origine Controllata e Garantia*) is allegedly a more rigorous classification, indicating that the wines not only conform to DOC standards, but are tested by government-appointed inspectors. At present few wines have been granted this status, but the number is planned to increase steadily. *Classico* means that a wine comes from the oldest part of the zone of production, though is not necessarily better than a *non-Classico*. *Riserva, superiore* or *speciale* denotes a wine that has been aged longer and is more alcoholic; *recioto* is a wine made from the outer clusters of grapes, with a higher sugar and therefore alcohol content.

Other Italian wine words are *spumante* (sparkling), *frizzante* (pétillant), *amabile* (semi-sweet), *abbocato* (medium dry), *passito* (strong sweet wine made from raisins). *Rosso* is red, *bianco* white; between the two extremes lie *rubiato* (ruby), *rosato*, *chiaretto* or *cerasuolo* (rosé). *Secco* is dry, *dolce* sweet, *liquoroso* fortified and sweet. *Vendemmia* means vintage, a *cantina* is a cellar, and an *enoteca* is a wine-shop or museum where you can taste and buy wines.

The regions of Piemonte, Tuscany and Veneto produce Italy's most prestigious red wines, while Friuli-Venezia Giulia and Trentino-Alto Adige are the greatest regions for white wines. King of the Tuscans is the mighty *Brunello di Montalcino* (DOCG), an expensive blockbuster. *Pinot Grigio* and the unusual *Tocai* make some of the best whites. But almost every other corner of Italy has its vinous virtues, be it the *Lambrusco* of Emilia-Romagna, the *Orvieto* of Umbria, the *Taurasi* of Campania or the *Frascati* of Lazio. The well-known *Valpolicella, Bardolino* and *Soave* are produced on the shores of Lake Garda. Even in the south, with much of its stronger, rougher wine shipped north for blending, you will find some wonderful varieties, such as the Sicilian *Corvo* (red and white).

Italy turns its grape harvest to other uses too, producing Sicilian *Marsala*, a famous fortified wine fermented in wooden casks, ranging from very dry to flavoured and sweet and *vin santo* (sacred wine), a sweet Tuscan speciality often served with almond biscuits. *Vermouth* is an idea from Turin made of wine flavoured with Alpine herbs and spices. Italians are fond of post-prandial brandies (to aid digestion) – Stock or Vecchia Romagna appear on the best-known Italian brandy bottles. *Grappa* is a rough, Schnapps-like spirit drunk in black coffee after a meal (a *caffè corretto*). Other drinks you'll see in any Italian bar include *Campari*, a red bitter drunk on its own or in cocktails; *Fernet Branca, Cynar* and *Averno* (popular aperitif/digestifs); and a host of liqueurs like *Strega*, the witch potion from Benevento, almond-flavoured *Amaretto*, cherry *Maraschino*, aniseed *Sambuca* or herby *Millefiori*.

Travel

Getting There

By Air from the UK and Ireland

Flying is obviously the quickest and most painless way of getting to Italy from the UK. There are direct flights to over 20 destinations from over half a dozen British airports. Rome, Milan, Pisa and Venice have the greatest choice of year-round services, though there are plenty of regular flights to the business cities of Genoa and Bologna too. Flights to coastal or island resort destinations may be much more seasonal. Florence and Turin have more limited air links with Britain, but are well connected by rail to Pisa, Milan and Rome. Scheduled services are, in the main, more expensive than charters, although there are a couple of low-cost airlines whose scheduled flight prices compete with the charter fares.

Scheduled return fares vary greatly, depending on the season. The best-value deals are usually **APEX** fares, which have to be booked seven to 14 days ahead, and must include a Saturday night in Italy – no alterations or refunds are possible without penalties. Return scheduled fares range from around £200 off-season to midsummer fares of well over £250. Full fares on the major carriers, especially to some of the less popular destinations such as Turin, can be as high as £500. There are cheaper fares on offer on scheduled airlines (around £150), but these often have restrictions and may involve flying via another European destination.

Many inexpensive charter flights are available to popular Italian destinations in summer, though you are unlikely to find the same sort of rock-bottom bargains as, say, to

Major Carriers

From the UK
Alitalia, London, t (0990) 448 259; Dublin, t (01) 677 5171, www.alitalia.co.uk.
British Airways, t (0845) 779 9977, www.britishairways.com.
KLM Direct, t (0870) 507 4074.
Meridiana, t (020) 7839 2222, www.meridiana.it
Sabena, t (0845) 601 0933, www.swissair.com.
Lufthansa, t (0345) 737 747, www.lufthansa.com.
Aer Lingus, Dublin, t (01) 886 8888; or Belfast, (0645) 737 747, www.aerlingus.ie.

From the USA
Alitalia, (USA) t (800) 223 5730, www.alitaliausa.com.
British Airways, t (800) AIRWAYS, TTY (1 877) 993 9997, www.britishairways.com.
Continental, t (800) 231 0856, (800) 343 9195 (hearing impaired), Canada (800) 525 0280, www.continental.com.
Delta, t (800) 241 4141, www.delta.com.
Air Canada, t (1 888) 247 2262, www.aircanada.ca.
Northwest Airlines, t (800) 225 2525, www.nwa.com.

TWA, t (800) 892 4141, www.twa.com.
United Airlines, t (800) 241 6522, www.ual.com.

Low-cost Carriers (UK)

Go, t (0845) 605 4321, www.go-fly.com. Operates flights between London Stansted and Bologna (7 times a week), Venice (7 times a week), Rome (14 times a week) and Milan (21 times a week).
Ryanair, t (08701) 569 569, www.ryanair.com. Flights from Stansted to Turin, Treviso, Ancona, Pisa, Brescia, Genoa and Rimini.
Buzz, t (0870) 240 7070, www.buzzaway.com. Flights from Stansted to Milan.

Charters, Discounts, Youth Fares and Special Deals

From the UK
Italy Sky Shuttle, 227 Shepherd's Bush Rd, London W6 7AS, t (020) 8748 1333.
Italflights, 125 High Holborn, London WC1V 6QA, t (020) 7405 6771.
Trailfinders, 215 Kensington High Street, London W8, t (020) 7937 1234.

Spain. You may find cheaper fares by combing the small ads in the travel pages, or from a specialist agent (use a reputable ABTA-registered one), which offer good student and youth rates too. The main problems with cheaper flights tend to be inconvenient flight schedules, and restrictions – especially on changing travel times. Take out good travel insurance, however cheap your ticket is.

By Air from the USA and Canada

The main Italian air gateways for direct flights from North America are Rome and Milan, though, if you're doing a grand tour, check fares to other European destinations (Paris or Amsterdam, for example) which may well be cheaper. It may be worth catching a cheap flight to London (New York–London

fares are always very competitive) and then flying on from there using some of the British low-cost carriers like **Go** and **Ryanair** (*see* box for websites). Prices are higher from Canada, so you may be better off flying via the States to reach Italy from any part of North America.

By Air from Mainland Europe

Air travel between Italy and other parts of Europe can be expensive, especially for short hops. Some airlines (for example **Alitalia, Qantas** and **Air France**) offer excellent rates on the European stages of intercontinental flights, and Italy is an important touchdown for many long-haul services to the Middle or Far East and some parts of Africa. Amsterdam, Paris and Athens are good centres to find cheap flights.

Budget Travel, 134 Lower Baggot Street, Dublin 2, **t** (01) 661 1866.

United Travel, Stillorgan Bowl, Stillorgan, County Dublin, **t** (01) 288 4346/7.

Besides saving 25 per cent on regular flights, young people under 26 have the option of flying on special discount charters.

Usit Campus Travel, 52 Grosvenor Gardens, SW1W 0AG, **t** (0870) 240 1010, with branches at most UK universities; *www.usitcampus.co.uk.*

STA, 6 Wright's Lane, London W8 6TA, **t** (020) 7361 6161, *www.statravel.com*, and branches.

USIT Now, 19-21 Aston Quay, Dublin 2, **t** (01) 679 8833, and other branches in Ireland, *www.usitnow.ie.*

From the USA

For discounted flights, try the small ads in newspaper travel pages (*e.g. New York Times, Chicago Tribune, Toronto Globe & Mail*). Numerous travel clubs and agencies also specialize in discount fares, but may require an annual membership fee.

Airhitch, 2790 Broadway, Suite 100, New York, NY 10025, **t** (212) 864 2000, *www.airhitch.org.*

Council Travel, 205 E 42nd Street, New York, NY 10017, **t** (800) 743 1823. Major specialists in student and charter flights; branches all

over the USA. Can also provide Eurail and Britrail passes for train travel.

Last Minute Travel Club, 132 Brookline Avenue, Boston, MA 02215, **t** (800) 527 8646.

Now Voyager, 74 Varick St, Suite 307, New York, NY 10013, **t** (212) 431 1616. Courier flights.

STA, *www.statravel.com*, **t** (800) 781 4040, with branches at most universities and also at 10 Downing Street, New York, NY 10014, **t** (212) 627 3111, and ASUC Building, 2nd Floor, University of California, Berkeley, CA 94720, **t** (510) 642 3000.

TFI, 34 West 32nd Street, NY, NY 10001, **t** (212) 736 1140, **t** (800) 745 8000.

Travel Cuts, 187 College St, Toronto, Ontario M5T 1P7, **t** (416) 979 2406. Canada's largest student travel specialists; with branches in most provinces.

You could also research your fare on some of the US cheap flight websites including:
www.priceline.com (bid for tickets)
www.bestfares.com
www.travelocity.com
www.eurovacations.com
www.cheaptrips.com
www.courier.com (courier flights)
www.ricksteves.com
www.xfares.com (carry on luggage only)
www.smarterliving.com

By Rail

Train travel, at whatever speed, has its benefits – escape from the brain-mushing awfulness of airports, and the chance to watch the changing scenery and gently acclimatize to new surroundings are two. With Eurostar from London the journey time to Rome is 15½ hours, or 12 hours 40 minutes to Milan. Services run daily in the summer and return fares range from £187 to £250. Travelling by train and ferry takes about 24 hours but you can stop off as often as you like. There are also Motorail links from Denderleeuw in Belgium to Milan, Rimini, Rome, Bologna and Venice (contact **Rail Choice**, *see* below).

Fares, Passes and Discounts

In an age of low-cost airlines rail travel is not much of an economy unless you're able to take advantage of student, youth, family, young children and senior citizen discounts. Interail (UK) or Eurail (USA/Canada) **passes** give unlimited travel for all ages throughout Europe for one or two months. A month's full Interail pass covering France, Switzerland and Italy costs £269, or £195 for the under-26s; for France and Italy only it costs £230, or £169 for the under-26s (contact **Rail Europe**, *see* box). Various **youth fares** and inclusive rail passes are also available within Italy, and if you're planning on doing a lot of rail travel in Italy you can organize these before leaving home at **Rail Choice** (*see* box). The **Kilometric** card currently costs £88 and is valid for up to 5 people for a maximum of 20 journeys or 3,000km. The **Italy Flexi Card** allows 4 days' unlimited travel in any month for £96, 8 days for £132 or 12 days for £172 (with no extra costs). The **Italy Rail Card** allows 8 days' travel for £128, 15 days for £158, 21 days for £186 and 30 days for £220. Rail Choice have further discounts for students and under-26s using Eurostar (*see* Getting Around, p.99, for details on purchasing the rail passes in Italy).

CIT offices, which act as agents for Italian State Railways, also offer various deals. In Italy, a good bet for discounted train tickets and flights is **CTS**, the Italian student agency.

Timetables

A convenient pocket-sized **timetable**, detailing all the main and secondary Italian railway lines, is available in the UK, costing £9 (plus 50p postage – contact **Italian Railways** or **Italwings**). If you wait until you arrive in Italy you can pick up the Italian timetable (in two volumes) at any station for about L4,500.

Venice-Simplon Orient Express

The Orient Express deserves a special mention: it whirls you from London through Paris, Zurich, Innsbruck and Verona to Venice in a cocoon of traditional twenties and thirties glamour, with beautifully restored Pullman/wagon-lits. It's fiendishly expensive but quite unforgettable for a once-in-a-lifetime treat. Prices (including meals) are around £1,200 per person one-way; Venice–London one-way tickets include a free flight out. Several operators offer packages including smart Venice hotels and return flights home (contact **Venice-Simplon Orient Express**, *see* box).

Rail Agencies

Rail Europe (tickets on Eurostar and interail passes), (UK) 179 Piccadilly, London W1V OBA, **t** (08705) 848 848, or see the website at *www.raileurope.co.uk*; (USA) 226–230 Westchester Ave, White Plains, NY 10604, **t** (914) 682 2999, or **t** (800) 438 7245, *www.raileurope.com*.

Rail Choice (rail passes within Italy and Motorail), 15 Colman House, Empire Square, High Street, Penge, London SE20 7EX, **t** (020) 7939 9915, *www.railchoice.co.uk* (UK), *www.railchoice.com* (USA).

CIT (agents for Italian state railways), (UK) Marco Polo House, 3–5 Lansdowne Rd, Croydon, Surrey, **t** (020) 8686 0677, *www.citalia.co.uk*; (USA) 15 West 44th Street, 10th Floor, New York, NY 10036, **t** (212) 730 2121; (Canada) 80 Tiverton Court, Suite 401, Markham, Toronto L3R O94, **t** (905) 415 1060.

CTS (flights, rail tickets), (Italy) Corso P. Ticinese 83, Milan, **t** (02) 837 2674, *www.cts.it*.

Italian Railways (tickets and timetables), (UK) **t** (020) 7724 0011, *www.fs-on-line.com*.

Italwings (travel & accommodation), (UK) 162–8 Regent St, London W1R 5TB, **t** (020) 7287 2117.

Venice-Simplon Orient Express, Sea Containers House, 20 Upper Ground, London SE1 9PF, **t** (020) 7928 6000, *www.orient-express.com*.

By Road

By Bus and Coach

Eurolines, 52 Grosvenor Gardens, London SW1Q OAU, **t** (0990) 808 080, *www.goby coach.com*, are booked in the UK through National Express (return ticket London–Rome £129; single £90; under 26s and senior citizens return £115 or single £80). Within Italy you can obtain more information on long-distance bus services from any CIT office.

By Car

Italy is the best part of 24 hours' driving time from the UK, even if you stick to fast toll roads. Calais–Florence via Nancy, Lucerne and Lugano is about 1042km. The most scenic and hassle-free route is via the Alps but if you take a route through Switzerland expect to pay for the privilege (around £15.50 or 40SFr for motorway use). In winter the passes may be closed and you will have to stick to those expensive tunnels (one-way tolls range from about 40–70SFr for a small car). You can avoid some of the driving by putting your car on the train. There are Motorail links from Denderleeuw in Belgium to Bologna, Rimini, Rome and Venice (infrequently in winter: for further details contact Rail Choice, **t** (020) 7939 9915, *www.railchoice.co.uk*). The **Italian Auto Club** (ACI), **t** 06 44 77, offers reasonably priced breakdown assistance.

To bring a GB-registered car into Italy, you need a **vehicle registration document, full driving licence**, and **insurance papers** (these must be carried at all times when driving). If your driving licence is of the old-fashioned sort without a photo you are also strongly recommended to apply for an international driving permit (available from the AA or RAC). Non-EU citizens should preferably have an **international driving licence,** which has an Italian translation incorporated. Your vehicle should display a nationality plate indicating its country of registration. Before travelling, check everything is in perfect order. **Red hazard triangles** and **headlight converters** are obligatory; also recommended are a spare set of bulbs, a first-aid kit and a fire extinguisher. Spare parts for non-Italian cars can be difficult to find. Before crossing the border, fill your car up; *benzina* is very expensive in Italy.

At the time of writing the Mont Blanc tunnel is still closed after a catastrophic fire in 1999. Current motorway tunnel tolls are:

Fréjus Tunnel, *www.tunneldufrejus.com*, from Modane (France) to Bardonècchia. Prices range from L31,000– L61,000.

Gran San Bernardo, *www.grandsaint bernard.ch*, from Bourg St Pierre (Switzerland) to Aosta. Small car or motorcycle L34,000 single, L47,000 return.

For more information on driving in Italy, contact the **AA, t** (0990) 500 600 or (0800) 444 500 (5-star breakdown cover), or **RAC**, **t** (0800) 550 550 in the UK, and **AAA, t** (407) 444 4000, in the USA.

Entry Formalities

Passports and Visas

EU nationals with a valid passport can enter and stay in Italy as long as they like. Citizens of the USA, Canada, Australia and New Zealand need only a valid passport to stay up to 90 days in Italy. If you mean to stay longer than 90 days in Italy you will have to get a *permesso di soggiorno*. For this you will need to state your reason for staying, be able to prove a source of income and medical insurance. After a couple of exasperating days at some provincial Questura office filling out forms you should walk out with your permit.

UK, 38 Eaton Place, London SW1X 8AN, **t** (020) 7235 9371 or (09001) 600 340 (visa information, 60p/minute), **f** (020) 7823 1609; 32 Melville Street, Edinburgh EH3 7HA, **t** (0131) 226 3631; 2111 Piccadilly, Manchester, **t** (0161) 236 9024, *www.embitaly.org.uk*.

Ireland, 63–65 Northumberland Road, Dublin, **t** (01) 660 1744; 7 Richmond Park, Stranmillis, Belfast BT9 5EF, **t** (02890) 668 854.

USA, 690 Park Avenue, New York, NY 10021, **t** (212) 737 9100; 12400 Wilshire Blvd, Suite 300, Los Angeles, CA, **t** (213) 820 0622, *www.italyemb.org*.

Canada, 136 Beverley Street, Toronto (ON) M5T 1Y5, **t** (416) 977 1566, **f** (416) 977 1119, *www.toronto.italconsulate.org*.

Australia, 61 Macquarie St, Sydney 2000 NSW, **t** (02) 9392 7900, **t** (02) 9252 4830, *www.ausitalian-embassy.it*.

New Zealand, 34 Grant Rd, PO Box 463, Thorndon, Wellington, **t** (04) 4735 339, **t** (04) 4727 255.

By law you should register with the police within eight days of your arrival in Italy. In practice this is done automatically for most visitors when they check in at their first hotel.

Customs

EU nationals over the age of 17 can now import an unlimited amount of goods for personal use. Non-EU nationals have to pass through the Italian Customs which are usually benign. How the frontier police manage to recruit such ugly, mean-looking characters to hold the sub-machine guns and dogs from

Courses for Foreigners and Special-interest Holidays

The Italian Institute, 39 Belgrave Square, London SW1X 8NX, **t** (020) 7235 1461, or 686 Park Avenue, New York, NY 10021, **t** (212) 879 4242, is the main source of information on courses for foreigners in Italy. Graduate students should also contact their nearest Italian consulate to find out about scholarships – apparently many go unused each year because no one knows about them.

A selection of specialist companies are listed below. Not all of them are necessarily ABTA-bonded; we recommend you check before booking.

In the UK

Abercrombie & Kent, Sloane Square House, Holbein Place, London SW1W 8NS, **t** (020) 7559 8686, **f** (020) 7730 9376, *info@aber crombiekent.co.uk, www.abercrombiekent. com*. City breaks in all the major cities, country retreats and island-hopping cruises plus a range of walking holidays in Tuscany, the Italian Lakes and Umbria and combi-holidays (Rome, Venice, Florence, and Sicily – Amalfi).

Ace Study Tours, Babraham, Cambridge CB2 4AP, **t** (01223) 835 055, **f** (01223) 837 394, *www.study-tours.org*. Cultural and garden tours all over Italy (Piero della Francesca, Vasari, the Visconti and the Sforza, popes and princes, etc).

Alternative Travel, 69–71 Banbury Road, Oxford OX2 6PE, **t** (01865) 31578, **f** (01865) 315 697, *info@atg-oxford.co.uk*. Walking, wild flower-spotting, garden and cycling tours. Piero della Francesca, the Palio in Siena, Renaissance Tuscany, Venice, Sardinia and Sicily art routes; also truffle hunts and painting courses.

American Express Europe, Destination Services, 19-20 Berners St, London W1P 4AE, **t** (020) 7637 8600 **f** (020) 7631 4803. City breaks and fly-drive.

Arblaster & Clarke Wine Tours, Farnham Road, West Liss, Petersfield, Hants GU33 6JQ, **t** (01730) 893 344, **f** (01730) 892 888, *www.winetours.co.uk*. Wine tours, truffle hunts and gourmet cooking tours in Rome, Southern Italy, Tuscany, Verona, the Veneto and northern and central Italy, also cruises.

British Airways Holidays, Astral Towers, Betts Way, Crawley, West Sussex, RH10 2XA, **t** (0870) 24 24 243/(01293) 723 100, **f** (01293) 722 702, *www.baholidays.co.uk*.

British Museum Traveller, 46 Bloomsbury Street, London WC1B 3QQ, **t** (020) 7323 8895, **f** (020) 7580 8677. Tours with guest lecturers, looking at art and architecture in Tuscany, Umbria – particularly Florence.

Brompton Travel, Brompton House, 64 Richmond Road, Kingston-upon-Thames, Surrey KT2 5EH, **t** (020) 8549 3334, **f** (020) 8547 1236, *www.BromptonTravel.co.uk*; tailor-made and opera tours in Verona, Naples, Venice, Milan, Turin and Genoa.

Citalia, Marco Polo House, 3–5 Lansdowne Road, Croydon CR9 1LL, **t** (020) 8686 5533, (020) 8681 0712, *ciao@citalia.co.uk*. Resorts, self-catering holidays and honeymoons throughout Italy including Florence, Rome, Venice, Puglia, Campania (Maori, Paestum and Positano), the Lakes, Umbria and Venice (the Carnival).

Cox & Kings, 4th Floor, Gorden House, 10 Greencoat Place, London SW1P 1PH, **t** (020) 7873 5027, **f** (020) 7630 6038, *www.coxand kings.co.uk*. Short breaks, gastronomic and escorted cultural tours with guest lecturers in Rome and the Lakes; also cruises.

Fine Art Travel, 15 Savile Row, London W1X 1AE, **t** (020) 7437 8553, **f** (020) 7437 1733. A mix of

such a good-looking population is a mystery, but they'll let you be if you don't look suspicious and haven't brought along more than 200 cigarettes or 100 cigars, or not more than a litre of hard drink or three bottles of wine, a couple of cameras, a movie camera, 10 rolls of film for each, a tape-recorder, radio, record-player, one canoe less than 5.5m, sports

equipment for personal use, and one TV. You can take the same items listed above home with you without hassle. US citizens may return with $400 worth of merchandise – keep your receipts.

Pets must always be accompanied by a bilingual Certificate of Health from your local Veterinary Inspector.

cultural, art and historical tours in Umbria, Venice and Naples.

Gordon Overland, 76 Croft Road, Carlisle, Cumbria CA3 9AG, **t** (01228) 526 795, **f** (01228) 523 724, *sierasgold@aol.com*. Annual month-long language and painting holidays in Tuscany and the Veneto, also garden and villa tours in northern Italy.

Inscape Fine Art Tours, Austins Farm, High Street, Stonesfield, Witney, Oxfordshire OX8 8PU, **t** (01993) 891 726, **f** (01993) 891 718. Escorted art tours with guest lecturers in Venice, the Veneto, Sicily, Umbria and Tuscany.

Italia 2000, 8 Timperley Way, Up Hatherley, Cheltenham, Gloucestershire GL51 5RH, **t/f** (01242) 234 215. Horse-riding, golf and sailing holidays all over Italy.

Italiatour, 9 Whyteleafe Business Village, Whyteleafe Hill, Whyteleafe, Surrey CR3 0AT, **t** (01883) 621 900, **f** (01883) 625 255, *italia tour@dial.pipex.com*. Resort holidays and city breaks all over Italy, also vegetarian cookery courses in Umbria, horse-riding in Umbria, football tickets, opera in Rome, Venice and Verona, and *agriturismo*.

JMB, Rushwick, Worcester WR2 5SN, **t** (01905) 425 628, **f** (01905) 420 219, *www.jmb travel.co.uk*. Opera holidays in Florence, Palermo, Milan, Turin, Torre del Lago, Rome and Venice.

Kirker, 3 New Concordia Wharf, Mill Street, London SE1 2BB, **t** (020) 7231 3333, **f** (020) 7231 4771, *cities@kirker.itsnet.co.uk*. City breaks, tailor-made tours throughout Italy, and trips to the Verona Opera.

Magic of Italy, 227 Shepherd's Bush Road, London W6 7AS, **t** (020) 8748 7575, **f** (020) 8748 3731, *www.magictravelgroup.co.uk*. City breaks and villa holidays throughout Italy.

Martin Randall Travel, 10 Barley Mow Passage, Chiswick, London W4 4PH, **t** (020) 8742 3355,

f (020) 8742 7766, *info@martinrandall.co.uk*. Imaginatively put-together cultural tours with guest lecturers: architecture and painting, history, Florence, Venice, Verona at Christmas, wines, Venice music festival, gardens and villas.

Page & Moy, 135-140 London Road, Leicester LE2 1EN, **t** (0116) 250 7000, **f** (0116) 250 7123. City breaks, gastronomy and cultural tours: Sicily, northern Italy, gardens of the Italian Lakes, plus river cruises and air and coach tours throughout the country.

Ramblers, Box 43, Welwyn Garden City, Hertfordshire AL8 6PQ, **t** (01707) 331 133, **f** (01707) 333 276, *info@ramblersholidays. co.uk*. Walking holidays in Abruzzo, Umbria, Tuscany, Sicily, Sorrento, Urbino, Assisi, Lake Garda, Florence, Venice, Siena and Liguria.

Simply Tuscany & Umbria, Kings House, Wood Street, Kingston-upon-Thames, Surrey KT1 1UG, **t** (020) 8541 2206, **f** (020) 8541 2280, *www.simply-travel.com*. Tailor-made itineraries, also art, architecture and vegetarian cookery courses, balloon flights, spa resorts and painting holidays.

Special Tours, 81a Elizabeth St, London SW1W 9PG, **t** (020) 7730 2297. Escorted cultural tours: art, architecture, gardens in Florence, Ravello, Naples, Sicily and Sardinia, plus opera holidays in Verona.

Swan Hellenic, 77 New Oxford Street, London WC1A 1PP, **t** (020) 7800 2200, **f** (020) 7800 2723, *www.swanhellenic.com*. Cruises.

Tasting Places, Unit 40, Buspace Studios, Conlan Street, London W10 5AP, **t** (020) 7460 0077, **f** (020) 7460 0029, *www.tasting places.com*. Cookery courses in Umbria, Sicily, the Veneto, Tuscany and Piedmont.

The Travel Club of Upminster, Station Road, Upminster, Essex RM14 2TT, **t** (01708) 225 000, **f** (01708) 229 678, *www.travelclub. org.uk*. Painting holidays, garden tours,

Getting Around

Italy has an excellent network of airports, railways, highways and byways and you'll find getting around fairly easy – until one union or another takes it into its head to go on strike (to be fair they rarely do it during the high holiday season). There's plenty of talk about passing a law to regulate strikes, but it won't happen soon, if ever. Learn to recognize the word in Italian: *sciopero* (SHO-per-o), and do as the Romans do – quiver with resignation. There's always a day or two's notice, and strikes usually last only a day, just long enough to throw a spanner in the works if you have to catch a plane. Keep your ears open – ask bartenders and hotel reception, and watch for notices in the stations.

art and gastronomy in Piemonte and the Italian Lakes.

Travelsphere, Compass House, Rockingham Road, Market Harborough, Leicestershire LE16 7QD, t (01858) 464 818, f (01858) 434 323. Themed air and coach cultural tours: art, gardens, food, wine, walking and house party singles holidays.

Venice Simplon-Orient Express, Sea Containers House, 20 Upper Ground, London SE1 9PF, t (020) 7928 6000, f (020) 7805 5908, *www.orient-express.com*.

Voyages Jules Verne, 21 Dorset Square, London NW1 6QG, t (020) 7616 1010, f (020) 7723 8629, *www.vjv.co.uk*. Swish resorts all over Italy, especially Venice, Venice Lido, Ravello, Sorrento, Taormina and Capri.

Wallace Arnold, Gelderd Road, Leeds LS12 6DH, t (0113) 2310 739, f (0113) 231 0749, *www.wallacearnold.com*. Coach holidays all over Italy including Tuscany, Riva del Garda and Venice, Lake Como, Italian Riviera, Sorrento and Capri.

In the USA/Canada

Abercrombie & Kent, 1520 Kensington Rd., Oak Brook, IL 60523 2141, t (630) 954 2944, (800) 323 7308, *www.abercrombiekent.com*. City breaks, walking holidays, country retreats and island-hopping cruises.

Archaeological Tours Inc., Suite 904, 271 Madison Avenue, New York, NY 10016, t (212) 986 3054. Expertly led archaeological tours for small groups, with an annual tour of Sicily & southern Italy, Ancient Rome and a biannual tour of Etruscan sites in Tuscany and Umbria.

Bike Riders' Tours, PO Box 130254, Boston, MA 02113, t (617) 723 2354, f (617) 723 2355, *www.bikeriders.com*. Cycling tours in Umbria, Tuscany, the Veneto, Emilia-Romagna and Sicily.

Certified Vacations, 300 Pinnacle Way, Norcross, GA 30093, t (800) 241 1700. Pre-packaged or tailor-made FIT tours.

CIT Tours (in the USA), 15 West 44th St, New York, NY 10173, t (212) CIT-TOUR, *www.cit tours.com*, and 9501 West Devon Ave, Rosemount, Il 60018, t (800) CIT-TOUR; (in Canada), 80 Tiverton Court, Suite 401, Markham, Ontario L3R 0GA, t (800) 387 0711. General and skiing holidays.

Dailey-Thorp Travel, 330 West 58th Street, New York, NY 10019, t (212) 307 1555. Luxury escorted tours to the Milan opera.

Esplanade Tours, 581 Boylston Street, Boston, MA 02116, t (617) 266 7465. (800) 426 5492, *www.specialtytravel.com*. Art and architecture and FIT itineraries.

Europe Train Tours, 198 E. Boston Post Rd, Mamaroneck, NY 10543, t (914) 698 9426, (800) 551 2085, f (914) 698 9516. Escorted tours by train and car.

Italiatour, 666 5th Avenue, New York, NY 10103, t (800) 845 3365 (US) and (888) 515 5245 (Canada), *www.italiatour.com*. Fly-drive holidays and sightseeing tours organized by Alitalia; three nights in Rome from $430.

Maupintour, 1421 Research Park Drive, Kansas 66049, t (785) 331 1000, or (800) 255 4266.

Travelguide International, 1145 Clark St, Stephen's Pt, Wisconsin 54481, t (715) 345 0505. Travel with a guide.

Trafalgar Tours, 11 East 26th Street, New York, NY 10010, t (212) 689 8977.

Travel Concepts, 307 Princeton, Mass 01541, t (978) 464 0411. Wine and food itineraries.

Worldwide Classroom, P.O. Box 1166, Milwaukee, WI 53201, t (414) 351 6311, (800) 276 8712, f (414) 224 3466, *www.worldwide. edu*. Database listing educational organizations around the world.

All (800) numbers are toll-free if calling from within the USA.

By Air

Air traffic within Italy is intense, with up to ten flights a day on popular routes. Domestic flights are handled by Alitalia, ATI (its internal arm) or Avianova. Air travel makes most sense when hopping between north and south. Shorter journeys are often just as quick (and usually much less expensive) by train or even bus, if you take travelling to the airport and check-in times into account.

Mainland cities with airports include Ancona, Bari, Bergamo, Bologna, Brindisi, Florence, Genoa, Lamezia Terme (near Catanzaro), Milan, Naples, Parma, Pisa, Reggio Calabria, Turin, Trieste, Venice and Verona, all of which have direct flights to and from Rome.

Domestic flight costs are comparable to those in other European countries, and a complex system of discounts is available. Each airport has a bus terminal in the city; ask about schedules when you purchase your ticket to avoid hefty taxi fares. Baggage allowances vary between airlines. Tickets can be bought at CIT and other travel agencies.

By Rail

FS national train information: t 1478 88 088 (open 7am–9pm); www.fs-on-line.com.

Italy's national railway, the **FS** (Ferrovie dello Stato) is well run, inexpensive and often a pleasure to ride. There are also several private rail lines that may not accept Interail or Eurail passes. On the FS, some of the trains are sleek and high-tech, but much of the rolling stock hasn't been changed for fifty years. Possible FS unpleasantnesses you may encounter, besides a strike, are delays, crowding (especially at weekends and in the summer), and crime on overnight trains: someone might rifle through your bags while you sleep. Reserve a seat in advance (*fare una prenotazione*): the fee is small and can save you hours standing in some train corridor. On the more expensive trains, and for sleepers and couchettes on overnight trains, **reservations** are mandatory. Check when you purchase your ticket that the date is correct; tickets are only valid the day they're purchased unless you specify otherwise. At sleepy rural train stations without information boards, the imminent

arrival of a train is signalled by a platform bell, triggering a Pavlovian rush for seats.

It is easiest to buy **tickets** at a travel agent in one of the city centres. Fares are strictly determined by the kilometres travelled. The system is computerized and runs smoothly, at least until you try to get a reimbursement for an unused ticket (usually not worth the trouble). Be sure to ask which platform (*binario*) your train arrives at or leaves from; the boards in the stations are not always correct. Always remember to stamp your ticket (*convalidare*) in the not-very-obvious yellow machines at the head of the platform before boarding the train. Failure to do so could result in a fine. If you get on a train without a ticket you can buy one from the conductor, with an added 20 per cent penalty. You can also pay a conductor to upgrade to first class or to get a couchette, if there are places available.

There is a fairly straightforward **hierarchy of trains.** At the bottom of the pyramid is the humble, sometimes excruciatingly slow, *Locale* (euphemistically known sometimes as an *Accelerato*), which often stops even where there's no station in sight. When you're checking the schedules, beware of what may look like the first train to your destination – if it's a *Locale*, it will be the last to arrive. A *Diretto* stops far less, an *Expresso* just at the main towns. *Intercity* trains whoosh between the big cities and rarely deign to stop. *Eurocity* trains link Italian cities with major European centres. Both of these services require a supplement – some 30per cent more than a regular fare.

Even higher up the train hierarchy are the *ETR 500 pendolino* trains, similar to the French TGV, which can travel at nearly 300 km/hr. Reservations are free, but must be made at least five hours before the trip, and on some trains there are only first-class coaches. The super-swish, super-fast (Florence–Rome in 1½ hours) *Eurostars* make very few stops, have both first and second class carriages, and carry a supplement which includes an obligatory seat reservation. Trains serving the most important routes have names such as the *Vesuvio* (Milan, Bologna, Florence, Rome, Naples), the *Adriatico* (Milan, Rimini, Pesaro, Ancona, Pescara, Foggia, Bari), or the *Colosseo/ Ambrosiano* (Milan, Bologna, Florence, Rome).

The FS offers several **passes**. The **Flexi Card** (marketed as a 'Freedom Pass' in the UK) allows unlimited travel for either four days within a month (L206,000), 8 days (within a month) (L287,000), 12 days (within a month) (L368,000) plus seat reservations and supplements on Eurostars. The **Kilometrico** allows 3000km of travel, on a maximum of 20 journeys, and is valid for two months (2nd Class L206,000, 1st Class L338,000). One advantage is that it can be used by up to five people at the same time, but supplements are payable on *Intercity* trains. Other discounts are available for day returns, families, senior citizens and the under-26s.

Refreshments on routes of any great distance are provided by bar cars or trolleys; you can usually get sandwiches and coffee from vendors along the tracks at intermediary stops. Station bars often have a good variety of take-away travellers' fare; consider at least investing in a plastic bottle of mineral water, since there's no drinking water on the trains.

Besides trains and bars, Italy's stations offer other **facilities**. Most have a *deposito*, where you can leave your bags for hours or days for a small fee. The larger ones have porters (who charge L1500–2000 per piece) and some even have luggage trolleys; major stations have an *albergo diurno* ('day hotel', where you can take a shower, get a shave and have a haircut, etc.), information offices, currency exchanges open at weekends (not at the most advantageous rates, however), hotel-finding and reservation services, kiosks with foreign papers, restaurants, etc. You can also arrange to have a rental car awaiting you at your destination – Avis, Hertz and Maggiore are the firms most widespread in Italy.

Beyond that, some words need to be said about riding the rails on the most serendipitous national line in Europe. The FS may have its strikes and delays, its petty crime and bureaucratic inconveniences, but when you catch it on its better side it will treat you to a dose of the real Italy before you even reach your destination. If there's a choice, aim for one of the older cars, depressingly grey outside but fitted with comfortably upholstered seats, Art Deco lamps and old pictures of the towns and villages of the country. The washrooms are invariably clean and pleasant. Best of all, the FS is relatively reliable, and even if there has been some delay you'll have an amenable station full of clocks to wait in; some of the station bars have astonishingly good food (some do not), but at any of them you may accept a well-brewed cappuccino and look blasé until the train comes in. Try to avoid travelling on Friday evenings, when the major lines out of the big cities are packed.

By Coach and Bus

Inter-city coach travel is sometimes quicker than train travel, but also a bit more expensive. The Italians aren't dumb; you will find regular coach connections only where there is no train to offer competition. Coaches almost always depart from the vicinity of the train station, and tickets usually need to be purchased before you get on. In many regions they are the only means of public transport and well used, with frequent departures. If you can't get a ticket before the coach leaves, get on anyway and pretend you can't speak a word of Italian; the worst that can happen is that someone will make you pay for a ticket.

City buses are the traveller's friend. Most cities (at least in the north) label routes well; all charge flat fees for rides within the city limits and immediate suburbs (L1,500). Bus tickets must always be purchased before you get on, at either a tobacconist, a newspaper kiosk, a bar, or from ticket machines near the main stops. Once you get on, you must 'obliterate' your ticket in the machines at the front or back of the bus; controllers stage random checks to make sure you've punched your ticket. Fines for cheaters are about L50,000, and the odds are about 12 to 1 against a check, so many passengers take a chance. If you're good-hearted, however, you'll buy a ticket and help some overburdened municipal transit line meet its annual deficit.

By Car

The advantages of driving in Italy generally outweigh the disadvantages, but, before you bring your own car or hire one, consider the kind of holiday you're planning. For a tour of Italy's great art cities, you'd be better off not driving at all: parking is impossible, traffic impossible, deciphering one-way streets, signals and signs impossible. In Naples, don't even think about it. But for touring the countryside a car gives immeasurable freedom.

Third-party **insurance** is a minimum requirement in Italy (and you should be a lot more than minimally insured, as many of the locals have none whatsoever!). Obtain a Green Card from your insurer, which gives proof that you are fully covered. Also get hold of a **European Accident Statement** form, which may simplify things if you are unlucky enough to have an accident. Always insist on a full translation of any statement you are asked to sign. Breakdown assistance insurance is obviously a sensible investment.

Petrol (*benzina*: unleaded is *benzina senza piombo*, and diesel *gasolio*) is still expensive in Italy (around L2200 per litre), though prices are comparable to France or Germany at the moment. Many petrol stations close for lunch in the afternoon, and few stay open late at night, though you may find a 'self-service' where you feed a machine nice, smooth L10,000 notes. Services can be hard to find in remote areas and are generally closed all afternoon. Motorway (*autostrada*) tolls are quite high (the journey from Milan to Rome on the A1 will cost you around L60,000). Rest stops and petrol stations along the motorways stay open 24 hours.

Italians are famously anarchic behind a wheel. The only way to beat the locals is to join them by adopting an assertive and constantly alert driving style. Bear in mind the maxim that he/she who hesitates is lost (especially at traffic lights, where the danger is less great of crashing into someone at the front than being rammed from behind). All drivers from boy racers to elderly nuns seem to tempt providence by overtaking at the most dangerous bends, and no matter how fast you are hammering along the *autostrada*, plenty will whizz past at apparently supersonic rates. North Americans used to leisurely speeds and gentler road manners may find the Italian interpretation of the highway code especially stressful. Speed limits (generally ignored) are officially 130km/hr on motorways, 110km/hr on main highways, 90km/hr on secondary roads, and 50km/hr in built-up areas. Speeding fines may be as much as L500,000, or L100,000 for jumping a red light (a popular Italian sport).

If you are undeterred, you may actually enjoy driving in Italy, at least away from the congested tourist centres. Signposting is generally good, and roads are well maintained. Some are feats of engineering that the Romans themselves would have admired: bravura projects suspended on cliffs, crossing valleys on vast stilts and winding up hairpins.

Buy a good road map (the Italian Touring Club series is excellent). The **Automobile Club of Italy** (ACI) is a good friend to the foreign motorist. Besides having bushels of useful information and tips, they can be reached from anywhere by dialling t 116 – also use this number to find the nearest service station. If you need major repairs, the ACI can make sure the prices charged are according to their guidelines.

Hiring a Car

Hiring a car (*autonoleggio*) is simple but not particularly cheap. Remember to take into account that some hire companies require a deposit amounting to the estimated cost

Car Hire

In the UK
Avis, t (0990) 900 500, f (0870) 606 0100.
Budget, t (0541) 565 656, f (01442) 280 092.
Europcar, t (0870) 607 5000, f (01132) 429 495, *www.europcar.com*.
Hertz, t (0990) 996 699, f (020) 8679 0181.
Thrifty, t (0990) 168 238, f (01494) 751 601, *thrifty@thrifty.co.uk*.

In the USA
Auto Europe, 39 Commercial St., Portland, ME 04101, t (207) 842 2000, (888) 223 5555, *www.autoeurope.com*.
Avis Rent a Car, 900 Old Country Rd., Garden City, NY 11530, t (516) 222 3000, (800) 331 1084, *www.avis.com*.
Europcar, 5330 E. 31st St., P.O. Box 33167, Tulsa, OK 74153 1167. t (918) 669 2823, (800) 800 6000, f (918) 669 2821, *www.europcar.com*.
Europe by Car, One Rockefeller Plaza, New York, NY 10020 NY, t (212) 581 3040, (800) 223 1516, f (212) 246 1458, California t (213) 272 0424, (800) 252 9401, f (310) 273 9247, *www.europebycar.com*.
Hertz, 225 Brae Blvd., Park Ridge, NJ 07656, t (800) 654 3001, *www.hertz.com*.

of the hire. The minimum age limit is usually 25 (sometimes 23) and the driver must have held their licence for over a year. Most major rental companies have offices in airports or main stations, though it may be worthwhile checking prices of local firms. If you need a car for longer than three weeks, leasing may be a more economic alternative. The National Tourist Office has a list of firms in Italy that hire caravans (trailers) or camper vans. Non-residents are not allowed to buy cars in Italy.

It is probably easiest to arrange your car hire with a domestic firm before you depart and, in particular, to check out fly-drive discounts.

Europ Assistance, Sussex House, Perrymount Road, Haywards Heath, West Sussex RH16 1DN, **t** (01444) 442 211, will help with car insurance while travelling abroad.

Hitch-hiking

It is illegal to hitch on the *autostrade*, though you may pick up a lift near one of the toll booths. Don't hitch from the city centres, head for suburban exit routes. For the best chances of getting a lift, travel light, look respectable and take your shades off. Hold a sign indicating your destination if you can. Risks for women are lower in northern Italy than in the more macho south, but it is not advisable to hitch alone. Two or more men may encounter some reluctance. On major roads, heading out of town, you may sometimes see some scantily clad women, usually of African origin, standing or sitting on stools on the edges of corn fields trying to attract your attention. These are not hitch-hikers, although you may still pick them up.

By Motorcycle or Bicycle

Mopeds, vespas and scooters are the vehicles of choice for a great many Italians. You will see them everywhere. In the traffic-congested towns this is a ubiquity born of necessity; when driving space is limited, two wheels are always better than one. Despite the obvious dangers, there are clear benefits to moped-riding in Italy. For one thing it is cheaper than car hire and can prove an excellent way of covering a town's sites in a limited space of time. Furthermore, because Italy is such a scooter-friendly place, car drivers are more conditioned to their presence and so are less likely to hurtle into them when taking corners. Nonetheless, you should only consider hiring a moped if you have ridden one before (Italy's hills and alarming traffic are no place to learn) and, despite local examples, you should always wear a helmet. Also, be warned that some travel insurance policies exclude claims resulting from scooter or motorbike accidents.

You can hire a bicycle in most Italian towns. Alternatively, if you bring your own bike, check the airlines' policy on transporting them. Bikes can be transported by train in Italy, either with you or within a couple of days: you'll need to apply at the baggage office (*ufficio bagagli*).

Practical A-Z

09

Children

Children are the royalty of Italy, pampered, often obscenely spoiled, probably more fashionably dressed than you are, and never allowed to get dirty. Surprisingly, most of them also manage somehow to be well-mannered little charmers. If you're bringing your own *bambini* to Italy, they'll receive a warm welcome everywhere.

Many hotels offer advantageous rates for children and most of the larger cities have permanent **Luna Parks**, or funfairs. Rome's version in the EUR is huge and charmingly old-fashioned (a great trade-off for a day in the Vatican Museums).

Apart from endless quantities of pizza, spaghetti and ice cream, children love the **Bomarzo Monster Park** in northern Lazio (a collection of huge, weird 16th-century follies); the Disneyesque amusement parks of **Edenlandia** near Naples and **Gardaland** on Lake Garda; **Minitalia** between Bergamo and Milan (a relief model of Italy studded with replica monuments); **Pinocchio Park** in Collodi, near Pisa; the fairy-tale playground of **Città della Domenica** in Perugia; and the whole city of **Venice**.

If a **circus** visits town, you're in for a treat: it will either be a sparkling showcase of daredevil skill or a poignant, family-run version of Fellini's *La Strada*. Try to catch one or two of Italy's more vivacious **festivals** or **carnivals** – famous ones are in Venice and Viareggio.

Climate and When to Go

'O Sole Mio' notwithstanding, all of Italy isn't always sunny; it rains just as much in Rome every year as in London, and Turin's climate in the winter is said to be about the same as that of Copenhagen. **Summer** comes on dry and hot in the south and humid and hot in much of the northern lowlands and inland hills; the Alps and high Apennines stay fairly cool, while the coasts are often refreshed by breezes, except for Venice, which tends to swelter. You can probably get by without an umbrella, but take a light jacket for cool evenings. For average touring, August is probably the worst month to tramp through Italy. Transport facilities are jammed to capacity, prices are at their highest, and Rome, Milan, Florence, Venice and the other large cities are abandoned to hordes of tourists while the

Average Temperatures in °C (°F)

	January	April	July	October
Bari	8.4 (46)	13.9 (57)	24.5 (76)	18.2 (64)
Florence	5.6 (42)	13.3 (55)	25.0 (77)	15.8 (60)
Genoa	8.4 (46)	14.5 (58)	24.6 (76)	18.1 (64)
Milan	1.9 (35)	13.2 (55)	24.8 (77)	13.7 (56)
Cortina	2.3 (28)	5.2 (41)	15.8 (60)	7.6 (44)
Naples	8.7 (47)	14.3 (58)	24.8 (77)	14.5 (58)
Rome	7.4 (44)	14.4 (58)	25.7 (79)	17.7 (63)
Venice	3.8 (38)	12.6 (54)	23.6 (74)	15.1 (59)
Lake Garda	4.0 (39)	13.2 (55)	24.5 (76)	14.7 (58)

Average Monthly Rainfall in Millimetres (inches)

	January	April	July	October
Bari	39 (2)	35 (1)	19 (1)	111 (4)
Florence	61 (3)	74 (3)	23 (1)	96 (4)
Genoa	109 (4)	82 (3)	35 (2)	135 (5)
Milan	62 (3)	82 (3)	47 (2)	75 (3)
Cortina	51 (2)	138 (5)	148 (6)	119 (4)
Naples	87 (3)	55 (2)	14 (1)	102 (4)
Rome	74 (3)	62 (3)	06 (3)	123 (5)
Venice	58 (2)	77 (3)	37 (1)	66 (3)
Lake Garda	31 (1)	62 (3)	72 (3)	89 (3)

locals take to the beach. In Milan, especially, so many restaurants close down that you could starve, and the few staff left behind to man the galleys are sullen captives.

Spring and **autumn** are perhaps the loveliest times to go; spring for the infinity of wild-flowers in Italy's countryside, autumn for the colour of the trees in the hills and the vineyards. The weather is mild, places aren't crowded, and you won't need your umbrella too much, at least until November.

From December to March the happiest visitors are probably those on skis in the Alps or Apennines, or opera buffs in La Scala, San Carlo or La Fenice – but it's the best time to go if you want the art and museums to yourself. Beware though, it can rain and rain, and mountain valleys can lie for days under banks of fog and mist. The Italian Riviera enjoys the mildest **winter** climate on the peninsula.

Crime

There is a fair amount of petty crime in Italy – purse-snatchings, pickpocketing, minor thievery of the white collar kind (always check your change) and car break-ins and theft – but violent crime is rare. Nearly all mishaps can be avoided with adequate precautions. Scooter-borne purse-snatchers can be foiled if you stay on the inside of the pavement and keep a firm hold on your property (sling your bag-strap across your body, not dangling from one shoulder). Pickpockets strike in crowded buses or trams and at gatherings; don't carry too much cash, and split it so you won't lose the lot at once. In cities and popular tourist sites, beware groups of scruffy-looking women or children apparently begging for money. They use distraction techniques to perfection: the classic trick is for one child to thrust a placard at you while other children rifle your pockets. The smallest and most innocent-looking child is generally the most skilful pickpocket.

If you are targeted, the best technique is to grab sharply hold of your possessions and pockets and shout furiously – the threat of fuss usually puts them off, and Italian passers-by or plain-clothes police may come to your assistance if they realize what is happening. Be extra careful in train stations, don't leave valuables in hotel rooms, and always park your car in garages, guarded car parks or on well-lit streets, with temptation well out of sight.

Purchasing small quantities of soft drugs for personal consumption is technically legal in Italy, though what constitutes a small quantity is unspecified: if the police don't like you to begin with, it will probably be enough to get you into big trouble.

Political terrorism, once the scourge of Italy, has declined greatly in recent years, mainly thanks to quasi-military squads of black-uniformed national police, the *Carabinieri* (who are, however, the butt of Italian jokes). Local matters are usually in the hands of the *Polizia Urbana*; the nattily dressed *Vigili Urbani* concern themselves with directing traffic, and handing out parking fines. If you need to summon any of them, dial **t** 113.

Disabled Travellers

Italy has been slow off the mark in provision for disabled visitors. Cobblestones, uneven or non-existent pavements, the appalling traffic conditions, crowded public transport and endless flights of steps in many public places are all inconveniences. Progress is gradually being made, however, and a national support organization in your own country may have specific information on facilities in Italy, or will at least be able to provide general advice.

The Italian tourist office, or CIT (travel agency) can also advise on hotels, museums with ramps, and so on. If you book rail travel through CIT, you can request assistance. Once in Italy, call the Disabled Cooperative, **t** 167 179 179, for advice on accommodation and travel.

Specialist Organizations

In the UK

RADAR (Royal Association for Disability & Rehabilitation), 12 City Forum, 250 City Rd, London EC1V 8AF, **t** (020) 7250 4119, *www.radar.org.uk*. For information and books on travelling abroad.

Holiday Care Service, Imperial Building, Victoria Rd, Horley, Surrey, RH6 7PZ, **t** (01293) 774 535, **f** (01293) 784 647, Minicom **t** (01293) 776 943, *www.holidaycare.org.uk*, *holiday.care@virgin.net*. Publishes information sheets on regional travel.

In the USA and Canada

Alternative Leisure Co, 165 Middlesex Turnpike, Suite 206, Bedford, MA 01730, t (718) 275 0023, *www.alctrips.com*. Organizes vacations abroad for disabled people.

Mobility International USA, PO Box 10767, Eugene, OR 97440, USA, t/TTY (541) 343 1284, f (541) 343 6812, *www.miusa.org*. Information on international educational exchange programmes and volunteer service overseas for the disabled.

SATH (Society for the Advancement of Travel for the Handicapped), 347 5th Avenue, Suite 610, New York NY 10016, t (212) 557 0027, f (212) 725 8253, *www.tenonline.com/sath*. Travel and access information; also details other access resources on the web.

Internet Sites

Access Tourism, *www.accesstourism.com*. Pan-European website with information on hotels, travel agencies and specialist tour operators aware of access issues affecting disabled travellers.

The Able Informer, *www.sasquatch.com/able-info*. On-line magazine with travel tips for disabled people abroad.

Emerging Horizons, *www.emerging horizons.com*. On-line travel newsletter for people with disabilities.

Global Access, *www.geocities.com*. On-line network with links, archives and information on travel guides for disabled travellers.

Embassies and Consulates

Bari, (UK) Via Dalmazia 127, t 080 554 3668.
Florence, (UK) Lungarno Corsini 2, t 055 284 133; (USA) Lungarno Vespucci 38, t 055 239 8276.
Milan, (Australia) Via Borgagna 2, t 02 7601 1330; (Canada) Via Vittorio Pisani 19, t 02 669 7451; (UK) Via San Paulo 7, t 02 723 001; (USA) Largo Donegani 1, t 02 2900 1841.
Naples, (UK) Via Crispi 122, t 081 663 511; (USA) Piazza Repubblica 2, t 081 583 8111.
Rome, (Australia) Via Alessandria 215, t 06 852 721; (Canada) Via Zara 30, t 06 440 3028; (Ireland) Largo Nazareno 3, t 06 678 2541; (New Zealand) Via Zara 28, t 06 440 2928; (UK) Via XX Settembre 80/a, t 06 482 5441; (USA) Via V. Veneto 119/a, t 06 46741.

Festivals

Every 50 years the Catholic Church celebrates a Holy Year (*Giubileo*) and thousands of pilgrims descend on Italy's holiest sights. The last Holy Year was in 2000.

There are literally thousands of other festivals answering to every description in Italy. Every *comune* has at least one or two honouring patron saints, at which the presiding Madonna is paraded through the streets decked in fairy lights and gaudy flowers. Shrovetide and Holy Week are great focuses of activity. *Carnival*, after being suppressed and ignored for decades, has been revived in many places, displaying the gorgeous music and pageantry of the *Commedia dell'Arte* with Harlequin and his motley crew. In Venice, the handmade carnival masks now constitute a new art form and make popular souvenirs.

Holy Week celebrations take on a dirgelike Spanish flavour in the south, when robed and hooded penitents haul melodramatic floats through the streets. Meanwhile, in Rome, the Supreme Pontiff himself officiates at the Easter ceremonies. Other festivals are more earthily pagan, celebrating the land and the harvest with giant phallic towers. Some are purely secular affairs sponsored by political parties (especially the Communists and Socialists), where everyone goes to hang out.

There are great costume pageants dating back to the Middle Ages or Renaissance, like the Sienese *Palio* (a bareback horse race), an endless round of carnivals, music festivals, opera seasons and antique fairs. Relaxed village *festas* can be just as enjoyable as (or more so than) the big national crowd-pullers. Outsiders are nearly always welcome. Whatever the occasion, eating is a primary pastime at all Italian jamborees, and all kinds of regional specialities are prepared. Check at the local tourist office for precise dates, which alter from year to year, and often slide into the nearest weekend.

Food and Drink

When you eat out, mentally add to the bill (*conto*) the bread and cover charge (*pane e coperto*, between L2,000 and L4,000), and a

Calendar of Events and Festivals

January–July Opera and ballet season at La Scala, **Milan**.

January 5–6 Child-oriented Epiphany celebrations throughout Italy, honouring the good stocking-filling witch La Befana, who brings lumps of coal and sweets.
Three Kings Procession, **Milan**.

Late January Festival of Italian Popular Song, **San Remo** – the Italian Eurovision, a must in any kitsch-lover's diary, at least on TV.

30–31 January Sant'Orso craft fair, **Aosta**.

February–March Shrovetide Carnivals all over Italy, especially in **Venice** – boat procession; **Viareggio**, Sa Sartiglia – medieval tournament and masquerade.

March Fashion collections shown, **Milan**.
Sant'Ambrogio carnival, **Milan**.

March–April Holy Week and Easter celebrations : processions in **Tàranto, Bari**, and **Brìndisi**; Scoppio del Carro (Explosion of the Cart), **Florence**; Good Friday procession from St Peter's to the Colosseum, led by the Pope, **Rome**; concerts at San Maurizio church in Monastero Maggiore, **Milan**.

April Ortafiori flower festival, **Orta San Giulio**.

May Feast of San Nicola, **Bari**.
Festival of Snakes, **Cocullo** (Abruzzo).
Palio del Carroccio, **Legnano** (Milan) – celebrates the defeat of Barbarossa by the Lombard League in 1176 (medieval parade and horse-race).
Feast of San Gennaro, the first of three such occasions when the faithful assemble in **Naples** cathedral to await the miraculous liquefaction of a phial of their patron saint's blood – it never fails.
Corsa dei Ceri (Race of the Candles), **Gubbio** (Umbria) – huge wooden shrines are raced up the town's steep hill to the basilica.
Palio della Balestra (Crossbow Palio), **Gubbio** – medieval contest with antique weapons.
Vogolonga, Venice – the 'long row' from San Marco to Burano.

May–June Maggio Musicale Fiorentino, **Florence**.

June Historical Regatta of the Four Ancient Maritime Republics (boat race between the rival ports and former rulers of the sea, **Pisa**,

Venice, **Amalfi** and **Genoa** – each takes it in turn to host the regatta.
Gioco del Ponte (Game of the Bridge), **Pisa** – mock battle.

June 21 Infiorata, **Genzano** (Rome) and **Spello** (Umbria) – Corpus Domini celebrations with flower decorations.
Feast of St Antonio, **Padua**.
Gioco del Calcio, **Florence** – football in medieval costume.
Festa dei Gigli, **Nola** (Naples) – 'lily' procession; the lilies here are actually large wooden towers.

Mid-June–July Festival of Two Worlds, **Spoleto** (Umbria) – Italy's biggest arts festival.

July Joust of the Bear, **Pistoia**.
Feast of the Redeemer (Il Redentore), **Venice** – fireworks and gondola procession.
Umbria Jazz Festival, **Perugia**.
Archery contest, **Fivizzano** (Massa).

July and August Palio, Siena – bareback horse race (held twice).
Summer Operetta Festival, **Trieste**.
Verona Outdoor Opera Season.

August Joust of the Quintana, **Ascoli Piceno** (The Marches).
Bravo delle Botti, **Montepulciano** – barrel race around the hill town's streets.
International Film Festival, **Venice**.
Regatta, **Ventimiglia**.
Wheat Festival, **Foglianise** (Benevento) – decorated tractors.

August–September Settimane Musicali (Musical Weeks), **Stresa** – concerts galore.

September Joust of the Saracen, **Arezzo** – knights in armour.
Historic Regatta, **Venice** – antics in boats.
Living Chess Game, **Maròstica** (Veneto) (even years).
Feast of San Gennaro, **Naples**.
Luminaria di Santa Croce, **Lucca** – torchlit procession.
Italian Grand Prix, **Monza**.
Neapolitan song contest, **Piedigrotta**.

October Truffle Fair, **Alba**.
Feast of St Francis, **Assisi**.

November Festa della Salute, **Venice**.

December Opera Lirica season opens throughout Italy.
Advent and Christmas celebrations.
Christmas Fair of the *presepi*, **Naples**.
Sausage and *polenta* festival, **Benevento**.

15 per cent service charge. This is often included in the bill (*servizio compreso*); if not, it will say *servizio non compreso*, and you'll have to do your own arithmetic. Additional tipping is at your own discretion, but never do it in family-run places (you may offend).

We have divided restaurants into price categories (*see* box, above).

When you leave a restaurant you will be given a receipt (*scontrino* or *ricevuto fiscale*) which according to Italian law you must take with you out of the door and carry for at least 60 metres. If you aren't given one, it means the restaurant is probably fudging on its taxes and thus offering you lower prices. There is a slim chance the tax police (*Guardia di Finanza*) may have their eye on you and the restaurant, and if you don't have a receipt they could slap you with a heavy fine.

For further information about eating in Italy, including local specialities, wines and a menu decoder, *see* the **Food and Drink** chapter, p.83.

Health and Emergencies

You can insure yourself against almost any possible mishap before you leave – cancelled flights, stolen or lost baggage and health. Check any current insurance policies you hold to see if they cover you while abroad, and under what circumstances, and judge whether you need a special **traveller's insurance** policy for the journey. Travel agencies, as well as insurance companies and banks, sell special travel packages; it's worth shopping around, but do read the small print.

EU citizens are entitled to **reciprocal health care** in Italy's National Health Service and a 90 per cent discount on prescriptions (bring **Form E111** with you, which you can obtain in the UK from any main post office). The E111 should cover you for emergencies, but does not cover all medical expenses (no repatriation costs, for example, and no private treatment); it is still advisable to take out travel insurance.

Citizens of non-EU countries should check carefully that they have adequate insurance for any medical expenses, and the cost of returning home. Australia has a reciprocal health care scheme with Italy too, but New Zealand, Canada and the USA do not. If you already have health insurance, a student card, or a credit card, any of these may entitle you to some medical cover abroad.

In an **emergency**, dial **115** for fire and **113** for an ambulance in Italy (*ambulanza*) or to find the nearest hospital (*ospedale*). Less serious problems can be treated at a *pronto soccorso* (casualty/first aid department) at any hospital clinic (*ambulatorio*), or at a local health unit (Unita Sanitarial Locale – USL). Airports and main railway stations also have **first-aid posts**. If you have to pay for any health treatment, make sure you get a receipt, so that you can make any claims for reimbursement later.

Dispensing **chemists** (*farmacie*) are generally open from 8.30am to 1pm and from 4 to 8pm. Pharmacists are trained to give advice for minor ills. Any large town will have a *farmacia* that stays open 24 hours; others take turns to stay open (the address rota is posted in the window).

No specific **vaccinations** are required or advised for citizens of most countries before visiting Italy; the main health risks are the usual travellers' woes of upset stomachs or the effects of too much sun. Take a supply of **medicaments** with you (insect repellent, anti-diarrhœal medicine, sun lotion and antiseptic cream), and any drugs you need regularly.

Most Italian doctors speak rudimentary English, but if you can't find one, contact your embassy or consulate for a list of English-speaking doctors. Standards of health care in the north are generally higher than in the deep south.

Living and Working in Italy

Registration and Residency

If you are planning to stay in Italy long-term without working, you should register with the police within eight days of arrival and apply for a *permesso di soggiorno* from the local **Questura** (police station). Get there early in the morning as most state offices close in the afternoon, though you'll probably still have to wait. However frustrating the process of obtaining documentation in Italy, try to appear calm and remain polite, or things will only get worse. You need a *permesso* in order to open a bank account in Italy, or to buy a car. It lasts for three months, after which you will need to renew it. If you can prove you have enough money to live on, permission is usually granted, though non-whites may have a harder time. Take your passport, photographs and as much ID as you can muster.

If you wish to be registered as a resident you should apply to the local **Ufficio Anagrafe** (registry office). If you are in Italy for work, your employer should help you with the red-tape, though many small businessmen prefer to take unregistered foreigners (so that they don't have to declare them and pay tax). Students attending courses at Italian universities must obtain a declaration from the Italian Consulate in their home countries before their departure, certifying their 'acceptability' for further study, and that they have adequate health insurance. A surprising number of scholarships are offered to foreign students (especially post-graduates) by the Italian Ministry of Foreign Affairs; ask your Italian embassy for details, or write to the Ministry directly (**Direzione Generale per la Cooperazione Culturale Scientifica e Tecnica**, Piazzale della Farnesina 1, Roma).

Maps

The maps in this guide are for orientation only and for exploring it is worth investing in a good, up-to-date regional map before you arrive from one of the following bookshops:
Stanford's, (UK) 12–14 Long Acre, London WC2 9LP, t (020) 7836 1321.
The Travel Bookshop, (UK) 13 Blenheim Crescent, London W11 2EE, t (020) 7229 5260.
The Complete Traveller, (USA) 199 Madison Ave, New York, NY 10016, t (212) 685 9007.
Excellent maps are produced by **Touring Club Italiano, Michelin** and **Istituto Geografico de Agostini**. They are available at major bookshops in Italy or sometimes on news-stands. Italian tourist offices are helpful and can often supply good area maps and town plans.

Money

It's a good idea to order a wad of local currency from your home bank to have on hand when you arrive in Italy, the land of strikes, unforeseen delays and quirky banking hours. Take great care how you carry it, however (don't keep it all in one place). Obtaining money is often a frustrating business involving much queueing and form-filling. The major banks and exchange bureaux licensed by the Bank of Italy give the best exchange rates for currency or traveller's cheques. Hotels, private exchanges in resorts and FS-run exchanges at railway stations usually have less advantageous rates, but are open outside normal banking hours.

Weekend Exchange Offices
Milan: Banca Ponti, Piazza del Duomo 19; Banca delle Comunicazioni, Stazione Centrale; American Express, Via Brera 3.
Florence: Thomas Cook, Lungarno Acciaioli 6r; American Express, Via de' Guicciardini 49r.
Rome: Banco Nazionale delle Comunicazione, Stazione Termini; Thomas Cook Piazza Barberini 21D.
Naples: CIT, Piazza Municipio 72; Ashiba, Piazza Municipio 1.
Venice: American Express, S. Moise 1471; CIT, Piazza S. Marco.

In addition there are exchange offices at most airports. Remember that Italians indicate decimals with commas and thousands with full points.

Most British banks have an arrangement with their Italian counterparts, whereby you can (for a significant commission) use your bank card to take money out of Italian ATMs (Bancomats), but check with your bank first. Bancomats also take Eurocheque cards and credit cards (as long as you know your PIN number). Banks will advance you cash on a credit card or Eurocheque with a Eurocheque card. Visa, American Express and Diner's are more widely accepted than MasterCard (Access). Large hotels, resort area restaurants, shops and car hire firms will accept plastic as well; smaller places may not.

The Euro
From 1 January 2002 the lira will be replaced by the euro. Prices are already quoted in both

currencies. The exchange rate between the lira and the euro is fixed at L1,936.27 to €1. Or, as the ad campaign in Italy says, drop 3 zeros and divide by half.

National Holidays

Most museums, as well as banks and shops, are closed on the following national holidays.

1 January (New Year's Day)
6 January (Epiphany)
Easter Monday
25 April (Liberation Day)
1 May (Labour Day)
15 August (Assumption, also known as *Ferragosto*, the official climax of the Italian holiday season)
1 November (All Saints' Day)
8 December (Immaculate Conception)
25 December (Christmas Day)
26 December (*Santo Stefano*, St Stephen's Day)

In addition to these general holidays, many towns also take their patron saint's day off.

Opening Hours and Museums

Although it varies from region to region, with the north bearing more resemblance to the rest of Europe than the Mediterranean south, most of Italy closes down at 1pm until 3 or 4pm to eat and properly digest the main meal of the day. Afternoon hours are from 4 to 7, often from 5 to 8 in the hot summer months. Bars are often the only places open during the early afternoon. Some cities (notably Milan) close down completely during August when locals flee to the hills, lakes or coast. In any case, don't be surprised if you find anywhere in Italy unexpectedly closed (or open), whatever its official stated hours.

Offices

Banks: open Mon–Fri 8.30–1 and 3–4, closed weekends and on local and national holidays (*see* above).
Shops: open Mon–Sat 8–1 and 3.30–7.30. Some supermarkets and department stores stay open throughout the day, and hours vary according to season and are shorter in smaller centres.

Government-run dispensers of red tape (*e.g.* visa departments) often stay open for quite limited periods, usually during the mornings (*Mon–Fri*). It pays to get there as soon as they open (or before) to spare your nerves in an interminable queue. Anyway, take something to read, or write your memoirs.

Museums and Galleries

Many of Italy's museums are magnificent, many are run with shameful neglect, and many have been closed for years for 'restoration' with slim prospects of reopening in the foreseeable future. With at least one work of art per inhabitant, Italy has a hard time financing the preservation of its national heritage; enquire at the tourist office to find out exactly what is open and what is 'temporarily' closed before setting off on a wild-goose chase.

Churches

Italy's churches have always been a prime target for art thieves and as a consequence are usually locked when there isn't a sacristan or caretaker to keep an eye on things. All churches, except for the really important cathedrals and basilicas, close in the afternoon at the same hours as the shops, and the little ones tend to stay closed. Always have a pocketful of coins for the light machines in churches, or whatever work of art you came to inspect will remain clouded in ecclesiastical gloom. Don't do your visiting during services, and don't come to see paintings and statues in churches the week preceding Easter – you will probably find them covered with mourning shrouds.

In general, Sunday afternoons and Mondays are dead periods for the sightseer – you may want to make them your travelling days. Places without specified opening hours can usually be visited on request – but it is best to go before 1pm. We have listed the hours of important sights and museums, and specified which ones charge admission. Entrance charges vary widely; major sights can be fairly steep (L12,000 plus), but others may be free; the Vatican continues a long papal tradition with its high admission charges. EU citizens under 18 and over 65 get free admission to state museums, at least in theory.

Packing

You simply cannot overdress in Italy; whatever grand strides Italian designers have made on the international fashion merry-go-round, most of their clothes are purchased domestically, prices be damned. Now, whether or not you want to try to keep up with the natives is your own affair. It's not that the Italians are very formal; they simply like to dress up with a gorgeousness that adorns their cities as much as those old Renaissance churches and palaces. The few places with dress codes are the major churches and basilicas (no shorts, sleeveless shirts or strappy sundresses – women should tuck a light scarf in a bag to throw over shoulders), casinos, and a few posh restaurants.

Your electric appliances will work in Italy if you adapt and convert them to run on 220 AC with two round prongs on the plug.

Post Offices

Usually open Mon–Sat 8–1; in large cities 8–6 or 7.

Dealing with *la posta italiana* has always been a risky, frustrating, time-consuming affair. It is one of the most expensive and slowest postal services in Europe. Even buying the right stamps requires dedicated research and saintly patience. One of the scandals that mesmerized Italy in recent years involved the minister of the post office, who disposed of literally tons of backlog mail by tossing it in the Tiber. When the news broke, he was replaced ; the new minister, having learned his lesson, burned all the mail the post office was incapable of delivering.

Not surprisingly, fed-up Italians view the invention of the fax machine as a gift from the Madonna. From these harsh judgements, however, we must exempt the Vatican City, whose special postal service (on angelic wings?) knocks spots off the rest of the country for speed and efficiency. If you're anywhere in Rome, be sure to post your mail in the Holy See. You need to buy special Vatican stamps, which provide a tidy profit for the papal coffers.

To have your mail sent *poste restante* (general delivery), have it addressed to the central post office (*Fermo Posta*) and expect it to take three to four weeks to arrive. Make sure your surname is clearly written in block capitals. To pick up your mail you must present your passport and pay a nominal charge. Stamps (*francobolli*) are available in post offices or at tobacconists (*tabacchi*, identified by blue signs with a white T). Prices fluctuate.

You can also have money telegraphed to you through the post office; if all goes well, this can happen in a mere three days, but expect a fair proportion of it to go into commission.

Shopping

'Made in Italy' has become a byword for style and quality, especially in fashion and leather, but also in home design, ceramics, pots and pans, jewellery, lace and linens, glass and crystal, chocolates, bells, Christmas decorations, hats, woven straw and baskets, art books, engravings, handmade stationery, gold and silver, bicycles, sports cars, woodwork, a hundred kinds of liqueurs, aperitifs, coffee machines, gastronomic specialities, and antiques. You'll find the best variety of goods in Milan, Rome, Florence and Venice – in other words, where the money is. Design-conscious Milan is Italy's major shopping centre and a cynosure of innovative style and fashion throughout the world.

If you are looking for antiques, be sure to demand a certificate of authenticity – reproductions can be very good. To get your antique or modern art purchases home, you will have to apply to the Export Department of the Italian Ministry of Education and pay an export tax as well; your seller should know the details. Non-EU citizens should save all receipts for Customs.

Italians don't much like department stores, but there are a few chains – the classiest is the oldest, Rinascente, while COIN stores often have good buys in almost the latest fashions. Standa and UPIM are more like Woolworths; they have good clothes selections, houseware and so on, and often contain supermarkets. The main attraction of Italian shopping, however, is to buy classy luxury items; for less expensive clothes and household items you can nearly always do better at home. Prices for clothes are generally very high.

Sports and Activities

Cycling

About three-quarters of Italy is hilly or mountainous, so a cycling holiday is no soft option. It is best to bring your own bike (a mountain bike if possible) and spare parts; cycling is growing fast, but is nowhere near as fanatically practised in Italy as, say, in France or Denmark. Facilities for hiring or repairing bikes are less widespread, but you can buy a good bike for L200–300,000. Good biking regions include Tuscany and Umbria, Puglia and the Alpine areas, where there are some good trails. Most airlines and rail companies will transport bikes quite cheaply. The spring Tour d'Italia is Italy's annual cycling event.

Fishing

You don't need a permit for sea-fishing (without an aqualung), but Italy's coastal waters, polluted and over-exploited, may disappoint. Commercial fishing has depleted stocks to such an extent that the government has begun to declare two- and three-month moratoria on all fishing to give the fish a break. Many freshwater lakes and streams are stocked, and if you're more interested in fresh fish than the sport of it, there are innumerable trout farms where you can practically pick the fish up out of the water with your hands. To fish in fresh water you need to purchase a year's membership card (currently L189,000) from the **Federazione Italiana della Pesca Sportiva**, which has an office in every province; they will inform you about local conditions and restrictions. Bait and equipment are readily available.

Football

Soccer (*il calcio*) is a national obsession. For many Italians its importance far outweighs tedious issues like the state of the nation, the government of the day, or any momentous international event – not least because of the weekly chance (slim but real) of becoming an instant lira billionaire in the Lotteria Sportiva. All major cities, and most minor ones, have at least one team of some sort. The sport was actually introduced by the English, but a Renaissance game, something like a cross between football and rugby, has existed in Italy for centuries. Rivalry between Italian teams is intense, and scandals – especially involving bribery and cheating – are rife; yet crowd violence is minimal. Big-league matches are played on Sunday afternoons (*Sept–May*). For information, contact the Federazione Italiana Giuoco Calcio, Via G. Allegri 14, 00198 Rome, t 06 84911.

Golf

Italians have been slower than some nationalities to appreciate the delights of biffing a small white ball into a hole in the ground, but they're catching on fast. The north is a good place to practise, particularly around Lake Como. Contact the Federazione Italiana Golf, Via Flaminia 388, 00196 Rome, t 06 323 1825, for more information.

Hiking and Mountaineering

These sports are becoming steadily more popular among native Italians every year. Walking in the Alps is generally practicable between May and October. Strategically placed **Alpine refuges** (*rifugi alpini*) provide shelter, but if you come in early June or October when the refuges are closed you'll need to carry camping gear. The refuges are open from the end of June to the end of September; in July and August it's wise to book a bed in advance to avoid disappointment. They vary dramatically. Many are owned by the Italian Alpine Club, while others are privately owned, primarily by ski resorts. Some are along trails, while others may be reached via cable car. All offer bed and board; nearly all now require that you bring a sleeping sheet, or buy one on the site. Prices vary by altitude: the higher up and more difficult the access, the more expensive. Besides the refuges, there are the *baite* (wooden huts), *casere* (stone huts) and *bivouacs* (beds but no food) along some of the higher trails: they have no custodians but offer shelter. For information, write to the Italian Alpine Club (CAI, Via Fonseca Pimental 7, 20121 Milan, t 02 2614 1378, f 02 2614 1395.

Some Alpine resorts have taken to offering Settimane Verdi (Green Weeks) – good-value accommodation and activity packages for summer visitors similar to skiers' White Weeks (*see p.113*). Tuscany and the Apennines (Abruzzo National Park) offer less strenuous but equally enjoyable walking country.

Hunting

Italy's most controversial sport pits avid enthusiasts against a growing number of environmentalists. The debate is fierce and the start of the season is marked by huge protests. Indiscriminate trapping, netting and shooting is responsible for the decimation of many migrant Mediterranean songbirds – thrushes and the like. Less controversial, at least from the conservation point of view, is duck, pigeon and wild-boar shooting.

Motor Racing

The homeland of Ferrari, Maserati and Alfa Romeo fosters a keen interest in motor sports, proof of which can be witnessed along any Italian road, which Italians regard as practice tracks. Monza, near Milan, hosts the Italian Grand Prix every September. The Formula Uno track, built in 1922, is 15km from town.

Riding Holidays

Riding holidays are now available in many parts of Italy, particularly in areas where *agriturismo* (*see* Where to Stay – Rural Self-Catering, p.118) is well represented, such as Tuscany, Umbria and Lazio; in these areas tours staying at country estates are organized. There are riding stables in most cities and resorts. For more information, contact the local Agriturist office, or the Associazione Nazionale per il Turismo Equestre, Via A. Borelli 5, 00161 Rome, **t** 06 444 1179. Rome's International Riding Show in the Villa Borghese draws a big crowd each May. Horse racing is staged in many large cities, but easily the most exciting race of all is Siena's bareback Palio (*see* p.107 and p.719), a medieval pageant that arouses huge local rivalries.

Rowing and Canoeing

The annual regatta between the four ancient maritime republics of Venice, Amalfi, Genoa and Pisa (held in turn at each city, *see* p.107) is a splendidly colourful event. Lake Piediluco in Umbria hosts an international rowing championship. If you prefer the DIY version, try the Arno or any of Lombardy's lakes. The mountain rivers provide exciting white-water sport. Kayak races are held in the Dolomites. For more information contact the Federazione Italiana Canoa e Kayak, Viale Tiziano 70, 00196 Rome, **t** 06 368 58215.

Skiing and Winter Sports

Italy still lacks the cachet of neighbouring Switzerland or Austria among the skiing fraternity, but has caught up significantly, and now has a better reputation for safety and efficiency than it once did, though erratic snow cover is always a problem. Its main resorts are obviously in the Alps, particularly the scenic Dolomites. Downhill and cross-country (*sci di fondo*) skiing are available, along with more exotic variants (for experts only) like helicopter skiing. Equipment hire is generally not too expensive, but lift passes and accommodation can push up the cost of a winter holiday. Some of the most fashionable (and expensive) resorts include **Cortina** and **Courmayeur**. The Sella Ronda links several resorts in an exhilarating day's circuit. The Marmolada glacier in Trentino-Adige and Cervinia at the foot of the Matterhorn provide year-round sources of snowy runs. Lombardy's most famous ski resort is **Bormio**, at the entrance to Italy's largest national park, which has hosted world events in recent years (glacier skiing above the Stelvio pass).

Prices are highest during Christmas and New Year holidays, in February and at Easter. Most resorts offer *Settimane Bianche* (White Weeks) – off-season packages at economical rates. Other winter sports such as ice-skating and bob-sleighing are available at resorts.

Tennis

If soccer is Italy's most popular spectator sport, tennis is probably the game most people actually play. Every *comune* has public courts for hourly hire, especially resorts. Private clubs may offer temporary membership to passing visitors, and hotel courts can often be used by non-residents for a reasonable fee. Contact local tourist offices for information. Italy's big tennis event is the Grand Prix tournament. held in Rome in May.

Water Sports

Despite Italy's notorious coastal pollution, watersports are immensely popular, especially sailing and windsurfing. The best areas for sailing include the Ligurian Riviera and the Tuscan or Lazio coasts. Lakes Como and Garda also have well-equipped sailing and windsurfing schools. Waterskiing is possible on all the major lakes, as well as at many coastal resorts. A few areas are good for diving, such as Alassio (Liguria) and Capri. Boat and equipment hire is often quite expensive. Mainland Italy is not remarkable for its **beaches**. Much of the coast is disappointingly flat and dull and many seaside resorts are plagued by that peculiarly Italian phenomenon, the concessionaire, who parks ugly lines of sunbeds and brollies all the way along the best stretches of coast, and charges all comers handsomely for the privilege of spending some time at the seaside. During the winter you can see what happens when the beaches miss out on their manicures; many get depressingly rubbish-strewn.

The beaches in the south (Calabria, Basilicata and Puglia) are generally cleaner and less developed than those further north; those around the Bay of Naples, Rome's Lido di Ostia and the Venetian Lido are best avoided for swimming. Head for the islands for cleaner water and prettier scenery. In Lombardy, the smaller, less crowded lakes like Viverone, Varese and Mergozzo are preferable to the larger lakes for swimming. No one bats an eye at topless bathing, though nudism requires more discretion.

For further information on sporting activities, contact the **Italian State Tourist Office** or write to the following organizations:
Federazione Italiana Vela (Italian Sailing Federation), Via Brigata Bisagno 2/17, Genoa, t 010 565 723.
Federazione Italiana Motonautica (Italian Motorboat Federation) and **Federazione Italiana Sci Nautico** (Italian Waterskiing Federation), Via Piranesi 44b, Milan, t 02 761 050.

Telephones

Public phones for international calls may be found in the offices of **Telecom Italia**, Italy's telephone company. They are the only places where you can make reverse-charge calls (*a erre*, collect calls) but be prepared for a wait, as calls go through the operator in Rome. Rates for long-distance calls are among the highest in Europe. Calls within Italy are cheapest after 10pm; international calls after 11pm. Italy's streets are dotted with orange phones.

Most phone booths now take either coins (L100, 200, 500 or 1,000) or phone cards (*schede telefoniche*), available in L5,000, L10,000 and sometimes 15,000 amounts at tobacconists and news-stands – you have to snap off the small perforated corner in order to use them. In smaller villages you can usually find *telefoni a scatti*, with a meter on it, in at least one bar (a small commission is generally charged). Try to avoid telephoning from hotels, which often add 25% to the bill.

Direct calls may be made by dialling the international prefix (for the UK 0044, Ireland 00353, USA and Canada 001, Australia 0061, New Zealand 0064). If you're calling Italy from abroad, dial +39 first. Many places have public fax machines, but the speed of transmission may make costs very high.

Time

Italy is on Central European Time, one hour ahead of Greenwich Mean Time and six hours ahead of Eastern Standard Time. From the last weekend of March to the end of September, Italian Summer Time (daylight saving time) is in effect – clocks go back one hour.

Toilets

Frequent travellers have noted a steady improvement over the years in the cleanliness of Italy's public conveniences, although as ever you will only find them in places like train and bus stations and bars. Ask for the *bagno*, *toilette* or *gabinetto*; in stations and the smarter bars and cafes there are attendants who expect a few hundred lire for keeping the place decent. You'll probably have to ask them for paper (*carta*). Don't confuse the Italian plurals; *signori* (gents), *signore* (ladies).

Tourist Offices

Tourist information offices: open 8–12.30 or 1 and 3–7, possibly longer in summer. Few open on Saturday afternoons or Sundays.

Known as EPT, APT or AAST, information booths provide hotel lists, town plans and terse information on local sights and transport. Queues can be maddeningly long. If

Hotel Price Categories

Category		Double with Bath	Price in Euros
luxury	★★★★★	L450–800,000	€225–400
very expensive	★★★★	L300–450,000	€150–225
expensive	★★★	L200–300,000	€100–150
moderate	★★	L120–200,000	€60–100
cheap	★	up to L120,000	€60

you're stuck, you may get more sense out of a friendly travel agency than an official tourist office. Nearly every city and province now has a web page, and you can often book your hotel direct through the Internet.

UK, Italian State Tourist Board, 1 Princes Street, London W1R 8AY, **t** (020) 7408 1254, **f** (020) 7493 6695, *www.enit.it/www.italian tourism.com*; Italian Embassy, 14 Three King's Yard, Davies Street, London W1Y 2EH, **t** (020) 7312 2200, **f** (020) 7312 2230, *www.embitaly.org.uk.*

USA, 630 Fifth Ave, Suite 1565, New York, NY 10111, **t** (212) 245 5095/4822, **f** (212) 586 9249; 12400 Wilshire Blvd, Suite 550, Los Angeles, CA 90025, **t** (310) 820 1898/9807, **f** (310) 820 6357; 500 N. Michigan Ave, Suite 2240, Chicago 1 IL 60611, **t** (312) 644 0996, **f** (312) 644 3019, *www.italiantourism.com.*

Australia, Level 26-44 Market Street, Sydney, NSW 2000, **t** (02) 92 621 666, **f** (02) 92 621677, *lenitour@ihug.com.au.*

Canada, 17 Bloor Street East Suite 907, South Tower, M4W 3R8 Toronto (ON), **t** (416) 925 4882/925 3725, **f** (416) 925 4799, *www.italian tourism.com.*

New Zealand, c/o Italian Embassy, 34 Grant Road, Thorndon, Wellington, **t** (04) 736 065.

Tourist and travel information may also be available from **Alitalia** (Italy's national airline) or **CIT** (Italy's state-run travel agency) offices in some countries.

Where to Stay

All accommodation in Italy is classified by the Provincial Tourist Boards. Price control, however, has been deregulated since 1992. Hotels now set their own tariffs, which means that in some places prices have rocketed. After a period of rapid and erratic price fluctuation, tariffs are at last settling down again to more predictable levels under the influence of market forces. Good-value, interesting accommodation in cities can be very difficult to find. Milan has the most expensive and heavily booked hotels in Italy; check the calendar of events with the tourist office – a major trade fair or conference could put all your travel plans in jeopardy.

The quality of furnishings and facilities has generally improved in all categories in recent years. Many hotels have installed smart bathrooms and electronic gadgetry. At the top end of the market, Italy has a number of exceptionally sybaritic hotels, furnished and decorated with real panache. But you can still find plenty of older-style hotels and *pensioni*, whose eccentricities of character and architecture (in some cases undeniably charming) may frequently be at odds with modern standards of comfort or even safety.

Hotels and Guesthouses

Italian *alberghi* come in all shapes and sizes. They are rated from one to five stars, depending what facilities they offer (not their character, style or charm). The star ratings are some indication of price levels, but for tax reasons not all hotels choose to advertise themselves at the rating to which they are entitled, so you may find a modestly rated hotel just as comfortable (or more so) than a higher rated one.

Conversely, you may find a hotel offers few stars in hopes of attracting budget-conscious travellers, but charges just as much as a higher-rated neighbour.

Pensioni are generally more modest, though the distinction between these and ordinary hotels is becoming rather blurred. *Locande* are traditionally an even more basic form of hostelry, but these days the term may denote somewhere fairly chic. Other inexpensive accommodation is sometimes known as *alloggi* or *affittacamere*. There are usually plenty of cheap dives around railway stations; for somewhere more salubrious, head for the historic quarters. Whatever the shortcomings of the décor, furnishings and fittings, you can usually rely at least on having clean sheets.

Price lists, by law, must be posted on the back of the door of every room, along with meal prices and any extra charges (such as air-conditioning, or even a shower in cheap places). Many hotels display two or three different rates, depending on the season. Low-season rates may be about a third lower than peak-season tariffs. Some resort hotels close down altogether for several months a year. During high season you should always book ahead to be sure of a room (a fax reservation may be less frustrating to organize than one by post or telephone, and certainly more likely to reach its destination).

If you have paid a deposit, your booking is valid under Italian law, but don't expect it to be refunded if you have to cancel. Tourist offices publish annual regional lists of hotels and *pensioni* with current rates, but do not generally make reservations for visitors. Major city business hotels may offer significant discounts at weekends.

Main railway stations have accommodation booking desks; inevitably, a fee is charged. Chain hotels or motels are generally the easiest hotels to book, though not always the most interesting to stay in. Top of the list is CIGA (*Compagnia Grandi Alberghi*) with some of the most luxurious establishments in Italy, many of them grand, turn-of-the-century places that have been exquisitely restored. Venice's legendary Cipriani is one of its flag-ships. The French consortium *Relais et Châteaux* specializes in tastefully indulgent accommodation, often in historic buildings. At a more affordable level, one of the biggest chains in Italy is *Jolly Hotels*, always reliable if not up to the same standard; these can be found near the centre of larger towns. Many motels are operated by the ACI (Italian Automobile Club) or by AGIP (the oil company) and usually located along major exit routes.

If you arrive without a reservation, begin looking or phoning round for accommodation early in the day. If possible, inspect the room (and bathroom facilities) before you book, and check the tariff carefully. Italian hoteliers may legally alter their rates twice during the year, so printed tariffs or tourist board lists (and prices quoted in this book!) may be out of date. Hoteliers who wilfully overcharge should be reported to the local tourist office. You will be asked for your passport to register.

Prices listed in this guide (*see* box, p.115) are for double rooms, and you can expect to pay about two-thirds the rate for single occupancy – though in high season you may be charged the full double rate in some popular beach resorts. Extra beds are usually charged at about a third more of the room rate. Rooms without private en suite bathrooms generally charge 20–30 per cent less, and most offer discounts for children sharing parent's rooms, or children's meals. A single room (*camera singola*) may cost anything from about L25,000 upwards. Double rooms (*camera doppia*) go from about L60,000 to L250,000 or more. If you want a double bed, request a *camera matrimoniale*.

Breakfast is optional in hotels, obligatory in *pensioni*. You can get better value by eating breakfast in a bar or café. In high season you may be expected to take half board in resorts if the hotel has a restaurant, and one-night stays may be refused.

Hostels and Budget Accommodation

There aren't many youth hostels (*alberghi* or *ostelli per la gioventù*) in Italy, but they are generally pleasant and sometimes located in historic buildings. The **Associazione Italiana Alberghi per la Gioventù** (Italian Youth Hostel Association, or AIG) is affiliated to the International Youth Hostel Federation. For a full list of hostels, contact AIG at Via Cavour 44, 00184 Roma (**t** 06 487 1152; **f** 06 488 0492). An international membership card will enable you to stay in any of them. You can obtain these in advance from:

UK, Youth Hostels Assocation of England and Wales, Trevelyan House, 8 St Stephen's Hill, St Albans, Herts AL1 2DY, **t** (01727) 855 215, **f** (01727) 844 126, *www.yha.org.uk*.

USA, American Youth Hostels Inc., 1009 11st Street NW, Washington DC 20001, **t** (202) 737 2333, *www.yha.org.usa*.

Australia, Australian Youth Hostel Association, PO Box 314, Camperdown 1450, NSW Australia, **t** (02) 9565 1699, *www.yha.org.au*.

Canada, Canadian Hostelling Association, 205 Catherine Street, Suite 401, Ottawa, ON K23 1C3, **t** (613) 237 7884.

Cards can be purchased on the spot in many hostels if you don't already have one.

Religious institutions also run hostels; some are single sex, others will accept Catholics only. Rates are usually somewhere between L15,000 and L20,000, including breakfast. Discounts are available for senior citizens, and some family rooms are available. You generally have to check in after 5pm, and pay for your room before 9am. Hostels usually close for most of the daytime, and many operate a curfew. During the spring, noisy school parties cram hostels for field trips. In the summer, book ahead. Contact the hostels directly.

Villas, Flats and Chalets

If you're travelling in a group or with a family, self-catering can be the ideal way to experience Italy. The Italian State Tourist Office has lists of agencies in the UK and USA which rent places on a weekly or fort-nightly basis. The small ads in the weekend papers are crammed with suggestions, especially for Tuscany.

If you have set your heart on a region, write to its tourist office for a list of agencies and owners, who will send brochures or particulars of their accommodation. Maid service is included in the more glamorous villas; ask whether bed linen and towels are provided. The agencies in the box below are all reliable.

Accommodation and Self-catering

In the UK and Ireland

Accommodation Line, 46 Maddox St, London W1R 9PB, **t** (020) 7499 4433, **f** (020) 7409 2606. Reservations for a selection of hotels from family-run *pensioni* to five-star *palazzi*.

Citalia, Marco Polo House, 3–5 Lansdowne Road, Croydon CR9 1LL, **t** (020) 8686 5533, **f** (020) 8681 0712, *ciao@citalia.co.uk*.

CUENDET (*see* International Chapters). Farmhouses and castles anywhere you might want to stay in Italy, including less well-represented Puglia and the Veneto.

Inghams, 10–18 Putney Hill, London SW15 6AX, **t** (020) 8780 4450/ 7700, **f** 020 8780 7705, *www.inghams.co.uk*.

Interhome, 383 Richmond Road, Twickenham, Middx TW1 2EF, **t** (020) 8891 1294, **f** (020) 8891 5331, *www.interhome.co.uk*

International Chapters, 47-51 St John's Wood High Street, London NW8 7NJ, **t** (020) 7722 0722, **f** (020) 7722 9140, toll free from USA only, 186 6493 8340 *www.villa-rentals.com*.

Italian Chapters (*see* International Chapters). Villas and converted farmhouses in Tuscany, Umbria, the Amalfi Coast and Sardinia.

Magic of Italy, 227 Shepherds Bush Road, London W6 7AS, **t** (020) 8748 7575, **f** (020) 8748 3731, *www.magictravelgroup.co.uk*.

Topflight, D'Olier Chambers, D'Olier Street, Dublin 2, **t** (01) 679 9177, *www.topflight.ie*.

Tuscan Enterprises (*see* International Chapters). Villas and apartments in Chianti, often on properties that share a pool.

Vacanze in Italia, Manor Courtyard, Bignor, Pulborough, West Sussex RH20 1QD, **t** (01798) 869 421/(0870) 0772 772, **f** (0870) 0780 190, *www.indiv-travellers.com*.

In the USA

At Home Abroad, 405 East 56th Street 6C, New York, NY 10022-2466, **t** (212) 421 9165, **f** (212) 752 1591, *www.athomeabroad.com*.

CIT Tours, **t** (800) CIT-TOUR, 15 West 44th St, New York, NY 10173, **t** (212) CIT-TOUR, *www.cit-tours.com*, and 9501 West Devon Ave, Rosemount, Il 60018, and, in Canada, 80 Tiverton Court, Suite 401, Markham, Ontario L3R 0GA, **t** (800) 387 0711.

Hideaways International, 767 Islington St., Portsmouth, NH 03802, **t** (603) 430 4433, (800) 843 4433, **f** (603) 430 4444, *www.hideaways.com*. Apartments, villas and farmhouses to let.

Rentals in Italy (and Elsewhere!), Suzanne T. Pidduck, 1742 Calle Corva, Camarillo, CA 93010, **t** (805) 987 5278 or **t** (800) 726 6702, **f** (805) 482 7976, *www.rentvillas.com*.

RAVE (Rent-a-Vacation-Everywhere), Market Place Mall, Rochester, NY 14607, **t** (716) 427 0259.

The Apartment Service, 5–6 Francis Grove, London SW19 4DT, **t** (020) 8944 1444, **f** (020) 8944 6744, *www.apartmentservice.com*. Selected city apartment accommodation.

Rural Self-catering

For a breath of rural seclusion, the gregarious Italians head for a spell on a **working farm**, in accommodation (usually self-catering) that often approximates to the French *gîte*. Often, however, the real pull of the place is cooking by the hosts: a chance to sample home-grown produce. Outdoor activities may include riding and fishing.

This branch of the Italian tourist industry is run by **Agriturist**. It has burgeoned in recent years, and every region now has several offices. Prices of farmhouse accommodation, compared with the over-hyped 'Tuscan villa', are still reasonable. To make the most of your rural hosts, it's as well to have a little Italian under your belt. Local tourist offices will have information on this type of accommodation in their areas; complete listings are compiled by the national organization **Agriturist**, Corso Vittorio Emanuele 101, 00186 Rome t 06 651 2342, or **Turismo Verde**, Via Mariano Fortuny 20, 00196 Rome t 06 366 9931. Both publications are available in Italian bookshops.

Alpine Refuges

The Italian Alpine Club operates refuges (*rifugi*) on the main mountain trails (some accessible only by *funivie*). These may be predictably spartan, or surprisingly comfortable. Many have restaurants. For an up-to-date list, write to the Club Alpino Italiano, Via Fonseca Pimental 7, Milan, t 02 2614 1378. Charges average L18,000–L25,000 per person per night, including breakfast. Most are open only from July to September, but those used by skiers are 20 per cent more expensive from December to April. Book ahead in August.

Camping

Life under canvas is not the fanatical craze it is in France, nor necessarily any great bargain, but there are over 2,000 sites in Italy, particularly popular with holidaymaking families in August, when you can expect to find many sites bursting point. Unofficial camping is generally frowned on. Camper vans (and facilities for them) are increasingly popular. You can obtain a list of local sites from any regional tourist office. Campsite charges generally range from about L6–8,000 per adult; tents and vehicles carry an additional cost of about

L7,000 each. Small extra charges may also be levied for hot showers and electricity.

To obtain a camping carnet and to book ahead, write to:

Centro Internazionale Prenotazioni Campeggio, Casella Postale 23, 50041 Calenzano, Firenze, t 055 882 381, f 055 882 3918 (ask for their list of campsites with the booking form).

Touring Club Italiano (TCI) publishes a comprehensive annual guide to campsites throughout Italy which is available in bookshops for L 29,500. Write to: TCI, Corso Italia 10, 20122 Milan, t 02 85261/02 852 6245.

Women Travellers

Italian men, with the heritage of Casanova, Don Giovanni, and Rudolph Valentino as their birthright, are very confident in their role as Great Latin Lovers, but the old horror stories of gangs following the innocent tourist maiden and pinching her bottom are way behind the times. Italian men these days are often exquisitely polite and flirt on a much more sophisticated level, especially in the more 'Europeanized' north: Milan or Venice are easier cities for women than Rome or Naples.

Still, women travelling alone may frequently receive hisses, wolf-whistles and unsolicited comments, 'assistance' from local swains – usually of the balding, middle-age-crisis variety. A confident, indifferent poise is usually the best policy. Failing that, a polite 'I am waiting for my *marito*' (avoiding damaged male egos which can turn nasty), followed by a firm '*no!*' or '*Vai via!*' (Scram!) will generally solve the problem. Flashers and wandering hands on crowded buses may be an unpleasant surprise.

Risks can be greatly reduced if you use common sense and avoid lonely streets or parks and train stations after dark. Choose hotels and restaurants within easy and safe walking distance of public transport. Travelling with a companion of either sex will buffer you considerably from such nuisances (a guardian male, of course, instantly converts you into an inviolable chattel in Italian eyes). Two women travelling together may still find they attract unwanted advances, particularly in the south. Avoid hitch-hiking alone in Italy.

Piemonte and Valle d'Aosta

10

Piemonte (Piedmont), 'the foot of the mountains', is not only the birthplace of the modern Italian state, the source of its greatest river, the cradle of its industry, and the originator of such indispensable Italian staples as vermouth, Fiats and breadsticks, but also a beautiful region full of surprises. To the north and west tower some of the most important peaks in the Alps such as Gran Paradiso and Monviso, while the small autonomous region of Valle d'Aosta is home to such world-class heavyweights as Mont Blanc, the Matterhorn and Monte Rosa. The south is walled off from Liguria and the Mediterranean by the lush green Maritime Alps which, like the rest of Piemonte, are unspoiled, ill-equipped with the amenities of international tourism, and utterly delightful. Between the Maritime Alps and the Po are miles of rolling hills clad in the noble pinstripe patterns of some of the world's most prestigious vineyards.

North of the Po the scenery changes again, into a flat plain criss-crossed by a complicated web of small canals that feed Europe's most important rice fields. And in the centre of the hills, plains and mountains lies the regional capital Turin, not an industrial by-product as one might suppose, but Baroque and strange.

If the Italy you seek includes sensational Alpine scenery – snowy peaks and emerald valleys – and mountain resorts, either ultra-sophisticated or rustic, or somewhere in between; if it includes un-hyped medieval hill villages and castles standing like islands above rolling seas of vines; if it includes fantastic wines and regional cuisine, with a French touch; or if you have a special interest in white truffles, caves, Saint Bernards, trout fishing, Egyptology, Romanesque architecture, rare flowers, wildlife or kayaking, you will love Piemonte and Aosta. On the other hand, if your Italy consists of Renaissance art, lemon groves and endless sunshine, you'd better do as Hannibal did and just pass right on through.

Wines, and a Drinker's Itinerary

Piemonte is one of Italy's finest wine regions, and rare in that its most celebrated vintages – Barbaresco, Barolo, Dolcetto and Barbera – age well. To promote them the region has eight regional cellars (*enoteche regionali*) in historic castles and buildings along the 'wine roads' in the provinces of Asti and Cuneo: in **Grinzane**, *t 0173 262 159*, in the castle that Cavour, the village mayor, used to call home (*open 9.30–12.30 and 2.30–6.30; closed Tues and Jan*); **Barbaresco**, Via Torino 8/a, *t 0173 635 251*, in the deconsecrated church of San Donato (*open 9.30–1 and 2.30–6; closed Wed, Jan and first week in July; wine-tasting L3,000–L5,000 per glass*); **Barolo**, Piazza Falletti, *t 0173 56277*, in the 18th-century castle where the wine was born (*open 10–12.30 and 3–6.30; closed Thurs and Jan; adm L3000; wine-tasting – only at weekends – L3000 per glass*); **Mango**, at the Enoteca del Moscato d'Asti e dell'Asti Spumante in Mango Castle, *t 0141 89291 (Wed–Mon 10.30–1 and 3–6; closed Jan; wine-tasting L3,000–L5,000)*; **Monferrato**, in the 17th-century Palazzo Callori, *t 0142 933 243 (open Mon–Fri 9–1 and 1.30–4.30, Sat 10–12 and 3–7, Sun 10–1 and 2–7; closed Jan)*; **Acqui Terme**, Piazza Levi 7, *t 0144 770 273/4*, in the ancient cellars of the Palazzo Robellini (*open 10–12 and 3–6.30; closed Mon, Wed, Thurs morning and Jan*). For more information on Piemonte's wine roads, contact the regional tourist board in Turin, Via Magenta 12, *t 011 43211*.

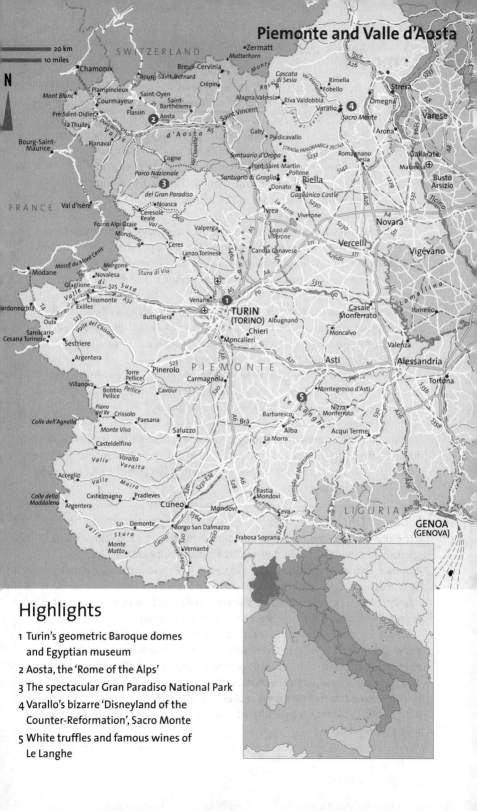

Highlights

1 Turin's geometric Baroque domes
  and Egyptian museum
2 Aosta, the 'Rome of the Alps'
3 The spectacular Gran Paradiso National Park
4 Varallo's bizarre 'Disneyland of the
  Counter-Reformation', Sacro Monte
5 White truffles and famous wines of
  Le Langhe

Piemonte

Historically Piemonte is one of Italy's newer regions, its name not even in existence until the 13th century, when it gradually came to encompass the former Marquisates of Monferrato, Ivrea and Saluzzo, and the County of Turin. The French dynasty of Savoy first got a foothold in Piemonte by marriage in the 11th century, and from the very beginning kept a much tighter reign on its realm than other Italian princes.

The rise of independent *comuni*, the republics and the heady ideas of the Renaissance failed to penetrate the Savoys' feudal fastness. For centuries the population didn't even consider itself Italian, and instead spoke Provençal, which still survives in many a remote valley.

Yet, as unprogressive and as uninspired as Piemonte remained throughout Italy's Golden Age, it was the first region to re-surface when the peninsula went under in the 16th-century tidal wave of invasions and looting; Piemonte's French occupation, begun in 1502, ended 60 years later when Duke Emanuele Filiberto won back his lands with a series of gritty battles.

From that point on the Savoys linked Piemonte's destiny with Italy, treading the troubled political waters of the day with an astute choice of alliances and cautious diplomatic manoeuvring that earned them the title of King of Sardinia in 1713, and then, in the Risorgimento, the crown of Italy herself.

There were violent riots in Turin when the first king of Italy, Vittorio Emanuele II, moved his capital to Florence, en route to Rome; the Piemontese rightly sensed that they had been relegated to the knick-knack shelf of history.

But rather than collect dust, they began Italy's industrial revolution, building the first wool and cotton mills in the torrent-sliced valleys of Biella, the first cars in Turin, the first typewriters in Ivrea, and creating a felt-hat empire in Alessandria. Piemonte's economy has always been one of the strongest in Italy, with tourism playing only an insignificant supporting role.

Food and Drink

The kitchens of Piemonte are famous for their flavoursome and sophisticated specialities, combining the best of northern Italian cuisine with the traditions of Provence. *Grissini* (breadsticks) were invented in Turin, and so charmed Napoleon that he introduced them over the border.

Tartufi bianchi (white truffles) are a local obsession, and are often served grated in a *fonduta* (with melted fontina cheese from the Valle d'Aosta).

The winter speciality, *bagna cauda*, a rich hot dip made with butter, olive oil, garlic, anchovies and cream, is often served with cardi, a raw artichoke-like thistle, or roasted meats. *Bolliti misti* (mixed boiled meats) and *fricandò* (Piemontese stew) are other popular *secondi*, while the classic first course is *agnolotti* – pasta squares similar to *ravioli* stuffed with meat or cheese. The pastries are among the best in Italy: the Bocca di Leone is a sinfully rich calorific heavyweight, *torta di nocciole* a divine hazelnut cake.

Turin

Detroit without the degradation; the aristocratic capital of the Savoys; an elegantly planned Baroque city of arcades and squares; frequent venue of international bridge tournaments; the home of the famous shroud, of Juventus, the Red Brigades and vermouth; and reputedly the centre of black magic in the Mediterranean – Turin (Torino) makes a rather unexpected 'Gateway to Italy'. It stands on the Po, so close to its Alpine sources that this longest and most benighted of Italy's rivers is almost clean. Its cuisine is influenced by France; its winters are colder than Copenhagen's; its most renowned museum is Egyptian.

As important Italian cities go, Turin is a relative newcomer. In 1574, a time when King Philip II of Spain held the rest of the peninsula by the bootstrap, feisty 'iron-headed' Emanuele Filiberto of Savoy, descendant of Europe's most ancient ruling house, drove the French and Spanish troops from his territory and moved his capital from Chambéry to Turin, previously little more than a fortified Roman outpost (*Augusta Taurinorum*) and medieval university town. It was a move symbolizing the dynasty's new identity with the Italian portion of Savoy, or Piemonte, a move that was to have the greatest impact on the future. No-one at the time suspected that the highly centralized duchy in this hitherto neglected corner of the peninsula would one day unite the land, and that Turin would be the first capital of the Kingdom of Italy.

It's a common cliché that the Agnelli family's Fiat Corporation is Turin's new dynasty; founded in 1899, it is not only Europe's largest car manufacturer, but one of the largest corporations in the world. While the historic centre of Turin retains its refined air of a courtly drawing room (no other Italian city looks anything like it), the glitter and sleekness of the shops are thanks mostly to Fiat money, which is also responsible for the vast suburb of Mirafiori south of Turin, built by the company to house the thousands of workers who have come up from Calabria, Sicily and other parts of the south.

Paradoxically, while Turin takes credit for Italy's unification, it has suffered the consequences of that union most acutely, plagued by perhaps the worst relations and bigotry between northern and southern Italians. The latter became Italy's first and most organized proletariat: during the First World War, Gramsci, the great philosopher of the Italian Communist party, led the workers' factory councils in occupying the Fiat works in what he hoped would become an Italian Petrograd. The failure taught him that Italians required a different solution, and made him rightly fear that extremism in one form or another would be the end result.

Gramsci died in a Fascist prison; fifty years after his factory councils experiment, the Red Brigades were born in the urban anonymity of Mirafiori. Their militant sympathizers and radical unionism crippled Fiat in the seventies. Since then, prosperity perhaps more than anything has exorcised most of Turin's extremist bogeys. Despite increasing European competition – and partly due to a far-sighted 'understanding' with Japanese car-makers not to intrude into each other's home markets – Fiat still supplies well over three-quarters of all the cars in Italy, through Fiat itself, or through Fiat-owned Lancia or Alfa Romeo.

Getting There

By Air

Turin's **Caselle airport** (t 011 300 0611) is 15km north of the city. Every 30 minutes an airport bus, run by SADEM, stops at Porta Susa Station, at the main bus terminal on Corso Inghilterra and outside Porta Nuova Station. Tickets can be bought from a kiosk in the arrivals hall or at the Café Negrita on the corner of Via Sacchi and Corso Vittorio Emanuele II (opposite Porta Nuova).

By Rail

Turin's massive neoclassical station, **Porta Nuova** (t 848 888 088), is near the centre, with connections to France and Genoa (2 hrs), Milan (1½ hrs), Aosta (2½ hrs) and Venice (5 hrs).

The **Porta Susa Station**, on the west side of town, can be a convenient getting-off point, while a third station, **DORA**, serves the regional line to Cirié, Lanzo and Ceres.

By Bus

The SADEM **bus terminal** is on Corso Inghilterra (t 011 300 0611), at the western end of Corso Vittorio Emanuele II, though many buses also stop near Porta Susa Station. Buses head out from here for Aosta's ski resorts as far as Chamonix and also provide year-round connections to towns in the province.

Getting Around

Turin is not a big city: most of its principal sites are clustered together within **walking** distance of each other.

Otherwise, its regular grid of streets is served by old-fashioned **trams** and **buses**. The city transport office at Porta Nuova Station provides a good free city transport map (also available from tourist offices). There is also a **tourist bus** offering city tours starting from outside the tourist office in Piazza Castello (one tour daily except Tuesday, at 2.30pm, L12,000). **Parking** in Turin is not as impossible as in most Italian cities, but is still very restricted in the old city centre.

Taxi ranks are in many of the main piazzas (t 011 5730, or t 011 3399).

Tourist Information

Piazza Castello 161, t 011 535 181/011 535 901, f 011 530 070 (open Mon–Sat 9.30–7, Sun 9.30–3). The main office, operates a free room-finding service; other offices are at Porta Nuova Station, t 011 531 327; Via Garibaldi 25, t 011 443 1806, f 011 442 3838; and Caselle Airport.

For information on concerts, film times and so on, check out the listings in La Stampa, or visit the InfoCulture booth, Piazza San Carlo 159, freephone t 800 015 475. Ask for the Torino Cultura Brochure, translated into English.

Shopping

Turin is a good city for shopping, particularly for **clothes**, with the smartest shops located around **Via Roma** and **Piazza Castello**. Two of the best places for strolling and window shopping are the city's great *gallerie* off the Via Roma – **Galleria San Federico** and **Galleria Subalpina**. The walls of **Pastificio Defilippis**, Via Lagrange 39, are lined with thousands of jars of **pasta**, sold by weight measured on an ancient pair of scales. A good buy in Turin is fine chocolates, **gianduiotti**, named after Gianduia, a comic figure associated with St John's Day; try them at **Giordano**, Piazza Carlo Felice 69. A few doors down is a shop selling Alessandria's famous **Borsalino hats**. For bargains, don't miss the Saturday morning **'Balôn' flea market** in Piazza della Repubblica, which is joined by the much bigger **'Gran Balôn'** every second Sunday of the month.

Sports and Activities

Football is Italy's second religion, played between September and May. The vast **Stadio delle Alpi**, Strada Altessano 131, on the northern outskirts of town (the no.9 tram stops just outside) is home to **Torino**, in the Italian second division, and **Juventus**, the 'old lady of Turin' – reigning first division champions. If you want to watch a game, steer clear of any match involving Juventus and Fiorentina (Florence), referred to in the Italian media as the 'derby of poison'. The rivalry started in 1990 when Roberto Baggio,

Fiorentina's star player, was transferred to Juventus – an everyday sporting transaction that prompted three solid days of rioting in Florence. It is generally acknowledged, however, that the Italian league produces the highest standard of football played anywhere in the world and that no one (except emergent Roma and Lazio, or perhaps AC Milan in a good year) plays it better than Juventus. (**t** 011 65631 for tickets; L55,000–L240,000).

Where to Stay

Turin ✉ 10100

Turin's hotels tend to be either modern, expensive and designed for business clients, or cheap and fairly seed. Most are within walking distance of Porta Nuova Station.

Luxury

★★★★Turin Palace, Via Sacchi 8, **t** 011 562 5511, **f** 011 561 2187. A traditional grand hotel across from Porta Nuova Station, the Palace has been in operation since 1872 and has the deserved reputation of being Turin's top hotel. The public rooms are sumptuous, the restaurant elegant and expensive, and the sound-proofed bedrooms luxurious.

Very Expensive

★★★★Villa Sassi, Via Traforo del Pino 47, **t** 011 898 0556, **f** 011 898 0095. The most evocative hotel in the city, located in the hills east of the Po in a lovely park. Converted from a 17th-century patrician villa, it has maintained most of its original features – marble floors, Baroque fireplaces and portraits – and each room has been individually designed. The Villa also has one of Turin's finest restaurants, **El Toulà**. You need a car. *Closed Aug; minimum stay three days.*
★★★★Grand Hotel Sitea, Via Carlo Alberto 35, **t** 011 517 0171, **f** 011 548 090. In a quiet street near the centre, with pleasantly luxurious bedrooms; rooms are half-price at weekends. Its restaurant **Carignano** (*expensive*) serves a variety of Piemontese fare.

Expensive

★★★Victoria, Via Nino Costa 4, **t** 011 561 1909, **f** 011 561 1806. Furnished with a delightful

hotchpotch of screens, chairs, tables and sofas, many Japanese, while the bedrooms are all determinedly singular. Each is decorated in a different style including one rendered largely in leopard skin. The staff are friendly and helpful. A superb, bright and airy breakfast room overlooks the garden. Excellent value.

Moderate

★★★Roma & Rocca Cavour, Piazza Carlo Felice 60, **t** 011 561 2772, **f** 011 562 8137. A somewhat impersonal choice. Although some of its rooms are lovely, with old-fashioned fittings and furnishings, others are merely adequate (but may be available at a special reduced rate for tourists) and some even have a balcony. All prices drop out of season.

Cheap

★★Sila, Piazza Carlo Felice 80, **t** 011 544 086. A great location and views, although the hotel itself is slightly gloomy. It is just twenty yards from the airport-bus stop, making it a good last-night stopover.
★Kariba, Via San Francesco d'Assisi 4, **t** 011 534 856. Comfortable and cheap. The bedrooms are clean and welcoming (but don't have bathrooms). *Closed Aug.*
Ostello Torino, Via Alby 1, **t** 011 660 2939, **f** 011 660 4445. The town's youth hostel, on the other side of the river, near the Piazza Crimea (bus no.52 from the station). It has decent very cheap rooms, bed and breakfast. *Reception open 7–10 and 3.30–11.30. Closed mid-Dec through Jan.*

Eating Out

Very Expensive

Vecchia Lanterna, Corso Re Umberto 21, **t** 011 537 047. Turin's temple of fine cuisine is a subdued and classy turn-of-the-century restaurant, where the food is an artistic achievement. Specialities include gourmet delights like quail pâté, *ravioli* filled with duck in a truffle sauce, shellfish salad, a wide variety of stuffed trout, sea bass in the old Venetian style – all accompanied by a perfect wine list. Reserve ahead of time. *Closed Sat lunch and Sun.*

Cambio, Piazza Carignano 2, t 011 546 690, or t 011 543 760. The 'exchange' opened in 1757 and offers a nostalgic trip back to the old royal capital, where the menu invites you every Friday 'to eat like a king' with dishes once served by the Savoys. The décor, the chandeliers, gilt mirrors, frescoes, red upholstery and even the costume of the waiters, have all been carefully preserved: Prime Minister Cavour's favourite corner, where he could keep an eye on the Palazzo Carignano (if he were urgently needed a handkerchief would be waved from the window), is immortalized with a plaque. The old recipes have, though, been lightened to appeal to modern tastes. *Antipasto* choices include *cardi in bagna cauda*; other specialities are *agnolotti*, trout with almonds, boar, beef braised in Barolo, and *finanziera* – Cavour's favourite dish (made of veal, sweetbreads, cock's combs and *porcini* mushrooms, cooked in butter and wine). Top it off with home-made *tarte tatin*, all for a kingly bill. *Closed Sun, Aug and first week of Jan.*

Expensive

El Toulà. A little way outside the city, in the Villa Sassi hotel. Another of Turin's best, its menus feature garden-fresh ingredients from the estate, and there is a renowned wine cellar containing over 90,000 bottles. *Closed Sun and Aug.*

Moderate

Montecarlo, Via San Francesco da Paola 37, t 011 888 763. One of Turin's most romantic restaurants, located in the atrium of the *palazzo* of the notoriously well-loved Contessa di Castiglione. Under the stone arches a delectable variety of *antipasti* (marinated swordfish, a flan of peas and scampi) may be followed by carrot soup with barley and well-prepared *secondi* like baked liver, lamb or duck. Excellent desserts and wines. *Closed Sat lunch, Sun and Aug.*
L'Arcimboldo, Via Santa Chiara 54, t 011 521 1816. An excellent choice north of the city centre, with over a hundred sauces to accompany your pasta; the hare *ravioli* and home-made lemon sorbet with vodka are particularly recommended. *Closed Mon, Aug and first 10 days of Jan.*

Cheap

Arcadia, Galleria Subalpina 16, t 011 561 3898. A popular lunchtime spot, with excellent *antipasti*, pasta and country-style meat dishes. *Closed Sun.*
Lullaby, Via XX Settembre 6, t 011 531 024. Serves delicious, filling local fare in a still-smart but unpretentious atmosphere. It's hard to spend much, and it's one of the few restaurants in Italy with no *coperto*. *Closed Sun and Aug.*

Entertainment and Nightlife

There's always something to do in Turin. The **Torino Film Festival** every November is a hugely popular showcase for new and up-and-coming directors of independent art-house movies: Via Monte di Pieta 1, t 011 562 3309, f 011 562 9796. The **Teatro Regio** in Piazza Castello was rebuilt after a fire in the 1970s and now stages ballet, symphony concerts and opera all year round: t 011 881 5241/2, or freephone t 800 807 064. The **Extra Festival** in July and August sees plays, ballets and concerts performed in Turin's parks. **Settembre Musica**, logically enough in September, is entirely devoted to classical music, featuring two concerts a day in the city's theatres and churches. **St John's Day** (24 June), on another plane entirely, is Turin's big folklore festival. If you'd like to know the future, Turin's sedate fortune-tellers and sorcerers run their operations around Porta Pila.

Cafés

No visitor to Turin, hot chocolate fan or not, should pass over the city's most distinctive and seductive catering establishments – its grand 19th-century cafés. They're not cheap, but their chocolate, cakes, sandwiches and ice cream are usually superb, and they're very much part of the atmosphere of the city. Classic cafés include **Baratti & Milano**, in the Piazza Castello near the Galleria Subalpina, largely unchanged since 1873; the **Caffè Torino**, Piazza San Carlo 204, famed for its cocktails; and the beautifully decorated **Mulassano**, Piazza Castello 15.

Via Roma

Central Turin is laid out in a stately rhythm of porticoed streets and squares. Few railway stations in Italy deposit the weary traveller in a piazza as inviting as Porta Nuova's manicured **Piazza Carlo Felice**, where even the traffic junctions are covered with pots of flowers. Fashionable **Via Roma**, lined with designer clothes shops, leads from here into the heart of the city, passing through an impressive 'gateway' of twin churches, **Santa Cristina** and **San Carlo**, designed by the Sicilian Baroque genius Filippo Juvarra, court architect to the King of Sardinia in the early 18th century.

Behind the churches lies Turin's finest square, **Piazza San Carlo**, a 17th-century confection with a flamboyant centrepiece in its bronze equestrian statue of Duke Emanuele Filiberto, 'the Iron Head', sheathing his sword after battle, by local sculptor Carlo Marochetti (1838). This is a city of elegant cafés, and in Piazza San Carlo you can sip your cappuccino in the most celebrated of them all, the 19th-century **Caffè Torino**, a veritable palace of java with chandeliers and frescoed ceilings. Just west, the **Museo della Marionetta** at Via S. Teresa 5 (*t 011 530 238; open daily by appointment; adm*) has a collection of Italian puppets from various periods. Nearby is the glass-roofed shopping arcade, **Galleria San Federico**.

The Egyptian Museum and Galleria Sabauda

These treasure troves are just off Piazza San Carlo, sharing the **Palazzo dell'Accademia delle Scienze**. This palace, designed as a Jesuit college, is the most ponderous of all the landmarks designed by the remarkable Guarino Guarini, a Theatine architect priest who came to work for Carlo Emanuele II in 1668 and changed the face of Turin.

The **Museo Egizio** (*t 011 561 7776; open Tues–Sun 8.30–7.30; adm exp*) is rated (except by the directors of the Louvre!) as the second most important in the world, after the museum in Cairo. It was begun as a collection of curios in 1628 by Carlo Emanuele I, but later Savoys took their pharaohs and mummies more seriously, especially Carlo Felice, who acquired the collection of Piemonte native Bernardo Drovetti – the French consul general of Egypt and a confidant of viceroy Mohammed Ali – and in 1824 founded the first Egyptian museum in the world. Two major 20th-century Italian expeditions added to the collections, and the museum played a major role in the Aswan Dam rescue digs. It was rewarded with one of the temples it had preserved – the 15th-century BC rock-cut **Temple of Ellessya**, with a relief of Thothmes III, now reconstructed on the ground floor of the museum – best seen in the early evening when the half-light allows the reliefs to stand out properly.

The same floor houses an excellent collection of monumental public sculpture, notably the 13th-century BC black granite Rameses II, the 15th-century BC Thothmes III, and the sarcophagus of Ghemenef-Har-Bak, a vizier of the 26th Dynasty. Upstairs, in the two main rooms, is an immense papyrus library, including copies of the *Book of the Dead* and the *Royal Papyrus*, listing all the kings of Egypt from the Sun itself down to the 17th dynasty; Turin's papyrus collection is so extensive that after Jean François Champollion cracked the Rosetta Stone he came here to complete his study of hiero-glyphics. Elsewhere upstairs you can spend hours wandering through the essentials and the trivialities of ancient Egypt: there are artefacts from the Egyptians' daily lives, notably a reconstruction of the 14th-century BC **tomb of the architect Khaiè and his wife Meriè** (18th Dynasty) that somehow managed to escape the grave robbers – even the bread and beans prepared for their afterlife remain intact. Other rooms contain mummies in various stages of déshabille, wooden models of boats and funerary processions, paintings, statuettes, jewellery, clothing and textiles.

The basement holds finds from the Gebelein, Assiut and Qau el Kebir sites first excavated by representatives of the museum between 1905 and 1920. There are reconstructed tombs, painted sarcophagi and dozens of beautifully preserved wooden models recovered from tombs: boats with crews and oars, kitchens and granaries, servants performing everyday tasks, as well as scale models of the dead.

On the top floor, the **Galleria Sabauda** (*t 011 547 440; open Tues–Sun 8.30–7.30; adm*) houses the principal collections of the House of Savoy. The Savoys liked Flemish and Dutch art just as much as Italian, which gives the Sabauda a variety most Italian galleries lack. Among the Italians are two fine Florentine works: *Tobias and the Archangel Raphael* by Antonio and Piero del Pollaiuolo, and a fine study of Botticelli's newborn *Venus*, thought to be by one of his students; other works are by Mantegna, Taddeo Gaddi, Il Sodoma, Tintoretto, Titian, Veronese and Bergognone. Among the northerners are Jan Van Eyck's *St Francis*, Memling's drama-filled *Scenes from the Passion*, Van Dyck's beautiful *Children of Charles I*, popular scenes by Jan Brueghel, *Portrait of a Doctor* by Jacobs Dirk, and Rembrandt's *Old Man Sleeping*. The French have a room to themselves, with works by Poussin, Claude and Clouet.

Across from the museum, the **Palazzo Carignano**, much more representative of Guarini's work, was begun in 1679 for the Savoy-Carignano branch of the royal family – the branch that was to produce Vittorio Emanuele II, who was born here. The palace presents two very different façades: the first, looming above Piazza Carignano, is a fine undulating Baroque concoction; the other, facing Piazza Carlo Alberto and the Biblioteca Nazionale, is dull and neoclassical. The palace is full of Italian historical fossils: the bedroom where freedom-fighting King Carlo Alberto died; Cavour's study; and the chamber of the Piemontese Subalpine Parliament preserved exactly as it appeared during its final session in 1860 – full of chandeliers, gilt furnishings and red plush. The palace also hosted the first Italian Parliament, which on March 14 1861 proclaimed Vittorio Emanuele II King of Italy. The themes are covered in more depth in the **Museo Nazionale del Risorgimento** (*t 011 562 1147; open Tues–Sun 9–7; adm*), one of the more interesting of Italy's scores of Risorgimento museums.

Piazza Castello

Parallel to Via Accademia Valentina, the Galleria Subalpina is Turin's other shopping arcade, inspired by the Galleria Vittorio Emanuele in Milan. It leads to the elegant Caffè Baratti & Milano, and the huge expanse of **Piazza Castello**, the main square of Turin, with the **Palazzo Madama** in the middle. Named for the two royal widows ('Madama Reale') who lived here, the palace dates back to the 15th century, though it incorporates in its structure fragments from the eastern Roman gate, the Porta Decumana, as well as the original 13th-century castle. In 1718 one of the Madamas had Juvarra give the old place a facelift – a task Juvarra responded to with a beautiful, serene façade that has little to do with the typical Baroque of this period.

The palace houses the **Museo Civico di Arte Antica** (*closed for restoration until 2004*), with a notable collection of medieval and Renaissance sculpture and painting, and of manuscripts. Among the highlights, when we're allowed in again to see them, are the illuminated 14th-century law codes of Turin, unique pieces of 15th-century glassware, copies of the *Book of Hours* of the Duc de Berry, illustrations by Jan Van Eyck, and the superb *Portrait of an Unknown Man* (1476) by Antonello da Messina.

Under the arcade flanking the north side of Piazza Castello, the **Armeria Reale** (*t 011 543 880; open Tues–Sun 8.30–7.30; adm*) contains one of the finest collections of medieval and Renaissance arms, armour and guns in the world; the library upstairs contains a famous self-portrait in red ink by Leonardo da Vinci.

The Palazzo Reale and the Duomo

The dark apricot **Palazzo Reale** (*t 011 436 1455; open Tues–Sun 8.30–7.30; adm*) lies just off the Piazza Castello, behind a gate of mounted 'Dioscuri' and Turin's largest parking lot, which doesn't do much for its already bureaucratic façade. This, however, was the main residence of the princes of Savoy from 1646 until 1865, and you can take the tour to learn that they lavished a considerable amount of their subjects' taxes on chandeliers and fluffy frescoes. The cases of Chinese porcelain try hard to relieve the anomie. The palace's **Giardino Reale** is a far more pleasant place to while away an afternoon, with the Mole Antonelliana rising above the horse chestnut trees like the headquarters of Ming the Merciless. The royal chapel of **San Lorenzo**, stands on the corner; although the outside is bland – an unusual octagonal dome its only distinguishing feature – the interior by Guarini (1668–80) is an idiosyncratic Baroque fantasia.

Around the corner, just off Via XX Settembre, is Turin's plain **Duomo di San Giovanni** built by three dry 15th-century Tuscan architects. What it lacks in presence it compensates for with one of the most provocative relics of Christendom: the **Turin Shroud**, brought to the city from the old Savoy capital of Chambéry in the 16th century by Emanuele Filiberto. To house the relic properly, Guarini designed the striking black marble **Cappella della Sacra Sindone** (Chapel of the Holy Shroud), crowned by a bold dome-cone zig-zagging to a climax of basketweave arches full of restless energy (*the chapel is closed for restoration, but much of it can be appreciated from the outside*).

The shroud, shown only on special occasions (the last was in the Holy Year, 2000), is kept in a silver casket in an iron box in a marble coffer in the urn on the chapel altar; an exact replica, however, is displayed along with a multilingual explanation of the results of several scientific investigations, which tried to determine whether it was possible that the shroud was used at Christ's burial. Although forensic scientists and their computers have concluded that it would have been impossible to forge the unique front and back impressions of a crucified man with a wound in his side and bruises from a crown of thorns, the shroud flunked a carbon-dating test in 1989, and is now believed by many to date from the 12th century. In 2000, however, a prominent Israeli researcher asserted that pollen trapped in the linen threads of the shroud belongs to wild flowers known to grow only in the Jerusalem countryside.

Besides the shroud, the cathedral contains in its second chapel a fine polyptych of *SS Crispin and Crispinian* by Defendante Ferrari, and a copy of Leonardo da Vinci's *Last Supper*, painted when the original began to crumble. Near the cathedral's campanile are the remains of a Roman theatre, while across the piazza stands the impressive Roman **Porta Palatina**, with its two unusual 16-sided towers. On Saturday mornings the circular Piazza della Repubblica is the site of the 'Balôn' antique and flea market.

More of ancient *Augusta Taurinorum* can be found on Via XX Settembre in the **Museo delle Antichità** (*t 011 521 1106; open Tues–Sun 8.30–7.30; adm*), and on Via Consolata, just off the Corso Regina Margherita, at the **Consolata Church**. The Consolata is a regular ecclesiastical hotchpotch, with a Roman tower adjacent to its apse, an 11th-century campanile inherited from the demolished church of Sant'Andrea, and two churches, a hexagon and an oval, knitted together by Guarini.

The Mole Antonelliana

Turin's idiosyncratic landmark, the **Mole Antonelliana** ('Antonelli's massive bulk'), on Via Montebello, was begun in 1863 by the quirky Piemontese architect-engineer Alessandro Antonelli. Intended originally as a synagogue, the project ran out of steam until 1897, when the city completed it and declared it a monument to Italian Unity. Standing some 549ft high, the Mole is a considerable engineering feat, and manages to be harmonious and bizarre at the same time – a vaguely Greek temple façade, stacked with a colonnade, a row of windows, a majestic sloping glass pyramid, a double-decker Greek temple, and a pinnacle crowned with a star, which the city illuminates at night.

The Mole has been a lightning rod of madness – Nietzsche thought it was marvellous, then permanently went over the edge. There is a lift up to the observation terrace (282ft up) for a fine view of Turin and the Alps beyond.

The recently opened **National Museum of Cinema** inside focuses on Italian movies from the 1940s to the present day (*t 011 812 5658; lift operates Jan–Feb Tues– Sun 11–5, Sat 11–11; Mar–Dec Tues–Sun 10–8, Sat 10am–11pm; museum open Tues–Sun 9–8, Sat 9am–11pm; guided tours in Italian; adm, cheaper combined ticket available*).

Lively, arcaded **Via Po**, two blocks from the Mole, is the main funnel from the centre down to the river; it is also the main artery of the city's student life. Although founded in the 14th century, Turin University never gained the prestige of the schools in Padua, Bologna, Naples, Salerno or Pavia. Its headquarters since 1720, the **Palazzo Università**, lies a block down from Piazza Castello on Via Po; in its courtyard there's a plaque to Erasmus, the most renowned of its alumni.

Via Po widens out to form the long and bewildering Piazza Vittorio Veneto, half street-half parking lot, giving on to the Ponte Vittorio Emanuele I over the Po. Across the river stands an imitation Pantheon, the Gran Madre di Dio church. The **Museo Nazionale della Montagna Duca degli Abruzzi** at Via Giardino 39 (*t 011 660 4104; open Mon–Sun 9–7; adm*), founded in 1874 by the Club Alpino Italiano, is dedicated to Italy's mountains, their geography and folk traditions.

Parco del Valentino

Back along the west bank of the Po stretches Turin's largest park, Parco del Valentino, named after the 1660 **Castello del Valentino**, built by Madama Reale Maria Cristina, who felt her royal dignity required a French château. The château now does time as the university's School of Architecture, with the city's Orto Botanico (Botanical Garden) laid out beneath it, but it isn't the only castle on the block; Turin built another one, along with a mock medieval hamlet, the **Castello e Borgo Medioevale**, as part of its 1884 Exhibition. The houses are modelled on traditional styles found in Piemonte, while the castle is furnished with baronial fittings (*t 011 443 1707; castle tours Tues–Sun 9–7; adm; borgo open Mon–Sun 9–8*). A place near the castle loans out bicycles by the day, while along the riverbank you can rent a rowing boat for a duck-eye view of Turin. At the end of the park are the massive buildings of the Torino Esposizioni, home of a famous springtime Auto Show in even-numbered years.

Museo Nazionale dell'Automobile Carlo Biscaretti di Ruffia

Three kilometres south of the Parco del Valentino, is the **Museo Nazionale dell'Automobile Carlo Biscaretti di Ruffia** (*Corso Unità d'Italia 40, t 011 677 666; open Tues–Sun 10–6.30; adm*). Founded in 1933, its present quarters are an elephantine vintage-1960s exhibition hall; highlights of the collection include the classics of the great age of Italian car design – Lancias, Maseratis, Alfa Romeos, Italicas and of course Fiats – as well as some oddities like the asymmetrical 1948 Tarf 1. Further along the Corso Unità d'Italia is another huge exhibition hall, the **Palazzo del Lavoro**, built in 1961 by Pier Luigi Nervi.

One last museum, the **Galleria Civica d'Arte Moderna e Contemporanea** (*Via Magenta 31, t 011 562 9911; open Tues–Sun 9–7; adm*) is in another corner of the city, off Corso Vittorio Emanuele II west of the Porta Nuova Station. It has one of Italy's best collections of modern art, with works by Klee, Chagall, Modigliani, Picasso and others.

Basilica di Superga

Northeast along the Po, on the metropolitan fringe, bus no.79 from Corso Casale will take you up to the stately Baroque **Basilica di Superga**. The delightful trip through the greenwood culminates with Juvarra's masterpiece, built on top of a commanding 2,205ft hill to fulfil a vow made by Vittorio Amedeo II during the French siege of Superga. Two fine towers flank a magnificent drum dome, set above a deep neoclassical porch; the crypt contains the tombs of Vittorio Amedeo II and subsequent kings of Sardinia, and the views stretch to the Alps. Another fine viewpoint east of Turin, the Colle della Maddalena (2,526ft), is also the site of the 2km-long **Parco della Rimembranza**, a memorial to Turin's First World War dead, planted with some 10,000 trees and crowned by a *Victory* with her torch (1928), the largest cast bronze statue in the world at nearly 60ft tall.

Turin, with its access to Alpine herbs, invented vermouth and remains Italy's top producer: Carpano, the oldest house (1786), bottles the popular bittersweet Punt e Mes, while the competition, Martini & Rossi and Cinzano, are known for their classic dry *bianco* and the popular reddish elixir of many an Italian happy hour. At **Pessione**,

19km east of Turin, the **Museo Martini di Storia dell'Enologia** (*t 011 941 9217; open Tues–Fri 2–5, Sat–Sun 9–12 and 2–5*) vividly recounts the history of wine-making, and sells some of the end products too.

Stupinigi

Nine kilometres southwest of Turin, past the dreary suburbs of Mirafiori and the Fiat works, Stupinigi is the site of Vittorio Amedeo II's hunting lodge, the **Palazzina Mauriziana di Caccia** (*t 011 358 1220; open Tues–Sun 10–5; adm*), built in 1730 on land belonging to the royal Mauritian Order. Designed by the great Juvarra, this magnificent, asymmetrically complex rococo palace has a statue of a stag perched on the top, frescoes of hunting scenes by Carle Van Loo, and trompe-l'œil scenes of hanging game to remind the visitor of the palace's raison d'être. The main oval salon is especially lovely, and was used for royal wedding receptions. The Mauritians run Stupinigi as a furniture museum.

West of Turin: the Valle di Susa

Some of the most spectacular and accessible scenery in Piemonte lies in the upper Valle di Susa. Skiing is the main attraction in the winter, and the resorts are especially popular among the French, who find the prices far more congenial than those on the

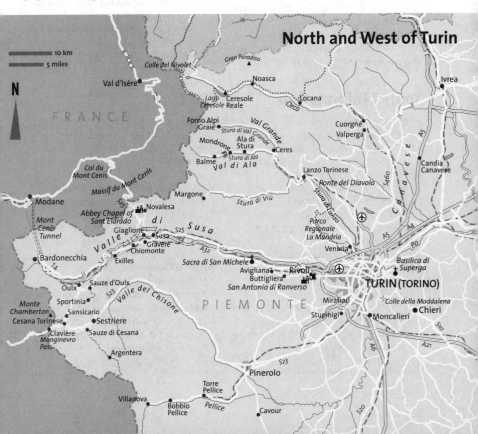

other side of the Alps. Old villages and churches are a constant reminder that this corner of Italy sat out the Renaissance; whereas Baroque dominates in Turin, Romanesque graces the Valle di Susa.

Turin to Susa

Rivoli, the first large town west of Turin, was a Savoy residence and preserves one of their typically Baroque, typically imposing castles. The family sold it to the municipal authorities in 1883 for the suitably regal sum of L100,000; after languishing for a century it reopened in 1984 as a **Museo dell'Arte Contemporanea** (*t 011 956 5220; open Tues–Fri 10–5, Sat–Sun 10–7, also first and third Sat of month 10–10; adm exp*).

In **Buttigliera Alta**, 5km west, the church of the 12th-century abbey of **Sant'Antonio di Ranverso** has a unique quattrocento façade, dominated by three high-pitched gables over the three doors; inside (*t 011 936 7450; open Mar–Oct Tues–Sun 9–12.30 and 2.30–6, Nov–April Tues–Sun 9–12.30 and 2–5; adm*), fine 15th-century frescoes by Giacomo Jaquerio adorn the walls, and the altar has a polyptych by Defendante Ferrari (1531). The next town, **Avigliana**, is a Romanesque gem, with two fine

Getting There

Trains from Turin go through the Valle di Susa to the French border at the Mont Cenis Tunnel (note that only local trains make more than a few stops *en route*).

There are frequent SADEM **buses** from Turin to Susa, Pinerolo, Sestriere and Claviere, which also call at most of the valley villages.

Tourist Information

Avigliana: Piazza del Popolo 24, t 011 932 8650, f 011 934 1584; for the Valle di Susa.
Susa: Corso Inghilterra 39, t 0122 62 2 470.
Sauze d'Oulx: Piazza Assietta 18, t 0122 858 009, f 0122 850 700.
Bardonecchia: Via della Vittoria 4, t 0122 99032, f 0122 980 612.
Claviere: Via Nazionale 30, t 0122 878 856, f 0122 878 888.
Sestriere: Via Louset, t 0122 755 444, f 0122 755 171.
Pinerolo: Viale Giolitti 7/9, t 0121 794 003, f 0121 794 932.

All the tourist offices in the area will be able to provide useful information on mountain excursions, walking routes, conditions and the like; most stock trail maps.

Where to Stay and Eat

Susa ✉ **10059**
★★★Napoleon, Via Mazzini 44, t 0122 622 855, f 0122 31900 (*moderate*). The top place to stay, but don't expect unbridled luxury. The hotel is unpretentious but friendly – the rooms are equipped with the bare three-star essentials – and the restaurant (*cheap*) is uninspiring and *closed Jan*.
Il **Sentiero dei Franchi** in Sant'Antonino di Susa, Borgata Cresto 16 (a couple of miles east of the Sacra di San Michele), t 011 963 1747 (*moderate*). For an excellent meal with a view of the countryside near Susa, try the 'Franks' path', where you can sample local specialties like *malfatti* (spinach and *ricotta* dumplings), *polenta concia* (laced with butter and cheese), wild boar and stuffed cabbage. On the ground floor, the restaurant doubles as a wine bar. *Closed Tues., 10 days in Jan, 10 days in June, and 10 days in Sept.*

Sauze d'Oulx ✉ **10050**
★★★★Capricorno, in Le Clotes, t 0122 850 273, f 0122 850 055 (*moderate*). A very intimate and quiet eight-room lodge, reached by chairlift. Half board L250,000 per person; reserve well in advance. *Closed May–mid-June and mid-Sept–Nov.*

churches and a 12th-century Savoy castle clustered around its heart, the medieval Piazza di Conde Rosso (Red Count Square).

From Avigliana it's 14km up to Piemonte's most provocative church, the **Sacra di San Michele**, an abbey founded around the year 1000 on the 2,018ft ridge of Monte Pirchiriano, overlooking the Dora Riparia Valley and the Alps beyond (*t 011 939 130; open mid-Mar–mid-Oct Tues–Sat 9.30–12.30 and 3–6, Sun and holidays 9.30–12 and 2.40–6; the rest of the year closes an hour earlier in the afternoon, at 5pm; adm*). Like all mountaintop shrines dedicated to God's archangelic aide-de-camp, the Sacra is a strange place, built like a seal over an ancient dragon's lair, full of mysterious, half-pagan nuances – in particular the **Porta dello Zodiaco**, a grand Romanesque archway featuring some rather alarming gargoylesque carvings of the zodiac. The air of spookiness is further enhanced by the sound of piped monastic chanting which filters down the stairs as you approach. Similar churches are thought to have had roles in medieval initiation rites, and it's significant that this one is located just off one of the main pilgrimage routes to Rome – the pilgrimage being an important rite of passage of the faith. The Sacra, piled on a complicated mass of 90ft substructures,

**Stella Alpina, Via Miramonti, t 0122 858 731 (*moderate*). English-run, and worth the slightly higher cost. *Open Dec–April and July–Sept.*

**Villa Daniela, Via Monfol, t 0122 850 196 (*cheap*). Small and personal, with a lovely little restaurant (also *cheap*).

Sestriere ✉ 10058
****Grand Hotel Sestriere, Via Assietta 1, t 0122 76476, f 0122 76700 (*moderate*). The most luxurious and elegant hotel on the slopes, with an indoor pool, spacious rooms and a fairly good restaurant. *Open Dec–April.*

**Duchi d'Aosta, t 0122 77123, f 0122 754 379 (*expensive*). The twin towers that dominate Sestriere belong to the Club Méditerranée; this is the ritzy twin, which has comfortable if functional rooms.

*La Torre, same t/f (*moderate*). The Dukes' more simply furnished twin. Book at the Club Med offices in Sestriere, t 0122 799 800. Full board only. *Open mid-Dec–April.*

La Baita, Via Louset 4/a, t 0122 77496 (*moderate*). Famous for its *polenta* – served with hare – boar or tamer dishes. *Closed Tues and May.*

La Tana della Volpe, Monte Banchetta Sestriere, t 0335 362 054 (*cheap*). For something completely different, try the 'fox's den',

set in the mountains above the town. After a delicious meal, guests ski back to town bearing flaming torches. Reserve. *Open Dec–April.*

Bardonecchia ✉ 10052
****Des Geneys-Splendid, Viale Einaudi 21, t 0122 99001, f 0122 999 295 (*expensive*). Enjoys a tranquil setting in the trees and has more character than many resort hotels. *Open mid-Dec–mid-April and July–mid-Sept.*

**Bucaneve, Viale della Vecchia 2, t 0122 999 332, f 0122 999 980 (*moderate*). At walking distance from the lifts, the traditionally-decorated 'snowdrop' is a large wooden chalet with ample guest rooms and that extra bit of warmth. Half board only. *Closed mid-Sept-Nov.*

**La Quiete, Viale San Francesco 26, t 0122 999 859, f 0122 999 859 (*cheap*). As quiet as its name. Inside it's warm and cosy, log-cabin style, with good-size rooms, some with balcony. Full board required in season.

Tabor, Via della Stazione 6, t 0122 999 857 (*cheap*). Restaurants in Bardonecchia are fairly simple; this is one place that does more than just slap out plates of mediocre pasta for the crowds. *Open Dec–Mar and July–Sept.*

is reached by the covered **Scalone dei Morti**, the 154-step 'Staircase of the Dead' hewn out of the rock – well-named, as the climb seems designed to test your mortality. The ceiling of the mostly 12th-century church is supported by a massive, 59ft stone pillar; in the crypt are buried the early dukes and princes of the House of Savoy-Carignano. The abbey was suppressed in 1622.

Susa

The fine old town of Susa (Roman *Segusio*) may sound Persian, but was actually the seat of the Gaulish chieftain Cottius. Cottius was the kind of fraternizing Gaulish creep that Asterix and Obelix would have liked to slap around with a menhir, one who so admired the Romans that he erected the **Arco di Augusto** in the emperor's honour, carved with reliefs of a triumphant procession. Augustus returned the compliment by making Cottius a prefect, and naming the Cottian Alps after him. Other remains of *Segusio* lie above the Arco di Augusto, including another arch, baths and the **Porta Savoia**, part of a 3rd-century aqueduct.

The **Castello della Contessa Adelaide** (who gave her hand to Otho of Savoy in 1045) looms over the pretty medieval Piazza della Torre; inside, a **Museo Civico** houses an archaeological collection (**t** *0122 622 694; castle open by request only; museum closed for restoration*). In the centre of Susa, in the shadow of its own massive tower, the **Duomo di San Giusto** dates from the 11th century, and contains the prized *Triptych of Rocciamelone*, a Flemish brass portraying the Virgin, saints and donor, made in 1358. Another chapel houses a polyptych by Bergognone. Note the rare 10th-century baptismal font, made of serpentine.

From Susa the Monte Cenis road leads to **Giaglione**, a tranquil hamlet spread out under the mountains; its **Cappella di Santo Stefano** has 15th-century exterior frescoes of the Virtues and Seven Deadly Sins. On 22 January, Giaglione celebrates its patron's feast day with a 'Dance of the Swordmaker'. Another medieval village near Susa, **Novalesa**, has the ruins of a Romanesque Benedictine abbey and chapels, one of which, **Sant'Eldrado**, is still in use and contains good 13th-century frescoes.

The Upper Valley

From Susa the road ascends steeply past the venerable villages of **Gravere** and **Chiomonte**, the latter also the first of the valley's important ski resorts. **Exilles**, further on, lies under a mighty fortress that long dominated the valley; lit at night, it seems to spill over the hill like molten gold. Exilles also has a fine 11th-century parish church.

Oulx, Sauze d'Oulx and Bardonecchia, at the crossroads of several valleys near the Mont Cenis Tunnel, are fashionable winter sport centres in what the Italians like to call the Via Lattea, or 'Milky Way'. **Sauze d'Oulx**, the 'Balcony of the Alps', and its plateau Sportinia, surrounded by a fine natural amphitheatre, are popular ski-package destinations. They are also adored by motorcyclists, some of whom attempt to scale the Chamberton, apparently the highest point in Europe accessible by bike. **Bardonecchia**, a pretty village of old stone houses known as *grangie*, is an even more developed resort, with summer skiing on the Sommeiller glaciers (9,843ft), and four separate ski areas with their own lifts; one, Fregiusia-Jaffereau, is for experts only. In the village, a small **Museo Civico** on Piazza Vittorio Veneto (*t 0122 902 612; open by request only*) houses local artefacts, old costumes and tools. The best views in the neighbourhood are from Monte Colomion (6,645ft), reached by a chairlift.

The **Mont Cenis Pass** has always been a favoured French route into Italy, used by conquerors from Hannibal (one of several possible routes proposed by scholars) to Charlemagne and Napoleon, who began the carriage road in 1808. The **Mont Cenis Tunnel**, or Traforo del Frejus, at 12.8km is the second-longest road tunnel in Europe, opened in 1980, though the rail tunnel was finished back in 1871. It was a bad business for Marseilles, which lost much of its importance as an eastern port, but a boon to the port of Brindisi and the rest of Europe in the increased speed in communications with that part of the world.

The Valle del Chisone

The Milky Way of winter resorts sweeps around the Upper Susa Valley to **Cesana** and its ultramodern satellite Sansicario, lying at the junction of the road to Oulx. Besides being a ski resort, Cesana is also a good base for summer walks, as is **Claviere**, lying just below the Col de Montgenèvre (Monginevro, the Roman *Mons Janus*). This was the favoured pass of the Roman emperors and Napoleon (again) in his frequent comings and goings. The Roman god Janus had two faces, and his mountain does, too – Italian Claviere on one face and French Montgenèvre on the other – which nevertheless share lifts and ski passes.

Sestriere, Piemonte's most fashionable playground, was never a real village, but planned as a summer and winter resort, with tall cylindrical hotels and modern flats and hotels, as charming as university dormitories. But the mountains are the main

Pinerolo and the Waldenses

The Valle del Chisone and the Val Péllice, south of Pinerolo, are commonly known as the **Valli Valdesi**, or Waldensean Valleys. The Waldenses were followers of Peter Waldo of Lyon – like St Francis of Assisi the son of a wealthy merchant who renounced all his possessions to preach the gospel; unlike Francis, however, Waldo criticized the corruption of the Church, and was branded a heretic instead of a saint. Condemned by a Lateran Council in 1184, his followers, many from the south of France, took refuge in Piemonte's secluded valleys. The Waldenses joined up with Protestantism during the Swiss Reformation but were frequently persecuted, especially under Carlo Emanuele and Louis XIV of France. They briefly took refuge in Switzerland, but returned in 1698 to reconquer their mountain valleys. Vittorio Amedeo of Savoy agreed to tolerate them as his subjects, although they had to wait until 1848 to gain complete freedom of religion. Today nearly every town in Northern Italy has a small community of Waldenses – Torre Péllice is their centre, with a Waldensean college and museum. It is also a base for scenic excursions up the valley to Bobbio Péllice and Villanova, which still has a flood embankment built with money sent by the Waldenses' great supporter Oliver Cromwell.

attraction, and Sestriere boasts exceptional slopes and lifts, cross-country trails, ice tracks for winter races, a skating rink and more; in summer you can tee off at Europe's highest golf course. Above Sestriere are the old villages of **Sauze di Cesana** and **Grangesises**, with traditional wooden Alpine houses, and the tiny village and lovely wooded valley of **Argentera**, a popular destination for cross-country skiers and hikers.

At the foot of the Valle del Chisone stands **Pinerolo**, once the capital of the Princes of Acaia, predecessors of the Savoys. Splendidly situated at the junction of two valleys, it preserves several memories of its glory days, including the 14th-century Palazzo dei Principi d'Acaia, the Romanesque San Maurizio, with the Acaia princes' tombs, the Gothic cathedral, and several streets of medieval houses. In the 17th century the fortress of Pinerolo belonged to the French (who called it Pignerol) and here, between 1668 and 1678, they imprisoned the never-identified Man in the Iron Mask. Further south, between Pinerolo and Saluzzo, lies **Cavour**, birthplace of the great Prime Minister and 'architect of Italian unity'.

North of Turin: the Valli di Lanzo and Ivrea

The Valli di Lanzo

The northern valleys are much less visited than the Valle di Susa and Valle del Chisone. The long arm of Turin's industry extends as far as Ciriè, but just beyond lies the beautiful park of **La Mándria**, once a royal hunting reserve, with a toy palace of a hunting lodge; grander digs were built in 1660 at nearby **Venaria**, with Baroque flourishes added later by Juvarra. Although now a barracks, part of it may be visited. **Lanzo Torinese** is a pretty town, and a base for excursions into the branching valleys; its most famous monument is the 1378 **Ponte del Diavolo**, spanning the River Stura, Impressive even today with its soaring single arch; like most medieval bridges the architect was none other than the devil himself.

The railway from Turin peters out at **Ceres**, a summer excursion centre at the fork of two pretty valleys. Buses from Ceres continue up the **Val Grande** to **Forno Alpi Graie**, the base for several good walks; another bus winds up the **Valle d'Ala** to the small ski resort of **Balme**, passing by way of **Ala di Stura** with a chairlift, and **Mondrone** with a lovely waterfall.

Turin to the Valle d'Aosta

The **Canavese**, a pretty glacier-carved amphitheatre, is a peaceful woody region. Its capital is **Ivrea** (Roman *Eporedia*), famous for its carnivals and typewriters. It reached its peak of influence in 1002, when its Marquis Arduin was crowned king of Italy; not long after, Ivrea built its cathedral, which, despite an unfortunate neoclassical façade, preserves its original towers by the apse and dome. Here and there you can pick out pieces from even older buildings, including Roman columns and a sarcophagus, while the interior has 12th-century frescoes and paintings in the sacristy by Defendante Ferrari. The mighty castle of Ivrea, built in 1358, guards the River Dora with four lofty

Getting There

Trains on a regional rail line head north from the DORA staton in Turin into the Valli di Lanzo, as far as Ceres, and to Cuorgné.

For the valleys further north, trains run from Turin to Aosta about every two hours, stopping at Ivrea.

Any destinations not on the rail line can easily be reached by SADEM **buses**.

towers. In 1908 the Olivetti office machine company was founded in Ivrea, and continues to dominate the town's economy.

South of Ivrea is the pretty lake of Candia, guarded by a 14th-century castle and surrounded by vineyards producing Doc Erbaluce and sweet Passito di Caluso. West of Ivrea, the N565 leads into the **Parco Nazionale del Gran Paradiso** by way of the ancient town of **Cuorgné** (also linked separately by rail from Turin), with a cluster of fine medieval buildings, especially on Via Arduino, where King Arduin once resided. **Valperga**, just to the south, has an attractive castle and church from the 15th century; both Valperga and Cuorgné are known for cottage industries producing beaten copper. From Cuorgné the road follows the River Orco, the scenery becoming increasingly splendid as it nears the waterfalls around **Noasca**. The peaks of Gran Paradiso rise up majestically around the meadows of **Ceresole Reale** at the park entrance; the 'Reale' in its name is derived from a battle in 1544, when the French troops of Francis I defeated the army of Emperor Charles V. It stands on the banks of a deep blue lake among the rough and tumble snowy giants that frown down from above.

Valle d'Aosta

At French-speaking **Pont-St-Martin**, the road from Turin enters the semi-autonomous Valle d'Aosta, one of the most spectacularly beautiful regions in Italy. Rimmed by the highest mountains in Europe – **Mont Blanc** (15,780ft), the **Matterhorn** (Cervino in Italian, 14,690ft), **Monte Rosa** (15,200ft) and **Gran Paradiso** (13,402ft) – the Aosta valleys are one of Europe's most popular summer and winter playgrounds, dotted with lakes and serenaded by rushing streams. Emerald meadows lie beneath great swathes of woodlands; hills and gorges are defended by fairy-tale castles. With Piemonte, Aosta shares one of Italy's most beautiful national parks, Gran Paradiso.

The **Valle d'Aosta** has been compared to a leaf, traversed by a main vein (the Dora Baltea valley) with a dozen smaller veins, or valleys, branching off on either side. Each valley has its own character; in most of them French or Provençal is the main language, although Italian is understood everywhere. English comes in a poor third outside the major resorts.

Although the Valle d'Aosta has traditionally owed allegiance to Savoy, from the 11th to the 18th century it had its own Assembly of the three estates, a Council and body of law, the *Coutumier*. Union with Italy aggravated linguistic differences, a wound which Mussolini proceeded to rub salt in with his policy of cultural imperialism. In defiance, the Aostans played a leading role in the Resistance, and in 1945 the region was granted cultural and a certain amount of administrative autonomy. Most towns are now officially bilingual.

Skiing

The major resorts are **Courmayeur, Breuil-Cervinia, St-Vincent, Brusson, Pila** and **Cogne**, but there are many smaller, quieter and less expensive bases; write ahead for the region's ski handbook with maps of the slopes, lifts and facilities in each of Aosta's valleys. Prices on the sunny side of the Alps are, like the weather, milder than in France or Switzerland, but can be very high by Italian standards. During high season at the resorts (*Christmas–1st week Jan, 2nd week Feb–mid-March, Easter holidays and July–Aug*) prices go up by about 15 per cent. If you come during the peak periods, reserve at least three months in advance. Although picking up a week's ski package (*settimana bianca*), including hotel and ski pass, from a travel agent is the easiest and least expensive way to go, families and groups of more than two may save money by writing in advance to the Aosta tourist office for its list of privately owned self-catering flats in the region (*elenco di appartamenti da affittare*).

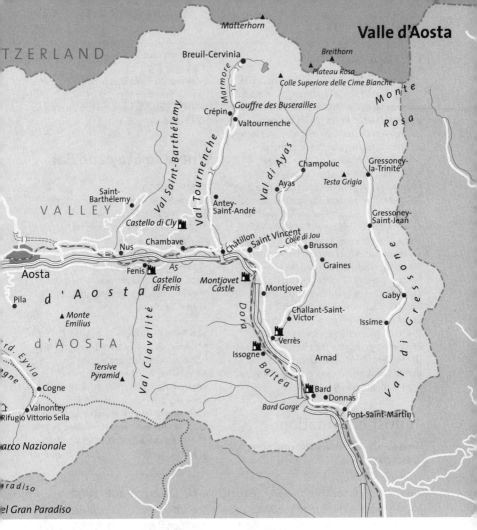

The Eastern Valleys

Pont-St-Martin and the Val du Gressoney

Besides Alpine splendour, the Valle d'Aosta is known for its picturesque castles and Roman remains that seem to mark every narrow defile and bend in the valleys. One of Italy's most remarkable Roman bridges, dating from the 1st century BC, lies just within the region, at **Pont-St-Martin** – yet another span later attributed to the devil. According to legend he made a pact with the village – the bridge for the first soul that wandered across – only to be cheated when St Martin sent a dog over at dawn. Pont-St-Martin is a fine old town, encompassed by vineyards that produce one of Aosta's finest wines.

At Pont-St-Martin two valleys meet: the main Valle d'Aosta along the River Dora, and the wide and pleasant **Val du Gressoney** (or Val de Lys), gracefully meandering up to crystal glaciers spilling off mighty Monte Rosa. The natives of the Val du Gressoney

Getting Around

Trains from Turin or Milan (a five-hour trip, changing at Chivasso) go through the main valley as far as Pré-St-Didier. The valleys are all served by SAVDA **buses** (**t** 0165 262 027), though services to some of the smaller valleys are infrequent. Regular **coach** connections include Turin or Milan to Courmayeur/ Chamonix; Turin–Chamonix–Geneva (two a day); Aosta– Val d'Isère–Col Iseran (one a day); Aosta–Martigny (two a day). In summer additional services include Genoa–Alessandria–Courmayeur; Courmayeur–San Remo–Rimini; and Aosta–Florence–Rome. There are regular **excursion buses** in summer from Aosta to Mont Blanc, Lake Geneva and the two Savoys/Annecy. The most breathtaking way to enter Aosta is by **cable car** from Chamonix over the glaciers of Mont Blanc to Courmayeur. It's expensive (L110,000 round trip) but unforgettable, especially if you're lucky enough to catch the mountain without its frequent veil of mist. The cable car runs during the ski season and in July and August, leaving roughly every hour.

Tourist Information

Gressoney-St-Jean: Villa Margherita, **t** 0125 355 185, **f** 0125 355 895.

Ayas-Champoluc: Via Varasc 16, **t** 0125 307 113, **f** 0125 307 785.
St Vincent: Via Roma 62, **t** 0166 512 239/0166 513 149, **f** 0166 511 335.
Breuil-Cervinia: Via J. A. Carrel 29, **t** 0166 949 136, **f** 0166 949 731.

Where to Stay and Eat

Verrès ✉ 11029
Da Pierre, Via Martorey 73, **t** 0125 929 376 (*expensive*). Elegant dining, with a menu that varies by season, as does the favoured spot to dine – in winter by the blazing hearth, in summer in the garden. Try the *agnolotti alla savoiarda* and venison in blueberry sauce, topped off by a warm slice of apple pie smothered in cream. *Closed Tues.*

Val d'Ayas ✉ 11020
★★★Castor, Via Ramey 2, **t** 0125 307 117, **f** 0125 308 040. An enchanting setting in Champoluc, with breathtaking views of Monte Rosa, panelled rooms with all mod cons, plenty of space and a very nice restaurant (*moderate*). English-run. Half board L125,000, full board L165,000. *Open all year.*
★★★Villa Anna Maria, Via Croues 5, **t** 0125 307 128, **f** 0125 307 884. A lovely old mountain

are Walser, who speak neither French nor Italian but an obscure dialect of German, having migrated here from the Swiss Valais in the 12th century. Their valley is utterly wholesome, with a solid family feel to it: their traditional Alpine chalets, with wooden balconies bursting with pots of geraniums, are a vision as fresh as childhood and Heidi. The main resorts of the valley are **Gressoney-St-Jean**, with its Castello Savoia, and the loftier, trendier **Gressoney-la-Trinité**, the latter with chairlifts up Monte Rosa and ski facilities shared with the Val d'Ayas, the next valley to the west. **Issime**, on the way up from Pont-St-Martin, merits a stop for its gabled parish church, the façade frescoed with a large 16th-century scene of sinners taking their licks in the Last Judgement as a warning to all passers-by. Issime is a small climbing centre and, like most of the valley, prefers to speak German; oddly the next village, **Gaby**, only 4km away, is an island of French Provençal.

Pont-St-Martin to Issogne
From Pont-St-Martin the main valley road continues past the **Donnaz** station, with the impressive remains of a Roman highway hewn 200 yards into the living rock, and

chalet, brimful of charm and simple, rustic bonhomie in a magnificent setting; the food is also delicious. Half board L100,000 *Open all year.*

St Vincent ✉ 11027

★★★★Grand Hotel Billia, Viale Piemonte 72, t 0166 5231, f 0166 523 799 (*luxury*). One of those elegant, terribly grand turn-of-the-century hotels, built to take advantage of St Vincent's curative mineral springs – which it still does, although it's a magnet for those who come to get soaked at its roulette tables too. Amenities include a sauna and outdoor pool in summer, tennis and lovely large park.

★★★Elena, Via Biavaz, t 0166 512 140, f 0166 537 459 (*moderate*). Has large pleasantly furnished rooms with balconies and good views of the surrounding countryside. Its only drawback is its proximity to the parish church with busy bells.

★★★Haiti, Via E. Chanoux 15/17, t 0166 512 114, f 0166 512 937 (*cheap*). The top inexpensive choice; modern rooms with lots of space and light.

Batezar da Renato, Via Marconi 1, t 0166 513 164 (*very expensive*). The place to celebrate a lucky streak at the roulette tables: in easy walking distance of the casino, with such delicacies as salmon mousse flavoured with wild fennel, duck with peaches, or pigeon stuffed with mushrooms, and a classy wine list. *Closed Wed, May and late June to mid-July.*

La Rosa Bianca, Via Chanoux 38, t 0166 512 691 (*moderate*). On the other hand, if your luck hasn't held out at the gaming tables try this small friendly diner in the centre.

Breuil-Cervinia ✉ 11021

★★★★Cristallo, Viale del Piolet 6, t 0166 943 411, f 0166 948 377 (*luxury*). The top hotel, standing above the town in all its smart, modern glory. It has bold brightcolours and styling, extremely comfortable rooms, a sauna, indoor swimming pool for rainy days and tennis courts. *Closed June and Sept–Nov.*

★★Les Neiges d'Antan, t 0166 948 775, f 0166 948 852 (*expensive*). The superbly named 'Snows of Yesteryear', 4km away at Perrères, is a pretty Alpine chalet in tranquil surroundings where the resort's skyscrapers are hidden from view. The restaurant (also *expensive*) is the best in the area so even if you don't stay at the hotel you may decide to drop by for a traditional meal of salt beef, *polenta*, cheeses, Valdostana wines and home-made desserts. *Open Dec–May and July–mid-Sept.*

then through the narrow **Gorge de Bard**. At the other end, the gloomy **fortress of Bard** looms up on its promontory, over the village of the same name; in 1800 Napoleon slipped his cannons past in the dead of night, spreading the road with sacking and straw to muffle their wheels. Picturesque **Arnad**, the next village, has a number of medieval houses and a Romanesque church built around the year 1000, adorned with 15th-century frescoes. Another old town, **Verrès**, lies at the junction of the Val d'Ayas, a crossroads defended by the massive, almost cubic, **Castello di Verrès** (*t 0125 929 067; open Mar–June and Sept, 9–7; July and Aug 9–8; Oct–Feb 10–12.30 and 1.30–5; closed Thurs only Oct–Feb; adm*). Built in the 14th century by the Lord of Verrès, Ibelto di Callant, it's a stiff climb up from the town (or a quick drive). Although a treat for castle fiends, most people will find the nearby residence of the Challant lords, the **Castello di Issogne** (*t 0125 929 373; open Mar–June and Sept, 9–7; July and Aug 9–; Oct–Feb 10–12.30 and 1.30–5; closed Wed only Oct–Feb; adm*), far more enchanting, with a frescoed courtyard that lacks only knights and fair ladies dallying by the fountain, in the shade of its mysterious iron pomegranate tree; the upper apartments, with their period furnishings and tapestries, are equally evocative.

Val d'Ayas

Thickly forested with pines and chestnut groves, the **Val d'Ayas** winds northwards with Monte Rosa on the right and the Matterhorn on the left, a walker's paradise and a good place to see traditional, massive Alpine chalets. The first comune of hamlets from Verrès, **Challant-St-Victor**, was the cradle of the Challant family who ran Aosta before the Savoys and their duke; their ruined castle still hangs over **Villa**, the main settlement. An even more impressive derelict castle stands further up the Val d'Ayas in **Graines** – an intriguing 13th-century ruin with a Romanesque chapel. You can reach it from the little resort of **Arcesaz**.

Brusson lies at the crossroads of the Val d'Ayas and the scenic road through the pine forests of the **Colle di Joux** from St Vincent; one of the best excursions is to walk up to the miniature mountain lakes under **Punta Valfredda**. From Brusson the road climbs steeply to the most important resort in the Val d'Ayas, **Champoluc**. Here, you can take the cable car and chairlift to the slopes just below **Testa Grigia** (10,875ft), one of the grandest belvederes of the western Alps. A guide is recommended if you want to continue all the way up to the summit, an ascent rewarded with a breathtaking panorama of Mont Blanc, the Matterhorn, Gran Paradiso and Monte Rosa, towering over a sea of peaks.

St Vincent and Châtillon

The valley widens at **St Vincent**, the 'Riviera of the Alps', an élite albeit slightly shabby spa for the rich and dissipated since the 18th century, boasting more than a mild climate and waters these days, with one of Europe's largest casinos (*open all year round daily 3pm–3am; adm exp, half price weekdays; hotel guests usually get in for free; bring your passport*). Besides blackjack and one-armed bandits, St Vincent offers excursions through the chestnut groves to St Germain Castle in Montjovet; or up the funicular to the Terme di St Vincent, a health spa built around a mineral spring, the *Fons Salutis*; or a cultural call at St Vincent's frescoed Romanesque church, built over the baths of a Roman villa (closed 12–2). The main road continues to the Valle d'Aosta's second city, **Châtillon**, given over to industry, but where many travellers leave the train to catch a bus up the Valtournenche.

Under the Matterhorn: Valtournenche and Breuil-Cervinia

The **Valtournenche** is Italy's picture window on the Matterhorn, its unique profile rising up majestically at the top of the valley, and visible from nearly every point. The first small resort in the Valtournenche, **Antey-St-André**, is known for its healthy, mild climate. For complete tranquillity, take the cable car from Buisson to the otherwise inaccessible hamlet of **Chamois**; from Chamois a chairlift continues up to the lovely green banks of the Lago di Lod. **Valtournenche**, the valley capital, is a popular ski resort, and hometown of the renowned Matterhorn guides – memorial plaques posted around the church are a grim reminder of the dangers they face. From Valtournenche you can get a cable car up the **Cime Bianche**, or take a dramatic walk along the specially constructed galleries through the **Gouffre des Buserailles**, a narrow gorge carved out by the River Marmore above Crépin.

The valley road ends at sparkling, smart **Breuil-Cervinia**, one of Italy's most renowned ski resorts. It enjoys a uniquely grand setting – the Matterhorn to the north, the sweep of the **Grandes Murailles** to the west, and the **Fruggen massif** to the east. The resort dates from the construction of the road up in the late 1930s, and although Breuil-Cervinia may look more like a frontier boom town, the mountains are everything, with 190km of ski run, and summer skiing on the glacier at **Plateau Rosa** (11,482ft); a cable car and lift from here can take you to the top of **Piccolo Cervino** (the little Matterhorn; 12,739ft), from where fantastic ski trails continue down to Zermatt in Switzerland, or along the valley to Valtournenche. The descents are so lengthy that the KL time trials for the world speed record are held here. Other winter sports at Breuil-Cervinia include ice skating, bob-sledding and hockey. In the summer months it is the base for ascents of the **Matterhorn** for experienced climbers, a feat first achieved from this side in 1867; the route's most precipitous passages are now fitted out with ropes.

Other far less demanding excursions include the easy hike from Plateau Rosa over the Colle Superiore delle Cime Bianche, either to emerald Lago Goillet and its view encompassing the Val d'Ayas, or to the summit of the **Breithorn** (13,684ft).

The Mian Valley: Chambave and Nus

West of Châtillon, **Chambave** lies under a crag draped with the ruins of the **Castello di Cly**; the vineyards that skirt the environs produce a rare and prized golden dessert wine called Passito di Chambave. More wine and a modest amount of tourism are the industries of **Nus**, the next town, where the Challants, the medieval Viscounts of Aosta, built their **Castello di Fénis** (*t 0165 764 263; open Mar–June and Sept, 9–; July and Aug 9–8; Oct–Feb 10–12.30 and 1.30–5; closed Tues only Oct–Feb; adm*).

More of a residence than a fortress, this is a genuine fairy-tale castle, all turrets and swallowtail crenellations. Only the ground floor is open to the public: a series of low-ceilinged rooms and alcoves filled with a random selection of medieval and modern furniture, all culminating in a beautifully preserved courtyard with wooden balconies and a 15th-century fresco of St George. From Nus you can visit two remote valleys – the **Val Clavalité**, with the striking Punta Tersiva at its head, or the **Val St-Barthélemy**, with its scattered villages lost in the trees – or continue 13km to Aosta.

Aosta: the 'Rome of the Alps'

Aosta's setting is pure enchantment, ringed by mountains that resemble divine emanations supporting the sky on their shoulders; on clear mornings they wrap Aosta in a total, shimmering blueness, while the bright snows of their peaks merge with the clouds to form a magic circle around the city. It grew up where the roads from the Mont Blanc and St Bernard passes meet – a piece of sunny Italy at the cross-roads of France and Switzerland.

Although ringed by industry, army installations and dull suburbs, the city's core, with its grand Roman and medieval monuments, retains its charm. The street plan

Tourist Information

Aosta: Place Chanoux 8, **t** 0165 236 627, **f** 0165 34657.

Rome (for Valle d'Aosta), Via Sistina 9, **t** 06 474 4104, **f** 06 482 3837. Both Aosta and Rome offices provide useful information on hiking routes in the Aosta valleys, and publish a monthly booklet with useful information.

Where to Stay and Eat

Aosta ✉ 11100

Aosta is not only the central transport hub for the region, but it's more likely than most of the resorts to have rooms available if you haven't booked in advance.

****Europe, Via Ribitel 8, **t** 0165 236 363, **f** 0165 40566 (*expensive*). An excellent, friendly hotel in the centre, with all mod cons, as well as a restaurant and piano bar.

***Rayon de Soleil, above Aosta in Saraillon, Viale Gran San Bernardo, **t** 0165 262 247, **f** 0165 236 085 (*moderate*). Convenient if you're driving, the 'sunbeam' is a pleasant, medium-sized hotel, with fine views, a garden and an indoor pool. *Closed Oct–mid-Dec.*

***Bus, Via Malherbes 18, **t** 0165 236 958, **f** 0165 236 962 (*moderate*). Back in town, a good choice is the oddly named Bus, located in a quiet street off Via Aubert, with rooms that are comfortable and tastefully decorated, and a good restaurant (*cheap*).

*Monte Emilius, Via G. Carrel 9, **t/f** 0165 35692 (*cheap*). Next to the station, with combination lovely/terrible views of mountains/railway tracks. is a little gem of a hotel with some large, high-ceilinged Art-Decoish rooms with balconies. The restaurant is also good.

Piemonte, Via Porta Praetoria 13, **t** 0165 40111 (*cheap*). A traditional favourite in the heart of town, featuring excellent, home-style Piemontese and French cuisine – *bagna cauda* upon request in the winter, boar steaks in the autumn, *crêpes* and apple pie, all at reasonable prices. *Closed Fri.*

Vecchia Aosta, Piazza Porta Praetoria 4, **t** 0165 361 186 (*moderate*). Built right into the Roman walls, with the most striking dining room in town. The food is good, too – home-made pasta, cured venison, trout with almonds – and lots of wines to help it down. *Closed Wed and two weeks in Feb and Nov.*

Vecchio Ristoro, Via Tourneuve 4, **t** 0165 33238 (*expensive*). Housed in a windmill that functioned until only a few years ago. The hot *antipasti*, smoked trout and salmon, and an especially good selection of local cheeses are all excellent. *Closed Sun, and Mon lunch.*

Papa Marcel's. Just off the main drag on Via Croix de Ville. Good place for a nightcap – The only place in town with any character, with graffiti scribbled all over the walls and hundreds of bottles containing weird liquids on the shelves. A must.

has changed little since 23 BC, when *Augusta Praetoria* was built after the conquest of the Salassian Gauls, the terror of the Alps. In the Middle Ages Aosta (a corruption of *Augusta*) was ruled by the Challant Viscounts, and then by the Dukes of Aosta, who owed allegiance to the Savoys. But here the French influence remained stronger than in Piemonte, and you are more likely to hear French or a French dialect in the streets than Italian. Aosta is touristy, but in a relaxed, easygoing way: it is part resort and part everyday workplace.

As the centre of transport in the Valle d'Aosta, the city makes a good base; it also has its 'own' ski resort at Pila. On 31 January it holds the famous **Sant'Orso Fair**, a market dating back to the year 1000, where Aosta's woodworkers sell everything from ladders to fine sculpture. In July there's a series of organ concerts, and in October the finals of a peculiar Valdostana sport, the **Bataille des Reines**, the 'Battle of Cows', in which heifers butt heads.

Place Emile Chanoux

Aosta is a hard town to get lost in, with its straight Roman streets branching out from the central Place Emile Chanoux, site of the French-style town hall, the tourist office and the IVAT (the local handicrafts association), where arts and crafts are displayed year-round. A short distance from the square tower are the mighty double arches of the **Porta Praetoria**, the original Roman gate, its impressive strength a compliment to the ferocity of the local Gauls. To the left of the gate stand the remains of the **Teatro Romano** (Roman Theatre), a four-storey section of the façade plus some of the central seating (*open daily Mar–Sept 9–8, Oct–Feb 9–6.30*). Next door the **Tour Fromage**, or tower of the cheesemakers, holds a small contemporary art gallery. Through the Porta Praetoria, **Via Sant'Anselmo** is Aosta's main drag, named after St Anselm (1033–1109), Archbishop of Canterbury, the founder of Scholasticism and a Doctor of the Church, who was born in the street now awash with stuffed Saint Bernards and garishly labelled bottles of mysterious Alpine elixirs.

Via Sant'Orso to the left leads shortly to the Romanesque-Gothic hybrid **Collegiata dei SS Pietro ed Orso** (*t 0165 262 026; open daily April–Sept 9–7, Oct–Mar 10–5*), founded in the late 10th century. The church is famous for rare Ottonian frescoes dating from its construction, and for its little cloister (1133), its short columns topped by capitals of white marble darkened with an artificial patina and carved with scenes both Biblical and mythological; cloisters were one of the few places where medieval sculptors could follow their fancies. The crypt contains the remains of Aosta's some-what apocryphal patron, Sant'Orso (St Bear). Across the lane, the excavations belong to the **Basilica di San Lorenzo**, built in the 6th and destroyed in the 9th century (*open Mar–June and Sept, 9–7; July and Aug 10–8, Oct–Feb 10–5*). Via Sant'Anselmo ends at the **Arco di Augusto**, built at the founding of the city to celebrate the victory over the Salassi; the incongruous roof was added in the 18th century. On the other side of the arch and above the River Buthier, a single-span Roman bridge has outlasted the channel it once crossed, but is still used by Aostans to pass over the river bed.

The Cathedral and Forum

From Place Emile Chanoux, Via Xavier de Maistre leads, on the right, to the scanty remains of the **Anfiteatro Romano** (Roman Amphitheatre) and the 12th-century **Torre dei Balivi**. To the left is the **Cathedral of the Assunta**, off Via Monseigneur de Sales, an ancient church rebuilt several times, with a neoclassical façade hiding a Gothic cross-vaulted interior. The 23 stained-glass windows are 15th and 16th-century Swiss workmanship, while the choir contains finely inlaid 15th-century stalls and two excellent mosaics, one a 12th-century *Labours of the Months*, the other a 14th-century scene featuring 'ferocious beasts' from Mesopotamia. The huge suspended wooden cross with life-size Jesus is the work of local Piemontese craftsmen from the end of the 14th century. Next to the choir, behind the glass doors, is the well-arranged **Museo del Tesoro** (*t 0165 40413; open in summer, weekdays 10–11.30 and 3–5.30, Sun and holidays 3–5.30 only; in winter holidays only; adm*), containing such outstanding treasures as an ivory diptych from 406 AD, portraying the Emperor Honorius; the 13th-century effigy of Tommaso II of Savoy, visible in the choir, and Romanesque reliquaries and statues, all described in a free audio guide in English.

Opposite, in Piazza Giovanni XXIII, are the remains of the **Foro Romano** (*currently under restoration*), and the huge 302ft by 285ft **Cryptoportico** or underground gallery that stretches out below. It may simply have been a storeroom or, perhaps, a walkway for the great and the good to perambulate on hot summer days – the temperature here is always several degrees cooler than outside. You can also make out the foundations of a Roman temple under the **Casa Arcidianale**. The **Museo Archeologico** on Piazza Roncas contains some good local finds (*t 0165 238 680; open daily 9–7*)

Beyond the forum stands a nearly intact portion of the Roman wall, with **La Tourneuve**, built by the Challants. Other sections of the walls remain in the south, near the station, with three towers: Roman **Torre Pailleron**, in a garden by the station; the impressive round **Torre di Bramafam**, a Challant defensive work; and the **Torre del Lebbroso** (*open for exhibitions Tues–Sun 9.30–12.30 and 2.30–6.30*), which earned its sad name from a family of lepers who were incarcerated here from 1733 until the last survivor died in 1803. It is used today to house temporary exhibitions.

Around Aosta

Pila, 20km south of Aosta, is the nearest winter/summer resort, with chairlifts up the **Col di Chamolé** (7,546ft) that operate all year round, though much less frequently in summer. There are trails up the slopes of **Monte Emilius** (11,677ft), by way of Chamolé, that offer stupendous views over the ranges to the north.

More castles bristle over the valley west of Aosta, beginning with the solemn 13th-century **Castello di Sarre**, rebuilt in the 18th century. After the Risorgimento the kings of Italy, who spent 99.5 per cent of their time hunting, used it as a lodge, and filled the interior with trophies bagged in the surroundings. Two other restored medieval castles guard the pretty village of **St Pierre**, a bit further on: one is home to the **Museo Regionale di Scienze Naturali** (*open daily Mar 9–12 and 2–6, April–Oct 9–7; closed in winter; adm*); the other, the 14th-century **Sarriod de la Tour**, is used for art exhibitions.

The Western Valleys

Aosta to the Great St Bernard Pass

From Aosta at least two buses a day make the 34km trip to the most famous of Alpine passes, the Great St Bernard Pass (Colle del Gran San Bernardo – *closed Nov–May*), its importance now diminished by a tunnel (*open all year*). Before St Bernard, the pass was known as Mont Jovis, after a temple of *Jupiter Poeninus*; Celts, Romans and Holy Roman Emperors marched to and fro on a regular basis, and in 1800 Napoleon moved 40,000 troops through to defeat the Austrians at Marengo. The road up (SS27) is uncommonly pretty, affording splendid vistas down the valleys and back towards Aosta itself. **Etroubles** is the main resort *en route*, and **Saint Oyen**, in the midst of emerald meadows, is a quieter holiday centre, with skiing at Flassin.

The legendary 11th-century **Hospice de St Bernard** (*t 0041 277 871 236*) lies just over the Swiss border (passports required). St Bernard, archdeacon of Aosta, founded the monastery at the exposed summit of the pass (8,100ft), and the canons from **Martigny** who run it made it their business to minister to weary travellers, many of them pilgrims or churchmen going to Rome. To help find people lost in the heavy snows the canons developed their famous hardy breed of dog. Magnificent specimens abound near the hospice, and when not engaged in saving the lives of intrepid skiers, they happily mug for the cameras of the intrepid tourist.

Val di Cogne and the Parco Nazionale del Gran Paradiso

From Aosta and St Pierre, the Val di Cogne stretches south towards the blunt peak of the **Gran Paradiso massif** (13,323ft). The valley's rich magnetite and iron mines were exploited long before its tourism potential; the latter began in earnest with the opening of the national park in the 1920s.

The mouth of the valley is defended by the Challant **Castello di Aymavilles** (*closed indefinitely for restoration*), its four round towers dating from the 18th century. Further up, at **Pondel** (Pont d'Ael), the stunning, torrential **Grand Eyvia** gorge is spanned by a steep Roman bridge, still in use today. A breathtaking drive, through forested ravines and lush valleys, leads to the *comune* of **Cogne**, a pleasant, busy town that commemorates the traditional source of its livelihood with a handsome cast-iron fountain, erected in 1819. Now a popular resort, Cogne is the main gateway to the Parco Nazionale del Gran Paradiso, which encompasses the entire massif. Set aside as a Savoy hunting reserve in the 19th century, the park was donated to the state by Vittorio Emanuele III in 1919. It played the lead role in preserving the ibex (or *stambecco*, or *steinbock*), a pretty deer-like creature with long, ridged horns, which numbered only 420 in 1945, all of them in the confines of the park. Since then their numbers have increased tenfold, and animals from the park have been reintroduced into many of their old Alpine haunts. Although ibex prefer high altitude and rugged crags, they may be seen around the valleys in the winter and early spring.

They share their paradise with the more numerous, shorter-horned chamois, who have a wider range and are more easily spotted – if not here, on local dinner menus. In November and December the males of both species may be seen furiously butting heads for the ladies. Among the birds you may be lucky enough to see a wall creeper, chough, golden eagle, ptarmigan, nutcracker or black grouse. The flowers are at their most spectacular in early June, all labelled in the **Giardino Alpino Paradisia** (*open mid-June–mid-Sept 10–5.30, July and Aug until 6.30; adm*), laid out in 1955 in the lovely **Valnontey** near Cogne.

Cogne has seven campsites, hotels and eight Alpine refuges, used as hostels during the ski season. The best one to aim for is the **Rifugio Vittorio Sella** (8,478ft), a gorgeous walk through Cogne's vast meadow of Sant'Orso, up into the deep, flower-spangled vale of **Losòn**, a favourite rendezvous of ibex and chamois now that the refuge is no longer a royal hunting lodge. You can return to Cogne through Valnontey.

There are well-marked trek routes through the park, from flat meanders along valley floors to lung-bursting hikes up mountain sides; the Cogne tourist office can

Tourist Information

Cogne: Place Chanoux 36, t 0165 74040,
f 0165 749 125.
Courmayeur: Piazzale Monte Bianco 13, t 0165
842 060, f 0165 842 072.

Where to Stay and Eat

Cogne ✉ 11012

★★★★Bellevue, Rue Grand Paradis 22, t 0165
74825, f 0165 749 192 (*expensive*). The best
location of any hotel in Cogne, if not the
whole of the Valle d'Aosta, with majestic
views of a glacial valley – carpeted with
meadow flowers in summer and littered
with cross-country skiers in winter – from
the hotel's excellent restaurant. It's family-
run and the super-friendly staff dress in
Cogne traditional costume. There's a limou-
sine service, and a swimming pool and
jacuzzi in the basement. Half boad
L160,000–300,000. *Open Christmas holidays–Oct.*
★★★Sant'Orso, Via Bourgeois 2, t 0165 74821,
f 0165 749 500 (*moderate*). Also enjoys
splendid views, at slightly more affordable
prices, and has an excellent restaurant
(*moderate*).
Lou Ressignon, Via Mines de Cogne, t 0165
74034 (*moderate*). Serves good, honest
Valdostan specialities in an attractive chalet

– chamois (*camoscio*) with *polenta* for something out of the ordinary – topped off by
good home-made desserts. *Closed Tues
and Nov.*
Brasserie du Bon Pec, Rue Bourgeois 72, t 0165
749 288 (*moderate*). An excellent cosy little
diner where big meaty grills and *fondues* are
served by waiters in Cogne national dress.
There is an extensive and expensive wine
list. It's very popular, so book ahead. *Closed
Mon only Nov–mid-Dec*

Courmayeur ✉ 11013

In Courmayeur Christmas, Easter, July,
August, and from the second week of February
through to the end of March are high season,
when reservations are a must. At other times,
if a place is open, you'll find lower prices and
more room.
★★★★Royal E Golf, Via Roma 87, t 0165 831 611,
f 0165 842 093 (*very expensive*). The top
choice: may look a little lopsided from
outside, but inside the facilities and service
are as balanced as you could wish. The
views, especially from the excellent restaurant, are fantastic, and rooms are beautifully
furnished. There is an indoor pool and piano
bar. Half board L195,000–375,000. *Open
Dec–April and end-June–Sept.*
★★★★Palace Bron, t 0165 846 742, f 0165 844
015 (*luxury*). A truly luxurious white chalet,
just over a kilometre above Courmayeur at
pine-forested Plan Gorret, with beautiful

provide maps and advice. One of the easiest walks starts in Valnontey and continues
up a gorgeous riverside trail towards the glaciers.

The western reaches of the park – the lush, unspoiled **Val Savarenche** and the **Val di
Rhêmes** – may be reached from Villeneuve on the Courmayeur road. In the Val
Savarenche, the ideal base is **Dégioz**; from here a track leads up to the Rifugio Vittorio
Sella, while another, an ex-royal hunting road, goes to the **Nivolè Pass**, site of yet
another hunting lodge, now the **Rifugio Albergo Savoia**; an alternative route diverges
at **Lake Djuan** for the **Entrelor Pass** and the prettily situated village of **Rhêmes-Notre-
Dame** in the Val de Rhêmes. The Valsavarenche bus terminus, at **Pont**, is the base for
ascents of **Gran Paradiso**.

The Main Valley: Villeneuve to Pré-St-Didier

Every medieval Tom, Dick and Harry built a castle in these parts. **Villeneuve** is
sprawled under the massive, ruined, 12th-century **Châtel-Argent**, while the next town,
Arvier, sits under the slightly later **Château de la Mothe** and makes a helluva wine,

views over the Mont Blanc massif from nearly every room. It's convenient for the slopes, but far enough away to enjoy a rarefied tranquillity. Next to the hotel is an outdoor, lake-like pool; the restaurant and piano bar are elegant. *Open Dec–April and July–Sept.*

★★★**Del Viale**, Viale Monte Bianco, t 0165 846 712, f 0165 844 513 (*expensive*). An old-fashioned Alpine chalet with nice views. The cosy, folksy lobby and restaurant have stripped wooden floors and an open fire. Most rooms have a balcony or sun terrace. *Closed May, Oct and Nov.*

★★★**Bouton d'Or**, SS26 No.10, t 0165 846 729, f 0165 842152 (*expensive*). Friendly and central, with small but comfortably furnished rooms; some have balconies with views of Mont Blanc.

Le Vieux Pommier, Piazzale Monte Bianco 25, t 0165 842 281 (*expensive*). Run by the same family as the Bouton d'Or; a tourist favourite with a rustic hyper-Alpine interior and solid Valdostana cuisine. *Closed Mon.*

★★★**Croux**, Via Circonvallazione 94, t 0165 846 735, f 0165 845 180 (*expensive*). In the centre of town, enjoys outstanding views. Its bedrooms are modern and well-equipped. *Open Dec–April and late June–Sept.*

Venezia, Via Delle Villette 2, t/f 0165 842 461 (*cheap*). Large rooms with fantastic views.

La Palud/Entrèves ✉ 11013

Hotels are generally more reasonable around La Palud:

★★★**La Brenva**, Strada La Palud 12, t 0165 869 780, f 0165 869 726 (*moderate*). Just over in Entrèves, was once a simple royal hunting lodge but has been a hotel since 1897. The décor has changed little since then, though the amenities are up-to-date.

★★★**Astoria**, Strada La Palud 23, t 0165 869 740, f 0165 869 750 (*moderate*). An excellent choice with big, modern rooms in a cosy old style.

★★**Funivia**, Via San Bernardo, t 0165 89924, f 0165 89636 (*cheap*). Big rooms, modern bathrooms, old wooden furniture and priceless views.

Maison de Filippo, t 0165 869 797, f 0165 869 719 (*moderate*). *The* place to dine: Philip's house has a fame that extends into France and Switzerland, and there are those who don't mind paying the tunnel fares just to come over to feast at this jovial temple of Alpine cuisine. And feast is no exaggeration: if Philip's all-you-can-eat doesn't bust your buttons, no place will. The décor is charming – rustic without fussiness – and the tables are laid out on three levels; in the summer you can dine out in the garden. The food, from the *antipasti* of salami and ham, to the *ravioli* stuffed with *porcini* mushrooms, the *fondue*, trout or game, and the *grand dessert finale*, is all delicious. *Closed Tues.*

Vin de l'Enfer. Here a road forks for the wild and rocky **Val Grisenche**, dominated by the melancholy **Castle of Montmayeur** high on its rock. The main villages in the Val Grisenche, **Valgrisenche** and **Planaval**, have the shimmering **Rutor Glacier** for a backdrop; just beyond them towers the massive Beauregard Dam and its artificial lake.

Back in the main valley, **Avise**, a charming village with two medieval castles, lies at the foot of a romantic gorge, where the **Pierre Taillée** has remains of the Roman road cut into the rock. On the far side you get your first memorable glimpse of Mont Blanc. Above the road to the left, **Derby** has a fine collection of fortified medieval houses, a little Gothic church, and a waterfall, the **Cascata di Linteney**. To the right of the road the landmark is the 13th-century **Châtelard tower** in La Salle.

The medieval town of **Morgex**, headquarters of the upper main valley, or Valdigne, was the administrative seat of the Savoys. The little resort of **Pré-St-Didier**, just beyond, lies at the confluence of the Dora de la Thuile and Dora Baltea rivers. Its warm chalybeate springs are used for skin complaints; its station is the last rail link in the Valle d'Aosta. From here you can pick up buses to La Thuile or Courmayeur.

Little St Bernard Valley

At Pré-St-Didier begins the scenic road up to the **Little St Bernard Pass** (Colle del Piccolo San Bernardo, 7,178ft – *open June–Oct*), threading forests and dizzily skirting the ravine of the Dora de la Thuile. The town of **La Thuile** is a growing winter resort, with excellent skiing on the slopes of Chaz Dura. In summer the most striking excursion is up to the **Colle San Carlo** and the **Testa d'Arp**, with an azure lake and remarkable view of Mont Blanc.

Above La Thuile, Mont Blanc also forms a stunning backdrop to pretty **Lac Verney**, a mirror in a setting of emerald meadows. A bit beyond, the Little St Bernard Pass is marked by a statue of St Bernard on a column, and a *cromlech* (neolithic stone burial circle), with the ruins of two structures on the side. Just over the French frontier, the ancient **Hospice du Petit St Bernard** was founded even before St Bernard, with the same purpose of sheltering destitute travellers. Bombed during the Second World War, it was ceded to France, and abandoned. In 1897, an abbot, Pierre Canous, planted an **Alpine botanical garden** here, which, after years of neglect, has been re-established and reopened. From the pass it's 31km to the first French town, Bourg-St-Maurice.

Courmayeur

In more ways than one Valle d'Aosta reaches its climax in **Courmayeur**, one of the most stunning, best equipped and most congenial resorts in the Alps. Lying at the foot of Mont Blanc, it is perhaps Italy's most fashionable winter and summer resort, rivalling Chamonix in chic, but warmer both in its climate and atmosphere. The skiing is matchless, the scenery mythic in its grandeur, and the accommodation and facilities among the best in the Alps.

Besides the 100km of downhill ski runs at **Chécrouit-Val Veny**, served by nine cable cars, seven chairlifts, 13 ski lifts, and helicopters for jet-set thrills, Courmayeur offers magnificent cross-country skiing, ice skating and an indoor swimming pool: in summer there is skiing on the glacier of **Colle del Gigante**, a rock-climbing school, golf, tennis, riding, hang gliding, fishing and spectacular walks, with some 20 Alpine refuges in the area.

One thing Courmayeur isn't is a bargain. A trip on the thrilling, unforgettable cable car from **La Palud**, just north of Courmayeur, to Chamonix over Mont Blanc is L110,000 (summer only; returning by bus; passports required), though for L52,000 you can go only part of the way to **Punta Helbronner** (11,358ft), stopping off on the way at an **Alpine botanical garden** to ponder the rocks, moss and lichen at the **Pavillion du Mont Frety** (6,988ft) and a small meteorite museum at the **Rifugio Torino** (11,073ft). Wrap up warm – even in summer the temperatures near the top are near freezing. Alternatively, a one-way trip through the **Mont Blanc tunnel** is a mere L44,000; the entrance is near La Palud, just beyond the medieval fortress-village of **Entrèves**. Another scenic summer excursion is to take the **Funivia Courmayeur** from the west side of town to the **Plan Chécrouit**, and from there up to Col Chécrouit. This pass is the base for climbing **Mont Chétif** (1½ hours), the peak just before Mont Blanc, offering tremendous views into the mighty abyss of the **Aiguille Noire**. An alternative is to take another cable car from the Col Chécrouit to Cresta d'Arp (9,039ft), with more fantastic views, and a ski run descending all the way to Dolonne. For a less adventurous outing there is a little **Alpine museum** (*closed for restoration*), at the top of town, housing the diaries, drawings and equipment of Alpine pioneers, and a collection of black and white photos of Alpine life in the 1930s and 1940s.

Two gorgeous valleys run in opposite directions from Entrèves. The **Val Veny** may be ascended by bus as far as the **Lago di Combal**, the base for an ascent of **Mont Blanc** or a fairly easy hike to the **Rifugio Elisabetta** and, from there, a three-hour walk up to the **Col de la Seigne** on the French border, with fabulous views in either direction. **The Val Ferret** is enchanting and serene, the site of trout streams and the finest cross-country walks; there is accommodation in **Plampincieux**, a quiet resort in the pines.

East from Turin: Vercelli and Novara

East of Turin and north of the Po is a landscape that encompasses the whole gamut of scenery from flood plain to Alpine splendour. This section includes the province of **Vercelli** and part of **Novara**; for convenience, the northern part of Novara – from Lake Orta and Lake Maggiore to Domodossola and the Simplon Pass – is dealt with in the chapter on Lombardy and the Italian Lakes (*see* pp.273-284).

Vercelli and its Rice Paddies

Several million plates of *risotto* are born every year on the plain between Turin and Milan, a region that is no less than Europe's greatest producer of rice. Its capital, **Vercelli**, is surrounded by a seemingly endless patchwork of paddies divided by hundreds of irrigation canals, dating back to the 15th century. In summer, when they're newly flooded, they become magical, reflecting the clouds and sunset in an irregular checkerboard of mirrors, a landscape bordering on the abstract: uncanny and desolate, melancholy and beautiful.

Of all the cities in Piemonte, only Vercelli stirred from its feudal hibernation in the Renaissance, producing in the 16th century a school of painters, even though the most brilliant of them, Il Sodoma (born in 1477), soon escaped to more promising territory in Tuscany. Even so, as a minor 'city of art' Vercelli is an old, atmospheric place. If you have only an hour between trains you can take in its chief marvel, the **Basilica di Sant'Andrea**, which looms up just across from the station. The basilica was begun in 1219 by Cardinal Guala Bicchieri, papal legate and guardian and 'saviour' of Henry III. To thank Cardinal Bicchieri for his aid in obtaining the throne, Henry gave him the revenues from the Abbey of St Andrew in Chesterton, near Cambridge, and the cardinal used the money to finance another St Andrew's in Vercelli. Completed nine years later – a lightning clip in those days – thanks to the Cardinal's resources, the basilica, though basically Romanesque, is famous in Italian architectural history as one of the first to display signs of the new Gothic style from the Île de France, first adopted by the Cistercian Order; it whispers in Sant'Andrea's twin bell towers, the flying buttresses, the vaulting in the nave and the plan of the church and cloister.

Getting Around

This area is especially well served by rail. Frequent **trains** travel to Vercelli and Novara from Turin and Milan; both cities are also linked with Biella (1 hour), base of a network of **buses** into the Alpine valleys. The main rail and **road** approach to the Valsesia is from Novara (if coming from Turin, change trains at Romagnano) and goes as far as Varallo (from Novara, 1½ hours), where you can catch a bus up to Alagna. Rail links from Vercelli continue south to Casale Monferrato, Asti and Alessandria, while Novara has trains to Lakes Orta and Maggiore and beyond.

Tourist Information

Vercelli: Viale Garibaldi 90, t 0161 58002, f 0161 257 899.
Novara: Baluardo Quintino Sella 40, t 0321 394 059, f 0321 631 063.
Biella: Piazza V. Veneto 3, t 015 351 128, f 015 34612.
Varallo: Corso Roma 38, t 0163 51280, f 0163 53091.

Where to Stay and Eat

Vercelli ✉ 13100
★★★**Il Giardinetto**, Via Sereno 3, t 0161 257 230, f 0161 259 311 (*moderate*). Vercelli isn't exactly a popular stopover, but the little garden will do for a night, with eight modern rooms and an attractive restaurant and bar. *Closed Aug.*
Il Paiolo, Via Garibaldi 72, t 0161 250 577 (*expensive*). The province isn't known for its cuisine either, in spite of its rice, but you can dine on hearty *risotti* at 'the cauldron'. *Closed Thurs.*

Novara ✉ 28100
★★★★**Italia**, Via Solaroli 8/10, t 0321 399 316, f 0321 399 310 (*expensive*). Central and elegant, very modern, well furnished and comfortable; also claims one of the best restaurants in Novara (*expensive*), with good rice dishes and some surprisingly untypical dishes, like chicken curry.
★★★**Parmigiano**, Via dei Cattaneo 4/6, t 0321 623 231 f 0321 620 500 (*moderate*). An old

façade conceals a sparkling modern interior with simple rooms and an excellent restaurant (*cheap*) – a good place to try out local specialities. *Restaurant closed Sun.*
Trattoria Tri Scalin, Via Sottile 23, t 0321 623 247 (*moderate*). The shrine of Novarese cuisine. The food – antipasti of the local *salame della duja*, *risotto al Barolo* or *pasta e fagioli*, and a wide variety of **secondi** – is excellent, and accompanied by a good list of Piemontese wines. *Closed Sat lunch, Sun and Aug.*

Biella ✉ 13900
★★★★**Astoria**, Viale Roma 9, t 015 402 750, f 015 849 1691 (*moderate*). Biella's grandest hotel specializes in what it terms 'sober elegance' – lots of comfort but little style. It has a bar, but no restaurant.
★★★★**Augustus**, Via Italia 54, t 015 27554, f 015 29257 (*moderate*). A no-nonsense business hotel in the centre with comfortable rooms. *Closed Christmas holidays and Aug.*
Ca'Verna, Via Avogadro 10, t 015 22724 (*moerate*). In Biella Piazzo, near the funicular. Serves superb veal and pizzas. It's popular with the locals, and the general air of bonhomie is shared by the helpful staff.
Il Baracca, Via Sant'Eusebio 12, t 015 21941 (*moderate*). On the road to Oropa. The oldest and best place to eat in the area, with Piemontese treats like *bagna cauda*, *salame della duja*, rice dishes and mixed roast or boiled meats. *Closed Sat and Sun.*

Roppolo/Lago di Viverone ✉ 13900
★★★**Castello di Roppolo**, Via al Castello 2, t 0161 980 000, f 0161 987 156 (*moderate*). Near the Lago di Viverone. Eleven elegant rooms in a former medieval castle in a lovely setting. It also houses the **Enoteca della Serra** wine cellar and restaurant, t 0161 98501 (*expensive*), which offers a wide selection of Piemonte's finest wines and local specialities. *Hotel closed first three weeks in Aug, enoteca closed Jan.*

Varallo ✉ 13019
★**Monte Rosa**, Via Regaldi 4, t/f 0163 51100 (*cheap*). A wonderful little family-run hotel. Behind the red façade wait large old-fashioned, beautifully furnished rooms, with balconies and lovely views.

The change of materials halfway up the façade at first gives the same incongruous impression as a 1960s demi-wood station wagon. The three arched portals are Romanesque, with lunettes attributed to the great 12th-century sculptor Antelami. The lofty interior is majestic and striking in its simple red and white decoration. The cloister, with its cluster columns and sculptural details, is lovely, and offers the best view of the unusual cupola and the basilica's Romanesque and Gothic features. The massive detached campanile was added in 1407.

Vercelli's grand 16th-century **cathedral** is a short way to the left, in Piazza Sant'Eusebio; of the original Romanesque construction only the bell tower remains. It has an especially valuable library of *codices*, including 11th-century Anglo-Saxon poems perhaps brought to Vercelli by Cardinal Bicchieri. The one saintly member of the House of Savoy, the Blessed Amedeo IX, who died in Vercelli Castle in 1472, is buried in an octagonal chapel. From the cathedral, Via Duomo leads past the **Castello d'Amedeo** (to the left, behind Santa Maria Maggiore), then to Via Gioberti and Via Borgogna, site of the **Pinacoteca Borgogna** (*t 0161 252 776; open Tues–Fri 3–5.30, Sat and Sun 9.30–12; adm*), with paintings by Vercelli natives – most famously Il Sodoma, Gaudenzio and Defendante Ferrari, as well as works by other Italians.

Via Borgogna gives onto old Vercelli's main street, Corso Libertà. At No.204 be sure to look in at the lovely courtyard of the 15th-century **Palazzo Centori**. The Corso continues to main Piazza Cavour, where markets are held under the **Palazzo Municipio**. Down Via Lucca, **San Cristoforo** is adorned with a famous series of frescoes (1529–33) by Gaudenzio Ferrari, including his masterpiece, the *Madonna of the Oranges*. In Via Verdi, off Piazza Cavour, Vercelli has an interesting archaeological and historical collection in the **Museo Leone** (*t 0161 253 204; open Tues, Thurs and Sat 3–5.30, Sun 10–12 and 3–6; adm*), located in a 15th-century house and Baroque palace. From Piazza Cavour, Corso Libertà continues into the newer part of town; in Piazza Zumaglini, rice prices are decided in the Rice Exchange, or **Borsa Risi**; here, too, is the national rice board's headquarters.

Novara

Novara is an ancient city, but one that has preserved only a few traces of the past. The cobbled Corso Cavour and Corso Italia, lined with tearooms and fashionable shops, are pleasant for whiling away an hour or two, perhaps after digesting Novara's landmark, looming high above the surrounding rooftops: the three-tiered tower and dome of **San Gaudenzio**. The main body of the church was designed in the 16th century by Pellegrino Tibaldi, while the tower is a 19th-century addition by Italy's most phallic architect, Antonelli, who designed the similarly tall and pointy Mole in Turin. He crowned this particular creation with a spire and a shining figure of the saint who seems to poke the very sky. San Gaudenzio's equally unusual 8th-century campanile makes an interesting companion piece. Inside, look for Il Tanzio's nightmarish *Battle of Sennacherib* (1627).

Central Piazza della Repubblica has Novara's much restored **Broletto**, or lawcourts, in four separate buildings on a central courtyard, built between the 12th and 18th centuries. It shares the piazza with the **Duomo**, built in the 1860s by the inimitable

Antonelli. This time, instead of building tall, he designed one of the largest doorways in Europe (38ft by 19ft). Parts of an earlier Romanesque cathedral survive, including the campanile, the 12th-century frescoed chapel of San Siro, the red brick cloister, and some mosaics in the chancel; in the main body are frescoes and paintings by Gaudenzio Ferrari and others of the Vercelli school, and a collection of 16th-century Flemish tapestries. The **Baptistry** dates back to the 5th century, and contains very unusual frescoes of the Apocalypse, added 500 years later.

Biella, the Santuario d'Oropa, and Around

Easily reached from Vercelli, Novara or Turin, the wool and textile town of **Biella** is divided into two – the lower half, **Biella Piano** and the upper, Biella Piazzo, linked since 1885 by a jaunty little incline railway (*open daily 7am–midnight, Fri and Sat till 2am; L1500 return; pay at the top*). Biella Piano's chief monuments are clustered in the Piazza Duomo: the lovely little baptistry, dating back to the late 10th century and constructed from parts of old Roman buildings, the mighty nine-storey Romanesque campanile of a now-demolished church, and the town's white elephant, the Gothic cathedral, unfortunately prettified in the last century.

Biella Piano also has a fine Renaissance church – unusual in Piemonte – San Sebastiano, begun in 1504, with a remodelled 19th-century façade, housing a number of works by the Vercelli school, especially Bernardino Lanino's *Assumption*, and beautifully carved choir stalls. The **Museo Civico**, Via P. Micca 36 *(currently closed prior to relocation)* houses archaeological finds, ceramics and paintings. Biella's social life, in the lower part of town, is centred around Via Italia, a pretty cobbled street where the great and the good come to promenade in the sunshine.

During the Renaissance wealthy textile merchants built their showy mansions up in **Biella Piazzo**, which retains much of its patrician air and offers fine views over the city and surrounding mountains. A three-storey cotton mill from 1859 stands near the centre, a reminder of what is still the region's lifeblood. Across the River Cervo, in the park of San Gerolamo, the former villa of the great Alpine explorer and photographer Vittorio Sella is now the **International Museum of Alpine Photography**, founded in 1948, with his old equipment and photographs of the world's greatest peaks (*t 015 23778; call in advance to visit*).

On the map the environs of Biella look like a plate of spaghetti, a confusing network of squiggly yellow valley roads winding between the mountains. The main attractions, all connected by bus, include the stately 16th-century castle in **Gaglianico**, 5km from Biella, and the most venerated hill shrine in Piemonte, the **Santuario d'Oropa**, 12km north, founded by St Eusebius in the 4th century when he returned from the Holy Land with the *Black Madonna and Child*, reputedly carved by St Luke. The sanctuary consists of three vast quadrangles, a new Baroque basilica, and a remnant of the original frescoed church, sheltering one of the most exotic statues in Italian Christendom, jet black and embellished with a towering golden crown, a starry halo and costly jewels.

A cable car near the sanctuary ascends **Monte Mucrone** (7,661ft), with its lake, hiking in summer and skiing in the winter. In the next valley to the east, **Piedicavallo** is a base for hikes into the Val Gressoney in Valle d'Aosta, or into the Valsesia (*see* below). A few kilometres south of Piedicavallo begins the **Strada Panoramica Zegna** (SS232), which winds across to the Valsesia, and is noted for its spectacular views of Monte Rosa. In late spring thick clusters of rhododendrons and azaleas burst into a dazzling pageant of colour on **Monte Burcina**, west of Biella, in the village of **Pollone**. From here the road twists around to another popular hill sanctuary, **Graglia**, dedicated to Our Lady of Loreto. To the southwest of Graglia, at **Donato**, begins a district called **La Serra**, of steep green moranic ridge. Oaks, chestnuts, birch, and vineyards grow here in arcadian harmony, dotted with unspoiled villages. At the end of the ridge lies the clear, spring-fed **Lago di Viverone**, an unglamorous but soothing place to camp, swim, fish or mess about on a boat.

Varallo and the Valsesia

The lower part of the lovely Alpine valley of **Valsesia** is dotted with textile mills, but at Varallo the scene begins to change. **Varallo** is a fine, friendly town embraced by wooded slopes; the River Sesia froths and tumbles here, making for exciting white-water kayaking. Varallo has a good **Pinacoteca**, with works by the Vercelli school, sharing space with the Natural History Museum in the **Palace of Museums** (*t 0163 51424; open June–Sept Tues–Sun 10–12.30 and 2–6, Oct–May by request; adm*), as well as a fine church, **San Gaudenzio**, artistically piled up on top of a stair, housing a polyptych by Gaudenzio Ferrari. An entire wall of his work, depicting the Life of Christ, is in the church of **Santa Maria delle Grazie**, located at the foot of the steps up to Sacro Monte.

A very stiff walk (or cable car ride) will bring you to **Sacro Monte**, Varallo's five-star attraction, with singularly beautiful views over the lush woodlands. It was founded as the Sanctuary of New Jerusalem in 1491 by the Blessed Bernardo Caimi, who wanted to recreate the Holy Shrines of Palestine. The idea caught the fancy of St Charles Borromeo, the Archbishop of Milan, and when the two holy men were done, the result is nothing tub-thumping less than the Disneyland of the Counter-Reformation: 45 chapels, set in beautifully manicured grounds, containing the world's first dioramas – 16th-century 3D scenes from the Bible with fresco backgrounds, featuring some 1,000 statues and 4,000 painted figures.

When you can pull yourself away from this sincere but slightly nutty extravaganza, visit the **Piazzale della Basilica**, a little gem of porticoes, palm trees and a fountain under a pavilion. The **Basilica** itself is a mass of gilded exploding Baroque; the crypt, its walls covered in heart-rending tributes to dead children, provides the final flourish of religious fervour.

North of Varallo extends the **Val Mastallone**, a scenic valley of deep ravines and Alpine scenery; **Rimella** and **Fobello**, the latter famous for its Walser lace-making and embroidery, with a lace museum and school, are two small resorts. The upper extension of the Valsesia, the **Val Grande**, is more touristy; the main resort at **Riva Valdobbia**, has Monte Rosa as a background and a parish church with curious exterior frescoes. A number of walks begin here, with the hike over the **Colle Valdobbia** to the Val Gressoney in Aosta the most popular. **Alagna**, the last town in the valley, is a popular summer and winter resort under **Monte Rosa**, with funiculars up into the massif. In the charming hamlet of **Pedemonte**, 3km from Alagna, the Walser population (who immigrated from the Swiss Valais in the 12th century) have converted one of their wooden 17th-century homes into the **Walser Museum** (*t 0163 922 935; open weekends Sept–late-June 2–6; late-June–July 10–12 and 2–6; July also daily 2–6, Aug daily 10–12 and 2–6; adm*), furnished in the traditional manner.

Southeast Piemonte: Alessandria and Asti

When the Turinese or Milanese come to this region on weekends their thoughts are more on victuals and drink than on sights. **Alba** and **Asti** are the main wine-growing centres of Piemonte, producing its most famous wines in a supremely civilized land-scape, characterized by lovely, rolling hills and winding roads, and dotted with small villages and fortifications. The region's other speciality, *tartufi bianchi* (white truffles), the pungent ambrosia of the Italians, are harvested in the autumn with a barrage of ecstatic festivals devoted to gluttony, and sold at daily auctions in the main towns.

Casale Monferrato and Alessandria

Between Vercelli and Alessandria, **Casale Monferrato**, Italy's biggest producer of cement, once held the more glamorous position as capital of the medieval and Renaissance duchy of Monferrato, though it retains few traces of the Paleologhi dukes who held court here – a fairly good Romanesque cathedral and some walls of the old castle across the piazza. Monferrato was one of the most important safe havens for Jews in Italy during the Renaissance and Counter-Reformation, and Casale's most striking monument is its Baroquely ornate **synagogue** at Vicolo S. Olper 44 (*open Sun and public hols 10–12 and 3–5*), built in 1595, which now doubles as a **Jewish museum**.

Alessandria, the provincial capital, was founded in the 12th century by disgruntled nobility from Monferrato who opposed Emperor Frederick Barbarossa and named their new town after his arch-enemy, Pope Alexander III. These days Alessandria is best known as the city of Borsalino hats, famed as the world's finest. But, after checking out the fedoras, there's little to see besides the 12-pointed Cittadella, built in 1728 by the Savoys and one of the best-preserved from the period. North of Alessandria, **Valenza** produces gold and silver jewellery; the goldsmiths' association has a permanent exhibition of their craft in the centre of town.

Just eight kilometres south of Alessandria, on the Genoa road, Napoleon defeated the Austrians on 14 June 1800 in what he considered the greatest battle of his career, **Marengo**. The battlefield is marked by a column, and in the village there are monuments to Napoleon and General Desaix, who perished on the field, as well as a **museum of the battle** in the **Villa di Marengo** (*t 0131 3041; open Wed–Sun 9–12 and 2–6*). Another six kilometres further south lies **Bosco Marengo**, birthplace of Pope Pius V (1504–72), whose reign was notable for the great victory over the Turks at Lepanto. Pius built the magnificent church of Santa Croce in the village to serve as his tomb, a masterpiece of green marble and porphyry. The Romans, however, interred him in Santa Maria Maggiore.

Tortona and Acqui Terme

Tortona, east of Alessandria, was the Roman *Dertona*, and still has a sprinkling of Roman remains, most importantly two monumental tombs at the corner of Viale De Gasperi and Via Emilia. The **Museo Civico**, in Piazza Marconi, is housed in a 15th-century palace and contains Roman artefacts and medieval art. More **Roman remains** may be seen at the spa south of Alessandria on the SS30 road, **Acqui Terme** (*Acquae Statiellae*), most notably the four arches of the aqueduct in the park near the hotel Antiche Terme. An archaeological museum (*currently closed for restoration*) in the half-ruined **Castello dei Paleologhi** contains mosaics and remains from the ancient baths. Next to the castle stands the fine Romanesque **cathedral**, with a good doorway and campanile. The most memorable sight in Acqui, however, is the **Bollente**, a hot sulphuric spring that bubbles up under an octagonal pavilion, leaving the earth amid a diabolical cloud of steam.

Asti

Former rival of Milan, **Asti** is an old and noble city that well repays a visit. Although nowadays synonymous with fizzy wine, Asti is proudest of its poet, Vittorio Alfieri (1749–1803), who ran off with the young wife of the not-so-bonny Prince Charlie. Corso Alfieri is the main street, and all of the city's monuments are within a block of its length. At the Corso's end stands the 15th-century church and cloister of **San Pietro in Consavia**, housing a small archaeological collection (*t 0141 353 072; open April–Sept, Tues–Sun 10–1 and 3–7, Oct–Mar Tues–Sun 10–1 and 3–6*). Most intriguing, however, is its round baptistry, perhaps as old as the 10th century, supported by eight thick columns with cubic capitals.

Six streets further west, the Corso passes by the large Piazza Alfieri, with the tourist office and Public Gardens; behind the piazza is the **Campo del Palio**, the site of Asti's bare-back horse race, a tradition of neighbourhood rivalry dating back to 1275 and revived in 1967. As in Siena, the Palio combines medieval pageantry, daredevil riding, and much feasting and celebration afterwards; it takes place on the third Sunday of September, coinciding with Asti's great wine fair. A week before the Palio, in the *Festival delle Sagre*, people from the surrounding villages parade in traditional 19th-century costumes, and recreate cooking and working practices from that era. Their produce is on sale in the Campo del Palio.

Just a short distance from Piazza Alfieri is the attractive Romanesque-Gothic **Collegiata di San Secondo;** it is home of the relics of Asti's patron saint; the *Palio Astigiano* (the banner awarded at the horse race); and a polyptych by Asti's greatest Renaissance artist, Gandolfino d'Asti. Medieval towers loom over the rooftops – the tall, elegant **Torre Troyana** across the Corso and, further down the Corso, the **Torre Comentina**, with the swallowtail merlins of the Ghibellines, and then the octagonal **Torre dei De Regibus**. Here, detour to the right for the tall cathedral, a 14th-century Gothic monument with Baroque frescoes, paintings by Gandolfino d'Asti and Holy Water stoups constructed from Roman and Romanesque capitals.

Back on the Corso there's a museum and wild-eyed bust devoted to Vittorio Alfieri, in the **Casa Alfieri**, at Corso Alfieri 375 (*closed for restoration*). In the basement of the

Southeast and Southwest Piemonte

Valle del Chisone

Po

Rivoli

TURIN
(TORINO)

S23

PIEMONTE

Pinerolo

S23

Carmagnola

S20

Racconigi

Pellice

A6

Brà

Piano
del Re

Crissolo

Ghisola
Paesana

Polle

Cherasco

Colle dell'Agnello

▲ *Monte Viso*

Revello

Saluzzo

Manta

Verzuolo

Casteldelfino

Sampéyre

Varaita

Valle Varaita

Villar San
Costanzo

S231-E74

S28

A6

Acceglio

Valle Maira

Dronero

S20

Bastia
Mondo

*Colle della
Maddalena*

Argentera

Stretta delle Barricate

Castelmagno

Pradleves

Monterosso
Grana

Grana

Cuneo

Mondovì

Ponte delle Barricate

Pietraporzio

Valle Stura

S21

Demonte

Borgo San
Dalmazzo

S564

Santuario di
Vicoforte

Bagni di
Vinadio

Gesso

S20

Vernenagna

Vernante

Certosa di
Pesio

Pesio

Frabosa
Soprana

Grotta
Bossea

Bossea

Monte
Matto ▲

Terme di Valdieri

Parco Regionale Alpi Marittime

Cima di Argentera ▲

Pallanfrè

Limone Piemonte

Parco Naturale
dell'Argentera

Cima di
Gelas ▲

Orme

N

10 km

5 miles

neighbouring Liceo at Via Gualtieri 1, you can visit the 8th-century **Crypt of Sant'Anastasio**, with notable carved capitals, and the **Museo Lapidario** (*t 0141 399 391; open Sat–Sun 10–1 and 3–6, other days by request*). On Via Mazzini, across from the Alfieri museum, the **Palazzo Malabayla** is the finest Renaissance palace in Asti.

The Corso ends by another medieval tower, the **Torre Rossa**, an unusual cylinder on a Roman foundation, with a checkerboard crown. Four kilometres north, the **Chiesetta di Viatosto** is a pretty little Romanesque-Gothic chapel on a hill, with quattrocento frescoes inside and enchanting views over the fertile countryside to the Alps.

North of Asti: Monferrato

The province of Asti divides itself into two sections, **Monferrato** in the north and **Le Langhe** in the south. The gastronomic capital of Monferrato is **Moncalvo** (bus from Asti), with famous wine and truffle festivals. The towers and moats remain of its castle; there's a good Gothic church, San Francesco; and most spectacularly, a view of the countryside from the large Piazza Carlo Alberto.

Just northeast of Moncalvo another *Black Madonna*, similar to the one at Oropa, is venerated at the **Santuario di Crea**. Its 23 chapels contain late 15th- to 17th-century

Getting Around

Alessandria, Casale Monferrato, Acqui Terme, Asti and Alba are all linked together by **rail**, and Alessandria and Asti also have good connections to Turin, Genoa and Milan. To explore the scenic 'wine roads' (*strade dei vini*), though, you need a **car**.

Tourist Information

Alessandria: Piazza di Santa Maria di Castello 14, **t** 0131 251 021, **f** 0131 220 546.
Casale Monferrato: Piazza Castello (in a kiosk) **t/f** 0142 444 330.
Acqui Terme: Via Ferraris 5, **t** 0144 322 142, **f** 0144 329 054.
Asti: Piazza Alfieri 29, **t** 0141 530 357, **f** 0141 538 200.
Alba: Piazza Medford 3, **t** 0173 35833, **f** 0173 363 878.

Activities

Organized **rambles** through the vineyards, villages and woods, on horseback or foot (known as 'trekking' in Italy), are popular, ranging from a one-day stroll to a more strenuous three days, spending the night in castles along the way. For details, call Signor Elio Sabena **t/f** 0173 366 734 or 0336 610 255, or English-speaking Signora Carmen Navello **t** 0335 701 2494.

Where to Stay and Eat

Casale Monferrato ✉ 15033
La Torre, Via Garoglio 3, **t** 0142 70295 (*expensive*). A restaurant that the Turinese and Milanese drive out of their way to patronize. The offerings are based almost entirely on fresh ingredients grown, produced and procured in the immediate environs, such as *risotto* with crayfish,

spinach-filled *tortelli*, or breast of duck. *Closed Wed and Aug.*

Alessandria ✉ 15100
****Alli Due Buoi Rossi**, Via Cavour 32, **t** 0131 445 252, **f** 0131 445 255 (*expensive*). The most comfortable hotel, also has the city's best restaurant (*expensive*). Located in the heart of town, the rooms are luxurious, and the meals feature the full range of Piemontese specialities. *Restaurant closed Sun.*
****Domus**, Via T. Castellani 12, **t** 0131 43305, **f** 0131 232019 (*moderate*). Centrally located with small, modern rooms.
Rex, Via S. Francesco d'Assisi 48, **t** 0131 252 297 (*cheap*). Bright and modern.
Il Grappolo, Via Casale 28, **t** 0131 253 217 (*expensive*). At the top end of town, is a smart, modern restaurant in a 19th-century *palazzo*, with a fine selection of local wines.

Acqui Terme ✉ 15011
***Nuove Terme**, Piazza Italia 1, **t** 0144 322 106, **f** 0144 324 909 (*moderate*). In Acqui Terme you can take the water or mud cure here in this pampered environment.
San Marco, Via Ghione 5, **t** 0144 322 456, **f** 0144 321 073 (cheap). Otherwise opt for the best deal in town, the family-run St Marks. Full board available. *Closed over Christmas and last two weeks in July.*
Schiavia, Vicolo della Schiavia, **t** 0144 55939 (*expensive*). The town offers a good choice of attractive restaurants, but you shouldn't miss this refined watering-hole on the first floor of an 18th-century building. Reserve. *Closed Sun and three weeks in Aug.*
Curia, Via alla Bollente 72, **t** 0144 356 049 (*moderate*). Lively, with the best cellar in town and a soft spot for *stoccafisso* (stock fish). *Closed Mon.*
Da Bigät, Via Mazzini 30, **t** 0144 324 283 (*cheap*). Famous for hearty *farinata* (a sort of flat chick pea bread, like a pizza without a topping) and local specialties, including Roccaverano cheese. No credit cards. *Closed*

frescoes and statues; the highest chapel, del Paradiso, has more fine views over the vineyards. Another town just northeast of Asti, **Castagnole Monferrato**, holds, on the second Sunday in October, *La Vendemmia del Nonno* (Grandpa's Grape Harvest), with old-fashioned grape-picking, barefoot wine-crushing, dancing and music. More

Wed, two weeks in July, and two weeks in Feb. No dinner on Sun.

Asti ✉ 14100

****Reale, Piazza Alfieri 6, **t** 0141 530 240, **f** 0141 34357 (*expensive*). Large, sumptuously decorated modern rooms enjoying the best position in town, all with balconies looking out on to the square; extremely good value. Reserve in advance for the Palio.

***Aleramo, Via E. Filiberto 13, **t** 0141 595 661, **f** 0141 30039 (*expensive*). An excellent hotel. The top two of its six floors enjoy superb views over the town's rooftops.

***Hasta, Valle Benedetta 25, **t** 0141 213 312, **f** 0141 219 580 (*moderate*). Just outside Asti (convenient for drivers), tranquil and very cosy, with tennis courts and a garden. It also has a good restaurant (*expensive*), featuring local dishes.

Cavour, Piazza Marconi 18, **t/f 0141 530 222 (*cheap*). Just off the Campo del Palio; a clean, modern hotel with well-equipped rooms.

Gener Neuv, Lungo Tanaro 4, **t** 0141 557 270 (*very expensive*). Dine extremely well overlooking the river; an elegant gourmet haven where you can enjoy a superb *menu degustazione*, based on Piemontese traditions and prepared in an imaginative and exquisite manner. The desserts are light and beautiful to behold, and the list of Piemontese wines is matchless. Reserve. *Closed Mon and Aug.*

Falcon Vecchio, Via Mameli 9, **t** 0141 593 106 (*moderate*). Nearly as well-known, in a wonderfully atmospheric old building. All dishes are *tipici Astigiani* – making it the place to try truffles or local meats. *Closed Sun eve and Mon.*

Monna Laura Pizzeria, Via Cavour 30, **t** 0141 594 159 (*cheap*). Buzzing, come the weekend, with people who come for the well-prepared if standard fare. *Closed Mon.*

Costigliole d'Asti ✉ 14055

Da Guido, Piazza Re Umberto 127, **t** 0141 966 012 (*very expensive*). One of the top

restaurants in Piemonte; reservations long in advance are essential to partake of the kitchen masterworks, all made of fresh local ingredients, with a predilection for *porcini* mushrooms and truffles. The wine cellar is one of the best endowed in the entire country. *Closed Sun and public holidays.*

Alba ✉ 12051

***Savona, Via Roma 1, **t** 0173 440 440, **f** 0173 364 312 (*moderate*). The best place to stay; recently refurbished with very stylish, comfortable and modern rooms, as well as a restaurant and bar.

Piemonte, Piazza Rosetti 6, **t/f 0173 441 354 (*cheap*). Nicely situated, small rooms.

Osteria dell'Arco, Piazza Savona 5, **t** 0173 363 974 (*moderate*). One of the best of a good selection of restaurants in Alba, in a historic building in the very centre of town. The small, excellent-value menu includes a tasty tarragon *risotto*, stuffed guinea fowl and a good selection of wine. *Closed Sun and Aug.*

Barolo ✉ 12060

Del Buon Padre, Via delle Viole 30, in the outskirts at Vergne, **t** 0173 56192 (*moderate*). The classic place to dine from among a substantial selection of restaurants in Barolo. The Piemontese cuisine is solid and simply very good, and the wines are divine. *Closed Wed, Jan and last two weeks of July.*

La Morra/Verduno ✉ 12064

The Belvedere, Piazza Castello 5, **t** 0173 50190 (*expensive*). Where, according to many, Piemonte's finest *agnolotti* are served; also a good place to try *finanziera*, good mushroom and truffle dishes in the autumn and, naturally wines. *Closed Sun eve and Mon.*

Real Castello, Via Umberto I 9, **t** 0172 470 125 **f** 0172 470 298 (*expensive*). Stay in Carlo Alberto's castle in Verduno and dine like a king on the region's favourite pasta, *tajarin* (tiny *tagliatelle*), roast guinea fowl and hazelnut torte. *Open mid-April–Nov.*

sophisticated features include a truffle auction, and stalls with Barbera and Grignolino, as well as Ruch 130, a new red dessert wine – accompanied by a buffet.

In the middle of the countryside near **Albugnano** (22km northwest of Asti, off the road to Chivasso), the **Abbazia di Vezzolano** (**t** *011 992 0607; open April–Sept Tues–Sun*

9–1 and 2–6, Oct–Mar Tues–Sun 9–1 and 2–5) is the finest Romanesque building in Piemonte, founded according to legend in 773 by Charlemagne, who had a vision on the site while out hunting. It has a remarkable façade from the early 12th century, adorned with blind arcades and sculpture, and an even more remarkable rood screen that divides the nave in two and is carved with two strips, the upper one depicting the *Four Evangelists* and the *Deposition, Assumption and Incarnation of the Virgin,* while the lower one has a cast of solid medieval characters sitting in a row, with their names draped over their chests like beauty contestants. On the high altar are 15th-century terracotta figures of the Virgin and Child, worshipped by kneeling figures of St Augustine and Charlemagne, all under a florid Gothic *baldacchino*. Part of the cloister is even older than the church, with sculpted capitals, while the newer section is adorned with frescoes of biblical scenes and Charlemagne.

Between the abbey and Turin, **Chieri** is a fine old town with an especially interesting Gothic cathedral, finished in 1436, and built over Roman and early medieval foundations; its frescoed baptistry dates back to the 13th century.

Le Langhe and Alba

South of Asti lie the beautiful, fertile hills of **Le Langhe**, swathed with the intricate woven patterns of the vines that produce Italy's finest red wines – *Barolo, Barbera, Barbaresco, Dolcetto* and *Nebbiolo*. Little villages are clustered on the tallest hills, crowned by their castles (many now regional *enoteche*). One, **Montegrosso**, is the main producer of *Barbera* wine; and **Costigliole d'Asti** and **Canelli**, surrounded by vineyards producing muscat grapes, are the centre of *Asti Spumante* production. **Nizza Monferrato** is the site of the **Museo Bersano** Piazza Dante 24 (**t** *0141 720 211; open by request; free guided tours also in English*), with a collection of artefacts related to the history of wine.

On the banks of the Tanaro river, the town of **Alba** is the capital of Le Langhe, an austere medieval city of narrow winding alleys and brick towers. At the beginning of the 16th century it produced its greatest painter, Macrino, whose *Vergine Incoronata* (1501) hangs in the council chamber of the Palazzo Comunale, along with the *Piccolo Concerto* by Mattia Preti. The highlight of the 14th-century Duomo is the choir stalls, inlaid in 1500 by Cidonio. Traditionally a bitter enemy of Asti, Alba is now content to send up its old rival in a donkey Palio complete with clown jockeys the first Sunday in October. But Alba can be serious when needs be: its resistance fighters were the bravest in Italy and defended the 'Free Republic of Alba' from the Germans for 23 days in 1944.

Around Alba

Around Alba, hilltop villages, ruined castles and vineyards are set in lovely rolling country. A few kilometres south of the town the oldest Piemontese *enoteca*, in the castle of **Grinzane di Cavour**, is also the meeting point of the 'Order of the Knights of the Truffle and Wines of Alba', and contains a restaurant and a museum dedicated to wine-making, folk traditions, and the castle's most famous former resident, Count

Camillo Cavour. **Barbaresco**, east of Alba, and **Barolo**, to the south, have respectively given their names to renowned red wines; in Barolo the 16th-century **Castello Falletti** is used as a wine museum and well-stocked *enoteca*.

The village of **La Morra**, the belvedere of Le Langhe, is a good base for walks through the vineyards, and for visiting the former Abbey of the Annunciation, now the **Ratti Wine Museum** – not as funny as it sounds (*t 0173 50185; open Mon–Fri 8.30–12 and 2.30–5 but call ahead; closed Jan and Aug*). Nearby **Verduno** is dominated by a 17th-century castle, in Juvarra's elegant Baroque style, that was used as a summer residence by King Carlo Alberto and is now a restaurant. Another castle, this one from 1340, guards the concentric village of **Serralunga d'Alba** to the east.

West of Alba, in **Brà**, odds and ends from Roman *Pollentia* (Pollenzo) may be seen in the Gothic **Palazzo Traversa**, on Via Serra, and in **Santa Chiara** (1742), designed by Bernardo Vittone, with its delightful rococo interior. **Pollenzo** itself retains a circular funerary monument, the foundations of the forum, theatre and amphitheatre (with seating for 17,000) which illustrate the fortune Roman *Pollentia* made in textiles.

Cherasco, south of Brà, is smaller and more atmospheric – its **Torre Civica** has a rare clock of the phases of the moon. The local museum houses historical items; the local castle is a comfortable residence built by the Visconti in the 14th century.

Southwest Piemonte: Cuneo and the Maritime Alps

Despite the long frontier this district shares with France, the difficult mountainous terrain has made this one of the least known corners of Italy. The French influence is strong, both in the dialect and kitchen. Isolation has also meant that traditions in handicrafts, costumes and festivals have lingered longer than almost anywhere else on the peninsula.

South from Turin to Saluzzo

Students of the French Revolution will recognize the name of one of the first towns south of Turin, **Carmagnola**, as the origin of the popular Parisian song of that period, the 'Carmagnole'. The song was originally sung by Piemontese minstrels about an early 15th-century condottiere nicknamed Il Carmagnola; how it made Danton's hit parade is anyone's guess. **Racconigi**, a silk-making town further south, is the site of the **Castello Reale** of the Savoys, begun in 1676 and finished in 1842; behind the castle extends a beautiful park with ancient trees and a lake (*t 0172 84005; open Tues–Sun 8.30–6.30; adm*).

Mellow old **Saluzzo** was the capital of a marquisate, founded in 1142, that knew its golden age in the 15th century; in the lanes below the castle it retains much of its character from those days. The church of San Giovanni (1280) has a good 14th-century Romanesque-Gothic campanile and contains among its treasures the tomb of Saluzzo's greatest marquis, Ludovico II, who died in 1503. On Via San Giovanni, the

Getting Around

Cuneo is linked by **rail** with Turin via Saluzzo, and with Genoa via Ceva and Mondovì. It is also linked by **one of Italy's most spectacular railways** to southwest Piemonte's main mountain resort, Limone Piemonte, and then via French territory to Ventimiglia, a 98km stretch that only reopened in 1979 after suffering grave damage in the Second World War. The journey takes roughly three hours, with all its windings and hairpin bends over the mountains.

Buses also run from Cuneo to all the towns in the province and to Turin and Genoa.

Tourist Information

Saluzzo: Via Torino 51, t 0175 46710, f 0175 46718.
Cuneo: Piazza Boves, t/f 0171 693 258.
Limone Piemonte: Via Roma 30, t 0171 926 757.
Mondovì: Via Vico 2, t 0174 40389, f 0174 47428.

Where to Stay and Eat

Carmagnola ✉ 10022
Carmagnole, Via Chiffi 31, t 011 971 2673 (*very expensive*). Like the rest of Piemonte, the southwest corner is a happy hunting ground for the galloping, or even the bus-riding gourmet. Carmagnole is a lovely restaurant in a 17th-century Piemontese mansion, featuring dishes based on the freshest of ingredients; the delicious *menu degustazione* includes pheasant *galantine* in Sauternes and raspberry vinegar, and local specialities like *ossobuco* and *porcini* mushrooms in cream. The desserts and wines, from Le Langhe and Friuli, are exceptional. *Closed Mon and Aug.*

Saluzzo ✉ 12037
★★Persico, Vicolo Mercati, t 0175 41213, f 0175 248 075 (*cheap*). A nice bohemian hotel (complete with resident artist) a stone's throw from the cathedral, with comfortable if slightly oddly furnished rooms, and a good restaurant (*cheap*). The wild boar stew is particularly recommended. *Closed Fri.*
La Gargotta del Pellico, Piazzetta dei Mondagli 5, t 0175 46833 (*expensive*). An exceptionally good restaurant in the birthplace of Saluzzo's great republican patriot, Silvio Pellico – try the quail in pastry, or the *raviolini* – little stuffed pasta parcels – with marjoram and mushroom butter, followed by superb and highly original desserts like pear mousse, and exquisite Piemontese cheese. *Closed Tues, and Wed lunch.*

charming 15th–16th-century Casa Cavassa is now used as the **Museo Civico** (*t 0175 41455; open April–Sept Wed–Sun 9–12.15 and 3–6.1; Oct–Mar afternoon closure one hour earlier, at 5.15; open Tues by request; adm*), which contains, amongst other things, a splendid carved altarpiece of the *Madonna of Mercy* by Hans Clemer.

Four kilometres south of Saluzzo, in the village of **Manta**, the marquises had one of their favourite castles. It's not much to look at, but contains in its baronial hall some excellent frescoes by Giacomo Jaquerio of Turin, of nine heroes and nine heroines, believed by some to be portraits of the marquises and their wives, all posing by the Fountain of Youth (1420s).

Western Valleys: the Po, Varaita and Maira

Buses calling at Saluzzo ascend the rugged Upper Valley of the Po just to the west. **Revello**, near the entrance to the valley, was fortified by the first Marquis of Saluzzo. Part of their palace has been incorporated in the Municipio, including their chapel, adorned with portraits of the marquises and a Leonardoesque fresco of the *Last Supper*. The fine 15th-century Collegiata has a Renaissance marble portal by Matteo

Cuneo ✉ 12100

★★★★Principe, Piazza Duccio Galimberti 5, **t** 0171 693 355, **f** 0171 67562 (*expensive*). One of the town's best hotels, right in the centre, with 42 modern rooms.

★★★Ligure, Via Savigliano 11, **t/f** 0171 634 545 (*cheap*). In the oldest quarter, itself a bit old and worn at the edges, but brightened with old-fashioned courtesy. Rooms vary in price, depending on the plumbing, and tasty meals of home-made pasta and roast meat or trout are equally cheap. *Closed Jan. Restaurant closed Sun eve.*

Tre Citroni, Via Bonelli 2, near Piazza Galimberti, **t** 0171 602 048 (*expensive*). A favourite in old Cuneo: a family-run citadel of fine dining, with delightful *agnolotti* and roast lamb, among other dishes.

Osteria della Chiocciola, Via Fossano 1, **t** 0171 66277 (*moderate*). Serves traditional Piemontese fare, including mouth-watering *agnolotti del plin* (stuffed with meat and vegetables), duck, and rabbit with olives. *Closed Sun and 2-3 wks. in Jan.*

Rododendro, Frazione San Giacomo, **t** 0171 380 372 (*very expensive*). For a real treat, head 9km south of Cuneo to Boves, where you'll find the wood-surrounded atelier of one of Italy's finest woman chefs. Her leek soup, truffles with eggs, and exquisitely tender *Chateaubriand* have put the restaurant on Italy's gourmet map, with an extensive wine list of French and Italian bottles. *Closed Sun eve, Mon, and some of June.*

★★Tre Verghe d'Oro, **t** 0171 986 116 (*cheap*). In the Cunean valleys there are many, often simple and rustic, places to stay and eat. Try this long-established, old-fashioned mountain inn in Pradleves in the Valle Grana, which serves *gnocchi al Castelmagno* and other mountain specialities. (*moderate*). *Hotel closed Jan, restaurant closed Tues.*

Limone Piemonte ✉ 12015

★★★Le Ginestre, Via Nizza 68, **t** 0171 927 596, **f** 0171 927 597 (*moderate*). Small, cosy and conveniently near the slopes.

Lu Taz, Località San Maurizio, **t** 0348 444 6062 (*expensive*). Limone has no lack of restaurants. The best bet is the attractive Lu Taz, in a stone house in the woods 1 km out of town, where traditional Piemontese dishes are prepared with a flair. *Closed Tues, two weeks. in June, and two weeks in Nov.*

Mac Miche, Via Roma 64, **t** 0171 92449 (*moderate*).Mac's offers a fairly standard but reliable Italian menu. *Closed June and Nov.*

La Crubarsela, Via Comm. Beltrandi 7, **t** 0171 92391 (*cheap*). Excellent and less expensive food. A family-run eatery just down from the tourist office, which serves fine local dishes in a homely setting, and has an unusually good wine selection. *Closed Mon, May and two weeks in Nov.*

Sanmicheli. According to ancient tradition, when Charlemagne exiled the last Lombard king of Italy, Desiderius, in 774, he took refuge in **Ghisola**, a tiny, ancient hamlet near Paesana, at the valley crossroads.

Further up the valley, **Crissolo** is a small resort under the pointed peak of Monviso (12,600ft), the highest peak in the Maritime Alps. From Crissolo, with a guide and a sense of adventure, you can visit the stalactite-packed **Grotta del Rio Martino**. The valley road ends at the **Piano del Re**, the source of the Po, Italy's longest river (652km). If you've always wanted to drink a glass of Po, this is the place to do it; by the time it joins the Adriatic it becomes one of the most toxic substances in Europe. Above Piano del Re, you can walk through the **Pertuis de la Traversette** (9,455ft), a 246ft tunnel dug in 1480 by the Marquis Ludovico II – a remarkable feat of Renaissance engineering undertaken to facilitate the passage of mule caravans between Saluzzo and the Dauphiny. The pass above Piano del Re is believed by some to have been used by even bigger freight – Hannibal's elephants.

Starting again from Saluzzo, from **Verzuolo** (south of Manta) you can take a lovely detour or an entire holiday in the luxuriant **Valle Varaita**, a Provençal-speaking valley that has retained many of its ancient ways. Aim for **Sampeyre**, manufacturer of iron-work and eiderdowns, where early frescoes have been discovered in SS. Pietro e Paolo. During Carnival, Sampeyre celebrates the Baio, a thousand-year-old pageant featuring historical characters and dramas in Napoleonic-era costumes, topped with brightly ribboned hats. Another village, **Casteldelfino**, recalls in its name the 14th century when it was the capital of the Dauphin's Cisalpine lands; in good weather you can continue along the road to France, over the **Colle dell'Agnello**.

The **Valle Maira**, the next valley to the south, is known for its lush fruit orchards. It begins at **Dronero**, with an attractive 15th-century bridge, yet another one built by Old Nick. Nearby, **Villar San Costanzo** has a beautiful 12th-century crypt, a survivor of a Benedictine Abbey, entered through the church of San Pietro in Vincoli. Villar San Costanzo is also the base for visiting the weirdly shaped chimney rocks, or *ciciu* (puppets), on the Pragamonti ridge. Formed by glacial erosion eons ago, and standing anywhere from 6-26ft high, they look like giant mutant mushrooms and are especially haunting in winter or at night. The upper part of the Valle Maira, around **Acceglio**, is completely unspoiled.

Cuneo: Piemonte's Cheesy Wedge

A pleasant provincial capital, **Cuneo** stands at the confluence of the rivers Gesso and Stura, which here form a wedge, or *cuneo*, which lends the city its unusual triangular shape. If you're coming by rail, you'll pass over the impressive **Viadotto Soleri**, dating from the early 1930s. Mostly rebuilt in the 18th and 19th centuries, Cuneo is arranged around its vast porticoed main square, **Piazza Galimberti**, site of an enormous market every Tuesday. Of the churches, the most interesting is **San Francesco** (1227), with a good Gothic portal from 1481, now housing a small collection of Piemontese paintings from the 18th and 19th centuries and prehistoric, Roman and medieval artefacts (*t 071 634 175; open Tues–Sat 8.30–1 and 2.30–5.30, Sun 10–12.30 and 2.30–6*). Each September, in odd years, Brà hosts the Piemontese cheese exhibition, starring 'art cheeses' – Castelmagno, Murazzano, Rashera and more, which you can nibble on while sipping the vintages of Le Langhe.

Buses from Cuneo will take you up the surrounding valleys, the closest of which, the little **Valle Grana**, has the tiny village of **Monterosso Grana**, spread under its ruined watchtower, with a 15th-century frescoed chapel, a small ethnographic museum and a school aimed at reviving the old crafts of furniture-making and weaving. **Pradleves** is a small resort, while **Castelmagno** makes its famous cheese. A serpentine road leads up to the **Santuario di San Magno**, dedicated to a Roman legionary martyred on this lonely site; its oldest section, the choir, dates back to the 15th century.

Borgo San Dalmazzo and its Three Valleys

South of Cuneo, **Borgo San Dalmazzo** is named after another Roman martyr, Dalmatius, but is more famous these days for its snails, the main attraction of the *Fiera Fredda* (the Cold Fair), an early December market founded by Emanuele Filiberto. Borgo's **Santuario della Madonna del Monserrato** is a miniature version of the famous Catalan shrine, accessible by foot in 20 minutes along a chapel-dotted Via Crucis.

Fungus fans have a **Mushroom Museum** to peruse in the nearby village of Boves (*t 0171 389 337; open on request*).

A trio of valleys convene at Borgo San Dalmazzo. The longest, the **Valle Stura**, is a botanical paradise for its rare flowers, and throughout history was a major route of salt merchants and armies. Its chief town is medieval **Demonte**; on the mountain of Podio stand the ruins of the once mighty **Fortezza di Consolata**, destroyed by the French in 1796. Further up the valley, **Terme di Vinadio** is a small, hot sulphur spring-spa (*open summers only*); at **Pietraporzio** begins the **Stretta delle Barricate**, a narrow ravine closed in by sheer walls. **Argentera**, the last and highest comune, is a cool summer resort; from May to mid-October the pass into France above Argentera, the **Colle della Maddalena**, is open, lined with pastures and brimful of flowers.

The second valley, the **Valle Gesso**, leads into the heart of the Maritime Alps, the southernmost to have snow all year round, with three peaks – Argentera, Gelas and Matto – at over 10,000ft, all encompassed in the **Parco Naturale dell'Argentera**, along with many refuges and huts for hikes and ascents. In the middle of the park, the old Savoy spa, **Terme di Valdieri**, was rebuilt in the 1950s and is famed for its hot sulphur springs; waters flow down a series of steps covered with a rare, multi-coloured algae called '*muffa*' (*Ulva labyrinthiformis*), which has special healing properties when applied to wounds.

East of Borgo San Dalmazzo, the **Valle Vermenagna**, the route taken by the railway and the SS20 road, is steep and wooded. From **Vernante** an 8km side road leads up to **Palanfre**, a small village on the fringe of an enchanting beech forest. The unusual circumstance of mountains over 10,000ft so close to the sea, and the high level of rainfall, combine to create a lush microclimate of extraordinary richness; over 650 different trees and flowers thrive within the limited confines of the **Parco Naturale di Palanfre**. Back in Valle Vermenagna, near the French border, Provençal-speaking **Limone Piemonte** is a popular winter sports centre, with the area's best nightlife in season. Its citrusy name actually derives from *leimon*, Greek for meadow, one of the village's most charming features. Amidst the new development stands the Gothic **San Pietro in Vincoli**, with examples of local 17th-century woodcarving.

There's another natural park at the head of the **Valle del Pesio**, the next valley, with interesting karstic formations and pine forests, spread under the loftiest peak, Marguareis. In the spring be sure to look for the **Piss del Pesio**, a spectacular 100ft jet of subterranean water into a void, which resembles just what it sounds like. The Certosa di Pesio, founded in 1173 and dominated by an oversize cloister, was abandoned after Napoleon, but is now once again used as a religious house, and the monks take in guests.

Mondovì

Like several other towns in Piemonte, **Mondovì** is divided into an older, upper half called Piazza, and a lower part known as Breo. **Piazza**'s heart beats in the attractive, asymmetrical **Piazza Maggiore** where, in contrast to the Renaissance buildings, the **Chiesa della Missione** (1675–1733) adds an elegant Baroque touch; inside, 17th-century *trompe-l'œil* figures by Andrea Pozzo float in the vault. The cathedral (1763), also up in Piazza, has a chapel dedicated to Universal Suffrage, a notion introduced in Italy by five-times-Prime Minister Giovanni Giolitti, a native of Mondovì. Down in mostly 18th-century **Breo**, the city's symbol, the 'Moor', sounds the hours atop the church of SS Piero e Paolo. Two other noteworthy churches are in the mountainous environs: near **Bastia Mondovì**, the inside of the 11th–15th-century San Fiorenzo is covered with a series of 51 late-Gothic frescoes in the Provençal style, while just east of Mondovì the huge 16th–18th-century sanctuary in **Vicoforte** has an unusual, enormous dome and suitably impressive interior.

To the south, **Frabosa Soprana** is a popular winter and summer resort, with ski slopes; from here the road continues south to **Bossea** (bus from Mondovì), site of the **Grotte di Bossea** among the most interesting and important in Italy, with a wide variety of beautiful stalactite formations, narrow passages and huge caverns, an underground river and lakes, and a skeleton of a prehistoric bear, *Ursus spelaeus*. The caves maintain a year-round temperature of 9°C, and can be visited daily with a guide.

From the rail junction at Ceva, you can take a train south along the Tanaro as far as Ormea, by way of **Garessio**, a picturesque collection of four hamlets, with ski slopes, mineral water cures, and a summer palace of the Savoys, the Castello di Casotto. Pretty **Ormea** is a woodsy summer resort, its ruined castle once a nest of Saracen corsairs in the 10th and 11th centuries, when they controlled the Ligurian coast.

Liguria
The Italian Riviera

11

Highlights

1 Genoa's piquant *centro storico* and new aquarium
2 Liberty-style San Remo, grand resort of the 1890s
3 Albenga's Romanesque cathedral
4 Exquisite Portofino and its promontory
5 Cliff-hanging villages of the Cinque Terre

'Riviera' in Italian simply means shore, but in Liguria the shore is *the* Riviera, a rugged, rock-bound rainbow of coast linking France to Tuscany, endowed with what is surprisingly one of the rarer Italian commodities – beautiful beaches. Usually not large, buxom, sandy beaches, but rather refined, slender strands in magical settings, beneath steep cliffs and hanging gardens, backed by old fishing towns squeezed between the rock, or palm-fringed resorts that fit like an old pair of shoes.

After Liguria, you'd have to continue all the way down to the Bay of Naples to find a shore of comparable interest and beauty. And if you're approaching from the

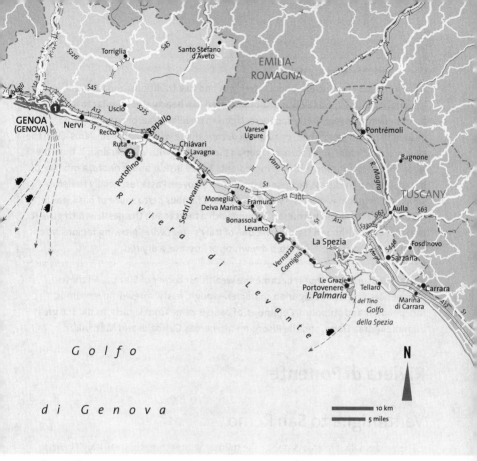

haughty French Riviera, the Italian Riviera comes as a pleasant surprise, genteelly relaxed and laid back – no one cares if your socks don't quite match, or you've brought the children. There are splendid grand hotels, but they are outnumbered by small and unpretentious *pensioni*.

Although August is peak season these days, people first came to this fabled shore for its sunny and mild winter climate. Sheltered by the Maritime Alps and Apennines from the fogs and chills of the north, Liguria has a sensuous growth of lemons, oranges and flowers – one of the region's principal exports. The olive oil from its ancient groves is legendary. Bathed in a luminous, warm light, the Riviera's colours are dazzling, the reds, blues, yellows like glistening newborns. Yet just a few dozen hairpin turns up into the hinterland, and you're in another world altogether, lush and cool and green; Liguria is the most forested region of Italy.

The delights of sun and sea are only part of what the region has to offer. Long isolated from the rest of Italy because of the mountains, Liguria has a distinct identity all its own. Poor in resources, but full of intrepid, tenacious seamen and merchants, it has looked to the sea for its survival since the early Middle Ages. After the Crusades, the Republic of Genoa grew to become a seapower and east-west wheeler-dealer rivalled only by Venice, and in the 17th century it did so well financing

> **Food and Wine in Liguria**
> In Liguria look for ancient popular festivals and folk traditions, and for great regional cuisine, especially fish dishes prepared in a hearty style similar to neighbouring Provence – try *cacciucco*, Ligurian bouillabaisse, or *cappon magro*, pickled fish with vegetables, or *zuppa di datteri*, made with razor shell clams. Even the snacks are different, like *focaccia*, Ligurian pizza, made with a softer dough than the Neapolitan version, and with the ingredients baked inside, and *farinata*, a mixture of baked, ground chickpeas best eaten hot from the oven. Pasta (especially *trenette*, similar to *linguine*) is often served with Genoa's famous *pesto* sauce of basil, garlic, pine nuts, olive oil and parmesan, ground with a mortar and the pestle which gave it its name. And, although Liguria isn't one of Italy's great wine-growing regions, you may want to try its best, Pigato, a dry white, or Rossese, a dry red.

Spain's treasure fleet that it became the wealthiest corner of Europe. All these experiences formed the Ligurian character – tough, feisty, shrewd, adventurous, independent and stubborn. Columbus, of course, came from Liguria, as did the great admiral Andrea Doria, and the Risorgimento heroes Garibaldi and Mazzini.

Riviera di Ponente

Ventimiglia to San Remo

The western Riviera enjoys one of the mildest winter climates in all Italy. Flowers thrive here even in February, and are cultivated in fields that dress the landscape in a brilliant patchwork (albeit increasingly shrouded in plastic), lending this stretch the well-deserved name of the 'Riviera of Flowers'. In the 19th century consumptive northerners flocked here every autumn, but you may want to avoid that particular season; in recent years, perhaps as a result of global warming, the area has been hit by tempestuous rains. In October 1998, San Remo endured its worst floods since 1875.

Ventimiglia

Ventimiglia is tricky: if you arrive by train it can seem seedy and dull. On the other hand, if you come by the coastal road from France it is pure enchantment, a garden-town by the sea where roses and carnations are the main crops, and in July they stage the 'Battle of the Flowers'.

Ventimiglia is also a garden of history, with the most ancient roots in Liguria. Between 100 and 200,000 BC, members of Europe's first sophisticated culture – the Neanderthal – lived in the **Balzi Rossi** caves, near the French frontier on the beach of Grimaldi. At the entrance to the caves, the **Museo Preistorico** displays the finds – seashell finery, tools, weapons and lumpy 'Venuses', the first sculptures, ever. The caves hold traces of elaborate burials, and the *Grotto del Caviglione* has an etching of a horse, of a breed now common only on the Russian steppes (*t 0184 381 113; museum and caves open Tues–Sat 9–7; closed Mon*).

A municipal bus from Ventimiglia serves Mortola Inferiore and the **Hanbury Gardens** (*open April–Sept 9–6; Oct–Mar 10–4; closed Wed*), a botanical paradise founded in 1867 by Sir Thomas Hanbury, who acclimatized some 5,000 rare and exotic plants from Africa and Asia to co-exist with native Mediterranean flora; acquired by the state in 1960, the gardens are among the most important in Italy. Near the gardens, a section of the ancient Via Aurelia has a plaque listing VIPs who have passed this way, from St Catherine of Siena to Napoleon. The main road, passing underneath the gardens, leads to the customs post at Ponte San Ludovico, with its **castle** where Serge Voronoff performed his experiments, seeking the Fountain of Youth in monkey glands.

Ventimiglia's Roman incarnation, **Albintimilium**, 1km east of the modern town, was an important stop on the Via Aurelia; best-preserved among its ruins is the small 2nd-century AD **theatre** (*open Wed and Fri 3–7, Thurs and Sat 9–1*), while the finds are on view in the nearby **Museo Archeologico**, Via Verdi 41 (*open Tues–Sat 9.30–12.30 and 3–5, Sun and hols 10–12.30; adm*). Ventimiglia itself is divided into old and new by the River Roja, the modern town built around the huge Friday market and lined with typical seaside promenades, while the old town, with its twisting medieval lanes, has the attractive 11th–12th-century **cathedral** and **baptistry** for a focal point. Another Romanesque church, **San Michele**, was built from Roman columns and milestones. Guarding the coast to the west of town, the ruined 12th-century **Castel D'Appio** was the headquarters of the piratical Counts of Ventimiglia.

Dolceacqua

Among the valleys cutting inland from Ventimiglia, the Val Nervia is perhaps the most appealing (buses hourly from Ventimiglia). Aim for Dolceacqua, a picturesque village linked by the single arch of a medieval bridge, and crowned by the 16th-century **Castello di Doria**, reputedly haunted by lordly villains who took full advantage of their *droit de seigneur* with the local brides. On St Sebastian's Day (20 January) Dolceacqua holds a unique religious procession led by the 'tree man', who bears a huge tree branch hung with large, coloured communion hosts, a curious mixture of Christianity and ancient fertility rites.

The hills around Dolceacqua are terraced with vineyards producing Rossese, a good red wine available in the local cafés. Further up, **Pigna**, the 'Pinecone', looks like one with its concentric walls, which shelter two fine churches with paintings by Giovanni Canevesio. Some 3km away, **Castelvittorio** has changed little since the 13th century, when its thick walls kept out arch enemy Pigna, with whom it conducted nonstop war in the Middle Ages.

Bordighera

Once a favourite winter retreat of chilblained Britons (who once outnumbered the locals), Bordighera is now one of the most jovial resorts on the Riviera, blessed with a good beach and regal promenades and a September festival of humour. As at

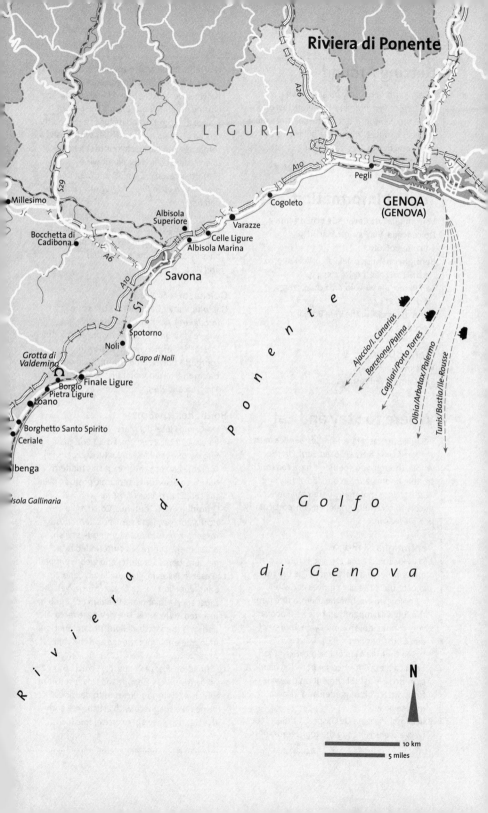

Riviera di Ponente

LIGURIA

A26

529

Pegli

GENOA
(GENOVA)

A10

Cogoleto

Millesimo

S29

Albisola
Superiore

Varazze

Bocchetta di
Cadibona

A6

Celle Ligure

Albisola Marina

A10

Savona

S1

Spotorno

Noli

Capo di Noli

Grotta di
Valdemino

Finale Ligure

Borgio

Pietra Ligure

Loano

Borghetto Santo Spirito

Ceriale

lbenga

sola Gallinaria

Riviera di Ponente

Golfo

di Genova

Ajaccio/I. Canarias

Barcelona/Palma

Cagliari/Porto Torres

Olbia/Arbatax/Palermo

Tunis/Bastia/Ile-Rousse

N

10 km

5 miles

Getting Around

Trains run frequently up and down the coast; from Ventimiglia a line branches off for Cuneo, in Piemonte, one of the country's most scenic rail routes. Inland, the hill towns are easily reached by **bus** from their nearest coastal towns.

Tourist Information

Ventimiglia: Via Cavour 61, **t** 0184 351 183.
Dolceacqua: Via Patrioti Martiri 58,
t 0184 206 681.
Bordighera: Palazzo del Parco, Via Roberto 1,
t 0184 262 322, **f** 0184 264 455.
San Remo: Via Nuvoloni 1, **t** 0184 571 571,
f 0184 507 649.
Arma di Taggia: in the Villa Boselli,
t 0184 43 333.

Market Days

Ventimiglia: Fridays
San Remo: Wednesdays

Where to Stay and Eat

San Remo has a hotel-finding service in the station, **t** 0184 80172 (closed Sun). On the whole, though, you shouldn't have too much trouble finding a room outside of July and August. Note that many hotels still prefer guests to take full or half pension, particularly in high season.

Ventimiglia ✉ 18039

★★★La Riserva, **t** 0184 229 533, **f** 0184 229 712, *info@lariserva.it* (*moderate*). The top hotel choice, up in the olive groves at Castel d'Appio, 5km west of the town, a fine family-run inn with magnificent views, a pool and very comfortable rooms. *Open April–Sept and Christmas hols only.*

★★★Sea Gull, Via Marconi 24, **t** 0184 351 726, **f** 0184 231 217, *info@seagullhotel.it* (*cheap*). A comfortable establishment on the waterfront, with a bit of garden and its own private beach.

Balzi Rossi, Piazzale De Gasperi, **t** 0184 38132 (*very expensive*). Long the top restaurant in

the Ventimiglia area, right on the frontier at San Lodovico, with a dining room full of flowers overlooking the Mediterranean. The cuisine magnificently blends the best of France and Liguria, and includes a legendary *terrina di coniglio*, pasta dishes with fresh tomatoes and basil, scallops of sea bass, divine desserts and excellent wines. Definitely reserve. *Closed Mon, Tues lunch; also Sun lunch in July and Aug; also half Mar and half Nov.*

Usteria d'a Porta Marina, Via Trossarelli 22, **t** 0184 351 650 (*moderate*). A more modest choice, specializing in fish, particularly sea bass in Rossese wine. *Closed Tues eve and Wed.*

Dolceacqua ✉ 18035

Gastone, Piazza Garibaldi 2, **t** 0184 206 577 (*moderate*). A relaxed and friendly place, where you can try *capron magro* or imaginative dishes such as *gnocchetti* with courgette flowers and shrimp, followed by a traditional baked rabbit in casserole. *Closed Mon eve and Tues.*

Bordighera ✉ 18012

★★★★Grand Hotel del Mare, Via Portico della Punta 34, **t** 0184 262 201, **f** 0184 262 394, *info@grandhoteldelmare.it* (*very expensive*). For real elegance check in at this modern hotel in a beautiful panoramic position over the sea. *Closed Nov–Christmas.*

★★★Bordighera & Terminus, Corso Italia 21, **t** 0184 260 561, **f** 0184 266 200, *terminus@rosenet.it* (*moderate*). A luminous, stylish hotel, in the centre but surrounded by a garden; rooms are pretty and well-equipped.

La Reserve Tastevin, Via Aurelia 20, Capo Sant'Ampelio, **t** 0184 261 322 (*expensive*). The most spectacular place to eat in Bordighera, inserted in the cliffs. The views are fantastic, and so is the food, a delightful combination of ingredients from the sea and the Valle Argentina.

Le Chaudron, Piazza Bengasi 2, **t** 0184 263 592 (*expensive*). Very elegant and tiny restaurant which will win your heart with delicious dishes like spaghetti with artichokes, and the Ligurian speciality, *pesce al sale* (fish baked in a bed of salt, skinned, then dressed with olive oil). Reserve.

Ristorante dei Marinai, Via Marinai 2, t 0184 261 511 (*moderate*). As the name would suggest, this restaurant specializes in all things marine, with the menu dependent on the day's catch. The *stoccafisso mantecato alla Liguria* is particularly good. *Closed Wed.*

San Remo ✉ 18038

★★★★★Royal, Corso Imperatrice 80, t 0184 5391, f 0184 661 445, *royal@royalhotelsanremo.com* (*luxury*). The top hotel in San Remo, near the casino, is more of a palace than accommodation for rent. Surrounded by lush gardens, with palms and flowers, this turn-of-the-last-century *grande dame* has rooms that vary from imperial suites to modest doubles. True to tradition, the hotel orchestra serenades guests in the afternoon and gets them dancing in the evening.

★★★★Astoria West End, Corso Matuzia 8, t 0184 667 701, f 0184 663 318, *astoria@tourism.it* (*very expensive*). One of the region's oldest hotels, it sounds as if it belongs in New York, but instead sits in all its confectionery elegance – grand chandeliers, elaborate stucco ceilings and carved lifts – opposite the sea in San Remo. It also has luxurious gardens with a pool and a pretty outdoor terrace.

★★★★Grand Hotel Londra, Corso Matuzia 2, t 0184 668 000, f 0184 668 073, *londra@tourism.it* (*expensive*). If you prefer something with a Liberty-style touch, the Grand Hotel Londra can oblige. Built around the turn of the last century, it has a lovely garden and pool, and fine original interior details. *Closed Oct–Nov.*

★★★Paradiso, Via Roccasterone 12, t 0184 571 211, f 0184 578 176, *Paradisohotel@sistel.it* (*moderate*). Perfect if you seek peace and quiet, set just back from the seafront, above most of the hurly-burly, and enveloped with flowers on the terrace and balconies. It has a distinguished, glass-enclosed restaurant and a lovely sunny breakfast room. *Closed Nov–early Dec.*

★★★Lolli Palace, Corso dell'Imperatrice 70, t 0184 531 496, f 0184 541 574, *lolli@tourism.it* (*moderate*). A lovely little seafront hotel with

a decent restaurant. The sea-facing rooms are superb: large, bright and airy with great big bay windows and cute little balconies – all tastefully decorated in white and wood.

★★★Eletto, Corso Matteotti 44, t 0184 531 548, f 0184 531 506 (*moderate*). A very pretty 19th-century hotel in the centre, furnished with antiques, and also blessed with a welcoming little garden.

★★Sole Mare, Via Carli 23, t 0184 577 105, f 0184 532 778 (*cheap*). Tiny and comfortable, with eight rooms, especially popular with Italians.

Da Giannino, Corso Trento e Trieste 23, t 0184 504 014 (*very expensive*). Exquisitely prepared dishes based on fresh, natural ingredients, including a speciality of the region, *tagliolini al sugo di triglia* (whole-wheat pasta with red mullet sauce), polenta with cheese and vegetable sauce, and pigeon with ginger, accompanied by an excellent wine list. *Closed Sun eve and Mon.*

Paolo e Barbara, Via Roma 47 (conveniently near the Casino, if you've hit the jackpot) t/f 0184 531 653 (*very expensive*). Another highly acclaimed restaurant, generally rated one of the tops in all Liguria, run by a couple dedicated to perfect food and all the trimmings. Paolo Masieri in the kitchen is a wizard of invention, which he deftly combines with Riviera traditions – home-made breads, the famous *gamberoni San Remo* flambéed in whisky, and more. Reserve. *Closed Wed, Thurs lunch, two weeks June and July, some of Dec and Jan.*

Bagatto, Via Matteotti 145, t 0184 531 925 (*expensive*). One of the brightest and most relaxed restaurants in San Remo, with tempting *antipasti, risotti* and other dishes using sun-ripened vegetables, as well as delicious seafood and lamb dishes. *Closed Sun and July.*

Arma di Taggia ✉ 18011

La Conchiglia, Via Lungomare 33, t 0184 43169 (*expensive*). One of the most highly regarded restaurants on the Riviera, which serves Ligurian delights based on seafood, local cheese and delicate olive oil – the prawn and white bean salad is delicious. There's a very good set lunch. Reserve. *Closed Wed, except July and Aug, closed 15 days in June and Jan.*

Ventimiglia, the environs contain fields of cultivated flowers, but here the speciality is palms; since Sant'Ampelio supposedly brought the first date palm seeds from Egypt in 411, Bordighera has had a monopoly in supplying the Vatican with fronds during Easter week. Monet painted here in 1884, captivated by 'this brilliance, this magical light'. In the summer the tourist office runs free tours that point out the Giardino Moreno, Valle di Sasso and other places that caught his eye.

The tiny medieval nucleus of Bordighera, above the Spianata del Capo, is shoehorned behind its gates; further up, the flower-bedecked **Via dei Colli** has excellent views of the shimmering coast. Below, the Romanesque church of **Sant'Ampelio** stands on its little cape above the grotto where the saint lived; from here you can walk along the pleasant Lungomare Argentina west to the spa, or east along the seaside Via Arziglia to Bordighera's palm and mimosa plantations at the **winter garden** and the **Giardino Madonna della Ruota**, a 45-minute walk. **Museo Bicknell** (Via Bicknell, *t 0184 263 601; open Mon–Fri 10–12 and 3–5; closed first two weeks of Aug*) has plaster casts of the curious Neolithic rock-engravings from the Valle delle Meraviglie (part of France since the Second World War), discovered by the Reverend Clarence Bicknell. This whole neighbourhood is packed with British hotels and villas.

San Remo

San Remo is the opulent queen of the Italian Riviera, her grand hotels and villas as beautiful and out-of-date as antimacassars on an armchair. Yet even if the old girl isn't young, she's a corker with a Mae West twinkle in her eye. Other resorts may have more glamour, but few have more character. San Remo also has considerable bargains – the French pour over to purchase designer clothes and furnishings that cost 20 to 30 per cent more in Paris.

Set on a huge, sheltered bay, San Remo was long a watering hole for a variety of drifting aristocrats, most famously Empress Maria Alexandrovna, wife of Czar Alexander II. She played the Pied Piper to a sizeable Russian colony, including Tchaikovsky, who composed *Eugene Onegin* and the Fourth Symphony during his stay here in 1878. The duke of nonsense, Edward Lear, ended his lifelong travels in the Mediterranean here in 1888, as did the father of dynamite and famous prizes, Alfred Nobel, who died in 1896 in the **Villa Nobel**, on the east edge of town, by the Parco Ormond (*t 0183 704 304; due to reopen in 2001 after restoration*). Modern San Remo consists of three distinct parts: the shopping district, the rather dusty old town and the smart west end, where the grandest hotels are situated. To get the full flavour take the *passeggiata* down the lovely, palm-lined **Corso dell'Imperatrice**; here, springing out of luxuriant, semi-tropical foliage, are the incongruous onion domes of a **Russian Orthodox church** (*open year-round Tues, Thurs and Sat 9.30–12.30 and 4–7; winter 3–6.30*), a dainty jewel box built in the 1920s by the exiled nobility and containing the tombs of the deposed members of the royal house of Montenegro.

This part of town reaches it zenith at the white brightly lit, Liberty-style **municipal casino**, a legacy from these golden days of fashion and still the lively heart of San

Remo's social life, with its gaming rooms, roof garden cabaret and celebrated restaurant with a live orchestra (*open 10am–3am; roulette wheels in operation from 2pm–3am; there is a dress code in the French gaming rooms but not the American; adm Mon–Thurs L5,000, Fri–Sun L15,000*). As you travel further east along Corso Matteotti, San Remo's main shopping street, you enter the lively, commercial heart of San Remo. In February the Corso's **Teatro Ariston** hosts the biggest event in the world of Italian pop, the unabashedly tacky *Festival della Canzone*, an extravagant five-day-long lip-synch ritual built of glitter and hype, where this once gloriously musical nation parades its contemporary talents with all the self-confidence of the Emperor in his new clothes. All year long, early risers can take in the intoxicating colour and scent of the **San Remo Flower Market** on Corso Garibaldi, just off Piazza Colombo – very much a working, wholesale market, but fascinating for visitors nonetheless.

The old town, **La Pigna**, is San Remo's 'casbah', a tangled, mystery-laden mesh of steep lanes and stairs weaving under archways and narrow tunnels, fortified around the year 1000 as a refuge against the Saracens. Get there by way of Piazza San Siro, site of the 12th-century, but much altered, **Duomo di San Siro**, with an unusual black crucifix by an unknown sculptor and the Baroque **Oratorio dell'Immacolata Concezione**. The large, covered food market is nearby on Piazza Eroi Sanremesi (*open Tues–Sat 8.30–1*). From here you can wend your way up through the casbah to the **Giardini Regina Elena**, which is rather dull as a garden but has fantastic views of the town and harbour.

Standing majestically at the top of La Pigna is the 17th-century **Santuario Madonna della Costa** (*open April–Sept daily 9–12 and 3–6.30; Oct–Mar daily 9–12 and 3–5.30; buses run regularly from San Remo*). The madonna inside saved a local sailor from shipwreck, who subsequently donated the first gold coin to establish the shrine. On Ferragosto, 15 August, this event is celebrated with fireworks and a feast, in one of the Riviera's most attractive traditional festivals. The panoramic **Corso degli Inglesi** begins at the casino, and passes the old funicular to **Monte Bignone**, the highest peak in the amphitheatre of hills around San Remo (4281ft). You can drive or take a bus part way to the top, past the **Ulivi Golf Club** (**t** 0184 557 093), for great views of the Riviera.

Around San Remo

San Remo has several interesting neighbours, all easily reached by buses departing from the train station. Just to the west, the quiet seaside resort of **Ospedaletti** is shaded by luxuriant pines, palms and eucalyptus; Katherine Mansfield lived here in the early-1900s. Its name comes from the Knights Hospitallers of Rhodes, who had a pilgrims' hospice here in 1300. They also bestowed their name on the nearby hill town of **Coldirodi**, known for its **Rambaldi Art Gallery** (*t 0184 670 131; open daily 10–12, Fri and Sat also 3.30–6; closed Mon and Wed; adm*), with great forgeries – of Veronese, Reni and Rembrandt (along with real paintings).

Then there's **Bussana Vecchia**, Italy's trendiest ghost town. On 23 February 1887 an earthquake killed thousands and turned Bussana into a picturesque ruin, while the inhabitants rebuilt a Bussana Nuova 2km closer to the sea. In a typical Italian contradiction, Bussana Vecchia officially no longer exists, but has a number of artistically minded inhabitants who are equally officially non-existent, but who have restored the interiors of the ruined houses and been hooked up with water, lights, phones and two mild-mannered llamas from Peru, and sell paintings and all sorts of arty-farty dust-magnets. The earthquake knocked in the roof of the Baroque church (packed at the time for the Ash Wednesday service), but nearly all the parishioners managed to escape death in the side chapels; one survivor, Giovanni Torre detto Merlo, went on to invent the ice-cream cone in 1902. The church is open to the sky, the stucco decorations sprout weeds, trees grow in the nave and apse, and cherubs smile down like broken dolls on a shelf.

Further inland, **Bajardo**, spread out over its conical hill with a backdrop of mountains and forests, was also devastated by the earthquake, but was rebuilt on the same site. Don't miss the ruined church, with intriguing 13th-century capitals carved roughly with the heads of Mongols, some of whom are believed to have accompanied the Saracens to Liguria. Bajardo celebrates the Festival della Barca on Pentecost Sunday, when a large tree trunk topped by a smaller pine tree is erected in the middle of the piazza, around which the people slowly dance and sing a tale of tragic love from the year 1200, when the Count beheaded his daughter rather than let her marry against his will.

To the east, **Arma di Taggia** has one of the finest sandy beaches in the area, lying at the mouth of the Valle Argentina; 3km inland, picturesquely medieval **Taggia** is the site of an antiques fair every fourth Saturday and Sunday of the month. The **Dominican Convent** (open daily 9–12 and 3.30–5; closed Thurs and Sun) contains a number of fine paintings of the 15th-century the Ligurian school; the monks introduced the olive trees that have made Taggia's fortune. Noble palaces with coats of arms line the streets in the walls, and a remarkable, dog-leg 16-arched **medieval bridge** crosses the Argentina. Come on the third Sunday of July for the ancient Festival of Mary Magdalen who, according to tradition, once paid Taggia a call, and is remembered by members of her red-capped confraternity with an eerie Dance of Death performed by two men, one playing the role of 'the man' and the other of Mary Magdalen, who dies and is brought back to life with a sprig of lavender.

There are a number of attractive hill villages above the Valle Argentina, most intriguing of which is **Triora**, the Riviera's very own Salem, a fortified 15th-century village where, in 1588, during a famine, 13 women and girls were denounced as witches before the Inquisition; five died before their accusers themselves were excommunicated. The **Museo Etnografico e della Stregoneria** (open daily 3–6; adm) tells the story. The **Collegiata** has a beautiful Baptism of Jesus (1397) by Taddeo di Bartolo, and in the summer you can bungee jump too!

Imperia to Savona

Imperia divides the 'Riviera of Flowers' from the more rugged, silvery 'Riviera of Olives'. Connoisseurs of olive oil rate Liguria's the tops in Italy, although of course there are plenty of other regions ready to dispute this most slippery of crowns.

Imperia

In 1923 two towns, Porto Maurizio and Oneglia, were married by Mussolini to form a slightly schizophrenic provincial capital, Imperia. The bustling oil port (olive oil, that is) of Oneglia was the birthplace of the great Genoese Admiral Andrea Doria, while the old quarter of Porto Maurizio has most of Imperia's charm, with steep lanes and steps and palatial hill, the Paraxio, though even here Imperia lacks the typical Riviera resort ambience, for better or worse.

The Porto Maurizio side of town has a **naval museum** (*Piazza Duomo 11, t 0183 651 541/t 0183 64572; open summer Wed–Sat 9pm–11pm; winter Wed–Sat 3pm–7.30pm*), which contains ships' models and nautical instruments, and, behind the train station in Oneglia, the **Museo dell'Olivo** (*Via Garessio 13, t 0183 295 762; open daily 9–12 and 3–6; closed Tues*), dedicated to the history and practice of olive-growing. Imperia is also the base for exploring old villages in the hinterland, like **Dolcedo**, the site of the most renowned olive groves in the region, with numerous *fantoios* (presses) that sell the local oil, as well as medieval bridges, one built by the Knights of St John in 1292. In another valley, further east, the main SS28 leads to pretty **Pontedassio**.

East of Imperia are a string of popular resorts: **Diano Marina**, with its long beach and palms, and site of a small **Museo Civico** (*t 0183 496 112; closed for restoration*), which contains items from a 1st-century BC Roman shipwreck; modern **San Bartolomeo al Mare**; and, prettiest of the three, **Cervo**, a curl of white, cream and pale yellow houses sweeping up from the sea with a delightful, sunny, Moorish atmosphere. At the top of the curl stands the cream pastry Baroque **Chiesa dei Corallini** (the coral fishers), its concave façade emblazoned with a stag, or *cervo* in Italian. Although it hosts a chamber music festival in July and August, Cervo has only three small hotels near its shingle beach (none of which is exceptional).

Andora, next along the coast, consists of a marine quarter with a beach and, up in the Merula Valley, a fortified hamlet, Castello Andora, reached by way of a medieval bridge, with a picturesque ruined castle, tower-gate and the lovely 13th-century Romanesque-Gothic church of **SS. Giacomo e Filippo**. On the other side of Capo Mele ('Cape Apples') lies the attractive old fishing town of **Laigueglia**, with a majestic Baroque church from 1754.

Alassio and Albenga

With its mild climate and fine beach, Alassio has long been a resort. Some old *palazzi* on its main street, the pretty 1597 church of **Sant'Ambrogio** with a Romanesque campanile, and a defence tower recall Alassio's pre-resort days. Visiting celebrities, beginning with Hemingway, have their autographs in ceramic plaques on the 'Muretto' ('little wall'), Alassio's Hollywood Boulevard; in August there's even a 'Miss Muretto' beauty contest.

Between 15 June and 15 September you can take an excursion boat to the tiny islet, **Isola Gallinaria**, a mile off the coast. Named after the wild hens which used to populate it, the island provided sanctuary for St Martin when he was fleeing Arian persecution in the 4th century. For over a thousand years it was home to a powerful abbey, of which only ruins remain; today it is a nature reserve, expecially popular with

Tourist Information

Imperia: Corso G. Matteotti 54/a, **t** 0183 660 140, **f** 0183 666 510, *www.apt.rivieradeifiori.it.*
Cervo: Piazza Castello 1, **t/f** 0183 408 197.
Alassio: Viale Gibb 26, **t** 0182 647 027, **f** 0182 647 874, *www.italianriviera.com.*
Albenga: Viale Martiri della Libertà 1, **t** 0182 558 444, **f** 0182 558 740.
Finale Ligure: Via San Pietro 14, **t** 019 681 019, **f** 019 681 804.
Savona: Via Guidobono 125/r, **t** 019 840 2321, **f** 019 840 3672.

Where to Stay and Eat

Imperia ✉ 18100

★★★★Hotel Miramare, Viale Matteotti 24 **t** 0183 667 120, **f** 0183 60635, *rhotel@tin.it* (*very expensive–expensive*). Set in a 19th-century villa with its own garden, this hotel has all the amenities including swimming pool. The dinning area offers great views of the *duomo* and the sea below.

★★★Croce di Malta, Via Scarincio 148, Porto Maurizio, **t** 0183 667 020, **f** 0183 63687, *info@hotelcrocedimalta.com* (*moderate*). Good comfortable, seaside hotel with a pretty breakfast terrace and, most importantly, phones in the bathrooms, just in case. There are any number of one- and two-star hotels around Viale Matteotti in Oneglia.

Lanterna Blù, Via Scarincio 32, Borgo Marina, in Porto Maurizio, **t** 0183 63859 (*very expensive*). Excellent restaurant, preparing fine dishes using ingredients from two local farms; be sure to try the hot seafood antipasti. *Closed Wed.*

Ristorante Beppa, Calata Cuneo 24, **t** 0183 294 286 (*moderate*). In the port of Oneglia, opposite the fishing boats, enjoy good fresh fish in a no frills, no fuss atmosphere.

Alassio ✉ 17021

★★★★Grand Hotel Diana, Via Garibaldi 110, **t** 0182 642 701, **f** 0182 640 304 (*very expensive*). Probably the finest hotel of Alassio (the biggest resort in the area), with its own beach, beach bar, beach restaurant, free bike hire and heated indoor pool. The seafront rooms are nice and large with balconies and there is a small restaurant serving decent fare (*7.30–9pm*). Rooms without a sea view are much cheaper.

★★★Beau Sejour, Via Garibaldi 102, **t** 0182 640 303, **f** 0182 646 391 (*expensive*). Directly on the beach, with well-furnished rooms, a terrace and garden. Good for a longer stay. *Open April–Sept.*

★★★Milano, Piazza Airaldi e Durante 11, **t** 0182 640 597, **f** 0182 640 598 (*moderate*). Excellent hotel right on the beach; its rooms are well-equipped, with balconies and fine sea views. There is also a very nice restaurant serving various Ligurian specialities.

★★Bel Air, Via Roma 40, **t** 0182 642 578, **f** 0182 640 238 (*cheap*). Wonderful value: its rooms are modern and it has its own beach.

La Palma, Via Cavour 5, **t** 0182 640 314 (*expensive*). What Alassio may lack in grand hotels it makes up for with this gourmet palace, where you can choose between two *menu degustazione*, one highlighting basil, the totem herb of Liguria, and the other Provençal-Ligurian specialities, with an emphasis on seafood. La Palma is not large, so be sure to reserve.

skin-divers. Another pleasant outing from Alassio is up to the 13th-century Benedictine church of **Santa Croce**, with one of the best view-points in the area. From here you can walk the Roman road down to Albenga.

East of Alassio, **Albenga** was the Roman port of *Album Ingaunum*. It remained prosperous throughout the Middle Ages, until its harbour shifted away with the course of the Cento River; nowadays the town stands 1km from the sea and grows asparagus in the old river bed. Albenga's impressive collection of 13th-century towers, built during its days as a *comune*, stand like bridesmaids around the elegant 1391 campanile of the Romanesque **cathedral**. One (*c.* 1300) belongs to the Palazzo Vecchio del Comune, and now houses the **Museo Civico Ingauno** (*open Tues–Sun 10–12 and 3–6*), which contains

La Cave, Passeggiata Italia 7, **t** 0182 640 693 (*expensive*). An atmospheric old restaurant in the heart of the old town, serving typical Ligurian cuisine like *troffie al pesto* and fish soups. *Closed Wed.*

Ristorante La Prua, Passeggiata Baracca 25, **t** 0182 642 557 (*expensive*). Presentation and service of Ligurian classics, such as *branzino alla ligurie* are second to none at this stylish restaurant. Reserve. *Closed Nov and Thurs.*

Garlenda ✉ 17033

★★★★**La Meridiana**, Via ai Castelli 11, **t** 0182 580 271, **f** 0182 580 150 (*very expensive*). A golfer's paradise, next to the course, amid pretty olive groves, ancient oaks and vineyards. A member of the Relais et Châteaux group, it is a contemporary building constructed with traditional stone walls and wooden ceilings, and simple but attractive furnishings. The restaurant is expectedly recherché, serving refined Franco-Italian gourmet dishes, including a delicious breast of duck with caramelized pears. *Open all year.*

Finale Ligure ✉ 17024

Hotels in Finale Ligure mainly cater to families, and if you arrive without a reservation, there's a hotel finding service, **t** 019 694 252 (*open June–Sept*).

★★★**Park Hotel Castello**, Via Caviglia 26, Finalmarina, **t** 019 691 320, **f** 019 692 775 (*moderate*). Near the top of the town, with more character than most and a pretty garden; it's also one of the few that remain open all year.

★★★**Conte**, Via Genova 16, Finalmarina, **t** 019 680 234, **f** 019 695 783 (*moderate*). A change from the fairly anonymous modern establishments, with its own secluded garden in a lovely setting. Inside, it's like stepping back in time 50 years – old prints line the walls and period furniture sits in reception.

Raffa, Via Concezione 64, Finalmarina, **t** 019 692 495 (*expensive*). Run by Raffaele Ciuffo, who prides himself on choosing only the freshest of local fish, which is served in an intimate atmosphere. Don't leave without trying the speciality, *pescespada alla Raffa*. *Closed Wed.*

Torchi, Via dell'Annunziata, Finaleborgo, **t** 019 690 531 (*expensive*). Warm antipasti, herb-filled *ravioli* and a couple of meat dishes as well as good fish dishes. *Closed Tues, out of season also Mon.*

Entertainment and Nightlife

During the summer this area is one of the liveliest on the Italian coast. Throughout summer, the **Musica nei Castelli di Liguria** classical music festival takes place in the castles of the region. Full details are available from local tourist offices. Anyone with children should also keep in mind that Ceriale, just to the east of Albenga, has the only **aquapark** in the region, at Le Caravelle, Via Sant'Eugenio, **t** 0182 931 755 (*open April–Sept daily 10–7*). Finale is the other hot-spot: plenty of **bars** line the seafront, including Clipper, with an old-style atmosphere. Of the **discos**, Caligola, on Via Colombo, plays mainly dance; and El Patio, Lungomare Italia, provides less frantic music for a slightly older crowd; the **outdoor clubs**, Covo and Covo Nord Est, are trendiest of all.

finds from Roman to medieval times. Steps lead down from the piazza to Albenga's celebrated 5th-century **baptistry** (*open Tues–Sun 10–12 and 3–6*). The first Christians were very fond of geometrical forms, and Albenga's baptistry is a minor *tour de force*, fitting a 10-sided exterior around an octagonal interior. The original blue and white mosaics depict 12 doves, symbols of the Apostles. To the north of the cathedral, the **Piazzetta dei Leoni** is named after the three 17th-century stone lions who stand guard here. Nearby on Via Episcopio, the Bishop's Palace, with exterior frescoes, houses the **Museo Diocesano** (*open Tues–Sun 10–12 and 3–6*), with 17th-century tapestries, paintings, reliquaries and illuminated manuscripts. The 13th-century **Loggia dei Quattro Canti**, nearby, marks the Roman town centre

Another tower, on Piazza San Michele, belongs to the **Palazzo Peloso Cipolla** ('Hairy Onion Palace'), built in the 14th century, with a Renaissance-era façade; it now contains the **Museo Navale Romana** (*open Tues–Sun 10–12 and 3–6*), featuring amphorae and other items salvaged from a 1st-century BC Roman shipwreck discovered near the Isola Gallinaria, as well as 16th–18th-century blue and white pharmacy jars from Albisola.

To the west and along the Cento you can stroll through the scattered remains of *Album Ingaunum* – the old Roman road and tombs on the hill, the amphitheatre below, and the foundations of the city on the river banks. A short walk from here, along the Viale Pontelungo, will take you to part of the ancient Via Aurelia and the impressive 13th-century 495ft-long **Ponte Lungo**; apparently it only spanned the Cento for a few years before the river changed its course. Along the road, note the ruins of the 4th-century basilica of **San Vittore**, one of the oldest in Liguria.

The Paleolithic Grottoes of Toirano

Heading east from Albenga, **Ceriale** is a small seaside resort with a long beach lined with palms. **Borghetto Santo Spirito**, the next coastal town, is the junction (and bus pick-up point) for **Toirano**, a medieval village that seems spanking new compared with the relics of its Middle Palaeolithic inhabitants (80,000 BC), discovered in the limestone cliffs just up the valley. These Cro Magnons, like modern Italians, had excellent taste, and chose as their abode the **Grotta della Basura**, one of the loveliest caves in the region, tarted up by Mother Nature, with draperies of pastel-coloured stalactites. Apparently they had company: the cave has a 'Bear Cemetery', full of the bones accumulated over thousands of years; a 'Corridor of Imprints', where human hand, foot and knee prints mingle with bear claws, as if left from a mad prehistoric boogie-woogie; and a 'Room of Mystery', where they threw clay balls at the walls, perhaps just to see if they'd stick. The tour includes the **Grotta di Santa Lucia**, with a miraculous eye-curing spring, and the pretty water-sculpted **Grotta del Colombo** (*open daily 9–12 and 2–5; 1½hr guided tours; adm*). Admission includes the **Museo Preistorico della Val Varatella**, containing remains found in these and other caverns in the valley, and a reassembled bear skeleton.

Another medieval village nearby, **Balestrino**, is still defended by a picturesque **Del Carretto** castle; other castles constructed by the same clan of local lordlings may be seen further up at **Castelvecchio di Rocca Barbena**, high on a crag, its castle dating from the 11th century (but altered since), encircled by the walled village, with magnificent views down the valley.

Loano to Noli

Loano is an attractive, palm-shaded town and resort, long a fief of the Doria; in their 16th-century **Palazzo Doria** (now the Municipio), you can see a rare 3rd-century AD mosaic pavement, and fine views from its Carmelite convent (1608). Another old seaside town and modern beach resort, **Pietra Ligure**, has the ruins of a Genoese fortress; from nearby Borgio, the next resort, you can dip inland to visit the **Grotta di Valdemino**, with more colourful stalactites (*open Tues–Sun 9–11.30 and 2.30–5; adm*).

Finale Ligure is the big news here, however, a lively resort spread between Finale Marina and the medieval village of Finalborgo, two kilometres inland. Finale is pocked with caves filled with the debris left by Palaeolithic man and woman – most famously the **Grotta delle Arene Candide** – and, although none is open to visitors, pottery, tools, tombs, Venuses and another huge bear skeleton are on display in the **Museo Civico**, housed in the cloister of Santa Chiara in Finalborgo (*open June–Sept Tues–Sun 10–12 and 3–6; Oct–May Tues–Sun 9–12 and 2.30–4.30*). Finalborgo itself is spread under an impressive if derelict Del Carretti **castle** and the splendid 13th-century octagonal campanile of the **Basilica di San Biagio**. One of the prettiest excursions from Finalborgo is to make your way along the **Roman Via Julia Augusta**, which weaves through the Valle di Ponci northeast of Finale Pia, traversing five Roman bridges from 124 AD; one, the **Ponte delle Fate**, is in perfect nick.

Although it never made the big time like Pisa or Genoa, **Noli** thrived as a small maritime republic from 1192 to 1796, celebrated every September in a regatta between its four neighbourhoods. Lying between Capo Noli and Monte Ursino, Noli still has eight of its original 72 medieval towers. Its most important monument is the 11th-century **San Paragorio**, founded in 820; its treasures include a 13th-century bishop's throne and a 12th-century crucifix called a *Volto Santo* because of the picture on it, said to be a true portrayal of Christ – similar to the more famous one in Lucca. Be sure to note Noli's antique street lamps. There's a good beach here, and an even better one nearby at **Spotorno**.

Savona

The provincial capital, Savona is a working city rather than a resort, as well as one of Italy's busiest ports; one of the most interesting things to do is hang around the docks and watch the aerial cablecars unload coal for the ironworks at San Giuseppe di Cairo. The harbour tower, the **Torre di Leon Pancaldo**, dates from the 13th century, but was renamed to honour Magellan's unlucky pilot who was born nearby. Other natives of Savona include the Della Rovere family, which gave the world two popes: Sixtus IV, who built the Sistine Chapel in the Vatican, and his nephew, Julius II, who hired Michelangelo to paint it. The two also left their mark on Savona. Giuliano da Sangallo designed the **Della Rovere Palace** (now the law courts; Via Pia 28) for Julius; in the next street back the **cathedral** is full of fine Renaissance marbles and a carved choir, flanked by another **Sistine Chapel**, built by Sixtus and redone *à la* rococo to house the marble tomb of his parents. The best art is tucked away in the **cathedral's treasury** (*open on request*), with a fine *Adoration of the Magi* by the Hoogstaeten master, 14th-century English alabaster statues, and items donated by the popes.

The cathedral's medieval predecessor was demolished by the Genoese in 1528 to build the **Fortezza Priamàr** – not to protect Savona, but to put a dampener on its considerable ambition. This now holds the **Pinacoteca Civico** (*open Mon–Sat 8.30–12.30*), with Renaissance works by Donato de Bardi and Giovanni Mazone and others from the Baroque era; also modern Italian paintings in the **Museo Sandro Pertini**, donated by the politician – one of Italy's most revered for his probity – and 20th-century works by Savonese sculptor Renata Cuneo.

From Savona, rail lines branch off for Turin and Milan. The first route passes the traditional boundary between the Alps and the Apennines at **Bocchetta di Cadibona** and **Millesimo** (bus from Savona), a charming, fortified hill town, where even the bridge, the **Gaietta**, has a watch tower. Now a popular excursion destination, it has a clutch of artisans' workshops and pastry shops selling scrumptious rum chocolates called *millesimini*.

Savona to Genoa

Although the bathing quality declines the closer you get to the big city, there are some tempting stopovers: **Albisola**, Liguria's ceramics centre, or **Celle Ligure** and **Varazze**, both resorts, the latter still partly surrounded by walls that incorporate the façade (but nothing else) of the 10th-century church of **Sant'Ambrogio**. The rebuilt Sant'Ambrogio (1535), with a lovely medieval campanile, contains fine Renaissance and Baroque art. Further east, **Cogoleto**, according to one tradition, was the birthplace of Columbus. At least everyone in the village thinks so, and they've erected a statue to him in the piazza.

Pegli, a longtime weekend retreat of the Genoese, has been sucked into the metropolis but, like Nervi to the east, maintains its beauty and most of its tranquillity. The grounds of two seigneurial villas are now used as parks. One, the **Villa Doria**, belonged to the frescoed 16th-century Villa Centurione Doria, which now houses the **Museo di Storia Navale** (*open Tues–Thurs 9–1, Fri and Sat 9–7, 1st and 3rd Sun 9–12.30*), with a fine collection of artefacts relating to Genoa's proud maritime traditions, including ships' models, paintings (among them a portrait of Columbus), compasses, astrolabes, weapons, armour and maps. Another park, the magnificent **Villa Durazzo-Pallavicini**, is an elegantly arranged 19th-century garden with statuary, rotundas, temples and ponds. The house itself contains an **archaeological museum** (*open Tues–Thurs 9–7, Fri and Sat 9–1, 2nd and 4th Sun 9–12.30*), with pre-Roman and Roman finds from the Ligurian coast, including Genoa, and especially the Palaeolithic caves. The star exhibit is the 'Young Prince', discovered in the Grotta delle Arene Candide, with a seashell headdress and a dagger in his hand.

Genoa

There's always a tingling air of danger, excitement, unexpected fortune or sudden disaster in real port cities. The streets are enlivened with sailors, travellers and vagrants of all nationalities, and there's always the volatility of the sea itself, ready to make or break a fortune. Of the country's four ancient maritime republics (Venice, Amalfi and Pisa are the others), only Genoa (Genova) has retained its salty tang and thrill. It is Italy's largest port, and any possible scenographic effect it could have, enhanced by its beautiful location of steep hills piling into the sea, has been utterly snuffed out by the more important affairs of the port: an elevated highway, huge docks, warehouses, stacks of containers and unloading facilites hog the shoreline for miles, so that from many points you can't even see the sea. And behind the docks wind dishevelled alleys lined with typical piquant portside establishments that cater to men of indeterminate nationality, old pirates and discreetly tattooed ladies.

Counterbalancing this fragrant zone of stevedores is the Genoa that Petrarch called *La Superba*, the Superb City (or 'Proud', as in one of the Seven Deadly Sins) of palaces, gardens and art; the city whose merchant fleet once reigned supreme from Spain to the southern Russian ports on the Black Sea, the city that gave the Spaniards Columbus but which in return controlled the contents of Spain's American silver fleets, becoming the New York City of the 16th century, flowing with money, ruled by factions of bankers and oligarchs, populated by rugged individualists and entrepreneurs, and leaving a mark in the fashion industry with its silks and sturdy blue cotton trousers the French called de Gênes.

Genoa is a neon-flashing, kinetic antidote to the Riviera's resortarama. Even its impossible topography is exciting: squeezed between mountains and sea, the city stretches for 30 kilometres – there are people who commute to work by lift or funicular, tunnels bore under green parks in the very centre of the city, and apartment houses hang over the hills so that the penthouse is at street level.

The old quarter is a bustling warren of alleys, or *carugi* – miniature canyons under eight-storey palaces and tenements, streaming with banners of laundry. There are streets of Renaissance palaces and Art Nouveau mansions, art (although the Genoese produced few painters or sculptors of note, they amassed some fine collections), and one of the most amazing cemeteries on earth. And since the Colombus fair in 1992, Genoa has a new razzmatazz, concentrated in the Porto Antico.

History

Genoa's destiny was shaped by its position, as not only the northernmost port on the Tyrrhenian Sea, but one protected and isolated by a ring of mountains. It was already a trading post in the 6th century BC, when the Phoenicians and Greeks came to barter with the Ligurians. Later the city was a stalwart outpost of the Roman Empire, and as such suffered the wrath of Hannibal's brother Mago; rebuilt after his sacking, it remained relatively happy and whole until the Lombards took it in 641, initiating a dark, troubled period. While the merchants of Amalfi, Pisa and Venice were creating their maritime republics in the 10th and 11th centuries, Genoa was still an agricultural backwater, far from the main highways of the Middle Ages, its traffic dominated by Pisa, its coasts prey to Saracen corsairs.

Adversity helped form the Genoese character. Once it rallied to defeat the Saracens in the 12th century, the city began a dizzy rise to prominence, capturing Sardinia and Corsica, and joining the Normans to conquer Antioch, where Genoa established its first of many trading colonies in the Middle East. In 1155 the walls had to be enlarged as the city expanded and competition with Pisa grew into a battle of blows as well as of trade. The turning point for their duel for supremacy in the western Mediterranean came in 1284, when Genoa soundly pummelled Pisa into naval obscurity at the Battle of Meloria – a victory Genoa followed up by defeating a more troublesome rival, Venice, at the Curzonali Islands in 1298.

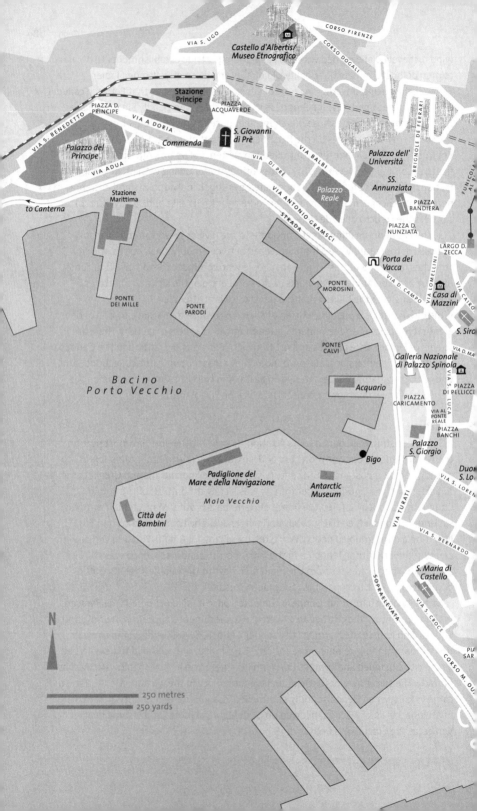

CORSO FIRENZE

VIA S. UGO

CORSO DOGALI

Castello d'Albertis/
Museo Etnografico

Stazione
Principe

PIAZZA D.
PRINCIPE

PIAZZA
ACQUAVERDE

VIA A. DORIA

V. BRIGNOLE DE' FERRARI

VIA S. BENEDETTO

Commenda

S. Giovanni
di Prè

VIA DI PRÈ

VIA BALBI

Palazzo dell'
Università

FUNICOLARE
AL P

Palazzo del
Principe

VIA ADUA

SS.
Annunziata

PIAZZA
BANDIERA

Palazzo
Reale

VIA ANTONIO GRAMSCI

PIAZZA D.
NUNZIATA

Stazione
Marittima

STRADA

Porta dei
Vacca

LARGO D.
ZECCA

to Canterna

PONTE
MOROSINI

VIA LOMELLINI

VIA D. CAMPO

VIA CAIRO

Casa di
Mazzini

PONTE
DEI MILLE

PONTE
PARODI

PONTE
CALVI

S. Siro

VIA D. MA

Galleria Nazionale
di Palazzo Spinola

VIA S. LUCA

PIAZZA
DI PELLICCE

Bacino
Porto Vecchio

Acquario

PIAZZA
CARICAMENTO

VIA AL
PONTE
REALE

PIAZZA
BANCHI

Bigo

Palazzo
S. Giorgio

Duom
S. Lo

VIA S. LOREN

Padiglione del
Mare e della Navigazione

Antarctic
Museum

Molo Vecchio

Città dei
Bambini

VIA TURATI

VIA S. BERNARDO

S. Maria di
Castello

SOPRAELEVATA

VIA S. CROCE

PIA
SAR

CORSO M. OU

N

250 metres
250 yards

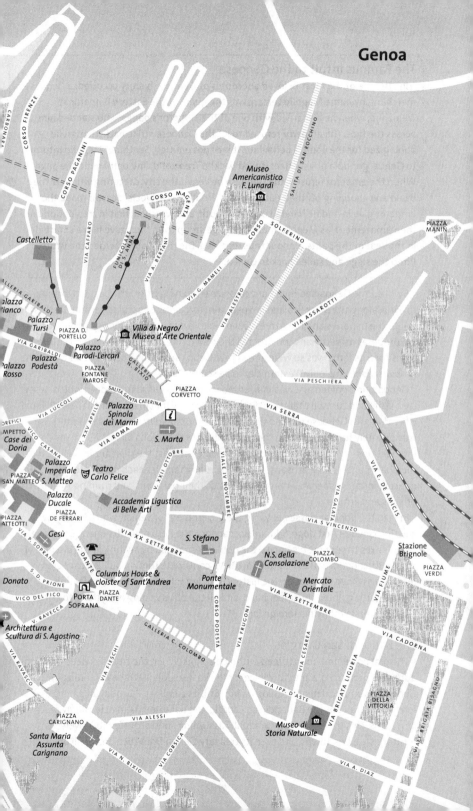

Genoa

CORSO FIRENZE

CARBONARA

CORSO PAGANINI

CORSO MAGENTA

VIA CAFFARO

FUNICOLARE DI S. ANNA

VIA A. BERTANI

Castelletto

Museo Americanistico F. Lunardi

SALITA DI SAN FOCCHINO

CORSO SOLFERINO

PIAZZA MANIN

GALLERIA GARIBALDI

Palazzo Bianco

Palazzo Tursi

PIAZZA D. PORTELLO

VIA G. MAMELI

VIA PALESTRO

VIA ASSAROTTI

Villa di Negro/ Museo d'Arte Orientale

Palazzo Parodi-Lercari

VIA GARIBALDI

Palazzo Podestà

Palazzo Rosso

PIAZZA FONTANE MAROSE

GALLERIA N. BIXIO

PIAZZA CORVETTO

VIA PESCHIERA

SALITA SANTA CATERINA

VIA SERRA

VIA LUCCOLI

V. XXV APRILE

Palazzo Spinola dei Marmi

VICO CASANA

VIA ROMA

S. Marta

OREFICI

MPETTO

Case dei Doria

V. XXII OTTOBRE

VIALE IV NOVEMBRE

VIA E. DE AMICIS

PIAZZA SAN MATTEO

Palazzo Imperiale

S. Matteo

Teatro Carlo Felice

Palazzo Ducale

Accademia Ligustica di Belle Arti

PIAZZA DE FERRARI

VIA GALATA

VIA S VINCENZO

Stazione Brignole

PIAZZA VERDI

PIAZZA ATTEOTTI

VIA P. SOPRANA

Gesù

V. DANTE

VIA XX SETTEMBRE

S. Stefano

N.S. della Consolazione

PIAZZA COLOMBO

Donato

S. D. PRIONE

Columbus House & cloister of Sant'Andrea

Ponte Monumentale

Mercato Orientale

VIA FIUME

VICO DEL FICO

PORTA SOPRANA

PIAZZA DANTE

VIA XX SETTEMBRE

VIA CADORNA

V. RAVECCA

Architettura e Scultura di S. Agostino

GALLERIA C. COLOMBO

CORSO PODESTA

VIA FRUGONI

VIA CESAREA

PIAZZA DELLA VITTORIA

VIA RAVASCO

VIA FIESCHI

VIA IPP. D'ASTE

VIA BRIGATA LIGURIA

VIALE BRIGATA BISAGNO

PIAZZA CARIGNANO

VIA ALESSI

Santa Maria Assunta Carignano

VIA N. BIXIO

VIA CORSICA

Museo di Storia Naturale

VIA A. DIAZ

The Famous Insult to the Genoese

In 1316 one of the most beloved anecdotes of Genoese history occurred: a Genoese merchant, by name Megollo Lercari, was the guest of the Eastern Emperor at Trebizond, when he disagreed with one of the emperor's pages, who slapped him across the face. The emperor refused to let the Genoese strike back, though he apologized for the youth's behaviour. It was not enough. Seething, Megollo returned to Genoa, got up a private fleet, sailed back to Trebizond, and demanded the page. When the emperor refused, the Genoese besieged the city, capturing whoever they could and chopping off their ears or noses. Finally his subjects' despair made the emperor give in and he handed over the youth, and watched, first in trepidation and then amazement, as Megollo made the page stoop over, then gave him a smart kick in the seat of the pants. Honour thus regained, the merchant returned the youth, lifted the siege and sailed back to Genoa.

By this time Genoa had merchant colonies stretching from the coast of North Africa to Syria, along the Black Sea and in Spain, where Genoese captains became the first to sail to the Canaries and the Azores. Genoa itself was the most densely populated city in Europe, as its patricians constructed their towering houses that seemed so 'superb' to visitors; its fame was so widespread that Genoa served as a setting for a tale in the *Arabian Nights*, the only Western city to be so honoured.

Genoa's first golden age was marred, however, as all subsequent ones would be, by civic strife and turmoil that were disgraceful even by Italian standards. The individual-istic, stubborn Genoese refused to accept communal unity; nearly every enterprise was privately funded, down to the city's military expeditions. Genoa itself was divided into factions – nobles against each other, nobles against the mercantile classes, the merchants against the artisans – while the ruling families each dominated their own quarter, forming *alberghi*, or brotherhoods, of their partisans, and running their own prisons and armies.

In 1339 the popular classes, envying the government of Venice, won a victory by electing Genoa's first doge, Simone Boccanegra, the hero of Verdi's opera. Boccanegra raised taxes to support his habits: the nobles responded by inviting in the Visconti of Milan; Boccanegra was exiled to Pisa; the Visconti were thrown out; Boccanegra returned as Doge – Genoese civic history is an ignoble chronicle of one faction momentarily gaining the upper hand, and all the others doing everything to under-mine it, even inviting in a foreign lord.

The Banco di San Giorgio

The real power in Genoa turned out to be a bank. When the city sank deep into debt during its prolonged war with Venice for the eastern Mediterranean (ending in Genoa's traumatic defeat at Chioggia in 1380), its creditors – Genoa's oligarchs – formed a syndicate, the Banco di San Giorgio, to guarantee their increasingly precar-ious loans. This the bank did by gradually assuming control of the city's overseas territories, castles, towns, and even its treasury. Genoa from then on, for all practical

Getting There

By Air

Genoa's international **airport**, Cristoforo Colombo (**t** 010 601 5410), 6km from the city in Sestri Ponente, has direct flights to Britain and many European destinations as well as to Italian cities. **Buses** to the airport depart an hour before each flight from Stazione Brignole and Piazza de Ferrari.

By Sea

You can sail away to exotic lands on a ferry from the **Stazione Marittima**, **t** 010 246 3686, just below the Stazione Principe.

By Rail

Genoa has two main train stations: **Principe**, in Piazza Acquaverde, just west of the centre, and **Brignole**, to the northeast. Principe in general handles trains from the north and France, while Brignole takes trains from the south, though most long-distance trains actually call at both. City bus no.37 links the two. For train information call **t** 147 888 088.

By Long-distance Bus

Intercity services and buses to the rest of the province and the Riviera depart from the Piazza della Vittoria, south of Stazione Brignole, or from Piazza Acquaverde, in front of Stazione Principe. For information, call **t** 010 599 7414.

Getting Around

Chances are you won't need to make much use of the city's public transport system, as most of Genoa's points of interest are in the centre between the two train stations. However, public transport is relatively cheap; an urban ticket, valid for ninety minutes' travel on **bus, train, metro, lift** or *funivia*, is L1,500. A day ticket with the same restrictions is L5,000. **Tickets** must be purchased before embarking, from tobacco shops or the transport authority (ATM) information kiosks at the rail stations.

The **funiculars** run from Piazza del Portello and Largo della Zecca to the city's upper residential quarters; the one served by the latter, **Righi**, has a splendid outlook over the city and harbour. A **lift** from Piazza Portello will also take you up to the nearer belvedere at Castelletto. **Taxis** are plentiful. For a radio taxi, **t** 010 5966. Genoa is one of several Italian cities with an unnecessarily complicated street-numbering system: any commercial establishment receives a red (r) number, but any residence a black or blue numberplate.

Tourist Information

Porto Antico; Palazzina Santa Maria B5, **t** 010 24871, **f** 010 246 7658, *www. apt.genova.it* There are branch offices at Stazione Principe, **t** 010 246 2633, and at the airport, **t** 010 241 5247.

For information about special events and what's on in general in Genoa, try the city's daily paper, *Il Secolo XIX*.

Activities

Genoa's main cultural event is its annual **Boat Show**, a celebration of all things nautical held in early October. Each year half a million people come to look at over 2000 boats of all shapes and sizes displayed in and around the port's exhibition area. To get a closer look at the sea itself, take the **tour of Genoa's port**. Excursions are run by the Cooperativa Battellieri, **t** 010 265 712, and by Alimar, **t** 010 256 775; both companies depart from the Calata Zingari, near the Stazione Marittima.

purposes, was run as a business proposition – once, in 1421, when the bank was short of cash, it sold Livorno to Florence for a tidy sum. The Genoese never had any reason to identify with their government, but, as Machiavelli noted, they were very loyal to their bank. Under its bankers, Genoa recovered from the defeat at Chioggia by transforming its economy from the mercantile to the financial sphere. The cinquecento

Where to Stay

Genoa ✉ 16100

Very Expensive

★★★★**Bristol Palace**, Via XX Settembre 35, **t** 010 592 941, **f** 010 561 756, *astorige@tin.it*, *www.hotelbristolpalace.com*. An elegant choice, near Brignole Station and the Teatro Carlo Felice, with sumptuous antique furnishings, beautiful rooms and a pleasant English bar.

★★★★**Britannia**, Via Balbi 38, **t** 010 26991, **f** 010 246 2942, *britannia@split.it*. Perhaps the best upper-range hotel near Principe Station. Very smart and slick, if maybe rather garishly designed in black and red. The top floor rooms enjoy fantastic views.

Expensive

★★★★**Astor**, Viale delle Palme 16, Nervi ✉ 16167, **t** 010 329 011, **f** 010 372 8486, *hotelastor@pn.itnet.it*. Fashionable and elegant hotel in an enchanting garden near the sea, far from the hurly-burly of the city centre.

Moderate

★★★**Agnello d'Oro**, Via Monachette 6, **t** 010 246 2084, **f** 010 246 2327. In a 17th-century property of the Doria family, near Via Balbi. Although most of the old-fashioned charm of the place is concentrated in the lobby, the bedrooms at the 'Golden Lamb' are very comfortable.

★★★**La Capannina**, Via T. Speri 7, **t** 010 317131, **f** 010 362 2692, *lacapannina@mclink.it*. Out in the eastern residential zone, near the charming fishing port of Boccadasse, with a lovely terrace where breakfast is served, and simple but tranquil rooms. In summer, the hotel's boat goes out on diving expeditions.

Cheap

★★★**Vittoria & Orlandini**, Via Balbi 33, **t** 010 261 923, **f** 010 246 2656, *vittorin@mbox.vol.it*. A charming, slightly eccentric hotel with rooms around an inner garden; comfortable bedrooms and a pretty breakfast room with views over the historic centre.

★★**Cairoli**, Via Cairoli 14/4, **t** 010 246 1454, **f** 010 246 7512, *cairoli@rdn.it*. Among the more respectable and hygienic of the city's inexpensive choices, and very centrally located, it's more like a three-star hotel, with sparkling, modern rooms and a relaxed, friendly and personal atmosphere. Excellent value.

★★**Villa Bonera**, Via Sarfatti 8, Nervi, **t** 010 372 6164, **f** 010 372 8565. Very attractive option with 26 charming rooms in a 17th-century villa surrounded by a pretty garden.

Eating Out

Besides various forms of pasta with *pesto*, the Genoese are fond of putting basil in numerous other dishes: *pansotti* are little *ravioli* filled with spinach and served in a walnut sauce; *torta pasqualina* consists of vegetables and hard-boiled eggs rolled in a pastry; *cima alla Genovese* is breast of veal filled with similar ingredients.

Expensive

Toe Drue, Via Corsi 441, **t** 010 650 0100. One of Genoa's most famous restaurants, in the working-class district of Sestri Ponente, west of the centre. *Toe Drue* means 'hard table', and this very fashionable restaurant has kept the furnishings of the rustic inn that preceded it. On these hard tables are served an array of delightful and unusual Ligurian specialities, many featuring seafood. Reservations necessary.

found the city Europe's leading economic power, a position Genoa maintained thanks to the foresight of Andrea Doria (1468–1560), the 'Saviour of Genoa' and the greatest admiral of his day.

During the Wars of Italy between Charles V of Spain and Francis I of France, Doria drove Genoa's traditional French allies from the city and welcomed Spanish protection. He then wrote a new Republican constitution for the strife-torn city,

Gran Gotto, Viale Brigata Bisagno (near Piazza della Vittoria), t 010 583 644. Another of the city's classic eateries, first opened in 1939, and it seems to be getting better all the time, featuring imaginative and delicately prepared seafood like turbot in radicchio sauce, warm seafood antipasti, famous *rognone* (kidney) dishes and delectable desserts. *Closed Sat lunch and Sun.*

Ristorante Da Rina, Mura delle Grazie 3/r, t 010 246 6475. Run by the same family since 1946. Rina, now 88, still maintains a watchful eye, although the day to day running has been assumed by her daughter-in-law. The preferred choice of Italy's ex-president Sandro Pertini, as well as countless stars from the big screen thanks to its simple, good food served in unpretentious surroundings. Try the *branzino in salsa di asparagi*, positively to die for. Reserve. *Closed Mon and Aug.*

Trattoria del Mario, Via Conservatori del Mare 35/r, t 010 246 2269. An old Genoese favourite in the old centre, near Piazza Banchi, that offers the freshest of fish prepared in authentic Genoese style, and pasta with *pesto* as well as *cima*; the delicious seafood salad is a popular starter. *Closed Sat and Aug.*

Pancetti Antica Osteria, Borgo Incrociati 22/r, t 010 839 2848. One of the best traditional choices in the old city, offering *pansotti* and some other Ligurian classics that are rarely prepared elsewhere, accompanied by the region's best vintages. *Closed Mon.*

Moderate

Trattoria Da Vittorio, Via Sottoripa 59, t 010 247 2927. If the beautiful display of fish and shellfish isn't enough to entice you in, then the knowledge that half a lobster with *linguine*, wine and coffee for under L40,000 should be. Reserve or be prepared to wait. No credit cards.

Archivolto Mongiardino, No.2, in the street of the same name, t 010 247 7610. The place to go for excellent seafood dishes, in the maze of streets in the southern old city. *Closed Sun and Mon.*

Cheap

Trattoria da Pino, in Piazza Caricamento, t 010 372 6395. One of Genoa's top portside greasy-spoon districts. Try the fresh fish.

Ostaja Do Castello, Salita Santa Margherita del Castello, t 010 246 8980. Some of the best cheap food in town, with good Genoese specialities. *Closed Sun.*

Trattoria da Maria, Vico Testadora 14/r, t 010 581 080. Wonderfully authentic *trattoria* just off Via XXV Aprile, near the Piazza de Ferrari, serving up filling three-course meals for under L20,000. *Closed Sat.*

Entertainment and Nightlife

In Paganini's home town there is bound to be plenty of music. The **Genoa Opera**, now back in the Teatro Carlo Felice in Piazza de Ferrari after years of being without a proper home, presents its main season from January to June, and in the summer sponsors the prestigious **Ballet Festival** in the park in Nervi. Every year Genoa competes with Venice, Pisa and Amalfi in the **Regatta of the Ancient Maritime Republics**, hosted by the previous year's winner.

The main centre of **café and bar** life is around Via XX Settembre, though a noisier and seamier choice of places waits around the port. Anyone needing an English drinking ambience can find it at the **Brittania Pub** on Vico della Casana just off Piazza de Ferrari, which is very popular with both foreigners and Italians.

institutionalizing the shared rule of the 28 *alberghi*. Charles V rewarded Doria with the title of Prince of Melfi, and he and other Genoese were given prominent posts throughout the Empire. Meanwhile the Banco di San Giorgio became fat and sleek financing the wars in the Low Countries for Charles V and Philip II, processing Spain's silver and taking over the international money market from Besançon and Antwerp: millions of *scudi* passed through Genoa every year. Doria was also Genoa's first great patron of the arts, introducing the Renaissance to the city that had formerly managed without it.

Nevertheless, after the crusty old admiral Genoa began to decline. Spain's bankruptcies came too frequently; Atlantic commerce overtook in importance the old Mediterranean trade; the Ottoman Empire gobbled up Genoa's last colonies in the east. The French besieged (1668), and the Austrians took briefly (1746), the city itself; Corsica, Genoa's last colony, revolted in 1768, and the Banco di San Giorgio could do nothing but sell it to France. By the 1815 Treaty of Vienna, Genoa and Liguria joined Piemonte, and almost at once the city became a hotbed of unification sentiment, led by the conspiring philosopher of the Risorgimento, Giuseppe Mazzini, and such patriot luminaries as Nino Bixio, Goffredo Mameli, the Ruffini brothers and, of course, Garibaldi himself.

Stazione Principe to Via Garibaldi

Both of Genoa's two main stations are lovely – the Stazione Principe could serve as a setting for a fancy-dress ball. In its Piazza Acquaverde visitors are greeted by a **statue of Columbus**, a view of the port, and the stately Via Balbi. If you're catching a ferry, Via Andrea Doria will take you down to the Stazione Marittima, passing the **Palazzo del Principe** on the way, the only 'royal' palace built during the secular history of the Genovese Republic. The royal in this instance was Andrea Doria whose decision in 1528 to commission Raphael's pupil, Perin del Vaga, to decorate the interior marked the beginining of Genoa's Renaissance (*open Sat 3–6, Sun 10–3; adm exp; guided tours outside opening hours, t 010 255 509*).

Afterwards, you might like to take in Genoa's most celebrated landmark, the **Lanterna**, a well-signposted 10-minute walk west around the port. The 384ft medieval lighthouse is now open for the first time in decades, and you can climb the 375 stairs to the top and admire the spectacular views of the city and coast (*guided tours by appointment only, t 010 246 5396, except Sun when you can just turn up at 2.30 at the Gran Bigo – the giant crane; the first 100 people will be admitted*). In the old days a huge fire would be ignited on top to guide vessels into the port. Back near the Stazione Principe, **La Commenda** is Genoa's oldest hotel, where pilgrims lodged on their way to the Holy Land. In 1180 the Knights of St John built a hospital and adjacent two-storey church, **San Giovanni di Pré**, with a spire-clustered campanile.

Via Balbi is lined with late-Renaissance palaces, among them the yellow and red **Palazzo Reale** (*open Sun–Tues 9–1.45, Wed–Sat 9–7; adm exp*), with its hyper-decorated 18th-century ballroom and Hall of Mirrors, and a *Crucifixion* by Van Dyck, who spent several years in Genoa. Via Balbi gives on to Piazza della Nunziata, site of **SS. Annunziata** (16th-century), a church with a grubby façade which hides a voluptuous rococo interior.

From the next square, **Largo della Zecca**, you have several options: browsing through the district's antique shops; a thrilling funicular ride to Righi, where you can dine at the top of the town; walking through the tunnel to Piazza Portello and taking the lift up to the Castelletto belvedere; or continuing round on Via Cairoli to Genoa's most famous street, **Via Garibaldi**. Via Garibaldi, the former *Strada Nuova* laid out in 1558, was for centuries Genoa's 'Millionaires' Row', with uninterrupted lines of 16th- and 17th-century *palazzi*. Many have since been converted into banks and offices, but the street's unique and elegant character has been carefully maintained.

Two of the palaces hold important art collections: the **Palazzo Bianco** (*open Tues, Thurs and Fri 9–1, Wed and Sat 9–7, Sun 10–6; closed Mon; adm*), at No.11, former residence of the Grimaldi, is no longer very white, but has the most noteworthy collection in the city, with a good assortment of Italian paintings, including Filippino Lippi's *Madonna with Saints*, Pontormo's *Florentine Gentleman*, Veronese's *Crucifixion*, and an even more impressive collection of Flemish art. Among the latter are Gerhard David's sweetly domestic *Madonna della Pappa*, paintings by Cranach, Van der Goes, Van Dyck and Rubens (who worked for a while in Genoa); there is also a fine *San Bonaventura* by Zurbarán. The portrait of Andrea Doria by Jan Matsys is remarkable for its hands.

Across the street at No.18, the **Palazzo Rosso** (*currently undergoing renovation, but still open Tues, Thurs and Fri 9–1, Wed and Sat 9–7, Sun 10–6; adm*), retains some of its palatial fittings, as well as a picture gallery with an especially good collection of portraits by Van Dyck, Pisanello and Dürer, and works by Caravaggio and his follower Mattia Preti to Veronese and Guercino.

Opposite the Palazzo Rosso, the former **Palazzo Tursi** is now Genoa's Municipio, with the city's most beautiful courtyard and such municipal treasures as native son Paganini's violin, in the Sala della Giunta, and three letters from Columbus in the Sala del Sindaco. You can enter the courtyard of No.7, the **Palazzo Podestà**, with an elaborate fountain in the shape of a grotto. The façade of No.3, the 16th-century **Palazzo Parodi-Lercari**, was built by the descendants of Megollo Lercari, who recalled the 'Insult to the Genoese' at Trebizond (*see* p.192) with earless and noseless caryatids.

The Villa di Negro

Via Garibaldi ends at Piazza Marose, with more palaces, especially the 15th-century **Palazzo Spinola dei Marmi**, embellished with black and white bands and statues of the Spinola family. From here Salita Santa Caterina leads into the circular **Piazza Corvetto**, a major junction of the city bus lines and the entrance to the **Villa di Negro**, an urban oasis that takes full advantage of Genoa's crazy topography, with streams, cascades, grottoes and walkways, culminating at the top with the **Museo di Arte Orientale** (*open Tues, Thurs, Fri and Sat 9–1; adm*), Italy's finest museum of Oriental art, a lovely collection of statues, paintings and theatre masks, and an extraordinary set of Samurai helmets and armour, all well displayed in a sun-filled modern building.

At the corner of Piazza Corvetto and Via Roma you can stop off for a history-imbued coffee break at the early 19th-century **Caffè Mangani**. Via Roma continues down to tumultuous **Piazza de Ferrari**, on one side marked by the neoclassical **Teatro Carlo Felice**, built in 1829, bombed in 1944, and then left crumbling until 1992, when it was restored for Columbus year; it now holds a year-round opera, dance and theatre programme (**t** 010 538 1226). Across the piazza is the giant, black and white mass of the 16th-century Palazzo Ducale. Next door Piazza de Ferrari and Piazza Matteotti are linked by a monumental staircase, formerly used for the city's processions.

The Old City

From Piazza de Ferrari you can descend into Old Genoa; the most picturesque way is to head down Via Dante to Piazza Dante and through the tall twin-towered **Porta Soprana**, built in 1155 as part of the Barbarossa walls designed to protect the city from the Frederick of that name. Columbus' father was gatekeeper here; the explorer's 'boyhood home' is nearby, as are the ruins of the 12th-century cloister of **Sant'Andrea**, set out on the lawn.

Within the Porta Soprana are the tall houses of old Genoa, sliced by corridor-like alleys, some so narrow that they live in perpetual shade. Partly bombed in the Second World War and now mostly restored, leaning ever so gently towards the harbour below, many houses have white marble and black slate portals, permitted only to those families who performed a deed of benefit to the city, while corners and wall niches are decorated with hundreds of shrines called *madonnette*, little Madonnas.

The old town is for exploring, although single women should exercise caution, especially after dark. To see the highlights of the quarter, take Via Ravecca down from Porta Soprana to the 13th-century Gothic church of Sant'Agostino, its ruined cloisters converted into the well-designed **Museo di Sant'Agostino** (*open Tues–Sat 9–7, Sun 9–12*), containing art and architectural fragments salvaged from Genoa's demolished churches. One of the finest works is the fragment of the tomb of Margherita of Brabant, wife of Emperor Henry VII, sculpted in 1312 by Giovanni Pisano. Margherita died suddenly in Genoa while accompanying her husband to Rome for his coronation, and Henry, whom Dante and many others had hoped would be able to end the feud between Italy's Guelphs and Ghibellines, died in Siena two years later, many believe of sorrow; his last request was that his heart be taken to Genoa to be interred with his wife. There are also Roman works, Romanesque sculpture, frescoes and the 14th-century wooden *Christ of the Caravana*.

From Sant'Agostino, the Stradone di Sant'Agostino leads to another good church, the 12th-century Romanesque **San Donato**, with an exceptionally lovely octagonal campanile, portal and interior, combining a mix of ancient and medieval columns. The nearby Via San Bernardo, one of the few straight streets in the old city, was laid out by the Romans. Their castle up the hill (take the Salita della Torre degli Embriaci) provided the foundations for Genoa's most venerable church, the evocative **Santa Maria di Castello**, incorporating Roman columns and stones in its Romanesque structure. The crusaders used Santa Maria's complex as a hostel. Fairest of its art is the 15th-century fresco of the *Annunciation* in the cloister, while the strangest is the *Crocifisso Miracoloso* in a chapel near the high altar – miraculous in that the Christ's beard is said to grow whenever Genoa is threatened with calamity.

Around Piazza Matteotti

Another entrance into the historic centre from Piazza de Ferrari is by way of Piazza Matteotti, dominated by the main yellow and red façade of the grandiose **Palazzo Ducale**. First built in the 16th century, it was greatly altered in the following century to serve as the city law courts. It stood neglected for years, but like the Carlo Felice theatre it was restored and renovated for 1992, and now you can walk through its attractive courtyards, one adorned with a fountain, or sample the restaurants, bars and shops, and visit the exhibitions (*Tues–Sun 9am–9pm; guided tours available of the monumental rooms, **t** 010 557 4000; adm exp*). Sharing the square is the Baroque church of the **Gesù**, designed in the 1600s by Jesuit Giuseppe Valeriani. The interior is pure Baroque fantasia, all lavish stuccoes, frescoes and *trompe l'œil* stage effects that highlight its frothy treasures: a *Circumcision* and *St Ignatius Exorcising the Devil* by Rubens, and an *Assumption* by the 'Divino' Guido Reni.

Just off the square stands the jauntily black-and-white-striped **Duomo di San Lorenzo**, begun in the 12th century, and modified several times; the façade was last restored in 1934. Odds and ends from the ages embellish the exterior – two kindly 19th-century lions by the steps, and a carving of St Lawrence toasting on his grill above the central of three French-Gothic-style portals. On the north side there's a pretty 12th-century **Portal of San Giovanni**; on the south, Hellenistic sarcophagi, another Romanesque portal and a 15th-century tomb. The rather morose interior also wears jailbird stripes (two sides are currently undergoing renovation). The first chapel on the right contains a good marble *Crucifixion* of 1443, and a British shell fired from the sea 500 years later that hit the chapel but miraculously failed to explode. On the left, note the sumptuous Renaissance **Cappella di San Giovanni Battista**, with fine sculptures and marble decorations, and a 13th-century sarcophagus that once held the Baptist's relics.

The well-arranged **Museo del Tesoro** (*open Mon–Sat 9–12 and 3–6; guided tours only*), in the vaults to the left of the nave, contains a number of genuine treasures acquired during the heyday of Genoa's mercantile empire: a crystal plate said to have been part of the dinner service of the Last Supper, the blue chalcedony dish on which John the Baptist's head was supposedly served to Salome, an 11th-century arm reliquary of St Anne, the golden, jewel-studded Byzantine *Zaccaria Cross*, and an elaborate 15th-century silver casket built to hold the Baptist's ashes.

The Salita del Fonaco follows the back of the Palazzo Ducale, then veers right for **Piazza San Matteo**, a beautiful little square completely clothed in the black and white bands of illustrious civic benefactors – and it's no wonder, for this was the public foyer of the Doria family, encompassed by their *palazzi* and their 12th-century church of **San Matteo**, inscribed with their great deeds and adorned with a charming early 14th-century cloister. Andrea Doria's palace was No.17 on the square, while No.14, belonging to Branca Doria, has a portal guarded by Genoa's patron St George.

Between Via San Lorenzo and Via Garibaldi

This northern section of the historic centre, built up mostly in the Renaissance, has survived somewhat better than the area around Porta Soprana, and has, amid its monuments, fine shops, pubs, restaurants and cafés. From Piazza San Matteo it's a short walk to the **Campetto**, a lovely square adorned with the ornate 16th-century **Palazzo Imperiale**; in the nearby Piazza Soziglia you can take a break at one of the oldest coffee-houses in Genoa, **Kainguti**, at No.98/r, or **Romanegro**, at No.74/r, both founded at the beginning of the 19th century. From Piazza Soziglia and the Campetto, pretty Via degli Orefici meanders down to the major intersection of medieval Genoa,

Piazza Banchi, with its Renaissance Loggia dei Mercanti. From here Via Ponti Reale descends to the harbourside **Piazza Caricamento**, lined with the ancient arcades of Via Sottoripa and dominated by the gaudily decorated **Palazzo San Giorgio**. This was originally built in 1260 for the Capitani del Popolo, but was taken over in 1408 by the Banco di San Giorgio, so the shrewd bankers could scrutinize the comings and goings of the port. It's now occupied by the Harbour Board, but you can ask the guard to show you the rooms that have been refurbished in 13th-century style.

Seawards, on the other side of the *Sopraelevata* from the Piazza Caricamento, the whole of the old quay (*Molo Vecchio*), known locally as the Porto Antico, was the showcase for the 1992 celebrations. Redevelopment has continued apace; it is now home to an Antarctic Museum; the largest cinema complex in Italy; the **Citta dei Bambini** (*open daily 10–6; closed Mon and Sept; adm exp*), the ne plus ultra of educational playgrounds – full of climbing frames and giant plastic insects, as well as a building site where children can dress up in hard hats and overalls and push around plastic wheelbarrows full of sand; and, housed in a converted ship, Europe's largest **aquarium** (*open Tues–Fri 9.30–6.30, Sat and Sun 9.30–8pm; ticket office closes 1½hrs earlier; adm very exp, children under 3 free*), with seals, dolphins, sharks and penguins, and reconstructions of coral reefs, visited by a million and a half people each year, making it Italy's third most attended 'museum'. There is also the **Gran Bigo**, or 'Great Crane', designed by Renzo Piano, which towers over the port; a panoramic, revolving lift goes to the top for the superb views (*adm*). Finally, there is the **Padiglione del Mare e della Navigazione** (Sea and Navigation Pavilion) (*open Mon–Fri 10.30–6, Sat and Sun 10.30–7; adm exp*), with artefacts from 16th- and 17th-century ships, and a reconstruction of a medieval shipyard.

Returning to the old city, **Via San Luca**, the main street passing through Piazza Banchi, was the principal thoroughfare of medieval Genoa and, in its day, home turf of another prominent Genoese family, the Spinola. They donated one of their palaces, just off Via San Luca in little Piazza di Pellicceria, with its 16th–18th-century décor and paintings to form the **Galleria Nazionale di Palazzo Spinola** (*open Tues–Sat 9–7, Sun 2–7*). The paintings, still arranged as in a private residence, include Antonello da Messina's sad, beautiful *Ecce Homo*, Joos Van Cleve's magnificent *Adoration of the Magi*, works by Van Dyck (*Portrait of a Child* and the *Four Evangelists*), and a statue of Justice, another fragment of Giovanni Pisano's tomb of Margherita di Brabante.

A little further to the north, back towards Largo Zecca, stands one of the chief shrines of 19th-century Italian history, the **Casa Mazzini**, Via Lomellini 11, where the romantic prophet of Italian unification, Giuseppe Mazzini, was born in 1805. It now houses Genoa's **Museo del Risorgimento** (*open Tues, Thurs, Fri and Sat 9–1*), with a collection centred on various relics of Mazzini himself.

East Genoa

East of the Piazza de Ferrari runs arcaded **Via XX Settembre**, the main thoroughfare of 19th-century Genoa, adorned here and there with Liberty-style touches. This is still the city's main shopping street, and it and the area around Stazione Brignole make up a lively neighbourhood, aglow with neon lights. Via XX Settembre is traversed by the

Ponte Monumentale, which carries the Corso A. Podesta overhead. Next to the bridge a lane leads up to another of Genoa's striped medieval churches, **Santo Stefano**, which contains a *Martyrdom of St Stephen* by a less flamboyant than usual Giulio Romano. Beyond the bridge the avenue continues to the large Piazza della Vittoria, a Fascist-era square presided over by a 1931 War Memorial Arch.

The Hills and Staglieno Cemetery

Some of the loveliest bits of Genoa are to be found up in the surrounding hills. The **Circonvallazione a Monte** is the scenic route, made up of several *corsi*, that skirts the slopes, a route followed by city bus no.33, from Stazione Brignole or Piazza Manin. The one attraction to stop for is at Corso Solferino 25, installed in the 17th-century Villa Grüber: the **Museo Americanistico F. Lunardi** (*open Tues–Sat 9.30–12 and 3–5.30, Sun 3–5.30*) housing an important collection of pre-Columbian art, especially strong in Mayan work. The hillside route continues along Corsos Magenta, Paganini, Firenze and U. Bassi, passing on the way the imposing medieval **Castello d'Albertis**, rebuilt in the 19th century.

Just over the mountains, along the Torrente Bisagno, lies Genoa's famous **Cimitero di Staglieno** (*open daily 8–5; bus no.34 from Piazza Acquaverde or Piazza Corvetto*). Founded in 1844, the cemetery covers 160 hectares, and even has its own internal bus system. The Genoese have a reputation for being tight-fisted, but when it comes to post-mortem extravagance they have few peers. Staglieno is a veritable Babylon of the dead, with miniature cathedrals, Romanesque chapels, Egyptian temples and Art Nouveau palaces and statuary – a fantastic, often surreal ensemble. In the centre of the hills, Genoa's great revolutionary idealist of the Risorgimento, Giuseppe Mazzini, is buried in a simple tomb behind two massive Doric columns, surrounded by laudatory inscriptions by Tolstoy, Lloyd George, D'Annunzio and others. After a life of plots, conspiracies and exile, Mazzini died in semi-exile in Pisa, hiding out under the assumed name of American abolitionist John Brown. Mrs Oscar Wilde is buried in the Protestant section.

Around Genoa

Nervi, one of the oldest resorts on the Riviera, is just east of Genoa, and has been incorporated into the metropolis and can be reached by bus no.17 from Piazza de Ferrari, or bus no.15 from the Piazza Caricamento. On the way, in Genova Quarto, is another monument to the Risorgimento, the **Museo Garibaldi** in Villa Garibaldi (*open daily 9–1; closed Thurs*), which houses some of the original red shirts of Garibaldi's Thousand (originally intended for slaughterhouse workers in South America), some of their bayonets and a variety of documents. In Nervi itself, two of the town's oldest Genoese villas have been converted to museums: the **Galleria d'Arte Moderna** in the Villa Serra Gropallo, Via Capolungo 3, contains a large collection of 19th- and 20th-century Italian art (*open Tues–Sat 9–7, Sun 9–1*). The other, the **Museo Giannettino Luxoro**, Viale Mafalda di Savoia 3 (*open Tues–Sat 9–1*), is further east in one of the Riviera's loveliest parks. It, too, has a small modern art collection, but is especially noteworthy for its decorative arts holdings: clocks (some of the first luminous time-pieces), furniture, fabrics and lace.

There are also two popular excursions into the hinterland from Genoa: **Casella**, a small mountain resort reached by electric train from Piazza Manin, and **Torriglia** (reached by bus, or by car on the SS45 road towards Piacenza), with an impressive if utterly derelict medieval castle, a small resort offering skiing in winter and pretty walks in summer.

Riviera di Levante

Recco to Sestri Levante

East of Genoa, the coast, fairly tame up to this point, becomes a creature of high drama and romance. The beaches aren't as prominent, nor the climate quite as mild, but from the Monte di Portofino to the once nearly inaccessible fishing villages of the Cinque Terre, the mountains and sea tussle and tumble in a voluptuous chaos of azure, turquoise and piney green. Against these deep-coloured coves, cliffs and inlets rise the villages of weathered pastels and ochres, with silvery groves of olives gazing out over bobbing fleets of fishing craft, sailing boats and sleek white yachts.

Recco and Camogli

Of all the nubs and notches in the Italian coastline, one of the best beloved is the squarish promontory of Monte di Portofino, which comes into view as you leave Nervi, and forms, on its western side, the Gulf of Paradise. **Recco**, at the crossroads to Camogli, was bombed into dust during the War, and has since been completely rebuilt, but **Camogli**, only a kilometre or so away on the promontory, was spared. Built on a pine-wooded slope, it is an old sea town, once home port of a renowned fleet that fought with Napoleon; its fishing and merchant vessels were equally prominent along the Riviera. Its name derives from *Casa Mogli* (home of wives), since the menfolk were almost always at sea. The old harbour, piled high with tall, faded houses with dark green shutters, is the site of the famous *Sagra del Pesce*, an ancient festival that takes place on the second Sunday in May, where Italy's largest frying pan (13ft across) is used to cook up thousands of sardines, which are distributed free to all comers – a display of generosity and abundance that carries with it the hope that the sea itself will be equally generous and abundant in the coming year.

A small promontory separates Camogli's little pebble beach from its fishing port. Near here, Castello della Dragonara, originally built in the Middle Ages to defend the port from Saracens, now contains the **Acquario di Camogli** (*open April–Sept 10–11.45 and 3–6.45; Oct–Mar 10–11.45 and 3–5.45; adm*), an aquarium with 22 tanks of Mediterranean creatures. Camogli recalls its own history in the **Maritime Museum** (*Via Gio Bono Ferrari 41; open April–Sept Wed–Mon 9–12 and 4–7; Oct–Mar Wed, Sat and Sun 9–11.45 and 3–5.40, Mon, Thurs and Fri 9–12*). The archaeological section (*open Wed–Mon 9–12*), contains artefacts from, and a reconstruction of, an Iron Age settlement discovered nearby; the maritime section contains an array of ship's models, nautical instruments, maps, paintings and documents that recall Camogli's thrilling days as a rough-and-tumble sea power.

San Fruttuoso

From Camogli there is a regular boat service (run by Golfo Paradiso, Via Scalo 2, **t** 0185 772 091, **f** 0185 771 263) to the tiny fishing hamlet of San Fruttuoso on the seaward side of the promontory. The hamlet is inaccessible save by sea or on foot (from Camogli it's a three-hour hike; there are also boats from Portofino, Santa Margherita and Rapallo, so in summer it can be elbow-room only). On the way from Camogli the boats pass the **Punta Chiappa**, a point famous for the changing colours of the sea, though unfortunately – thanks to the quantity of rubbish floating around nowadays – the water is no longer as clear as it once was.

San Fruttuoso is named after its **abbey**, founded in 711 by the Bishop of Tarragona, who fled Spain from the Moors, bringing with him the relics of San Fruttuoso. The Benedictines subsequently took over, under the protection of Genoa's powerful Doria family; Andrea Doria added the **Torre dei Doria** in the 16th century, when Turkish corsairs plagued the coast in the name of the king of France. In 1981 the modern Dorias donated the abbey and surrounding land to the Italian National Trust; you can stroll through the abbey, and the pretty white 11th-century church with a Byzantine cupola and tiny cloister (*open Mar–April Tues–Sun 10–1 and 2–4; May–Oct till 6; Nov–Feb public hols only*).

San Fruttuoso is surrounded by a lush growth of palms and olives, and from here it's a two-hour walk through these groves to Portofino. Another sight, best appreciated by skin-divers, is the 1954 bronze **Cristo degli Abissi** (Christ of the Depths), off-shore, and eight fathoms under the sea, a memorial to those lost at sea and protector of all who work underwater.

Portofino

The stunning **Monte di Portofino** (2,001ft) is easiest reached from **Ruta** and **Portofino Vetta** (buses from Camogli). Protected as a natural park, it offers several lovely walks, especially up to the summit (one hour from Ruta), with its priceless views of the Riviera and out to sea as far as Elba, or in another hour to the lighthouse on the cliffs (the Semaforo Nuovo), or in two hours to Portofino.

One of Italy's most romantic little nooks, Portofino itself was discovered long ago by artists, then by the yachting set, who fell in love with its delightful little port framed by mellowed, narrow houses, and then by the rich and trendy, who fell in love with its spectacular beauty and seclusion and made it a favourite setting for illicit trysts, far, they hoped, from the paparazzi. This exclusiveness still exists to a certain extent – it's certainly a difficult place to get to, especially if you have left the yacht at home. The nearest railway station is in Santa Margherita, 9km away, the only means of access a single coastal road – a steeply meandering ribbon of tarmac roughly one and a half cars wide. Buses make the journey (with constant horn accompaniment) from Santa Margherita Station every twenty minutes or so for a minimal charge. Despite

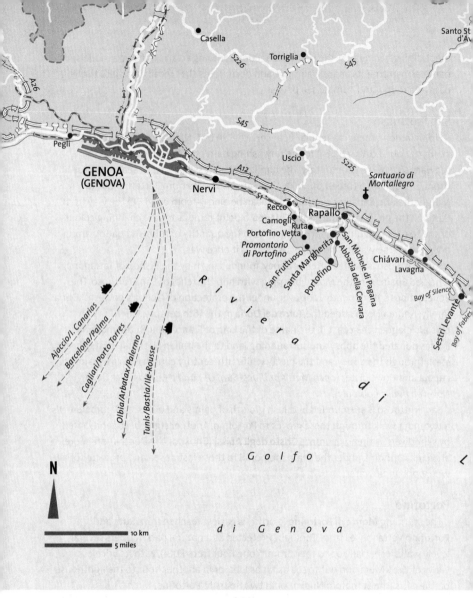

this, and the fact that there are only a handful of hotels, Portofino's hard-fought seclusion vanishes every weekend and every day in summer when thousands of trippers pour in for an afternoon's window-shopping in the smart boutiques (some selling the district's famous lace), a drink in the portside bar or even a walk in the cyprus-lined hills. In the evening, though, the yachtsmen and the residents of the hillside villas descend once again to their old haunts and reclaim Portofino as their own.

Portofino's name is derived from the Roman *Portus Delphini*, which had a *mithraeum* (an initiatory sanctuary dedicated to the popular Persian god Mithras, a favourite of Roman soldiers) on its isthmus. This is now the site of the church of

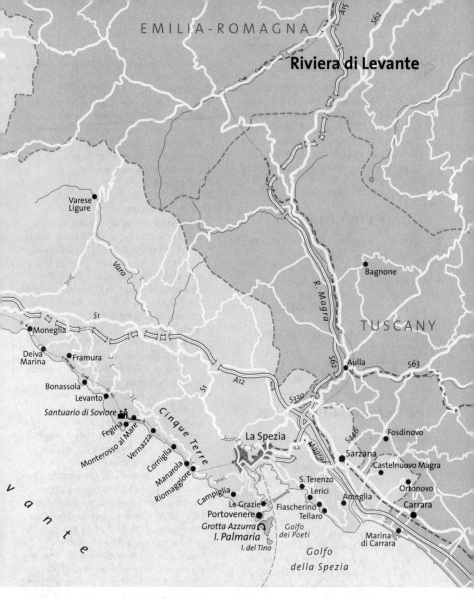

S. Giorgio, rebuilt after war damage in 1950 but still housing the relics of the defrocked St George; as often as not there's a cat sleeping under the altar. Further up, **Castello Brown**, built in the 1500s as a defence against the Turks, affords enchanting views of the little port (*open Tues–Sun 10–6; adm*). Another lovely walk, beyond the castle, is to Punta del Capo and the **Faro**, the old lighthouse, taking in magnificent views of the Gulf of Tigullio through the pine forest. The other thing to do in Portofino is find a table at one of the two portside drinking holes which have long competed for the biggest celebrities: **La Gritta American Bar** and **Scafandro American Bar**, both elegant, glamorous, studiously laid-back and very expensive.

Getting Around

The Genoa–Pisa **railway** hugs the coast, but in many places you can only get glimpses of the scenery between the tunnels. The most scenic road is the old coastal Via Aurelia (SS1), which is also the route used by most of the buses. Camogli, San Fruttuoso, Portofino, Santa Margherita and Rapallo are linked by **boat** services.

Tourist Information

Camogli: Via XX Settembre 33, **t/f** 0185 771 066 (very helpful).

Portofino: Via Roma 35, **t** 0185 269 024.

S. Margherita Ligure: Via XXV Aprile 2/b, **t** 0185 287 485, **f** 0185 283 034.

Rapallo: Via A. Diaz 9, **t** 0185 51282, **f** 0185 230 346.

Chiávari: Corso Assarotti 1, **t** 0185 325 198, **f** 0185 324 796.

Sestri Levante: Piazza S. Antonio 10, **t** 0185 457 011, **f** 0185 459 575.

Where to Stay and Eat

Recco ✉ 16036

Though lacking in scenic attractions, Recco is something of a gourmet mecca, famous for its *focaccia* with cheese, and *trofie* with *pesto* sauce and *pansotti*. The mayor of Recco runs some of the best places to stay and eat.

★★★★**La Villa**, Via Roma 278, **t** 0185 720 779, **f** 0185 721 095, *manulina@omninet.it* (*expensive*). A typical Genoese pleasure villa with all mod cons, prettily set in a garden with pool. Pre-dating the hotel is its restaurant, the celebrated **Manuelina**, where you can try exquisite *trofie* with *pesto*, and seafood in a variety of styles for *secondo*. *Closed Wed.*

Focacceria, next door to Manuelina (*expensive*). Dine on one of the town's famous *focaccia*, or on other Ligurian dishes such as *cima. Closed Wed.*

Da-o Vittorió, Via Roma 160, **t** 0185 74029 (*expensive*). Another renowned restaurant in Recco is a hundred years old. Its specialities include utterly superb *minestrone di verdura alla Genovese* and *trofie al pesto*.

Recco has good budget-price restaurants, too, particularly along the seafront and around the Via Roma.

Camogli ✉ 16032

★★★★**Cenobio dei Dogi**, Via Cuneo 34, **t** 0185 7241, **f** 0185 772 796 (*luxury*). A lovely former palace of Genoa's doges, at the water's edge with fantastic views of the gulf – on a clear day you can see the steady winking of Genoa's lighthouse. The bedrooms are light and airy and tastefully decorated in white and wood, and there are two excellent restaurants, one on the hotel's private pebble beach, both open to the public and both with superb views. There are various sun terraces, a flower-filled park, a heated swimming pool and tennis courts.

★★★★**Hotel Portofino Kulm**, Viale Bernardo Gaggini 23, Portofino Vetta. **t** 0185 7361, **f** 0185 776 622, *kulm@ifree.it, www.portofinokulm.it* (*very expensive*). Built in 1905 this sumptuous, if oddly named hotel ('kulm' is German for summit) was reopened in April 2000 having been closed for restoration for six years. Set in a forest at the top of the Monte di Portofino, overlooking the beautiful village of Camogli, this is a far cry from the madness that is Portofino during the summer months. With a fitness centre, indoor pool, sauna and Jacuzzi available as well as Internet access, rest and relaxation is assured. Regarding the restaurant, suffice it to say that it is run by Zefferino.

★★★**Casmona**, Salita Pineto 13, **t** 0185 770 015, **f** 0185 775 030 (*moderate*). For something more affordable: a quiet, tidy place with a restaurant and a shady little patio.

Santa Margherita

Santa Margherita, with its beautiful harbour, is not as spectacular as Portofino, but friendly and lively, a popular winter hideaway for the British, and a summer resort with accommodation priced for all budgets. The main sight in town is the **Basilica di**

**Pensione La Camogliese, Via Garibaldi 55, t 0185 771 402, f 0185 774 024 (*cheap*). Very pleasant and also has an attractive restaurant, with a veranda overlooking the port, and good, reasonably priced fish dishes. *Closed Wed. Hotel closed Nov and half Dec.*

Vento Ariel, Calata Porto 1, t 0185 771 080 (*expensive*). A tiny, charming place on the harbour that bases its existence entirely on the luck of the town's fishing fleet. Only fish and seafood are served, with daily set menus or *à la carte*. Reservations are essential in summer. *Closed Wed.*

San Fruttuoso ✉ 16030

There are a couple of good seafood restaurants here.

Da Giovanni, t 0185 770 047 (*expensive*). A small, charming place, which also doubles as an inexpensive hotel.

La Cantina, t 0185 772 626 (*expensive*). On the beach, serving fish cooked to order at very reasonable prices.

Portofino ✉ 16034

****Splendido, Viale Baratta 16, t 0185 267 801, f 0185 267 806, *www.orient-expresshotels.com* (*luxury*). The management believe they run the best hotel in Liguria, if not Italy. It's an arrogant assumption but one with which precious few people would disagree. The views alone, of olive- and cypress-clad hills gently framing the town, its tiny harbour and the deep blue sea beyond, are well worth the astronomical fees. The bedrooms are sumptuous, the restaurant refined and the breakfast terrace, sheltered beneath a huge sub-tropical canopy, simply delightful. Take a swim in the heated outdoor pool or, for a mere L1,000,000 per day, go for a ride in the hotel's own speedboat. If you are still not impressed, the staff will point you towards their wall of fame where you will find numerous signed photographs of the various film stars, pop stars

and members of minor European royal families who have sampled the Splendido and found it to their liking (Winston Churchill, Groucho Marx, Elizabeth Taylor and Richard Burton, Humphrey Bogart and Lauren Bacall, Wallis Simpson and Edward, Duke of Windsor, Liza Minnelli, Barbra Streisand, Madonna and Bill Gates, to name-drop a few). In essence, this is the sort of place where, for just one night, you can be Grace Kelly. Its secluded location high on a hillside preserves its air of exclusivity.

Splendido Mare, Via Roma 2, t 0185 267 802, f 0185 267 807 (*luxury*). The Spendido's smaller and newer sibling on the Piazza by the harbour. A less grand, slightly cheaper version of the original with a delightful al fresco restaurant, the Chufley Bar. A shuttle service links the two hotels. *Both closed Feb.*

****Nazionale, Via Roma 8, t 0185 269 575, f 0185 269 138, *www.nazionale portofino.com* (*luxury*). Smack on the port, with a slightly faded charm, furnished with antiques or reproductions. The best rooms, rather more expensive, have Venetian furniture and overlook the harbour. It has no parking, which can be a big problem in Portofino.

***Eden, Vico Dritto 18, t 0185 269 091, f 0185 269 047 (*very expensive*). Far from cheap, but the least expensive hotel in town. A charming 12-room establishment in the centre, endowed with a fine garden and good Ligurian restaurant.

Dining out in Portofino can be a rarefied experience. Most of the restaurants are clustered around Portofino's little piazza and port.

Il Pitosforo, Molo Umberto I 9, t 0185 269 020 (*very expensive*). The Ligurian cuisine is among the finest anywhere, whether you order bouillabaisse, spaghetti with prawns and mushrooms, the red mullet or sea bream with olives. A tree grows out of the middle of the dining room, and one whole wall is lined with a collection of spirits from

Santa Margherita, a rococo extravaganza with Italian and Flemish art. Just outside the town, towards Portofino, is the **Abbazia della Cervara**, where King Francis I was imprisoned after the Battle of Pavia. Boat excursions run to Portofino, San Fruttuoso and the Cinque Terre.

around the world that will make any serious drinker's eyes glaze over in delight. Every night at 10pm all the lights are switched off to highlight the magical view of the golden lights in the port. *Closed Tues.*

Da Puny, Piazza Martire Olivetta 7, **t** 0185 269 037 (*expensive*). Delicious pasta and seafood dishes for starters, and well-prepared main fish dishes, like sea bass baked in salt. *Closed Thurs.*

Taverna del Marinaio, Piazza Martire Olivetta 36, **t** 0185 269 103 (*moderate*). Although by no means cheap, it's as reasonable as you'll find in Portofino. The fish and pasta are excellent. *Closed Tues.*

Santa Margherita ✉ 16038

★★★★★**Imperiale Palace**, Via Pagana 19, on the edge of town, **t** 0185 288 991, **f** 0185 284 223, *info@hotelimperiale.it, www.hotelimperiale.com* (*luxury*). Formerly a private villa, converted into a hotel at the turn of the last century; in 1922, in one of the palatial marble- and gilt-encrusted public rooms, the Weimar Republic signed an agreement with Russia to re-open diplomatic relations. Antiques litter the hallways, public rooms and more expensive bedrooms, and concerts are held in the music room some afternoons. There's a heated outdoor pool, a lush tropical garden and a seafront terrace. The **restaurant** is rich and refined and leads on to a wonderful breakfast room overlooking the garden. *Closed Nov–Feb.*

★★★★**Grand Hotel Miramare**, Via Milite Ignoto 30, **t** 0185 287 013, **f** 0185 284 651, *miramare@pn.itnet.it, www.grandhotelmiramare.it* (*very expensive*). Shining white and almost as palatial, though purpose-built as a posh winter hotel in the early 1900s. Surrounded by a lovely garden, with a heated salt-water pool (and a pebbly beach across the road), it has lovely, many with fine views of the gulf from their balconies.

★★★**La Vela**, Via N.Cuneo 21, **t** 0185 284 771, *info@lavela.it, www.lavela.it* (*moderate*). A former villa located a bit above town, with a friendly, intimate atmosphere and 16 rooms with good sea views. *Closed Nov–Christmas.*

★★**Albergo Fasce**, Via L. Bozzo 3, **t** 0185 286 435, **f** 0185 283 580, *www.hotelfasce.it* (*moderate*). Santa Margherita's best value option in this category, and very friendly and welcoming. Part of the 'family hotel' chain. Its rooms are modern and immaculately maintained, and it also offers a laundry service, free bike hire, sun roof and a small garden. There's an excellent **restaurant**, where you can enjoy a full meal of delicious Ligurian specialities for not much more than L20,000 a head (*high season only*). *Closed Nov–Christmas.*

★**San Giorgio**, Via N. Cuneo 59, **t** 0185 286 770, **f** 0185 280 704 (*cheap*). A bit outside the centre, with nine pleasant rooms and an agreeable garden.

Cesarina, Via Mameli 2/c, **t** 0185 286 059 (*very expensive*). The finest restaurant in Santa Margherita, located under an arcade in the old part of town. The décor is fresh and modern, and goes well with such specialities as *zuppa di datteri* (razor clam soup) or Liguria's famous spaghetti with red mullet (*triglie*) sauce. Reservations are advisable. *Closed Tues.*

L'Ancora, Via Maragliano 7, **t** 0185 280 599 (*moderate*). Seafood specialities (an excellent *insalata di pesce*), and a good-value set tourist menu. *Closed Tues.*

Rapallo ✉ 16035

Rapallo has more hotels than any other resort on the Riviera di Levante.

★★★**Riviera**, Piazza IV Novembre 2, in the centre of Rapallo, **t** 0185 50248/9, **f** 0185 65668 (*expensive*). A converted villa near the sea. Remodelled inside, it has a popular glass terrace in the front and a garden at the rear.

★**Pensione Bandoni**, Via Marsala 24/3, **t** 0185 50423, **f** 0185 57206 (*cheap*). A good value,

Rapallo and Inland

After Portofino, Rapallo, tucked in the innermost corner of the Gulf of Tigullio, is the most famous resort on the Riviera di Levante, enjoying a mild year-round climate, and counts among its blessings a fairly good beach, an 18-hole golf course, busy tourist harbour, indoor pool, tennis, riding school, stables, and marvellous natural surround-

comfortable, simple hotel close to the seafront and right in the middle of town.

Osteria U Bansin, Via Venezia 105, **t** 0185 231 119 (*cheap*). Open since 1907, this truly authentic *osteria* attracts both blue and white-collar workers due to its quick service and wonderfully good, local food. *Closed Sun*. Otherwise the best cheap eateries are around Piazza Garibaldi and Via Venezia.

Chiávari ✉ 16043

Ca' Peo, Strada Panoramica, in Leivi, 6km from Chiávari, **t** 0185 319 696 (*very expensive*). One of the best restaurants on the Riviera. The atmosphere is elegant and charming, and the food imaginatively and delicately prepared, featuring ingredients like radicchio from Treviso, truffles from Alba, *porcini* mushrooms and very fresh fish, followed by excellent desserts and accompanied by noble wines. Reservations are a must. *Closed Mon, Wed lunch and Nov*.

Lord Nelson Pub, Corso Valparaiso 27, **t** 0185 302 595 (*very expensive*). May have dark woods and bottles, but the resemblance to a pub ends there: this is the most elegant gourmet restaurant in town, with delicate seafood dishes such as *ravioli* with smoked ricotta and shrimp and *dentice* (similar to sea bream) with pine nuts, olives and potatoes. Save room for the exquisite desserts. *Closed Wed*.

Felice, Via L. Risso 71, **t** 0185 308 016 (*moderate*). Serves a delicious *zimino* (fish soup) and other Ligurian dishes; it's small, so book. *Closed Mon*.

Sestri Levante ✉ 16039

★★★★★Grand Hotel dei Castelli, Via Penisola 26, **t** 0185 487 220, **f** 0185 44767 (*very expensive*). Built in the 1920s at the tip of the Isola peninsula on the site of a Genoese castle, and constructed from the castle's stone. The views of both bays and the sea crashing against the cliffs all around the hotel's park are magnificent, especially from the dining terrace. There's also a natural sea pool cut into the rock for safe swimming. *Closed Nov–April*.

★★★★Villa Balbi, Viale Rimembranza 1, **t** 0185 42941, **f** 0185 482 459, *www.villabalbi.it* (*very expensive*). Supremely stately pink palace on the seafront, built at the beginning of the 17th century for the Brignole family and full of unexpected treasures: a preserved library and a room decorated entirely with paintings of fish, as well as oak-beamed bedrooms and antique-laden public rooms. Much of the original garden remains, including a large camphor tree growing in the middle (indeed, through the roof) of the restaurant. *Closed Nov–Mar*.

★★★Helvetia, Via Cappuccini 43, **t** 0185 41175, **f** 0185 457 216, *www.hotelhelvetia.it* (*expensive*). A welcoming little hotel in the prettiest part of town, right on the Bay of Silence, with a large terraced garden.

★★★Mira, Via Rimembranza 15, **t** 0185 41576, **f** 0185 41577 (*moderate*). Family-run hotel with rooms with a view and a restaurant serving excellent fish specialities, including *riso marinara* and *nasello alla mira*, on a covered terrace overlooking the sea. *Closed Mon*.

Fiammenghilla Fieschi, Via Pestella 6, **t** 0185 481 041 (*very expensive*). Seafood and traditional Ligurian cuisine. A great place to try marinated swordfish, lobster, *focaccia* or *pansotti*. There's also a very good Ligurian wine list and a very expensive *menu degustazione* on offer. *Open evenings only*. *Closed Mon*.

Angiolina, Piazza Matteotti 51, **t** 0185 41198 (*expensive*). the place to go for excellent seaside dining: an exquisite *zuppa di pesce* and other delicious denizens of the deep. *Closed Tues*.

Polpo Mario, Via XXV Aprile 163, **t** 0185 480 203 (*moderate*). A nice cosy family restaurant a few streets back from the Bay of Silence.

ings. Rapallo was the longtime home of Max Beerbohm, who lived in the Villino Chiaro and attracted a notable literary circle; it is also a venue for conferences – at the **Villa Spinola**, Italy and Yugoslavia signed the Treaty of Rapallo in 1920. This villa lies along the Santa Margherita road, as does **San Michele di Pagana** containing a *Crucifixion* by Van Dyck, and the site of large festivals in July and September.

In Rapallo itself, the **castle**, surrounded by the harbour's waters, is now used for changing exhibitions. Further along the shore, there's the **Museo del Pizzo al Tombolo** in the Villa Tigullio (*open daily 3–6, Thurs 10–11.30; closed Mon*), dedicated to Rapallo's proudest age-old craft. Rapallo's main attraction is its **funivia** (*Mar–Oct 8–sunset; Nov–Feb 8.30–5; cars leave every 30mins*). The seven-minute trip will take you up 7,707ft, to the 16th-century **Santuario di Montallegro**, on the site where a vision of the Madonna appeared to a local farmer, with a Byzantine icon which miraculously flew here from Dalmatia and a spectacular view of the coast.

Inland from this stretch of coast there are two attractive hill resorts: one is **Uscio**, reached by the SS333 road from Recco, a health spa and manufacturer of large campanile clocks. From Rapallo and the Montallegro, a long, winding road arrives after about an hour at **Santo Stefano d'Aveto**, up in the Ligurian Apennines, where Rapallo's wintertime visitors head for a taste of snow and a bit of skiing at just over 1000m, as well as a scenic 8km cablecar excursion. Santo Stefano's landmark is the imposing **Castello Malaspina**.

Chiávari and Lavagna

East of Rapallo, **Zoagli** is a small seaside village that has produced patterned velvets ever since they were fashion's rage in the Middle Ages, although nowadays people prefer it for dressing their furniture instead of themselves; most of the velvet factories are open for visits. A seaside path cut into the rock offers lovely views over the gulf. **Chiávari**, the next town, was founded as a colony of Genoa in 1178, and is a craft centre for straw chairs, and macramé, an art brought back by the town's sailors from the Middle East, and still used to adorn towels and tablecloths with intricate fringes, although easy money from tourism leaves them by wayside. Orchids are another local speciality, their blooms best seen at the annual show at the end of February.

The centre of life in Chiávari is **Piazza Mazzini**, with a lively morning market, tower and stern palaces and a monument dedicated to Liguria's favourite revolutionary. A few streets away, the **Palazzo Rocca**, Via Costaguta 2, has a beautiful garden designed by Bartolomeo Bianco (1629), and houses two museums: the **Civica Galleria** (*open Sat and Sun 10–12 and 4–7.30*), with works by the Genoese school, and the **Civico Museo Archeologico** (*open daily 9–1.30*), with items found in the nearby 8th–7th-century BC necropolis, demonstrating trade links with the Phoenicians, Greeks and Egyptians. Another place to aim for, **Caffè Defilla**, Via Garibaldi 4, founded in 1883, has excellent ice-cream and pastries. In Chiávari's newer quarters, there's a small pleasure port near the long sandy beach. A road leads from here to Santo Stefano d'Aveto.

Lavagna, which is separated from Chiávari by a bridge over the Entella, has an equally long beach. It was ruled in the Middle Ages by the Fieschi, who produced a 13th-century pope, Innocent IV, and Count Opizzo Fieschi, whose marriage to Bianca dei Bianchi in 1230 made such an impression on Lavagna that the anniversary (14 August) is re-enacted each year, finishing with the communal eating of the gargantuan *Torta dei Fieschi*. Innocent IV, on the other hand, is remembered in the beautiful early Gothic church he built, the **Basilica di San Salvatore dei Fieschi**, half an hour's walk inland near Cogorno.

Sestri Levante

Sestri Levante overlooks a lovely, curving peninsula called the Isola, dividing the 'Bay of Silence' from what Hans Christian Andersen himself christened the 'Bay of Fables'. It has a picturesque sandy beach, and more than its share of touristic development. The magnificent garden on the peninsula belongs to Albergo dei Castello, where Marconi performed his first experiments with radio waves; below it stands the fine Romanesque church of **San Nicolò**, with views of the two bays. The **Galleria Rizzi**, on the Bay of Silence (*Via Cappuccini 8; open April–Oct Wed 4–7, Fri and Sat 9pm–11pm, Sun 10–1*), contains works by the Florentine, Emilian and Ligurian schools, ceramics and a small furniture collection.

From Sestri a bus heads inland along the tortuous SS523 to **Varese Ligure**, the chief town of the Val di Vara, an agricultural and market centre and summer resort. It has an unusual core, the perfectly circular Borgo Rotundo, laid out in the late 15th century by the Fieschi, who offered land to any merchant who would build a house in a ring around the market. The Fieschi also owned the recently restored 15th-century castle. North of Varese, the scenery is lush and rolling, dotted with tiny slate-roofed hamlets.

The Cinque Terre and La Spezia

Before sliding down to the comparatively dull and flat coast of Tuscany, the Riviera bows out with a dramatic flourish around the rugged, almost inaccessible cliffs of the Cinque Terre, the rocky peninsula of Portovenere, and La Spezia's lovely 'Gulf of Poets'. One particular plus point of this area is that prices, especially for accommodation, are noticeably more reasonable than elsewhere along the Riviera.

Sestri Levante to the Cinque Terre

After Sestri Levante, the Apennines move in and crowd the coast, admitting here and there little glens and sandy strands – at sleepy **Moneglia** (from the Latin *monellia*, or jewel), with its quiet stretch of beach framed by two medieval castles, Monleone and Villafranca, **Deiva Marina**, near the pretty village of Framura, **Bonassola**, and, most importantly, **Levanto**, which has a good sandy beach, flower gardens, and several monuments from the 13th century – the **Loggia** (town hall), the church of **Sant'Andrea**, and chunks of its walls.

Next on the coast, **Monterosso al Mare** is the first of the towns of the **Cinque Terre** ('The Five Lands'), as they've been known since the Middle Ages. Perched wherever the cliffs and hills permitted enough space to build, surrounded by steep slopes corrugated by hundreds of terraces laboriously carved out of the earth and rock, the Cinque Terre towns are visually stunning. They also enjoy a fine, mild climate, and the vineyards that occupy the near-vertical terraces produce the region's finest (and most potent) wines – the ones labelled Sciacchetrà are made from raisins, and can be either dry or sweet. Formerly accessible only by sea or by a spectacular series of cliff-skirting footpaths, the towns have maintained much of their charm, even though nowadays they are far from being undiscovered.

Getting Around

The easiest way to reach the Cinque Terre is by **train** from Genoa or La Spezia. Each of the five towns has a station, only a few minutes apart and separated by long tunnels; afterwards the train drills through the mountains straight to La Spezia and Sarzana, from where you can continue on towards Parma or Pisa.

There are **buses** from Piazza Chiodo in La Spezia to Riomaggiore and Manarola, Portovenere (every 15 minutes), Lerici, Sarzana and Florence.

There are also several **boat** lines serving the area, linking La Spezia, Lerici, Portovenere and the Cinque Terre; **NGP** goes as far as Portofino to the north, and Marina di Massa and Marina di Carrara in Tuscany; **Fratelli Rossignoli**, sails between Monterosso and Viareggio during summer. Ferries sail between La Spezia and Bastia, Corsica daily in summer, and less frequently at other times.

Tourist Information

Lévanto: Piazza Cavour, t 0187 808 125.
Monterosso al Mare: Via Fegina 38, t 0187 817 506 (*summer season only*).
La Spezia: Viale Mazzini 45, t 0187 770 900, f 0187 770 908; in the station, t 0187 718 997.
Portovenere: Piazza Bastreri 1, t 0187 790 691, f 0187 790 215.
Lerici: Via Biaggini 6, t 0187 967 346.
Sarzana: in the town hall, Piazza Matteotti, t 0187 6141, f 0187 614 225.

Where to Stay and Eat

Moneglia ✉ 16030

★★★**Villa Edera**, Via Venino 12, t 0187 492 291, f 0187 49470, *www.villaedera.com* (*moderate*). Nice, quiet, bright pink, family-run hotel set in the hills a few minutes from the beach, directly next to the medieval Castello Monleone. The rooms are basic but comfortable, with good views of the countryside. It also has a lovely **restaurant** featuring homemade regional specialities.
Rocca Incatenata, Punta Rospo, t 0185 49476 (*expensive*). The 'Enchanted Citadel' is a bit

hard to reach through the tunnels, but lives up to its name, a lovely spot directly on the wine-dark sea, with a menu based on the day's catch. *Closed Mon except in summer.*

Monterosso al Mare ✉ 19016

Of the five towns of the Cinque Terre, Monterosso has the best accommodation.
★★★★**Porto Roca**, Via Corone 1, t 0187 817 502, f 0187 817 692, *www.portoroca.it* (*very expensive*). The top choice, on the headland, with lovely views of the sea from all the rooms.
★★★**Degli Amici**, Via Burranco 36, t 0187 817 544, f 0187 817 424 (*moderate*). Probably the best budget option, in the old part of town and 150m from the beach. The rooms are light and airy, some with balcony, and there's an excellent restaurant.
Il Gigante, Via IV Novembre, t 0187 817 401 (*moderate*). The best food in Monterosso. Especially good Ligurian specialities – *pansotti*, *trenette al pesto* and fresh fish.

Vernazza ✉ 19018

★**Sorriso**, Via Gavino 4, t 0187 812 224 (*cheap*). An honest little inn with very inexpensive rooms and a well-known restaurant.
Gambero Rosso, Piazza Marconi 7, t 0187 812 265 (*moderate*). Well-known restaurant that's partly carved out of the rock; try the *tegame di acciughe*, a dish made with the Cinque Terre's special anchovies, but there's plenty of less piquant seafood, too.
Da Capitano, t 0187 812 201 (*moderate*). Fine fish fare on the square – try the *linguine ai granchi*, washed down with a glass of the genial Captain's own wine.

Manarola ✉ 19010

★★★**Marina Piccola**, t 0187 920 103, f 0187 920 966 (*cheap*). A good place to get away from it all, with 10 simple rooms and a very nice restaurant. Rooms are better in the main hotel than in the annexe.
Aristide, Via Roma, t 0187 920 000 (*moderate*). The choice *trattoria*, serving a delicious *minestra* and fish dishes, also rabbit, game and other meat in season.

La Spezia ✉ 19100

★★★★**Jolly**, Via XX Settembre 2, t 0187 739 555, f 0187 22129 (*very expensive*). La Spezia's finest accommodation. A modern and rather stylish member of the Italian hotel chain, with views stretching to the gulf.

★Flavia, Vicolo dello Stagno 7, **t** 0187 736 060, off Via del Prione (*cheap*). One of the best bargains, not far from the station.

Parodi, Viale Amendola 210, **t** 0187 715 777 (*expensive*). Elegant restaurant just off the seafront, serving the best gourmet dishes in the city, with a tempting menu of market-fresh ingredients featuring all the best from the land and sea; great choice of wines and spirits too. *Closed Sun.*

There are a good number of low-price restaurants, much patronized by the naval personnel who are everywhere in the town, mainly concentrated around Via del Prione.

Osteria All'Inferno, Via Lorenzo Costa 3, **t** 0187 29 458 (*moderate*). Housed in an old coal cellar, this inconspicuous restaurant has been run by the same family since 1905. Though originally just an *enoteca* (wine bar) they have been serving local delights such as *mesciua* and *porcetta al forno* since 1945. *Closed Sun and whole of Aug.*

Portovenere ✉ 19025

★★★★Grand Hotel Portovenere, Via Garibaldi 5, **t** 0187 792 610, **f** 0187 790 661, *ghp@village.it* (*expensive*). In a 17th-century Franciscan convent, beautifully set by the sea with views across the gulf and Palmaria. The former cells have been converted into stylish rooms; there's a restaurant with terrace.

★★★Paradiso, Via Garibaldi 34, **t** 0187 790 612, **f** 0187 792 582 (*moderate*). Little family-run hotel with lovely views from its seaside terrace, and cosy, well-equipped rooms.

★★Genio, Piazza Bastreri 8, **t** 0187 790 611 (*cheap*). The cheapest rooms in town, and a nice little garden, too.

Iseo, in Calata Doria, **t** 0187 790 610 (*expensive*). Portovenere's best known restaurant, featuring accurate renditions of the classics, and an especially delicious spaghetti with seafood. *Closed Wed, Jan, Feb.*

La Taverna del Corsaro, Lungomare Doria 182, **t** 0187 790 622 (*expensive*). In one of the most delightful locations in town at the beginning of the promontory, where you can savour delicacies like prawn in bell-pepper sauce and *zuppa di datteri* (razor clams).

Lerici ✉ 19032

★★★Shelley & Delle Palme, Lungomare Biaggini 5, **t** 0187 968 204, **f** 0187 964 271, *www.charmerelax.it* (*moderate*). One of the largest and most comfortable hotels on the 'Gulf of Poets', with fine views of the sea.

★★★Byron, Via Biaggini 19, **t** 0187 967 104, **f** 0187 967 409, *hbyron@cdh.it* (*moderate*). Also a good choice, on the left as you approach the town, where the smallish rooms are compensated for by views across the bay and some huge balconies.

★★Hotel del Golfo, Via Gerini 37, **t** 0187 967 400, **f** 0187 965 733 (*cheap*). The only inexpensive hotel in Lerici, just up from the tourist office. Some rooms have balconies.

Due Corona, Via G Mazzini, **t** 0187 967 417 (*very expensive*). The best restaurant in Lerici, beside the port, the deserving winner of two culinary awards. Seafood is, of course, a speciality; try their *cocktail di antipasti mare* and *grigliata mista*. *Closed Thurs.*

Ameglia ✉ 19031

Ameglia is the gourmet vortex for this far east end of the Riviera.

★★★Paracucchi Locanda dell'Angelo, at Ca' di Scabello, Viale V Aprile 60, **t** 0187 64391/2, **f** 0187 64393 (*moderate*). The pioneer establishment, comprising a modern, stylish and slick hotel, with a pool and the sea only a couple of minutes away; the **restaurant** (*very expensive*), founded by one of Italy's most famous chefs and cookbook writers, Angelo Parcucchi – and now run by son Marco – is top notch, although not as good as Tamerici; the menu changes often, but each dish is superb and often amazingly simple. Great desserts, especially the fruit flambée, and excellent wine list. *Closed Sun eve and Mon out of season.*

★★★Locanda delle Tamerici, Via Litoranea 116, **t** 0187 64262, **f** 0187 64627 (*rooms moderate, restaurant very expensive*). Also down by the sea at Fiumaretta, with cosy, adorable, tranquil rooms and a romantic flower-filled garden; the restaurant rivals Angelo's for its lovely, flavour-enhanced seafood and vegetable dishes. A few days here on full board, unwinding by the sea, is one of the nicest and most effective possible cures for stress. *Closed Tues.*

Monterosso is the most touristy of the five, with beaches (free and 'organized'), hotels, rooms in private houses, and so on, and boats to hire for personal tours of the coast. Most of the facilities are in the new half of town, Fegina, separated from the old by a hill crowned with the **Convento dei Cappuccini** (1622) and a medieval tower; the 18th-century **Santuario di Soviore**, built over an older church, hosts a music festival in the summer. From Monterosso it's a momentary train ride or a lovely hour-and-a-half walk to the next town, **Vernazza**, founded by the Romans on a rocky spit, a striking vision from the footpath above. Its parish church, Santa Margherita of Antioch, was built in 1318.

The hour-and-a-half walk from Vernazza to **Corniglia** is one of the most strenuous, for Corniglia, unlike the other towns, is high up on the cliffs and not on the sea, though it does have the longest (though pebbly) beach. From Corniglia another hour's walk through splendid scenery leads to **Manarola**, a colourful fishing village built along steep lanes, all piled on a great black rock. It is linked in 20 minutes or so to Riomaggiore by the most popular section of the footpath, the 'Via dell'Amore', carved into the cliff face over the sea. **Riomaggiore**, one of the prettiest towns, also sees plenty of visitors, who crowd its lively cafés and rocky beaches.

La Spezia

The largest city in the region, the provincial capital, and a major naval base, La Spezia was bombed heavily in the Second World War and presents a modern but cheerful face to the world, standing at the head of one of Italy's prettiest gulfs. Mostly used by visitors as a base for visiting the Cinque Terre and Portovenere, it has a number of attractions in its own right – among them a promenade of swaying palms and lush public gardens.

On the hill, the recently restored medieval Castello San Giorgio, now the **Museo del Castello** (*Via XXVII Marzo,* **t** *0187 751 142; open summer daily 9.30–12.30 and 5–8; winter daily 9.30–12.30 and 2–5; closed Tues; adm*), houses the Ubaldo Formentini Collection, an important archaeological section, with prehistoric finds from Palmaria's Grotta dei Colombi, pre-Roman and Roman material from Luni and, most notably, Ligurian stelae from the Bronze and Iron Ages. The excellent **naval museum**, in Piazza Chiodo, next to the Naval Arsenal (*open Tues–Thurs and Sat 9–12 and 2–6, Mon and Fri 2–6; adm*) contains a fine collection begun in 1560 by Emanuele Filiberto, with relics of the ships sent by the Savoys to the Battle of Lepanto, as well as models, figureheads and mementos from Italy's naval battles. **The Museo Amedeo Lia** (*Via Prione 234; open daily 10–6; closed Mon; adm exp*), housed in a former convent in the centre of town, contains works by Giovanni Mazone, Giacomo Recco and Titian.

Portovenere and Palmaria

South of La Spezia the road is delightful but winding (if you're prone to car sickness, take the boat), and passes by way of the pretty cove of **Le Grazie** before ending at **Portovenere**. With its long promontory, castle and pastel houses, Portovenere is fittingly named after the goddess of love herself, a protectress of fishfolk. The temple of Venus stood at the tip of the promontory, until it was upstaged by a church dedicated to Christianity's top fisherman, **San Pietro**. This strange little church of black and white striped marble dates from 1277, while below are a few colourful remains of its 6th-century predecessor. It enjoys splendid views of Palmaria and the Cinque Terre coast; the lovely bay below once held the Grotta Arpaia, where Byron wrote *The Corsair*, and from where he swam across the gulf to Lerici and Shelley's villa. It collapsed in the 1930s.

The best thing to do in Portovenere is wander through its narrow, cat-crowded lanes (this is Italy's champion kitty city), past tall ancient houses on the waterfront with interesting details on the doorways, built by the Genoese, who fortified the town in the early 12th century (as the Pisans had fortified Lerici across the gulf).

A lane leads up to the lovely church of **San Lorenzo** (1130), with a bas-relief of St Lawrence being toasted on his gridiron over the door; inside is Portovenere's most precious relic, the *Madonna Bianca*, said to have floated to the town encased in a cedar log in the 13th century (the log, too, is on display). Further up, a steep but worthwhile walk leads to the 16th-century Genoese *castello*, with marvellous views (*open April–Oct daily 10–12 and 2–6; Nov–Mar daily 3–5*).

From Portovenere you can cross the 400m channel to **Isola Palmaria** and visit its famed **Grotta Azzurra** – though a much cheaper proposition is to book a passage from La Spezia. Palmaria, site of a Neolithic settlement, produces the black, gold-veined marble you may have noticed in Portovenere. The much smaller **Isola del Tino**, with a lighthouse and the ruins of an 8th-century monastery, and the even tinier **Tinetto**, lie further out.

Lerici

Lerici, on its own little bay, is the most important town on the east shore of the 'Golfo dei Poeti'. Tit for Portovenere's tat, its imposing *castello* (*open daily 9–12 and 2–midnight; adm*), towering up on its promontory, was built by the Pisans, and enlarged by the Genoese in the 15th century; inside you can visit the Chapel of Sant'Anastasia (1250). Lerici has a nice beach and mild winter climate, and its environs were beloved by Shelley, whose last home was the Casa Magni in **San Terenzo**, the charming fishing village across the bay; it was from here that he sailed, in 1822, to meet Leigh Hunt at Livorno, only to shipwreck and drown by Viareggio. To the south is the enchanting, tranquil, tiny cove and beach of **Fiascherino**, where D. H. Lawrence lived from 1913 to 1914; beyond is the unspoiled medieval hamlet of **Tellaro**. Another scenic road continues around the gulf and begins to climb up the Val di Magra to **Ameglia**, with its 10th-century castle, and the slate portals of the older houses.

Sarzana and Ancient Luni

From La Spezia, bridges cross the River Magra for **Sarzana**, once the easternmost edge of the Republic of Genoa: an ancient town guarded by a Medici citadel and the **Fortezza di Sarzello** (a mile east), a great stone steam iron built in the early-14th century by the tyrant of Lucca, Castruccio Castracani. The 14th-century **cathedral** contains one of the best works of Master Guglielmo: a *Crucifixion* of 1138; other churches of note include **Sant'Andrea** and **San Francesco**, which have good sculptures.

To the north in **Fosdinovo**, the Malaspina castle which hosted Dante in 1306; he is also said to have visited the ruined 13th-century castle in **Castelnuovo Magra**. The church contains a *Calvary* by Brueghel the Younger.

Ortonovo lies near the site of the ancient Roman town and marble-shipping port of **Luni**, founded in 177 BC as a bulwark against the fierce Ligurians. The city survived until 1204, when its bishopric was moved to Sarzana and malaria led to its desertion. Excavations have revealed a sizeable amphitheatre, forum, houses, temples and so on; on the site the **Museo Nazionale di Luni** (*open April–Sept Tues–Sun 9–12 and 3–7; Oct–Mar Tues–Sun 2–7; adm*) has marble statuary, coins, jewellery, portraits, etc., as well as a display of archaeological techniques used in excavating the site. If you're continuing down the coast from here, *see* 'The Tuscan Coast', p.695.

Lombardy and the Lakes

Lombardy and the Lakes

SWITZERLAND

Highlights

1 Milan's cathedral, Galleria and museums

2 Gonzaga frescoes in Mantua

3 Resort villages and Borromean islands of Lake Maggiore

4 The refined art city of Bergamo

5 Lake Garda: palms, lemon groves and castles at the foot of the Alps

Of all the barbarians who desecrated the corpse of the Roman Empire, none was more barbaric than the Lombards (or Longobards), a tall Germanic tribe who bled much of the peninsula dry before settling down in the region that still bears their name. Even today the Milanese are taller than the average Italian, although whether it's because of their Lombard blood or prosperity is anyone's guess. Since the Middle Ages Lombardy has been the economic powerhouse of Italy. The complaint that Milan makes money while Rome wastes it is almost as old as the city itself.

Frenetic Milan, the pounding, racing economic heart of modern Italy, is the centre of gravity for the entire north. It always has been, for its geography has meant that the destinies of entire empires and kingdoms have been decided here, not to mention religions – Christianity was made the religion of the Roman Empire in Milan.

Lombardy has its gentle side as well. This was the homeland of epic Virgil and lyric Catullus, of composers Donizetti and Monteverdi, of the great violin masters, Amati, Guarneri and Stradivarius. And since the 18th century countless poets, composers and weary aristocrats have come for the peace and beauty of the Italian Lakes – which, although partially in Piemonte, Switzerland and the Veneto, have all been included here for convenience's sake.

Milan

Most tourists don't come to Italy looking for slick, feverish Milan, and most of those who find themselves here take in only the obligatory sights – Leonardo's *Last Supper*, La Scala, the Duomo, the Brera, and the shops. Most Italians (apart from the almost two million Milanese, that is) have little good to say about their second city either: all the Milanese do is work, all they care about is money, and they refuse to indulge the myth of *la dolce vita*. The Italians who deride Milan (many of whom work just as many hours themselves) are mostly envious, and the tourists who whip through it in a day are mostly ignorant of what this great city has to offer. Milan is indeed atypical, devoid of the usual Italian daydreams and living-museum mustiness. Like Naples it lives for the present, but not in Naples' endearing anarchy; as one of Europe's financial centres and a capital of fashion, Milan dresses in a well-tailored, thoroughly cosmopolitan three-piece suit. The skills of its workers, above all in the luxury clothing trades, have been known for centuries – as evoked in the English word 'millinery'.

And yet, as the Milanese are the first to admit, Milan has made its way in the world not so much by native talent as through the ability to attract it, from St Ambrose and Leonardo da Vinci to the designer of the moment. It has produced no great music of its own, but La Scala is one of the world's most prestigious places to sing; it has produced very few artists of its own but has amassed enough treasures to fill four superb galleries. Milan is the Italian melting pot, Italy's picture window on the modern world, where the young and ambitious gravitate to see their talents appreciated and rewarded. Here history seems to weigh less; here willowy Japanese models slink down the pavement with natty young gents whose parents immigrated from Calabria. Roiling, moiling, toiling, constantly evolving, Milan is *sui generis*; in Milanese dialect they have said, since long before Gertrude Stein's 'a rose is a rose', *Milan l'e Milan*, Milan is Milan.

History

Milan was born cosmopolitan. Although located far from any sea or river, in the midst of the fertile Lombard plain, it occupies the natural junction of trade routes through the Alpine passes, from the Tyrrhenian and Adriatic ports and the River Po. This commercially strategic position has also put Milan square in the path of every

St Ambrose (Sant'Ambrogio)

No sooner had Christianity received the imperial stamp of approval than it split into two hostile camps: the orthodox, early-Catholic traditionalists and the followers of the Egyptian bishop Arius. Arians denied that Christ was of the same substance as God; the sect was widespread among the peoples on the fringes of the Roman Empire. An early bishop of Milan was an Arian and persecutor of the orthodox, and a schism seemed inevitable when he died. When the young consular governor Ambrose spoke to calm the crowd during the election of the new bishop, a child's voice suddenly piped up: 'Ambrose Bishop!' The cry was taken up, and Ambrose, who hadn't even been baptized, suddenly found himself thrust into a new job.

According to legend, when Ambrose was an infant in Rome, bees had flown into his mouth, attracted by the honey of his tongue. Ambrose's eloquence as bishop (374–97) is given much of the credit for preserving the unity of the Church; when the widow of Emperor Valentine desired to raise her son as an Arian, demanding a Milanese basilica for Arian worship, Ambrose and his supporters held the church through a nine-day siege, converting the empress' soldiers in the process. His most famous convert was St Augustine, and he also set what was to become the standard in relations between Church and Empire when he refused to allow Emperor Theodosius to enter church until he had done penance for ordering a civilian massacre in Thessalonika.

Ambrose left such an imprint on Milan that to this day genuine Milanese are called Ambrosiani. Their church, which was practically independent from Rome until the 11th century, still celebrates Mass according to the Ambrosian rite and holds its own carnival of Sant'Ambrogio in March.

conqueror tramping through Italy. Mediolanum, as it was called for its first millennium and a half, first became prominent in the twilight of Rome when, as the headquarters of the Mobile Army and the seat of the Western government, it became the de facto capital of the Empire; Diocletian preferred it to Rome, and his successors spent much of their time here. The official Christianization of the empire began here in 313, when Constantine established religious toleration with his Edict of Milan.

The Rise of the Comune

During the next few centuries 'Mediolanum' was shortened to Mailand, the prized Land of May, for so it seemed to the frostbitten Goths and Lombards who came to grab it. In the early 11th century Milan became Italy's first comune under the leadership of another great bishop, Heribert, who organized a parlamento of citizens and a citizen militia. The new comune – Guelph in defiance of imperial pretensions – at once began subjugating its Ghibelline rivals Pavia, Lodi and Como. To inspire the militia, Heribert also invented that unique Italian war machine, the carroccio, a huge ox-drawn cart that bore the city's banner, altar and bells into battle, to remind the soldiers of the city and church they fought for.

It was Lodi's complaint to Emperor Frederick Barbarossa about Milan's bullying that first brought old Red Beard to Italy in 1154. It was to prove a momentous battle

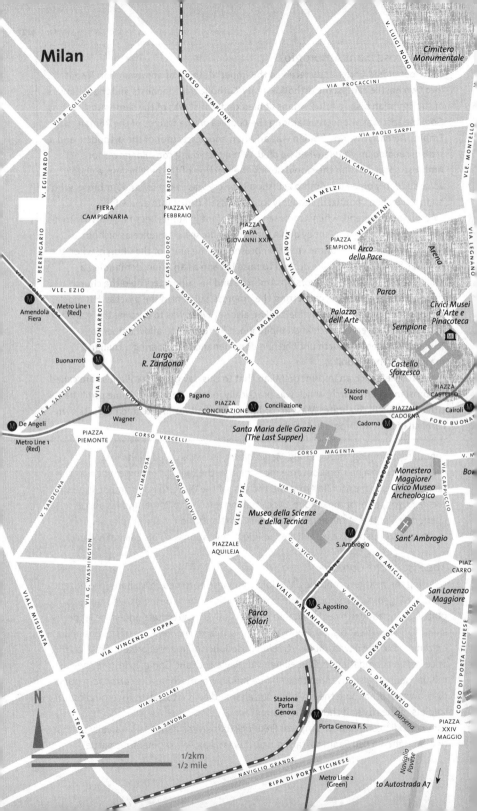

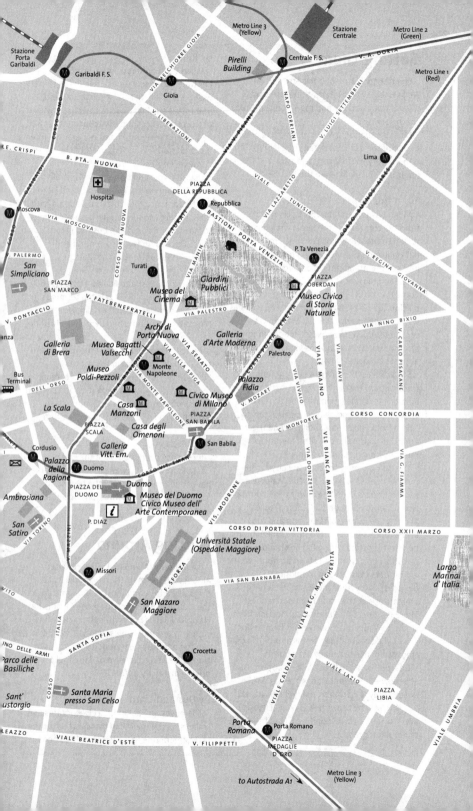

Getting There

The transport hub of northern Italy, Milan is well served by two international **airports**, several **train** stations and many long-distance **coach** services.

Milan's expanding **Metro** network is, as well as one of the quickest means of getting from A to B, a very useful orientation aid, and stops (indicated Ⓜ) are listed in the text below.

From the Airport

Milan has two main airports, **Linate** (8km from the centre) and the larger **Malpensa** (50km to the west), both of which receive national and international flights. As a rule, intercontinental flights use Malpensa while Linate handles most of the European and domestic traffic – but check. For **flight information** call t 02 7485 2200 or visit the website *www.sea-aeroportimilano.it*. Malpensa's second *terminal ovest* (west) opened in 1998 after 10 years' work and has increased the airport's capacity by half.

STAM buses (L5,000) run every 30 minutes from 5.40am to 9pm between Linate and Stazione Centrale (running time 20 minutes approx). **City bus** no. 73 (L1,500) also runs to Linate from Piazza San Babila (Ⓜ line 1), corner Corso Europa, in the city centre, every 10 minutes from 5.30am to 2am.

The quickest way to reach the city centre from Malpensa is by rail shuttle **Malpensa Express** (t 02 20222). The journey to Cadorna North Railway Station (Ⓜ Cadorna) takes about 40 minutes, costs L15,000 and runs every 30mins from 5am to 11pm. **Air Pullman** bus shuttles (t 02 5858 3185) link Malpensa to the Stazione Centrale in about an hour every 20 minutes from 4.15am to midnight (L13,000). Every hour there is a bus service which stops at the Trade Fair upon request. There is a direct Air Pullman connection from Linate to Malpensa, hourly from 6am to 8pm (cost L18,000, duration 75mins approx). Taxis from Malpensa to Milan cost a bomb.

Charter flights may use a third airport, **Orio al Serio**, near Bergamo, t 035 326 323. STAB buses –they're harmless, really (t 035 318 472) link it to Milan's Stazione Centrale (L13,000) and vice versa, corresponding to the timetable of regular flights.

By Rail

Milan's splendiferous main **Stazione Centrale** (Ⓜ lines 2, 3), designed in the thirties with the travelling Fascist satrap in mind, dominates the Piazza Duca d'Aosta northeast of the centre. Centrale (switchboard t 147 888 088, open 7am–11pm) handles nearly all international trains, as well as most of the domestic routes.

Useful trams and buses from Centrale include tram no. 1 to Piazza Scala and Nord Station, and no. 33 to Stazione Garibaldi and the Cimitero Monumentale; bus no. 60 goes to Piazza del Duomo and bus no. 65 runs down Corso Buenos Aires, Corso Venezia and through the centre to Corso Italia.

Left Luggage, t 02 6371 2212. Open 4am–1.30am. **Lost and Found**, t 02 6371 2667.

Stazione Garibaldi (Ⓜ 2) is the terminus for car-train services, as well as trains for Pavia, Monza, Varese, Como and Bergamo. Stazione Lambrate (Ⓜ 2), on the east side of the city, has connections to Genoa, Bergamo and towards the Simplon Pass. Stazione Cadorna (Ⓜ Cadorna) is the main station of Lombardy's regional Milan Nord railway (t 02 20222, open 24hrs) with connections to Como, Varese, Saronno, Erba and Laveno (Lake Maggiore).

By Coach

Inter-city coaches arrive in the Piazza Castello (Ⓜ Cairoli), where several companies have their offices. Contact the tourist office for information on destinations, schedules and prices.

Getting Around

Even though Milan looks like a bloated amoeba on the map, the city marks its age in rings, like a tree, and most of its sights are in the walkable innermost ring, the Cerchia dei Navigli. Milan is not a difficult place to find your way around – unless you've brought a car: the one-way system, no traffic zones in the centre and expensive parking make driving distinctly unfun.

By Bus and Tram

The buses and dashing Art Deco trams and trolleys run by the **Milan transport authority** (ATM, freephone from within Italy t 800

016857, *www.atm-mi.it*) are convenient and their routes well marked. Purchase **tickets** (L1,500, or carnets of 10 tickets, L14,000) in advance at tobacconists, news-stands, metro stations or in the coin-gobbling machines at the main stops, and stamp them in the machines on board; a ticket is valid for 75 minutes' travel anywhere on the network above ground, regardless of how many transfers you make, but tickets can only be used once on the metro. Most bus routes run from about **6am to midnight**, after which time special **night bus** routes operate with reasonable frequency. If you plan to be riding around a fair bit, buy a **one-day pass** (L5,000), or two-day pass (L9,000), valid for buses, trams and the metro. The ATM also publishes a very useful **map** showing all the bus routes and metro stops, the *Guida Rete dei Trasporti Pubblici*, available at the tourist office and the Stazione Centrale.

By Metro

The Metropolitana Milanese (Ⓜ), begun in the sixties, is sleek and well run, and a boon for the bewildered tourist. There are three lines, the **Red** (Ⓜ 1), **Green** (Ⓜ 2), and **Yellow** (Ⓜ 3), the last of which was completed in 1990. The Metro is open from **6am to midnight** daily, and tickets are the same as those used for the buses or trams.

By Taxi

Milanese taxis are white and their drivers generally honest and reliable. They can be found waiting at ranks in the Piazza del Duomo, by the Stazione Centrale, and in several other central piazzas. Alternatively, **book a taxi** on **t** 02 8383, **t** 02 6767, **t** 02 3100 or **t** 02 5353. On entering the taxi you pay a charge of L6,000.

Tourist Information

Piazza del Duomo on Via Marconi 1, **t** 02 7252 4301/2/3, **f** 7252 4350 (*open Mon–Fri 8.30–7; Sat 9–1 and 2–6; Sun 9–1 and 2–5*).
Stazione Centrale (*open Mon–Sat 8am–7pm, Sun 9–12.30 and 1.30–6*). Both provide an updated list of accommodation, good city maps and other practical information.

Milan Hotelliers Association, Corso Buenos Aires 77, **t** 02 674 8031, *www.traveleurope.it.*
Milano Hotels Central Booking, **t** 02 805 4242, *www.hotelbooking.com.* Hotel reservations.

Shopping

Most shops are closed all day Sunday and Monday mornings (except during the Christmas period), and in August. Food stores close on Monday afternoons.

Milan is Italy's best shopping city hands down, and most especially for clothes and everything else capable of being designed in one way or another. Italians have always liked to put on the dog, *la bella figura*; it's in their blood. The hype machine has turned this traditional trait into a national obsession. After an hour of window-shopping only a die-hard fashion slave would disagree with Walter Benjamin's 'Monotony is nourished by the new'. The big **sales** begin the second week of January and around 10 July.

The Quadrilateral

Missoni, Valentino, Armani, Laura Biagiotti, Versace, Byblos, Krizia, Luciano Soprani, Dolce e Gabbana, Alberta Ferretti, Ferragamo, Prada, Gucci, Chanel, Helmut Lang, Fendi, Ferre, Gigli, Krizia, Moschino – you'll find them all in the Quadrilatero, defined by Via Monte Napoleone, Via della Spiga, Via S. Andrea and Via Borgospesso (Ⓜ Monte Napoleone). Nearly all the shops here have branch offices elsewhere in Milan and in other cities. You may just find the latest of the latest designs on Monte Napoleone, but be assured they'll soon show up elsewhere. The **jewellers** were actually here first, in the 1930s; have a look in the windows at **Buccellati**, considered by many the best designer in Italy, featuring exquisitely delicate gold work and jewels, each piece individually crafted. Other Quadrilateral shops worth a browse include **Lorenzi**, Monte Napoleone 9, the city's most refined pipe and male accessories shop. **Il Salumaio** has nearly every gourmet item imaginable.

City Centre

Besides the great **Galleria Vittorio Emanuele**, several minor *gallerie* branch off the Corso Vittorio Emanuele, each a shopping arcade lined with good quality and reasonably priced shops.

In Piazza del Duomo a monument almost as well known as the cathedral itself is Milan's biggest and oldest department store, **La Rinascente**; it's also the only one to have been christened by Gabriele D'Annunzio. La Rinascente has six floors of merchandise, with especially good clothing and domestic sections, offering a wide array of kitchen gear dear to the heart of an Italian cook. The cafeteria on the top floor has great views over the cathedral.

Other shops in the centre include **Guenzati**, Via Mercanti 1, which will make a velvet-lover's heart flutter; they also do made-to-order. Near the Duomo, Via Spadari and Via Speroni are a food shopper's heaven, beginning with the **Casa del Formaggio**, Via Speronari 3, where the best cheeses, from the most exotic to the most everyday, have been sold since 1894. At Via Spadari 9 stop at **Peck**, the home of Milanese gastronomy, where you can queue for a wide choice of Italian and foreign deli-catessen delights.

Rizzoli, Galleria Vittorio Emanuele 79, is one of the city's best-stocked bookshops (with many English titles), owned by the family that founded the *Corriere della Sera*. In the Galleria del Corso, **Messaggerie Musicali** is one of the best for musical scores and recordings.

Elsewhere in Milan

Brera offers some of Milan's most original shops and boutiques, as well as old standbys like **Surplus**, Corso Garibaldi 7, with a marvellous array of second-hand garments.

On Corso Buenos Aires (🚇 Lima), one of Milan's longest and densest shopping thoroughfares, you can find something of every variety and hue; one unusual shop is **Le Mani d'Oro**, Via Gaffurio 5 (near Piazzale Loreto), which specializes in *trompe l'œil* objects and decorations. Another shopping street with excellent merchandise and reason-able prices is Via Paolo Sarpi (🚇 Moscova), formerly the city's Chinatown. For books in English, try **The English Bookshop**, Via Mascheroni 12, **t** 02 469 4468 🚇 Conciliazione), or **The American Bookstore**, Via Camperio 16 in the historical centre, **t** 02 878 920 (🚇 Cairoli).

Markets

The tourist office publishes a complete list of markets in Milan: most are open mornings from 9 to 1, with the exception of the huge Saturday clothes markets in Viale Papiniano (🚇 S. Agostino) and Via Osoppo (🚇 Gambara) that continue until 6pm.

Flea markets include the **Fiera di Senigallia**, in Viale d'Annunzio every Saturday from 8.30 to 5 (🚇 S. Agostino) and the **San Donato** market on Sunday mornings (🚇 San Donato). For antiques, there's the enormous **Mercatone dell'Antiquariato** every last Sunday of the month (except July) along the Naviglio Grande (🚇 Porta Genova) and the **Mercato Antiquariato di Brera** in Via Fiori Chiari on the third Saturday of each month (🚇 Lanza).

Sports and Activities

A dip in one of Milan's public swimming pools can make a hot day of sightseeing far more tolerable: two of the nicest and most convenient are situated in the **Parco Solari**, Via Montevideo 11 (🚇 Sant'Agostino; closed Aug), and the **Lido di Milano**, Piazzale Lotto 15 (🚇 Lotto), with two large outdoor pools and water slides.

East of town, the **Parco dell'Idroscalo**, built around an artificial lake designed as a 'runway' for seaplanes in the 1920s, has a lovely complex of three pools known as Milan's Riviera (Viale dell'Idroscalo 1), reached by a special bus no.ID departing from San Babila. The **Luna Park** at Idroscalo has water slides and rides for the kids.

A popular **bicycle excursion** from Milan is to pedal along the Naviglio Grande canal from the Darsena to the Ticino river (around 40km), passing by way of Cassinetta di Lugagnano, home of one of Italy's top restaurants (the Antica Osteria del Ponte, *see* p.229). Like the Venetians with their villas along the Brenta Canal, the 18th-century Milanese built sumptuous summer houses along the Naviglio. Only one, the 15th-century frescoed **Villa Gaia** in Robecco, is open to visitors (call ahead, **t** 02 947 0512). Bicycles to rent at Vittorio Comizzoli, Via Washington 60, **t** 02 498 4694 (🚇 Wagner), and AWS, Via Ponte Seveso 33 (🚇 Gioia), (**t** 02 6707 2145).

Milan's two first-division **football** clubs, **AC Milan** and **Inter**, play on alternate Sundays during the Sept–May season at San Siro stadium, Via Piccolomini 5 (**Ⓜ** *Lotto, then walk, or tram no. 24 or buses no. 95, 49 or 72*). San Siro Stadium is open for visits (*daily 10–6 excluding match days; adm exp*), **t** 02 404 2432. **Tickets** for matches are available at the stadium, or from Milan Point, Via P. Verri 8, **t** 02 780398. For Inter matches, you can also buy tickets at branches of Banca Popolare di Milano; for AC games from branches of the Banca Cariplo.

Where to Stay

Milan has two types of accommodation: smart hotels for expense accounts, and seedy dives for new arrivals from the provinces. This bodes ill for the pleasure traveller, who has the choice of paying a lot of money for an up-to-date modern room with little atmosphere, or paying less for a place where you may not feel very comfortable (or, worse, very safe). Reserve in advance, because the exceptions to the rule are snapped up fast. In August much of Milan closes down, so that at this time it can be surprisingly easy to find a hotel. On the other hand, during the trade fairs (especially the big fashion shows in spring and autumn, and the April Fair) you may find no room at the inn. (*see* Tourist Information for booking agencies.)

Luxury

★★★★★Four Seasons, Via Gesù 8, ✉ 20121, **t** 02 77088, **f** 02 7708 5000, *www.fourseasons. com*. A beautiful hotel in a 15th-century monastery. The church is the lobby, breakfast is served in the refectory, and most of the spacious rooms look over the cloister; enormous bathrooms, great plush sofas around the blazing fire in the winter.

★★★★★Principe di Savoia, Piazza della Repubblica 17, ✉ 20124, **t** 02 6230, **f** 02 659 5838. Elegant and prestigious, this hotel was originally built in 1927 and has since been lavishly redecorated. When the Duke of Windsor, Charlie Chaplin, Eva Peron, Onassis, Maria Callas and the Aga Khan visited Milan, they stayed here. The hotel has its own airport bus and a divine restaurant.

★★★★★Grand Hotel et de Milan, Via Manzoni 29, ✉ 20121, **t** 02 723 141, **f** 02 8646 0861, *www.grandhoteletdemilan.it*. A favourite with everyone from Verdi to Hemingway and Nureyev since it opened in 1863. Nowadays the Grand is the fashion head-quarters of Naomi Campbell and Kate Moss. Rooms are individually furnished with antiques, and the atmosphere is grand and gracious without being stuffy.

★★★★★Excelsior Gallia, Piazza Duca d'Aosta 9, ✉ 20124, **t** 02 67851, **f** 02 6671 3239, *www.excelsiorgallia.it*. Around the corner from the Stazione Centrale; has hosted visiting potentates including music composer Arturo Toscanini and Mikhail Gorbachev since it first opened in 1932. Spruced up with briarwood furnishings and oriental rugs, its rooms are spacious and elegant, and it offers Turkish baths.

Very Expensive

★★★★Cavour, Via Fatebenefratelli 21, ✉ 20121, **t** 02 657 2051, **f** 02 659 2263, *www.hotel-cavour.it*. An elegantly furnished hotel in the Brera, a few blocks from Via Monte Napoleone. Note the elegant public halls, the design of the spiral steps and the collection of drawings of costumes at La Scala Theatre by Gio Ponti.

★★★★De La Ville, Via Hoepli 6, ✉ 20121, **t** 02 867 651, **f** 02 866 609. Modern, located between the Duomo and La Scala, it has antique furnishings and courteous service, comfortable lounges, bar and excellent restaurant; great weekend rates.

★★★★Sheraton Diana Majestic, Viale Piave 42, ✉ 20129, **t** 02 20581, **f** 02 20582058 (**Ⓜ** Porta Venezia). A fashionable, stylish Liberty-style hotel built at the turn of the century, with charming rooms, views over a garden and a lovely breakfast buffet.

★★★Ariosto, Via Ariosto 22, ✉ 20145, **t** 02 481 7844, **f** 02 498 0516, *www.brerahotel.com*. More character than most, and conveniently close to **Ⓜ** Conciliazione. An early 20th-century mansion, it has a lovely little courtyard, overlooked by the nicer rooms. Special weekend and children's rates.

★★★Ariston, Largo Carrobbio 2, ✉ 20123, **t** 02 7200 0556, **f** 02 7200 0914, *www.brerahotel. com*. At the south end of Via Torino. An environmentalist's dream, with 100% cotton futons, hydro-massage water-saving showers, recycled everything, ion-emitting machines in every room, and a no-smoking floor. There are bicycles to borrow. Special weekend and children's rates. *Closed Aug.*

★★★**Manzoni**, Via Santo Spirito 20, ✉ 20121, **t** 02 7600 5700, **f** 02 784 212, *www.hotel. manzoni@tin.it*. Book in advance for this pleasant hotel, one of the most privileged locations in Milan – on a quiet street within easy walking distance of Monte Napoleone and La Scala, with bright baths. *Closed late July–Aug.*

★★★**Antica Locanda Dei Mercanti**, Via San Tomaso 6, ✉ 20121, **t** 02 805 4080, **f** 02 805 4090, *www.locanda.it*. As discreet as its sign-post, hidden in a building entrance, this charming inn is situated in a pedestrian street within easy walking distance of the Castello Sforzesco, the Duomo, La Scala, and the Brera district. Rooms are individually furnished in classic style with fine white fabrics. The top floor rooms have dramatic canopy beds and individual roof terraces.

Expensive

★★**Antica Locanda Solferino**, Via Castelfidardo 2, ✉ 20121, **t** 02 657 0129, **f** 02 657 1361. This atmospheric 19th-century inn in Brera hass 11 rooms, all different, though the baths are spartan. Book well in advance to be sure of a room. *Closed Aug.*

★★**London**, Via Rovello 3, ✉ 20121, **t** 02 7202 0166, **f** 02 805 7037, *hotel.london@ traveleurope.it*. On a quiet street near the castle. *Closed Aug.*

Moderate

★★**Casa Mia**, Viale Vittorio Veneto 30, ✉ 20124, **t** 02 657 5249, **f** 02 655 2228, *hotelcasamia@ libero.it*. An excellent value hotel just north of the Giardini Pubblici, recently renovated. (ⓜ Repubblica/ Porta Venezia).

★**Alba d'Oro**, Viale Piave 5, ✉ 20129, **t** 02 7602 3880 (ⓜ Metro Palestro/Porta Venezia). 'The Golden Dawn' is small and safe; baths down the hall.

★**Speronari**, Via Speronari 4, ✉ 20123, **t** 02 8646 1125, **f** 02 7200 3178. Adequate and just southwest of the Duomo; rooms with bath cost a bit more.

San Francisco, Viale Lombardia 55, ✉ 20131, **t** 02 236 1009, **f** 02 2668 0377. A safe and acceptable choice close to ⓜ Loreto.

Cheap

La Cordata (Casa Scout), Via Burigozzo 11, **t** 02 5831 4675 (ⓜ Missori). Private hostel where you can also use the kitchen facilities.

Eating Out

In moneyed Milan you'll find some of Italy's finest restaurants and the widest range of international cuisine; on the down side, an average meal will cost you considerably more than it would almost anywhere else in Italy. That said, you will still pay less than you would in comparable London restaurants. Presume unless otherwise stated that all are closed in August; so few restaurants remain open that their names are printed in the paper. At other times, the best places to find a selection of cheaper restaurants are in the Brera, Ticinese and Navigli districts.

Saffron is Milan's fetish spice, and appears in most dishes *alla milanese*. The origins of its use go back to a Belgian stained-glass maker, working on the Duomo in 1574, who was called 'Saffron' by his fellows because he always sprinkled a bit of the stuff in his mixes to make the glass colours deeper and richer. The other glassworkers laughed and joked that he loved saffron so much that he would soon be adding it to his food. During the wedding of Saffron's daughter, his apprentice, meaning to play a prank, actually had the chef put saffron in the rice; everyone was astonished at the yellow concoction, but it was delicious, and the Milanese have been making their saffron *risotto alla milanese* ever since – or so the serendipitous legend goes.

Very Expensive

Savini, Galleria Vittorio Emanuele, **t** 02 7200 3433. A bastion of Milanese tradition (since 1867), where you can try Lombard classics at the pinnacle of perfection – especially the *secondi*. The often-abused *cotoletta* and *risotto* retain their primordial freshness, as do the more earthy *cassoeula* and *ossobuco*. *Closed Sat lunch, and Sun.*

La Scaletta, Piazzale Stazione Porta Genova 3, t 02 5810 0290. Another culinary bastion: the workshop of Italy's *nuova cucina* sorceress, Pina Bellini, who does exquisite things to pasta and *risotto*, fish and rabbit, all beautifully presented. Excellent desserts and wines finish off a truly memorable meal. In the Navigli district. *Closed Sun and Mon; reservations advised.*

Peck, Via Victor Hugo 4, t 02 876 774. A name that has meant the best in Milan for over a hundred years, either in its epicurean delicatessen and shop at Via Spadari 9, or here at its modern cellar restaurant, which offers such a tantalizing array of delights that you hardly know where to begin. Their unctuous *risotto alla milanese* is hard to beat. *Closed Sun and hols and 3 weeks in July, but open in Aug.*

Nino Arnaldo, Via Carlo Poerio 3, t 02 7600 5981. One of Milan's most elegant restaurants, the base of one of the city's most creative chefs: his pasta dishes are original and the limited dessert selection holds some real jewels – the cinnamon ice-cream and *zabaione* are exquisite. In the Central Station area. *Closed Sat noon and Sun.*

Antica Osteria del Ponte, along the Naviglio Grande in Cassinetta di Lugagnano, t 02 942 0034. Although it's 20km from Milan, this is a holy temple of Italian cuisine that shouldn't be missed by any serious gourmet, featuring heavenly dishes such as *ravioli* filled with lobster and *zucchini*, fresh foie gras, marvellously prepared fish, *cassata* with pistachio sauce and perfect little pastries The décor is beautiful, intimate and elegant. *Closed Sun and Mon.*

Expensive

Aurora, Via Savona 23 (in the Navigli), t 02 8940 4978. Lovely *belle époque* dining rooms and equally lovely Piemontese cuisine, with an emphasis on mushrooms and truffles; another speciality is the cart of boiled meats, from which you can choose a vast array of sauces. Another cart will overwhelm you with its bewildering array of cheeses. Exceptional value, and lovely on summer evenings in the cool shade. *Closed Mon.*

Bice, Via Borgospesso 12, t 02 7600 2572. Sophisticated, traditional cuisine and impeccable service; the traditional favourite restaurant of VIPs in Milan. *Closed Mon.*

Antica Trattoria della Pesa, Viale Pasubio 10, t 02 655 5741. Close to Porta Comasina (central station). This *trattoria* dates back to 1880, and has fed generations of Milanese publishers and journalists, as well as Maria Callas and Visconti. Traditional cooking, to the point where you can eat an original Italian cuisine academy *risotto alla milanese*, *ossobuco*, *casseuola* with *polenta*, as well as 'new' dishes such as home-made *cappelletti* in capon broth and *tagliolini* with butter and truffle, introduced by the new owners. Among the new desserts is vanilla with ratafia liqueur. *Closed Sun.*

13 Giugno, Via Carlo Goldoni 44, t 02 719 654. Sicilian seafood recipes in a 1930s ambience and a piano bar every evening. Expensive *menu degustazione* available. A pleasant garden for summer dining. *Closed Sun.*

Centro Ittico, Via Aporti 35, t 02 614 3774 (Ⓜ Loreto, Buemos Aires). Fish comes directly from the market counter to your plate. Expect only a lemon sorbet for dessert. *Closed Sun and Mon.*

Moderate

The **Ticinese** quarter has several restaurants offering good affordable regional dishes.

Ponte Rosso, 23 Via Ripa di Porta Ticinese, t 02 837 3132. Soak in a romantic old-world bistro atmosphere, where the cuisine is excellent and mixes traditional dishes from Trieste in Veneto with Lombard specialities. *Closed Sun and Wed eve.*

Al Pont de Ferr, 55 Via Ripa Ticinese, t 02 8940 6277. Try the smoked salami, and dishes such as pigeon with mushrooms and *polenta*. The delicious wines are selected by *sommelier* and host Maida Mercuri. Arrive early to avoid the queues. *Closed every day for lunch and Sun.*

Trattoria Toscana, 58 Corso Porta Ticinese, t 02 8940 6292. A jolly place, with music and drinks in the garden, and dishes like *gnocchi* filled with *ricotta* and swordfish with thyme. *Open until 3am (but kitchen closes at 1); closed every day for lunch and Sun.*

Trattoria all'Antica, Via Montevideo 4, t 02 5810 4360. Still in the Ticinese; serves abundant Lombard fare prepared simply, but with the very freshest of ingredients. *Closed Sat lunch and Sun.*

Trattoria Milanese, Via Santa Marta 11, t 02 864 51991. In the city centre; a family-run *trattoria* which offers true Milanese dishes in a sober, yet homely ambience. *Closed Tues.*

Innocenti Evasioni, Via Bindellina, t 02 3300 1882. In the San Siro area; true to its name, it offers an escape from the city with its country-style rooms overlooking a garden. Eclectic, ever-changing dishes; four types of *menu degustazione* to choose from. *Closed lunch and Sun–Mon eves.*

Tre Pini, Via Tullio Morgagni 19, t 02 6680 5413. Hidden behind a monumental pine in the Maggiolina, the journalists' district close to the station, this is the place to go for roasted meat and fish. Cooking takes place in a chimney which burns olive wood in the middle of the conservatory in winter and in the garden pergola in summer. *Closed Sat.*

Cheap

Besides the places listed below, Milan is well endowed with American and Italian fast-food places for those without the money or time for an Italian sit-down feast. Highly recommended are self-service chain Brek and Pastarito (pasta dishes only, so large that one portion often feeds two people).

Da Rino Vecchia Napoli, Via Chavez 4 (between Stazione Centrale and Parco Lambro), t 02 261 9056. Prize-winning championship pizzas, with a vast selection to choose from, are the speciality here. They also do good *antipasti, gnocchi*, and fish dishes; it's best to book. *Closed Sun lunch and Mon.*

Geppo, Viale Brianza 30, t 02 284 6548. Another name in Milanese pizza lore, with 50 kinds to choose from, including a Milanese with saffron, rocket and *porcini* mushrooms (🅜 Loreto). *Closed Sun.*

Osteria del Treno, Via S. Gregorio 46, t 02 669 1706. At lunchtime, this atmospheric former railway workers' club has an excellent very cheap self-service, although the excellent sit-down dinners are in moderately priced (🅜 Lima). *Closed Sat.*

Osteria Tagiura, Via Tagiura 5, t 02 4895 0613. In the San Siro area; open at lunchtime only. At this friendly family-run *osteria* you can have a full meal or just a piece of cake or a dish of salami, but the full menu is very affordable, and very good. Fish on Fridays, home-made pasta every day, different daily traditional dishes. *Closed Sun, no credit cards.*

Joya, Via P. Castaldi 18, t 02 2952 2124. Considered one of the best vegetarian restaurants in Italy: cheap at lunchtime, more expensive in the evening. *Closed Sat lunch and Sun.*

Entertainment and Nightlife

Check listings in the daily *Corriere della Sera* and *La Repubblica*'s Wednesday *Tutto Milano* magazine. For clubs with live music check under the heading '*Ritrovi*'. If you want to see a film in English, make sure it says *versione originale*. Other sources include the free *Milano Mese*, available at the tourist office.

Tickets are sold at **Virgin Megastore**, Piazza Duomo 8; **Ricordi**, Galleria Vittorio Emanuele at Corso Buenos Aires 33; **La Biglietteria**, Via Molino delle Armi 3; **Box Ticket**, Largo Cairoli; and in a kiosk in Stazione Cadorna.

Opera, Classical Music and Theatre

For many people, an evening at **La Scala** is in itself the reason for visiting Milan. The season runs from 7 December, St Ambrose's Day, to mid-July; and mid-September through mid-November. Telephone bookings can be made on t 02 860 775 (24hrs), approx two months in advance of the show, for two-week periods. The best way to check for tickets on sale is to consult the website, *www.teatroallascala. org*, which also provides an internet booking service. The CIT office, in the Galleria Vittorio Emanuele, t 02 863 701, has a certain number of tickets to sell to foreign tourists who make hotel reservations through them. Finding a good seat at a moment's notice is all but impossible; you could try through your hotel's concierge, or just show up at the box office an hour or so before the performance starts to see what's available; standing tickets were recently abolished because of security concerns, but comparably cheap tickets can be bought for the upper galleries.

Giuseppe Verdi Conservatorio, Via del Conservatorio 12, t 02 762 1101 or t 02 7600

1854. More classical music is performed here. *Closed July–mid-Sept*.

The city sponsors a series of Renaissance and Baroque music concerts in the lovely church of **San Maurizio** on Corso Magenta and in **San Marco**, Piazza San Marco; adm free or around L20,000.

Piccolo Teatro, Via Rovello 2, near Via Dante, t 7233 3222. *www.piccoloteatro. org*. Milan is the home of Italy's best theatre company. Founded after the Second World War and run by brilliant director Giorgio Strehler for years , the Piccolo is ideologically sound, with a repertory from *commedia dell'arte* to the avant-garde. Tickets are cheap so anyone can go – but do book. The Piccolo Teatro divides its performances between the historical venue of Via Rovelli, Teatro Giorgio Strehler, Largo Greppi and Teatro Studio, Via Rivoli 6.

Teatro Nazionale, Piazza Piemonte 12, t 02 4800 7700, *www.teatronazionale.com*. Stages plays and musicals.

Jazz

Jazz clubs are in the Navigli district.

Scimmie, Via Ascanio Sforza 49, t 02 8940 2874. One of the best, with diverse but high-quality offerings from Dixieland to fusion; in the summer the action moves to a canal barge. *Closed Tues*.

Tangram, Via Pezzotti 52, t 02 8950 1007. A mix of jazz, funk, rhythm and blues. *Closed Sun*.

Blues House, 26 Via S. Uguzzone, t 02 2700 3621. Plays exclusively blues. *Closed Mon*.

Grilloparlante, Alzaia Naviglio Grande 36. Enter an old Navigli house, cross the courtyard and you'll find alternate jazz and blues by amateurs and professionals. Also country, rock and even classical music.

Gelaterie

Rossi, Viale Romagna 23. Even the Milanese like to take an evening promenade topped off with a stop at the *gelateria*. Some of the best ice cream in Milan is scooped out here at this minuscule place. Exquisite chocolates and *tiramisù*. *Closed Tues*.

Viel, Foro Buonaparte 71. The most surprising flavours of ice cream in Milan. *Closed Wed*.

Ecologica, Corso di Porta Ticinese 40. Totally natural ingredients go into the ice cream treats. *Closed Wed*.

Cafés and Bars

Jamaica, Via Brera 26. The old rendezvous of artists and intellectuals in the twenties and thirties, this used to be the meeting place of the *Scapigliati* (the Wild-Haired Ones).

Moscatelli, Corso Garibaldi 93. A beloved oasis for the fashion-weary. Milan's oldest *bottiglieria* (wine bar) at 150 years old.

Magenta, Via Carducci 13. A historic Art Nouveau bar and beer house. *Closed Mon*.

Grand Café Fashion, Corso di Porta Ticinese. One of the Navigli area's most popular bars.

Cocquetel, Via Vetere 14. Also popular, with hundreds of cocktails.

Bar Basso, Via Plinio 39 (Città Studi area). The place for happy hour: over 500 cocktails and home-made ice creams, in a 19th-century *salotto* and a country-style area. *Closed Tues*.

Havana, Viale Bligny 50. A Cuban venue with live music, salsa and *merengue* dancers.

Atiemme, Bastioni Porta Volta 15. Brera's Corso Garibaldi/Corso Como area jumps at night: in-spots include this fashionable former train station with good cocktails and music.

Lollapaloosa, Corso Como 15. Loud and Irish.

Clubs and Discos

The club scene in Milan, as in the rest of Italy, is concerned more with appearance than dancing and having a good time. It is possible to find places where the emphasis is reversed – though you have to look hard. Generally, clubs open every day until 3am (later at weekends), and the pricey admission fee entitles you to one free drink.

Hollywood, Corso Como 15 . At the time of writing, Hollywood is one of two discos hot among fashion victims, models and designers. *Closed Mon*.

Shocking, Via Bastioni di Porta Nuova 12. Other fashion victims' choice. *Closed Sun and Mon*.

Propaganda, Via Castelbarco 11 (Navigli). Alternates disco and live concerts. *Wed eve free for students. Closed Thurs*.

Tropicana Club Latino, Viale Bligny 52 (Ⓜ Porta Romana), is the place for Latin American dancing. *Closed Sun, Mon and Wed*.

Plastic, Viale Umbria 120. Wonderful, bizarre and very chic, small and shiny with a very eclectic clientele, drag-queen shows and fussy doormen; Thursday is gay night. *Open Thurs–Sat; adm*.

between the emperor and Milan that would define the relationship of Italy's *comuni* towards their nominal overlord. Barbarossa besieged and sacked Milan in 1158; the Ambrosiani promised to behave, but attacked his German garrison as soon as he was back safely over the Alps. Undaunted, Barbarossa returned and for two years laid waste to the countryside around Milan, then grimly besieged the defiant city. When it surrendered he demanded the surrender of the *carroccio*, forced the citizens to kiss his feet with ropes around their necks, and invited Lodi and Como to raze the city to the ground, sparing only the churches of Sant'Ambrogio and San Lorenzo.

But this total humiliation of Milan, meant to *encourager les autres*, had the opposite effect; it galvanized Italy's *comuni* to form the Lombard League against the foreign oppressor (only Pavia hated Milan too much to join). On his next foray over the Alps in 1176, Barbarossa was soundly defeated by the Lombard League at Legnano and found his empire on the verge of total revolt. To preserve it, Barbarossa had to do a little foot-kissing himself in Venice, the privileged toe in this case belonging to Pope Alexander III, whom Barbarossa had exiled from Rome in order to set up another pope more malleable to his schemes. To placate the Lombard *comuni* the Treaty of Constance was signed in 1183, in which the signatories of the Lombard League received all they desired: their municipal autonomy and the privilege of making war – on each other! The more magnanimous idea of a united Italy was still centuries away.

The Age of the Big Bosses

If Milan invented government by *comune*, it was also one of the first cities to give it up. Unlike their counterparts in Florence, Milan's manufacturers were varied in their trades; they limited themselves to small workshops, and failed to form the companies of merchants and trade associations that were the power base of a medieval Italian republic. The first to fill the vacuum at the top were the Torriani (della Torre), feudal lords who became the city's *signori* in 1247, losing their position to the Visconti in 1277.

The Visconti, created dukes in 1395, made Milan the strongest state in Italy, and marriages with French and English royalty brought the family into European affairs. Most ambitious of all the Visconti was Gian Galeazzo (1351–1402), married first to the daughter of the king of France and then to the daughter of his powerful and malevolent uncle Bernabò, whom Gian Galeazzo sent to prison before conquering northern Italy, the Veneto, Romagna and Umbria. His army was ready to march on Florence when he died of the plague. In his ruthlessness and his dependence on astrology, his love of art and letters (he founded the Certosa of Pavia, began the Duomo, held a lavish court and supported the University of Pavia), Gian Galeazzo was one of the first 'archetypal' Renaissance princes. The Florentines and Venetians took advantage of his demise to carry off pieces of his empire; while his sons, the obscene Giovanni Maria (who fed his enemies to the dogs) and the gruesome, paranoid Filippo Maria, tried to regain their father's conquests, Milan's influence was reduced to Lombardy.

Filippo Maria left no male heirs but he betrothed his wise and lovely daughter, Bianca, to his best *condottiere*, Francesco Sforza (1401–66). After Filippo's death the Golden Ambrosian Republic was declared by the Milanese, but it crumbled after three years, when Francesco Sforza returned peacefully to accept the dukedom. One of

Milan's best rulers, he continued the scientific development of Lombard agriculture, navigable canals and hydraulic schemes, and kept the peace through an alliance with the Medici. His son, Galeazzo Maria, was assassinated, but not before fathering Caterina Sforza, the great Renaissance virago, and a son, Gian Galeazzo II.

Lodovico il Moro

It was, however, Francesco Sforza's second son, Lodovico il Moro (1451–1508), who took power and ran one of Italy's most sparkling courts, helped by his wife, the delightful Beatrice d'Este until her early death in childbirth. Lodovico hired Leonardo to paint the *Last Supper* and design engineering schemes and magnificent theatrical pageants. But Lodovico also bears the blame for one of the greatest political blunders in Italian history, when his quarrel with Naples grew so touchy that he invited Charles VIII of France to come and claim Naples for himself. Charles took him up on it and marched unhindered down Italy. Lodovico soon realized his mistake, and joined the last-minute league of Italian states that united to trap and destroy the French at Fornovo. They succeeded, partially, but the damage was done: the French invasion had shown the Italian states, beautiful, rich, in the full flower of the Renaissance, to be disunited and vulnerable. Charles VIII's son, Louis XII, took advantage of a claim on Milan through a Visconti grandmother and captured the city, and Lodovico with it. Lodovico died a prisoner in a Loire château, an unhappy Prospero, covering the walls of his dungeon with bizarre graffiti that perplexes visitors to this day. After more fights between French and Spanish, Milan ended up a province of Charles V's empire, ruled by a Spanish viceroy.

In 1712 the city came under the Habsburgs of Austria and, with the rest of Lombardy, profited from the enlightened reforms of Maria Theresa, who did much to improve agriculture (especially the production of rice and silk), rationalize taxes and increase education; her rule saw the creation of La Scala, the Brera Academy and most of central neoclassical Milan. After centuries of hibernation the Ambrosiani were stirring again, and when Napoleon arrived the city welcomed him fervently. With a huge festival Milan became the capital of Napoleon's 'Cisalpine Republic', linked to Paris via the new Simplon Highway.

The Powerhouse of United Italy

After Napoleon's defeat in 1814 the Austrians returned, but Milan was an important centre of Italian nationalist sentiment during the Risorgimento and rebelled against the repressive Habsburg regime in 1848. The city's greatest contribution during this period, however, was the novelist Manzoni, whose masterpiece *I Promessi Sposi* caused a sensation and instilled a sense of unity in a peninsula that had unravelled after the fall of Rome (*see* p.78).

After joining the new kingdom of Italy, Milan rapidly took its place as the country's economic dynamo, attracting thousands of workers from the poorer sections of Italy. Many of these workers joined the new Socialist Party, which was strongest in the regions of Lombardy and Emilia-Romagna. In Milan, too, Mussolini founded the Fascist Party and launched its first campaign in 1919. The city was bombed heavily during the war. In May 1945 Milan's own partisans liberated it from the Germans before the Allies arrived, and when Mussolini's corpse was strung up in the Piazzale Loreto the Milanese turned out to make sure that the duke of delusion was truly dead before beginning to rebuild their battered city on more solid ground.

Milan became, again, the centre of Italy's postwar economic miracle when it took off in the late fifties, drawing in still more thousands of migrants from the south. Despite a few hiccups, its wealth has continued to grow steadily ever since, while its political affairs were dominated from the seventies onwards by the Socialists and their ineffable boss Bettino Craxi. Since the beginning of the nineties, however, as anyone exposed to any of the Italian media has not been allowed to forget for even one minute, the whole structure has come crashing down, for it was in Milan, too, that the first allegations of the large-scale taking of *tangenti* (bribes) came to light, initially involving the Socialists, though the mud later spread to touch all the established parties. Craxi and his cronies have disappeared from the political map (Craxi disappeared from Italy altogether, and spent his last years holed up in Tunisia) and power in Milan is now held by a rightist government after being disputed between a Left/Green alliance and Umberto Bossi's Lega Nord.

Piazza del Duomo

In the exact centre of Milan towers its famous **Duomo**, a monument of such imposing proportions (third largest in the world after St Peter's and Seville Cathedral) that on clear days it is as visible from the distant Alps as the Alps are visible from its dome. Bristling with 135 spires, defended by 2,244 marble saints and one cheeky sinner (Napoleon, who crowned himself King of Italy here in 1805), guarded by 95 leering gargoyles, energized by sunlight pouring through the largest stained-glass windows in Christendom, Milan Cathedral is a remarkable bulwark of the faith. And yet for all its monstrous size, for all the hubbub of its busy piazza, traversed daily by tens of thousands of Milanese and tourists, the Duomo is utterly ethereal, a rose-white vision of pinnacles and tracery woven by angels. In Vittorio de Sica's *Miracle in Milan* (1950) it serves its natural role as a stairway (or rather launching pad) to heaven for the broomstick-riding heroes.

Gian Galeazzo Visconti began the Duomo in 1386 as a votive offering to the Mother of God, hoping that she would favour him with an heir. His prayers for a son were answered in the form of Giovanni Maria, a loathsome degenerate assassinated soon after he attained power; as the Ambrosiani have wryly noted, the Mother of God got the better of the deal. For, along with the money to build the church, Gian Galeazzo threw in the Candoglia quarries (source of the fine marble still used by the Cathedral Building Company) and hired the finest architects and masons of the day, including the Campionese masters of Lake Lugano. However, before the cathedral was completed, the Gothic style – which the Italians never liked much to begin with – had become unfashionable, and the bewildered façade went through a Renaissance and a Baroque stage, then back to Gothic, with the end result, completed in 1809 under

Napoleon's orders, resembling a shotgun wedding of Isabelline Gothic with Christopher Wren. In the 1880s there were plans to tear it down and start again, but no one had the heart, and the Milanese have become used to it. The subjects of the bas-reliefs on the bronze doors, all cast in this century, are a Milanese history lesson: the Edict of Constantine, the Life of St Ambrose, the city's quarrels with Barbarossa, and the history of the cathedral itself. To see what the original builders were about, walk around to the glorious Gothic **apse**.

The remarkable dimensions of the interior challenge the eyes to take in what at first seems like infinity captured under a canopy. Its tremendous volume is defined into five aisles by 52 pillars of titanic dimensions, crowned by rings of niches and statues, and is dazzlingly lit by acres of stained glass; the windows of the apse, embellished with flamboyant Gothic tracery, are among the most beautiful anywhere. In them you can see the mysterious alchemical symbol adopted as the Visconti crest, and now the symbol of the city: a twisting serpent in the act of swallowing a man.

All other decorations seem rather small afterthoughts, but you may want to seek out in the right transept Leoni's fine Mannerist tomb of Gian Giacomo de' Medici, better known as Il Medeghino, the pirate of Lake Como – erected by his brother Pope Pius IV. Near Il Medeghino's tomb is the most disconcerting of the cathedral's thousands of statues: that of San Bartolomeo being flayed alive, with an inscription saying that it was made by Marco Agrate and not by Praxiteles, just in case you were confused. Other treasures include the 12th-century Trivulzio Candelabrum, by Nicola da Verdun, as well as ivory, gold and silverwork in the Treasury, located by the crypt, where St Charles Borromeo (nephew of Il Medeghino) lies in state.

Near the cathedral entrance a door leads down to the **Baptistry of San Giovanni delle Fonti** (*open Tues–Sun 9.45–5.45; adm; tickets at the bookshop, closed 1–3pm*), excavated in the 1960s, containing the octagonal baptismal font where St Ambrose baptized St Augustine. Throughout the Duomo you can see the alchemical symbol adopted as the Visconti crest, now the symbol of Milan: a twisting serpent in the act of swallowing a man; the story goes that in 1100, in the Second Crusade, the battling bishop Ottone Visconti fought a giant Saracen, and when he slew him he took the device from his shield.

For a splendid view of Milan, take a walk through the enchanted forest of spires and statues on the **cathedral roof** (*open Nov–Feb daily 9–4.45, Mar–Oct daily 9–5.45, steps or lift from outside the cathedral; adm; combined ticket with the Museo del Duomo available*). The 15th-century dome by Amadeo of Pavia, topped by the main spire with the gilt statue of *La Madonnina* (who at 12ft really isn't as diminutive as she seems 354ft from the ground), offers the best view of all – on a clear morning, all the way to the Matterhorn.

Museo del Duomo and Palazzo Reale

On the south side of the cathedral, the Palazzo Reale was for centuries the headquarters of Milan's rulers, from the Visconti down to the Austrian governors, who had the place redone in their favourite neoclassical style. In one wing, the **Museo del Duomo** (*open daily 9.30–12.30 and 3–6; adm*) contains art and artefacts made for the cathedral over the past six centuries, including some of the original stained glass and fine 14th-century French and German statues and gargoyles, tapestries, and a Tintoretto. Other rooms document the cathedral's construction: a magnificent wooden model from 1519, designs from the 1886 competition for the façade, and castings from the bronze doors.

The main core of the Palazzo Reale used to accommodate the **Civico Museo dell'Arte Contemporanea (CIMAC)**, which displayed Italian art of this century. The museum is now closed for major restructuring and and its collections are divided between the Civica Galleria d'Arte Moderna and the Esposizione Permanente at the Società per le Belle Arti, both in the Giardini Pubblici area (*see* pp.238-9). Behind the palace, on Via Palazzo Reale, be sure to note the beautiful 14th-century **campanile di San Gottardo**, formerly belonging to the palace chapel. The porticoes around the Piazza del Duomo are occupied by some of the city's oldest bars; in the centre of the square old Vittorio Emanuele II on his horse looks ready to charge into action.

North of the Duomo

The Galleria and La Scala

The king lent his name to Milan's majestic drawing room, the elegant **Galleria Vittorio Emanuele**, a glass-roofed arcade linking Piazza Duomo and Piazza della Scala. It was designed by Giuseppe Mengoni, who tragically slipped and fell from the roof the day before its inauguration in 1878. Here are more elegant bars (especially the venerable **Salotto**, serving perhaps Milan's best cup of coffee) and some of the city's finest shops. In the centre, under a marvellous 48m (157ft) glass dome, is a mosaic figure of Taurus; the Milanese believe it's good luck to step on the bull's testicles.

The Galleria opens up to the Piazza della Scala, address of one of the world's great opera houses, the neoclassical **Teatro alla Scala**, its name derived from the church of Santa Maria alla Scala which formerly stood on the site. Inaugurated in 1778 with Salieri's *Europa Riconosciuta*, La Scala saw the premieres of most of the 19th-century classics of Italian opera; when bombs smashed it in 1943, it was rebuilt as it was in three years, reopening under the baton of its great conductor Arturo Toscanini. The **Museo Teatrale alla Scala** (*open June–Oct daily 9–12 and 2–5, Nov–May Mon–Sat only; adm*), entered through a door on the left, has an excellent collection of opera memorabilia (especially on Verdi) including scores, letters, portraits and photos of legendary stars, and set designs; there's even an archaeological section related to ancient Greek and Roman drama. From the museum you can look into the beautiful 2,800-seat theatre, with its great chandelier; try to imagine the scene in 1859, when the crowded house at a performance of Bellini's *Norma* took advantage of the presence of the Austrian governor to join in the rousing war chorus.

An unloved 19th-century statue of Leonardo stands in the middle of the Piazza della Scala, while opposite the theatre the imposing **Palazzo Marino** is a fine 16th-century building hiding behind a 19th-century façade; now the Palazzo Municipale, it has one of the city's loveliest courtyards. A few steps away, on Via Catena, the unusual 1565

Casa degli Omenoni was built by sculptor Leone Leoni for his retirement, and is held up by eight uncomfortable telamones. Around the corner of cobblestoned Piazza Belgioioso, at Via Morone 1, the handsome old home of Alessandro Manzoni (1785–1873) is now a shrine, the **Museo Manzoniano** (*open Tues–Fri 9–12 and 2–4*), filled with items relating to the Milanese novelist's life and work, including illustrations from *I Promessi Sposi* and an autographed portrait of his friend Goethe.

Museo Poldi-Pezzoli

Open Tues–Sun 10–6; adm; combined ticket for Poldi-Pezzoli and Bagatti-Valsecchi museums available.

In front of La Scala runs one of Milan's busiest and most fashionable boulevards, the **Via Manzoni**. Verdi lived for years and died in a room in the Grand Hotel (No.29); at No.10 is the lovely 17th-century palace of Gian Giacomo Poldi-Pezzoli, who rearranged his home to fit his fabulous art collection, then willed it to the public in 1879. Repaired after bomb damage in the war, the **Museo Poldi-Pezzoli**, Ⓜ Monte Napoleone, houses an exquisite collection of 15th- to 18th-century paintings, including one of Italy's best-known portraits, the 15th-century *Portrait of a Young Woman* by Antonio Pollaiuolo, depicting an ideal Renaissance beauty. She shares the most elegant room of the palace, the **Salone Dorato**, with the other jewels of the museum: Mantegna's Byzantinish *Madonna*, Giovanni Bellini's *Pietà*, Piero della Francesca's *San Nicolò* and, from a couple of centuries later, Guardi's *Grey Lagoon*. Other outstanding paintings include Vitale da Bologna's *Madonna*, a polyptych by Cristoforo Moretti and works by Botticelli, Luini, Foppa, Turà, Tiepolo, Crivelli, Lotto, Cranach (including portraits of Luther and wife) and a crucifix by Raphael. The collection is also rich in decorative arts: Islamic metalwork and rugs – note the magnificent Persian carpet (1532) depicting a hunting scene in the Salone Dorato – medieval and Renaissance armour, Renaissance bronzes, Flemish tapestries, Murano glass, antique sundials, lace and much more.

Via Monte Napoleone

Just up Via Manzoni is the entrance to Milan's high-fashion vortex, concentrated in the palace-lined **Via Monte Napoleone** and elegant **Via della Spiga**. Even if you're not in the market for astronomically priced clothes by Italy's top designers, these exclusive lanes make for good window-shopping and perhaps even better people-watching. It's hard to remember that up until the 1970s Florence was the centre of the Italian garment industry. When Milan took over this status – it has the airports Florence lacks – it added the essential ingredients of business savvy and packaging to the Italians' innate sense of style to create a high-fashion empire rivalling and often surpassing Paris, London and New York.

There are three museums in the sumptuous 18th-century Palazzo Morando Bolognini, on Via S. Andrea 6, between 'Montenapo' and Via della Spiga: the **Civico Museo di Milano** and the **Civico Museo di Storia Contemporanea** (*both open Tues–Sun 9–1 and 2–6*), the first with paintings of old Milan, the second devoted to Italian history between the years 1914 and 1945; the third, the **Civico Museo Marinaro Ugo Mursia** (*open Tues–Sun 9–12.45 and 1.45–5*), has a collection of nautical models, English figureheads, scrimshaw and mementos, founded by a Milanese scholar obsessed with Joseph Conrad. A fourth museum, still in the ozone of chic, the **Museo Bagatti-Valsecchi**, Via Santo Spirito 10 (*open Tues–Sun 1–5; adm*), was the life's work of two brothers, Fausto and Giuseppe Bagatti-Valsecchi, who built a neo-Renaissance palace to integrate the period fireplaces, ceilings and friezes that they had collected, carefully disguising such 19th-century conveniences as the bathtub. Some of the city's top designers have made unique creations inspired by the displays in the museum, which are sold in the shop in the lobby.

Near the intersection of Via della Spiga and Via Manzoni, the **Archi di Porta Nuova**, the huge stone arches of a gate, are a rare survival of the 12th-century walls. The moat around the walls was enlarged into a canal to bring in marble for building the cathedral; it was covered in the 1880s when its stench outweighed any economic benefit. (A useful bus, no.94 from the Piazza Cavour, makes the circuit of the former canal and is convenient for the Castello Sforzesco, Santa Maria delle Grazie or Sant'Ambrogio.)

The Giardini Pubblici

From Piazza Cavour, Via Palestro curves between the two sections of Milan's public gardens. The romantic **Giardini di Villa Reale** (**◍** Palestro) were laid out in 1790 for the Belgioioso family by Leopoldo Pollak, who later built the Villa Reale, Napoleon's residence while in the Cisalpine Republic. The neoclassical villa is now the **Civica Galleria d'Arte Moderna** (*open daily 9.30–5.30*) where, at the time of writing, the ground floor houses the Vismara collection of paintings (works by Picasso, Matisse, Modigliani, de Pisis, Tosi, Morandi and Renoir) and the Marino Marini sculpture collection; Marini (d. 1980), generally acknowledged as the top Italian sculptor of the 20th century, spent most of his career in Milan, and in 1973 he gave the city many of his sensuous, acutely observed bronzes, as well as paintings and graphic works. The first floor of the gallery hosts a collection of Italian art of the 1800s, which includes the famous painting of *The Fourth State* by Pelizza da Volpedo and, temporarily, 40 contemporary works of the Jucker collection (from the Civico Museo d'Arte Contemporanea), with paintings by Picasso, Klee, Kandinsky and Modigliani. The gallery's fine paintings of the self-consciously romantic *Scapigliati* (the Wild-Haired Ones) of Milan and Italian Impressionists were not on show at the time of writing. The second floor hosts the Grassi collection of French painters Gauguin, Bonnard, Manet and Toulouse Lautrec and paintings by Italian futurists Balla and Boccioni.

The Giardini Pubblici proper, a shady Arcadia between Via Palestro and the Corso Venezia, was laid out in 1782; artificial rocks compensate for Milan's flat terrain. A good place to take children, with its zoo, swans, pedal cars and playgrounds, it is also the site of Italy's premier **Natural History Museum** (*open Mon–Fri 9.30–6, Sat–Sun 9.30–6.30*), near the Corso Venezia; another victim of the war, it has been rebuilt in its original neo-medieval style. Look out for the Canadian cryptosaurus, the colossal European lobster, the Madagascar aye-aye and the 40-kilo topaz. The gardens also contain the recently reopened **Museo del Cinema**, Viale Manin 2 (*open Fri–Sun 3–6;*

Lo Stile Liberty

'Liberty style' is the name given in Italy to Art Nouveau, the short-lived artistic and architectural movement that flourished in many European countries around the turn of the 19th–20th centuries. It refers, curiously, to Liberty's, the London shop, whose William Morris-influenced, flower-patterned fabrics and ceramics were some of the first articles in the style imported into Italy, and became enormously popular at the time (the style is also, less commonly, known as the *stile floreale*). The ethos behind the movement was an avoidance of architectural precedents, an embracing of 'naturalistic' ornament and smooth, flowing lines, and a desire to 'integrate' all the arts – hence the importance given not just to painting and fine art, but also to architecture and interior design. Decoration, an integral part of every design, was key.

Liberty style was never as important in Italy as were its equivalents in France, Austria or Catalunya – nor was it usually as extravagant as they often were – but it did for a time become the vogue among the newly wealthy middle classes of Italy's industrializing north. As the prosperity of this class grew in the 1900s, so too did demand for Liberty buildings and products – seen most notably in the hotels and villas around the lakes or along the Riviera. Perhaps the most important figure working in the style in Italy was Giuseppe Sommaruga (1867–1917), whose achievements include the Palazzo Castiglione, a pair of villas at Sárnico on Lake Iseo, and Hotel Tre Colli near Varese, characterized by their richly ornamental lines and an uninhibited use of space. In a similar but more refined style, is the architecture of Raimondo D'Aronco (1857–1932), who worked mainly on public buildings, particularly for exhibitions. His most famous work is the Palazzo Comunale in Udine.

adm), located in the Palazzo Dugnani, with a small collection on early animation techniques, posters, cameras and so on.

Close to the gardens, in a classy palace of the 1800s, the **Società per le Belle Arti ed Esposizione Permanente**, Via Turati 34 (Ⓜ Turati; *open Tues–Fri 10–1 and 2.30–6.30, Thurs until 10pm; Sat, Sun and holidays 10–6.30; adm exp*) temporarily displays 100 sculptures and paintings of the 20th century from the Civico Museo dell'Arte Contemporanea, including paintings by Boccioni, De Chirico, Modigliani and Fontana.

Corso Venezia itself is lined with neoclassical and Liberty-style palaces – most remarkably, the 1903 **Palazzo Castiglione** at No.47 and the neoclassical **Palazzo Serbelloni**, Milan's press club, on the corner of Via Senato. The district just west of the Corso Venezia was the city's most fashionable in the 1920s, and there are a smattering of rewarding buildings: the **Casa Galimberti** with a colourful ceramic façade at Via Malpighi 3, off the Piazza Oberdan; the good Art Deco foyer at Via Cappuccini 8; the eccentric houses on Via Mozart (especially No.11); and the romantic 1920s **Palazzo Fidia** at Via Melegari 2.

Northwest of the Giardini Pubblici, the **Piazza della Repubblica** has many of the city's hotels; the Mesopotamian-scale **Stazione Centrale** (1931), blocking the end of Via Vittor Pisani, is the largest train station in Italy. The nearby skyscraper, the Pirelli Building, known as **Pirellone** (big Pirelli), is one that the Milanese are especially proud of, built in 1960 by Gio Ponti, while Pier Luigi Nervi designed the concrete structure.

It's now the seat of Lombardy's regional government, and you can see most of the city from its terrace (*call ahead,* **t** *02 67651*). A new panoramic tower, the steel **Fernet Branca**, was opened briefly in summer 2000 in the park behind the Castello Sforzesco, and is expected to open permanently to the public in 2001. Named after one of the city's famous *digestivi*, this metal structure, reminiscent of the Eiffel Tower in Paris, was also designed by Gio Ponti, and erected in 1933, in the record time of two and a half months, in time for a Triennale. Closed to the public in 1972 for security reasons, the tower was abandoned, but, following Branca's tradition of sponsoring cultural events, will have Italy's most panoramic literary café on top when it reopens.

Further to the northwest, at Via Petteri 56, the Palazzo Martinitt houses the **Museo del Giocattolo e del Bambino** (**Ⓜ** *Lambrate; open Tues–Sun 9.30–12.30 and 3–6*) with a beautiful display of toys dating back to 1700.

Brera and its National Gallery

Another street alongside La Scala, Via G. Verdi, leads into the **Brera**, one of the few old neighbourhoods to survive in central Milan. Although some of the old cobblestoned streets of Brera have maintained their original flavour (especially Corso Garibaldi), local trendies are busily turning the remainder into Milan's version of Greenwich Village, full of curiosity shops, late-night haunts and art galleries.

At the corner of Via Brera and the piquantly named Via Fiori Oscuri ('Street of the Dark Flowers') is the elegant courtyard of the **Galleria Nazionale di Brera** (**Ⓜ** *Lanza or Monte Napoleone; open Tues–Sun 8.30–7.15, closes at 6pm in winter; adm*), one of the world's finest hoards of art. The collection was compiled by Napoleon, whose bronze statue, draped in a toga, greets visitors as they enter; a believer in centralized art as well as centralized government, he had northern Italy's churches and monasteries stripped of their treasures to form a Louvre-like collection for Milan, the capital of his Cisalpine Republic. The museum first opened in 1809; ongoing improvements and restorations since 1988 may lead to certain sections being closed.

Perhaps the best known of the Brera's scores of masterpieces is Raphael's *Marriage of the Virgin*, a Renaissance landmark for its evocation of an ideal, rarefied world, where even the disappointed suitor snapping his rod on his knee performs the bitter ritual in a graceful dance step, all acted out before a perfect but eerily vacant temple in the background. In the same room hangs Piero della Francesca's last painting, the *Pala di Urbino*, featuring among its holy personages Federico da Monfeltro, Duke of Urbino, with his famous nose. The Venetian masters are well represented: Carpaccio, Veronese, Titian, Tintoretto, Jacopo Bellini and the Vivarini, but especially Giovanni Bellini, with several of his loveliest Madonnas and the great *Pietà*, as well as a joint effort with his brother Gentile of *St Mark Preaching in Alexandria*; there are luminous works by Carlo Crivelli and Cima da Conegliano; and several paintings by Mantegna, including his remarkable study in foreshortening, the *Cristo Morto*. Other famous works include *Christ at the Column* by Bramante; Caravaggio's striking *Supper at Emmaus*; the *Pala Sforzesca* by a 15th-century Lombard artist, depicting Lodovico il Moro and his family; a polyptych by Gentile da Fabriano; and fine works by the Ferrarese masters Da Cossa and Ercole de' Roberti.

Outstanding among non-Italians are Rembrandt's *Portrait of his Sister*, El Greco's *St Francis* and Van Dyck's *Portrait of the Princess of Orange*. When Great Masters become indigestible, take a breather in the 20th-century wing of the gallery, populated mainly by futurists like Severini, Balla and Boccioni, who believed that speed was success, and the metaphysical followers of De Chirico, who believed just the opposite.

Brera's other principal monument is **San Simpliciano**, just off Corso Garibaldi to the north. Perhaps founded by St Ambrose, it retains its essential palaeo-Christian form in a 12th-century wrapping, with an octagonal drum. The apse has a beautiful fresco of the *Coronation of the Virgin* (1515) by Bergognone, and the larger of the two clois-ters, from the mid-16th century, is especially charming with its twin columns.

Castello Sforzesco

Marking the western limits of the Brera quarter, the **Castello Sforzesco** (Ⓜ Cairoli or Cadorna) is one of Milan's best-known landmarks. It was originally a fortress within the walls; the Visconti made it their base, and as a symbol of their power it was razed to the ground by the Ambrosian Republic in 1447. Three years later, under Francesco Sforza, it was rebuilt; after air raids in the war damaged it and its treasures it was rebuilt again, this time disguising water cisterns in its stout towers.

Today the castle houses the city's excellent collections, the **Civici Musei d'Arte e Pinacoteca del Castello** (*open Tues–Sun 9–5.30*). The entrance, by way of a tower rebuilt on a design by Filarete (1452) and the huge Piazza d'Armi, is through the lovely Renaissance **Corte Ducale** and the principal residence of the Sforza. There are intriguing fragments of Milanese history – the equestrian tomb of Bernabò Visconti and a beautiful 14th-century monument of the Rusca family; reliefs of Milan's triumph over Barbarossa, and the city's gonfalon. Leonardo designed the ilex decorations of the **Sala delle Asse**; the next room, the **Sala dei Ducali**, contains a superb relief by Duccio from Rimini's Tempio Malatestiano; the **Sala degli Scarlioni** contains the two finest sculptures in the museum, the *Effigy of Gaston de Foix* (1525) by Bambaia and Michelangelo's unfinished *Rondanini Pietà*, a haunting work that the aged sculptor worked at off and on during his last nine years, repudiating all of his early ideals of physical beauty in favour of such blunt, expressionistic figures; the difference between this and his Pietà in St Peter's could not be greater.

Upstairs, most notable among the fine collection of Renaissance furnishings and decorative arts are the 15th-century Castello Roccabianca frescoes illustrating the popular medieval tale of Patient Griselda. The **Pinacoteca** contains a tender *Madonna with Child* by Giovanni Bellini, his brother-in-law Mantegna's more austere, classical *Madonna* in the Pala Trivulzio, and the lovely *Madonna dell'Umiltà* by Filippo Lippi. Lombards predominate: Foppa, Solario, Magnasco (who spent most of his life in Milan), Bergognone (especially the serene *Virgin with SS. Sebastian and Gerolamo*) and Bramantino, with an eerie *Noli me tangere*. There are Leonardo's followers, and the *Primavera*, by Milanese Giuseppe Arcimboldo (1527–1593), who was no one's follower at all, but the first surrealist – the *Primavera* is a woman's face made up entirely of flowers. From 18th-century Venice, Francesco Guardi's *Storm* looks ahead to another school – Impressionism.

The castle's third court, the beautiful **Cortile della Rocchetta**, was designed by the Florentines Bramante and Filarete, both of whom worked for several years for Francesco Sforza. The basement of the courtyard is filled with an extensive Egyptian collection of funerary artefacts and the prehistoric collection of items found in Lombardy's Iron Age settlements, most notably the 6th-century BC bronzes from the tomb of the warrior of Sesto Calende. The first floor houses the **Museum of Musical Instruments** with a beautiful collection of 641 string and wind instruments, and a spinet that was played by Mozart. The **Sala della Balla**, where the Sforza danced, now contains the *Tapestries of the Months* designed by Bramantino.

Parco Sempione and Cimitero Monumentale

Behind the Castello stretches the Parco Sempione, Milan's largest park, where you can find De Chirico's **Metaphysical Fountain**; the 1930s Palazzo dell'Arte, used for exhibitions, especially the Milan Triennial of modern architecture and design; the **Arena**, designed in 1806 after Roman models, where 19th-century dilettantes staged mock naval battles; and an imposing triumphal arch, the **Arco della Pace**, marking the terminus of Napoleon's highway (Corso Sempione) to the Simplon Pass. Originally intended to glorify Napoleon, the Austrians changed the dedication to peace. At Corso Sempione 36 the **Casa Rustici** (1931), designed by Giuseppe Terragni of Como on the proportions of the Golden Rule, is considered Milan's finest modern building.

Further out (*tram no. 14 from Via degli Orefici, Duomo*), the **Cimitero Monumentale** (*open Tues–Sun 8.30–5*) is the last rendezvous of Milan's well-to-do burghers. Their lavish monuments – Liberty-style temples and pseudo-ancient columns and obelisks – are just slightly less flamboyant than those of the Genoese, the Italian champs for post-mortem splendour. The cemetery keeper has guides to the tombs – Manzoni, Toscanini and Albert Einstein's father are among the best-known names. The central structure called The Temple of Fame hosts some illustrious citizens. Newer acquisitions include Italian novelists Eugenio Montale and Elio Vittorini and opera singer Maria Callas. The memorial to the 800 Milanese who perished in German concentration camps is the most moving.

West of the Duomo

Santa Maria delle Grazie and the *Last Supper*

Open Tues–Sun 8.15–6.45, in summer until 10pm on Thurs and Sat; adm exp: booking compulsory, t 02 8942 1146; only 15 visitors are admitted at a time.

Milan's greatest painting, Leonardo da Vinci's *Last Supper* (or the *Cenacolo*), is in the refectory of the convent of **Santa Maria delle Grazie** (Ⓜ *Cadorna, then Via Boccaccio and left on Via Caradosso*). But before entering, get into the proper Renaissance mood by walking around the 15th-century church and cloister. Built by Guiniforte Solari, with later revisions by Bramante under Lodovico il Moro, it is perhaps the most beautiful Renaissance church in Lombardy, its exterior adorned with fine brickwork and terracotta. Bramante's greatest contribution is the majestic Brunelleschi-inspired

The *Last Supper*

Leonardo painted three of his masterpieces in Milan, the two versions of the mystery-laden *Virgin of the Rocks* and the *Last Supper*. The former two are in London and the Louvre; the latter would have been in Paris too, had the French been able to figure out a way to remove the wall.

Unfortunately for posterity, the ever-experimental genius was not content to use proper, established fresco technique (where the paint is applied quickly to wet plaster) but painted with tempera on glue and plaster as if on wood, enabling him to return over and over to achieve the subtlety of tone and depth he desired. The result was exceedingly beautiful, but almost immediately the moisture in the walls began its deadly work of flaking off particles of paint.

Although it was considered a 'lost work' by the 17th century, various restorers have tried their hand at this most challenging task, with mixed success. In the Second World War the refectory was massively damaged by a bomb, and the *Last Supper* was preserved thanks to piles of mattresses and other precautionary measures. In 1977 restorers began cleansing the work of its previous restorations and stabilizing the wall to prevent further damage; in April 1995 the last scaffolding was taken down.

Deterioration or no, the *Last Supper* still thrills. Painted at the moment when Christ announces that one of his disciples will betray him, it is a masterful psychological study, an instant caught in time, the apostles' gestures of disbelief and dismay captured almost photographically by one of the greatest students of human nature.

According to Vasari, the artist left the portrait of Christ purposely unfinished, believing himself unworthy to paint divinity; Judas was another problem, but Leonardo eventually found the proper expression of the betrayer caught guiltily unawares but still nefariously determined and unrepentant.

tribune, added in 1492; he also designed the choir, the unusual crossing under the hemispherical dome, the sacristy and the cloister, all simple, geometric and pure.

Monastero Maggiore and the Archaeological Museum

From Santa Maria delle Grazie the Corso Magenta leads back towards the centre; at the corner of Via Luini stands the Monastero Maggiore. The monastery's pretty 16th-century church of **San Maurizio** (*open Sept–June 4–6pm*) contains exceptional frescoes by Bernardino Luini, one of Leonardo's most accomplished followers. The former Benedictine convent (*entrance at Corso Magenta 15*) houses the city's Etruscan, Greek and Roman collections in the **Civico Museo Archeologico** (*open Tues–Sun 9–5.30*). As important as Milan was in the late Roman Empire (there's a model of the city inside), little has survived the frequent razings and rebuildings: the 3rd-century tower in the garden, Roman altars, sarcophagi, *stelae*, glass, ceramics, bronzes and mosaics. Other parts are Greek, Etruscan, Indian (from Gandhara), Goth and Lombard.

Sant'Ambrogio

Located just off San Vittore and Via Carducci (Ⓜ Sant'Ambrogio), the stern towers of the 12th-century gate, the **Pusterla di Sant'Ambrogio**, bristle, perhaps appropriately enough, with the armour, antique weapons and torture instruments of the **Museo della Criminologia e Armi Antiche** (*open daily 10–7; adm*). The Pusterla guards the last resting place of Milan's patron saint and the city's holy of holies, the beautiful church of Sant'Ambrogio. Founded by Ambrose himself in 379, it was enlarged and rebuilt several times (most notably by Archbishop Anspert in the 870s, becoming a prototype Lombard Romanesque basilica). Its current appearance dates from the 1080s.

The church (*open daily 9–12 and 2–8*) is entered through a porticoed atrium, which in 1140 replaced the original Carolingian paved court or parvis. It sets off the simple, triangular façade with its rounded arches and towers; the one to the right, the Monks' Campanile, was built in the 9th century, while the more artistic Canons' Campanile on the left was finished in 1144. The bronze doors, in their decorated portals, date from the 10th century. In its day the finely proportioned if shadowy interior was revolutionary for its new-fangled rib vaulting; rows of arches divide the aisles, supporting the women's gallery or *matroneum*. On the left, look for the 10th-century bronze serpent (the ancient symbol of health, or perhaps representing Moses' staff) and the richly sculpted pulpit, a vigorous masterpiece carved in 1080, set on an enormous late Roman sarcophagus. The apse is adorned with 10th–11th-century mosaics of the Redeemer and saints, while the sanctuary contains two ancient treasures: the 9th-century *Ciborium* on columns, and a magnificent gold, silver, enamel and gem-studded altarpiece (835), both signed by a certain '*Wolvinus magister phaber*'. In the crypt below moulder the bones of Saints Ambrose, Gervasio and Protasio. At the end of the south aisle the 4th-century **Sacello di San Vittore in Ciel d'Oro** ('chapel of Saint Victor in a sky of gold') contains brilliant 5th-century mosaics in its cupola and a presumed authentic portrait of St Ambrose.

After working on Santa Maria delle Grazie, Bramante spent two years on Sant'Ambrogio, contributing the unusual **Portico della Canonica** (*entered from the door on the left aisle*) and the two cloisters, now incorporated into the adjacent Università Cattolica; these display Bramante's new interest in the ancient orders of architecture, an interest he was to develop fully when he moved to Rome. In the upper section of the portico is the **Museo della Basilica di Sant'Ambrogio** (*open Mon–Fri 10–12 and 3–5; closed Tues; Sat and Sun 3–5; adm*), housing illuminated manuscripts, the saint's bed, Romanesque capitals, ancient fabrics and vestments called the 'Dalmatiche di Sant'Ambrogio' dating back to the 4th century, tapestries, and frescoes by Luini and Bergognone. The 1928 **War Memorial** in the Piazza Sant'Ambrogio was designed by Giovanni Muzio and inspired by Athens' Tower of the Winds.

Museum of Science and Technology

Open Tues–Sun 9.30–5, weekends till 6.30; adm.

From Sant'Ambrogio, Via San Vittore leads to the Olivetan convent of San Vittore, repaired after the War to house the **Leonardo da Vinci Museo Nazionale della Scienza e Tecnica** (Ⓜ *S. Ambrogio,*). Most of this vast and diverse collection, still arranged in its original 1950s format, is rather mysterious for the uninitiated, and if you're not keen on smelting and the evolution of batteries you may want to head straight for the Leonardo da Vinci Gallery, lined with pretty wooden models and explanations of his machines and inventions. Other rooms display musical instruments and optics, radios, computers, clocks and astronomy; downstairs you can push buttons and make waterwheels turn. Other buildings are devoted to trains, ships and naval history.

Milan's Financial District

For centuries, the area between Sant'Ambrogio and the Duomo has been the headquarters of Milan's merchant guilds, bankers, and financiers, concentrated in the bank-filled **Piazza Cardusio** (Ⓜ Cardusio), Via degli Affari and Via Mercanti, just off Piazza del Duomo. Milan's imposing **Borsa** (stock exchange) in Piazza Affari was founded by Napoleon's viceroy Eugène de Beauharnais and is now the most important in Italy. On Via Mercanti, the **Palazzo della Ragione** (1233), the old Hall of Justice, was given an extra floor with oval windows by Maria Theresa.

On the side facing Piazza Mercanti, look for a beautiful early 13th-century equestrian relief; while facing Via Mercanti don't miss the bas-relief of a sow partly clad in wool, discovered when the foundations for the *palazzo* were dug. According to legend, a tribe of Gauls under their chief Belloveso defeated the local Etruscans in the 6th century BC and wanted to settle in the area. An oracle told them to found their town on the spot where they found a sow half-covered in wool, and to name it after her. The sow was eventually discovered, and when the Romans conquered the Gauls, they translated the Celtic name of the town into the Latin *Mediolanum*, 'half-woolly'.

The Ambrosiana

Still in the financial district, in Piazza Pio XI (off Via Spadari and Via Cantù), the Ambrosiana is Milan's most enduring legacy of its leading family, the Borromei. Cardinal Federico Borromeo (cousin of St Charles) founded one of Italy's greatest libraries here in 1609, containing 30,000 rare manuscripts, including ancient Middle Eastern texts to aid the cardinal's efforts to tranlsate the Bible; a 5th-century illustrated *Iliad*; Leonardo da Vinci's famous *Codex Atlanticus*, with thousands of his drawings; early editions of *The Divine Comedy*; and much more (*the library is open for study, for occasional special exhibits, or by appointment; t 02 8645 1436*).

After years of restoration, the cardinal's art collection or **Pinacoteca** (*open Tues–Sun 10–5.30; adm*), housed in the same building, has recently been reopened. Although paintings have been added over the centuries, the gallery is essentially a monument to one man's taste – which showed a marked preference for the Dutch, and for the peculiar, and ranges from the truly sublime to some of the funniest paintings ever to grace a gallery. Here are Botticelli's lovely *Tondo*, and his *Madonna del Baldacchino* nonchalantly watering lilies with her milk; a respectable *Madonna* by Pinturicchio; paintings by Bergognone (including the altar from Pavia's San Pietro in Ciel d'Oro), a lovely portable altar by Geertgen tot Sint Jans, and the strange, dramatic *Transito della Vergine* by Baldassarre Estense. Further along, an *Adoration of the Magi* by the Master of Santo Sangue is perhaps the only one where Baby Jesus seems properly thrilled at receiving the very first Christmas presents. A small room, illuminated by a pre-Raphaelite style stained-glass window of Dante by Giuseppe Bertini (1865), contains the glove Napoleon wore at Waterloo, a 17th-century bronze of Diana the

Huntress, so ornate that even the stag wears earrings, and entertaining paintings by the Cardinal's friend Jan Brueghel the Younger, who delighted in detail and wasn't above putting a pussycat in Daniel's den of lions.

These are followed by more masterpieces: a *Page*, perhaps by Giorgione, Luini's *Holy Family with St Anne* (from a cartoon by Leonardo), Leonardo's *Portrait of a Musician*, a lovely portrait of *Beatrice d'Este* attributed to Ambrogio da Predis, and then Bramantino's *Madonna in Trono fra Santi*, a scene balanced by a dead man on the left and an enormous dead frog on the right. Challenging this for absurdity is the nearby *Female Allegory* by 17th-century Giovanni Serodine, in which the lady, apparently disgruntled with her lute, astrolabe and books, is squirting herself in the nose.

The magnificent cartoon for Raphael's *School of Athens* in the Vatican is as interesting as the fresco itself; the copy of Leonardo's *Last Supper* was done by order of the Cardinal, who sought to preserve what he considered a lost work (the copy itself has recently been restored). A 16th-century *Washing of Feet* from Ferrara has one Apostle blithely clipping his toenails. Another room contains pages of drawings from Leonardo's *Codex Atlanticus*. The first Italian still-life, Caravaggio's *Fruit Basket*, is also the most dramatic; it shares the space with more fond items like Magnasco's *The Crow's Singing Lesson*. Further on is Titian's *Adoration of the Magi*, painted for Henri II of France, and still in its original frame.

San Satiro

On the corner of Via Spadari and busy Via Torino, a 19th-century façade conceals the remarkable Renaissance church of **San Satiro**, rebuilt by Bramante in 1476, his first project in Milan. Faced with a lack of space in the abbreviated, T-shaped interior, Bramante came up with the ingenious solution of creating the illusion of an apse with *trompe l'œil* stucco decorations. Bramante also designed the beautiful octagonal baptistry, decorated with terracottas by Agosto De Fondutis. The 9th-century Cappella della Pietà is one of the finest examples of Carolingian architecture in north Italy, even though it was touched up in the Renaissance, with decorations and a *Pietà* by De Fondutis. San Satiro's equally antique **campanile** is visible on Via Falcone.

South of the Duomo: Porta Romana

This corner of Milan, the main traffic outlet towards the *autostrada* to the south, can be busy. Trams no.4 and no.24 (Via Orefici, Duomo) will take you to **San Nazaro Maggiore** on Corso Porta Romana, a church that has undergone several rebuildings since its 4th-century dedication by St Ambrose, and was last restored in the Romanesque style. The most original feature of San Nazaro is the hexagonal *Cappella Trivulzio* by Bramantino, built to contain the tomb of the *condottiere* Giangiacomo Trivulzio, who wrote his own epitaph, in Latin: 'He who never knew rest now rests: Silence.' Trivulzio did have a busy career; a native Milanese who disliked Lodovico Sforza enough to lead Louis XII's attack on Milan in 1499, he became the city's French governor, then went on to lead the League of Cambrai armies in thumping the Venetians at Agnadello (1509).

On Corso Italia, another main artery south, **Santa Maria presso San Celso** (1490–1563) offers a fine example of the Lombard love of ornament, which reaches almost orgiastic proportions in the Certosa di Pavia. Within, beyond an attractive atrium, the interior is paved with an exceptional marble floor and decorated with High Renaissance paintings by Paris Bordone, Bergognone and Moretto; on the day of their marriage Milanese brides and grooms traditionally stop by to pray in the chapel of the Madonna. The adjacent 10th-century church of **San Celso** has a charming interior restored in the 19th century and a good original portal.

South Milan: The Ticinese and Navigli Districts

Southwest of the city centre, Via Torino leads into the artsy quarter named for the Ticino river, traversed by the main thoroughfare, Corso di Porta Ticinese (*tram no.3 from Via Torino*). In the Ticinese you can find pieces of Roman *Mediolanum*, which had its forum in modern **Piazza Carrobbio**. There's a bit of the Roman circus on Via Circo, off Via Lanzone, and the **Colonne di San Lorenzo**, on the Corso: 16 Corinthian columns, now a favourite teenage hangout but originally part of a temple or bath, were transported here in the 4th century to construct a portico in front of the **Basilica di San Lorenzo Maggiore**. The oldest church in Milan, it acquired its octagonal form, encircled by an ambulatory and crowned with a dome, in the 4th century, predating the church it resembles most, San Vitale in Ravenna. Carefully spared by Barbarossa in the sack of Milan in 1164, it has since suffered severe fires, and in the 16th century, when it was near total collapse, it was rebuilt, conserving as much of the old structure as possible. Luckily, the beautiful **Cappella di Sant'Aquilino** (*adm*) has come down intact, with 4th- or 5th-century mosaics of Christ and his disciples and an early Christian sarcophagus.

A green walkway, the Parco delle Basiliche, links San Lorenzo to the **Basilica di Sant'Eustorgio**, rebuilt in 1278 along the lines of Sant'Ambrogio, with a lofty campanile (1309). The pillars along the naves are crowned with good capitals, and the chapels, added in the 15th century, are finely decorated with early Renaissance art. One chapel is dedicated to the Magi, where a large Roman sarcophagus held the relics of the Three Kings until Frederick Barbarossa hauled them off to Cologne.

The highlight of the church, however, is the pure Tuscan Renaissance **Cappella Portinari** (1468) built for Pigello Portinari, an agent of the Medici bank in Milan (*open Tues–Sun 9.30–12 and 3.30–6; adm*). Attributed to Michelozzo and often compared with Brunelleschi's Pazzi Chapel in Florence in its elegant cubic simplicity and proportions, the chapel is crowned by a lovely dome, adorned with stucco reliefs of angels. This jewel is dedicated to the Inquisitor St Peter Martyr (who was axed in the head on the shores of Lake Como in 1252), whose life of intolerance was superbly frescoed on the walls by Vincente Foppa and whose remains are buried in the magnificent marble Arca di San Pietro Martire (1339) by the Pisan Giovanni di Balduccio. Balduccio also added the relief of saints on the nearby 14th-century **Porta Ticinese** built in the Spanish walls.

The colourful **Navigli** district (**Ⓜ** *Porta Genova, tram no.2 or no.14*) is named for its navigable canals, the Naviglio Grande (linking Milan to the river Ticino, Lake Maggiore and the Candoglio marble quarries) and Naviglio Pavese (to Pavia) that meet to form the docks, or Darsena, near Porta Ticinese. Up until the 1950s Milan, through these canals, handled more tonnage than seaports like Brindisi, and, like any good port, the Navigli was then a lively working-class district of warehouses, workshops, sailors' bars and public housing blocks. Although some of this lingers, the Navigli is now a relaxed, fashionably bohemian zone, where many of the city's artists work, where the restaurants are cheaper and you can hear jazz in the night.

Short Excursions from Milan

Monza

Only 15 minutes by train from Milan's Garibaldi Station, or 20 minutes by ATM bus from the same place, Monza seems to be unfairly slighted by most visitors to Lombardy. Monza attracts throngs in early September when it hosts the Italian Grand Prix; otherwise you may have its venerable monuments to yourself.

Back in the late 6th century Monza was the darling of the Lombard Queen Theodolinda, who founded its first cathedral after her conversion from Arianism by Pope Gregory the Great. Rebuilt in the 13th century, the **Duomo** on Via Napoleone bears a lovely green and white striped marble façade by the great Matteo da Campione (1396). The massive campanile dates from 1606, when the interior was given its Baroque facelift. To the left of the presbytery, **Theodolinda's chapel** has charming 1444 frescoes by the Zavattari brothers, depicting the life of the queen who left Monza its most famous relic, preserved in the high altar: the gem-encrusted **Iron Crown of Italy** (*open Tues–Sat 9–11.30 and 3–5.30, Sun and holidays 10.30–12 and 3–5.30; adm*). The story goes that when his mother Helena unearthed the True Cross in Jerusalem, Emperor Constantine had one of its iron nails embedded in his crown. It became a tradition in the Middle Ages for every newly elected emperor to stop in Monza or Pavia to be crowned King of Italy before heading on to Rome to receive the Crown of Empire from the pope – a tradition Napoleon briefly revived when he had himself crowned in Milan's Duomo in 1805. The cathedral's **museum** (*same hours; combined adm available*) contains Theodolinda's treasure: a processional cross given to her by Gregory the Great, the 5th-century ivory diptych of Stilicho, her crown and the famous silver hen and seven chicks symbolizing Lombardy and its provinces, as well a precious Syriac cross belonging to her son Agilgulfo (it's not hard to see why Lombard names soon fell out of fashion) and Gian Galeazzo Visconti's goblet.

Just north of the Duomo, the 13th-century Palazzo Comunale or **Arengario** is the city's finest secular building. From here, Via C. Alberto leads north to the beautiful 800-hectare **Parco di Monza** (*open 7–7, till 8.30 in summer*) one of greater Milan's 'lungs', home to a horse-racing course, the 1922 Autodromo and site of the Italian Grand Prix. Until 1806 the park was the grounds of the neoclassical **Villa Reale** (*open to groups of 20 or more by appointment; book 10 days ahead on t 323222; adm*), built by

Archduke Ferdinand of Austria and the favourite residence of Napoleon's viceroy Eugène de Beauharnais. The single sombre note is struck behind the 18th-century residence – an expiatory chapel built by Vittorio Emanuele III that marks the spot where his father Umberto was assassinated by an anarchist in 1900.

Alfa Romeos and Saronno

Northwest of Milan, on the road and rail line to Varese, **Arese** has since 1910 been the home town of Lombardy's car industry, the *Associazione Lombarda Fabbrica Automobilistiche*, or Alfa Romeo, when a group of Lombard magnates bought up the French Darracq manufacturer. Alfa, in turn, has recently been bought up by Fiat, but in Arese you can visit the six floors of the 'family album', the **Museo Storico dell'Alfa Romeo** (*open Mon–Fri 9–12.30 and 2–4.30, closed Aug and Christmas holidays*).

Further along towards Varese, **Saronno** is synonymous with *amaretto*, either in the liqueur glass or in the biscuits, but students of Lombard Renaissance art will recognize it at once for its **Santuario della Madonna dei Miracoli**, built by Giovanni Antonio Amadeo in 1498. The façade with its trumpeting angels was added in the next century by Pellegrini, while highlights in the rich interior include the dome's startling, innovative fresco, the *Concert of Angels* by Gaudenzio Ferrari (1534) and Bernadino Luini's beautiful frescoes in the chapel of the Madonna (1531).

The Lombard Plain

The three provincial capitals of the Lombard plain are among Italy's most rewarding art cities. **Pavia**, the capital of the ancient Lombards and the region's oldest centre of learning, embellished with Romanesque churches and its famous Renaissance Certosa. **Cremona**, the graceful city where the raw medieval fiddle was reincarnated as the lyrical violin. And **Mantua**, the dream shadow capital of the wealthy Gonzaga dukes and Isabella d'Este.

Pavia

Pavia is a serious no-monkey-business town. It is one of those rare cities that had its golden age in the three-digit years, that misty half-legendary time that historians have shrugged off as the Dark Ages. But these were bright days for Pavia, when it served as capital of the Goths and saw Odoacer proclaimed King of Italy after defeating Romulus Augustulus, the last Roman Emperor in the West. In the 6th century the heretical Lombards led by King Alboin captured Pavia from the Goths and formed a state the equal of Byzantine Ravenna and Rome, making Pavia the capital of their *Regnum Italicum*, a position the city maintained into the 11th century. Charlemagne came here to be crowned (774), as did the first King of Italy, Berengar (888), and Emperor Frederick Barbarossa (1155). At the turn of the millennium the precursor of Pavia's modern university, the *Studio*, was founded; one of its first law students was first Norman Archbishop of Canterbury, Lanfranc, born in Pavia in 1005.

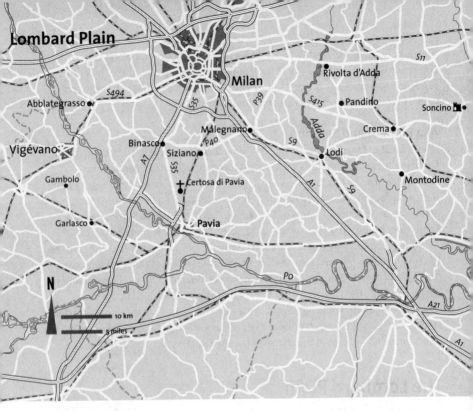

Pavia was the Ghibelline 'city of a hundred towers' and a rival of Milan, to whom it lost its independence in 1359. It was favoured by the Visconti, especially by Gian Galeazzo, who built the castle and founded the Certosa. It bears the mark of Pavia's great, half-demented sculptor-architect, Giovanni Antonio Amadeo.

The Duomo and San Michele

Pavia's core retains its street plan from the days when it was Roman *Ticinum*. The *cardus* (Corso Cavour) and the *decumanus* (Corso Strada Nuova) intersect by the town hall or **Broletto**, begun in the 12th century, and the **Duomo**, a front-runner for the ugliest church in Italy. Begun in 1488, it owes its imposing design to Leonardo da Vinci, Bramante, Amadeo and a dozen others (proof that too many cooks spoil the broth), and its corrugated cardboard façade to an understandable lack of interest in finishing it. The last apses were added only in 1930. Next to the cathedral, a stump recalls the singularly unattractive 12th-century **Torre Civica**, whose sudden collapse in 1989 prompted serious attention to its famous Pisan relation. From here, Strada Nuova continues down to the **covered bridge**, a replacement for the original Renaissance model damaged in the last war. Off Strada Nuova, Via Maffi leads to 12th-century **San Teodoro**, where a fresco shows Pavia with its forest of towers and original bridge.

East of Strada Nuova, Via Capsoni leads to the Romanesque **Basilica di San Michele Maggiore**, founded in 661 but rebuilt in the 12th century after its destruction by lightning. Unlike the other churches of Pavia, San Michele is made of sandstone,

mellowed into a fine golden hue, though the weather has been less kind to the intricate friezes that cross its front like comic strips, depicting a complete 'apocalyptic vision' with its medieval bestiary, monsters and human figures involved in the never-ending fight between Good and Evil. The solemn interior, where Frederick Barbarossa was crowned with the Iron Crown of Italy, contains more fine carvings on the capitals; the most curious, the fourth on the left, portrays the 'Death of the Righteous'. Along the top runs the women's gallery, while the chapel to the right of the main altar contains the church's most valuable treasure, a 7th-century silver crucifix.

The University and Castello Visconteo

The yellow neoclassical quadrangles of the **University of Pavia**, famous for law and medicine, occupy the northeast quadrant of the ancient street plan. First a *Studio*, it was officially made a university in 1361. In the 18th century Maria Theresa worked hard to bring the university back to life after scholarship had hit the skids, and financed the construction of the main buildings. Three of Pavia's medieval skyscrapers or **Torri** survive in the middle of the university in Piazza Leonardo da Vinci; the roof in the piazza shelters the crypt of the demolished 12th-century **Sant'Eusebio** church. You can meet some of the university's 17,000 students at the Bar Bordoni, on Via Mentana. In Piazza San Francesco d'Assisi, northeast of the main university, **San Francesco d'Assisi** was one of the first churches (1228) in Italy dedicated to the saint; it has a façade adorned with lozenge patterns and a triple-mullioned window.

Getting There

There are **buses** roughly every 30 minutes between Milan and Pavia, and this is also the best way to travel if you wish to stop off and visit the Certosa, some 8km north of Pavia. Buses arrive in and depart from Via Trieste, in the brand-new station-cum-shopping centre. Frequent **trains** link Pavia to Milan (30mins) and Genoa (1½ hours), and there are less frequent services to Cremona and Mantua, Alessandria and Vercelli, and Piacenza. The train station is a 10-minute walk from the centre, at the end of Corso Cavour and Viale Vittorio Emanuele II.

Tourist Information

Via Filzi 2 (a couple of streets from the station), t 0382 22156, f 0382 32221, www.apt.pv.it.

Where to Stay

Pavia ✉ 27100

★★★★**Castello di San Gaudenzio**, Via Mulino 1, t 0383 3331, f 0383 333409, info@castellosan-gaudenzio.com (very expensive). Thirty minutes' drive from Pavia in the hamlet of San Gaudenzio, near Cervesina in the Oltrepò area, this 14th-century castle is set in the middle of a century-old Italian-designed park. The central, oldest part contains the beautifully decorated Sala Cavour and Sala delle Cariatidi, and three charming suites, including one on two floors in the tower. Most rooms are in the modern building next door.

★★★★**Moderno**, Viale Vittorio Emanuele II 41, t 0382 303 401, f 0382 25225, www.hotel moderno.it (very expensive). The most comfortable, if expensive, hotel in town, next to the railway station.

★★★**Ariston**, Via A. Scopoli 10/d, t 0382 34334, f 0382 25667 (moderate). Centrally located and with a slightly more old-fashioned touch, for much less than you'd pay in Milan.

★★★**De La Ville**, Via Ticino 44, t/f 0382 928 100, www.hotel-delaville.com (moderate). In the tiny village of Bereguardo, 8km from the city centre. A good choice for families and countryside-lovers. In the Ticino park, within walking distance of Italy's only surviving pontoon bridge, with a playground for children as well as a good, reasonably priced restaurant.

★★**Aurora**, Via Vittorio Emanuele II 25, t 0382 23664, f 0382 21248 (cheap). Another hotel near the station; showers in all the rooms.

Locanda della Stazione (ring the bell), Viale Vittorio Emanuele II 14, t/f 0382 29231

At the top of Strada Nuova looms the **Castello Visconteo**, built in 1360 for Gian Galeazzo II, but partially destroyed in the Battle of Pavia on 24 February 1525 when Emperor Charles V captured Francis I of France, who succinctly described the outcome in a letter to his mother: 'Madame, all is lost save honour.' Three sides of the castle and its beautifully arcaded courtyard with terracotta decorations managed to survive, and now house Pavia's **Museo Civico** (open Tues–Fri 10–1.30, Sat and Sun 10–7; Dec–Jan, July–Aug open Tues–Sun 9–1pm only). The archaeological and medieval sections contain finds from Gaulish and Roman Pavia, robust Lombard carvings and colourful 12th-century mosaics. The picture gallery contains works by Giovanni Bellini, Correggio, Foppa, Van der Goes and others.

San Pietro in Ciel d'Oro

Behind the castle, Via Griziotti (off Viale Matteotti) leads to Pavia's second great Romanesque temple, **San Pietro in Ciel d'Oro** ('St Peter in the Golden Sky'), built in 1132 and named for its once-glorious gilded ceiling, mentioned by Dante in Canto X of the *Paradiso*. The single door in the façade is strangely off-centre; within, the main altar is one of the greatest works of the Campionese masters, the **Arca di Sant'Agostino**, a

(*cheap*). A good budget option in a private house with rooms to rent. Bathrooms are shared, but the homely rooms are spacious, clean and decorated with old-style furniture. It is advisable to call ahead.

Eating Out

Pavia is well endowed with good restaurants. Specialities include frogs, salami from Varzi and *zuppa pavese* (a raw egg on toast drowned in hot broth). Good local wines to try are from the Oltrepò Pavese region, one of Lombardy's best. Cortese is a fresh dry white, Bonarda a meaty, dry red, Pinot a more fruity white.

Locanda Vecchia Pavia al Mulino, Via al Monumento 5, t 0382 925 894 (*expensive*). Located in the restored 16th-century mill of the Certosa. Brings former chic gourmet restaurant Locanda Vecchia Pavia and country inn Vecchio Mulino together under one roof. The restaurant mantains the tradition, style (and prices) of the former, with refined dishes such as truffle-filled home-made *ravioli*, or prawn with *lardo* of Colonnata and *porcini* mushrooms, and delicate desserts. *Closed Mon and Wed lunch.*

Al Cassinino, Via Cassinino 1, t 0382 422 097 (*expensive*). Pavia's temple of fine cuisine is just outside the city on the Giovi highway.

Sitting on the Naviglio, the restaurant is done out in the style of a medieval inn. Dishes are whatever the market provides. *Closed Wed, and Christmas.*

La Zelata, Zelata in Parco di Ticino, t 0382 928 178 (*expensive*). Not far from Bereguardo, this family-run restaurant has been serving delightful traditional Lombard dishes for the last 20 years. Various types of *risotto* are the house speciality, but save room for chocolate mousse or *tarte tatin*. After the meal take some time to go heron-watching: this is the biggest nesting area of the Ticino Park. *Closed Sun, and Mon lunch.*

Antica Osteria del Previ, Via Milazzo 65, t 0382 26203 (*moderate*). Situated on the banks of the Ticino, this is an old-fashioned place serving home-made salami, *risotto* with frog or *radicchio* and *speck*, and for *secondi* river-fish, frog and snails. The menu does vary seasonally – when frogs are out of season there's a good selection of meats. *Closed Sun.*

Osteria della Madonna del Peo, Via Cardano 63 corner Via dei Liguri, t 0382 302 833 (*cheap*). In the city centre, located in a homely vaulted inn. Serves typical Lombard dishes, such as *risotti*, roasted and braised meats, or stuffed guinea-fowl, which require lengthy cooking. Cheap menu at lunchtime and a good selection of Oltrepò wines.

magnificent 14th-century monument built to shelter the bones of St Augustine, retrieved in the 8th century from Carthage by the Lombard king Luitprand (so the legend goes), staunch ally of Pope Gregory II against the iconoclasts of Byzantium. Luitprand is buried in a humble tomb to the right, and in the crypt lies another Dark Age celebrity, the philosopher Boethius, slain by Emperor Theodoric of Ravenna in 524.

Outside the centre, to the west (Corso Cavour to Corso Manzoni and Via della Riviera) it's a 15-minute walk to the rather plain, vertical, 13th-century **San Lanfranco**, notable for its lovely memorial, the Arca di San Lanfranco, sculpted by Amadeo in 1498, his last work (though Archbishop Lanfranc was actually buried in Canterbury); the same artist helped design the church's pretty cloister.

The Certosa di Pavia

Open Tues–Sun, Oct–Mar 9–11.30 and 2.30–4.30; April 9–11.30 and 2.30–5.30; May–Sept 9–11.30 and 2.30–6.

The pinnacle of Renaissance architecture in Lombardy, and according to Jacob Burckhardt 'the greatest decorative masterpiece in all of Italy', the Certosa or

Charterhouse of Pavia was built over a period of 200 years. Gian Galeazzo Visconti laid the cornerstone in 1396, with visions of the crown of Italy dancing in his head, and the desire to build a splendid pantheon for his hoped-for royal self and his heirs. Although many architects and artists worked on the project (beginning with the Campionese masters of Milan cathedral), the greatest imprint it bears is that of Giovanni Antonio Amadeo, who with his successor Bergognone worked on its sculptural programme for 30 years and contributed the design of the lavish façade.

Napoleon disbanded the monastery, but in 1968 a small group of Cistercians reoccupied the Certosa. The monks of today live the same style of contemplative life as the old Carthusians, maintaining vows of silence. A couple, however, are released to take visitors around the complex. If you arrive by the Milan–Pavia bus, the Certosa is a 1½km walk from the nearest stop, a beckoning vision at the end of the straight, shaded land, surrounded by well-tended fields and rows of poplars once part of the vast game park of the Castello Visconteo in Pavia.

Once through the main gate and **vestibule** adorned with frescoes by Luini, a large grassy court opens up, lined with buildings that served as lodgings for visitors and stores for the monks. At the far side rises the sumptuous, detailed façade of the **church**, a marvel of polychromatic marbles, medallions, bas-reliefs, statues, and windows covered with marble embroidery from the chisel of Amadeo, who died before the upper, less elaborate level was begun. The interior plan is Gothic but the decoration is Renaissance, with later Baroque additions. Outstanding works of art include Bergognone's five statues of saints in the chapel of Sant'Ambrogio (sixth on the left); the tombs of Lodovico il Moro and his young bride Beatrice d'Este, a master-piece by Cristoforo Solari; the beautiful inlaid stalls of the choir; and the tomb of Gian Galeazzo Visconti, all works of the 1490s and surrounded by fine frescoes. The old sacristy contains a magnificent early cinquecento ivory altarpiece by the Florentine Baldassarre degli Embriachi, with 94 figures and 66 bas-reliefs.

From the church, the tour continues into the **Little Cloister**, with delicate terracotta decorations and a dream-like view of the church and its cupola, a rising crescendo of arcades. A lovely doorway by Amadeo leads back into the church. The **Great Cloister** with its long arcades is surrounded by the 24 house-like cells of the monks – each contains a chapel and study/dining room, a bedroom upstairs and a walled garden in the rear. The frescoed **Refectory** contains a pulpit for the monks who read aloud during otherwise silent suppers.

Around Pavia: Lomello and Vigévano

West of Pavia and the Certosa lies the little-known Lomellina, a major rice-growing and frog-farming district, irrigated by canals dug by the Visconti in the 14th century. The feudal seat, **Lomello**, has some fine early medieval buildings, most notably a lovely little 5th-century polygonal baptistry near the main church, the 11th-century Basilica di Santa Maria.

Also in the Lomellina is the old silk town of **Vigévano** (better known these days for its high-fashion shoes), the site of another vast castle of the Visconti and Sforza clans; it was the birthplace of Lodovico il Moro, and has been undergoing a lengthy restoration. Below it lies the majestic Piazza Ducale, designed in 1492 by Bramante (with help from Leonardo) as Lombardy's answer to Venice's Piazza San Marco. Originally a grand stairway connected the piazza to one of the castle towers; now the three sides are adorned with slender arcades, while on the fourth stands the magnificent concave Baroque façade of the cathedral, designed by a Spanish bishop, Juan Caramuel de Labkowitz. Inside there's a 15th-century Lombard polyptych on St Thomas of Canterbury, and a rich treasury (*open Sun and hols only 3–6, or on request*), containing illuminated codices, Flemish tapestries and golden reliquaries.

Cremona

Cremona is famous for four things that have added to the sum total of human happiness: its Romanesque cathedral complex, Claudio Monteverdi, nougat, and violins. It has been the capital of the violin industry since 1566, when Andrea Amati invented the modern violin from the old medieval fiddle. It quickly became fashionable, and demand across Europe initiated a golden age of fiddle-making, when Andrea's son Nicolò Amati, and his pupils Stradivarius and Giuseppe Guarneri, made the best violins ever. Walking around Cremona you can easily pick out in the elegant curves and scrolls on the brick and terracotta palaces that inspired the instrument's Baroque form, while the sweetness of the violin's tone seems to have something of the city's culinary specialities in it, not only nougat but *mostarda di Cremona* – candied cherries, apricots and melons in a sweet or piquant mustard sauce, served with boiled meats. Today some 50 *liutai* (violinmakers) keep up the tradition, using similar methods and woods (poplar, spruce, pear, willow and maple); a school and research institute are devoted to the craft, and every third October (next in 2003) the city hosts a festival of stringed instruments.

Milan captured the once feisty *comune* of Cremona in 1344 and in 1441 gave the city to Bianca Maria Visconti as her dowry when she married Francesco Sforza, marking the change of the great Milanese dynasties. The city enjoyed a happy, fruitful Renaissance as the apple of Bianca's eye, producing Monteverdi, the father of opera, the prolific Campi family of painters, and Sofonisba Anguissola, the recently rediscovered Renaissance portrait painter admired by Michelangelo, Van Dyck and Philip II (who summoned her to work in Spain) for her ability to depict a sitter's soul.

Via Palestro to the Piazza del Comune

Cremona can be easily visited on foot, starting from the station and the Via Palestro. Here, behind a remodelled Baroque façade at Via Palestro 36, the **Palazzo Stanga Trecco**'s 15th-century courtyard is an excellent introduction to the Cremonese fondness for elaborate terracotta ornament.

The **Museo Stradivariano** nearby at No.17 (*open Tues–Sat 8.30–6, Sun and holidays 10–6; closed Aug; adm*) is an equally good introduction to the cream of Cremona's best-known industry, featuring casts, models, items from the master's workshop and drawings explaining how Stradivarius did it. Just around the corner, on Via U. Dati 4,

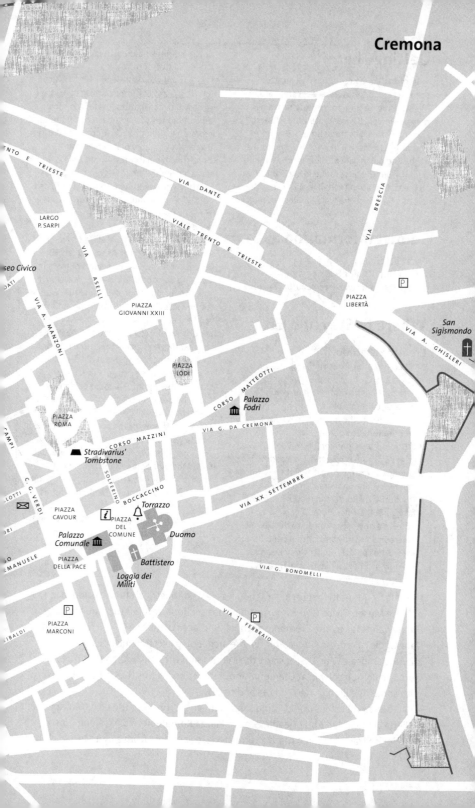

Cremona

VIA DANTE

VIALE TRENTO E TRIESTE

ENTO E TRIESTE

VIA BRESCIA

LARGO
P. SARPI

VIA ASELLI

seo Civico

DATI

VIA A. MANZONI

PIAZZA
LIBERTÀ

P

San
Sigismondo

VIA A. GHISLERI

PIAZZA
GIOVANNI XXIII

PIAZZA
LODI

CORSO MATTEOTTI

Palazzo
Fodri

PIAZZA
ROMA

CORSO MAZZINI

VIA G. DA CREMONA

CAMPI

C. G. VERDI

Stradivarius'
Tombstone

SOLFERINO

BOCCACCINO

VIA XX SETTEMBRE

LOTTI

PIAZZA
CAVOUR

Torrazzo

PIAZZA
DEL
COMUNE

URI

Palazzo
Comunale

Duomo

EMANUELE

PIAZZA
DELLA PACE

Battistero

VIA G. BONOMELLI

Loggia dei
Militi

SO

P

PIAZZA
MARCONI

VIA 11 FEBBRAIO

P

IBALDI

Getting There

Cremona's **railway** station is delightful: there are frequent train services from Milan (fast trains take 1hr 15mins, regional trains may be slower), Pavia, Mantua, Brescia and Piacenza, as well as three times a day from Bergamo. The station lies north of the centre, at the end of Via Palestro. Buses arrive at and depart from the bus station in Via Dante, next to the train station. Exchange your **car** for free use of a bicycle at the Via Villa Glori car park.

Tourist Information

Piazza del Comune 5, t 0372 23233, freephone from within Italy t 800 655 511, f 0372 534 080, *www.cremonaturismo.com*.

Where to Stay and Eat

Cremona ✉ 26100

******Continental**, Piazza della Libertà 26, t 0372 434 141, f 0372 454 873, *reception.hc@hotelcontinental.cremona.it* (*expensive*). Modern, comfortable, friendly and central, this hotel sets the mood with its display of Cremona-made fiddles.

*****Duomo**, Via Gonfalonieri 13, t 0372 35242, f 0372 458 392 (*moderate*). On a pedestrian-only street facing the cathedral, the Duomo has a very nice restaurant and *pizzeria*.

*****Astoria**, Via Bordigallo 19, t 0372 461 616, f 0372 461 810 (*moderate*). A very pleasant hotel in a quiet street close to the Duomo. The rooms are tidy and comfortable. Be careful not to interrupt the owners, two friendly brothers, while they play cards.

Cheaper rooms have baths en suite but shared showers.

*****La Locanda**, Via Pallavicino 4, t 0372 457 834, f 0372 457 835 (*moderate*). Just off the pedestrian area; bathrooms less comfortable than the Astoria but a good restaurant.

Ristorante Il Violino, Via Sicardo 3, t 0372 46101 (*expensive*). Located just behind the baptistry, this classy restaurant enjoys an enviable reputation for its regional dishes, starting with melt-in-your-mouth *antipasti*, *tortelli di zucca* and zesty *secondi* featuring meat or seafood. Book in advance. *Closed Mon eve and Tues.*

Trattoria La Prima, Via Cavitelli 8, t 0372 411 383 (*moderate*). Truly local dishes and attitude: its owner, host and chef selects punters by keeping half of the tables reserved even if they aren't, but if you overcome the selection process the service is very hospitable and the cooking excellent. *Closed Mon.*

Trattoria Mellini, Via Bissolati 105, t 0372 30535 (*moderate*). An older, rather more traditional restaurant on the west end of town, featuring dishes to make animal-lovers foam at the mouth – casseroled donkey and baby horse, or raw baby horse with truffle. Less controversial dishes includes a kind of *risotto* with salami and savoy cabbage, fresh pasta with sausage, and other hearty regional fare. *Closed Sun eve, Mon and Aug.*

Porta Mosa, Via Santa Maria in Betlem 11, t 0372 411 803 (*moderate*). A tiny family-run place serving delicious traditional dishes such as *tortelli* stuffed with squash and locally caught sturgeon steamed with herbs and capers. They also concoct a mean *tiramisù*. Best to reserve. *Closed Sun, and mid-Aug–mid-Sept.*

the Palazzo Affaitati (begun in 1561) houses a grand theatrical staircase added in 1769 and the **Museo Civico** (*same hours*), which has sections devoted to some amazingly dreary paintings by the Cremonese school (Boccaccino and the Campi family) and Caravaggio's *Francesco in Meditation*. The archaeology section includes a fine labyrinth mosaic with Theseus and the Minotaur in the centre (*c.* 2nd century AD) from the Roman *colonia* at Cremona; another section houses the cathedral treasury, with some fine illuminated codices and corals.

Via Palestro becomes Corso Campi, and at an angle runs into the boxy, Mussolini-era Galleria Venticinque Aprile, leading to the **Piazza Roma**, a little park; along Corso Mazzini is Stradivarius' red marble tombstone, transferred from a demolished church.

Corso Mazzini forks after a block; near the split, at Corso Matteotti 17, is Cremona's prettiest palace, the 1499 **Palazzo Fodri** (owned by the Banca Cariplo; ask the guard to open the gate), with a courtyard adorned with frescoed battle scenes and terracottas.

Piazza del Comune: The Torrazzo and Duomo

Cremona's lovely medieval Piazza del Comune is seductive enough to compete in any urban beauty contest. By now you've probably caught at least a glimpse of its biggest feature, the curious pointed crown of the tallest belltower in Italy, the 370ft **Torrazzo** (*open April–Oct Tues–Sun 10.30–12 and 3–6, until 7pm Sun and holidays; Nov–Feb weekends and holidays only 10.30–12 and 3–6; adm*). Only slightly shorter than Milan cathedral, the Torrazzo was built in the 1260s, has battlements as well as bells, and even tells the time thanks to a fine astronomical clock added in 1583 by Giovanni Battista Divizioli (*the astronomical clock room can be visited by appointment only, call t 0372 27633; adm exp*). The stout-hearted can ascend 487 steps to the top for an eye-popping view; the less ambitious can purchase a famous Cremona TTT post-card (Torrazzo, *torrone* and *tette* – tits) to send home. The lower level houses a reproduction of a violinmaker's shop of Stradivarius' time (*this too can be visited by request, call t 0372 27633; adm exp*).

Linked to the Torrazzo in 1525 by a double loggia, the **Portico della Bertazzola**, the **Duomo** is the highest and one of the most exuberant expressions of Lombard Romanesque, with a trademark Cremonese flourish in the graceful scrolls added to the marble front. Built by the Comacini masters after an earthquake destroyed its predecessor in 1117, the main door or **Porta Regia** remains as it was originally, flanked by two nearly toothless lion telamones and four flat prophets, and crowned by a small portico known as the Rostrum, where 13th- and 14th-century statues of the Virgin and two saints silently but eloquently hold forth above a frieze of the months by the school of Antelami.

The cathedral was begun as a basilica, but when Gothic came into fashion the arms of a Latin cross were added; the new transepts, especially the north one, are almost as splendid from the outside as the main façade. Restoration of the interior has revealed primitive frescoes under the opulent 16th-century works by Romanino, Boccaccino and Pordenone (who painted the *Crucifixion* under the rose window); the right transept has some endearing sweet and simple paintings on the ceiling; the twin pulpits have nervous, delicate reliefs attributed to Amadeo or Pietro da Rho; the choir has exquisite stalls inlaid in 1490 by G.M. Platina – with secular scenes, still lifes and views of Cremona. In the crypt, with the tomb of Ombrono Tucenghi, patron saint of tailors (d. 1197), note the painting of old Cremona with its Manhattanesque skyline.

Completing the sacred ensemble in Piazza del Comune is the octagonal **Battistero di San Giovanni** (1167) (*open Sat 3.30–7, Sun and holidays 10.30–12.30 and 3.30–7*), with another pair of lions supporting the portico, and two sides of marble facing to match the cathedral. Across from the Duomo, the **Loggia dei Militi** (1292) was used as a rendezvous by the captains of the *comune*'s citizen militia; the outdoor pulpit between two of the arches is a relic of the charismatic, itinerant preachers like San Bernadino of Siena, whose sermons were so popular they had to be held outside.

Behind it, the **Palazzo del Comune** (*open Tues–Sat 8.30–6, Sun and holidays 10–6; adm*) was begun in 1206 as the lavish seat of the Ghibelline party and now serves as Cremona's town hall. On show are paintings salvaged from churches, a superb marble fireplace of 1502 by Giovan Gaspare Pedone, Baroque furniture – and the **Saletta dei Violini**, with the town's violin collection, starring Stradivarius' golden 'Cremonese 1715', which retains its original varnish – as mysterious as the embalming fluids of ancient Egypt. Another of the master's secrets was in the woods he used for his instruments; like Michelangelo seeking just the right piece of marble in the mountains of Carrara, Stradivarius would visit the forests of the Dolomites looking for perfect trees that would one day sing. Other violins include 'Charles IX of France' by Andrea Amati, one of 24 violins commissioned in the 1560s by the French sovereign from the father of modern fiddles; the 'Hammerle', by Nicolò Amati (1658); Giuseppe Guarneri's 'Del Gesù' (formerly owned by Pinchas Zukerman); and the 1689 'Quarestini', also by Guarneri. To hear the unique sound of such rare instruments, you can book a listening session, held in the Saletta (*t 0372 22138*). Once you are in the Palazzo, take some time to visit the Sala Rossa and Sala della Giunta (if there is not a plenary session) for their original décor.

Back Towards the Station

Behind the Palazzo del Comune lie Piazza Cavour and Corso Vittorio Emanuele, leading to the River Po. En route it passes one of Italy's earliest and most renowned small-town theatres, the **Teatro Ponchielli** (*to visit, by appointment only, call t 0372 407275*), built in 1734 and rebuilt after a fire in 1808, named for Amilcare Ponchielli, who premiered several of his operas on its little stage. A street to the right of the theatre leads back to Piazza San Pietro and **San Pietro al Po**, coated with 16th-century stuccoes and frescoes by Antonio Campi.

Cremona has several lofty churches with interiors that look like nothing as much as ancient Roman basilicas. One is the 14th-century church of **Sant'Agostino**, north of the Corso Vittorio Emanuele, on Via Plasio. Its striking red brick façade is adorned with fine terracotta decorations, and the centre nave is lined with statues of the virtues. There are good Renaissance frescoes in the right aisle by Bonifacio Bembo and a lovely *pala* of the *Madonna with Saints* (1494) by Perugino (*under restoration*).

For something different, seek out the sinuous terracottas on the Liberty-style building nearby at Via Milazzo 16. Further up Via Plasio joins the Corso Garibaldi, site of the 11th-century church of **Sant'Agata**, hiding behind a neoclassical façade; the interior, a perfect Roman basilica, contains excellent frescoes by Giulio Campi of the singularly unpleasant *Martyrdom of St Agata* in the choir, a painting in the left aisle of the holy family by Lucia Anguissola, sister of the more famous Sofonisba, and a 13th-century masterpiece, the wooden panel painted with the life of St Agatha.

Opposite, the recently restored Gothic **Palazzo Cittanova** (1256) was the head-quarters of the Guelph party: adjacent, note the flamboyant but phoney façade of the **Palazzo Trecchi**. Continuing along, at Corso Garibaldi 178 the pink and white **Palazzo Raimondi** (1496) houses the Scuola Internazionale di Liuteria, where students learn to make violins (*can be visited by appointment, t 0372 38689, but visits are selected and* *tourists come second to music schools*). If you are interested in the art of fiddle-making the school's **Museo Organologico-Didattico** (*open Mon–Fri 9–12 and 3–5, Sat 9–12*) is worth a look. Across the street stands the city's most peculiar palace, crowned with strange iron dragons. Near the station, **San Luca** has a beautiful terracotta façade and a detached octagonal temple of 1503, a votive offering for the end of a plague.

One last church, **San Sigismondo**, is 1km east beyond the Piazzale Libertà, on Via A. Ghisleri (*take bus no.2*). Built in 1463 by Bianca Maria Visconti to commemorate her marriage to Francesco Sforza, the interior is delicious proof that fake is better than real: rich pastel frescoes and *trompe l'œil* décors by Giulio, Antonio and Bernardino Campi, Camillo Boccaccino and Bernardino and Gervasio Gatti coat the interior. The choir stalls are by Domenico and Gabriele Capra (1590). In the cloister look for a fresco of the *Last Supper* by Tommaso Aleni (1508). Bianca's marriage also occasioned the invention of *torrone*, made of almonds, honey and egg whites – the gastronomical equivalent to the Torrazzo (and hence the name) and still made in Cremona.

Around Cremona

Soncino and Paderno Ponchielli

Lying between the rivers Po and Oglio, the rich and strategic agricultural province of Cremona is well fortified with castles and towers that recall the glorious days when the Italian *comuni* had nothing better to do than beat each other up. The most imposing of the surviving castles, the **Rocca Sforzesca** (*open Tues–Fri 10–12, Sat, Sun and holidays 10–12.30 and 2.30–5.30, April–Oct 3–7 ; adm*) rears up over Soncino, a walled town north of Cremona on the Oglio. Built in the 12th century, it was greatly enlarged in 1473 by Galeazzo Maria Sforza as an advance base against the Venetians, who were holed up in the Brescian town of Orzinuovi directly across the river. The moat and sinister beetling towers survive intact, as well as the dungeon, which in 1259 hosted the most ferocious and hated man in Italy: Emperor Frederick II's henchman, Ezzelino da Romano. Ezzelino was severely wounded when his own army and Ghibelline allies turned on him as he crossed the Oglio on his way to surprise Milan; at age 65, he kept his reputation as a tough *hombre* to the end, refusing to speak or receive any medical treatment, ripping the bandages from his wounds until he died in agony.

On a more cheerful note, admire the watermill under the castle walls, and the delicious painted terracottas and frescoes (*c.*1500) by Giulio Campi and others that cover the interior of **Santa Maria delle Grazie**. In the late 15th century the Sforza invited a community of Jewish refugees to settle in Soncino, one of whom, Israel Nathan, founded a press and printed his first ornate book in Hebrew in 1483, and the first complete Old Testament in Hebrew in 1488: the site of the press is now a little **Museo della Stampa** (*open same hours as the castle*).

Between Cremona and Crema (the two Italian towns that most sound like dairy products) you'll find **Paderno Ponchielli**, birthplace of 'the Italian Tchaikovsky', Amilcare Ponchielli (1834–86). Italy has produced scores of one-opera composers, but

Ponchielli can claim two that are performed with some frequency: *La Gioconda* and *Marion Delorme*; and as the teacher of Puccini and Mascagni can claim to be grandfather of many others. His humble birthplace is now the **Museo Ponchiellano** (*open Tues and Thurs 2–5, other days/times by appointment t 0374 367200*).

Crema

It was in 1159, during Frederick Barbarossa's third war with Milan, that the emperor, realizing that he lacked suffecient troops to besiege the big city, turned his German army on little Crema, Milan's staunch ally. Four hundred Milanese came to Crema's defence, but Frederick wasn't in the mood for a fair fight. He hung adult hostages from Crema and Milan outside the gates, hoping to horrify Crema into surrendering, and when that didn't work he strapped their infants to moving siege towers, so that the Cremaschi could not repulse the towers without harming their own children. The parents asked their fellow citizens to kill them, to avoid witnessing their children's torture, while at the same time shouting to their children to be brave and boldly give up their lives for their country. Crema held out for six more months against Frederick's merciless tactics, but at last, starving and exhausted, it surrendered on the condition that the citizens could withdraw to Milan as their town was razed to the ground.

Three hundred years later, in 1449, Francesco Sforza offered the most loyal town of Crema to Venice when the Serenissima offered to support his dukedom. It proved to be a more pleasant occupation, enduring for three centuries and endowing Crema with a tidy elegance rare in the Lombard plain. To this day it bears a white Istrian marble lion of St Mark on its gates and town hall, the latter by the pink brick **Duomo**, a delightful Romanesque Gothic work built after Barbarossa sent the original up in flames. Its high 'wind façade' from the 1300s has windows finely decorated with curling vines, little turrets and blind arcading: next to it stands the whimsical, almost Moorish campanile of baked clay that so ravished John Addington Symonds.

Crema's narrow streets are lined by neat but secretive façades that often hide pretty courtyards and gardens. If you happen to be in Crema in late September or October,

Tourist Information

Pro Loco Crema, Via Benzoni 11, t 0373 81020, f 0373 255 728. Very helpful.

Where to Stay and Eat

Crema ✉ 26013
★★★★**Ponte di Rialto**, Via Cardorna 7, t 0373 82342, f 0373 83520 (*moderate*). One of Crema's three hotels. Small but pleasant.
★★★★**Palace**, Via Cresmiero 10, t 0373 81487, f 0373 86876 (*moderate*). Also reasonable.
★★★★**Park Hotel Residence**, Via IV Novembre, t 0373 86353, f 0373 83520 (*moderate*). Hotel with a good restaurant, the **Openhouse**,

t 0373 82341, whose Sicilian chef prepares excellent fish (*expensive*). *Closed Fri.*

As for **food**, the local speciality, *tortelli cremaschi*, is decidedly different: pasta filled with *amaretti*, raisins, citron, peppermint, nutmeg and cheese, and served in melted butter, sage and cheese.

Mario, Via Stazione 118, t 0373 204 708 (*moderate*). A good choice for local dishes. *Closed Tues eve and Wed.*

Trattoria Gobbato, Via Podgora 2, t 0373 80891 (*cheap*). A funky place that has been feeding local workers for decades. As well as local specialities, it also serves great local salami, *pasta e fasoi* (pasta with beans), vegetable lasagne and hare with *polenta. Closed Mon.*

ask the tourist office if they are organizing special visits to private palaces and villas. There are quite a few tidy palaces, and the uncompleted but utterly romantic Baroque **Palazzo Terni de' Gregori** (or Bondenti) in Via Dante, opposite the former convent of Sant' Agostino. This now houses the library and **Museo Civico** (*open Mon 2.30–6.30, Tues–Fri 9–12 and 2.30–6.30, Sat, Sun and holidays 10–12 and 4–7*) with everything from medieval Lombard armour discovered in *Aufoningum* (Offanengo) in 1963, Risorgimento mementoes, and scores by local composers, to two dramatic paintings of the *Miracles of Christ* by Alessandro Magnasco with backgrounds by Clemente Spera, an expert on painting theatrical landscapes of ruins, and other works by local talent, including a really gross 17th-century *Martyrdom of San Erasmo* and aquafortes by Federica Galli, who lives just outside town. Ask the curators to unlock the refectory to see the recently restored frescoes of the *Last Supper* and *Crucifixion* (1498) by Giovan Pietro da Cemmo. Just north of the walls, at the end of a long tree-lined avenue, stands the basilica of **Santa Maria della Croce** (1490–1500), a lovely Renaissance drum church inspired by Bramante, encircled by three orders of loggias.

West of Crema, **Rivolta d'Adda** has an 11th-century church of San Sigismondo, dwarfed by its battlemented campanile and containing some good carvings. Rivolta also offers Jurassic-era fun in its **Parco della Preistoria** (*open Mar–Nov daily 9–dusk; adm*), where a zoo train chugs past 23 life-size reproductions of dinosaurs, prowling the wooded banks of the Adda.

Mantua

Mantua's setting hardly answers to one's great expectations of Italy, sitting in the midst of a table-flat plain, on a wide thumb of land protruding into three swampy, swollen lakes formed by the River Mincio. Its climate is moody: soggy with heat and humidity in the summer and frosty under blankets of fog in the winter. The local dialect is harsh, and the Mantuans, when they feel chipper, dine on braised donkey with macaroni. Verdi made it the sombre setting of his opera *Rigoletto*. And yet this former capital of the art-loving, fast-living Gonzaga dukes is one of the most atmospheric old cities in the country – 'a city in the form of a palace' as Castiglione called it – masculine, dark and handsome, with few of Cremona's sweet architectural arpeggios – poker-faced, but holding a royal flush of dazzling Renaissance art.

History

Mantua gained its fame in Roman times as the home town of Virgil, who recounts the legend of the city's founding by the Theban soothsayer Manto, daughter of Tiresias, and her son Ocnus. Virgil was born around 70 BC, and not much else was heard from Mantua until the 11th century, when the city formed part of the vast domains of Countess Matilda of Canossa. Matilda was a great champion of the pope against the emperor; her advisor, Anselmo, Bishop of Lucca, became Mantua's patron saint. Even so, as soon as Mantua saw its chance it allied itself with the opposition, beginning an unusually important and lengthy career as an independent Ghibelline *comune*, dominated first by the Bonacolsi family and then the Gonzaga.

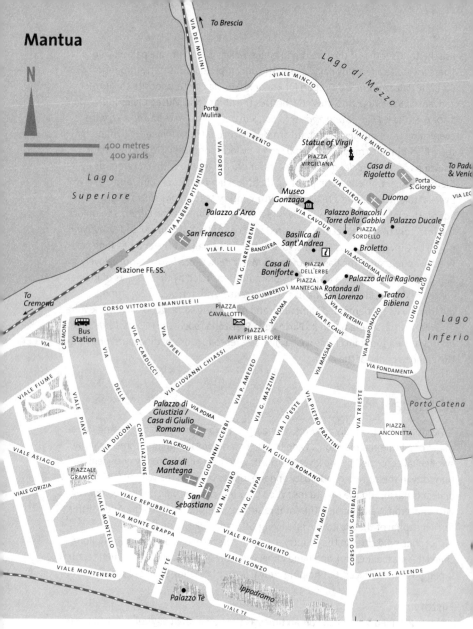

Mantua

N

400 metres
400 yards

To Brescia

VIA DEI MULINI

Lago di Mezzo

VIALE MINCIO

Porta
Mulina

VIA TRENTO

VIALE MINCIO

Statue of Virgil

PIAZZA
VIRGILIANA

Casa di
Rigoletto

To Padu
& Venio

Porta
S. Giorgio

VIA LEC

VIA CAIROLI

VIA PORTO

Lago

Superiore

VIA ALBERTO PITENTINO

Museo
Gonzaga

Duomo

Palazzo d'Arco

VIA CAVOUR

Palazzo Bonacolsi /
Torre della Gabbia

Palazzo Ducale

San Francesco

Basilica di
Sant'Andrea

PIAZZA
SORDELLO

VIA F. LLI

VIA G. ARRIVABENE

Broletto

VIA ACCADEMIA

Stazione FF. SS.

Casa di
Boniforte

PIAZZA
DELL'ERBE

Palazzo della Ragione

LUNGO LAGO DEI GONZAGA

To
Cremona

CORSO VITTORIO EMANUELE II

PIAZZA
MANTEGNA

Rotonda di
San Lorenzo

Teatro
Bibiena

Lago

Inferio

PIAZZA
CAVALLOTTI

C.SO UMBERTO I

VIA G. BERTANI

VIA CREMONA

Bus
Station

VIA G. CARDUCCI

VIA SPERI

PIAZZA
MARTIRI BELFIORE

VIA ROMA

VIA P. F. CALVI

VIA MASSARI

VIA PONPONAZZO

VIA FONDAMENTA

Portó Catena

VIALE FIUME

VIALE PIAVE

VIA DELLA

VIA DUCONI

CONCILIAZIONE

VIA GIOVANNI CHIASSI

VIA POMA

VIA P. AMEDEO

VIA GIOVANNI ACERBI

VIA G. MAZZINI

VIA I. D'ESTE

VIA PIETRO FRATTINI

VIA TRIESTE

PIAZZA
ANCONETTA

Palazzo di
Giustizia /
Casa di Giulio
Romano

VIA GRIOLI

Casa di
Mantegna

VIALE ASIAGO

VIALE GORIZIA

PIAZZALE
GRAMSCI

San Sebastiano

VIA N. SAURO

VIA G. RIPPA

VIA GIULIO ROMANO

VIA A. MORI

CORSO GIUS GARIBALDI

VIALE MONTELLO

VIALE REPUBBLICA

VIA MONTE GRAPPA

VIALE RISORGIMENTO

VIALE ISONZO

VIALE S. ALLENDE

VIALE MONTENERO

VIALE TE

Palazzo Tè

Ippodromo

VIALE TE

Naturally defended on three sides by the Mincio, enriched by river tolls and enjoying the protection of the emperor, Mantua became prominent as a neutral buffer state between Milan and Venice. The three centuries of Gonzaga rule, beginning in 1328, brought the city unusual peace and stability, while the refined tastes of the marquesses brought out artists of the highest calibre: Pisanello, Alberti and Andrea Mantegna, who was court painter from 1460 until his death in 1506. Gianfrancesco I Gonzaga invited the great teacher Vittorino da Feltre to open a school in the city in 1423, where his sons and courtiers, side by side with the children of Mantua's poorer families, were taught according to Vittorino's advanced theories, which gave equal emphasis to the intellectual, the physical and the moral. His star pupil was Ludovico (1412–78), one of the most just princes of his day, who tried to recreate Mantua according to Florentine humanist principles. Ludovico's grandson, Gianfrancesco II, was a military commander who led the Italians against the French at Fornovo, but is perhaps best known in history as the husband of the brilliant Isabella d'Este, the foremost culture-vulture of her day as well as an astute diplomat, handling Mantua's affairs of state for her not very clever husband.

The family fortunes reached their apogee under Isabella's two sons. Federico II (1500–40), godson of Cesare Borgia, married Margherita Palaeologo, the heiress of Monferrato, acquiring that duchy for the family as well as a ducal title for the Gonzaga. He hired Raphael's assistant, Giulio Romano ('that rare Italian master', Shakespeare called him in *The Winter's Tale*), to design and adorn his pleasure dome, the Palazzo Tè. When he died, his brother, Cardinal Ercole, served as regent for his son Guglielmo, and both of these men, too, proved to be busy civic improvers. The last great Gonzaga, Vincenzo I, was a patron of Rubens, Fetti and Monteverdi, who composed the first modern opera, *L'Orfeo*, for the Mantuan court in 1607.

But times grew hard and in 1628 Vincenzo II sold off many of the Gonzaga's treasures to Charles I, including Mantegna's *Triumphs of Caesar*, now at Hampton Court in the UK. It's just as well that he did; two years later Mantua suffered a near mortal blow when the Gonzaga's claims to Monferrato came into conflict with the Habsburgs, who were never ones for legal niceties and sent troops to sack the city. The duchy, under a cadet branch, limped along until the Austrians snatched Mantua in 1707, eventually making it the southwest corner of their Quadrilateral.

Piazza Mantegna

From the station, Corso Vittorio Emanuele and Corso Umberto I lead straight into the Renaissance heart of Mantua, where the narrow cobbled streets are lined with inviting porticoes. Rising above it all in Piazza Mantegna is the great basilica of **Sant'Andrea**, designed by Leon Battista Alberti in 1472 to house the Gonzaga's most precious relic: two ampoules of Christ's blood, said to have been given to St Andrew by St Longinus, the Roman centurion who pierced Christ's side. Ludovico Gonzaga had asked Alberti to create a truly monumental edifice to form a fitting centrepiece for the city, and Alberti came up with the goods. In Florence, Alberti had found himself constrained by his patrons' tastes, but in Mantua he was able to experiment with the ancient forms he loved. Sant'Andrea is based on Vitruvius' idea of an Etruscan temple, with a single barrel-vaulted nave supported by side chapels, fronted with a unique façade combining a triumphal arch and a temple. The lofty dome, designed by Juvarra, was completed in 1782. Andrea Mantegna (d. 1506) is buried in the first chapel on the left, with decorations by his followers and a rather stern self-portrait in bronze. The other chapels have fine altarpieces as well, especially the second one on the left, by Lorenzo Costa.

On the east side, the unfinished flank of the basilica is lined with the porticoes and market stalls of the delightful **Piazza dell'Erbe**. Sunk below the level of the modern

Getting There and Around

Mantua, 25km from Verona's **airport**, is linked directly by **train** with Verona, Milan, Modena, and Cremona, and indirectly with Brescia (change at Piadena). There are also **buses** (t 0376 327 237) to Lake Garda and towns in the province. Both the bus and train stations are near Piazza Porta Pradella, close to Giardini Belfiore, about 10 minutes' walk from the centre.

Tourist Information

On the corner of Piazza dell'Erbe/Piazza Mantegna 6, t 0376 328 253, f 0376 328 253, *www.aptmantova.it.*

Activities

Several **boat** companies operate on Mantua's lakes and the River Mincio, including Motonavi Andes, Piazza Sordello 8, t 0376 322 875, f 0376 322 869, *www.motonaviandes.it.* A pleasant 1½hr trip past Gonzaga castles, a beautiful bridge designed by Nervi, waterlilies, water chestnut farms and flocks of egrets costs L18,000, children L16,000 (weekdays), Sun and holidays L20,000. Motonavi also sails to San Benedetto Po, the delta of the river Po, Ferrara and Venice (book in advance).

Where to Stay

Mantua ✉ 46100

Make sure to reserve in advance, as Mantua's few hotels tend to fill up fast.

*****Villa dei Tigli**, Via Cantarana 20, t 0376 650 691, f 0376 650 649, hotel.villadeitigli@ interbusiness.it (*very expensive*). Situated in Rodigo, 15km from Mantua, this is the only five-star hotel in the area. A patrician villa from the beginning of the century set in its own park, it has all modern facilities, including a swimming pool.

****San Lorenzo**, Piazza Concordia 14, t 0376 220 500, f 0376 327 194, *www.hotelsan lorenzo.it* (*expensive*). Housed in a restored late Renaissance building in the central pedestrian zone, with views over the Piazza dell'Erbe. The rooms have most comforts; from the terrace there are views across to the dome of Sant'Andrea.

****Rechigi**, Via Calvi 30, t 0376 320 781, f 0376 220 291, *info@rechigi.com* (*expensive*). Conveniently located in the historic centre. The hotel also holds contemporary art exhibitions. Bikes for hire.

***Broletto**, Via Accademia 1, t 0376 326 784, f 0376 221 297, hotelbroletto@tin.it (*moderate*). A cosy family-run hotel in the centre. Rooms are smallish but modern.

***Due Guerrieri**, Piazza Sordello 52, t 0376 321 533, f 0376 329 645 (*moderate*). Housed in an older building overlooking the Palazzo Ducale, its location is its best attribute.

***Bianchi Stazione**, Piazza Don Leoni 24, t 0376 326 465, f 0376 321 504 (*moderate*). Near the station. Recently renovated with soberly furnished rooms and nice bathrooms. Most of the rooms open on a quiet inner courtyard. From the top floor you can see the water lilies of Lago Superiore.

*Maragò**, just outside the centre at Virgiliana, t 0376 370 313 (*cheap*). Thirteen simple rooms, not all with bath.

Eating Out

During the reign of the Gonzaga the Mantuans developed their own cuisine, which other Italians regard as a little peculiar. The notorious *stracotto di asino* (donkey stew)

pavement, the **Rotonda di San Lorenzo**, modelled on the Church of the Holy Sepulchre in Jerusalem, was built by Countess Matilda in 1082; an ambulatory supports a *matroneum*. Opposite the tourist office, **Casa di Boniforte da Concorezzo** has elegant stucco decoration, almost unchanged since it was built in 1455, while the 13th-century **Palazzo della Ragione** has a stout clock tower topped by an odd little temple and astronomical clock, added during Ludovico's restoration in 1475. The piazza is closed by the **Broletto** (1227), facing Piazza del Broletto; note the niche holding a 13th-century statue of Virgil seated near the door.

heads the list, but the Mantuans also have a predilection for adding Lambrusco to soup. Classic *primi* include *agnoli* stuffed with bacon, salami, chicken livers and cheese cooked in broth, *risotto alla pilota* (with onion, butter and *grana* cheese), or *tortelli di zucca* (pasta parcels stuffed with pumpkin, mustard and cheese, served with melted butter). Catfish, eel, crayfish, bass, pike (the delicious *luccio in salsa*, prepared with peppers and capers) – and crispy-fried frog's legs are typical *secondi*. Mantua is also the place to taste true Lambrusco; the foam should vanish instantly when poured. There are three main kinds: the grand Lambrusco di Sorbana, the mighty Lambrusco di Santa Croce and the amiable Lambrusco di Castelvetro.

Aquila Nigra, Vicolo Bonaclosi 4, t 0376 327 180 (*expensive*). A lovely place with its marble and traces of frescoes, serving exquisitely prepared regional dishes; the pasta courses (*ravioli* filled with truffled duck, for instance) are a joy, and there's a wide choice of seafood as well as meat dishes. A great wine list, cheeses and delicious desserts like chestnut *torte* round off a special meal. *Closed Sun, Mon, Aug.*

Trattoria dei Martini, Piazza d'Arco, t 0376 327 101 (*expensive*). Overlooks an inner garden. Has a menu that changes according to the season, although solidly based on local cuisine – *tagliatelle* with duck, lamb casseroled with herbs, or roast guinea fowl. *Closed Mon, Tues, and first half of Jan.*

San Gervasio, Via San Gervasio 13, t 0376 327 077 (*moderate*). Located in a superbly renovated 14th-century palace, this restaurant offers an excellent moderate *menu mantovano. Closed Wed and Aug.*

Ristorante Pavesi dal 1918, Piazza delle Erbe, t 0376 323 627 (*moderate*). In the summer the tables fill up early here; service is friendly and they do a particularly good *gnocchi alla gorgonzola. Closed Thurs.*

Trattoria Quattrotette, Vicolo Nazione, t 0376 329 478 (*moderate*). Away from the obvious tourist areas, this small restaurant squeezes in hordes of local clientele who relish the dishes of vegetables and salads, hot bowls of pasta, and *pasticceria. Closed Sun.*

Ai Garibaldini, Via S. Longino 7, t 0376 328 263 (*moderate*). In the historic centre, in a fine old house with a shady garden for al fresco dining. The menu features many Mantuan dishes, with especially good *risotto* and *tortelli di zucca. Closed Wed, Jan.*

Antica Osteria Fragoletto, Piazza Arche 5, t 0376 323 300 (*cheap*). This former *trattoria* has become a trendier restaurant, with a nice atmosphere and good cuisine, appreciated by the local clientele. *Closed Mon.*

Due Cavallini, Via Salnitro 5 (near Lago Inferiore, off Corso Garibaldi), t 0376 322 084 (*cheap*). The place to come if you want to bite into some donkey meat – though it has other less ethnic dishes as well. *Closed Tues, and late-July–late-Aug.*

Il Portichetto, Via Portichetto 14, t 0376 360 747 (*cheap*). Run by a former left-wing activist who has turned his hand to cooking; the results are excellent. The menu revolves around local river-fish – mixed *antipasti*, *tagliatelle* with perch or pike in *salsa verde* – and there are lots of vegetarian dishes. *Closed Sun eve, and Mon.*

L'Ochina Bianca, Via Finzi 2, t 0376 323 700 (*cheap*). An ever-changing menu which might include smoked beef dressed with superb olive oil, deep-fried *zucchini* flowers, delicate home-made pasta and succulent meat dishes. The autumn menu offers pumpkins even as a dessert (ice cream *neve nel bicchiere*, snow in the glass). *Closed Mon and Tues lunch.*

An archway leads into the grand cobbled **Piazza Sordello**, traditional seat of Mantua's bosses. On one side rise the sombre palaces of the Bonacolsi, the Gonzaga's predecessors, with their **Torre della Gabbia**, named for the iron cage they kept to suspend prisoners over the city (though the Mantuans claim it was only used once). At the head of the piazza stands the **Duomo**, with a silly 1756 façade, topped by wedding-cake figures, that hides a lovely interior designed by Giulio Romano in 1545. Renaissance tapestries hang in the choir, and the enormous *Trinity* in the apse is by Domenico Fetti, another Roman painter who worked in Mantua in the early 1600s.

The 15th-century house at No.23 has been named the '**Casa di Rigoletto**' to satisfy the longings of Verdi buffs; opposite, a new archaeology museum is in the works.

The Palazzo Ducale

Open Tues–Sun 8.45–7.15, but if you arrive after 6pm you will get a shorter tour; Jun–Sept open Sat 8am–11pm; to see the Camera degli Sposi groups must book on t 0376 382150.

Opposite the Bonacolsi palaces stands that of the Gonzaga, its unimpressive façade hiding one of Italy's most remarkable Renaissance abodes, both in sheer size and the magnificence of its art. The insatiable Gonzaga kept on adding on until they had some 500 rooms in three main structures – the original **Corte Vecchia**, first built by the Bonacolsi in 1290, the 14th-century **Castello**, with its large towers overlooking the lake, and the **Corte Nuova**, designed by Giulio Romano. Throw in the Gonzaga's **Basilica di Santa Barbara** and you have a complex that occupies the entire northeast corner of Mantua. If you go in the winter, dress warmly – it's as cold as a dead duke.

Although stripped of its furnishings and most of its portable art, the Palazzo Ducale remains imposing and seemingly endless. One of the first rooms on the tour, the former **chapel**, has a dramatic, half-ruined 14th-century fresco of the *Crucifixion*, attributed by some to Tommaso da Modena, while another contains a painting of a battle between the Gonzaga and the Bonacolsi in the Piazza Sordello, in which the Gonzaga crushed their rivals once and for all in 1328 – although the artist, Domenico Monore, painted the piazza as it appeared in 1494. Even more fascinating than this real battle is the vivid **fresco of Arthurian knights** by Pisanello, Italy's International Gothic master. Recorded as damaged in the 1480s, the fresco was believed lost until 1969, when layers of plaster were stripped away to reveal a remarkable work commissioned by Gianfrancesco Gonzaga in 1442 to commemorate his receiving from Henry VI the concession to use the heraldic SS collar of the House of Lancaster, an insignia that forms the border of Pisanello's mural, mingled with marigolds, a Gonzaga emblem.

Beyond this are the remodelled **neoclassical rooms**, holding a set of Flemish tapestries from Raphael's *Acts of the Apostles* cartoons (now in the V&A Museum, London). Woven in the early 1500s, these copies of the Vatican originals are in a much better state of preservation. Beyond, the **Sala dello Zodiaco** has vivacious 1580 frescoes by Lorenzo Costa; the **Sala del Fiume** is named for its fine views over the river; and the **Galleria degli Specchi** has mirrors and mythological frescoes and, by the door, a note from Monteverdi on the musical evenings he directed there in the 1600s.

The Gonzaga were mad about horses and dogs and had one room, the **Salone degli Arcieri**, painted with *trompe l'œil* frescoes of their favourite steeds standing on upper ledges; the family used to play a kind of guessing game with them, when curtains would be drawn over the figures. Sharing the room are works by Tintoretto and a family portrait by Rubens, court painter under Vincenzo I, a picture so large that Napoleon's troops had to cut it up to carry it off. The duke's apartments hold a fine collection of classical statuary: busts of the emperors, a Hellenistic torso of Aphrodite, and the 'Apollo of Mantova', inherited from Sabbioneta after Vespasiano's death. The

Sala di Troia has vivid 1536 frescoes by Giulio Romano and his pupil, Rinaldo
Mantovano, while another ducal chamber has a 17th-century labyrinth painted on the
ceiling, each path inscribed in gold with 'Maybe Yes, Maybe No'.

The oldest part of the palace complex, the 14th-century **Castello San Giorgio**, is
reached by a low spiral ramp, built especially for the horses the Gonzaga could never
bear to be without. Here, in the famous **Camera degli Sposi**, are the remarkable
frescoes painted by Mantegna in 1474, who like a genie captured the essence of the
Gonzaga in this small bottle of a room. Restored to their brilliant original colours, the
frescoes depict the life of Ludovico Gonzaga, with his wife Barbara of Brandenburg,
his children, dwarves, servants, dogs and horses, and important events – greeting his
son Francesco, recently made a cardinal, and playing host to Emperor Frederick III and
King Christian I of Denmark. The portraits are unflattering and solid, those of real
people not for public display, almost like a family photo album. The effect is like
stumbling on the court of the Sleeping Beauty; only the younger brother, holding the
new cardinal's hand, seems to suspect that he has been enchanted. Wife Barbara and
her stern dwarf stare out, as if determined to draw the spectator into the eerie scene.
And there is a lingering sorcery here, for these frescoes are the fruit of Mantegna's
fascination with the mysterious new science of perspective. The backgrounds of
imaginary cities and ruins reflect Mantegna's other love, classical architecture, but
add an element of unreality in their vividness, as do his *trompe l'œil* ceiling frescoes.

From here the tour continues to the **Casetta dei Nani**, residence of the dwarves, tiny
rooms with low ceilings and shallow stairs, although there are party-poopers who say
the rooms had a pious purpose, and were meant to bring the sinning dukes to their
proud knees. The last stop is the **rooms of Isabella d'Este**, designed by her as a retreat
after her husband's death. Her fabulous art collection has long gone to the Louvre,
but the inexplicable emblems and symbols she devised with her astrologers remain
like faint ghosts from a lost world on the ceiling.

Around Town

There are several sights within easy walking distance of the Palazzo Ducale. At Via
Accademia 47, east of the Broletto, the **Teatro Accademico Bibiena** (*open Tues–Sun
9.30–12.30 and 3–6; adm*) is a gem built by Antonio Galli Bibiena, a member of the
famous Bolognese family of theatre builders. Mozart, aged 13, performed at the
inaugural concert in 1770; his father Leopold said it was the most beautiful theatre he
had ever seen.

West of the Piazza Sordello, Via Cairoli leads to the city's main park, the **Piazza
Virgiliana**, with a marble statue of Virgil from 1927 (in time for the poet's 2,000th
birthday) and the **Museo Gonzaga** (*open April–June Tues–Sun 9.30–12 and 2.30–5; July
and Aug Thurs, Sat and Sun only; Nov–Mar Sun only; adm*), containing artefacts and
treasures that once belonged to the family. Further west, in the Piazza d'Arco, the
Palazzo d'Arco (*open Nov–Feb Sat 10–12.30 and 2–5, Sun 10–5; Mar–Oct Tues–Sun and
holidays 10–12.30 and 2.30–5.30; adm*) was rebuilt in 1784 over a 15th-century palace
for the arty counts from Garda's north shore and has been left more or less as it was,
complete with furnishings, paintings, instruments, a superb kitchen and, in a room

preserved from the original palace, fascinating frescoes of the zodiac, attributed to Giovanni Maria Falconetto of Verona and painted c. 1515 in the period between Mantegna's death and Giulio Romano's arrival. The nearby **church of San Francesco** (1304) was rediscovered in 1944, when a bomb hit the arsenal that had disguised it for a century and a half. Restored to its original state, it contains frescoes by the excellent Tommaso da Modena in the last chapel on the right.

South of the medieval nucleus, just off main Via Principe Amedeo at Via Poma 18, the **Casa di Giulio Romano** was designed by the artist himself in 1544 while working on the Palazzo Tè. He also gets credit for the quaint palace decorated with monsters nearby; the heavy **Palazzo di Giustizia** at No. 22 was built in the 1620s. Mantegna also designed his dream house, the **Casa del Mantegna**, in the same neighbourhood, at Via Acerbi 47 (*open Tues–Sun 10–12.30 and 3–6 when an exhibition is on; otherwise Mon–Fri 10–12.30*). Designed as a cube built around a circular courtyard, he intended it partially as his personal museum and embellished it with classical 'Mantegnesque' decorations. Opposite stands the rather neglected San Sebastiano (1460), the second church in Mantua designed by Alberti, this one in the form of a Greek cross.

A Renaissance Pleasure Dome: the Palazzo Tè

Open Tues–Sun 9–6, Mon 1–6; adm exp.

At the end of Via Acerbi is Giulio Romano's masterpiece, the marvellous Palazzo Tè, its name derived not from tea, but from the rather less savoury *tejeto*, a local word for a drainage canal. On a former swamp, drained for a horsey Gonzaga pleasure ground, work began in 1527 when Federico II had Giulio Romano expand the stables to create a little palace for his mistress, Isabella Boschetti, of whom his mother, Isabella d'Este, disapproved. The project expanded over the decades to become a guest house suitable for the emperor Charles V, who visited twice.

Giulio Romano had moved from Rome to Mantua in 1524 to escape prison for designing a series of pornographic prints. In his Palazzo Tè, one of the very first great Mannerist buildings, he had the same desire to shock and amaze and upset the cool classicism exemplified in Mantua by Alberti, and along the way he created one of the great Renaissance syntheses of architecture and art, combining *trompe l'œil* with a bold play between the structure of the room and the frescoes. Most of the art still has classical themes: the **Sala della Metamorfosi** is inspired by Ovid and Roman frescoes, which Giulio discovered with his master Raphael in Nero's Golden House in Rome. Gonzaga emblems fill the **Sala delle Imprese**: putti holding a cup, a belt, a bird catching fish, a muzzle, Mount Olympus, the salamander (a symbol of Federico's love, which is consumed, but doesn't burn); the chariot of the sun on the ceiling is a first hint of Giulio's love of wacky perspectives. The next room has more life-size Gonzaga horses up on ledges, and in the next, the **Sala di Psiche**, all glory bursts forth in the intense colours and exuberance of the scenes from *The Golden Ass* of Apuleius. The **Camera dei Venti** was Federico's private study, designed with the most precious materials and with a complex iconographic programme based on ancient astrological texts, each scene illustrating a prediction linked to a rising constellation.

The **Loggia di Davide**, quickly thrown up for Charles V's second visit in 1532, is decorated with scenes dear to Federico's heart – he identified himself with the king, and his Isabella with Bathsheba, both of whom were relieved of their husbands in suspicious circumstances. The next room has incredible antiquizing stuccoes by Francesco Primaticcio, who later went on to Fontainebleau to work for François I. The climax, however, is the famous **Sala dei Giganti**, Giulio's most startling work, entirely frescoed from floor to ceiling. Above, Zeus and Co. rain lightning, thunder, boulders and earthquakes down on the uppity Titans, creating so powerful an illusion of chaos that it seems as if the very room is about to cave in around the spectator.

Around Mantua

Mantua's western lake, **Lago Superiore**, is noted for its delicate lotus blossoms, planted in the 1930s as an experiment. They have since thrived, and turn the lake violet and pink in July and August around the city's park, the **Valletta Belfiore**. Another park, the **Bosco della Fontana** (*open Mar–Oct daily excluding Tues and Fri 9–7; Sun and holidays adm; Nov–Feb 9–5*) lies 5km to the north off the road to Brescia. Once a Gonzaga hunting reserve, with a moated little castle built as a hunting lodge in 1595, the Bosco's ancient, broad-leafed trees are a last relic of the ancient forest that once covered the Po plain, and its shady paths and streamlets are a tempting retreat from the afternoon heat. If you're in Mantua on 15 August be sure to visit the **Sanctuary of the Madonna delle Grazie**, on the banks of Lago Superiore at Curtatone, and see the contest of *madonnari* – artists who draw sidewalk chalk portraits of the Madonna – among other diversions. Built as a votive offering by Francesco I after the plague of 1399, the church has a 15th-century frescoed ceiling, paintings by Lorenzo Costa, and a hotchpotch of votive offerings, including a stuffed crocodile.

San Benedetto Po

Some 22km southeast of Mantua, and connected in the summer by boats sailing down the Mincio to the Po, San Benedetto Po grew up around the Benedictine abbey of **Polirone** (*open daily 8–12 and 2.30–7*), touted as the 'Monte Cassino of the North', established in the year 1007 by the Canossa counts of Tuscany. It was especially favoured by the last of their line, the feisty Countess Matilda (d. 1115), whose alabaster sarcophagus survives in the richly decorated Basilica di San Benedetto, rebuilt in the 1540s by Giulio Romano and linked to the 12th-century church of **Santa Maria**, which preserves a fine mosaic of 1151. There are three cloisters and a refectory with frescoes by Correggio, now part of the **Museo dell'Abbazia** (*open Mar–May Tues–Fri 9–1 and 2.30–6; June–mid Nov Tues–Fri 9.30–1 and 3–6.30; Sat and Sun 9.30–12.30 and 3–7; mid Nov–Feb call t 0376 623036 to arrange a visit; adm*).

Sabbioneta

An hour's bus ride southwest of Mantua on the Parma road, Sabbioneta was built as a capital and ideal dream city by the prince of Bozzolo, Vespasiano Gonzaga, member

Tourist Information

Ufficio del Turismo del Comune: Piazza d'Armi, t 0375 22104, *comune.sabbioneta@unh.net* *(open April–Sept Tues–Sat 9.30–12.30 and 2.30–6, Sun 9.30–12.30 and 2.30–7; Oct–Mar Tues–Sat 9.30–12.30 and 2.30–5, Sun 9.30–12.30 and 2.30–6)*
Pro Loco: Via Gonzaga 31, t 0375 52039, f 0375 220295.

Where to Stay

Sabbioneta ✉ 46018
**Al Duca, Via della Stamperia 18, t 0375 52474, f 0375 22021 *(cheap)*. There's not a lot of choice in Sabbioneta, but the Duke is a fairly large, central hotel, with comfortable modern rooms and bathrooms.

Eating Out

Sabbioneta's two best restaurants are outside the city walls:
Parco Cappuccini, Via Santuario 30, t 0375 52005, f 0375 220 056 *(expensive)*. This elegant restaurant occupies an 18th-century villa with a verandah on the park, an inviting place to linger over classic Italian cuisine. *Closed Mon and Wed eve.*
Il Capriccio, Via Solazzi 51, t/f 0375 52722 *(moderate)*. Serves delicious creative dishes based on Mantuan tradition, with a cheap lunch menu. *Closed Mon eve and Tues.*

of a cadet branch of the Gonzaga family. Vespasiano was a firm believer that the city should be a rational expression in the measure of man, and had the streets of his 'Little Athens' laid out straight and square within its irregular hexagonal walls; his humanistic philosophy attracted many Jewish settlers, who founded a famous printing press. To see the interiors, contact one of Sabbioneta's two tourist offices: the newly created Ufficio del Turismo del Comune, for civic buildings, or the privately run Pro Loco for religious ones; two may seem excessive for such a small place, but a legal quarrel divides them – the state versus the church, just as in olden times. Things may change, but for now the civic office runs 1½-hour-long tours of Vespasiano's dream palaces, in English on request, and the Pro Loco covers church and synagogue.

The classical utopian vision of Vespasiano was out of fashion before Sabbioneta was even built, and its spark died with its creator, leaving a little museum city. In the last 15 years, however, interest in Sabbioneta has been rekindled, and much has been restored; antique shops and restaurants have begun to fill some of the houses. Around central Piazza Castello, Vespasiano constructed a long frescoed corridor, the **Galleria degli Antichi**, to display his classical statues (now in Mantua's Palazzo Ducale). At one end stands the **Palazzo del Giardino**, his pleasure palace, adorned with frescoes and stuccoes by the school of Giulio Romano. The next stop on the tour is the small 1588 **Teatro Olimpico**, designed by Vincenzo Scamozzi after Palladio's theatre in Vicenza. Twelve plaster statues of the ancient Olympians grace the balcony, and some of the original Venetian frescoes have recently been rediscovered. The second piazza contains the symmetrical **Palazzo Ducale**, with its five arches housing wooden equestrian statues of Vespasiano and his kin; other rooms, with fine frescoes and ceilings, include the **Sala d'Oro**, the **Sala degli Elefanti** and the **Sala delle Città Marinare**, with paintings of port towns. Behind the palace, the church of the **Incoronata** houses Vespasiano's mausoleum, with a bronze statue of the prince in classical Roman garb. Also in the centre of town is the 16th-century **synagogue**, derelict since it was destroyed during the Second World War.

The Italian Lakes

Just to mention the Italian Lakes is to evoke a soft, dreamy image of romance and beauty, a Latin Brigadoon of gentlemen and gentle ladies strolling through gardens, sketching landscapes, and perhaps indulging in a round of whist on the villa verandah in the evening. The backgrounds to their fond pleasures are scenes woven of poetry, of snow-capped peaks tumbling steeply into ribbons of blue, trimmed with the silver tinsel of olives and the daggers of dark cypress; of mellowed villas gracing vine-clad hillsides and gold-flecked citrus groves; of spring's excess, when the lakes become drunken with colour, as a thousand varieties of azaleas, rhododendrons and camellias spill over the banks. For even though the Swiss border is just around the corner, the lakes cover enough area to create their own climatic oases of Mediterranean flora, blooming even at the foot of the Alps.

Lake holidays faded from fashion in the post-War era, when a suntan became a symbol of leisure not manual labour, and summer's mass trek to the seashore became as fixed a ritual as the drowning of lemmings. But the lakes are simply too lovely to stay out of fashion for long, and today a new generation is busily rediscovering what their grandparents took for granted. For better or worse, the Italians have ringed the lakes with finely engineered roads, making them perhaps too accessible, although all still have their leisurely steamers.

Between July and September rest and relaxation, or even peace and quiet, may seem a Victorian relic, unless you book into one of the grander villa hotels. Quiet havens, however, still exist on the smaller, less developed lakes of Iseo and Orta, the east shores of Maggiore and Como.

Lake resorts are generally open between April and October. The best times to visit are in spring and autumn, not only to avoid the crowds, but because the lakes themselves are less subjected to winter mists and summer haze. In the restaurants, look for lake fish, served either fresh or sun-dried. The finest wines from the lake district come from the Franciacorta near Iseo, Bardolino on Lake Garda, the Valtellina, and La Brianza near Lake Como.

Below, the lakes are described geographically from west to east, from Piemonte's Lake Orta and the valleys around Domodossola, through Lombardy's lakes and the Valtellina, Bergamo and Brescia, and then to Lake Garda on the border of the Veneto.

Lake Orta

The green waters of Lake Orta run still and quiet, and in the centre they hold a magical isle, illuminated on summer nights like a golden fairy-tale castle. A mere 13km long, Orta is a lake 'made to the measurements of man'. Nietzsche, who never fell in love, did so on its soft green shores. He didn't get the girl, but the world got *Thus Spake Zarathustra*. On a more mundane level, Orta's villages produce bathroom taps, saxophones, coffee pots and chefs; so many come from Armeno that the second Sunday each November it holds an annual reunion of cooks.

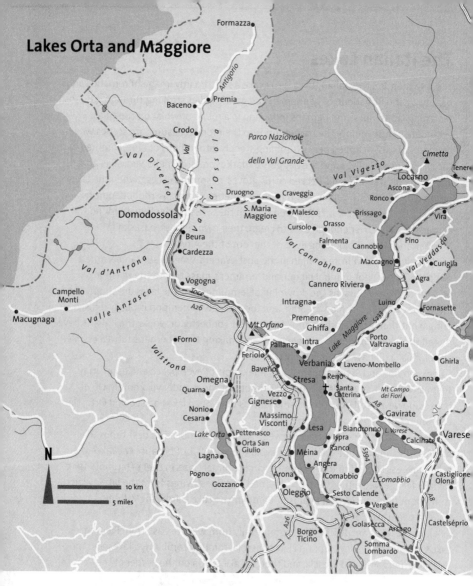

Lakes Orta and Maggiore

Orta San Giulio, its Island, and Omegna

Blithely set on its own garden peninsula, the lake's 'capital', Orta San Giulio, is a fetching little town. Lanes too narrow for cars all lead into handsome lakeside **Piazza Motta**, a cosy rendezvous nicknamed the *salotto* or drawing room, with the bijou 1582 **Palazzotto** as a centrepiece, its stuccoed exterior decorated with now-faded frescoes. In April and May, Orta opens the season with the Ortafiori flower festival, when you can visit the superb gardens of the Villa Motta.

From Orta, steamboats run to the ports of Pella, Oira and Omegna, and to **Isola San Giulio**, once the lair of loathsome serpents and monsters. They were banished by Orta's answer to St Patrick – St Julius – who arrived in 390 and founded the precursor to the island's **basilica**. Most of what you see today dates from the 12th century, including the black marble pulpit, carved with the banished griffons and serpents. There are some good 15th-century frescoes by Ferrari and his school, and a marble sarcophagus of Lombard Duke Meinulphus, who had betrayed the island to the Franks and was beheaded by Agilulf; a decapitated skeleton was found inside in 1697.

On the northern tip of the lake, **Omegna** (Roman *Vomenia*) is the biggest town on the lake, which specializes in making pots and pans and coffee pots In the pleasant centre of town, the Piazza del Municipio gives on to a bridge spanning the river that drains Orta – the Nigoglia – the only river in Italy that flows *towards* the Alps.

From Lake Orta to Domodossola

Valle Anzasca

From Omegna, the railway and *autostrada* continue into the northernmost reaches of Piemonte. Between Omegna and Domodossola, the enchanting Valle Anzasca diverges to the west. Little villages lie scattered in the woods, like tiny **Colombetti**, its slate roofs huddled under a cliff; **Bannio-Anzino**, the 'capital' of the valley, with modest skiing facilities – and a 7ft-tall, 16th-century bronze Christ from Flanders in its parish church; and **Ceppo Morelli**, with a famous, vertiginous bridge over the Anza, which traditionally divides the valley's Latin population from the Walser. Beyond Ceppo the road plunges through a gorge to **Pestarena**, an old gold-mining town.

The various hamlets that comprise **Macugnaga**, the Valle Anzasca's popular resort, lie under the majestic frowning face of **Monte Rosa** (15,213ft). As in the Val Gressoney on the southern side of Monte Rosa, Macugnaga was settled by German-speaking Swiss from the Valais (the Walser) in the 13th century. A small museum in **Borca** is devoted to Walser folklore, while other old Swiss traces remain in the 13th-century parish church.

Macugnaga has a number of ski lifts, and a chairlift that operates in the summer as well, to the magnificent **belvedere** with views over the Macugnaga glacier; a *funivia* from Staffa to the **Passo Monte Moro** (9,407ft) is used by skiers in both the winter and summer seasons. From Macugnaga, fearless alpinists can attempt the steep east flank of Monte Rosa, one of the most dangerous ascents in the Alps; serious walkers can make a three-day trek over the mountains to Gressoney-St-Jean and other points in the Valle d'Aosta (trail map essential, *see* p.139). North of the Valle Anzasca, the pretty wooded **Val d'Antrona** is famed for its old-fashioned ways: the older women still wear their traditional costumes every day and make Venetian lace.

Domodossola

The largest town in the Valle d'Ossola, Domodossola lies at the foot of the **Simplon Pass** (Passo del Sempione), through which, after the Battle of Marengo, Napoleon constructed his highway from Geneva to Milan, completed in 1805. Exactly 100 years later the even more remarkable 19.8km Simplon Tunnel was completed – the longest in the world. Domodossola itself is a pleasant old town with an arcaded main square.

Getting Around

The main lake resorts, Orta San Giulio, Pettenasco and Omegna, are easily reached from Turin or Milan on **trains** heading north to Domodossola and the Simplon Pass. Orta is also easy to reach from Lake Maggiore: **buses** run from Stresa to Orta, from Arona to Borgomanero with connections to Orta, and from Verbania to Omegna.

Navigazione Lago d'Orta, t 0322 844 862, provides a **boat** service at least twice a day between the ports of Oria, Omegna, Punta di Crabbia, Pettenasco, L'Approdo, Orta, Isola San Giulio, Pella, San Filiberto and Lagna (Lagna closed for repairs at the time of writing). The company also offers midnight cruises from Orta, Pella and Pettenasco in August, and to and from Omegna for the San Vito festival.

Tourist Information

Orta San Giulio: Via Panoramica, t 0322 905614, f 0322 905800; ortatl@tin.it.
Pettenasco: Piazza Unità d'Italia, t 0323 89593.
Omegna: Piazza XXIV Aprile 17, t/f 0323 61930, *proloco.omegna@gse.it* (open summer only).
Macugnaga: Piazza Municipio, t 0324 65119, f 0324 65775, *www.macugnaga-online.it* (open summer only).
Domodossola: Piazza Matteotti, at the train station, t/f 0324 248265, *ufficioiat@libero.it*.
Santa Maria Maggiore: Piazza Risorgimento 28, t 0324 95091, *www.vallevigezzo.vb.it*.

Where to Stay and Eat

Orta San Giulio ✉ 28016
****Villa Crespi**, Via G. Fava 8/10, t 0322 911 902, f 0322 911 919, *www.lagodortahotels.*

com (*very expensive*). Orta San Giulio is awash in lovely hotels, and this is the lake's most luxurious, in a garden at the top of the town: a Moorish folly built in 1880 and now painstakingly restored and furnished with period pieces. The eight suites and six bedrooms each have romantic canopied beds, marble baths and jacuzzis. The elegant dining room is equalled by the ravishing dishes prepared by top chef Antonino Cannavacciuolo, mixing Mediterranean and alpine flavours: macaroni with lobster ragout, cherry tomatoes and light *pesto* sauce or pigeon breast stuffed with foie gras and wrapped in the savoy *labrage*. Menus are surprisingly good value (L130,000 for a gourmet menu, L85,000 for regional and foreign menus). *Closed Tues in winter, Jan and Feb.*

****San Rocco**, Via Gippini 11, t 0322 911 977, f 0322 911 964, *www.hotelsanrocco.it* (*very expensive*). Down in Orta's historic centre, and located in a former 17th-century monastery, traces of which remain in the structure, some public halls and windows. Rooms are modern and there's a pretty garden and a heated outdoor pool right on the water. In August it hosts jazz and classical music concerts.

***Orta**, Piazza Motta, t 0322 90253, f 0322 905 646, *www.orta.net/hotelorta* (*moderate*). Brimming over with old-fashioned Italian character, the Orta has been run by the same family for over a century, with big rooms and bathrooms and a charming dining terrace directly on the lake.

***Leon d'Oro**, Piazza Motta, t 0322 911 991, f 0322 90303, , *www.orta.net/leondoro* (*moderate*). In 1882, Nietzsche and Lou Salomé spent their love-troubled week here and to this day the lake terrace and bar are

---

Its **Museo G.G. Galletti** has exhibits relating to to the flight of Peruvian Jorge Chavez, the first man to fly over the Alps (29 September 1910), only to die in a crash near Domodossola. He also has a monument in Piazza Liberazione.

A narrow-gauge electric railway, **La Vigezzina**, makes the picturesque journey in an hour and a half between Domodossola and Locarno on Lake Maggiore through the **Val Vigezzo**, a romantic beauty nicknamed the Valley of Painters. The place to stay if you're tempted to paint a landscape is the main town, **Santa Maria Maggiore**; from nearby Maleco a road descends the Val Cannobina to Cannobio on Lake Maggiore.

especially amenable to such breaks from philosophy; rooms, recently remodelled, are small but immaculate.

Olina, Via Olina 40, **t 0322 905 656, **f** 0322 90377 (*moderate*). Very pleasant rooms, some with whirlpool shower, and an elegant restaurant (*moderate*); specialities are home-made pasta and lake fish. *Closed Wed.*

Taverna Antico Agnello (*moderate*). A couple of steps up, this is a charming and cosy restaurant with fish from the lake and more unusual fare such as venison *cotoletta* with juniper berries; also a good selection of cheeses, sliced hams and salami of the neighbouring regions, delicious *torte di verdura*, home-made pasta, *confiture* and desserts and a good wine list; book, and order *risotto*, in advance. *Closed Tues.*

Venus, Piazza Motta, **t** 0322 90362 (*moderate*). Always packed for lunch due to its position in the *salotto* of Piaza Motta, but standards have dropped and prices risen.

Pettenasco ✉ 28028
***Giardinetto, Via Provinciale 1, **t** 0323 89118, **f** 0323 89219, *www.lagodortahotels.com* (*expensive*). Right on Lake Orta, a friendly family hotel with views of the Isola San Giulio. Prices drop out of season, and there are reduced rates for children, a swimming pool and private beach. The excellent restaurant is expensive, but has a convenient cheap *menu degustazione* for two. *Open April–Oct only.*

Macugnaga ✉ 28876
***Zumstein, Via Monte Rosa 63, **t** 0324 65118, **f** 0324 65490, *sviva@bbs.infosquare.it* (*moderate*). The largest and most luxurious choice, with attractive rooms near the centre of Staffa. *Closed May, Oct and Nov.*

Chez Felice, Via alle Ville 14, **t 0324 65229, **f** 0324 65037. Chez Felice is the best restaurant in the valley, a haven of mountain *nuova cucina*, where you can sample salmon mousse with herbs, warm artichokes with a sauce of anchovies and capers, *risotto* with almonds, cheese and herb soufflé and many other delights; for afters, there's a magnificent array of local cheeses and exquisite desserts. Reserve if you're not staying at the hotel. *Closed Thurs.*

Domodossola ✉ 28845
***Corona, Via Marconi 8, **t** 0324 242 114, **f** 0324 242 842, *htcorona@tin.it* (*moderate*). The most stylish hotel in town has very comfortable rooms. Ask for the top-floor rooms at the back to enjoy the views over the old city centre and to the Sacro Monte. The restaurant has both local and international dishes.

Trattoria Piemonte da Sciolla, Piazza Convenzione 5, **t** 0324 242 633 (*moderate*). In the centre, highly recommended for its regional dishes such as *polenta* with milk and poppyseeds and its home-made desserts. *Closed Wed and late Aug.*

Santa Maria Maggiore ✉ 28857
***Miramonti, Piazzale Diaz 3, **t** 0324 95013, **f** 0324 94283, *www.miramontihotels.com* (*moderate*). You can sleep and eat in style up near the station at the bigger hotel building, or, preferably, at the cosy chalet with flowers flowing over the balconies. Candlelit dinners at the hotel restaurant with finely prepared and served local dishes, including traditional *pane e latte* cake (stale bread, milk, raisins – like an English bread and butter pudding) are rounded off with the local S. Giacomo *digestivo*, poured from tall narrow bottles.

Buses from Domodossola also plunge north into the spectacular scenery that leads up into the **Val Formazza**, colonized by German-speaking families from the Valais. Their charming, scattered, villages are small summer and winter resorts offering excursions to the Alpine lakes. If you come between 9 and 5 on a Sunday or holiday from June until September, or any day between 10 and 20 August, you can take in one of the most breathtaking waterfalls in all the Alps at the end of the road: the thundering 985ft veil of mist, the **Cascata del Toce**. At other times, like all of Italy's best waterfalls, its bounding, splashing energy spins hydroelectric turbines.

Lake Maggiore

Have you not read in books how men when they see even divine visions are terrified?
So as I looked at Lake Major in its halo I also was afraid ...

Hilaire Belloc, *The Path to Rome*

Italy's second-largest lake, Maggiore winds majestically between Piemonte and Lombardy, its northern corner lost in the snow-capped Swiss Alps. In Roman times Maggiore was called *Lacus Verbanus*, for the verbena that still grows luxuriantly on its shores. What really sets the lake apart, though, are the fabled Borromean Isles and their gardens, still the property of the Borromeo family of Milan, who also own all the lake's fishing rights – as they have since the 1500s. Otherwise, the western shore, especially the triad of resorts – Stresa, Baveno, and Verbania – are the most scenic places to aim for. Unless you book well in advance, however, avoid July and August.

Arona

Arona is the southernmost steamer landing, and even if you're just passing through it is hard to avoid San Carlone, a 115ft-high copper and bronze jug-eared colossus

The World's Biggest Saint

Charles Borromeo – son of Count Gilbert Borromeo and a Medici mother – was the most influential churchman of his day, appointed 'Cardinal Nephew and Archbishop of Milan' at the age of 22 by his maternal uncle, Pope Pius IV. In Rome he was a powerful voice calling for disciplinary reform within the Church, and he instigated the Council of Trent, that decade-long Counter-Reformation strategy session in which he played a major role. There was one legendary point in Trent when the cardinals wanted to ban all church music, which by the 16th century had degenerated to the point of singing lewd love ballads to accompany the *Te Deum*. Charles and his committee, however, decided to let the musicians have one more chance, and asked Palestrina to compose three suitable Masses that reflected the dignity of the words of the service (Charles reputedly told the composer that the cardinals expected him to fail). To their surprise, and to the everlasting benefit of Western culture, Palestrina succeeded, and sacred music was saved.

After the death of his uncle-pope, Charles went to live in his diocese of Milan, the first archbishop to do so in 80 years. Following the codex of the Council of Trent to the letter (that's the book under the arm of the San Carlone statue), he at once began reforming the once-cosy clergy to set the example for other bishops. The Milanese weren't exactly thrilled: Charles escaped an assassination attempt in the cathedral, when the bullet bounced off his brocade vestments. He was a bitter enemy of original thought and not someone you would want to have over for dinner; if New York has a Statue of Liberty, Arona has a Statue of Tyranny. For a queer sensation walk up the steps through his hollow viscera (access for people aged 8+ only, due to its steep steps): his head can hold six people, who can peer out of his eyes, each a foot and a half wide. The plastic doodahs in the souvenir shop below are worth a special trip.

towering above the old town (*open April–Sept daily 8.30–12.30 and 2–6.30; Oct–early Nov 9–12.30 and 2–5; Nov–Mar open Sat and Sun only 9–12.30 and 2–5 and Christmas period; adm*). San Carlone (St Big Chuck) is perhaps better known as Charles Borromeo (1538–84), born in the now-ruined Castello di Arona; his family erected the statue in 1697. The Borromeo chapel in Santa Maria contains a 1511 altarpiece by Ferrari.

More Borromeana awaits at **Angera**, across the lake in Lombardy and the first steamer call. Its mighty **Rocca di Angera** (*open April–Oct daily 10.30–12.30 and 4–6; July and Aug 9.30–12.30 and 3–7; adm*) commands the whole southern half of the lake. The 11th-century builders, the Della Torre, lost it to the Visconti, who frescoed it in 1277 with battle scenes of their victory. The Borromei picked it up again in 1439.

Stresa, the 'Pearl of Verbano'

Beautifully positioned on the lake overlooking the Borromeo islands, under the majestic peak of Mottarone, Stresa is Maggiore's most beautiful town, bursting with flowers and sprinkled with fine old villas. A holiday resort since the last century, famous for its lush gardens and mild climate, it soared in popularity after the construction of the Simplon Tunnel in 1906; Hemingway used its **Grand Hôtel des Iles Borromées** as Frederick Henry's refuge from war in *A Farewell to Arms*. The little triangular **Piazza Cadorna** in the centre, shaded by age-old plane trees, is Stresa's social centre, the numbers of its habitués swollen by international congress participants and music lovers attending the *Settimane Musicali di Stresa*, featuring orchestras from around the world from the last week of August through September.

Two of Stresa's lakeside villas are open to the public: **Villa Pallavicino** (1850) and its colourful gardens, where saucy parrots rule the roost (*open Mar–Oct, daily 9–6; adm*) and the **Villa Ducale** (1771), once the property of Catholic philosopher Antonio Rosmini (d. 1855); besides the gardens, there's a Rosmini museum (*open daily 9–12 and 3–6*).

From Stresa you can ascend **Monte Mottarone** (4,920ft), via the cableway beginning at Stresa Lido (*9.20, then every 20 mins until 12 and 1.40–5.30, the last descent; adm exp, cheaper for under-12s*) The views are famous, on a clear day taking in not only all seven major Italian lakes, but also glacier-crested peaks from Monte Viso (far west) and Monte Rosa over to the eastern ranges of Ortles and Adamello, as well as much of the Lombard plain. If you drive, walk or take the bus from Stresa, you can also visit the Alpine rock gardens of the **Giardino Alpinia** (*open April–15 Oct Tues–Sat 9.30–6*), or **Gignese**, where the **Museo dell'Ombrello** (*open April–Sept Tues–Sun 10–12 and 3–6*) waits to tell you all about the history and making of umbrellas and parasols.

The Borromean Islands

Lake Maggiore became a private fief of the Borromei in the 1470s, and to this day they own some of the finest bits, including the sumptuous gardens and villas of the **Isole Borromei**. There are frequent boats from Stresa, Baveno, Pallanza and Laveno, or you can hire a boat and row there. The three islands have restaurants.

The closest island to Stresa, **Isola Bella** (*guided tours daily end Mar–end Oct: end Mar–end Sept 9–12 and 1.30–5.30; Oct 9.30–12 and 1.30–5; adm exp*) was a scattering of barren rocks until the 17th century, when Count Carlo III Borromeo decided to make it

Getting Around

Trains from Milan's Stazione Centrale to Domodossola stop at Arona and Stresa; others from Milan's Porta Garibaldi station go to Luino on the east shore. A third option is the regional railway from Milano-Nord, which passes by way of Varese to Laveno. Trains from Turin and Novara go to Arona and Stresa; a train also links Stresa to Orta four times a day.

From Lake Orta, there are **buses** from Omegna to Verbania every 20 minutes. Buses that connect the two lakes also run from Stresa and Arona stations, while others serve all the villages along the west shore.

Navigazione Lago Maggiore, t 0322 46651, *www.navlaghi.it*, runs **steamers** to all corners of the lake, with the most frequent services in the central lake area, between Stresa, Baveno, Verbania, Pallanza, Laveno and the islands; **hydrofoils** buzz between the main Italian ports and Locarno (in Switzerland). Frequent services by steamer or hydrofoil from Stresa, Baveno and Pallanza sail to the Borromean Isles – a ticket for the furthest, Isola Madre, entitles you to visit all. **Car ferries** run year round between Intra and Laveno.

Tourist Information

Lake Maggiore: *www.lagomaggiore.it*.
Arona: Piazzale Duca d'Aosta, t/f 0322 243 601.
Stresa: Via Canonica 3, t 0323 30150, f 32561.
Baveno, Piazza Dante Alighieri 14, t/f 0323 924 632, *www.comune.baveno.vb.it*.
Pallanza: Corso Zanitello 8, t 0323 503 249, f 0323 556 669; there are also summer kiosks at the Intra and Pallanza steamer landings.
Maccagno: Via Garibaldi 1, t 0332 562 009.

Where to Stay and Eat

Arona ✉ 28041
Taverna del Pittore, Piazza del Popolo, t 0322 243 366 (*very expensive*). One of the finest restaurants on Lake Maggiore; enjoy lovely views from the lake terrace while feasting on seafood *lasagnette* with saffron, fragrant *ravioli* with mushrooms, lamb in pastry, and exceptional hot or cold desserts. *Closed end of Dec–Jan*.

Ranco ✉ 21020
****Il Sole, Piazza Venezia 5, t 0331 976 507, f 0331 976 620, *soleranco@relaischateaux.fr*, (*very expensive*). A superb retreat from the cares of the world; a lovely old inn surrounded by gardens with a charming terrace and one of the finest restaurants on the lake. Ask for room 20 to see the lake through the branches of a lush magnolia. The exquisitely and imaginatively prepared lake fish and crayfish are worth the journey. *Closed Mon lunch and Tues, Dec and Jan*.

Stresa ✉ 28838
*****Des Iles Borromées, Corso Umberto I 67, t 0323 938 938, f 0323 32405, *www.stresa.net / hotel/borromees* (*luxury*). Opened in 1861; stylish in both its aristocratic *belle époque* furnishings and its modern conveniences. Overlooking the islands, and a lovely flower-decked, palm-shaded garden, the hotel has a pool, beach and *Centro Benessere* ('Wellbeing Centre').

***Regina Palace, Corso Umberto I, t 0323 933 777, f 0323 933 776 (*very expensive*). Some 40 years younger, this is a lovely, bow-shaped Liberty-style palace, conserving its original décor and furniture in the halls; its rooms are decorated in style. It has a heated pool, bath, beach, and splendid views over its tranquil park. *Open mid-Mar–Oct*.

****Milan au Lac, Piazza Marconi, t 0323 31190, f 0323 32729, *hotmispe@tin.it* (*expensive*). Another lake-front hotel, with good-size rooms, many with balconies. wonderful views, and a pool. *Open Mar–Oct*.

***Primavera, Via Cavour 39, t 0323 31286, f 0323 33458 (*moderate*). A friendly hotel with a touch of style, and pretty balconies.

***Moderno, at Via Cavour 33, t 0323 933 773, f 0323 933 775, *moderno@hms.it* (*expensive*). Rooms are set round an inner patio. There are two good restaurants. *Open Mar–Oct*.

***Du Parc, Via Gignous 1, t 0323 30335, f 0323 33596 (*expensive*). A charming family-run hotel in a period private villa set in its own grounds right below the railway tracks and 300 yards from the lakeside.

*Elena, Piazza Cadorna 15, t 0323 31043, f 0323 33339, *www.hotelelena.com* (*moderate*). A good budget option, with big modern rooms, most with balconies.

★La Locanda, Via Leopardi 19, **t/f** 0323 31176 (*cheap*). Close to the Mottarone cableway, just a short walk along the lake from Stresa's centre, this is a new, quiet family-run hotel and an excellent budget option: most of the 14 rooms have have their own balcony, although with no lake view.

Piemontese, Via Mazzini 25, **t** 0323 30235 (*expensive*). Find a table in the garden to tuck into the divine spaghetti with melted onions, basil and *pecorino* and the excellent fish dishes. *Closed Mon, Jan and half of Feb.*

Isole Borromei ✉ 28838

★★★Verbano, Isola dei Pescatori, **t** 0323 30408, **f** 0323 33129, *www.hotelverbano.it* (*expensive*). Offers the chance to see the island after the hordes return to the mainland, and has a restaurant (*moderate* set menu, *expensive à la carte*), where romantic views compensate for brusque service and average food. Quiet and nicely decorated.

Ristorante Belvedere, **t** 0323 32292. On the opposite side of the isle; has a cheap menu appreciated by hordes of tourists.

Delfino, on Isola Bella, **t** 0323 30473 (*moderate*). Better views than food.

La Piratera, on Isola Madre, **t** 0323 31171 (*moderate*). Again, the views beat the food.

Baveno ✉ 28831

★★★Hotel Beau Rivage, **t** 0323 92434, **f** 0323 925 253 (*moderate*). On the lake-front road in Baveno's centre is this family-run hotel with a nice back garden, and old-style furniture and atmosphere on the ground floor. Rooms are neat; the best are the top floor lake-front suites (*expensive*), with nice terraces.

★★Elvezia, Via Monte Grappa 15, **t** 0323 924 106, *www.elveziahotel.com* (*cheap*). The charming Monica and Marco run this bright hotel up by the church, with a little garden and lots of wine-tasting. *Open April–Oct.*

Verbania-Pallanza ✉ 28922

★★★★Majestic, Via Vittorio Veneto 32, **t** 0323 504 305, **f** 0323 556 379, *www.grandhotel majestic.it* (*expensive*). Right on the lake, a comfortable grand old hotel Suites 4 and 6 have a corner terrace overlooking the lake and the private Isolino San Giovanni. Has a private beach. *Open April–Oct.*

★★★Pace, Via Cietti 1, **t** 0323 557 207, **f** 0323 557 341 (*moderate*). Excellent value, with old-style writing desks. *Open Mar–Oct.*

★Meublé Matilde, Via Vittorio Veneto 63, **t** 0323 503805 (*moderate*). An old lake-front villa in a quiet central position with a view.

Milano, Corso Zanitello 2, **t** 0323 556 816 (*expensive*). A fine old lake-front villa, with romantic dining on the terrace. The food is some of the finest on Maggiore: delicious *antipasti* and lake fish. *Closed Tues.*

Osteria dell'Angolo, Piazza Garibaldi 35, **t** 0323 556 362 (*moderate*). Also on the lake front, with lovely food – *crespelle* (little crêpes) stuffed with *scamorza*, and *risotti that* have to be ordered in advance. *Closed Mon.*

Cannero Riviera ✉ 28821

★★★Cannero, Lungolago 2, **t** 0323 788 046, **f** 0323 788 048, *www.hotelcannero.com* (*expensive*). Balconies overlook the lake. Restaurant, with a cheap set menu. A pool, free boats and bikes for guests. Minimum three-day stay. *Open mid-Mar–Oct.*

★Miralago, Via Dante 41, **t** 0323 788 282, **f** 0323 787 075 (*cheap*). Simpler, with views. Baths and showers down the hall. *Open Mar–Nov.*

Ca' Bianca, north of Cannero (*moderate*). The garden terrace overlooking the castle ruins and islet is a fine place to linger over a meal.

Cannobio ✉ 28822

★★★Pironi, Via Marconi 35, **t** 0323 70624, **f** 0323 72184, *hotel.pironi@cannobio.net* (*expensive*). In a frescoed 15th-century palace in the historic centre shaped like the Flatiron building in New York, with rooms all different shapes; a few top-floor ones have a lake view. Room 12 has a romantic frescoed balcony all to itself. *Open Mar–Oct.*

Del Lago, Via Nazionale 2, Carmine, **t** 0323 70595 (*expensive*). One of the best in the area. Try the *risotto* with saffron, *zucchini* and mussels, turbot with caviar, or duck breast with honey-roasted sesame seeds. *Closed Tues and Wed lunch, and Nov–Mar.*

Maccagno ✉ 21010

Al Pozzo, **t** 0332 560 145 (*cheap*). Simple but enchanting, on the mountain road to Lake Delio. Enjoys a spectacular view and offers a basic but cheap menu. *Open daily.*

a garden in the form of a ship for his wife Isabella (hence the name Isola Bella). Angelo Crivelli was put in charge of designing this pretty present, and arranged it in ten terraces to form a pyramid-shaped 'poop deck', to create the kind of perspectives beloved by Baroque theatre. The project was continued by Vitaliano VI Borromeo (d. 1670), who added the grottoes and **palace**, completed by the Borromei according to the original plans between 1948 and 1959.

The Borromei opened the delightful, larger **Isola Madre** (*open as Isola Bella*) to the public in 1978. Here they planted a luxuriant botanical garden, dominated by Europe's largest Kashmir cypress; its camellias begin to bloom in January. On its best days few places are more conducive to a state of perfect languor, at least until one of the isle's bold pheasants, peacocks or parrots tries to stare you out. The 16th-century villa has a collection of 18th- and 19th-century puppet theatres, marionettes, portraits and furnishings. The third island, **Isola dei Pescatori**, is home to an almost too quaint and picturesque fishing village. A fourth islet called **San Giovanni**, just off the shore at Pallanza, is privately owned; its villa once belonged to Toscanini.

Beyond Stresa

Baveno is Stresa's quieter sister, connected by a beautiful, villa-lined road. It has been fashionable among the international set ever since 1879, when Queen Victoria spent a summer at the Villa Clara, now Castello Branca. A pretty road leads up **Monte Camoscio**, behind Baveno, while another leads back to the little Lake Mergozzo, a corner of Lake Maggiore that has been cut off in the last hundred years by silt from the river Toce. The main shore road carries on to **Pallanza**, which has a famously mild winter climate. Pallanza was united with Suna and Intra in 1939 to form **Verbania** (from the old Roman name of the lake), now the capital of a province. Here is the celebrated **Villa Taranto**, some 50 acres planted with 20,000 kinds of plants by a Scot, Captain Neil McEacharn. The aquatic plants, including giant Amazonian water lilies and lotus blossoms, the spring tulips and autumn colour are exceptional, as are some of the rarer species – the handkerchief tree, bottle bush, and copper Japanese maple. The house is used by the Italian prime minister for special conferences (*open, if he's not in, April–Oct daily 8.30–7.30; adm exp*). Intra is the departure point for a ferryboat across to Laveno, and buses up to the mountain resort of **Premeno**.

North of Intra, **Ghiffa** is a pretty, rural village with an attractive castle and 13th-century Lombard Gothic church. **Cannero Riviera**, further up the shore, is a quiet resort amid the citrus groves, facing two picturesque islets, haunts of medieval pirates. **Cannobio**, the last stop before Switzerland, is an ancient town famous, though in Piemonte, for adhering to the Milanese Ambrosian Rite, revived by Cardinal Charles Borromeo to promote local pride. It has a fine Bramante-inspired **Santuario della Pietà**, with an altarpiece by Ferrari. The village lies at the foot of Val Cannobina, where you can hire a boat to visit the pretty **Orrido di Sant'Anna** with its waterfall.

The Eastern Shore and Santa Caterina del Sasso

Interest on the Lombard shore is concentrated around the romantic, deserted Carmelite convent of **Santa Caterina del Sasso** (*open daily 8.30–12 and 2–6*), hanging on a sheer cliff over the water. The convent is visible only from the lake; boats call here between April and September. According to legend, in the 12th century a wealthy merchant and usurer named Alberto Besozzi was sailing on the lake when his boat sank. He prayed to St Catherine of Alexandria, who cast him upon this rock-bound shore. Alberto repented of his usury and lived as a hermit in a cave; when his prayers brought an end to a local plague, he asked that as an ex voto the people construct a shrine to St Catherine. Over the centuries, other buildings were added as the cave of Beato Alberto – Blessed Albert – became a popular pilgrimage destination, especially after a huge boulder fell on the roof, only to be miraculously wedged just above the altar, sparing the priest who was saying Mass. The boulder finally crashed through in 1910 without harming anyone, because nobody was there; the monastery had been suppressed in 1770 by Joseph II of Austria. In 1986 the restoration was completed, revealing medieval frescoes (one in the Sala Capitolare showing armed men). There's also a 16th-century fresco of the *Danse Macabre* in the loggia of the Gothic convent.

Laveno, the most important town in the district, is well known for its ceramics. If you're taking the train from Milan or Varese, the Milano-Nord line will leave you right next to the lake. The best thing to do in Laveno is to take the cable car up to the **Sasso del Ferro** (3,483ft), from where you can walk up for a marvellous view over the lake. Or come at Christmas-time, when Laveno can claim Italy's only underwater *presepio* (Christmas crib) – floodlit and visible from *terra firma*. The northern reaches of the lake on the eastern side are not very exciting. **Luino**, the largest town, was the birthplace of Bernardino Luini. To the north, **Maccagno Inferiore** and **Maccagno Superiore** are more pleasant places to take refuge from the crowds.

Lake Varese and Castiglione Olona

Between Lake Maggiore and Milan lies the quiet **Lago di Varese**, 8½km long and the big sleepyhead of the 'minor lakes'. The main town, **Gavirate**, makes hand-carved pipes. Just south in **Voltorre**, the cloister of the 11th-century monastery of San Michele (now a cultural centre) has splendid, older carvings on the capitals, attributed to Lanfranco. From Biandronno boats depart for little Isolino Virginia, site of the **Museo Preistorico di Villa Ponti** (*open April–Oct Sat and Sun 2–6*), which chronicles a prehistoric lake settlement (3000 BC–Roman times).

The little Renaissance nugget of **Castiglione Olona**, southeast of the lake and 8km from Varese, is an islet of Tuscany in Lombardy, but it's an islet in a huge lake of suburban sprawl around an aeronautics plant; locate the ghastly new church and take the steep road down to the bottom of the valley to find the Borgo – the Castiglione Olona you want. It owes its quattrocento charm to Cardinal Branda Castiglioni (1350–1443), a son of the local nobility who went on to serve as a bishop in Hungary and briefly in Florence, where he was so enchanted by the blossoming Renaissance that he brought Masolino da Panicale (after his work with Masaccio in Florence's Brancacci Chapel) and Lorenzo di Pietro (Il Vecchietta) home with him to do up Castiglione, and incidentally introduced the new humanism into Lombardy.

The Borgo, the Cardinal's 'ideal citadel', is essentially unchanged since 1440. In tiny central Piazza Garibaldi, the **Chiesa di Villa** was inspired by Brunelleschi, a cube surmounted by an octagonal drum, its exterior decoration limited to framing bands of grey and two giant statues on either side of the door, of St Christopher and St Anthony Abbot. Inside, nearly all the art dates from the 1400s: the *Annunciation*, the tomb of Guido Castiglioni by the school of Amadeo, and the four terracotta *Doctors of the Church*.

Opposite, the **Palazzo Branda Castiglioni** is now a museum (*open April–Sept Tues–Sat 9–12 and 3–6, Sun and holidays 10.30–12.30 and 3–6; Oct–Mar Tues–Sat 9–12 and 3–6, Sun 3–6 only, except the first Sun of each month, during the Fiera del Cardinale, open 10.30–12.30 and 3–6; adm*). The cardinal's bedroom has charming frescoes of children playing under the fruit trees by an unknown Lombard painter, while below are various emblems and sayings – mnemonic devices? – probably designed by the cardinal himself. Il Vecchietta frescoed the chapel (1437); in the study, Masolino painted a scene of Veszprem, Hungary, as described by the cardinal from memory.

Ancient plane trees line the steep Via Cardinal Branda that leads up to the Gothic **Collegiata** (*open Oct–Mar Tues–Sun 10–12 and 2.30–5; April–Sept Tues–Sun 9.30–12 and 3–6.30*), built in 1421 over the Castiglioni castle. The brick church contains beautiful frescoes, especially Masolino's *Life of the Virgin* in the vault, while Il Vecchietta painted the *Life of St Stephen*, and Paolo Schiavo frescoed the *Life of St Lawrence*; the *Crucifixion* in the apse is attributed to Neri di Bicci. In 1435 Masolino frescoed the entire **baptistry** (once the castle tower), a work commonly considered his life's masterpiece, the culmination of his evocatively lyrical and refined style.

The Olana valleys hold a pair of other surprises. The **Monastero di Torba** (*open Feb–Sept 10–1 and 2–6; Oct–mid-Dec 10–1 and 2–5; closed end of Dec–Jan; adm; extra fee for special events*), set in the woods just off the road in Gornate Olana, was founded in the 5th century as a Lombard defence tower, but three centuries later it found new use as a monastery. Acquired by the Fondo per l'Ambiente Italiano, the 8th-century frescoes in the tower have been restored, along with the original crypt and tombs. The tower defended **Castelséprio** to the south, a Lombard *castrum* designed on the Roman model. Destroyed in the 13th century, ruins of the walls, churches and castle moulder under the trees 1.5km from the centre, but the main reason to stop is little **Santa Maria Foris Portas**: its unique 8th-century frescoes in an Eastern Hellenistic style were discovered during the Second World War by a partisan hiding here (*all part of a Zona Archeologica; open Mon–Sat 9–6; Sun and holidays 9–5*).

Varese

A garden city of shoe-manufacturers, Varese serves as a departure point for lakes Maggiore or Lugano, Castiglione Olona or **Sacro Monte**, reached by bus from the station. Founded by St Ambrose in gratitude for Lombardy's deliverance from the Arian heresy, Sacro Monte's church of Santa Maria was lavishly rococo-ed; pilgrims ascend along the Sacred Way, marked by 14 11th-century chapels dedicated to the Mysteries of the Rosary. There are fine views from Sacro Monte, and even finer ones if you continue up to the karst massif of the **Parco Naturale di Campo dei Fiori**. If you have an hour to kill in Varese, head for the **Giardino Pubblico**, the 18th-century park of the Este dukes of Modena; there's a hotchpotch of archaeology and art in the **Musei Civici** (*open Tues–Sun 9.30–12.30 and 2–5; adm*), housed in the Villa Mirabello.

Lake Lugano

Zigzagged Lake Lugano with its steep, wooded fjord-like shores is more than half Swiss; the Italians, when they want to make a point about it, call it Lake Ceresio. Its most important town, Lugano, is the capital of the Canton of Ticino. The Swiss snatched it from Milan way back in 1512, and when the canton had a chance to return to Italy a couple of centuries later it stalwartly refused. Nevertheless, Italy maintains a wee island of territory in the middle of the lake, Campione d'Italia, which is just big enough to support a casino inviting Swiss francs: if you can't beat 'em, soak 'em.

Lake Lugano slowly drains its waters into Lake Maggiore through the Tresa, a river that forms the border between the Italian and Swiss halves of the village of **Ponte Tresa**. There's not much to see in either half beyond the steamer landing, but if from Varese you head instead to Lugano's other Italian landing at **Porto Ceresio**, you can take in along the way the 16th-century **Villa Cicogna Mozzoni**, on the SS244, just north of Arcisate (*open Sun and public hols April–Oct 9.30–12 and 2.30–7, and every afternoon in Aug; adm*) at Bisuschio, near the little resort of **Viggiú**; the villa has frescoes by the Campi brothers, and a fine garden.

From Porto Ceresio the steamer enters Swiss territory (bring your passport), passing the pretty village of **Morcote** on route to **Campione d'Italia**. In the Middle Ages, before state-sanctioned gambling was invented, the once-independent fief of Campione was celebrated for its master builders, who worked anonymously and are known to history only as the Campionese Masters. They had a hand in most of Italy's great Romanesque cathedrals – in Cremona, Monza, Verona, Modena and Sant'Ambrogio in Milan – and such was their reputation that when the Hagia Sophia in Constantinople began to sag, the Byzantine Emperor hired the Campionese Masters to prop it up. In their hometown they left only a small sample of their handiwork, **San Pietro** (1326). A later Baroque-coated church of the **Madonna dei Ghirli** (Our Lady of the Swallows) has a fine exterior fresco of the Last Judgement from 1400. Campione uses Swiss money and postal services and has no border formalities.

Lugano

Warm, palmy Lugano is an arty resort city piled between Monte Brè and Monte San Salvatore, a lovely setting that has been compared to Rio de Janeiro; in Switzerland at any rate it's as close as you can get to Paradise (a residential suburb, 10 minutes west by bus). To go with its sumptuous lake views, it has a sumptuous Renaissance gem, in waterfront Piazza Luini: the plain church of **Santa Maria degli Angioli**, frescoed by Bernardino Luini – his masterpiece. Ruskin, who called Luini 'ten times greater than Leonardo', wrote of these frescoes, 'Every touch he lays is ethereal; every thought he conceives is beauty and purity…'

Lakes Lugano and Como

Lugano's **Villa Favorita** (*open Easter–Oct Fri–Sun 10–5; adm exp*) was home to Baron Heinrich von Thyssen-Bornemisza's fabulous collection of Old Masters, now on loan in Madrid and Barcelona (thanks to the Baroness, a former Miss Spain), although the villa retains the Thyssen collection of European and American modern art, with a special emphasis on the Luminists and Hudson River School. A popular excursion is to continue down the south arm of the lake to **Capolago** and take the rack railway up to the summit of Monte Generoso.

East of Lugano the lake returns to Italy. **Santa Margherita**, on the south shore, has a cableway up to the panoramic belvedere. **San Mamete**, a steamer landing on the north shore, is the prettiest village in the area, with its castle and the quiet Valsolda

Getting Around

Lugano's **airport** in Agno is served by Crossair (**t** 0041 91 610 1212) linked up to Swissair flights from London, Paris, Nice, Rome, Florence and Venice as well as the major Swiss airports. A shuttle service (**t** 079 221 4243) connects the airport with the city centre.

Lugano is also easily reached from Milano's Malpensa, with a shuttlebus service via Chiasso (**t** 682 8820).

From Varese, **trains** go as far as Porto Ceresio on the west end of Lugano; from Milan trains to Como continue to Lugano by way of Chiasso, while Lugano itself is linked by a local train line (the FLP) to points west as far as Ponte Tresa.

Porlezza, on the east end of the lake, is linked by **buses** to Como or Menaggio; buses from Lugano or Como go directly to Campione d'Italia.

All the lakeside towns are served by **steamers** on the Società Navigazione Lago di Lugano line, run with the precision of Swiss clockwork, except when the wind's up (**t** 971 5223; a variety of passes are available).

Tourist Information

Note: for Lugano telephone numbers, dial 004191 from outside Switzerland, or dial 0191 from within Switzerland.
Lugano: Riva Albertolli 5, **t** 913 3232, **f** 922 7653, *www.lugano-tourism.ch*.
Campione d'Italia: Via Volta 3, **t** 649 5051, **f** 649 9178, *aptcampione@ticino.com*.

Where to Stay and Eat

Lugano ✉ CH6900
*****Villa Principe Leopoldo, Via Montalbano 5, **t** 985 8855, **f** 985 8825, *www.leopoldo-hotel.com* (*luxury*). If money's no object, this 19th-century Relais & Châteaux in a beautiful hillside park overlooking the city will keep you in the style you'd like to be accustomed to. Gourmet Mediterranean and international cuisine at the restaurant and café.
***International au Lac, Via Nassa 68, **t** 922 7541, **f** 922 7544, *www.hotel-international.ch*

(*very expensive*). More than comfortable, with a pool and garden terrace near the lake in the city centre.
Fischer's Seehotel, Sentiero di Gandria 10, **t 971 5571, **f** 970 1577 (*expensive*). Simple and pleasant; smack on the lake far from the traffic. Cheaper rooms available without bath. A nice restaurant, but beware, the kitchen closes at 8.30pm for dinner.
*Montarina, Via Montarina 1, **t** 966 7272, **f** 966 1213, *www.montarina.ch* (*cheap*). Hotel and hostel, which welcomes families and backpackers in a 19th-century villa set in a palm garden not far from the station with pretty views over the lake. Comfortable rooms; private bathrooms available at an extra fee. There is a chicken farm and a swimming pool in the garden.

Lugano is chock-full of top-notch restaurants where you can seriously strain your overdraft facilities, but lunch at some of these temples of cuisine can be quite reasonable.
Parco Saroli, Via Stefano Franscini 6, **t** 923 5314. This fashionable eatery serves excellent and unusual home-made pasta dishes, seafood, a wide choice of superb breads, cheeses, desserts and an award-winning wine list. A *moderate* set menu, or *expensive* six-course *menu degustazione* available. *Closed Sat and Sun*.
Antica Osteria Gerso, Piazzetta Solaro 24 at Massagno, **t** 966 1915 (*moderate*). An intimate, utterly simple restaurant serving a limited but discriminating menu: favourite dishes include onion soup with tangy *pecorino* cheese, *tortelli di zucca alle mandorle* and duck with oranges, all accompanied by a fair wine choice from the adjacent *enoteca*. Book a day or two ahead. *Closed Sun and Mon*.

San Mamete (Valsolda) ✉ 22010
***Stella d'Italia, **t** 0344 68139, **f** 0344 68729, *www.stelladitalia.com* (*expensive*). A lovely lakeside hotel with a lido, garden, good restaurant under the pergola, nice library inside, and waterside terraces. Every room has a balcony, and you can borrow the hotel's boat for outings. Minimum three-days' stay. *Open April–Oct*.

behind. **Osteno** has fine views of the lake, and boat excursions up the ravine of the River Orrido. From **Porlezza** you can catch a bus for Menaggio on Lake Como, passing tiny, enchanting Lago di Piano.

Lake Como

Sapphire Lake Como has been Italy's prestige romantic lake ever since the earliest days of the Roman Empire, when the Plinys wrote of the luxuriant beauty surrounding their several villas on its shores. It was just the sort of luxuriant beauty that enraptured the children of the Romantic era, inspiring operas from Verdi, Rossini and Bellini, as well as enough good and bad English verse to fill an anthology. And it is still there, the Lake Como of the Shelleys and Wordsworths, the villas and lush gardens, the mountains and wooded promontories. The English still haunt their traditional English shore, but most of the visitors to Como these days are Italian, and there are times when the lake seems schizophrenic, its mellowed dignity battered by modern expectations of a Milanese Riviera. Even so, Como is large and varied enough to offer retreats where, to paraphrase Longfellow's ode to the lake, no sound of Vespa or high heel breaks the silence of the summer day.

Third largest of the lakes, 50km long but only 4.4km at its widest point, Como (or Lario) is one of the deepest lakes in Europe, plunging down 1,345ft near Argegno. It forks in the middle like a pair of legs, the east branch known as the **Lago di Lecco** for its biggest town, while the prettiest region is the centre, where Como appears to be three separate lakes, and where towns like Tremezzo and Bellagio have been English enclaves for 200 years. One legacy of the English are the seven golf courses in the province, while the waters around Domaso are excellent for windsurfing. The further you go from the city of Como, the cleaner the lake.

The City of Como

Magnificently located at the southern tip of the lake's left leg, Como is a lively little city that has long had a bent for science, silk and architecture. In AD 23 it was the birthplace of Pliny the Elder, compiler of antiquity's greatest work of hearsay, the *Natural History,* and later it produced his nephew and heir Pliny the Younger, whose letters are one of our main sources for information on the cultured Roman life of the period. From *c.* 1050 to 1335, when Como enjoyed a period as an independent *comune*, it produced a school of master builders, known generally as the Maestri Comacini, rivals to Lugano's Maestri Campionesi.

Como's historic centre, its street plan almost unchanged since Roman times, opens up to the lake at **Piazza Cavour**, with its cafés, hotels, steamer landing and pretty views. Two landmarks in the public gardens just to the west offer an introduction to Como's more recent scientists and architects. The first, the circular **Tempio Voltiano** (*open April–Sept Tues–Sun 10–12 and 3–6; Oct–Mar Tues–Sun 10–12 and 2–4; adm*), was built in 1927 to house the manuscripts, instruments and inventions of Como's electrifying native son, the self-taught physicist Alessandro Volta (1745–1827), who lent his name to volts in a hundred languages. A bit further on, the striking

Getting Around

There are frequent FS **trains** from Milan's Centrale or Porta Garibaldi stations, taking you in some 40 minutes to Como's main San Giovanni station (**t** 147 888 088). Slower trains run on the regional Milano-Nord line to the lakeside station of Como-Lago. From Como, trains to Lugano and Lecco depart from San Giovanni. **Buses** from Como run to nearly every town on the lake.

A **steamer** (the 1926 *Concordia*, running July and August only), motor boats and hydrofoils are operated by Navigazione Lago di Como, based in Como at Piazza Cavour (**t** 031 304 060) and in Lecco at Lungolario C. Battisti, (**t** 031 579 211, or freephone from within Italy **t** 800 551801), where you can pick up schedules and tourist passes (one and three days' validity). In the summer night cruises with dinner and dance on board depart from Como, Bellagio, Menaggio, Varenna and Lecco. The most frequent connections are between Como, Tremezzo, Menaggio, Bellagio, Varenna and Cólico, with additional services in the central lake, and at least one boat a day to Lecco. Note that **hydrofoil** tickets cost about half as much again as the more leisurely steamers. **Car ferries** run between Bellagio, Menaggio, Varenna and Cadenábbia. Some services stop altogether in the winter.

Tourist Information

Piazza Cavour 17, **t** 031 269 712, **f** 031 240 111, *www.lakecomo.com, www.lagodicomo.com.*

Where to Stay

Como ✉ 22100
★★★★**Le Due Corti**, Piazza Vittoria 15, **t** 031 328 111, **f** 031 265 226 (*expensive*). The place to stay in Como for character, charm and history, located just in front of Porta Vittoria, main entry to the walled city centre. Converted from a monastery into a post house, it reopened in 1992 as a hotel. Rooms are arranged around the former cloister and all are individual, there's a small outdoor pool in the cloister. Good restaurant and piano bar.
★★★★**Palace Hotel**, Lungo Lario Trieste 16, **t** 031 303 303, **f** 031 303 170, *www.palacehotel.it, aproser@tin.it, (expensive)*. On the lake, this luxurious hotel partly occupies the former archbishop's palace, with big, modern rooms. *Moderate* lunches at the restaurant.
★★★★**Barchetta Excelsior**, Piazza Cavour, **t** 031 3221, **f** 031 302622, *www.villadeste.it, (expensive)*. A grand old hotel, many rooms boasting balconies over the lake;offers special gourmet and shopping weekends. *Open all year.*
★★★★**Albergo Terminus**, Lungo Lario Trieste 14, **t** 031 329 111, **f** 031 302 550, *larioterminus@ galactica.it, (expensive)*. An elegant, recently reopened 1902 hotel right in the heart of town, carefully restored to mantain the original Liberty style in the halls, reading room and charming Bar delle Terme, with a panoramic terrace on the lake. Rooms are decorated in style and have all modern comforts.

Monumento ai Caduti – a memorial to the fallen of the First World War – was designed by the young futurist architect Antonio Sant'Elia of Como (1888–1916), who himself died in action on the Front; his plans and drawings of futuristic cityscapes in particular have established him as one of the most important visionary planners of the 20th century. The monument was built by Giuseppe Terragni (1904–34), a Como native and the most inspired Italian architect to work during the Fascist period; ask the tourist office for a special Terragni town plan.

From Piazza Cavour, Via Plinio leads back to Como's elegant salon, the Piazza Duomo. Unusually, the chief monuments are all attached: the **Torre del Comune** to the charming white, grey and red marble striped town hall or **Broletto** (both built in 1215), one of the rare Romanesque (and not Gothic) symbols of civic might in the north; and this in turn to the magnificent **Duomo** (1396), the whole now looking

★★★★**Villa Flori**, Via Cernobbio 12, **t** 031 573 105, **f** 031 570 379 (*expensive*). Classy and romantic 19th-century hotel just outside Como on the west shore, which has Como's finest restaurant to boot. All rooms have a terrace overlooking the lake, and you can spend a night in the Garibaldi Suite, part of the original one-storey villa built by Marquis Flori as a gift upon the marriage of his 18-year-old daughter Giuseppina to the Hero of the Two Worlds.

★★★**Park Hotel**, Viale Fratelli Rosselli 20, **t** 031 572 615, **f** 031 574 302 (*moderate*). Medium-sized and welcoming, near the lake and close to S. Giovanni railway station. Recently renovated.

★★★**Marco's**, Via Lungo Lario Trieste 62, **t** 031 303 628, **f** 031 302 342 (*moderate*). Eleven small rooms, all with balcony, strategically located near the lake front, the city centre and the cableway to Brunate.

★★**Posta**, Via Garibaldi 2, **t** 031 266 012, **f** 031 266 398, *www.hotelposta.net* (*cheap*). You can dream about the glories of the corporate state here at a hotel designed in 1930 by Terragni, although recent refurbishment has changed the original interiors.

Eating Out

Terrazzo Perlasca, Piazza de'Gasperi 8, **t** 031 300 263 (*expensive*). Como is one of those towns where the restaurants tend to process clients with slipshod food and service, especially in summer. This is one that doesn't. It's run by four brothers, two in the kitchen and two out front. The menu changes almost every day and features typical dishes like *filetto di laverello* (whitefish fillets) and *fettuccine e funghi* (pasta with local mushrooms), all accompanied by wonderful views over the lake. *Closed Mon.*

Sant'Anna, Via Filippo Turati 1/3, **t** 031 505 266 (*expensive*). This used to be a family establishment frequented by silk toilers and featuring typical Lombard dishes. The new managment offers ever-changing seasonal menus of nouvelle cuisine: from the *expensive* seasonal menu to the *very expensive menu degustazione*, wine included. You need a car to get here. *Closed Fri and Sat lunch, and late July–late Aug.*

Villa Flori's Ristorante Raimondi, **t** 031 573 105 (*expensive*). Join Como society at Marquis Flori's villa, where exquisite renditions of classic Italian and Lombard cuisine are served on the lakeside terrace or in the luminous dining room. *Closed Mon.*

Locanda dell'Oca Bianca, Via Canturina 251 (5mins drive on the road to Cantù), **t** 031 525 605 (*moderate*). Further out of the city centre is another winner, serving sit-up-and-take-note dishes, out on its summer terrace, from a variety of Italian regions and some French, especially foie gras, loyal to the restaurant's name of 'White Goose'. *Closed Mon, lunch by reservation only.*

Ristorante Teatro Sociale, near the cathedral at Via Maestri Comacini, **t** 031 264 042 (*cheap*). Traditional post-theatre inn, with a good *cheap* menu including wine. *Closed Tues.*

spanking new thanks to a thorough 700th birthday cleaning. The **Duomo** is Italy's most harmonious example of transitional architecture, although Gothic dominates in the façade and lovely rose window and pinnacles. The sculpture and reliefs are mainly by the Rodari family (late 15th–early 16th century) who also sculpted the lateral doors – the most ornate one, facing the Broletto, is known as the frog door, although half the frog was hacked away by vandals. Even more unexpected than frogs are the two statues of famous pagans flanking the central door, under delicate stone canopies: Pliny the Elder (on the left) and Pliny the Younger. Although Pliny the Younger did write a letter to Trajan on the subject of Christians, praising their hard work and suggesting that they be left in peace, the fact is that Renaissance humanists regarded all noble figures of antiquity as honorary saints, especially if they were local boys – pagan or not.

Inside, the three Gothic aisles combine happily with a Renaissance choir and transept, crowned by a dome designed by the great late Baroque master Filippo Juvarra in 1744. Nine 16th-century tapestries hang along the nave, lending an air of palatial elegance; a pair of Romanesque lions near the entrance are survivors from the cathedral's 11th-century predecessor. But most of the art is from the Renaissance: in the right aisle six reliefs with scenes from the Passion by Tommaso Rodari, and fine canvases by two of Leonardo's followers, Gaudenzio Ferrari (*Flight into Egypt*) and Luini (*Adoration of the Magi*); Luini's famous *Madonna with Child and four saints* adorns the high altar. The left aisle has more by the same trio: Rodari's *Deposition* on the fourth altar, Ferrari's *Marriage of the Virgin* and Luini's *Nativity*.

For a contrast, go behind the Duomo and across the train tracks to the Piazza del Popolo, where Giuseppe Terragni's ex-Casa del Fascio, now the **Palazzo Terragni,** stands out in all its functional, luminous beauty. Built in 1931 but completely unlike the typically ponderous travertine buildings constructed under Mussolini, it is 50 years ahead of its time, practically transparent, an essay in light and harmony, the masterpiece of the only coherent architectural style Italy has produced in the 20th century. Its present occupants, the Guardia di Finanza, allow visits to the ground floor.

From the cathedral, main Via Vittorio Emanuele leads to Como's old cathedral, **San Fedele**, on this site since 914. It has a unique pentagonal apse and a doorway carved with chubby archaic figures and a griffon; the interior is lavishly decorated with 18th-century frescoes. Further up, in the Piazza Medaglie d'Oro Comasche, the **Museo Civico** (*open Tues–Sat 9.30–12.30 and 2–5; Sun 10–1; adm*) is the city's attic of artefacts, from the Neolithic era until the Second World War, with interesting Roman frescoes along the way. From the piazza, continue down Via Giovio to the **Porta Vittoria**, a striking skyscraper of a gate from 1192, its immaculate tiers of arches rising 72ft.

Near here, Como's small **Pinacoteca**, Via Diaz 84, contains carved capitals and wonderful medieval paintings from the old monastery of Santa Margherita del Broletto (*currently closed for restoration; medieval and Renaissance parts of the collection scheduled to reopen in March 2002*). A short walk away from the Porta Vittoria, at the beginning of the Via della Regina (the road built by Lombard queen Theodolinda around Lake Como), is Como's Romanesque gem **Sant'Abbondio**, consecrated by Pope Urban II in 1095. The façade is discreet, and the twin campaniles are believed to be of Norman inspiration, while the interior, with its lofty vaults and forest of columns forming five aisles, offers a kind of preview of coming great events in Italian architecture. The elegant apse is decorated with 14th-century frescoes: note the knights in armour arresting Christ in Gethsemane.

For great views take the funicular up **Brunate**, the hill overlooking Como (*every 15–30 minutes; call **t** 031 303 608 for exact times; combined ferry/funicular ticket*). The station is on the Lungolario Trieste, by the beach. **Cantù**, a short hop away on the train towards Lecco, has a rare 10th-century basilica, **San Vicenzo**, decorated with a remarkable fresco cycle painted just after the first millennium (*contact the parish, **t** 031 714 126, before setting out; the basilica is a 20-minute walk east of the station in Galliano; follow the signs*).

Around Lake Como

Zigzagging back and forth from shore to shore, the steamer is the ideal way to travel around the lake, allowing you to drink in the marvellous scenery. The first steamer landing, **Cernobbio**, is an old resort, the 1816–17 retreat of Queen Caroline of England, who held wild parties in what is now the fabulous Hotel Villa d'Este. Across the lake, at **Torno**, stands the 16th-century **Villa Pliniana**, which so charmed Shelley that he tried to buy it; its name is derived from its peculiar intermittent spring, described in a letter of Pliny the Younger. The area has been fertile soil for operas; Rossini composed *Tancredi* in the Villa Pliniana, while Bellini composed *Norma* in other villas nearby.

Back on the west shore, **Argegno** enjoys a privileged positions on the lake, with views of the snow-clad mountains to the north and access to the west into the pretty Val d'Intelvi, which ascends to Lake Lugano. North of Argegno lies the pretty islet of **Comacina**, sprinkled with the ruins of ancient churches, the entrance to the lush and balmy mid-lake district of **Tremezzina**, where calling Como the 'mirror of Venus' hardly seems extravagant, especially in the spring. **Lenno**, the southernmost village, was the site of Pliny the Younger's villa 'Comedia'; in one of his letters he describes fishing from his bedroom window. It was in this idyllic spot, in front of a posh villa in nearby Mezzegra, that Mussolini and his mistress Claretta Petacci were executed by partisans. They had been captured on the north shore of the lake, attempting to flee in a German truck to Switzerland. Claretta was killed trying to shield Il Duce from the bullets.

Beautiful villas are chock-a-block along the shore at **Tremezzo**, including two of the finest: the early 18th-century **Villa La Quiete** at Bolvedro, with its stone balustrades, and, from the same period, the celebrated **Villa Carlotta** (*open Mar and Oct daily 9–11.30 and 2–4.30; April–Sept daily 9–6; adm exp*), on the north end of Tremezzo. Originally built in 1747, the villa took its name from Princess Carlotta of the Netherlands, who received it as a wedding gift from her mother in the 1850s. But most of what you see was the work of the former owners, the Counts Sommariva, who laid out the magnificent gardens and park, where in April and May the thousands of azaleas, camellias and rhododendrons put on a dazzling display of colour. No matter when you come you can also take in the neoclassical interior, filled with cool, virtuoso neoclassical statuary that the Sommarivas couldn't get enough of: a copy of Antonio Canova's St Petersburg *Cupid and Psyche*, *Venus and Paris*, *Mary Magdalene* and *Palmedes* (rebuilt by Canova after someone understandably smashed it), and in the drawing room the Dane Bertel Thorvaldsen's marble frieze of *Alexander's Triumphant Entrance of Babylon*, commissioned by Napoleon but completed after Waterloo for the Sommarivas. After the Villa Carlotta, look for 'the leafy colonnade' of trees described by Longfellow which marks the entrance to **Cadenábbia**, still served by an Anglican church built in the 19th century when the English came here in droves.

Bella Bella Bellagio

High on the headland where the lake forks, enjoying one of the most scenic positions in all Italy, Bellagio (from the Latin *bi-lacus*) is a beautiful old town that has managed to maintain an air of quiet dignity through the centuries. A bus from the

Tourist Information

Cernobbio: Via Regina 33b, t/f 031 510 198, *cernobbio@tin.it (open May–Oct)*.
Tremezzo: Via Regina 3, t/f 0344 40493.
Bellagio: Piazza della Chiesa 14, t/f 031 950 204, *www.bellagiolakecomo.com*, or *www.fromitaly.net* for all the central Lake Como area *(closed Tues and Sun in winter)*.
Menaggio: Piazza Garibaldi, t 0344 32924, *www.menaggio.com*.
Varenna: in the centre close to the church, t/f 0341 830 367, *www.varenna.net*.
Lecco: Via Nazario Sauro 6, t 0341 362 360, f 286 231, *www.vol.it./pvlecco*.

Where to Stay and Eat

Cernobbio ✉ 22012

★★★★★**Grand Hotel Villa d'Este**, t 031 3481, f 031 348 844, *www.villadeste.it (luxury)*. Lake Como's fabulous, most glittering showcase, it was built in 1557 by Pelligrini for Cardinal Tolomeo Gallio, the son of a Como noble family who went on to become one of the most powerful men in the Vatican – besides this villa, he had seven along the road to Rome so he never had to spend a night 'away from home'.
Since 1873 it has been a hotel. Each room is individual, furnished with antiques or fine reproductions, the public rooms are regal; the food is superb and served on the panoramic verandah or in the slightly more informal grill room.
The glorious gardens are in themselves a reason to stay, with a floating swimming pool and another indoor pool, a sybaritic spa, a nightclub and more too. The hotel has a long list of regal guests and Hollywood stars, as well as fashion moguls on their visit to the capital of silk. Be warned that the rooms cost a king's ransom too, at L800,000 or more for a double; non-guests are welcome at the restaurant, where the average bill is L150,000. *Open April–Oct*.

★★★★**Asnigo**, Piazza S. Stefano, t 031 510 062, f 031 510 249, *asnigo@galactica.it (very expensive)*. A nice hotel above the city centre, built in 1914 with a beautiful terrace overlooking Cernobbio and Como and pretty rooms, friendly service, and a good restaurant with a moderate daily menu.
★★**Terzo Crotto**, Via Volta 1, t 031 512 304 *(moderate)*. Just behind the centre, set in its own green and peaceful grounds, with nine rooms and an excellent family-run restaurant *(moderate)*. *Closed Mon and Tues lunch*.
★**La Vignetta**, Via Monte Grappa 32, t 031 334 7055, f 031 342 906, *lavignetta@tin.it (cheap)*. An excellent value choice, clean, cosy and with a nice restaurant *(moderate)*. Not all the rooms have bathrooms. Convenient family rooms with three/four beds.
Trattoria Gatto Nero, Via Monte Santo 69, t 031 512 042 *(expensive)*. Rustic restaurant with lovely lake views and delicious food; five minutes' drive from the city in Rovenna hamlet, it has lovely lake views, plenty of character and little rooms and terraces full of nice furniture, objects and pictures as well as delicious food. *Closed Mon and Tues lunch*.

Ossuccio ✉ 22018

Locanda dell'Isola Comacina, t 0344 57022 *(expensive)*. The Isola Comacina is deserted except for this 50-year-old restaurant. For one fixed price *(expensive)* you are picked up in a boat at Cala Comacina or Ossuccio, and regaled with a set meal of *antipasti* followed by grilled trout, fried chicken, wine and dessert, and a rendition of poetry while you sip your flambéed coffee called *caffè all'uso delle canaglie in armi* (coffee for the armed blackguards – ask the host why) and a return trip to the mainland. *Open Mar–Oct, closed Tues except summer*.

Tremezzo ✉ 22019

★★★★★**Grand Hotel Tremezzo**, t 0344 42491, f 0344 40201, *www.grandhoteltremezzo.com (luxury)*. Next door to Villa Carlotta, it couples the generous comforts and charm

pier will take you to the **Villa Serbelloni**. Most scholars believe this stands on the site of Pliny's villa 'Tragedia', higher over the lake than his villa 'Comedia'; tragedy was considered a loftier art, because in his day tragic actors wore higher heels. The villa is now the Rockefeller Foundation centre (*two daily guided tours of the grounds*

of a large 19th-century hotel set in a large park, with all modern facilities, a swimming pool, own mooring and helipad. The 1930s film *Grand Hotel* starring Greta Garbo was shot here, John Irving's *A Month by the Lake* had the Grand Hotel as a background, while George Lucas 'secretly' stayed here while filming the last episode of the *Star Wars* saga in Villa Balbianello. The lakeside restaurant offers an expensive five-course menu. *Open Mar–mid-Nov.*

★★★Villa Marie, Via Regina 30, **t** 0344 40427 (*expensive*). An intimate Victorian hotel with 15 pleasant rooms and an outside pool. Overlooks the lake and a shady garden. *Open April–Oct.*

Cadenábbia ✉ 22011

★★★Bellevue, **t** 0344 40418, **f** 0344 41466 (*moderate*). A large but very pleasant place to stay, with plenty of sun terraces, garden and pool, right on the lake. Charmingly old-fashioned; rooms have modern fittings. *Open mid-Mar–mid-Oct.*

★★★Britannia Excelsior, **t** 0344 40413, **f** 0344 42068 (*moderate*). A cosy old hotel in Cadenábbia's piazza overlooking the lake, with lots of rooms with balconies. *Open April–Oct.*

Bellagio ✉ 22021

★★★★★Grand Hotel Villa Serbelloni, Via Roma 1, **t** 031 950 216, **f** 031 951 529, *www.villaserbelloni.it* (*luxury*). Romantic Bellagio has several fine hotels, among them this magnificent, ornate one set in a flower-filled garden at the very tip of the headland. The frescoed public rooms are glittering and palatial, and there's a heated pool and private beach and boating. You can also swim in the lake and bask on an anchored raft. *Open April–Oct.*

★★★Hotel Du Lac, Piazza Mazzini, **t** 031 950 320, **f** 031 951 624, *dulac@tin.it* (*expensive*). Genial and family-run, this hotel occupies a 16th-century building near the centre, with fine views from the rooftop terrace and a traditional restaurant. The bar under the arcades is one of the nicest in town. Ask for one of the rooms with wonderful lake views.

★★★Firenze, Piazza Mazzini 42, **t** 031 950 342, **f** 031 951 722, *hotflore@tin.it* (*expensive*). Located in a 19th-century villa right next to Bellagio's harbour, owned by the same family for over a century; rooms are nicely decorated in style, the corner American and coffee bar is full of atmosphere and has live music in the evening once a week. The terraces and many of the rooms have lake views, there's a cosy lobby with heavy beams and a Florentine fireplace, and a restaurant under an arbour by the lake. *Open April–Oct.*

★★★Excelsior Splendide, **t** 031 950 225, **f** 031 951 224, *splendide@interfree.it* (*expensive*). A lake-front hotel with touching, faded Liberty-style charm, big old rooms (most with a view, though be sure to ask), a pool and its own garden. The restaurant has cheap or moderate menus.

★★Silvio, Via Carcano 12, **t** 031 950 322, **f** 031 950 912, *www.bellagiosilvio.com* (*moderate*). A few kilometres from the centre in Loppia, on the road to Como. A must for good value accommodation, friendly service, peaceful surroundings and home cooking. Rooms are comfortable, and all with lake or garden view. Fresh fish is caught daily by father and son, or try the home-made pasta, fish *ravioli* and *tiramisù* which have already been approved by Pavarotti and Robert de Niro.

★★La Pergola, Piazza del Porto, **t** 031 950 263, **f** 031 950 253 (*moderate*). Situated in the tiny fishing harbour of Pescallo, ten minutes' walk from Bellagio – follow the path among the vineyards – this is a small, charming olde-worlde place with stylish rooms. Its waterside restaurant with a nice pergola above the lake has a cheap menu. *Closed Tues out of season.*

Barchetta, Salita Mella 13, **t** 031 951 389 (*expensive*). The best place to eat in Bellagio, where you can feast on Lombard cuisine creatively revisited by chef Armando Valli on the terrace overlooking Bellagio's narrow and deep streets. Try the foie gras and pasta

April–Oct Tues–Sun at 11 and 4; tickets from the tourist office up to 10mins beforehand; in season the morning tour is often booked by groups). Another villa in Bellagio open for visits, the Villa Melzi *(open late Mar–Oct daily 9–6.30; adm)*, also has a fine garden and greenhouse, while the villa itself contains a collection of Egyptian sculpture. Back

dishes, rigorously home-made, or the lake delicacies. *Moderate* menu at lunchtime. *Closed Tues, Nov–Feb.*

Bilacus, Salita Serbelloni 9, t 031 95080 (*moderate*). One of the nicest places to dine in Bellagio's centre; on a romantic terrace, feasting on excellent, intense *spaghetti alle vongole*, saffrony mushroom *risotto* or simple grilled fish. *Closed winter.*

Mella, Via J. Rezia, San Giovanni, t 031 950 205 (*moderate*). A pleasant half-hour walk through the Villa Melzi and beyond. The place to go for a feast of fish – starve yourself first. Order the mixed fish *antipasto*, the mixed grilled fish and a bottle of lemony Soave. *Closed Tues and winter.*

Menaggio ✉ 22017

★★★★Grand Hotel Victoria, Lungolago Castelli 7, www.palacehotel.it, t 0344 32003, f 0344 32992 (very expensive). Built in 1806 next to the lake; during recent renovation its original décor was carefully preserved and complemented with creature comforts like designer bathrooms. The public rooms are elegant and there's a pool in the garden.

★★★★Grand Hotel Menaggio, t 0344 30640, f 0344 30619, *www.grandhotelmenaggio. com* (very expensive). Stands in its own grounds on the lake; most rooms have stunning views. Heated pool. *Open Mar–Oct.*

★★★Bellavista, t 0344 32136, f 0344 31793, *hotel.bellavista@cash.it*, (expensive). On the lake, with nice rooms; at the heart of the action in Menaggio's centre. *Open Mar–Dec.*

Vecchia Menaggio, Via al Lago 13, t 0344 32082, f 0344 30141 (*cheap*). A friendly low-key restaurant with great pizzas and pasta – calmer and better than the tourist havens by the lake. There are also cheap rooms to stay in, four with baths. *Closed Tues and Wed.*

Varenna ✉ 22050

★★★★Hotel du Lac, t 0341 830 238, f 0341 831 081 (very expensive). On the lakeside in the quiet medieval part of the city centre, with nicely decorated rooms, suites and bathrooms with marvellous views. Nice terrace, pergola, own mooring and a good if very pricey restaurant at lake level.

★★★Albergo Milano, Via XX Settembre 29, t/f 0341 830 298, *hotelmilano@varenna.net*, (*moderate*). Family-run hotel that enjoys an exquisite setting in the village, with eight rooms with balconies and wonderful views. The ones to request (months in advance) are numbers 1 or 2 with their large terraces, ideal for couples and incurable romantics.

Vecchia Varenna , Via Scoscesa 10, t 0341 830 793 (*moderate*). For gastronomic joy book a table here, where the sumptuous views are matched by dishes prepared with the finest ingredients from France and Italy: the lake fish is exquisite. *Closed Mon.*

Lecco ✉ 22053

★★★★Il Griso Via Provinciale 51, t 0341 202 040, f 0341 202 248, *hgriso@aol.it* (expensive). Lecco doesn't brim over with hotels; this elegant one, 1km away at Malgrate, has fine views of the lake from its wide terrace. The food and views compensate for the faded charm and 1970s interior décor. There's a pool in the garden, and one of the region's best gourmet restaurants – *very expensive menu degustazione*. Reservations essential.

Al Porticciolo, Via Valsecchi 5, t 0341 498 103 (*very expensive*). Lecco's best restaurant; you can pick your fish from the tanks. The chef concentrates on bringing out the natural flavours of the seafood. *Very expensive menus. Closed Mon, Tues, Aug and early Jan.*

Viganò Brianza ✉ 22048

Pierino Penati, Via XXIV Maggio 36, Viganò Brianza, t 039 956 020 (*very expensive*). The tiny village of Viganò Brianza, 9km south of Lake Annone, is worth a trip for this restaurant. Delicious regional specialities and a superb wine list complement the chef's own innovations (*gnocchetti* in a saffron-scented prawn bisque, for instance). *Closed Sun eve and Mon, Aug, Jan.*

on the west shore, **Menaggio** is another pleasant resort, with a beach. It lies at the head of two valleys: the Val Menaggio, an easy route to Lake Lugano, and the **Valle Sanagra**, from where you can make one of the finest ascents on the lake, the day-long walk up to panoramic **Monte Bregagno** from the Villa Calabi.

Varenna, on the east shore of the lake, is near Lake Como's most curious natural wonder, the **Fiumelatte**, Italy's second shortest river, running only 250m before hurtling down in creamy foam into Lake Como. For the Fiumelatte, as its name implies, is as white as milk. Not even Leonardo da Vinci, who delved deep into the cavern from which it flows, could discover its source, or why it abruptly begins to run in the last days of March and abruptly ceases at the end of October. Varenna also has a couple of lovely gardens: **Villa Monastero** (*open spring and autumn daily 10–6, summer 9–7, closed winter; adm*), built on the site of a 13th-century monastery with a garden especially known for its citrus trees, and **Villa Cipressi** (*same hours as Villa Monastero, combined ticket*).

High above Varenna, the ruined **Castello Vezio** was founded by Queen Theodolinda; you can drive up for the fantastic view. Another east shore village, **Bellano**, lies at the bottom of the steep gorge of the River Pioverna. It has a fine church, **Santi Nazzaro e Celso** (1348), by the Campionese masters (*open most days for religious services*), and a walkway through the gorge over the river.

Across on the west shore, visitors to Venice will recognize the name **Rezzonico**, cradle of the family that built one of the grandest palaces on the Grand Canal. Further up, looming over Musso, the lofty, almost inaccessible **Rocca di Musso** was the stronghold of Como's notorious pirate, Gian Giacomo de' Medici, 'Il Medeghino', born during the Medici exile from Florence in 1498. He gained the castle from Francesco II, Duke of Milan, for helping to remove the French from Milan and assassinating the duke's best friend; he made it the base for his fleet that patrolled the lake and extorted levies from towns and traders. He ended his career as the Marquis of Marignano, helping Charles V oppress the burghers of Ghent. His brother became the intriguing Pope Pius IV, while his nephew was St Charles Borromeo.

Next on the lake, **Dongo**, **Gravedona** and **Sorico** once formed the independent republic of the Three Parishes that endured until the arrival of the Spaniards. In the Middle Ages the little republic was plagued by the attentions of the inquisitor Peter of Verona, who sent scores of citizens to the stake for daring to doubt that the pope was Christ's representative on earth. Peter got a hatchet in his head for his trouble – and a quick canonization from the pope as St Peter Martyr. Gravedona was and still is the most important town of the three; it has a 12th-century church, the small **Santa Maria del Tiglio**, believed to have been originally a baptistry, with frescoes of St John the Baptist; it has some fine carvings (the centaur pursuing a deer is Early Christian symbolism, representing the persecution of the Church), and an unusual tower. Nearby is another ancient church, **San Vicenzo**, with a 5th-century crypt.

Lecco and its Lake

The Lago di Lecco, the less touristy east leg of Lake Como, resembles a brooding fjord, with granite mountains plunging down steeply into the water, a misty landscape beloved by Leonardo. **Lecco** itself is an industrial but pleasant city, lying at the foot of jagged Monte Resegone, where the River Adda continues its journey south (a typical entry in Pliny's *Natural History* records how the River Adda passes through the entire lake without mingling its waters).

Lecco was the birthplace of Alessandro Manzoni (1785–1873) and the setting of his novel, *I Promessi Sposi* ('The Betrothed'), the 19th-century Italian classic that embodies Manzoni's liberal, pro-unification attitudes. Literary pilgrims flock to the museum in Manzoni's boyhood home, the **Villa Manzoni**, now lost amid the urban sprawl at Via Guanella 7 (*from Piazza Manzoni, walk up Viale Dante; open Tues–Sun 9.30–2; adm*). Also to see in Lecco are the 14th-century fortified bridge over the Adda, built by the Visconti, which survives without its towers, and Lecco's **basilica**, adorned with 14th-century Giottoesque frescoes. The prettiest square is Piazza XX Settembre, just under the Visconti tower.

La Brianza

Between Lecco and Como are five baby-sized lakes in the pretty, wine-growing, furniture-making region called La Brianza. The first town, **Civate**, is the site of a famous Benedictine abbey, **San Calocero**, founded in 705, with 11th-century frescoes and nothing less than the keys of St Peter given him by Christ. It's an hour's walk to 10th-century **San Pietro al Monte** (*open Sun 9–3; ask the sacristan at Civate's parish church for the key before setting out, or contact Mario Canali, Via Monsignor Gilardi 3, t 0341 551 576*), with its remarkable frescoes of the Apocalypse, rare baldaquin from 1050 and ornate crypt. The adjacent **Oratorio di San Benedetto** has an unusual 12th-century painted altar.

Beyond Como: the Valli del Sondrio

North and east of Lake Como lies the mountainous province of Sondrio, sandwiched between the Orobie Alps and Switzerland. Its glacier-fed rivers flow in three directions: into Como and the Mediterranean, through the Danube to the Black Sea, and through the Rhine into the North Sea. Only four roads link the two main valleys, the **Valchiavenna** and the **Valtellina**, with the rest of Italy. The province is among the least-exploited Alpine regions, offering plenty of opportunities to see more of the mountains and fewer of your fellow creatures.

When the Spanish Habsburgs took Milan, the Valtellina, with its many Protestants, joined the Swiss Confederation. It was of prime importance to the Spaniards during the Counter-Reformation, assuring the route between Milan, Austria and the Netherlands. In 1620 the Spanish in Milan instigated the 'Holy Butchery' of 400 Protestants in the valley by their Catholic neighbours. The valley rejoined Italy only in the Napoleonic partition of 1797.

The Valchiavenna

In Roman times Lake Como extended as far north as **Samolaco**; between here and Cólico lies the marshy Piano di Spagna and shallow Lake Mezzola, an important breeding ground for swans. On the west shore of the lake stands the 10th-century Romanesque chapel of **San Fedelino**; on the east, **Novate Mezzola** is the base for walks in the enchanting **Val Codera**.

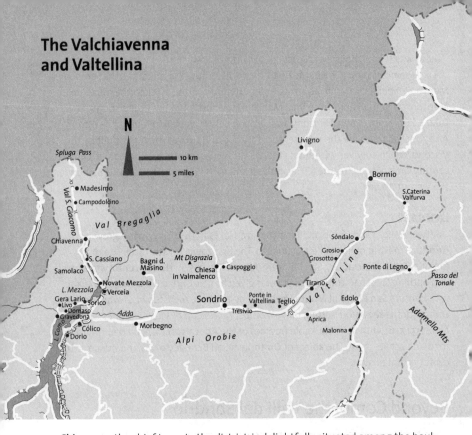

The Valchiavenna and Valtellina

Chiavenna, the chief town in the district, is delightfully situated among the boulders of an ancient landslide in a lush valley. Amidst the rocks are natural cellars, the *crotti*, which maintain a steady, year-round temperature and have long been used for ripening cheeses and hams; some have been converted into wine cellars. The most important church, **San Lorenzo**, was begun in the 11th century and now guards its treasure: a 12th-century golden 'Pax' cover for the Gospels; also note the carved octagonal font (1156) in the Romanesque Baptistry. Above the Palazzo Baliani you can walk up to the **Parco Botanico Archeologico Paradiso** (*open Tues–Sun 10–12 and 2–6; adm*), an ancient pot-stone quarry where workers once cut out pots and stone for architectural details. Further up, **Parco Marmitte dei Giganti** ('Giants' Kettles') is named for its remarkable glacial potholes, the finest collection in Europe. The path up to the park passes *crotti* under the horse chestnuts and charming meadows; beyond the potholes a sign directs the way to the ***incisioni rupestri*** – etchings in the boulders left by centuries of passers-by.

East of Chiavenna in the Val Bregaglia, a magnificent waterfall, the **Cascate dell'Acqua Fraggia**, is just above **Borgonuovo**; 2,000 leg-aching steps lead up past *crotti* to the ancient hamlet of Savogno atop the waterfall. In 1618 a landslide off Monte Conto buried the town of Piuro, next to Borgonuovo; you can visit the excavations of this humble 17th-century Pompeii, once an important pot-stone quarrying town. Before it was buried Piuro had fine mansions like the 16th-century **Palazzo**

Vertemate Franchi in nearby **Prosto di Piuro** (*open Mar–Oct; guided tours only, Tues–Fri 10, 11, 2, 3 and 4, Sat and Sun 10, 11, 3, 4 and 5; adm*), its rooms decorated with carved ceilings and lush mythological frescoes by the Campi brothers of Cremona.

North of Chiavenna, the **Valle San Giacomo** becomes increasingly rugged and steep, with dramatic landslides, glaciers and waterfalls. The village of **Campodolcino**, with a Roman bridge and a church with florid rococo altars, shares the 45km 'Skirama' ski slopes with Madesimo, watched over by a 43ft gilt statue of the **Madonna d'Europa**. **Madesimo**, further up, is a high-rise, high-altitude international resort (skiing and trekking) – before the 6,948ft **Splügen Pass**, generally closed six months of the year.

The Valtellina

East of Cólico and Lake Como the thoroughly unpleasant, traffic-swollen SS38 enters the Valtellina, giving a false first impression: the rest of the great valley of the Adda, where villages and vineyards hang precariously on the faces of the mountains, is as pure and unadulterated and fresh as any, a great Alpine playground only a couple of hours from smoggy Milan.

The old, vine-wrapped villages and numerous churches along the lower valley are part of the **Costiera dei Cèch**, referring to its Cèch inhabitants, whose origin is as mysterious as the name. Their main town is **Morbegno**; from here buses make excursions south into two scenic valleys, the **Valli del Bitto**, with iron-ore deposits that made them a prize of the Venetians for two centuries, and the rural **Val Tartano**, a 'lost paradise' dotted with Alpine cottages, woods and pastures. The road through the valley was only finished in 1971, but many hamlets even today are accessible only by foot or mule. A third valley running north, the wild granite **Val Másino**, is traversed by the magnificent 'Sentiero Roma', and also serves as the base for the ascent of Monte Disgrazia (12,070ft), one of the highest peaks in the region. Near the village of Cataéggio, the landmark is an awesome granite boulder, the **Sasso Remenno**.

The provincial capital **Sondrio** (from *sundrium*, the land Lombard lords gave to their peasants) is mostly modern, built on the flood-prone Torrente Mallero which devastated the city in 1987. Many of Sondrio's surviving mansions have found new uses: one 18th-century *palazzo* holds the **Museo Valtellinese di Storia e Arte**, Via M. Quadrio 27 (*open Tues–Sat 10–12 and 3–6; t 0342 526 270*), with art and frescoes salvaged from churches, and an exceptional collection of rococo drawings, etchings and oils by the 18th-century Ligari family. At Via del Gesù 6, Palazzo Sertoli (with a fancy-pants *trompe l'œil* ballroom) houses the **Collezione Fulvio Grazioli** (*open Tues–Sat 9–10 and 2–3*), one of Italy's most important collections of rocks and minerals, nearly all from the Val Malenco. Opposite Palazzo Sertoli, Via Scarpaletti leads up into old Sondrio, dominated by **Castello Masegra**, founded in 1041. On the other side of the Torrente Mallero, the **Palazzo Carbonera** (1533) is Sondrio's finest.

The best excursion from Sondrio is to head north into the **Val Malenco**, lined with deep chestnut forests and glacier lakes. It is a paradise for rock hounds – no valley in the Alps comes close to matching the 260 different minerals that have been found here; **Chiesa in Valmalenco** is a fine base for exploring or the seven-day Alta Via trail.

Getting Around

At Cólico the railway from Milan and Lecco forks, one line heading north as far as Chiavenna. **Buses** from there link up to Madesimo and other valley towns. **FS trains** from Milan and Lecco serve the valley as far east as Tirano, where you can pick up the 'Trenino Rosso del Bernina' for St Moritz, 70km away, **t** 0342 701 353 (in winter you can get a combined train ticket and ski pass). A network of **buses**, connecting with the trains, serves the villages and points east, and there are direct **coach** connections to Sondrio from Milan, as well as direct summer and winter services to Bormio and Stelvio National Park from Milan, Varese and Como.

Tourist Information

Chiavenna: Piazza Caduti della Libertà, **t/f** 0343 36384, *www.valchiavenna.com*.
Sondrio: Via C. Battisti 12, **t** 0342 512 500, **f** 0342 212 590, *www.valtellinaonline.com*.
Bormio: Via Roma 131, **t** 0342 903 300, **f** 904 696, *aptbormio@provincia.so.it*.
Livigno: Via Gesa 55, **t** 0342 996 379, **f** 996 881, *info@aptlivigno.it*.

Sports and Activities

Stelvio National Park is administered by the provinces of Sondrio, Trento and Bolzano, all of which have **park visitor's centres**. Bormio's is at Via Roma 26, at Torre Alberti, **t** 0342 901 654 (*open July–10 Sept daily 9–12 and 3–6*); they can tell you where to find the 1,500km of marked trails at all levels of ability, or the best place to watch for the park's chamois, the not very shy marmots, golden eagles,

lammergeyers and other wildlife, including the ibex, reintroduced in 1968. The last bear in these mountains was bagged in 1908, but hunting is now illegal, at least in the Lombard section of the park. Above the visitor's centre, the **Giardino Botanico Alpino Rezia** (open daily July and Aug, or call **t** 0342 927 370) contains many of the 1,800 species of plants and flowers that grow in Stelvio. The local tourist offices have plenty of information on summer and winter sports and activities in the area.

Where to Stay and Eat

Chiavenna ✉ 23022
La Lanterna Verde, Via S. Barnaba 7, Villa di Chiavenna, **t** 0343 38588. *lanver@tin.it* (*expensive*). 10km west of Chiavenna, this family-run restaurant is the best place to taste regional cuisine elevated to a gourmet level. Leave some appetite for the beautifully served desserts: if you are a chocolate addict, do not miss the *mousse au chocolat fondant* with a passionfruit heart in a rum sauce. Menus range from *moderate* (trout menu) to *expensive* (gourmet, two main dishes) and change seasonally. Be sure to book. *Closed Wed, Thurs lunch*.

Morbegno ✉ 23017
★★★**Margna**, Via Margna 36, **t** 0342 610 377, **f** 0342 615 114 (*moderate*). In business since 1886, but completely remodelled and modernized, with a nice roof terrace solarium. The restaurant is particularly well looked after; recently renovated with style, it features the likes of *crespelle* (pancakes) filled with *bitto* cheese, *risotto* with wild mushrooms, and venison cutlets in juniper berry sauce. Ask about special wine and food

The Upper Valtellina

The highway rises relentlessly through the valley; but take the scenic 'Castel road' running north of the highway from Sondrio, past Tresivio and the melancholy ruins of Grumello Castle, then on to the old patrician town of **Ponte in Valtellina,** birthplace of astronomer Giuseppe Piazzi (1746–1826), discoverer of the first asteroid; the parish church of **San Maurizio** has an unusual bronze *cimborio* (1578), and frescoes by Luini.
Further east, charming **Teglio** gave its name to the entire valley (from Tellina Vallis). Its Renaissance **Palazzo Besta** is the finest in the region (*guided tours May–Sept 9, 10,*

weekends (except during high season) comprising visits to the city and neighbouring wine cellars.

Sondrio ✉ 23100

★★★★Della Posta, Piazza Garibaldi 19, **t** 0342 510 404, **f** 0342 510 210, *www.hotelposta.so.it* (*expensive*). Garibaldi is only one of the illustrious guests to have slept here. Formerly the old stage post, this grand old family-run hotel offers big rooms with lots of charm. It also has a cosy reading room, American bar and excellent restaurant Sozzani, with a moderate menu, otherwise expensive.

Chiesa in Valmalenco ✉ 23023

★★★★Tremoggia, Via Bernina 6, **t** 0342 451 106, **f** 0342 451 718, *tremoggia.so@bestwestern.it* (*moderate*). A warm and welcoming place; the restaurant serves good cheesy *sciatt* and beef marinated in juniper berries. *Closed Wed and Nov.*

La Volta, Via Milano 48, **t** 0342 454 051, (*expensive*). Serves local cuisine creatively revisited. *Closed Wed and Thurs lunch except summer and Christmas.*

Il Vassallo, in Vassalini hamlet, **t** 0342 451 200 (*moderate*). An old stone chalet restaurant, which couples traditional and original recipes. Excellent home-made *gnocchi* and *pappardelle. Closed Mon.*

Ponte in Valtellina ✉ 23026

Cerere, Via Guicciardi 7, **t** 0342 482 294 (*moderate*). One of the region's best restaurants, occupying a 17th-century palace, it has long set the standard of classic Valtellina cuisine with dishes like *sciatt* and *pizzoccheri*; the wine list includes the valley's finest. *Closed Wed, Jan and July.*

Grosio ✉ 23022

★★★Sassella, **t** 0342 847 272, **f** 0342 847 550 (*moderate*). A fine old hotel and restaurant run by friendly chef and owner Jim Pini, the chef who feeds the Italian ski team, and his family. The restaurant serves a refined version of local specialities like *bresaola condita* (served with olive oil, lemon and herbs), *crespelle* with mushrooms and local cheese, an unparalleled *sciatt*, smoked trout and Valtellina wines; excellent *moderate* menu changes daily. *Closed Mon in winter.*

Bormio ✉ 23032

★★★★Rezia, Via Milano 9, **t** 0342 904 721, **f** 0342 905 197, *hotelrezia@valtline.it* (*expensive*). In the centre of Bormio, this is one of the town's cosiest hotels, furnished throughout with locally handcrafted furniture; the restaurant (*moderate*) is especially good, serving up delicious mushroom dishes in season, as well as solid Valtellina home-cooking. *Closed Mon.*

★★★★Palace, Via Milano 54, **t** 0342 903 131, **f** 0342 903 366 (*very expensive*). Modern and upmarket; swimming pool and very comfortable rooms. *Closed May.*

★★★★Baita dei Pini, Via Don Peccedi 15, **t** 0342 904 346, **f** 0342 904 700, *www.baitadeipini. com* (*expensive*). Central and pleasant, with very good rooms. *Open Dec–April, 15 June–Sept.*

★★Everest, Via S. Barbara 11, **t** 0342 901 291, **f** 0342 901 713 (*cheap*). Flowery balconies, a little back garden and standard rooms. *Closed Oct, Nov.*

Kuerc, Piazza Cavour 8, **t** 0342 904 738 (*moderate*). Situated in the heart of old Bormio and named after the ancient council of Bormio, this is a good place to try local dishes in an attractive setting. *Closed Tues.*

11, 12, 2.30, 3.30 and 4.30; closed 2nd and 4th Sun and 1st and 3rd Mon of the month; in winter call the tourist office at Teglio for details; adm). Built in 1539, the arcaded courtyard is embellished with *chiaroscuro* frescoes from the *Aeneid* and *Orlando Furioso*; inside, the Sala della Creazione has a world map dated 1549. Downstairs, the **Antiquarium Tellinum** houses the Stele di Caven or the Mother Goddess, an exceptional example of the prehistoric rock incisions common in these parts, which the locals once believed were made by the claws of witches. Among the old lanes in the centre, look for 11th-century **San Pietro**, with geometric decorations and a Byzantinish fresco of Christ Pantocrator in the apse; the **Oratorio dei Bianchi**, its exterior frescoed with a ruined 15th-century *danse macabre*; and the **Ca' del Boia**, with blackened arcades, once the home of a particularly adept executioner. These days Teglio takes pride in its wines and *pizzoccheri*, once described as 'narcotic grey noodles with butter and vegetables', served up at the autumn *Sagra dei Pizzoccheri*. **Aprica**, to the east of Teglio, is a well-equipped winter and summer resort.

The vines begin to give way to lush apple orchards as you approach **Tirano**, a historic crossroads: mule trains from Venice and Brescia would pass up the Valle Camonica and at Tirano either turn west to trade in the Valtellina or continue north into Switzerland and Germany. Today the town is the terminus of the FS trains from Milan and the narrow-gauge **Trenino Rosso del Bernina** that plunges and twists 70km through dramatic gorges to St Moritz; in July and August special open cars make it even easier to drink in the stupendous scenery. Once the site of a major annual Swiss-Italian fair, Tirano has a fine clutch of 16th- and 17th-century buildings in its centre, but its most famous, the **Santuario della Madonna di Tirano** (1505), is a kilometre away, marking the spot where the Virgin appeared, in September 1504. It became the focal point of Catholicism during the Counter-Reformation, and was exuberantly baroqued, painted and stuccoed and given an impressive wood-inlaid organ.

The Stelvio road continues up to **Grosotto**, with the 17th-century **Santuario della Beata Vergine delle Grazie**, with an even better 18th-century organ and, in the sacristy, a painting by Michelangelo's friend Marcello Venusti.

The large old village of **Grosio**, another 2km on, was long the fief of the Visconti Venosta family, whose ruined castle sits on top of town. Just below the castle, however, is evidence that Grosio was important long before their arrival, in the curious stick-man engravings (2200–1000 BC) on the whaleback rock of its **Parco delle Incisioni Rupestri**. Art in Grosio took another step forward in the 16th century with the birth of Cipriano Valorsa, the 'Raphael of the Valtellina', who frescoed **San Giorgio** and his own house, the **Casa di Cipriano Valorsa**.

The early 20th-century Villa Visconti Venosta contains the **Museo Civico** (*open summer Tues–Sun 10–12 and 2–5; winter Tues–Sat 10–12 and 2–4*); among the exhibits are Venetian-inspired costumes, with bright kerchiefs and Burano-embroidered aprons that the older women still wear. **Sóndalo**, the next town, has courtly 16th-century frescoes in its 12th-century church of Santa Marta.

Bormio and Stelvio National Park

The seat of an ancient county, not unjustifiably called the 'Magnifica Terra', **Bormio** is a fine old town with many frescoed palaces, recalling the days of prosperity when Venice's Swiss trade passed through. Splendidly situated in a mountain basin, it is a major ski centre: nearby **Santa Caterina Valfurva**, 'the skier's last white paradise', is a cradle of champions, most recently of Olympic gold medalist Deborah Compagnoni. Bormio is the main entrance into the **Parco Nazionale dello Stelvio**, Italy's largest national park, founded in 1935 and encompassing the grand Alpine massif of Ortles-Cevedale. A tenth of the park's area is covered with glaciers, including one of Europe's largest, the *Ghiacciaio dei Forni*. The peaks offer many exciting climbs, on **Grand Zebrù**

(12,631ft), **Ortles** (12,811ft) and **Cevedale** (12,395ft) among other peaks. It also includes Europe's second-highest pass, the **Passo di Stelvio** (9,048ft) through which you can continue into the Süd Tirol between June and October (*see* p.475); the pass is also an important winter and summer ski centre.

From Bormio the **Valdidentro** heads east up towards the **Valle di Livigno**, another ski area, noted for its traditional wooden houses and trout fishing. Before reaching the valley, you must pass through Italian customs – it's a bustling duty-free zone, though the Forcola di Livigno, another pass into Switzerland, is open in summer only.

Bergamo

At the end of *A Midsummer Night's Dream*, Bottom and his mechanical pals who played in 'Pyramus and Thisbe' dance a bergomask to celebrate the happy ending. Bergamo itself has the same happy, stomping magnificent spirit as its great peasant dance, a city that mixes a rugged edge with the most delicate refinement: it has given the world not only a dance but the maestro of *bel canto*, Gaetano Donizetti, the Renaissance painter of beautiful women, Palma Vecchio, and the great master of the portrait, Gian Battista Moroni.

Piled on a promontory on the edge of the Alps, the city started out on a different foot, founded by mountain Celts who named it *Bergheim* or hill town. To this day the Bergamasques speak a dialect that puzzles their fellow Lombards; their language, courage and blunt up-front character are all a part of the essential *bergheimidad* that sets them apart. Although old Bergamo owes many of its grace notes to the long rule of Venice (1428–1797), the culture traffic was by no means one-way: Bergamo contributed not only artists, but the Serenissima's most brilliant and honourable *condottiere*, Bartolomeo Colleoni (1400–75), as well as many of Venice's servants, porters and stock comic characters.

Bergamo also contributed so many men to Garibaldi in its enthusiasm for the Risorgimento that it received the proud title 'City of the Thousand'.

Up to the Piazza Vecchia

There are two Bergamos: the **Città Alta**, the medieval and Renaissance centre up on the hill, and the **Città Bassa**, pleasant, newer and more spacious on the plain below, most of its streets laid out at the beginning of this century. The centre of the Lower Town is the large, oblong **Piazza Matteotti** (from the station, walk up Viale Giovanni XXIII), with the grand 18th-century **Teatro Donizetti** and, on the right, the church of **San Bartolomeo**, containing a fine 1516 altarpiece of the *Madonna col Bambino* by Lotto. Further up Viale Vittorio Emanuele II is the funicular up to the Higher Town; once you're at the top, Via Gombito leads from the upper station in a short distance to beautiful **Piazza Vecchia**.

Architects as diverse as Frank Lloyd Wright and Le Corbusier have praised this square as one of Italy's finest for its magnificent ensemble of Renaissance and medieval buildings, all overlooking a low, dignified lion fountain. At the lower end

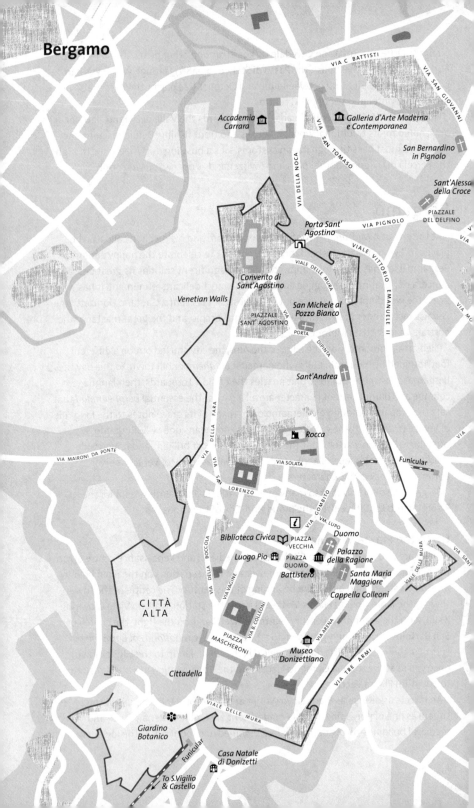

Bergamo

Accademia Carrara

Galleria d'Arte Moderna e Contemporanea

San Bernardino in Pignolo

VIA C BATTISTI

VIA SAN GIOVANNI

VIA SAN TOMASO

VIA DELLA NOCA

Sant'Alessa della Croce

PIAZZALE DEL DELFINO

Porta Sant' Agostino

VIA PIGNOLO

VIALE VITTORIO EMANUELE II

Convento di Sant'Agostino

VIALE DELLE MURA

Venetian Walls

PIAZZALE SANT' AGOSTINO

San Michele al Pozzo Bianco

PORTA

VIA DIPINTA

Sant'Andrea

VIA DELLA FARA

VIA MAIRONI DA PONTE

Rocca

VIA S. LORENZO

VIA SOLATA

Funicular

VIALE DELLE MURA

VM. LUPO

VIA GOMBITO

Biblioteca Civica

PIAZZA VECCHIA

Duomo

Luogo Pio

PIAZZA DUOMO

Palazzo della Ragione

Battistero

Santa Maria Maggiore

CITTÀ ALTA

VIA DELLA BOCCOLA

VIA VAGINE

VIA B. COLLEONI

Cappella Colleoni

VIA DELLE MURA

VIA SANT

PIAZZA MASCHERONI

VIA ARENA

Museo Donizettiano

VIA TRE ARMI

Cittadella

VIALE DELLE MURA

Giardino Botanico

Funicular

Casa Natale di Donizetti

To S.Vigilio & Castello

Getting There

Bergamo is an hour's **train** ride from Milan. It has frequent connections to Brescia, but only a few trains a day to Cremona and Lecco (freephone **t** 1478 88088). Bergamo's **airport**, Orio al Serio, has flights to Rome and Ancona.

There are regular **bus** services (**t** 035 289 011) to Milan, Como, Lake Garda (via Brescia), the Bergamasque Valleys and Boario in the Valle Camonica. Lecco can be reached by train. Both train and bus stations are located near each other at the end of Viale Papa Giovanni XXIII.

Tourist Information

Bergamo has two tourist offices, one in a 1900s villa set in its own grounds, **Viale Vittorio Emanuele 20**, **t** 035 210204, **f** 035 280184, a few hundred yards from the funicular station to the Città Alta; the other in the **Città Alta**, at Vicolo dell'Aquila Nera 3, **t** 035 242 226, **f** 035 242 994, *www.apt.bergamo.it*.

Where to Stay and Eat

Bergamo ✉ **24100**

★★★★**Excelsior San Marco**, Piazzale della Repubblica 6, **t** 035 366 111, **f** 035 366 175, *www.hotelsanmarco.it* (*very expensive*). The city's most comfortable hotel, a few minutes from the funicular, with modern rooms, and an excellent restaurant **Colonna** (*expensive*). The hotel has a beautiful roof terrace with a 360-degree view over old and new Bergamo.

★★★★**Cappello d'Oro**, Viale Giovanni XXIII 12, **t** 035 232 503, **f** 035 242 946 (*expensive*). Modern rooms with lovely bathrooms, and a very good restaurant, but beware that extra rooms in annexes, drafted into use when the hotel is full, may not meet the category's standards. Check in advance.

★★★**San Vigilio**, Via S. Vigilio 15, **t** 035 253 179, **f** 035 402 081, *www.sanvigilio.it* (*moderate*). Above the Città Alta, reached by the S. Vigilio cable car – this hotel was built last century by a local bank for employees' holidays. It has just seven rooms – five with magnificent views – and an old-fashioned feel.

★★**Agnello d'Oro**, Via Gombito 22, **t** 035 249 883, **f** 035 235 612, *www.agnellodoro.it*

(*moderate*). The most atmospheric hotel in the Città Alta, built in 1600 – but rooms are modern. The excellent restaurant (*moderate*) offers regional dishes including *casoncelli*, *maize foiade* and rice dishes, and beef stew, sausages and quails with *polenta*. Outside dining in the square in front. *Closed Mon.*

★★**San Giorgio**, Via S. Giorgio 10, **t** 035 212 043, **f** 035 310 072, *sangiorgio@infinito.it* (*cheap*). Near the station; quiet rooms nonetheless.

Bergamo prides itself on its cooking: look for *casoncelli* (*ravioli* filled with tangy sausage-meat, in a sauce of melted butter, bacon and sage), *polenta taragna* (with butter and cheese) or *risotto* with wild mushrooms. Many restaurants, surprisingly, feature seafood – Bergamo is a major inland fish market. In August you might have to resort to a picnic.

Da Vittorio, Viale Papa Giovanni XXIII 21, **t/f** 035 218 060 (*expensive*). The classic for fish, specializing in seafood prepared in a number of exquisite ways, as well as a wide variety of meat dishes, *polenta*, *risotto* and pasta. *Closed Wed, and three weeks in Aug.*

Taverna del Colleoni, Piazza Vecchia, **t** 035 232 596, **f** 035 231 991 (*expensive*). A celebrated restaurant featuring exquisite classical Italian cuisine, including delicate dishes such as *ravioli* filled with leek and potato in a toasted pine nut *pesto*. *Moderate* lunch menu. *Closed Mon and two weeks in Aug.*

Da Ornella, Via Gombito 3, **t** 035 232 736 (*moderate*). The place to come for *polenta taragna* with rabbit, chicken and *porcini* mushrooms, served in hot cast-iron bowls (their speciality) and *casoncelli*, local *affettati* and braised meats. *Closed Thurs.*

La Colombina, Borgo Canale 12, **t** 035 261 402 (*moderate*). Near Donizetti's birthplace; the almost perfect restaurant, with stunning views from its dappled terrace, and a pretty Liberty-style dining room. Try the salad of local *taleggio* cheese with slivers of pear, a plate of cured meats, and the best *casoncelli* in town. Leave room for a slice of deep, dark caramelized apple cake. *Closed Mon and Aug; and one week in Jan and June.*

Antica Hosteria del Buon Vino, Piazza Mercato delle Scarpe, in Bergamo Alta, in front of the exit of the *funivia*. A hearty cheap meal serving *polenta* (try the *tris*) and local hot and cold dishes. *Closed Mon.*

stands the **Biblioteca Civica** (1594), designed after Sansovino's famous library in Venice. Directly opposite, an ancient covered stair leads up to the 12th-century **Torre Civica**, with a 15th-century clock and curfew bell that still warns the Bergamasques to bed at 10pm; there is a lift to take visitors up for the fine views over Bergamo (*open April–Sept daily 9–12 and 2–8, Fri and Sat till 11pm, Sun 9–8pm; March daily 10–12 and 2 to 6; Oct weekends and holidays only 10–12 and 2–6; Nov–Feb weekends and holidays only, 10–12 and 2–4; adm*). Next to the stair, set up on its large rounded arches, is the 12th-century **Palazzo della Ragione**, with a Lion of St Mark added recently to commemorate the city's golden days under Venice.

Through the dark, tunnel-like arches of the Palazzo della Ragione are glimpses of a second square resembling a jewel box. This is **Piazza del Duomo**, and the jewel box reveals itself as the sumptuous, colourful façade of the 1476 **Colleoni Chapel** (*open daily 9–12 and 2–6.30; Nov–Mar till 5.30; closed Mon*), designed for the old *condottiere* by Giovanni Antonio Amadeo while he worked on the Certosa at Pavia.

The Colleoni Chapel is even more ornate and out of temper with the times, disregarding all the fine proportions and serenity of the Tuscans for the Venetian love of flourish. Amadeo also sculpted the fine tombs within, a double decker for Colleoni and his wife; the golden equestrian statue on top by Sixus of Nuremberg makes him look like a wimp compared to Verrocchio's version in Venice (*see p.382*).

His young daughter Medea's tomb is much calmer, and was brought here in the 19th century from another church. The ornate ceiling is by Tiepolo, and there's a painting of the *Holy Family* by Goethe's constant companion in Rome, the Swiss artist Angelica Kauffman.

Flanking the chapel are two works by Giovanni, a 14th-century Campionese master: the octagonal **baptistry** (*open by appointment only, t 035 278 111*) and the colourful porch and equestrian statue of St Alexander on the otherwise austere **Basilica of Santa Maria Maggiore** (1137).

The palatial interior with its sumptuous tapestries hits you like a gust of lilac perfume, but the the 33 Old Testament scenes designed by Lorenzo Lotto and executed in *intaglio* by Capodiferro ('Ironhead') di Lovere are off limits. However four of the scenes can be seen on Sundays; their locked wooden covers, with unfathomable allegories, are food for thought. Donizetti's tomb, near the back of the church, has mourning putti and a keyboard. The third building on the square is an insipid neoclassical **cathedral**.

The rest of the Città Alta deserves a stroll; walk along the main artery, Via Colleoni (the *condottiere* lived at No.9) to the old fortress of the Cittadella, which houses the city's **Museo di Scienze Naturale** (*open Tues–Sun 9–12.30 and 2.30–7.30; until 5.30 in winter*) and **Museo Civico Archeologico** (*open Tues–Thurs 9–12.30 and 2.30–6; Fri–Sun 9–6*). Near the Cittadella is the bottom station of another funicular, up to **San Vigilio** where there is another fortress, the **Castello**, with superb views. Back at the Cittadella, quiet, medieval Via Arena leads around to the back of the cathedral, passing by way of the **Museo Donizettiano** (*open Tues–Sat 10–1, by appointment; Sun 10–1 and 2.30–5*), with a collection of artefacts and instruments once owned by the great composer of *bel canto*, who died syphilitic and mad in 1848.

The Accademia Carrara

Open daily 9.30–12.30 and 2.30–5.30; adm; Sun free.

This is one of the top provincial art museums in Italy, and certainly one of the oldest, founded in 1796 by Count Giacomo Carrara and housed in this neoclassical palace since 1810. It has exquisite portraits – Botticelli's haughty *Giuliano de' Medici*, Pisanello's *Lionello d'Este*, Gentile Bellini's *Portrait of a Man*, Lotto's *Portrait of Lucina Brembati* with a vicious weasel under her arm and a sickly moon overhead, and another strange painting of uncertain origin, believed to be of Cesare Borgia, with an uncannily desolate background. Other portraits (especially the *Young Girl*, one of the most beautiful portraits of a child ever painted) are by Bergamo's Giovan Battista Moroni (1520–78), the master to whom Titian sent the *Rectors of Venice* for their portrait, saying that only Moroni could 'make them natural'. There are beautiful *Madonnas*, three superlative ones by Giovanni Bellini, others by Mantegna (who couldn't do children), Fra Angelico, Landi and Crivelli (with his cucumber signature). The anti-plague saint Sebastian is portrayed by three contemporaries in very different aspects – naked and pierced with arrows before a silent city, by Giovanni Bellini; well-dressed and sweetly contemplating an arrow, by Raphael; and sitting at a table, clad in a fur-trimmed coat, by Dürer. Other paintings are by Bergognone, Cariani, Fra Galgario, Palma Vecchio and Prevetali (all from Bergamo), the Venetians Carpaccio, Vivarini, Titian, Veronese, Tintoretto, Tiepolo and Guardi; also Cosmè Tura, Foppa, Luini, Savoldo, Moretto, Clouet, Van Dyck and Brueghel.

Around Bergamo

The year after Bartolomeo Colleoni was appointed Captain General of Venice, he purchased the ruined **Castello di Malpaga in Cavernago**, 8km southeast of Bergamo, which he had restored for his old age; his heirs added a series of frescoes by Romanino or someone like him, commemorating a visit by Christian I of Denmark in 1474, portraying Colleoni hosting the *de rigueur* splendid banquets, jousts, hunts and pageants of Renaissance hospitality (*to visit, call t 030 840 003*).

At **Trescore Balneario**, 14km east of Bergamo on the road to Lovere, the chapel of the **Villa Suardi** (*call t 035 944 777 to arrange a visit*) has an utterly charming fresco cycle by Lorenzo Lotto, painted in 1524 during his 15-year stint in Bergamo, when he was driven from his home in Venice by the merciless 'Triumvirate' of Titian, Sansovino and the poison-pen Aretino. The subject of the frescoes is the story of St Barbara, patroness of artillerymen, architects and gravediggers. Her apocryphal life reads like a fairy-tale – her pagan father locked her in a tower, and after various adventures had her martyred for being a Christian, although he paid for his wickedness by being struck down by a bolt of lightning – and Lotto gave it just the treatment it deserved.

Southwest of Bergamo, **Caravaggio** was the birthplace of Michelangelo Merisi da Caravaggio, who left not a smear of oil paint here, not even in the popular pilgrimage shrine of the **Santuario della Madonna del Fonte**, designed in a cool Renaissance style by Pellegrino Tibaldi (1575) on the site of a 1432 apparition of the Virgin. In **Capriate San Gervasio**, off the *autostrada* towards Milan, the **Parco Minitalia Fantasy World** (*open Mar–Oct daily 9–6; winter opening hours vary; adm*) cuts Italy down to size – 1,310ft from tip to toe, with mountains, seas, cities and monuments all arranged in their proper place. Due east of Bergamo, **Sotto del Monte** was the birthplace of the beloved Pope John XXIII, and is an increasingly popular pilgrimage destination; there's a **Museo Papa Giovanni** near his birthplace, filled with memorabilia (*open Tues–Sun 8.30–11.30 and 2.30–6.30; until 5.30 only in winter*).

The Bergamasque Valleys

North of Bergamo two valleys plunge into the stony heart of the Orobie Alps. The western **Val Brembana** was the main route for Venetian caravans carting minerals from the Valtellina; the eastern **Valle Seriana** is Bergamo's favourite summer retreat.

Val Brembana

North of Bergamo, just off the main road, in Almenno San Bartolomeo, the tiny, round 12th-century church of **San Tomè** (*open Sun and hols only 2–4; summer until 6*) is a jewel of Lombard Romanesque, composed of three cylinders, one atop the other, and prettily illuminated at night; its isolation makes it especially impressive. Zogno, further up the valley, has the **Museo della Valle Brembana** (*open Tues–Sun 9–12 and 2–5; adm*), with artefacts relating to the district's life and history and **La Grotta delle Meraviglie**, with a long gallery of stalactites and stalagmites. **San Pellegrino Terme**, next up the valley, means mineral water to millions of Italians. Lombardy's most fashionable spa, it developed at the turn of the century around two Baroque/Liberty-style confections, the Grand Hotel and the Casino. Excursions include a ride up the funicular for the view, and a visit to the **Grotta del Sogno** ('Dream Cave'). According to legend, the humorously frescoed **Casa dell'Arlecchino** at Oneta in San Giovanni Bianco was the birthplace of Harlequin. The role, they say, was invented by a *commedia dell'arte* actor named Ganassa who lived there, lumping together the experience of the many men and women who, like Harlequin, chose to forsake their poor hills to become servants in Venice or Bergamo. There are any number of lovely, forgotten hamlets like Oneta in these mountains; many of them lie in a mini-region called the Val Taleggio, on the other side of the gorge of the **Torrente Enna**.

The next town north, **Cornello dei Tasso**, may be down to 30 inhabitants, but it preserves as if in aspic its appearance as a medieval relay station, with an arcaded lane to protect the mule caravans. In the 13th century the business of expediting merchandise here was in the hands of the Tasso family, whose destiny, however, was far bigger than Cornello. One branch went on to run the post between Venice and Rome; another moved to Germany in the 1500s to organize for Emperors Maximilian I and Charles V the first European postal service and give us the word *taxi*. Their network of postal relay stations was still in use into the 19th century. Another branch of the family in Sorrento produced the loony, melancholy Renaissance poet Torquato Tasso. Cornello preserves the ruins of the Tasso ancestral home.

Beyond **Piazza Brembana** the road branches out into several mountain valleys. The most important and developed resort is **Foppolo**; besides winter sports it offers an easy ascent up the **Corno Stella**, with marvellous views to the north and east. Other ski resorts include **Piazzatorre** and **San Simone** near Branzi; **Carona** is a good base for summer excursions into the mountains and Alpine lakes. Another important village on the merchants' road, the prettily situated **Averara**, was the first station after the Passo San Marco; besides the covered arcade for the caravans, there are a number of 16th-century exterior frescoes.

Valle Seriana

Bergamo's eastern valley, the Valle Seriana, is industrial in its lower half and ruggedly Alpine in the north. At the bottom of the valley, some 8km from Bergamo, **Alzano Lombardo** is worth a brief stop for the Basilica di San Martino, containing one of Italy's most striking rococo pulpits, covered with reliefs and soaring cherubs by Antonio Fantoni, along with some fine 17th-century inlaid and *intarsia* work. **Gandino** is another town to aim for; in the Middle Ages it was the chief producer of heavy bergamasque cloth. It too boasts a fine basilica, a 17th-century garlic-domed church, with works by Fantoni and a museum housing relics of the medieval textile industry.

Clusone, further up, is the capital and prettiest town of the Valle Seriana, with many frescoes, a beautiful 16th-century astronomical clock in Piazza dell'Orologio, and a market every Monday. Near the clock, the Oratorio del Disciplini is adorned with an eerie 1485 fresco of the *Danse Macabre* and the *Triumph of Death*, where one skeleton mows the nobility and clergy down with arrows, while another fires a blunderbuss. There are more frescoes inside, and a *Deposition* by Fantoni. Winter and summer resorts further north include the **Passo della Presolana** and **Schilpàrio**, both located near dramatic Dolomite-like mountain walls.

Lake Iseo, Franciacorta and the Valle Camonica

Lake Iseo (the Roman *Lacus Sebinus*) is the fifth lake in size but one of the first in charm, well endowed with what it takes to get under your skin; even back in the 1750s it was the preferred resort of Italophile Lady Montagu, who disdained the English who 'herd together' by the larger lakes. The southeast shore borders on the lovely wine-growing region of Franciacorta; the lake's main source, the river Oglio, runs through the lovely Valle Camonica, the rocky palette for some of the world's most intriguing prehistoric art.

Franciacorta and Lake Iseo

Between Brescia and Iseo lies the charming wine-growing region known as **Franciacorta**, the 'free court', which, owing to its poverty, paid no taxes, a fact that endeared it to the villa-building patricians of Lombardy. Today the name of the region is also synonymous with one of Italy's best-known varieties of sparkling wine, as well as with mellowing old estates surrounded by vineyards producing a fine DOC red and Pinot Bianco. Places to stop include the **Villa Lana da Terzo** in Colombaro, where Italy's oldest cedar of Lebanon grows in the garden. The Romanesque Olivetan abbey church at **Rodengo** has three cloisters and frescoes by Romanino and Moretto, and in

Provaglio, monks from Cluny founded **San Pietro in Lamosa** in 1083, overlooking an emerald peat bog called **Le Torbiere**, which blossoms into an aquatic garden of pink and white waterlilies in late spring; the tourist office in Iseo rents out rowing boats to enable you to paddle through.

Near Le Torbiere, **Iseo** is a charming little town and the main resort on the lake, with beaches and a venerable 12th-century church, Pieve di Sant'Andrea. **Clusane**, just south of Iseo, is crowned by an abandoned Castello di Carmagnola – it briefly belonged to the famous Venetian captain – and has a fishing fleet of white-, blue- and pink-rimmed boats called *naêcc* in the local dialect. The fleet spends the day bagging the ingredients of *tinca al forno* (baked lake tench with *polenta*), a dish based on a recipe invented in 1800, and served in 20 restaurants, seating 4,000 – in a village with a population of 1,500!

Steamers link Iseo town with **Sàrnico**, a smaller resort to the south, sprinkled with Liberty-style villas, and with the island of **Monte Isola**, a fair-size copy of Gibraltar soaking in its own tub, with just some 200 souls in genteelly decaying fishing villages; it has a number of inviting walks through olive and chestnut groves. Another steamer port, **Sale Marasino**, is one of the prettier spots on the lake, ringed by mountain terraces. From the nearby village of **Marone** you can hike up to the panoramic view point of **Monte Guglielmo** (6,393ft, with an Alpine refuge), passing along the way **Zone** and its spiky 'erosion pyramids'. Next along the shore, the old village of **Pisogne** has the last train station on the lake shore, and bus connections to Lovere. Pisogne's church of Santa Maria della Neve is covered with excellent frescoes by Romanino, who spent two years on the project. **Lovere**, the oldest resort on Lake Iseo, has a 15th-century frescoed church, Santa Maria in Valvendra, and a handful of paintings in its **Galleria dell'Accademia Tadini** (*open late-April–Oct Mon–Sat 3–6, Sun 10–12 and 3–6*), especially a *Madonna* by Jacopo Bellini. The highlight of Iseo's west shore is **Riva di Solto**, with odd little bays and views across the water of the formidable Adamello Mountains. **Tavèrnola Bergamasca** has a steamer to Sàrnico.

Valle Camonica

From Pisogne the road and railway continue northeast into the lovely Valle Camonica. Its name is derived from a Rhaetian tribe, the Camuni, whose artistic ancestors used the smooth, glacier-seared permian sandstone of their valley as tablets to engrave solar discs, labyrinths, mysterious figures, geometric designs, animals, weapons and people. What is especially remarkable is the unbroken length of time during which the engravings were made: the oldest are from the Neolithic era (before 2200 BC) and the latest date from the arrival of the Romans – a period spanning 25 centuries, from the random scratched symbols of the late Stone Age to the finely drawn, realistic and narrative figures of the Bronze and Iron Ages. Although it's impossible to understand the significance these etchings had for their makers, their magic must have been extraordinary: in the valley 180,000 have been discovered so far. Some are beautiful, some ungainly, some utterly mystifying, while a few are fuel for crackpot theories. UNESCO has put the Valle Camonica on its list of sites to be protected as part of the artistic heritage of humanity.

Some 12km from Pisogne, rock incisions from the 3rd millennium BC may be seen in a lovely park at Luine, near the spa of **Boario Terme**. Unfortunately the rock here has weathered, and the graffiti are often hard to decipher. Boario also offers a scenic detour up the **Valle d'Angolo** and its wild **Dezzo Ravine**. When the Romans conquered the valley their capital was **Cividate Camuno**, and it remembers their passing with mosaics and tomb stones in its small **Museo Archeologico** (*open Tues–Sun 9–2*). It also

Lakes Garda, Iseo and the Valle Camonica

has a fine 12th-century tower, and churches with frescoes by the excellent quattro-cento painter Da Cemmo in the environs, at **Esine** and **Bienno** (Santa Maria Annunziata). **Breno**, the modern capital of the valley, lies under an imposing medieval castle; its 14th-century church of **Sant'Antonio** contains frescoes by Romanino, and its **Museo Civico Camuno** (*open Tues and Thurs 2–4; Wed and Fri 9.30–11.30,* **t** *0364 22042*), in the town hall, has an ethnographic collection from the valley.

Getting Around

Buses run quite frequently from Bergamo to the lake towns of Tavèrnola and Lovere.

For a special treat, on summer Sundays and holidays, FS **trains** run from Bergamo to Palazzolo sul Oglio to link up to the little **steam train** Ferrovia del Basso Sebino to Sárnico, with direction connections on to the lake steamers; call **t** 035 910 900 for more information.

Iseo town is served by frequent buses from Brescia, and a regional railway, the FNME, runs along the entire east shore of Lake Iseo from Brescia or the FS rail junction at Rovato, between Bergamo and Brescia.

From Pisogne at the northern end of the lake several FNME trains a day continue up the Valle Camonica as far as Edolo.

Steamers run by Navigazione Lago d'Iseo, Via Nazionale 16, Costa Volpino, Bergamo, **t** 035 971 483, ply the lake between Lovere and Sárnico, calling at 15 ports and Monte Isola. Timetables are posted by the quays.

Tourist Information

Iseo: Lungolago Marconi 2, **t** 030 980 209, **f** 030 981 361.

Clusane OTC (private), Via Punta 14, **t** and **f** 030 982 9142.

Boario Terme: Piazza Einaudi 2, **t** 0364 531 609, **f** 0364 532 280.

Capo di Ponte: by the highway, **t** 0364 42080.

Edolo: Piazza Martiri della Libertà 2, **t/f** 0364 71065.

The website *www.bresciaholiday.com* covers the whole province.

Where to Stay and Eat

Iseo ✉ 25049

★★★★I Due Roccoli, in the hills above the town in Frazione Invino, **t** 030 982 2977, **f** 030 982 2980, *www.idueroccoli.com* (*expensive*). 4km from Iseo (direction Polaveno). Iseo's top choice occupies part of an old hunting lodge, set in its own large gardens. The suites, rooms and bathrooms are beautifully designed and have either garden views or breathtaking views of the lake. There's a sun terrace and pool. Much of the superb food in the restaurant is freshly harvested from the hotel's own farm. Favourite dishes include an *antipasto* of salad and truffles, a delicious green pasta with mushrooms known as *pappardelle verdi con funghi porcini* and, for dessert, a *mousse di cioccolato bianco* that is

Capo di Ponte and its National Park

In the centre of the Valle Camonica, within a 6km radius of Capo di Ponte, are the most extensive and best-preserved prehistoric engravings: pick up a map in the tourist office. The most notable and accessible are in the **Parco Nazionale delle Incisioni Rupestri Preistoriche** (*open Tues–Sun 8.30–4.30; adm*), where the enormous **Naquane rock** attracted artists from the Neolithic to Etruscan periods. Over a thousand figures, often superimposed, are etched into the rock: labyrinths, dogs, hunters and deer; enigmatic processions, armed warriors and horsemen, priests, a funeral; looms, carts, huts, even an Iron Age smithy. Certain symbols are repeated so often as to suggest a code: 'blades', slashes and four-petalled, dotted 'Camuna roses'.

Capo di Ponte's **Centro Studi Preistorici** has a small museum, with plans of Camuni sites among other explanatory items (*open Mon–Fri 9–4*), while just up beyond a car park two great lumps of sandstone, the **Massi di Cemmo**, once formed part of a much longer megalithic alignment, covered with engravings of deer, oxen, other animals and human figures, all dating from the 3rd millennium BC. A bit further up, the **Archeodromo** (*open daily 8.30–12.30 and 1.30–5.30, June–Sept 1.30–6; adm*), 'Centre of Experimental Archaeology', has a reconstruction of an Iron Age Camuni village; above this, a path leads to the lovely 11th-century Romanesque **San Siro**, its three tall apses

one of the best in the country. *Closed Oct–Mar. Restaurant open to non-residents Thurs–Mon only.*

****Iseolago, Via Colombera, **t** 030 98891, **f** 030 988 9299, *www.iseolagohotel.it* (*expensive*). An ideal retreat for families, south of Iseo's centre, with a swimming pool, a children's playground, beach volleyball galore, and an *enoteca* for parents. Surfing and canoeing courses available, as well as pedalos and bikes to hire.

Albergo Rosa, Via Roma 47, **t 030 980 053, **f** 030 982 1445 (*cheap*). On the provincial road, but better than it appears. A neat family-run hotel, recently refurbished.

Il Volto, Via Mirolte 33, **t** 030 981 462 (*expensive*). Dine in an old-fashioned inn, serving a mix of Italian and French cuisine. Dishes feature lake fish (excellent with *tagliolini*) and also tasty land dishes such as roast pigeon in a mustardy cream sauce. Best to reserve. *Closed Wed and Thurs lunch, and two weeks in July and Jan.*

Monte Isola ✉ 25050

Bellavista, **t/f 030 988 6106 (*cheap*). One of two wonderful places in Siviano. Comfortable rooms, small and simple with outstanding views, and there's a nice little restaurant (*cheap*).

Canogola, **t/f 030 982 5310 (*cheap*). Slightly more expensive. A quiet and romantic hotel, with only seven rooms in the trees by the lake. Beautiful wisteria in April. *Closed Nov–Feb.*

Boario Terme ✉ 25041

****Rizzi, Via Carducci 11/Corso Italia 12, **t** 0364 531 617, **f** 0364 536 135, *rizzi@boarioterme.com* (*moderate*). The most comfortable rooms in town, 100m from the Terme. The Rizzi has its own garden, with an outside verandah overlooking it and a very nice restaurant featuring local dishes. *Open April–Oct.*

***Diana, Via Manifattura 12, **t/f** 0364 531 403 (*moderate*). Opposite the Terme. Stylish and modern, with good-sized rooms, large bathrooms and wonderful views of the mountains, as well as a restaurant and garden. Candle-lit dinners in the evening.

Ariston, **t/f 0364 531 532, **f** 0364 536 066, *ariston@boarioterme.com* (*cheap*). Small, clean rooms and old-fashioned hospitality. A good budget option, in the station forecourt.

Capo di Ponte ✉ 25044

Cumili, Via Italia 27, **t 0364 42034 (*cheap*). Small, simple rooms with baths and with a restaurant.

rising over the River Oglio (*open Mon and Fri 9–12 and 2–6; Sat 9–12, Sun 9–12 in summer, or call Pro Loco at Capo di Ponte, **t** 0364 42080*). Across the river, the Cluniac church of **San Salvatore** was built in the late 11th century in the Burgundian style, its monastic grounds still protected by walls (*open 9–11 and 3–5, or call the Pro Loco*).

A few kilometres south, another great concentration of engravings was discovered in 1975 in what is now the **Riserva Regionale Incisioni Rupestri Ceto-Cimbergo-Paspardo** (*open Mon–Sun 9–12 and 2–6; adm*). The main entrance is in tiny **Niardo**, where from the small museum a path leads up to Foppe di Niardo, dotted with rocks etched from Neolithic to Etruscan times: scenes of solar worship, five-pointed stars, weapons, a village, footprints and what looks like a god by praying figures. The reserve also encompasses the rocks of Campanine, just under the ruined castle and village of **Cimbergo**, where Iron Age graffiti mingle with a Latin dedication to Jove and early Christian symbols, and Iron Age etchings in three different sites in **Paspardo**.

Down on the main Valle Camonica road below Ceto is the crossroads for **Cerveno**, up in the hills to the west, where the Sacro Monte-style chapels of the **Santuario della Via Crucis-San Martino** (*open daily 8–12 and 2.30–5 Oct–May; 8–12 and 2.30–7 June–Sept*) contain 198 life-sized figures carved and painted in the 18th century – the Passion of Christ.

Further up the valley the scenery becomes grander as the Adamello group of the Brenta Dolomites looms up to the right. Beautiful excursions into the range are possible from **Cedegolo** into the **Val di Saviore**, with its mountain lakes Arno and Salarno under Mount Adamello (11,660ft).

From **Malonno** you can drive along a scenic road through the chestnut woods of the **Valle Malga**, with more lakes and easy ascents (Corno delle Granate, 10,204ft). Surrounded by majestic mountains, **Edolo** stands at the crossroads of the valley and the Valtellina road to the Passo di Tonale. It is a base for excursions, and for the ski resorts of the **Valle di Corteno**, **Ponte di Legno** (the most developed) and Passo di Tonale. From the **Passo di Tonale** you can continue east into Trentino's Val di Sole (*see* p.461), or from Ponte di Legno north through Stelvio National Park to Bormio.

Brescia

Lombardy's second city, Brescia is a busy and prosperous place but somehow it's no one's favourite town, even though it has a full day's supply of fine art, architecture and historic attractions: Brescia's Roman and Lombard relics are among the best preserved in northern Italy. Perhaps it's the vaguely sinister aura of having been Italy's chief manufacturer of arms for the last 400 years. Perhaps it's because the local Fascists saw fit to punch out the heart of the old city and replace it with a piazza as frosty and heavy as an iceberg. The Brescians seem to detest it, but it's hard to avoid; they would do well to raze it. Give them credit, however, for preserving the rest of their historic centre by spawning Brescia Due, a mini-version of Paris's La Défense, to quarantine all its new gangly office buildings.

History

Brescia was founded by the Gauls, an origin remembered only in its name *Brixia*, from the Celtic *brik* ('hill'). *Brixia* saw the inevitability of Rome early on, collaborated, and in 26 BC achieved the favoured status of a *Colonia Civica Augusta*, when it was embellished with monuments. By the 8th century Brescia had recovered enough from the barbarian invasions to become the seat of a Lombard duchy under King Desiderius, whose daughter Ermengarda was wed by Charlemagne – the condition imposed by the Italians before they crowned him emperor. He later repudiated her, and the forlorn Ermengarda returned to Brescia to die in the Abbey of San Salvatore.

When Brescia joined the Lombard League against Frederick Barbarossa, its opposition had a voice: that of a Benedictine monk, Arnold of Brescia, who studied under Peter Abelard in Paris and went to Rome, preaching eloquently against the tyranny of the emperor and the corrupt, worldly materialism of the Church. In 1155, Barbarossa, in collusion with Adrian IV, handed the troublesome monk over to the pope, who burned Arnold alive at the stake in front of Castel Sant'Angelo.

Brescia itself was too tempting a prize to be left in peace. Firmly in the Guelph camp, for the freedom of cities against imperial pretensions, it held tight when Frederick II besieged it for 68 days, then suffered under his lieutenant, the unspeakable Ezzelino da Romano, in 1258; in 1421, when the detested Visconti horned in, the weary Brescians turned to Venice for relief and asked to be adopted. The Venetians didn't have to be asked twice; Brescia meant access to the unusually pure iron deposits in the valleys to the north. By the 16th century Brescia had become Italy's major producer of firearms, and the Republic imposed severe emigration restrictions to keep skilled workers from wandering.

Venice not only brought peace and prosperity, it initiated an artistic flowering. The Brescian Vincenzo Foppa (1485–1566) was a key figure in the Lombard Renaissance; his monumental paintings were among the first to depict a single, coherent atmosphere. The individualistic linear style of Girolamo Romanino (1485–1566) may stand somewhat apart, but Romanino's contemporary Alessandro Bonvincino (better known as 'the little Moor' or Moretto; 1498–1554), an ardent student of Titian, contributed the first Italian full-length portrait and taught Giovanni Battista Moroni of Bergamo. His contemporary Giovanni Girolamo Savoldo, a Brescian who later worked in Venice, was neglected in his day but is now recognized for his lyricism, especially in his use of light. Recently Giacomo Antonio Ceruti (1698–1767) has aroused interest for his realistic genre paintings of Brescia's humble, demented and down-and-out – a unique subject for the time. His nickname was Il Pitocchetto ('the little skinflint').

The Central Squares

Hurry, as the Brescians do, through the deathly pale **Piazza della Vittoria**, designed in 1932 by Marcello Piacentini; that frigid, Fascist square that melts each May, when it acts as the starting gate for the famous *Mille Miglia* vintage car race across Italy. Duck behind the post office to enter into a far more elegant display of power, the closed, Venetian-style **Piazza della Loggia**, named for the **Palazzo della Loggia**, Brescia's town hall, a neo-Roman confection begun in 1492 and designed in part by Venice's top architects, Sansovino and Palladio; its great white roof swells over the old city like Moby Dick on the prowl. The public areas can be visited during office hours. Opposite the Palazzo della Loggia, the **Torre dell'Orologio** is a copy of the clock tower in St Mark's Square, complete with two bell-ringing figures on top. The Brescians must have been hopeless spendthrifts: the other chief buildings on the square are the old and new municipal pawn shops, the **Monte di Pietà Vecchia** (1489) and the **Monte di Pietà Nuova** (1590s); the Roman inscriptions embedded in the façade of the former constitute Italy's very first lapidary collection.

Looming up behind the clock tower rises the third-highest dome in Italy, the green-lead-roofed crown of the **Duomo**, built in 1602 by Gianbattista Lantana (*open Mon–Sat 7.30–12 and 4–7.30, Sun 8–1 and 4–7.30*). From the **Piazza Paolo VI** itself, however, the dome is hidden by a high marble front – a Lombard 'wind-breaker' façade. Over the door a bust of Brescia's great Cardinal Querini 'winks mischievously, as if inviting the faithful to enter'. You should take him up on it, not so much for the few paintings by Romanino (by the bishop's throne) and Moretto that try to warm the cold interior, as to visit the adjacent **Duomo Vecchio** or La Rotonda (*open April–Oct Wed–Mon 9–12 and 3–7; Nov–Mar Sat and Sun only, 9–12 and 3–6*). Built in the 11th century over the ruins of the Basilica of San Filastrio and the ancient Roman baths,

Getting Around

Brescia is conveniently reached from three **airports**: Verona's Catullo, Bergamo's Orio al Serio and Montichiari's Gabriele D'Annunzio, half way between Brescia and Lake Garda.

Brescia is on the main Milan–Venice **rail** line, 55 minutes from Milan, an hour from Verona, and less to Desenzano del Garda, the main station on Lake Garda. There are also frequent services to Bergamo (1 hour) and Lecco (2 hours); to Cremona (just over an hour); and to Parma via Piadena (2 hours). For FS rail information, call freephone from within Italy, **t** 147 888 088. The regional FNME railway line, **t** 030 46027, wends its way north along the east shore of Lake Iseo and up the Valle Camonica to Edolo (2½ hours).

There is an even more extensive **bus** network, with frequent links to the towns of Lakes Garda and Iseo and less frequently to Idro; also to Turin and Milan, Padua and the Euganean Hills, Marostica, Bassano del Grappa and Belluno; to Trento via Riva and to the resorts of Pinzolo and Madonna di Campiglio in Trentino, as well as to all points within the province.

The **bus** and **railway** stations are located next to each other just south of the city centre: on Viale Stazione, the railway station and the SIA bus station serving the Brescia province, **t** 030 377 4237; just around the corner, in Via Solferino 6, the other bus services serving all other destinations including Garda, Cremona, etc., **t** 030 34915. Bus C connects them to the centre, or you can walk there in 10 minutes up the Corso Martiri della Libertà.

Tourist Information

Corso Zanardelli 34, **t** 030 43418/45052, **f** 030 293 284, *www.bresciaholiday.com*, near the central Piazza del Duomo.

Where to Stay

Brescia caters mainly to business clients, and its best hotels are comfortable if not inspiring. *****Vittoria**, Via X Giornate 20, **t** 030 280 061, **f** 030 280 065 (*very expensive*). The city's premier hotel has everything it should – large, sumptuous rooms, palatial bathrooms of French Rosa marble, banqueting suites, marble and chandeliers. But the severe Fascist-era architecture is a bit soulless. ***Master**, Via L. Apollonio 72, **t** 030 399 037, **f** 030 370 1331 (*expensive*). Near the centre by the castle. Family-run, with a nice gazebo in the garden, cheap menu in the restaurant, and spacious if simple rooms. ****Ambasciatori**, Via Crocifissa di Rosa 92, **t** 030 399 114, **f** 030 381 883, *ambascia@tin.it* (*moderate*). A bit further out of the centre, very modern, but offering a warm welcome.

this singular old cathedral is the only one in Italy designed in the shape of a top hat, low and rotund, with a massive cylindrical tower rising from its centre, supported by eight pillars, the light diffused through its upper windows. Inside, its simple form is broken only by a 15th-century raised choir; the altarpiece, an *Assumption* by Moretto, is one of his greatest works. The crypt of San Filastrio, a survival of the ancient basilica, contains a mixed bag of Roman and early medieval columns, and mosaics from the Roman baths. Several medieval bishops are entombed around the walls, most impressively Bishop Mernardo Maggi in his sarcophagus of 1308; the treasury holds two precious relics – the 16th-century *Stauroteca* containing a bit of the True Cross, and the 11th-century banner once borne on the *carroccio* (sacred ox cart) of the Brescian armies.

On the other side of the new Duomo, the 12th-century **Broletto** was the civic centre of Brescia prior to the construction of the Palazzo della Loggia which later became the seat of the Venetian governor; its formidable tower, the **Pegol**, predates it by a century. Just behind the new cathedral, on Via Mazzini 1, the 18th-century **Biblioteca**

Trento, Piazzale Cesare Battisti 31, off Porta Trento, **t 030 380 768 (*moderate*). Recently opened and conveniently located within walking distance of the city centre and castle. Cheap restaurant.

Eating Out

Brescians are rather stolid conservatives at table: kid, stews, *risotti*, meat on a skewer and *polenta* have been in vogue since the Renaissance.

La Sosta, Via San Martino della Battaglia 20, **t** 030 295 603 (*expensive*). This elegant restaurant is set in a 17th-century stable that has been stripped and completely over-hauled. A second menu features fish and Italian classics. *Closed Mon, Sun eve, and Aug.*

Castello Malvezzi, Via Colle San Giuseppe 1, **t** 030 200 4224 (*expensive*). A lovely medieval place north of the centre. Serves delicious food, cooked by a French and an Italian chef, to go with a superb selection of wines. *Closed Mon and Tues, 15 days Aug and Jan.*

I Templari, Via Matteotti 19, **t** 030 375 2234 (*expensive*). Fresh seafood with a Tuscan touch. *Closed Sat lunch, Sun and Mon lunch.*

L'Artigliere, Via Forcella 6, **t** 030 277 0373, at Gussago, 5km west of Brescia (*expensive*). Emerging chef Davide Botta and his wife Silvana offer gourmet local cuisine in an old country *osteria*, refurbished with care, with a portico for outdoor dining in summer and a cellar to visit.

Duomo Vecchio, Via Trieste 3, **t** 030 40088 (*moderate*). An intimate place near the Duomo Vecchio itself, serving excellent southern Italian dishes; moderate lunch menu. *Closed Tues.*

Locanda dei Guasconi, Via Beccaria 11/G, **t** 030 377 1605 (*moderate*). In the city centre. A medieval setting for traditional dishes such as *polenta* and lamb, but also more unusual fare such as ostrich meat. Attracts a young crowd. Book in the evening. *Closed Mon.*

Al Graner, **t** 030 375 9345 (*moderate*). In the summer Piazzale Arnaldo is very lively in the evenings. This is a popular meeting place, specializing in meat, including Fiorentina steak. *Closed Mon.*

La Vineria, Via X Giornate 4, **t** 030 280 477 (*cheap*). Here you can feast on excellent dried and cured meats and salami, herby *risotto*, *casoncelli* and home-baked tarts. *Closed Mon.*

Due Stelle, Via San Faustino 48, **t** 030 42370 (*cheap*). One of Brescia's oldest *osterias*, situated in the city centre, with a nice cellar to taste wine and an inner courtyard with fountain for dining in the summer. Local versions of tripe, *casoncelli* and old peasant dishes revisited, such as chicken and bread dumplings in broth. Good *antipasti*. Dried cod from Thurs to Sun. *Open Tues–Wed lunch only, Thurs–Sun eves too.*

Queriniana (*closed to the public*) contains 300,000 rare books and manuscripts, including the 6th-century 'Purple Evangeliary' with silver letters, from San Salvatore, and Eusebius' 11th-century *Concordances of the Gospels*; Cardinal Querini, the library's founder, enriched his own collection at the expense of the Vatican library.

Roman and Lombard *Brixia*

Flanking the Broletto, the ancient *Decumanus Maximus*, now the Via dei Musei, leads to the heart of Roman *Brixia*. Its forum, now the narrow **Piazza del Foro**, lies under the mighty columns of the **Capitoline Temple**, erected by the Emperor Vespasian in AD 73 and preserved for posterity by a medieval mud-slide that covered it until its rediscovery in 1823. In 1955 an earlier, Republican-era Capitoline temple was discovered beneath Vespasian's, with unusual mosaics of natural stone. The Temple is divided into three *cellae*, which were probably dedicated to the three principal Roman deities – Jupiter, Juno and Minerva. The *cellae* contain the lapidarium, tablets, altars and architectural fragments of the Roman age. The central *cella* has inscriptions on display. More Roman remains are on display in the Museo della Città. Next to the temple is the unexcavated *cavea* of the **Roman Theatre**, while down Via Carlo Cattaneo, in Piazza Labus, you can make out the columns and lintels of the third building of the forum: the **Curia**, or senate, imprinted like a fossil in a house wall.

From Piazza del Foro, Via dei Musei continues to the **Monastero San Salvatore-Santa Giulia** (*open end Oct–May Tues–Sun 9.30–5.30; July–Sept Tues–Sun 10–6; adm: combined ticket includes the museums of Santa Giulia, Armi Antiche Luigi Marzoli, Risorgimento and the Pinacoteca Tosio-Martinengo*), founded in the 700s by the wife of the Lombard king Desiderius, disbanded at the end of the 18th century and now the **Museo della Città**. At the entrance are the remains of a large Roman *domus*, with original mosaics and frescoes. The museum documents the various layers of Brescian history, from the prehistoric period to the Venetian age through the Roman, the Lombard, the Carolingian and the medieval age of the *comuni* and *signorie*, with over 11,000 finds on display. The heart of the complex, the 8th-century **Basilica of San Salvatore**, was modelled on the 6th-century churches of Ravenna. In the nave, the capitals are either ancient Roman or made of stucco, an art at which the Lombards excelled. Some Carolingian frescoes remain under the arcades; others were painted by Girolamo Romanino in 1530. The semi-circular crypt, where the relics of St Giulia were laid in 762, was enlarged in the 12th century, with vigorous capitals sculpted by the school of Antelami: the one on the life of Giulia is a serene masterpiece. The same century saw the addition of another church, sturdy **Santa Maria in Solario**, crowned with an octagonal dome or tiburium, its lower vaults supported on an ancient Roman altar, its upper level frescoed by Floriano Ferramola (1480–1528). In the 16th century a third church, **Santa Giulia**, was built; the nuns' choir has more frescoes by Ferramola.

The **Civico Museo Romano** (*open Tues–Sun 9–12.30 and 3–5, summer 10–12.30 and 3–6; adm*) contains a collection of Roman remains preserved thanks to the foresight of the 1485 municipal council, which forbade the sale of antiquities outside Brescia. Treasures include: six gilded bronze busts of emperors and a 6ft bronze *Winged Victory*, all found in the temple; the *Victory*, bereft of what she once held, seems to be snapping her fingers in a dance. There's a gilt bronze figurine of a Gaulish prisoner, believed to be Vercingetorix, a Greek amphora from the 6th century BC and a facsimile of the 25ft-long Peutringer Map of Vienna, itself a 12th-century copy of a Roman road map. Of the museum's two other exceptional pieces, one is the 8th-century golden Lombard *Cross of Desiderius*, studded with 212 gems and cameos, including one from the 4th century of a Roman woman with her two children, peering warily into the approaching Dark Ages; the Brescians like to believe it is the great Galla Placidia of Ravenna. The other is a 4th-century ivory coffer called the *Lipsanoteca*, adorned with beautiful bas-reliefs of scriptural scenes. One of the superb 5th-century ivory diptychs originally belonged to the father of the philosopher Boethius. Lombard jewellery, medieval art and Renaissance medals round out the collection.

The Cydnean Hill

The poet Catullus, who considered *Brixia* the mother of his native Verona, was the first to mention the Cydnean hill that rises behind the Via dei Musei. Named after the

Ligurian king Cidno, the legendary founder of *Brixia*, the site has been inhabited since the Bronze Age. It was the core of Gaulish and early Roman *Brixia* – along Via Piamarta are the ruins of the city's last surviving **Roman gate**, as well as the attractive 1510 **San Pietro in Oliveto** (*open Sun 8.30–12 and 3–6 except during Mass; on other days ask the Padri Carmelitani*), named after the ancient olive grove around the church.

Up on top an imposing Venetian gate in Istrian marble, still guarded by the Lion of St Mark, is the entrance to the **Castello**, with its round 14th-century Mirabella Tower, sitting on a Roman foundation. Built in 1443, during the brief reign of the Visconti, the donjon houses the **Museo Civico delle Armi Antiche Luigi Marzoli** (*open June–Sept Tues–Sun 10–5; Oct–May 9.30–1 and 2.30–5; adm*), an extensive collection of Brescia's industry, with a special display of 15th–18th-century firearms. The castle's Venetian granary now houses the **Museo del Risorgimento** (*same hours*), with special honours going to Brescia's Ten Day revolt in 1849, bloodily suppressed by Austria.

The Pinacoteca and Around

From the Capitoline Temple, Via Crispi descends to Piazza Moretto, site of the **Pinacoteca Civica Tosio-Martinengo** (*open June–Sept Tues–Sun 10–5; Oct–May 9.30–1 and 2.30–5; adm*), housed in a 16th-century patrician palace. It showcases Brescia's local talent, including Foppa (*Madonna and Saints*), Savoldo, Moretto (his *Salome* is a portrait of the great Roman courtesan-poetess Tullia d'Aragona), Romanino, Moroni and Ceruti; there's also a lovely *Adoration of the Magi* by Lorenzo Lotto, a *Senator* by Tintoretto, a *Portrait of Henri III* by Clouet and two early works by Raphael – a not altogether wholesome, beardless *Redeemer* and a lovely *Angel*, and an anonymous golden fairytale picture of *St George and the Princess*, painted around 1460.

South on Via Crispi, there's more art in little 16th-century **Santa Angela Merici**, by Tintoretto and Francesco Bassano (*open Mon–Sat 7.30–9.30, Sun 3–5.30, or ask the Compagnia S. Angela Merici*), and at Via Monti 9, in the Istituto Paolo VI's **Museo Arte e Spiritualità** (*open Sat and Sun 4–7; other days upon request; t 030 375 3002*), devoted to contemporary religious art, something that Pope Paul VI sincerely believed wasn't an oxymoron. **Sant'Alessandro**, in Via Moretto (*open Mon–Sun 6.30–11 and 5.30–7.30*), contains a pretty *Annunciation* by Jacopo Bellini; further north, in elegant, porticoed Corso Zanardelli, the **Teatro Grande** with its luscious foyer and five tiers of boxes is one of the most lavish theatres in Lombardy; here in 1904 Puccini's *Madam Butterfly* was wholeheartedly vindicated by the public after its disastrous premiere.

West Side Churches

The piquant quarters west of the Piazza della Loggia are rich in interesting old churches. Just west of Via S. Faustino (off Piazza della Loggia) there are two strikingly unusual ones – **San Faustino e Giovita** (*open Mon–Sat 7.30–11 and 3–7, Thurs 7.30–10 only, Sun 7.30–12 and 3.30–7*), a cylindrical, steep-roofed drum of a church from the 12th century (near the intersection with Via dei Musei) and, further up, on Contrada Carmine, the 14th-century **Santa Maria del Carmine**, crowned with a set of Mongol-like brick pinnacles; it contains frescoes by Foppa, among his finest work, and a 15th-century terracotta *Deposition* by Mazzoni (*temporarily closed, call t 030 40807*).

Just off Corso G. Mameli, Renaissance **San Giovanni Evangelista** (*open daily 7–11 and 4–6.30*) has good works by Moretto, Romanino and the Bolognese painter Francia. Further along the Corso stands the giant **Torre della Pallata**, a survivor from the rough-and-tumble 13th century, with a travesty of a 16th-century fountain like a bunion on its foot. From here Via della Pace heads south to the venerable 1265 **San Francesco** (*church open Mon–Sun 7–11.30 and 3–5; cloister Mon–Sat 8–12 and 2.30–6.30*) with its cloister in red Verona marble and frescoes (a few by Romanino and Moretto), and the nearby **Santa Maria dei Miracoli** (*open Mon–Sun 6–12 and 3–6*) with a 15th-century Lombard Renaissance marble façade that survived even though the interior was blown to smithereens in the last war. Further south, on Corso Matteotti, the 18th-century **Santi Nazzaro e Celso** (*open during Mass only, Sat 6pm and Sun at 9, 10, 11 and 6; otherwise call t 030 375 4387*) houses the Averoldi polyptych (1522), the masterpiece of Titian's youth, with a gravity-defying, virtuoso *Risen Christ* that soars into the numbing bathos of spiritual banality. The chapels hold works by Moretto.

Around Brescia

Besides Lakes Garda and Iseo, there are a number of worthwhile excursions into the mountains – as well as one to the south in the plain, to Montirone and its fine **Villa Lechi**, built in 1740 by Antonio Turbino, and little changed since Mozart slept there. It has frescoes by Carlo Carloni, period furnishings, and well-preserved stables and park.

To the north stretches the **Valtrompia**, a scenic agricultural valley. Its main town, **Gardone Val Trompia**, produced firearms for Venice, and enjoyed the special protection of the Republic; it still makes hand-crafted sports rifles. North of Gardone the valley narrows as the road climbs to two summer resorts, **Bovegno** and **Collio**. Beyond Collio a new road continues up to the scenic **Passo del Maniva** and over to the Passo di Croce Domini. Long, narrow **Lake Idro** lies over the mountains from Collio, at the head of the Val Sabbia. Surrounded by rugged mountains and rural villages, it is the highest of the Lombard lakes, and one of the best for trout fishing. Named after the small resort town of **Idro**, its sandy beaches are all low-key, family-orientated places. **Anfo** is another resort, while the most interesting lake settlement is **Bagolino**, on the trout-filled River Caffaro, with its peaceful medieval streets and the 15th-century church of San Rocco, frescoed in the 1400s by Da Cemmo. From Lake Idro you can continue up the Chiese River into Trentino's Valli Giudicarie (*see p.460*).

Lake Garda

The Italian lakes culminate in Garda, the largest (48km long, and 16km across at its widest point) and most dramatic, the Riviera of the Dolomites. With the profile of a tall-hatted witch, its romantic shores have enchanted poets from the days of Catullus and Virgil, who both knew it by its Roman name, *Lacus Benacus*. For travellers from the north, its olive and lemon groves, its slender cypress and exotic palm trees have long signalled the beginning of their dream Italy. No tourist office could concoct a more scintillating Mediterranean oasis to stimulate what the Icelanders call 'a longing for figs' – the urge to go south.

Lake Garda

Arco
Varone
Riva del Garda
Torbole

Bezzecca
Molina
di Ledro
Lake
Ledro
Val di Ledro

Condino

Valli Giudicarie

Limone sul Garda

Passo de
Maniva

Lodrone

Bagolino

Tremosine
Malcésine

Campione
Tignale

Lake
Idro

Anfo

Assenza

Lavenone
Idro

Brenzone

Gargnano

Bogliaco

Lake Garda

Sabbio

Vobarno

Pai

Toscolano-
Maderno

S. Zeno

Gardone Riviera

Caprino

Salò

Torri del
Benaco

Gavardo

Is. di
Garda

S.Felice del Benaco

Costermano

Garda

Polpenazze

Manerba

Bardolino

Affi

Cavernago
Cisano

Moniga

Padenghe

Lazise

Sirmione

Desenzano del Garda

Lonato
Colombare

Pacengo

Rivoltella

Peschiera del Garda

S. Martino d. Battaglia

A4

A22

Castiglione
d. Stiviere

N

Solferino

Carpenedolo

Sigurta
Gardens

Valeggio
sul Mincio

5 km
2.5 miles

Getting Around

There are two **train** stations at the southern end of Lake Garda, at Desenzano and Peschiera, both of which are also landings for the lake's **hydrofoils** (*aliscafi*) and **steamers**. **Buses** from Brescia, Trento and Verona go to their respective shores; Desenzano, the gateway to Lake Garda, is served by buses from Brescia, Verona and Mantua. Frequent buses connect Sirmione to Desenzano and Peschiera. Other local bus lines run up and down the road that winds around the lake shores – a marvel of Italian engineering, called *La Gardesana*, Occidentale (SS45) on the west and Orientale (SS249) on the east. In summer, however, their splendour sometimes pales before the sheer volume of holiday traffic.

All **boat services** on the lake are operated by Navigazione sul Lago di Garda, Piazza Matteotti 2, Desenzano, t 030 9141 9511, f 030 914 9520, freephone from within Italy, t 800 551801, where you can pick up a timetable; the tourist offices have them as well. The one **car ferry** crosses from Maderno to Torri; between Desenzano and Riva there are several hydrofoils a day, calling at various ports (2 hours the full trip), as well as the more frequent and leisurely steamers (4½ hours). Services are considerably reduced from November to March. Full fare on the 4-hour sail from Desenzano to Riva on the steamer is L16,600, on the hydrofoil L22,300. Children travel for free (up to 4 years) or at reduced rates (4–12 year olds). 20% discount for EU over-60s.

Tourist Information

Desenzano del Garda: Via del Porto Vecchio 34, t 030 914 1510, f 914 4209, *www.desenzano.net*
Sirmione, Viale Marconi 2, t 030 916 114, f 030 916 222, *www.sirmione.net*.
Salò: Lungolago Zanardelli 39, t/f 0365 21423.

Gardone Riviera: Corso Repubblica, t/f 0365 20347.
Gargnano: Piazza Feltrinelli 2, t/f 0365 712 224, *www.prolocogargnano.com*.
Limone sul Garda, Via Comboni 15, t 0365 954 070, f 0365 954 689.

There is also a seasonal tourist office at Piazzale A. De Gasperi. Riva del Garda, Giardini di Porta Orientale 8, t 0464 554 444, f 0464 520 308.

Local website *www.rivadelgarda.com* has an indexed seach for hotels and a list of Lake Garda local websites.

Where to Stay and Eat

Sirmione ✉ 25019

Keep the confirmation of your reservation handy to get past castle guards.
★★★★★**Villa Cortine**, Via Grotte 12, t 030 990 5890, f 030 916 390, *www.villacortine.com* (*luxury*). A neoclassical villa built by an Austrian general and converted into a hotel in 1954. It offers an immersion in romance, and perhaps the rarest amenity in the town – tranquillity. Its century-old garden occupies almost a third of the entire peninsula. Inside, all is plush and elegant under frescoed ceilings; it's ideal for a break from the real world, with private beach, dock and pool. Half board compulsory during high season (Easter and mid-June–Sept). *Open April–Oct.*
★★★★★**Grand Hotel Terme**, Viale Marconi 7, t 030 916 261, f 030 916 192, *www.terme-disirmione.com* (*very expensive*). Another top choice, with a private beach and pool as well as a lovely lakeside restaurant. *Open April–Oct.*
★★★**Catullo**, Piazza Flaminia 7, t 030 990 5811, f 030 916 444 (*expensive*). Refurbished in 1991 and situated in the heart of the old town, offering good-sized rooms with beautiful views and all modern amenities.

Lake Garda is less status-conscious than the other lakes, and draws a wide range of visitors, from beach bums to package tourists; sailors and windsurfers come to test their mettle on Garda's unusual winds, first mentioned by Virgil: the *sover* which blows from the north from midnight and through the morning, and the *ora*, which blows from the south in the afternoon and evening.

Panoramic terrace and solarium. *Open April–Nov.*

Speranza, Via Casello 6, **t** 030 916 116, **f** 030 916 403, *hsperanza@jumpy.it* (*moderate*). No lake views, but all the fittings of a three-star hotel, including marble bathrooms, at significantly lower prices. *Open Mar–Nov.*

****Grifone**, Via Bocchio 4, **t** 030 916 014, **f** 030 916 548 (*cheap*). More attractive on the outside than in the rooms, but has a great location overlooking the Rocca Scaligera. *Open April–Oct.*

Vecchia Lugana, Via Verona 71, **t** 030 919 012 (*expensive*). One of Garda's finest and classiest restaurants, near the base of Sirmione's peninsula. The menu changes with the seasons and the food, based on lake fish, is exquisite – try the divine asparagus *tagliatelle* in a ragoût of lake fish, or the mixed grill of fish and meat. *Expensive* and *very expensive* menus available. Dining is in the hall overlooking the lake in winter, on the lakeside terrace in the summer. *Closed Mon eve and Tues.*

La Rucola, Via Strentelle 7, **t** 030 916 326 (*expensive*). An intimate and classy atmosphere to go with its gourmet fish and meat specialities, changing seasonally and according to the genius of young chef and patron Gionata Bignotti, who creatively mixes aromatic herbs and fruit flavours with traditional Mediterranean cuisine. A range of *very expensive menu degustazione*, accompanied by an excellent selection of wines (over 700 labels) and grappas. Near the Scaliger castle. Reserve in advance. *Closed Thurs.*

Osteria al Torcol, Via San Salvatore 30, **t** 030 990 4605 (*cheap*). For a late snack or meal and excellent wines – and oils! – to taste. Try local cheeses and *affettati* or be treated to home-made pasta or *ravioli al bagoz* close to the old wine press inside or outside, your table placed in the *osteria*'s kitchen garden. *Open 6pm–2am; closed Wed.*

Salò ✉ 25087

****Laurin**, Viale Landi 9, **t** 0365 22022, **f** 0365 22382, *www.laurinsalo.com* (*expensive*). One of the loveliest places to stay on the lakes: an enchanting Liberty-style villa converted into a hotel in the 1960s, retaining the elegant period décor in the public rooms. The charming grounds include a pool and beach access. For stylish dining, amid frescoes, Art Nouveau windows and beautifully presented gourmet dishes, indulge at the hotel's restaurant (*expensive*). *Closed Jan.*

****Duomo**, Lungolago Zanardelli 63, **t** 0365 21026, **f** 0365 290 418, *hotel.duomo@tin.it* (*expensive*). The first-floor rooms are the ones to request here – all lead out to a huge geranium-laden balcony overlooking the lake; rooms with no lake view are cheaper. Rooms are big and modern, and there's a fine restaurant.

***Vigna**, Lungolango Zanardelli 62, **t** 0365 520144, **f** 0365 20516, *www.hotelvigna.it* (*moderate*). Recently refurbished with comfortable and modern rooms, and views that really steal the show.

Lepanto, on the lake at Lungolago Zanardelli 67, **t** 0365 20428, **f** 0365 20428 (*cheap*). This is Salò's best kept secret. The signpost advertises the restaurant, in a nice garden terrace, but there are also six rooms to stay in, all overlooking the lake, for the lucky few who book in advance.

Antica Trattoria delle Rose, Via Gasparo da Salò 33, **t** 0365 43220 (*expensive*). Run by the same family as the Osteria dell'Orologio (*see below*). Go for *pasta e fagioli*, or lake fish with fresh pasta. *Closed Wed.*

Il Melograno, Via del Panorama 5, **t** 0365 520 421 (*expensive*). A hidden jewel, in Campoverde hamlet, south of Salò. The young chef experiments with home-made foie gras dishes with excellent results – try for instance the *scaloppa* filled with foie gras – and also cooks mouthwatering *risotti* and

Storms are not uncommon, but on the other hand the breezes are delightfully cool in the summer. In the winter Garda enjoys a mild climate, less oppressed by clammy fogs and mists than the other lakes; the jagged peaks that rim it shimmer with snow and you can better take in the voluptuous charms that brought visitors to its shores in the first place.

lake fish soups. Good selection of local wines to go with the foie gras. *Closed Mon eve and Tues, Nov and June.*

Osteria dell'Orologio, Via Butterini 26, **t** 0365 290 158 (*moderate*). Another extremely good value place: an old, beautifully restored inn where you can indulge in local dishes such as *tonno del Garda* (not tuna, but pork cooked in wine and spices), lake fish and skewered wild birds. A very popular place, so book in advance and be prepared to wait for service. *Closed Wed.*

Gardone Riviera ✉ 25083

Gardone Riviera and its suburb Fasano Riviera have competing Grand Hotels, both attractive old pleasure domes:

★★★★Grand Hotel, Via Zanardelli 84, Gardone, **t** 0365 20261, **f** 0365 22695, *www. grngardone.it* (*very expensive*). With its 180 rooms this was one of the largest resort hotels in Europe when built in 1881. It is still recognized as a landmark, and its countless chandeliers glitter as brightly as when Churchill stayed here in the late 1940s. Almost all the palatial rooms look on to the lake, where guests can swim in the heated outdoor pool or off the sandy beach, or simply luxuriate on the garden terraces. The dining room and delicious food match the quality of the rooms. *Open April–mid-Oct.*

★★★★★Fasano Grand Hotel, Fasano Riviera, **t** 0365 290 220, **f** 0365 290 221, *www.grand-hotel-fasano.it* (*very expensive*). Fasano's alternative was built in the early 19th century as a Habsburg hunting palace and converted into a hotel around 1900. Surrounded by a large park, it's furnished with *Belle Époque* fittings; there is also a heated pool and private beach, and the restaurant is one of Lake Garda's best. *Open May–Oct.*

★★★Villa Fiordaliso, Corso Zanardelli 150, **t** 365 20158, **f** 0365 290 011, *www.relaischateaux. fr/fiordaliso* (*very expensive*). A Liberty-style palace set in luxuriant gardens directly on the lake, with a private beach and pier. It has only seven rooms, all finely equipped. You can request (for a price) the suite where Mussolini and his mistress Clara Petacci spent their last few weeks. It also boasts an elegant restaurant, the best in Gardone, featuring classic Lombard dishes; very expensive *menu degustazione. Closed Nov–mid-Feb.*

★★★Monte Baldo, Via Zanardelli 110, **t** 0365 20951, **f** 0365 20952, *www.hotelmontebaldo. com* (*expensive*). A less pricey lakeside hotel; its a well-aged outer shell hides a modern stylish interior. The hotel also has a pool. Breakfast, meals and drinks are served on the lakeside terrace. *Open April–Oct.*

★★★Bellevue, Via Zanardelli **t** 0365 20235, **f** 0365 290 080, *hotelbellevuegardone.com* (*moderate*). Above the main road overlooking the lake, with a garden sheltering it from the traffic. Modernized rooms and a swimming pool. *Open April–Oct.*

★Hohl, Via dei Colli 4, **t** 0365 20160 (*moderate*). Halfway up to Il Vittoriale, this is another atmospheric 19th-century villa in a pleasant garden. The rooms don't have a bath but are quiet and big, with old rather bohemian-looking furniture.

Gargnano ✉ 25084

★★★Baia d'Oro, Via Gamberera 13, **t** 0365 71171, **f** 0365 72568 (*expensive*). Situated in Villa, just outside Gargnano, this is a small but charming old place on the lake front with an artistic inn atmosphere (owner Giovanbattista Terzi is a painter). It has a private beach and picturesque terrace. *Open mid-Mar–Oct.*

★★★Du Lac, Via Colletta 21 in Villa, **t** 0365 71107, **f** 0365 71055, *www.hotel-dulac.it* (*moderate*). A salmon-tinted charmer smack on the water, with individually furnished rooms. The restaurant with panoramic terrace features local cuisine, and they've also fitted

The South Shore: Desenzano and Solferino

Lively, colourful and delightful, **Desenzano del Garda**, on a wide gulf dotted with beaches, is Garda's largest town, built up in the 15th and 16th centuries. Life centres around its busy portside cafés, presided over by a statue of Sant'Angela, foundress of the Ursuline Order, who seems appalled at all the carryings-on. Another statue on the

a bar and a piano into the tiny hotel. *Open April–mid Oct.*

La Tortuga, Via XXIV Maggio 5, t 0365 71251 (*expensive*). A celebrated gourmet haven near the port, specializing in delicate dishes based on seasonal ingredients and lake fish, perfectly prepared; there are also delicious vegetable soufflés, innovative meat courses, mouth-watering desserts and fresh fruit sherbets, and an excellent wine and spirits cellar. *Closed Mon eve, Tues and mid Jan–Feb.*

Lo Scoglio, Via Barbacane 3, in Bogliaco di Gargnano, t 0365 71030 (*expensive*). Highly recommended restaurant featuring chef Agnese Bertolini. Specialities include all kinds of lake fish, home-made pastas and cakes. *Closed Fri.*

Osteria del Restuaro, on the main square, t 0365 72643 (*cheap*). Overlooks the small harbour; good for both hot and cold dishes. *Closed Wed.*

Limone Sul Garda ✉ 25010

★★★★**Le Palme**, t 0365 954 681, f 0365 954 120 (*moderate*). Housed in a pretty Venetian villa in the historic city centre, preserving much of its original charm alongside modern amenities. Named after its two ancient palm trees, it has a fine terrace and a good fish restaurant. *Open April–Oct.*

★★★**Hotel Coste**, Via Tamas 11, t 0365 954 042, f 0365 954 393, *www.hotelcoste.com* (*moderate*). Ten minutes from the city centre, in an olive grove, a family-friendly hotel with its own outdoor pool, boules area and playground. Minimum three days' stay.

★★**Villa Margherita**, Via Luigi Einaudi 3, t/f 0365 954 149 (*moderate*). Further out. Staying here is like entering Ms Margherita's private house, spotless and carefully decorated – each room has a different coloured flowery decor; the corner ones are particularly nice with windows on two sides and a private terrace onto the olive groves, a peaceful retreat with stunning views.

★★**Mercedes**, Via Nanzello 12, t 0365 954 073, f 0365 914961 (*cheap*). Above the lake in another olive grove, with a pool and lovely views. *Open April–Nov.*

Riva del Garda ✉ 38066

★★★★**Hotel du Lac et du Parc**, Viale Rovereto 44, t 0464 551 500, f 0464 555 200, *hoteldulac@anthesi.com* (*very expensive*). When German intellectuals from Nietzsche to Günter Grass have needed a little R&R in Italy they have for decades flocked to Riva del Garda to check in here: a spacious, airy and tranquil hotel, set in a large lakeside garden, now with indoor and outdoor pools and a beach. *Open April–Oct.*

★★★★**International Hotel Liberty**, Viale Carducci 3/5, t 0464 553 581, f 0464 554 908, *liberty@tecnoprogress.it* (*very expensive*). A stylish stay in a Liberty villa set in its own grounds at the back of the city centre. Indoor pool and whirlpool baths.

★★★★**Grand Hotel Riva**, Piazza Garibaldi 10, t 0464 521 800, f 0464 552 293, *ghr@anthesi.com* (*expensive*). A turn-of-the-last-century hotel majestically positioned on the main square, with 87 bedrooms overlooking the lake. The rooftop restaurant combines fine food with incomparable views. *Open Mar–Oct.*

★★★★**Sole**, Piazza III Novembre, t 0464 552 686, f 0464 552 811, *www.hotelsole.net* (*expensive*). Right on the port in Riva's main square. Plenty of atmosphere and a beautiful terrace, though refurbishment inside has lost some of the character.

★**Restel de Fer**, Via Restel de Fer 10, t 0464 553 481, f 0464 552 798 (*moderate*). Built in 1400; only five rooms and a good restaurant, with summer dining in the cloister.

★**Villa Moretti**, 3km up in Varone, t 0464 521 127, f 0464 559 098 (*cheap*). If you want peace and quiet, a garden and pool in a panoramic spot, this family-run hotel fits the bill to perfection.

lake front, the whooshing high speed monument, celebrates an air speed record (709km per hour) set here in 1934 by Francesco Agello.

On the lower end of the technological scale, Desenzano's Bronze Age (2200–1200 BC) inhabitants lived in pile dwellings, recently discovered in the peat bogs southwest of town and yielding the contents of the **Museo Archeologico**

Rambotti in the cloister of Santa Maria de Senioribus, Via Anelli 7 (*open Tues, Fri, Sat, Sun and hols 3–7*). There are models of houses and, among the ornaments, little 'pearls' of amber: Desenzano was on the ancient trade route between the amber-rich Baltic and the Mediterranean, which endured until the end of the Roman period.

Desenzano, also on the Bergamo–Verona *Via Gallica*, became popular with the Romans towards the end of the empire, when the rich and powerful retreated from the growing anarchy to their massive country estates, maintained by hundreds of slaves and retainers – the origins of feudalism.

One of the most important was Desenzano's **Villa Romana**, just in from the Lunglago at Via Crocifisso 22 (*open Mar–mid Oct Tues–Fri 8.30–7, Sat and Sun 9–6; end Oct–Feb Tues–Fri 8.30–4.30, Sat and Sun 9–4.30; adm*). Although begun in the 1st century BC, the villa was given its present form in the 4th century, fitted with sumptuous heated baths, a *triclinium* (dining hall) with three apses, and the most extensive mosaic floors in northern Italy. Nearby, along Via Roma, **Santa Maria Maddalena** has 27 huge canvases by a transplanted Venetian, Andrea Celesti (d. 1712), and a strikingly different *Last Supper* by Giandomenico Tiepolo.

As well as Lake Garda, Desenzano is also the base for visiting the low, war-scarred hills to the south. The two most important battles occurred on the same day, 24 June 1859, when the Italians and their French allies pounded the Austrians from two sides. Napoleon III defeated Emperor Franz Joseph at **Solferino** and King Vittorio Emanuele defeated the Austrian right wing at **San Martino della Battaglia**, 8km away. It was the beginning of the end for the proud Habsburgs in Italy, but the Battle of Solferino had another consequence as well – the terrible suffering of the wounded so appalled Swiss citizen Henry Dunant that he founded the Red Cross.

At San Martino you can climb the lofty **Torre Monumentale** (*open end Mar–Sept Mon–Sat 9–12.30 and 2–7; Sun and holidays 9–7; Oct–mid March daily 9–12.30 and 2–7; closed Tues and 1–15 Dec; adm*), erected in 1893, which contains paintings and mementos from the battle. Solferino saw the single bloodiest battle in the whole war; the **Cappella Ossuaria** behind the church of S. Pietro (*same hours as the Torre, but closed Mon; adm*) contains the remains of 7,000 mostly French and Austrian troops; memorabilia are housed in an old tower of the Scaligeri of Verona, the **Spia d'Italia**.

Sirmione

> *Sweet Sirmio! thou, the very eye*
> *Of all peninsulas and isles*
> *That in our lakes of silver lie*
> *Or sleep enwreathed by Neptune's smiles.*

Thus spake Catullus, Rome's greatest lyric poet, born in Verona in 84 BC. Like many well-to-do Romans, he had a villa out on the narrow 4km-long peninsula of Sirmione that pierces Lake Garda like a pin, just over 280ft across at its narrowest point. Sirmione is the most visually striking resort on the lake. On the very tip of the rocky promontory, the **Grotte di Catullo** (*open Mar–mid-Oct Tues–Sat 8.30–7, Sun 9–6; end Oct–Feb Tues–Sun 9–6; adm*), entwined with ancient olive trees are Romantic ruins with a capital R, not of Catullus' villa, but of a Roman bath complex (Sirmione is still famous today for its spa). The views across the lake to the mountains are magnificent; there's also a small **museum** on the site, with mosaics and frescoes. The medieval centre of Sirmione is dominated by one of the most memorable of Italian castles, the fairytale **Rocca Scaligera** (*open Nov–Mar Tues–Sun 8.30–4.30; April–Oct 9–6; adm*), built by Mastino I della Scala of Verona in the 13th century, and surrounded almost entirely by water. There's not much to see inside, but there are fine views from its swallowtail battlements. Also worth a look is the ancient Romanesque church of **San Pietro in Mavino**, with 13th-century frescoes. The best swimming is off the rocks on the west side of the peninsula.

Peschiera del Garda, Gardaland and the Sigurtà Gardens

East of Sirmione, Peschiera is an old military town, near the mouth of the River Mincio that drains Lake Garda. Its strategic position has caused it to be fortified since Roman times, though the imposing walls that you see today are actually 16th-century Venetian, reinforced by the Austrians when Peschiera was one of the corners of the empire's 'Quadrilateral'. Today Peschiera is mainly a transit point to the lake from the Veneto but its massive purifying plant, the ultimate destination of what goes down every drain in every lakeside town (thanks to an underwater pipeline) still helps it to fulfil its ancient role as a defender of the lake's status as the cleanest in all Europe.

Here, too, you can treat the children – at **Gardaland** (*t 045 644 9777, www.gardaland. it*) Italy's largest, and most massively popular, Disney-clone theme park with a green dinosaur named Prezzemolo or 'Parsley' as official mascot (*open late Mar–June and Sept–Oct daily 9.30–6.30; July–mid-Sept daily 9am–midnight; adm*).

The region south of Peschiera is known for its flavourful dry white wine, Bianco di Custoza, and for the pretty gardens and groves that line the Mincio all the way to the lakes of Mantua. The most amazing of these, the **Sigurtà Gardens**, 8km from Peschiera (*open Mar–Nov daily 9–7; adm*), were the 40-year project of Dr Count Carlo Sigurtà, known as 'Italy's Capability Brown' – who, granted water rights from the Mincio, used them to transform a barren waste of hills into 500,000 square metres of Anglo-Italian gardens along 7km of lanes; 13 parking areas have been provided on the route so you can get out and walk as much as you like. The Sigurtà Gardens are near **Valeggio sul Mincio**, an attractive town in its own right, with a castle and a bridge built by the Visconti, and a pair of competing water fun parks, open until midnight.

Up the West Shore to Salò

From Sirmione the steamer passes the lovely headlands of Manerba and Punta San Fermo and the **Isola di Garda**, the lake's largest, where there was a monastery once visited by St Francis. Long ruined, it provided the base for a monumental 19th-century Venetian-Gothic-style palace, now owned by the Borghese family, whose Scipione made the famous drive from Peking to Paris in the early days of the automobile.

Salò (the Roman *Salodium*) enjoys one of the most privileged locations on the lake, but is best known internationally for having given its name to Il Duce's last dismal stand, the puppet 'Republic of Salò' of 1943–45, formed after the Nazis rescued him from his prison in an Abruzzo ski lodge. It also has a number of fine buildings, including a late-Gothic cathedral with a Renaissance portal (1509), and paintings within by Romanino and Moretto da Brescia, and a golden polyptych by Paolo Veneziano. There's also a small museum, the **Museo del Nastro Azzuro** (*open Easter–Sept Sat 4–6; Sun and holidays 10–12.30 and 4–6; adm*), containing information on the history of the region. **L'Ateneo**, in the Renaissance Palazzo Fantoni, contains a collection of 13th-century manuscripts and early printed books. North of Salò begins the **Brescia Riviera**, famous for its exceptional climate and exotic trees and flowers.

Gardone Riviera and D'Annunzio's Folly

Vittoriale open Oct–Mar Mon–Fri 9–5, Sat and Sun 9–5.30; April–Sept daily 8.30–8. D'Annunzio house open Oct–Mar Tues–Sun 9–1 and 2–5; April–Sept Tues–Sun 10–6; ticket office closes one hour earlier; adm exp but you can buy a cheaper ticket for the museum and grounds only; expect queues.

North of Salò, sumptuous old villas, gardens and hotels line the lovely promenade at **Gardone Riviera**. Gardone became the most fashionable resort on Lake Garda in 1880, when a German scientist noted the almost uncanny consistency of its climate. One place that profits most from this mildness is the **Giardino Botanico Hruska** (*open Mar–Oct daily 9–6.30; adm*), a botanical garden with 8,000 exotic blooms and plants growing between imported tufa cliffs and artificial streams.

Above the garden waits Il Vittoriale degli Italiani (1863–1938), the home of Gabriele D'Annunzio. This luxurious Liberty-style villa in an incomparable setting, designed for a German family by Giancarlo Maroni, was presented to the extravagant writer by Mussolini in 1925. D'Annunzio immediately dubbed his new home 'Il Vittoriale' after Italy's victory over Austria in 1918; with Maroni's help he recreated it in his own image, leaving posterity a remarkable mix of eccentric beauty and self-aggrandizing kitsch.

D'Annunzio made the Vittoriale his personal monument, suspecting (correctly) that one day crowds would come tramping through the estate to marvel at his cleverness and taste, if not sheer acquisitiveness: the villa is a pack rat's paradise, its every nook and cranny filled with quirky, desirable and hilarious junk, left as it was in 1938, when a sudden brain haemorrhage put an abrupt end to the poet's hoarding.

Once past the entrance gate to the Vittoriale, note the double arch, a copy of the bridge pier on the Piave, where the Italians held the line against the Central Powers in 1917–18. Like many a jerk, D'Annunzio loved fast cars and two of his favourites are parked near the courtyard – one is the the 1913 Fiat he drove in triumph to Fiume.

The tour begins with the 'cool reception' room for guests D'Annunzio disliked – it is austere and formal, compared to the comfy one reserved for favourites. When Mussolini came to call he was entertained in the former. Like Aubrey Beardsley and movie characters usually played by Vincent Price, D'Annunzio hated the daylight and had the windows painted over, preferring low-watt electric lamps.

The ornate organs in the music room and library were played by his young American wife, who gave up a promising musical career to play for his ears alone. In his bedroom, the Stanza della Leda, he kept a cast of Michelangelo's slave, the naughty bits veiled by a skirt. He designed the entrance to his study low so that

More Italian than Any Other Italian

Born Gaetano Rapagnetta into a very modest family in the Abruzzo, the self-styled angel Gabriel of the Annunciation (one wonders what he would have thought of Madonna!) went on to become the greatest Italian poet of his generation, a leading figure in the fin-de-siècle Decadent school who managed to have nearly all of his works placed on the pope's Index.

But Gabriele D'Annunzio scoffed at the idea that the pen is mightier than the sword. A fervent right-wing nationalist, he clamoured for Italy to enter the First World War, and when it was over he was so furious that Fiume (Rijeka), a town promised as a prize to Italy, was actually to be ceded by the Allies to Yugoslavia that he took matters into his own hands and invaded Fiume with a band of volunteers (September 1919). In Italy D'Annunzio was proclaimed a hero, stirring up a diplomatic furore before being forced to withdraw in January 1921.

Luigi Barzini has described D'Annunzio as 'perhaps more Italian than any other Italian' for his love of gesture, spectacle, and theatre – what can you say about a man boasted that he had once dined on roast baby? Yet for the Italians of his generation, whatever their politics, he exerted a powerful influence in thought and fashion; he seemed a breath of fresh air, a new kind of 'superman', hard, passionate yet capable of writing exquisite, intoxicating verse; the spiritual father of the technology-infatuated futurists, ready to destroy the old bourgeois *Italia vile* of museum curators and parish priests and create in its stead a great modern power, the 'New Italy'.

He lived a life of total exhibitionism – extravagantly, decadently and beyond his means, at every moment the trend-setting, aristocratic aesthete, with his borzois and melodramatic affairs, with the 'the Divine' actress Eleanora Duse and innumerable other loves (preferably duchesses). Apparently he thought the New Italians should all be as flamboyant and clever, and he disdained the corporate state of the Fascists. For Mussolini, the still-popular old nationalist was a loose cannon and an acute embarrassment, and he decided to pension him off into gilded retirement on Lake Garda, correctly calculating that the villa would appeal to his delusions of grandeur.

visitors would have to bow as they entered; here he kept a bust of Duse, but covered, to prevent her memory from distracting his genius.

In the **museum**, located in the Art Deco Casa Schifamondo ('escape the world') that D'Annunzio built but never moved into, you can ponder his death bed and death mask, more casts of Michelangelo's sculptures, paintings and biographical memorabilia. The recently opened **private garden** occupies an 18th-century lemon terrace, where a magnolia grove contains D'Annunzio's war memorial, with a throne and stone benches for nationalist legionary ceremonies, which must have been a hoot. The open-air theatre, designed by Maroni after the ancient Greek theatre in Taormina, has a magnificent view from the top seats, stretching from Monte Baldo to Sirmione; in July and August it hosts D'Annunzio's plays. There's a nice surreal touch nearby: the prow of the battleship *Puglia* from the Fiume escapade. Walk up to the **mausoleum**, the poet's last ego trip, a perverse wedding cake in white travertine.

Toscolano-Maderno and Gargnano

The double-barrelled *comune* of **Toscolano-Maderno** has one of the finest beaches on Lake Garda, and the car ferry to Torri. Toscolano traces its origins to the Etruscans, and Maderno was the site of Roman *Benacum*. In the 12th century many of Maderno's Roman bits were incorporated into the extremely elegant **Sant'Andrea**, a Romanesque beauty benignly restored in the 16th century by St Charles Borromeo; inside, the capitals, some retaining their original paint, are sculpted with fighting animals. The 18th-century parish church has a *Sant'Ercolano* by Paolo Veronese and a *Martyrdom of St Andrew* by Palma Giovane. Toscolano was the chief manufacturer of nails for Venice's galleys and had a famous printing press in the 15th century; to this day the Cartiera di Toscolano mill is Garda's largest industry. The cool **Valle delle Cartiere** – the valley of the papermills – is a favourite excursion.

To the north, **Gargnano**, the last town before the towering cliffs, means sailing. Since 1950 it has hosted the colourful Centomiglia regatta the second week of September, attracting yachts from as far away as New Zealand. The Franciscans were among the first to live here in the 13th century; their church has been baroqued inside and the cloister's capitals have carvings of lemons and oranges, a reminder that the Franciscans were the first to cultivate citrus in Europe. After the Borghese pile on Isola di Garda, the largest villa on the lake is just south of Gargnano: the 18th-century **Villa Bettoni** in Bogliaco, used as a set in a dozen films.

Limone sul Garda

North of Gargnano the lake narrows, the cliffs plunge sheer into the water and the Gardesana road pierces tunnel after tunnel like a needle. In the morning, when the wind's up, windsurfers flit across the waves like a swarm of crazed one-winged butterflies. On weekends their cars are parked all along the road around **Campione**, a tiny hamlet huddled under the cliffs. For tremendous views, take one of the several turnings inland that wind precipitously up to the cliffs: to **Tignale** or **Tremósine**, atop a 1,000ft precipice.

The inland route from Tremósine rejoins the lake at **Limone sul Garda**, a popular resort with a teeny tiny port and a beach over 3km long. Its name comes from the Latin *limen* (border), although by happy coincidence Limone was one of the main citrus towns, and to this day its lemon terraces with their white square pillars are a striking feature of the landscape: D. H. Lawrence, who lived south of Limone for a spell, liked to see them as the ruins of ancient temples.

Riva del Garda

North of Limone, the charming town of Riva sits snug beneath an amphitheatre formed by Monte Brione. An important commercial port for the bishops of Trento beginning in 1027, it was much sought and fought after, and ruled by Verona, Milan and Venice before it was handed back to the bishop-princes of Trent in 1521. In 1703, during the War of the Spanish Succession, the French General Vendôme sacked it and all the surroundings, leaving only a ghost of the former town to be inherited by Napoleon in 1796. Riva revived as a resort during the days of Austrian rule (1813–1918) as the 'Southern Pearl on the Austro-Hungarian Riviera', a pearl especially prized by writers: Stendhal, Thomas Mann, D. H. Lawrence and Kafka were among its habitués. The centre of town has a plain **Torre Apponale** (1220) and the **Palazzo Pretorio**, built by Verona's Cansignorio della Scala in 1376, while the lake front was defended by the sombre grey bulk of the 12th-century castle, the **Rocca**, surrounded by a swan-filled moat. This now houses Riva's **Museo Civico** (*open Tues–Sun 9.30–6.30, until later in July and Aug; adm*), with finds from the Bronze Age settlement at Lake Ledro, six statue-*stelae* from the 4th–3rd millennia BC, Roman finds, paintings, frescoes and sculpture. Riva's best church, the **Inviolata** (1603), is by an unknown but imaginative Portuguese architect, who was given a free hand with the gilt and stucco inside. It also has paintings by Palma Giovane.

Only 3km north, a dramatic 287ft waterfall, the **Cascata del Varone**, crashes down a tight grotto-like gorge by the village of Varone; walkways allow visitors to become mistily intimate with thundering water (*open May–Aug daily 9–7, April and Oct daily 10–12.30 and 2–5; Nov–Feb Sun and holidays only 10–12.30 and 2–5; Mar daily same hours; adm*). From the west side of Riva the exciting Ponale Road (N240) rises to **Lake Ledro**, noted not only for its scenery but also for the remains of a Bronze-Age settlement (*c.* 2000 BC) of pile dwellings, discovered in 1929. One has been reconstructed near the ancient piles around **Molina di Ledro**, where the **Museo delle Palafitte** houses the pottery, axes, daggers and amber jewellery recovered from the site (*open mid-June to mid-Sept daily 10–1 and 2–6; end Sept–Nov and Mar–mid-June Tues–Sun 9–1 and 2–5; Dec, Sat and Sun only, same hours; closed Jan–Feb; adm*); the visit includes a botanical garden, dedicated to the plants cultivated by northern Italian farmers in the Bronze Age.

One of the most dramatic sights on Garda is just behind Riva: the jagged crag and **Castello d'Arco** (*open April–Sept 10–7 (lawn) 10–6 (upper towers); Oct and Mar 10–5 and 10–4; Nov and Feb 10–4 and 10–3; adm*), dramatically crowned with ancient, dagger-sharp cypresses and the swallowtail crenellations. The path up is lovely and, despite the damage wrought by Vêndome's troops, there are a few frescoes left, including one of a courtly game of chess. **Arco** itself, once heavily fortified and moated (the only surviving gate has a drawbridge), became, like Riva, a popular resort in the 1800s, prized for its climate. In the centre, a Baroque fountain dedicated to Moses splashes before the Palladian-inspired **Collegiata dell'Assunta** (1613) by Giovanni Maria Filippi, who went on to become court architect of Emperor Rudolph II in Prague. There's a public garden full of Mediterranean plants, and a pretty 19th-century casino.

The East Shore: Riva to Peschiera

Garda's east shore belongs to the province of Verona. The silvery groves that grace the hills gave it its name, the Riviera degli Olivi, but its most outstanding feature is Monte Baldo, a massive ridge of limestone stretching 35km between Lake Garda and the Adige Valley, cresting at 6,989ft. Baldo is anything but bald: known as 'the botanical garden of Italy', it supports an astonishing variety of flora from Mediterranean palms to Arctic tundra; some 20 different flowers first discovered on Monte Baldo

Getting Around

APT **buses** run up the east coast from Verona and Peschiera as far as Riva, **t** 045 800 4129. The **car ferry** crosses year-round from Torri del Benaco to Maderno.

Tourist Information

Malcésine, Via Capitanato 6/8, **t** 045 740 0044, **f** 045 740 1633.
Torri del Benaco, Viale F.lli. Lavanda, **t** 045 722 5120, **f** 045 629 6482.
Garda, Via Don Gnocchi 23, **t** 045 627 0384, **f** 045 725 6720.
Bardolino, at Piazzale Aldo Moro, **t** 045 721 0078, **f** 045 721 0872. www.aptgardaveneto.com.

Where to Stay and Eat

Malcésine ✉ 37018

★★★★Val di Sogno, **t** 045 740 0108, **f** 045 740 1694 (very expensive). About three minutes out of town in a beautiful setting in its own grounds on the lake shore., with a pool and private beach, a lakeside restaurant, and modern rooms with balconies. Minimum three-day stay.
★★★★Uphill Park Hotel at Campiano, **t** 045 740 0344, **f** 045 740 0848 (very expensive). Situated south of the centre, this is a romantic place to stay, with lovely views, a pool, garden, and one of the best restaurants in the area; the cuisine is light and seasonal. Closed Nov–Mar.
★★★Vega, Viale Roma, **t** 045 657 0355, **f** 045 740 1604 (expensive). An inviting lake-front hotel in the city centre with big, modern rooms and a private beach.
★★★Sailing Centre, Molini Campagnola 3, **t** 045 740 0055, **f** 045 740 0392 (expensive). A hotel with rooms in low houses in a lake-front garden, each room with private balcony or access to garden. Minimum three-day stay. Open end Mar–end Oct.
★★★Malcésine, Piazza Pallone, **t/f** 045 740 0173 (moderate). Beautifully positioned, on the lake in the city centre; has a garden with pool.
★★San Marco, Via Capitanato, **t/f** 045 740 0115 (moderate). In the centre, you can sleep in a simple room where Goethe snoozed in 1786.

The town of Malcésine has only 35,000 inhabitants but 17,000 hotel beds. Once a playground for the elite, it is now a typical tourist destination with the obvious result that restaurant food is generally dreadful – overcooked spaghetti with meat sauce.

Trattoria Vecchia Malcesine, Via Pisort 6, **t** 045 7400469 (expensive). An exception to the above: a charming escape from the hurly-burly, on a panoramic terrace, with high quality food cooked by young chef Leandro Lippi and served by his wife Lidia. Leandro's

bear its name. The southern third of the Riviera degli Olivi is more grapey than olivey, the land of one of Italy's finest reds – Bardolino.

Torbole

Back on Garda's northeast shore, **Monte Baldo** looms over **Torbole** and the mouth of the Sarca, the most important river feeding the lake. An old fishing village and a pleasant resort, Torbole is famous in the annals of naval history. In 1437, during a war with the Visconti, the Venetians were faced with the difficulty of getting supplies to Brescia past the southern reaches of Lake Garda, then controlled by Milan. A Greek sailor made the suggestion that the Venetians sail a fleet of provision-packed warships up the Adige to its furthest navigable point, then transport the vessels over Monte Baldo on to Lake Garda. Anyone who has seen Herzog's film *Fitzcarraldo* will appreciate the difficulties involved, and the amazing fact that, with the aid of 2,000 oxen, the 26 ships were launched at Torbole only 15 days after leaving the Adige. But after all that trouble, the supplies never reached Brescia. The same trick, however,

Alto Adige origins make him lean towards smoky flavours and spices like cumin, combined with Garda's best ingredients: try the *canederli di speck* (ham-flecked dumplings), seasoned with Monteveronese cheese from Veneto, or butterfly pasta with *porcini* mushrooms and *ricotta*. Lake recipes include sardines with *tagliolini*, mint and pine nuts, or poached pike with a cape sauce. Reserve. *Closed lunch, Wed, Feb.*

Torri del Benaco ✉ 37010
***Gardesana**, Piazza Calderini 20, **t** 045 722 5411, **f** 045 722 5771, *www.hotel-gardesana.com* (*expensive*). A comfortable hotel, built in 1442, on the harbour with splendid views of the lake, old harbour and castle. King Juan Carlos, Vivien Leigh and Laurence Olivier, Kim Novak, Maria Callas and André Gide all sojourned here. The fame of the hotel is also due to its restaurant (*open eves only*), the best on the Veronese shore according to many, which serves lake specialities revisited with a creative touch: the soup of Garda lake fish is worth the journey alone, but also the fillets of lake sardine marinated in cider, the trout *carpaccio*, pike with *polenta*, or pike in a tart with peppers and ginger.
***Al Caval**, Via Gardesana 186, **t** 045 722 5666, **f** 045 629 6570, *www.alcaval.com* (*moderate*). A plain and simple hotel near the lake, with a very good restaurant

(*moderate*). *Hotel closed Jan–Mar. Restaurant closed Mon.*

Garda ✉ 37016
****Locanda San Vigilio**, Punta San Vigilio, **t** 045 725 6688, **f** 045 725 6551, *sanvigilio@gardanews.it* (*very expensive*). This little inn hidden out by Sammichele's villa by a little private harbour has seven romantic rooms and a beach. Delicious food is served in the romantic old tavern. *Open Mar–Nov.*
****Hotel Regina Adelaide**, Via Francesco D'Assisi 23, **t** 045 725 5977, **f** 045 725 6263, *www.regina-adelaide.it* (*very expensive*). In Garda's centre, with carefully decorated rooms. The annexe has been recently restored with a nice old touch.
***Flora**, Via Giorgione 22 and 27, **t** 045 725 5348, **f** 045 725 6623 (*expensive*). Excellent value, above the town in its own grounds, slick and modern spacious rooms with pine fittings, all with balcony. *Open Easter–Oct.*
Ancora, Via Manzoni 7, **t** 045 725 5202 (*moderate*). In the centre of the action, a good-value lake-front option. Clean and comfortable rooms.
Stafolet, Via Poiano 12, **t** 045 725 5427 (*moderate*). On the landward side of Garda; it's worth asking directions to, for its *tagliolini* with truffles and grilled meat.
Al Pontesel, Via Monte Baldo 71, **t** 045 725 5419. Less distinguished, but good and cheap, featuring stout local cooking.

perhaps even suggested by the same Greek, enabled Mohammed II to bring the Ottoman fleet into the upper harbour of Constantinople the following year and capture the city.

Malcésine and Monte Baldo
South of Torbole, the forbidding cliffs of Monte di Nago hang perilously over the lake, attracting scores of Lycra-bright human flies, before Malcésine, the loveliest town on the east shore. The Veronese lords always took care to protect this coast and in the 13th century, over the old Lombard castle, they built their magnificent **Rocca Scaligera** (*open April–Oct 9.30–7; until 9 in summer; winter Sat and Sun only; adm*) rising up on a sheer rock over the water; inside are natural history exhibits, prehistoric rock etchings and a room dedicated to Goethe, who was accused of spying while sketching the castle. As well as the Scaliger castle, note the 16th-century **Palazzo dei Capitani del Lago** in the centre of Malcésine's medieval web of streets.

Every half-hour a pair of cableways run vertiginously over 1,700m up **Monte Baldo** (*t 045 740 0206 for information; adm exp*); the views are ravishing, and the ski slopes very popular with the Veronese.

Torri del Benaco and Garda

Further south, past a steep, sparsely populated stretch of shore, there are two pretty towns, one on either side of Punta di San Vigilio, that played minor roles in the 10th century. The first, laid-back **Torri del Benaco**, owes its name to a rugged old tower in the centre which served as the headquarters of Berengario, the first king of Italy, in his 905 campaign against the Magyars. Later, it was defended by another **Scaliger castle** (1383), now a museum (*open April, May and Oct 9.30–12.30 and 2.30–6; June–Sept 9.30–1 and 4.30–7.30; adm*) with displays on olive oil, citrus, fishing, and rock engravings found in the area from *c.* 2000 BC, similar to those in the Valle Camonica. The church of **Santa Trinità** has good 14th-century Giottoesque frescoes.

Laurence Olivier, for his part, preferred enchanting **Punta di San Vigilio** with its Sirens' rocks, occupied by the beautiful **Villa Guarienti** by the great Venetian Renaissance architect Sammicheli, the old church of San Vigilio, and a 16th-century tavern, now an inn. In Punta San Vigilio, the Mermaid Bay, a private beach accessible by walking through a park shaded with olive trees, has playgrounds for children and two refreshment bars. On the other side of a green soufflé of a headland, the Rocca del Garda, lies **Garda** itself, a fine old town with Renaissance *palazzi* and villas. It gave the lake its modern name, from the Lombard *Warthe*, 'the watch'. After Charlemagne defeated the Lombards, Garda became a county, and in its long-gone castle the wicked Count Berenguer secretly held Queen Adelaide of Italy prisoner in 960, after he murdered her husband Lotario and she refused to marry his son. After a year she was discovered by a monk, who spent another year plotting her escape. She then received the protection of Otto I of Germany, who defeated Berenguer, married the widowed queen, and became Holy Roman Emperor.

Bardolino

To the south, Bardolino is synonymous with its lively red wine with a bitter cherry fragrance that goes so well with fishy *antipasti*; you can learn all you want to know about it at the Cantine Zeni's **Museo del Vino**, Via Costabella 9 (*open Mar–Oct daily 9–1 and 2–6*). There are two important churches in Bardolino itself: the 8th-century **San Zeno** and the 12th-century **San Severo**, with frescoes and a landmark campanile. **Cisano**, to the south, has the **Museo dell'Olio d'Oliva**, Via Peschiera 54 (*open 9–12.30 and 3–7, closed Sun and Wed pm*), dedicated to the Riviera degli Olivi's other cash crop.

The next town, **Lazise**, was the main Venetian port and near the harbour retains an ensemble of Venetian buildings, as well as another castle, this one built in the 9th century by the Magyars and taken over and rebuilt by the Scaligers. Just inland from Lazise, at Bussolengo, the **Parco Natura Viva** is a private foundation devoted to the protection of endangered species, and is divided into a zoo (*open 9–6*) and a drive-through safari park (*open Mar and Oct Thurs–Tues 9.30–4; April, May and Oct daily 9.30–4; Aug daily 9.30–6; closed Jan and Feb*). Near here too is Gardaland (see p.329).

Venetia

Venetia

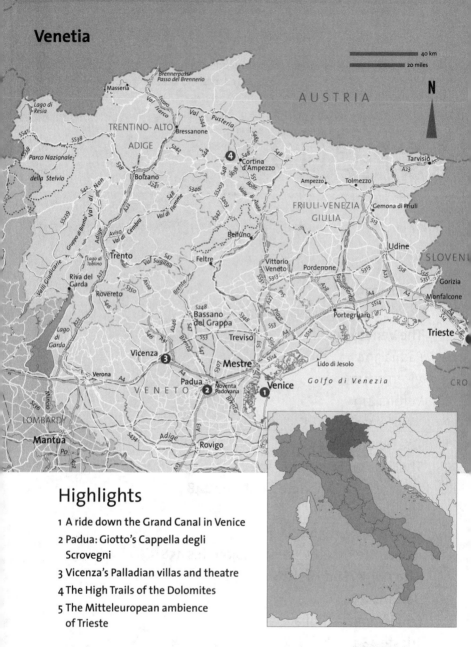

AUSTRIA

N

Brennerpass
Passo del Brennerio

Masseria

Lago di
Resia

TRENTINO- ALTO
ADIGE

Bressanone

Pusteria

Parco Nazionale
della Stelvio

Bolzano

Cortina
d'Ampezzo

Tarvisio

Ampezzo

Tolmezzo

FRIULI-VENEZIA
GIULIA

Gemona di Friuli

Belluno

Udine

SLOVENI

Trento

Feltre

Vittorio
Veneto

Pordenone

Lago di
Toblino

Val Sugana

Gorizia

Riva del
Garda

Monfalcone

Rovereto

Bassano
del Grappa

Portegruaro

Trieste

Lago
di
Garda

Treviso

Vicenza

Mestre

Lido di Jesolo

Golfo di Venezia

CRO

Verona

Padua

Noventa
Padovana

Venice

VENETO

LOMBARDY

Mantua

Rovigo

Highlights

1 A ride down the Grand Canal in Venice
2 Padua: Giotto's Cappella degli
  Scrovegni
3 Vicenza's Palladian villas and theatre
4 The High Trails of the Dolomites
5 The Mitteleuropean ambience
  of Trieste

Venetia – in Italian the Tre Venezie – encompasses three regions, two of them double-barrelled – the Veneto, the autonomous region of Trentino-Alto Adige (including a good part of the Dolomites), and Friuli-Venezia Giulia, stretching east to Slovenia. As the local economic powerhouse for over a thousand years, the Venetian influences are strong everywhere; in wealth Venetia rivals Lombardy, in culture it rivals Tuscany itself: Venice, Verona, Vicenza, Treviso, Padua, Trento and Ùdine are major art cities. Lagoons and sandy beaches line the coast, while the Dolomites, arguably the most beautiful mountains in the world, are dotted with fairy-tale castles and vineyards, as well as resorts equipped for every summer and winter sport, including one, Cortina d'Ampezzo, with Olympic facilities. In between, landscapes are lush and green, and littered with thousands of villas built in the 16th–18th centuries, including 18 by Palladio, the master of the genre. Friuli is one of Italy's top wine regions, and has a variety of other attractions, especially its Roman-medieval capital Aquileia, the most important archaeological site in northern Italy, and the fascinating Lombard town of Cividale.

Because Venetia has so much to offer, especially for families (the seashore, Lake Garda and its theme parks, and the mountains), avoid coming in August if you possibly can, when the crowds and prices can be overwhelming. At any time of year you can get along without a car, although a car does come in handy for visiting villas or castles. Venice is the obvious place to start, and has frequent links to Padua and Treviso; Verona, with quick connections to Lake Garda, is another good base, although Palladiophiles will want to stay in Vicenza. The Dolomites are served by an excellent bus system; Trento, Bolzano and Cortina are important hubs and have beautiful routes to explore in all directions. Ùdine makes a good base for Friuli-Venezia Giulia, with connections to Aquileia, Trieste and the coast.

Venice

Venice seduces, Venice irritates, but Venice rarely disappoints. She is a golden fairy-tale city floating on the sea, a lovely mermaid with agate eyes and the gift of eternal youth. On the surface she is little changed from the days when Goethe called her the 'market-place of the Morning and the Evening lands', when her amphibious citizens dazzled the world with their wealth and pageantry, their magnificent fleet, their half-Oriental doges, their crafty merchant princes, their splendidly luminous art, their silken debauchery and decline and fall into a seemingly endless carnival. One can easily imagine Julius Caesar bewildered by today's Rome, or Romeo and Juliet missing their rendezvous in the traffic of modern Verona, but Marco Polo, were he to return from Cathay today, could take a familiar gondola up the familiar Grand Canal to his house in the Rialto, astonished more by the motor-boats than anything else. Credit for this unique preservation goes to the Lagoon, the amniotic fluid of Venice's birth, her impenetrable 'walls' and the formaldehyde that has pickled her more thoroughly than many far more venerable cities on the mainland.

For a thousand years Venice called herself the Most Serene Republic (*la Serenissima*), and at one point she ruled 'a quarter and a half' of the Roman Empire. The descent to an Italian provincial capital was steep and bittersweet; sensitive souls find gallons of melancholy, or, like Thomas Mann, even death, brewed into the city's canals that have nothing to do with the more flagrant microbes. In the winter, when the streets are silent, Venice can be so evocative that you have to kick the ghosts out of the way to pass down the narrower alleys (*Don't Look Now*). But most people (some million or so

Venice

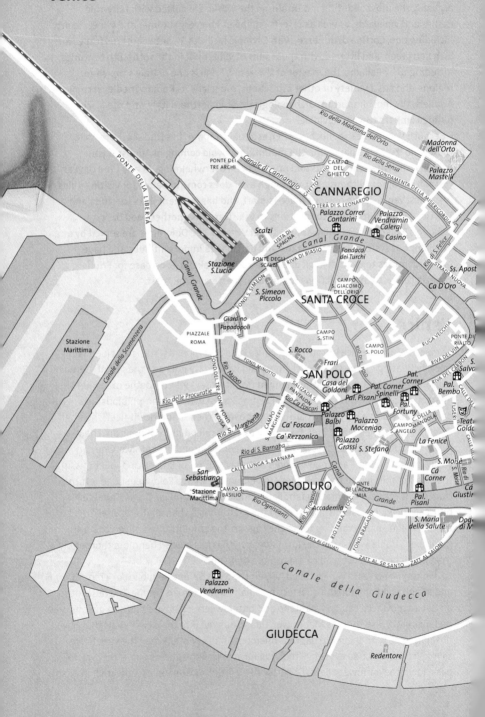

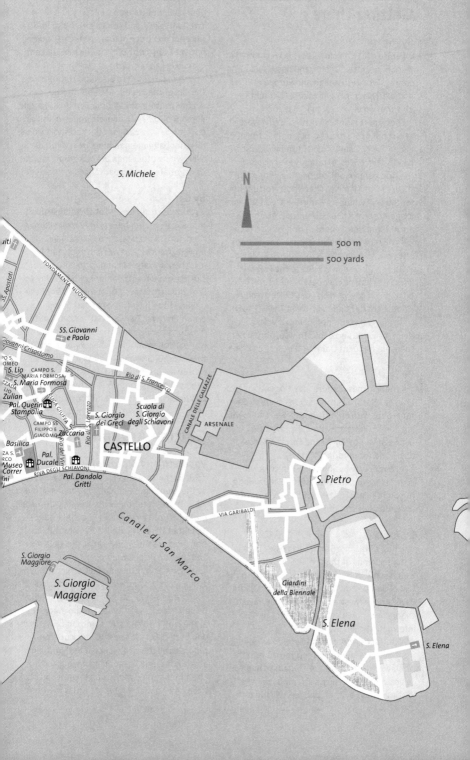

S. Michele

N

500 m
500 yards

SS. Apostoli

FONDAMENTA NUOVE

Giovanni Crisostomo

SS. Giovanni
e Paolo

PO S.
OMEO
S. Lio
CAMPO S.
MARIA FORMOSA
S. Maria Formosa
Rio di S. Francesco
IO
Zulian
Pal. Querini
Stampalia
CAMPO SS
FILIPPO E
GIACOMO
S.
Zaccaria
S. Giorgio
dei Greci
Scuola di
S. Giorgio
degli Schiavoni

CANALE DELLE GALEAZZE

ARSENALE

Basilica
ZA S.
CO
Museo
Correr
ni
Pal.
Ducale
RIVA DEGLI SCHIAVONI
Pal. Dandolo
Gritti

VIA GIUFFA
Rio di S. Lorenzo

CASTELLO

S. Pietro

VIA GARIBALDI

Canale di San Marco

S. Giorgio
Maggiore

S. Giorgio
Maggiore

Giardini
della Biennale

S. Elena

S. Elena

Getting There

By Air

Venice's Marco Polo Airport is 13km north of the city near the Lagoon, and has regular connections with Italian and European cities, and with New York (via Milan).For flight information in Venice, call **t** 041 260 9260.

The airport is linked with Venice by water-taxi (**t** 041 966 870 or **t** 041 523 5775), the most expensive option (L150,000); or by *motoscafi* to San Marco (Zecca) roughly every hour (L17,000 per person), connecting with most flights from March to October. Unfortunately for those catching an early flight, you can no longer reserve a departure; boats start at 4.50 am and run hourly until midnight. Call **t** 041 541 5084 for information. The journey time is one hour ten minutes to or from San Marco.

There is also an ATVO bus to the Piazzale Roma (L7,000) or, cheapest of all, the ACTV city bus no.5 (L1,500), which goes twice an hour.

Some charter flights arrive at Treviso, 30km away. If a transfer is not included with your ticket, catch bus no.6 into Treviso, from where there are frequent trains and buses to Venice.

By Sea

Adriatica lines (Zattere 1412, **t** 041 520 4322 or **t** 041 522 8018) has connections every 10 days June–Sept with Split (15 hours) and Dubrovnik (24 hours). There are also daily car-ferries between Venice, Corfu and Patras, Greece (2 days), and Alexandria (3½ days).

An easier way to approach Venice on water is by taking the Burchiello from Padua along the Brenta Canal (Siamic Express, Via Trieste 42 (by Padua bus station), **t** 049 660 944).

By Train

Venice's Stazione Santa Lucia (the Ferrovia) is the terminus of the Venice Simplon-Orient Express, and of less glamorous trains from the rest of Europe and Italy. All trains from Santa Lucia stop in Mestre, where you may have to change for some destinations. For rail information call **t** 1478 88088.

Water-taxis, *vaporetti* and gondolas wait in front of the station to sweep you off into the city. If you've brought more luggage than you can carry, one of Venice's infamous **porters** (distinguished by their badges) will lug it to your choice of transport and, if you pay his fare, will take it and you to your hotel (official price for one piece of luggage is L20,000 between any two points in the historic centre, extra bags are L10,000).

Porter stands are to be found throughout the city at the main tourist points and *vaporetto* stops; Accademia, Ferrovia, Piazzale Roma, Rialto, San Marco, etc. You can also call a porter, **t** 041 522 4891 or **t** 041 520 5308. Since rates for baggage-handling are unregulated everywhere other than at the station, be sure to negotiate a price in advance.

By Car

All roads to Venice end at the monstrous municipal parking towers in Piazzale Roma, **t** 041 523 7763, L30,000 a day, or its cheaper annexe, Tronchetto, **t** 041 520 7555, nothing less than the largest car park in Europe. You can leave your car there for L25,000 a day, or less for longer stays. Otherwise consider the Italian Auto Club's three car parks (open to non-members): Fusina, **t** 041 547 0160, at the mouth of the Brenta Canal south of Marghera (car park open summer only; *vaporetto* no.16 to Venice); S. Giuliano, in Mestre near the causeway (bus service to Venice), and Punta Sabbioni, **t** 041 530 1096, in between the Lido and Jesolo (ferry no.17 from Tronchetto).

Getting Around

Vaporetti and Motoscafi

Public transport in Venice means by water, by the grunting, canal-cutting *vaporetti* (the all-purpose water-buses), or the sleeker, faster *motoscafi*, run by the ACTV (**t** 041 528 7886). Note that the only canals served by public transport are the Grand Canal, the Rio Nuovo and the Canale di Cannaregio; between them, you'll have to rely on your feet, which is not as gruelling as it sounds, as Venice is so small.

Single **tickets** (a flat rate of L6,000) should be purchased and validated in the machines at the landing-stages. As some landing stages don't sell tickets, it's best to stock up (most *tabacchi* sell them in blocks of ten). You can also buy a single ticket on board, but tell the attendant immediately you get on. If you plan to be on a boat at least three times in a one day, purchase a **24-hour tourist pass**, for L18,000, valid for unlimited travel on all lines, or the **3-day pass**, for L35,000. Most lines run until midnight. There is also an all-night line. Schedules are listed in the free monthly tourist office guide, *Un Ospite di Venezia*.

At San Marco you can also find **excursion boats** – more expensive than public transport, but useful if you're pressed for time.

Water-taxis

These are really more tourist boats – they work like taxis, but their fares are de luxe. Stands are at the station, Piazzale Roma, Rialto, San Marco, Lido and the airport. These jaunty motor boats can hold up to 15 passengers, and fares are set for destinations beyond the historic centre, or you can pay L150,000 per hour. Within the centre the minimum fare for up to four people is L50,000; additional passengers are up to L10,000 each, and there are surcharges for baggage, holiday or nocturnal service (after 10pm), and for using a radio taxi (t 041 522 2303 or 041 723 112).

Gondolas

Gondolas, first mentioned in the city's annals in 1094, have a stately mystique that commands all other boats to give way. Like Model Ts, gondolas come in any colour as long as it's black, still obeying the Sumptuary Law of 1562, though nowadays –sadly – hardly any have cabins for clandestine trysts.

Once used by all and sundry, gondolas now operate frankly for tourists (and weddings). Official prices are L120,000 for a 50-minute ride (L150,000 after 8pm). Before setting out, agree with the gondolier on where you want to go and how long you expect it to take to avoid any unpleasantness later on.

In addition, gondolas retired from the tourist trade are used for *gondola traghetti* services across the Grand Canal at various points between its three bridges – your only chance to enjoy an economical, if brief, gondola ride for L700. *Traghetti* are signposted in the streets nearby. For appearance you'll have to stand: only sissies sit on *traghetti*.

Hiring a Boat

Perhaps the best way to spend a day in Venice is by hiring your own boat – a small motor boat or a rowing boat – though beware of the Venetian type of oar, which requires practice to use. It can be difficult to find a boat for hire, but ask in the Piazza San Marco tourist office for suggestions. Try Sport e Lavoro, Fondamenta della Misericordia, t 041 522 9535, L160.000 per day, 7 people maximum. *Motoscafi* for hire are easier to find, especially with chauffeurs: try Cooperativa San Marco, S. Marco 4267, t 041 240 6736; Veneziana Motoscafi, S. Marco 2828, t 041 716 000; or Serenissima Motoscafi, Castello 4545, t 041 522 4281.

Tourist Information

The main information office is in one corner of Piazza San Marco, to the far left as you face the square from the basilica (Ascensione 71/c). Branch offices at Palazzetto Selva, right by the S. Marco *vaporetto* stop, the railway station and the bus station in Piazzale Roma offer accommodation services. There are also offices on the Rotonda Marghera, Marco Polo Airport, on the Lido at Gran Viale 6, and in Mestre at Corso de Popolo 65 (t 041 975 357). There is now one central tourist information telephone number in Venice; t 041 529 8711, f 041 523 0399, *www.turismovenezia.it*.

The main source in English on any current events is the fortnightly magazine *Un Ospite di Venezia*, distributed free at tourist offices and in hotels. Otherwise, the two local papers *Il Gazzettino* and *Nuova Venezia* both have listings of films, concerts and so on in Venice and the *terra firma*. Another detailed source of information is the monthly city magazine *Marco Polo*, with articles written in Italian but summarized in English. The APT publishes a quarterly magazine called *Leo* with articles and useful information in English.

For L5,000, people between the ages of 14 and 29 can buy a *Rolling Venice* card, which gives discounts on the city's attractions, from films at the Film Festival to museums, hostels, shops and restaurants (and access to the university canteen in Palazzo Badoer, Calle del Magazen 2840). It also allows you to buy a special reduced-price ticket for travelling on the *vaporetti*. Apply at one of these three associations: the Assessorato alla Gioventù, Corte Contarina 1529, San Marco, t 041 274

7650/1 (*Mon–Fri 9.30–1, Tues and Thurs also 3–5*); Agenzia Arte e Storia, Corte Canal 659, Santa Croce, t 041 524 0232 (*Mon–Fri 9–1 and 3.30–7*); or Associazone Italiana Alberghi per la Gioventù, Calle del Castelforte 3101, San Polo, t 041 520 4414 (*Mon–Sat 8–2*), or at the Rolling Venice booth at S. Lucis Stratia (t 041 524 2852). Take a photo and your passport.

If you lose something, try the Municipio, t 041 274 8111; or if you lost it on a train, t 041 785 238; or on a *vaporetto*, t 041 272 2179.

Shopping

Venice is a fertile field for shoppers, whether you're looking for tacky bric-a-brac to brighten up the mantelpiece (just walk down the Lista di Spagna) or the latest in hand-crafted Italian design – but be warned that bargains are hard to find. Everything from fresh fish to lovely inlaid wooden boxes and huge quantities of tourist junk can be found at the **Rialto markets**; especially colourful is the Rialto fish market, La Pescheria – follow your nose and marvel at the incredible range of seafood on display (*closed Sun and Mon*). You will also come across food stalls in any number of squares and on barges along the smaller canals, but there is another large food and produce market in Castello, on **Via Garibaldi** (*Mon–Sat am*). The main public auction house is **Franco Semezato**, Palazzo Giovanelli, Cannaregio 2292.

Antiques

A flea market appears periodically in Campo San Maurizio, near Campo Santo Stefano, a week before Easter and Christmas and in the third week of September. This is also the area with the largest concentration of antique shops. **Antonietta Santomanco della Toffola**, Frezzeria 1504, S. Marco, has Russian and English silver, prints, and antique jewellery and glass, while the establishments of the print dealer **Pietro Scarpa** at Campo S. Moisè 1464 and Calle XXII Marzo 2089, S. Marco, are as much museums as shops. Away from the San Marco area, **Salizzada**, S. Lio 5672, in Castello, has old prints of Venice, clocks, and many other curious odds and ends, and **Xanthippe**, Dorsoduro 2773, near Ca' Rezzonico, is a highly eclectic shop specializing in the

19th century and Art Deco Venetian glass. A general market (food, clothes, hardware and the like) is held every Tuesday morning on the Lido and Friday morning at Sacca Fisola.

Books

Venice has a good selection of bookshops. **Fantoni Libri Arte**, Salizada di S. Luca 4121, S. Marco, has a monumental display of monumental art books, while **Sansovino**, Bacino Orseolo 84, S. Marco (just outside the Procuratie Vecchie), also has a large collection of art and coffee-table books combined with a huge stock of postcards. The best stock of books in Italian about every aspect of Venice, including some rare editions, is in **Filippi**, Calle del Paradiso 5763, Castello. If you're looking for books in English, try **San Giorgio**, Calle Larga XXII Marzo 2087, S. Marco; **Studium**, Calle Canonica, S. Marco, for books in English and travel books; **Alla Toletta**, Sacca della Toletta 1214, Dorsoduro, or **Serenissima**, Merceria dell'Orologio 739, San Marco.

Fashion, Fabrics and Accessories

Most of Venice's high-fashion designer boutiques are located in the streets to the west of Piazza San Marco; fashion names like **Missoni**, with some of Italy's most beautiful knitwear, at Calle Vallaresso 1312, S. Marco, near Harry's Bar; **Krizia**, Mercerie del Capitello 4949, S. Marco, for more youth-oriented, colourful knits; **Laura Biagiotti**, Via XXII Marzo 2400/a, S. Marco; **Roberta di Camerino**, Lungomare Marconi 32, on the Lido, one of Venice's home-grown designers; and Giorgio Armani, at both **Giorgio Armani da Elysée**, Frezzeria 1693, S. Marco, and **Emporio Armani**, Calle dei Fabbri 989, S. Marco, with more accessible prices. For fashions by maverick Italian and French designers, try **La Coupole**, Via XXII Marzo, or its sister shop, **La Fenice**, 1674, for more everyday-wear designers. Then there's **M. Antichità**, S. Marco 1691, offering velour dresses of Renaissance richness, and jewels to match.

Most Venetians, however, buy at least some of their clothes at the **COIN** department store, Salizzada San Giovanni Crisostomo, just north of Campo San Bartolomeo, part of a national chain, and a variety of cheap clothes stalls spread along Rio Terra San Leonardo, Cannaregio. Fashionable second-hand clothes are the mainstay at **Aldo Strausse**, Campo S. Giustina, in Castello, but **Emilio Ceccato**, Sottoportico di Rialto, S. Polo, is the place to find something very typically Venetian – gondoliers' shirts, jackets and tight trousers. Meanwhile, at the **Camiceria San Marco**, at Calle Vallaresso 1340, S. Marco, they will make up men's shirts and women's dresses to order for you within 24 hours.

For sensuous and expensive lingerie, visit **Jade Martine**, S. Marco 1762. There is also luxurious and expensive lingerie at **La Perla**, Campo San Salvador 4828. The great place to find Venetian lace, whether for lingerie or tablecloths, is on Burano (*see* p.390), although beware that the bargains there are neither handmade nor even Buranese. Back in Venice itself, **Jesurum**, Piazza S. Marco 60/61, has a vast quantity of Venetian lace and linen of all kinds on display in a 12th-century former church behind St Mark's Basilica, as well as a selection of swimwear and summer clothes.

Not just lace but also other luxurious fabrics have figured among Venice's traditional specialities, using skills that in many cases have been reinvigorated in recent years. **Trois**, Campo S. Maurizio, S. Marco 2666, is an institution selling colourful pleated Fortuny silks, invented in Venice and made to traditional specifications on the Giudecca. Modern designs in silks and fabrics can be found at **Valli**, Merceria S. Zulian 783, S. Marco.

For posh shoes, **La Fenice**, Via XXII Marzo 2255, S. Marco, has a good selection by French and Italian designers. The greatest name in Venetian leather is **Vogini**, Via XXII Marzo 1300, S. Marco, which has a comprehensive selection of bags and luggage, and a complete range by Venetian designer Roberta di Camerino. For Wellington boots to help you throught the *aqua alta* try **Fratelli Regini**, Calle al Ponte di S. Antonio, Cartello

Jewellery in Venice tends to be expensive and conservative – particularly in the many shops in and around San Marco – and so may be of more interest for looking than buying. **Codognato**, S. Marco 1295, is one of the oldest jewellers in Venice, with some rare Tiffany, Cartier and Art Deco items; at **Missiaglia**, Piazza S. Marco 125, you can see some of the most elegant pieces produced by Venetian gold and silversmiths working today.

Food and Drink

As well as in the markets, other good places to pick up local specialities include **Pastificio Artigiano**, Strada Nuova 4292, Cannaregio, where Paolo Pavon has for fifty years created Venice's tastiest and most exotic pastas, among them *pasta al cacao* (chocolate pasta) and lemon, beetroot and curry varieties. Similarly, **Il Pastaio**, Calle del Varoteri 219, in the Rialto market, offers pastas in over a score of different colours.

For a staggering choice of dried goods (including coffees and spices), go to the pungently smelling **Drogheria Mascari** in the Ruga dei Speziali ('spice lane'), San Polo. It is the only shop of its kind left on a street that was once full of them. The smell of chocolate as you enter **Pasticceria Marchini** at Ponte San Maurizio (just off Campo Santo Stefano) is almost overwhelming; it has a fabulous, prize-winning Torta del Doge.

If you do want to picnic as you make your way round Venice then **Rizzo Pane**, Calle delle Botteghe, S. Marco, just off Campo F. Morosini, is an *alimentari* where you'll find all you need. For wines and spirits, **Cantinone Già Schiavi**, Fondamenta S. Trovaso 992, Dorsoduro, has plenty to choose from. Scattered throughout the city are shops that sell regional wines by the litre – Tocai, Merlot, Pinot Grigio, and the rest. Bring your own bottles and have them filled at **Vineria Nave de Oro**, Campo Santa Margherita and Calle del Mondo Nuevo.

Gifts

Anyone seeking unusual gifts will find plenty to look at in Venice, though, again, prices sometimes need to be handled with care. At **La Scialuppa**, Calle Seconda dei Saoneri 2695, S. Polo, you can buy the wares of woodworker Gilberto Penzo, who makes beautiful *forcole* (gondola oar locks, made of walnut), replicas of Venetian guild signs and many other things. **Calle Lunga 2137**, in Dorsoduro, is a workshop specializing in decorative wrought-iron, and **Fondamenta Minotto 154**, S. Croce, near S. Nicolò Tolentino and the railway station, has all sorts of gold and brass items, such as Venetian door-knockers. For children, **Signor Blum**, Calle Lunga S. Barnaba 2864, Dorsoduro, has beautiful jigsaw puzzles and brightly painted wooden toys. For an overview, the **Consorzio Artigianato Artistico Veneziano**, Calle Larga S. Marco 412, S. Marco, has a fair selection of all kinds of handmade Venetian crafts. For wooden models of traditional Venetian boats including gondolas and sandolos, try **Gilberto Penzo**, Calle Secondo dei Saoneri, San Polo.

Fabulously rich decorative and furnishing fabrics, tapestries, brocades and trimmings are sold at **Mario Bevilacqua**'s shops in Campo Santa Maria and Fondamenta Canonica; the family business has been running for more than 200 years. For beautiful silk and velvet scarves and evening bags in every imaginable colour, some of them made with the original Fortuny technique, head for **Venetia Studium**, San Polo 3006 and Mercerie 723, San Marco. They also make delicate, Moorish Fortuny lamps to original designs.

The most renowned of Venice's ancient crafts is, of course, an obvious choice. As Burano is the centre for lace, so too Murano is still the place to go for glassware, but in the city one of the grand names in Venetian glass is **Pauly**, at the end of Calle Larga, near Ponte Consorzi, S. Marco, which has 30 rooms of both traditional and contemporary designs in glass housed in a former doge's *palazzo*. At a less exalted level, **Paolo Rossi**, Campo S. Zaccaria 4685, S. Marco, has attractive reproductions of ancient glassware at still-reasonable prices, and **Arte Veneto**, Campo S. Zanipolo 6335, Castello, offers glass and ceramic trinkets that escape looking tacky or ridiculous. You can find glass beads of all kinds at **Perle e Dintorni**; buy them individually or have them made into necklaces and bracelets to order in a couple of hours (Calle della Bissa 5468 and Calle della Mandorla, both in San Marco). Upmarket glass designs (beads, jewellery, lamps, sculpture) by American **Leslie Genniger** can be found at Calle del Traghetto, Dorsoduro and Calle del Fruttariol, S. Marco.

If you can contemplate carrying them home then mosaics, one of the oldest Venetian crafts, are also available, as individual *tessere* or larger items. Try **Arte del Mosaico**, Calle Erizzo 4002, Castello, or **Angelo Orsoni**, Campiello del Battello 1045, Cannaregio.

For exquisite handmade paper, blank books and photo albums try **Paulo Olbi**, Calle della Mandorla 3653 (near Campo S. Angelo), and for paper designs, silk ties and masks made by Alberto Valese fusing Persian and Italian styles, visit **Alberto Valese-Ebrû**, Campo S. Stefano 3471, S. Marco (nearly opposite the church door). Another wonderful paper shop, crammed with handmade paper, leather-bound books and picture frames of all kinds, is **Legatoria Polliero**, Campo dei Frari 2994.

Mondo Novo, at Rio Terrà Canal in Dorsoduro, is one of Venice's most famous mask shops; Stanley Kubrick came here to choose the masks for the surreal orgy scene in *Eyes Wide Shut*. Masks of every shape and size are made on the premises at **Tragicomica** where they also supply theatres with masks and costumes. Prices start at L25,000/L40,000 for the simplest models and from there the sky's the limit (between Campo San Polo and Campo S. Tomà at Calle de' Nomboli 2800).

Where to Stay

The rule of thumb in Venice is that whatever class of hotel you stay in, expect it to cost around a third more than it would on the mainland, even before the often outrageous charge for breakfast is added to the bill. Reservations are near-essential from about April to October and for Carnival; many hotels close in the winter, although many that do stay open offer substantial discounts at this time. Single rooms are always hard to find. If you arrive without reservations, tourist offices at the station and Piazzale Roma have a free room-finding service (a deposit is required, which is deducted from your hotel bill), though they get very busy in season. Also, the tourist office in Piazza San Marco has a list of agencies that rent self-catering flats.

Luxury

*******Cipriani**, Giudecca 10, t 041 520 7744, f 041 520 3930, *www.orientexpresshotels. com*. Since 1963 this has been one of Italy's most luxurious hotels, a villa isolated in a lush garden at one end of the Giudecca that's so quiet and comfortable you could forget Venice exists, even though it's only a few minutes away by the hotel's 24-hour private launch service. An Olympic-size pool, sauna, jacuzzis in each room and a superb restaurant are just some of its facilities.

*******Danieli**, Riva degli Schiavoni 4196, **t** 041 522 6480, **f** 041 520 0208, *www.sheraton. com*. The largest and most famous hotel in Venice, in what must be the most glorious location, overlooking the Lagoon and rubbing shoulders with the Palazzo Ducale. Formerly the Gothic *palazzo* of the Dandolo family, it has been a hotel since 1822; Dickens, Proust, George Sand and Wagner checked in here. Nearly every room has some story to tell, in a setting of silken walls, Gothic staircases, gilt mirrors and oriental rugs. The new wing, much vilified ever since it was built in the 1940s, is comfortable but lacks the charm and the stories.

*******Gritti Palace**, S. Maria del Giglio 2467, S. Marco, **t** 041 794 611, **f** 041 520 0942, *RES073_grittipalace@ittsheraton.com*. The 15th-century Grand Canal palace that once belonged to the dashing glutton and womanizer, Doge Andrea Gritti, has been preserved as a true Venetian fantasy and elegant retreat, now part of the CIGA chain. All the rooms are furnished with Venetian antiques, but for a real splurge do as Somerset Maugham did and stay in the Ducal Suite. Another of its delights is the restaurant, the **Club del Doge**, on a terrace overlooking the canal.

******Londra Palace**, Riva degli Schiavoni 4171, Castello, **t** 041 520 0533, **f** 041 522 5032, *info@hotellondia.it*. Tchaikovsky wrote his *Fourth Symphony* in room 108 of this hotel, and it was also a favourite of Stravinsky. The hotel was created by linking two palaces together, and it has an elegant interior; over half the rooms have a stunning canal view, it has one of the cosiest lobbies in Venice, and exceptionally good service. There is also an excellent restaurant, **Les Deux Lions.**

******Concordia**, Calle Larga S. Marco 367, **t** 041 520 6866, **f** 041 520 6775, *venezia@hotel concordia.it*. The only hotel overlooking Piazza S. Marco, the Concordia was swishly renovated in 1994 with a touch of Hollywood in some of its furnishings. Central air conditioning is an added plus, as well as substantial off-season discounts.

******Saturnia & International**, Via XXII Marzo 2398, S. Marco, **t** 041 520 8377, **f** 041 520 7131. A lovely hotel in a romantic quattrocento *palazzo* that has preserved centuries of

accumulated decoration. Very near S. Marco, it has a garden court, faced by the nicest and quietest rooms. Off-season discounts.

******Ca' Pisani**, Dorsoduro 979/a, **t** 041 2771478, **f** 041 2771061. Located in a 17th-century *palazzo* just behind the Zattere, the newly opened Ca' Pisani flies in the face of Venetian hotel tradition by being designer-minimalist. Original 1930s pieces (beds, mirrors, wardrobes, chests) are scattered around and blend well with contemporary pieces and a colour scheme where silver, orange, grey, pale violet and browns dominate. There is a roof terrace, Turkish bath and basement wine bar, and not a scrap of flock wallpaper in sight.

Very Expensive

*****Accademia** 'Villa Maravege', Fondamenta Bollani 1058, Dorsoduro, **t** 041 521 0188, **f** 041 523 9152. A hotel that offers a generous dollop of slightly faded charm in a 17th-century villa with a garden, just off the Grand Canal. Its 26 rooms are furnished with a menagerie of antiques, some of which look as if they were left behind by the villa's previous occupant – the Russian Embassy. The Accademia is a favourite of many, so book well in advance. Off-season discounts.

*****La Fenice et Des Artistes**, Campiello de la Fenice 1936, S. Marco, **t** 041 523 2333, **f** 041 520 3721. A favourite of opera buffs in Venice (not much use until La Fenice reopens). Inside there are lots of mirrors, antiques and chandeliers to make *artistes* feel at home.

*****Flora**, Calle Bergamaschi 2283/a, S. Marco, **t** 041 520 5844, **f** 041 522 8217. A small hotel on a little street that's remarkably quiet so near to Piazza San Marco, with a charming garden and patio, spilling flowers. It's comfortably furnished, but ask for a large room. Off-season discounts.

*****Do Pozzi**, Corte do Pozzi 2373, S. Marco, **t** 041 520 7855, **f** 041 522 9413. With a bit of the look of an Italian country inn, this hotel has 29 quiet rooms on a charming little square, only a few minutes from Piazza San Marco. It's friendly and well run.

*****Sturion**, Calle del Sturion 679, San Polo, **t** 041 523 6243, **f** 041 522 8378. A popular choice, as it's one of the least expensive hotels actually on the Grand Canal. It's advisable to book well ahead for one of its eight large, finely furnished rooms. Also it has nice extras such as a small library of books, a video library and an internet point, all for guests' use – but there is no lift and the climb up the stairs is steep!

***Pausania**, Fondamenta Gherardini, Dorsoduro 2824, **t** 041 522 2083, **f** 041 522 2989. Just up-canal from a floating vegetable shop in the picturesque San Barnaba area, this Gothic *palazzo* has a sunny living room overlooking the canal and a breakfast room overlooking a quiet garden. Bedrooms are refreshingly unfussy.

***San Cassiano-Ca' Fevretto**, Calle della Rosa, Santa Croce 2232, **t** 041 524 1768, **f** 041 721 033. In a pretty *palazzo* on the Grand Canal right opposite the glorious Ca' d'Oro, most of the rooms in this hotel are a bit disappointing; exceptions are those on the canal which are quite grand and no more expensive than the others.

Expensive

Agli Alboretti, Rio Terrà Foscarini 884, Dorsoduro, **t 041 523 0058, **f** 041 521 0158. A charming little hotel, recently refurbished, on a rare tree-lined lane near the Accademia; 19 rooms.

***La Calcina, Zattere ai Gesuati 780, Dorsoduro, **t** 041 520 6466, **f** 041 522 7045. Near the Gesuati church and overlooking the Giudecca canal, this was Ruskin's *pensione* in 1877. Totally refurbished in 1996 with all mod cons; has a beautiful breakfast terrace. Book well ahead.

Falier, Salizzada S. Pantalon 130, S. Croce, **t 041 710 882, **f** 041 520 6554. A small hotel near Campo San Rocco. Elegantly furnished, it has two flower-filled terraces to lounge around on when your feet rebel; one room has its own terrace.

Messner, Salute 216, Dorsoduro, **t 041 522 7443, **f** 041 522 7266. A nice hotel only a hop from the Salute, highly recommended for families. Great showers, awful coffee.

Mignon, SS. Apostoli 4535, Cannaregio, **t 041 523 7388, **f** 041 520 8658. In a fairly quiet area, not far from the Ca' d'Oro, the Mignon boasts a little garden for leisurely breakfasts, though the rooms are rather plain. It has a loyal following all the same.

La Residenza, Campo Bandiera e Moro 3608, Castello, **t 041 528 5315, **f** 041 523 8859. Located in a lovely 14th-century palace in a quiet square between San Marco and the Arsenale. The public rooms are flamboyantly decorated with 18th-century frescoes, paintings and antique furniture, though the bedrooms are simpler.

Serenissima, Calle Goldoni, San Marco 4486, **t 041 520 0011, **f** 041 522 3292. A delightful little hotel a stone's throw from S. Marco with neat rooms and a friendly reception.

Antico Locanda Al Gambero, Calle dei Fabbri 4687, San Marco, **t 041 522 4384, **f** 041 520 0431. Between San Marco and Rialto, the Gambero has surprisingly smart rooms for a two star hotel.

Salute da Cici, Fondamenta di Ca' Balla, Dorsoduro, **t 041 523 5404, **f** 041 522 2271. Near the Accademia and the Guggenheim Collection, an elegant, 50-room hotel with a tiny garden and a bar for guests' use. Some of the white-painted rooms overlook the canal: those in the modern annexe are actually more comfortable.

*Casa Verardo, Ruga Giuffa 4765, Castello, **t** 041 528 6127, **f** 041 523 2765. A classy, 9-room *locanda* with friendly owners.

Moderate

The largest concentration of cheaper hotels in Venice is around the Lista di Spagna, running eastwards into Cannaregio from the train station, though they can be pretty tacky and noisy. A more relaxed, pleasant and attractive area in which to find less expensive accommodation is in Dorsoduro, particularly around Campo S. Margherita.

*Antico Capon, Campo S. Margherita 3004/b, Dorsoduro, **t/f** 041 528 5292. Being refurbished by new management at the time of writing, this hotel has seven simple rooms, and, thankfully, no breakfast. It owes most of its charm to its sociable Campo.

*Casa Petrarca, Calle delle Fuseri 4393, S. Marco, **t** 041 520 0430. Petrarch didn't really sleep in one of these six friendly rooms near the Piazza, but who cares?

*Sant'Anna, Corte Bianco 269, Castello, **t/f** 041 528 6466. A fine little hotel popular with those who want to escape tourist Venice, located just north of the Giardini Pubblici. Only eight rooms, including some triples.

★Silva, Fondamenta Rimedio 4423, Castello, t 041 522 7643, f 041 528 6817. A bit hard to find – on one of the most photographed little canals in Venice, between the S. Zaccaria *vaporetto* stop and S. Maria Formosa. The rooms are fairly basic, but quiet, and the staff are friendly.

★Ca' Foscari, Calle della Frescada, Dorsoduro, t 041 710401, f 041 710817. Near Campo San Tomà in a bustling, residential area, this 11-roomed hotel is a cut above other one-stars. The modest but pretty bedrooms are spotless; not all have bathrooms.

★Locanda Fiorita, Campiello Nuovo, Santo Stefano, S. Marco 3457/A, t 041 523 4754, f 041 522 8043. With a central location just off Campo Santo Stefano, this hotel is more comfortable than many in its category. A pretty, flower filled terrace runs along the front of the house for use in summer.

Eating Out

The Venetians themselves are traditionally the worst cooks in Italy, and their beautiful city bears the ignominy of having a highest percentage of dud restaurants per capita. Not only is cooking in general well below the norm in Italy, but prices tend to be about 15 per cent higher, and even the moderate ones can give you a nasty surprise at *conto* time with excessive cover charges. Pizza is a good standby if you're on a budget. The restaurants listed have a history of being decent or better, so chances are they still will be when you visit.

Luxury

Antico Martini, Campo S. Fantin 1983, S. Marco, t 041 522 4121. This is a Venetian classic, all romance and elegance. It started out as a Turkish coffeehouse in the early 18th century, but is better known now for its seafood, a superb wine list and the best *pennette al pomodoro* in Venice. The intimate piano bar-restaurant stays open until 2am. Its romantic flavour is temporarily swallowed up by La Fenice's rebuilding operations directly outside. *Closed Tues, Wed midday, Dec and Feb.*

Danieli Terrace, in the Danieli Hotel, Riva degli Schiavoni 4196, Castello, t 041 522 6480. The Danieli's rooftop restaurant is renowned for classic cuisine (try the *spaghetti alla Danieli*, prepared at your table) and perfect service in an incomparable setting overlooking Bacino San Marco.

Da Fiore, Calle del Scaleter, San Polo, t 041 721 308. People 'in the know' believe that Da Fiore is now the best restaurant in Venice. Food is taken seriously here; the atmosphere is sober without any of the pretentious frills of many other Venetian eateries. You can begin a meal with a plate of *misto crudo* or marinated raw fish or scallops *gratinati* in the oven with thyme before moving on to the classic *bigoli in salsa* (handmade spaghetti in a sauce of mashed anchovies and onions), penne with scallops and broccoli, or a wonderful, silky black squid ink *risotto*. Main courses include *involtini* of sole wrapped round radicchio, and a superb meaty tuna steak flavoured with rosemary. *Closed Sun and Mon.*

La Caravella, Calle Larga XXII Marzo 2397, S. Marco, t 041 520 8901, in an annexe to the Saturnia Hotel. For sheer variety of seasonal and local dishes, prepared by a master chef, few restaurants in Italy can top this merrily corny repro of a dining hall in a 16th-century Venetian galley. Try gilthead with thyme and fennel. Despite the décor, the atmosphere is fairly formal. *Open Oct–April, closed Wed.*

Harry's Bar, Calle Vallaresso 1323, S. Marco, t 041 523 6797. In a class by itself, a favourite of Hemingway and assorted other luminaries, this is as much a Venetian institution as the Doge's Palace, though food has become secondary to its celebrity atmosphere. Best to avoid the restaurant upstairs and just flit in for a quick hobnob with the rich and famous while sampling a sandwich or the justly famous cocktails (a Bellini, Tiziano or Tiepolo – delectable fruit juices mixed with Prosecco), at a table downstairs near the bar. *Closed Mon.*

Very Expensive

Do Forni, Calle dei Specchieri 468, S. Marco, t 041 523 2148. For many Italians as well as foreigners, this is *the* place to eat in Venice. There are two dining rooms, one 'Orient

Express'-style and the other rustic, and both are always filled with diners partaking of its excellent seafood antipasti, *polenta*, and seafood. *Closed Thurs in winter.*

Dall'Amelia, Via Miranese 113, Mestre, **t** 041 913 955. A restaurant that, despite its inconvenient mainland location, has to be included, as all Italian gourmets cross the big bridge to dine here at least once. The oysters are delicious and there's a divine *tortelli di bronzino* (sea bass), plus wine from one of Italy's most renowned cellars. *Closed Wed.*

Expensive

Corte Sconta, Calle del Pestrin 3886, Castello, **t** 041 522 7024. It may be off the beaten track, but the reputation of this *trattoria* rests solidly on its exquisite molluscs and crustaceans, served in a setting that's a breath of fresh air after the exposed beams and copper pots that dominate the typical Venetian restaurant. The Venetians claim the Corte Sconta is even better in the off-season; be sure to order the house wine. *Closed Sun, Mon, and most of July and Aug.*

Antica Locanda Montin, Fondamenta di Borgo or Eremite 1147 (near S. Trovaso), Dorsoduro, **t** 041 522 7151. This has long been Venice's most celebrated artists' eatery – Peggy Guggenheim was a one-time regular – with a vast garden, but the food ranges erratically in quality from first to third division. *Closed Tues evening, Wed, and half of Aug.*

Trattoria Vini da Arturo, Calle degli Assassini 3656, S. Marco, **t** 041 528 6974. In an infamous little street near La Fenice, this is a tiny *trattoria* that marches to a different drum from most Venetian restaurants, with not a speck of seafood on the menu. Instead, try the *pappardelle al radicchio* or Venice's best steaks; its *tiramisù* is famous. *Closed Sun and half Aug.*

Da Remigio, Salizzada dei Greci 3416, Castello, **t** 041 523 0089. A neighbourhood favourite, with solid Venetian cooking. Very popular with the locals. *Closed Mon, and Tues eve.*

Le Bistrot, Calle dei Fabbri, San Marco, **t** 041 523 6651. This cosy restaurant presents poetry readings, live music and other cultural events as well as specializing in historical Venetian dishes which, reflecting the city's multicultural past, are full of unusual herbs and spices. The menu, complete with helpful notes on the origins of each dish, features such choices as pumpkin and cheese *gnocchi* flavoured with cinnamon, spicy pheasant soup, *baccalà* in a sweet and sour sauce, sturgeon cooked with prunes, grapes and balsamic vinegar and spicy Turkish spiced rice pudding. *Stays open till 1am.*

Moderate

Altanella, Calle della Erbe 268, Giudecca, **t** 041 522 7780. A delightful old seafood restaurant with an attractive setting on the Rio del Ponte Longo and a sideways glimpse of the Giudecca canal thrown in. Any of the grilled fish will be superb, and the *risotto di pesce* and *fritto* are worth the trip. Reserve. *Closed Mon eve, Tues, and half of Aug.*

Antica Mola, Fondamenta degli Ormesini 2800, Cannaregio, **t** 041 717 492, near the Ghetto. All the old favourites – fish, *risotto*, *zuppa di pesce* – and tables by the canal. *Closed for three weeks in Aug.*

Alla Madonna, Calle della Madonna 594, S. Polo (off Fond. del Vin, Rialto), **t** 041 522 3824. A large, popular, and very Venetian fish restaurant. *Closed Wed and Jan.*

Alle Testiere, Calle del Mondo Novo, Castello, **t** 041 522 7220. A tiny *osteria* situated between Campo Santa Maria Formosa and Rialto which only has seating for 20, so book well ahead. *Cicchetti* and wine are served up to a certain point, but if you are lucky enough to secure a table, more substantial fare – all fish based and a bit different from the norm – is available for lunch and dinner: delicious and varied *antipasti, gnocchetti* with baby squid or scampi and rocket, monkfish tails with capers and turbot with red radicchio. Puddings are homemade and well worth leaving room for. *Closed Sun and three weeks in Aug.*

Al Mascaron, Calle Lunga S. Maria Formosa, Castello, **t** 041 522 5995. A favourite Venetian *osteria*, now somewhat spoilt by too many tourists, but nonetheless full of atmosphere and serving good food. Wine is served out of huge containers in the front room and the atmosphere is noisy and unpretentious. Traditional Venetian specialities – both fish and meat – are served at marble-topped tables. Liver, as well as the more usual sardines, is served *in saor* –with pine nuts, raisins and marinated onions. *Closed Sun.*

Sacro e Profano, Sottoportego dei Orefici, t 041 520 1931. On the western side of the Rialto, hidden away behind the jewellery stalls, this friendly squeeze of an *osteria* is run by Gabriele and Simone who serve up both snacks and hot dishes accompanied by good wines to a young, arty crowd.

L'Incontro, Dorsoduro 3062, t 041 522 2404. If you can't start the sight of another fish, head for this restaurant, where the menu is entirely meat and vegetable based. *Gnocchi* with tomato and *pecorino* cheese, *ravioli* flavoured with saffron, steaks (beef or horse) and roast suckling pig are among the temptations for carnivores.

Dal Ciuffo, Calle Priuli 106, t 041 714 651. Of all the dozens of third-rate restaurants round the station, this place with its larger-than-life chef stands out. You can have *cicchetti* and a glass of wine at the bar or sit for the usual Venetian fare. *Closed Mon.*

Cheap

Aciugheta, Campo SS. Filippo e Giacomo, Castello, t 041 522 4292. One of the best cheap restaurants and bars near the Piazza San Marco, with good pizzas and atmosphere to boot. Operates on two levels – touristy pizzeria at the front, but go with a local and get in early to the back room for great *chiccheti*, cheese and excellent wines. *Closed Wed; open daily in summer.*

Pizzeria alle Oche, Calle del Tentor 1552, S. Croce, t 041 524 1161, just before Ponte del Parucheta, south of S. Giacomo dell'Orio. Cheery, young atmosphere with 85 types of pizza, and take-away. *Closed Mon in winter.*

Rosticceria San Bartolomeo, Calle della Bissa 5424, San Marco, t 041 522 3569. Honest cooking for honest prices, a no-frills *trattoria* with an cheaper snack bar downstairs. You can either eat in or take away.

San Tomà, Campo San Tomà 2864, San Polo, t 041 523 8819. A good *trattoria/pizzeria* with convivial outdoor tables.

Casa Mia, Calle dell'Oca 4430, Cannaregio, t 041 528 5590, near Campo SS. Apostoli. A lively *pizzeria* full of locals, and six courtyard tables. *Closed Tues.*

Vino Vino, Campo S. Fantin 1983, S. Marco, t 041 523 7027. A trendy offspring of the next door élite Antico Martini, where you can eat a well-cooked, filling dish (cooked by the same chefs!) with a glass of good wine at prices even students can afford. Also does good *chicchetti*. *Closed Tues.*

Entertainment and Nightlife

Sadly, in a city that's clearly made-to-order for pleasure, revelry and romance, life after dark is notoriously moribund. The locals take an evening stroll to their local *campo* for a chat with friends and an *aperitivo*, before heading home to dinner and the TV – though the hotblooded may go on to bars and discos in Mestre, Marghera or the Lido. Visitors are left to become even poorer at the **Municipal Casino**, t 041 529 7111, out on the Lido from April to October, and at other times in the Palazzo Vendramin on the Grand Canal (*hours are 3pm–2am, dress up and take your passport*). You might prefer to spend less more memorably on a moonlit gondola ride, or you can do as most people do – wander about.

Even so, there are places to go among all this peace and quiet, and stacked against the absence of everyday nightlife there's Venice's packed calendar of special events. For an up-to-date calendar of current events, exhibitions, shows, films, and concerts in the city, consult *Un Ospite di Venezia*.

Opera, Classical Music and Theatre

Venice's music programme is heavily oriented to the classical. Opera (the season runs from December to May), ballet, recitals and symphonic concerts, at **La Fenice** until it burned down, are currently performed in a pavilion at Tronchetto while restoration goes on; tickets are available through the Cassa di Risparmio, Campo S. Luca, t 041 521 0161.

At Venice's main theatre **Teatro Goldoni**, Calle Goldoni 4650/b, S. Marco, t 041 520 7583, the Goldoni repertory holds pride of place, but there are other plays, as well as concerts; in summer performances are often moved to Campo S. Polo.

Two other concert venues, worth visiting as much for the décor as the music, are the **Palazzo Labia**, Campo S. Geremia, Cannaregio (call ahead for tickets, **t** 041 524 2812), and Vivaldi's lovely rococo church of **La Pietà** (information and tickets, **t** 041 520 8711), where prices are usually high but the acoustics are well-nigh perfect. Concerts are also held regularly in the Frari church (early music), Scuola Grande di San Giovanni Evangelista, and Scuola Grande di San Rocco. Details can be obtained from the tourist offices.

English films are shown every Tuesday at the **Giorgione**, Canareggio 4612, **t** 041 522 6298.

Cafés and Bars

The classic **cafés** of Venice face each other across Piazza San Marco: **Florian's** and its great rival **Quadri**, both beautiful, and both correspondingly exorbitant.

Harry's Dolci, Fondamenta S. Biagio 773 on the Giudecca. Fashionable with smart Venetians today, particularly on Sundays, and noted for its elegant teas, ice creams and cakes.

Cips at the Cipriani. Open for scrumptious sandwiches and cakes.

Caffè Costarica, Rio Terrà di S. Leonardo, Cannaregio. Brews Venice's most powerful *espresso* and great iced coffee (*frappé*), and also sells ground coffees and beans over the counter.

Between 5pm and dinner is the time to indulge in a beer and *tramezzini*, sandwiches that come in a hundred varieties.

Bar alla Toletta, Calile della Toletta 1191, Dorsoduro. Some of the best *tramezzini* are to be found here at this eccentric bar run by a temperamental middle-aged couple with a voracious appetite for jazz.

Paolin, on the Campo Santo Stefano, S. Marco. The title of best *gelateria* in the city has by convention been accorded to Paolin, above all for their divine pistachio.

Boutique del Gelato on Salizada San Lio. However, many locals think that this tiny *gelateria* is the best. *Open 10.30–8 daily*.

Nico, on the Zattere ai Gesuati, Dorsoduro. Also a must on anyone's ice-cream tour, if the late-night queues are anything to go by.

Caffè Rosso, Campo Santa Margherita, **t** 041 528 7998. Simply known as 'The Red Bar', this is a lively local hang-out in trendy Campo Santa Margherita. Cocktails, coffee, pastries and snacks. *Open until 1.30am, closed Sun.*

Alla Mascareta, Calle Lunga Santa Maria Formosa, **t** 041 523 0744. Under the same ownership as the famous Al Mascaron, this *enoteca* has an exceptional wine list (some 400 labels) and wonderful choice of cheeses, hams and salamis. *Open 6pm–1am.*

Rosa Salva, Campo Santi Giovanni e Paolo, **t** 041 522 7949. Have breakfast in one of Venice's best cake shops with tables on the square.

Bacari

If you don't want a full meal, a *bacaro*, Venice's answer to a tapas bar, is a perfect solution. Many of them also serve complete meals (in which case you can have some *cicchetti* as an *antipasto*) – often at long tables in a back room.

Originally drinking places with the atmosphere of port drinking holes the world over, they now come in all shapes and sizes, from gloomy holes in the wall with standing room only and seemingly full of Venetian men speaking their unrecognizable dialect to the slick, new-generation establishments with trendy décor and lighting.

What they will all have in common, however, is a choice of wines by the glass (*un ombra*) which range from the rough-and-ready local white *tocai* or red *raboso* to more sophisticated labels, and an array of *cicchetti* or little snacks which are usually arranged on the counter in a mouth-watering display.

These can consist of just about anything from fishy tit-bits (crab claws, baby squid, *sarde in saor*, scampi, fishy mixtures spread on bread or toast and all those uniquely Venetian fish) to grilled vegetables, artichoke hearts, deep-fried pumpkin or courgette flowers, chunks of salami, ham or cheese, little sandwiches, squares of fried *polenta*...the inventiveness of these little snacks knows practically no bounds.

They are often speared with a toothpick off the main serving dish, or you can ask for a selection to be put on a plate, pointing at what takes your fancy even if you have no idea what it is. Venetian *bacari*-men have an astonishing capacity to keep tabs of just how many *bacari* and *ombre* have slipped down your gullet while you sink into a contented blur. One word of warning; prices are not usually displayed on each item and it's amazing how the bill adds up.

Venice is full of *bacari* and they are much too numerous to list here. They are usually hidden away down narrow alleyways and off the main drags, so a little exploration will probably turn up good results. Most are open all day (some have a couple of hours siesta in mid-afternoon) but close at around 8pm; some of the newer ones stay open late. They rarely accept credit cards.

Al Volto, Calle Cavalli di S. Marco 4081, S. Marco. The greatest variety of wines and Venice's oldest wine bar, with over 2,000 Italian and foreign labels to choose from and a sumptuous array of *cicchetti*. *Open 10–2.30 and 5–10.30; closed Sun.*

Da Pinto, Campo delle Beccerie, San Polo, t 041 718 308. *Closed Mon.* The best places to try fish *chicchetti* are at any of the *bacari* near the Rialto fish market-for obvious reasons. Accompany your snack with a glass or two of the house *tocai.*

Da Codroma, Fondamenta Briati, Dorsoduro, t 041 524 6789. Near the Carmine church, this is one of Venice's historic *osterie* with a real old-fashioned feel to it. At *ombra e chicchetti* time, the marble-topped counter groans with tempting tit-bits while customers are instructed (through various signs) not to spit on the floor or sing. *Closed Sat and Sun and Mon eve.*

Cantina Do Mori, Calle dei Do Mori, San Polo, t 041 522 5401. Near the Rialto market area and one of the oldest *osterie* in Venice (it claims to be *the* oldest) and with 20 different wines by the glass at any given time, the Do Mori has plenty of atmosphere and is always heaving. Try the *francobolli* (postage stamps), tiny sandwich squares stuffed with yummy fillings. *Closed Sun.*

Al Bottegon, San Trovaso 992, Dorsoduro, t 041 523 0034. An old-fashioned place near the Zattere with an 18th-century atmosphere, antique furniture and roof beams. *Closed Sun afternoon.*

Alla Patatina, Ponte San Polo 2742, San Polo, t 041 523 7238. A lively place, which is famous for its chunky fried potatoes.

Jazz, Clubs and Nightspots

Venice's few late-night bars and music venues can be fun, or just posey and dull, and what you find is pretty much pot luck, as places change constantly, going in and out of fashion at the whim of their ever-changing clientele of entrenched locals, expats, students, and people just passing through.

Paradiso Perduto, Fondamenta della Misericordia 2540, Cannaregio, t 041 720 581. The city's best-known and most popular late-night bar/restaurant with inexpensive though variable food, and a relaxed, bohemian atmosphere popular with a mix of locals and English visitors; live concerts (jazz and roots music), parties, art exhibitions. *Open 7pm–2am; also open Tues lunchtime; closed Wed.*

Taverna l'Olandese Volante (Flying Dutchman), Campo S. Lio 5658, Castello, t 041 528 9349. A current favourite for young trendies and one of Venice's answers to a pub, open late with snacks and simple food.

The Fiddler's Elbow, Corte dei Pali, Cannaregio, t 041 523 9930. An Irish pub serving Guinness on tap and piped Irish music. They do have live concerts in summer in the piazza outside.

Osteria da Codroma, Fondamenta Briati 2540, Dorsoduro, t 041 524 6789. A relaxed and informal wine bar which hosts art shows, a backgammon club, and occasional live jazz on Tuesdays. *Open 7pm–2am; closed Sat.*

Ai Canottieri, Ponte Tre Archi 690, Cannaregio, t 041 715 408. Another restaurant/bar with music, dancing and sometimes live rock or jazz. *Open 7pm–2am; closed Sun.*

Cantina Vecia Carbonera in Strada Nova just behind the Casinò, t 041 710 376. Live jazz or blues every evening to accompany wines and delicious-looking snacks.

Margaret Duchamp, Campo Santa Margherita, Dorsoduro, t 041 528 6255. A designer 'disco bar' (as it calls itself), one of the few in Venice and frequented by a trendy mix of black-clad Venetians and foreigners. Open until the wee hours (2am), it serves sandwiches and snacks and a range of beers.

Linea d'Ombra, Zattere ai Saloni, near the Salute, t 041 528 5259. A fairly glitzy piano bar. *Open 8pm–1am; closed Wed.*

Sound Code, Via delle Industrie 32, **t** 041 531 3890. The best disco within spitting distance of Venice. *Open Fri and Sat until 4am.*

Acropolis, Lungomare Marconi 22, **t** 041 526 0466. In July and August there's a disco here on the Lido.

Al Delfino. Take in a late-night game of billiards at this 'American Bar' at the Lido, with music and snacks at Lungomare Marconi 96. *Open until 2am.*

Villa Eva, Gran Viale 49. Music and snacks from midnight until 4am. *Closed Thurs except in the summer.*

The main **late-night drinking** holes are:

Osteria ai Assassini, Calle degli Assassini, S. Marco. Wines, beers, and good *cicchetti*. *Open till midnight; closed Sat lunch and Sun.*

Creperia Poggi, Cannaregio 2103. Has music and also stays open till 2am, flipping *crespelle* until midnight. *Closed Sun.*

Gelateria Bar Maleti, Gran Viale 47. The last chance for an ice cream is at 3am at this Lido *gelateria*. *Closed Wed.*

Exhibitions and Art Festivals

Venice is one of Europe's top cities for art exhibitions: major international shows fill the **Palazzo Grassi**, Campo S. Samuele, S. Marco, which Fiat has transformed into a lavishly equipped exhibition and cultural centre.

High calibre art and photographic exhibitions also appear frequently at the **Palazzo Querini-Stampalia**, the **Peggy Guggenheim Collection**, and **Ca' Pésaro**.

Then there's the **Biennale**, the most famous contemporary art show in the world, founded in 1895 and now held, in principle, in even-numbered years. The main exhibits of the forty or so countries officially represented are set up in the permanent pavilions in the Giardini Pubblici, but there is also an open section for younger and less-established artists, in venues across the city.

The city's other great cultural junket is the **Venice Film Festival**, held in the Palazzo del Cinema and the Astra Cinema on the Lido every year in late August and September. As well as spotting the stars, you can sometimes get in to see films if you arrive at the cinemas really early – tickets are only sold on the same day as each showing.

Traditional Festivals

Venice's renowned **Carnival**, first held in the ten days preceding Lent in 1094, was revived in 1979 after several decades of dormancy. It attracts huge crowds, but faces an uphill battle against the inveterate Italian love of *bella figura* – getting dressed up in elaborate costumes, wandering down to San Marco and taking each other's picture is as much as most of the revellers get up to. Concerts and shows are put on all over Venice, with city and corporate sponsorship, but there's very little spontaneity or serious carousing, and certainly no trace of what Byron called the 'revel of the earth'.

In 1988 Venice revived another crowd pleaser, **La Sensa**, held on the first Sunday after Ascension Day, in which the doge married the sea (*see* p.356). Now the mayor plays the groom, in a replica of the state barge or *Bucintoro*. It's as corny and pretentious as it sounds, but on the same day you can watch the gondoliers race in the **Vogalonga**, or long row, from San Marco to Burano and back again – much more energetic and fun.

Venice's most spectacular festival, **Il Redentore** (*see* p.385), is held on the third Sunday of July, with its bridge of boats. The greatest excitement happens the Saturday night before, when Venetians row out for an evening picnic on the water, manoeuvring for the best view of the fabulous fireworks display over the Lagoon. For landlubbers (and there are thousands of them) the prime viewing spots are towards the eastern ends of either the Giudecca or the Zattere.

More perspiration is expended in the **Regatta Storica** (first Sunday in September), a splendid pageant of historic vessels and crews in Renaissance costumes and hotly contested races by gondoliers and a variety of other rowers down the Grand Canal.

Another bridge of boats is built on 21 November, this time across the Grand Canal to the Salute, for the feast of **Santa Maria della Salute**, which also commemorates the ending of another plague, in 1631. This event provides the only opportunity to see Longhena's unique basilica as it would have been when it was built, with its doors thrown open on to the Grand Canal.

When to Go

Venice (Venezia) is as much a character as a setting, and the same may be said of its weather. In no other city will you be so aware of the light; on a clear, fine day no place could be more limpid and clear, no water as crystal bright as the Lagoon. The rosy dawn igniting the domes of St Mark's, the splash of an oar fading in the cool mist of a canal, the pearly twilit union of water and sky are among the city's oldest clichés.

If you seek solitude and romance with a capital R, go in January. Pack a warm coat, water-resistant shoes and an umbrella, and expect frequent fogs and mists. It may even snow – in 1987 you could even ski jump down the Rialto bridge. But there are also plenty of radiant diamond days, brilliant, sunny and chill; any time after October you take your chances.

As spring approaches there is Carnival, a game and beautiful but rather bland attempt to revive a piece of old Venice; Lent is fairly quiet, though in the under-current the Venetians are building up for their first major invasion of sightseers at Easter. By April the tourism industry is cranked up to full operational capacity; the gondolas are un-mothballed, the café tables have blossomed in Piazza San Marco, the Casino has re-located to the Lido. In June even the Italians are considering a trip to the beach.

In July and August elbow-room is at a premium. Peripheral camping grounds are packed, queues at the tourist office's room-finding service stretch longer and longer, and the police are kept busy reminding the hordes that there's no picnicking in St Mark's Square. The heat can be sweltering, the ancient city gasping under a flood of cameras, shorts, sunglasses and rucksacks. Scores head off to the Lido for relief; a sudden thunderstorm over the Lagoon livens things up, as do the many festivals, especially the Redentore and its fireworks in July. In the autumn the city and the Venetians begin to unwind, the rains begin to fall, and you can watch them pack up the parasols and cabanas on the Lido with a wistful sigh.

As far as hotels are concerned, high season is from Carnival to mid-November, with prices coming down a bit in midsummer.

a year) show up in the summer and, like their ancestors, have a jolly good time. For Venice is a most experienced old siren in her boudoir of watery mirrors. International organizations pump in the funds to keep her petticoats out of the water and smooth her wrinkles. Notices posted throughout the city acknowledge that she 'belongs to everybody', while with a wink she slides a knowing hand deep into your pocket. Venice has always lived for gold, and you can bet she wants yours – you might just as well give it to her, in return for the most enchanting, dream-like favours any city can grant.

History

Venice has always been so different, so improbable, that one can easily believe the legend that the original inhabitants sprang up from the dew and mists on the mud banks of the Lagoon. Historians who don't believe in fairies say that Venice was born of adversity: the islands and treacherous shallows of the Lagoon provided the citizens of the Veneto with a refuge from Attila the Hun and the Arian heresies sweeping the mainland. According to Venetians' own legends, the city was founded at exactly noon, 25 March 413, when the refugees laid the first stone on the Rialto. Twelve Lagoon townships grew up between modern Chioggia and Grado; when Theodoric the Great's secretary Cassiadorus visited them in 523 he wrote that they were 'scattered like sea-birds' nests over the face of the waters'.

In 697 the 12 townships united to elect their first duke, or doge. Fishing, trading – in slaves, among other things – and their unique knowledge of the Lagoon brought the Venetians their first prosperity, but their key position between the Byzantine empire and the 'barbarian' kings on the mainland also made them a bone of contention. In 810, the Franks, who had defeated the Lombards in the name of the Pope and claimed dominion over the whole of northern Italy, turned their attention to the last hold-out, Venice: Doge Obelario de'Antenori, engaged in a bitter feud with other Venetian factions, even invited Charlemagne's son Pepin to send his army into the city.

The quarrelling Venetians, until then undecided whether to support Rome or Constantinople, united at the approach of Pepin's fleet, deposed the Doge, declared for Byzantium, and entrenched themselves on the Rialto. The shallows and queer humours of the Lagoon confounded Pepin, and after a gruelling six-month siege he threw in the towel. A subsequent treaty between the Franks and the Eastern Emperor Nicephorus (814) recognized Venice as a subject of Byzantium, with important trading concessions. As Byzantine authority over the city was never more than words, it in effect marked the birth of an independent republic.

The Venetians lacked only a dynamic spiritual protector; their frumpy St Theodore with his crocodile was simply too low in the celestial hierarchy to fulfil the destiny they had in mind. In 829, Venetian merchants, supposedly on secret orders from the Doge, carried off one of the Republic's greatest coups when they purloined the body of St Mark from Alexandria, smuggling him past Egyptian customs by claiming that the saint was pickled pork. To acquire an Evangelist for themselves was, in itself, a demonstration of the Venetians' new ambition.

Marriage to the Sea

As the East–West trade expanded, the Venetians designed their domestic and external policies to accommodate it. At home they required peace and stability, and by the beginning of the 11th century had squelched all notions of an hereditary doge-ship by exiling the most hyper-active families; Venice would never have the despotic *signori* who plagued the rest of Italy.

Raids by Dalmatian pirates spurred the Venetians to fight and win their first major war in 997, under Doge Pietro Orseolo, who captured the pirates' coastal strongholds. The Venetians were so pleased with themselves that they celebrated the event with a splendidly arrogant ritual every Ascension Day, the Sensa or 'Marriage of the Sea', in which the Doge would sail out to the Lido in his sumptuous barge, the *Bucintoro*, and cast a diamond ring into the sea, proclaiming 'We wed thee, O sea, in sign of our true and perpetual dominion'.

Venice, because of her location and fleet, supplied a great deal of the transport for the first three Crusades, and in return received her first important trading concessions in the Middle East. Arch-rival Genoa became increasingly envious, and in 1171 convinced the Byzantine Emperor to all but wipe out the Venetian merchants in Constantinople. Rashly, the Doge Vitale Michiel II set off in person to launch a revenge attack upon the Empire, and failed utterly, and on his return he was killed by an angry mob. The Venetians were always sore losers, but they learned from their mistakes: the Great Council, the Maggior Consiglio, was brought into being to check the power of the Doge and avert future calamities.

Vengeance stayed on the back-burner until the next Doge, the spry and crafty Enrico Dandolo, was contracted to provide transport for the Fourth Crusade. When the Crusaders turned up without their fare, Dandolo offered to forgo it in return for certain services: first, to reduce Venice's rebellious satellites in Dalmatia, and then, in 1204, to sail to Constantinople instead of Egypt. Aged 90 and almost blind, Dandolo personally led the attack; Christendom was scandalized, but Venice had gained, not only a glittering hoard of loot, but three-eighths of Constantinople and 'a quarter and a half' of the Roman Empire – enough islands and ports to control the trade routes in the Adriatic, Aegean, Asia Minor and the Black Sea.

To ensure their dominance at home, in 1297 the merchant élite limited membership in the Maggior Consiglio to themselves and their heirs (an event known in Venetian history as the Serrata, or Lock-out), their names inscribed in the famous *Golden Book*. The Doges were reduced to honorary chairmen of the board, bound up by an increasingly complex web of laws and customs to curb any possible ambitions; for the patricians, fear of revolution from above was as powerful as fear of revolt from below.

A Rocky 14th Century

First the people (1300) and then the snubbed patricians (the 1310 Tiepolo Conspiracy) rose up against their disenfranchisement under the Serrata. Both were unsuccessful, but the latter threat was serious enough that a committee of public safety was formed to hunt down the conspirators, and in 1335 this committee became a permanent institution, the infamous Council of Ten. Because of its secrecy and speedy decisions, the Council of Ten (in later years it was streamlined into a Council of Three) was more truly executive than the figurehead Doge: it guarded Venice's internal security, looked after foreign policy and, with its sumptuary laws, kept tabs on the Venetians' moral conduct as well.

Away from home the 14th century was marked by a fight to the death with Genoa over eastern trade routes. Each republic annihilated the other's fleet on more than one occasion before things came to a head in 1379, when the Genoese, fresh from a victory over the Venetian commander Vittor Pisani, captured Chioggia and waited for Venice to starve, boasting that they had come to 'bridle the horses of St Mark'. As was their custom, the Council of Ten had imprisoned Pisani for his defeat, but Venice was now in such a jam, with half of its fleet far away, that the people demanded his release to lead what remained of their navy. A brilliant commander, Pisani exploited his familiarity with the Lagoon and in turn blockaded the Genoese in Chioggia. When the other half of Venice's fleet came dramatically racing home, the Genoese surrendered (June 1380) and never recovered in the East.

Fresh Prey on the Mainland

Venice was determined never to feel hungry again, and set her sights on the mainland – not only for the sake of farmland, but to control her trade routes into the west that were being increasingly harried and taxed by the *signori* of the Veneto. Treviso came first, then opportunity knocked in 1402 with the sudden death of the Milanese duke Gian Galeazzo Visconti, whose conquests became the subject of a great land grab. Venice picked up Padua, Bassano, Verona and Belluno, and in 1454 added Ravenna, southern Trentino, Friuli, Crema and Bergamo. In 1489 the republic's overseas empire reached its greatest extent when it was presented with Cyprus, a somewhat reluctant 'gift' from the king's widow, a Venetian noblewoman named Caterina Cornaro who received the hilltown of Àsolo as compensation (*see* p.407).

But just as Venice expanded, Fortune's wheel gave a creak and conspired to squeeze her back into her Lagoon. The Ottoman Turks captured Constantinople in 1453, and although the Venetians tried to negotiate trading terms with the sultans (as they had previously done with the infidel Saracens, to the opprobrium of the West), they would be spending the next three centuries fighting a losing battle for their eastern territories. The discovery of the New World was another blow, but gravest to the merchants of Venice was Vasco da Gama's voyage around the Cape of Good Hope to India in 1497, blazing a cheaper and easier route to Venice's prime markets that broke her monopoly of oriental luxuries; Western European merchants no longer had to pay Venice for safe passage to the East. In just 44 years nearly everything that Venice had worked for over 500 years was undermined.

On the mainland, Venice's rapid expansion had excited the fear and envy of Pope Julius, who rallied Italy's potentates and their foreign allies to form the League of Cambrai to humble the proud republic. They snatched her *terra firma* possessions after her defeat at Agnadello in 1509, but quarrelled amongst themselves afterwards, and before long all the territories they conquered voluntarily returned to Venice. Venice, however, never really recovered from this wound inflicted by the very people who should have rallied to her defence, and although her Arsenal produced a warship a day, and her captains helped to win a glorious victory over the Turks at Lepanto (1571), she was increasingly forced to retreat.

A Most Leisurely Collapse

The odds were stacked against her, but in her heyday Venice had accumulated enough wealth and verve to cushion her fall. Her noble families consoled themselves in the classical calm of Palladio's villas, while the city found solace in masterpieces of Venice's golden age of art. Carnival, ever longer, ever more licentious, was sanctioned by the state to bring in moneyed visitors, like Lord Byron, who dubbed it 'the revel of the earth, the masque of Italy'. In the 1600s the city had 20,000 courtesans, many of them dressed as men to whet the Venetians' passion. It didn't suit everyone: 'Venice is a stink pot, charged with every virus of hell,' fumed one Dr Warner, in the 18th century.

In 1797, Napoleon, declaring he would be 'an Attila for the Venetian state', took it with scarcely a whimper, ending the story of the world's longest-enduring republic, in the reign of its 120th doge. Napoleon took the horses of St Mark to Paris as his trophy, and replaced the old *Pax tibi, Marce, Evangelista Meus* inscribed in the book the lion holds up on Venice's coat of arms with 'The Rights of Men and Citizens'. Reading it, a gondolier made the famous remark, 'At last he's turned the page'. Yet while many patricians danced merrily around his Liberty trees, freed at last from responsiblity, the people wept.

Napoleon gave Venice to Austria, whose rule was confirmed by the Congress of Vienna after the Emperor's defeat in 1815. The Austrians' main contribution was the railway causeway linking Venice irrevocably to the mainland (1846). Two years later, Venice gave its last gasp of independence, when a patriotic revolt led by Daniele Manin seized the city and re-established the republic, only to fall to the Austrian army once again after a heroic one-year siege.

Modern Venice

The former republic did, however, finally join the new kingdom of Italy in 1866, after Prussia had conveniently defeated the Austrians. Already better known as a magnet to visitors than for any activity of its own, Venice played a quiet role in the new state. Things changed under Mussolini, the industrial zones of Mestre and Marghera were begun on the mainland, and a road was added to the railway causeway. The city escaped damage in the two World Wars, despite heavy fighting in the environs; according to legend, when the Allies finally occupied Venice in 1945 they arrived in a fleet of gondolas.

But Venice was soon to engage in its own private battle with the sea. From the beginning the city had manipulated nature's waterways for her own survival, diverting a major outlet of the Po, the Brenta, the Piave, the Adige, and the Sile rivers to keep her Lagoon from silting up. In 1782, Venice completed the famous *murazzi*, the 4km-long, 20ft-high sea walls to protect the Lagoon. But on 4 November 1966 a deadly combination of wind, torrential storms, high tides and giant waves breached the *murazzi*, wrecked the Lido and left Venice under record *acque alte* (high waters) for 20 hours, with disastrous results to the city's architecture and art. The catastrophe galvanized the international community's efforts to save Venice. Even the Italian state, notorious for its indifference to Venice (historical grudges die slowly in Italy) passed a law in 1973 to preserve the city, and contributed to the construction of a new flood barricade similar to the one on the Thames.

This giant sea gate, known as 'Moses', has now been completed, but arguments continue over whether it will ever be effective if needed, and what its ecological consequences might be. Venice today is perennially in crisis, permanently under restoration, and seemingly threatened by a myriad potential disasters – the growth of algae in the Lagoon, the effects of the outpourings of Mestre on its foundations, the ageing of its native population, or perhaps most of all the sheer number of its tourists. Fears of an environmental catastrophe have, though, receded of late; somehow, the city contrives to survive, as unique as ever, and recent proposals to give it more of a function in the modern world, as, for example, a base for international organizations, may serve to give it new life as well.

Architecture

At once isolated but deeply linked to the traditions of East and West, Venice developed her own charmingly bastard architecture, especially in a style called Venetian Gothic, adopting only the most delightfully visual elements from each tradition. Ruskin's *The Stones of Venice* is the classic work on the city's buildings, which harsher critics – and Ruskin was one – disparage for being all artifice and show. The Venetians inherited the Byzantines' love of colour, mosaics, rare marbles and exotic effects, epitomized in the magnificently gaudy **St Mark's**. Venetian Gothic is only slightly less elaborate, and achieved its best products in the great palaces, most notably **Palazzo Ducale** and the **Ca' d'Oro**, with their ogival windows and finely wrought façades.

The Renaissance arrived in Venice relatively late, and its early phase is called Lombardesque, after the **Lombardo** family (Pietro and sons Tullio and Antonio) who designed the best of it, including **Santa Maria dei Miracoli** and the rich **Scuola di San Marco**. Later Renaissance architects brought Venice into the mainstream of the classical revival, and graced Venice with the arcaded **Piazza San Marco**, the **Libreria** of Sansovino, the **San Michele** of Mauro Codussi (or Coducci), and two of **Palladio's** finest churches. Venice's best Baroque works are by **Longhena**, the spiritual heir of Palladio.

To support all this on the soft mud banks, the Venetians drove piles of Istrian pine 16½ft into the solid clay – over a million posts hold up the church of Santa Maria della Salute alone. If Venice tends to lean and sink, it's due to erosion of these piles by the salty Adriatic, pollution, and the currents and wash caused by the deep channels dredged into the Lagoon for the large tankers sailing to Marghera. Or, as the Venetians explain, the city is a giant sponge. Most Venetian houses are four to six storeys high. On the tops of some you can see the wooden rooftop loggias, or *altane*, where the Renaissance ladies of Venice were wont to idle, bleaching their hair in the sun; they wore broad-brimmed hats to protect their complexions, and spread their tresses through a hole cut in the crown.

Venetian Art

Venice may have been a Renaissance Johnny-come-lately, but the city and its hinterland are rivalled only by Tuscany when it comes to first-notch painting. Before the 14th century the Venetians excelled primarily in mosaic, an art they learned from the Byzantines, shown at their very best in St Mark's and Torcello. In 1306 **Giotto** painted his masterpiece in Padua's Cappella Scrovegni and gave local painters a revolutionary eyeful. His naturalism influenced a school of artists in Padua and **Paolo Veneziano**, the first great Venetian painter of note, although many artists would continue painting decorative Gothic pieces for a long time to come, notably **Jacobello del Fiore**, **Michele Giambono** and the **Vivarini** family.

Things began to change in the mid 15th century, with the advent of two great masters. **Andrea Mantegna** (1431–1506), trained in Padua, influenced generations with his strong interests in antiquity, perspective and powerful sculptured figures. His more lyrical and humane brother-in-law, **Giovanni Bellini** (1440?–1516) founded the Venetian school. Bellini learned the technique of oil painting from **Antonello da**

Messina during his visit in 1475, and he never looked back: his use of luminous natural light and colour to create atmosphere ('tonalism') and sensuous beauty are characteristics all of his followers adopted – and not one of them equalled. Giovanni's brother, **Gentile Bellini**, and **Vittore Carpaccio** (1470–1523) avoided tonalism altogether in their charming and precise narrative works.

The Cinquecento–Settecento

For the heavy hitters of Venice's 16th-century Golden Age, however, tonalism was a religion: while other Italians followed the Romans in learning drawing and anatomy, the Venetians went their own way, obsessed by the dramatic qualities of atmosphere. The tragically short-lived **Giorgione of Castelfranco** (1475–1510) was the seminal figure in the new manner: his *Tempest* in the Accademia is a remarkable study in brooding tension. Giorgione also invented the genre of 'easel painting' – art that served neither Church nor State nor patron's vanity, but stood on its own for the delectation of the viewer.

Giorgione's colleague, Tiziano Vecellio, or **Titian** (1485/90–1576), was the greatest master of the Venetian school. Known for his bold, spiralling compositions, his rich colours and his luscious mythologies, he was a revolutionary in his old age, using increasingly free brushstrokes and even applying paint with his fingers.

Tintoretto (1518–94), of the quick brushstrokes, took his Mannerist compositions to unforgettable extremes, while his contemporary, **Paolo Veronese** (1528–88), painted lavish *trompe l'œil* canvases and frescoes that are the culmination of Venice at her most decorative. This was also the period of **Palma Vecchio**, the sensuous painter of Venetian blonde goddesses, **Cima da Conegliano**, author of some of the loveliest landscapes, and **Lorenzo Lotto**, of the famous psychologically penetrating portraits, who was run out of Venice by Titian and his buddies.

Venetia and its art enjoyed a revival in the twilight years of the 18th century, when its art was in great demand at home and abroad. Much of the thanks goes to **Giambattista Tiepolo** (1697–1770), the first to cast Baroque gloominess aside to create an effervescent, light-filled, brilliantly coloured style; he was also the last great frescopainter in Italy. His chief follower was his son Giandomenico, although his influence can also be seen in the luminous palettes of **Antonio Canaletto** (1697–1768) and **Francesco Guardi** (1712–93), who produced the countless views of Venice that were the rage among travellers on the Grand Tour; even now most of their works are in Britain and France. **Pietro Longhi**, their contemporary, devoted himself to genre scenes that offer a delightful insight into the Venice of 200 years ago.

Around the City

The Grand Canal

A ride down Venice's bustling and splendid main artery is most visitors' introduction to the city, and there's no finer one. The Grand Canal has always been Venice's status address, and along its looping banks the patricians of the Golden Book, or *Nobili*

Venice Transport

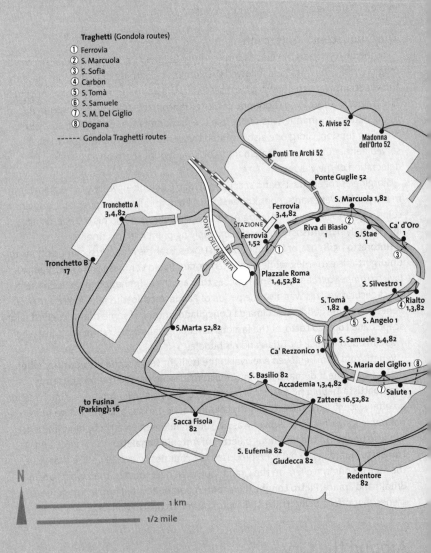

Traghetti (Gondola routes)
- ① Ferrovia
- ② S. Marcuola
- ③ S. Sofia
- ④ Carbon
- ⑤ S. Tomà
- ⑥ S. Samuele
- ⑦ S. M. Del Giglio
- ⑧ Dogana
- ------ Gondola Traghetti routes

S. Alvise 52

Madonna dell'Orto 52

Ponti Tre Archi 52

Ponte Guglie 52

S. Marcuola 1,82

Tronchetto A
3,4,82

PONTE DELLA LIBERTÀ

STAZIONE

Ferrovia
3,4,82

Riva di Biasio
1

② S. Stae
1

Ca' d'Oro
1

Ferrovia
1,52

①

Tronchetto B
17

Plazzale Roma
1,4,52,82

③

S. Silvestro 1

Rialto
1,3,82

S.Marta 52,82

S. Tomà
1,82

④

⑤ S. Angelo 1

⑥ S. Samuele 3,4,82

Ca' Rezzonico 1

S. Basilio 82

Accademia 1,3,4,82

S. Maria del Giglio 1 ⑧

⑦ Salute 1

to Fusina
(Parking): 16

Zattere 16,52,82

Sacca Fisola
82

S. Eufemia 82

Giudecca 82

Redentore
82

N

1 km

1/2 mile

Regular Lines

1: (*accelerato*) Piazzale Roma–Ferrovia–Grand Canal–San Marco–Lido: stops every where; around the clock, every 10min (20mins after 9pm). The entire one-way journey takes an hour.

6: (*diretto motonave*) S. Zaccaria–Lido; every 20mins.

11: (the 'mixed' line) Lido–Alberoni (by bus)–Pellestrina (by boat)–Chioggia (by boat); about once an hour. (Not shown.)

12: Fondamente Nuove–Murano–Torcello–Burano–Treporti; about once an hour.

13: Fondamente Nuove–Murano–Vignole–S. Erasmo; about once an hour.

14: S. Zaccaria–Lido–Punta Sabbioni–Treporti–Burano–Torcello (every half-hour).

17: (car ferry) Tronchetto (Piazzale Roma)–Giudecca–Lido–Punta Sabbione; every 50mins.

52: (green) (*motoscafo*) Lido–S. Zaccaria–Zattere–Piazzale Roma–Ferrovia–Fondamente Nuove–Murano; every 20mins.

82: (orange) (*diretto*) S. Zaccaria (S. Marco)–Lido–Giudecca–S. Giorgio Maggiore; every 10min during the day, approx. once an hour at night.

N: (*servizio notturno*) Lido–S. Zaccaria–Accademia–S. Toma–Rialto–Piazzale Roma–Zattere–Zitelle–S. Giorgio Maggiore; every 20mins from about 11pm all night.

Summer only

3: Tronchetto–Grand Canal–S. Zaccaria–Tronchetto

4: S. Zaccaria–Grand Canal–Tronchetto–S. Zaccaria

16: (private service L8,000) Zattere–Fusina car park; every 50mins.

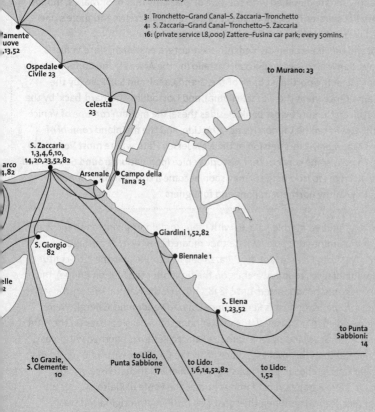

to Murano: 12,13,
to Mazzorbo, Burano,
Murano,Burano,Torcello: 12
to Vignole, S. Erasmo,
Treporti: 13

S. Michele
(Cimitero)
23, 52

'amente
uove
,13,52

Ospedale
Civile 23

to Murano: 23

Celestia
23

S. Zaccaria
1,3,4,6,10,
14,20,23,52,82

arco
1,82

Arsenale ● Campo della
1   Tana 23

S. Giorgio
82

elle
2

Giardini 1,52,82

Biennale 1

S. Elena
1,23,52

to Punta
Sabbioni:
14

to Grazie,
S. Clemente:
10

to Lido,
Punta Sabbione
17

to Lido:
1,6,14,52,82

to Lido:
1,52

The Face of Venice

Venice stands on 117 islets, divided by over 100 canals that are spanned by some 400 bridges. The longest bridges are the 4.2km rail and road causeways that link Venice to the mainland. The open sea is half that distance across the Lagoon, beyond the protective reefs or *lidi* formed by centuries of river silt and the Adriatic current. The Grand Canal, Venice's incomparable main street, was originally the bed of a river that fed the Lagoon; the other canals, its tributaries (called *rio*, singular, or *rii*, plural), were shallow channels meandering through the mud banks, and are nowhere as grand – some are merely glorified sewers.

A warren of 2,300 alleys, or *calli*, handle Venice's pedestrian-only traffic, and they come with a colourful bouquet of names – a *rio terrà* is a filled-in canal; a *piscina* a filled-in pool; a *fondamenta* or *riva* a quay; a *salizzada* is a street that was paved in the 17th century; a *ruga* is one lined with shops; a *sottoportico* passes under a building. A Venetian square is a *campo*, recalling the days when they were open fields; the only square dignified with the title of 'piazza' is that of St Mark's, though the two smaller squares flanking the basilica are called *piazzette*, and there's one fume-filled *piazzale*, the dead end for buses and cars.

All the *rii* and *calli* have been divided into six quarters, or *sestieri*, since Venice's earliest days: San Marco (by the piazza), Castello (by the Arsenal) and Cannaregio (by the Ghetto), all on the northeast bank of the Grand Canal; and San Polo (by the church), Santa Croce (near the Piazzale Roma), and Dorsoduro, the 'hard-back' by the Accademia, all on the southwest bank. Besides these, the modern *comune* of Venice includes the towns on the Lagoon islands, the Lido, and the mainland *comuni* of Mestre and Marghera, Italy's version of the New Jersey Flats, where most Venetians live today. There is some concern that historic Venice (population around 60,000 and falling, down from 170,000 in 1946) may soon become a city of second homes belonging to wealthy northern Italians and foreigners.

Homini, built a hundred marble palaces with their front doors giving on to the water, framed by peppermint-stick posts where they moored their watery carriages.

The highlights, from Piazzale Roma to Piazza San Marco, include: the 12th-century **Fontego dei Turchi** (with rounded arches, on the right after the Station Bridge), the Ottoman merchants' headquarters until 1838, and now the Natural History Museum. Nearly opposite, Mauro Codussi's Renaissance **Palazzo Vendramin-Calergi**, where Richard Wagner died in 1883, is now the winter home of the casino. Back on the right bank, after the San Stae landing, the Baroque **Palazzo Pésaro** is adorned with masks by Longhena. And then the loveliest palace of all, the **Ca' d'Oro**, with a florid Venetian Gothic facade, once etched in gold, housing the Galleria Franchetti (*see* p.383).

After the Ca' d'Oro Europe's most famous bridge, the **Ponte di Rialto**, swings into view. 'Rialto' recalls the days when the canal was the Rio Alto; originally it was spanned here by a bridge of boats, then by a 13th-century wooden bridge. When that was on the verge of collapse, the republic held a competition for the design of a new stone structure. The winner, Antonio da Ponte, was the most audacious, proposing a single arch spanning 157ft; built in 1592, it has defied all the dire predictions of the day and still stands, even taking the additional weight of two rows of shops. The reliefs over the arch are of St Mark and St Theodore.

To the right stretch the extensive **Rialto Markets**, and on the left the **Fóndaco dei Tedeschi** (German Warehouse), once the busiest trading centre in Venice, where merchants from all over the north lived and traded. The building (now the post office) was remodelled in 1505 and adorned with exterior frescoes by Giorgione and Titian, of which only fragments survive (now in the Ca' d'Oro).

Beyond the Ponte di Rialto are two Renaissance masterpieces: across from the S. Silvestro landing, Sanmicheli's 1556 **Palazzo Grimani**, now the Appeals Court, and Mauro Codussi's **Palazzo Corner-Spinelli** (1510) just before Sant'Angelo landing stage. A short distance further along the left bank are the **Palazzi Mocenigo**, actually three palaces in one, where Byron lived for two years. A little way further on the same side, the wall of buildings gives way for the Campo San Samuele, dominated by the **Palazzo Grassi,** an 18th-century neoclassical residence, renovated by Fiat as a modern exhibition and cultural centre.

On the right bank, just after the bend in the canal, the lovely Gothic **Ca' Foscari** was built in 1437 for Doge Francesco Foscari: two doors down, by its own landing-stage, is Longhena's 1667 **Ca' Rezzonico**, where Browning died. Further on the canal is spanned by the wooden **Ponte dell'Accademia**, built in 1932 to replace the ungainly iron 'English bridge'. On the left bank, before S. Maria del Giglio landing, the majestic Renaissance **Palazzo Corner** (Ca' Grande) was built by Sansovino in 1550.

On the right bank, Longhena's Baroque masterpiece **Santa Maria della Salute** is followed by the Customs House, or **Dogana di Mare**, crowned by a golden globe and weathervane of Fortune, guarding the entrance to the Grand Canal. The next landing-stage is S. Marco.

Signs, Directions, Piles and Hair

The Venetian language, Venetic or Venet, is still commonly heard – to the uninitiated it sounds like an Italian trying to speak Spanish with a numb mouth – and it turns up on the city's street signs. Your map may read 'San Giovanni e Paolo' but you should inquire for 'San Zanipolo'; 'San Giovanni Decollato' (decapitated John) is better known as 'San Zan Degola'.

Still, despite the impossibility of giving comprehensible directions through the tangle of alleys (Venetians will invariably point you in the right direction, however, with a blithe *sempre diritto!* – straight ahead!), it's hard to get hopelessly lost in Venice. It only measures about 1.5 by 3 kilometres, and there are helpful yellow signs at major crossings, pointing the way to San Marco, Rialto and the Accademia, or the Piazzale Roma and the Ferrovia if you despair and want to go home.

When hunting for an address in Venice, make sure you're in the correct *sestiere*, as quite a few *calli* share names. Also, beware that houses in each *sestiere* are numbered consecutively in a system logical only to a postman from Mars; numbers up to 5,000 are not unusual.

Piazza San Marco

Venice's self-proclaimed Attila, Napoleon himself, described this asymmetrical showpiece as 'Europe's finest drawing-room', and no matter how often you've seen it in pictures or in the flesh, its charm never fades. There are Venetians (and not all of them purveyors of souvenirs) who prefer it in the height of summer at its liveliest, when Babylonians from the four corners of the earth outnumber even the pigeons, who swoop back and forth at eye level, while the rival café bands provide a Fellini-esque accompaniment. Others prefer it in the misty moonlight, when the familiar seems unreal under hazy, rosy streetlamps.

The piazza and its two flanking *piazzette* have looked essentially the same since 1810, when the 'Ala Napoleonica' was added to the west end, to close in Mauro Codussi's long, arcaded **Procuratie Vecchie** (1499) on the north side and Sansovino's **Procuratie Nuove** (1540) on the south. Both, originally used as the offices of the 'procurators' or caretakers of St Mark's, are now filled with jewellery, embroidery and lace shops. Two centuries ago they contained an equal number of coffee-houses, the centres of the 18th-century promenade. Only two survive – the **Caffè Quadri** in the Procuratie Vecchie, the old favourite of the Austrians, and **Florian's**, in the Procuratie Nuove, its hand-painted décor unchanged since it opened its doors in 1720, although with espresso at L7,000 a head the proprietors could afford to remodel it in solid gold.

St Mark's Basilica

Open to visitors Mon–Sat 10–5, Sun and hols 1–5. No shorts, women must have their shoulders covered and a minimum of décolletage, or risk being peremptorily dismissed from the head of the queue, which can be diabolically long in season. There are separate admission charges for many of the smaller chapels and individual attractions; different sections are frequently closed for restoration. There is disabled ramp access from Piazzetta dei Leoncini.

This is nothing less than the holy shrine of the Venetian state. An ancient law decreed that all merchants trading in the East had to bring back from each voyage a new embellishment for St Mark's. The result is a glittering robbers' den, the only church in Christendom that would not look out of place in Xanadu. Until 1807, when it became Venice's cathedral, the basilica was the private chapel of the doge, built to house the relics of St Mark after their 'pious theft' in 828, a deed sanctioned by a tidy piece of apocrypha that had the good Evangelist mooring his ship on the Rialto on the way from Aquileia to Rome, when an angel hailed him with the famous '*Pax tibi...*' or 'Peace to you, Mark, my Evangelist. Here your body shall lie.'

The present structure, consecrated in 1094, was begun after a fire destroyed the original St Mark's in 976. Modelled after Constantinople's former Church of the Apostles, five rounded doorways, five upper arches and five round Byzantine domes are the essentials of the exterior, all frosted with a sheen of coloured marbles, ancient columns and sculpture ('As if in ecstasy,' wrote Ruskin, 'the crests of the arches break into marbly foam...'). The spandrils of the arches glitter with gaudy, Technicolor mosaics – the High Renaissance, dissatisfied with the 13th-century originals, saw fit to commission new painterly scenes, leaving intact only the *Translation of the Body of St Mark* on the extreme left, which includes the first historical depiction of the basilica itself. The three bands of 13th-century **reliefs** around the central portal, among Italy's finest Romanesque carvings, show Venetian trades, the Labours of the Months, and Chaos in the inner band.

Front and centre, seemingly ready to prance off the façade, the controversial 1979 copies of the bronze **horses of St Mark** masquerade well enough – from a distance. The ancient originals (cast some time between the 3rd century BC and 2nd century AD, and now inside the basilica's Museo Marciano) were one of the most powerful symbols of the Venetian Republic. Originally a 'triumphal quadriga' taken by Constantine the Great from Chios to grace the Hippodrome of his new city, it was carried off in turn by the artful Doge Dandolo in the 1204 Sack of Constantinople. Another prize from Byzantium are the four porphyry 'Moors' huddled in the corner of the south façade near the Doge's Palace; according to legend, they were changed into stone for daring to break into St Mark's treasury, though scholars prefer to believe that they are four chummy 3rd-century Roman Emperors, the Tetrarchs.

The Interior

The best mosaics, most of them from the 13th-century, cover the six domes of the **atrium**, or narthex, their old gold glimmering in the permanent twilight. The oldest mosaic in St Mark's is that of the *Madonna and Saints* above the central door, a survivor of the original 11th-century decoration of the basilica. A slab of red marble in the pavement marks the spot where the Emperor Barbarossa knelt and apologized to 'St Peter and his pope'– Alexander III, in 1177. This, a favourite subject of Venetian state art, is one of the few gold stars the republic ever earned with the papacy; mistrust and acrimony were far more common.

The interior, in the form of a Greek cross, dazzles the eye with the intricate splendour of a thousand details. The domes and upper vaults are adorned with golden mosaics on New Testament subjects, the oldest dating back to the 1090s, though there have been several restorations since. Ancient columns of rare marbles, alabaster, porphyry and verdantique, sawn into slices of rich colour, line the lower walls; the 12th-century pavement is a magnificent geometric mosaic of marble, glass and porphyry. Like a mosque, the nave is partially covered with carpets.

The first door on the right leads to the 14th-century **baptistry**, much beloved by John Ruskin and famous for its mosaics on the life of John the Baptist, with a lovely Salome in red who could probably have had just as many heads as she pleased. (*The baptistry is no longer open to the general public, but you can get in by asking one of the caretakers who will take you to the 'Ufficio Technico'. From there, you will be given a private tour*). Attached to the baptistry, the **Cappella Zen** was designed by Tullio Lombardo in 1504 to house the tomb of one Cardinal Zen, who had left a fortune to the Republic on condition he be buried in St Mark's. Further along the right transept you can visit the **treasury** (*open winter Mon–Sat 9.45–4, Sun 2–4, open until 5 in summer; adm*), containing the loot from Constantinople that Napoleon overlooked:

1 *Translation of the Body of St Mark* (1270)

2 *Venice Venerating the Relics of St Mark* (1718)

3 Central door, with magnificent 13th-century carvings in arches

4 *Venice Welcoming the Relics of St Mark* (1700s)

5 *Removal of St Mark's Relics from Alexandria* (1700s)

6 Pietra del Bando, stone from which the Signoria's decrees were read

7 *Scenes from the Book of Genesis* (1200) and 6th-century Byzantine door of S. Clemente

8 *Noah and the Flood* (1200s), tomb of Doge Vitale Falier (d. 1096)

9 *Madonna and Saints* (1060s); red marble slab where Emperor Barbarossa submitted to Pope Alexander III (1177); stair up to the Loggia and Museo Marciano

10 *Death of Noah and the Tower of Babel* (1200s)

11 *Story of Abraham* (1230s)

12 *Story of SS. Alipius and Simon, and Justice* (1200s)

14 Tomb of Doge Bartolomeo Gradenigo (d. 1342)

15 *Story of Joseph*, remade in 19th century

16 Porta dei Fiori (1200s); Manzù's bust of Pope John XXIII

17 *Christ with the Virgin and St Mark* (13th century, over the door)

18 Pentecost Dome (the earliest, 12th century)

19 On the wall: *Agony in the Garden* and *Madonna and Prophets* (13th century)

20 Baptistry, *Life of St John the Baptist* (14th century) and tomb of Doge Andrea Dandolo

21 Cappella Zen, by Tullio and Antonio Lombardo (1504–22)

22 On the wall: *Christ and Prophets* (13th century)

23 In arch: *Scenes of the Passion* (12th century)

24 Central Dome, the *Ascension* (12th century)

25 Tabernacle of the Madonna of the Kiss (12th century)

26 On wall: *Rediscovery of the Body of St Mark* (13th century)

27 Treasury

28 Dome of S. Leonardo; Gothic rose window (15th century)

29 In arch, *Scenes from the Life of Christ* (12th century)

30 Altar of the Sacrament; pilaster where St Mark's body was rediscovered, marked by marbles

31 Altar of St James (1462)

32 Pulpit where newly elected doge was shown to the people; entrance to the sanctuary

33 Rood screen (1394) by Jacopo di Marco Benato and Jacobello and Pier Paolo Dalle Masegne

34 Singing Gallery and Cappella di S. Lorenzo, sculptures by the Dalle Masegnes (14th century)

35 Dome, *Prophets Foretell the Religion of Christ* (12th century); baldaquin, with Eastern alabaster columns (6th century?)

36 Pala d'Oro (10th–14th century)

37 Sacristy door, with reliefs by Sansovino (16th century)

38 Sacristy, with mosaics by Titian and Padovanino (16th century) and Church of St Theodore (15th century), once seat of the Inquisition, and now part of the sacristy: both are rarely open

39 Singing Gallery and Cappella di S. Pietro (14th century): note the Byzantine capitals

40 Two medieval pulpits stacked together

41 *Miracles of Christ* (16th century)

42 Dome, with *Life of St John the Evangelist* (12th century)

43 Cappella della Madonna di Nicopeia (miraculous 12th-century icon)

44 Cappella di S. Isidoro (14th-century mosaics and tomb of the Saint)

45 Cappella della Madonna dei Máscoli: *Life of the Virgin* by Andrea del Castagno, Michele Giambono, Jacopo Bellini

46 On wall: *Life of the Virgin* (13th century)

47 Finely carved Greek marble stoup (12th century)

48 *Virgin of the Gun* (13th century – rifle ex-voto from 1850s)

49 Il Capitello, altar topped with rare marble ciborium, with miraculous Byzantine Crucifixion panel

St Mark's Basilica

Note how crooked it is!
In the Middle Ages symmetry was
synonymous with death.

Captions in *italics* refer to mosaics.

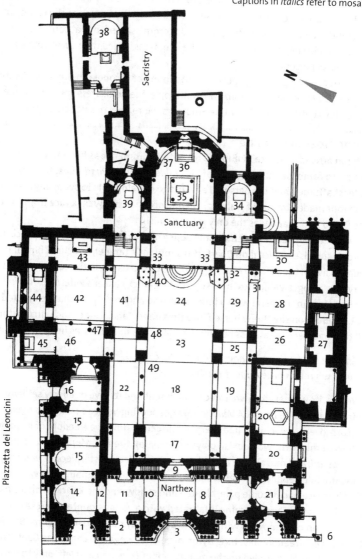

golden bowls and crystal goblets studded with huge coloured gems, straight from the cavern of Ali Baba. Near the Altar of the Sacrament, at the end of the right transept, a lamp burns 'eternally' next to one pillar: after the 976 fire, the body of St Mark was lost, but in 1094 (after Bari had beaten Venice to the relics of St Nicolaus) the good Evangelist staged a miraculous reappearance, popping his hand out of the pillar during Mass. St Mark is now safely in place in a crypt under the high altar, in the **sanctuary** (*open 9.45–5; adm*). You can't visit his relics, but you can see the altar's retable, the fabulous, glowing **Pala d'Oro**, a masterpiece of medieval gold and jewel work. The upper section may originally have been in the Church of the Pantocrator in Constantinople, and the lower section was commissioned in that same city by Doge Pietro Orseolo I in 976. Over the years the Venetians added their own scenes, and the Pala took its present form in 1345.

In the left transept, the **Chapel of the Madonna of Nicopeia** shelters a venerated 10th-century icon hijacked from Constantinople, the *Protectress of Venice*, formerly carried into battle by the Byzantine Emperors. More fine mosaics are further to the

Byron Goes Swimming

Byron arrived in Venice in 1816, his heart full of romance as he rented a villa on the Brenta to compose the last canto of his *Childe Harolde's Pilgrimage*. The city's canals at least afforded him the personal advantage of being able to swim anywhere (his club foot made him shy of walking); on one occasion he swam a race from the Lido to the Rialto bridge and was the only man to finish.

It wasn't long before the emotional polish of *Childe Harolde* began to crack. To Byron's surprise, Venice didn't perfect his romantic temper, but cured him of it. He went to live in the Palazzo Mocenigo on the Grand Canal, in the company of 14 servants, a dog, a wolf, a fox, monkeys and a garlicky baker's wife, *La Fornarina*, who stabbed him in the hand with a fork – which so angered Byron that he ordered her out, whereupon she threw herself into the Grand Canal. Under such circumstances, all that had been breathless passion reeked of the ridiculous, as he himself admitted:

And the sad truth which hovers o'er my desk
Turns what was once romantic to burlesque

Venice, its women, its own ironic detachment and its love of liberty set Byron's mind free to write *Beppo: A Venetian Story*, spoofing Venice's *cavalieri serventi* (escort-lovers – even nuns had them) while celebrating the freedom of its people. He followed this with two bookish plays on Venetian themes, *Marino Faliero* and *The Two Foscari*, and most importantly began his satirical masterpiece, *Don Juan*.

Meanwhile debauchery was taking its toll: an English acquaintance wrote in 1818 that 'His face had become pale, bloated and sallow, and the knuckles on his hands were lost in fat'. Byron became infatuated with a young Countess, Teresa Guiccioli, and left Venice to move in with her and her elderly husband in Ravenna. But, having tasted every freedom in Venice, Byron once more began to chafe; the Contessa was 'taming' him. He bundled up the manuscript of *Don Juan* and left, only to die of fever at the age of 36 in the Greek War of Independence.

left in the Chapel of St Isidore (the Venetian bodysnatchers kidnapped his relics from Chios – and in the mosaic he seems happy to go, grinning like a chimp). In the **Chapel of the Madonna dei Máscoli**, the mosaics on the *Life of the Virgin* by Tuscan Andrea Castagno and Michele Giambono (1453) were among the first harbingers of the Renaissance in Venice.

Before leaving, climb the steep stone stair near the west door of the narthex, to the **Museo Marciano, Galleria and Loggia dei Cavalli** (*open summer 9.45–5, winter 9.45–4; adm*) for a closer look at the dome mosaics from the women's gallery and a visit to the loggia, where you can inspect the replica horses and compare them with the excellently restored, gilded, almost alive originals in the museum.

The Campanile

Open summer 9–7.30; winter 9.30–3.30; adm.

St Mark's bell tower, to those uninitiated in the cult of Venice, seems like an alien presence, a Presbyterian brick sentinel in the otherwise delicately wrought piazza. But it has always been there, at least since 912; it was last altered in 1515, and when it gently collapsed into a pile of rubble on 14 July 1902 (the only casualty a cat) the Venetians felt its lack so acutely that they began to construct an exact replica, only a few hundred tons lighter and stronger, completed in 1912. It is 332ft tall, and you can take the lift up for a bird's-eye vision of Venice and its Lagoon; from up here the city seems amazingly compact. Though you have to pay for the view, misbehaving priests had it for free; the Council of Ten would suspend them in cages from the windows. Under the campanile, Sansovino's elegant **loggetta** adds a graceful note to the brick belfry. Its marbles and sculptures glorifying Venice took it on the nose when the campanile fell on top of them, but they have been carefully restored.

Piazzetta San Marco

To the south of the basilica, the Piazzetta San Marco was the republic's foyer, where ships would dock under the watchful eye of the doge. The view towards the Lagoon is framed by two tall Egyptian granite **columns**, trophies brought to Venice in the 1170s. The Venetians had a knack for converting their booty into self-serving symbols: atop one of the columns several Roman statues were pieced together to form their first patron saint, St Theodore with his crocodile (or dragon, or fish), while on the other stands an ancient Assyrian or Persian winged lion, under whose paw the Venetians slid a book, creating their symbol of St Mark.

Opposite the Doges' Palace stands the **Biblioteca** (*entry via Correr Museum*), built in 1536 by Sansovino and considered by Palladio to be the most beautiful building since antiquity, especially notable for the play of light and shadow in its sculpted arcades. Sansovino, trained as a sculptor, was notorious for paying scant attention to architectural details, and the library was scarcely completed when its ceiling collapsed. The goof-up cost him a trip to the Council of Ten's slammer, and he was only released on the pleading of Titian. Scholars with permission from the director can examine such treasures as the 1501 *Grimani breviary*, a masterwork of Flemish illuminators, Homeric *codices*, the 1459 world map of Fra Mauro, and Marco Polo's will. But not the famous library Petrarch willed to the Republic – the Venetians misplaced it.

Next to the library, at No.17, Venice's **Archaeology Museum** (*entry via Correr Museum*) is one of the few museums in the city heated in the winter. It has an excellent collection of Greek sculpture, including a violent *Leda and the Swan* and ancient copies of the famous *Gallic Warriors of Pergamon*, all given to the city by collector Cardinal Grimani in 1523. On the other side of the Libreria, by the waterfront, is another fine building by Sansovino, the 1547 **Zecca**, or Old Mint, which once stamped out thousands of gold *zecchini*, and gave English a new word: 'sequin'.

The Palace of the Doges (Palazzo Ducale)

Open 15 April–Oct 9–7; winter 9-5; other months somewhere in between; adm exp – includes entry to the Museo Correr. Ticket office (closes 5.30 summer, 3.30 winter) through Porta della Carta and in the courtyard.

What St Mark's is to sacred architecture, the **Doges' Palace** is to the secular – unique and audacious, dreamlike in a half-light, an illuminated storybook of Venetian history and legend. Like the basilica, it was founded shortly after the city's consolidation on the Rialto, though it didn't begin to take its present form until 1309 – with its delicate lower colonnade, its loggia of lacy Gothic tracery, and the massive top-heavy upper floor, like a cake held up by its own frosting. Its weight is partly relieved by the diamond pattern of white Istrian stone and red Verona marble on the façade, which from a distance gives the palace its wholesome peaches-and-cream complexion. Less benign are the two reddish pillars in the loggia (on the Piazzetta façade) said to have been dyed by the blood of Venice's enemies, whose tortured corpses were strung out between them.

Some of Italy's finest medieval sculpture crowns the 36 columns of the lower colonnade, depicting a few sacred and many profane subjects – animals, guildsmen, Turks, and Venetians. Beautiful sculptural groups adorn the corners, most notably the 13th-century *Judgement of Solomon*, near the palace's grand entrance, the 1443 **Porta della Carta** (Paper Door), a Gothic symphony in stone by Giovanni and Bartolomeo Bon.

Fires in 1574 and 1577 destroyed much of the palace, and at the time there were serious plans afoot to knock it down and let Palladio start again *à la* Renaissance. Fortunately, however, you can't teach an old doge new tricks, and the palace was rebuilt as it was, with Renaissance touches in the interior. Just within the Porta della Carta, don't miss Antonio Rizzo's delightful arcaded courtyard and his finely sculpted grand stairway, the **Scala dei Giganti**, named for its two Gargantuan statues of *Neptune* and *Mars* by Sansovino.

Visitors enter the palace via another grand stairway, Sansovino's **Scala d'Oro**. The first floor, once the private apartments of the doge, is now used for frequent special exhibitions (*separate adm*), while the golden stairway continues up to the *Secondo Piano Nobile*, from where the Venetian state was governed. After the fire that destroyed its great 15th-century frescoes, Veronese and Tintoretto were employed to paint the newly remodelled chambers with mythological themes and scores of allegories and apotheoses of Venice – a smug, fleshy blonde in the eyes of these two.

A Doge's Life: Gormenghast with Canals

Senator in Senate, Citizen in City were his titles, as well as Prince of Clothes, with a wardrobe of gold and silver damask robes, and scarlet silks. Once the Doge was dressed, the rest of his procession would fall in line, including all the paraphernalia of Byzantine royalty: a naked sword, six silver trumpets, a damask parasol, a chair, cushion, candle and eight standards bearing the Lion of St Mark in four colours symbolizing peace, war, truth and loyalty. Yet for all the pomp this was the only man in Venice not permitted to send a private note to his wife, or receive one from her, or from anyone else; nor could he accept any gift beyond flowers or rose-water, or go to a café or theatre, or engage in any money-making activity, while nevertheless having to meet the expenses of his office out of his own pocket. Nor could he abdicate, unless requested to do so.

The office was respected, but often not the man. When a Doge died he was privately buried in his family tomb before the state funeral – which used a dummy corpse with a wax mask. First, an 'Inquisition of the Defunct Doge' was held over the dummy, to discover if the Doge had kept to his *Promissione* (his oath of coronation), if his family owed the state any money, and if it was necessary to amend the *Promissione* to limit the powers of his successor still further. Then the dead Doge's dummy was taken to St Mark's to be hoisted in the air nine times by sailors, to the cry of '*Misericordia!*' (Mercy), and then given a funeral service at the church of Santi Giovanni e Paolo.

These paintings are the palace's chief glory, and signboards in each room identify them. Visiting ambassadors and other foreign official guests would be required to wait in the first room, the **Anticollegio**, so the frescoes (Tintoretto's *Bacchus and Ariadne* and Veronese's *Rape of Europa*) had to be especially impressive; in the next room, the **Sala del Collegio**, with several masterpieces by both artists, they would be presented to the hierarchy of the Venetian state.

Tintoretto's brush dominates in the **Sala del Senato** – less lavish, since only Venetians were admitted here – while the main work in the **Sala del Consiglio dei Dieci** is Veronese's ceiling, *Old Man in Eastern Costume with a Young Woman*. Under this the Council of Ten deliberated and pored over the accusations deposited in the *Bocche dei Leoni* – the lions' mouths spread over the Republic. To be considered, an accusation had to be signed and supported by two witnesses, and anyone found making a false accusation would suffer the punishment that would have been meted out to the accused had it been true. Next to the Ten's chamber, the old **Armoury** (Sala d'Armi) houses a fine collection of medieval and Renaissance arms and armour.

From here the visit continues downstairs, to the vast and magnificent **Sala del Maggior Consiglio**, built in 1340 and capable of holding the 2,500 patricians of the Great Council. At the entrance hangs Tintoretto's crowded, and recently restored, *Paradiso* – the biggest oil painting in the world (23 by 72ft), all the Blessed looking up at Veronese's magnificent *Apotheosis of Venice* on the ceiling. The frieze along the upper wall portrays the first 76 doges, except for the space that would have held the portrait of Marin Falier (1355) had he not led a conspiracy to take sole power; instead, a black veil bears a dry note that he was decapitated for treason. The portraits of the last 44 doges, each painted by a contemporary painter, continue around the **Sala dello Scrutinio**, where the votes for office were counted. Elections for doge were Byzantine and elaborate – and frequent; the Maggior Consiglio preferred to choose doges who were old, and wouldn't last long enough to gain a following.

At the end of the tour the **Bridge of Sighs** (*Ponte dei Sospiri*) takes you to the 17th-century **Palazzo delle Prigioni**, mostly used for petty offenders. Those to whom the Republic took real exception were dumped into uncomfortable *pozzi* (wells) in the lower part of the Palazzo Ducale, while celebrities like Casanova got to stay up in the *piombi* (leads) just under the roof.

The Secret Itinerary

In 1984 the section of the palace where the real nitty-gritty business of state took place, a maze of narrow corridors and tiny rooms, was restored and opened to the public. Because the rooms are so small the 1½-hour guided tour, the Itinerari Segreti ('Secret Itinerary'), is limited to 20 people, and the reason why it's not better known is that it has previously only been available in Italian, but is now available in French and English too (*mornings at 10 and 12; book at least a day in advance at the director's office on the first floor, or ring t 041 522 4951*).

The tour begins at the top of the Scala d'Oro, with the snug wood-panelled offices of the **Chancellery** and the 18th-century **Hall of the Chancellors**, lined with cupboards for holding treaties, each bearing the arms of a Chancellor. In the justice department is the **Torture Chamber**, where the three Signori della Notte dei Criminali (judges of the night criminals) would 'put to the question' anyone suspected of treason, hanging them by the wrists on a rope that is still in place. This ended in the early 1700s, when Venice, along with Tuscany, became one of the first states in Europe to pass a law abolishing torture.

Next is the ornate **Sala dei Tre Capi**, the chamber of the three magistrates of the Council of Ten, who had to be present at all state meetings. As this chamber might be visited by foreign dignitaries, it was lavishly decorated with works by Veronese, Antonello da Messina and Hieronymus Bosch. From here it's up to the notorious **Piombi**, which despite their evil reputation appear downright cosy, as prisons go. Casanova's cell is pointed out, and there's an elaborate explanation of his famous escape through a hole in the roof. Near the end of the tour comes one of Venice's marvels: the **attic of the Sala del Maggior Consiglio**, where you can see how the Arsenale's shipwrights made a vast ceiling float unsupported over the room below; built in 1577, it has yet to need any repairs.

San Marco to Rialto

The streets between the piazza and the market district of the Rialto are the busiest in Venice, especially the **Mercerie**, which begin under the clock tower and are lined with some of the city's smartest shops. It was down the Mercerie that Baiamonte Tiepolo, miffed at being excluded from the Golden Book, led his rebel aristocrats in 1310, when an old lady cried 'Death to tyrants!' from her window and hurled a brick at his standard-bearer, killing him on the spot, and causing such disarray that Tiepolo was forced to give up his attempted coup. It was a close call that the republic chose never to forget: the site, above the Sottoportego del Capello Nero, is marked by a stone relief of the heroine with her brick.

The Mercerie continue to the church of **San Zulian**, redesigned in 1553 by Sansovino, with a façade most notable for Sansovino's statue of its pompous and scholarly bene-factor, Tommaso Rangone. Sansovino also had a hand in **San Salvatore** in the next *campo*, adding the finishing touches to its noble Renaissance interior and designing the monument to Doge Francesco Venier. An 89-year-old Titian painted one of his more unusual works for this church, the *Annunciation*, which he signed with double emphasis *Titianus Fecit* – his patrons refused to believe that he had painted it.

Humming, bustling **Campo San Bartolomeo**, next on the Mercerie, has for centuries been one of the social hubs of Venice, and still gets packed with after-work crowds every evening. Its centre is graced by the **statue of Goldoni**, whose comedies in Venetian dialect still make the Venetians laugh; and by the look on his jolly face he still finds their antics amusing. Follow the crowds up to the **Ponte di Rialto** (*see* Grand Canal, p.364), the geographical heart of Venice, and the principal node of its pedes-trian and water traffic.

The city's central markets have been just across the bridge for a millennium, divided into sections for vegetables and for fish. Near the former you may pay your respects to Venice's oldest church, little **San Giacomo di Rialto**, founded perhaps as long ago as the 5th century and substantially reworked in 1071 and 1601. In the same *campo* stands a famous Venetian character, the 16th-century granite hunchback, **Gobbo di Rialto**, who supports a little stairway and marble podium from which the decrees of the Republic were proclaimed.

San Marco to the Accademia

Following the yellow signs 'To the Accademia' from the Piazza San Marco (starting by the tourist office), the first *campo* belongs to Baroque **San Moisè** (1668), Italy's most grotesque church, with a grimy opera-buffa façade, rockpile and altarpiece. For more opera and less buffa, take a detour up Calle Veste (the second right after Campo San Moisè) to monumental Campo San Fantin and **La Fenice** (1792), the Republic's last hurrah and one of Italy's most renowned opera houses, which saw the premieres of Verdi's *Rigoletto* and *La Traviata*. A fire set by a contractor during renovations ripped it apart in 1996, so expect to see a lot of scaffolding. Work on La Fenice will take another four years minimum. It has been held up by endless bureaucratic and political wran-glings, not to mention lack of money. Venice has a venerable musical tradition, albeit one that had become more tradition than music by the time of the era of grand opera – although Mozart's great librettist, Lorenzo da Ponte, was a Venetian.

Back en route to the Accademia, in the next campo stands **Santa Maria Zobenigo** (or del Giglio), on which the Barbaro family stuck a fancy Baroque façade in 1680, not for God but for the glory of the Barbari; the façade is famous for its total lack of religious significance. The signs lead next to the Campo Francesco Morosini, named after the doge who recaptured the Morea from the Turks, but who is remembered everywhere else as the man who blew the top off the Parthenon. Better known as **Campo Santo Stefano**, it's one of the most elegant squares in Venice, a pleasant place to sit outside at a café table – particularly at **Paolin**, Venice's best *gelateria*. At one end, built directly over a canal, the Gothic church of **Santo Stefano** has the most gravity-defying campanile of all the leaning towers in Venice (most alarmingly viewed from the adjacent Campo Sant'Angelo). The interior is worth a look for its striking wood ceiling, soaring like a ship's keel, as well as its wooden choir stalls (1488).

The Accademia

Open daily; hours vary slightly throughout the year; summer Tues–Sat 8.30am–7.30pm, Sun 9am–7pm, Mon 9–2; closed 1 May, 25 Dec and 1 Jan; adm exp, free for under-18s and over-60s if members of the EU. It's a good idea to get there early since only 300 visitors are allowed at a time.

Just over the bridge and Grand Canal from Campo Santo Stefano stands the Galleria dell'Accademia, the grand cathedral of Venetian art, ablaze with light and colour. The collection is arranged chronologically, beginning in the former refectory of the Scuola (**Room I**): among them, 14th-century altarpieces by Paolo and Lorenzo Veneziano, whose half-Byzantine Madonnas look like fashion models for Venetian silks. Later altarpieces fill **Room II**, most importantly Giovanni Bellini's *Pala di San Giobbe*, one of the key works of the quattrocento: the architecture repeats its original setting in the church of San Giobbe; on the left St Francis invites the viewer into a scene made time-less by the music of the angels at the Madonna's feet. Other beautiful altarpieces in the room are by Carpaccio, Basaiti, and Cima da Conegliano (the subtle *Madonna of the Orange Tree*).

The next rooms are small but, like gifts, contain the best things: Mantegna's confi-dently aloof *St George*, the little allegories and a trio of Madonnas by Giovanni Bellini (including the lovely, softly coloured *Madonna of the Little Trees*) and Piero della Francesca's *St Jerome and Devotee*, a youthful study in perspective. In **Room V** you will find Giorgione's *La Vecchia*, with the warning '*Col Tempo*' ('With Time') in her hand, and the mysterious *The Tempest*, two of the few paintings scholars accept as being indisputably by Big George, but how strange they are! It is said Giorgione invented easel painting for the pleasure of bored, purposeless courtiers in Caterina Cornaro's Àsolo (*see* p.407), but the paintings seem to reflect rather than lighten their *ennui*.

Highlights of the next few rooms include Lorenzo Lotto's *Gentleman in his Study*, which catches its sitter off-guard before he could clear the nervously scattered scraps of paper from his table, and Paris Bordenone's masterpiece, *Fisherman Presenting St Mark's Ring to the Doge* (1554) celebrating a miracle of St Mark.

The climax of the Venetian High Renaissance comes in **Room X**, with Veronese's *Christ in the House of Levi* (1573), set in a Palladian loggia with a ghostly white imagi-nary background, in violent contrast to the rollicking feast of Turks, hounds, midgets, Germans and the artist himself (in the front, next to the pillar on the left). The painting was originally titled *The Last Supper*, and fell foul of the Inquisition, which took umbrage (especially at the Germans). Veronese was cross-examined, and ordered to make pious changes at his own expense; the artist, in true Venetian style, saved himself both the trouble and the money by simply giving it the title by which it has been known ever since.

Room X also contains Veronese's fine *Annunciation*, and some early masterworks by Tintoretto – *Translation of the Body of St Mark*, and *St Mark Freeing a Slave*, in which the Evangelist, typically Tintoretto-esque, nosedives from the top of the canvas. The last great painting in the room was also the last ever by Titian, the sombre *La Pietà*, which he was working on when he died in 1576, aged about 90, from the plague; he intended it for his tomb, and smeared the paint on with his fingers.

Alongside several more Tintorettos, the following few rooms mainly contain work from the 17th and 18th centuries (Tiepolo, Sebatiano and Marco Ricci, Piazzetta, Longhi, Rosalba Carriera). Canaletto and Guardi, whose scenes of 18th-century Venice were the picture postcards of the British aristocracy on their Grand Tour, are represented in **Room XVII**.

The final rooms of the Accademia were formerly part of the elegantly Gothic church of Santa Maria della Carità, and house more luminous 15th-century painting by Alvise Vivarini, Giovanni and Gentile Bellini, Marco Basaiti and Crivelli. **Room XX** has a fascinating series depicting the *Miracles of the True Cross* with Venetian backgrounds, painted by Gentile Bellini, Carpaccio and others. **Room XXI** contains the dreamily compelling and utterly charming *Cycle of S. Ursula* by Carpaccio, from the former Scuola di Sant'Orsola. Finally, the last room, **Room XXIV**, the former *albergo* of the church, contains two fine paintings that were originally made for it: Titian's striking *Presentation of the Virgin* (1538) and a triptych by Antonio Vivarini and Giovanni d'Alemagna (1446).

Dorsoduro

The Accademia lies in the *sestiere* of Dorsoduro, which can also boast the second-most-visited art gallery in Venice, the **Peggy Guggenheim Collection** (*open Wed–Mon 10–6, Sat 10–10; adm exp*), just down the Grand Canal from the Accademia in her 18th-century Venetian Palazzo Venier dei Leoni. In her 30 years as a collector, until her death in 1979, Ms Guggenheim amassed an impressive quantity of brand-name 20th-century art – Bacon, Brancusi, Braque, Calder, Chagall, Dali, De Chirico, Duchamp, Dubuffet, Max Ernst (her second husband), Giacometti, Gris, Kandinsky, Klee, Magritte, Miró, Moore, Mondrian, Picasso, Pollock, Rothko and Smith. Administered by the Solomon R. Guggenheim Foundation in New York, the collection can come as a breath of fresh air after so much high Italian art, and also sponsors temporary exhibitions, even in winter; look out for posters.

From here it's a five-minute stroll down to the serene, octagonal basilica of **Santa Maria della Salute** 'of Health' (1631–81, *open Mon-Sat 10–5, Sun 1–5*), on the tip of Dorsoduro. One of five votive churches built after the passing of plagues (Venice, a busy international port, was particularly susceptible), La Salute is the masterpiece of Baldassare Longhena, its snow-white dome and marble jelly rolls dramatically set at the entrance of the Grand Canal. The interior is a relatively restrained white and grey Baroque, and the **sacristy** (*adm*) contains the *Marriage at Cana* by Tintoretto and several works by Titian, including his *St Mark Enthroned Between Saints*. Almost next to the basilica, on the point, stands the distinctive profile of the **Dogana di Mare**, the Customs House (*see* Grand Canal, p.365).

The **Fondamenta delle Zattere**, facing away from the city towards the freighter-filled canal and the island of Giudecca, leads around to the **Gesuati**, the only church in Venice decorated by Umbrian artists. For a more elaborate feast, take the long stroll along the Fondamenta (or take *vaporetto* Line 5 to San Basegio) to Veronese's parish church of **San Sebastiano** on Rio di San Basilio. Veronese, it is said, murdered a man in Verona and took refuge in this neighbourhood, and over the next 10 years he and his brother Benedetto Caliari embellished San Sebastiano – beginning in 1555 with the ceiling frescoes of the sacristy and ending with the magnificent ceiling, *The Story of Esther*, and illusionistic paintings in the choir (*the lights are always lit*).

From San Sebastiano you can head back towards the Grand Canal (Calle Avogaria and Calle Lunga S. Barnaba); turn left up Calle Pazienza to visit the 14th-century church of the **Carmini** with a landmark red campanile and lovely altars by Cima da Conegliano and Lorenzo Lotto. The **Scuola Grande dei Carmini** (*open Mon–Sat 9–6, Sun 9–4; adm; sometimes open for concerts*), next door, was designed by Longhena in the 1660s, and contains one of Tiepolo's best and brightest ceilings, *The Virgin in Glory*.

The Carmini is on the corner of the delightful **Campo Santa Margherita**. Traditionally the main marketplace of Dorsoduro, it's also a good spot to find relatively inexpensive pizzerias, restaurants and cafés that are not aimed primarily at tourists. It is also close to **Ca' Rezzonico** (Rio Terrà Canal down to the Fondamenta Rezzonico), home to the **Museo del Settecento Veneziano** (*currently closed*), Venice's attic of 18th-century art, with bittersweet paintings by Giandomenico Tiepolo, some wild rococo furniture by Andrea Brustolon, a pharmacy, genre scenes by Longhi (*The Lady and Hairdresser*), and a breathtaking view of the Grand Canal. The house was owned in the last century by Robert Browning's son Pen, and the poet died there in 1889. One of the palaces you see opposite belonged to Doge Cristoforo Moro, whom the Venetians claim Shakespeare used as his model for Othello, confusing the doge's name with his race.

San Polo and Santa Croce

From the Ponte di Rialto, follow the yellow signs to Piazzale Roma, passing the pretty **Campo** and church of **San Polo** (*open Mon–Sat 10–5, Sun 1–5; adm*), with Giandomenico Tiepolo's dramatic *Stations of the Cross* in the Oratory of the Crucifix. The signs next take you before a venerable Venetian institution: the huge brick Gothic church of the **Frari** (*open Mon–Sat 9–6, Sun and hols 1–6; adm*), one of the most severe medieval buildings in the city, built between 1330 and 1469. Monteverdi, one of the founding fathers of opera and choir director at St Mark's, is buried here, as is Titian, whose tomb follows the Italian rule – the greater the artist, the worse the tomb (see Michelangelo's in Florence). The strange pyramid with a half-open door was intended by Antonio Canova to be Titian's tomb, but it eventually became the sculptor's own last resting place. The Frari is celebrated for its great art, and especially for the most overrated painting in Italy, Titian's *Assumption of the Virgin* (1516–18), in the centre of the Monk's Choir. Marvel at the art, at Titian's revolutionary Mannerist use of space and movement, but its big-eyed, heaven-gazing Virgin has as much artistic vision as a Sunday school holy card.

That, however, is not true of Giovanni Bellini's *Triptych of Madonna with Child and Saints* in the sacristy, or Donatello's rustic statue of *St John the Baptist* in the choir chapel. In the north aisle Titian's less theatrical *Madonna di Ca' Pésaro* was modelled on his wife Celia; the painting had a greater influence on Venetian composition than the *Assumption*. Also note the beautiful Renaissance **Tomb of Doge Nicolò Tron** by Antonio Rizzo in the sanctuary, from 1476.

The Scuola di San Rocco

Next to the Frari, the **Scuola di San Rocco** (*open summer 9–5.30, winter 10–4; adm*) was one of Venice's most important *scuole*. San Rocco, renowned for his juju against the Black Death, was so popular among the Venetians that they stole his body from Montpelier and canonized him before the pope did. The *scuola* has a beautiful, lively façade by Scarpagnino, and inside it contains one of the wonders of Venice – or rather, 54 wonders – all painted by Tintoretto, who worked on the project from 1562 to 1585 without any assistance.

Tintoretto always managed to look at conventional subjects from a fresh point of view; while other artists of the High Renaissance composed their subjects with the epic vision of a Cecil B. de Mille, Tintoretto had the eye of a 16th-century Orson Welles, creating audacious, dynamic 'sets', often working out his compositions in his little box-stages, with wax figures and unusual lighting effects. In the *scuola*, especially in the upper floor, he was at the peak of his career, and painted what is considered by some to be the finest painting cycle in existence, culminating in the *Crucifixion*, where the event is the central drama of a busy human world. Vertigo is not an uncommon response – for an antidote, look at the funny carvings along the walls by Francesco Pianta. In the same room there are also several paintings on easels by Titian, and a *Christ* that some attribute to Titian, some to Giorgione.

Just north, beyond Campo San Stin, the **Scuola Grande di San Giovanni Evangelista** (*open on request, call t 041 718 234*) deserves a look for its beautiful Renaissance courtyard and double-ramp stairway (1498), Mauro Codussi's masterpiece, noted for the rhythms of its domes and barrel vaults.

From Campo San Stin, if you start along Calle Donà and keep as straight as possible, you should end up at Ca' Pésaro on the Grand Canal, a huge 17th-century pile by Longhena that is occupied by the **Galleria d'Arte Moderna** (*still closed*), with a collection principally of works exhibited in the Biennale exhibitions. Italian contemporary art, much of it unfamiliar to a foreign audience, is the mainstay, but some international figures are also represented, such as Gustav Klimt. Ca' Pésaro also houses a **Museum of Oriental Art** (*open daily 8.15–2; closed Mon; adm*), with a higgledy-piggledy collection of Asian artefacts collected in the last century. If you really want to escape the crowds, however, head further up the canal to the stuffed Lagoon fowl in the **Natural History Museum** (*closed for restoration at the time of writing; due to re-open spring 2002; call t 041 524 0885 to check*) in the Venetian-Byzantine **Fóndaco dei Turchi**.

San Marco to Castello

From Piazzetta San Marco, the gracefully curving, ever-thronging **Riva degli Schiavoni** took its name from the Slavs of Dalmatia; in 1782, Venice was doing so much business here that the quay had to be widened. A few steps beyond the Palazzo Ducale, one of the city's finest Gothic *palazzi* was converted in 1822 to the famous **Hotel Danieli**, its name a corruption of the 'Dandolo' family who built it. The quay also has a robust **Memorial to Vittorio Emanuele II** (1887) where two of Venice's over 10,000 lions shelter – as often as not with members of Venice's equally numerous if smaller feline population between their paws.

From Riva degli Schiavoni, the Sottoportico San Zaccaria leads back to the lovely Gothic-Renaissance **San Zaccaria** (*open Mon–Sat 10–12 and 4–6, Sun 4–6*), begun by Antonio Gambello in 1444 and completed by Mauro Codussi in 1515. Inside, look for Bellini's extraordinary *Madonna and Saints* in the second chapel to the right, and the refined Florentine frescoes by Andrea del Castagno in the chapel of San Tarasio. Another church, back on the Riva itself, **La Pietà**, served the girls' orphanage which the red-headed priest Vivaldi made famous during his years as its concert master and composer (1704–38). The church was rebuilt shortly afterwards by Giorgio Massari with a remarkable oval interior, in luscious cream and gold with G. B. Tiepolo's extravagant *Triumph of Faith* on top. It has particularly fine acoustics – Vivaldi helped design it – and is still frequently used for concerts.

Due north of La Pietà stands the city's Greek Orthodox church, the 16th-century **San Giorgio dei Greci**, with its tilting tower and *scuola*, now the **Museum of Byzantine Religious Painting** (*open Mon–Sat 9–12.30, 1.30–4.30, Sun 10–5; adm*). Run by the Hellenic Centre for Byzantine Studies, many of its icons were painted in the 16th and 17th centuries by artists who fled the Turkish occupation. In Venice the Greeks came into contact with the Renaissance; the resulting Venetian-Cretan school nourished, most famously, El Greco.

Close by, another ethnic minority, the Dalmatians – present in Venice almost throughout the history of the Republic – began their tiny **Scuola di San Giorgio degli Schiavoni** in 1451 (*open summer Wed–Sun 9.30–12.30; winter Tues–Sat 9.30–12.30, 3.30–6.30, Sun 9.30–12.30; adm*). Its minute interior is decorated with the most beloved art in all Venice: Vittore Carpaccio's frescoes on the lives of the Dalmatian patron saints – Augustine writing, watched by his patient little white dog; Jerome bringing his lion into the monastery, George charging a petticoat-munching dragon in a landscape strewn with maidenly leftovers from lunch, and more. Some of the greatest paintings by Carpaccio's more serious contemporaries, the Vivarini and Cima da Conegliano, hold pride of place in **San Giovanni in Brágora** (between San Giorgio degli Schiavoni and the Riva); the best work, Cima's *Baptism of Christ*, is in the sanctuary.

The Arsenale

From the Riva degli Schiavoni, the Fondamenta dell'Arsenale leads to the twin towers guarding the **Arsenale**. Founded in 1104, this first of all arsenals derived its name from the Venetian pronunciation of the Arabic *darsina'a*, or workshop, and up until the 17th century these were the greatest dockyards in the world, the very foundation of the Republic's wealth and power. In its heyday the Arsenale had a payroll of 16,000, and produced a ship a day to fight the Turks. Dante visited this great industrial complex twice and, as Blake would later do with his Dark Satanic Mills, found its imagery perfect for the *Inferno*.

Today the Arsenale is occupied by the Italian military, but you can look at the **Great Gateway** next to the towers, built in 1460 – almost entirely from marble trophies nicked from Greece. Among the chorus line of lions is an ancient beast that Doge Francesco Morosini found in Piraeus, with 11th-century runes carved in its back in the name of Harold Hardrada, the member of the Byzantine Emperor's Varangian Guard who was later crowned king of Norway. Other very innocent-looking lions, eroded into lambs, were taken from the island of Delos in 1718 when the Turks weren't looking.

Venice's glorious maritime history is the subject of the fascinating artefacts and models in the **Museo Storico Navale** (*open Mon–Fri 8.45–1.30, Sat 8.45–1, closed Sun and hols; adm*) – most dazzling of all is the model of the doge's barge, the *Bucintoro*. The museum is just past the gateway to the Arsenale, near the beginning of Via Garibaldi; in a neighbouring house lived two seafarers, originally from Genoa, who contributed more to the history of Britain than that of Venice, Giovanni and Sebastiano Caboto.

Via Garibaldi and Fondamenta S. Anna continue to the Isola di San Pietro, site of the unmemorable **San Pietro di Castello** (*open Mon–Sat 10–5, Sun 1–5; adm*), until 1807 Venice's cathedral, its lonely, distant site a comment on the Republic's attitude towards the papacy. The attractive, detached campanile is by Codussi, and inside there is a marble throne incorporating a Muslim tombstone with verses from the Koran, which for centuries was said to have been the Throne of St Peter in Antioch. To the south are the refreshing pines and planes of the **Public Gardens**, where the International Exhibition of Modern Art, or Biennale, takes place in even-numbered years in the artsy pavilions. This, and the **Parco delle Rimembranze** further on, were a gift to this sometimes claustrophobic city of stone and water by Napoleon, who knocked down four extraneous churches to plant the trees. From here you can take Line 1 or 2 back to San Marco, or to the Lido.

San Marco to Santi Giovanni e Paolo

The *calli* that lead from the Piazzetta dei Leoncini around the back of San Marco and over the Rio di Palazzo will take you to the Romanesque cloister of Sant'Apollonia and one of Venice's newest museums, the **Museo Diocesano** (*open Mon–Sat 10.30–12.30*), containing an exceptional collection of trappings and art salvaged from the city's churches. Through a web of alleys to the north there's more art in the 16th-century Palazzo Querini-Stampalia, home of the **Fondazione Querini-Stampalia** (*open Tues, Wed, Thurs and Sun 10–1 and 3–6, Fri and Sat 10–1 and 3–10; closed Mon; adm exp*), which has an endearing assortment of genre paintings – scenes of 18th-century Venetian convents, dinner parties, music lessons, etc. by Pietro Longhi and Gabriel Bella, as well as works by Bellini, Palma il Vecchio, Vincenzo Catena (a 16th-century merchant and the first known amateur to dabble in painting) and G. B. Tiepolo – all in a suitably furnished 18th-century patrician's *palazzo*.

Santa Maria Formosa (*open Mon–Sat 10–5, Sun 1–5; adm*), in its charming *campo* just to the north, was rebuilt in 1492 by Codussi, who made creative use of its original Greek-cross plan. The head near the bottom of its campanile is notorious as being the most hideous thing in Venice, while, inside, Palma il Vecchio's *Santa Barbara* is famed as the loveliest of all Venetian blondes, modelled on the artist's own daughter. Another celebrated work, Bartolomeo Vivarini's *Madonna della Misericordia* (1473), is in the first chapel on the right; the parishioners shown under the protection of the Virgin's mantle earned their exalted position by paying for the painting.

The next *campo* to the north is dominated by **Santi Giovanni e Paolo** (or San Zanipolo in dialect), after St Mark's the most important church on the right bank (*open 7.30–12.30 and 3.30–7; Sun 3–6*). A vast Gothic brick barn begun by the Dominicans in 1246, then almost entirely rebuilt after 1333, and finally completed in 1430, it could be accused by no one of being beautiful, despite its fine front doorway.

San Zanipolo was the pantheon of the doges; all their funerals were held here after the 1300s, and some 25 of them went no further, but lie in splendid Gothic and Renaissance tombs. Scattered among them are monuments to other honoured servants of the Venetian state, such as Marcantonio Bragadin, the commander who in 1571 was flayed alive by the Turks after he had surrendered Famagusta, in Cyprus, after a long siege; his bust sits on an urn holding his neatly folded skin. The adjacent chapel contains Giovanni Bellini's polyptych of *St Vincent Ferrer*, a fire-eating subject portrayed by the gentlest of painters; nearby there's a buoyant Baroque ceiling by Piazzetta in St Dominic's chapel, and a small shrine containing the foot of St Catherine of Siena.

The right transept has paintings by Alvise Vivarini, Cima da Conegliano and Lorenzo Lotto; the finest tomb is in the chancel, that of Doge Andrea Vendramin, by Tullio and Antonio Lombardo (1478), while the **Chapel of the Rosary** in the north transept, which was severely damaged by fire in the last century, has a ceiling by Veronese from the church of the Umiltà, long demolished.

Adjacent to San Zanipolo, the **Scuola Grande di San Marco** has one of the loveliest Renaissance façades in Italy, the fascinating *trompe-l'œil* lower half by Pietro and Tullio Lombardo, the upper floor by Mauro Codussi, and finished in 1495. The *scuola* is now used as Venice's municipal hospital, but it is possible to enter to see the lavish coffered ceiling in the library with the permission of the Direttore di Sanità.

Opposite stands the superbly dynamic **Equestrian Statue of Bartolomeo Colleoni**, the *condottiere* from Bergamo (1400–76) who had served the Republic so well on the mainland. In his lifetime proud of his emblem of *coglioni* (testicles – a play on his name), Colleoni envied Donatello's statue of his predecessor Gattamelata erected by the Venetians in Padua (*see p.400*), and in his will he left the Republic 100,000 ducats if it would erect a similar statue of him in front of St Mark's. Greedy for the money but unable to countenance a monument to an individual in their sacred piazza, the wily Venetians put the statue up before the *scuola* of St Mark. Verrocchio, the master of Leonardo and Botticelli, had only finished the plaster moulds when he died in 1488, leaving Alessandro Leopardi to do the casting. Verrocchio never saw a portrait of his subject, and all resemblances to Klaus Kinski are purely accidental.

Santa Maria dei Miracoli and the Ca' d'Oro

From Campo San Zanipolo, Largo G. Gallina leads to the perfect little Renaissance church of **Santa Maria dei Miracoli** (*open Mon–Sat 10–5, Sun and hols 1–5; adm*), built by Pietro Lombardo in the 1480s and often compared to an exquisite jewel box, elegant, graceful, and glowing with a soft marble sheen, inside and out. Just to the south are two enclosed courtyards, known as the **Corte Prima del Milion** and the **Corte Seconda del Milion**, where Marco Polo used to live. The latter in particular looks much as it did when the great traveller lived there; 'Million', his nickname in Venice, referred to the million tall tales he brought back with him from China. Nearby, Codussi's **San Giovanni Crisostomo** (1504) was his last work, a seminal piece of Renaissance architecture that contains Giovanni Bellini's last altar painting (*SS. Jerome, Christopher, and Augustine*), as well as a beautiful high altarpiece by Sebastiano del Piombo.

Further towards the railway station up the Grand Canal, signposted off the Strada Nuova (Via 28 Aprile), stands the enchanting Gothic **Ca' d'Oro**, finished in 1440 and currently housing the **Galleria Franchetti** (*open daily 8.15–2; adm*). In its collection are Mantegna's stern *St Sebastian*, Guardi's series of Venetian views, an excellent collection of Renaissance bronzes and medallions by Pisanello and Il Riccio, Tullio Lombardo's charming *Double Portrait*, and now sadly faded fragments of the famous frescoes by Giorgione and Titian from the Fóndaco dei Tedeschi. Also present are minor works by Titian, including a voluptuous *Venus*. The building itself is famous for the intricate traceries of its façade, best appreciated from the Grand Canal, and the courtyard, with a beautifully carved well-head by Bartolomeo Bon.

Due north, near the Fondamente Nuove, stands the unloved, unrestored church of the **Gesuiti** (*open daily 10–12 and 5–7*), built by the Jesuits when the republic relaxed its restrictions against them, in 1714–29: a Baroque extravaganza, full of *trompe l'œil* of white and green-grey marble draperies that would make a fitting memorial for Liberace. A previous church on this same site was the parish church of Titian, to which he contributed the *Martyrdom of St Lawrence* – the saint on a grill revered by Titian's patron, Philip II of Spain.

Cannaregio

Crumbling, piquant Cannaregio is the least visited *sestiere* in Venice, and here, perhaps, more than anywhere else in the city, you can begin to feel what everyday life is like behind the tourist glitz – children playing tag on the bridges, old men in shorts messing around in unglamorous, unpainted boats on murky canals, neighbourhood greasy spoons and bars, banners of laundry waving gaily overhead.

Northern Cannaregio was Tintoretto's home, and he is buried in the Venetian Gothic **Madonna dell'Orto** (*open Mon–Sat 10–5, Sun and hols 1–5; adm*). It also houses several of his jumbo masterpieces, such as the *Sacrifice of the Golden Calf*, in which Tintoretto painted himself bearing the idol – though he refrained from predicting his place in the *Last Judgement*, opposite. He also painted the highly original *Presentation of the Virgin* in the south aisle, near one of Cima da Conegliano's greatest works, *St John the Baptist*. The first chapel by the door has a *Madonna* by Giovanni Bellini.

From the Campo Madonna dell'Orto, take a short walk down the Fondamenta Contarini, where, across the canal, in the wall of the eccentric **Palazzo Mastelli** you can see one of Venice's curiosities: an old, stone relief of a Moor confronting a camel. There are three more 'Moors' in the **Campo dei Mori**, just in front of the Madonna dell'Orto. The original identities of these mysterious figures has long been forgotten, although a fourth one, embedded in one corner of the square and with a metal nose like Tycho Brahe, is named Signor Antonio Rioba. He featured in many Venetian pranks of yore: anonymous satires or denunciations would be signed in his name, and new arrivals in the city would be sent off to meet him.

Also in the area is another church, **Sant'Alvise** (*open Mon–Sat 10–5, Sun 1–5*), which must be the loneliest church in Venice. Its main features are a forceful *Calvary* by Giambattista Tiepolo and a set of charming tempera paintings that Ruskin called the 'Baby Carpaccios', but are now attributed to Carpaccio's master, Lazzaro Bastiani, as Carpaccio would only have been about eight years old when they were painted.

Three *rii* to the south of Sant'Alvise is the **Ghetto** – the Ghetto, for, like '*Arsenal*', the Venetians invented the name: *ghetto* derives from the word '*getto*' meaning 'casting in metals', and there was an iron foundry here which preceded the establishment of a special quarter to which all Jews were ordered to move in 1516. The name is poignantly apt, for in Hebrew 'ghetto' comes from the root for 'cut off'. And cut off its residents were in Venice, for the Ghetto is an island, surrounded by a moat-like canal, and at night all Jews had to be within its windowless walls. Cramped for space, the houses are tall, with very low ceilings, which, as many people have noted, eerily presage ghetto tenements of centuries to come.

But the Venetians did not invent the mentality behind the Ghetto; Spanish Jews in the Middle Ages were segregated, as were the Jews of ancient Rome. In fact, Venetian law specifically protected Jewish citizens and forbade preachers from inciting mobs against them – a common enough practice in the 16th century. Jewish refugees came to Venice from all over Europe; here they were relatively safe, even if they had to pay for it with high taxes and rents. When Napoleon threw open the gates of the Ghetto in 1797, it is said that the poor residents who remained were too weak to leave.

The island of the **Ghetto Nuovo** – in fact the oldest section – is a melancholy place, its small *campo* often empty and forlorn. The **Scuola Grande Tedesca** is the oldest of Venice's five synagogues, built by German Jews in 1528, and is in the same building as the small **Museo Comunità Israelitica/Ebraica** (*open 1 Oct–31 May 10–5.30, 1 June–30 Sept 10–7, closed Sat and Jewish hols; guided tour at 30mins past the hour, adm exp*). The museum organizes informative tours (in English), which visit this synagogue and two others, the **Scuola Spagnola** – an opulent building by Longhena – and the **Scuola Levantina**.

Light years from the Ghetto in temperament, but only three minutes away on foot, the **Palazzo Labia** (next to the 1580 **Ponte delle Guglie**), has a ballroom with Giambattista Tiepolo's lavish, sensuous frescoes on the *Life of Cleopatra*. The *palazzo* is now owned by RAI, the Italian state broadcaster, and the ballroom is open for concerts (*or call t 041 781 277/781 203 well in advance to arrange an appointment between 3 and 4pm on Wed, Thurs or Fri*). Away from the *palazzo* towards the railway station runs the garish, lively **Lista di Spagna**, Venice's tourist highway, lined with restaurants, bars, hotels and souvenir stands that are not as cheap as they should be.

San Giorgio Maggiore and the Giudecca

The little islet of San Giorgio Maggiore, crowned by Palladio's church of **San Giorgio Maggiore** (*open daily 9.30–12.30 and 2.30–6.30; adm, including the* campanile), dominates the view of the Lagoon from the Piazzetta San Marco (*vaporetto* Line 82). Built according to his theories on harmony, with a temple front, it seems to hang between the water and the sky, bathed by light with as many variations as Monet's series on the Cathedral of Rouen. The austere white interior is relieved by Tintoretto's *Fall of Manna* and his celebrated *Last Supper* on the main altar, which is also notable for the fine carving on the Baroque choir stalls. A lift can whisk you to the top of the **Campanile** for a remarkable view over Venice and the Lagoon. The old monastery, partly designed by Palladio, is now the headquarters of the Giorgio Cini Foundation, dedicated to the arts and the sciences of the sea, and venue for frequent exhibitions.

La Giudecca (Lines 41, 42, 82, N) actually consists of eight islands that curve gracefully like a Spanish *tilde* just south of Venice. Prominent among its buildings is a string of empty mills and factories – the product of a brief 19th-century flirtation with industry – and for the most part the atmosphere is relatively quiet and homely. Like Cannaregio, it's seldom visited, though a few people wander over to see Palladio's best church, **Il Redentore** (*open Mon–Sat 10–5, Sun 1–5; adm*). In 1576, during a plague that killed 46,000 Venetians, the doge and the senate vowed that if the catastrophe ended they would build a church and visit it once a year until the end of time. Palladio completed the Redentore in 1592, and on the third Sunday of each July a bridge of boats was constructed to take the authorities across from the Zattere. This event, the *Festa del Redentore*, is still one of the most exciting events on the Venetian calendar. The Redentore itself provides a fitting backdrop; Palladio's temple front, with its interlocking pediments, matches it basilican interior, with curving transepts and dome. The shadowy semi-circle of columns behind the altar adds a mystical effect.

The Lagoon and its Islands

Pearly and melting into the bright sky, iridescent blue or murky green, a sheet of glass yellow and pink in the dawn, or leaden, opaque grey: Venice's Lagoon is one of its wonders, a desolate, often melancholy and strange, often beautiful and seductive 'landscape' with a hundred personalities. It is 56km long and averages 8km across, added up to some 448sq km; half of it, the Laguna Morta ('Dead Lagoon'), where the tides never reach, consists of mud flats except in the spring, while the shallows of the Laguna Viva are always submerged, cleansed by tides twice a day.

To navigate this treacherous sea the Venetians developed an intricate network of channels, marked by *bricole* – wooden posts topped by orange lamps – that kept their craft from running aground. When threatened, they only had to pull out the *bricole* to confound their enemies; the Lagoon was thus always known as 'the sacred walls of the nation'. Keeping the Brenta from silting it up kept engineers busy for centuries.

Once the largest of the 39 Lagoon islands were densely inhabited, each occupied by a town or at least a monastery. Now all but a few have been abandoned. Occasionally one hears of plans to bring them back to life, only to wither on the vine of Italian bureaucracy. If you think you have a good idea, take it up with the Revenue Office (Intendenza di Finanza).

The Lido and South Lagoon

The Lido, one of the long spits of land that forms the protective outer edge of the Lagoon, is by far the most glamorous of the islands, one that has given its name to countless bathing establishments, bars, amusement arcades and cinemas all over the world. On its 12 kilometres of beach, poets, potentates and plutocrats at the turn of the century spent their holidays in palatial hotels and villas, making the Lido the pinnacle of *belle époque* fashion, so brilliantly evoked in Thomas Mann's *Death in Venice*, and Visconti's subsequent film. The story was set and filmed in the **Grand Hotel des Bains**, just north of the Mussolini-style **Municipal Casino** and **Palazzo del Cinema**, where Venice hosts its annual Film Festival.

The Lido is still the playground of the Venetians and their visitors, with its bathing concessions, riding clubs, tennis courts, golf courses and shooting ranges. The free beach, the **Spiaggia Comunale**, is on the north part of the island, a 15-minute walk from the *vaporetto* stop at San Nicolò (go down the Gran Viale, and turn left on the Lungomare d'Annunzio), where you can hire a hut and frolic in the sand and sea.

Further north, the **Porto di Lido** is maritime Venice's front door, the most important of the three entrances into the Lagoon, where you can watch the ships of the world sail by. This is where the Doge would sail to toss his ring into the waves, in the annual 'Marriage of the Sea'. It is stoutly defended by the mighty **Forte di Sant'Andrea** on the island of Le Vignole, built in 1543 by Venice's fortifications genius Sanmicheli. In times of danger, a great chain was extended from the fort across the channel.

One of the smaller Lagoon islands just off the Lido, with its landmark onion-domed campanile, is **San Lazzaro degli Armeni** (*vaporetto no.20 from San Zaccharia, open to visitors daily 3.25–5pm*). It was Venice's leper colony in the Middle Ages, but in 1715 the then-deserted island was given to the Mechitarist Fathers of the Armenian Catholic Church after they were expelled from Greece by the Turks. Their monastery is still one of the world's major centres of Armenian culture and its monks, noted as linguists, run a famous polyglot press able to print in 32 languages, one of the last survivors in a city once renowned for its publishing. Tours of San Lazzaro include a museum of relics of the ancient Christian history of Armenia, as well as memorabilia of Lord Byron, who spent a winter visiting the fathers and bruising his brain with Armenian. The fathers offer inexpensive prints of Venice for sale; or else they would appreciate a donation.

From the Lido to Chioggia

Buses/ferries from the Lido or quicker buses from Piazzale Roma will take you to Chioggia at the southernmost end of the Lagoon. The seldom used bus/ferry route (leaving roughly every hour) allows you to take in **Malamocco**, a tranquil fishing village named after the first capital of the Lagoon townships, a nearby islet that lost

Sports and Activities

Despite dire reports about the state of the waters of the Adriatic, people still swim off the Lido without becoming mutants, but there is an alternative in the swimming pool on Sacca Fisola, at the west end of the Giudecca, **t** 041 528 5430 (*closed July and August*). Another swimming pool (*closed July*), is Piscina Communale Sant' Alvise, Campo Sant' Alvise, Connaregio, but be warned the hot pools here have limited hours as they are used mainly for lessons. If you're interested in sailing, enquire at the sailing club, the Compagnia della Vela, near the Giardinetti in S. Marco, **t** 041 522 2593, for information on lessons and boat hire.

The Lido has an 18-hole golf course - the Alberoni, Via del Forte Alberoni, **t** 041 731 015, and three tennis clubs, the Tennis Club Venezia, Lungomare Marconi 41/d, **t** 041 526 0335, the Campi Comunali di Tennis, and the Cai del Moro, Via Ferrucio Parri 6, **t** 041 770 801, which also has a pool and a gym. You can also ride along the Lido, like Byron and Shelley, though it's no longer a romantic hooves-in-the-surf affair – enquire at Circolo Ippico Veneziano, Ca' Bianco, Lido, **t** 041 526 1820.

If you prefer to cycle on the Lido, you can hire a bike at Giorgio Barbieri, Via Zara 5, **t** 041 526 1490.

Where to Stay and Eat

Luxury

★★★★★Excelsior Palace, Lungomare Marconi 41, Lido di Venezia, **t** 041 526 0201, **f** 041 526 7276. An immense confection, built in 1907 as the biggest and most luxurious resort hotel in the world and recently redesigned with as much flamboyance as ever. The outrageous exterior is part-Hollywood and part Moorish neo-Gothic. Private beach, swimming pool, tennis courts, golf, night-club and private launch service to Venice are some of its amenities. Ogling the stars at the film festival is another. The restaurant, **t** 041 526 0201 (*very expensive*), offers the classic turn-of-the-last-century Lido experience, with everything you could desire – including a traditional Venetian meal. *Closed mid-Nov–mid-Mar.*

★★★★Des Bains, Lungomare Marconi 17, Lido di Venezia, **t** 041 526 5921, **f** 041 526 0113. A grand old luxury hotel, now part of the Sheraton empire, that preserves much of the feel of its *belle époque* revelries in its magnificent Liberty-style salon, private cabanas, and large garden designed for dalliance. Thomas Mann stayed here on several occasions, and has Aschenbach sigh his life away on the private beach. There's also a salt-water swimming pool, perfect service, and a launch service into Venice. *Closed Dec–mid-Mar.*

★★★★Quattro Fontane, Via delle Quattro Fontane 16, Lido di Venezia, **t** 041 526 0227, **f** 041 526 0726. The best of the smaller Lido hotels, it was formerly the seaside villa of a Venetian family. Its cool walled-in courtyard is inviting and tranquil, and the public and private rooms are furnished with antiques. Book well in advance. *Closed Nov–Mar.*

Very Expensive

★★★★Villa Mapaba, Riviera S. Nicolò, **t** 041 5260590, **f** 041 5269441. Lovely situation overlooking the lagoon, but some of the rooms (particularly those in the annexe) are rather banal; the best are on the first floor. The villa is set in a tranquil garden, and dinner is served on the terrace in summer.

★★★Villa Parco, Via Rodi 1, Lido di Venezia, **t** 041 526 0015, **f** 041 526 7620. A recently renovated villa a short way from the beach with a fine little garden for a bit of privacy. Children are welcome.

Cheap

Bar Trento, Via San Gallo 82. **t** 041 526 5960. The Lido is not really the place to look for cheap, or even moderate-priced places to stay and eat. This is one cheap and cheerful place to eat, however, unfrequented by tourists – an especially rare find. You can stand at the bar and graze on excellent traditional *cicchetti*, or sit down and eat a whole meal; *baccalà* (salt cod) in various ways (especially on Fri), *risotti*, pasta with fish sauce, *pasta e fagioli*, *fegato alla veneziana* (basically liver and onions, though prepared with a finer touch) and fish of the day. *Open for lunch only, closed Sun.*

its status after Pepin and his Franks nabbed it in 810. The capital moved to the Rialto, leaving the original Malamocco to sink poetically into the sea during a tremendous storm in 1106. Next to it, the small resort of **Alberoni** is home to the Lido golf course and the ferry to the next island reef, Pellestrina, which is even thinner. It has two sleepy villages, San Pietro in Volta and Pellestrina, where the *murazzi* or sea walls begin, the last great public works project of the Republic's Magistrato alle Acque. Built in response to to increased flooding in the 18th century, the 4km-long *murazzi* are constructed of huge, white Istrian blocks and built, as their plaque proudly states: *Ausu Romano–Aere Veneto* ('With Roman Audacity and Venetian Money'). From 1782 until 4 November 1966 they succeeded in holding back the flood.

Dusty **Chioggia** is one of the most important fishing ports on the Adriatic, a kind of populist Venice where the streets and canals are arrow-straight and full of working craft, many with brightly painted sails. The morning fish market, the *mercato ittico*, brimming with exotic denizens of the deep, is one of the wonders of Italy. On the map the town on its islands even resembles a fish, gutted and spread out flat, its straight narrow lanes lined up like bones.

The Venetians like to poke fun at Chioggia, which they consider a grumpy old place, and they like to wind it up by calling the little Lion of St Mark on its column in Piazzettta Vigo (where the ferry deposits you) the 'Cat of St Mark'. Goldoni was amused enough by it all to make the town the setting of one of his comedies, *Le Baruffe Chiozzotte*. Almost nothing remains of medieval Chioggia thanks to the blockade and siege by the Genoese in the 1380 Battle of Chioggia. But if you take the first bridge left from the port and continue straight, you will eventually reach the church of **San Domenico**, containing Carpaccio's last painting, *St Paul*, signed and dated 1520, and a beautiful quattrocento crucifix on the altar.

Tourist Information

Chioggia: Viale Po 16, Lido di Sottomarina, t 041 554 0466, t 041 554 0855.

Where to Stay

Chioggia ✉ 30015
★★★**Florida**, Viale Mediterraneo 9, t 041 491 505, f 041 496 6760 (*expensive*). Typical family-run seaside lodgings. *Closed Nov–Jan.*
★★★**Park**, Lungomare Adriatico, t 041 496 5032, f 041 490 111. At Sottomarina. (*expensive*).

Eating Out

Chioggia
El Gato, right behind the fish market in Campo S. Andrea 653, t 041401806 (*expensive*).

Seafood lovers flock to 'The Cat' (*el gato*), where the chef prepares the freshest of fish in the tastiest of Venetian styles. *Closed Mon and Tues lunch, Jan and mid Feb.*
Trattoria Buon Pesce, Stradale Ponte Caneva 625, t 041 400 861 (*moderate*). Start with *gnocchetti alla marinara* and follow it with oysters or crab. Prices at this old-fashioned *trattoria* are half what you'd pay in Venice.
Osteria Penzo, Calle Largo Bersaglio 526. t 041 400 992 (*moderate*). In the old town near the Vigo column, this was once a simple *bacaro*. Now you can sit comfortably, alongside plenty of locals, and eat traditional dishes such as black squid-ink *tagliolini* with scampi and tomato sauce, scallops with *porcini* mushrooms and radicchio and an excellent *fritto misto*, made only with fish in season. *Closed Tues and Mon evening in winter.*

Chioggia's other monuments are strung along the main **Corso del Popolo** (the fish spine). The fish market is just beyond a large 14th-century grain warehouse, the **Granaio**, with a relief of the Madonna on the façade by Sansovino. Further up the Corso, past a couple of low-key churches, is the **Duomo**, built by Baldassare Longhena after the 14th-century original, except for the campanile, burned in 1623. In the chapel to the left of the altar are some murky, unpleasant 18th-century paintings of martyr-doms, one of which is attributed to Tiepolo, although it's hard to swallow. However, the Gothic chapel of San Martino has a lovely polyptych (1349) that really might be by Paolo Veneziano.

And when you've had your fill of fish and the locals, you can stroll along the long bridge (or catch the bus at the *duomo*) for a swim among the vivacious Italian families at Chioggia's lido, **Sottomarina**, which attracts mainly Italian families; from here it's a short drive down into the Po Delta, now a natural park (*see* p.404).

Islands in the North Lagoon

Most Venetian itineraries take in the islands of Murano, Burano and Torcello, all easily reached by inexpensive *vaporetti*. Lines 41 and 42 from Fondamente Nuove to Murano call at the cypress-studded cemetery island of **San Michele**, with its simple but elegant church of **San Michele in Isola** by Mauro Codussi (1469), his first-known work and Venice's first taste of the Florentine Renaissance, albeit with a Venetian twist in the tri-lobed front. It contains the tomb of Fra Paolo Sarpi, who led the ideo-logical battle against the pope when the republic was placed under the Great Interdict of 1607. Venice, considering St Mark the equal of St Peter, refused to be cowed and won the battle of wills after two years, thanks mainly to Sarpi, whose *Treatise on the Interdict* proved it was illegal. In return, he was jumped and knifed by an assassin: '*Agnosco stylum romanae curiae*,' he quipped ('I recognize the method or the "dagger" of the Roman court'). His major work, the critical *History of the Council of Trent*, didn't improve his standing in Rome, but made him a hero in Venice. Sarpi's main interest however, was science; he supported Copernicus and shared notes with Galileo, then lecturing at Padua, and 'discovered' the contraction of the iris.

The **cemetery** itself is entered through the cloister next to the church (*open daily 8.30–4*). The Protestant and Orthodox sections contain the tombs of some of the many foreigners who preferred to face eternity from Venice, among them Ezra Pound, Sergei Diaghilev, Frederick Rolfe (Baron Corvo) and Igor Stravinsky. The gate-keeper provides a basic map.

Murano

The island of Murano (*vaporetti nos. 41 and 42 from Ferrovie or Fondamente Nuove, 71 and 72 from Piazzale Roma, Ferrovia, S. Zaccharia and Fondamente Nuove*) is synony-mous with glass, the most celebrated of Venice's industries. The Venetians were the first in the Middle Ages to rediscover the secret of making crystal glass, and especially mirrors, and it was a secret they kept a monopoly on for centuries by using the most drastic measures: if ever a glassmaker let himself be coaxed abroad, the Council of Ten sent their assassins after him in hot pursuit. However, those who remained in

Venice were treated with kid gloves. Because of the danger of fire, all the forges in Venice were relocated to Murano in 1291, and the little island became a kind of republic within a republic – minting its own coins, policing itself, even developing its own list of NHs (*nobili homini* – noblemen) in its own *Golden Book*.

But glass-making declined like everything else in Venice, and only towards the end of the 19th century were the forges once more stoked up on Murano. Can you visit them? You betcha! After watching the glass being made, there's the inevitable tour of the 'Museum Show Rooms' with their American funeral parlour atmosphere, all solicitude, carpets and hush-hush – not unfitting, as some of the blooming chandeliers, befruited mirrors and poison-coloured chalices begin to make Death look good. There is no admission charge, and there's not even too much pressure to buy. It wasn't always so kitschy. The **Museo Vetrario** or Glass Museum (*open 10–5; closed Wed; adm included in San Marco museums admission*), in the 17th-century Palazzo Giustinian on Fondamenta Cavour, has a choice collection of 15th-century Murano glass.

Nearby stands the another good reason to visit this rather dowdy island, the Veneto-Byzantine **Santi Maria e Donato** (*open daily 8–12 and 4–7*), a contemporary of St Mark's basilica, with a beautiful arcaded apse. The floor is paved with a marvellous 12th-century mosaic, incorporating coloured pieces of ancient Murano glass, and on the wall there's a fine Byzantine mosaic of the Virgin. The relics of Bishop Donato of Euboea were nabbed by Venetian body-snatchers, but in this case they outdid themselves, bringing home not only San Donato's bones but those of the dragon the good bishop slew with a gob of spit; you can see them hanging behind the altar. Back on the Fondamenta dei Vetrai, the 15th-century **San Pietro Martire** has one of Giovanni Bellini's best altarpieces, *Pala Barbarigo* (1484), a monumental *Sacra conversazione* of the Madonna enthroned with SS. Mark and Augustine, and Doge Barbarigo.

Burano

Burano (*vaporetto no.12 from Fondamente Nuove*) is the Legoland of the Lagoon, where everything is in brightly coloured miniature – the canals, the bridges, the leaning tower, and the houses, painted with a Fauvist sensibility in the deepest of colours. Traditionally on Burano the men fish and the women make Venetian point, 'the most Italian of all lace work', beautiful, intricate and murder on the eyesight. All over Burano you can find samples on sale (of which a great deal are machine-made or imported), or you can watch it being made at the **Scuola dei Merletti** in Piazza Galuppi (*open daily exc Tues 10–5; adm included in San Marco museums admission*). 'Scuola' in this case is misleading; no young woman in Burano wants to learn such an excruciating art. The school itself was founded in 1872, when traditional lacemaking was already in decline. In the sacristy of the church of **San Martino** (with its tipsily leaning campanile) look for Giambattista Tiepolo's *Crucifixion*, which Mary McCarthy aptly described as 'a ghastly masquerade ball'.

From Burano you can hire a *sandola* (small gondola) to **San Francesco del Deserto**, some 20 minutes to the south. St Francis is said to have founded a chapel here in 1220, and the whole islet was subsequently given to his order for a **monastery** (*visitors welcome daily 9–11 and 3–5.30*). In true Franciscan fashion, it's not the buildings you'll remember (though there's a fine 14th-century cloister), but the love of nature evident in the beautiful gardens. Admission is free, but donations are appreciated.

Torcello

Though fewer than 100 people remain on Torcello (*vaporetto no.12*), this small island was once a serious rival to Venice herself. According to legend, its history began when God ordered the bishop of Roman *Altinum*, north of Mestre, to take his flock away from the heretical Lombards into the Lagoon. From a tower the bishop saw a star rise over Torcello, and so led the people of *Altinum* to this lonely island to set up their new home. It grew quickly, and for the first few centuries it seems to have been the real metropolis of the Lagoon, with 20,000 inhabitants, palaces, a mercantile fleet and five townships; but malaria decimated the population, the *Sile* silted up Torcello's corner of the Lagoon, and the bigger rising star of Venice drew its citizens to the Rialto.

Torcello is now a ghost island overgrown with weeds, its palaces either sunk into the marsh or quarried for their stone; narrow paths are all that remain of once bustling thoroughfares. One of these follows a canal from the landing stage past the picturesque Ponte del Diavolo to the grass-grown piazza in front of the magnificent Veneto-Byzantine **Cathedral of Santa Maria Assunta** with its lofty campanile, founded in 639 and rebuilt in the same Ravenna basilica-style in 1008. The interior (*no longer a cathedral, although mass is celebrated every Sunday during the summer; open daily 10–5.30; adm*) has the finest mosaics in Venice, all done by 11th- and 12th-century Greek artists, from the wonderful floor to the spectacular *Last Judgement* on the west wall and the unsettling, heart-rending *Teotoco*, the stark, gold-ground mosaic of the thin, weeping Virgin portrayed as the 'bearer of God'. Next to the cathedral is the restored 11th-century octagonal church of **Santa Fosca**, surrounded by an attractive portico, a beautiful and rare late Byzantine work. Near here stands an ancient stone throne called the **Chair of Attila**, though its connection with the Hunnish supremo is nebulous. Across the square, the two surviving secular buildings of Torcello, the Palazzo del Consiglio and Palazzo dell'Archivio, contain the small **Museo dell'Estuario** (*open daily 10.30–5.30 summer, shorter hours winter; closed Mon and hols; adm*).

Cavallino and Jesolo

One suspects these beach resorts closest to Venice owe part of their success to their total lack of any cultural 'obligations'. On the other hand, they have every facility for fun, Italian-style, from windsurfers and rollerblades for hire to water parks, horse-riding along the lagoon, bike trails and even covered *bocce* courts.

There are two ports on the *litorale* linked to Venice: **Punta Sabbioni** (*vaporetto no. 14, from Riva degli Schiavoni and the Lido; car ferry no. 17, from Tronchetto*) and **Treporti** (*vaporetto no. 12*); frequent buses ply the strip between Jesolo with Punta Sabbioni. The **Litorale del Cavallino**, the 10km sliver of land that protects the northern part of the Lagoon, was long known as a semi-wild place of beach, dunes and pine forests. There's still some of that left, among its 28 camping grounds and umpteen hotels and restaurants. **Lido di Jesolo**, north from Punta Sabbioni, is a densely packed resort on a wide sandy beach, attracting some six million tourists a year.

The Veneto

Memories of Venice are strong in the Veneto, but each city has a distinct personality, formed in the rambunctious Middle Ages when each was an independent *comune*. **Padua**, the brain of the Veneto, has nearly as much fine art as Venice, as well as a saint who in modern polls beats Mark hands down. Petrarch practically invented villa life when he retired to the **Euganean Hills**. **Vicenza**, the city of Palladio, is full of architectural bravura, with a score of famous villas within an hour's drive; **Verona**, the city of the Scaliger, is a rose-tinted medieval beauty on the Adige. The minor art capital of **Rovigo** rules the Po flatlands; **Treviso** with its canals is a Venice in miniature; **Belluno** enjoys a beautiful setting in the foothills of the Dolomites.

Venice to Padua and Verona: the Brenta Canal

From Venice to Padua: Villas along the Brenta

In *The Merchant of Venice*, Portia, disguised as a young lawyer, leaves her villa of Belmont on the Brenta Canal and boats down to Venice to preserve Antonio's pound of flesh. Over the years, the River Brenta had made itself universally detested by flooding the surrounding farmland and choking the Lagoon with silt, and in the 14th century the Venetians decided to control its antics once and for all. They raised its banks and dug a canal to divert its waters, and when all the hydraulic labours were completed in the 16th century they realized that the new canal was the ideal place for their summer *villeggiatura*; their gondoliers could conveniently row them straight to their doors, or, as Goethe and thousands of other visitors have done, they could travel there on the *burchiello*, a water bus propelled by oars or horses. Over seventy villas

and palaces sprouted up along this extension of the Grand Canal, and they were famous for their summer parties – one of the choicest locations for Venetian patricians to go a-squiring in the country, and still be within easy communication of the city. (Nowadays you just need a magic wand to make the traffic disappear: you can follow the Brenta along the S11, by car, take the half-hourly bus to Padua from Piazzale Roma, or, to reach La Malcontenta, you must take a different bus from Piazzale Roma that leaves only once an hour.)

One of the first villas you reach is Palladio's celebrated **Villa Foscari** (1560), or **La Malcontenta** (*between Fusina and Oriago; open May–Oct, Tues and Sat 9–12 or by appointment, t 041 520 3966; guided tours; adm exp*), named, they say, for Foscari's wife, the sad lady in one of the frescoes . La Malcontenta epitomizes the classical dream world of the Renaissance and harmonic proportions that Palladio understood better than any other. Viewed from the canal, the villa is a vision begging for Scarlett O'Hara to sweep down the steps – it's no coincidence: Palladio's *Quattro Libri dell'Architettura* was the bible for 18th-century builders in America.

Further up the canal, **Mira Ponte** is the site of the 18th-century **Villa Widmann-Foscari** (*guided tours Tues–Sun, 9–6; adm exp*). If you only have time for one villa, don't make it this one – redone soon after its construction in the French Baroque style; it contains some of its original furniture and bright, gaudy murals by two of Tiepolo's pupils, but not much of real interest. Mira's post office occupies the **Palazzo Foscarini**, Byron's address from 1817 to 1819, while working on the fourth Canto of *Childe Harold*.

The grandest villa in the Veneto is further up at Strá: the **Villa Nazionale** (or **Pisani**), enlarged by Alvise Pisani to celebrate his election as Doge in 1735 (*hour-long guided tours June–Sept Tues–Sun 9–6; until 7.30pm many days in Aug; Oct–May Tues–Sun 9–1.30; t 049 502 074; adm*). Modelled on Versailles, it was completed in 1760, then purchased by Napoleon in 1807 for his viceroy in Italy Eugène Beauharnais; in 1934 Mussolini chose it as a suitable stage for his first meeting with Hitler. Inside, the villa has lost most of its decoration, but the ballroom makes up for the boredom with Giambattista Tiepolo's shimmering *Apotheosis of the Pisani Family*, a fresco as lovely as its subject matter is ridiculous. The park contains a fiendish garden maze.

Padua

Although only half an hour from Venice, Padua (Padova) refuses to be overshadowed by the old dowager by the sea, and can rightly claim its own place among Italy's most interesting and historic cities. Nicknamed *La Dotta*, 'The Learned', it is home to one of Europe's oldest universities, founded in 1221 and attended by Petrarch, Dante and Galileo. Padua's churches, under the brushes of Giotto, Altichiero, Giusto de' Menabuoi and Mantegna, were virtual laboratories in the evolution of fresco. But what Padua attracts most of all are pilgrims of a more pious nature; its exotic landmark, a seven-domed mosque of a basilica, is the last resting place of St Anthony of Padua, whom the locals call simply *Il Santo*, the Saint. Although the north of Padua was bombed in the last war, some of the arcaded southern streets could still serve as a stage for *The Taming of the Shrew*, which Shakespeare set in this lively, student-filled city.

Getting There

Padua is easily reached by **train** from Venice (40mins), Vicenza (45mins) and other cities on the Milan–Venice line. Outside the train station, a booth dispenses tickets and directions for the city buses.

The **bus station** is a 10-minute walk away in the Piazzale Boschetti, Via Trieste 40, **t** 049 820 6844, and has buses every half-hour to Venice, and good connections to Vicenza, Treviso, Este, Monsélice, Bassano and Rovigo; **ACAP** city buses (**t** 0498 206 811) from the station serve Àbano Terme, Montegrotto Terme and Torreglia. **Landomas, t** 049 860 1426, has direct connections to Marco Polo or Treviso airports from Padua and the Euganean hills – they'll pick you up at your door if you book a day in advance. **Radio taxi: t** 049 651 333.

Delta Tours offer **cruises** along the Brenta Canal, and mini-cruises aboard *La Padovanella* around Padua itself on the River Piovego.

Tourist Information

In the railway station, **t** 049 875 2077 (*open Mon–Sat 9–7.30, Sun 8.30–12.30; Nov–Mar 9.20–5.45, Sun 9–12*); Riviera Mugnai 8, **t** 049 875 0655, **f** 049 650 794, *www.padovanet.it*

If you plan to visit most or all of the main attractions in Padua, a *biglietto unico* will save you money on admissions; you can buy it from any one of the participating sites.

Activities

Every summer a series of concerts, exhibitions, open-air films and shows takes place. The tourist office's *Padova Today* lists events. The Prato della Valle sees a large general market every Saturday, and an antique market every third Sunday of the month.

Where to Stay

Padua ✉ 35100

Expensive
★★★★**Donatello**, Via del Santo 102, **t** 049 875 0634, **f** 049 8675 0829. By the basilica of Sant'Antonio, you can't miss this hotel: Donatello's Gattamelata points right to it. Rooms have been recently renovated.
★★★★**Majestic Toscanelli**, Via dell'Arco 2, **t** 049 663 244, **f** 049 876 0025. Also in the historic centre, newer and more comfortable, with every luxury and a popular restaurant specializing in Brazilian dishes.
★★★★**Grande Italia**, Corso del Popolo 81, **t** 049 876 111, **f** 049 875 0850. A beautiful Liberty building, opposite the railway station.

Moderate
★★★**Leon Bianco**, Piazzetta Pedrocchi 12, **t** 049 875 0814, **f** 049 875 6184. Small and cosy, right in the heart of Padua. From the roof terrace – where breakfast is served in summer – you overlook the Caffè Pedrocchi.
★★★**Al Cason**, Via Paolo Scarpi 40, **t** 049 66236, **f** 049 875 4217. Cheaper and near the station, this hotel will make you feel at home, and fill you up with the classics in its restaurant.

Cheap
★★**Sant'Antonio**, Via S. Fermo 118, **t** 049 875 1393, **f** 049 875 2508. Between the station and centre by the Porta Molino, providing a friendly, family atmosphere.

Giotto's Cappella degli Scrovegni and the Museo Civico Eremitani

*Both open 9–6, until 7 in summer, museum closed Mon; adm exp; visits to the chapel timed, book in advance; **t** 0498 204 550.*

Padua deserves at least a day but, if you only have a couple of hours, it's a short walk from the bus or railway station to the jewel in its crown: Giotto's extraordinary, recently restored frescoes in the **Cappella degli Scrovegni** (or *Madonna dell'Arena*), a church sheltered by the crusty shell of Padua's Roman amphitheatre. Enter with the same ticket as the adjacent **Museo Civico Eremitani**. The chapel was built by Enrico Scrovegni in 1303, in expiation for the sins of his father, Reginaldo the usurer.

★★Arcella, Via J. D'Avanzo 7, **t** 049 605 581. Near the station but on the wrong side of the tracks; friendly owners.

★Pavia, Via del Papafava 11, **t** 049 661 558. Popular, clean, central and friendly.

★Junior, Via L. Faggin 2, **t** 049 811 756. A 10-minute walk from the station in the same area. A homey hotel, with no en suite baths.

Eating Out

La cucina padovana features what the Italians call 'courtyard meats' (*carni di cortile*) – chicken, duck, turkey, pheasant, capons, goose and pigeon. Pork, rabbit and freshwater fish are other favourites. Try one of the various *risotti* for *primo*.

Expensive

Antico Brolo, Corso Milano 22, **t** 049 664555. Not far from the historic centre and occupying an elegant 15th-century building. There's a garden for outdoor dining on Veneto and Emilian specialities: try the *chateaubriand* with balsamic vinegar. *Moderate* tourist menu. *Closed Mon and Sun lunch, some of Aug*. There's a good *pizzeria* down in the old wine cellar where you'll spend a lot less.

Moderate

Dotto di Campagna, Via Randaccio, **t** 049 625 469. In the suburb of Torre, 2km from the Padua-Est *autostrada* exit, offering elegant surroundings and inventive cookery based on the freshest of ingredients; for a first course try their famous *risotti* or *pasta e fagioli*. *Cheap* tourist menu available. *Closed Sun eve, Mon, Aug*.

Da Giovanni, Via Maroncelli 22, **t** 049 772 620. The crowds venture outside the city walls (bus no.9 from the railway station) for this classic Paduan home cooking, featuring succulent boiled and roast meats. The home-made pasta is especially good, as are the locally raised capons. *Closed Sat lunch, Sun, Aug*.

La Corta Dei Leoni, Via Pietro D'Abano 1, **t** 049 815 0083. For a truly sumptious meal in a walled courtyard in the historic centre of Padua. The menu is changed weekly in line with the seasons, imaginatively combining all the best seasonal ingredients, while the extensive wine list reflects the best that Italy has to offer . Specialities include *lardo di colonata* (wafer-thin lard, spiced and salted – a speciality protected by law since the 16th century) and *scaloppa di rombo con finocchi gratinata* (fillet of turbot with fennel au gratin). *Closed Sun eve, Mon; good disabled access*.

Cheap

Bertolini, Via Antichiero 162, **t** 049 600 357. Just north of the station, this restaurant has been a favourite for 150 years; go for the hearty vegetarian and seasonal dishes and home-made desserts. *Closed Sat*.

Bastioni del Moro, Via Bronzetti 18, **t** 049 871 0006. A restaurant serving up delicious *gnocchi* with scallops and *porcini* mushrooms, beyond Padua's western walls (take Corso Milano from the centre). It has had a recent facelift and you can eat indoors in winter or in the summer garden on balmy summer days. *Cheap* tourist menu available, although prices soar if you order fish. *Closed Sun*.

Fortunately, he left enough money behind for Enrico to commission Giotto, then at the height of his career, to fresco the interior with a New Testament cycle (1304–07). In sheer power and inspiration, Giotto's masterpiece was as revolutionary in its day as Michelangelo's Sistine Chapel would be 200 years later – a fresh, natural narrative composition, with three-dimensional figures solidly anchored in their setting.

Dante visited Giotto while he worked, and as a compliment placed Reginaldo in the seventh ring of the *Inferno* (Canto XVII). Giotto, however, had no doubt where he was going in the end; you'll find him fourth from the left in the front row of the elect in the *Last Judgement*.

Padua's vast **Museo Civico**, installed in the adjacent convent of the Eremitani, combines archaeology (coins and vases from the Veneto, and 14 rare funerary *stelae* from the 6th to 1st centuries BC) and acres of fine art. Here you'll find Giotto's *Crucifixion*, designed for the altar of the Cappella Scrovegni, works by his follower Guariento, founder of the medieval Paduan school, and others by nearly every Venetian who ever applied brush to canvas: Bellini, Tintoretto, Titian, Vivarini, Veronese, Tiepolo and down the line. Don't miss what must be the most camp portrait in all Italy: the 17th-century *Venetian Captain* by Sebastiano Mazzoni, framed among cupids, lions and a giant artichoke. The small Renaissance bronzes that fill the halls were a speciality of Padua, especially those by Il Riccio (Andrea Briosco).

Next to the museum, the church of the **Eremitani** (1306; *open Mon–Sat 8.15–12.15, 4–6; Sun 9.30–12, 4–6; same ticket as the Cappella Scrovegni*) was shattered in an air raid in 1944. What could be salvaged of the frescoes has been painstakingly pieced together, most importantly Andrea Mantegna's remarkable Ovetari chapel, frescoed from 1454 to 1457 when he was in his early twenties; *The Martyrdom of St Christopher and St James* still astonishes, thanks to Mantegna's depiction of the cold might of Rome, and his wizardly use of perspective to foreshorten the action from below. Padua's oldest church, the 9th-century **Santa Sofia**, is to the east at the corner of Via S. Sofia and Via Altinate; rebuilt in the 11th century, it has a lovely Byzantine apse.

Central Padua: The University and Palazzo della Ragione

A short walk from the Eremitani takes you to Piazza Cavour, historic heart of Padua and site of what resembles an Egyptian-revival mausoleum with columned stone porches at either end. This is the **Caffè Pedrocchi**, built in 1831 by Giuseppe Jappelli, famous in its day for never closing (it couldn't – it had no doors), and for intellectuals and students who came here to debate the revolutionary politics of Mazzini; it still serves coffee today. In Jappelli's adjacent neo-Gothic, bullet-scarred **Pedrocchino**, students turned words into deeds in 1848, clashing with the Austrian police.

Cater-corner on Via VIII Febbraio is the seat of the **University of Padua**, the 16th-century **Palazzo del Bo'** ('of the ox'), a nickname derived from a tavern that stood here in 1221. Galileo delivered his lectures from its old wooden pulpit; the Great Hall is coated with the arms of its alumni, and the claustrophobic **Anatomical Theatre** (1594) is believed to be the first permanent one anywhere, designed by Fabricius, tutor of William Harvey, who went on to discover the circulation of blood. Other professors included Vesalius, author of the first original work on anatomy since Galen (1555), and Gabriello Fallopio, discoverer of the Fallopian tubes.

Around the corner, **Piazza Antenore** has two sarcophagi for a centrepiece. The one on columns supposedly contains what remains of Antenor, hero of the Trojan War and founder of ancient *Patavium*, according to the great Roman historian Livy. Livy himself was born in the nearby Euganean Hills, and the other sarcophagus commemorates his 2,000th birthday. Perhaps he'll get something nicer for his 3,000th!

Opposite the Palazzo del Bò and behind the 16th-century **Municipio**, with its uncomfortable fascist-era façade, the delightful **Piazza delle Erbe** and **Piazza delle Frutta** still see bustling markets every morning. They are separated by the massive **Palazzo della**

Ragione (*open 9–7 closed Mon; adm*). Constructed as Padua's law courts in 1218 and then rebuilt in 1306, its upper storey, *Il Salone*, is one of the largest medieval halls in existence, measuring 260ft by 88ft, the 85ft ceiling like a 'vaulting over a market square', as Goethe described it. Its great hull-shaped roof was rebuilt after a fire in 1756 – an earlier blaze, in 1420, destroyed the frescoes by Giotto, which were replaced a few years later with over 300 biblical and astrological scenes by Niccolò Miretto. Exhibitions are frequently staged in the Salone, but two exhibits never change: the *pietra del vituperio*, a cold stone block where debtors were made to sit bare-bottomed, and a giant **wooden horse**, built for a joust in 1466, its fierce glance complemented by testicles the size of bowling balls.

Just to the west, Padua's stately **Piazza dei Signori** saw many a joust in its day, and can still boast Italy's oldest astronomical clock, built by Giovanni Dondi (1344) in the tower of the **Palazzo del Capitaniato**. On the left is the fine Lombard-style **Loggia della Gran Guardia** (1523), while behind Dondi's clock you'll find the university's Arts Faculty, the **Liviano**, built in 1939 by Gio Ponti. The Da Carrara, Padua's medieval *signori*, lived here in the 1300s, and the Liviano incorporates their palace's **Sala dei Giganti** and its giant frescoes of ancient Romans, repainted by Domenico Campagnola in the 1530s; Altichiero added the more intimate 14th-century portrait of Petrarch sitting at his desk. Around the corner from the square stands Padua's rather neglected **Duomo**, begun in the 12th century but tampered with throughout the Renaissance – Michelangelo was only one of several cooks who spoiled the broth here before everyone lost interest. The **baptistry** (*open 9.30–1 and 3–6, adm*), however, was beautifully frescoed by Florentine Giusto de' Menabuoi in the 1370s. The dome, with its multitude of saints in the circles of paradise, is awesome, but chilling.

St Anthony, Donatello, and the Biggest Square in Italy

Below the commercial heart of Padua rise the exotic domes of the **Basilica di Sant'Antonio**. St Anthony of Padua was a Portuguese missionary inspired by St Francis. He was shipwrecked in Italy en route to the heathen lands, but stayed, preached, and was canonized only ten months after his death, in 1232. The basilica was begun in the same year and finished the following century. For pure fantasy it is comparable only to St Mark's, a cluster of seven domes around a lofty, conical cupola, two octagonal *campanili* and two smaller minarets – perhaps not what a friar vowed to poverty might have ordered, but certainly a sign of the esteem in which he is held.

Inside, pilgrims queue patiently to press their palm against his tomb and to study the votive testimonials and photos (happy babies, wrecked cars) thanking the busy saint – who also runs Heaven's Lost Property Office. No one pays much attention to the 16th-century marble reliefs lining St Anthony's chapel, although they are exquisite works of the Venetian Renaissance: the fourth and fifth are by Sansovino, the sixth and seventh by Tullio Lombardo, and the last by Antonio Lombardo. Behind the chapel, the **Cappella di Conti** has rich frescoes by Giusto de' Menabuoi (1382).

The **high altar**, much rearranged over the centuries, is the work of Donatello and his helpers (1445–50), crowned by a famous *Crucifixion*, with bronze statues of the *Madonna* and *Six Patron Saints of Padua* and reliefs of the *Miracles of St Anthony* below. The great **Paschal Candelabrum** is the masterpiece of Il Riccio, who also, with his master Bellano, cast the 12 bronze reliefs of Old Testament scenes on the choir walls. Behind the high altar, in the ambulatory, don't miss the **treasury** of gold reliquaries, one containing Anthony's tongue and larynx, found perfectly intact when his tomb was opened in 1981.

In the right transept, the **Cappella di San Felice** contains more beautiful frescoes and a remarkable *Crucifixion*, painted in the 1380s by Altichiero. The basilica complex includes several other exhibitions and museums: one, the **Museo Antoniano** (*open 10–1 and 2.30–6.30, closed Mon; adm*) houses art made for the basilica over the centuries, including a lunette frescoed by Mantegna and a delightful 15th-century German reliquary in the shape of a ship.

Sharing the large piazza in front of the basilica, a bit lost among the pigeons and souvenir stands, is one of the key works of the Renaissance, Donatello's **statue of Gattamelata** (1453), the first large equestrian bronze since antiquity. The cool 'Honeyed Cat' *condottiere* from Narni in Umbria served Venice so well and honestly that the usually tightwadded Republic paid for this monument, which Donatello imbued with a serene humanistic spirit, in marked contrast to Verrocchio's arrogant Colleoni statue in Venice (*see* p.382).

Flanking the piazza opposite Gattamelata, the **Oratorio di San Giorgio** (*open 9–12.30 and 2.30–7; adm*) has beautiful frescoes by two heirs of Giotto: Altichiero and Jacopo Avanzi. Visit the adjacent **Scuoletta del Santo**, with paintings on the *Life of St Anthony* by a variety of artists in the panelled upstairs room, including some – not his best – by a teenage Titian (*open 9–12.30 and 2.30–7, closed Mon; adm*).

A few streets south of Piazza del Santo, the **Orto Botanico** (*open April–Sept, Mon–Sat 9–1 and 3–6; adm*) is Europe's oldest botanical garden, established in 1545; it retains the original layout, and even a few original specimens. At 'Goethe's palm', planted in 1585 and still flourishing, the poet speculated on his Theory of the Ur-plant, that all plants evolved from one universal specimen.

Beyond, 'Italy's largest piazza', the **Prato della Valle** (1775), does service as car park and pantheon for 78 illustrious men (and one woman) associated with Padua. On one side stands the **Basilica of Santa Giustina** (*open daily, 8.30–12 and 3–7*), designed by Il Riccio, its domes similar to St Anthony's, but its façade unfinished and its interior still-born Baroque, if brightened by a Veronese altarpiece; off the right aisle, don't miss the 5th-century **Sacellum di San Prosdocimo**.

South of Padua: the Euganean Hills and Around

The landscape south of Padua is as flat as any of the prairies of the Po, with the exception of the lush Euganean Hills, a retreat of poets and the world-weary since Roman times; dotted with villas, spas, walking trails and country restaurants, they remain Padua's favourite playground. South of the hills wait a handsome trio of medieval towns: Monsélice, Este and Montagnana – all 'with pasts' – as people used to say of women who dared to have fun.

The Euganean Hills

As soon as you leave Padua you'll spot them: the *Colli Euganei*, ancient volcanic islands, once surrounded by sea and now basking in the middle of the plain. Fertile, well-watered and defensible, they attracted the region's first settlers, the Paleoveneti, who made Este their chief stronghold. A few thousand years later, the Romans discovered the two key secrets of the Euganean Hills: wine (now DOC Colli Euganei) and hot mud. Livy, Suetonius and Martial all recommended the virtues of their springs, which flow from the ground at 87°C, and they have been appreciated ever since: some 130 hotels built over thermal swimming pools provide health or beauty cures at **Ábano Terme** and **Montegrotto Terme**, where the old Roman spa has been excavated. At nearby **Torréglia**, the vast **Villa dei Vescovi** (*open Mar–Nov Mon, Wed and Fri 10.30–12 and 2.30–6; adm*), was designed by Giovanni Maria Falconetto (1579) for holidaying bishops, and was a major influence on Palladio.

From Torréglia, there's a road west to **Teolo**, Livy's birthplace. Because of their unusual micro-climate, the Euganean Hills are home to some interesting flora, now protected in a regional park; from Teolo you can join a 42km circular nature trail around the district or visit the Benedictine **Abbazia di Praglia**, founded in 1117 but given the full Renaissance treatment by Tullio Lombardo, Bartolomeo Montagna, Giambattista Zelotti and others (*tours every half hour, 3.30–5.30 summer, closed Mon*).

South of Torréglia towards Galzignano Terme, the **Villa Barbarigo** at **Valsanzibio** (*open 9–1 and 1.30 until sunset Mar–Nov; adm exp*) has the grandest gardens in the Veneto, laid out in the mid 1600s in the style of the Tivoli Gardens near Rome, with fountains, waterfalls, nymphaeums, pools and another wicked garden maze. Beyond, medieval **Arquà Petrarca** is the gem of the Euganean Hills, where the world-weary Petrarch, accompanied by his daughter Francesca and his stuffed cat, Laura II, retired in 1370. His charming villa, the **Casa del Petrarca** (*t 0429 718 294; open Feb–Sept 9–12 and 3–7; Oct–Jan 9–12.30 and 2.30–5.30; adm*), preserves much of its 14th-century furnishings; with the exception of a radio mast, the view from the poet's study remains the same. Petrarch died here in 1374, and now occupies a marble sarcophagus in front of the church.

Monsélice, Este and Montagnana

Spilling like an opera set down the southern slopes of the Euganean Hills, the natural citadel of **Monsélice** was first fortified by the Romans, and in 1239 by Ezzelino da Romano, the cruel tyrant of the Veneto. His beautifully restored Ca' Marcello is now part of the **Castello Monsélice** (*t 0429 72931; open April–11 Nov, guided tours from 9–12 and 3–6 all year, some tours in English; adm*) and houses a superb collection of medieval and Renaissance arms and antiques. The castle lies near the base of Vincenzo Scamozzi's striking **Via Sacra delle Sette Chiese** (1605), zigzagging up the hill, past the sumptuous **Villa Nani**, the Romanesque **Duomo**, seven **chapels** built by Scamozzi and frescoed by Palma Giovane, and the elegant 16th-century **Villa Duodo** and **Esedra di San Francesco Saverio**, also by Scamozzi, now a university centre of hydraulic studies. A path continues up to the **Mastio Federiciano** (**Rocca**), built over a Lombard fort by Frederick II, Ezzelino's boss (*open Sat and Sun, book, t 042 972 931*).

Getting Around

The spas and towns in the **Euganean Hills** are easily reached by **bus** from the main station in Padua.

There are also regular **trains** from Padua to Monsélice (23km), Este (32km), Montagnana (52km) and Rovigo (45km), which can take about the same time as the buses, although allow for the vagaries of the Italian train system. You may have to change trains at Monsélice. Buses from Monsélice go to Arquà Petrarca once a day, not Sun (10km).

Tourist Information

Ábano Terme: Via Pietro d'Abano 18, t 049 866 9055, f 049 866 9053.

Montegrotto Terme: Viale della Stazione 60, t 049 793 384, f 049 795 276.

Monsélice: Piazza Mazzini, t 0429 783 026.

Este: Piazza Maggiore, t 042 93635.

Montagnana: Castel S. Zino, t 044 298 1320 (*closed Mon pm and Tues*).

Where to Stay and Eat

Ábano Terme ✉ 35031

★★★★★Grand Hotel Orologio, Viale delle Terme 66, t 049 866 9111, f 049 866 9841 (*very expensive*). All the spa hotels in the Euganean Hills have private mineral water pools, therapists and gardens, but none can match the class of this one, built by Giuseppe Jappelli in 1825. A large park and landscaped pools attract many guests seeking tranquillity instead of magic mud. *Closed Dec–Feb*.

★★★Verdi, Via F. Busonera 200, t 049 667 600, f 049 667 025 (*moderate*). A friendly hotel, offering more pools and mud for a quarter of the price.

In nearby Torréglia, join the hungry Paduans at their favourite country restaurants.

Da Taparo, Via Castelletto 42, t 049 521 1060 (*moderate*). This restaurant has a beautiful terrace overlooking the hills to match its delicious Veneto cuisine. *Closed Mon*.

Antica Trattoria Ballotta, Via Carromatto 2, t 049 521 2970, f 049 521 1385 (*moderate*).

In business since 1605 and one of the oldest restaurants in Venetia, with fine dining inside or in the garden. *Closed Tues*.

Rifugio Monte Rua, Via Mone Rua 29, t 049 521 1049 (*moderate*). A panoramic location, where dishes change according to season. *Closed Tues*.

Arquà Petrarca ✉ 35032

La Montanella, Via Costa 33, t 0429 718 200 (*expensive–moderate*). Near the centre of Arquà, you can enjoy not only the garden and views, but exquisite *risotti* and duck with fruit; select your wine, olive oil and vinegar from special menus. *Closed Tues eve, Wed, 2 weeks each in Aug and Jan*.

★Roncha, Via Costa 132, t 0429 718 286 (*moderate*). A little way down the same road as La Montanella, serving local specialities and fine wines.

Monsélice ✉ 35043

★★★Ceffri Villa Corner, Via Orti 7, t 0429 783 111, f 0429 783 100 (*moderate*). A modern hotel, with a pool and well-equipped rooms, and a good restaurant featuring home-made pasta and a cheap tourist menu.

La Torre, Piazza Mazzini 14, t 0429 73752 (*moderate, expensive for truffles*). An elegant place where *funghi* fiends can head for gratification. *Closed Sun eve, Mon, and part of July and Aug*.

Venetian Palace Hostel, 'Citta di Monsélice', Via Santo Stefano Superiore 33, t 0429 783 125 (*cheap*). For somewhere more stylish try this hostel, once used by the dukes of Padua as a guest house. It now offers comfortable rooms with modern convieniences.

Montagnana ✉ 35044

★★★Aldo Moro, Via G. Marconi 27, t 0429 81351, f 0429 82842 (*moderate*). Stay in fine rooms beside the *duomo*, and visit the restaurant serving local *prosciutto dolce del montagnanese*. *Closed Mon*.

Da Stona, Via Carrarese 51, t 0429 81532 (*cheap*). For lunch or dinner, try this excellent *trattoria* with tasty home cooking – *pasta e fagioli*, *prosciutto dolce* and so forth – and a good local wine list; *cheap* tourist menu available. *Closed Mon*.

Monsélice's old rival, **Este** (ancient *Ateste*), is only 9km to the west; its name was adopted by its 11th-century rulers, who moved on to greater glory in Ferrara. Like Monsélice, Este was a hotly contested piece of real estate, and bristles with the towers of the 1339 **Castello dei Carraresi,** now put out to pasture in a public garden.

Abutting the garden, the 16th-century Palazzo Mocenigo houses the excellent **Museo Nazionale Atestino** (*t 0429 2085; open 9–7; adm*), covering the Paleoveneto civilization from the 10th century BC up to Roman times. Don't miss the outstanding 7th-century BC *Situla Benvenuti*, a bronze vase decorated with warriors and fantastic animals. There is also a superb collection of 6th–5th-century BC bronzes, and – a bit out of place – a luscious red-dressed *Madonna and Child* by Cima da Conegliano.

Behind the castle, the **Villa De Kunkler** was Byron's residence from 1817 to 1818. Here Shelley, his guest, penned 'Lines written among the Euganean Hills', after the death of his little daughter, Clara. Don't miss the startlingly tilted 12th-century campanile of **San Martino**, just off Piazza Maggiore, and Giambattista Tiepolo's altarpiece of *Santa Tecla versus the Plague* in the **Duomo**.

Montagnana, 15km to the west, boasts some of the best-preserved medieval fortifications in Italy, the handiwork of Ezzelino da Romano and Padua's Carrara family. The walls extend two kilometres, defended by 24 intact towers – impressive but not effective; Venice lost and regained the town 13 times during the War of the Cambrai.

The walls now form a picturesque backdrop to Montagnana's colourful *palio* in September. Jutting asymmetrically into the main piazza, the **Duomo** has a portal by Sansovino, a *Transfiguration* by Veronese and a huge painting of *The Battle of Lepanto*. Palladio mavens won't want to miss his **Palazzo Pisani**, by the Porto Padova.

Little Mesopotamia

About 20km south of Monsélice, Rovigo is the capital of the province wedged between the mighty Adige and the mightier Po, known as the Polèsine or 'Little Mesopotamia'. Like ancient Mesopotamia it has been blessed and cursed by its rivers, which make it fertile but often spill over their banks, while miles of silt have left its ancient capital Adria high and dry.

Rovigo and Adria

The other inhabitants of the Veneto may sneer '*Rovigo no m'intrigo*', but this prosperous little provincial capital doesn't give a damn. For a landmark, Rovigo can match Bologna with its odd couple of leaning towers, the 11th-century **Torri Donà**, one tall, one stubby. Nearby (nothing is far), central Piazza Vittorio Emanuele II is a handsome trapezoid dotted with palaces, one containing the **Pinacoteca dell'Accademia dei Concordi** (*open Mon–Fri 9.30–12 and 3.30–7, Sat 9.30–12; July and Aug, Mon–Sat 10–1; adm free*), founded by local scholars in 1580, with a fine collection of works by Giovanni Bellini, Lorenzo Lotto, Palma Vecchio and others. From adjacent Piazza Garibaldi, follow Via Silvestri back to the octagonal **La Rotonda**, by Francesco Zamberlan, a pupil of Palladio, with a detached tower by Longhena and walls covered with 17th-century paintings glorifying Venetian bureaucrats.

Getting Around

From **Rovigo** there are frequent buses to Adria and the Delta towns; trains also run from Rovigo to Adria and Chioggia (1hr 20mins), or south to Ferrara (30mins) and Bologna (1hr). Rovigo's **bus station** is on the Piazzale G. Di Vittorio; the **train station** is on the Piazza Riconoscenza. Fratta Polèsine can be reached by bus from Rovigo.

Tourist Information

Rovigo: Via J. H. Dunant 10, t 0425 361 481, f 0425 30416, apt@gal.adigecolli.it
Rosolina Mare: Via dei Ligustri 3, t 0426 68012.

Where to Stay and Eat

Rovigo ✉ 45100
★★★★**Villa Regina Margherita**, Viale Regina Margherita 6, t 0425 361 540, f 0425 31301.

A few steps from Rovigo's centre, this Liberty-style villa is far and away the most stylish place to stay; bedrooms are well equipped, if lacking the high tone of the public rooms.

Tre Pini, Viale Porto Po 68, t 0425 421 111 (*moderate*). A little villa in the pines, serving delightful homemade *tortellini* and fresh salmon. *Closed Sun, Aug.*

Tavernetta Dante dai Trevisani, Corso del Popolo 212, t 0425 26386 (*moderate*). Here you can try that famous medieval Veneto favourite, *pappardelle all'anatra* (broad flat noodles with duck sauce) as well as other treats. *Closed Sun.*

Degli Amici, Via Quirina 4, t 0425 91045 (*moderate*). The best place of all, 8km south of Rovigo in Arquà Polèsine, where fresh- and salt-water fish share the tempting menu with locally reared duck and goose, prepared in an old wood-burning oven. *Closed Wed, and in summer Sat and Sun lunch.*

From Rovigo it's 18km southwest to **Fratta Polèsine**, where Palladio's pretty temple-fronted **Villa Badoera** (1570) is now property of the city of Rovigo, with its frescoes of pseudo-Roman grotesques by Giallo Fiortino (*currently closed for restoration*).

Buses and trains from Rovigo also head east for **Adria**, a dusty place dominated by a radio mast, founded by the Etruscans and colonized by the Greeks in the 6th century BC, when it stood on the shore of the sea that took its name. The Venice of its day, Adria has but one canal now, and a **Museo Archeologico Nazionale** at Piazzale degli Etruschi (*t 0426 21612; open 9–7 daily, Thurs, Fri and Sat also 8.30–11pm; adm*), with lovely Roman glass and a 3rd-century BC iron chariot of Gaulish workmanship, found entombed with three tiny horses.

The Po Delta

After travelling over 652km, the Po splits into six major branches, creating a reed-filled delta, a marshy wonderland of a thousand islets, haven for waterfowl and migratory birds. Before it became the **Parco del Po**, a few resorts sprung up along the sandy, pine-shaded shores – **Rosolina Mare** and **Isola Albarella**; they now try hard to be ecologically correct. There are several **boat cruises** that explore the delta, departing from **Porto Tolle** or **Taglio di Po**. Contact the tourist office for details.

North of Padua: up the Valley of the Brenta

Some of the Veneto's best-known sites are north of Padua, in the foothills of the Dolomites: Castelfranco, birthplace of Giorgione, Àsolo, where the Queen of Cyprus held her fabled Renaissance court, and several outstanding villas, including Masèr, where Palladio and Veronese collaborated to create a unique work of art.

Castelfranco and Cittadella

Piombino Dese, just off the main SS307 from Padua to Castelfranco, is a sprawling rural *comune*, and a must-detour for Palladiophiles. Its 1554 **Villa Cornaro**, a block from the Piombino Dese train station (*t 049 936 5017; garden only, interior by appointment*) is one of the master's most innovative and well-preserved structures, the first with a double loggia; it was frescoed in 1717 by Mattia Bortoloni with biblical scenes.

Castelfranco Vèneto, further north, basks in the glory of having given the world Giorgione, in 1478. Big George in return gave Castelfranco a masterpiece: the **Duomo**'s *Castelfranco Madonna* (1504), a triangular composition of the Virgin, St Francis and the local soldier-saint Liberalis, their remote figures inhabiting the same ineffable, dreamlike world as his paintings in the Accademia in Venice. Next to the *duomo*, the **Casa del Giorgione** (*open Tues–Sun, 9.30–12.30 and 3–6 during the summer months; adm*) is decorated with a *chiaroscuro* frieze of scientific instruments attributed to Giorgione, and has copies of all this most elusive of painters' works.

Castelfranco itself is a walled city, built by Treviso in 1199 to counter the ambitions of Padua. The Paduans, tit for tat, founded the egg-shaped **Cittadella** 15km to the west; one tower in its mighty 13th-century walls was Ezzelino's infamous torture chamber (*cf. Paradiso* IX, 54). The Venetians added the fine lion with a kinky tail in the square.

From Castelfranco you can also nip up to **Fanzolo**, 5km to the northeast, for another of Palladio's finest: **Villa Emo** (*t 0423 476 334; open April–Oct 3–7, Sun and hols 10–12.30*

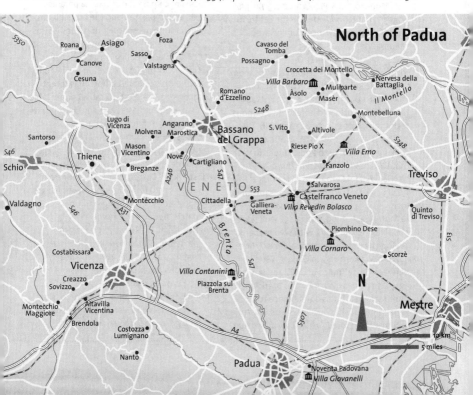

Getting Around

From Padua there are **buses** and **trains** to Bassano del Grappa via Castelfranco (40mins); from Vicenza change trains at Castelfranco, passing Cittadella on the way. From Venice, change in Treviso. Bassano's **bus station** is in Piazzale Trento, near the tourist office, t 0424 30850, while the **train station** is at the top of Via Chilesotti. Frequent buses from Montebelluna, Bassano or Treviso serve Àsolo (14km) and Masèr (6km further); others, from Bassano and Vicenza, run to Maròstica (20 buses daily), Lonedo di Lugo, Thiene (25km) and Asiago (36km).

Tourist Information

Castelfranco Veneto: Via Francesco Maria Preti 39, t 0423 495 000.
Àsolo: Piazza G. D'Annunzio 2, t 0423 529 046, f 0423 524 137.

Where to Stay and Eat

Castelfranco Veneto ✉ 31033
★★★**Al Moretto**, Via S. Pio X 10, t 0423 721 313, f 0423 721 066 (*moderate*). In the centre of Castelfranco, in a 17th-century palace.
★★★**Roma**, Via Fabio Filzi 39, t 0423 721 616, f 0423 721 515 (*moderate*). Outside the fortifications but with a good view of them.
★★★**Ca' delle Rose**, on the Circonvallazione Est, Salvarosa, t 0423 490 232, f 0423 490 261 (*moderate*). A little old hotel with a famous restaurant, **Barbesin**, t 0423 490 446. The setting is as idyllic as its fresh and seasonal cooking; the veal with apples melts in your mouth. *Closed Wed eve and Thurs.*
★★★★**Fior**, Via dei Carpani 18, t 0423 721 212, f 0423 498 771 (*expensive*). In the same area, in an old villa and park, with pool.
Alle Mura, Via Preti 69, t 0423 498 098 (*expensive*). Next to the walls, with well prepared seafood dishes and a garden. *Closed Thurs.*
Palazzino, Via Roma 29, in Galliera Vèneto, between Castelfranco and Cittadella, t 049 596 9224 (*expensive*). A former patrician hunting lodge that is a great place to try Renaissance dishes such as pheasant stuffed with truffles. *Closed Tues eve, Wed, and Aug.*

Fanzolo ✉ 31050
★★★**Villa Emo**, Via Stazione 5, t 0423 476 414, f 0423 487 043 (*expensive*). A few elegant rooms in the wing of a Palladian villa; peace and quiet guaranteed. Fine dining too (*expensive) Closed Mon, Tues lunch*).

Masèr and Around ✉ 31010
Da Bastian, Via Cornuda, t 0423 565 400 (*moderate*). Just up the road from Palladio's villa, dine in enchanting surroundings, where the pâté, *risotto*, Venetian-style snails and desserts are renowned. *Closed Wed eve and Thurs, some of Aug.*
Al Ringraziamento, Via S. Pio X 107, t 0423 543271 (*expensive*). Just north in Cavaso del Tomba, you can dine at this romantic restaurant, where the creative chef is a master at concocting delicious dishes. *Closed Mon, Tues lunch, some of Aug.*

Àsolo ✉ 31011
★★★★★**Villa Cipriani**, Via Canova 298, t 0423 952 166, f 0423 952 095 (*very expensive*). One of Italy's most evocative hotels, in a 16th-century house that once belonged to Robert Browning, decorated with Eleonora Duse's Persian carpets. It overlooks a paradise of hills and cypresses, and the hotel has an enchanting rose garden full of song birds; some of its 32 rooms are in garden houses.
★★★★**Al Sole**, Via Collegio 33, t 0423 528 111, f 0423 528 399 (*expensive*). In the historic centre, this celebrated hotel has recently had an overhaul and is now more comfortable than ever, but hasn't lost any charm, or its memories of famous past guests.
★★★**Duse**, Via Browning 190, t 0423 55241, f 0423 950 404 (*expensive). Overlooking Àsolo's central piazza, with a little garden.
Hosteria Ca' Derton, Piazza D'Annunzio 11, t 0423 52730 (*moderate*). In one of Àsolo's oldest houses, featuring traditional dishes to match the setting. *Closed Mon.*
Ai Due Archi, Via Roma 55, t 0423 952 201 (*moderate*). Wood-panelled, intimate, elegant and antique like Asolo itself; serves delicious *polenta* in various guises. *Closed Wed eve and Thurs.*
Caffè Centrale, Via Roma 72. Every passing celebrity has had a drink at this historic café; it's a great place to watch the world go by.

and 3–7; Oct–Mar, Sat and Sun only 2–6; adm exp), and the only villa still owned by the family that commissioned it. Like most, this ranch was designed as a working farm, and was one of the first in Europe to grow maize (1536), used primarily to fatten pigeons before it was used for *polenta* to fatten Venetians. The main rooms were frescoed with brightly coloured mythologies by Giambattista Zelotti; the *barchesse* or storage wings are now a hotel. Palladio also designed the long rows of workers' cottages that are slowly being restored.

Villa Barbaro at Masèr

t 0423 923 004; open Mar–Oct, Tues, Sat, Sun and hols 3–6;
Nov–Feb, Sat, Sun and hols, 2.30–5; adm exp.

Montebelluna, also northeast of Castelfranco, was another favourite area for building summer villas, including the lovely Villa Barbaro at Masèr. Begun in 1568 for brothers Daniele and Marcantonio Barbaro (the former was Patriarch of *Aquileia* and one of Venice's most distinguished humanistic scholars), Masèr is a unique synthesis of two great talents: Palladio and his friend Paolo Veronese.

Palladio taught Veronese about space and volume, and nowhere is this so evident as in these ravishing, architectonic *trompe l'œil* frescoes, populated by the original owners and their pets, who linger as if the villa lay under the same spell as Sleeping Beauty's castle – an effect heightened by the slippers passed out to visitors at the door (to protect the original floors). Signora Barbaro and her sons gaze down from painted balconies; a little girl opens a door; a dog waits in a corner; painted windows offer views of imaginary landscapes; the huntsman in the far bedroom is Veronese, gazing across the row of rooms at his mistress.

Behind the villa, the nymphaeum is guarded by giants sculpted by Marcantonio himself. The striking, if crumbling, **Tempietto**, just across the road, is a miniature pantheon designed by Palladio in 1580 and decorated by Alessandro Vittoria.

Àsolo, the 'Town of a Hundred Horizons'

The old walled hilltown of **Àsolo** was the consolation prize given by Venice in 1489 to Queen Caterina Cornaro after demanding her abdication from the throne of Cyprus. It could have been worse: Àsolo is one of the most enchanting spots in Italy, and Caterina's Renaissance court lent it a high degree of refinement and art. Pietro Bembo used it as a setting for his dialogues on love, *Gli Asolani*, and Giorgione strolled through its rose-gardens strumming his lute; the enforced idleness in Àsolo perhaps inspired his invention of art merely for the sake of pleasure. In the last century, Àsolo was also a beloved retreat of Robert Browning (his last volume of poems was entitled *Asolando*; 'Pippa Passes' was set here as well). Eleonora Duse and the great traveller Freya Stark lived and are buried here.

Some people never get beyond Àsolo's perfect piazza with its 16th-century **Fontana Maggiore**, but you can look at the **Castello** with its watch tower (in both senses of the word – it tells the time) and what little remains of the garden where Queen Caterina lived in 'lace and poetry'; the courtyard has a modern *bocce* court. In 1700 the great hall was replaced with a theatre, but in 1930 the John Deere tractor heir bought and rebuilt it in his villa in Sarasota, Florida.

Near the castle, the frescoed **Loggia del Capitano** contains a museum dedicated to Queen Caterina, Browning and La Duse (*closed until kingdom come for restoration*). The **Duomo** has works by Lotto, Jacopo da Bassano and Vivarini. For the famous view over Àsolo of 'a hundred horizons' climb (or drive – the road is halfway down the hill) up to the **Rocca**, built over a Roman fort (*t 0497 710 977; open Sat, Sun, or any day by appointment for groups, or ask in the tourist office; closed for bad weather; adm*).

Possagno, 10km north at the foot of Monte Grappa, was the birthplace of Antonio Canova (1757–1822), the ultimate neoclassical sculptor, the favourite of Napoleon and several popes. You can visit his house, and clay and plaster models, in the **Gypsoteca** (*t 0423 544 323; open daily exc Mon, 9–12 and 3–6; Oct–April 9–12 and 2–5; adm*).

Most artists leave a work or two in their home towns, but Canova left nothing less than a full-scale model of the Pantheon with the Parthenon stuck on front as his last resting place. The town itself describes the **Tempio** as 'one of the greatest monuments that man on earth has ever erected – in praise of God – to himself'. You can climb up the dome (*open Tues–Sun 9–12 and 2–5; adm*); or study the leaning bell tower, and try to figure out if it was built that way.

Bassano del Grappa, Maròstica and Asiago

Carry on west for more Veneto essentials: Bassano del Grappa with its covered bridge, Maròstica, where they play chess with human players, more villas by Palladio and the mountains of Asiago.

Bassano del Grappa

Sprawled over the foothills of the Alps where the Brenta begins its flow down the plain, the colourful bustling town of Bassano celebrated its first millennium in 1998. Palladio gets credit for its picturesque landmark, the **Ponte degli Alpini**, the unique covered wooden bridge. First constructed in 1599, the bridge has been rebuilt several times to the master's design – lastly in 1969, after it was swept away in the Brenta's flood. At one end, in the Palazzo Beltrame-Menarola, the grappa distillery Poli operates a **Museo della Grappa** where you can taste and buy (*t 0424 524 426; open 9–1 and 2.30–7.30; closed Mon am; adm free*).

Bassano's centre is made up of a string of squares: first is medieval Piazzotto Montevecchio, where the old **Monte di Pietà** (municipal pawn shop) is covered with the coats of arms of 120 Venetian *podestà*. This is linked to piquant Piazza Libertà, hogged by the neoclassical façade of the mastodontic church of **San Giovanni**, while the next square, Piazza Garibaldi, is guarded, both physically and spiritually, by a medieval **Torre Civica** and the Gothic church of **San Francesco**. Its cloister contains the **Museo Civico** (*open Tues–Sat 9–6.30, Sun 3.30–6.30; adm; same ticket for the ceramics museum*), with an excellent archaeological section of finds from Magna Graecia, and paintings with an emphasis on the dark and/or stormy by the Bassano family, and

Tourist Information

Bassano: Largo Corona d'Italia 35, t 0424 524
351, f 0424 525 301.
Maròstica: Piazza Castello, t 0424 72127, f 0424
72800, *proloco@telemar.it*.
Asiago: Via Stazione 5, t 0424 462 661, f 0424
462 445; they also have information about
visits to the University of Padua's astro-
physical observatory, t 0424 462 221,
apt-asiago@ascom.vi.it.

Where to Stay and Eat

Bassano del Grappa ✉ 36061

As you may have noticed wandering
through town, dried mushrooms and honey as
well as grappa are specialities of Bassano, but
it's yet another treat that attracts droves of
hungry gourmets every April: Asparagi DOC di
Bassano, long fat white asparagus, delicate
and full of flavour, and perfect for spring-
cleaning one's internal plumbing. Anyone can
grow white asparagus by shielding the stalks
from the sun with mounds of dirt. But in
Bassano they somehow do it better: try it the
local way, *asparagi alla bassanese*, blanched
and topped with a hollandaise-type sauce

made with cooked eggs and olive oil, or
simply *alla parmigiana*.

****Belvedere**, in a 15th-century house in
Piazzale Gen. Giardino 14, t 0424 529 845,
f 0424 529 849 (*expensive*). This central hotel
has the best rooms in town: convenient, if
not always quiet; ask for one in the back.
The hotel's elegant restaurant, at Viale delle
Fosse 1, t 0424 524 988, serves Bassano's
finest gastronomic delights, both Veneto
and Italian classics, with the promised view.
Closed Sun.

***Brennero**, near the station at Via Torino 7,
t 0424 228 538, f 0424 227 921 (*moderate*).
Traditional and comfortable for a short stay.

****Villa Palma**, Via Chemin Palma 30, t 0424
577 407, f 0424 87687 (*expensive*). A lovely,
award-winning hotel, just east of Bassano at
Mussolente. It occupies an elegant 17th-
century villa, with plush rooms full of
high-tech gizmos and a gourmet restaurant.

Al Sole-Da Tiziano, Via Vitorelli 41, t 0424 523
206 (*moderate*). Besides Bassano's hotel
restaurants, there's this beautiful dining
room, which offers a perfect *risotto*,
delicious duck, and Bassano's favourite
seasonal ingredients: mushrooms, white
asparagus and radicchio.
Closed Mon, July.

especially Jacopo (his masterpiece, the twilit *Baptism of St Lucia*). Alessandro
Magnasco weighs in with the uncanny *Burial of a Trappist Monk* and *Franciscan
Banquet*, full of racing, wraith-like friars. There are calmer works too: Michele
Giambono's *Madonna* and a beautiful recently restored *Crucifix* by Guariento.

In the mid 17th century Bassano and the nearby town of Nove became the Veneto's
top ceramics manufacturers, a status they maintain to this day, thanks to 56 firms. In
the 18th-century Palazzo Sturm, just up Via Ferracina from the bridge, the **Museo
della Ceramica** (*open April–Oct 9–12.30 and 3.30–6.30, closed Sun am, Mon; June–Sept
same hours, also Sun 10–12.30 ; Nov–Mar Tues–Sat 9–12.30 Fri, Sat and Sun 3.30–6.30;
same adm as Museo Civico*) has a display of local ware and porcelain knicknacks.

The 'Grappa' was added to Bassano's name in 1928, not for its fire water, but in
memory of the terrible fighting in the First World War at Cima Grappa, where the
Italians held the line after Caporetto. The road up to **Cima Grappa** (5,822ft), the Strada
Cadorna, was built during the conflict and begins in Romano d'Ezzelino. On top, the
Galleria Vittorio Emanuele II was the enormous trench dug by the Italian military to
shelter its battery of guns; displays and a museum describe the conflict. The
monumental cemetery holds the remains of 12,615 Italians; the slightly smaller
Austro-Hungarian cemetery contains 10,590 dead (*open mid-May–Sept 10–12 and 2–5;
Oct–mid-May 10–12 and 1–4*).

Maròstica ✉ 36063

Maròstica is famous for its cherries and a rather unusual dish, *paetarosta col magaragno*, young turkey roasted on a spit and served with pomegranate sauce.

Ristorante al Castello, t 0424 73315 (*moderate*). Such a delicious dish may appear on the menu in this restaurant. In a renovated castle, there are lovely views and lovely food, with an emphasis on fresh local ingredients. Top it off with a *caffè corretto*, 'corrected' with one of a score of different grappas.

★★★La Rosina, 2km north in Valle San Florian, Contrà Narchetti 4, t 0424 75839, f 0424 470 290 (*moderate*). Located in a superb hilltop setting, the restaurant here is run by a talented chef; rooms are modern and comfortable. *Closed Aug.*

Asiago ✉ 36012

Asiago is synonymous with its low-fat cow's milk cheese with a bit of a bite, one of the few in Italy to achieve DOC status – and surprisingly little known outside Italy. There are two kinds: fresh *asiago pressato*, delicate and soft, often used in cooking, fried or in salads, and *asiago d'allevo*, ripened like cheddar, and sold either *mezzano, vecchio* and *stravecchio* (middle-aged, old and extra old), becoming more intensely flavoured with age.

★★★Erica, Via Garibaldi 55, t 0424 462 113, f 0424 462 861 (*moderate*). A long-established hotel that is a cosy bet for a summer or winter stay. *Open Dec–mid-April, June–mid-Sept.*

★★★Da Barba, t 0424 463 363, f 0424 462 888 (*moderate*). A little place in Kaberlaba, 5km from Asiago, offering magnificent views, a warm welcome and good food not far from the pistes. *Closed May and mid-Oct–Nov.*

Lepre Bianca da Pippo (Phil's White Hare), at Camona, t 0424 445 666 (*moderate, restaurant expensive*). Just northeast of Asiago in the comune of Gallio. Not only are the rooms cosy, but there's opportunity for memorable dining in an elegant English-style dining room; seasonal dishes, exquisitely fresh seafood (rare up in these hills) and delicate desserts. *Closed Mon.*

★★★La Bocchetta, t 0424 704 117, f 0424 700 024 (*moderate*). Midway between Bassano del Grappa and Asiago, at Conco. An old mountain inn and restaurant from the early 18th century, rebuilt in over-the-top Tyrolean style, but with a handy indoor pool, sauna and mountain bike hire as well.

West of Bassano

More colourful ceramics wait in **Nove**, where budding potters learn the ropes at the national school: part of the complex includes the **Museo Istituto Statale d'Arte per la Ceramica**, Via Giove 1 (*open school hours*); the far larger **Museo Civico della Ceramica** in the 19th-century Palazzo De Fabris (*open Tues–Sun 9–1; adm*) has works from the last three centuries by local masters and foreign artists, including Picasso.

Maròstica, 7km west of Bassano, is a striking storybook town enclosed in 13th-century walls, its upper castle sprawled over the hill and a lower castle, abode of the Venetian lord and now the town hall, sitting like a giant rook in the main piazza. This provides the perfect setting for the storybook event that has put Maròstica on the map: the *Partita a Scacchi*, the human chess match, which takes place on even-numbered years, the second weekend in September. The game, played with its human (and horse) 'pieces' in medieval costume on a 72 sq ft board, commemorates the contest in 1454 for the hand of Lionora Parisio. Her father, the Venetian governor, refused to let her two suitors fight the traditional duel 'in sad memory of the unhappy lovers Madame Juliet Capuleti and Master Romeo Montecchio' – and even offered the loser his younger daughter. The level of play matches the gorgeous costumes; each game is a reproduction of a grand masters' duel, although things can go wrong when the pieces misunderstand their commands, announced in archaic Venet. At other times the Renaissance finery is on display in the castle's **Museo dei Costumi** (*open Sun 9–6; or ask at the Pro Loco; adm*).

Further west, in **Lonedo di Lugo**, near the town of Lugo (about 6km north of Breganze), there are two important villas by Palladio. **Villa Godi Valmarana Malinverni**, Via Palladio, 44 (*open Mar–May, Sept and Oct, Tues, Sat, Sun and hols 2–6; June–Aug daily 3–7; adm*), built in 1540, was his very first, with the central portion, usually the most prominent and decorated part of his villas, recessed behind two large wings. The interior was frescoed by Padovano and assistants, and contains a fossil collection and rooms of Italian 19th-century painting.

The later and more classically elegant **Villa Piovene Porto Godi** is a couple of doors down, in a neoclassical park (*gardens only; open daily 2.30–7*).

In the centre of pleasant **Thiene**, 10km to the west, the quattrocento **Villa de Porta Colleoni** (*t 0445 366015; open 12 Mar–Nov except July, Sun only for tours at 3, 4 and 5, groups every day if booked; adm*) is an attractive castle-villa, with towers, battlements and Venetian Gothic windows; inside there are frescoes, antique ceramics and jumbo paintings of the former residents of the 18th-century stables on the grounds. Opposite note the flamboyant little church of the **Natività**, its roofline studded with flames of curly kale. Thiene's slender **Torre Civica** dates from the 1600s.

North of Thiene you can climb into the cool green high plain of **Asiago** (3,257ft), known for its salubrious climate, cheese, pretty walks and skiing. Like all the villages, the main town of Asiago had to be completely rebuilt after its use as a battlefield in the war to end all wars. Its focal point is a massive pink stone **Municipio**, with an enormous tower and lion and, in the park behind, a delightful **fountain** features Pan and all the animals of the forest. A ghastly number of war dead – 12,795 identified, 21,491 nameless, 19,999 Austro-Hungarians – lie in the hilltop **Sacrario**, which also houses a small **Museo Storico** (*open daily 9–12 and 3–5*).

A Grappa Digression

Although a lot of grappa does come from Bassano del Grappa, its name doesn't derive from the town or its mountains but from *graspa*, the residue left at the bottom of the wine vat after the must is removed; it can be drunk unaged and white, or aged in oak barrels, where it takes on a rich, amber tone. First mentioned in a 12th-century chronicle, grappa, or aqua vitae ('the water of life'), was chugged down as a miracle-working concoction of earth and fire to dispel ill humours. In 1601 the Doge created a University Confraternity of Aqua Vitae to control quality; during the First World War Italy's Alpine soldiers adopted Bassano's enduring bridge as their symbol and its grappa to keep them on their feet. One of their captains described it perfectly:

Grappa is like a mule; it has no ancestors and no hope of descendants; it zigzags through you like a mule zigzags through the mountains; if you're tired you can hang on to it; if they shoot you can use it as a shield; if it's too sunny you can sleep under it; you can speak to it and it'll answer, cry and be consoled. And if you really have decided to die, it will take you off happily.

Vicenza

'The city of Palladio', prettily situated below the Monte Bérici, is an architectural pilgrimage shrine and knows it; where other Italians grouse about being a nation of museum curators, the prim Vicentini glory in their city, the intellectual product of a gentry immersed in humanistic and classical thought (a gentry, they gently remind you, that was far better educated than those merchants by the lagoon, who ruled Vicenza in its heyday). Their pride was recently vindicated when UNESCO placed Vicenza on its list of World Heritage Sites. Although it was heavily damaged during the Second World War, restorers have tidied up all the scars. Vicenza's other name now is the 'City of Gold', thanks to its gold-working industry, the most important in Europe; it is also the birthplace of Federico Faggin, inventor of the silicon chip. Add machine tools, textiles and shoes, and you have one of Italy's wealthiest cities.

Getting There

Vicenza is on the main **rail** line between Verona (45mins), Padua (35mins) and Venice (1hr); there is also a branch line up to Thiene; trains always run, if not on time. The station is on the south side of the town, at the end of Viale Roma. The FTV **bus station**, t 0444 223115, is alongside it: buses depart from here for Bassano and Maròstica as well as for Asiago, Rovigo, Este, Lonigo and other destinations in the region. You can rent a **bike** at the train station's *deposito bagagli* – part of the deal includes a free map with bike routes.

Leave your **car** in one of the two attended car parks, one at the west end of the town by the Mercato Ortofrutticolo and the other to the east by the stadium. Both are linked to the centre by special bus every five minutes.

Tourist Information

Piazza Matteotti, 12; also Piazza Duomo 5, t 0444 320 854, f 0444 327 072. (*open Mon–Sat 9–1 and 2.30–6, Sun 9–1*).

Where to Stay

Vicenza ✉ 36100

Vicenza has a limited selection of hotels.
****Campo Marzo, Viale Roma 21, t 0444 545 700, f 0444 320 495 (*expensive*). Near the railway station, providing modern, comfortable rooms.

***Cristina, Corso B. Felice 32, t 0444 323 751, f 0444 543 656 (*moderate*). For comfort in a central location.
**Casa Raffaele, Viale X Giugno 10 (through an arch in the Portici), t 0444 545 767, f 0444 542 2597 (*cheap*). Up on the slopes of Monte Bérico, offering good value, as well as tranquillity and great views.
**Due Mori, Contrà da Rode 26 (near the Piazza dei Signori), t 0444 321 888, f 0444 326 127 (*cheap*). Located on a quiet street in the historic district.
*Vicenza, t/f 0444 321 512. More basic than Due Mori, a few doors down the street.
****Genziana, Via Mazzini 75, Selva, t 0444 572 398, f 0444 574310 (*moderate*). If you're driving, 6km west of town in Altavilla towards Montecchio Maggiore, this hotel is warm and welcoming and full of art; there's a pool too. *Closed some of Aug*.
***Locanda Grego, Via Roma 24, t 0444 350 588, f 0444 350 695 (*moderate*). Going in the other direction, to Bolzano Vicentino in the hills above the Vicenza Nord *autostrada* exit, a hotel in an old postal relay station, with well-furnished rooms and a good family-run restaurant. *Closed some of Aug*.

Eating Out

Whatever airs Vicenza puts on in the culture department become somewhat draughty in the kitchen – this is *polenta* and *baccalà* (salt cod) country. The hearty and filling fare is not the most subtle on the stomach. But the locals

Porta Castello to the Piazza dei Signori

From the station, Viale Roma enters the historic centre through the **Porta Castello**, with its powerful 11th-century tower. The palace with the columns the size of sequoias is the **Palazzo da Porto Breganze,** designed by Palladio and partly built by his pupil Scamozzi, before the very monumentality of the design defeated him. Scamozzi also built the less exciting **Palazzo Bonin** at No.13, after his master's designs.

From Piazza Castello, Contrà Vescovado leads to the Gothic **Duomo**, which was carefully pieced together after the war and houses a beautiful polyptych by Lorenzo Veneziano, painted in 1356, in the 5th chapel on the right. Excavations have revealed the Duomo's 8th-century ancestor and a stretch of Roman road and, under the square, a **Criptoportico**, a subterranean passage from a 1st century AD palace. Down Contrà Porti, turn at Via Pigafetta for the fine eclectic **Casa Pigafetta** (1444), birthplace

beg to differ: their *baccalà alla vicentina*, made of top-quality cod endlessly pummelled with a wooden hammer, soaked for 36 hours, sprinkled with cheese and browned in a mix of butter, oil, anchovies and onions, then cooked over a slow flame, and seasoned with parsley, pepper and milk, is 'a whole refined civilization...simmering in the pot' according to writer Guido Piovene. A favourite way to eat *polenta* is sliced and grilled, accompanied with *sopressa* sausage from Valli del Pasubio and Recoaro, or pigeon roasted on embers. Other specialities are *gnocchi* made with cinnamon and raisins, and *bigoli con l'arna*, fat spaghetti with duck sauce, delicious with a glass of red Tocai. Montecchio Maggiore is known for its *mostarda*, a spicy condiment of fruit.

Nuovo Cinzia & Valerio, t 0444 505 213 (*expensive*). For perfectly prepared seafood, take a walk to Piazzetta Porta Padova, where you can find this restaurant serving *tagliatelle* with salmon, cuttlefish *risotto* or grilled sole, followed by home-made ice cream and crisp biscuits. *Closed Sun eve, Mon, Aug.*

Antica Decchio Trattoria Tre Visi, Corso Palladio 25, **t** 0444 324 868 (*moderate*). Luigi Da Porto, author of the original version of *Romeo and Juliet*, was born in this 15th-century palace that was converted into an inn some 200 years ago. It still serves exquisite food today and, with its fireplace and rustic fittings, is a charming place to enjoy good, high quality Veneto cooking and home-made pasta dishes. Be sure to try the local delicacies; the ambience here, while

busy, is always very friendly. *Closed Sun eve, Mon, July.*

Trattoria Framarin, Via Battista Framarin 48, **t** 0444 570 407 (*moderate*). Just west of the city walls at this family-run place you'll also find delicious homemade pasta and a warm welcome. *Closed Sun, some of Aug.*

Vecchia Guardia, Contrà Pescherie Vecchie 11, **t** 0444 321 231 (*cheap*). Located near Piazza delle Erbe, for pizza and straightforward meals. *Closed Thurs.*

Antica Casa della Malvasia, Contrà delle Morette 5, near Piazza dei Signori, **t** 0444 543 704 (*cheap*). Basic, lively and very popular, with real home cooking.

Righetti, Piazza Duomo (*cheap*). A popular stop for a cheap lunch, this bustling self-service canteen has seats spilling on to the piazza. *Closed Sat, Sun.*

Antica Offelleria della Meneghi, Contrà Cavour 18. If you need something sweet and stylish, Vicenza has two historic *pasticcerie* near the Basilica: this one, and **Sorarù**, Piazzetta Palladio 17.

Principe, Via S. Caboto 16, **t** 0444 67131, **f** 0444 675 921 (*hotel moderate, restaurant expensive*). The real gastronomic fireworks await just east of Montecchio Maggiore at this restaurant (also a small hotel) in Arzignan. One of Italy's top young chefs – trained in France – prepares superb, imaginative meals, accompanied by a selection of homemade breads, a chariot of fine and unusual French cheeses and delightful pastries. *Closed Sun, some of Aug.*

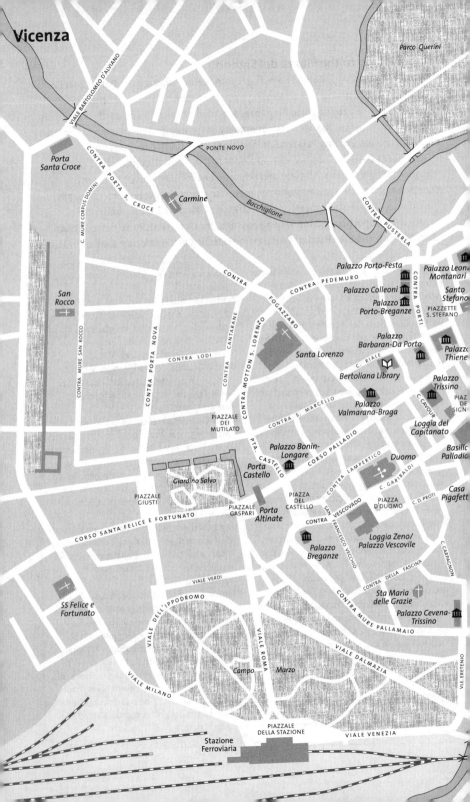

Vicenza

Parco Querini

Porta Santa Croce

PONTE NOVO

CONTRA PORTA S. CROCE

Carmine

Bacchiglione

CONTRA PUSTERLA

C. MURE CORPUS DOMINI

San Rocco

Palazzo Porto-Festa

Palazzo Leoni Montanari

CONTRA PEDEMURO

Palazzo Colleoni

Santo Stefano

CONTRA PORTI

CONTRA

Palazzo Porto-Breganze

PIAZZETTE S. STEFANO

CONTRA MURE SAN ROCCO

CONTRA PORTA NOVA

FOGAZZARO

Palazzo Barbaran-Da Porto

Palazzo Thiene

Santa Lorenzo

CONTRA LODI

CONTRA CANTARANE

CONTRA MOTTON S. LORENZO

C. RIALE

Bertoliana Library

Palazzo Trissino

C. CAVOUR

PIAZ DE SIGN

CONTRA S. MARCELLO

Palazzo Valmarana-Braga

PIAZZALE DEI MUTILATO

Loggia del Capitanato

PTA. CASTELLO

Palazzo Bonin-Longare

CORSO PALLADIO

Duomo

Basilic Palladia

CONTRA LAMPERTICO

Porta Castello

Giardino Salvo

PIAZZA DEL CASTELLO

C. GARIBALDI

PIAZZA D'DUOMO

Casa Pigafett

PIAZZALE GIUSTI

PIAZZALE GASPARI

Porta Altinate

CONTRA SAN VESCOVADO

C. D. PROTI

CORSO SANTA FELICE E FORTUNATO

Palazzo Breganze

CONTRA SAN FRANCESCO VECCHIO

Loggia Zeno/ Palazzo Vescovile

C. CARPAGNON

CONTRA DELLA FASCINA

VIALE VERDI

Sta Maria delle Grazie

SS Felice e Fortunato

VIALE DELL'IPPODROMO

CONTRA MURE PALLAMAIO

Palazzo Cevena-Trissino

VIALE ROMA

VIALE DALMAZIA

V.LE ERETENIO

VIALE MILANO

Campo Marzo

PIAZZALE DELLA STAZIONE

Stazione Ferroviaria

VIALE VENEZIA

of Antonio Pigafetta, who happened to be in Spain in 1519 when Magellan was setting out for the first of all world tours. Pigafetta went along, and wrote the definitive account of the voyage three years later. Note his motto '*Il n'est rose sans espine*' by the door. Beyond, to the left, lies the Piazza dei Signori.

Piazza dei Signori

This kingly square is the heart and soul of Vicenza, its public forum from Roman times to this day. In the 1540s the Vicentines decided that the piazza's crumbling old medieval Palazzo della Ragione needed a facelift to match their Renaissance-humanist aspirations. Having rejected designs by such luminaries as Sansovino and Giulio Romano, they surprisingly hired a young unknown called Palladio to give it a facelift. The city would never be the same.

In 1549 Palladio began working on the building, ever since known as the **Basilica** – 'hall of justice', as in Latin (*open Tues–Sun 9–5; adm*), and kept at it off and on until his death. Two tiers of rounded arches interspersed with Doric and Ionic columns give an appearance of Roman regularity, although Palladio had to vary the size of the arches to compensate for the irregularities in the Gothic structure. The roof is concealed behind a pediment lined with life-size statues; stare at them long enough and the urge to shoot them off like ducks in a penny arcade becomes almost irresistible. To see what Palladio was disguising, go behind the basilica to the Piazza delle Erbe, home to Vicenza's daily market, and its Torre del Tormento, the medieval prison.

The basilica shares Piazza dei Signori with the needle-like **Torre di Piazza** (12th–15th century), and Palladio's **Loggia del Capitanato** (1571), built to celebrate the victory at Lepanto. If its grand columns and arches seem confined in too narrow a space, it's because the loggia was meant to extend over several more bays. The neighbouring 16th-century **Monte di Pietà**, built in two sections, was frescoed in the 1900s with Liberty-style pin-up girls, some of whom still faintly survive moral outrage, war damage and Father Time.

As in Venice, this piazza has two columns: of the Redeemer (1640) and of St Mark (1473). A right turn here down Via San Michele leads to the Retrone, one of Vicenza's two rivers, spanned here by the **Ponte S. Michele** (1620). There are lovely views of the Retrone lapping the houses and, on the opposite bank, the **Oratorio di S. Nicola** is remarkable for the creepiest altarpiece in Italy, *La Trinità* by the 17th-century Vicentine painter Francesco Maffei, whose feverish brush infected the Oratorio's walls as well, with the assistance of Giulio Caprioni.

Corso Palladio, Contrà Porti and Around

Returning to the Piazza dei Signori, step behind the Loggia del Capitanato to **Corso Palladio**, once called 'the most elegant street in Europe, not counting the Grand Canal in incomparable Venice'. Just to your right is Vincenzo Scamozzi's masterpiece, **Palazzo Trissino**, with an Ionic portico and superb courtyard (begun in 1592, now the Municipio), the city's prettiest, and the late-Gothic **Palazzo Da Schio** (1470s), or 'Ca' d'Oro'. Palladio himself is only dubiously linked to a couple of works on the street named after him; to find his work, turn up **Contrà Porti**, another elegant street:

Palazzo Iseppo Da Porto, at No.21, is one of his earlier works (1552), influenced by Raphael. Next door, the sombre Gothic **Palazzo Porto-Colleoni** (No. 19) hides an internal garden courtyard and an airy asymmetrical loggia; next to it, the late-Gothic **Palazzo Porto-Breganze** (No.17) has a beautiful door added in 1481 and a precious mullioned window, the only one in Vicenza with Venetian reversed arches.

The vast medieval **Palazzo Thiene** (now the Banca Popolare) was, like the basilica, a facelift project for Palladio, who was to make it the most imposing residence in all Vicenza; it was never completed – like many of Palladio's projects. The Contrà Porti side is a fine work by Lorenzo da Bologna. Around the corner is Palladio's work, with its weighty sculpted windows, rustication and Mannerist classicizing – his homage to Giulio Romano. Some of the interior retains its original and rather magnificent decoration; if the bank isn't too busy, ask to see the first floor's Rotonda with a domed vault and statues. Its neighbour on the corner of Contrà Riale, **Palazzo Barbaran-da Porto**, built from scratch by Palladio in 1570, now holds the **Museo Palladiano**, opening to coincide with a big exhibition on Palladio's influences in Europe (*contact the Institute for Palladian Studies, t 0444 323 014, courses@cisapalladio.org*).

Diagonally across the Contrà Zanella from the Palazzo Thiene, the church of **Santo Stefano** contains one of Palma Vecchio's most beautiful paintings, *Madonna with SS. George and Lucy and Musical Angel*. More fine art waits just at the other end of the Contrà S. Stefano in the chapels of the early Gothic **Santa Corona**: it contains, among other works, Veronese's *Adoration of the Magi* (1573) and Giovanni Bellini's *Baptism of Christ*, a late masterpiece set in a rugged landscape. Alongside the church, the **Museo Santa Corona** contains natural history exhibits and Paleoveneti, Roman and Lombard relics discovered in the area (*open Tues–Sat 9–12.30 and 2.15–5, Sun 9–12.30; adm*).

Vicenza's Perfect Architect

A Paduan by birth, Andrea di Pietro della Gondola (1508–80) had worked in Vicenza as a stonemason from the age of 16. When he was 29, he met the great humanist Giangiorgio Trissino, who saw a spark in the young man no one else had noticed, and gave him a Renaissance education, took him on a two-year tour of Rome, and gave him a new name: Palladio.

His first major commission, the Basilica, so captured the hearts of the Vicentines that they commissioned him to build their palaces and villas. He was, for them, the perfect architect, able to produce classical grandeur for very little money – mainly by using cheap brick coated with a marbly sheen of stucco.

Towards the end of his career, he summed up everything he knew in *I Quattro Libri dell' Architettura*, of which Sir Reginald Blomfield, in his *Studies in Architecture*, wrote pointedly, 'With the touch of pedantry that suited the times and invested his writings with a fallacious air of scholarship, he was the very man to summarize and classify, and to save future generations of architects the labour of thinking for themselves.'

The book contributed greatly to the Palladian movement in Britain and America that began in 1603, when Inigo Jones visited Vicenza, and reached its peak in the 1700s under its 'high priest', Lord Burlington, and its great admirer, Thomas Jefferson.

At the north end of the Corso, Palladio's open, airy **Palazzo Chiericati** (1550–1650) is one of his masterpieces, and now home to the **Pinacoteca** (*open Tues–Sat 9–5 June-Aug 9–9; adm*). The ground floor retains its original frescoes, including a hilarious ceiling by Domenico Brusasorci, who took it upon himself to portray the sun god and his steeds from the viewpoint of earthlings at noon – all bums and bellies. Upstairs are 24 rooms of art from the 14th to the 20th centuries, by Paolo Veneziano, Memling, Bartolomeo Montagna, Cima da Conegliano, Lorenzo Lotto, Sansovino, Tintoretto, Van Dyck, Jan Brueghel the Elder, Bassano, Veronese, Tiepolo *père* and *fils*, and the irrepressible Francesco Maffei (*Glorification of the Inquisitor Alvise Foscarini*).

Teatro Olimpico

Open Tues–Sun 9–5; between June and Aug 9–9; t 0444 222 800; adm. Tickets also cover the Basilica, Pinacoteca, the Museo del Risorgimento and the Museo Naturalistico.

Across Piazza Matteotti from the museum, the Teatro Olimpico was Palladio's swan-song, one of his most original works, a unique masterpiece of the Italian Renaissance, and the oldest operational indoor theatre in the world (1580). Palladio himself was a member of the group of 25 literati and dilettantes who formed the high-minded 'Olympic Academy' that built the theatre for their own plays and lectures. For the seating and stage, Palladio as always went back to his Vitruvius and the Roman theatres he had seen during his sojourns, while after his death Scamozzi added the stage set of a square and radiating streets in flawless, fake perspective – designed especially for the theatre's first production in 1585, Sophocles' *Oedipus Rex*, and meant to represent the city of Thebes. But here Thebes has become a pure ideal, a Renaissance dream city, so perfect that no one ever thought to change the set, or bothered, as the Council of Trent banned theatrical representations not long after. Now, however, it has been brought back to life, and is used for plays and ballets.

Outside the Historic Centre

Vicenza's oldest church, **SS. Felice e Fortunato** (a 10min walk from Piazza Castello), was built just after Constantine officialized Christianity. Since then the church has taken its licks from barbarians and earthquakes, but has been un-restored as much as possible to its 4th-century appearance, revealings mosaics in the right aisle and a martyr's shrine. Two other churches full of art are north of the *duomo* and Corso Palladio, up **Corso Fogazzaro**, an atmospheric street lined with porticoes: first, the 13th-century Franciscan **San Lorenzo**, with a lovely marble portal, and further on, **Santa Maria del Carmine**, a Gothic church decorated with 15th-century bas reliefs and altars by Veronese and Jacopo Bassano.

Monte Bérico and the Villa Rotonda

Vicenza's holy hill, Monte Bérico, rises just to the south of the city. Buses make the ascent every half-hour from the bus station, or you can walk up under the half-mile-long **Portici**, built in the 18th century to shelter pilgrims climbing to the Baroque **Basilica di Monte Bérico** (*open weekdays 6.15–12.30 and 2.30–7.30, holidays 6.15–8*).

This commemorates two 15th-century apparitions of the Virgin, and contains two first class paintings: *La Pietà* by Bartolomeo Montagna, and the *Supper of St Gregory the Great* by Veronese, hung in the refectory (down the steps to the left), and carefully pieced together after Austrian soldiers sliced it to shreds in 1848. Outside, there are superb views of the city and the Villa Rotonda.

From here, walk back down the Portici as far as Via M. D'Azeglio; not far down on the right is an alley to the **Villa Valmarana**, nicknamed 'dei Nani' after the stone dwarfs on the wall, arty ancestors of the garden gnome (*open 15 Mar–April daily 2.30–5.30; May–Sept Wed, Thurs, Sat, Sun 10–12 and daily 3–6; Oct–15 Nov daily 2–5; adm exp*). The villa's main draw is its sumptuous decoration by Giambattista Tiepolo, who frescoed the *Palazzina* with scenes of love versus duty from the *Iliad, Aeneid, Orlando Furioso* and *Jerusalem Delivered*. Son Giandomenico's intimate, ironic scenes of rural life in the *Foresteria* (guest house) undermine his father's Grand Manner under his nose.

From here, a further five-minute walk along the Stradella Valmarana (alternatively, by bus no.8 from the railway station) brings you to the **Villa Rotonda** (*gardens open 15 Mar–4 Nov, Tues, Wed and Sat 10–12; adm; interior open Wed only, same times; adm exp*), designed by Palladio for Cardinal Capra in 1551 and completed after his death by the faithful Scamozzi. Unlike Palladio's other villas, which were farmhouses with outbuildings, the Villa Rotonda was built for sheer delight, the occasional garden party – and the perfect setting for Joseph Losey's film, *Don Giovanni*. One of the main interests of the Accademia Olimpica was mathematics, and the Villa is an exercise in geometrical form – a circle in a cube, complemented by four symmetrical porches.

Around Vicenza: More Villas

The tourist office publishes a map listing the most important of the hundreds of villas of Vicenza province. Only a handful are open, and the ones that are often have bizarre hours, so be sure to check before setting out. Most are in the north (*see* p.404) or south in the Colli Berici; otherwise, it's easy to take a bus from Vicenza out to **Montecchio Maggiore**, 13km west along the road to Verona, defended by two Scaliger castles that in Da Porto's 1529 tale of *Romeo and Juliet* belonged to the Montagues and Cappelletti. Just before the village, the 18th-century **Villa Cordellina-Lombardi** (*open April–Oct Tues–Fri 9–1; Sat, Sun and hols 9–12, 3–6; f 0444 399 111; adm*), built in 1760 by Giorgio Massari, has colourful frescoes by a young Giambattista Tiepolo.

Verona

There is no world without Verona walls
But purgatory, torture, hell itself
Hence banished is banish'd from the world;
And world's exile is death.
                    Romeo and Juliet, Act III

Well, love leads one to extremes. When Cupid's pilgrims descend on Verona they sigh over 'Juliet's balcony' and other places concocted in response to a demand for

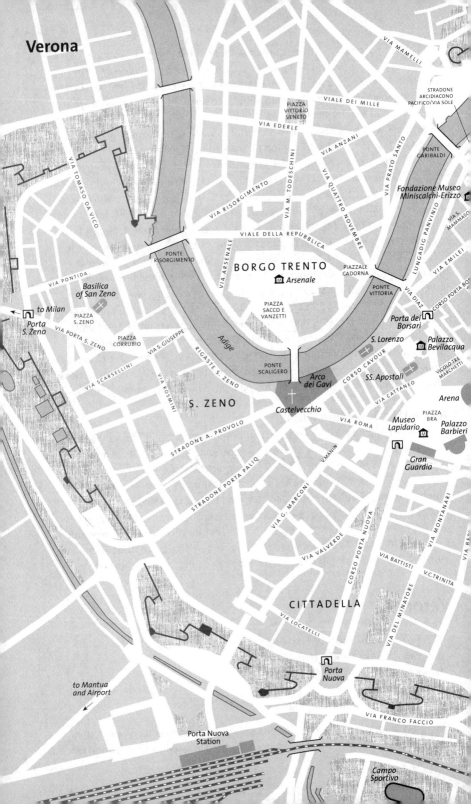

Verona

VIA MAMELLI

STRADONE ARCIDIACONO PACIFICO/VIA SOLE

VIALE DEI MILLE

PIAZZA VITTORIO VENETO

VIA EDERLE

VIA ANZANI

VIA PRATO SANTO

PONTE GARIBALDI

VIA TOMASO DA VICO

VIA RISORGIMENTO

VIA M. TODESCHINI

VIA QUATTRO NOVEMBRE

Fondazione Museo Miniscalchi-Erizzo

VIA S. MAMMASO

VIALE DELLA REPUBBLICA

PONTE RISORGIMENTO

VIA ARSENALE

BORGO TRENTO

Arsenale

PIAZZALE CADORNA

LUNGADIG PANVINIO

VIA EMILEI

VIA PONTIDA

Basilica of San Zeno

PIAZZA SACCO E VANZETTI

PONTE VITTORIA

VIA DIAZ

CORSO PORTA BO

to Milan

Porta S. Zeno

PIAZZA S. ZENO

PIAZZA CORRUBIO

VIA PORTA S. ZENO

VIA S. GIUSEPPE

Adige

S. Lorenzo

Porta dei Borsari

Palazzo Bevilacqua

VICOLO TRE MARCHETTI

VIA SCARSELLINI

VIA ROSMINI

RIGASTE S. ZENO

S. ZENO

PONTE SCALIGERO

Arco dei Gavi

Castelvecchio

CORSO CAVOUR

SS. Apostoli

VIA CATTANEO

Arena

STRADONE A. PROVOLO

VIA ROMA

Museo Lapidario

PIAZZA BRA

Palazzo Barbieri

VMANIN

Gran Guardia

STRADONE PORTA PALIQ

VIA G. MARCONI

VIA MONTANARI

VIA BEN

VIA VALVERDE

CORSO PORTA NUOVA

VIA BATTISTI

V.C.TRINITA

CITTADELLA

VIA DEL MINATORE

VIA LOCATELLI

to Mantua and Airport

Porta Nuova

Porta Nuova Station

VIA FRANCO FACCIO

Campo Sportivo

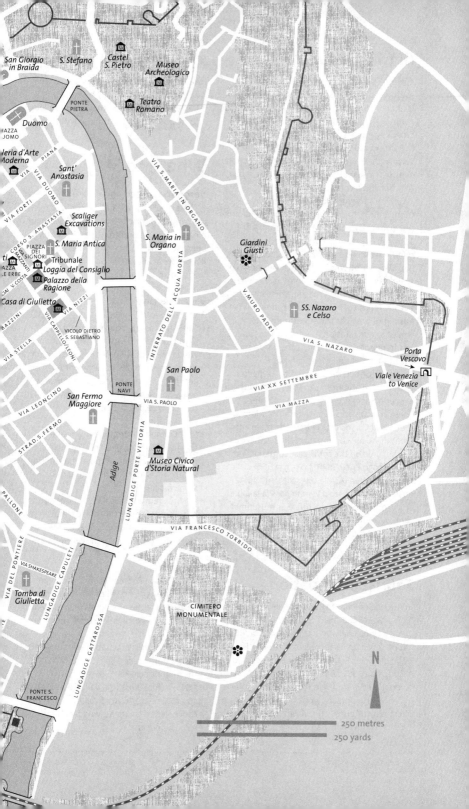

San Giorgio
in Braida

S. Stefano

Castel
S. Pietro

Museo
Archeologico

PONTE
PIETRA

Teatro
Romano

MAZZA
IOMO

Duomo

leria d'Arte
Moderna

Sant'
Anastasia

VIA S. MARIA IN ORGANO

VIA PIANA

VIA DUOMO

VIA FORTI

Scaliger
Excavations

S. Maria
in Organo

Giardini
Giusti

CORSO S. ANASTASIA

S. Maria Antica

PIAZZA
DEI
SIGNORI

ti

PIAZZA
DELLE ERBE

MAZZANTI

Tribunale

Loggia del Consiglio

Palazzo della
Ragione

VIA V. COSTA

Casa di Giulietta

VIA NIZZI

SS. Nazaro
e Celso

V MURO PADRI

INTERRATO DELL' ACQUA MORTA

VIA S. NAZARO

Porta
Vescovo

VICOLO DIETRO
S. SEBASTIANO

VIA CAPPELLO/LEONI

San Paolo

Viale Venezia
to Venice

VIA MAZZINI

VIA STELLA

VIA S. PAOLO

VIA XX SETTEMBRE

VIA MAZZA

San Fermo
Maggiore

PONTE
NAVI

VIA LEONCINO

STRAD.S.FERMO

Adige

LUNGADIGE PORTE VITTORIA

Museo Civico
d'Storia Natural

PALLONE

VIA DEL PONTIERE

Tomba di
Giulietta

VIA SHAKESPEARE

LUNGADIGE CAPULETI

VIA FRANCESCO TORBIDO

CIMITERO
MONUMENTALE

LUNGADIGE GATTAROSSA

PONTE S.
FRANCESCO

N

250 metres

250 yards

Getting Around

Verona's **airport** Valerio Catullo, to the southwest at Villafranca, has daily flights to London on British Airways, and direct flights to Rome, Naples and Bari. For information cal t 045 809 5666. Every 20 minutes buses link the airport to Porta Nuova train station in Verona; there are also three direct connections daily to the respective bus stations in Brescia, Mantua and Trento.

Verona is the junction of major **rail** lines from Venice (1hr 45mins), Milan (2hrs), Bologna (1hr 40mins), Trento (1hr) and Bolzano (1hr 40mins). The station, **Porta Nuova**, is a 15-minute walk south of Piazza Brà, along Corso Porta Nuova; alternatively, city buses nos.71 or 72 link the railway station with Piazza delle Erbe and Piazza Brà. A machine dispenses bus tickets opposite the station. The provincial APT **bus depot** is across the street from Porta Nuova railway station (t 045 800 4129) and has frequent departures to Lake Garda and the mountains, and Mantua (1 hour).

The historic centre is closed to traffic from 7.30 to 10am and from 1.30 to 4.30pm with the exception of cars going directly to hotels. There are **car parks** near the train station, Arena and Corso Porta Nuova, the main entry point if you are coming from the A4. **Bicycles** can be hired on the southeast corner of Piazza Brà, t 045 504 901. **Taxis:** t 045 532 666

Verona urban (ATM, t 045 588 7111) and APT buses offer an *Invito a Verona* pass (available at the bus depot, tourist office or museums) from mid-June–Oct, a daily or weekly scheme that includes unlimited travel and museum admissions.

Tourist Information

In the side of Palazzo Barbiera, Via Leoncino 61, t 045 806 8680 (next to the Arena) and Porta Nuova railway station, t 045 800 861 (*both open daily, closed Sun in winter*). For the province: Piazza delle Erbe 38, t 045 800 6997, f 045 801 0682, *www.verona-apt.net*, *veronapt@mbox.vol.it*. Youth information: Corso Porta Borsari 17, t 045 801 0795.

There is an internet cafe, Internet Train, in the centre of town on Via Roma 17, but it's always busy; try across the street in the telephone shop (it has a faster connection). Note: on the first Sunday of every month admission is free to the Museo Castelvecchio, the Teatro Romano, Juliet's tomb and the Museo Lapidaro Maffeiano.

Where to Stay

Verona ✉ 37100

There are plenty of soulless chain hotels on the fringes of the city, but not really enough nice places in the centre, especially during opera season in July or August, so do book. Rooms are also tight in March, when Verona hosts an agricultural fair.

Very Expensive

★★★★★**Due Torri Baglioni**, Piazza Sant'Anastasia 4, t 045 595 044, f 045 800 4130. Goethe and Mozart slept here, and would feel just at home today, at least in the rooms appointed with 18th-century antiques. The public rooms are equally resplendent: the ceilings adorned with 17th-century frescoes, the banquet rooms with circus scenes.

★★★★★**Colomba d'Oro**, Via C. Cattaneo 10, t 045 595 300, f 045 594 974. Located in a quiet, traffic-free street near the Arena, offering very comfortable rooms behind its old stone façade.

★★★★**Accademia**, Via Scala 12, t/f 045 596 222. A restored 16th-century palace houses another excellent, atmospheric choice of places to stay, smack in the centre.

Expensive

★★★**Giulietta e Romeo**, Vicolo Tre Marchetti 3, t 045 800 3554, f 045 801 0862. Centrally located near the Arena, this recently renovated hotel is on a quiet street and offers fine rooms.

★★★**De' Capuleti**, Via del Pontiere, t 045 800 0154. Another good Shakespearean choice in the historic centre.

★★★**Novo Hotel Rossi**, Via delle Coste 2, t 045 569 022, f 045 578 297. *Simpatico* and very convenient if you're arriving by train; some rooms *moderate*.

***Italia**, Via Mameli 58, t 045 918 088, f 045 834 8028. On the other side of the Adige, near the Roman Theatre: the rooms are tranquil, modern, comfortable and priced right.

Moderate

**Sammicheli, Via Valverde 2, t 045 800 3749, f 045 800 4508. About 150 yards from the Arena, this is a convenient hotel for operagoers.

**Torcolo, Vicolo Listone 3, t 045 800 7512, f 045 800 4058. A welcoming hotel in the same area, convenient and not too noisy, on a quiet little square.

**Scalzi, Via Scalzi 5, t 045 590 422, f 045 590 069. Just south of the Castelvecchio, this family-run establishment has similar amenities to the Torcolo, located in a fairly quiet spot.

Cheap

*Catullo, Via Valerio Catullo 1, t 045 800 2786. Try this hotel for cheaper rooms with or without bath, in the centre, some even have balconies.

Eating Out

The Veronese have long gastro-memories. They've been fond of potato *gnocchi* (served with melted butter and sage) since the late 16th century, when the ingredients were distributed after a great famine, and, like the Parisians, attribute their weakness for horse-meat to a siege when horses were all there was left to eat; it's served in stew called *pastissada de caval*. In summer look for Italy's finest peaches.

Very Expensive

Il Desco, Via dietro San Sebastiano 7, t 045 595 358. This king of the Veronese restaurant scene occupies a 15th-century palace, not far from the Ponte Nuovo. Expect exquisite dishes based on seasonal ingredients: *gnocchi* with ewe's milk cheese, red mullet with black olives and rosemary, goose liver in a sauce of sweet wine and grapes. *Closed Sun, hols, part of Jan and June.*

Arche, Via delle Arche Scaligere 6, t 045 800 7415. Run by the same family for over a

hundred years, and located near the Scaliger tombs, a restaurant which has long been the classic place to go for a special meal in an aristocratic setting. The freshest of fish is brought in daily from Chioggia and imaginatively prepared by the maestro in the kitchen. Excellent wine list. *Closed Sun, Mon lunch.*

Expensive

I Dodici Apostoli, Corticella San Marco 3, t 045 596 999. An even older favourite, located a couple of streets from Piazza delle Erbe, offering a traditional Renaissance setting – complete with frescoes of Romeo and Juliet. The name is derived from twelve 18th-century 'apostles' of the kitchen who gathered here to dine. Some of the delicacies served today are adapted from Roman or Renaissance recipes; the *salmone in crosta* (marinated salmon in pastry) is famous. *Closed Sun eve, Mon, two weeks June and July.*

Nuovo Marconi, Via Fogge 4, t 045 591 910. For a glamorous gourmet experience, sit outside in Piazza dei Signori and have your every culinary care tended to by elegant waiters. The food is as rooted in tradition as the surroundings: *tagliolini* with crab, *gnocchi* with pumpkin, and fine scampi and duck. *Closed Sun, part of June and July.*

Bottega del Vino, Via Scudo di Francia 3 (off Via Mazzini), t 045 800 4535. A century-old restaurant, preparing traditional recipes using organically grown ingredients, and pasta made on the premises, all customized to accompany a huge list of wine from around the world. *Closed Tues, except during opera season.*

Maffei, Piazza delle Erbe 38, t 045 801 0015. Another beauty, both ancient and elegant, which serves a melt-in-the-mouth cheese flan and *risotto* with pumpkin and *amarone*. *Closed Sun, Mon in July and Aug.*

Moderate

Greppia, Vicolo Samaritana 3, t 045 800 4577. Serves up traditional and Veronese favourites in a quiet little square near Juliet's house. *Closed Mon, June.*

Alla Strueta, Via Redentore 4 (near the Roman Theatre), t 045 803 2462. Prices are lower over the Adige in Veronetta, where this old workers' *osteria* now features delights in the order of smoked goose breast, *gnocchi* and, yes (or rather, neigh!), *pastissada de caval*. *Closed Mon and Tues lunch, Aug.*

Alla Pergola, Piazzetta Santa Maria in Solaro 10, t 045 800 4744. A traditional and reliable old favourite, housed in a deconsecrated medieval church off Via Garibaldi. *Closed Wed, Aug.*

Cheap

Giardino, Via G. Giardino 2, t 044 834 330. You'll find a number of places around the Liston offer cheap, run-of-the-mill tourist menus. But for something special head north into the Borgo Trento quarter to this exceptionally friendly *trattoria* serving delicious homemade *tortelli di formaggio*, grilled cutlets and Italian cheesecake (*tortine di ricotta*). Tables are few, so book.

Osteria Morandin, Via XX Septembre 144, just off Interrato dell'Acqua Morta. This is another old standby in Veronetta, with a good choice of wines and a few dishes to go with it. *Closed Sun.*

Antico Café Dante, Via Fogge 1. Stop for a coffee at this historic café.

Cordioli, Via Cappello 39. This takes some beating for traditional Veronese pastries. *Closed Wed.*

Entertainment and Nightlife

Verona bills itself as the 'city for all seasons' and offers a wide-ranging cultural programme throughout the year.

Opera, Classical Music and Theatre

Stagione Lirica. Big events take place in the Arena, especially this opera and ballet festival, founded in 1913, with performances almost daily in July and August.

If you're travelling on a tight schedule, it's best to reserve your seat before coming to Italy, which you can do through an agency.

Liaisons Abroad, London, t 020 7376 4020. Will arrange tickets before you go.

Ente Lirico Arena di Verona, Piazza Brà 28, t 045 8051811, *www.arena.it*. An alternative place

to contact for programme details and reservation. Tickets sales are next to the Arena at Via Dietro Anfiteatro 6/b, t 045 800 5151, f 045 801 3287. If you get an unnumbered seat, plan on arriving an hour earlier to get yourself situated. And bring a cushion.

From December to April there is drama in the **Teatro Nuovo**, and also more opera and concerts in the **Teatro Filarmonico**, sponsored by the Ente Lirico.

Festivals and Carnivals

Verona also hosts a **Shakespeare festival** (in Italian) in the Roman Theatre: tickets and information from the Ente Lirico. From mid-December to mid-January, the arcades of the Arena are used for a show of Christmas cribs (*presepi*) from around the world.

In the spring the city hosts one of Italy's oldest **carnivals**, first recorded in 1530; the last Friday of carnival is known as the 'Bacchanal of *Gnocchi*', presided over by the Papà dello Gnoco who walks about with a giant potato dumpling on a fork.

All listings are in the tourist office's free *Passport Verona. Siri-Sera*, fly-posted weekly in cafés and around town, has information on discos, films and more casual artistic events.

Art and Antiques

There are a number of **art galleries** around the Piazza delle Erbe, while the area between the Via Ponte Pietra, Via Duomo, Sottoriva, and Corso S. Anastasia is called the 'little city of antiques'. Beware: the region is Italy's largest producer of reproductions.

Bars

Unlike the Venetians, the Veronese like to be out and about in the evening and have their own expression for pub-crawling, '*andar per goti*' (going Goth-ing), after a memorable binge by Theodoric's gang back in the 5th century. The bars in Piazza Brà and Piazza delle Erbe are the busiest.

Al Carro Armato, Via San Pietro Martire 2a, t 045 803 0175. An old-fashioned bar near the Piazza de' Signori, and one of the most atmospheric.

Le Vecete, near Piazza delle Erbe at Via Pellicciai 32, t 045 594 681. A favourite wine bar. *Closed Sun.*

shrines to the unlucky teenage lovers. But the gorgeous rose-pink city curling along the banks of the Adige has far more to offer than Romeo and Juliet and other star-crossed lovers singing their hearts out in its popular summer opera in the Roman Arena: evocative streets and romantic piazzas, sublime art, magnificent architecture, and all the *gnocchi* you can eat.

History

Blessed with a navigable river at the bottom of a busy Alpine pass, Verona was favoured by the Romans from the time of its colonization in 89 BC, a period when it produced Vitruvius, the spiritual father of Palladio and Renaissance architecture, and the lyric poet Catullus. The city maintained its status as a regional capital under the Ostrogoths and Franks, and in 1107 it became a free *comune*.

The freedom of government by *comune* inaugurated the most violent era of Verona's history, when the city's nobility spiced Italy's Guelph and Ghibelline battles with a sideshow of purely domestic feuds and vendettas. Their notoriety inspired the story of *Romeo and Juliet* (first written by Luigi Da Porto in 1529), and led to the *comune* in despair actually inviting the 'son of Satan' himself, the tyrant Ezzelino da Romano, to take power, which he did until 1259, when the reins of the city were taken over by the Della Scala family.

The Della Scalas (or the Scaligeri) were a typical late-medieval Italian family of exquisite gangsters, combining a bloodthirsty passion for power with a taste for the arts. Their names were, however, uniquely canine: Cangrande I ('Big Dog'; 1311–29) both greatly expanded the family's claims in northern Italy and gave such generous hospitality to Dante that the poet dedicated his *Paradiso* to him (although one may well wonder if Dante's famous 'Letter to Cangrande' on how to read poetry ever arrived; any modern postman who saw the name 'Big Dog of the Stair' written on the door would have walked straight past). Cangrande's heir, Mastino II ('the Mastiff') consolidated his gains while his own successor, the fratricidal Cansignorio ('Lord Dog'; 1359–75) presided over the construction of the family's last great monuments. In 1387 the city was seized by the Milanese warlord Gian Galeazzo Visconti.

By the time of Visconti's death in 1402, Verona had had enough of *signori* and joined up with the Serenissima. After Venice's defeat in the Wars of the Cambrai, Verona opened its gates to the German army and didn't return to St Mark's fold until 1517. The jilted Venetians retaliated by making Verona foot the bill for a vast new system of walls designed by Sammicheli. However (and notably unlike Venice), Verona had the spunk to resist Napoleon in 1797 – only to be partly destroyed for its presumption. Bombed in the Second World War, Verona quickly rebuilt and remains a *città d'arte* of the first rank. It has also, since the war, become one of the economic boom towns of modern Italy.

Porta Nuova to the Arena

The first thing most people see of Verona, whether arriving by rail or road, is Sammicheli's Renaissance gate, the **Porta Nuova**, now stranded on a traffic island at the head of the Corso Porta Nuova. This avenue leads straight under the **Portoni della Brà**, built under Gian Galeazzo Visconti's tenure, and into the heart of tourist Verona: the large, irregular **Piazza Brà**, a favourite promenade of the Veronese and tourists, milling about a broad swathe of café-filled pavements (the Liston) and the **Arena** (*open daily 9–7; closed Mon; during opera season 8.15–3.30; adm*). Built in the 1st century AD and, after the Colosseum, the best-preserved amphitheatre in Italy, the elliptical Arena measures 456ft by 364ft and seats 25,000, and has been kept in an excellent state of preservation since the 16th century. Earthquakes, however, have downed the original outer arcade except for the four arches of the wing, or '*ala*'. As amphitheatres go, the Arena is exceptionally lovely in its pink and white stone, enough to make one almost forget the brutal sports it was built to host; since 1913, the death and mayhem has been purely operatic, with sets in Karnak proportions.

Opposite the Arena in Piazza Brà rises the 17th-century **Palazzo della Gran Guardia**, with a Visconti tower peeking over its shoulder. The **Museo Lapidario Maffeiano**, on the corner of Via Roma, at No. 28 (*open Tues–Sun 9–2.30; adm*) was one of the first such museums in the world, established in 1714, with an important collection of ancient inscriptions.

Piazza delle Erbe and Piazza dei Signori

From Piazza Brà, **Via Mazzini** (the first street in Italy to ban cars) is the most direct route to the core of medieval and Roman Verona, **Piazza delle Erbe**, occupying the old forum and still fulfilling its original purpose, selling fast food, souvenirs and over-priced vegetables. Four old monuments on the piazza's spine poke their heads above the rainbow lake of parasols – a Lion of St Mark; a 1368 fountain built by Cansignorio topped by a Roman statue known as the 'Madonna Verona'; an elegant Gothic stone lantern; and a 16th-century loggia called the 'Berlina', where malefactors used to be tied and pelted with rotten produce.

A colourful variety of buildings encases the square, including the charming **Casa Mazzanti**, formerly part of a Scaligeri palace, brightened with 16th-century frescoes, and the 12th-century **Torre dei Lamberti**, 275ft high, with a lift to the top from the courtyard of the Palazzo della Ragione (*open Tues–Sun 9–6; adm*). The smaller **Torre del Gardello**, at the other end of the square, was another work of Cansignorio. Six ancient gods pose atop the adjacent Baroque **Palazzo Maffei**, while the battlemented red-brick palace, built in 1301 for a merchants' association, still does duty as Verona's Chamber of Commerce after 700 years.

From bustling Piazza delle Erbe, the **Arco della Costa** ('of the rib' – named after a whalebone hung in the arch) leads into stately **Piazza dei Signori**, the civic centre, presided over by a rather severe 1865 statue of Dante, and the striped **Palazzo della Ragione**, with a Romanesque-Gothic courtyard (*Cortile del Mercato Vecchio*) and striking grand staircase. Behind Dante, the **Loggia del Consiglio** (1493), with yellow and red frescoes and statues of five ancient citizens of Verona (including Pliny the Elder, pinched from Como), is the city's finest Renaissance building. The adjacent crenellated **tribunale** (law courts), formerly a Scaliger palace, has a portal by Sammicheli; in the courtyard, and adjacent to Via Dante, you can peer down through glass into Verona's Roman streets, revealed in the **Scaliger excavations**. The underground corridors are used for photo exhibitions (*open daily 10–6.30; closed Mon*).

The arch adjoining the Tribunale leads to the grandiose Gothic pantheon of the Della Scala, the **Scaliger Tombs** or Arche Scaligere. The three major tombs portray their occupants in warlike, equestrian poses on top and reposing in death below, although a copy has replaced the statue atop the Tomb of Cangrande (d. 1329), built into the wall of the 12th-century church of **Santa Maria Antica**. Don't miss the crowned dogs next to Cangrande's effigy, holding up ladders, the family emblem. More ladder motifs can be seen in the fantastical pinnacles of the tomb of 'Lord Dog' Cansignorio (d. 1375), in the more sedate one of Mastino II (d. 1351), and in the web of their wrought-iron enclosure. The rather plain 14th-century house in the same Via delle Arche Scaliger belonged to the Montecchi family (Shakespeare's Montagues), and has been known ever since as the **Casa di Romeo**.

The tour groups, however, are all over at the **Casa di Giulietta**, Via Cappello 23, near the Piazza delle Erbe (*open daily 9–6.30; closed Mon; adm*). Although the association is slim (the 13th-century house was once an inn called 'Il Cappello', reminiscent of the Dal Cappello aka Capulet family), it was restored on the outside in 1935 to fit the bill, with lovely windows and *de rigueur* balcony; inside you can peruse lovelorn grafitti, ripe postcards and photos of Italian girlhood's new Romeo, Leonardo di Caprio.

Sant'Anastasia, Modern Art and the Duomo

North of the Scaliger Tombs, it's hard to miss Gothic **Sant'Anastasia**, Verona's largest church, begun in 1290 but never completed; of its woebegone façade, only the fine portal, with frescoes and reliefs of St Peter Martyr, gives an idea of what its builders intended. The interior, is beautiful but, just coming in from the sun, many people start at what appears in the dim light to be two men loitering under the holy water stoops; these are the *Gobbi*, or 'hunchbacks'. There are frescoes by Altichiero from 1390 in the Cavalli Chapel (note how the horse-head helmets the worshippers wear on their backs are similar to the dragon head on Cangrande's statue); terracottas by Michele da Firenze; paintings by the school of Mantegna in the Pellegrini chapel; and, best of all, in the sacristy, a fresco of *St George at Trebizond* (1438) by Pisanello, Italy's unrivalled maestro of international Gothic; his watchful, calculating princess seems more formidable than any dragon. Nearby, in Corso Sant'Anastasia, the medieval Palazzo Forti now houses the **Galleria d'Arte Moderna** (*t 0458 001 903; open 9–7 for the permanent exhibition, 9–10 for the summer exhibitions, closed Mon*), where temporary exhibits share the walls with Italian masters (Hayez, Fattori, De Pisis, Boccioni, Birolli, Vedova and Manzù) of the 19th and 20th centuries.

A few streets down Via Duomo, almost at the tip of the river's meander, stands Verona's **Duomo**, consecrated in 1187 – Romanesque at the roots and Renaissance in the octagonal crown. The portal, supported on the backs of griffons, was carved by the 12th-century Master Nicolò of San Zeno. Look for the chivalric figures of Roland and Oliver by the west door, and on the south porch a relief of Jonah and the Whale.

Inside, in the Cappella Mazzanti is the beautifully carved Tomb of St Agatha (1353), and in the first chapel on the left is an *Assumption* by Titian. Painted in 1540, it shows us a very different Virgin from the heaven-gazing goddess in Venice's Frari – this one looks down sympathetically at her friends on earth. The pretty cloister has a few remains of the *duomo*'s pre-Romanesque predecessor, and the ancient baptistry, **San Giovanni in Fonte**, has an eight-sided font big enough to swim in (1200), carved from a single piece of marble and decorated with beautiful reliefs. The chapter library, the **Biblioteca Capitolare**, Piazza del Duomo 10 (*open daily 9.30–12.30; also Tues and Fri 4–6; closed Thurs, Sun and July*), originated in the 5th century as a *scriptorium* and justifiably claims to be the oldest library still operating in Europe; it contains a magnificent collection of medieval manuscripts.

North of the Adige: Veronetta

The north bank of the Adige is known locally as 'Veronetta', and it's worth a whole morning unto itself: if you cross over the Ponte Garibaldi, just down from the *duomo*, the large dome of **San Giorgio in Braida** (1477) looms to your right, sheltering a number of first-rate paintings, especially Paolo Veronese's *Martyrdom of St George.* Follow the Adige down to **Santo Stefano**, an important Paleo-Christian church pieced together in the 12th century from 5th–10th-century columns and capitals, and brightened with 14th-century frescoes, some by Altichiero. In front, the **Ponte Pietra**, built by the Romans, was blown up in the Second World War, but partly reconstructed from its original stone dredged up from the Adige.

In ancient times the citizens of Verona would trot over this bridge to attend the latest plays at the **Teatro Romano** (*open summer 9–6.30, winter 9–3; adm*), carved out of the cypress-clad hill of San Pietro in the time of Augustus. They still do: the cavea and arches are in good enough nick to host Shakespeare in the summer. A lift goes up to the **Museo Archeologico** (*same hours and ticket*), occupying a convent built on top of the theatre and containing small bronzes, portrait busts and a few mosaics. Above it, the **Castel San Pietro** was built by the Austrians over Roman fortifications, and has famous views over Verona at sunset.

South, on the Interato dell'Acqua Morta, **Santa Maria in Organo** has a façade (1533) by Fra Giovanni da Verona; the talented friar also made the charming *trompe l'œil* intarsia choir stalls, lectern and cupboards (in the sacristy) depicting scenes of old Verona – as well as birds, animals and flowers.

Across the street that runs at the back of the church, behind the façade of the Palazzo Giusti, are the cool **Giardini Giusti** (*open 9am–dusk in summer, 9am–8pm in winter; adm*), described by the Bavarian Thomas Coryat as 'a second paradise, and a passing delectable place of solace'. That was in 1611, the date of the enormous cypresses, formal box hedge parterres, the fountains and grotto topped with a leering mask; the hillside was re-landscaped in the 19th century in the more romantic and informal English style.

Further south, **Santi Nazaro e Celso** (1484), on Via Muro Padri, contains 16th-century frescoes and a painting of the eponymous saints by Montagna, while **San Paolo** (rebuilt 1763), south on Via San Paolo, contains Veronese's beautiful *Madonna and Saints*, one of the few works he left in his home town before he had to move on to Venice, supposedly after committing a murder. On the river bank, at Lungadige Porta

Vittoria 9, there's the elegant Palazzo Pompei, built in 1530 by Sammicheli and now housing the **Museo Civico di Storia Naturale** (*open Mon–Sat 9–7; Sun 2–7; closed Fri; adm*), with an excellent fossil collection.

San Fermo Maggiore and Juliet's Tomb

From Piazza delle Erbe, Via Cappello/Leoni leads past the picturesque ruins of the Roman **Porta dei Leoni** (incorporated in a building) to the splendid vertical apse of **San Fermo Maggiore**, an architectural club sandwich of two churches, one atop the other. The Romanesque bottom was begun in the 11th century by the Benedictines, while the upper Gothic church, with its attractive red and white patterns, was added by the Franciscans. The interior is covered with fine 14th-century frescoes, works by Caroto (*Madonna and Saints*), and a graceful *Annunciation* by Pisanello (1462).

The so-called **Tomba di Giulietta** (*open daily 9–6.30; closed Mon; adm*) is back near the river on Via del Pontiere, not far from the Piazza Brà. Even the Veronese admit no plausible connection, but the Romanesque cloister and the 14th-century red marble sarcophagus would make a fine set for the tragedy's last scene. A small **museum of frescoes** is an added attraction, including lovely 16th-century allegorical and mythological scenes by Paolo Farinati.

Piazza delle Erbe to Castelvecchio

From Piazza delle Erbe, Corso Porta Bórsari leads to an impressive Roman gate, **Porta dei Bórsari**, built in the 1st century AD and named after the *borsarii*, who collected duties on goods entering the city on the Via Postumia. Beyond the gate, the street becomes Corso Cavour, embellished with palaces from various epochs, including Sammicheli's refined 1588 **Palazzo Bevilacqua** (No.19), noted for its ornate, rhythmic alteration of large and small windows, columns and pediments.

Opposite, the lovely Romanesque **San Lorenzo** (1117) preserves its upper, women's gallery (matroneum), reached by way of its two cylindrical towers. Further down, Corso Cavour opens up into a small square with yet another Roman arch: the simple but elegant **Arco dei Gavi**, designed by Vitruvius in honour of a local family. The French demolished it in 1805, but in 1932 the local *Fascisti* put it back together again.

Castelvecchio and its Museum of Art

Next to the arch, Cangrande II's fortress of **Castelvecchio** (1355) has weathered centuries of use by other top dogs, from the Venetians to Napoleon and the Nazis, to become Verona's excellent and well-arranged civic **museum of art** (*t 0455 94734; open Tues–Sun 9–6.30; adm*). The ground floor features a sarcophagus (1179) carved with vivid reliefs of SS. Sergius and Bacchus, as well as expressive 14th-century Veronese sculpture, especially a stark, painful *Crucifixion*. The museum is rich in lovely Madonnas, beginning with two straight out of fairy tales: the *Madonna of the Quail* by Pisanello, and the *Madonna of the Rose-garden* by Stefano da Verona; there are fine paintings by Crivelli and Mantegna, followed by another beautiful *Madonna* by Giovanni Bellini, and Carpaccio's *SS. Caterina and Veneranda*.

Next comes Verona's mascot, the striking 14th-century equestrian **statue of Cangrande I** from the Arche Scaligere, displayed outside the first floor window. The pyjama-clad steed, complete with an equine hood ornament and deathly eyes, and the moronically grinning 'Big Dog' himself, with his ghastly dragon-helmet slung over his back, make an unforgettable pair, straight out of a malevolent pantomime. Beyond Cangrande are paintings by Veronese, Tintoretto, Giovan Francesco Caroto (including his well-known *Child with Sketch*, a happy insight into Renaissance childhood), both Tiepolos, Guardi and Longhi. Behind the castle, Cangrande II's **Ponte Scaligero**, spanning the Adige, repeats the attractive 'swallowtail' battlements of the Castelvecchio; like the Ponte Pietra, it was meticulously reconstructed from the original stones after the War.

The Basilica of San Zeno Maggiore

A 15-minute walk west from the Castelvecchio, mostly along the riverbank (or bus no.32 or 33 from Corso Porta Borsari), will take you to the superb **Basilica di San Zeno** (*open daily 7–12.30 and 3.30–6.30*), the belle of Verona's churches and one of the finest Romanesque buildings anywhere. First built in the 4th century, the church took its present form in the mid-14th century. Its magnificence demanded a legend: beneath its lofty campanile (finished in 1149) lies the tomb of a personage no less than the Frankish King Pepin the Short.

The rich façade of San Zeno has a perfect centrepiece: a 12th-century rose window of the *Wheel of Fortune* by Maestro Brioloto. Below, the beautifully carved porch (1138) by Masters Nicolò and Guglielmo shows scenes from the months, the miracles of San Zeno, the Hunt of Theodoric and other allegories. The **bronze doors**, with their 48 panels, are a 'poor man's Bible' and one of the wonders of 11th-century Italy, and still, after a millennium, have an unmatched freshness and vitality: in the Annunciation scene Mary covers her face in fear and anguish while the angel Gabriel does his best to comfort her; in the Descent into Hell, Christ and a large, leering Satan fight a tug-of-war for souls. Other scenes seem a bit strange to us, especially the one of two nursing mothers on the lower lefthand door, one suckling twin children, the other, what look to be twin crocodiles.

The vast interior, divided into three naves by Roman columns and capitals, has a beautiful Gothic ceiling, 13th- and 14th-century frescoes and, on the altar, the magnificent triptych of the *Madonna col Bambino tra Angeli e Santi* (1459) by Andrea Mantegna, a work that brilliantly combines the master's love of classical architecture and luminous colouring. Although the French returned the painting after Napoleon took it, they kept the predella as a souvenir; the originals are in the Louvre. In the crypt below, the body of St Zeno glows in the dark.

Around Verona: Soave, Valpolicella and Lessinia

Verona's province is awash in wine, the sloshing cradle of four of Italy's best-known DOC wines: white Soave and Bianco di Custoza, and red Valpolicella and Bardolino. And each has at least one *strada del vino* if you want to spend a lazy hour or two touring and tasting. Bianco di Custoza and Bardolino grow on the shores of Lake

Garda (*see* p.329 and p.336), while east along the Vicenza road (SS11), vines literally engulf the old town of **Soave**, distinguished by the well-preserved crenellated **Scaliger castle** (*open daily 9–12 and 3–6; closed Mon; adm*), first built in the 10th century. On Via Roma, try a Soave Classico or the sweet Recioto di Soave, a dessert wine made from raisins at the **Enoteca del Castello**.

Valpolicella, northwest of Verona, has twin nuclei, **Negràr** and **Sant'Ambrogio**. The latter produces Verona's famous red marble – in addition to red wine; nearby, in the lovely old hilltop hamlet of **San Giorgio**, the parish church was founded in the 7th century. The ciborium over the altar also dates from the 600s, and among the frescoes there's a fascinating 12th-century *Last Judgement*. Northern Valpolicella melts seamlessly into **Lessinia**, the foothills of the Dolomites, famous for rocks – in formations, flintstones and fossils. And falls – at Molina's Parco delle Cascate. North, beyond **Fosse**, the slopes of Corno d'Aquilio are pierced by the **Spluga della Preta**, one of the world's deepest chasms, its floor 2,906ft down. Lessinia's flint attracted the first people in *c.* 500,000 BC. Finds from the period are in the prehistory museum at **Sant'Anna d'Alfaedo**, along with a 20ft fossilized shark. South of Sant'Anna, not far off the road to Fane, don't miss the **Ponte di Veja**, a spectacular, natural 170ft arch, the inspiration for the Malebolge bridge in Dante's *Inferno*. A winding road loops east to **Bosco Chiesanuova**, Lessinia's modest winter sports centre. From here follow the road to **Velo Veronese**, the starting point for a visit to the **Valley of the Sphinxes** (*Valle delle Sfingi*), named for its striking chasms and landforms, made of layers of red ammonite.

In 17th-century Lessinia, flintlocks were big business. Many of these were made by Bavarians who had settled here in the 13th century. Their roots are remembered in their language, costumes, and the huge *tromboni*, a kind of arquebus that they blast on holidays. You can learn more about them at the museum in **Giazza**, one of Lessinia's prettiest villages with its medieval German houses. **Bolca**, southeast of Giazza, caused a sensation in the Renaissance when the discovery of a rich bed of fossilized fish was cited as scientific proof of Noah's Flood. They are also extremely beautiful and delicate, and in the local fossil museum.

Treviso

Although famous for radicchio and Benetton, Treviso is still one of the Veneto's best kept secrets, laced with little canals (or *canagi*) diverted from the River Sile, languorous with willows, lazy water wheels, swans and mossy walls, yet all humming with more than a little discreet prosperity. Like Verona, it formed its character in the century preceding its annexation by Venice (1389), when it was ruled by the Da Camino and embellished by one of Giotto's greatest pupils, Tommaso da Modena, who did little outside of Treviso.

Colours were an obsession in Treviso long before Benetton united them. Attractive building stone was scarce, so it became the custom to cover the humble bricks walls with plaster and frescoes – in the 1300s with simple colours and patterns and, by the 1500s, with heroic mythologies and allegories. Although faded and fragmented since

Getting Around

Treviso **airport** (t 0422 230 393) is southwest of the town; bus no.6 runs from there to the railway station; Ryan Air links it several times a week to London Stansted.

Both the train and bus stations (t 0422 412 222) are in Via Roma south of the centre. **Trains** run from Venice or Mestre to Treviso (30mins) and Belluno (2 hours), either directly or by changing at Padua or Conegliano. One line to Belluno goes via Conegliano and Vittòrio Vèneto; the other, longer but more scenic, via Montebelluna (also a getting-off point for Masèr and Àsolo).

Cars. It's very simple: don't try to take a car into Treviso. In July 2000 the local council changed the traffic system in and around Treviso and the result is mayhem. There are 35,000 residents and 140,000 commuters in Treviso, and like true Italians, they all drive. Abandon your car at the hotel and walk; many of the surrounding roads are one-way so get a decent map.

Tourist Information

Piazza Monte di Pietà 8, t 0422 547 632, f 0422 419 092, *tvapt@sevenonline.it*.

Where to Stay

Treviso ✉ 31100
★★★**Al Foghèr**, Viale della Repubblica 10, t 0422 432 950, f 0422 430 391 (*expensive–moderate*). There's not a lot of choice, but this is the pick of the bunch. Outside the walls but in walking distance of the centre, with parking, well-equipped rooms, a warm welcome, and a good restaurant.
★★★★**Continental**, Via Roma 16, t 0422 411 662, f 0422 411 620 (*expensive*). A convenient modern hotel near the station.
★★★**Scala**, Viale Felissent 1, near the exit for Conegliano, t 0422 307 600, f 0422 305 048 (*expensive*). If you're driving you may prefer one of the 20 rooms just north of town in this attractive patrician hotel, set in a pretty park.
★★**Campeol**, Piazza Ancillotto 8, t 0422 56601, f 0422 540 871 (*moderate*). Smack in the

historic centre, a hospitable and long-established hotel with good views.
★★★**La Fattoria**, Via Callalta 83, t 0422 361 770, f 0422 460 150 (*moderate*). Near the Treviso Sud exchange on the A27 in Silèa, offering cosy rooms in a restored farmhouse. *Closed part of Aug.*

Eating Out

Cichorium intybus, otherwise known as *radicchio trevignana*, is not only a local obsession, but a salad vegetable that has the same quality control as wine; to be DOC *radicchio trevignana* it must have sprouted up in one of eight *comuni* and grown under certain organic conditions. You can taste the difference (or so they claim!), especially in December, when it's at its best. Another speciality is *sopa coada*, a baked pigeon casserole.

Alfredo, Via Collalto 26, t 0422 540 275 (*expensive*). If money's no object, try *sopa coada* here at Treviso's most acclaimed restaurant, in a lovely, elegant *belle époque* setting. The imaginative menu otherwise has an emphasis on seafood. Reserve. *Closed Sun eve, Mon, Aug.*

Al Bersagliere, Via Barberia 21, t 0422 579 902 (*moderate*). Occupying a beautiful 12th-century building, and offering a full selection of delicious *antipasti*, *sopa coada* and other Venetian specialities such as squid in its own ink, *risotto*, and liver Venetian-style. *Closed Sun, Sat lunch, Aug.*

Beccherie, Piazza Anchillotto 10, t 0422 540 871 (*moderate*). One of Treviso's bastions of local atmosphere and cooking – a great place to try *pasta e fagioli* with radicchio. *Closed Sun eve, Mon and July.*

Toni del Spin, Via Inferiore 7, t 0422 543 829 (*moderate–cheap*). An old favourite for its Veneto dishes (*bigoli, risi e bisi*, and the like) topped off with American apple pie. *Closed Sun and Mon lunch.*

Il Dominicale, Via Postumia 51, t 0422 969 360 (*moderate*). If you have a car, it's a very short drive north to Ponzano Veneto and this charming restaurant, where you can linger in the garden on warm summer evenings over delicious Italian classics. *Closed Sun, Mon, some of Aug.*

then – on Good Friday 1944 an air raid destroyed half of Treviso in five minutes – one of the delights of visiting the city is to pick out frescoes under the eaves, or hidden in the shadows of an arcade.

Piazza dei Signori and the Duomo

From the bus or train station, it's a 10-minute walk over the Sile along the Corso del Popolo and Via XX Settembre to the Piazza dei Signori, the heart of Treviso. Here stands the city's only surviving *comunale* palace, the huge brick **Palazzo dei Trecento**, 'of the Three Hundred', built in the 1200s and rebuilt after wartime bombing; Treviso café society shelters below. The adjacent **Palazzo del Podestà** was rebuilt in 1877, along with the Torre Civica looming over its shoulder. Behind the Palazzo dei Trecento, the **Monte di Pietà** (pawn shop) contains the Renaissance **Sala dei Reggitori** (*t 0422 654 320; open for group tours only Mon–Fri 9–12 and 3–5*), with walls of gilt leather, a painted, beamed ceiling and canvases by Sebastiano Ricci and Luca Giordano.

The arcaded main street, Calmaggiore, leads from the square to the **Duomo**, a Venetian Romanesque building with a cluster of domes (12th century); the adjacent baptistry gives an idea of what the cathedral looked like before its many alterations. Besides fine Renaissance tombs of local prelates, much of the cathedral's best art is concentrated in the **Cappella Malchiostro**, just right of the altar, designed by Tullio and Antonio Lombardo, with works by Paris Bordone (*Adoration of the Shepherds*) and Girolamo da Treviso (*Madonna del Fiore*). The frescoes are by native son Pordenone, while his mortal enemy Titian contributed *The Annunciation* on the altar; Vasari wrote that Pordenone always painted with his sword at his hip in case Titian showed up while he was working. Behind the cathedral, the **Museo Diocesano** (*open Mon–Thurs 9–12, Sat 9–12 and 3–6*) has one of Tommaso da Modena's masterpieces, the detached fresco, *Cristo Passo*.

Museo Civico and San Nicolò

From Piazza Duomo, Via Canova leads past the 15th-century **Casa Trevigiana** (*open for special exhibitions*), a reliquary of the city's architecture. Via Canova meets Borgo Cavour near the **Museo Civico Luigi Bailo** (*open Tues–Sat 9–12.30 and 2.30–5, Sun 9–12; adm*), with Bronze-Age swords and 5th-century BC bronze discs from Montebelluna; and an excellent collection of masters from the Veneto: Giovanni Bellini, Titian, Lotto, Jacopo Bassano, Cima da Conegliano, the Tiepolos, Rosalba Carriera, Guardi, Longhi – and Joshua Reynolds. Borgo Cavour makes a grandiose exit through the great Venetian gate, **Porta dei Santi Quaranta** (1517), encompassed by an impressive stretch of the ramparts. However, if you turn instead down Via S. Liberale and right in Via Absidi, you'll come to Treviso's best church, Gothic **San Nicolò** with its polygonal apse. The interior is a treasure house of lovely frescoes – from a huge *St Christopher* on the south wall to the charming pages by Lorenzo Lotto by the d'Onigo tomb. Tommaso da Modena contributed the saints standing to attention on the columns, but even better are his perceptive portraits of 40 Dominicans (1352), some using medieval reading glasses, in the **Capitolo dei Domenicani**, in the adjacent Seminario (*open April–Sept daily 8–6; Oct–Mar daily 8–12.30 and 3–5.30; ring the bell at the porter's lodge*).

San Francesco

Treviso's east end is separated by one of its wider streams, the Cagnàn; on a little islet (take Via Trevisi–Via Pescheria from the Monte di Pietà), the lively and colourful **fish market** (1851) is open every morning except Sunday. San Nicolò's near twin, the tall brick, Romanesque-Gothic **San Francesco**, is just up Via S. Parisio, and has a fresco of the Madonna by Tommaso da Modena, as well as the tombs of Francesca Petrarch (d. 1384) and Pietro Alighieri (d. 1364), the children of Italy's two greatest poets, whose final meeting-place here in Treviso was purely a coincidence.

Back along the walls to the east, Viale Burchiellati leads shortly to the city's other great gate, Guglielmo Bergamasco's exotic **Porta San Tommaso** (1518). From here follow Borgo Mazzini to the deconsecrated church of **Santa Caterina**, with Tommaso da Modena's detached frescoes on *The Life of St Ursula*, a series that's just as delightful as Carpaccio's St Ursulas in the Accademia in Venice (*closed for restoration*).

North of Treviso: the Marca Trevigniana

You can drive straight up to the Dolomites in less than two hours from Treviso, or spend a day exploring the fine towns of Marca Trevigniana province along the way.

Oderzo and Conegliano

A delightful town crisscrossed by canals and devoted to wine-making, **Oderzo** may not be a household name, but in its Roman heyday, as *Opitergium* it was recorded as far away as Egypt. Piazza Vittorio Emanuele II marks the old forum, overlooked by the late-Gothic **Duomo**; in Via Garibaldi, the **Museo Civico Opitergino** (*closed for restoration*) has a good assortment of Roman finds and mosaics. Nearby, the **Pinacoteca Alberto Martini**, Via Garibaldi 63 (*open by appointment only, Mon–Fri 3–7, Sun 3–7*) has works by Oderzo-born surrealist painter Alberto Martini, as well as other contemporary Italian painters, mostly from Oderzo. Make the short detour north of Oderzo to picturesque **Portobuffolè**, a village of frescoed buildings and three very funny Venetian lions (especially the spooked one with a pie pan face, sticking out its tongue on the 15th-century Monte della Pietà, now the Cassa Marca). The oldest house, 13th-century **Casa di Gaia da Camino**, houses a bicycling museum.

Conegliano, a town neatly divided into old and new, with the Accademia cinema and its giant sphinxes in the centre, was the birthplace of Giambattista Cima (1460–1518) – 'the sweet shepherd among Venetian painters' as Mary McCarthy called him – the son of a seller of hides, who often painted his native countryside in his backgrounds. If you haven't seen the originals, reproductions are displayed at his birthplace, the **Casa di Cima**, on quiet Via Cima 24 (*ring ahead, t 0438 21660*). An original and beautiful Cima, a *Sacra Conversazione* in an architectural setting (1493), forms the altarpiece of the 14th-century **Duomo**. In the 16th century Ludovico Pozzoserrato and Francesco da Milano collaborated on the frescoes of Old and New Testament scenes in the adjacent **Sala dei Battuti**, the hall of a flagellants' confraternity (*open Sun 3–7, other days exc Wed 9–12 if you ring ahead; t 0438 22606*). Be sure to stroll

Tourist Information

Oderzo: Piazza Castello 1, t 0422 815 251,
f 0422 814 081.
Conegliano: Via Colombo 1, t/f 0438 21230.
Vittòrio Vèneto: Piazza del Popolo 18, t 0438
57243, f 0438 53629.

Where to Stay and Eat

Oderzo ✉ 31046
***Villa Revedin**, Via Palazzi 4, t/f 0422 800
033 (*moderate*). The nicest place to sleep
near Oderzo is 5km east at Gorgo al
Monitcano, at this 15th-century villa set in a
park. Rooms are well equipped and the
breakfasts superb.
Gellius, Calle Pretoria 6, t 0422 713 577
(*moderate*). Here in the centre, you have the
chance to dine in an atmospheric Roman
prison, but the food has improved dramatically in the last 2,000 years. *Closed Mon,
Tues lunch.*

Conegliano ✉ 31015
***Canon d'Oro**, Via XX Settembre 129,
t/f 0438 34246 (*moderate*). Behind an
exterior frescoed in the 1500s, this hotel
provides a warm welcome and plush rooms
overlooking the town's main street.
***Sporting Hotel Ragno d'Oro**, Via Diaz 37,
t 0438 412 300, f 0438 412 310 (*moderate*). For
an alternative, try this hotel set in parkland

on Conegliano's outskirts, boasting a
sizeable swimming pool.
Tre Panoce, Via Vecchia Trevigiana 50, t 0438
60071 (*expensive*). Just outside Conegliano, a
lovely restaurant occupying a seicento farmhouse crowning a hill of vineyards, with
outdoor tables in summer (if you're not
driving, bus no.1 stops outside). You can try a
number of little dishes by ordering the
menu veneto, followed by delicious desserts.
Closed Sun evenings, Mon, Aug.
Al Salisà, Via XX Settembre 2, t 0438 24288
(*expensive*). An elegant restaurant in a 13th-
century building, featuring succulent snails
(*lumache*) and game specialities in season,
especially venison. There's also a good local
wine list, and special menus for lunch.
Closed Tues evenings, Wed, Aug.

Vittòrio Vèneto ✉ 31029
***Hotel Terme**, Via della Terme 4, t 0438 554
345, f 0438 554 347 (*moderate*). Not too many
choices in Vittòrio, but this is the best, with
good, comfortable rooms near the station.
Postiglione, Via Cavour 39, t 0438 556 924
(*moderate*). Dine on hearty mountain
specialities at this popular restaurant in an
old post house. *Closed Tues and two weeks in
July–Aug.*
Il Capitello, Via S. Francesco, Cobranese, t 0485
564 279 (*moderate*). For the finest dining in
the region try this restaurant, west in Tarzo,
featuring all that's exquisite, with a modern
flair. *Closed Wed, Thurs lunch, Jan and Aug.*

down arcaded **Via Venti Settembre**, lined with old frescoed palaces; the **castle** on the
hill, begun in the 10th century, has a small **Museo Civico** with paintings and other
odds and ends. Conegliano produces a delightful Prosecco which you can go a-tasting
along the pretty 42-kilometre **Strada del Prosecco** – from the castle to **Valdobbiadene**
to the west, then back east to Vittòrio Vèneto. On the way have a look at **San Pietro di
Feletto**, its exterior frescoed in the 15th century by an unknown painter, who pictures
Jesus in a unique fashion: lines from his wounds are connected to chickens, wine,
people lying in bed, and farm tools.

Vittòrio Vèneto

The Venetian pre-Alps saw heavy action in the First World War, and the hills around
Asiago, Monte Grappa and the Piave are often crowned with dispiritingly huge Italian,
British or French war cemeteries. **Vittòrio Vèneto**, north of Conegliano, was the site of
Italy's final victorious battle (October 1918). Vittòrio's name, however, is for Vittorio

Emanuele II; in 1866, to celebrate the birth of Italy, the two rival towns of Cèneda and Serravalle were united. The **Castello di San Martino**, dating back to the Lombards, hovers over **Cèneda**, where the main Piazza Giovanni Paolo I holds the **Loggia del Cenedese**, designed by Sansovino in 1538, now home to a museum of the Battle of 1918 (*t 0438 57695; open May–Sept 10–12 and 3.30–7; Oct–April 10–12 and 2–5; closed Mon; adm*); Albino Luciani (John Paul I) was a longtime bishop of Vittòrio Vèneto and founded the **Museo Diocesano** in the seminary, with works by Palma Giovane and Titian (*open by request, t 0438 948 411*). Another church, **Santa Maria del Meschio**, has a beautiful altarpiece of the *Annunciation* by Andrea Previtali.

Serravalle begins with a clock tower up the poetic street (Via Dante/Virgilio/Petrarca) which links the two halves of Vittòrio Vèneto. Serravalle has conserved its atmospheric old palaces and houses, especially in Piazza Flaminio, where the 15th-century **Loggia Serravallese** houses, confusingly, the **Museo del Cenedese** (*open May–Sept 10–12 and 4.30–6.30; Oct–April 10–12 and 3–5; closed Mon; same ticket as the Museo della Battaglia*), with a collection of Roman finds, sculpture and minor paintings. The **Duomo** has a fine altarpiece by Titian, the *Madonna col Bambino* (1547). Vittòrio Vèneto's playground is the lovely **Bosco del Cansiglio**, a vast forest of fir, larch and beech on a lofty karstic plateau set aside by Venice in 1548 as its 'Forest of St Mark's Oars'; Monte Cansiglio itself offers the closest downhill skiing to Venice.

Towards the Dolomites: Belluno and Feltre

Belluno

A provincial capital at the junction of the Piave and Ardo rivers, Belluno is one of those small, perfectly proportioned Italian cities: urban, urbane and yet never far from magnificent views over the countryside – here of the Venetian Dolomites.

The old civic and religious centre of town, **Piazza del Duomo**, has two of Belluno's finest buildings, the ornate **Palazzo dei Rettori** (1491), residence of the Venetian governors, and the **Duomo**. Founded in the 7th century, and last redesigned by Pietro Lombardo, work on the church dragged on until the 1600s, and tends to be overshadowed by the magnificent detached **Campanile**, designed by Filippo Juvarra (1742); when restoration is complete, you may be able to go up again for the bird's-eye views.

In Via Duomo, the **Museo Civico** (*t 0437 944 836; open mid-April–Sept, Tues–Sat 10–12 and 4–7, Sun 10–12, closed Mon; Oct–mid-April Tues–Fri 3–6 only; adm*) is a treat for fans of extrovert womanizing Baroque painter Sebastiano Ricci, with some of his greatest work; it also provides a chance to learn about some interesting if obscure local painters from the 1300–1800s. Via Mezzaterra/Via Rialto follow the ancient Roman *castrum*, by way of atmospheric **Piazza del Mercato**, a picture-perfect little square, with arcades and a fountain from 1410. To the south Via Mezzaterra ends at the 12th-century **Porta Ruga** and a postcard view of the Piave Valley and the mountains. Also have a look at the Gothic church of **Santo Stefano** (1468) in Via Roma, where a 15th-century relief of the Madonna in her merciful umbrella pose guards the door, leading into a handsome striped interior.

Tourist Information

Belluno: Via Rodolfo Pesaro 21, **t** 0437 940 083, **f** 0437 94 0073.
Feltre: Piazza Trento-Trieste 9, **t** 043 92540, **f** 043 92839.
National Park t 0439 3328 or *info@ dolomitipark.it*.

Where to Stay and Eat

Belluno ✉ 32100

Most people head straight up into the mountains, but if you want to stay, there are a few choices.

★★★★Villa Carpenada, Via Mier 158, **t** 0437 948 343, **f** 0437 948 345 (*expensive*). Just west of the centre, this well-run hotel offers quiet rooms in an 18th-century villa.

★★★Astor, Piazza dei Martiri 26-E, **t** 0437 942 094, **f** 0437 942 493 (*moderate*). Good value and comfortable, central rooms.

★★★Delle Alpi, Via J. Tasso 13, **t** 0437 940 545, **f** 0437 940 565 (*moderate*). Within walking distance of the station, with large welcoming rooms and one of the best restaurants in town, specializing in seafood ferried up from the coast. *Closed Sun, some of Aug*.

Al Borgo, Via Anconetta 8, **t** 0437 926 755 (*moderate*). Set in an 18th-century villa south of the Piave, and another favourite place to eat, serving traditional favourites. *Closed Mon eve and Tues*.

Pieve d'Alpago ✉ 32010

Dolada, Via Dolada 9, **t** 0437 479 141, **f** 0437 478 068 (*very expensive*). Just outside Pieve in the hamlet of Plois, and one of the top restaurants in all Venetia, overlooking Lago di Santa Croce and its surroundings. Wood panelling, candlelight and romance accompany inspired dishes in the best Italian tradition: home-made pasta, the celebrated *zuppa dolada*, superb fish, duck and lamb dishes and an exceptional wine list. It also has rooms. *Closed Mon lunch and Tues, exc in July and Aug*.

If you don't have time for a foray into the Dolomites, take the bus to the **Alpi del Nevegàl**, 12km south of Belluno, for gorgeous views and a chairlift to the Rifugio Brigata Alpina Cadore (5,248ft), with an Alpine garden. From the refuge it's an easy three-hour walk up to the **Col Visentin**, where another refuge commands a unique panorama: north across the sea of Dolomite peaks and south to the Venetian Lagoon. The hills of the **Alpago** are another popular weekend destination, especially the **Lago di Santa Croce**, the focal point for its small villages: aim for **Pieve d'Alpago** in a lovely setting, famous for its restaurant.

Feltre: the Dead Man and SS. Vittore e Corona

West from Belluno the SS50 skirts the Piave on its way to hilltop Feltre. Sacked by the troops of Emperor Maximilian in 1510 during the War of the Cambrai, Feltre was immediately rebuilt and has changed little since, especially the houses along **Via Mezzaterra**, with their faded frescoes and dozens of marble plaques hammered into illegibility by someone who had it in for Feltre's memories. The jewel on Via Mezzaterra is the picturesque **Piazza Maggiore**, where a very quizzical Lion of St Mark stands vigil over the castle; the church of San Rocco has a fountain by Tullio Lombardo, and the superb 16th-century **Palazzo dei Rettori** (now the Municipio) is decked out with a Palladian portico. Inside, a wooden theatre built in 1684 saw the production of Goldoni's first plays. In the centre of Piazza Maggiore, a statue honours the famous educator, Vittorino da Feltre (*see* Mantua, pp.264–265).

The Palazzo Villabuono, by the town's east gate, now houses the **Museo Civico**, Via L. Luzzo 23 (*currently closed for restoration*) which has among its archaeological collections an altar to the *anna perrena* (the year), and among its paintings works by Gentile Bellini, Cima da Conegliano and Feltre's own contribution to the Renaissance, Lorenzo Luzzo, better known by his punk nickname, *Il Morto da Feltre*, the 'Dead Man', given to him because of his unusual pallor. The *Transfiguration*, the Dead Man's most acclaimed work, is nearby in the sacristy of the church of **Ognissanti**.

Five kilometres from Feltre, signposted off the Treviso road (SS473), the Romanesque **Santuario di SS. Vittore e Corona** (*open April–Sept daily 8–12 and 3–7; Oct–Mar daily 9–12 and 3–6*) is up a steep little road. Built in 1100 and unchanged since, it shelters the remains of Vittore, a Roman soldier martyred in Syria in 171, and Corona who converted at the sight and was martyred too. The apse is filled with their elevated sarcophagus, decorated with windblown acanthus. Note the relief of Vittore on the underside, and behind, capitals inscribed with Kufic script, reading 'the Universe is God'. The frescoes are by the schools of Tommaso da Modena and Giotto, with figures copied directly from Padua's Scrovegni Chapel – Giotto sold the reproduction rights. Don't miss the *Last Supper*, in which the artist's prawns look like scorpions.

The Dolomites

...the most beautiful 'constructions' in the world.
Le Corbusier

There are mountains, and then there are the Dolomites. Born as massive corals in the primordial ocean, and heaved up from the seabed 60 million years ago, tempests and blizzards over the aeons have whittled away at the dolomitic limestone and porphyry to form an extraordinary landscape. Other-worldly and majestic peaks claw and scratch at the sky between the valleys of the Adige and the Piave rivers, each monumental range a petrified tempest of jagged needles, cloud-tickled pinnacles and sheer cliffs, dyed rose by the dawn and glowing red by the setting sun.

These most romantic and beautiful of mountains were named after a wandering French mineralogist with a fantastical name, Dieudonné Sylvain Guy Tancrède de Gratet de Dolomieu, who in 1789 was the first to describe their mineral content. Marmolada (10,959ft), the highest peak in the range (17 others top 10,000ft) has glaciers even in summer, but elsewhere the snow fields convert in July to a massive bouquet of wild flowers, streaked with blue gentians, yellow Alpine poppies and buttercups, edelweiss and pink rhododendron. The air and light in autumn are so sharp and fine they can break your heart.

The Eastern Dolomites: the Cadore

Although mostly Italian-speaking, much of the Cadore, the district north of Belluno along the upper Piave, was incorporated into Italy only after the First World War. Its

Mountain Sports

Hiking

One is tempted to lapse into Italian hyperbole about hiking in the Dolomites – but suffice to say it's as close as some of us will ever get to heaven. There are routes for everyone from semi-couch-potatoes to rock-grappling daredevils, and eight **High Trails of the Dolomites** (Alte Vie delle Dolomiti) designed for those 'vagabonds of the path' who fall in between the two extremes. The trails range from 120–180km in length, and are designed to take average walkers two weeks.

Equipment

The High Trails have the virtue of keeping you on top of mountains and plateaux for most of their length. While they do not require special climbing skill, they do demand a stout pair of hiking boots with good rubber soles (80 per cent of accidents are caused by slipping), and protection against sudden storms, even in the middle of summer. A telescopic walking stick for descents and a mobile phone in case of emergencies are also recommended.

Maps

There are two good sets of maps that include the Alte Vie and other paths as well, and point out the location of the Alpine refuges: *Carta dei Sentieri e Rifugi*, Edizioni Tabacco Udine, and *Maps Kompass-Wanderkarten*, Edizioni Fleishmann-Starnberg. Both are scale 1:50,000, and are readily available at news-stands in the region. The relevant tourist offices have booklets on each trail in English that contain all the basic information, including phone numbers of the refuges. They also give a good idea of the level of difficulty of each trail (*see* maps, Practical A–Z, p.109).

Refuges

Strategically placed *rifugi alpini* provide shelter, but if you come when they are closed you'll need to carry camping gear. The refuges are open from the end of June to the end of September; in July and August it's wise to book a bed in advance to avoid disappointment.

They vary dramatically. Many are owned by the Italian Alpine Club; others are privately owned, primarily by ski resorts. Some are along trails; others may be reached via cable car. All offer bed and board; nearly all now require that you bring a sleeping sheet, or buy one on the site. Prices differ mainly according to altitude: the higher up and more difficult the access, the more expensive. Besides these refuges, there are the *baite* (wooden huts), *casere* (stone huts) and bivouacs (beds but no food) along some of the higher trails: they generally have no custodians but offer shelter at any time.

Write to the tourist offices in Belluno (*see* p.437), Trento (*see* p.453) and Bolzano (*see* p.465) for more information, or try the **Italian Alpine Club** (CAI), Via Fonseca Pimental 7, 20121 Milan, t 02 2614 1378, f 02 2614 1395.

Many of the 200 alpine refuges in Trentino are operated by the Società degli Alpinisti Tridentini (SAT), a branch of the CAI, at Via Manci 57, 38100 Trento, t 04 6198 1871, f 04 6198 6462. In the Alto Adige, the address is CAI, Piazza dell'Erbe 46, 39100 Bolzano, t 0471 971 694.

Skiing

The Dolomites are like a candy shop for winter sports junkies. As the sunny side of the Alps they enjoy good clear weather, and when it snows, it falls delightfully dry and powdery. There is a variety of slopes of all levels of difficulty, and country trails, toboggan and bobsled runs, ice rinks and speed-skating courses; if all of the ski runs were ironed out flat they would stretch from the Brenner Pass to Reggio Calabria. There are other bonuse too: ski schools in July, and heated indoor pools in midwinter.

Write ahead to the tourist offices in Belluno, Trento or Bolzano, or book a week's *Settimana Bianca* package (a week's room and board at a hotel, ski-pass and instruction) from CIT (Citalia) or other travel offices all over Italy.

If you want to try as many resorts as possible, the *Dolomiti Superski* pass, 'the world's most extensive ski pass', gives unlimited access (for about L100,000 a day) to 464 lifts and 1180km of ski runs for periods of one, two, or three weeks.

For the latest information and prices, call t 04 7179 5397, f 04 7179 4282, *www.Dolomiti Superski.com*.

The Dolomites

AUSTRIA

SWITZERLAND

Brennerpass
Passo del
Brennerio

Val Ridanna

Vipiteno

Novace

Bressanon

Lago di
Resia

Gruppo
di Tessa ▲

Parcines

Merano

Chiusa

Laudes
Malles Venosta
Sluderno
Spondigna
Silandro
SS38
Naturno
Castelrotto
Val Ga
Collalbo
Siusi

Müstair
Tarres
TRENTINO ALTO
Soprabolzano
Fiè
Sciliar
Prato
Alpe

SS38
Val Venosta
Parco Nazionale
ADIGE
Bolzano

Passo delle
Stelvio
Solda
Val di Fassa
Val d'Eg
SS41

Val Martello
Val di Senales
SS38

della Stelvio
Bagni di Rabbi
Fondo
Caldaro
Ponte Nova

Peio
Val di Rabbi
Val di Sole
SS42
L. di Sta Giustina
Lago di Caldaro
Látemar ▲

Pellizzano
Ossana
Malé
Cles
Coreda
Termeno
Ora
Predazzo

Val di Non
Tassullo
Egna
Cavalese
Tesero

Grosotto
Lago di
Tovel
Pradalago
Val di Pan
Madonna di
Campiglio
Mezzocorona
S.
Alpe Cermis ▲
Catena del La

Tirano
Cascata di
Nardis
SS239
Gruppo di Brenta
Spormaggiore
Michele all'Adige
Lisignago
Val di Cembra
Cembra
Segonzano

Edolo
S39
Val di Genova
Carisolo
Pinzolo
Molveno
Aviso
Palù del Fersina

Aprica
Adamello Mts
Monte
Paganella
Civezzano
Baselga di
Piné

Capo
di Ponte
S. Lorenzo
in Banale
Sardagna
Vanéze
Vason
Trento
Pergine
Valsugana
Pieve Te
Castell

Schilpario
Valle Camonica
Tione di Trento
Ponte Arche
M. Bondone
Vetriolo
Terme
Val Sugana

Valli Giudicarie
Fiave
Cornetto ▲
Lago di
Caldonazzo
Levico
Terme

Boario
Terme
Val di Daone
Varone
Molina
di Ledro
Arco
Calliano
Lavarone
Altopiano d

Riva del Garda
Volano
Rovereto
Folgaria
S350

Torbole
Val Lagarina
A22
Asso

Lago
d'Idro
Limone sul Garda
Sette Con

Malcésine
Camposilvano
Santorso
Thiene
Brega

Lago
di
Garda
M. Baldo
Avio
S46
Recoaro Terme
Schio

Gardone Val
Trompia
Gargnano

somewhat overripe, fashionable heart is the glossy resort of Cortina d'Ampezzo, host of the 1956 Winter Olympics, which did much to introduce the Dolomites to the world. The Alte Vie – the High Roads of the Dolomites – pass through this region as well, winding their way at high altitudes across some of the most renowned ridges and peaks in the range.

AUSTRIA

N

20 km
10 miles

Valle Aurina
Riva di Tures
Campo Tures
Val di Tures
Chienes
Brunico
Val Pusteria
Monguelfo
Rienza
Dobbiaco
V. di Landro
Sesto
Val di Sesto

Carbonin
Rif. Auronzo
Lago di Misurina
Comelico Superiore
Misurina
Auronzo di Cadore
Sto Stefano di Cadore
Sappada

La Villa
S. Cassiano
Tofane
Corvara
Cortina d'Ampezzo
M. Agudo

Passo di Sella
Arabba
Col di Lana
Cinque Torri
Campitello di Fassa
Andraz
Selva di Cadore
S. Vito di Cadore
Calalzo di Cadore
Forni di Sopra
Sauris di Sopra
Lago di Sauris
Ampezzo

Canazei
Marmolada
Caprile
Colle Sta Lucia
Borca di Cadore
Pieve di Cadore
Tolmezzo
di Fassa
Fassa

Alleghe
M. Pelmo
Boite

Canale d'Agordo
M. Civetta
Cencenighe
Dont
Valle di Zoldo
Forni di Sotto
Socchieve

Falcade
neveggio
di Rolle
Cordevole
Agordo
Gemona di Friuli

no di ozza
Pale di S. Martino
Frassene
Longarone
Lago del Vaiont
M. Toc
S. Daniele di Friuli

Fiera di Primiero
Parco Nazionale
delle Dolomiti
M. Dolada
Val Cellina
Lago di Barcis
Tagliamento

Bellunesi
Belluno

Feltre
Bosco del Cansiglio
FRIULI VENEZIA-GIULIA

Polcenigo

Vittorio Veneto
Caneva
Livenza
Sacile
Pordenone

Conegliano

Romano d'Ezzelino
Asolo
Maser
Montebelluna
Oderzo
Summaga
Portegruaro

Bassano del Grappa
Piave
Treviso

The Piave Valley

The roads north along the River Piave from Belluno (SS50) and Treviso (SS51) meet at the junction of Ponte nelle Alpi before continuing up through scenery marked by the steep pyramids of **Monte Dolada** and **Piz Gallina**. A less benign mountain, **Toc** (6,301ft), looms over the town of **Longarone**. In 1963 a landslide from its slopes crashed into the local reservoir, Lake Vaiont, creating a tidal wave that killed 1,917

Getting Around the Dolomites

Even the heirs of the Romans can only make the **trains** go so far in the mountains. The line north from Venice, Treviso and Belluno passes through Pieve di Cadore before petering out in Calalzo di Cadore, 35km from Cortina d'Ampezzo (2½ hours from Venice). The western Dolomites are linked by the main line between Verona and Munich, by way of Trento (1½ hours) and Bolzano (2½ hours) to the Brenner Pass (4 hours). Branch lines run from Bolzano to Merano and Malles Venosta, to the west, and from near Bressanone to Brunico and San Candido to the east.

To make up for the lack of trains, the Dolomites are exceptionally well served by two bus companies – Dolomiti-Bus in the east (with, for example, daily routes to Agordo, Arabba, Falcade, and Colle S. Lucia from Venice) and the cheerful SAD Buses in the west.

Besides their normal runs, the companies add special scenic tours in July and August from the major centres.

When to Go

Prices skyrocket in the Dolomites during their high-season periods (Christmas holidays, end of January to Easter, mid-July to mid-September).

To avoid high prices and the crowds, try to go in June, early July or late September–October, when the alpine refuges are open but not packed to the gills, or immediately after the New Year holidays for skiing, when everyone else has to go back to work and the resorts offer big discounts.

But from March–June and September–December beware: you should expect to look fairly hard for a hotel, because the area does use this time – neither summer nor winter season – to catch its breath.

people in Longarone; a memorial church, unfortunately resembling a parking garage, documents the disaster and has a few poignant bits salvaged from the mud. A road runs along the path of the disaster, the lofty and narrow **Gola del Vaiont**, to the lake, 6km to the east. From Longarone there's also the option of turning west on the SS251 for the **Val Zoldana**, a lovely valley lining the River Maè, with typical hamlets in wood and stone, the cradle of Italy's best *gelato* makers. The valley road passes the stunning peaks of Civetta and Pelmo on the way to Selva di Cadore (*see* p.448).

The main road from Longarone skirts the high banks of the Piave north into the foothills of the Antelao and Marmarole and **Pieve di Cadore**. *Pieve* means parish, and from Roman times on this was the most important one in the Cadore, a status that grew with the reputation of that mighty wielder of the brush, Tiziano Vecellio (Titian), born here c. 1483. His statue stands in the main piazza, just up from his birthplace, the pretty **Casa Natale di Tiziano** (*open 9.30–12.30 and 4–7; closed Mon; adm; if it's not open, the museum listed below should be able to let you in*), containing drawings, studies and some original furnishings. In the church of **Santa Maria Nascente**, the last chapel on the left holds his *Madonna with SS. Andrew and Titian*, starring his own family – his daughter as the Virgin, his son as Titian the Bishop, his brother as St Andrew and Titian himself looking in from the left. The most important building in Pieve doesn't leave room for any false modesty but calls itself the **Palazzo della Magnifica Comunità Cadorina** (*same hours as Titian's Birthplace*). Built in 1525, it now houses the local historical museum, with pre-Roman weapons and 2nd-century BC bronze figurines. Towards Tai, at the crossroads, the **Museo degli Occhiaia** (*open daily 9.30–12 and 3.30–7; adm*) contains a collection of antique spectacles. But what Pieve is proudest of these days is Babbo Natale (the Italian Santa Claus), who has made the town his home, with a Christmas-letter-answering service for the *bambini*.

The road and the Piave continue north past the end of the rail line at **Calalzo**, where you can catch a bus for the resort **Santo Stefano di Cadore**, located in the beautiful **Comelico Valley**. From here you can continue northwest to Cortina, or take another beautiful road east towards the popular resort of **Sappada**, a town more Austrian in feel than Italian.

From Pieve di Cadore there is also a direct road to Cortina d'Ampezzo, the SS51, which winds through the **Valle del Boite** with its many rustic wooden chalets, between the Antelao massif, the 'King of Cadore' and **Pelmo**, one of the most unusual and striking peak clusters in the Dolomites. The road passes through **Borca di Cadore** and the more important resort of **San Vito di Cadore**, an excellent base for ascending Pelmo and nearby peaks.

Tourist Information

Pieve di Cadore: Via XX Settembre 18, in Tai, t 0437 31644, f 0435 31645.
Santo Stefano di Cadore: Via Venezia 40, t 0435 62230, f 0435 62077.
Sappada: Borgata Bach 20, t 0435 469 131, f 0435 66233.
San Vito di Cadore: Via Nazionale 9, t 0436 9119, f 0436 99345.

Where to Stay and Eat

Sappada ✉ 32047

★★★Haus Michaela, Borgata Fontana 40, t 0435 469 377, f 0435 66131 (*moderate*). One reason for Sappada's popularity is its abundance of reasonably priced accommodation. At this little hotel the emphasis is on fitness, with an indoor pool, sauna and gym. *Open Dec–Easter and June–Sept.*

★★Corona Ferrea, Borgata Kratten 11, t 0435 469 442, f 0435 469 103 (*cheap*). A cheaper choice, which has comfortable rooms, all with bath. *Open July–20 Sept, 20 Dec–15 April.*

★★★Sierra Hof, Borgata Soravia 110, t 0435 469 110, f 0435 469 647 (*cheap*). A small place, near the centre of the village.

Keisn, Borgata Kratten 8, t 0435 469 070 (*expensive*). A tiny and romantic little place, offering the best food in the area (try the delicious - and surprising for the area – *formatino di zucchine* if it's on the menu)

and wonderful desserts. *Closed Wed, Thurs lunch, June and Oct.*

Baita Mondschien, Via Bach 96, t 0435 469585 (*moderate*). For some really authentic cooking try this pretty alpine chalet situated at the bottom of Sappada's slalom course. Serving wonderful grills and some interesting desserts, as well as home-made ice cream. *Open all year, closed Mon.*

★★★Belvedere, Piazza Cima 93, t/f 0435 469 112 (*moderate*). Located in Cima Sappada, 4km away, this hotel has only 14 rooms, but does have its own sauna and a good restaurant (*open to non-residents*): mountain specialities include variations on venison and desserts. *Open Dec–Mar, mid-June–Sept.*

★★★Bellavista, Via Cima, t 0435 469 175, f 0435 66194 (*moderate*). Also in Cima Sappada, a hotel which has been recently remodelled; lovely views and mountain bike hire. *Open Dec–Easter, mid-June–Sept.*

San Vito di Cadore ✉ 32046

★★★★Marcora, Via Roma 28, t 0436 9101, f 0436 99156 (*very expensive*). The best of a number of comfortable hotels here, in a fine setting with a pool. *Open 20 June–10 Sept, 20 Dec–20 Mar.*

★★★Cima Belprá, Via Calvi 1, at Chiapuzza, t 0436 890 441, f 0436 890 418 (*moderate*). A welcoming place with the best restaurant in the whole area, La Scaletta (*open to non-guests*), with beautiful views, and traditional *polenta* and beef dishes. *Closed Mon out of season, and Nov.*

The Eastern Dolomites

Cortina d'Ampezzo

Cortina's the sort of place where David Niven and Audrey Hepburn in turtlenecks and sunglasses would sit on a café terrace, but it also enjoys the best location in the Dolomites: a lofty (4,015ft–10,637ft), sunny, cross-shaped meadow at the junction of the Boite and Bigontina valleys, in the centre of a ring of extraordinary mountains – Tofane, the great mount 'owl' (scene of the 1997 World Cup); Cristallo; Sorapis, licked by stony flames; and the Cinque Torri, the 'five towers'.

Devoted heart and soul to fun and the sporting life, Cortina is almost as well known for its night-time activities, when the *après ski* crowd fills its clubs to trip the light fantastic until the wee hours of dawn. But whatever worldly pleasure and delight this snowy fleshpot offers, it comes at a price, rating right up there with Capri, Portofino and Venice herself on the bottom line of the tab.

Getting Around

Cortina's **bus** station is just off Via Marconi, and is served by SAD (**t** 1678 46047) and Dolomiti buses (**t** 0435 332 155). Services are greatly augmented from June to September, when buses serve virtually every paved road in the region; SAD buses make the Great Dolomites Road once a day. There's one bus a day direct from Venice or Treviso (**t** 042 15944).

The nearest **train** stations are Dobbiaco, 32km north (on the Bolzano–Lienz line), or Calalzo di Cadore, 35km south; both have regular bus connections to Cortina.

Tourist Information

Cortina d'Ampezzo: Piazzetta S. Francesco 8, near Piazza Venezia, **t** 0436 3231, **f** 0436 3235, *apt1@sunrise.it*. Accommodation, trail maps, information about walks and the *Dolomiti Superski* pass. The alpine guides are next door (*July, Aug and Sept*) **t** 0436 868505.

Where to Stay

Cortina d'Ampezzo ✉ 32043

Expect to run up against the full or half board requirement nearly everywhere in Cortina in its high season (it's an old tradition; the ancient Greek writer Polybius wrote that in Cisalpine Gaul travellers at inns requested the price for their whole stay, rather than have itemized accounts). It may be mortifying to the pocketbook, but not to the flesh; the local cuisine is usually as *haute* as the price.

Luxury–Very Expensive

★★★★★Miramonti Majestic, Via Miramonti 103, **t** 0436 4201, **f** 0436 867 019. If you're putting on the dog in Cortina, this is the place to do it. Warm, traditional and rustic, it has pretty wooden balconies with magnificent views. The rooms have all imaginable creature comforts, and there's an indoor pool and sauna. *Open July–Aug, Christmas–Mar.*
★★★★De La Poste, Piazza Roma 14, **t** 0436 4271, **f** 0436 868 435. If you'd rather be in the heart of the action, try this large, historic alpine chalet with classy rooms and balconies. The Poste's terrace and bar see much of Cortina's

social round, especially in the evening; half-pension mandatory in high season.

Expensive

★★★★Corona, Via Val di Sotto 10, **t** 0436 3251, **f** 0436 867 339. Another alpine chalet, 10 minutes from the centre, at the bottom of the valley beside the river. A modern art collection more extensive than the museums'. More convenient than most for the ski lift. *Open June–Sept, Dec–Mar.*
★★★Da Beppe Sello, Via Ronco 68, **t** 0436 3236, **f** 0436 3237. Award-winning, warm and welcoming, and serving some of the best food in Cortina, with game in season. *Open Nov–Easter, mid-May–mid-Sept.*

Moderate

★★★Menardi, Via Majon 110, **t** 0436 2400, **f** 0436 862 183. A charming 800-year-old farmhouse that's been run as an inn by the same family for the past century, furnished with antiques and bedecked with flowers. *Open 20 June–20 Sept, 20 Dec–10 April.*
★★Cavallino, Corso d'Italia 142, **t/f** 0436 2614. Small and friendly.

Cheap

★★★Imperio, Via C. Battisti 66, **t** 0436 4246, **f** 0436 4248. An unpretentious hotel with no restaurant but adequate rooms, all with bath. *Closed May.*
★★Montana, Corso Italia 94, **t** 0436 860 498, **f** 0436 868 211. As a second choice try here.

Eating Out

El Toulà, Via Ronco 123, **t** 0436 3339, near Pocol (*expensive*). An elegant place to eat, in a wooden farmhouse. It specializes in grilled meats, roast lamb, and Tyrolean desserts, with a renowned wine list. *Open Christmas–Easter, 15 July–30 Aug only; closed Mon.*
Tivoli, Via Lacedel 34, **t** 0436 866 400 (*expensive*). Its rival, northeast of the centre, offers lovely views and innovative, ultra-refined cuisine. *Closed Mon.*
Al Camin, Via Alverà 99, **t** 0436 862 010 (*moderate*). A brief walk up the hill behind town brings you to this cosy restaurant with lots of wood and a fireplace, serving local versions of *polenta* and goulash. *Closed Mon.*

The Sporting Life

The 1956 Olympics endowed Cortina with superb winter sports facilities; here you can ski-jump, speed-skate, fly down bobsled and luge runs, and cut figures of eight in the ice stadium, not to mention the thousand and one downhill and cross-country ski runs in the vicinity. In the summer, it's an excellent base for hiking, rock-climbing, delta-planing and more, while in town there's a riding school, tennis, both summer and winter swimming pools, and activities like the Ice Disco Dance in the Olympic Ice Stadium.

Cortina has its share of trendy shops, and a museum of contemporary art you can take in if it rains – the **Museo Ciasa de Ra Regoles**, Via del Parco, on the corner of Corso d'Italia (*open daily 10.30–12.30 and 4–7.30; closed Mon; adm*) which has sections on palaeontology and ethnography, and art by De Pisis, Morandi, De Chirico and others. Two cablecars from Cortina wait to whisk you up to the mountains, both at the end of the town bus lines: in the north, near the Olympic stadium, to **Tofana di Mezzo** (10,637ft) where there are privately run Alpine refuges, and in the west, to **Tondi di Faloria** (7,685ft).

Excursions From Cortina

As a major crossroads, Cortina offers numerous forays into the surrounding mountains. For the classic Great Dolomites Road between Cortina and Bolzano, *see p.470.*

Lake Misurina and Around

For a beautiful short trip from Cortina, take the SS48 and SS48b over the lofty **Tre Croci Pass** to **Lake Misurina**, shimmering below the jagged peaks of Sorapis and the remarkable triple-spired **Tre Cime di Lavaredo**, 15km northeast of Cortina. The colours of Misurina are so brilliant they look touched-up on the postcards; as a resort it makes a quiet alternative to Cortina, especially if ice-skating is your sport. From Misurina it's a magnificent 7km drive up to the **Rifugio Auronzo**, located just beneath the Tre Cime di Lavaredo, where you can make the easy walk to the 1916 **Bersaglieri memorial**, honouring Italy's famous sharpshooters. More fine views await from **Monte Piana**, a lofty meadow 6km north of Misurina.

Circular Routes from Misurina to Cortina

There are two possible circular routes from Misurina back to Cortina that make rewarding full-day excursions. Both begin to the east on the SS48 via **Auronzo di Cadore**, past a peak known as the **Corno del Doge** for its resemblance to the Doge's bonnet. Auronzo, on the shores of an artificial lake, surrounded by fragrant spruce forests, makes another fine base, and has a cablecar and chairlifts up **Monte Agudo**.

From Auronzo you can circle south around Pieve di Cadore and the Valle del Boite (161km; *see p.443*) or take the longer route around to the north (224km) through **Comelico** and the beautiful **Val di Sesto**. The route passes into the Alto Adige, through **San Candido/Innichen**, a resort on the River Drava; it has a Benedictine monastery and a Romanesque collegiate church, the 13th-century **SS. Candidus e Corbinian**, its altar decorated with a superb early 13th-century *Crucifixion* in polychrome wood.

Tourist Information

Auronzo: Via Roma 10, **t** 0435 9359,
f 0435 400 161.
Dobbiaco: Via delle Dolomiti 3, **t** 0474 972132,
f 0474 973730, *toblach@dnet.it.*
Alleghe: Piazza Kennedy 17, **t** 0437 523 333,
f 0437 723 881.
Agordo: Via Sommariva 10, **t** 0437 62105,
f 0437 65205.

Where to Stay and Eat

Misurina ✉ 32040

★★★Lavaredo, Via Monte Piana 11, **t** 0436 39227,
f 0436 39127 (*moderate*). Offers tennis courts
and a good restaurant. *Closed Nov–mid-Dec.*
★★Dolomiti des Alpes, Via Monte Piana, **t** 0436
39031, f 0436 39216 (*cheap*). Situated just
above the lake, with a sauna-solarium.
Closed Oct–mid-Dec.
★Sport, Via Monte Piana 18, **t/f** 0436 39125
(*cheap*). Views of Lake Misurina; simple
rooms.

Auronzo di Cadore ✉ 32041

★★★Auronzo, Via Roma 30, **t** 0435 400 202,
f 0435 99879 (*moderate*). Auronzo has far
more choices. This is a cosy old place with
tennis and a park on the lake shore. *Open
Dec–Mar and June–Sept.*
★★Vienna, Via Verona 2, **t** 0435 9394 (*cheap*).
Near the lake with views of the mountains.
Cavaliere, on the road east of Auronzo at Cima
Gogna, **t** 0435 9834 (*moderate*). Delicious
suckling pig and *risotto* with herbs or mushrooms, amid wood-panelling. *Closed Wed.*

San Candido/Innichen ✉ 39038

★★★Orso Grigio, Via Rainer 2, **t** 0474 913 115,
f 0474 914 182 (*expensive*). An award-
winning hotel with charming, modern
rooms in a handsome 18th-century building.
Open Jan–April, mid-June–mid-Oct.

★★★Posthotel, Via Sesto 1, **t** 0474 913 133,
f 0474 913 635 (*expensive*). Central and traditional, with plenty of activities, including a
games room for children, Turkish bath, pool
and solarium, and excellent local and
international cuisine.
Uhrmacher's Weinstube, Via Tintori 1, **t** 0474
913 158. A special treat for wine or spirit
lovers; visit the cellar and choose a wine to
go with a snack, or try a glass from one of
the thirty or so bottles they open every day.
Closed Wed, exc summer.

Dobbiaco/Toblach ✉ 39034

★★★★Cristallo, Via S. Giovanni 37, **t** 0474 972
138, f 0474 972 755 (*expensive*). The same
family has run this fine resort hotel since
1911; recently renovated. In a beautiful
setting, with an indoor pool and sauna.
Open Christmas–Easter, June–mid-Oct.
Winkelkeller, Via Conte Künigi 8, **t** 0474 972
022 (*moderate*). Dine on refined mountain
cuisine. *Closed Wed, June and part of Oct.*

Selva di Cadore ✉ 32020

★★★Giglio Rosso, at Pescul, **t** 0437 720 310,
f 0437 521 110 (*moderate*). A fine place both
to stay and to eat. The kitchen does a fine
mulberry *risotto* and turkey in beer. *Open
Dec–Mar, June–Sept.*

Àlleghe/Caprile ✉ 32022

★★★Coldai, Via Coldai 13, **t** 0437 523 305, f 0437
523 438 (*moderate*). A hotel with lovely views
over the lake and pleasant rooms. *Closed
May–mid-June, Oct, Nov.*
★★★★Alla Posta, Piazza Dogliani 19, in Caprile
t 0437 721 171, f 0437 721 677 (*expensive*). This
130-year-old hotel is the most prestigious in
the area, with comfortable rooms, indoor
pool, sauna and good restaurant. *Open 20
Dec–15 April, 15 June–30 Sept.*
★★Marmolada, Corso Veneto 27, **t** 0437 721 107
(*cheap*). Simple, but adequate – who wants
to be indoors anyway? *Closed May, Oct.*

The turn back to Cortina (SS51) is at **Dobbiaco/Toblach**, one of the original Dolomite
resorts, thanks to its magnificent setting and lake, and a railway station built by the
Habsburgs. The large **castle** in the old part of town was built for Emperor Maximilian
in 1500. In July Dobbiaco holds a series of concerts in honour of Mahler, who spent his
summers here; in summer, too, you can visit the little **Museo Gustav Mahler**, 4km

from the centre at Casa Trenker (*ring the tourist office for hours*). From Dobbiaco the road heads south past wooded Lake Dobbiaco and enters the dramatic **Val di Landro**, where the Cristallo group looms over **Carbonin/Schluderbach**. Beyond are a pair of little lakes, and the lonely ruins of the **Castel Sant'Umberto**. The road then circles around castle-crowned **Podestagno**, before descending into the Ampezzo with the Le Tofane group storming up to the right.

Cortina to Colle Santa Lucia and Agordo

There are two routes to these mountains southwest of Cortina: the main one follows the Great Dolomites Road (*see* p.470) through the Falzarego Pass, before taking the SS203 south at Andraz; a lesser-known but equally pretty route takes the smaller SS638 road through the **Passo di Giau**, where in recent years some of the most important Mesolithic tombs in Europe (5000 BC) have been discovered.

The artefacts of 'Mondeval man' can now be seen down in **Selva di Cadore**, in the **Museo Storico** (*open July and Aug daily 4–6.30*). Selva is a growing resort in the lovely Val Fiorentina, where a road crosses into the Valle di Zoldana and ends up at Longarone (*see* p.441). Above Selva, **Colle Santa Lucia** is a pretty place with its old agricultural hamlets and a beautiful belvedere.

Continuing south from Colle the road passes **Caprile** and the mighty north wall of Civetta en route to **Àlleghe** with its lovely lake, formed in 1771 by a landslide from Civetta. At **Cencenighe** you have the option of turning off for Falcade and San Martino di Castrozza (*see* p.458). **Àgordo** (45km) is an attractive town and resort in the Val Cordévole, along one of the principal branches of the Piave.

The Passo Duran above Àgordo leads back to Cortina via the Valle di Zoldo and the village of **Dont** (another 21km) – there are splendid views of Civetta and Pelmo, and you can buy local woodcarvings.

The Western Dolomites: Trentino

The autonomous province of Trentino encompasses the western Dolomites, as beautiful as the eastern mountains, especially the Val di Fassa and the isolated but hauntingly majestic Brenta Group, to the west of the Adige. Unlike the Alto Adige/Süd Tirol further north, Trentino is mostly Italian in language and heritage, sprinkled with a Ladin minority in the valleys. Trento is a fine little art city, worth a day on its own.

From Verona to Trento: Val Lagarina and Rovereto

Following the Adige up from Verona, the A22 and SS12 enter Trentino near **Avio**, dominated by the proud 14th-century **Castello di Sabbionara** (*open Tues–Sun 10–1 and 2–6, till 5 in winter; closed Jan; adm*). Its guardhouse preserves a wonderful fresco cycle of battling knights, while in the keep the frescoes depict scenes of courtly love.

Further up the Adige, past a sea of vineyards, **Rovereto**, 'the Athens of the Trentino', is an evocative old place, the second city of the Trentino, built around an imposing Venetian castle; between 1416–87 the city formed the northern extent of the

Getting Around

Frequent **trains** and **buses** follow the Adige from Verona to Trento, stopping at the main towns. Getting off at the station in Rovereto is more fun than it used to be, with three life-size dinosaurs as a welcoming committee.

Tourist Information

Rovereto: Via Dante 63, **t** 0464 430 363, **f** 0464 435 528.
Lavarone: Municipio, **t** 0464 784 151, *aptlavarone@seldati.it*.

Where to Stay and Eat

Rovereto ✉ 38068

★★★Rovereto, Corso Rosmini 82/d, **t** 0464 435 522, **f** 0464 439 644 (*expensive*). A fine central hotel, with comfortable rooms in a variety of styles, and an excellent restaurant, **Novecento** (*moderate*), featuring regional dishes, delicious homemade pasta, and a vegetarian menu. *Closed Sun*.

Al Borgo, Via Garibaldi 13, **t** 0464 436 300 (*expensive*). The best place to eat is this surprisingly sophisticated little restaurant in the heart of town. The menu features delicious dishes like ham and spinach in puff pastry, *risotto* with lemon, or turbot with artichokes, followed by fantastic desserts, and all accompanied by piano music in the evening. Unusually for Italy, they even bake their own bread. *Closed Sun eve and Mon, part of Feb and July*.

Lavarone/Folgaria ✉ 38046

★★★Hotel du Lac in Frazione Chiesa, **t** 0464 783 112 **f** 0464 783 255 (*moderate*). Freud stayed here; its pretty setting on the lake (and an indoor swimming pool) make it a fine place to forget your neuroses.

★★★Camminetto, near the chairlift Bertoldi, **t/f** 0464 783 214 (*cheap*). Lots of wood and flowers give this hotel its cosy charm. *Open Dec–mid-April, mid-June–Sept*.

L'Antico Pineta, Via de Gasperi 66 in Folgaria, **t** 0464 720 327 (*moderate*). A good place to dine and try *polenta* laden with melted Asiago cheese.

Serenissima, before the Trentini, with the aid of the Tyroleans, shoved the Venetians back to Verona. This area was also hotly contested in the First World War, and the castle contains an extensive **war museum** devoted primarily to that conflict (*open Mar–Nov Tues–Sun 8.30–12.30 and 2–6; July–Sept 8.30–6.30; adm*). Cannons from each of the 19 belligerents were melted down to make the largest ringing bell in the world, the **Campana dei Caduti**, located in the southern quarter of Rovereto; it rings in memory of the fallen every day at sundown.

The futurist Fortunato Depero (1892–1960) worked for many years in the town, and bequeathed it the **Museo Depero**, Via della Terra 53 (*open daily 9–12.30 and 2.30–6; closed Mon; adm*), near the castle, a rather striking little museum designed by the artist himself as a showcase for his tapestries, puppets and paintings. Rovereto was also the home town of archaeologist Paolo Orsi, who willed his statues and vases from Magna Graecia to the city. They are displayed in the new **Museo Civico**, Borgo S. Caterina 43 (*open Tues–Sat 9–12 and 3–6*).

Just southeast of Rovereto, you can walk the 'Path of the Dinosaurs', marked by footprints planted 200 million years ago. The 'Path of Peace', a long-distance walk along the front line of the First World War, ends at Mount Zugna, further the south, by the Campana dei Caduti.

Across the Adige from Rovereto, **Isera** is the centre for the production of Marzemino, one of Trentino's finest red wines. To the north, seen from the Trento road, the ruined but imposing **Castel Beseno** (*open April–Oct daily 9–12 and 2–5.30; closed Mon; adm*)

The Western Dolomites

Parco Nazionale

Val di Fassa

TRENTINO - ALTO ADIGE

della Stelvio

N

10 km
5 miles

M. Cevedale

Bagni di Rabbi

Val di Rabbi

Malé

Val di Sole

S42

Fondo

Passo di Mendola

Appiano

S38

Caldaro sulla Strada del Vino

Romeno

L. di Sta Giustina

Cles

S. Romedio

Sanzeno

Coreda

Lago di Caldaro

Termeno

Val di Non

Ossana

Pellizzano

Folgarida

Marilleva

Tassullo

Tueno

Taio

Ton

Eg

Val di

Lago di Tovel

Pradalago

Madonna di Campiglio

Campo Carlo Magno

Spormaggiore

Mezzocorona

Persanella

Cascata di Nardis

Val di Genova

Carisolo

Pinzolo

SS239

C. Tosa

Gruppo di Brenta

Andalo

Fai della Paganella

Michele all'Adige

Segonzano

Cembra

Adamello Mts

Molveno

Monte Paganella

Lisignago

Aviso

Baselga di Piné

Val di

Lago di Molveno

S. Lorenzo in Banale

Monte Paganella

Adige

Civezzano

Pergine

Valsugar

Stenico

Cast. Toblino

Sardagna

Trento

L. Lev

Val di Daone

Tione di Trento

Sarche

Ponte Arche

Dasindo

Fiavé

Lago di Toblino

Vaneze

Vason

M. Bondone

Cornetto

Lago di Caldonazzo

Lago di Cavedine

Drena

Dro

Lavarone

Folgaria

Calliano

Cast. Beseno

Val di

Arco

Cascata

Caneve

Villa Lagarina

Volano

Castèl Pietra

Varone

Isera

Rovereto

Riva del Garda

Cast. Dante

Molina di Ledro

Torbole

Lago di Ledro

Valli Giudicarie

Val Lagarina

A22

Limone sul Garda

Camposilvano

Tremosine

Malcésine

Campione

Avio

S46

Lago d'Idro

Lago di Garda

Gargnano

Ferrara di M. Baldo

Recoaro Terme

is the largest castle in the region, and has rooms frescoed with scenes of the months. Two small resorts on a 3,280ft plateau below Monte Cornetto can be reached by the SS350 from Calliano: **Folgaria**, with its 17th-century Maso Spilzi, restored to its original appearance (*open June–Sept*), and the larger **Lavarone**, near the lake of the same name, where Freud spent three summers.

Trento

In the 16th century Emperor Charles V, ruler of much of Europe and the Americas, found his Germanic possessions in the throes of the Reformation, and his Catholic domains braced for a hysterical reaction. Charles sought to heal the rift in his realm by asking Pope Clement VII to call a council to look into some urgently needed reforms. Clement demurred until Charles sacked Rome in 1527, but years would pass before one of his successors, Paul III, actually convoked the prelates, after quibbling about venue – Charles wanted it on Imperial turf, while the Pope insisted on an Italian city. Italian Trento, ruled by a powerful bishop-prince in the Holy Roman Empire, proved to be the perfect compromise, thanks to the lobbying efforts of the city's great Renaissance patron, Bernardo Cles, Prince-Bishop from 1514 to 1539. By the time it started, the Council of Trent (1545–63) was too late to bring the Protestants back into the fold, although it did provide the doctrinal ammo for the Counter-Reformation.

The Council put Trento on Europe's map, but it doesn't put on airs. Lying at the foot of Monte Bondone, between the banks of the Adige and the Fersina, it is refreshingly unpretentious and charming; many of its gently winding streets are embellished with *al fresco* frescoes, and its bishop's palace has a fresco cycle of the months that alone is worth the trip.

To the Duomo

Trento's points of interest can easily be seen on foot. **Piazza Dante**, in front of the station, is a convenient place to start (and find a place to park); the statues of the eponymous poet and other Italian celebrities were erected here amid the public gardens in 1896 by Trento's irredentist societies, in defiance of their Austrian rulers. Next to the station itself, the attractive 12th-century collegiate church of **San Lorenzo** stands in a sunken lawn.

From San Lorenzo, Via Andrea Pozzo and Via D. Orfane lead to the gracious pink **Santa Maria Maggiore** (1520), a simple and elegant Renaissance church with ornate portals, commissioned by Bernardo Cles. It was large enough to be used for several sittings of the Council of Trent, has a beautiful organ gallery by Vincenzo Grandi (1534), and the *Dispute with the Doctors* by Giambattista Moroni from Bergamo.

One block east of S. Maria Maggiore runs **Via Belenzani**, forced through the medieval quarters by Bernardo Cles who wanted a proper straight street to the cathedral. It is lined with fine palaces: the best, **Palazzo Pona Geremia**, is entirely covered with recently restored 16th-century frescoes of the locals receiving the Emperor Maximilian and mythological subjects. Via Belenzani ends with the handsome

Getting Around

The **bus** and FS **railway** station are next to each other on the Piazza Dante. *Atestina* buses go up all the valleys in the Trentino, t 0461 821 000. For the Trento-Malè station, with trains up the Val di Non to Cles, turn left out of the main station, and walk 500m to Via Seconda da Trento 7, t 0461 238 350.

Tourist Information

Trento: Via Alfieri 4, across Piazza Dante from the station, t 0461 983 880, f 0461 984 508. **Trentino** region: Via Romagnosi 3, t 0461 839 000, f 0461 260 245; *apt@provincia.tn.it*. Freephone from within Italy, t 1678 45034.

Where to Stay

Expensive

****Accademia, near Santa Maria Maggiore at Vicolo Collico 4/6, t 0461 233 600, f 0461 230 174. Some of the cardinals attending the Council of Trent are said to have slept at predecessor of this hotel. The wood-panelled rooms are comfortable and the restaurant is excellent, with a menu that changes every month.

****Buonconsiglio, Via Romagnosi 16/18, t 0461 272 888, f 0461 272 889. A fine, recently revamped place to stay in the historic centre – though with a little less history than the 'Academy'.

Moderate

***America, Via Torre Verde 50, t 0461 983 010, f 0461 230 603. A comfortable 1920s hotel, in walking distance of the train station.

***Aquila d'Oro, Via Belenzani 76, t/f 0461 986 282. Right in the centre with extremely comfortable rooms, as well as café tables spilling out into the street.

***Villa Madruzzo, 3km east of Trento in Cognola, Via Ponte Alto 26, t 0461 986 220, f 0461 986 361. If you have a car, one of the nicest places to stay is this charming 19th-century villa located in a leafy park. It has modern, comfortable rooms, fine views and a very good traditional restaurant.

Cheap

**Venezia, Via Belenzani 70, t 0461 234 559. On Trento's prettiest street.

*Venezia, Piazza Duomo 45, t/f 0461 234 144. Another Venezia, which has small, basic rooms; ask for one overlooking the *duomo* and Fountain of Neptune.

Eating Out

Trentino cuisine is basically alpine: popular dishes include *canederli*, *gnocchi* made from breadcrumbs, egg, cheese and bacon; *patao*, a minestrone of yellow flour and sauerkraut, and *osei scampadi*, veal 'birds' with sage.

Chiesa, in the 17th-century Palazzo Wolkenstein, Parco San Marco (near the Castello di Buonconsiglio) t 0461 238 766 (*expensive*). Trento's most celebrated restaurant is famous for its 'Apple Party Menu' in which Trentino's favourite fruit appears in every course; other choices include smoked trout and a tempting cheese strudel, or even a 1500s menu based on the preferred dishes of Bernardo Cles, accompanied by an extensive wine list and scrumptious desserts. Reservations essential. *Closed Sun, Mon lunch, Aug.*

Osteria a Le Due Spade, Via Don Rizzi 11, t 0461 234 343 (*expensive*). In business since 1545, serving refined dishes in a delightful dining room, decorated with mosaics. *Closed Sun, Mon lunch.*

Port'Aquila, Via Cervara 66, t 0461 230 420 (*moderate*). Right under the Castello di Buonconsiglio, this retro restaurant serves good *canederli*, *polenta* and other traditional dishes, served with well-aged Trentino vintages. *Closed Sun and Aug.*

Forst, Oss Mazzurana 38, t 0461 235 590 (*cheap*). Located in the middle of Trento, in a 16th-century palace. A popular place to drink beer and Trentino's wines, eat a pizza *tirolese* (with mushrooms and *speck*) or a *piatta trentino* (a mixture of local specialities). *Closed Mon, July.*

Al Vo', Vicolo del Vo' 11 (off Via Torre Verde) t 0461 985 374 (*cheap*). Serving good regional dishes and unusual specialities, but prices can mount if you're not careful. *Closed Sun, two weeks in July.*

porticoed **Casa Cazuffi**, decorated with monochrome frescoes from the 1530s. These overlook **Piazza Duomo** and the 18th-century **Fountain of Neptune**, the region's sea god symbol – not an obvious mascot until you focus on the trident he wields and remember the city's Roman name, *Tridentum*.

The Duomo and Museo Diocesano Tridentino

Trento's beautiful **Duomo** was designed in the 13th century and completed in 1515. Although it took 300 years to build, the style is all monumental Romanesque, richly decorated with galleries along its three apses and dome. The Council of Trent held its three major sessions here, and its decrees were blessed before the huge crucifix, still there in a right-hand chapel. The baldaquin over the high altar is a replica of St Peter's. Excavations unearthed a 6th-century basilica under the *duomo*, first home of the relics of Trento's patron, San Vigilio.

Next to the cathedral, the **Palazzo Pretorio**, crowned with swallowtail battlements, and a medieval **Torre Civica** house the excellent **Museo Diocesano Tridentino** (*open daily 9–12.30 and 2.30–6, closed Sun; adm*), renovated, and opened by John Paul II in 1995. There are paintings of the Council of Trent; a 16th-century portrayal of a *Mass of St Gregory*, its nonchalant congregation including a large band of pious skeletons; three 12th-century ivory caskets made by Islamic craftsmen and other treasures; and four charming 15th-century wooden altarpieces from the Val di Non, portraying three local martyrs in scenes observed by a man in a beaver hat. The museum's greatest prize, a cycle of six early 15th-century Flemish tapestries by Peter Van Aelst – woven masterpieces of portraiture and detail – were brought to Trento by Bernard Cles. (*The ticket also includes access to the excavations.*)

Castello di Buonconsiglio and its Museums

From Via Belenzani, Via Roma/Via Gian Antonio Manci leads to the magnificent residence of the bishop-princes, **Castello di Buonconsiglio** (*open Tues–Sun 9–12 and 4–5.30; adm exp*). Because of Trento's strategic location on the main highway to Rome, the medieval German emperors sought to keep the city's favour by granting its bishops a near-regal temporal status. Their castle consists of two buildings – the 13th-century Castelvecchio, with its Venetian Gothic loggia, and the Magno Palazzo, added by Bernardo Cles (1528–36). Today they house the provincial museum of art: medieval manuscripts, statues (especially fine wooden 15th- and 16th-century wooden sculptures) and paintings, although these are overshadowed by the castle's own 16th-century frescoes by Marcello Fogolino, Gerolamo Romanino and Dosso Dossi. Dossi painted the Olympian gods to conform to Counter-Reformation modesty levels – the gods model what look like turn-of-the-last-century bathing costumes, and the goddesses resemble Tarzan's Jane.

Best of all are the ravishing, detailed **frescoes of the months** in the Torre dell'Aquila, painted around the year 1400. While the nobility sports and flirts in the foreground, peasants perform their month-by-month labours, tending their flocks, making cheese, planting and harvesting, and making wine. One scene has the oldest-known depiction of Trento, dominated by the castle itself.

Vigilio and the Ciusi-Gobj Masquerade

Vigilio was a Roman patrician who studied in Athens, then moved to Trent with his family, where he was made bishop. His persuasive powers were good enough to convert his diocese, but when he went further afield to the Val Rendena and tipped over a statue of Saturn he was stoned to death.

He is celebrated every 20–26 June with an enthusiastic *Palio dell'Oca*, in which teams from each of the city's districts don 17th-century costumes and race down the Adige on rafts, trying to slip a ring over the neck of a papier-mâché goose suspended over the river. The climactic moment comes on 26 June, commemorating the same day back in the Middle Ages when Trento hired workers from Feltre to reinforce the town walls. Food supplies being low, Trento's bishop realized that the city could not afford to feed the workers and sent them home – only the Feltrese returned in the night to raid the stores. The ensuing battle is re-enacted in costume in the Piazza Duomo – the *Ciusi* are from Feltre, and they have five chances to break the ranks of Trento's *Gobj* to make off with the prize: a pot of hot, bubbling *polenta*.

Buonconsiglio also has an historical collection from the Napoleonic era to the Second World War; the idea for this museum was suggested in 1903 by local patriot Cesare Battisti, who, 13 years later, was executed for high treason in this same castle, by the Austrians. His and his companions' cells, the courtroom, and the ditch where they were shot and hanged, are shrines. You've probably already noticed Battisti's memorial – a marble circle of columns on the hill over the Adige. The present is illustrated by the new **Galleria Civica d'Arte Contemporaneo** (*open 10–12 and 4–7; closed Mon; adm*), which hosts temporary exhibitions.

More Museums: Art and Planes

Prince-Bishop Cristoforo Madruzzo did not feel quite at ease in the Castello di Buonconsiglio, and built a suburban residence on the Adige where he could get away from it all. This, the Palazzo delle Albere, 'of the poplars' – named for the trees that once lined the road out – now shelters the **Museo d'Arte Moderna e Contemporanea**, Via R. da Sansoverino 45 (*open 10–6; closed Mon; adm*), devoted to 19th–20th-century art, mostly Italian with a high concentration of futurists, who offer a stark contrast to the Renaissance frescoes by Fogolino.

The **Museo dell'Aeronautica Gianni Caproni**, Via Lidorno 3, by Trento's airport (*open 9–1 and 2–5, Sat, Sun 10–1 and 2–6, closed Mon; adm*) began in 1929 as the private collection of Gianni Caproni, a native of Trentino and one of Italy's leading aviation engineers in the 1910s and 20s, and whose aviation factory in Trento only closed in the 1950s; the museum contains a number of unique specimens, as well as a model of Leonardo da Vinci's flying machine.

Around Trento: Monte Bondone and Lake Caldonazzo

The slopes of Trento's own mountain, Bondone, can be easily reached by road or cablecar (*Mon–Sat 7am–9pm, Sun 9–6*), departing from the Ponte di San Lorenzo in

Trento (behind the bus station) and climbing as far as **Sardagna**. At least three buses a day continue on to **Vaneze** and **Vason**, both ski resorts; from Vason another cablecar ascends to one of Bondone's three summits (6,881ft). Further on, **Viotte** has an Alpine refuge and **Botanical Garden** (*open June–Sept daily 9–12 and 2–5*), one of the richest in Europe, founded in 1938 on the banks of two artificial lakes and planted with over two thousand species of high-altitude flora. Keep your eyes peeled for the pair of golden eagles who have recently nested nearby.

Another popular excursion is to head east up the Val Sugana along the Brenta to warm **Lago di Caldonazzo**, 'Trento's Lido', ideal for swimming, sailing and windsurfing. From lakeside **Vetriolo Terme** you can hike up to the summit of Panarotta for splendid views over Caldonazzo and its equally warm neighbour, **Lake Levico**.

East of Trento

The magic mountains wait, whether you turn east, west or north of Trento. San Martino di Castrozza and Paneveggio National Park are the main attractions to the east, along with two lovely valleys and a score of lovely lakes.

Val di Fiemme and Val di Fassa

These two northeasternmost valleys of Trentino, running between the Pale di San Martino, Rosengarten and the western slopes of the Marmolada, are among the most stunning and well-known among the cross country skiing fraternity. From Trento the road ascends the Val di Cembra, passing through a striking region of rocks eroded into spiky 'pyramids' near **Segonzano**. The once autonomous **Val di Fiemme** begins at **Cavalese**, where the elected *Regolani* held their parliament by the parish church; you can still see their stone benches, the **Banc de la Reson**. The *Magnifica Comunità* of Cavalese still has considerable say in local affairs, running the Val di Fiemme from the grand old frescoed **Palazzo della Comunità**, rebuilt in the 1500s by Bernardo Cles. Inside, a **museum** (*open July, Aug and Christmas daily 4.30–7.30*) documents Fiemme's proud past, and has works by the 17th–18th-century Fiemme school, a group of harmless painters who travelled about the smaller courts of Europe. A cablecar from Cavalese ascends to **Mount Cermis** (7,311ft).

Other places to aim for in the Val di Fiemme include **Tesero**, a village with a 15th century bridge, where furniture- and instrument-makers still ply their old trades, perhaps too well – the chapel of **San Rocco** (1528) is frescoed with a 'Sunday Christ', surrounded by all the tools that are taboo on the Sabbath. In **Predazzo** the **Civico Museo di Geologia** (*under restoration*), founded in 1899, takes the subject of Dolomitic rocks and marine fossils in hand, with geological paths at Doss Cappèl, reached by the Predazzo chair lift. Predazzo is the turn off for San Martino di Castrozza (*see p.458*).

Otherwise, continue straight into the beautiful **Val di Fassa**; **Moena**, the largest town and winter sports centre, is the 'boundary'. It has two churches of note: the large 12th-century **San Vigilio**, with paintings by local artist Valentino Rovisi, a pupil of Tiepolo; and **San Volfango**, richly frescoed by one of the anonymous, itinerant artists who travelled around the Trentino in the 15th century.

Tourist Information

Cavalese: Via F.lli Bronzetti 60, t 0462 241 111,
f 0462 230 649.
Canazei: Via Costa 79, Alba, t 0462 601 113,
f 0462 602 502.
San Martino: Via Passo Rolle 165, t 0439 768
867, f 0439 768 814.
Fiera di Primiero: t 0439 62407, f 0439 62992.

Where to Stay and Eat

Cavalese ✉ 38033
★★★**San Valier**, t 0462 341 285, f 0462 231 020
(*moderate*). Located in a pretty setting with
an indoor pool and sauna. *Closed Nov.*
★★★**Villa Trunka Lunka**, Via Degasperi 4, t 0462
340 233, f 0462 231 433 (*moderate*). One of
the nicest hotels, with the funniest name,
24 rooms, a sauna and solarium.
★★★**Sporting-Club Grand Chalet des Neiges**,
t/f 0462 341 650 (*moderate*). Right on the
pistes of Mt Cermis, superbly positioned at
6,562ft, this hotel has a pool and sauna to go
with its magnificent views. *Open mid-
Dec–mid-Apr.*
Cantuccio, Via Unterberger 14, t 0462 340 140
(*expensive–moderate*). Restaurants sometimes have *caronzèi*, the valley's unique
ravioli, filled with potatoes, *puzzone* cheese,
nutmeg and chives, topped with cheese,
sage and poppyseeds. Try this place, where
mushrooms are king, and they make a mean
rabbit in garlic cream and artichokes. *Closed
Mon eve and Tues out of season.*

Moena ✉ 38035
Moena is famous for its *puzzone* or 'stinky
cheese' which, in spite of its name, tastes
pretty good with toasted *polenta*.
★★★**Catinaccio Rosengarten**, Via Someda 6,
t 0462 573 235, f 0462 574 474 (*expensive*). A
hotel near the centre, with an indoor pool
and plenty of mountain atmosphere. *Open
Christmas–mid-April, July–mid-Sept.*
★★★**Post Hotel**, Piazza Italia, t 0462 573 760,
f 0462 573 281 (*moderate*). A classy choice,
with fine rooms and a good restaurant,
Tyrol. *Open Dec–Easter, mid-June–mid-Sept.*
Malga Panna, Via Costalunga 29, t 0462 573
489 (*expensive*). Long one of the best

restaurants in the region, with a variety of
menus, from *polenta* with a selection of
local cheeses and cold meats to the *menu
degustazione* of trout, rabbit, *tortelli ai
porcini*, *speck*, venison and strawberries.
Open Dec–April, July–Sept; closed Mon.
★★★★**Monzoni**, t 0462 573 352, f 0462 574 490
(*expensive*). Up above Moena at Passo di San
Pellegrino, this is a great place to stay: an old
mountain refuge converted into a hotel,
with an emphasis on nightlife and fun. *Open
Christmas–mid-April, mid-July–Aug.*

Canazei ✉ 38032
★★★**La Perla**, Via Pareda 103, t 0462 602 453,
f 0462 602 501 (*expensive*). In a panoramic
position near the ski slopes; a comfortable
spot, with a pool and sauna. *Closed Nov.*
★★**Dolomites Inn**, Via Arntersies 35, at Penia,
t 0462 602 212, f 0462 602 474 (*moderate*). A
little place with two squash courts. *Open
Dec–April, mid-June–mid-Sept.*
★★★**Bellevue**, t 0462 601 104, f 0462 601 527
(*moderate*). Great mountain views and
pleasant rooms. *Open all year.*
El Ciasel, t 0462 62190 (*moderate*). If you have
yet to try *strangolopreti* ('priest-stranglers'),
they're one of the specialities at this restaurant, along with game dishes and *polenta*.

San Martino di Castrozza ✉ 38058
★★★★**Des Alpes**, Via Passo Rolle, t 0439 769
069, f 0439 769 068 (*expensive*). The place to
soak up a turn-of-the-century Dolomites
feel. *Open Christmas–Mar, July–mid Sept.*
★★★**San Martino**, Via Passo Rolle 277, t 0439
68011, f 0439 68550 (*moderate*). Has an
indoor pool and sauna.
★★★**Venezia**, t 0439 68315, f 0439 769 159
(*moderate*). This hotel sits astride the Passo
di Rolle north of San Martino, has fantastic
views stretching across the valley, and
provides a great base for the National Park.
★★**Suisse**, Via Dolomiti 1, t/f 0439 68087
(*cheap*). Five minutes' walk up the hill from
San Martino brings you to this simple and
comfortable B&B.
Malga Ces, Loc. Malga Ces, t 0439 68223
(*moderate*). The best dining around; specialities include *canederli*, *polenta* with venison,
village cheeses and fruits of the forest. *Open
Dec–mid-April, mid-June–Sept.*

Seven *comuni* in the Val di Fassa preserve their Ladin language (a cross between Celtic and Latin introduced by Roman settlers; *see* p.461) and culture, especially **Vigo di Fassa**, site of the Ladin Cultural Institute and several *tabià* – the Ladini's traditional wooden cabins. A 20-minute walk leads up to the Gothic church of **Santa Giuliana a Vigo.** For a big thrill, take the three chairlifts from nearby Pozzo di Fassa up the flanks of Rosengarten, leaving you at the path to the **Torri del Vaiolet**, a sheer triple pinnacle.

Campitello di Fassa, the next town up the valley, has a *funivia* to the **Col Rodella** (8,151ft) – a famous viewpoint and winter sports centre. Further up the Val di Fassa, **Canazei**, rebuilt after 1912 when a fire destroyed the town, is the base for exploring the other magnificent peaks in the area – Marmolada, Sassolungo and Sella. The passes above lead to Arabba and Cortina, or north into the Val Gardena (*see* p.468).

San Martino di Castrozza and Paneveggio National Park

Predazzo is the main turn off for the stunning, pinnacle-crowned **Pale di San Martino** (Altars of St Martin; 10,466ft) – the principal group of the southern Dolomites. **San Martino di Castrozza**, lies dramatically at its feet – the biggest and best-equipped resort south of Cortina d'Ampezzo (complete with helicopters, and a bobsled run). But don't expect much character; the Austrians demolished the medieval town in the First World War, leaving only the ancient church. A popular excursion is the ascent by cablecar and chairlift to the summit of **Rosetta** (8,997ft).

Most of the big scenery around San Martino lies within the **Parco Naturale Paneveggio–Pale di San Martino**, a wilderness of emerald meadows, rushing streams, wildflowers and wildlife. Access to the park is from the visitors' centre in **Paneveggio**, north of San Martino, beyond the **Passo di Rolle**. Two paths take in tremendous vistas, not only of the Pale di San Martino, but also the distinctive peaks of **Marmolada**, **Pelmo** and **Civetta**. The forests here provided Stradivarius and co. with the resonant wood for their fiddles until the Venetians replanted trees in straight lines for masts and punished tree-poachers with death. Rules are still strict: there are only a few camp sites and no one may stay longer than 24 hours.

The Pale di San Martino are encircled by a road of scenic grandeur. The southern route, via Agordo (SS347), passes through **Frassene**, then climbs through the forests of Gosaldo to the **Passo di Cereda** and **Fiera di Primiero**, with a 15th-century centre. Fiera stands at the crossing of two valleys, the Cismon and the Canali, and has good skiing; a popular summer outing is the hour's walk up to sinister ruined **Castel di Pietra**, balancing on a jagged rock – built, according to legend, by Attila the Hun.

West of Trento: the Brenta Dolomites

The Brenta Group, though a bit distant from the other Dolomites, is just as marvellous and strange, and a challenge for experienced alpinists, although there are numerous less demanding walks for ordinary folk as well. The Adamello-Brenta Park is the last refuge of brown bears in the Alps, but you'd have to be very lucky, if that's the word, to see one. The following section circles them, a round trip of 175km from Trento.

Tourist Information

Molveno: t 0461 586 924, f 0461 586 221.
Pinzolo: t 0465 51007, f 0465 502 778.
Madonna di Campiglio: Via Pradalago 4,
t 0465 442 000, f 0465 540 404
Folgarida: t 0463 986 113, f 0463 986 594.
Malè: Viale Marconi 7, t 0461 901 280,
f 0463 901 563.

Where to Stay and Eat

San Michele all'Adige ✉ 38010

Da Silvio, Via Nazionale 1, Masetto de Faedo,
t 0461 650 324 (*moderate*). An ultra-modern
setting and an imaginative kitchen; try the
delicious *altamira*, a selection of mixed
meats grilled at your table, with a choice of
sauces. *Closed Sun eve and Mon, part of Jan
and June.*

Molveno ✉ 38018

★★★Belvedere, Via Nazionale 9, t 0461 586 933,
f 0461 586 044 (*expensive*). Fine rooms with
exquisite views over the lake and
mountains, an indoor pool and solarium.
Open Christmas, Feb, April–Oct.
★★★Miralago, Piazza Scuole 3, t 0461 586 935,
f 0451 586 268 (*moderate*). An older hotel,
offering an outdoor heated pool, garden and
superb terrace.
Alpotel Venezia, Via Nazionale 8, t 0461 586
920 (*cheap*). The place for good Trentino
home-cooking in the *centro storico*; try the
strangolopreti alla trentina – Trent-style
priest-stranglers.

Madonna di Campiglio ✉ 38084

Madonna di Campiglio is the one resort in
the Brenta Dolomites with accommodation
and facilities to please even the most
demanding customers, and prices are
correspondingly high.
★★★★Golf Hotel, up at the Passo Carlo Magno,
t 0465 441 003, f 0465 440 294 (*very expensive*). You can tee off at altitude while
staying at the one-time summer residence
of the Habsburg emperors, now beautifully
converted into a hotel. *Open mid-Dec–Mar
and mid-June–mid-Sept.*
★★★★Spinale Club Hotel, Via Monte Spinale 39,
t 0465 441 116, f 0465 442 189 (*very
expensive*). Down in Madonna di Campiglio
itself, a very attractive, elegantly appointed
hotel with a large indoor pool; the hotel also
takes special care of children. *Open Dec–April
and June–Sept.*
★★★Palù, Via Vallesinella 4, t 0465 441 695,
f 0465 443 183 (*expensive*). An older hotel,
with a blazing fireplace to sit around in the
winter. *Open Dec–Easter and July–Sept.*
★★Hermitage, Via Castelletto 65, t 0465 441
558, f 0465 441 618 (*moderate*). Small and
cosy, with a fine panoramic terrace and good
food. *Open Dec–mid-April and July–Sept.*
★★Gianna, Via Vallesinella 16, t 0465 41106,
f 0465 40775 (*moderate*). A family-run
bargain, with a bus that runs every half hour
into town and up to the ski lifts. *Open
Dec–Easter and July–Sept.*
Artini, Via Cima Tosa 47, t 0465 440 122
(*expensive*). For a special meal, this is a
modern and luminous restaurant,
specializing in wild mushroom dishes.
Open Dec–April and July–Sept.
Malga Montagnoli, Spinale, t 0465 42141
(*moderate*). Dine on venison with redcurrant
compôte or *risotto* with mushrooms.
La Fontanella, Via Dolomiti del Brenta 127,
t 0465 41398 (*moderate*). Filling *polenta*
dishes or *tagliatelle* with hare sauce.

Around Monte Paganella

To reach Monte Paganella, the eastern flank of the Brenta group, first head north to
San Michele all'Adige, home to the **Museo degli Usi e Costumi della Gente Trentina**, a
fascinating ethnographic collection, occupying 40 rooms in a former Augustinian
monastery (*open daily 9–12.30 and 2.30–6; closed Mon; adm*). Nearby **Mezzocorona**
produces Teròldego; the 'prince of Trentino wines' and lies at the start of the Bolzano
wine road (*see* p.464).

From Mezzocorona follow the signs to three well-equipped resorts, served by four
buses a day from Trento: **Fai della Paganella**, **Andalo** (both with cablecars to the

summit of Monte Paganella – 6,970ft) and Molveno, near Lago di Molveno, and a good base for hiking. From Molveno the road continues south to **Ponte Arche**, passing Fiavé, where a 5,000-year-old settlement of lake dwellers was discovered. East of Ponte Arche is picture postcard **Lake Toblino**, with its enchanting 12th-century castle, set on a tiny peninsula amid trees planted by Attila the Hun. Or so they say.

The Valli Giudicarie

The Brenta Group's southern flanks rise over the Giudicarie Valleys, a network encompassing several rivers and torrents, running from lake to lake – from Molveno down to Idro. Just south of Molveno, **San Lorenzo in Banale** has a road rising north up the **Val d'Ambiez** and the Rifugio al Cacciatore, providing a quick route for hikers to approach the highest peaks of the Brenta group. Further down, the Giudicarie is defended by the lovely castle at **Stenico**, founded in the 12th century. It retains some faded but good Renaissance frescoes; part of it now houses the archaeological collections of the **Trentino Provincial Museum** (*open Tues–Sun 9–12 and 2–5.30; adm*).

One of the Giudicarie's rivers, the Sacra, feeds Lake Garda. The main road follows it up to **Pinzolo**, an attractive town where the exterior of the cemetery church, **San Vigilio**, was frescoed in 1539 by Simone Baschenis with a vividly eerie medieval-style *Dance of Death*. Placid, businesslike skeletons conduct princes, popes, soldiers and everyone else to their end, with a couplet of elegant poetry for each. More of Simone Baschenis' precise work can be seen inside the church and at **Carisolo**, 2km away, where he painted another *Danse Macabre* on **Santo Stefano**. Frescoes within tell of an apocryphal visit by Charlemagne.

Carisolo is just in the lovely **Val di Genova**, one of the most beautiful valleys in the Alps, once the haunt of ogres and witches, all of whom were turned to stone after the Council of Trent. Part of the **Parco Naturale Adamello-Brenta**, the Val di Genova is graced by the lofty **Cascate di Nardis**, a woodland waterfall flowing from the glacier on **Presanella** (10,673ft) – in Pinzolo you can find a guide to make the ascent. To the east a chairlift (the world's fastest, they claim, so hold on to your hat) rises to the lower slopes of **Cima Tosa**, the highest peak of the Brenta Dolomites.

Madonna di Campiglio

From Pinzolo the SS289 zigzags up to the most important resort in the Brenta Dolomites, the superbly sited **Madonna di Campiglio**, with facilities that include a ski-jump, 31 lifts, speed-skating, skating rink and an indoor pool; in the summer it offers experienced climbers a chance to test their mettle on ice and a wild, rocky terrain; for walkers it has the most scenic trails. Even if you only have enough spunk to get into a chairlift, you can enjoy the marvellous views from the **Passo del Grostè**, some 7,413ft above Madonna to the east, or from **Pradalago** to the west. Get the tourist office's map to take the classic walk through the beautiful Val di Brenta and Valsinella just to the south. A far more difficult path, the fabulous **Via Bocchette**, takes in the region's most bizarre naked pinnacles and fantastic cliffs. North of Madonna the road passes through **Passo Campo Carlo Magno**, named after Charlemagne, who stopped here on his way to Rome to receive the Emperor's crown.

Val di Sole

Still circling the Brenta Group, the **Val di Sole**, occupies the upper reaches of the Noce River and the Trentino sector of the Stelvio National Park (*see* p.475). Italy's 'Sun Valley' is a cosy region of soft green meadows with lofty Monte Cevedale as a backdrop; valley churches have exterior frescoes by Simone Baschenis and kin; an *Annunciation* at Pellizzano and a *St Christopher* at Peio. The scenic roads up the **Val di Peio** and **Val di Rabbi** lead into the Stelvio; there is a **park visitors' centre** in Bagni di Rabbi. **Malè** is the site of the **Museo della Civiltà Solandra** (*open mid-June–mid-Sept daily 10–12 and 4–7; closed Sun*) – a civilisation of handicrafts and agricultural implements; these days, the town is a woodworking centre, and has good skiing in winter.

Down the Val di Non: Lake Santa Giustina to Trento

The wooded Val di Non, the enchanting valley along the lower Noce, produces some of Italy's finest apples, especially Golden Delicious and 'Renetta del Canada', which look more like potatoes. The valley is especially lovely in the spring, when its apple blossoms, emerald meadows and snow-clad mountains glow with colour.

Cles, the main town of the Val di Non (linked by local train to Trento), stands on the large artificial lake of Santa Giustina. Prince-bishop Bernardo Cles was born in the 11th-century **Castello Cles**, but the most striking building is across the lake, 6km from **Sanzeno**: the remarkable **Santuario di San Romedio** (*open daily 7.30–6*), reached by way of a road up a narrow gorge. The hermit Romedio lived as a kind of Alpine St Jerome with his pet bear on the cliff; his sanctuary consists of chapels stacked one atop another down the rock over the centuries, the end result somewhat resembling a doll's house in the forest. Don't miss the 11th-century barbaric reliefs on the portal, the disarming home-made ex-votos, or the ghastly souvenir shop.

South of Cles a 15km road leads to **Lago di Tovel**, lying deep in the folds of the Brenta Dolomites. Unlike other mountain lakes celebrated for their sapphire hue, Tovel was until recently famous for its ruby redness at certain periods when a rare algae, *Glendodinium sanguineum*, covered its surface. Nowadays Tovel is perhaps the only case in the world where one regrets that pollution has made the water turn blue.

From Lake Santa Giustina you can head east to Bolzano through the **Passo Mendola** (with a cablecar up to the view), or continue down the Val di Non past its orchards and old castles to **Vigo di Ton**, where the **Castel Thun**, was transformed into the most sumptuous palace of the Trentino. When restored, it will be a provincial museum; its paintings, long ignored, were recently found to be early 17th-century works by Crespi and the Bologna school. The road continues south to Trento via San Michele all'Adige.

Alto Adige/Süd Tirol

Everything has two names on the sunny side of the Alps, in the bilingual province of Alto Adige/Süd Tirol. In isolated mountain valleys people speak German and little Italian, while others still converse in Ladin, a language that owes its origins to the days when Tiberius sent Roman soldiers to crush the Celts of the mountain valleys of

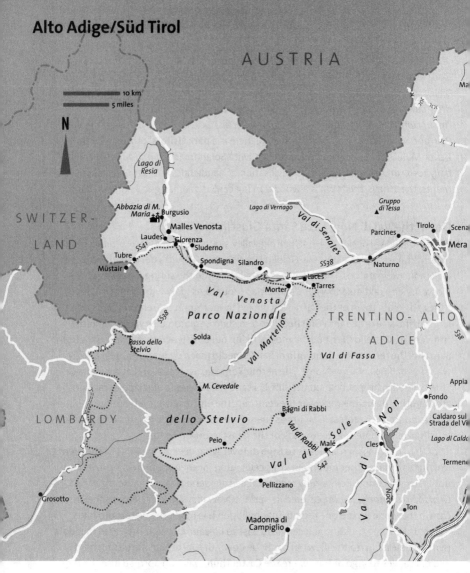

Alto Adige/Süd Tirol

AUSTRIA

10 km
5 miles

N

SWITZER-
LAND

Lago di
Resia

Abbazia di M.
Maria   Burgusio
Malles Venosta
Laudes   Glorenza
Sluderno
Tubre   Spondigna   Silandro
Müstair   SS41

Lago di Vernago   Val di Senales   Gruppo
di Tessa
Parcines   Tirolo   Scena
Mera
Naturno
SS38

Val   Venosta   Laces
Morter   Tarres
Parco Nazionale   TRENTINO- ALTO
Solda   ADIGE
SS38   Val Martello   Val di Fassa   SS38

Passo dello
Stelvio
M. Cevedale   Appia
Fondo
dello Stelvio   Bagni di Rabbi   Caldaro sul
Strada del Vi
Peio   Val di Rabbi   Val di Sole   Cles   Lago di Calda
Termene
Val di   S42   Male
Pellizzano   Ton
Grosotto
LOMBARDY   Madonna di
Campiglio   Noce
Val di Non

Switzerland and the Tyrol. Some stayed, and their descendants became known as the Ladini, or Latins: the Ladin language they speak is a fusion of Latin and Celtic dialect. In the Middle Ages all were ruled by the bishop of Bressanone and the counts of Tyrol, based near Merano. After the abdication of the 'Ugly Duchess', Margaret of Tyrol, in 1363, the whole region passed to the Habsburgs. Northern influence was hence much stronger here than in Trentino, and when Napoleon gave the Süd Tirol to Austria it had no objection – unlike Trentino, which chafed to join Italy.

After the First World War, however, Italy gained Trentino, and in the 1920s absorbed the lands up to the Brenner Pass as the natural frontier. Mussolini, a dedicated cultural imperialist, immediately invented Italian names for all the towns in the

Alto Adige and tried to ram the language of Dante down the inhabitants' throats – until Hitler told him to lay off. Still, things were so bad that in 1939, when German citizenship was offered to anyone who didn't want to be Italian, most people left, leading to severe depopulation of the rural areas. It was hardly an auspicious beginning, and if it weren't for the Italian vote from Trentino, the southern half of the autonomous region, separatism would have been a serious problem. As far as language goes, the figures are presently 69 per cent German-speaking, 27 per cent Italian and 4 per cent Ladin. Rome has done much to mollify the region, granting it a great deal of autonomy, and enough economic perks to make it one of the country's wealthiest areas.

Its position at one of the great historical crossroads between north and south, its brilliant Alpine scenery, its winter sports and its renowned climatic spa at Merano made the Süd Tirol a tourist destination long before the other Dolomite provinces. The region also has an exceptional collection of frescoes in its castles and churches, and produces fine wines, especially whites – there are some 40 vines for every inhabitant. Try the light and smooth Riesling Renano, dry and snappy Gewürztraminer, Weissburgunder (Pinot Bianco), Welschriesling (Riesling Italico), Sylvaner (with a dry, delicate perfume) and Müller-Thurgau (light and fruity), all of which may be sampled along the wine road south of Bolzano.

Bolzano/Bozen

Bolzano, the lively, cultured capital of Alto Adige, with its high, narrow-gabled houses, beer cellars and arcaded streets, is an excellent base for visiting the mountains on either side. Located on the banks of the Isarco and Talvera, which merge just downstream to form the Adige, Bolzano has been an important market town since the Middle Ages. And as of March 1998, the city has a new symbol, although one far, far older than itself: Ötzi the Ice Man.

Piazza Walther, the Duomo and Via dei Portici

Bolzano's cultural fusion manifests itself unexpectedly in its pretty parlour, **Piazza Walther**. In the centre stands a statue of the great *minnesinger* from these parts, Walther von der Vogelweide (1170–1230), and at his feet slouch travellers from around the world munching on Big Macs. In front of Walther stands Bolzano's Gothic **Duomo**, with its green and yellow roof and pretty tower. The art, however, is a block behind the cathedral in the church of the **Domenicani** (*open Mon–Sat 9.30–5.30*), now the Music Conservatory, where the chapels of San Giovanni and Santa Caterina contain lovely 14th-century Giottoesque frescoes by artists from Padua, the best medieval work in the Alto Adige.

From here Via Goethe leads up to the jovial **Piazza delle Erbe**, Bolzano's commercial hub, where Neptune and his trident (nicknamed *Gabelwirt* – 'Mine host with fork') watch over the daily fruit and vegetable market. On Via Argentieri, off Piazza delle Erbe, the 18th-century Palazzo Mercantile has a lovely courtyard; it now houses a **Museo Mercantile** (*open Mon–Fri 10–5; adm*), where a collection of period furniture and paintings attest to Bolzano's old flair for business.

This is still readily apparent if you return to Piazza delle Erbe to stroll up the city's main street, **Via dei Portici**, lined with smart shops. Via dei Portici passes the old heart of the city, Piazza del Grano (the former cornmarket) and ends in Piazza Municipio, where the ornate neo-Baroque town hall of 1907 holds court. Take Via dei Bottai, a street of beer cellars, to the Casa di Massimiliano (1512), the old Imperial customs house, now the new **Museo Provinciale di Scienze Naturali** (*open Tues–Sun 9–5*), with displays on glaciers and the first people to move into the valleys after they melted. From here Via Vintler leads around to Piazza della Madonna and Via dei Francescani,

Getting Around

Trains for Trento, Bressanone, Vipiteno, Brenner and Innsbruck, to the north; Merano and Malles/Venosta, to the northwest; and for Brunico, Dobbiaco and Lienz, to the east, all depart from the FS station, a short distance from Piazza Walther down Viale Stazione.

The **bus station** is across Via Garibaldi: **t** 1678 46047, with connections to Cortina and to nearly every town in the Alto Adige.

Tourist Information

Bolzano: Piazza Walther 8, **t** 0471 307 0001/2/3, **f** 0471 980 128, *bolzano@sudtirol.it*.

Alto Adige/Süd Tirol region: Piazza Parrochia 11, **t** 0471 993 808, **f** 0471 993 899, with an extremely efficient website at *www.sudtirol.com/bolzano*.

Alpine information service: **t** 0471 993 809. Another source of information on **mountaineering**, **hiking** and organized **day-trips** is the Club Alpino Italiano (CAI), Piazza delle Erbe 46, **t** 0471 971 694.

Where to Stay and Eat

Bolzano/Bozen ✉ 39100

Note that in the summer you may want to base yourself higher up; the humidity in the valley can turn Bolzano into a sauna.

★★★★**Parkhotel Laurin**, Via 4 Laurino, **t** 0471 311 000, **f** 0471 311 148 (*very expensive*). The best here: CIGA chain's lavish hotel built at the turn of the century in Viennese *Jugendstil*, located in a fine old park and rose garden near the centre. It has a heated swimming pool, and the public areas are furnished with antiques clustered around black marble fireplaces; don't miss the beautiful frescoed bar and exquiste dining in the restaurant **Belle Epoque**.

★★★★**Luna-Mondschein**, Via Pieve 15, **t** 0471 975 642, **f** 0471 975 577 (*expensive*). A modern hotel, also in the centre, set next to a park, with cosy rooms, parking garage, and indoor/outdoor restaurant serving Tyrolean classics.

★★★**Città-Stadt**, Piazza Walther, **t** 0471 975 221, **f** 0471 976 688 (*moderate*). In the very heart and soul of Bolzano.

★★★**Eberle**, Passeggiata Sant'Osvaldo 1, **t** 0471 976 125, **f** 0471 982 334 (*moderate*). Outside the centre, this 11-room hotel offers guests peace and quiet, a pool and sauna, in addition to cosy rooms; there's also an excellent restaurant.

★★**Hotel Feichter**, right in the centre of town (*moderate*). A wonderful place to stay. It has fine rooms, all with balconies, and a nice *fin-de-siècle* feel.

★**Croce Bianca-Weisses Kreuz**, Piazza del Grano 3, **t** 0471 977 552, **f** 0471 972 273 (*cheap*). Cheerful and welcoming. Its lobby is a café that opens on to the pavement.

★**Klaushof**, Colle 14, **t** 0471 329 999 (*cheap*). For peace and quiet, take the Colle cable car (Italy's oldest) from the opposite bank of the

where the church of the **Francescani** (*open Mon–Sat 10–12 and 2.30–6*) has a pretty Gothic cloister, a 14th-century fresco of the Franciscan Doctors, and a beautiful altarpiece of the Nativity, by woodcarver Hans Klocker (1500). The street leads back to Piazza delle Erbe.

Museo Archaeologico dell'Alto Adige: the Ice Man Cometh

On Via Museo, around the corner from Piazza delle Erbe. Open May–Sept, Tues–Sun 10–6, Thurs 10–8; Oct–April Tues–Sun 9–5, Thurs 9–8; adm exp. Audio guides in English available for a small fee.

You might recall reading about the discovery in the papers. In 1991 Erika and Hermert Simon were walking along the Similaun Glacier northwest of Merano when they chanced upon a body. There hadn't been an accident or murder there in years:

Isarco (bus no.11 or a short walk from the train station) up to the refreshing breezes of Colle, where you'll find this old farmhouse of 10 rooms, some without en suite bathroom.

Like the language, the cuisine of Alto Adige/Süd Tirol is a bit more than half Austrian – instead of *prosciutto*, expect *speck* (smoked Tyrolean ham) on pizza. Other specialities are Wiener schnitzel, *sauerkraut*, goulash, *knödel* (breadcrumb dumplings in a variety of styles), *Terlaner* (wine soup) with apple, cheese, and poppy-seed strudels, Sachertorte, and rich mousse for dessert.

Amandè, Viacolo Ca' de Bezzi 8 (off Via Cavour), t 0471 971 278 (*expensive*). Where Bolzano cuisine, stylishly prepared according to the market, holds pride of place; near the Ice Man. *Closed Sun.*

Da Abramo, Piazza Gries 16, t 0471 280 141 (*expensive–moderate*). Offering contemporary elegance and very good Italian food; seafood is a speciality, and among their offerings are a divine *risotto*, turbot with rosemary, and escalopes in a white pepper sauce. *Closed Sun, some of Aug.*

Cesare, Via Perathoner 15, t 0471 976 638 (*moderate*). Situated in the centre, and a fine place to tuck into fresh pasta and succulent grilled meats.

Cavallino Bianco/Weisses Rossel, Via dei Bottai 6, t 0471 973 267 (*cheap*). This jovial 400-year-old place is still extremely popular, with an eclectic menu stretching from ham and eggs to *Bolognerschnitzel* and a very tasty onion soup. *Closed Sat eve and Sun.*

Patscheiderhof, at Signato, t 0471 365 267 (*moderate*). Up the cable car (or road) in Renon. A favourite of many Sunday lunchers, but the food – pure traditional home-cooking – is perhaps better on other days when they aren't so rushed; tasty pasta and roast pork dishes, topped off with poppy-seed cake. *Closed Tues and July.*

Appiano sulla Strada del Vino/Eppen an der Weinstrasse ✉ 39057

★★★★**Schloss Korb**, at Missiano, t 0471 636 000, f 0471 636 033 (*expensive*). Close to Bolzano and the wine road, a fairytale 11th-century castle surrounded by vines. 53 spacious rooms, heated outdoor and indoor pools, tennis, and a fine restaurant. *Open Easter–Nov.*

★★★★**Schloss Freudenstein**, at San Michele, t 0471 660 638, f 0471 660 122. A smaller, elegant hotel, enjoying another beautiful setting; also has a pool. *Open April–mid-Nov.*

Zur Rose, at San Michele, t 0471 662 249 (*expensive*). Book a table at this award-winning restaurant for a gourmet epiphany based on Tyrolean traditions in a 12th-century house. *Closed Sun, Mon lunch and July.*

Stroblhof, Via Piganò 25, San Michele, t 0471 662 250 (*moderate*). A mansion houses this *osteria*, serving tasty *Schlutzkrapfen* filled with seasonal treats and other regional specialities to accompany their Pinot Nero and other wines. *Closed Mon and Nov–Mar.*

the man they found mummified in the ice had died long before living memory – 5,300 years ago, at the start of the Copper Age.

It was the first time ever that scientists had such an ancient body in such excellent condition, and after years of study and analysis, Ötzi, as he's been baptized, has become the magnet of this new museum which opened in March 1998. He was about 46 years old, they estimate, an experienced mountaineer who got caught in a sudden storm. He had tattoos on his torso and legs, that might have served as a kind of acupuncture map. A room reproducing the cold and humidity of the glacier was specially built to house him. And a curious, rather poignant sensation it is, peering through the window at the body of a man who could be one's grandfather, 250 generations removed.

Ötzi, in short, was a lot like us. They've made a model of what he looked like, dressed in all his gear, which is spread out in the next cases. His clothing is cunningly designed for the weather, using the materials at hand in 3700 BC, from bearskin hat to goatskin underwear, and a mantle woven of grasses; he had a bow and arrows, and in his pouch he carried bone tools and lucky talismans. The museum's other exhibits – prehistoric to Roman – pale somewhat after the Ice Man, but don't miss the statue steles nor the cast of the Mithraic altar of Bressanone (*see* p.469 for the real thing).

Museo Civico and Over the Talvera to Gries

Nearby, on the corner of Via Museo and Via Cassa di Risparmio, the **Museo Civico** (*open Tues–Sat 9–12 and 2.30–5.30, closed Sun, Mon and hols; adm*) houses Gothic altarpieces by local masters Hans Klocker and Michael Pacher, Baroque art and ethno-graphic items. Via Museo ends at the bridge over the Talvera, a river lined with parks and promenades; to the right, in its own field, the stout-towered 13th-century **Castel Mareccio** no longer guards Bolzano, but hosts conventioneers. Just across the Talvera, the imposing fascist **Monumento alla Vittoria** celebrates Italy's victory in the First World War and was purposely placed where the Austrian monument was slated to go; in 1978 Tyrolean nationalists attempted to blow it to smithereens. On Saturday morning it hosts an enormous market.

Corso Libertà leads through Mussolini's dreary industrial suburb (1937), purposely built as a contrast to old Bolzano and everything it stood for. The Corso ends in **Gries**, an old health resort. The old **parish church** of Gries (*open April–Oct Mon–Fri 10.30–12 and 2.30–4*) houses a beautifully carved Gothic wooden altar with doors by Michael Pacher (1475) and a masterful 13th-century *Crucifix*. (Bus no.10 returns to the centre.)

Around Bolzano

There are two fine walks around Bolzano. Beyond the Gries parish church, at the end of Via Knoller, begins the 1½km **Passeggiata del Guncina**, with an inn at the top for refreshments. A bit longer but more dramatic, the **Passeggiata Sant'Osvaldo** begins near the train station at Via Renico and descends by the head of the Lungotalvera promenade. Further up the Talvera, **Castel Roncolo** (*open Mar–Nov Tues–Sat 10–5*) has guarded the passage on its impregnable rock since 1237. The city gave it to Emperor Maximilian; it preserves 14th-century frescoes of chivalric knights, some of which were 'touched up' in 1508.

Three cablecars ascend from Bolzano, the most rewarding one from Via Renon, near the station, which climbs 4,005ft up the slopes of Bonzano's playground, Mt Renon/Rittner to **Soprabolzano/Oberbolzen** (*cablecar runs daily 7am–8pm*). The views are splendid, but continue from here on the rack railway to **Collabo/Klobenstein**, and follow the path to the **Longomoso Pyramids** – rocks eroded to form a dense forest of needles and bizarre stone drapery. More fine views of the Dolomites can be had from **San Genesio/Jenesien**, a hamlet easiest reached by cablecar from Via Sarentino (just before the Castel Roncolo).

La Strada del Vino/Der Weinstrasse

Folks on the west bank of the Adige south of Bolzano have been making wine since before the Romans, and this lovely road through the vine-carpeted hills is so well known that the towns along it have taken its name. Specific places to aim for include **Castel d'Appiano**, one of *forty* castles and manor houses in **Appiano sulla Strada del Vino/Eppen an der Weinstrasse**. In 1158 one of its lords, Federigo d'Appiano, had the cheek to hijack a precious treasure the Pope was sending to the Holy Roman Emperor, only to have his castle obliterated in response. The castle was rebuilt shortly after, but the holy armies left the original chapel, **Santa Caterina**, untouched, with its beautiful frescoes from the dawn of the 13th century (*open daily April–1 Nov; closed Tues in July*).

The winemaking capital, **Caldaro sulla Strada del Vino/Kaltern an der Weinstrasse**, overlooks Lago di Caldaro, which is warm enough for a dip from May to September. The **Museo Provinciale del Vino** in Castel Ringberg (*open April–7 Nov Tues–Sat 9.30–12 and 2–6, Sun and hols 10–12*) is full of vinous lore and carved barrels. **Termeno sulla Strada del Vino/Tramin an der Weinstrasse** owes its fame to its blood-heating wine, Gewürztraminer Aromatico, of reputed aphrodisiacal qualities; try it at the **Cantina Hofstätter**, in Piazza del Municipio, which claims to possess the largest wine cask in Europe. Termeno's neo-Gothic church conserves a quattrocento choir with elegant Renaissance frescoes. Just outside of town, rising out of a sea of vineyards, tiny **San Giacomo in Castelaz** has remarkable frescoes spanning the 13th–15th centuries.

East of Bolzano: the Val Gardena and Rosengarten

Bolzano lies just to the west of the Süd Tirol's most celebrated Dolomite scenery, taking in the pinnacles of Pelmo, Civetta and Marmolada. Scores of Alpine refuges, chairlifts and cablecars, and fast buses from Bolzano to the valleys, make access easy.

Val Gardena/Grödnertal

The most accessible and certainly one of the most beautiful excursions from Bolzano is to take the Brenner road north into the Ladin-speaking Val Gardena, lying between the jagged Odle group and **Alpe di Siusi**, a magnificent plateau noted for its sunny skiing and world-class ski schools, and endless meadows of flowers in the late spring; there are numerous lifts up from the Val Gardena, or a road up from the resort town of **Siusi**. A classic but not strenuous hike from Siusi is the 4-hour trek up **Monte Pez**, including a stay at one of the *grandes dames* of 19th-century Alpine refuges, the **Rifugio Bolzano di Monte Pez**.

The SS242 turns off the main highway and enters the Val Gardena at **Ponte Gardena/Waidbrück**, in the shadow of the medieval **Castel Trotsburg**, perched on a crag, with Gothic and late-Renaissance decor (*t 0471 654 401; open Easter–end Oct Tues–Sun, guided tours only at 11, 2, 3 and 4*). The largest town in the valley, elegant **Ortisei/St Ulrich**, and the next two villages, **Santa Cristina** and **Selva di Val Gardena/Wölkenstein**, are all well-equipped resorts with cablecars to the Alpe di Siusi; skiers should make time for the Saslonch-Ruacia piste which passes right below the 17th-century **Castel Fischburg**. Santa Cristina has lifts into the Odle group and up to the foot of the most distinctive peak in the region, the spiralling, dream-like **Sassolungo** (10,430ft) to the south.

Tourist Information

Val Gardena: *www.val-gardena.com.*

Ortisei/Sankt Ulrich in Gröden: Via Rezia 1, t 0471 796 328, f 0471 796 749, *ortisei@val-gardena.com.*

Santa Cristina: Via Chemun 9, t 0471 793 046, f 0471 793 198, *s.cristina@val-gardena.com.*

Selva di Val Gardena/Wölkenstein: Via Meisules 213, t 0471 795 122, f 0471 794 245, *selva@val-gardena.com.*

Corvara: Ciasa de Comun 198, t 0471 836 176, f 0471 836 540.

Nova Levante/Welschnofen: Lago di Carazza, t 0471 613 126, f 0471 613 360; *www.sudtirol.com/rosengarten.*

Where to Stay and Eat

Ortisei / Sankt Ulrich in Gröden ✉ 39046

****Adler**, Via Rezia 7, t 0471 796 203, f 0471 796 210 (*very expensive*). This historic hotel is also the most glamorous place to indulge; set in a large park, with an indoor pool and beauty treatments, and the best restaurant in town. *Open mid-Dec–mid-April, mid-May–Oct.*

***Hotel Snaltnerhof**, Piazza S. Antonio 142, t 0471 796 209 (*moderate*). You could also try this place in the central square, just a stone's throw from the museum. The rooms are modern and overlook the main square.

***La Perla**, Via Digon 1, t 0471 796 421, f 0471 798 198 (*expensive*). Located just outside town, and a year-round pleasure to visit, with its park and indoor pool. *Open mid-June–mid-Oct and mid-Dec–mid-April.*

Selva di Valgardena/Wölkenstein in Gröden ✉ 39048

****Alpenroyal**, Via Meisules 43, t 0471 795 178, f 0471 794 161 (*expensive*). Small but very comfortable, and one of the few hotels in the area that is open all year, with plenty of facilities to keep its guests fit and happy – indoor pool, whirlpool baths, sauna, solarium, beauty centre and fitness room. *Open mid-Dec–mid-April and June–Oct.*

****Europa**, Via Nives 50, t 0471 795 157, f 0471 796 445 (*moderate*). A typical little family-run mountain hotel. *Closed Ma and Nov.*

****Freina**, Via Centro 403, t 0471 795 110, f 0471 794 318 (*moderate*). Another choice convenient for the slopes, with 12 rooms with bath. Half board, if not full board, is required, but the food is excellent – stop here to eat if you're just passing through.

Santa Cristina in Valgardena/Sankt Christina in Gröden ✉ 39047

*****Diamant**, Via Skasa 1, t 0471 796 780, f 0471 793 580 (*very expensive*). Lovely mountain views, an indoor pool and sauna, all in a quiet park. *Open mid-Dec–Mar and mid-June–mid-Oct.*

****Cendevaves**, t 0471 792 062, f 0471 793 567 (*moderate*). There are several hotels up at Monte Pana: this one has an indoor pool and good views.

Nova Levante/Welschnofen ✉ 39056

*****Posta Cavallino Bianco/Weisses Roessel**, Strada Carezza 30, t 0471 613 113, f 0471 613 390 (*expensive*). A name that recalls the former postal relay station ('Little White Horse Staging Post'), though its facilities – indoor and outdoor pools, tennis, and much more – are up to date. *Open mid-Dec–mid-April and mid-May–mid-Oct.*

****Rosengarten**, Via Catinaccio 43, t 0471 613 262, f 0471 613 510 (*moderate*). A pleasant place to stay, and also the best place to eat in town; the restaurant uses the freshest local ingredients, garden herbs and home-made pasta. *Closed Mon, Tues lunch and Nov.*

From the crossroads in Selva di Val Gardena you have a choice of two spectacular routes, either over the fabulous **Passo di Sella** to Canazei in Trentino (*see* p.458), where you can pick up the Great Dolomites Road, or over the grand **Passo di Gardena** down into the **Alta Badia** to the east, another beautiful valley that has retained its Ladin culture. **Corvara in Badia** and **La Villa** are its main resorts, which were good enough to host the Alpine Ski World Cup. Another treat in the Alta Badia is the famous **Sella**

The Woodcarvers of the Val Gardena

Ortisei has specialized in wood carving for centuries, and if you're buying you'll find a wide range of works to choose from, from the artistic to cheesy alpine schlock, some of it just awful. Farmers took up carving to while away the long winter evenings, using soft pine from the valley's slopes. In the 1640s some began to neglect their land to hike over the mountains, selling carved toys, ornaments, household furniture and implements. By 1820, 300 craftsmen were working in the valley, and a school was set up in 1872 to consolidate skills and encourage trade.

Today over 3,000 wood-carvers whittle away in the Val Gardena. Ask the tourist office for their list of workshops, and stop by Ortisei's parish church and museum to look at permanent exhibitions of their craft created over the past three centuries.

If you're really inspired, Ortisei's school of wood-carving holds weekly courses in July and August: contact the tourist office for details.

Ronda, a circuit of the entire Sella group, entirely on skis, thanks to a series of refuges and lifts. To the north the SS244 leads to San Lorenzo near Brunico, while to the south the road descends to Arabba.

Catinaccio/Rosengarten

The other main group accessible from Bolzano, Catinaccio/Rosengarten, is enchanting – and enchanted. Its name first appears in a 13th-century Tyrolean epic describing how King Lauren of the Dwarves was made prisoner and dragged away from his mountain realm. Furiously Lauren put a curse on the roses that had betrayed him, that no one would ever see them again, neither by night nor by day. But he neglected to mention the dawn or the twilight, when the enchanted roses make the stony face of Rosengarten blush a deep red.

From Bolzano the road to Rosengarten (SS241) begins at Cardara/Kardaun, just east of town, and passes through the breathtaking narrow and deep red gorge – like a giant sore throat – of the **Val d'Ega**. As the road nears **Nova Levante/Welschnofen**, the main resort, the craggy peaks of the **Latemar** group loom up to the right, while the massive wall of Rosengarten rises to the left. You can reach the slopes of Rosengarten from Nova Levante or the Passo di Costalunga near aquamarine **Lake Carezza**, a popular stop on the road from Nova Levante. For an even more spectacular approach, continue along the SS241, to **Pozza di Fassa** on the eastern slopes of Rosengarten.

The Great Dolomites Road: Bolzano to Cortina d'Ampezzo

The above stretch of road from Bolzano, the SS241 through the Val d'Ega to Rosengarten and Pozza, is the first leg of the fabled 110km Great Dolomites Road, laid out in 1909. Buses from Bolzano or Cortina make the journey, and you should take one – it's torture, it really is, to have to keep your eyes on the road. On the other hand, driving allows you to linger for as long as you like at the passes and other belvederes.

After Pozza di Fassa the road (now the SS48) continues up Trentino's Val di Fassa to **Canazei** (see p.458), the best base for the ascent of the Dolomites' mightiest peak, **Marmolada** (10,962ft). The road from Canazei climbs past the peculiar tower of

Sassolungo and Sella glowering on the left, on its way to the **Passo Pordoi**, affording stupendous views of Sella and Marmolada. From the pass the road writhes down towards **Arabba**, a ski resort dwarfed by Sella, and **Pieve di Livinallongo**, below the odd-shaped **Col di Lana**, its summit blown off by an Italian mine in the First World War. The road then climbs again, past the haunting, eroding **Castello d'Andraz** (just after the settlement of Andraz) to the **Sasso di Stria** (Witch's Rock) and the tunnel at **Passo di Falzarego**, where a cablecar on threads ascends the vertiginous cliffs. From the pass the road begins the descent to Cortina, with views of the strange **Cinque Torri** (Five Towers) and nearly vertical slopes of Tofane, before reaching the top of the Valle del Boite, with beautiful views over Cortina (*see* pp.443–446).

North Towards the Brenner Pass

North of Bolzano and Ponte Gardena lies the Val Isarco/Eisacktal, the main route to the Brenner Pass. Bressanone, Vitipeno and Novacella are the man-made highlights.

Val Isarco: Bressanone

On the way up from Bolzano the road passes the ancient town of **Chiusa/Klausen**, under the **Monastero di Sabiona**, founded in the 4th century – 'the Tyrol's Cradle of Christianity', immortalized in Albrecht Dürer's engraving, *The Great Fortune* (*Nemesis*) *c.* 1497. Nearly all rebuilt in the 17th century after a fire, you can visit the church, **Santa Croce** (*open daily 7–6.30*) with curious *trompe l'œil* frescoes of landscapes and architecture painted in 1679. From Chiusa a side road climbs to the 16th-century **Castel Velturno** (*t 0472 855290, info@felthurns.com; guided tours Mar–Nov at 10, 11, 2.30 and 3.30, closed Mon; adm*), the summer residence of the bishop of Bressanone, decorated with frescoes and wood intarsio.

Bressanone/Brixen is the most charming city in the Alto Adige, capital of the region for a millennium and seat of a powerful prince-bishop, similar to Trento's. Although the *duomo* was metamorphosed into a dull Baroque church in the 18th century, the remodellers neglected the Romanesque cloister and its magnificent 14th-century frescoes, covering nearly every incident in the Bible. The bishops' palace has an exquisite arcaded, three-storey courtyard, and houses the **Museo Diocesano** (*open 15 Mar–Oct 10–5; closed Sun; cribs only 1 Sept– 31 Jan 2–5; all closed 24–25 Dec; adm*), with the cathedral treasure and a fine collection of *presepi* (Christmas cribs).

Three kilometres north of Bressanone, the wine-making **Abbazia di Novacella** (*guided tours Easter–Oct Mon–Sat at 10, 11, 2, 3 and 4; Nov–Easter Mon–Fri 10 and 3, Sat at 11; adm*), begun in 1142, is a fascinating study in the evolution of architecture, with its 12th-century tower, Baroque church, beautiful frescoed 14th-century cloister and the round, crenellated 12th–16th century-chapel of San Michele.

The Pusteria

The Pusteria, the wide and pleasant valley running eastwards along the River Rienza towards Dobbiaco/Toblach, is dotted with typical Tyrolean villages and castles. Many

Tourist Information

Bressanone/Brixen: Viale Stazione 9, **t** 0472 836 401, **f** 0472 36067, *brixen.info@acs.it*.
Brunico/Bruneck: Via Europa 22, **t** 0472 555 722, **f** 0472 555 544, *bruneck@Dolomiti Superski.com*.
Vipiteno/Sterzing: Piazza Città 3, **t** 0472 765 325, **f** 0472 765 441.

Where to Stay and Eat

If you come between September and late November, you can join in with the locals in their *Törggelen* (from the Latin *torculum*, or wine press) – going from *maso* to *maso* to try the unfermented grape juice (*Sußer*) and the new wine (*Nuie*), with roast chestnuts, speck, rye bread, and smoked salami (*Kaminwurz*), sometimes accompanied by music. But beware: if alcohol is not your forte, take lots of water with you, this stuff isn't for children.

Bressanone ✉ 39042

★★★★Dominik, Via Terzo di Sotto 13, **t** 0472 830 144, **f** 0472 836 554 (*very expensive*). Stay in the lap of luxury at a prestigious Relais & Châteaux member; these spacious rooms have lovely views, and there's an indoor pool and sauna. *Open April–mid-Nov, Christmas holidays*. The restaurant, one of the best in the entire region, serves regional and Italian specialities. *Closed Tues*.
★★★★Elefant, Via Rio Bianco 4, **t** 0472 832 750, **f** 0472 836 579 (*expensive*). This hotel recalls a gift from the King of Portugal who, in 1550, sent an Indian elephant to Emperor Maximilian for his menagerie. En route, the pachyderm spent a week in Bressanone's post house, so impressing the locals that they had its portrait done, and there it remains to this day, on the front of this old Renaissance inn. Only the fresco remains, but inside, the ceilings and walls still have antique panelling and beautiful tile stoves.

Many of the lovely rooms are furnished with antiques, though no one remembers which one the elephant slept in. There's also a pool, tennis and pleasure garden, as well as a dairy and vegetable garden that provides many of the ingredients for the Tyrolean dishes served in the restaurant. *Open Mar–Nov, Christmas; restaurant closed Mon out of season*.
★★★Bel Riposo, Via dei Vigneti 1, **t** 0472 836 548, **f** 0472 836 548 (*moderate*) By the river, a little turn-of-the-century hotel, charming and welcoming, with a gourmet restaurant, **Zum Auenhaus**, **t** 0472 838 344, for ultra-refined Tyrolean cuisine. *Closed Mon*.
★★Goldene Traube, Via Portici Minori 9, **t** 0472 836 552, **f** 0472 834 731 (*cheap*). Inside the city walls; it fills up fast.
Fink, Via Portici Minori 4, **t** 0472 834 883 (*moderate*).The old walls are ringed with cafés. This one, a century old, has a restaurant upstairs, serving traditional Südtirolese cooking: saddle of venison, *polenta nera* (made from buckwheat) and a wide variety of cold meats and cheeses, as well as vegetarian dishes. Simpler, less pricey dishes are served downstairs in the Arkade. *Closed Tues eve, Wed, July*.

Vipiteno/Sterzing ✉ 39049

★★★★Aquila Nera, Piazza Città 1, **t** 0472 764 064, **f** 0472 766 522 (*expensive*). You can relax in the heart of town in this 16th century hotel and take a dip in the indoor pool.
★★★Albergo Post, Citta Nuova 14, **t** 0472 766 664, **f** 0472 762 189 (*moderate*). Located between the two towers that mark the length of the main street. The rooms are wood lined with creaky floorboards – but comfortable.
Pretzhof, **t** 0472 764 455, 8km away in Tulve (*moderate*). A favourite place to eat, which will fill you up on delicious traditional dishes, prepared with ingredients from the family's farm. *Closed Mon, Tues, some of June and July*.

of its churches contain works by the valley's 15th-century master woodcarver Michael Pacher, most notably the 13th-century parish church of **San Lorenzo di Sebato**, with an ancient crypt (*closed Mon and Tues*). The capital of the Pusteria, medieval **Brunico/Bruneck**, has two lovely old gates, along with a 13th-century bishop's castle; along elegant Via di Città, even the city pharmacy has frescoes. From here you can head up a wooded valley north to **Campo Tures**, clustered under the baronial **Castel di Tures**, guarding the entrance to the Val Aurina. Tours take in the hall of mirrors, two dozen rooms of tapestries, a chapel frescoed in 1482 by the school of Pacher and a beautiful library (*tours Jan–Oct Tues, Fri and Sun at 4; June–Aug 10–11 and 2–4.30; adm*). Glacier alpinists come here for the **Vedrette Giganti** (or di Ríes), reached from Riva di Tures, and its waterfall, while extremists may carry on north up the Val Aurina to **Casere** and its hamlet, **Pratomagno** – the northernmost houses in Italy.

East of Brunico, **Monguelfo/Welsberg** is a resort under a 12th-century castle; from here a road turns south into the Val di Braies, where the **Lago di Braies**, fast in the Dolomites' embrace, is celebrated for its perfect stillness and intense green colour. East of Monguelfo the road continues to Dobbiaco (*see* p.447).

The Upper Val Isarco to the Brenner Pass

The main town between Bressanone and the pass, **Vipiteno/Sterzing** formerly belonged to the great banking dynasty, the Fuggers. The attraction it held for them was its mines, especially silver; although abandoned in 1979, they were lucrative enough in the Renaissance for the residents to build splendid battlemented houses after a fire devastated the town in 1443 – the tall **Torre di Città** was built to celebrate the reconstruction. The mines are remembered in the **Museo Provinciale delle Miniere Jöchlsthurn** (*open Easter–15 Nov Tues–Sat 10–12 and 2–5; adm*). The best houses are along Via Città Nuova; pop into the courtyard of the Municipio to see an impressive Mithraic altar from the 3rd century BC. In Piazza Città, the **Museo Multscher** (*open April–Oct Mon 2–5, Tues–Fri 10–12 and 2–5, Sat 10–12; adm*) is devoted to elegant works by the 15th-century painter Hans Multscher. Three kilometres southeast, the Counts Thurn und Taxis' 11th–14th century frescoed **Castel Tasso** has Gothic decoration (*guided tours Easter–Nov 1 at 9.30, 10.30, 2 and 3; closed Fri; adm*).

Further north, **Colle Isarco/Gossensass** is another resort, with skiing and hiking on Cima Bianca and in the Val di Fleres. Beyond this lies the **Brenner Pass** (4,510ft), the lowest of the Alpine passes, and the route of countless invaders from the north, heavily bombed during the Second World War. From here it is 125km to Innsbruck.

Merano and the Upper Adige

A famous spa, vineyards and lots of castles follow the road and Adige up to to the Resia Pass, near the Austrian and Swiss frontiers.

Merano

Just 28km up the Adige from Bolzano, Merano is an attractive town of gardens and flowers, a favourite spa for central Europeans with respiratory complaints since the 1830s, basking in a balmy microclimate. The benefits of the waters, clean air and graded mountain walks are complemented by specific cures, such as the notorious grape cure in September and October; eating two pounds of Merano grapes a day, taking care to chew them well, apparently keeps the doctor away. Their juice usually works wonders for the rest of the year.

Tourist Information

Merano: Corso Libertà 35, t 0473 235 223, f 0473 235 524; *info@meraninfo.it*.

Where to Stay and Eat

Merano ☑ 39021

As one might expect of an old-world spa like Merano, there are a good number of luxury hotels, but not much in the lower ranges.

****Kurhotel Castel Rundegg, Via Scena 2, t 0473 234 100, f 0473 237 200 (*very expensive*). You can sleep like a lord in this picturesque 12th-century castle near the centre. With every luxury, including an indoor pool and fitness centre and a lovely park.

*****Palace, Via Cavour 2, t 0473 211 300, f 0473 234 181 (*very expensive*). Kafka preferred this aristocratic hotel in the heart of Merano. Set in beautifully maintained grounds with a spa and beauty centre, the restaurant is considered the best in town.

***Castello Labers, Via Labers 25, t 0473 234 484, f 0473 234 146 (*expensive*). Set among the vines above Merano, a castle-villa from the 1200s. A little more modest, but has a pool and views too. *Open April–Nov*.

***Westend, Via Speckbacher 9, t 0473 447 654, f 0473 222 726 (*moderate*) Another atmospheric choice, also near the centre: 22 lovely rooms in a 19th-century villa, tucked back in a garden.

*Pension Tyrol, Via 30 Aprile 8, t 0473 449 719 (*cheap*). A quiet hotel near the spa, in a big garden, with free parking.

Laubenkeller, Via dei Portici 118, t 0473 237 706 (*moderate*). Merano's restaurants are concentrated around this street: try this one for *typische Südtiroler* cooking. *Closed Thurs*.

Sissi, Via Galilei 44, t 0473 231 062 (*expensive*). One of the best in town, up by the Castello Principesco, where the delicious food has a Piemontese touch. *Closed Mon*.

Apart from inflicting digestive disorders, Merano has other attractions: along the Adige, there's the striking Liberty-style casino and **Kursaal** topped with dancing maidens, now a congress centre. Two streets back, the arcaded Via dei Portici was the main street in the medieval town; the stern 15th-century Gothic *duomo* contains International Gothic frescoes in the style of Trento's Castello di Buonconsiglio.

Via Cassa di Risparmio leads back to the little 15th-century **Castello Principesco** (*open Tues–Sat 10–5, Sun 10–1; July and Aug also Sun 4–7; adm*), built by Archduke Sigismond and containing Gothic furnishings, arms, and swords. Opposite, you can take a chairlift up to Tirolo or pick up the 4km **Passeggiata Tappeiner**, the Meraners' favourite promenade, a botanical wonderland overlooking the city. At Via delle Corse 42 – the next street over – the **Museo Civico** (*same hours*) has four Bronze-Age statue steles, Gothic sculptures and a *Pietà* by the school of Michael Pacher.

For centuries the landowners of these valleys were generally left alone to defend their turf, and as a result the area bristles with a large proportion of the Alto Adige's more than 350 castles. The big cheese, however, lived just above Merano in **Tirolo**, at **Castel Tirol** (*closed for renovations, expected to reopen in 2001*) balanced on the precipice. The castle gave its name to the region and to this day remains a symbol of Tyrolean identity, the headquarters of the independent Counts until 1363, when Margherita di Maultasch, the 'Ugly Duchess', ceded Tyrol to the Habsburgs. Adorned with medieval monsters and frescoes, it houses different exhibitions every year. Also in Tirolo, **Castel Fontana** (*open mid-Mar–Nov 10–5; closed Tues; adm*), a rather imaginary reconstruction of a 12th-century castle, has a collection of farm instruments and memorabilia related to poet Ezra Pound (d. 1972), who was found too crazy to stand trial for treason (he made pro-Mussolini radio broadcasts during the War) and retired here in 1958, after his release from a Washington hospital.

The Val Venosta

West of Merano, the Val Venosta follows the Adige west towards Austria. At **Naturno**, the little church of **San Procolo** has some fresco fragments that go back to the 8th century, the oldest in any German-speaking territory (*open Tues–Sun 9.30–12 and 2.30–5*). In the upper valley, an hour's drive from Merano, **Sluderno/Schludrens**, was long ruled by the Trapps, whose magnificent 13th/16th-century **Castel Coira** (*open late Mar–1 Nov Tues–Sun 10–12 and 2–4.30; adm*) has gloriously painted Renaissance loggias and the largest private collection of armour in all Europe. At the other extreme, nearby **Glorenza/Glurns** is the smallest walled city in Europe, and looks much as it did in the 15th century.

At Sluderno the SS41 branches off west to Switzerland; the main road continues to ancient **Malles Venosta**, before turning north to Austria. Malles also has very old frescoes, colourful and Carolingian, in the chapel of **San Benedetto** (*key at Via S. Bemedeo 31, Mon–Sat 9–11.30 and 1.30–5; adm*). Just up in **Burgusio**, the beautiful 17th-century Benedictine **Abbazia di Monte Maria** has a gleaming white crown of towers and gables, in a woodland setting; the crypt from the original church has rare, excellently preserved 12th-century frescoes of Jerusalem (*guided tours daily exc Sat pm and Sun, 15 June–15 Sept at 10, 11, 3 and 4.30; Oct–May at 10.45 and 3; adm*). On the way to Austria the road passes the romantic ruins of **Lichtenburg** castle and the artificial **Lago di Resia**, with the church spire of a submerged village poking above its surface.

Parco Nazionale dello Stelvio

If you leave the main valley road (the SS40) at Spondigna, just before Sluderno, and stay on the SS38, you'll enter the **Stelvio National Park**, the largest in Italy and administered by the provinces of Sondrio, Trento and Bolzano, all of which have **visitors' centres** that can tell you where to find the trails, Alpine refuges and the best flowers and wildlife: chamois, marmots, eagles and the ibex, reintroduced in 1968. As well as offering endless possibilities for climbers, the park has fifty lakes, a hundred glaciers (a tenth of the 134,620 hectares is ice) and Europe's second-highest pass, the **Passo di Stelvio** (*open June through October*). Through it the road makes its way down towards Bormio and the Valtellina (*see pp.209–303*).

Friuli-Venezia Giulia

For many British or American visitors, this elongated region east of Venice is *terra incognita*, a jumbly name that turns up on the wine list in Italian restaurants. Trieste, at the far end of Italy, evokes cloudy images of pre- and post-War intrigue, a kind of Third Man on the Mediterranean. From Trieste to Venice the imagination fails.

It doesn't help that the region is burdened with a history as messy as its name. In Roman days *Aquileia* was the most important city and seat of the oldest patriarchate

Friuli-Venezia Giulia

outside Rome. Its authority was gradually usurped by Cividale del Friuli, the Lombard capital, in the Dark Ages, and then in the Middle Ages by Ùdine, before Venice took over in 1420. Trieste was Venice's bitter rival under the Counts of Gorizia and the Austrians. Napoleon threw the region in with the 'Kingdom of Illyria', a piece of real estate subsequently picked up by the Austro-Hungarian Empire, until 1918 when Italy inherited it, as well as all of Istria down to Fiume (modern Rijeka). After the Second World War, Tito took Trieste from the Germans; the western Allies then forced them to leave, occupying the city themselves as a neutral free port until 1954, when it was readmitted into Italy, leaving the rest of Istria to Yugoslavia. The region's troubles were

> ## Wine in Friuli
>
> The Friuli region has seven DOC regions. The best is the Collio (around Gorizia), famous for its whites, especially Pinot Bianco and Riesling. The Collio Orientale, a much larger region, also produces good whites and a brisk red, Refosco. Rochi di Cialla and Giovanni Dri are just two of the best-known labels. The other DOC regions – Aquileia, Isonzo, Carso, Latisana and Grave del Friuli – produce good reds; names to look out for are Schiopettino, Carso Terreno, and Riva Rossa.

hardly over: two disastrous earthquakes in 1976 (6.5 and 6.1 on the Richter scale) shook Friuli to the core, killing a thousand people, levelling entire towns, and leaving 70,000 buildings in need of major structural repair.

Weary of being marginal, Friuli-Venezia Giulia is now creating an identity of its own, but it's like trying to put together pieces from several different jigsaw puzzles. The population in the east speaks Slovenian, while the north has a sizeable German minority. In Trieste there are large Jewish, Greek and Serb minorities, and in the middle, around Údine, is a majority Friulian ethnic group, like the Ladini in the South Tyrol, who speak a language similar to the Swiss Rhaeto-Romansch. In the 1990s, with the reopening of Central and Eastern Europe, Friuli Venezia-Giulia stopped being eastern Italy's dead end and became an important link to its future.

From Venice to Lignano-Sabbiadoro

Altino and Càorle

The SS14 from Venice passes first Marco Polo airport and then **Altino**, the modern name of Roman *Altinum*. Once renowned for its wealth, it was put to the sack by Attila the Hun – only the first of many hardships that led its inhabitants to give up and found a new city on the island of Torcello in the Venetian Lagoon. They took whatever Attila and the Lombards didn't wreck, so that all that remains in the **Museo Nazionale** (*open Tues–Sun 9–2*) are mosaics and a few odds and ends.

The route continues over the Piave near **San Donà di Piave**, a town that had to be completely rebuilt after the First World War; it was here that Hemingway, then an ambulance-driver for the Red Cross, was wounded in 1918, an experience that became the germ of *A Farewell to Arms*. From San Donà, a detour to the old fishing town and modern seaside resort of **Càorle** is tempting, for its isthmus, beaches and lagoon beloved of wildfowl, and its *duomo*, built in 1038, with a charming cylindrical campanile and a splendid Venetian *Pala d'Oro* (12th–14th centuries). **Bibione**, to the east, is an even bigger resort, with a long strand of sand.

Portogruaro and Around

Portogruaro is a seductive old town, dreaming away under its palm trees and jauntily tilted 193ft campanile, built in the 12th century. The *duomo* is a wallflower, but the neighbouring 14th-century **Loggia Comunale** is shaped like a mountain, the roofline

Getting Around

Trains from Venice along the coast run roughly every two hours (journey time to Trieste two hours). **Buses** are less frequent, though Càorle can most easily be reached by direct bus from Venice. An alternative is to take the train to S. Donà di Piave and the local bus to Càorle from there. For Lignano-Sabbiadoro, take the train to Latisana, linked by bus to the coast in about 30 minutes.

Tourist Information

Càorle: Calle delle Liburniche 11, **t** 0421 81085, **f** 0421 84251.
Portogruaro: Borgo S. Agnese 57, **t** 0421 274 230, **f** 0421 274 600.
Lignano-Sabbiadoro: Via Latisana 42, **t** 0413 71821, **f** 0431 70449, *www.aptlignano.it*.

Where to Stay and Eat

In the beach resorts, high season prices run from mid-June to the end of August; book ahead, especially for the first three weeks of August. Expect the freshest fish, landed daily. In the evenings the docks are awash with squid ink, which features heavily in local menus.

Càorle ✉ 30021

★★★**Diplomatic**, Via Strada Nuova 19, **t** 0421 81087, **f** 0421 210 089 (*moderate*). A comfortable hotel, set on its own little port. Featuring the area's best restaurant, **Duilio**, justifiably celebrated for its succulent seafood *antipasti*, seafood pasta, and seafood *secondi*. A charming setting, a huge wine list and reasonably priced menus are added attractions. *Closed Mon, Jan.*

★★★**Garden**, Piazza Belvedere, **t** 0421 210 036, **f** 0421 210 037 (*moderate*). Immersed in pines, right by the beach, with a pool and sauna; nearly all rooms have balconies. *Open April–Sept.*

Al Cacciatore, Corso Risorgimento 25, **t** 0421 80331 (*expensive*). Up the Livenza river in San Giorgio di Livenza. A popular family-run restaurant of long standing, featuring the freshest of fish and mushrooms in season. *Closed Wed, some of Aug.*

Lignano ✉ 33054

★★★★★**Greif**, Arco del Grecale 27, **t/f** 0431 422 261 (*very expensive*). Near the pines in shady Lignano-Pineta. A large resort hotel with a pool and park, sauna and private beach.

★★★★**Medusa Splendid**, Raggio dello Scirocco 33, **t** 0431 422 211, **f** 0431 422 251 (*expensive*). This more intimate hotel also has a pool, very good rooms and a garden. *Open mid-May–mid-Sept.*

★★★★**Eurotel**, Calle Mendelssohn 13, **t** 0431 428 991, **f** 0431 428 992 (*expensive*). A fashionable hotel in Lignano Riviera, enjoying perhaps the most beautiful setting in the area and offering lovely rooms, a heated pool and more. *Open mid-May–mid-Sept.*

★★★★**Miramare**, Via Aquileia 47/B, **t** 0431 71260, **f** 0431 720051 (*expensive*). Built up in the last 25 years, Lignano-Sabbiadoro is a good place to look for self-catering bungalows as well as hotels, although none really stands out. For comfortable rooms try this place with parking and a garden, as well as its own beach. *Open mid-May–Sept.*

★★★**Vittoria**, Lungomare Marin 28, **t** 0431 71221, **f** 0431 73292 (*moderate*). A fine older hotel, which has recently had a face lift. *Open mid-May–Sept.*

Bidin, Via Europa 1, **t** 0431 71988 (*expensive*). Good restaurants include this small but convivial place, with a separate *menu degustazione* for either fish or meat. *Closed Wed.*

Al Bancut, Via Friuli 32, **t** 0431 71926 (*moderate*). In the centre of town, featuring fine grilled fish, traditionally prepared. *Closed Tues eve, Wed.*

crested with fantail Ghibelline battlements, which lend it a curiously organic appearance. The **Museo Nazionale Concordiese**, in Via del Seminario (*open daily 9–8; adm*) is crowded with an assortment of bronzes and coins, among other finds excavated in *Concordia Sagittaria*, just to the south. This was an arrow-manufacturing (*sagittae*)

Roman colony, and has a Romanesque cathedral standing next to a ruined basilica (389) and a frescoed Byzantine baptistry of 1089.

In **Summaga**, 3km west of Portogruaro, the abbey of Santa Maria Maggiore, t 0421 205 126, was built around a 6th-century votive chapel. The walls are covered with a fascinating cycle of 12th- and 13th-century frescoes, all recently restored; in the votive chapel, don't miss the fighting griffins and lions, chivalrous deeds, virtues and vices.

More fond old things await in **Sesto al Règhena**, 9km north of Portogruaro, a quaint medieval village with a moat in the centre, originally part of the defences of **Santa Maria in Silvis** (*open daily 8–8*), a Lombard foundation that grew to become one of the most powerful abbeys in the area. The current basilica dates from the 12th century and is decorated with 14th-century frescoes, one showing Christ crucified on a voluptuous pomegranate tree. Among the bas-reliefs is a beautiful 13th-century *Annunciation*, while the crypt contains an 8th-century Lombard-Byzantine sarcophagus of St Anastasia. Lastly, to the west near **Fossalta di Portogruaro**, by the little church of Sant'Antonio in Vilanova, grows one of the oldest oak trees in Europe, already three hundred years old when they signed the Magna Carta.

Lignano-Sabbiadoro

From a few kilometres east of **Latisana**, where a new road (the SS354) branches off to the coast, you can follow the crowds south to the Laguna di Marano and the fastest-growing resort area on the Adriatic, **Lignano-Sabbiadoro**, the 'Austrian Riviera'. Set on the tip of the peninsula, with a lovely 9km sandy beach and scores of new hotels, apartments, bungalows and campsites, Lignano-Sabbiadoro and its two adjacent resorts of **Lignano-Pineta** (the prettiest section, under the pinewoods) and smart **Lignano Riviera** offer fun in the sun and Wiener schnitzel just like Mutti makes. Some of the smaller islands are dotted with *casoni*, steep thatched fisherman's cottages – some real, some recreated for visitors.

Pordenone and Around

There's not a lot to say about Pordenone, provincial capital and manufacturer of domestic appliances. Its name is only familiar thanks to the Renaissance artist G. A. Sacchiense, who adopted it and whose works may be seen in the **Museo Civico d'Arte**, housed in the pretty 15th-century Palazzo Richiere (*open Tues–Fri 9.30–12.30 and 3–6; t 0434 392 312; adm*), and in the salmon-pink *duomo*, where his odd masterpiece, the *Madonna della Misericordia* (1515) hangs.

The lofty campanile is Pordenone's landmark, a refined tower of Romanesque brickwork of 1347. The bijou **Palazzo Comunale**, focal point of Pordenone's arcaded, palace-lined Corso Vittorio Emanuele, has a Venetian clock tower topped by two bell-ringing Moors, superimposed on a graceful 13th-century building. And that about sums it up.

Hanging over the willowy banks of the Livenza, **Sacile** (west of Pordenone) is famous for its bird festival (the *Dei Osei*), held on the last Sunday in August ever since 1351. Thousands of songbirds are assembled in the main piazza, and prizes are awarded to the birds and the person who can best imitate their songs.

Tourist Information

Where to Stay and Eat

Pordenone ✉ 33170

★★★★Villa Ottoboni, Piazzetta Ottoboni 2,
t 0434 208 891, f 0434 208 148 (*expensive*).
This elegant hotel is right near the centre
and offers fully furnished rooms; the restaurant dates from the late 15th century.

★★★Park, Via Mazzini 43, t 0434 27901, f 0434
522 353 (*moderate*). For modern, comfortable
rooms in the centre.

Da Zelina, Piazza San Marco, t 0434 27290
(*moderate*). Dine here in an early
Renaissance palace, with succulent meat
dishes and pizzas in the evening. *Closed Sat
lunch, Mon, part of Aug.*

Gildo, Viale Marconi 17, in Porcia, 4km west,
t 0434 921 212 (*expensive*). Head out to this
imposing Venetian palace in a large park.
The menu is equally divided between meat
and fish dishes; prices are considerably
lower at lunch. *Closed Sun eve, Mon, Aug.*

Alla Cantina, Piazza Cavour 3, t/f 0434 520 358
(*cheap*). If you like your classic Italian dishes
in opulent surroundings try this place right
in the centre of town. *Closed Tues.*

Antica Trattoria La Primula, Via San Rocco 47,
t 0434 91005, f 0434 919 280 (*expensive*).
Nine kilometres north of Pordenone, at San
Quirino. This hotel has for six generations
served up the best food in the province,
superb, classic and simply prepared, from
the *antipasti* through the fresh seafood to
the elegant desserts, served in the simple
but elegant dining room. It has 7 rooms if
you over-indulge (it's easily done) although
you would need to book.

Osteria Alle Nazioni. The same folks run this
place, adjacent to the hotel and frescoed,
with good food and kinder prices. *Closed Sun
eve, Mon, part of Jan and July.*

Spilimbergo ✉ 33097

★★Michielini, Viale Barbacane 3, t/f 0427
50450 (*cheap*). An old family-run hotel in the
centre of town, with restaurant.

La Torre, Piazza Castello, t 0427 50555
(*moderate*). Alternatively, dine in this castle
on the likes of *ravioli* filled with pumpkin in
mushroom sauce and strudels. Anyone fond
of wine will have a field day with the selection in its cellar. *Closed Sun eve and Mon.*

Enoteca La Torre, Via di Mezzo 2, t/f 0427 2998,
higamp@tin.it (*cheap*). If you're looking for
something lighter try this place, located in
the castle gate house. It has a wonderful
cellar of Friulian wines and of course San
Daniele ham. Staff are friendly and helpful
and more than happy to guide you through
the Friulian vineyards. *Open 10–2 and 5–2am,
closed Tues.*

Osteria Al Bachero, Via Pilacorte 5, t 0427 2317
(*cheap*). The authentic taste of Friulian
dining. Try the *baccalà e trippe con polenta*
(salted cod and tripe with *polenta* – not
everyone's kettle of fish) or any number of
local dishes, and dine around an open fire
with simple wooden furniture. They have
one menu in English – and you won't have
to wait for it. *Closed Sun.*

Towards Ùdine: the Villa of the Last Doge, Spilimbergo and San Daniele

On the road to Ùdine, Codroipo is the site of the **Villa Manin** (1738), the biggest villa
in all Venetia, the swan blast of a way of life (*open Tues–Sun 9–12.30 and 3–6; winter
9–12 and 2–5*). When owner Ludovico Manin was elected doge in Venice, his chief rival
declared, 'A Friulian as Doge! The republic is dead.' The prediction was no sooner
proved correct than Napoleon himself stayed at this massive ranch as a guest, if not a
welcome one. A painting by David hangs in the room he slept in; also to see are airheaded frescoes, an elegant horseshoe exedra (a secular version of Bernini's
colonnade in St Peter's Square), a museum of arms and carriages and a park.

Medieval **Spilimbergo**, on the west bank of the Tagliamento, has a discreet charm, a pretty 12th-century castle complex with exterior frescoes, a Gothic cathedral with a Romanesque portal and paintings by Pordenone, and a mosaic school, founded in 1922 (*open 9–12.30 Mon–Sat by reservation only, made through the secretary, t 0427 2077, f 0427 3903*). Off to the north of Spilimbergo, near Clauzetto, the **Grotte Verdi di Pradis** (*open July and Aug daily daylight hours; other months sunny Sundays only; adm*) is as weirdly green as its name; walkways follow the torrential Cosa up a high narrow gorge. In 1968 it was made a church, the 'National Temple of Speleology'.

Surrounded by fields of maize and *prosciutterie*, **San Daniele del Friuli** is the 'Siena of Friuli', an ochre-tinted medieval market town famous for its sweet-cured hams. Don't miss the recently restored frescoes by Pellegrino di San Daniele (1498–1522) in the church of **Sant'Antonio**, his masterpiece. There are other good churches to see, and the **Biblioteca Guarneriana**, Via Roma 1 (*open Tues–Sun 9–12*), founded in the 15th century by a canon of Aquileia, with lovely medieval manuscripts. Every August, at the *Aria di Festa*, hundreds of hams are lined up in the piazza for tasting.

Palmanova, Aquileia and Grado

In a beeline from north to south, you have the planned military town, the ancient capital and the modern seaside resort – the only one in the Adriatic entirely facing south – offering a strikingly varied and full day.

Palmanova

In the Renaissance, despite all Alberti's theories on town planning, only a handful of new towns were ever constructed. One of the most remarkable, **Palmanova**, was built in 1593 by the Venetians as their eastern bulwark against the Austrians and Turks, and populated by 'volunteers'. Perhaps because it was never actually needed for anything, Palmanova remains intact, a perfect example of 16th-century 'ideal' radial military planning and a geometrical *tour de force*: the star formed by its walls has nine points. Even though most of the walls and moat are now overgrown, their stone softly moulded into serpentine hills and gullies, they are still defended by young conscripts. At the **Museo Storico**, Borgo Ùdine 4 (*open 10–12 and 3–6; closed Wed; adm*), ask about the torchlight tour of the walkways within the walls.

Aquileia

If Palmanova is unique in its plan, Aquileia, directly south, is unique in that it was the only major Roman city in Italy to die on the vine. While most other Roman metropolises are still notable towns, Aquileia has dwindled from an estimated 200,000 in its heyday to 3,500 inhabitants, who no longer receive emperors but tend vineyards, and the tourists who flock to see the most important archaeological site in northern Italy. Founded as a Roman colony in 181 BC, *Aquileia* ('Eagle') earned its name from the eagles that flew over the town while plans were being laid for Augustus'

Getting Around

For Aquileia and Grado, take the train to Cervignano del Friuli and then a bus, or take a direct bus from Trieste. Local buses link Palmanova, Aquileia and Grado.

Tourist Information

Aquileia: Piazza Capitolo, t 0431 919 491 (April–Nov).
Grado: Viale Dante Alighieri 72, t 0431 899309, f 0431 899 210.

Where to Stay and Eat

Aquileia ✉ 33051

★★★**Patriarchi**, Via Julia Augusta 12, t 0431 919 595, f 0431 919 596 (*moderate*). Overlooking the Roman excavations; air-conditioned.

★**Aquila Nera**, Piazza Garibaldi 5, t 0431 91045 (*cheap*). An old hotel in the quiet main square, offering small rooms without bath. The restaurant is traditional and homely, with good *gnocchi* and basic meat dishes.

La Colombara, Via S. Zilli 34, t 0431 91513 (*moderate*). 2km out on the Trieste road, serving up fine cuisine, and specializing in seafood prepared in various ways, accompanied by good wines from the Collio. *Closed Mon, June.*

Grado ✉ 34073

★★★★**Antica Villa Bernt**, Via Colombo 5, t 0431 82516, f 0431 82517 (*very expensive*). There are lots of nice hotels in Grado, but a couple stand out, within sight of one another in the centre of the town. The first is this refurbished villa from the 1920s with 22 lovely rooms. *Open April–Oct.*

★★★★**Savoy**, Via Carducci 33, t 0431 897 111, f 0431 83305 (*very expensive*). Also try this hotel, which has a pool, garden, parking and comfortable rooms. *Open June–Oct.*

★★★**Eden**, Via M. Polo 2, t 0431 80136, f 0431 82087 (*expensive*). By the beach; a typical holiday hotel. *Open April–mid-Oct.*

★★★**Cristina**, Viale Martiri della Libertà 11, t 0431 80989 (*moderate*). Similar to the Eden, a bit further from the beach but in a shady garden. *Open May–Sept.*

Convento di Barbana, t 0431 80453. If you seek tranquillity, there's a pilgrims' hostel on the island, with 24 single rooms; it's quite popular so book to be sure of a room.

Albergo Ambriabella, Riva Slataper 2, t 0431 81479 f 0431 82257 (*moderate*). Alternatively try this hotel facing the Isola Della Schiusa. It provides some welcome personal touches missing from some of the larger hotels.

All'Androna, Calle Porta Piccola 4, t 0431 80950 (*expensive*). In the winding streets around the cathedral, with a menu of fresh fish that changes according to the day's catch, and home-made bread and pasta. *Closed Tues out of season, Dec–Mar.*

De Toni, Piazza Duca D'Aosta 37, t 0431 80104 (*moderate*). Overlooking the Roman excavations; offering fresh fish prepared in a variety of local styles, along with a long wine list. *Closed Wed.*

German campaign. It proved to be a good augury. Augustus himself was in and out of Aquileia and received Herod the Great here. Christianity found an early foothold in the city; the Patriarchate of Aquileia was founded in 313, the year that Constantine the Great issued the Edict of Milan, tolerating the religion, and its patriarch was given jurisdiction that extended to the Ukraine. It didn't last long; after Aquileia was sacked by Attila (452) and the Lombards (568), the patriarch moved to a safer home in Grado, an island on its outer port. When Aquileia wanted the title back in the 7th century, Grado refused to surrender it, and for 400 years rival patriarchs sat in Grado and in Cividale del Friuli, the Lombard capital. When they were reconciled in 1019, Aquileia's great basilica was rebuilt, but it was the city's last hurrah. Aquileia's port on the Natissa silted up, malaria killed the population, the patriarchate moved to Cividale, then to Ùdine, and was ultimately demoted to an archbishopric.

The Basilica

Aquileia's magnificent **Basilica** (*open April–Sept daily 8.30–7; Oct–Mar daily 8.30–12.30 and 2.30–5.30*) is a landmark on the Friulian plain for miles around. It was founded in 313 by the first Patriarch Theodore, and when Poppone rebuilt it in 1023 he covered Theodore's old-fashioned floor, leaving it intact for discovery in 1909.

The pavement is vast – 837 sq yards – the largest Paleochristian mosaic in the west, a vivid and often whimsical carpet of portraits, animals and geometric patterns happily mingling with Christian and pagan scenes. Original frescoes from 1031 survive in the apse, showing Patriarch Poppone dedicating the basilica, accompanied by Emperor Conrad II and Gisela of Swabia.

Set next to the wall, the 11th-century marble **Santo Sepolcro** is a reproduction of the Holy Sepulchre in Jerusalem. Next to this, the so-called **Cripta degli Scavi** (the excavations around the belltower) contains more mosaics from 313, sandwiched in between pagan Roman mosaics and others from the 8th century. The **crypt** proper, under the altar, is adorned with colourful 12th-century Byzantine-style frescoes (*one adm for both crypts*). The **Museo del Patriarcato**, opposite the Basilica (*open April–Oct 9.30–12.30 and 3–6; closed Mon*), contains fancy medieval reliquaries, sculptures and other works from the Basilica, including bas-reliefs of Christ with St Thomas of Canterbury, carved only a few years after his martyrdom, showing just how fast news of church politics travelled in the 1170s.

The Museo Archeologico

Open April–Sept Tues–Sun 9.30–7, Mon 9–2; Oct–Mar Tues–Sun 9–2; adm.

On the same road, but down to the left, an old palace houses a fascinating collection of artefacts from Roman *Aquileia*, including a fine set of highly individualized Republican portrait busts; unlike the Greeks who idealized in marble (or perhaps were just better-looking), the Romans insisted that all their warts, cauliflower ears and crumpled noses be preserved for posterity. Among the bas-reliefs there's a smith with his tools, amber and gold ornaments, and a thousand household items that breathe life into ancient *Aquileia*. The Aquileians could be light-hearted: there are flies made of gold, and a wee bronze figurine of a springing cat.

The Excavations

A circular walk, beginning on the Via Sacra behind the basilica, takes in most of *Aquileia*'s excavations; an unfortunate proximity to that quarrying magpie Venice has shorn them of most of their grandeur. The Via Sacra first passes by **Roman houses** and **Palaeo-Christian oratories** (some with mosaics intact), then continues up through the considerable ruins of the ancient harbour, marked by cypresses: in the 1st century AD this was a bustling commercial port. Continue straight and bear right after the crossroads on Via Gemina to the **Palaeo-Christian Museum** (*same hours as Museo Archeologico*), with reliefs and sarcophagi, and a walkway over the undulating mossy mosaics of a huge 4th-century basilica; ancient *Aquileia* required not one but two enormous churches.

Return by way of Via Gemina to Via Giulia Augusta. To the right you can see the old Roman road, and on the left, the **Forum** with its re-erected columns. Just off a fork to the right, the **Grand Mausoleum** (1st century AD) was brought here from the distant suburbs. The meagre ruins of the amphitheatre, the baths and the **Sepolcreto** (five Roman family tombs) are on Via XXIV Maggio and Via Acidino, north of the village's central Piazza Garibaldi.

Grado: Up to Your Neck in Sand

Aquileia had an inner port and an outer port, or *grado*, on the island that still bears its ancient name. Today Grado is linked by a causeway, and reigns as the queen of its own little lagoon and archipelago. The narrow alleys of the old town, the **Castrum Gradense**, are called *calli* as in Venice, and most are as happily traffic-free. In the 6th century the Patriarch of Nova Aquileia, as he fashioned himself, moved to the *duomo* (Basilica of Sant'Eufemia). Here Corinthian capitals sit atop exotic marble pillars, and the 11th-century domed pulpit is carved with four Evangelists; the painted baldachin could easily be the tent of the sheikh of Araby.

The mosaic floor is from the 6th century, although its scriptural adages and geometrical patterns may seem austere after the garden of delights in Aquileia's Basilica. One scene on the altar depicts *Castrum Gradense* and its islands; in the back glows a silver *pala* donated by the Venetians in 1372. An alley of sarcophagi separates Sant'Eufemia from the octagonal 5th-century baptistry, with a full immersion font, and another smaller basilica, the 5th-century **Santa Maria delle Grazie**, with its original altar screeens and mini-theatre for the clergy behind the altar – a common feature of early-Byzantine basilicas.

Grado owes its origin as a beach resort to medicine. Keen to bring children with TB to the seaside, doctors sought a fresh-water spring on the peninsula of Grado. In 1892 a spring was duly discovered, and Emperor Franz Josef at once included Grado on his official list of curative resorts in the Habsburg empire.

A new town grew up to accommodate the nobility, who have since been replaced by athletes, models and business people undergoing specific treatments, including the 'sand cure' – being buried up to one's neck in warm sand. If the free beaches are dirty or crowded, walk east to **Pineta**, or catch the boat to **Barbana**, an island in the lagoon with a resident religious community (*boats run frequently every day in summer; Nov–May Sat and Sun only*). There are also daily sea connections to Trieste and the Istrian coast in summer, and to the fishing village of **Porto Buso**.

Trieste

Once the main seaport of the Austro-Hungarian Empire, two world wars left Trieste to become the woebegone widow of the Adriatic. With the fall of the Berlin Wall, all this has changed: Trieste is now a very merry widow, courted across Central Europe and quickly regaining its old cosmopolitan lustre, something that the inhabitants accept as simply another twist in a knotted history. The streets and shops bubble with

Slovene, Serbo-Croat, German, Hungarian and Czech, and a bewildering variety of car licence plates clog up the very Central European 19th-century streets. Trade is picking up, too: not from tourists who once passed through on their way to points east, but from Slovenes and Hungarians flashing new-found wealth, and Austrian and Czech businessmen seeking new Mediterranean markets. Don't come to Trieste for art or beautiful buildings: its capitalist swag has been firmly invested in banks, shipping-lines and stocks. Instead, come to sense the energy and excitement of a city shaking off decades of nostalgic sloth, and picking up the threads of its most vibrant time, the beginning of this century. Or you could just come for the breasts: plastered with naked statues, Trieste must have more perky size Ds than any other city in the world.

History

Founded as the Celtic port of *Tergeste*, Trieste first became an important city under Augustus. From the 9th to the 13th centuries it maintained precarious independence under its prince-bishops; in the 14th and 15th centuries it was Venice's chief rival in the Adriatic. Austria, always longing for a port, is deeply woven into Trieste's history. It first offered the city its protection in 1382, and in 1719 Charles VI granted it free-port status, initiating a golden age. Trieste returned to Austrian rule after the fall of Napoleon in 1815, although bereft of free-port status. Their heavy-handed govern-ment turned the majority Italian population into ardent 'Irredentists' – unredeemed – turbulently desiring union with Italy.

Italian troops were welcomed in 1918, but Italian government all too soon proved to be another disappointment for Trieste, when Mussolini tried to force the hetero-geneous population into a cultural strait-jacket. The real disaster came in the aftermath of the Second World War, when Trieste found itself permanently divorced from its Istrian hinterland in Slovenia and Croatia. Tito only gave up his claims to Trieste itself in 1954, and the border was not finally settled until 1975. In the mid-1960s, the city, lacking direction, decided to create a new role for itself as a scientific and research centre – Trieste has institutes of theoretical physics, genetic engi-neering, experimental geophysics and marine biology, among others.

At the turn of the last century Trieste sparkled not with scientists, but literati. Sir Richard Burton, translator of the *Arabian Nights*, was consul here from 1870 until his death in 1890 – virtually in exile from his Middle Eastern interests. James Joyce, after eloping with Nora Barnacle, taught English in Trieste from 1904 to 1915 and 1919 to 1920; here he wrote *The Dubliners* and began *Ulysses* (fans can pick up a Joycean itin-erary at the tourist office, marking all his old haunts). Joyce befriended and translated Ettore Schmitz (Italo Svevo), a member of Trieste's once-thriving Jewish community, and author of comedy neurosis novel *La Coscienza di Zeno*. Unknown to either of them, Rainer Maria Rilke was living and working nearby at Duino.

Along the Port to Piazza dell'Unità d'Italia

If you only have an hour or two at Trieste's train or bus station, you can pop over to the **Galleria Nazionale d'Arte Antica**, Piazza della Libertà 7 (*open 9–1.30; closed Sun;*

Getting There

By Air

Trieste's **airport**, served by daily flights from Rome and Milan, and weekly flights from London on British Airways, is at Ronchi dei Legionari, **t** 0481 773 224, 30km to the north near Monfalcone; the airport bus departs from the main bus station in Piazzale Libertà. Alitalia's office is at Piazza Sant'Antonio 1, **t** 040 631 100.

By Sea

The *Marconi* links Trieste every day except Tuesday from late May–Sept, to Grado and Lignano, Piran (Slovenia) and Umag, Porec, Rovinj and Pula (Croatia). Remember to take a passport for Slovenia and Croatia. Tickets from Piazza Unità d'Italia 6, **t** 040 367 529 or Piazza Duca degli Abruzzi 1/a, **t** 040 363 737.

In the summer Anek runs four weekly **ferries** to Igoumenitsa, Patras and Corfu in Greece; for information, **t** 040 363 242. Sem Ferries sail to Split on the Dalmatian coast once a week (Via Milano 4, **t** 040 760 033). For more details, try the harbourmaster: Riva Tre Novembre 13, **t** 040 366 666.

By Rail

There are frequent trains to Venice, Gorizia and Ùdine, as well as to Austria, Slovenia and other destinations in Eastern Europe, from the **Stazione Centrale** on Piazza della Libertà 8.

By Long-distance Bus

The main **bus station** is in front of the Stazione Centrale, in Piazza della Libertà, **t** 040 425 001. It has bus services to Venice, Treviso, Padua, Belluno, Trento, and Cortina and Sappada in the Dolomites; long-distance coaches to Milan, Mantua and Genoa; international services to Ljubljana, Rijeka, Zagreb, Athens, Istria and more.

Getting Around

Trieste's long, straight Habsburger streets mean that finding one's way around on foot is relatively simple, although use the crossings carefully, as these streets can make even Rome appear pedestrian. City **buses** are frequent,

and most routes run from or by the central bus station; for information, **t** 167 016 675. A **funicular railway** (*tranvia*) runs every 22 minutes from Piazza Oberdan to Villa Opicina.

Cars have been banished from the city centre and parking can be diabolical; it's best to just surrender your *macchina* to one of the garages or car parks (near Piazza della Libertà and Piazza Unità d'Italia) and get it over with. Radio **taxi**, **t** 040 307 730.

Tourist Information

Trieste: Via San Nicoló 20, **t** 040 679 6111, **f** 040 679 6299; also at the Stazione Centrale, **t** 040 420 182 (ask for their Joyce itinerary).
Friuli's regional tourist office is at Via G. Rossini 6, **t** 040 363 952, **f** 040 365 496; freephone from within Italy **t** 167 016 044, *www.triestetourism.it.*

Where to Stay

Trieste ✉ 34100

Very Expensive
★★★★Duchi d'Aosta, Piazza dell'Unità d'Italia 2, **t** 040 760 0011, **f** 040 366 092. The city's finest hotel, on Trieste's finest square, in a neo-Renaissance palace erected in 1873. Now owned by the CIGA chain, it exudes a dignified *belle époque* ambience; the luxurious rooms are fitted with all modern comforts. It has an excellent restaurant, **Harry's Grill.**

Expensive
★★★Novo Hotel Impero, Via S. Anastasia 1, **t** 040 364 242, **f** 040 365 023. Conveniently located near the train station, a short walk from the centre; some rooms are cheaper.

Moderate
★★★San Giusto, Via C. Belli 3, **t** 040 762 661, **f** 040 7606 585. By the historic hill, a modern hotel with everything you need.
★★Al Teatro, Via Capo di Piazza G. Bartoli 1 (near Piazza dell'Unità), **t** 040 366 220, **f** 040 366 560. In a neoclassical building, this hotel served as British headquarters after the Second World War and is a bit of a nostalgic trip back to the Trieste of yore.

***Milano**, Via Ghega 17, t 040 369 680, f 040 369 727. Comfortable, near the station.

***Nuovo Hotel Daneu**, Via Nazionale 11, t 040 214 241, f 040 214 215. If you don't like the hurly-burly of a big city, take the tram up to Opicina where this hotel has a good restaurant and indoor pool.

Cheap

There are many less expensive choices in the centre of Trieste – look around Via Roma, Via della Geppa, or Via XXX Ottobre.

*Alabarda-Flora, Via Valdirivo 22, t 040 630 269, f 040 639 284. Clean, comfortable and good value.

Around Trieste

***Duino Park**, near the old citadel t 040 208184, f 040 208 526 (*moderate*). Along the coast, at Duino, a modern hotel with its own pool and a private piece of beach.

****Belvedere**, t 040 299 256 (*moderate*). With a garden and views over the sea.

***Lido**, Via Battista 22, t 040 273 338, f 040 271 979 (*moderate*). Another modern hotel, in Muggia, on the edge of town and the sea, with a restaurant serving local seafood.

Eating Out

Trieste is a good place to eat dumplings instead of pasta – Slovenian and Hungarian influences are strong in the kitchen. A famous first course is *jota*, a bean, potato and *sauer-kraut* soup, or you could try *kaiserknödel* (bread dumplings with grated cheese, ham, and parsley). For *secondo*, there's a wide variety of fish like *sardoni* (big sardines), served fried or marinated, and both tasty and cheap. Goulash, roast pork and *stinco* (veal knuckle) are also popular. The middle-European influence is especially noticeable in the desserts: the lovely strudels, the *gnocchi di susine* (plums), or *zavate*, a warm cream pastry.

Expensive

Antica Trattoria Suban, Via Comici 2, t 040 54368. The place to partake of *cucina Triestina* is this wonderful old inn in the suburb of San Giovanni (quite hard to find, so take a taxi). Founded out in the country in 1863, it has since been absorbed by urban growth, though it maintains much of its old feel and fine views over Trieste. Suban offers a famous *jota*, *sevapcici* (Slovenian grilled meat fritters), sinful desserts and good wines. Quality depends, however, on the presence of the regular chef; when booking ask if he's on duty, and if not, wait till he is. *Closed Mon lunch, Tues, part of Jan, Aug.*

Hosteria Bellavista, Via Bonomea 52, t 040 411 150. A wine lover's paradise, with hundreds of bottles from around the world to go with delicate renditions of Trieste's favourites. *Closed Sun, Mon lunch, some of Jan.*

Moderate

Scabar, Via dell'Istria at Erta di S. Anna 63, t 040 810 368. Take a taxi into the hills for gourmet fish and mushroom dishes; the day's special is usually fantastic. *Closed Mon, Tues, Feb, mid-July–Aug.*

Città di Cherso, Via Cadorna 6, t 040 366 044. Convenient to Piazza Unità d'Italia and the museums, serving delicious seafood Friulian-style, topped off with heavenly desserts. *Closed Tues, some of July and Aug.*

Cheap

Buffet da Pepi, Via Cassa di Risparmo 3, t 040 366 858. Founded in 1903; its been thriving ever since, serving up Trieste's specialities. *Closed Sun, half of July.*

Birreria Forst, Via Galatti 11, (near Piazza Oberdan) t 040 365 276. Another old favourite; goulash and beer. *Closed Sun.*

Re di Coppe, Via Geppa 11, t 040 370 330. The waiters still write orders on the tablecloths here; you can eat a classic *jota* and boiled meats. *Closed Sat, Sun, mid-July–mid-Aug.*

Entertainment

The **opera** season at Trieste's Teatro Comunale Verdi runs from November to March; in summer the theatre and the Sala Tripcovich in Piazza della Libertà see an International Operetta Festival (for schedules and bookings, t 040 672 2500, f 040 672 2249).

Carnival is celebrated with a Venetian flair in Muggia, with a lavish parade that's well beyond what you would expect in a small coastal town.

adm), with a second-division collection of Italian paintings from the 15th–19th centuries, and a charming *Diana and Actaeon* by Lucas Cranach the Elder. Otherwise, take Corso Cavour into the **Borgo Teresiano**, the neoclassical commercial centre laid out in 1750 by Maria Theresa's planners with a pair of rulers, and planted with neoclassical architecture.

The street passes over the **Canale Grande**, an inlet with moorings for small craft; the adjacent Piazza Ponterosso is the site of the daily **market**. At the head of the canal stands the temple-fronted Roman Catholic church of **Sant'Antonio** and, near it, the blue-domed Serbian Orthodox **Santo Spiridone**, an exotic orchid in the regimented garden. Just over the canal, overlooking the sea on Riva Tre Novembre, Trieste's oldest coffee house, **Caffè Tommaseo** (1830) has recently been restored, along with its *belle époque* furnishings.

Trieste's whale of a heart, **Piazza dell'Unità d'Italia**, is one of Italy's largest squares. It faces the harbour, framed by the **Palazzo del Comune**, topped by two Moors who ring the bell in the clock tower; on one side the **Palazzo del Governo** glows in its bright skin of neoclassical mosaics, on the other broods the **Palazzo di Lloyd Triestino**, now the seat of Friuli-Venezia Giulia's regional government. In one corner, a pile of rocks and statuary purported to represent the *Four Continents* (1750) may send you staggering off for a drink at the piazza's **Caffè degli Specchi**, in business since 1839 and once an Irredentist meeting place.

Trieste keeps its art a few blocks south of Piazza dell'Unità d'Italia, around Piazza Venezia. The **Museo Revoltella**, Via Diaz 27 (*open 9–12 and 3–6, tours at 9, 10.30, 12, 3 and 6; closed Tues and Sun; adm*), was founded by Baron Pasquale Revoltella, one of the financiers of the Suez Canal (which was a big boon to Trieste's port). Full of original furnishings, it contains 18th- and 19th-century paintings by Triestine artists that evoke the city's golden days, as well as modern works by Morandi and De Chirico. Up a block, on Largo Papa Giovanni XXIII, the **Museo Sartorio** (*open 9–1, closed Mon; at the time of writing only the rooms used as appartments viewable; adm*), housed in an 18th-century villa, offers a glimpse into Triestine bourgeois life in the 19th century, along with a mix of new and old art, including a triptych by Paolo Veneziano.

Up the Capitoline Hill

Catch bus no.24 from the station or Piazza dell'Unità to ascend Trieste's very own Capitoline Hill, the nucleus of the Roman and medieval city. In the 5th century the Triestini raised the first of two basilicas here to their patron San Giusto. An adjacent basilica, built in the 11th century, was linked to the earlier church in the 14th century, thus giving the **Cathedral of San Giusto** (*closed 12–3*) its curious plan. The doorway, under a splendid Gothic rose window, is framed by the fragments of a Roman sarcophagus: six funerary busts gaze solemnly ahead like a corporate board of directors, while a Roman frieze embedded in the adjacent, squat campanile resembles a fashion plate for armour. The interior has some fine mosaics, especially the 13th-century *Christ with SS. Giusto and Servulus*, as well as good 12th-century frescoes. Buried on the right is Don Carlos, the Great Pretender of Spain's 19th-century Carlist Wars, who died as an exile in Trieste in 1855.

Next to San Giusto are fragments of the Roman forum and a 1st-century basilica, of which two columns have been re-erected. The excellent view over Trieste from here is marred by a 1933 **Monument to the Fallen,** which extols the principal Fascist virtues of strength and vulgarity. The 15th-century **Castello di San Giusto** was begun by the Venetians and finished by the Austrians, and offers more views from its ramparts and a small **Museo Civico** (*open Tues–Sun 9–1; adm*) of armour and weapons.

Just down the lane from the cathedral is the **Civico Museo di Storia ed Arte e Orto Lapidario** (*t 040 308 686; open Tues–Sun 9–1, adm*), housing finds from ancient Tergeste, and a famous 5th-century deers' head rhyton from ancient *Tarentum.* The Orto Lapidario contains a red granite Egyptian sarcophagus and the tomb of J. J. Winckelmann, the famous art historian who was murdered in Trieste in 1768 by a cook. On the way down to the centre, have a look at the 1st-century **Roman theatre** on Via Teatro Romano.

More Cafés and Museums

The Grand Cafés, once the symbol of Triestine society and filled with fervent cross-cultural conversation, ideas and spies, have mostly vanished, or deal primarily in nostalgia. Joyce was an habitué of the **Caffè Pirona,** Largo Barriera Vecchia 12, north of the castle hill and south of Piazza Goldoni (at the bottom of the 'Giant's Stair' from the Castello); the locals say he conceived Ulysses over its *pinzas* and *putizzas.* On the other side of Piazza Goldoni, **Caffè San Marco,** Via Cesare Battisti 18, opened in 1914 but was rebuilt after it was blown up in the First World War, complete with Venetian murals that betrayed the owner's pro-Italian sentiments. According to the *Triestini,* the masked figures in the oval over the bar portray Vittorio Emanuele and Mussolini. One street away, on Via S. Francesco, stands the most beautiful **synagogue** in Italy, and the biggest in Europe, built in 1910 on ancient Syriac models.

In sombre counterpoint, Trieste had the only concentration camp in Italy used for mass exterminations, the **Risiera di San Sabba** at the southern extreme of the city (Ratto della Pileria 1), a rice-husking factory that was taken over by the Nazis in September 1943 to 'process', among others, 837 Triestine Jews. The building now houses a small **museum** (*bus nos. 20, 21, 23 or 19; open Tues–Sun, 9–1*). In the same area, the **Museo Ferroviario,** in the Campo Marzio (*t 040 379 4185; open daily 9–1; closed Mon*) has a display of retired locomotives. It also runs summer excursions in period trains: three-hour electric train journeys around the city, and steam train excursions around the region and neighbouring countries; call for schedules.

Excursions from Trieste

You can't go too far without running into Slovenia. For a short jaunt, take the **Opicina Tranvia,** built in 1902, up the cliffs from Piazza Oberdan for the fine panorama from the **Vedetta d'Opicina.** Another popular excursion is to **Miramare,** 7km up the beach-lined Riviera di Barcola (bus no.36 from Piazza Oberdan or Stazione Centrale). On the way stands the **Faro della Vittoria,** a lofty lighthouse and 1927 war memorial to sailors, crowned by a heavy-sinewed, big-busted Valkyrie in a majorette's costume.

Miramare: Habsburg Folly by the Sea

*Open April–Sept 9–6; Oct–Mar 9–4; also Thurs, Fri, and Sat
from 8.30–10.30pm in July, Aug, and early Sept; adm exp.
Miramare Park, open daily in summer 9–sunset, winter 8–4; free.*

Set on its own little promontory by the sea, the castle of Miramare hides a dark history behind its charming 19th-century façade. It was built by the Habsburg Archduke Maximilian and his Belgian wife Carlotta, and visitors are greeted by a stone sphinx with a cryptic smile that seems to ask the world, 'Why did Maximilian leave this pleasure palace and, like a *dummkopf*, let Napoleon III's financiers con him into becoming Mexico's puppet emperor in 1864, and why did he linger around there to face a firing squad three years later? Was he an idealist as his apologists claim, or too much of a Habsburg to know any better?'

Carlotta, after desperately trying to rally European support for her husband, went mad after his execution and survived him for another 50 years in Belgium; while Miramare acquired the ominous reputation of laying a curse on anyone who slept within its walls, when another Habsburg – the Archduke Ferdinand – stayed here on his way to assassination in Sarajevo. When the Americans occupied the palace in 1946, their superstitious commander insisted on sleeping out in the park in a tent.

You can hear the whole sad story in the sound and light show 'Miramare's Imperial Dream' (*in Italian only, Mon, Tues and Wed at 9.30 or 10.45 pm in July, Aug and Sept, but ring t 040 679 6111 for possible performances in English*). The charming park was designed by Maximilian, who made a better botanist than emperor of Mexico; the gardens and coastal waters are now managed by the Worldwide Fund for Nature and shelter the rare Stella's otter and marsh harriers.

The Carso

Most of Trieste's slender province lies within the Carso, named from its karst or pliable limestone, easily eroded by the rain into remarkable shapes – and here, pale cliffs that form Italy's most dramatic Adriatic coastline north of Monte Cònero.

Inland the karst has been buffeted by the 90mph *bora* into petrified waves of rock dotted with *dolinas* (swallow holes), while, underground, aeons of dripping water have formed vast caverns, ravines and subterranean lakes and rivers. Vineyards grow wherever there's room, and elsewhere the landscape is dominated by sumac, which autumn ignites into a hundred shades of scarlet.

Between Miramare and the industrial shipbuilding town of Monfalcone lies the fishing village of Duino, with its 15th-century **Castello Nuovo**, perched on a promontory over the sea. Castello Nuovo has long been owned by the Princes von Thurn und Taxis, one of whom played host to Rilke here from 1910 to 1911, when the poet began his 'Duino Elegies'. The castle is now a school, and off limits, but you can follow the beautiful 2km **Rilke walk** along the promontory, beginning in nearby **Sistiana**, a pretty resort with yacht harbour in its own little bay; peregrine falcons nest on the cliffs.

Born in a karstic abyss in Slovenia, the **Timavo River** continues underground for 30km before reappearing near the winsome Romanesque church of **San Giovanni al**

The Duino Elegies

When Princess Marie von Thurn und Taxis left Rilke alone in the castle that winter of 1910–11, the poet was in a restless mood. One day he received a nasty business letter, and despite the blustery winds he went for a walk along the castle bastions to sort out his thoughts before replying. In the wind and waves crashing far below he heard a voice: 'Who, if I cried, would hear me among the angelic orders?'

It was the muse Rilke had anxiously been waiting for; he jotted the words down, and by the evening the first of his ten 'Duino Elegies' was finished. Another followed, but eleven years and the terrible war intervened before his 'voice' returned and he completed the Elegies.

As the expression of Rilke's very personal and prophetic vision of reality, the Elegies were notoriously as difficult to write as they are to read. Rilke felt that in the 20th century it was impossible to find adequate external symbols to express our inner lives and, like Blake, he used angels in a highly personal way.

On one level, as he wrote to his Polish translator, Rilke felt a responsibility and foreboding that many Europeans of his generation dimly understood. 'Now there comes crowding over from America empty, indifferent things, pseudo-things, dummy life... The animated, experienced things that share our lives are coming to an end and cannot be replaced. We are perhaps the last to have still known such things. On us rests the responsibility of preserving not merely their memory (that would be little and unreliable), but their human and laral worth...'

Hence, in part, the Elegies.

Timavo, above Duino. The main attraction in the Carso is the **Grotta Gigante** (*t 040 327 312; bus no.45, every half-hour from the Piazza Oberdan; guided tours April–Sept 10–6; closed Mon exc in July and Aug; Oct–Mar 10–12 and 2–4; adm exp*). The name for once is no exaggeration: this is the largest cavern in the world open to visitors – its main hall could swallow the entire basilica of St Peter's. A pair of stalactites measuring 346ft are the biggest anywhere. The ceiling is so high that drops of water disintegrate before reaching the floor, forming curious leaf-shaped stalagmites. A belvedere overlooks a sheer 360ft drop. The cave is in Sgonico, site of a beautiful botanical garden, the **Carsiana** (*open 24 April–15 Oct, Tues–Fri 10–12, Sat, Sun and holidays 10–1 and 3–7, closed Mon*).

Bus no.40 from Piazza Oberdan offers an excursion through some fine scenery to the perilous karstic cliffs in the **Val Rosandra**, south of Trieste. Bus no.20 heads along the coast from Trieste to **Muggia**, a higgledy-piggledy Venetian fishing port at the end of Italy. The lion in its square looks most disapproving, however, and holds a closed book. The pretty tri-lobed *duomo* has a peculiar relief over the door, showing God holding a grown-up Jesus on his lap – a refreshing change from the Madonna and baby Jesus; the frescoes inside date from the 13th century.

The best views around are enjoyed by the **Basilica di Santa Maria Assunta**, a 10th-century frescoed church overlooking Muggia.

Gorizia and Around

The frontier town of Gorizia was for centuries ruled by a powerful dynasty of counts, who were always ready to stir up trouble against Venice, with the approval of the Kings of Hungary. When the last count died in 1500, the city was briefly controlled by Venice before being taken over by the Habsburgs. As in Trieste, the Austrians gave Gorizia broad, straight boulevards and parks and pronounced the result an 'Austrian Nice' (minus the seashore).

The city saw fierce fighting in the First World War, but it was after the Second World War that Gorizia became Italy's Berlin, divided between Italy and Slovenia in such a thoughtless manner that it almost choked. Things were improved in 1979, when residents were granted a 16km zone around the city to transact their affairs freely. In 1991 Gorizia saw the first shots of the Balkan War, when Slovenia declared independence and the Yugoslav army was sent in to wrest back the lucrative border posts. Today, as independent Slovenia prospers, the town has flashy boutiques catering for cross-border traffic.

Borgo Castello

Crowning Gorizia, Borgo Castello is a little medieval village within the city, all enveloped by a Venetian fortress of 1509. In the centre stands the **Castle of the Counts**

Tourist Information

Gorizia: Via Roma 5, t 0481 386 222/5/4 f 0481 386 277, *giubileo11@adriacom.it*.
Gradisca d'Isonzo: Palazzo Torriani, Via M Ciotti, t 0481 99217, f 0481 99880.

Where to Stay and Eat

Gorizia ✉ 34170

****Golf Hotel, Via Oslavia 2, t 0481 884 051, f 0481 884 052 (*expensive*). Just north of Gorizia at San Floriano del Collio, this 17th-century manor house has 15 rooms furnished with antiques and every amenity; pool, tennis and golf too.
***Palace, Corso d'Italia 63, t 0481 82166, f 0481 31658 (*moderate*). The most attractive place to stay in town, with large modern rooms on the main street.
Lanterna d'Oro al Castello, t 0481 82007 (*moderate*). In Borgo Castello, you can sup here in medieval splendour. The menu features Friuli specialities like *prosciutto di San Daniele*, and well-prepared dishes of venison, kid and boar. *Closed Mon*.

Cormòns ✉ 34071

***Felcaro, Via S. Giovanni 45, t 0481 60214, f 0481 630 255 (*moderate*). The nicest place to sleep in the Collio. It began life as an Austrian villa and is spread out over several buildings, with a pool and a fine restaurant, specializing in game dishes to go with its enormous wine list.
**La Subida, Monte 22, t 048 60531, f 0481 61616 (*cheap*). In a charming rural setting on a hill, with a handful of rooms, many sleeping up to five, with an outdoor pool and riding, and excellent restaurant.
Il Cacciatore, Monte 22, t 048 60531, f 0481 61616 (*expensive*), the restaurant of La Subida, serves excellent regional dishes, with extensive borrowings from nearby Slovenia: the cold breast of pheasant in mushroom cream is a popular summer dish. Excellent Collio wines. *Closed Tues, Wed, Feb*.
Al Giardinetto, Via Matteotti 54, t 0481 60257, f 0481 630 704 (*expensive*). Twin chefs have put this restaurant firmly on the gastronomic map with their innovative Friulian dishes – *millefoglie di polenta* and *gnocchi* with crinkly cabbage and game sauce. *Closed Mon eve, Tues, July*.

> ## Wine Around Gorizia
>
> The hills around Gorizia, the Collio, are a lost bit of Tuscany as well as the most prestigious wine region in Friuli, producing exquisite white wines since the Middle Ages. The pleasant, leafy town of Gradisca d'Isonzo straddles the blue-green River Isonzo, neat and tidy with pastel houses and little 17th-century *palazzi*. It also offers the chance to taste any or all of the Friulian wines at the Enoteca Regionale Serenissima, in business since 1965 (*open daily 10–1 and 4–11pm; closed Mon*). Cormòns, another major wine town, was the only one in Italy to erect a statue to Emperor Maximilian. Visit its Cantina Prodottori Vini del Collio e Isonzo, **t** 0481 60579 (*closed Sun*), which produces a Vino della Pace, made from vines gathered from around the globe, and sent out annually to the world's heads of state.

of Gorizia, first mentioned in 1001, but completely rebuilt after the First World War. It now houses the **Museo del Medioevo Goriziano** (*open Tues–Sun 9.30–1 and 3–7.30; adm*), with a display dedicated to Gorizia's complicated history.

Just below stands the pretty church of **Santo Spirito** (1386) and the Casa Formentini, now the **Museo Provinciale** (*open daily 10–8; closed Mon; adm*), featuring local artists, especially Giuseppe Tominz, painter of the bourgeoisie of Gorizia and Trieste (d. 1866); don't miss his self-portrait with his brother (fully grown) sitting on his lap, about to receive Giuseppe's fully laden palette on the back of his frock coat. Best of all are the basement rooms, dedicated to the Isonzo front and its trenches, evoking the horror and some of the black humour of the First World War.

In 1990 Guglielmo Coronini, the last Count of Gorizia, died, and now his home, **Villa Coronini Cronberg** (1594), Viale XX Settembre 14, is open for tours (*Tues–Sat 10–1 and 4–8, Sun 10–12 and 4–8; adm*). There's the bedroom where Charles X, the last King of France, died in 1836 and the Count's collection: paintings by Tintoretto, Strozzi, Magnasco, Rubens, Monet, Rosalba Carriera and, of course, Giuseppe Tominz; plus prints by Titian and Rembrandt – and Japanese masters; you can also wander through the villa's English park.

Ùdine

Legend states that Ùdine's *castello* sits on a mound erected by Hunnish warriors who carried the soil in their helmets so that Attila could watch the burning of Aquileia. The story is apocryphal, as Ùdine took Aquileia's place as seat of the patriarchate from 1238 to 1751. In 1420 its leading family gave it to the Serenissima. In the Second World War it was the last city in Italy to be liberated (May 1945).

Ùdine is something of a best-kept secret – scorned even by Italians from further south, who don't know what they're missing; artistically, you'll see much that looks Venetian and much by lagoonland's greatest 18th-century painter, Giambattista Tiepolo, thanks to his first important patron, Patriarch Dionisio Delfino, who kept GB here with commissions between 1726 to 1730, a period when he took up the brilliant colours that became his trademark.

Getting Around

Ùdine's **railway station** (with connections to Venice, Trieste and Gorizia) is on Viale Europa Unità; a private local railway links Ùdine station with Cividale (20mins). The **bus station** is not far away on the other side of the same street, **t** 0432 506941.

Tourist Information

Ùdine: Piazza 1 Maggio 7, **t** 0432 295 972, **f** 0432 504 743, *arpt1.ud@adriacom.it*.
Cividale del Friuli: Corso Paolino d'Aquileia 10, **t** 0432 731 461, **f** 0432 731 398, *arpt.cividale@ redione.fvg.it*.

Where to Stay and Eat

Ùdine ✉ 33100
★★★★Astoria Hotel Italia, Piazza XX Settembre 24, **t** 0432 505 091, **f** 0432 509 070 (*very expensive*). The *grande dame* of the city's hotels, located in the heart of town; it has air-conditioning, a garage, rooms with all the mod cons, and a fine restaurant, specializing in Venetian meat and fish

dishes. Ask to have a peek in the frescoed conference room, designed by Japelli in 1833.
★★★La' di Moret, just north of the centre at Viale Tricesimo 276, **t** 0432 545 096, **f** 0432 545 096 (*expensive*). This elegant turn-of-the-century hotel has won awards for its rooms; the restaurant, one of the best in the region, features seafood Friuli-style. *Closed Sun eve and Mon.*
★★★San Giorgio, Piazzale Cella 2, **t** 0432 505 577, **f** 0432 506 110 (*moderate*). Just outside the centre of Ùdine, five minutes' walk from the train station, with modern rooms.
★★Quo Vadis, Piazzale Cella 28, **t** 0432 21091, **f** 0432 21092 (*cheap*). Good clean rooms with balcony.
★Da Brando, Piazzale Cella 16, **t/f** 0432 502 837 (*cheap*). No en suite baths.
Alla Vedova, Via Travagnacco 9, **t** 0432 470 291 (*moderate*). The oldest restaurant in Ùdine, quite a way from the historic centre, off the SS13 to Tarvisio; but what better way to spend an evening than at a table near the great hearth (or outdoors in the summer), dining on wild duck *risotto*? The house's red Refosco is famous. *Closed Sun eve, Mon.*
Vitello d'Oro at central Via Valvason 4, **t** 0432 508 982, **f** 0432 508 982 (*expensive*). Another

Piazza della Libertà

The heart of Ùdine, Piazza della Libertà, has been called 'the most beautiful Venetian square on *terra firma*'. Its most striking building, the candy-striped **Loggia del Lionello**, a mini doges' palace, was built by a goldsmith in 1448 and faithfully reconstructed after a fire in 1876.

A second loggia, the **Loggia di San Giovanni** (1533), supports a clock tower and a bell rung by two Venetian-inspired 'moors'. There is the usual Venetian column topped by a Lion of St Mark, accompanied by statues of Heracles and Justice, with unusual Bette Davis eyes. The **Municipio**, all in white Istrian stone, is a fine piece of Art Deco by Raimondo D'Aronco (1910–31) that blends right in.

Palladio's rugged **Arco Bollari** (1556) is the gateway to the sweeping **portico**, built in 1487 to shelter visitors to the **Castello**, former seat of the Patriarch and the Venetian governor. Rebuilt in 1517, and restored after the earthquake, it now houses the **Civici Musei** (*open 9.30–12.30 and 3–6; closed Mon; adm, free Sun am*); sections include prints and a large and excellent collection of paintings, with especially good works by Carpaccio, Giambattista Tiepolo and a painter little-known outside his hometown, but well worth looking at, Luca Carlefarijs of Ùdine (1662–1730).

historic inn, serving traditional specialities, with an emphasis on fish. *Closed Wed and three weeks in July.*

Vecchio Stallo, Via Viola 7, t 0432 21296 (*cheap*) This charming restaurant is Ùdine's best value for money; good food, and wine by the glass. *Closed Wed.*

Boschetti, Piazza Mazzini 9, t 0432 851 230 (*very expensive*). For an exceptional meal, head 7km north of Ùdine to Tricesimo and this gourmet haven, where the innovative chef bases his dishes entirely on the availability of fresh ingredients and old Friulian traditions – try *pappardelle* with *porcini* mushrooms, scallops with French beans in almond oil, or steamed salmon with vegetables, followed by exquisite desserts. Book well in advance. *Closed Sun eve, Mon, half of Aug.*

Cividale del Friuli ✉ 33043

★★★Locanda al Castello, Via del Castello 20, t 0432 733 242, f 0432 700 901 (*moderate*). Slightly outside the town in the suburb of Fortino, this ivy-covered hotel is not really in a castle but a former fortified Jesuit seminary. It now offers Cividale's most atmospheric rooms, as well as a fine restaurant with views from its balcony. *Closed Nov, Feb.*

★★★Roma, Via G. Gallina, t 0432 731 871, f 0432 701 033 (*moderate*). Other choices are in the centre and include this modern hotel without a restaurant but with parking.

★★Locanda Pomo d'Oro, Piazza S. Giovanni 20, t/f 0432 734 189 (*cheap*). A romantic place set in an 11th-century hostel.

Alla Frasca, Via di Rebeis 8a, t 0432 731 270 (*moderate*). A restaurant with a charming Renaissance atmosphere and tasty Friulian dishes, including a *menu di funghi* that offers truffles and mushrooms with everything. *Closed Mon.*

Al Fortino, Via Carlo Alberto 46, t 0432 731 217 (*moderate*). Also pleasant, with typical Friuli fare and home-made pasta. *Closed Tues.*

Trattoria Al Paradiso, Via Cavour 21, t 0432 732 438. Behind the Duomo in Cividale and always full of locals. *Closed Mon.*

Eleforte, Piazza Paulo Diacono 4, t 0432 700 966. If you are looking for more of a snack, then this place could be perfect. It serves over 40 different kinds of Friulian wines and an impressive selection of *bruschetta*. This is a lovely corner of Cividale to watch the world go by.

Down in the City

Just east of Piazza Libertà along Via Vittòrio Vèneto, the oft-altered **Duomo** has a charming 14th-century lunette over the door with figures so weathered they look like gingerbread. The interior, a dignified Baroque symphony of grey and gold, has two frescoes by Tiepolo. In the campanile, the small **Museo del Duomo** is adorned with excellent 1349 frescoes of the *Funeral of St Nicolas* by Vitale da Bologna, and a 14th-century sarcophagus. Even after Tiepolo become world famous he never forgot his first fans, and in 1759 when he was at the height of his powers he returned to fresco the **Oratorio della Purità**, added to the cathedral in 1680; he also painted the altarpiece of the *Immaculate Conception*; the *chiaroscuro* frescoes on the walls are by his son Giandomenico. Near the *duomo* on Piazza Venerio, 14th-century **San Francesco** has good frescoes in the apse. From here take a left on Via Savorgnana for the more ornate **San Giacomo**, with its clock tower and life-size figures gazing over the arcaded **Piazza Matteotti**, Ùdine's old market square. Note the outdoor altar over the door of San Giacomo, used to celebrate mass on market days – as convenient for shoppers in its day as a drive-in church in California.

And there's more on the Tiepolo trail: from Piazza Libertà take Via Manin to Piazza Patriarcato and the **Palazzo Arcivescovile**, now the **Museo Diocesano** (*open Wed–Sun*

10–12 and 3.30–6.30), with an entire gallery of Old Testament scenes frescoed by GB in the 1720s. More recent art (Severini, Carrà, De Chirico, De Kooning, Segal, Lichtenstein, Dufy, and the brothers Afro, Mirko and Dino Basaldell of Ùdine) is in the **Galleria d'Arte Moderna** *(open 9.30–12.30 and 3–6; closed Mon; adm, free Sun am)*: take bus no.2 from the station.

Cividale del Friuli

Only a hop and a skip from Ùdine in the valley of the Natisone, Cividale del Friuli is a fine old town with an impressive pedigree. Caesar founded it in 50 BC and named it for his family, *Forum Iulii*, a name condensed over the centuries into 'Friuli'. The Lombards invaded in 568, liked what they saw, and made Cividale the capital of their first duchy. The Patriarch of Aquileia moved here in 737, initiating a magnificent period, documented by Paulus Diaconus, the Lombard historian born in Cividale and one of the brightest beams of light we have on the 'Dark Ages' in northern Italy.

The Duomo and Archaeology Museum

The centre of Cividale is a series of squares around the old forum. In the most important, **Piazza Duomo**, you'll find the rebuilt 13th–15th-century **Palazzo Comunale**, a statue of founder Julius Caesar and the **Duomo** *(open 9.30–12 and 3–7, till 6 in winter)*, begun in 1453 and given its plain but attractive Renaissance façade by Pietro Lombardo. It contains unique treasures: the 12th-century silver altarpiece, the *Pala di Pellegrino II*, with its 25 saints and two archangels; a fine gilded equestrian monument (1617); and the Renaissance sarcophagus of Patriarch Nicolò Donato.

Off the right aisle, the **Museo Cristiano** *(t 0432 731 144; open 9.30–12.00 and 3–7)* contains the octagonal Baptistry of Callisto and the Altar of Ratchis, dating back to 749, when there was still considerable confusion about lion anatomy (the one on the Baptistry is part fish, part hedgehog) and how hands and arms are attached to the human body. In the scene of the Magi, Mary and baby Jesus frown as if they didn't like their presents – what's a baby going to do with a pot of myrrh anyhow? Yet compare its barbaric charms with the Tempietto.

Next to the *duomo*, the **Museo Archeologico Nazionale** *(t 0432 700 700; open all year Tues–Fri 8.30–7.30, Mon 9–2; adm)* is housed in Palladio's Palazzo Pretorio. This vast treasure trove has Roman items, especially the unique Zuglio bronzes – an enormous shield with a man's portrait in the centre – as well as objects from Lombard tombs of the 6th and 7th centuries: crosses, *fibulae*, swords and shield-holders (*ambone*). There are ivory pieces for a game called *ad tabulam*, the 8th-century Carolingian *Pax del Duca Orso*, adorned with an ivory crucifix and studded with jewels; a 5th-century *Evangelical of St Mark*, autographed by Lombard nobles who thought it was written in the apostle's hand; and architectural bits from the Romanesque **Duomo** – mermaids, monsters and a man in a funny hat.

The Ipogeo Celtico and Tempietto Longobardo

Corso Ponte d'Aquileia descends to the pretty turquoise Natisone and the lofty 1442 **Ponte del Diavolo**. In the Middle Ages it was a common folk belief that bridges were magical, and stories grew up on how they were erected overnight by the Devil in exchange for the first soul that ventured across in the morning. But of course Satan is a sucker in every instance; the wily Cividalesi sent over a cat at dawn.

Just up from the bridge is the mysterious **Ipogeo Celtico**, Via Monastero 21 (*the Bar All'Ipogeo on Via Paolino d'Aquileia, t 0432 701 211, has the key; on Mon pick it up at the tourist office*). This creepy pit, the perfect setting for a nasty cult, may have served as a funeral chamber in the 3rd century BC, although no one's sure, because there's nothing to compare it to. The Romans and Lombards used it as a prison, where unfor-tunates would have had to look at the three monstrous carved heads that peer out of the walls, seemingly from the dawn of time.

Follow the Natisone up to the happier **Tempietto Longobardo**, or Santa Maria in Valle (*open summer daily 9–1 and 3–6.30; winter daily 10–1 and 3.30–5.30; adm*), the finest 8th-century work in Italy, despite the fact that it had to be restored in the 13th century after an earthquake shattered three-quarters of its ornamentation and all of its mosaics. The stuccoes that remain, however, are a love letter from the Dark Ages: ravishing, uncanny and perhaps even miraculous: a sextet of gently smiling saints and princesses in high relief, standing at either side of a beautiful and intricately carved window, all positioned over an even more intricately carved arch with a vine motif. Artistically, Europe wasn't to see the like again for 400 years.

North of Ùdine: the Julian and Carnia Alps

The mountainous north of Ùdine is now linked to the city by a bright new *autostrada*. It has yet to bring in the crowds. The Julian Alps are Slovene-speaking, their church towers crowned with colourful garlic domes. If the peaks lack the romance of their Dolomite neighbours, they also lack their crowds and lofty prices.

Into Friuli's Mountains

Just off the *autostrada*, **Gemona** and **Venzone** were the epicentre of the powerful 1976 earthquake. Rather than move on, residents rebuilt them with meticulous care, a labour of love that after 23 years is almost completed. Set in the Julian foothills, Gemona del Friuli's gem is a 13th-century cathedral with a façade featuring a remarkable St Christopher, sculpted by a Nordic artist in 1331. Nearby Venzone, a smaller, double-walled town, began as a crossroads stop on the Julia Augusta road. A display under the painted ceiling of the loggia has astonishing 'before and after' photographs of the earthquake zone.

The *autostrada* continues northeast into the Julian Alps. The mountains south of **Tarvisio** (near the Austrian and Slovenian borders) cradle an up-and-coming resort, **Sella Nevea**, near two pretty lakes. Tri-national ski passes are available.

The Carnia Mountains rise to the west, next door neighbours to the Dolomites. **Tolmezzo**, an 18th-century producer of damasks and taffetas, is the main town and transportation hub of the mountains. In a 16th-century palace in Piazza Garibaldi, the **Museo Carnico Delle Arti Popolari** (*t 0433 43233; open 9–1 and 3–6, closed Mon*) has a fine ethnographic collection, covering mountain life from the 14th to the 19th centuries. Beyond Tolmezzo the scenery grows increasingly delightful. From **Comeglians** there is a lovely scenic road up to **Sappada** in the Cadore (*see* p.443). West of Tolmezzo, at **Ampezzo**, you can pick up the road to isolated **Sauris** with its beautiful lake. The road west to Pieve di Cadore (*see* p.442) passes **Forni di Sotto**, a village rebuilt after the Nazis burnt it down in reprisal for partisan activities, and **Forni di Sopra**, in a beautiful setting, with a fine 15th-century triptych in the Romanesque church of San Floriano.

Emilia-Romagna

14

Highlights

1 Parma, city of Correggio, music and *prosciutto*

2 The Romanesque cathedral in Modena

3 Bologna: the little brick universe of porticos, *tortellini* and leaning towers

4 The frescoed Abbey of Pomposa

5 Golden Byzantine mosaics of Ravenna

Between the sparkling wines of Lombardy, the elegant Soave of the Veneto and the full-bodied Chianti of Tuscany, Emilia-Romagna seems like a glass of warm beer. It is mostly flat, on the southern plain of the Po, hot and humid in the summer, and cold and fog-bound in the winter. Most tourists see it only from the train window when chugging between Venice and Florence.

Emilia-Romagna

But for anyone interested in cracking the surface of this glossiest and most complex of nations, Emilia-Romagna is an essential region to know. For this is Middle Italy: agricultural, wealthy, progressive, a barometer of Italian highs and lows – the birthplace of the country's socialist movement, but also of Mussolini and Fascism. In Emilia-Romagna hard-working cities like Modena, Parma and Bologna share space with Rimini, Italy's vast, madcap international resort, with Ravenna, the artistic jewel of the region with its stupendous Byzantine mosaics, and with traditional Apennine villages. Emilia-Romagna is the cradle of innovative film directors – Fellini, Bertolucci and Antonioni; of musical giants like Verdi, Toscanini, Pavarotti, Tebaldi and Bergonzi; and of such diverse talents as Marconi, Correggio, Savonarola, Ariosto, Pavarotti, Parmigianino and Ferrari.

As a united region, Emilia-Romagna is a child of the Risorgimento. Emilia, west of Bologna, was named after the Via Aemilia, built by M. Aemilius Lepidus in 187 BC between Piacenza and Rimini, running almost dead straight for hundreds of kilometres along the course of the Apennines. Nearly all of Emilia's cities grew up at intervals along the road, like beads on a string. Romagna, east of Bologna, recalls the period from the 5th century to 751 when this was 'Rome', when Ravenna was the last

The Gourmet in Emilia-Romagna

Nothing sums up this area so well as food and, beside the wonderful experiences waiting in restaurants, it's easy to find tastes to take home. Cheese, meat, wine, liqueurs or sweets travel well. Most Parmesan cheese, called *grana* on account of its grainy quality, is actually *Parmigiano-Reggiano*, and is produced around Parma, Modena and Reggio Emilia. A true Parma ham is first left to dry in the sweet air of the Magra Valley, to lose its excessive saltiness and gain the scent of pine and olives, then taken down the Cisa Pass to take the chestnutty air of the Apennines. Yet even more revered is *culatello*, a sausage made from a pig's buttocks, which can be prepared only in the humid lowlands of the Po Valley.

Nocino is a liqueur which tradition states must come from Sassuolo, near Modena, and be made from unripe walnuts picked on St John's Day, 24th June. Alcohol is poured over the crushed nuts, then sugar, cinnamon, cloves and lemon rind are added; the mixture is left for forty days before being sieved through cotton. The other great specialities of Modena are balsamic vinegar – the finest of which is as prized and precisely regulated as any DOCG wine – and cherries, from Vignola. In Bologna delicatessens sell fresh *tortellini*, stuffed with any combination of *ricotta* cheese, minced beef or veal, bread, chicken, nutmeg and fresh herbs. Bologna is also famous for its desserts and pâtisserie, the most specialized of which is *torta di riso*, a sweet, thick rice pudding. It is also the home of Lambrusco which, if it's the right stuff, should foam like a beer when it's first poured, only to reveal a sparkling, elegant and full-bodied wine below.

enclave of the Roman Empire in the west, ruled by the exarchs of the Eastern Roman Empire in Byzantium. By the Middle Ages these cities had gone their own way, controlled by dukes or *signori* – the Farnese, Este, Malatesta, Bentivoglio and Da Polenta – who claimed allegiance to the pope, and held the front line between the Papal States and the Venetians and Milanese.

In Emilia-Romagna you'll find, besides the remarkable art of the Byzantines and Ostrogoths in Ravenna, exceptional Romanesque churches (Parma and Modena), two of Italy's crookedest towers (Bologna), beautiful Renaissance art (Parma, Bologna and Ferrara) and the Renaissance's strangest building, the Malatesta Temple in Rimini. You can ski, hike, ride or hang-glide in the Apennines, sunbathe in style on the Adriatic, visit the ancient Republic of San Marino or Italy's ceramics capital at Faenza, or attend grand opera in Parma, Reggio, Bologna or Modena. You'll also find Italy's best food (*see* above).

Piacenza

Competing with the more famous charms of nearby Parma and Cremona, Piacenza is the unassuming wallflower of Renaissance cities. Nevertheless, it can boast of two of the most gallant horses in Italy, a Botticelli, and an amazing bronze liver. A Roman colony established in 218 BC at the conjunction of the Via Aemilia and the Po, Piacenza was an important *comune* in the 12th and 13th centuries, and a member of the Lombard League in 1314. It spent much of its history under the Farnese thumb, as part of the Duchy of Parma. In 1848, after a plebiscite, Piacenza became the first city to unite with Piedmont in the new nation of Italy, earning itself the nickname of *Primogenita* or 'first-born'.

Piazza Cavalli

Piacenza's excellent Piazza Cavalli (to get there from the station, cut across the park to Via G. Alberoni and Via Roma, then turn left on Via Carducci) takes its name from its two bronze horses with flowing manes, masterpieces of the early Baroque, cast in the 1620s by Francesco Mochi. Riding them are two members of the Farnese clan: Alessandro, the 'Prince of Parma', one of the key figures of the 1500s, who was Philip II

Getting Around

The **train** station, on Piazzale Marconi, a 10-minute walk from the centre, has frequent connections to Milan, Parma and Cremona. The **bus** station, **t** 0523 337 245, in Piazza Cittadella, near the Palazzo Farnese, has buses to Cremona, Bobbio (10 a day), Grazzano Visconti, Castell'Arquato and other towns in the province. Buses to the *Velleia* excavations are infrequent; if you go make sure you don't get stranded. STAT Turismo will take you long-distance to Genoa and the Riviera, Bolzano or Trento, **t** 0142 781 660.

Tourist Information

Piazzetta dei Mercanti 10 (off Piazza Cavalli), **t/f** 0523 32924; *www.piacenzaTurismi.net*.

Where to Stay

Piacenza ✉ **29100**
****Grande Albergo Roma**, Via Cittadella 14, **t** 0523 323 201, **f** 0523 330 548, *hotelroma@altimedia.it* (*expensive*). Piacenza's most prestigious hotel, just off Piazza Cavalli, equipped with soberly elegant woodwork and furnishings, old-fashioned service and the good **Ristorante Panoramico**, with pretty views over the city.
***Hotel City**, Via Emilia Parmense 54, **t** 0523 579 752, **f** 0523 579 784 (*moderate*). Southeast of town on the Parma road, modern with 60 quiet rooms.

Eating Out

Antica Osteria del Teatro, Via Verdi 16, near Sant'Antonino, **t** 0523 384 639 (*very expensive*). Piacenza boasts one of Italy's very best restaurants, an intimate and exceptional gourmet pleasure dome. Local recipes merge delectably with French nouvelle cuisine under chef Filippo Chiappini Dattilo's magic touch: the *tortelli del Farnese* with butter and sage are as light as a summer's breeze; *secondi* include sea or land food, including heavenly *foie gras* in pastry, layered with honey and Calvados, or a bit of Sardinia in the roast suckling pig perfumed with myrtle. For dessert, splurge on one of the heavenly chocolate concoctions. There's a choice of two *menu di degustazione*. Be sure to book well in advance to get a table here. *Closed Sun, Mon and Aug*.
Vecchia Piacenza, San Bernardo 1, **t** 0523 305 462 (*expensive*). Just west of the *centro*, off Via Taverna. Tasty *antipasti* (try the *porcini* if they're on the menu) and a constantly changing list of *primi* and *secondi*, based on the market and the chef's whim. *Closed Sun and first half of July*.
La Pireina, Via Borghetto 137, **t** 0523 338 578 (*cheap*). A traditional *trattoria* near the old city walls, which serves typical local and regional dishes in a simple, unpretentious way: *tortelli d'erbette* (stuffed with spinach and *ricotta* cheese), *tagliolini al ragù*, or *faldia* (a type of schnitzel made with horse steak). *Closed Sun, Mon eve, and first half of Aug*.

of Spain's governor in the Low Countries during the Dutch War of Independence (not a position that won him any popularity contests, despite the fine statue, his lack of religious fanaticism and his aversion to gratuitous violence and massacres), and his son Ranuccio, a bad Duke and a paranoid waster. The piazza also contains the Gothic Palazzo del Comune, better known to the Piacentini as **Il Gotico** for its pointed arches (*open to visitors during temporary exhibitions*), built in 1280, with swallowtail crenellations, mullioned windows and a rose window, and the 13th-century church of San Francesco, noted for its Gothic interior.

Rising up at the end of the main Via XX Settembre, the Lombard-Romanesque **Duomo** (1122–1233) is an imposing pile begun four years before the *comune*; a picturesque confusion of columns, caryatids and galleries in the shadow of an octagonal cupola and campanile (1333). The transitional interior (Romanesque to Gothic) has a striking striped marble floor and good 15th-century frescoes. The relics of the city's patron, obscure 4th-century martyr Santa Giustina, are in the impressive crypt, with its 108 columns.

From here Via Chiapponi leads to **Sant'Antonino**, Piacenza's oldest church, with an 11th-century octagonal lantern believed to be the first built in Italy, and a lofty Gothic porch called the Paradiso. Just southwest on Via San Siro and Via Santa Franca, opposite a picturesque but derelict Art Nouveau theatre, is the Ricci-Oddi Gallery (*under restoration, due to reopen some day in the misty future*), a huge collection that shows a keen eye for what Italian artists were up to between 1800 and 1930.

The Palazzo Farnese

From Piazza Cavalli, Corso Cavour leads to the pachydermic, uncompleted Palazzo Farnese, local headquarters of the ducal family (begun in 1558 by Vignola). Inside is the **Museo Civico** (*open Tues, Wed and Thurs 8.30–1, Fri, Sat and Sun 8.30–1 and 3–6; closed Mon; guided tours offered at 9.30, 10.15 and 11; adm*). Botticelli's lovely Tondo from the 1480s, when he was trading in mythological fancies for Christian piety, is the highlight of the paintings; you can also see the most famous Etruscan bronze of them all: the *fegato di Piacenza*, a model of a sheep (or some say human) liver, designed for apprentice haruspices, or augurs, diagrammed and inscribed with the names of the Etruscan deities. The Etruscans regarded the liver as a microcosm of the sky, ruled over by the gods, and looked in it for blemishes to see which deity had anything to communicate. The carriage museum contains a wonderful piece of folk art, a Sicilian cart painted with scenes from the operas of Verdi.

Across the courtyard stands the scanty remains of the 14th-century **Cittadella**; the Farnese pulled most of it down, as no doubt the place was an embarrassment to them: Pier Luigi, the first Duke, met his end here in 1547 when rebellious Piacentini nobles murdered him and threw his corpse out of a window into the moat.

About 2km southwest of the city is the Collegio Alberoni (*visits by appointment only, t 0523 613 198*), dedicated to San Lazzaro, which contains a fine collection of Flemish tapestries and a rare work by Sicilian Antonello da Messina, Italy's first oil-painter: his *Ecce Homo* is an unusual composition and the Renaissance's most sorrowful Christ.

Environs of Piacenza

The rarely visited hills and mountains south of Piacenza offer several possibilities for excursions or road stops. The main SS45 to Genoa follows the Trebbia Valley to **Bobbio** (46km), where St Columbanus founded a monastery in 612, shortly before his death. Columbanus, one of several scholarly Irishmen who came to the illiterate continent as missionaries in the Dark Ages, had also founded the great abbey of Luxeuil (Vosges), but been forced to leave because of his outspoken views of the Frankish barons and his Celtic observances. Another, later abbot became Pope Sylvester II in 999 – despite being accused of sorcery for constructing planetary spheres and mechanical clocks. Bobbio began to decline in the 1400s, and the abbey was largely rebuilt, but the Basilica retains traces of its medieval splendours – a 9th-century campanile and apse; 12th-century mosaics of mythological beasts in the crypt, conveniently labelled for the perplexed, including a dragon and a 'quimera' (chimera); and an intricate wrought-iron screen – as well as Columbanus' Renaissance sarcophagus. The **Museo dell'Abbazia** (*open all year Sat and Sun 4.30–6; July and Aug Tues, Wed, Fri and Sat 4.30–6, Sun 11–12 and 3–6; adm*) contains a famous 4th-century *teca*, an ivory urn with reliefs, and Romanesque statuary and painting; in the town of Bobbio, clustered around the monastery and castle, there are many fine old stone houses.

Emilia's best-preserved Roman town, prettily situated on a hillside, is **Velleia**, 33km south of Piacenza between Bobbio and Salsomaggiore. It was never very large, but retains its forum, temple, amphitheatre and mysterious large carved stones that resemble bathplugs. Most of the finds are now in Parma, though bits and pieces remain in the *antiquarium* on the site (*open daily 9am–sunset*). If you're driving you can cut over the hills from here to Lugagnano and **Castell'Arquato**, a lovely walled hill town built around an asymmetrical Palazzo del Podestà (1293), a picturesque Romanesque church of the same period with a Paradiso portico and some barbaric carved capitals, and its Rocca. Just as picturesque, closer to Piacenza but not as authentic, **Grazzano Visconti** was recently rebuilt in the medieval style. The village is a good place to purchase ornamental wrought iron. Just north of Castell'Arquato, **Vigolo Marchese** has a Romanesque church and a rare 11th-century circular baptistry; inside it are some rare bits of frescoes from the same period.

Piacenza to Parma

North of the Via Aemilia between Piacenza and Parma lies the flat Po Valley known as the **Bassa**, a favourite landscape in Italian films. Down the Via Aemilia itself, 30km east of Piacenza, the Cistercian Abbey of **Chiaravalle della Colomba** (*open daily 8–12 and 2.30–6*), 4km north of Alseno, has a Romanesque church, Giottesque frescoes and a beautiful brick cloister. More of the same awaits at **Fidenza**, Roman *Fidentia Iulia*, owned by the Pallavicini for 600 years and known for centuries as Borgo San Donnino – until Mussolini resurrected its more imperial-sounding name. Of interest, it has a 13th-century **Duomo**, with a beautiful porch by the followers of Antelami, the master of Parma's baptistry.

Where to Stay and Eat

Salsomaggiore ✉ 43039

★★★★★Grand Hotel et de Milan, Via Dante 1, **t** 0524 572 241, **f** 0524 573 884 (*very expensive*). The plushest of the scores of hotels here to take the waters at, in a large 19th-century country villa once owned by the Dukes of Parma. The public rooms have retained their old-fashioned charm, while the many of the bedrooms are equipped with private spas. There's a heated pool in a pretty garden, a solarium and beauty farm; the restaurant serves regional cuisine and meals for guests on special diets. *Open April–Dec.*

★★★★Grand Hotel Porro, Viale Porro 10, **t** 0524 578 221, **f** 0524 577 878, *thernet@polaris.it* (*expensive*). Liberty-style, set in a 12-acre park, dedicated to life in the slow lane, with comfortable rooms to relax in after visits to the spa and sauna; it too has special menus for special diets, and is one of the few in Salsomaggiore that stays open all year.

★★★Valentini, Viale Porro 10, **t** 0524 578 251, **f** 0524 578 266 (*moderate*). Salsomaggiore has a vast choice of less expensive hotels: next to the Porro, this is another old hotel, with its own spa and swimming pool in a quiet park setting. *Closed 10 Nov–20 Dec.*

Osteria Bellaria, Via Bellaria 14, **t** 0524 573 600 (*moderate*) West of town on the Piacenza road; puts *porcini* mushrooms and truffles in as many dishes as possible – *sott'olio* as an *antipasto*, in the *tortelli*, in the *tortino*, on the grill, by a steak. All are simply prepared and delicious – provided you like mushrooms and truffles, that is. Home-made desserts and local wines accompany the feast. *Closed Mon, most of Jan, and late July–mid-Aug.*

Busseto ✉ 43011

★★★I Due Foscari, Piazza Carlo Rossi 15, **t** 0524 930 031, **f** 0524 91625 (*moderate*). The finest place to stay in Busseto is, naturally, named after one of Verdi's operas, and is owned by the family of a tenor who often performs in them, Carlo Bergonzi: neo-Gothic and neo-Moorish, it's small, very comfortable (the public rooms in particular have lovely ceilings and furnishings) and will probably have no vacancies unless you reserve in advance. Here, too, you can find one of Busseto's best **restaurants**, featuring solid, traditional Parmigiano cooking. *Closed in Jan, Aug.*

★★★★Palazzo Calvi, Località Sambosetto 26, **t** 0524 90211, **f** 0524 90213 (*expensive*) Just outside the centre, with six welcoming rooms in the guest house of an 18th-century villa, in a lovely garden setting with a pool. The management is friendly and an added bonus is the excellent restaurant and *enoteca* for Verdian wine-tastings. *Closed Aug.*

South of Fidenza, **Salsomaggiore** ('Big Salt'), with its 109 hotels, is the largest and best-known of a cluster of saline water spas specializing in arthritic and rheumatic cures. It was popular with Italian royalty at the turn of the century, and is now favoured by opera singers. Its baths, the Terme Berzieri, are concentrated in a half-baked Liberty-style palace, while the Palazzo dei Congressi on Viale Romagnosi was once the grand hotel, owned by Cesar Ritz; past clients included Caruso, Toscanini and Queen Margherita of Italy. The lobby is still one of the grandest in Italy – a Liberty-arabesque fantasy with fabulously colourful frescoes by Galileo Chini. Another important spa nearby is **Tabiano Bagni**, with stinky sulphur springs.

Busseto and its Swan

Some 15km north of Fidenza on the road to Cremona, Busseto is the attractive, neatly rectangular walled town that gave the world Joe Green – Giuseppe Verdi. To Italians Verdi is not just another great composer, but the genius who expressed the national spirit of the Risorgimento in music: Italy's answer to Richard Wagner. In the

Campanini, Via Roncole Verdi 136, **t** 0524 92569 (*moderate*). Just outside Busseto, at Madonna Prati. It's been in the same family for generations. One of their concerns is producing *culatello*, made from the finest hind cuts of pork; the humid environment essential for its curing is supplied in spades by the winter fogs (the famously misty, moisty *culatello* capital, Zibello, is just up the road). Try it, and the other cold meats made by the family, as well as their exquisite home-made pasta. In spring they serve sturgeon in parchment, at other times *bolliti* and roast duck. No credit cards. *Closed Tues and Wed, and from mid-July to mid-Aug.*

Soragna ✉ 43019

★★★★**Locando del Lupo**, Corso Garibaldi 64, **t** 0524 597 100, **f** 0524 597 066, *locanda@polaris.it* (*expensive*). Occupies the charming 18th-century coach house and outbuildings belonging to the castle of the Meli Lupi princes. Exquisitely restored from its terracotta floors to its old oak beams. Baroque paintings hang on the walls, and special pride is taken in the wrought iron beds, with their dreamy mattresses and linen sheets. The excellent restaurant serves regional and international dishes; bike hire is another plus.

Antica Osteria Ardenga, at Via Maestra 6 in nearby Diolo, **t** 0524 599 337 (*moderate*).

Another atmospheric place and former possession of the Meli Lupi. (Bertolucci shot several scenes of La Luna here). All of the *salumi* is made *in casa*; follow this with *agnolini* in capon broth or *bomba di riso*, and roast duck or goose. *Closed Tues and Wed, and half of July.*

Fontanellato ✉ 43012

Locanda Nazionale, Via A. Costa 7, **t** 0521 822 602 (*cheap*). A small hotel with six simple rooms overlooking the castle; the **restaurant** (*moderate*) is excellent, offering Parmigiano home-cooking. All the pasta is home-made (try the *maltagliati* with asparagus), and hearty second courses include roast duck, *stracotto* (beef braised in red wine and stewed) and *tagliata* (steak) cooked with balsamic vinegar.

Sacca di Colorno ✉ 43052

Stendhal-Da Bruno, Via Sacca 80, **t** 0521 815 493 (*moderate*). In Sacca, north of Colorno on the banks of the Po, there is the perfect complement to a visit to the Farnese palace, inhabited in Stendhal's time by Marie Louise. Fish is the speciality here – eels and small fry from the Po, and denizens of the deep brought in daily from Chioggia. Great charcuterie, home-made desserts and wine, all served in a serene setting.

1850s, crowds at the opera screamed 'Viva Verdi!' – but not just as a tribute to the composer: everybody knew it was also a not-too-subtle demand for Vittorio Emanuele, Re D'Italia! Opera buffs can take in the complete 'Swan of Busseto' tour, beginning in the house at **Roncole**, 9km southeast of Busseto, where the composer was born in 1813 (the same year as Wagner), son of a grocer and tavern-keeper (*open April–Sept Tues–Sun 9.30–12.30 and 3–6; Oct and Nov Tues–Sun 9.30–12.30 and 2.30–5.30; adm*). While in Roncole, you can also visit the parish church where little Giuseppe was baptized and played the organ.

In Busseto proper a statue of Verdi relaxes in an armchair near the medieval castle, or **Rocca**, built by Pallavicini lord Oberto, who became the subject of Verdi's first and seldom-heard opera, Oberto. The Rocca contains the **Teatro Verdi**, modelled after La Scala, built in the composer's honour in 1845; Verdi frequently attended performances. The Rocca's Palazzo Pallavicino is now the **Museo Civico** (*t 0524 92487; castle, theatre and museum open Mar–Oct daily and the last two Sundays in Feb; guided tours at 9.45, 10.45, 11.45, 2.45, 3.45 and 4.45; adm*), full of Verdian memorabilia. With the proceeds from Rigoletto, Verdi built the **Villa Verdi**, in Sant'Agata di Villanova, 3km north of Busseto (*open April–Oct daily exc Mon, 8–12 and 2.30–6; adm*); it has a replica of the hotel room in Milan where Verdi died in 1901.

The Castles of Parma

The province of Parma is known for its beautiful castles, some of which lie between Busseto and Parma. The **Palazzo di Soragna** (*guided tours April–Oct Tues–Sun 9.30–12.30 and 3–7; Nov–Mar Tues–Sun 9–12 and 2.30–6; adm*), begun in the 8th century as a castle, was converted into a palace ten centuries later by its current owners, the Princes of Meli Lupi, and was frescoed by the likes of Parmigianino and Gentile da Fabriano. In Fontanellato the moated Renaissance **Castello di Sanvitale** (*open Nov–Mar daily for guided tours 9.30–12.30 and 3.30–7; April–Oct Mon–Sat 9.30–11.30 and 3–6, Sun 9.30–12 and 2.30–6; adm*) is much more of a fairy-tale castle. It is adorned inside with frescoes; the rich, sensuous Diana and Actaeon in the boudoir was painted by Parmigianino, hiding here on the run from the police after a spat with some monks in Parma. Another imposing fortress nearby, **Castel Guelfo** (*visible from the outside only*), once belonged to the Ghibelline Pallavicini family of Busseto, but was renamed as an insult by its Guelph captors in 1407.

In **Colorno**, just north of Parma on the road to Mantua, one of the Farnese dukes, Ranuccio II, converted an old castle into a 'miniature Versailles' in 1660 (*temporarily closed; ask at the Parma tourist office if it has reopened yet, or ring t 0521 312 545*). It has beautiful gardens, with canals, an *orangerie* – and tunnels: the later Bourbon rulers – who spent much time here – must have been nervous, for they installed escape hatches leading all over the countryside, one supposedly running all the way to Parma. Nearby **Castelnuovo Fogliani** (*open by appointment, t 0523 947 112*) is a medieval stronghold that was reshaped into an up-to-date palace with sumptuously decorated rooms and a large park by Luigi Vanvitelli, 18th-century court architect to the King of Naples and builder of the 'Italian Versailles' at Caserta. One other must-see castle in these parts is the **Rocca dei Rossi** at San Secondo Parmense (*t 0521 873 214; guided tours summer Tues, Wed, Fri 9–12, and Sun and hols 3–6; winter Tues–Sun 10, 11 and 3–6; adm*). Troilo Rossi I of the Rossi family made it into an elegant pleasure dome, commissioning the frescoes of the 'Wolf Room', and an original cycle on the *Golden Ass* of Apuleius. Troilo Rossi II added 12 scenes on the glory of the Rossi family.

Parma

Le Monde rates Parma as the best of all Italian cities to live in. Besides its general air of well-being and contentment, Parma's many admirers can cite her splendid churches and elegant lanes, her art and antiquities, the lyrical strains of grand opera that waft from her Teatro Regio – a house that honed the talents of the young Arturo Toscanini – and the glories of its famous cheese and ham at table as reasons not only to visit, but to return again and again. Parma is the place to see the masterpieces of Benedetto Antelami (1177–1233), the great sculptor trained in Provence whose

Getting Around

Parma has a small **airport** northwest of the city, t 0521 982 626, with services to Rome and a few other destinations, mostly within Italy (plus flights to London in summer).

The city is easy to reach by **rail**, on the main lines from Turin and Milan via Bologna to Florence and Rome. There are also lines to Brescia and to La Spezia on the Ligurian coast, and Rimini on the Adriatic. The station is north of the centre, on Piazzale Carlo Alberto Dalla Chiesa, at the end of Via Verdi; buses no.1 and no.8 link it to the city centre (though it's only a ten-minute walk).

The **bus** station, t 0521 273 251, is also on Piazzale C.A. Dalla Chiesa (which most people still call by its old name, 'Piazzale della Stazione'). TEP buses serve the villages of the province (there is an office on the west side of the piazza); Zani Autoservizi serves Venice, Rimini and the other resorts (t 0521 242 645); Autolinee Lorenzini, Viareggio and the Ligurian coast (t 0521 273 251).

Tourist Information

Strada Melloni 1/6, just off the main Strada Garibaldi, t 0521 218 889, f 0521 234 735 (*open Mon–Sat 9–7, Sun 9–1*).

Shopping

There are plenty of antique shops in Parma, around Via Nazario Sauro; on the third Sunday of every month a huge antiques fair, the **Mercatino dell'Antiquariato**, takes place at Fontanellato. **Fashion shops** cluster around Borgo Angelo Mazza, along with perfume shops that will sell you a bottle of *Violetti di Parma* – the essence of violets worn by Marie Louise, who commissioned her hairdresser Borsari to come up with something nice – or one of Borsari's 300 other scents.

Then there's **food**: this is the city that hosts a biannual world food fair, the Cibus, in even-numbered years; a more convenient place to stock up for a picnic or pick up some local specialities to take home is the main market in Piazza Ghiaia, by the river. Otherwise, try **Specialità di Parma**, Strada Farini 9/c, a magnificently stocked emporium supplying all the regional delicacies.

For tours of the establishments that make Parma's prime products – prosciutto, wine and Parmesan cheese – ask at the Parma tourist office, or at one of the cooperatives: the **Consorzio Prosciutto**, t 0521 243 987, and the **Consorzio Parmigiano**, t 0521 292 700.

Where to Stay

Parma ✉ 43100

Parma's trade fair grounds are bustling in May and September, when you should reserve a couple of months in advance.

Very Expensive

****Grand Hotel Baglione, Viale Piacenza 12/c, t 0521 292 929, f 0521 292 828, *ghb.parma@beedit.it*. Overlooking the Parco Ducale, slightly outside the centre; the public rooms are Liberty-style, full of lovely furniture, and bedrooms are quiet.

Expensive

****Hotel Villa Ducale, Via del Popolo 35, t 0521 272 727, f 0521 780 756. Two kilometres from the centre of Parma, at Moletolo, lies this 18th-century country villa that belonged to Marie Louise. A quiet haven set in its own park of lawns and century trees, it deftly combines old and new.

****Park Hotel Stendhal, Via Bodoni 3, t 0521 208 057, f 0521 285 655, *stendhal.htl@rsad-vnet.it*. Right in the heart of town alongside the Piazza Pilotta, this is an older hotel with good facilities. Prices are higher in season.

baptistry here introduced the Italians to the idea of a building as a unified work of architecture and sculpture. Parma's distinctive school of art began relatively late, with the arrival of Antonio Allegri Correggio (1494–1534), whose highly personal and self-taught techniques of *sfumato* and sensuous subtlety deeply influenced his many followers, most notably Francesco Mazzola, better known as Parmigianino.

Moderate

★★★Torino, Borgo Angelo Mazza 7, **t** 0521 281 046, **f** 0521 230 725. Centrally located with ample, comfortable rooms and very friendly staff; have your morning coffee in a Liberty-style breakfast room, or in the flower-filled courtyard. Free bicycles for clients will get you about town, Parma-style. *Closed most of Aug, and two weeks in Jan.*

★★★Button, Borgo della Salina 7, **t** 0521 208 039, **f** 0521 238 783. In the knot of small streets behind the Palazzo del Comune, almost as cute as its name; rooms are small but very comfortable. *Closed in July.*

★★★Brenta, Via Gambattista Borghesi 12, **t** 0521 208 093, **f** 0521 208 094, *stebrenta@iol.it*. A little family-run place, also near the station, simple and fairly quiet.

Cheap

★Lazzaro, Via XX Marzo 14, **t** 0521 208 944. Near the cathedral and baptistry, an old-fashioned *locanda* – a good solid *trattoria* with well-kept rooms upstairs – the only cheap rooms in the centre.

Eating Out

The pig is like the music of Verdi; nothing in it of waste.
old Parma saying

Music and food are the Parmigiani's ruling passions; a perfect aria is greeted with the same rapt silence as a perfect dish of pasta, dusted with freshly grated Parmesan cheese. Dishes to look out for, besides the city's famous ham and cheese, are *stracotto* (stewed beef), *carpaccio* (raw beef or sometimes horse), the various methods of serving *carciofi* (artichokes) – in fritters, pasta dishes and in crêpes – and the famous pasta dishes: *tortelli di erbetta* (stuffed with *ricotta* and spinach, and served with melted butter and Parmesan), or *di zucca* (with pumpkin), or with potato.

Very Expensive

La Greppia, Strada Garibaldi 39, **t** 0521 233 686. Housed in a former stable, 'The Manger' presents some of Parma's most modern and innovative cuisine, based on local traditions. There's a delicious selection of *pasta di verdure* (made with spinach or tomatoes) and other original vegetable dishes, and good *secondi*, all prepared before your eyes in the glass kitchen. *Closed Mon, Tues and July.*

Angiol d'Or, Vicolo Scutellari 1, **t** 0521 282 632. Near the Duomo, with seating outside that allows you to contemplate the baptistry while enjoying a steaming plate of *tortelli d'erbetta*, *tortellini di zucca*, pasta with sea bass and peas, or tripe with *parmigiano*. For dessert, try the *tortino di riso* with grape must. *Closed Sun, and part of Aug.*

Expensive

Cocchi, Via Gramsci 16, **t** 0521 981 990. Elegant but not fussy, dedicated to bringing out the finest in Parma's fine ingredients: *culatello di Zibello* and *prosciutto*, rich *minestrone*, various *bolliti*, delicately stewed *baccalà*, stuffed veal, and old-fashioned home-made ice cream. *Closed Sat all year, Sun in June and July; all August.*

Il Cortile, Borgo Paglia 3, **t** 0521 285 779. Stylish, intimate, located in a covered interior courtyard, and serves a delicious mix of traditional and modern dishes – pasta with asparagus tips, or pistachios, or shellfish, sea bass cooked in salt, sturgeon grilled with chives. *Closed Mon lunch, Sun and Aug.*

Il Trovatore, near the station, Via Affò 2/a, **t** 0521 236 905. Recently opened: an elegant restaurant run by a talented young chef, who serves the classics along with a choice of less traditional dishes, such as venison with fruits of the forest, or turbot *involtini* accompanied by lemon and potatoes sautéed with rosemary. Dessert wines by the glass; and a good value four-course menu with wine available. *Closed Sun.*

History

Parma is a fine example of how Italians can adapt and even prosper in the face of continual political uncertainty. After starting out as a small Roman way-station on the Via Aemilia, the fledgling medieval town of Parma found itself insecurely poised on the edge of the spheres of influence of pope and emperor, a conflict echoed

Al Tramezzino, Via del Bono 51/b (on the east side of town, at San Lazzaro Parmense). One of Parma's most popular eateries. It started as a sandwich bar and has kept its friendly atmosphere, while serving some of the city's most creative cuisine, with an emphasis on seafood, based on the finest ingredients. Excellent list of wines and spirits. *Closed Mon, and first half of July.*

Moderate

Antica Cereria, Borgo Rodolfo Tanzi 5, **t** 0521 207 387. Near the Parco Ducale, occupies an old candle factory and serves one of the region's famous dishes, *bomba di riso con il piccione* (a moulded round of rice around boned pigeon in mushroom sauce, baked in the oven), and delicious home-made desserts. *Closed Mon, Aug.*

Vecchio Molinetto, Viale Milazzo 39, **t** 0521 253 941, near the Villetta cemetery; an unpretentious place offering good honest local cuisine – great *risotto* baked with veal and *involtini alla Molinetto. Closed Mon and Aug.*

Trattoria dei Corrieri, Strada del Conservatorio 1, **t** 0521 234 426. Traditional Parma cuisine at very reasonable prices
served in an old postal relay station near the University; the walls are a veritable museum of old Parma photos and relics. The menu usually features salami and ham *antipasti, carpaccio* with rocket, *pasta alla parmigiana,* quail, and a filling *bollito misto* (boiled meats). This is the place, and everybody knows it; get in early for a seat at lunch. *Closed Sun.*

Antica Osteria Fontana, Strada Farini 24a, **t** 0521 286 037. Has been there for donkey's years; although wine is the main focus, there's a small menu of typical dishes at lunch time, while in the evening the Fontana becomes a wine bar, with a good selection of sandwiches and charcuterie to make up a light meal around a bottle. *Closed Sun and Mon, most of Aug.*

Trattoria Qui Cosi', Borgo San Biagio 6, **t** 0521 230 584. Near the cathedral, a new place that aims to please; *tortellini all'erbe* or with pumpkin, and a very nice *brasaole al barolo* with fried *polenta. Closed Thurs.*

Lazzaro, Borgo XX Marzo, **t** 0521 208 944 (with rooms, *see above*). All the *tortelli* and the usual favourites; for a light lunch there are big salads (*insalatone*) and crêpes.

Bottiglia Azzurra, Borgo Felino 63, **t** 0521 285 842. Very popular; in the evening it draws a young crowd to its long narrow dining rooms crammed with tables. Good food on a menu that changes every week, a wide choice of Italian and French cheeses and other things that go well with the big wine list. Stays open late. *Closed Sun, July and Aug.*

Entertainment and Nightlife

Opera mobilizes a more enthusiastic local audience in Parma than just about anywhere else in Italy. The main season at the **Teatro Regio** runs from December to March, with some concerts during the rest of the year: **t** 0521 218 678, *www.teatroregioparma.org* (*box office open weekdays 10–2 and 5–7, Sat 9.30–12.30 and 4–7*). There are occasional performances at the **Teatro Farnese**.

Parma also hosts two **music competitions**, one for conductors at the end of August, and another for opera singers in October. In September there's also the **Verdi Festival**; for information, contact Fondazione Verdi Festival, Strada Farini 34, **t** 0521 289 028, **f** 0521 282 141. In the **summer concerts** are also held in the surrounding **castles** – the tourist office provides a full list of forthcoming events.

Nearby **Busseto**, Verdi's home, has its own **philharmonic** and chorus, and puts on its own small opera season in December and January; for information and tickets contact the tourist office, Piazzale Verdi 10, **t** 0524 92487.

internally by the factions of the Da Correggio and Rossi families. The *popolo* began to assert itself in 1250 with the aid of a tailor called Barisello, and commoners ran the town for a whole nine years. From then on various *signori* – the Visconti, Della Scala, Este, Sforza and others – ruled the city until its incorporation in the Papal States in 1521. Even this endured only until 1545, when Pope Paul III (otherwise known as

Alessandro Farnese) required a tax farm for his natural son, Pier Luigi Farnese, and created the Duchy of Parma and Piacenza to fit the bill.

Pier Luigi's own ambitions led shortly to his assassination by a Spanish-led conspiracy, but all in all the Farnese duchy gave Parma a measure of stability. In 1748, with the extinction of the male Farnese line, it passed to a branch of the French Bourbons, who ruled it until the Napoleonic era. The year 1815 saw the arrival of Parma's best-loved ruler, Napoleon's estranged Empress Marie Louise, who was given the duchy by the Congress of Vienna. In 1859 mass unrest forced her to abdicate; a year later, after a plebiscite, the city was incorporated into the Kingdom of Italy.

Palazzo della Pilotta

Arriving by train or bus in Parma, the **Museo Archeologico Nazionale** (*open Tues–Sun 9–7; adm*), one of the first buildings you notice is also, unfortunately, the most pathetic: the ungainly, unfinished and, since 1944, bomb-mutilated Palazzo della Pilotta, built for the Farnese. Begun in 1602 by gloomy Duke Ranuccio, it was named after *pelote*, a ball game once played in its courtyard. But looks are deceiving, for within this patched-together shell are Parma's greatest treasures. A grand staircase leads to the museum, founded in 1760 and containing finds from the excavations at Roman *Velleia* (*see p.505*). The single most important exhibit is the *Tabula Alimentaria*, a large bronze tablet that records private citizens' dole contributions in Trajan's time, as well as Egyptian sarcophagi, Greek vases from Etruscan tombs, and Roman statues including one of Nero as a boy.

On the second floor, the **Galleria Nazionale** (*open daily except Mon, 9–1.30; adm*) was founded even earlier, in 1752. To reach it, you pass through the fine wooden **Teatro Farnese**, built in a hurry in 1618–19 by Palladio's pupil, Giambattista Aleotti to honour Duke Cosimo of Florence – who never showed up. In 1944 a bomb tore the theatre into splinters and sawdust, but it has since been restored according to the motto of Italian restorers: '*dov'era, com'era*'.

Most of the gallery's paintings are from Emilia-Romagna and Tuscany. Early Renaissance works are by the Tuscans Gaddi, Giovanni di Paolo and Fra Angelico, and the Emilians Simone de' Crocefissi and Loschi – top dog of the Parma quattrocento (his St Jerome holds a toddler of a lion paternally by the paw). Further along there's a lovely portrait sketch by Leonardo, *La Scapigliata*, paintings by Venetian Cima da Conegliano, and Sebastiano del Piombo's portrait of the handsome if calamitous Medici pope, Clement VII.

Some of Correggio's most celebrated works are here – the tender *Madonna di San Gerolamo* and the *Madonna della Scodella* – as well as Parmigianino's *Marriage of St Catherine* and the flirtatious *Turkish Slave*; Sebastiano Ricci's huge mythological *Rape of Helen* came here after two centuries entertaining the nurses of Parma's Foundlings' Hospital. Non-Italians include El Greco's *Guarigione del Cieco*, Peter Brueghel the Younger, Van Dyck, and Holbein's portrait of the sharp-featured Erasmus. Alongside gigantic classical statues of Hercules and Bacchus – looted by the Farnese clan from Palatine in Rome – are portraits of the looters, and Canova's statue of Marie Louise on her throne. On the same floor as the gallery, the **Palatine Library** (*open Mon,*

Wed, Fri 8.30–5.30, Tues, Thurs 8.30–6.45, Sat 9–12.30) has a vast collection of incunabula, codices, manuscripts and editions published by the city's famous printer, Bodoni, who gave his name to the popular type he invented.

Piazza della Pace and Around

Once a car park, the piazza facing Palazzo della Pilotta has become the subject of a controversial planning project, providing Parma with an interminable soap opera for most of the 1990s while the politicians argued over various plans and counter-plans for its redevelopment. More complications were added when the builders – inevitably – uncovered some important archaeological remains, and the piazza spent years closed off behind an ugly board fence. The new design is now well under way, trees are being planted, and all should be complete in 2001.

In the meantime, the fat and not-so-fat ladies still sing at the celebrated **Teatro Regio** (*entrance in Strada Garibaldi; tours Mon–Fri 10–1, 4–6, except during the opera season*), built by Marie Louise in 1829. This is one of operatic Italy's holy-of-holies, and the best place to hear Parma's favourite son, Verdi. Its audiences are contentious and demanding, and each year tenors and sopranos from all over the world submit either to avalanches of flowers or catcalls from the famous upper balconies, the *loggioni*. Toscanini began his career playing in its orchestra, since re-named in his honour.

Across Strada Garibaldi stands one of Parma's grand churches, the **Madonna della Steccata,** begun in 1521 though not entirely completed until 1730; inside are some hyper-elegant frescoes by Parmigianino, including the *Wise and Foolish Virgins, Adam and Eve, Aaron* and *Moses.* He never finished his commission, and the church canons briefly had him jailed for breach of contract; gossips said the artist's obsession with his alchemical experiments was taking up all his time.

Just to the north, the huge palace called the Riserva, once used for entertainments and to house guests of the dukes, now is shared by the post office, several shops and the **Museo Glauco Lombardi** (*open Tues–Sat 10–3, Sun 9–1; adm*). Few museums are so successful in summoning up the spirit of a distant age. Its grand Empire-style salons are filled with art and the personal possessions of Marie Louise from the days when Napoleon was still on top and she was empress of most of Europe.

Just off the piazza on Via Melloni is one of the most remarkable sights of Parma: the **Camera di San Paolo** (*open daily except Mon 9–1.30; adm*), in the ex-convent of San Paolo. In 1519 its worldly abbess, Giovanna Piacenza, hired Correggio to fresco her refectory with mythological scenes representing the theme of 'the conquest of moral virtue', along lines discussed by her learned circle of humanist friends; he portrayed the abbess herself as a sensuous goddess Diana over the fireplace, with the enigmatic inscription *Ignem Gladio ne Fodias,* 'Do not use the sword to poke the fire'– leading the pope to cloister the nuns in 1524.

The decorative scheme in the vault is unique, with sixteen putti set over sixteen emblems, of mysterious import. The abbess wasn't the only woman in the Renaissance to hide her meaning in secret code: Isabella d'Este did the same in Mantua. Another room contains equally mysterious allegorical frescoes and grotesques by Araldi (1514).

Piazza Duomo

Strada Pisacane connects Piazza della Pace to Piazza Duomo, the heart of medieval Parma and the site of its superb cathedral and baptistry. The **Duomo** (*open daily 9–12.30 and 3–6*) is ambitious, angular Romanesque, embellished with rows of shallow arches; three tiers cross the façade, creating an illusion of depth around the central arched window. The pattern continues in the rich decoration of the apses and dome, but the campanile is Gothic. Reliefs of the Labours of the Months decorate the façade's central portal; frescoes cover every inch of the interior, which has two masterpieces: a relief of the *Deposition from the Cross* by Antelami and, in the dome, Correggio's *Assumption* (1526–30), celebrated since Vasari wrote of its three-dimensional portrayal of clouds, angels and saints – one of the first illusionistic dome frescoes, anticipating the Baroque. Come on a sunny morning to get the full effect.

The octagonal **Baptistry** (*open daily 9–12.30 and 3–6; adm*), built of pale rose-coloured marble from Verona, is one of the jewels of the Italian Romanesque (it may be familiar from *panettone* boxes), designed in 1196 by Antelami, who also carved the remarkable ribbon frieze of animals and allegories encircling it. Its architect planned the mystic octagon with a decorative *summa theologica* meant to represent everything on earth and in the heavens, but the meaning behind all the winged cats, archers, griffons and sea serpents is as elusive as Correggio's ceiling at San Paolo; the Tale of Barlaam, portrayed over the south door, was a popular medieval legend that migrated from India – based on a moral fable told by Buddha. Antelami also carved the doorways dedicated to the Virgin Mary and the Last Judgement, and the statues in the niches. Inside are his famous reliefs of the Months, with the Labours and zodiacal signs, Spring and Winter. The 16-sided interior is almost entirely covered with paintings, one of the most complete ensembles of Italian medieval art: those in the upper portion, from the 1200s, are tempera, not true fresco. The vault is divided into six zones with a starry heaven; below is a grab-bag of biblical figures.

San Giovanni Evangelista, the church just behind the cathedral (*open daily 9–12 and 3–6, Sun 10–1 and 3.30–6*), shelters a key work of the High Renaissance under its Baroque skin: Correggio's fresco in the dome of the *Vision of St John*. This is one of the most carefully planned ceiling frescoes ever: starting from the door, the composition gradually reveals itself as you walk down the nave. Sadly, when the church was remodelled in 1587 Correggio's reputation was at a low, and the rest of his ceiling was destroyed, though a fresco of St John survives over the door north of the altar. Some of the other frescoes are by Parmigianino. Near the church you can visit the historic **Spezieria di S. Giovanni** on Borgo Pipa (*open daily except Mon 9–1.30; adm*), which dispensed drugs non-stop from 1298 until 1881; its grand Renaissance-Baroque interior contains alembics, medieval pharmaceutical instruments and paintings of great doctors of antiquity – real and mythological – from Apollo to Hippocrates.

Piazza Garibaldi

In company with the other old gents of Parma, Garibaldi and Correggio, or at least their statues, spend the day in the modern centre of the city, Piazza Garibaldi. Here, too, stands the yellow 17th-century **Palazzo del Governatore**, with its intricate sundials telling you when noon reaches towns from Quebec to Constantinople. South of the piazza on Via Cavestro, the **Pinacoteca Giuseppe Stuard** (*open Tues–Sat 9–6.30, Sun 9–1.20; adm*) holds a small collection that ranges from trecento Tuscans to 19th-century Parma salon painters. East of the Piazza, on Via della Reppublica, have a look inside **Sant'Antonio Abate** for the bizarre late Baroque vaulting and false ceiling – the architect, Ferdinando Bibiena, was also a stage designer.

South of the city centre, the **Cittadella** was Alessandro Farnese's only gift to Parma. Most of this huge fortress has been demolished, and the ground converted into a park, though some of the ornate Baroque gates survive.

Paganini, Toscanini and Stendhal

Parma's west end, across the river, is called the Oltratorrente. It is home to some interesting churches, notably the proto-Baroque **SS Annunziata** (1561), just over the Ponte di Mezzo on Via d'Azeglio, and **Santa Maria del Quartieri** (1604) in Piazza Picelli. Here too is the **Parco Ducale**, built by the Farnese.

There are three musical and literary pilgrimages to make in Parma, and two of them are in the Oltratorrente. The first is to the **tomb of Paganini**, the embalmed wizard of catgut and bow who lies decked out in virtuoso splendour in Villetta cemetery, after the rest of Europe, suspecting his talents were diabolic, refused him Christian burial (*15min walk from the centre, on the west side of the river; open daily all year 7.45–12.30; May–Sept also 6–7; Oct and Feb–April also 2.30–5.30; Nov–Jan also 2–5*).

The **birthplace of Arturo Toscanini** (1867–1957) is a modest house at Borgo Rudolfo Tanzi 13 (*open Tues–Sat 10–1 and 3–6, Sun 10–1; adm*), between the Ponte di Mezzo and the Parco Ducale; it contains memorabilia and a copy of every record he ever made. He became an enthusiastic Fascist in 1919, but later turned against the movement's violent *squadre* and Mussolini's dictatorship, and was beaten up for refusing to play the Fascist anthem at a concert in Bologna.

Stendhal aficionados will be glad to know that there really is a **Charterhouse of Parma**, the Certosa (*open Mon–Fri 8–12 and 2–5, Sat and Sun 8–12*), although it bears no resemblance to the novelist's invention. Located 4km east of town (bus no.10), it was founded in 1281 but rebuilt in the 17th century, and now serves as a military school. The cloister is out of bounds, but you can visit the church's frescoed interior.

Four More Castles

Further afield there are Parma's famous castles, each reachable by bus from the city. In the foothills to the south – where Parma hams and Parmigiano cheeses are produced aplenty – and visible from miles around (on the Langhirano road), towers **Torrechiara** (*open April–Sept Tues–Fri 8.30–3.30, Sat and Sun 10–6.30; Oct–Mar Tues–Sun 8.30–3.30; adm*), a castle of brick and fantasy almost unchanged since the 15th century, and defended by four mighty towers. Inside there is an elegant courtyard with ornate terracotta tiles; frescoes of acrobats performing impossible feats with hoops on the backs of lions; and a fresco cycle by Bembo in the 'Golden Bedchamber' depicting the tragic tale of the original owner and his young lover Bianca, who died in his arms in this room.

Another castle, the 15th-century **Bardi**, perches atop its own hill southwest of Parma and has beautiful beamed ceilings (*open Mar and Oct Sat 2–6, Sun 10–6; April–May Sat 2–7, Sun 10–7; June and Sept Mon–Sat 2–7, Sun 10–7; July daily 10–7; Aug Mon–Sat 10–7, Sun 10–8; Nov Sat 2–5, Sun 10–5; adm*). On the local road to Reggio Emilia via Montecchio lies **Montechiarugolo** (*open Mar–Nov Sun only, 10–12.30 and 3–6.30*), built by the Visconti in 1313 with a Torrechiara-style tower; it too has a lavish bedchamber with frescoed scenes of farming, study, navigation and war. **Compiano** (*open July and Aug daily 3–6.30; April, May, June and Sept Sun 3–6.30; rest of the year by appointment, t 0525 825 125; adm*), in the mountains on the SS513, has something rare in Italy – ghosts – and a curious museum of English freemasonry.

Reggio Emilia

A bright, prosperous agricultural city, Reggio Emilia was the Roman *Regium Lepidi*. It passed a Middle Ages notable for its violent factionalism, and from 1409 to 1796 was ruled by the Este family of Ferrara, during which time its most famous son, Ludovico Ariosto (1474–1533), author of *Orlando Furioso*, was born. Nowadays it is noted for its numerous ballet schools, its balsamic vinegar and its version of Parmesan cheese, Parmigiano-Reggiano, which tastes exactly the same as Parma's to any sane person.

Piazza Prampolini

Reggio grew up on the Via Aemilia, which now divides the old and new parts of the city. In the older, southern half, Piazza Prampolini is the civic and ecclesiastical heart of Reggio, with its peculiar **Duomo** topped by a single octagonal tower. Most of its Romanesque features were remodelled away in the 16th century, although fine statues of Adam and Eve were added to the façade, and in the tower niche there is a copper Madonna flanked by the cathedral donors. On the same piazza, **Palazzo del Monte di Pietà** has a lofty Torre dell'Orologio. The **Palazzo Comunale** is where the Tricolore was first proclaimed the Italian national flag in 1797, during the second congress of Napoleon's Cispadane Republic, a very short-lived entity that covered the area between Reggio, Mantua, Ferrara and Bologna. A covered arcade called the **Broletto**, where the bishops of Reggio used to grow their cabbages, leads behind the cathedral to **Piazza San Prospero**, the main market square and a wonderful place to see and stock up on local produce. The 16th-century **Basilica di San Prospero** (*currently under restoration*) is noted for its fine choir, with frescoes and inlaid stalls.

North of the Via Aemilia

Via Aemilia is now Reggio's main shopping street, passing through **Piazza Cesare Battisti**, roughly the site of Roman Reggio's forum. To its north Reggio's vast Piazza Cavour has the 19th-century **Teatro Municipale**, the town's opera house. Crowned by a surplus of musing statuary, it is one of Italy's most lavish theatres, built to upstage the Regio in Parma. It largely succeeds: performances of opera, concerts and plays (*from December to March*) are of a high quality, if not quite as prestigious as Parma's.

Tourist Information

Piazza Prampolini 5, by the cathedral: t 0522 451 152, f 0522 436 739; www.municipio.re.it.

Where to Stay and Eat

Reggio Emilia ✉ 42100

****Delle Notarie, Via Palazzolo 5, t 0522 435 500, f 0522 453 737 (*expensive*). Recently opened. Offers discreet luxury and lovely old wooden floors in a palace close to the cathedral. Spacious bedrooms. *Closed Aug.*

****Posta, Piazza del Monte, t 0522 432 944, f 0522 452 602, *hotelposta@citynet.it* (*expensive*). For a historic stay in the heart of Reggio, you can't beat the 'Post', in the 14th-century Palazzo del Capitano del Popolo, later home to Francesco d'Este. In the 1500s the palace became an inn; the public rooms still have frescoes. Bike hire available.

***Park, Via de Ruggiero 1, t 0522 292 141, f 0522 292 143 (*moderate*). Delightful, comfortable and friendly small hotel, 4km from the centre of town in a tranquil setting with garden and restaurant, and a minibus service into town.

Like Parma, Reggio is a major producer of Parmesan cheese (Parmigiano-Reggiano), and like Modena distils *aceto balsamico*. Reggio produces a savoury vegetable tart ideal for a picnic lunch, called *erbazzone*; good ones come from **Forno Katia**, Via Terrachini 35/c.

Convivium, Vicolo Trivelli 2, t 0522 453 534 (*expensive*). In the heart of town, run by a family from Liguria; plenty of excellent seafood dishes and pesto side by side with Emilian favourites. *Closed Sun lunch, Tues, and late Aug–early Sept.*

Trattoria della Ghiara, Vicolo Folletto 1/c, t 0522 435 755 (*moderate*). Near Piazza Roversi, a bastion of tradition but one where the heavier dishes are given a light modern touch so you can walk rather than waddle out; *salumi* and delicious *cappelletti in brodo*. There's a small but good selection of regional wines. *Closed Sun, last two weeks in June and most of Aug.*

Canossa, Via Roma 37, t 0522 454 196 (*moderate*). A fine place to try the various hams of this area, served together as an antipasto; other specialities include *tortelli* made on the premises. *Closed Wed.*

Sotto Broletto, Via Broletto 1, t 0522 439 676 (*cheap*). A thriving pizzeria in the arcade leading off Piazza Prampolini. *Closed Thurs.*

Correggio ✉ 42015

****Dei Medaglioni, Corso Mazzini 8, t 0522 632 233, f 0522 693 258 (*expensive*). Housed in a converted palace, with stylish rooms. *Closed much of Aug and Christmas.*

Brescello ✉ 42041

La Tavernetta del Lupo, Piazza M. Pallini at Località Sorbolo Levante, t 0522 680 509 (*expensive*). Not your typical Emilian restaurant; come here for skilful Italian *cucina nuova* that will surprise your tastebuds with dishes such as *gnocchi* made from carrots with basil and pine nuts, or salmon with raspberry vinegar and poppyseeds. *Closed Mon, early Jan, and Aug.*

Guastalla ✉ 42016

***Old River, Viale Po 2, t 0522 838 401, f 0522 824 676 (*moderate*). The best place to stay north of Reggio; excellent rooms in a pleasant green setting.

Rigoletto, in Reggiolo, east of Guastalla, Piazza Martiri 29, t 0522 973 520 (*very expensive*). The best restaurant in these parts. Set in a late 18th-century villa with a pretty garden, its talented chef works wonders with fine ingredients. Raisin and *gorgonzola* bread, *tortelli* filled with catfish in a buttery dill sauce, stuffed baby squid in a salad of toasted almonds and crispy bacon, lamb in grape must, or cray- and shell-fish *zuppa*. For the sweet of tooth there are sublime desserts, and the wine list is superb. Two special menus are offered, one featuring seafood and the other land food. *Closed Jan and Aug.*

Canossa ✉ 42026

La Cueva, Località. Giarretta 7, t 0522 876 316 (*moderate*). Just south of Canossa at Currada, an old country mill on the banks of the Enza has been converted into a lovely country restaurant, featuring the beloved *gnocco frito* with the *salumi*, *tortellini* and grilled meats. *Closed Mon, Tues, Jan.*

The **Museo Civici** (*open Tues–Fri 9–12, Sat and Sun 9–12 and 3–6; 1 Jul–15 Aug also 9pm–midnight; last two weeks of Aug Sat and Sun 3–6 only*), a block east on Via Secchi near a powerful monument to the Martyrs of the Resistance, is a charmingly old-fashioned museum containing everything from Roman mosaics of the two-faced god Janus to stuffed crocodiles, from the buxom Neolithic *Chiozza Venus* to the works of obscure Emilian painters; one room is dedicated to the humorous socialist 'painter of the Resistance' Mazzacurti. In Reggio's **Giardino Pubblico**, site of an Este castle, is the imposing 1st-century AD funerary monument of a Roman family, the **Tomb of the Concordii**. Near here is the very eclectic **Galleria Parmeggiani** (*same hours as Museo Civici*), with a 16th-century Moresco doorway brought over from Valencia.

In San Maurizio, 3km east of Reggio, **Villa Il Mauriziano** was the home of Ariosto's family; some of the rooms have been restored to the appearance they had when the poet came to visit from Ferrara – charming frescoes of love scenes and literati (*open Tues–Sun 9–11; for visits outside these hours, call t 0522 456 5271; adm free*).

Around Reggio

Some 15km northeast of Reggio, **Correggio** is a pretty town with old arcaded streets which suffered an earthquake in October 1996; all the damage now seems to have been repaired. It is the birthplace of the painter Antonio Allegri, better known as Correggio (d. 1534); his home on Borgo Vecchio was reconstructed in 1755. The brick Renaissance Palazzo dei Principi, contains the **Museo Civico** (*open the 1st and 3rd weekends of each month, Sat and Sun 10.30–1 and 3–7*), with a Christ by Mantegna and some lovely cinquecento Flemish tapestries. The Renaissance church of **San Quirino** is attributed to the Farnese's favourite architect, Vignola. Northwest in **Novellara**, the Gonzaga dukes of Mantua built a fine castle (14th century), now the town hall and **Museo Gonzaga** (*closed for restoration, but should reopen soon; t 0522 655 426*), with frescoes and faience chemists' jars of crabs' eyes and ground stag horn.

On the banks of the Po, **Gualtieri**, once Lombard *Castrum Walterii*, has the grand arcaded Piazza Bentivoglio – spacious enough to fit the humble village's 6,000 people and their cars and tractors too – and the 16th-century brickwork Palazzo Bentivoglio. The palace (*closed for restoration*) has some fine frescoes in its Sala dei Giganti, depicting scenes from Tasso's *Gerusalemme Liberata*. Another old Lombard town, **Guastalla** (originally *Warstal*) – much sought afer for its strategic position on the Po – was subsequently held by the Canossa, Visconti, da Coreggio and Gonzaga dynasties. It conserves many Gonzaga mementos: the grid of streets centred on the 'noble sreet', Via Gonzaga; the sad, abandoned Ducal Palace; and a bronze statue of the *condottiere*, Ferrante Gonzaga, who shaped the town. Outside Guastalla is a fine 10th-century Romanesque church, the Basilica della Pieve. Further down the Po, on the outskirts of Luzzara, the former convent has been converted into the charming **Museo Comunale dei Pittori Naïf**, with a permanent collection of naïf art starring Antonio Ligabue of Gualtieri (*open 15 June–15 Sept Tues–Sat 10–12 and 3.30–6.30, Sun 3.30–6.30; adm*).

Back west along the Po, **Brescello** is famous in Italian popular culture as the home-town of Giovanni Guareschi's Don Camillo, the priest of the post-war era, eternally, fraternally at war with the Communist mayor Peppone. The pair are immortalized in Fernandel's films, gentle parables that perfectly captured the mood of a recovering postwar Italy, which had seen enough of the bleakness of *cinema verità*. For fans, there is a **Museo Don Camillo e Peppone** (*open in winter daily 3–6, Sun 10–12 and 3–6; rest of the year ring* **t** *0522 962 158*).

All of these villages are accessible by bus or train from Reggio; for **Canossa**, south of Reggio, you'll have to drive, or else walk 7km from the nearest bus stop. Its name will ring a bell with anyone who ever studied medieval history: it's the spot where an emperor once humbled himself before a pope, kneeling in the snow for three days begging forgiveness. It all started in 951, when a knight named Atto Adalbert gave Queen Adelaide refuge here from a usurper, Berengar of Ivrea. German King Otto I came over the Alps to defeat Berengar, married Adelaide, and had them crowned Holy Roman Emperor and Empress – the birth of the post-Charlemagne empire that was the mainspring of Italian history for the next 700 years. Meanwhile, Atto's descendants, the di Canossa dynasty, were gaining their own fame: the most powerful was the charismatic and warlike Countess Matilda. In 1077, Emperor Henry IV deposed Pope Gregory VII; when the pope in turn excommunicated the emperor, Matilda was instrumental in bringing Henry to Canossa on his knees in the snow to apologize. Gregory later saw Rome sacked by imperial forces, and died in exile, but Canossa was a turning point – for the next two centuries, the popes held the moral high ground over the kings and barons of Europe. Today the impregnable eyrie of the **Castello di Canossa** is a scenic and tranquil ruin; historic pageants are sometimes staged inside.

Modena

Modena puts on a class act – 'Mink City' they call it, the city with Italy's highest per capita income, a city with 'a psychological need for racing cars' according to the late Enzo Ferrari, whose famous flame-red chariots compete with the shiny beasts churned out by cross-town rival Maserati. Sleek and speedy, Modena also has a lyrical side of larger-than-life proportions: Luciano Pavarotti was born here, and its scenographic streets take on an air of mystery and romance when enveloped in the winter mists rising from the Po.

Known in Roman days as *Mutina*, Modena first came to note in the 11th–12th centuries under Countess Matilda, powerful ally of the pope (*see* above); under her rule the city began its great cathedral (1099). When it became an independent *comune*, however, Modena's Ghibelline party dominated in response to the Guelph policies of arch rival, Bologna. In 1288 the city came under the control of Obizzo II d'Este, duke of Ferrara, and the Este Duchy of Modena endured until 1796; with the building of the Ducal Palace, the Corso Canalgrande and other projects under Francesco I (1629–58) and his successors, Modena was transformed into a model Baroque city. A feebly independent duchy was recreated by the Vienna Congress in 1815, only for Modena, like Parma, to be swept into the Kingdom of Italy by the wave of nationalistic feeling in 1859–60.

Duomo di San Geminiano

Via Aemilia is Modena's main thoroughfare, and it is in the centre of this city that the old Roman highway picks up one of its loveliest gems, the cobbled and partially porticoed Piazza Grande, site of Modena's celebrated Romanesque **Duomo di San Geminiano**. Begun with funds from Countess Matilda in 1099, the cathedral was designed by a master-builder named Lanfranco and completed in the 13th century. Curiously, its main features are Ghibelline-Lombard; Lanfranco followed the bidding of Modena's burghers to show their independence both from Matilda and from the powerful Abbey of Nonantola. Complementing the Duomo's fine proportions are the magnificent carvings by the 12th-century sculptor Wiligelmo above the three main entrances and elsewhere around the church. His followers, and after them the anonymous Lombard sculptors and architects known as the Campionese masters, carried on the work, making this cathedral a living museum of medieval sculpture.

Wiligelmo's friezes on either side of the main **Lion Portal** illustrate scenes from the medieval mystery play on the Book of Genesis, the Jeu d'Adam. His **South Portal** depicts the life of Modena's 4th-century patron, St Geminiano. The weights and measures carved into the façade, where a Medusa hides amid the foliage, recall the days when the daily market was held in the square.

Another contemporary, the 'Master of the Metopes', executed the eight fascinating relief panels of mythological creatures and allegorical subjects on top of the buttresses – monsters relegated to the ends of the cathedral just as they are relegated to the ends of the earth: an upside-down inhabitant of the antipodes, a hermaphrodite and a nude woman with a dragon, a three-armed woman, a bearded crouching man, a giantess with an ibis and a sphinx, and a fork-tailed siren. These are copies; the originals, which deserve a much closer look, are in the adjacent **Museo Lapidario** on Via Lanfranco (*soon to reopen after long restoration, ask at the tourist office or t 059 216 078*). Yet another 12th-century sculptor put King Arthur in the lunette over the **Porta della Pescheria**.

Later 12th-century work, including the rose window, was done by the Campionese masters of Lake Lugano, who also added the final touches to Lanfranco's charming interior, with its rhythm of arches supported by slender columns and ponderous piers. To decorate the wall the masters created the great Pontile, carved with lion pillars and polychromed reliefs of the life of Christ, and incorporating the ambone, a pulpit with pillars with excellent capitals. Underneath is a crypt of 32 columns with capitals carved by Wiligelmo and his followers, with more lions and a chimaera. San Geminiano is buried here, in a Roman sarcophagus.

The mighty if slightly askew campanile, called the **Ghirlandina**, houses a famous trophy – an ancient wooden bucket stolen during a raid on Bologna in 1325, and the subject of a 17th-century mock-heroic epic, *La Secchia Rapita*. The Bolognese make periodic attempts to steal it back; according to rumour, they have it now and the one you see is only a replica. It *is*, in fact, a replica: behind the Duomo, Modena's **Palazzo Comunale** (*open Tues–Sat 7–7, Sun 8–1 and 3–7, adm on Sun, otherwise free*) contains the real one, along with some fascinating Baroque frescoes on the history of the city. Outside, the enormous slab of red Verona marble in the angle of the Palazzo

Getting Around

There are frequent **rail** connections with Bologna, Parma and Milan, and also to Mantua via Carpi. The station is on Piazza Dante, a 10-minute walk from the centre (or take bus no.1 or no. 3). The **bus** station (t 059 308 801) on Viale Monte Kosica, 1km west of the train station (any no. 1, 2, 9, 10 or 11 city bus will take you from one to the other), has frequent connections to Bologna, Ferrara and destinations in Modena province (Vignola, Sestola and Fiumalbo). There is a shuttle service to Bologna **airport**, a 55-min run nine times daily, and municipal **bike rental** at Parco Novi Sad, near the bus station, open 7–7pm.

Tourist Information

Piazza Grande 7, t 059 206 660, f 059 206 659. The efficient city tourist office.

Modenatur, Via Scudari 10, t 059 206 686 or t 059 220 022, f 059 206 688. Offers bookings for hotels, restaurants, shows and events, and visits to wine and cheese producers.

Shopping and Activities

The concert, ballet and opera season at the **Teatro Comunale** on Corso Canal Grande (t 059 206 093) runs from September to May. **Pavarotti** gives a **concert** in Piazza Grande, in September. Crowds sit in the neighbouring bars, and listen to the music while watching the show on TV. The Pavarotti **singing competition** takes place in Modena in June.

Vignola celebrates is Cherry Blossom Festival in April with horse races, bicycle tours and other events. On 15 August there's a traditional festival at Pievepelago, and in nearby Riolunato the Maggio delle Ragazze and Maggio delle Anime, both celebrated in May

Where to Stay

Modena ✉ 41100

Expensive

****Canalgrande**, Corso Canalgrande 6, t 059 217 160, f 059 221 674, www.canalgrande-hotel.it. Named after Modena's long-gone medieval canal, it's palatial: once the palazzo of the Marchesi Schedoni, it has richly decorated and stuccoed 18th-century public rooms, with crystal chandeliers, ceiling frescoes and plush bedrooms. Ancient trees grace the hotel's pretty inner garden.

Moderate

***Principe**, Corso Vittorio Emanuele 94, t 059 218 670, f 059 237 693. The first of three good hotels in a row near the station and the Giardini Pubblici; bedrooms vary.
***Milano**, Corso Vittorio Emanuele 68, t 059 223 011, f 059 225 136. Number two; modern and functional with posh bathrooms.
***Europa**, Corso Vittorio Emanuele 52, t 059 217 721, f 059 222 288. Number three; occupying a peaceful 19th-century palazzo.
***Centrale**, Via Rismondo 55, t 059 218 808, f 059 238 201. Near the cathedral.

Cheap

*Sole**, Via Malatesta 45, t 059 214 245. A clean, old-fashioned locanda in a small ancient street; offers seven basic but spacious rooms without bathrooms.
*Del Torre**, Via Cervetta 5, t 059 222 615. Right in the centre, most rooms en suite, a few very cheap ones without bath.

Eating Out

Modena is nearly as mad for food as Parma: There are consorzi dei prodotti tipici for aceto

Comunale's façade is the *Preda Ringadora*, a speakers' platform in use since the 1200s (an *arringadore* meant an orator; that's where we get our word 'harangue').

Palazzo dei Musei

The other main sight in Modena is the **Palazzo dei Musei** (with your back to the cathedral, turn left along Via Aemilia). Upstairs, the **Galleria Estense** (open Tues, Fri, Sat 9–7, Wed and Thurs 9–2, Sun 9–1, closed Mon; adm) was founded by Francesco I d'Este,

balsamico, Lambrusco, cherries, cheese and hams quite as tasty as Parma's. In the heart of Emilia's pig country, Modena prides itself on its variety of *salumeria;* minced pork fills its *tortellini* and its famous main course, *zampone* (pig's trotter, boiled and sliced).

It is also the best place to taste true Lambrusco, which must be drunk young to be perfectly lively and sparkling; the test is to see if the foam vanishes instantly when poured into a glass. It's often possible to visit the traditional farms around the city: tours can be booked through Modenatur.

At weekends, the Modenesi embark on gastronomic voyages into the Apennines: stop at any roadside restaurant (choose the one with the most cars outside) and you'll find simple meals of smoked meats, cheeses, raw vegetables and freshly baked breads known as *tigelle* (a flat, baked muffin), or *crescente* (thin dough fried in fat). During the week you won't have to wait for a table.

Modena ✉ 41100

Very Expensive

Fini, Largo San Francesco, **t** 059 223 314. The cathedral of Modenese cuisine. Founded in 1912, Fini has an almost endless menu of hearty regional pasta (*lasagne* and *tortellini* prepared in a variety of ways – the *pasticcio di tortellini* is exceptional), meat dishes (the famous *zampone* or *bollito misto*), and appetizers, all deliciously prepared. *Closed Mon, Tues and most of Aug.*

Expensive

Osteria La Francesca, Via Stella 22, **t** 059 210 118. One of Modena's more innovative places, offering delicious food served in arty décor, with a changing menu. Artichoke lovers should not miss the *mousseline di carciofi*; great wine list. *Closed Sat lunch, Sun, Aug.*

Vinicio, Via Emilia Est 1526, **t** 059 280 313. A short drive out of the centre, does an excellent job of adapting the rather heavy local cooking to modern tastes – try *tortelli* with *ricotta* and spinach. There are very fine salads and vegetables, meat courses prepared with balsamic vinegar, and an excellent wine list. *Closed Sun and Mon.*

Moderate

Osteria Ruggera, Via Ruggera 18, **t** 059 211 129. A 150-year-old establishment near the cathedral, has delicious daily specials – try the *gnocchi* with *gorgonzola* and walnuts, pasta dishes and chops made with balsamic vinegar, and the famous and enormous *cotoletta alla Ruggera. Closed Tues and Aug.*

Stallo del Pomodoro, Largo Hannover 63, **t** 059 214 664. The 'Tomato Stall' takes its name from the former tomato market held here; the menu varies with the market and season. One of the springtime specialities is smoked goose breast with asparagus. Wide selection of wine and cheese and desserts. Outdoor tables. *Closed Sat lunch and Sun.*

Cheap

Aldina, Via Albinelli 40, **t** 059 236 106. Opposite the Mercato Coperto, resolutely old-fashioned but good, and attracts a wide range of customers, all happy to plunk down a small sum for a plate of fresh pasta, roast meat, dessert and a bottle of Lambrusco. *Open for lunch only, closed Sun and Aug.*

Ermes, Via Ganaceto 89 (no phone). A simple family-run place with a fixed-price menu, which includes a dish of home-made pasta, a main course (*bollito misto* always on Saturday), a side dish, Lambrusco and coffee. *Open lunch only, closed Sun and Aug.*

Compagnia del Taglio, Via Taglio 12, **t** 059 210 377. A classy wine bar in the *centro storico* .

whose excellent bust by Bernini greets visitors at the entrance. His taste and budget weren't quite as elevated as that of some other dukes, but here's your chance to see works by Modena's greatest medieval painter, Tommaso da Modena, as well as other good early Emilian works, bronzes by Il Riccio of Padua, a good Flemish collection, works by the Venetians Palma Vecchio, Cima da Conegliano, Veronese and Tintoretto (a set of ceiling paintings by Tintoretto called the *Ottagoni,* depcting energetic scenes from Ovid's *Metamorphoses,* was brought here from Venice in 1658), and Velázquez's

Portrait of Francesco I d'Este. The Florentines really steal the show, especially Botticelli's ripe Technicolor *Madonna con il Bambino*, but for all that, the painting you can't stop staring at will be the masterpiece and last known work of the great quattrocento eccentric Cosmè Tura, the cadaverous, beautiful, horrific *St Anthony of Padua* (1484), a life-sized vision of spiritual and anatomical deformity, captured in a garish pink sunset, which will send any good Catholic out in search of a stiff drink.

Besides the museum, the *palazzo* houses the **Biblioteca Estense** (*open Mon–Thurs 9–7.15, Fri and Sat 9–1.45*). Among its famous collection of illuminated manuscripts is one of the most fabulous anywhere, the *Bible of Borso d'Este*, made for the Duke of Modena, a gorgeously coloured 1,200-page marvel illustrated in the 15th century by the Emilians Taddeo Crivelli and Franco Rossi. On the way back to Piazza Grande, stop by to see the terracotta *Deposition* by Guido Mazzoni (1476) in **San Giovanni Battista**.

From Piazza Grande, Via C. Battisti leads to the huge Baroque **Palazzo Ducale**, once the home of the Este dukes and now the **National Military Academy**; some surviving frescoes and 18th-century rooms are on the guided tours (*open Sun only, except in Aug or when the Sunday is also a holiday; guided tours at 10 and 11; reservations necessary, book at the tourist office, or call* **t** *059 206 660*). The dukes' gardens have a botanical garden with a greenhouse of tropical plants. Between this behemoth and the station the main landmark is the neo-Romanesque Tempio Monumentale, erected in 1923.

The streets south of the Piazza Grande, around porticoed Corso Canal Chiaro and Via Canalino, are some of Modena's oldest and loveliest. The 'canal' street names recall that Modena was once a city full of canals, built by the medieval *comuni* to drain water from the marshy land, via the Canale Naviglio, into the Po. Modena's dukes started bricking over the canals in the 1600s, and the last of them was gone by 1800. In this neighbourhood too you'll find the city markets, including the delightful glass and iron **Mercato Coperto**, on Piazza XX Settembre just south of Piazza Grande.

North of Modena: Carpi and Nonántola

North of Modena buses and trains run to Carpi, a wealthy, workaholic town dominated by the oceanic **Piazza dei Martiri**; formerly called the Borgogioioso, this is the third largest piazza in Italy. Beside it stands the equally remarkable 16th-century **Castello del Pio**, which holds the **Musei Civici** (*open Thurs, Sat and Sun 9–12.30 and 3–6.30*), including some brilliant High Renaissance frescoes, a tribute to Ugo da Carpi, inventor of the *chiaroscuro* tinted woodcut (which made possible mass reproductions of paintings), and a museum remembering the Italian Jews deported to Germany from a Nazi camp here. Carpi's real treasure is hidden behind the *castello*'s bulk: **Santa Maria in Castello** (1120), one of the many churches built by Countess Matilda of Canossa; among the medieval and quattrocento frescoes inside is a lovely cycle on the *Life of St Catherine* by followers of Giovanni da Modena.

Eleven kilometres northeast of Modena, the important **Abbey of Nonántola** (*open daily 7.30am–8pm*) was founded in 752 by the Lombard abbot Anselmo, rebuilt in the 12th century and later given the Baroque one-two. The portal, however, retains its beautiful carving by the workshop of Wiligelmo. The church contains relics of the 4th-century St Sylvester, pope under Constantine, while the crypt contains 64 columns

Where to Stay and Eat

Nonántola ✉ 41015

Osteria di Rubbiara, Via Risaia 2, **t** 059 549 019 (*moderate*). Near Nonántola at Rubbiara. This hostelry has been in the Pedroni family since 1861. There's no menu for the good home cooking, in generous portions. For a reasonable price you'll get whatever's on offer; at least one dish will come with the family's balsamic vinegar. They also make a huge variety of liqueurs. *Open lunch only except Fri and Sat eves; closed Tues and Aug.*

Sestola ✉ 41029

★★★★San Marco, Via delle Rose 2, **t** 0536 62330, **f** 0536 62305, *sanmarco@cimone.it*

(*expensive*). St Mark's has a pine wood for a backdrop, and is set in a large 19th-century villa with a panoramic terrace. *Closed Oct.*

★★★Tirolo, Via delle Rose 19, **t** 0536 62523 (*cheap*). Very comfortable rooms. *Open June–Sept and mid-Dec–mid-May only.*

★★Sport Hotel, Via delle Ville 116, **t** 0536 62502 (*cheap*). A pleasant small hotel that's open all year; it has double rooms only, with or without baths.

San Rocco, Corso Umberto I 47, **t** 0536 62382 (*expensive*). The food is lavishly good; the chef does wonders with vegetables and pasta dishes (try the *pecorino* cheese with onions and balsamic vinegar, or *tagliatelle* with pine nuts); also tender roast meats. *Closed Mon, May and Oct.*

with carved capitals, and the tomb of another pope, St Adrian III, who died here in 885 en route to the Diet of Worms. The abbey has two cloisters, and a refectory with frescoes from the 11th and 12th centuries.

South of Modena

From Modena you can break away from the flatlands of the Po by heading south into the Apennines, which achieve majestic proportions on the Tuscan border. The region has perfect updraughts for hang-gliding and sailplanes, especially around **Pavullo** and **Montecreto**. In April the emerald-green foothills of **Vignola** and **Savignano** are covered with the lacy blossoms of Vignola's famous cherry trees; these are celebrated in a Cherry Blossom Festival in April, with horse races and medieval costumes. (you can get there from Bologna by way of the free seasonal Cherry Train, the 'Treno dei Ciliegi', laid on specially for the occasion).

From here continue further south to **Guiglia** and the peculiar pinnacles of **Rocca Malatina** in the **Parco Naturale di Sassi**. Just south of Guiglia, don't miss the 11th-century church at **Pieve Trebbio**, with primitive capitals inside.

Motorheads won't want to miss **Maranello**, where the **Galleria Ferrari** (*daily except Mon 9.30–12.30, 3–6; adm exp*) is dedicated to the legendary marque, with scale models, trophies, vintage cars and a reconstruction of Enzo Ferrari's office. **Sassuolo**, southwest of Modena, is the centre of Italy's ceramic tile industry, which has been booming since Italian designers have discovered that people spend money on decorating their bathrooms and kitchens as well as their persons. Under the rule of the Este family it produced more artistic tiles.

The most striking scenery is up at **Sestola**, a winter and summer resort near the highest peak of the Northern Apennines, **Monte Cimone** (7,100ft) (*for a ski report, call* **t** *0536 62350*). From Sestola you can visit the pretty glacial Lago della Ninfa and the **Giardino Esperia** at the Passo del Lupo, a botanical frontier where Alpine and Apennine species grow side by side (*June, July and Aug open daily 9.30–12.30 and*

2.30–6; May and Sept daily except Mon 9.30–12.30 and 2.30–5.30; adm). Another excursion from Sestola is to **Pian Cavallaro**, and from there to the summit of Monte Cimone for a unique view – on a clear day you can see both the Tyrrhenian and Adriatic seas, and all the way north to the Julian Alps and Mont Blanc.

You can also make the ascent from **Fiumalbo**, just below the **Passo Abetone** that separates Emilia from Tuscany. There is an unusual mountain lake in the meadows south of Fanano, a little to the east of Sestola: the small **Lago Pratignano.** In spring its banks are strewn with wild flowers and carnivorous plants – bring your waders.

Bologna

'You must write all the beautiful things of Italy,' said the Venetian on the train, but the man from Bologna vehemently shook his finger. 'No, no,' he insisted. 'You must write the truth!' And it is precisely that – a fervent insistence on the plain truth as opposed to the typical Italian *bella figura* – that sets Bologna apart. A homespun realism and attention to the detail of the visible, material world are the characteristics of the Bolognese school of art (recall Petrarch's comment that while only an educated man is amazed by a Giotto, anyone can understand a Bolognese picture).

The city's handsome, harmonic and well-preserved centre disdains imported marble or ornate stucco, preferring honest red brick. Bologna's municipal government, long in the hands of the Italian Communist Party (now the PDS), was long considered the least corrupt and most efficient of any large city in the whole country. In the 11th century it was the desire for truth and law that led to the founding of the University of Bologna, whose first scholars occupied themselves with the task of interpreting the law codes of Justinian in settling disputes over investitures between pope and emperor. And it is Bolognese sincerity and honest ingredients in the kitchen that has made *la cucina bolognese* by common consent the best in all Italy.

La Dotta, La Grassa and *La Rossa* (the Learned, the Fat and the Red) are Bologna's sobriquets. It may be full of socialist virtue, but the city is also very wealthy and cosy, with a quality of life often compared to Sweden. The casual observer could well come away with the impression that the reddest things about Bologna are its telephone booths and street names like Via Stalingrado, Via Yuri Gagarin and Viale Lenin. But Bologna is hardly a stolid place – its bars, cafés and squares are brimming with youth and life, and there's a full calendar of concerts from rap to jazz to Renaissance madrigals, as well as avant-garde ballet, theatre and art exhibitions; visitors, though, should be aware that in July and August Bologna can be as exciting as the cheap supermarket salami that bears its name.

History

Born as the prosperous Etruscan outpost of *Felsina*, and renamed *Bononia* by the Gauls, Bologna grew up at the junction of the Via Aemilia and the main road over the Apennines from Florence. Dominated by Ravenna for centuries, Bologna emerged from the Dark Ages around 1000 AD to start the new millennium with a bang, founding one of Italy's first free *comuni* and starting what became Europe's first university. By the 1100s Bologna was a hemp-, wool- and linen-trading boom town on an American scale, with tower-fortresses of the urban nobility zooming up like modern skyscrapers – some 180 of them, more than any city outside Florence. With 50,000 inhabitants by 1200, it was one of the great cities of Europe; thanks to its university it became the intellectual centre of Italy, and was the first city where books were copied for sale. Bologna's golden age continued through the 12th and 13th centuries, when it was one of the Guelph leaders of the Lombard League. As such it warred with Ghibelline Modena, and defeated that city in the Battle of Fossalta in 1249, capturing the talented Enzo, King of Sardinia and natural son of Emperor Frederick II. Defying custom, Bologna refused to ransom him and kept him in a castle until he died in 1272.

Bologna became part of the Papal States in 1278, though for the next few centuries real power was held by 'first citizens', most famously the Bentivoglio ('wish-you-well') family (1401–1506), who gained control after a brief period of reform. They heralded a flowering of local culture, despite a sensational family saga of assassination, high-living and questionable legitimacy – the paternity of Annibale, father of the great art patron Giovanni II, was decided by a throw of the dice. Giovanni II ruled for 43 years until ousted by Pope Julius II (patron of Michelangelo), after which Bologna was ruled directly by a papal legate, putting an end to its independence once and for all.

Bologna witnessed one of the key turning points in Italian history in 1530 when Charles V insisted on being crowned Holy Roman Emperor in its basilica of San Petronio instead of in Rome, which his troops had sacked three years previously. Charles felt that going to Rome would seem like an act of contrition, and such was the low standing of papal authority that when he told Pope Clement VII that he 'did not need to seek crowns, but that crowns ran after him', the humbled pope could only agree. Charles' coronation, both as Emperor and King of Italy, was celebrated with tremendous pomp, but marked the death knell for the Renaissance and the begin-ning of three centuries of foreign domination for Italy. Luigi Barzini notes that from then on the Italians put away their bright clothes and began to wear black in the Spanish style, as if they were in mourning – just as the *Fascisti* donned black shirts under Mussolini. A great age of post-Bentivoglio palace-building rapidly gave way to the totalitarian Church of the Counter Reformation – although it also gave expression to Bologna's local artistic talent like the Carracci and Guido Reni.

Modern Bologna

In the 19th century Bologna was the birthplace of Marconi, who carried out his first experiments with radio at the Villa Grifone. It was also at this time that Bologna took the lead in the Italian socialist movement; in the 20th century it endured the brunt of the Fascist reaction. It was on the Germans' 'Gothic Line' (1944–45), and the scene of fervid partisan activity – leading to brutal Nazi reprisals such as the massacre at Marzabotto – but emerged from the Second World War relatively unscathed. After the war, Bologna's Communists got their chance to run the city, and made the most of it, making it a showcase for the Italian brand of communism.

250 metres
250 yards

N

VIA BAROZZI

VIA GANDUSIO

VIALE MASINI

VIA MUGGIA

VIA STALINGRADO

PIAZZA
XX SETTEMBRE

PIAZZA
DI PORTA
MASCARELLA

VIALE BERT PICHAT

Parco della
Montagnola

PIAZZA
VIII AGOSTO

VIA DEL BORGO SAN PIETRO

VIA IRNERIO

VIA MASCARELLA

VIA CENTOTRECENTO

PIAZZA
DI PORTA
S. DONATO

Pinacoteca
Nazionale

Palazzo
Bentivoglio

VIA RIGHI

VIA PIELLA

A DELL'INDIPENDENZA

VIA DELLE BELLE ARTI

S.
Martino

VIA MARSALA

VIA ZAMBONI

Università

VIALE FILOPANTI

Teatro
Comunale

PIAZZA
VERDI

VIA

VIA BIBIENA

VIA SELMI

Duomo

VIA OBERDAN

PIAZZA
ROSSINI

S. Giacomo
Maggiore

VIA ALTABELLA

Palazzo di Re Enzo

Torre
Garisenda

PIAZZA DI
P.TA RAVEGNANA

VIA SAN VITALE

PIAZZA
DI PORTA
S. VITALE

VIA RIZZOLI

Pal. d. Podestà

S. Bartolomeo

AZZA
GGIORE

Palazzo
dei Banchi

Torre
degli Asinelli

VIA ARCHIGINNASIO

S. Maria
della Vita

Pal. d. Mercanzia

VIA BROCCAINDOSSO

VIALE ERCOLANI

VIA CLAVATURE

Casa
Isolani

Pal. dei Giganti

Museo Civico
Archeologico

STRADA MAGGIORE

etronio

PIAZZA
MINGHETTI

PIAZZA
SANTO
STEFANO

S. Stefano

AZZA
LVANI

Archiginnasio

VIA GUERRAZZI

S. Maria
dei Servi

VIA FARINI

VIA FARINI

PIAZZA
SAN GIOVANNI
IN MONTE

PIAZZA
DI PORTA
MAGGIORE

PIAZZA
CAVOUR

VIA CASTIGLIONE

S. Giovanni
in Monte

VIA SANTO STEFANO

VIA SAN PETRONIO VECCHIO

S. Domenico

VIA CARTOLERIA

PIAZZA
S. DOMENICO

PIAZZA
D. TRIBUNALI

PIAZZA
CARDUCCI

Getting There

By Air

Bologna's Guglielmo Marconi **airport** is to the northwest in the Borgo Panigale, **t** 051 647 9615; the **Aerobus** (**t** 051 290 290) runs from there to the railway station every 15 minutes 8am–8pm but can take an hour in traffic. There is also a direct bus to the Fiera district during trade shows (30mins). Bologna has flight connections with major Italian and European cities.

By Rail

Bologna is one of the prime nodes of the FS rail network, with frequent and fast trains to Venice, Florence, Milan, Ravenna, Rimini,Rome and almost everywhere else in Italy from the **Stazione Centrale** in Piazza Medaglie d'Oro, **t** 1478 88088. It's on the north side of the city centre, about a 10–15-minute walk from Piazza Maggiore, or buses no.11 and no.27 go straight there.

By Bus

The **bus station** is near the rail station at Piazza XX Settembre (**t** 051 350 301), and has services every hour for Ferrara, Imola, Modena and Ravenna.

Getting Around

Most of Bologna's sights are within easy walking distance of one another, but the city also has an efficient **local bus** system (ATC). There are offices that dispense tickets, bus maps and information at the main bus station, at a booth outside the railway station, and in the centre at Via IV Novembre 16, **t** 051 290 290; tickets must be bought before boarding the bus and are also available from *tabacchi* and newspaper kiosks. You can hire bicycles near the Porta Galliera, at Piazza XX Settembre 7, **t** 051 630 2015. For a taxi, call **t** 051 372 727, or **t** 051 534 141.

Tourist Information

Emilia's tourist information office is very central, at Piazza Maggiore 6, **t** 051 239 660 (*open Mon–Sat 9–7, Sun 9–1*). There's also an office at the railway station, **t** 051 246 541 (*open Mon–Sat 9–12.30 and 2.30–7*) and one at the airport.

Anyone planning serious museum-hopping might conside a one- or three-day *Biglietto Unico*, which gets you in free or cheap at some places. or a *Biglietto Integrato* that also works as a bus pass; you can buy them at larger museums and ATC bus ticket outlets.

Shopping

Via Rizzoli and Via dell'Indipendenza are the main centres for **chic boutiques** and **fashion chains**. But Bologna's most interesting buy is **food**: there are bustling **markets** at Via Ugo Bassi 2, and Via Clavature, just off the Piazza Maggiore (mornings Mon–Sat). La Piazzola market sells just about everything in Piazza VIII Agosto and along Via dell'Indipendenza (Fri and Sat). The windows of Bologna's general food stores present a dazzling array of delicacies; there's a string of them in the streets around Piazza Maggiore, particularly towards the Due Torri. **Paolo Atti & Figli**, Via Caprarie 7 or Via Drapperie 6, in business since 1880, sell excellent home-made pasta and pastries. For perfect cheeses, try **Al Regno della Forma**, Via Oberdan 45a. One of the ultimate food shops, **Tamburini**, Via Caprarie 1, is famous for its exquisite *salumeria* and other gastronomic highlights of Emilia-Romagna.

Where to Stay

When booking in Bologna, avoid nasty surprises by confirming the price of your room. Prices vary enormously depending on the room, time of year, and what's cooking at Bologna Fiera.

Luxury

★★★★Grand Hotel Baglioni, Via dell' Indipendenza 8, **t** 051 225 445, **f** 051 234 840, *ghb.bologna@bcedit.it*. Right in the centre, in the 16th-century Palazzo Ghisleri-Fava, embedded in Bologna's history; antiques and luxurious rooms, and a beautiful restaurant frescoed by the Carracci, specializing in authentic Bolognese cuisine. Morandi's paintings were first exhibited here in 1914.

Very Expensive

****San Donato, Via Zamboni 16, **t** 051 235
395, **f** 051 230 547. In a 17th-century palace
near the Due Torri; has a loyal clientele, who
appreciate the location, comfortable rooms
and lovely summer terrace.

***Dei Commercianti, Via Pignattari 11, **t** 051
233 052, **f** 051 224 733, *hotcom.tin.it*. A
recently revamped little hotel within spitting distance of San Petronio and Bologna's
ritziest shopping streets, occupying
Bologna's 12th-century town . All rooms are
different, most have balconies; the nicest
rooms, with attic ceilings, ancient beams
and the odd piece of fresco, are at the top.

Expensive

***Roma, Via D'Azeglio 9, **t** 051 226 322, **f** 051
239 909. In the medieval *centro storico*, a
minute from Piazza Maggiore, is one of
Bologna's all-round nicest, friendliest hotels,
offering large rooms with floral wallpaper
and fabrics.

***Orologio, Via IV Novembre 10, **t** 051 231 253,
f 051 260 552, *hotoro@iperbole.bologna.it*.
Occupying an atmospheric aged *palazzo*
with a big clock on the façade in a pleasant
square beside San Petronio, the 'Clock' has
cosy rooms with views of the city's streets.

***Touring, Via Mattuiani 1/2, **t** 051 584 305,
f 051 334 763, *htouring@iperbole.bologna.it*.
Fairly central, on the corner of Piazza de'
Tribunale, with comfortable rooms and bikes
for guests.

Moderate

***Palace, Via Monte Grappa 9/2, **t** 051 237
442, **f** 051 220 689. Central and genteely
faded, occupies a handsome old *palazzo*; try
to get one of the large old rooms that
haven't changed much since the early
1900s. *Closed Aug.*

Centrale, Via della Zecca 2, **t 051 265 827,
f 051 235 162. Another old *palazzo*, which is as
central as its name suggests, by Piazza
Maggiore; rooms are simple but pleasant,
and nearly all en suite; some triples.

Cheap

Rossini, Via Bibiena 11, **t 051 237 716, **f** 051
268 035. Cheaper accommodation is thin on
the ground in Bologna, and you'd do well to

book ahead. What exists is mostly central.
Tucked away in the university quarter,
Rossini offers clean, comfortable rooms and
very friendly management.

*Apollo, Via Drapperie 5, **t** 051 223 955, **f** 051
238 760. Just off Piazza Maggiore in a nest of
shopping streets; the rooms are small, and
the market outside starts up early, but you
couldn't be better placed.

Eating Out

In Italy's self-acclaimed gastronomic capital,
eating out is a pleasure whether you plump
for a meal at a fancy restaurant or head for
one of the city's traditional late-night inns or
osterie; the *cucina petroniana*, as they call it,
rarely disappoints. Besides famous pasta
dishes, the city is known for the best pâtés in
Italy, for its veal dishes and, of late, for culinary
innovations. The Bolognesi do love their
restaurants. Even on week-nights in the
winter, you might find it hard to walk into a
good one in the city centre and get a table
without a reservation.

Luxury

Pappagallo Piazza delle Mercanzia 3, **t/f** 051
232 807. You can join film stars and other
celebrities or just study the photos of past
diners at the most famous restaurant in
Bologna, in a quattrocento *palazzo*. Named
for its brightly painted parrot, it is extremely
elegant and slightly eccentric: instead of
flowers, bowls of handsome vegetables
adorn the tables. Munch on home-made
olive *ciabattas* as you choose from the
menu. The food is Italian with some French
influences: prawns with red *risotto* (makes a
good *antipasto*); fresh pasta; a wide range of
secondi seafood; meat dishes including
Chateaubriand and rabbit (the house
speciality). Vast wine list. *Closed Sun.*

Very Expensive

Antica Trattoria del Cacciatore, Via Caduti di
Casteldebole 25, **t** 051 564 203. North of the
centre, near the banks of the river Reno;
founded in the early 19th century for
hunters, who would wade there through the
shallow river. Well known for its heaving

carts of delicious *antipasti*, side dishes and desserts that come trundling to your table; there are excellent pasta dishes and plenty of game, as well as seafood. In the summer you can dine on the garden verandah (as long as you've booked – a necessity at any time of year). *Closed Sun eve, Mon.*

Torre de Galluzzi, Corte Galluzzi 5/a, **t** 051 267 638. An atmospheric place in a medieval tower behind the cathedral, serving original dishes executed with finesse, including plenty of seafood, *tortellini* with black truffles, *risotto* with *porcini* mushrooms, rabbit glazed in sweet Albana, guinea fowl grilled with mustard and mushrooms, and exquisite desserts. Big wine list, with Italian and French bottles. *Closed Sun and most of Aug.*

Expensive

Da Cesari, Via de' Carbonesi 8, **t** 051 237 710. Has been around for more than thirty years, and the *ambiente* has changed little in that time. However, innovative additions have been made to classic Bolognese dishes so you might find *ravioli* stuffed with rabbit and smoked *ricotta* on the menu alongside standards like tripe *alla parmigiana. Closed Sun and Sat in June and July.*

Silverio, Via Mirasole 19, **t** 051 585 857. South of San Domenico. A delightful place to dine, with a charming summer terrace and original inventive cuisine, available *à la carte* or on a choice of constantly changing gourmet menus: as far as we know, this is the only place in town where you can get Parmesan cheese ice cream. Great wine and spirits list. *Closed Sun and Aug.*

Rosteria Luciano, Via N. Sauro 19, (north of Via Ugo Bassi), **t** 051 231 249. Slightly old-fashioned, combines agreeable old-fashioned service and cuisine: *sformato di carciofi, tagliatella al ragù*, old fashioned *fritto misto* and a good wine list. *Closed Wed, and late July–late Aug.*

Re Enzo, Further north, at Via Riva di Reno 77, **t** 051 281498. Does Emilian cooking with a touch of Umbria: pasta with Umbrian black truffles, stewed boar, even the famous lentils from Castellucio; other game dishes include venison goulash. *Closed Sun.*

Moderate

Da Leonida, Vicolo Alemagna 2, **t** 0512 39742. Near the Due Torri; an elegant and popular *trattoria* where they do just about everything one could possibly do with *tortellini* and *tagliatelle*; also roast pheasant, rabbit with *polenta* and a choice of home-made desserts. *Closed Sun.*

Caminetto d'Oro, Via dè Falegnami 4, **t** 051 263 494. Just off Via dell'Indipendenza. It has the golden fireplace of its name and some of the more unusual of Emilia-Romagna's specialties, especially in the pasta department: *rigatoni con formaggio di fossa* and *spaghetti alla chitarra* in lamb sauce; good *zuppa inglese* for dessert. *Closed Tues eve, Wed, Jan and Aug.*

Serghei, Via Piella 12, **t** 051 233 533. Not far from the university is a typical little rustic Bolognese family-run *trattoria*. The menu, unchanged for years, features home-made pasta (meat-filled *tortellini* in tasty broth, rocket-filled *agnolotti*), pork cooked in milk, *ossobuco*, and a wonderful *ricotta* tart to finish. *Closed Sat eve, Sun and Aug.*

Belle Arti, 6 Via Belle Arti, **t** 051 225 581. Also near the University, the lively 'fine arts' splits its menu between the Bolognese and the Mediterranean, with pasta with *cozze* (mussels) or *bottarghe* (fish roe, preferred in Sardinia); good home-made desserts; stays open weekends until 2am. *Closed Wed.*

Gigina, Via Stendhal 1b (north of the centre), **t** 051 322 300. A classic Bolognese *trattoria*, in business since 1956, where they make the traditional favourites with fidelity: *lasagne, tortellini* and *tagliatelle*, roast guinea fowl and *bollito misto*, and the famous old-fashioned desserts: *torta di riso, zuppa inglese* and *crema fritta*. You need to book a couple of days in advance. *Closed Sat, most of Aug.*

Cantina Bentivoglio, 4 Via Mascarella, **t** 051 265 416. Another good wine bar, the 'wish-you-well cellar' has all the vintages great and small, as well as a small menu, with *bruschetta* and *crostini, pasta e fagioli*, and good main dishes (*involtini con scamorze*). Also jazz some nights. *Closed Mon.*

Cheap

Antica Trattoria Spiga, Via Broccaindosso 21/a (just east of the centre off Via San Vitale), t 051 230 063. It's been run by the same family since 1933, and is still doing well thanks to its traditional Bolognese dishes, including tripe and *maltagliati* in bean soup. No credit cards. *Closed Sun and Aug.*

Osteria del Sole, Vicolo Ranocchi, just off Piazza Maggiore, still has no phone. An institution, founded in 1468; there are long wooden tables where you can eat your own food bought at the surrounding market and sample the excellent wine. *Weekdays only, open until 9pm, closed Aug.*

La Farfalla, Via Bertiera 12 (near the church of San Martino), t 051 225 656. Rustic, authentic and good, serving delicious *tortellini in brodo*, aubergine *parmigiana*, stuffed courgettes, *bollito misto* and some dishes for bold diners, such as donkey with *polenta*, all accompanied by jugs of house wine. Arrive early for a seat. No credit cards. *Closed Sat eve and Sun.*

Entertainment and Nightlife

Not surprisingly, a thousand-year-old university city like Bologna stays up later than most other Italian cities. People here eat late – often around 10pm – and there are plenty of bars and cafés open till 3am. You only have to take a look at the student bars around the university and the posters in their windows to find out about concerts, films, exhibitions, performances and clubs; or check out the listings in Bologna's oddly named local paper, *Il Resto del Carlino* (which does not mean 'the remains of little Charles', as many foreigners suspect, but the change from an old coin called a Carlino – when you bought a cigar, instead of change you got a newspaper). The local fortnightly *Zero in Condotta* has better listings on more youth-orientated events.

Opera, Classical, Theatre and Cinema

The drama season at the **Teatro Duse**, Via Cartoleria 42, t 051 226 606, runs from November to May, while operas are performed at the **Teatro Comunale**, t 051 529 011, from December to May. Other classical music venues are the **Basilica di Santa Maria dei Servi**, t 051 261 710, and the **Accademia**

Filarmonia, Via Guerrazzi 13, t 051 554 715. In July and August, as an alternative to the usual Italian mid-summer shutdown, Bologna's local authorities organize the **Bologna Sogna festival,** featuring open-air theatre and cinema; dance performances and concerts are presented in Piazza Maggiore. In winter films are shown in *versione originale* at Tiffany, Piazza di Porta Saragozza 5, t 051 585 253, and Adriano, Via S. Felice 52, t 051 555 127. The Cinema Lumière, Via Pietralata 55, t 051 523 812, shows art-house movies all year, many of which have never been dubbed into Italian.

Cafés and Bars

Pasticceria Impero, Via dell'Indipendenza 39. A good place for breakfast; the speciality of the house are *certosini*, cakes with pine nuts, candied fruit, almonds and honey.

Pasticceria Majani, Via dei Carbonesi 5. Another institution, it's been a 'laboratory of sweet things' since 1796, and is especially famous for its *cioccolata scorza*.

La Torinese, Piazza Re Enzo 1. A century old, and famous for hot chocolate and pastries.

Live Jazz, Blues, Rock, Alternative

Every visitor to Bologna should drink in one of the city's traditional *osterie*, which serve food, with live music, and stay open late.

Cantina Bentivoglio, Via Mascarella 4, t 051 265 416. A lively, smart cellar for live acoustic jazz, with snacks or full meals and an endless wine list; open til 2am.

The **Osteria dell'Orsa**, near the university at Via Mentana 1, t 051 231 576. A beer cellar with jazz twice a week.

Officina Estragon, Via Calzoni 6, t 051 365 825, *www.estragon.it*. Features ska, hip-hop and reggae, by Italian and foreign bands .

Le Stanze, Via del Borgo di San Pietro 1, t 051 228 767. One of Bologna's more unusual cafés, housed in a Bentivoglio chapel of 1500.

Clubs and Discos

Palanord (Parco Nord, entrance on Via Michelino). Many of the clubs are outside the centre: Palanord is a big winter venue. **Sottotetto Sound Club** (out on Viale Zagabria 1) is another, or try **Il Covo**, t 051 505 801. In summer the ever-generous Bologna city council sponsors cheap, open-air raves.

Like the rest of Italy, Bologna in the late 1960s and '70s had more than its share of troubles. Italy was making a sharp left turn and a new generation sought radical alternatives to the PCI. In the so-called '*anni di piombo*' (leaden years) shadowy rightist groups in the security police and army infiltrated the 'Red Brigade' and fomented terrorism: Bologna's Communists and the city itself were prime targets. In 1980 the rightist terrorists made their bloodiest strike ever – a bomb in Bologna's Stazione Centrale that killed 85 people and wounded over 200. Things gradually calmed down after that, but by the 1990s a sharp increase in crime and drug addictions made many Bolognesi discontented with their city government. The 'catastrophe', as local leftists call it, came in the mayoral election of 1998, when a conservative squeaked in, Giorgio Guazzaloca. The right crowed and cackled across Italy: the great Red bastion had capitulated. So far, however, Guazzaloca's most controversial move has been to allow cars back into the *centro storico*.

This historic centre is one of the best preserved and maintained in Italy, to the credit of the city's policy of 'active preservation' since the 1970s – old houses in the centre are gutted and renovated for municipal public housing, maintaining the character and diversity of the old quarters. Nor is this the first time that Bologna has found a creative solution to its housing needs: you will soon notice every street is lined with arcades, or *portici*; the original ones date from the 12th century, when the *comune*, faced with a housing shortage caused by its 2,000 students, allowed rooms to be built on to existing buildings over the streets. Over time the Bolognese became attached to these overhanging additons and the shelter they provided from the weather; now it claims 70km of *portici*, more than any other city in the world.

Piazza Maggiore

The centre stage of Bolognese public life is Piazza Maggiore and its antechamber, Piazza Nettuno, graced with the virile and vaguely outrageous **Fountain of Neptune**, 'who has abandoned the fishes to make friends with the pigeons', designed in the 16th century by Tomaso Laureti of Palermo and embellished with the statue by Giambologna. Adjacent, and occupying part of both squares, are the **Palazzo di Re Enzo** of 1244 (where Frederick II's son was kept prisoner in some luxury, writing love poetry), and the **Palazzo del Podestà**, begun in 1212 and remodelled in 1484 by Aristotele Fioravanti, who went on to design parts of the Kremlin. The corners of the **Voltone** (the big *portico*) contain 16th-century statues of Bologna's four patron saints.

Filling the western side of the Piazza Maggiore, the crenellated **Palazzo Comunale** (*open Tues–Sun 10–6; adm*) incorporates the **Casa Accursio** of 1287 (the arcaded section), and the 1425 annexe by Fioravante Fioravanti, father of Aristotele. Over the door presides a bronze statue of Pope Gregory XIII, creator of the Gregorian calendar and a native of Bologna. Under a canopy to the left is a beautiful terracotta *Madonna* by Nicolò dell'Arca, a Renaissance sculptor from Puglia whose best work is in Bologna. Inside are two museums: the **Collezioni Comunali d'Arte**, reached via Bramante's grand staircase, with works by the Bolognese school, and the **Museo Morandi**, devoted to Bologna's greatest modern painter, Giorgio Morandi (1890–1964). He rarely left the city and, although a friend of futurists and metaphysicists in Ferrara, kept to himself, quietly producing some of the 20th century's best paintings. The subject matter – jars and jugs – is mundane, but Morandi's fierce gaze transforms it with startling intensity; as Umberto Eco put it, he 'made the dust sing'. There are also landscapes of Grizzana, where Morandi spent his summers.

Opposite the Palazzo del Podestà, the **Basilica di San Petronio** by Antonio da Vicenza (1390) is the largest structure on the square. Had the Bolognese had their way, this temple to their top patron would have been even larger than St Peter's in Rome. However, Pope Pius IV in 1565 ordered them to spend their money on the university's Archiginnasio instead, leaving even the façade unfinished; the white and red marble stripes recalling the city's heraldic emblem only made it up to the portals – perhaps sparing the city the embarrassment of another 'cathedral wearing pyjamas' like the one in Florence. The remarkable main door has reliefs by Jacopo della Quercia of Siena, begun in 1425. Like Ghiberti's doors to the baptistry in Florence (for which della Quercia was an unsuccessful candidate), they are landmarks in the visual evolution of the early Renaissance, and seem strangely modern – almost Art Deco in sensibility.

Missing from the front of San Petronio, however, is Michelangelo's colossal bronze statue of Pope Julius II, commissioned by him in 1506 after he regained the city for the Papal States. Julius also built a large castle in the centre of Bologna. Both were torn to bits by the population as soon as the Pope's luck changed; and to rub salt into his wounded pride the bronze was sold as scrap to his arch-enemy, Alfonso I of Ferrara, who melted it down to cast an enormous cannon – which he fondly named 'Julius'.

The lofty interior saw the crowning of Charles V and, according to tradition, the conversion of a visiting monk named Martin Luther who became so sickened by papal pomp and pageantry that he decided to start the Reformation. In 1655 astronomer Cassini designed the huge astronomical clock, which tells the time with a shaft of light through an *oculus* in the roof. Two of the chapels (third and fourth on the left) are noteworthy – one with 15th-century frescoes of Heaven and Hell, the other containing Lorenzo Costa's *Madonna and Saints*. In the **museum** at the end of the aisle are models of Bologna's basilican pipe dreams (*open daily 10–12.30; closed Tues*).

Via dell'Archiginnasio

The eastern side of Piazza Maggiore is closed by the **Palazzo dei Banchi**, with a long, elegant façade designed by Vignola (1568). Beyond is Bologna's excellent **Museo Civico Archeologico** at Via dell'Archiginnasio 3 (*open Tues–Fri 9–2, Sat and Sun 9–1 and 3.30–7; adm*). Into its dim and dusty wooden cases is crammed one of Italy's best collections of antiquities – beautifully wrought items from the Iron Age Villanova culture, native Italics who were eventually conquered by the Etruscans, and artefacts from Bologna's beginnings as Etruscan *Felsina. Felsina* may have been a frontier town, but it is richly represented here with tomb art, circular gravestones 10ft in diameter carved with proud warriors and ships, and an embossed bronze urn, the *Situla di Certosa*, similar to others found in Tuscany. The Etruscans traded extensively with the Greeks, whose Attic vases are one of the highlights of the museum. There are a few items from Gallic *Bononia*, Roman artefacts (a lovely copy of Phidias's bust of Athena Lemnia), and an excellent Egyptian collection.

The next long porticoed façade is the seat of the old university, the **Archiginnasio** (*open Mon–Sat 9–1*), its walls covered with the escutcheons and memorials of famous alumni. Bologna's university is the oldest in Europe, but was not provided with a central building until 1565 – at the expense of San Petronio. After 1803 this became the **Biblioteca Comunale**. Upstairs is the ornate old **anatomical theatre**, shattered by a bomb in the Second World War and painstakingly rebuilt in 1950. The monument in the piazza in front commemorates Luigi Galvani, the 18th-century Bolognese discoverer of electrical currents in animals, who gave his life and name ('galvanize') to physics. Just off Piazza Maggiore on Via Clavature, stop in **Santa Maria della Vita** to see the terracotta *Lament Over the Dead Christ* by Nicolò dell'Arca, a work harrowing in its grief and terror, a 15th-century version of Edvard Munch's *Scream*.

Two Leaning Towers

In the passage under Via Rizzoli, you can see remains of the Via Aemilia. The end of Via Rizzoli is framed by **Piazza Porta Ravegnana** and a pair of towers that might have wandered off the set of *The Cabinet of Dr Caligari*. After the initial shock wears off, however, fondness invariably sets in for this odd couple, the Laurel and Hardy of architecture. The taller one looks respectable only because the other is so hilarious.

The **Due Torri** were built in 1119 in a competition between two families. The winner, the svelte 318ft **Torre degli Asinelli** (*open summer daily 9–6; winter daily 9–5; adm*), is still the tallest building in Bologna. It tilts about three feet out of true, though the 500 steps that lead to the top are more likely to make your head spin than the tilt. The view over Bologna is worth the trouble, however. Its sidekick, the **Torre Garisenda**, sways tipsily to the south, 10ft out of true; the Garisenda contingent failed to prepare a solid foundation and, when they saw their tower pitching precariously, they threw in the towel. In 1360 it became such a threat to public safety that its top was lopped off, leaving only a squat 157ft stump; inscribed in its base you can read what Dante wrote about it in the *Inferno*.

Dante's mention of the Garisenda Tower comes in Canto XXXI of the *Inferno*, when he and Virgil encounter the giant Antaeus frozen in ice at the bottom of Hell:

Qual pare a riguardar la Garisenda
Sotto 'l chinato, quando un nuvol vada
Sovr'essa si, che ella incontro penda

Tal parve Anteo a me, che stava a bada
Di vederlo chinare, e fu tal ora
Ch'i' avrei voluto ir per altra strada.

('...like looking at the Garisenda, under the leaning side, when a cloud comes; so seemed Antaeus to me, about to fall – to see him leaning so, I wished I had taken another path.'). Dante is referring to an optical illusion that every child in Bologna knows – stand under the lean of the tower when clouds are moving in the opposite direction, and you'll see it.

Beyond the towers five streets fan out to gates in the eastern walls of the old city. One of these, the palace-lined Strada Maggiore, follows the route of the Via Aemilia, passing **San Bartolomeo**, notable for its two works by Bolognese masters: Albani's *Annunciation*, in a chapel on the south aisle, and Guido Reni's *Madonna*. In the 19th century Italians considered the 'Divine Guido' as their greatest artist; since then he has taken a precipitous and admittedly deserved fall from fashion. At Strada Maggiore 13, the **Casa Isolani**, home of the British Council, is one of the best-preserved 13th-century houses left in Bologna; at No.44 the 18th-century **Palazzo dei Giganti** (or Davia) (*open Tues–Sat 9–2, Sun 9–1*) contains the **Galleria Davia-Bargelli**, housing Vitale da Bologna's famous *Madonna with Teeth*, the patroness of dentists and perhaps the most characteristic and earnest work of the earnest Bolognese school. At this point the *portici* of the street intermingle with those of the arcades of the city's Gothic jewel, **Santa Maria dei Servi**, which contains among its works of art a rare *Madonna* by Cimabue (in the apse) which you'll need to illuminate to see.

Santo Stefano

Via Santo Stefano, another street radiating from the two towers, may also be reached from Santa Maria dei Servi via Via Guerrazzi (where, at No.13, the 14-year-old Mozart was elected to the Accademia Filarmonica). Via Santo Stefano has a curious quartet of churches, with a cloister and two chapels thrown in (*all open daily 9–12 and 3.30–6, Sun 9–12.45 and 3.30–6*), all part of the monastery of Santo Stefano founded by St Petronius, who reproduced here the seven holy sites of Jerusalem (over a temple of the Egyptian goddess Isis) and dedicated the ensemble to the first Christian martyr. Three of the churches of this unique and harmonious 8th–12th century Romanesque ensemble face Piazza Santo Stefano – the largest is the **Crocefisso**, begun in the 11th century, with an altar in its façade and an ancient crypt below its raised choir. To the left is polygonal **San Sepolcro**, modelled on the Holy Sepulchre, containing the **Edicola di San Petronio**, a large pulpit adorned with reliefs and encircled by the columns of Isis's circular temple. **SS. Vitale e Agricola**, further to the left, is Bologna's oldest church, built in the 5th century, with bits and pieces of old Roman buildings, and alabaster windows.

Beyond it is the **Cortile di Pilato**, containing an 8th-century Lombard bathtub that somehow gained the sinister reputation of being the basin in which Pontius Pilate washed his hands. From here you can enter the fourth church, the 13th-century **Trinità**, with a lovely 10th-century cloister and works by Simone de' Crocefissi. Up Via Santo Stefano towards the Due Torri is the lovely Gothic **Palazzo della Mercanzia** (1384); it has an ornate loggia by the architect of San Petronio, Antonio da Vincenzo.

Via Zamboni

Again from the towers, Via Zamboni leads shortly to **Piazza Rossini**. Rossini, composer of the *Barber of Seville* and *William Tell*, studied from 1806 to 1810 at the **Conservatorio G. B. Martini** (*open Mon–Sat 9–1*), and spent much of his life in a nearby *palazzo*. The Conservatory houses original scores by Mozart, Monteverdi and Rossini, and, oddly, a portrait by Thomas Gainsborough. Also on the square is **San Giacomo**

Maggiore, begun in 1267. It was the parish church of the Bentivoglio, one of whom, Giovanni II, hired Lorenzo Costa to paint the frescoes in the Cappella Bentivoglio – the *Triumph of Death*, the *Apocalypse* and *Madonna Enthroned* – with himself and family in their midst. In these pictures the Bentivoglio seem benign enough, but the Bolognese hated them and tore their palace apart brick by brick when they were deposed. The fresco itself was commissioned in thanksgiving for the thuggish Giovanni's escape from hired assassins. The fine altarpiece in the chapel is by Francesco Francia, a native of Bologna, while the high-mounted tomb opposite, of Anton Galeazzo Bentivoglio (1435), is by della Quercia.

The **Oratory of Santa Cecilia** (*open in summer 10–1 and 3.30–6.30, in winter 10–1 and 3–6*), entered from Via Zamboni, is frescoed by Costa and Francia. The **Teatro Comunale**, further up in Piazza Verdi, was built by Antonio Bibiena in 1763 over the Bentivoglio Palace. The Bibiena clan of theatre and stage designers were in demand all over Europe in the 17th and 18th centuries, and did much to popularize the typical Baroque tiers of boxes, which the Teatro Comunale preserves behind its 1933 façade.

The University

Beyond the theatre is the University, which was moved in 1803 from the too-central Archiginnasio (where the students could cause trouble) into Pellegrino Tibaldi's Mannerist **Palazzo Poggi**, topped by the eclectic astronomers' observation tower, the **Torre della Specola** – part of Luigi Ferdinando Marsigli's attempt to bring new empirical sciences to Bologna in 1720 – and adorned with Tibaldi's frescoes of Ulysses, an influential Mannerist illusionistic *quadratura* painting. Famed for medicine and astronomy (Copernicus studied here), Bologna was and is known best for jurisprudence, ever since its founding by the *glossatori* (who 'glossed' or annotated Justinian's codes). One student, Vacarius, went on to found the law school at Oxford in 1144.

There are a number of small museums connected to the university in the Palazzo Poggi (*all open Mon–Fri 8.30–5.30*) including the **Museo Aldovrandi**, housing the collections of the great Renaissance naturalist who established botany, zoology and entomology, and the **Museo di Astronomia**. Further north on Via Irnerio is the **Orto Botanico**, one of the world's oldest botanical gardens, and one of the most popular oddball attractions in Bologna, the **Museo di Anatomia Umana Normale** (*open Mon–Fri 9–1*), which houses wax anatomical models made by the most talented artists of the 18th cenury as medical teaching aids. For a sobering look at Fido sans skin, there's also the **Museo Anatomico di Animali Domestici**.

Pinacoteca Nazionale

Via Belle Arti 56, t 051 243 222; open Tues–Sat 9–2, Sun 9–1 (there are plans to open it some evenings in summer until 11pm); adm.

Across from the university, Bologna's most important art is stored here: 14th-century Bolognese artists – of whom Vitale da Bologna emerges as the star with his intense *St George and the Dragon* – and 'foreigners', the pride of which is a Giotto polyptych; fine Renaissance works by the Vivarini brothers and Cima da Conegliano of

Venice; works by the Ferrara school; and later Bolognese paintings. The most famous painting in the entire museum is Raphael's *Ecstasy of St Cecilia*, which the artist sent from Rome to his friend Il Francia. Parmigianino represents Emilia-Romagna's Mannerist decades, sharing space with Perugino and Titian. The Carracci brothers, who initiated Bologna's move into the forefront of Italian art, and the perfect little world of Guido Reni, Bologna's favourite son, each earn a room of their own.

Via Belle Arti, heading back towards the centre, passes several fine palaces and ends at the intersection of Via Mentana. Turn left for **San Martino**; Paolo Uccello painted a fresco here which was believed completely lost until 1981, when a *Nativity* fragment was found. The church also contains fine works by Francia, Costa and the Carraccis.

North and West of Piazza Maggiore

Via dell'Indipendenza links Piazza Maggiore to the station; on it is Bologna's 10th-century cathedral, **San Pietro**, rebuilt in the Baroque era. As with Venice's San Pietro di Castello, this symbol of the papacy received scant affection – the basilica of the city's patron saint was far more important. Hence San Pietro is not too interesting, unless you are a devotee of St Anne, whose skull is the chief treasure, a gift of Henry VI of England. The Romanesque campanile is a survivor of the original church. For a taste of medieval Bologna with all its towers stroll down Via Altabella and its adjacent lanes.

Opposite the cathedral, Via Manzoni leads to the **Palazzo Fava**, site of the **Museo Civico Medioevale e del Rinascimento** (*open Mon, Wed–Fri 9–2, Sat and Sun 9–1 and 3.30–7; adm*), one of the unmissable sights of the city, containing tombs of medieval scholars carved with life-like images of professors expounding to perplexed, earnest, daydreaming students; a colossal bronze propaganda statue of the most grasping and arrogant of popes, Boniface VIII; a collection of armour, ceramics, majolica, ivory, glass, and a 13th-century English cope. Several rooms of the old *palazzo* have recently been opened to the public, where Annibale Carracci and other Bolognese painters frescoed scenes from the *Aeneid* and classical mythology (*Jason and the Argonauts*).

Via Ugo Bassi, the westerly section of the Via Aemilia, leads to narrow and lively **Piazza Malpighi**, home to some odd little pavilions with pyramidal roofs raised off the ground on slender columns – the 13th-century **Tombs of the Glossatori**, tombs of noted doctors of the Law. The apse and rare flying buttresses of the lovely Gothic **San Francesco** back on to the piazza; begun in the saint's lifetime in 1236, the church has a striking, lofty interior, all white with brick piers and vaulting, and a beautiful 14th-century sculpted marble ancona. Back towards the centre, Via C. Battisti runs south from Via Ugo Bassi to the 17th-century San Salvatore, with a striking Mannerist *Marriage of St Catherine* (1534), the masterpiece of Girolamo da Carpi.

South of Piazza Maggiore

From the Archiginnasio, Via Garibaldi leads south to **San Domenico**, built in 1251 to house the relics of St Dominic, founder of the Dominican order of preaching friars. He built a convent on this site and died here in 1221; his tomb, the **Arca di San Domenico**, is a masterwork. Many chisels contributed to it, including those of Nicolò Pisano and his school, who executed the beautiful reliefs of the saint's life, and Nicolò dell'Arca, who gained his name from it – adding the eight patron saints of Bologna on top; when he died mid-work a 20-year-old refugee from Florence called Michelangelo finished them off, sculpting SS Petronius and Proculus and an angel holding a candle.

From San Domenico, Via Marsili leads to Via D'Azeglio, with the **Palazzo Bevilacqua**, a 15th-century Tuscan-style palace where the Council of Trent took refuge from a plague in Trent in 1547. Just north of here at Via Val D'Aposa 6 is the lovely brick and terracotta façade of **Spirito Santo**. Via Marsili, now Via Urbana, continues to the **Collegio di Spagna** (*visits by appointment, t 051 330 408*) the Spanish college founded in 1365 by Cardinal Albornoz, the papacy's top man in Italy while the popes were hiding out in Avignon. In the Middle Ages Bologna had many such colleges, but this one (an official corner of Spanish territory) is the only one to survive. Cervantes studied here, as did St Ignatius. From here Via Saragozza wends down to the **Porta Saragozza**, starting point for the portico to beat all porticoes – winding 4km up the hill to the **Santuario della Madonna di San Luca**. The church was built to house an icon attributed to St Luke, and the 666-arch portico added between 1674 and 1793.

There are fantastic views of the Apennines from the sanctuary (if you can't face the hike, bus no.20 from Via dell'Indipendenza covers some of the route). Other famous viewpoints in the hills south of Bologna are from **San Michele in Bosco**, a hospital in a former convent (bus no.30), and from **Villa Aldini** (bus no.52A), built on the site where Napoleon admired the panorama of the city. From this villa you can walk down towards the Porta San Mamolo and the fine 15th-century church of the Annunziata.

East of Bologna

Between Bologna and the Adriatic are a hotchpotch of attractions – Italy's most important trotting course and the Imola motor-racing course, the fine medieval town of Brisighella, Italy's top ceramics town, Faenza, and Forlì, decorated by Mussolini.

Imola

Nearest to Bologna, Imola is synonymous with the San Marino Grand Prix, held on the race track here, and for a restaurant, the San Domenico, a pilgrimage shrine for grand gourmets. Otherwise, in the cathedral you can pay your respects at the tomb of Imola's patron, San Cassiano, a schoolteacher whose martyrdom was particularly unpleasant: he was stabbed with the pens of his students. The **Rocca Sforzesca**, to the south of the Via Aemilia, was defended by Caterina Sforza, from the time of her husband Girolamo Riario's assassination in 1488 (for his role in the unsuccessful Pazzi conspiracy against Lorenzo de' Medici) until its capture by Cesare Borgia in 1499. As she rallied her supporters to help defend the castle, they pointed out that her six children were still in the hands of the enemy, leaving the family with no heirs; Caterina reportedly hoisted up her skirts and told the crowd she could still make plenty more. However the final, losing, battle may have been a little unbalanced: the Borgia side had a renowned expert on fortifications to assist their siege, a certain Leonardo da Vinci – who later drew a town plan of Imola, made for improving the defences, that is now at Windsor Castle. Caterina's life came full circle: she ended it married to a Medici. Her other castle, at **Dozza**, a few kilometres back towards Bologna, houses the **Enoteca Regionale Emilia-Romagna** (*t 0542 678 089, f 0542 678 073; open April–Oct Mon–Sat 10–12 and 3–6, Sun and holidays 10–12 and 3–7; Nov–Mar Mon–Sat 2–5, Sun and holidays 2–6*), a treasure-trove where you can sample 600 wines of the region.

Faenza

'Faience ware' was born in the 16th century in Faenza with the invention of a new style of majolica: a piece was given a solid white glaze then rapidly, almost impressionistically, decorated with two tones of yellow and blue. It caused a sensation, and was in such demand throughout Europe that Faenza became a household name. Today, though rather a shabby place, Faenza has regained much of its 16th-century lustre as a ceramics centre. There are 500 students enrolled in its Istituto d'Arte per la Ceramica and some 60 artists from around the world run workshops in the town. The **Associati Ente Ceramica**, Voltone della Molinella 2, **t** 0546 22308, issues a list of studios that you may visit and buy from. Among several buildings and palaces adorned with majolica the most splendid is the Liberty-style **Palazzo Matteucci** in Corso Mazzini. Every year from September to October Faenza hosts an international ceramics exhibition; the theme is contemporary in odd years, and antique in even.

The **Museo Internazionale delle Ceramiche** at Viale Baccarini 19 (*open April–Oct Tues–Sat 9–7, Sun 9.30–1, 3–7; Nov–March Tues–Fri 9–1.30, Sat and Sun 9.30–1 and 3–6; adm; if you're going to Ravenna, buy a biglietto cumulativo, which includes the main monuments there*) was founded in 1908 and restored after bombing in the War. It houses a magnificent collection, centred on 16th- and 17th-century Italian ceramics; pieces from Faenza adorned with giraffe-necked Renaissance ladies were typical nuptial gifts. There are fine Liberty-style pieces by Domenico Baccarini and Francesco Nonni, and downstairs you'll find pieces by Picasso, Matisse, Chagall and Rouault.

North of Faenza, nobody knows how **Bagnacavallo** ('horse-bath') got its name, but it has the distinction of having been the property of Sir John Hawkwood, the English mercenary captain of the 1300s whose monument you can see in Florence's Duomo.

Some 12km south of Faenza on the Florence road, **Brisighella** is a charming village and thermal spa in the Lamone Valley. The sharp cliffs overhead are crowned by the splendid towers of the 12th-century Rocca and the Torre dell'Orologio, the latter originally a respectable guard tower (1290) with a clock slapped on its front in the 18th century. Brisighella produces much of the clay fired in Faenza's kilns – next to the village you can see the gashes left in the hills by the old quarries. So precious was this cargo borne by mule caravans that a protected, elevated passageway, the Via degli Asini (Mule Road), was built. Several ceramics workshops still operate in Brisighella; from the end of June to the first week of July the city hosts an elaborate Medieval Festival, with music, games, feasts, plays – and absolutely gorgeous costumes.

Forlì

The *Forum Livii* on the Via Aemilia was elided over the years into Forlì, a city split between an attractive old town and the architectural legacy of Mussolini, who was

Getting Around

Between Bologna and Rimini **trains** are fast, frequent and occasionally packed, particularly in August. A slow local train runs from Faenza to Florence and stops at Brisighella; to continue to Florence you may have to change at Borgo San Lorenzo. Bagno di Romagna and other towns near the Tuscan frontier can best be reached by **bus** from Forlì or Florence.

Tourist Information

Imola: Via Mazzini 14, **t** 0542 602 207, **f** 0542 602 310; *www.comune.imola.bo.it.*
Faenza: Piazza del Popolo 1, **t** 0546 25231.
Brisighella: Piazzetta Porta Gabolo, **t** 0546 81166 (*summer only*).
Forlì: Corso della Repubblica 23, **t** 0543 712 435, **f** 0543 712 434, *www.delfo.forli-cesena.it.*

Where to Stay and Eat

Imola ✉ 40026
San Domenico, Via G. Sacchi 1, **t** 0542 29000 (*very, very expensive*). It's been a place of veneration for gastronomes from around the world for the past 30 years. This holy temple of Italian culinary traditions offers a constantly changing menu of the day, sublimely prepared with the lightest and most delicate of touches. The 1970s dining room may be slightly dated, but the food is as fresh and wonderful as ever, and the wine list is exquisite enough to shatter a credit card. Several set price menus are available, from an expensive lunch to the extremely expensive *menu degustazione. Closed Mon, Sun eve and late July–late Aug.*
Osteria del Vicolo Nuovo, Vicolo Coldronchi 6, **t** 0542 32552 (*expensive*). In a 17th-century cellar, serves delicious modern dishes based on local traditions: cheese soufflé with *porcini* mushrooms, home-made pasta (*gnocchi* with *porcini, tortellini* with asparagus), rabbit roasted in Sangiovese wine, tongue with *salsa verde*, an assortment of vegetarian dishes, and a delicious assortment of cheeses. *Closed Sun and Mon.*
è Parlaminté, Via G. Mameli 33, **t** 0542 30144 (*moderate*). The cheerful family-run 'parliament' is a favourite in Imola, a place where everyone comes to eat *passatelli in brodo* or *baccalà*, and discuss the affairs of the day. *Closed Thurs, and Sun in summer.*

Faenza ✉ 48018
★★★★**Hotel Vittoria**, Corso Garibaldi 23, **t** 0546 21508, **f** 0546 29136, *www.connectivy.it* (*expensive*). An attractive hotel in the centre, with 19th-century furnishings and the occasional frescoed ceiling; rooms are large; laundry service available.

For cheaper accommodation, there are now many *affittacamere* (rooms for rent) in private houses. Call the tourist office for details.
Le Volte, Corso Mazzini 54, **t** 0546 661 600 (*moderate*). Near the Pinacoteca, hidden in the old wine cellars, now under the Galleria Gessi arcade. Surrounded by antique furniture, eat *tortelloni al radicchio*, duck breast roasted with cabbage and pepper, or rack of lamb in a herb crust. *Closed Sun.*

Brisighella ✉ 48013
★★★★**Gigiolè**, Piazza Carducci 5, **t** 0546 81209 (*expensive*). In the centre of Brisighella, the excellent restaurant has long been a mecca for foodies. The rooms have been brought up to ★★★★standard, but the raison d'être continues to be the superb food created by a chef who has done detailed research into Romagna's medieval culinary traditions – a classic *borlonga*, filled with greens and cheese; *ravioli* stuffed with rabbit and mint, veal with wild fennel, chestnut-flour pasta with *porcini* mushrooms, and a rich dessert cart. *Restaurant closed Mon; everything closed mid-Feb to mid-March, half of July.*

born in nearby Predappio. The old centrepiece of old Forlì is the striking 12th-century **Basilica di San Mercuriale**, with a good campanile (1180), a fine lunette of the Magi by the school of Antelami, and an interesting interior. The **Duomo** on Corso Garibaldi has a temple façade; inside, note the painting of 15th-century firemen. On Corso della

***Valverde**, Via Lamone 14, **t** 0546 81388, **f** 0546 80445 (*cheap*). Other hotels are down by the river near the baths; the 'green valley' is a good choice, in a garden setting.

Trattoria di Strada Casale, Fraz. Strada Casale, **t** 0546 88054 (*moderate*). Thanks to the lead of the Gigiolè, and to the qualities of Brisighella's olive oil, the town has become something of a pilgrimage destination for gourmets. Here's another reason to linger; Remo Camurani and Andrea Spada offer superb creative food based on the finest ingredients on a menu that changes every day, and a fabulous five-course moderately priced *menu degustazione;* you can also get a more expensive one with three different wines. *Open weekday eve only, except Wed; also open for lunch on Sat and Sun.*

Cantina del Bonsignore, Via Recupeati 4a, **t** 0546 81889 (*moderate*).The atmospheric wine cellar of the *monsignore*'s palace, in the *centro storico*, where you can dine well on delicacies such as poppyseed *ravioli* and a *tortino di polenta* with *porcini* mushrooms. *Open eves only, closed Thurs, two weeks in Aug, two weeks in Jan.*

Forlì ✉ 47100

***Vittorino**, Via Baratti 4, **t** 0543 21521, **f** 0543 25933 (*cheap*). Central; small, simple rooms.

La Volpe e l'Uva, Via. G. Saffi, **t** 0543 33600 (*moderate*). Near the Pinacoteca, serves traditional dishes in a variety of forms: *tigelle*, green *garganelli*, fish and salads. *Closed Mon, and between July and Aug.*

La Casa Rusticale dei Cavalieri Templari, Via Bologna 275, **t** 0543 701 888 (*moderate*). Occupies a house built as a Templar lodge in the 13th century, which went through incarnations as a church and farmhouse. Now it's the place to come for delicious *piadine*, home-made pasta dishes and classic Romagnoli *secondi*. A selection of cheap and moderate lunchtime *menu degustazione. Closed Sun and Mon.*

Bagno di Romagna ✉ 47021

****Hotel Tosco Romagnolo**, Piazza Dante Aligheri 2, **t** 0543 911 260, **f** 0543 911 014 (rooms range from *very expensive* to *cheap*). Peaceful and modern, a charming place to stay and relax, with a garden on the banks of a *torrente*, a pool, and one of Italy's most enchanting restaurants, **Paolo Teverini**. The menu is based on Tuscan and Romagnolo country traditions, but with a very special touch: Teverini is considered the top vegetable chef in the country, a man who can make a gastronomic Mona Lisa from an onion. To accompany his masterpieces, seven special varieties of bread are baked daily, and if you can't decide what to choose *à la carte* there are four *menu degustazione* from *moderate* (the 'garden menu') to *very expensive* (the 'creative menu'); fabulous desserts and dessert wines served by the glass. *Closed Mon and Tues, except in July and Aug.*

Cesena ✉ 47023

****Casali**, Via B. Croce 81, **t** 0547 22745, **f** 0547 22828 (*expensive*). The nicest hotel here, traditional and luxurious although it's more convenient for motorists.

Osteria Michiletta, Via Fantaguzzi 26, **t** 0547 24691 (*moderate*). Popular and the oldest in town; serves good healthy dishes, based on vegetables and freshly ground wheat and other cereals – not perhaps your traditional Romagnolo food, but popular. There are also meat dishes, including tasty rabbit in *porchetta* with wild fennel. *Closed Sun.*

La Circolino, Via Corte Dandini 10, **t** 0547 21875 (*moderate*). Right in the centre of town, serves delicious starters and pasta dishes – mushrooms with *formaggio di fossa* (literally 'pit' or 'ditch' cheese), anchovies with sun-dried tomatoes and pink *cappelletti*, and dishes made with veal and rabbit to follow. *Closed Tues, Jan.*

Repubblica, the **Pinacoteca Saffi** (*open Mon–Fri 9–2 and 3–8, Sat 9–2; closed Aug*) has works by local artist Marco Palmezzano, Fra Angelico, and Canova's marble Hebe, a rarefied neoclassical fantasy. Nearby, **Santa Maria dei Servi** contains the finely sculpted tomb of Luffo Namai (1502). South of the centre, Forlì's castle, the highly picturesque 15th-century **Rocca di Ravaldino**, also belonged to Caterina Sforza, and was the birthplace in 1498 of her son Giovanni de' Medici ('Giovanni delle Bande Nere', a famous *condottiere* and father of Cosimo I, first Duke of Tuscany). It is now a prison.

At the eastern edge of the centre, on and around Piazza della Vittoria, you'll find the centre of an entire district laid out between 1925 and 1932 called the **Città del Duce.** Plenty of nonsense has been written about architecture and design under the Fascist regime. But for the inscriptions and pasted-on fasces and slogans Mussolini's architecture was no more 'authoritarian' than that of Paris in the 1930s. A little Bauhaus and a discreet touch of travertine Roman monumentalism are the main ingredients, with recurring conceits like the open porticos of tall square columns, seen all over Italy. The entire ensemble is a reminder of how much Fascism, like the Baroque, depended on mass spectacles in appropriate settings. Appearance was everything.

The Local *Palio*

Siena's *palio* (traditional horse race) may be the most famous, but it's neither unique in Italy, nor the only one to claim the longest history. However, whereas Siena's has continued virtually uninterrupted for centuries, the others, particularly in Emilia-Romagna, have resurrected themselves over the past few decades, and so lack the pomp, vast crowds and deep emotional response of that gallop around the Campo. The *palii* in Montagnana, Ferrara, Faenza (last two Sundays in July) or Forlimpopoli may be less vital, violent, cosmopolitan and crooked, but they do have other charms: no tourists, few police, small crowds, and a chance to see an Italian community expressing its self-love. Older traditions do remain (the tug of war to decide placings at the race's start), but the lack of formality and crowds allow a relaxed atmosphere; kids in medieval finery spend the afternoon tearing round the streets, beating on drums.

Siena provides the framework which lesser *palii* copy. The day begins with a procession in medieval costume, probably led by the town's standard, followed by a delegation from each district: 'landowners' on horseback, young married couples holding hands, a matron in the middle of a crowd of urchins, a criminal in the stocks, massed ranks of young men clasping spears and pushing a catapult, a cart piled with geese, and troupes of teenage *sbandierati* twirling long, silken flags from one hand to the other, tossing them into the air and, as they unfurl, catching them again.

By comparison the race itself is chaotic. Bales of hay line wooden barriers which shield the crowds from the thundering horses. Each bareback rider carries a *nerbo*, a whip with which he may hit any horse or opponent, and wears a small coat named *giacchetto*, from which we derive the English word 'jockey' (and 'jacket'). The horses, fired up, take several minutes to form a regular starting-line. The race is brief and furious. Its aftermath depends on where you are: in Montagnana, near Rovigo, the victor will be carried home for a beer and barbecue. In Siena supporters will try to kill the losers for having lost and the victor for having won; the entire city weeps for joy or shame at the outcome; casks of wine are splintered open on the pavement and goblets handed out to any passer-by.

Into the Apennines

South of Forlì three principal routes lead into Tuscany. Some of the best scenery is in the **Montone Valley**, the main route to Florence (along the SS67) passing the Renaissance planned village of **Terra del Sole**, begun in 1564 in the form of a perfect rectangle. Ruined medieval castles haunt the next towns of **Dovadola** and **Rocca San Casciano**. Dante's beloved Beatrice spent several summers in the very pretty old medieval town of **Portico di Romagna**; the Portinari house where she stayed can still be seen in the main street. Near the Tuscan frontier the 9th-century abbey at **San Benedetto in Alpe** sheltered Dante after his unsuccessful bid to return to Florence from exile (*Inferno*, Canto XVI, 94–105). In San Benedetto you can hire horses to explore the region's valleys, especially the lovely **Valle dell'Acquacheta** with its bucolic, stepped waterfall. The rapid Brusia river is popular with canoeists, and this is a marvellous area for hill walking.

The narrow alternative route just east (SS9 ter) passes through the **Sangiovese** wine country around **Predappio**, where Mussolini was born in 1883; in 1957 his remains were re-buried in the cemetery near his wife Rachele's, and are a pilgrimage site for creeps. Mussolini made Predappio the seat of the local *comune*, and embellished it with public buildings, leaving the old comune, Predappio Alto, alone beneath its overgrown castle. In Predappio Alto, you can taste the local ruby-red Sangiovese or 'blood of Jove' at the Cà de Sanvès (*open daily 10–12 and 3–midnight; closed Tues*).

From **Forlimpopoli**, with its well-preserved medieval castle, a third road heads south for **Bertinoro**, an old town famous for its wine and hospitality. Such were the squabbles over guests that a column was erected in front of the 14th-century Palazzo Comunale and hung with rings, one belonging to each family. The ring a stranger tethered his horse to decided which family got to be his host. Nearby **Polenta** has a fine 9th-century Byzantine-Romanesque temple.

The main SS310 from Forlì continues into the scenic, heavily forested Upper Bidenta Valley. There are ski facilities at Monte Campigna, near the old Tuscan town of Santa Sofia. Much further south, near Balze, there's more skiing at Monte Fumaiolo, on whose slopes the Tiber begins its 418km journey to Rome. San Piero in Bagno and Bagno di Romagna, with thermal and mud baths, are popular summer resorts in the region.

Cesena and the Crossing of the Rubicon

In the 14th–15th centuries Cesena, site of the European Trotting Championships in August, was one of the jewels of the Malatesta clan. Their castle still dominates the town, while a 1452 basilica built for Domenico Malatesta Novello is the main sight, housing the **Biblioteca Malatestiana** (*open Mon–Sat 9–12.45 and 4–6, Sun 10.30–12.30; closes at dusk; adm*), with a priceless collection of manuscripts. Between Cesena and Rimini at Savignano, the road crosses a poor excuse for a stream that most authorities accept as the shadowy Rubicon, which divided what was then Gaul from Roman Italy, and which Julius Caesar crossed with his army in 49 BC, thereby defying the Senate and declaring his intention to take over the Roman state. Today it separates respectable Emilia-Romagna from the beach Babylon of Rimini.

Ferrara

There's been a certain mystique attached to Ferrara ever since Jacob Burckhardt called it 'the first modern city in Europe' in his classic *Civilization of the Renaissance in Italy*. Whether or not Burckhardt was right can be debated endlessly; what is certain is that the famous 'additions' to the medieval city in the Renaissance were far too ambitious. Ferrara, even in the most brilliant days of the Este family, never mustered more than 30,000 citizens – not enough to fill the long, straight, rational streets laid out within the 9km circuit of the walls.

But what was a failure in the Renaissance is a happy success today; if Italian art cities can be said to come and go in fashion, Ferrara is definitely in, popularized by a well-received international campaign to save its unique walls, and a rebirth of interest in its great quattrocento painters. Thanks to the tyrannical Este, the charming city they enclose was one of the brightest stars of the Renaissance, with its own fine school of art led by Cosmè Tura, Ercole de' Roberti, Lorenzo Costa and Francesco del Cossa. Poets patronized by the Este produced three great Italian Renaissance epics – Boiardo's *Orlando Innamorato* (1483), Ariosto's continuation of the story, *Orlando Furioso* (1532), and Tasso's *Gerusalemme Liberata* (1581), all praising the ducal family.

History

Ferrara grew up on a formerly navigable branch of the Po River, and until the 17th century based its economy on river tolls, the salt pans of the Comacchio and the rich agricultural land of the Delta. It was always ruled by one family or the other, but it was the rise of the Este in 1250 that made Ferrara a great city, an outpost of papal power in the north. The Este clan produced and married some of the most interesting characters of the Renaissance: there was Nicolò II (1361–88) 'the Lame', a friend of Petrarch; Alberto (1388–93), who founded the University of Ferrara; Nicolò III (1393–1441), reputedly the father of hundreds of children on both banks of the Po, as well as being the villain who perpetrated one of the tragic love stories of his day – he found that his young wife Parisina and his son by another woman, Ugo, were lovers, and had both of them executed.

The legitimate sons of Nicolò III – Leonello, Borso and Ercole I (1471–1505) – met happier fates, and were responsible for the city's great cultural flowering. Ercole I had the first addition to the city (known as the Herculean Addition) designed by his architect Rossetti; his offspring, Isabella (wife of Francesco Gonzaga), Beatrice (married to Lodovico Sforza, Il Moro), and Cardinal Ippolito, were among the most cultured and influential people of their day. His heir, Alfonso I (1505–34), married the beautiful and unjustly maligned Lucrezia Borgia, who ran a brilliant and fashionable court, patronizing Ariosto and Titian, while her husband spent his days casting huge cannons. With the guns, and some carefully crafted marriages, Alfonso's skilful diplomacy helped Ferrara avoid invasion and emerge from the Wars of Italy with its independence intact. Their son, Ercole II (1534–59), married Renée, daughter of Louis XII of France, and a Calvinist, who sheltered John Calvin in Ferrara under an assumed name; eventually relations with Rome became so touchy that she had to be sent away.

The last Duke, Alfonso II (1559–97), patron of the unstable Tasso, was considered the best-educated and most courtly ruler of his day, but at the expense of his people. When he died without issue, Ferrara, sick and tired of paying the bills, was glad to see the last of the Este, and be ruled by a papal legate. The city soon became a backwater, and its population declined. In this century, however, the modern 'Metaphysical School' of painting (De Chirico, Carrà, De Pises, Morandi, and others) had its origins in the city, inspired at least in part by the great frescoes in the Palazzo Schifanoia.

The Castle and the Cathedral

At the very centre of Ferrara towers the imposing **Castello Estense** (*open Tues–Sun 9–5; adm*), which would look like a Victorian factory building were it not for its moat and drawbridges. It was begun as a fortress in 1385 by Nicolò II after a tax revolt, but later the Este transformed it into their chief residence, its crenellations replaced by white marble balustrades, and its great halls adorned with art. A few decorated rooms survive: the *Salone* and *Saletta dei Giochi* (the games room, the latter belonging to the children) and the fine *Sala dell'Aurora* (Ercole II's study) and *Camerina dei Baccanali* are the most interesting. The tour includes Renée's Calvinist chapel; and the Torre dei Leoni, where Ugo and Parisina languished before their beheading, and Giulio and Ferrante, brothers of Alfonso I, spent their lives after attempting a coup. The dukes weren't the forgiving kind: Ferrante died after 34 years in the tower, while Giulio came out with a pardon after 53 years, aged 81.

From the *castello*, Corso dei Martiri leads first to the **Palazzo Comunale,** built in 1243 and adorned with statues of Nicolò III and Borso; next to it in Piazza della Repubblica stands a statue of Savonarola, a native of Ferrara. Opposite the *palazzo* is the handsome rose-coloured **Duomo**, begun in 1135 by Wiligelmo of Modena fame and his follower Nicolò, and finished by 1300. Its glory is a marble portico: Nicolò executed the relief on the tympanum of *St George* and various Old Testament scenes; the pediment above the loggia on top is carved with a magnificent 13th-century Last Judgement. The candy-striped campanile is said to be Alberti's work. The upper loggia on the south side is a bit of show-offish Romanesque bravura, with twisted columns; the picturesque portico below, flanking the Duomo, was added in 1473. The interior was catastrophically remodelled in the 17th century, but you can see the best art in the **Museo della Cattedrale** on Via San Martino (*open Tues–Sat 10–12 and 3–5, Sun 10–12.30 and 3.30–5.30; adm*), including a marble *Madonna of the Pomegranate* by Jacopo della Quercia and two painted organ shutters by Cosmè Tura that rank among his greatest works: a naturalistic *Annunciation* and a surreal *St George*.

Renaissance Palaces

From behind the cathedral in Via Voltapaletto, Via Savonarola will take you to the **Casa Romei** (*open Tues–Sun 8.30–2; adm*), a fine example of the typical Renaissance palace, built for a banker who won the sweepstakes by marrying an Este in 1445. As well as its charming frescoes, terracotta fireplaces and elegant courtyards, there are expressive detached frescoes moved here from Sant'Andrea and other disused churches. To the south on Via Pergolato, behind the church of San Girolamo, the

Getting Around

Ferrara's **railway station** is just outside the city walls, a 15-minute walk west of the centre along Viale Cavour (or take local bus no.1, 2, 3c or 5). There are frequent rail connections to Bologna, Venice and Ravenna. The **bus station** is near the corner of the Rampari di San Paolo and Corso Isonzo; a network of lines serves the coast, Bologna, Modena, Ravenna and local destinations; ACFT Punto Bus **t** 0532 599 490.

Pancake-flat, Ferrara has the second-largest ratio of bicycles to humans in Europe (after Copenhagen). Hire one at the *deposito* just outside the train station, **t** 0532 772 190, or try Itinerando, Via Kennedy, just off Piazza Travaglio, **t** 0532 202 003.

Tourist Information

The office is inside the Castello Estense, **t** 0532 299 303, **f** 0532 209 370.

Activities

Ferrara has its own **Palio** or traditional horse race, every year on the last Sunday in May. In fact there are four *palii* – one for boys, one for girls, one for horses and one for donkeys. The Ferrara **Buskers' Festival** is held in the last week in August; buskers from all over the world perform in the streets in the centre of town. **Ferrara Musica** is an international season of **concerts** and **opera** which runs from September to May. Venues include the stunning Teatro Comunale.

Where to Stay

Ferrara ✉ 44100

Luxury
★★★★★**Duchessa Isabella**, Via Palestro 70, **t** 0532 202 121, **f** 0532 202 638, *isabella@tin.it*. Occupies a magnificent Renaissance palace in the heart of the city. When it was converted into a hotel, no detail was overlooked; antiques, linens and crystals furnish the old rooms, some of which still have frescoes by the Ferrara school and coffered ceilings. There's a private park; guests can use the hotel's bicycles and its own horse-drawn carriage to visit the city. *Closed Aug.*

Expensive
★★★★**Ripagrande**, Via Ripagrande 23, **t** 0532 765 250, **f** 0532 764 377, *ripa@mbox.4net.it*. Set in the Renaissance Beccari-Freguglia palace in the medieval quarter, this offers Ferrara's most memorable accommodation. Its ground floor has the original décor, old brick walls, marble stair and heavy-beamed ceiling. There is also a pleasant inner courtyard. Bicycle hire is another plus.

★★★★**Annunziata**, Piazza della Repubblica 5, **t** 0532 201 111, **f** 0532 203 233, *annunziata@ tin.it*. Our Lady of the Annunciation has big windows overlooking the Castello Estense and very comfortable rooms; there are free bikes for guests.

★★★★**Astra**, Viale Cavour 55, **t** 0532 206 088, **f** 0532 247 002, *astra@mbox.4net.it*. On the main street to the station, a sturdy, well-furnished hotel, with a fine restaurant.

Moderate
★★★**Europa**, Corso Giovecca 49, **t** 0532 205 456, **f** 0532 212 120. When Verdi stayed in Ferrara, he checked into this 17th-century palace designed by Rossetti. Bedrooms are fairly simple but have everything you need – some have frescoes. The lobby is full of 18th-century antiques and there's also a pretty garden courtyard.

★★★**Carlton**, Via Garibaldi 93, **t** 0532 211 130, **f** 0532 205 766, *hotelcarlton@sestantenet.it*. Peaceful, family-run place near the Duomo; fine rooms, a range of prices.

★★★★**Villa Regina**, Via Comacchio 402, at Cocomaro di Cona, **t** 0532 740 222, **f** 0532 761 085, *villaregina@tin.it*. If you want to escape

---

Corpus Domini church (*open Mon–Fri 9.30–12 and 3.30–5.30*) contains the austere tombs of Alfonso I, Alfonso II and Lucrezia Borgia. North of Via Savonarola, up Via Ugo Bassi, the late-Renaissance **Palazzina di Marfisa d'Este** is in a garden at Corso della Giovecca 170 (*open Mar–Oct daily 9–1 and 3–6; Nov–Feb daily 9–1 and 2–5; adm*).

from urban life while remaining within reach of it, try the beautiful 'queen's villa' outside the city, in a converted villa in a park.

Cheap

San Paolo, Via Baluardi 9, **t/f 0532 762 040. Pleasantly situated near the city walls by Piazza Travaglio, with rooms and service beyond what you'd expect for its price.

*Casa Degli Artisti, Via Vittoria 66, **t** 0532 761 038. The best of the cheapest options, right in the centre of town, on a quiet side street near the Duomo.

Eating Out

Ferrara's most famous dish (the favourite of Lucrezia Borgia) is spicy *salama da sugo* – a sausage that is cured for a year, then gently boiled for about four hours and eaten with a spoon. The bakers of Ferrara are famous for their X-shaped bread, *ciupèta*; little caps of pasta, *cappelletti*, filled with pumpkin, are another speciality. Renée of France brought her own vines to Ferrara, the origin of the local viticulture and the delicious Vino di Bosco.

Expensive

Il Don Giovanni, 17km south of Ferrara at Località Marrara, Via del Primaro 86, **t** 0532 421 06. A menu that changes weekly to take advantage of fresh seasonal produce and the day's catch; the sea and land food is imaginative, often full of delicious surprises and combinations (*ravioli* filled with seabass and fresh coriander in an onion sauce) ; great desserts, cheese and wine list. Reserve. *Closed Mon lunch, Sun, Jan and July.*

Moderate

L'Oca Guiliva, Via Boccacanale–Santo Stefano, **t** 0532 207 628. Lovers of good wine and food will find both here: the traditional menu includes *pasticcio di maccheroni alla ferrarese*, *salama da sugo* and *cappellacci di zucca*; the other menu changes every two weeks. There are 250 wines to choose from, including many by the glass. *Closed Mon, Tues lunch.*

Quel Fantastico Giovedì, Via Castelnuovo 9 (near Piazza del Travaglio), **t** 0532 760 570. Reservations are essential to get a table in the intimate dining rooms of 'What a Wonderful Thursday', where you'll be regaled with creative dishes prepared with a light touch – salmon marinated in herbs, or squid stuffed with aubergines in a yellow pepper sauce, and game dishes in season. Save room for dessert – the chocolatey ones especially. In case you're wondering, the name comes from a story by John Steinbeck. *Closed Wed, late Jan and mid-July–mid-Aug.*

Il Testamento del Porco, Via Putinati 24, **t** 0532 760 460. Just outside the walls by the hippodrome, 'the Pig's Will' is a popular place, for its delicious minestrone, home-made *tagliatelle* with *porcini* mushrooms; pork in various guises, ostrich and fillet of beef with balsamic vinegar. *Closed Sat lunch and Tues, and mid-Feb–mid-Mar.*

Cheap

Antica Trattoria Il Cucco, Via Voltacasotto 3, off Via C. Mayr, **t** 0532 760 026. A good place to indulge in Ferrara's traditional classics: *cappellacci con la zucca* and, if you book ahead, *salama da sugo* or *pasticcio alla ferrarese*, followed by the traditional *ciambella* and sweet wine. *Closed Wed.*

Trattoria da Noemi, **t** 0532 671 715. Also in the centre, on Via Bagno, cheap and cheerful, offers a simple menu with good *tortellini*.

Enotria, 41 Via Saracena. One of a number of *enoteche* in the city centre where you can stop for a glass or two and a snack. A fine selection as well as *bruschetta* and *crostini*.

Al Brindisi, Via Adelardi. Hidden behind the cathedral, it claims to be the oldest hostelry in the world (there's been an *osteria* on this spot since 1453). Now it's a convivial wood-panelled *enoteca* with fine cheeses, *salama del sugo* and other treats. *Closed Mon.*

Marfisa, a friend of Tasso, was beautiful and eccentric, and the subject of several ghost stories; it seems that she enjoyed post-mortem midnight rides through Ferrara in a wolf-drawn carriage. The interior of her little palace has unusual *grotteschi* frescoes on the ceiling. Outside is a loggia with frescoes of two little girls: one is Marfisa.

Palazzo Schifanoia

Ferrara's most famous palace, the 1385 Palazzo Schifanoia (*open daily 9–1 and 3–6; adm*), is a couple of streets away at Via Scandiana 23 (follow Via Ugo Bassi to Via Madama). Schifanoia means 'disgust with boredom', and it would be hard to stay bored in the utterly delightful **Salone dei Mesi**, frescoed for Borso d'Este c. 1475 by Ferrara's finest – Cosmè Tura, Ercole de' Roberti and Francesco del Cossa. The mythological and allegorical scenes, peopled by amiable aristocrats, are believed to have been inspired by Petrarch's Triumphs – in each month a different god is seen to triumph, most famously the Triumph of Venus for the month of April, with a rare Renaissance kiss. Another inspiration comes from the occult astrology that shaped so much of Renaissance thought and life. The palace has several other rooms with beautiful ceilings, and houses an eclectic collection of medieval art (note the alabaster *Passion of Christ* from Nottingham) and ancient art.

Palazzo di Lodovico il Moro

Turn right at the walls at the end of Via Scandiana and continue to Via XX Settembre for No.124, the elegant Palazzo di Lodovico il Moro designed by Biagio Rossetti and named after Beatrice d'Este's Milanese husband, although it never belonged to him. It has frescoes on the ground floor by Raphael's pupil, Garofalo, and upstairs an excellent **Museo Archeologico Nazionale** (*open Tues–Sat 9–2, Sun 9–1; adm*), with artefacts from the necropolis of the Graeco-Etruscan seaport of Spina, including Attic vases, a splendid gold diadem and two pirogues carved from tree trunks in the later Roman period. Nearby in Via Beatrice d'Este, the convent of **Sant'Antonio in Polèsine** has fine frescoes dating back to the 13th century and inlaid choir stalls. Just outside the walls (through the Porta Romana), **San Giorgio** was Ferrara's cathedral until the 12th century, and is worth a look for the sumptuous 1475 tomb of Lorenzo Roverella, Pope Julius II's physician. On the way back towards the centre, on Via delle Scienze, the 13th-century **Palazzo Paradiso** was the former seat of the university and is now the Ariosto library, with the complete manuscript of *Orlando Furioso* and Ariosto's tomb.

Just north of here is a labyrinth of narrow, cobbled streets, brick arches and alleyways – Modena's former ghetto. A **Jewish Museum** (*open for guided tours Sun–Thurs 10–2; adm*) has opened in Via Mazzini, where once there were three synagogues; the building has been the focus of Jewish life in Ferrara since 1485, when it was purchased by a rich financier from Rome employed at the Estense court: he left it in his will 'forever for the common use of the Jews'. Jewish refugees from Spain and the Papal State were subsequently welcomed in Ferrara, and made up a thriving community – until the popes locked them up in a ghetto from 1627 to 1859. Most of Ferrara's Jews were deported in the late stages of the Second World War; only five came back.

The Herculean Addition

North of the Castello Estense stretches the Herculean Addition, laid out by Biagio Rossetti for Ercole I, which more than doubled the size of 15th-century Ferrara. Not long after the fall of the Este dynasty travellers noted that many of the streets here were abandoned and overgrown, and even today they feel somewhat melancholy and quiet. Corso Ercole I was intended as the new district's 'noble street' and it attracted many to build their palaces in the area, including the new home of the Este dukes, Rossetti's showpiece **Palazzo dei Diamanti**. In the very centre of the Addition, it takes its name from the 8,500 pointed, diamond-shaped stones that stud the façade – diamonds being an emblem of the Este. It houses the **Pinacoteca Nazionale** (*open Tues–Sat 9–2, Sun 9–1; adm*), a fine collection by the Ferrara school – Tura, Cossa, Costa, Roberti, the sweet Raphaelesque Garofalo (a favourite of the 18th century) and Dossi – and detached frescoes from churches and palaces. There's also a Carpaccio *Death of the Virgin*, and works by two local artists known only as the 'Maestro degli Occhi Spalancati' (Master of the Wide-open Eyes) and a 'Maestro degli Occhi Ammicanti' (Master of the Winking Eyes). On the ground floor is a **Galleria Civica d'Arte Moderna** and the **Museo Michelangelo Antonioni**, containing a multi-media fantasy called the 'Enchanted Mountain' by the famous director (*open daily 9–1 and 3–6; adm*).

The palace lies at the junction of two main streets; Via Ariosto leads off Corso Biagio Rossetti to the right, to the **Casa di Ariosto** (*open Tues–Sun 9–2, Wed and Sat also 3–6pm; adm*), which the poet built for himself. 'Small,' he described it modestly, 'but suited to me.' To the east, the **Palazzo Massari** at Corso Porta Mare 9 (*open daily 9–1 and 3–6; adm*) houses two more museums: the first is the **Musei Civici d'Arte Moderna e Contemporanea**, dedicated to Ferrara's Metaphysical School. Pass through the courtyard to reach the **Palazzina dei Cavalieri di Malta**, formerly seat of the Knights of Malta 1826–1834, and now seat of the fascinating **Museo Giovanni Boldini**, a shrine to a flagrant and very fashionable salon painter of the mauve decades, a man born to paint society ladies in evening gowns. Verdi dedicated an opera to him.

Ferrara's well-preserved 9km circuit of red-brick walls is most easily seen by bicycle. They date from the 15th and 16th centuries, one of the prototypes for the new model fortifications of the Renaissance. The best stretch is between the Porta Mare and the former Porta degli Angeli, built by Rossetti on the north side of the city. Cycle paths run along their length, linking with routes out to the Po.

Around Ferrara

The region around Ferrara is flat and somewhat dreary. **Argenta**, southeast of the city, has an attractive quattrocento church of San Domenico, which houses a small art gallery, with works by Garofalo and others.

Between Ferrara and Modena, **Cento**, under its 14th-century castle, was the birthplace of Disraeli's ancestors and painter Giovanni Francesco Barbieri, better known by his nickname Guercino or 'Squinty' (1591–1666); a collection of his work is in the Pinacoteca Civica, Via Matteotti 10.

The Coast: from the Po to Ravenna

For most people the main attractions along this coast are the Po Delta and magnificent Romanesque Abbey of Pomposa, though there are plenty of Italian family lidos in the vicinity if you're tempted to join the summer ice-cream and parasol brigades.

The Southern Po Delta

Alfonso II d'Este was the first to start draining the marshes south of the Po Delta. Much of the land was planted with rice; a large part of the rest now belongs to the **Parco del Delta del Po**, one of Italy's most important wetlands, and a birdwatcher's paradise. Part of the primordial coastal pine forest survives intact in the **Bosco di Mésola**, now a nature reserve (*visitors are admitted Sun and holidays 8am–sunset*). Not far to the west, near Italba, this varied and ever-changing coastline offers something completely different – a marooned 100-acre patch of dunes, once part of the coast, called the '**Moraro**'. Excursion boats ply the narrow canals between the reeds explore the mouth of the Po di Goro and the Valle di Gorino, departing from the picturesque fishing hamlets of Gorino, Goro or Mésola; for information, contact Freccia del Delta, **t** 0533 999 817, or Principessa, **t** 0533 999 815, in Gorino.

The Abbey of Pomposa

The main coast road from the north, SS309, follows the old Roman coastal road, the Via Romea. Just south of the Po di Goro it passes through **Mésola**, with an old hunting lodge, the 'Delizia Estense' of Alfonso I d'Este, then continues down to the haunting and serene **Abbey of Pomposa**, an 8th-century Benedictine foundation, formerly on its own islet; in this atmosphere of total tranquillity the monk Guido d'Arezzo invented the modern musical scale in the early 11th century. Uninhabited since the 17th century, the abbey is dwarfed by its campanile (1063), adorned with mullioned windows, which progress tier by tier from a narrow slit on the bottom to a grand *quadrifore* (four arches) on top; the colourful ceramic plaques are replacements for the originals, made by monks in Egypt. The church (7th–11th centuries) has a lovely Byzantine atrium, done in patterned bricks and relief panels. Inside is a magnificent pavement, in maze-like patterns of stone and mosaics, and above it walls covered with the entire Old and New Testaments in colourful 14th-century frescoes. Some of the best (*Life of Sant'Eustachio*) are by the charming Vitale da Bologna; there are other frescoes by his school in the monks' Chapter House. The abbot governed from the beautifully austere 11th-century Palazzo della Ragione (*all open daily 7–12 and 2–7*).

The resorts along the sandy **Lidi di Comacchio** begin at the Lido di Volano on the other side of the wetlands of the Valle Bertuzzi, where the setting sun ignites the waters in a thousand colours. Of the resorts, the **Lido delle Nazioni** and **Porto Garibaldi** are the most interesting. The name of the latter recalls the defeated hero's attempt to escape from here after the collapse of the Roman Republic in 1849, in a desperate guerrilla movement that cost the life of his pregnant wife Anita. The most important town is **Comacchio,** the Romagna's 'Little Venice', with its monumental triple bridge, the Trepponti, spanning three of the town's many canals. Comacchio used to make its living on salt, but now it is famed for its eels, farmed in the Valli di Comacchio – if you're in the area between September and December you can watch the fishermen scoop them up. On the Canale Maggiore, an old hospital is being restored to house a new **Museo delle Culture Umane nel Delta del Po**. Just west of Comacchio stood the Graeco-Etruscan Spina, for centuries the main port of *Felsina* (Bologna), but now miles from the sea. Almost nothing remains of it.

Ravenna

Innocently tucked away among the art towns of Emilia-Romagna there is one famous city that has nothing to do with Renaissance popes and potentates, Guelphs or Ghibellines, sports cars or socialists. Little, in fact, has been heard from Ravenna in the last thousand years. Before that time, however, this city's career was simply astounding – heir to Rome itself, and the leading city of western Europe for centuries. For anyone interested in Italy's shadowy progress through the Dark Ages, this is the place to visit.

There's a certain magic in three-digit years; history guards their secrets closely, giving us only occasional glimpses of battling barbarians, careful monks 'keeping alive the flame of knowledge' and local Byzantine dukes and counts doing their best to hold things together. In Italy, the Dark Ages were never quite so dark. This can be seen in Rome, but much more clearly here, in the only Italian city that not only survived but prospered all through those troubled times. In Ravenna's churches, adorned with the finest mosaics ever made, such an interruption as the Dark Ages seems to disappear, and you experience the development of Italian history and art from ancient to medieval times as a continuous and logical process.

History

On an important route to Dalmatia and the Danube, Ravenna and its port of Classe first became prominent during the reign of Augustus. With their nearly impregnable

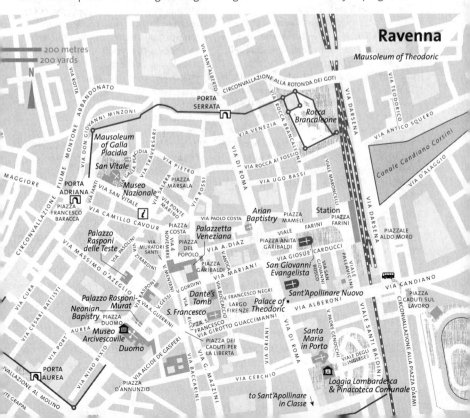

Getting There and Around

Ravenna is not on the main Adriatic railway line, but there are several **trains** a day from Florence, Venice, Ancona and Bologna (change at Faenza or Ferrara from other cities). The station is in Piazza Farini, east of the old town next to the ship channel, a short walk from the centre. The **bus station** is just across the tracks on Via Darsena.

The no.2 bus from the train station or Piazza del Popolo goes past Theodoric's Mausoleum, otherwise a half-hour walk from the centre. Bus no.1 or 70 goes to Marina di Ravenna. Buses no. 4 and 44 (and not minibuses 4 and 44) from the station or Piazza del Popolo go to S. Apollinare in Classe. Other buses from the train station or from Piazza del Popolo will take you to Classe or any of Ravenna's nearby lidos. You can hire **bicycles** in the Piazza Farini in front of the station, and in the ACI car park near San Vitale.

Tourist Information

The main office is Via Salaria 8, **t** 0544 35404, **f** 0544 35094; there is another at the Mausoleo Teodorico (*open Easter–end Sept*).

You can buy a *Biglietto Cumulativo* that will get you into combinations of sights for a discount. The ticket that includes San Vitale, Sant' Apollinare and the Battistero Neoniano, is worth buying if you're going to all of them, or there's one including Faenza's ceramics museum too. Note that Ravenna's sights have an old tradition of infernally complex opening hours, which change annually or even by the season; even the tourist office can't keep track, so don't be surprised if they've changed when you visit.

Festivals

The Ravenna Festival is an important music festival which runs from mid-June to mid-July. Internationally renowned musicians perform concerts, recitals and opera in some of the city's historic churches and palaces. For information call **t** 0544 32577.

Where to Stay

Ravenna ✉ 48100

Expensive

★★★**Cappello**, Via IV Novembre 41, **t** 0544 219 813. There are only seven rooms here, but they are located in a 14th-century *palazzo* reputed to have been the home of Francesca da Rimini. Added charms are frescoes, wood-panelled ceilings, antique fireplaces and a romantic little restaurant. *Hotel open all year; restaurant closed Mon lunch and Sun and Aug.*

Moderate

★★★**Diana**, Via G. Rossi 4, **t** 0544 39164, **f** 0544 30001. In an 18th-century palace, near the tomb of Galla Placidia; a delightful, comfortable hotel with a charming Baroque lobby and bicycles for clients.

★★★**Centrale Byron**, Via IV Novembre 14, **t** 0544 33479, **f** 0544 551 070. An older favourite, ageing gracefully just off the Piazza del Popolo, with some very nice rooms and some very plain ones in the cheap range.

★★★**Columbia**, Viale Italia 70, **t** 0544 446 038, **f** 0544 447 202. A beautiful modern hotel in attractive Marina Romea, to the north and a little way out of the city; it's a 10-minute walk from the beach.

setting, surrounded by marshes, the military advantage was clear, and Classe became Rome's biggest naval base on the Adriatic. As conditions in Italy grew unsettled in the 5th century, Ravenna's relative safety began to look very inviting to scared emperors.

Honorius moved the capital of the Western Empire here in AD 402 – just in time, with Alaric's sack of Rome coming eight years later. Honorius' sister, Galla Placidia, ruled the city in the emperor's absence, and began to embellish it with churches and monuments befitting its new status. When the Visigoths attacked Ravenna, Galla Placidia was taken hostage, and married the Visigothic king Ataulf. They got on

Cheap

★★★Roma, Via Candiano 26, **t** 0544 421 515, **f** 0544 420 505. Ravenna has plenty of budget accommodation but much of it is around the port, a long walk from the centre along Via delle Industrie. 'Rome' is in a more convenient, if not particularly pleasant, location on the other side of the tracks from the railway station.

★Al Giaciglio, Via Rocca Brancaleone 42, **t** 0544 39403. Another budget option, with good home cooking in the restaurant, and a cheap lunch menu that changes daily; pizza too.

Eating Out

Expensive

Tre Spade, Via Faentina 136, **t** 0544 500 522. Ravenna doesn't exactly boogie after dark, but it does shelter some good restaurants. Don't miss this, in the suburbs west of the centre, where they like to innovate and never miss a step. Most of Ravenna comes here for the seafood, but the adventurous try the vegetable/pastry concoctions, stuffed pigeon or some pasta combinations never seen before on this planet. Moderate seafood and meat menus available. *Closed Sun evenings, Mon and Aug.*

Saporetti Trattoria al Pescatore, Via N. Zen 13, **t** 0544 530 208. If you have a hankering for delicious seafood, head out to Marina di Ravenna and the *trattoria* run by the *simpatico* Saporetti family. In the summer you can dine in the garden. *Closed Tues.*

Moderate

Taverna San Romualdo, Via Sant' Alberto 364, **t** 0544 483 447. Not far from San Vitale is a typical rustic Romagnolo *osteria* which

serves hearty dishes. Mixed *antipasti* vary according to the season: *tortellacci* stuffed with nettles and served with *mascarpone* and pine nuts, *minestrone* flavoured with truffles, octopus stewed with balsamic vinegar and served tepid with rocket and *cannellini* beans, or a good choice of game in winter. Try nougat *semifreddo* with chocolate sauce for dessert. *Closed Tues.*

Capannetti, Vicolo Capannetti 21, **t** 0544 66681. An experienced chef who knows what to do with truffles, duck, mushrooms and desserts, though the choice is limited. *Closed Sun eve and Mon.*

La Gardela, Via Ponte Marino 3, **t** 0544 217 147. In the centre of Ravenna, makes its own *tortelloni*; follow it with *scaloppine* with taleggio and rocket, and sample the large collection of *grappas. Closed Thurs.*

Cheap

Renato Guidarello, with entrances at both Via Mentana 33 and Via Gessi 9, **t** 0544 213 684. Has a pleasant, traditional atmosphere and local cuisine, with fish still the main item every Friday. In a beautiful building with painted ceilings.

Ca' de Ven (the 'house of wine'), Via Corrado Ricci 24, **t** 0544 30163. An *enoteca* with a huge selection of Emilia-Romagna wines and snacks using local cheeses, hams and sausages. Suitably calm and dark, it's a great local favourite, the perfect place to while away an afternoon after a morning with the Byzantines. *Closed Mon.*

La Rustica, Via Alberoni 55, **t** 0544 28128. Practically a museum of old country kitchen gear; it's fun speculating just what some of the stuff hung on the walls might be for. Cuisine to match – traditional Romagnolo cooking and especially good pasta dishes.

well together in Toulouse, and before his assassination she rode at his side everywhere, even in battle. She returned eventually to Ravenna, however, and ruled it until she died in 450.

By the 6th century, with sheep grazing in the Roman Forum, Ravenna had become accepted as the metropolis of Italy. The Ostrogothic kings, Odoacer and Theodoric, made it their capital; during the reign of the latter the last flowering of Latin letters took place, under the influence of his famous councillors: Boethius, Symmachus and Cassiodorus. Boethius, one of the Fathers of the Church, wrote The *Consolation of*

Philosophy in Theodoric's dungeon, where the king had consigned him after suspecting the philosopher of intrigues with Constantinople.

The terrible wars for control of Italy, between the Ostrogoths and the Eastern Emperor, were beginning. Ravenna was spared the destruction the Byzantine generals Belisarius and Narses spread through the rest of Italy; after their victory the city became the seat of the exarchs, the Byzantine viceroys who were to rule increasingly smaller bits of Italy over the next 500 years. It was this period that would see the city's golden age. The Greek exarchs, never popular among their new subjects, performed the occasional service of obtaining Constantinople's aid in keeping the Lombards at bay. While tolerating the exarch's presence, the people of Ravenna were coming to rely increasingly on their own resources; when help from the east failed to appear, it was their own militia that defended the city against invaders. So, in the worst times, the city survived as a sort of cultural time-capsule, protected by its own efforts – and its swamps – still maintaining trade and cultural relations with the east, and carrying on the best traditions of classical culture single-handedly.

In 751 the Lombards finally succeeded in taking Ravenna, chasing out the last exarch. Only six years later, however, Pepin the Short's Frankish army snatched it back, and the city was placed under the rule of the popes. Ravenna declined slowly and gracefully in the following centuries. Venice took over its role as leading port of the Adriatic as Classe silted up and was abandoned. The newer cities of Romagna, such as Ferrara and Faenza, assumed a larger role in the region's economy, and even Ravenna's ancient school of Roman law was transferred to Bologna, there to become the foundation of Europe's first university.

Despite its declining fortunes, Ravenna still managed to rouse itself in 1177, becoming a free *comune*. During the 13th century government fell into the hands of the Da Polenta family, famous for offering refuge to Dante in his exile from Florence. Dante finished the *Divine Comedy* in Ravenna, and died here in 1321. In 1441 Ravenna came under the rule of Venice, and enjoyed a brief period of renewed prosperity which lasted until the popes came back in 1509; the economic decadence brought by papal rule has been reversed only since the 1940s. Parts of the city were heavily damaged in the Second World War, but in the last few decades, with the construction of a ship channel and new port, the discovery of offshore gas deposits and the intro-duction of large chemical industries, Ravenna has become a booming modern city – just coincidentally one with a medieval centre full of Byzantine mosaics.

San Vitale

Via San Vitale, near Porta Adriana, the western gate of the centro storico. Open summer daily 9–7; winter daily 9–4.30; Mar and Oct 9–5.30.

At first this dark old church may not seem like much, but as soon as the lights come on, the 1,400-year-old mosaics ignite into an explosion of colour: the mosaics of San Vitale, Ravenna's best, are one of the last great works of art of the ancient world.

The octagonal church, begun in AD 525 during the reign of Theodoric, is itself a fine example of the surprisingly sophisticated architecture of a troubled age. By the time

Mosaics

Either light was born here,
or reigns here imprisoned.
Latin inscription, Sant'Andrea chapel

In Byzantine times the greatest gift an emperor could bestow on any dependent town was a few tons of gold and enamel *tesserae* and an artist. From Justinian's time the art became almost a trademark of Byzantine civilization.

Before Christianity, mosaics were a favourite Roman medium, usually reserved for the decoration of villas, and in particular floors. Some reached the level of fine art (examples are in the Naples museum, the great villa at Piazza Armerina, Sicily, or Antakya in Turkey – ancient Antioch), but more often the productions were on the level of the famous 'beware of the dog' mosaic in Pompeii, or prophylactic images of Priapus. It was the early Christians, with a desire to build for the ages and a body of scriptures that could best be related pictorially, who made mosaics the new medium of public art in the 6th century. Mostly it was the Greeks who still had the talent and the resources for it; we don't know for certain, but it's most likely that Greek artists from the court of Constantinople created the celebrated mosaics in the churches and baptistries of Ravenna.

Western Christian art was born here, developing from simple images – the Good Shepherd and the Cross and Stars – to the iconic Christ in Sant'Apollinare Nuovo and the scriptural scenes in San Vitale. Never, though, did the early mosaicists turn their back on the idea of art; with the ideals of the ancient world still in their minds, they naturally thought of art and religion as going hand in hand, and found no problem in serving the cause of both. Using a new vocabulary of images and the new techniques of mosaic art, they strove to duplicate, and surpass, the sense of awe and mystery still half-remembered from the interiors of the pagan temples.

Try to imagine a church like San Vitale in its original state, with lots of lamps and candles flickering below the gold ground and gorgeous colours. You may see that same light that enchanted the Byzantines – the light of the Gospels, the light from beyond the stars.

the church was finished, in AD 548, the city was in the hands of Belisarius' Byzantine army; portraits of Justinian and Theodora represent the traditional imperial style of political propaganda. But far from being the sorry recapitulation of old forms and styles you might expect, San Vitale was a breathtakingly original departure in architecture. While the world was falling around their ears, late-Roman architects were making advances, using complex geometry and new vaulting techniques.

Take some time to admire the exterior, with its beautiful interplay of octagons, arches, gables and *exedrae* – pure proportional geometry done in plain solid brick. Inside, the curious double capitals on the columns are no design conceit, but an important 5th-century invention; the trapezoidal impost block on top is a capital specially designed to support the weight of arches. Holding up the second-floor galleries and large octagonal cupola was an unusual design problem; these capitals and the eight stout piers around the dome were the solution.

We do not know whether San Vitale's architects were Latins or Greeks, but the year after it was begun work commenced on the similar church of SS. Sergius and Bacchus in Constantinople, the prototype for the Hagia Sophia 10 years later. In its structure the great dome in Constantinople owes everything to the little dome of Ravenna: the innovation of the galleries, for example, in which the women were segregated, and the elongated apse cleverly combining the central plan favoured by eastern Christians with the basilica form needed for a court's religious ceremonies.

Nowhere in Constantinople, however, or anywhere in the east, will you find anything as brilliant as San Vitale's mosaics. Much was undoubtedly lost during the iconoclastic troubles of the 8th century, though iconoclasm was fiercely resisted in Italy – it was one of the first causes of the rupture between the Roman and Greek churches – and most of Ravenna's art was fortunately left in peace.

The colours are startling. Almost all the other surviving Byzantine mosaics, in Sicily, Greece and Turkey, are simple figures on a bright gold ground, dazzling at first but somewhat monotonous. There is plenty of gold on the walls of San Vitale, but the best mosaics, in the **choir,** have deep blue skies and rich green meadows for backgrounds, highlighted by brightly coloured birds and flowers. (The usual nomenclature is misleading here: the 'choir' is the site of the main altar, while the clergy sat on a bench around the apse.)

The two **lunettes** over the arches flanking the choir, each a masterpiece, show the two events in the Old Testament that prefigure the Transfiguration of Christ: the hospitality of Abraham and the sacrifice of Isaac, and the offerings of Abel and Melchisedek, set under fiery clouds with hands of benediction extended from Heaven. Around the two lunettes are scenes of Moses and Jeremiah; note, above the lunettes, the delicately posed pairs of angels holding golden crosses – almost identical to the fanciful figures from earlier Roman art displaying the civic crown of the Caesars.

In front of the choir the **triumphal arch** has mosaic portraits of the Apostles supported by a pair of dolphins; the galleries have portraits of the four evangelists.

The **apse** is dominated by the famous mosaic portraits of Justinian and Theodora – mostly, of course, of Theodora, the dancing girl from Constantinople who used her many talents to become an empress, eventually coming to wear poor Justinian like a charm on her bracelet. Here she is wearing a rich crown, with long strings of fat diamonds and real pearls. Justinian, like Theodora, appears among his retinue offering a gift to the new church; here he has the air of a hung-over saxophone player, badly in need of a shave and a cup of coffee. His cute daisy slipper steps on the foot (a convention of Byzantine art to show who's boss) of his General Belisarius, to his left. The likenesses are good – very like those in Constantinople – suggesting that the artist may have come from there, or at least have copied closely imperial portraits on display at Ravenna.

It can easily be imagined how expensive it was in the 5th century to make mosaics like these. It is said that the Hagia Sophia in Constantinople had over four acres of them, and even the treasury of Justinian was not bottomless; consequently most of

San Vitale remained undecorated until the 17th-century bishops did the rest in a not-too-discordant Baroque. The bishops' floor has been pulled up to reveal the original, of inlaid marble in floral and geometric patterns, the direct ancestor of medieval pavements in the churches of Tuscany and the south.

Mausoleo di Galla Placidia

Open same hours as San Vitale.

This small chapel, set in the grounds of San Vitale and originally attached to the neighbouring church of Santa Croce, never really held the tomb of Ravenna's great patroness – she is buried near St Peter's in Rome, and it's anyone's guess who occupies the three huge stone sarcophagi, traditionally the resting places of Galla Placidia and two emperors, her second husband Constantius III and her son Valentinian. Galla Placidia did construct the chapel, a small, gabled and cross-shaped building that is almost 7ft shorter than when it was built; the ground level has risen 7ft in 1,400 years.

The simplicity of the brick exterior, as in San Vitale, makes the brilliant mosaics within that much more of a surprise. The only natural light inside comes from a few tiny slits of windows, made of thin sheets of alabaster. The two important mosaics, on **lunettes** at opposite ends of the chapel, are coloured as richly as San Vitale. One represents St Lawrence, with his flaming gridiron; the other is a beautiful and typical early Christian portrait of Jesus as the Good Shepherd, a beardless, classical-looking figure in a fine cloak and sandals, stroking one of the flock. On the lunettes of the cross-axis, pairs of stags come to drink at the fountain of life; around all four lunettes, floral arabesques and maze patterns in bright colours cover the arches and ceilings. Everything in the design betrays as much of the classical Roman style as the nascent Christian, and the unusual figures on the **arches** holding up the central vault seem hardly out of place. They are SS. Peter and Paul, dressed in togas and standing with outstretched hands in the conventional pose of Roman senators.

The **vault** itself, a deep blue firmament glowing with hundreds of dazzling golden stars set in concentric circles, is the mausoleum's most remarkable feature. In the centre, at the top of the vault, a golden cross represents the unimaginable, transcendent God above the heavens. At the corners, symbols of the four evangelists provide an insight into the origins of Christian iconography. Mark's lion, Luke's ox and Matthew's man occupy the places in this sky where you would expect the constellations of the lion, the bull and Aquarius, 90 degrees apart along the zodiac. For the fourth corner, instead of the objectionable scorpion (or serpent, as it often appeared in ancient times) the early Christians substituted the eagle of St John.

The Museo Nazionale

The medieval and Baroque **cloisters** attached to San Vitale now house the large collection of antiquities found in Ravenna and Classis (*open Tues–Sat 8.30–6.30, Sun 8.30–5; adm*). There's a little bit of everything: good Roman plumbing, a boy's linen shirt from the 6th century, Byzantine forks (they invented them) and no end of coins and broken pots. The well-labelled coin collection is interesting even to the non-specialist, providing a picture history of Italy from Classical times into the early Middle Ages. Exceptional works of art include the 6th-century Byzantine carved screens, and a possibly unique sculpture of *Hercules capturing the Cerynean hind*. This, too, is from the 6th century, perhaps the last piece of art made in ancient times with a classical subject, possibly a copy of an earlier Greek work. Lovely, intricately carved ivory chests and plaques from the Middle Ages and Renaissance, with charming tableaux of medieval scenes such as tournaments and banquets, fill an entire room.

Ravenna's Centre

Piazza del Popolo at the centre of Ravenna was built by the Venetians during their brief period of rule, along with the twin columns bearing statues of Ravenna's two patrons, San Vitale and Sant'Apollinare. A little way south, off porticoed Piazza San Francesco, a modest neoclassical pavilion was built in the 18th century over the tomb of Dante. Ravenna is proud of having sheltered the storm-tossed poet in his last years, and the city will gently remind you of it in its street names, its tourist brochures, its Teatro Alighieri and its frequent artistic competitions based on themes from the *Divina Commedia*. Coming here may help explain just what Dante means to Italy; in all the country's more recent wars, for example, soldiers have come here for little rituals to 'dedicate their sacrifice' to the poet's memory.

Today there are always wreaths or bouquets from organizations of all kinds and private citizens from all over Italy. Beside the tomb is the **Museo Dantesco** (*open Tues–Sun 9–12; adm*), with a collection of paintings, sculptures and books connected with the poet.

Behind the tomb, the church of **San Francesco** was founded in the 5th century but rebuilt in the 11th and thoroughly baroqued in the 1700s. Greek marble columns and a fine 4th-century altar survive, and there are some fine Renaissance tombs. Some of the beautiful original mosaic pavement is visible through a hole in the floor – under eight feet of water. In the church itself and the Braccioforte oratory (behind the iron gate, by Dante's tomb) are fine early Christian sarcophagi, one familiarly called the 'Tomb of Elijah'.

North of Piazza del Popolo, Ravenna has a fine example of a medieval leaning tower: the tall, 12th-century **Torre Pubblica**, now supported by steel struts. This one seems good evidence for those who believe such things to be intentional. Despite the angle of the tower, the windows near the top were built perfectly level. Byron lived in nearby Via Cavour during his affair with Countess Teresa Guiccioli; his home now houses the Carabinieri.

In a little square between Via Paolo Costa and Via Armando Diaz, the **Battistero degli Ariani** (Arian Baptistry) (*open summer daily 8.30–6; winter daily 8.30–6; adm*) recalls church struggles of the 5th century. Theodoric and his Ostrogoths, like most of the Germanic peoples, adhered to the Arian heresy, a doctrine that mixed in elements of pagan religion and was condemned by more orthodox Christians as denying the absolute divinity of Christ. Like all heresies, this one is really the story of a political struggle, between the Gothic kings and the emperor in Constantinople. Unlike Justinian, a great persecutor, the Goths tolerated both faiths; the baptistry belonged to the adjacent Santo Spirito church (rebuilt in the 16th century), once the Arians' cathedral, while the Athenasians (orthodox) worshipped at what is now the cathedral of Ravenna. The Arian Baptistry preserves a fine mosaic ceiling, with the 12 Apostles arranged around a scene of the Baptism of Jesus. The old man with the palm branch, across from John the Baptist, represents the River Jordan.

There is another leaning tower – an even tipsier one – nearby on Viale Farini, two streets up from the railway station. It is the 12th-century campanile of **San Giovanni Evangelista**, a much-altered church that was begun by Galla Placidia in 425. Bombings in the last War destroyed the apse, with its original mosaics, but some parts of the 13th-century mosaic floor, with scenes of the Fourth Crusade and some fantastical monsters, can be seen in the aisles.

Sant'Apollinare Nuovo

Open summer daily 9.30–7; winter daily 9.30–6; Mar and Oct daily 9.30–4.30; adm.

After those of San Vitale, the mosaics of this 6th-century church are the finest in Ravenna. Theodoric built it, and after the Byzantine conquest and the suppression of Arianism it was re-dedicated to St Martin, another famous persecutor of heretics. The present name comes from the 9th century, when the remains of Sant'Apollinare were moved here from the old Sant'Apollinare in Classe. The tall, cylindrical campanile, a style that is a trademark of Ravenna's churches, was added in the 10th century.

Unlike San Vitale, Sant'Apollinare was built in the basilican form, with a long nave and side aisles. The two rows of Greek marble columns were probably recycled from an ancient temple.

Above them are the mosaics on panels that stretch the length of the church. On the left, by the door, you see the city of Classe, with ships in the protected harbour between twin beacons, and the monuments of the city rearing up behind its walls. On the right, among the monuments of Ravenna, is the Palatium, Theodoric's royal palace. The curtains in the archways of the palace cover painted-over Gothic notables and probably Theodoric himself, effaced by the Byzantines. Beyond these two urban scenes are processions of martyrs bearing crowns: 22 women on the left side, 26 men on the right. The female procession is led by colourful, remarkable portraits of the Magi (officially enrolled as Saints of the Church, according to the inscription above), offering their gifts to the enthroned Virgin Mary.

Above these panels, more mosaics portray Old Testament prophets, doctors of the Church, and scenes from the life of Jesus. These mosaics, smaller and not as well executed, are from Theodoric's time. Next door are the remains of the 6th-century building known as the **Palace of Theodoric** (*open daily 8.30–1.30*); more likely it was a governmental building of some sort – it may in fact have been the palace of the Byzantine exarchs.

The Battistero Neoniano and the Museo Arcivescovile

Open summer daily 9–7; winter daily 9.30–4.30; Mar and Oct daily 9.30–5.30; adm.

An earthquake in 1733 wrecked Ravenna's cathedral, west of Piazza del Popolo, and there's little to see in the replacement but another round medieval tower. Somehow the disaster spared the 'Orthodox' or **Neonian Baptistry**, named after the 5th-century bishop Neon who commissioned its splendid mosaics.

Unlike the Arian Baptistry, here almost the entire decoration has survived: a scene of the Baptism of Jesus and portraits of the 12 Apostles on the ceiling under the dome, while below the eight walls bear four altars and four empty thrones. The *etimasia*, the preparing of the Throne for Jesus for the Last Judgement, is an odd bit of Byzantine mysticism; interestingly enough, classical Greek art often depicts an empty throne as a symbol for Zeus, only with a pair of thunderbolts instead of a cross. In the 1500 years since its construction the ground level here has risen over 10ft – so has the baptistry's floor. In the side niches are a 6th-century Byzantine altar and a huge, thoroughly pagan marble vase. The 13th-century marble font is big enough for the immersion baptism of adults.

The **Archiepiscopal Museum**, behind the cathedral, comes as a real surprise. Its little-known treasures include the ivory throne of Bishop Maximian, a masterpiece of 6th-century sculpture thought to have been a gift from Emperor Justinian, and an 11th-century reliquary, the silver 'Cross of Sant'Agnello'. Among the fragments of sculpture and mosaics are works saved from the original cathedral. The large marble disc by the wall, divided into 19 sections, is an episcopal calendar, regulated to the 19-year Julian cycle to allow Ravenna's medieval bishops to calculate the date of Easter and other holy days.

The biggest surprise, however, is finding that the nondescript Archbishop's Palace in which the museum is located is, in parts, as old as anything in Ravenna. A little door at the back leads to a small chapel called the **Oratorio di Sant'Andrea**, built around 500 during the reign of Theodoric.

The mosaics on the vaults are among Ravenna's best: in the antechamber a fanciful scene of multicoloured birds and flowers, and an unusual warrior Christ in full Roman armour and wielding the cross like a sword, treading a lion and snake underfoot. In the chapel itself, four angels and the four evangelists' symbols surround Christ's monogram on the dome, and the apse bears a beautiful starry sky around a golden cross, like the one at the Galla Placidia mausoleum.

The best mosaics, however, are the excellent portraits of saints decorating the arches. Early Christian representations of the saints are often much stronger than the pale, conventional figures of later art. Such portraits as these betray a fascination with the personalities and the psychology of saints; such figures as St Felicitas or St Ursicinus may be forgotten now, but to the early Christians they were not mere holy myths, but near contemporaries, the spiritual heroes and heroines responsible for the miraculous growth of Christianity, the exemplars of a new age and a new way of life.

Mausoleo Teodorico

Via Cimitero, near the industrial zone; open Mon–Fri 8.30–1.30, Sat and Sun 8.30–4.30; adm.

For the real flavour of the days of the Roman twilight, nothing can beat this compellingly strange, sophisticated yet half-barbaric building outside the old city. To reach it, walk north from the railway station, past the new port and the Venetian fortress called the **Rocca di Brancaleone,** which now has a park inside. Theodoric's tomb, perhaps the only regular 10-sided building in Italy, is in another small park. Downstairs, there is a cross-shaped chamber of unknown purpose. The second storey, also decagonal though smaller, contains the porphyry sarcophagus, now empty. It is a comment on the times that scholars believe this is a recycled bathtub from a Roman palace. Theodoric was hardly broke, though; he could afford to bring the stone for his tomb over from Istria – and note the roof, a single slab of stone weighing over 300 tons. No one has yet explained how the Goths brought it here and raised it – or why.

Sant'Apollinare in Classe

Open daily 9–5; adm.

If you have the time, there is another important monument to Ravenna's golden age to be seen at the site of Classe, 5km from town; any local train towards Rimini or the regular bus service (most no.4 or 44 buses, and no.176 from the train station) can take you there. Sant'Apollinare in Classe, in fact, is literally all that remains of what was once the leading port of the northern Adriatic. The little River Uniti began to silt up Classe's harbour in classical times; when the port ceased to be a Roman military base and the funds for yearly dredging were no longer there, the city's fate was sealed. By the 9th century Classe was abandoned. The people of Ravenna carted away most of its stone and encroaching forests and swamps erased the rest. Today the former port is good farmland, 6km from the sea.

Sant'Apollinare, a huge basilica-form church completed in 549, survives only because of its importance as the burial place of Ravenna's patron. The plain brick exterior is another finely proportioned example of Ravenna's pre-Romanesque, with another tall cylindrical campanile. Inside it's almost empty, with only a few early-Christian sarcophagi lining the walls. The Greek marble columns have well-carved capitals in a unique style. Above them are 18th-century portraits of Ravenna's bishops – important to this city where for centuries the bishops defended local autonomy against emperors, exarchs and popes. But the real attraction is the mosaics in the apse, an impressive green-and-gold-ground allegorical vision of the *Transfiguration of Christ,* in a flower-strewn Mediterranean landscape, with Sant'Apollinare in attendance and three sheep representing Peter, James and John, who were with Christ on Mount Tabor. As at San Vitale, there are scenes of the sacrifices of Abel, Melchizedek and Abraham, opposite a mosaic of the Byzantine Emperor Constantine IV bestowing privileges on Ravenna's independent church. Archangels Gabriel and Michael appear in Byzantine court dress, under a pair of palm trees, the 'tree of life'.

Elsewhere around Classe there's little to see; bits of Roman road, pine groves, some foundations. Excavations began only in 1961, and continue today. Sant'Apollinare is near the centre of an immense necropolis with some half-million burials. Some interesting things could turn up here in coming years (*visiting hours at the excavations, daily 9am–dusk, Sun 9–12; adm*).

The Adriatic Riviera

From Ravenna and Classe the long stretch of small resorts that began at Comacchio straggles on towards the beach-Babylon of Rimini – forty miles long and a few blocks deep, a mass of compacted (and mostly quite attractive) urbanity, with the SS16 on one side and a solid line of beach on the other. It's the place where Italians come because their grandparents did, where Germans come to look for Italians, the British come to fill shopping trolleys with British gin, and Russians finally get a chance to wear their designer sunglasses.

The fall of the Iron Curtain made it possible for Czechs, Poles, Russians, Hungarians and everyone else in eastern Europe to get out for a holiday again, and only one place was close, friendly and relatively inexpensive. They only add to the charm of the biggest, funkiest, most unpretentious and most cosmopolitan lido in Europe. On any given night in August, over 100,000 people will be sitting down to *tagliatelle al ragù* in their *pensioni* and thinking that life is pretty damn sweet.

The beaches nearest Ravenna suffer somewhat from industrial pollution, but there has been a big effort to clean them up. Marina Romea, a spit of land with a broad beach and a pine forest, is perhaps the nicest; all are an easy day's outing from Ravenna. The first big centre on the coast is **Cervia-Milano Marittima**, which earned its living with 'white gold' or salt from the time of the ancient Greeks.

The next, **Cesenatico**, was built around a pretty, canal-like harbour designed for Cesare Borgia in 1502 by Leonardo da Vinci. The Museo della Mariniera in the harbour itself is a floating maritime museum, a display of the traditional fishing and trading boats used in the northern Adriatic; colourful sails are raised in summer.

Rimini

At first glance Italy's biggest resort may strike you as strictly cold potatoes, a full 15km of peeling skin and pizza, serenaded by the portable radios of ten thousand teenagers and the eternal whines and giggles of their little brothers and sisters. To many Italians, however, Rimini means pure sweaty-palmed excitement. In the sixties, following the grand old Italian pastime of *caccia alle svedesi*, a staple of the national film industry was the Rimini holiday movie, in which a bumbling protagonist with glasses was swept off his feet by some incredible Nordic goddess, who was as bouncy as she was adventurous. After many complications, embarrassing both for the audience and the actors, it could all lead to true love.

Getting Around

In summer there are regular **flights** from Milan and London Stansted and a stream of foreign charters to Rimini's airport (t 0541 715 711) behind the beaches at Miramare.

On this stretch of coast, the FS Adriatic **rail** line works almost like a tram service, with lots of trains and stops near the beaches in all the resorts. Rimini **city buses** run regularly up and down the long beach strip in summer. A 24-hour or eight-day discounted 'Orange Ticket' is available, giving unlimited travel within Rimini and to Riccione. From the railway station in Rimini, on Piazzale Cesare Battisti, there are **buses** to most nearby towns, including San Marino. For taxis, t 0541 50020.

Cultural day-trippers who shudder at the thought of Rimini's beach madness can dip in easily – the Tempio Malatestiano is only a 10-minute walk from the station.

Tourist Information

In summer Rimini and its suburbs have as many information offices as ice-cream stands. The main ones are at Piazzale C. Battisti, next to the station, t 0541 51331, and on the beach at Piazza Fellini 3, t 0541 56902, f 0541 56598. Next to both you'll find the Promozione Alberghiera, the local accommodation service. There are five information desks along the 15km beach.

Where to Stay

Rimini ✉ 47900

A holiday in Rimini usually means a standard package: Don't expect any surprises,

good or bad: you'll probably get a pleasant enough modern room with a balcony. You may as well take pot luck at the **Promozione Alberghiera**, Piazza Tripoli, t 0541 390 530, or in the railway station, Piazzale Fellini 3, t 0541 53399, and let them find you a vacancy. They also have four other well-marked offices around town, as well as in Bellaria, t 0541 340 060, and Riccione, t 0541 693 628. People do not come to Rimini for the scenery or charming inns but to join the crowd and seek out endless fun. If that sounds good, make sure to get a place in the centre where the action is. The places below are close to both the beach and the town.

Luxury

★★★★★**Grand Hotel**, Via Ramusio 1, t 0541 56000, f 0541 56866, *ghotel@iper.net*. An old-fashioned Grand Hotel might seem out of place in Rimini, but that's exactly what you'll find on Parco dell'Indipendenza at Marina Centro. This imposing turn-of-the-century dream palace helped make Rimini what it is today. Young Federico Fellini was fascinated with it, and it gets a starring role in *Amarcord* – even though a hotel nearer Rome actually played the part. The place hasn't slipped at all, with rooms that are almost indecently luxurious, all the brass well-polished, and the enormous crystal chandeliers well-dusted. It's the only hotel in Rimini with its own dance orchestra, as well as a pool and private beach.

Expensive

★★★★**Milton**, Viale C. Colombo 2, t 0541 54600, f 0541 54698, milton@iper.net. In a residential area and right on the beach; offers elegant rooms. The restaurant is good;

For the bumbling protagonists of real life, whether from Milan or Munich, all this may only be wishful thinking but they still come in their millions each year. As a resort Rimini has its advantages. Noisy as it is, it's a respectable, family place, relatively cheap for northern Italy, convenient and well organized.

Also, tucked away behind the beachfront is a genuine old city, dishevelled, damaged in the Second World War, but inviting, and offering one first-rate Renaissance attraction.

there's a garden bar, pool, and bicycles for guests. *Closed mid-Dec–mid-Jan.*

★★★★**Savoia**, Lungomare Murri 13, **t** 0541 393 322, **f** 0541 386 462. Right in the centre of the action; a brand new splashy building by celebrated architect Paolo Portoghesi that seeks to recapture the elegance of the old days with a modern twist; private beach, pool and solarium.

Moderate

★★★**Esedra**, Viale Caio Duilio 3, **t** 0541 23421, **f** 0541 24424. In a handsome remodelled seaside villa from the 1890s, offers 42 spacious up-to-date rooms, surrounded by a garden and pool. *Closed Nov and Dec.*

★★★**Primalba**, Via Regina Elena 86, **t** 0541 387 207, **f** 0541 392 266. Built in the early 1900s; located just in from the sea, it has a nice shady garden and pool; rooms are simple.

★★★**Napoleon**, Piazza C. Battisti 22, **t** 0541 27501, **f** 0541 50010, *napoleon@iper.net*. Near the station, a pleasant hotel vintage 1973, with big bathrooms and bicycles and laundry service.

Cheap

★★★**Saxon**, Via Cirene 36, **t/f** 0541 391 400. One of hundreds of cheap hotels. Central, pleasant and friendly.

★★**Cardellini**, Via Dante 50, **t** 0541 26412, **f** 0541 54374. Near the station, close to the Tempio Malatestiano, and open 24 hours in case you have a late flight or train.

Eating Out

Expensive

Acero Rosso, Viale Tiberio 11 (just outside the historic centre), **t** 0541 53577. You don't come to Rimini for a gourmet experience, but you won't do too badly here. It's one of the most elegant places in Rimini, and offers a choice of three *menu degustazione:* fish, meat, or vegetarian, all well prepared, and followed by masterful desserts. Moderately priced lunch menus and a good wine list. *Closed Sun eve and Mon, late July–mid-Aug.*

Lo Squero, Lungomare Tintori 7, **t** 0541 53881. Near the Grand Hotel, with an outdoor terrace overlooking the beach: shellfish are a speciality. *Closed Tues.*

Taverna degli Artisti, Viale Vespucci 1, **t** 0541 28519. With its colourful menu, best known for its seafood, along with some imaginative light pasta openers and something unexpected – a little *degustazione* of whisky; they have almost every brand from around the world. *Closed Wed.*

Moderate

Il Quartino, Via Coriano 161, **t** 0541 731 215. In an old farmhouse on the edge of Rimini (take the Via Flaminia), where you can dine very well – not seafood but the likes of *carpaccio* with *formaggio di fossa* and *ravioli* Parma-style, filled with herbs, and other regional delights on the excellent menu. *Closed Tues.*

Saraghina's, Via Poletti 32, **t** 0541 783 794. A popular and friendly spot in the heart of town, serving seasonal dishes and seafood with a light touch. *Open evenings only and Sun lunch, closed Mon.*

Dallo Zio, Via S. Chiara 16, **t** 0541 786 74. An excellent seafood palace in the old town, offering marine *lasagne*, fishy vol-au-vent and other surprises; very popular with locals and tourists alike. *Closed Mon.*

Osteria di Santa Colomba, Via Agostino di Duccio 2, **t** 0541 780 048. Near the market

The Tempio Malatestiano

Open 8–12.30 and 3.30–6.30; Sun 9–1 and 3.30–7; adm free.

Sigismondo Malatesta ('Headache'), tyrant of Rimini, went into the books as one bad hombre. According to Jakob Burckhardt, 'the verdict of history...convicts him of murder, rape, adultery, incest, sacrilege, perjury, and treason, committed not once, but often.' The historian adds that his frequent attempts on the virtue of his children, both male and female, may have resulted from 'some astrological superstition'. In

and Piazza Malatesta there is an old favourite (they say Napoleon slept here), with simple traditional fare – the best possible antidote to the cosmopolitanism of beach Rimini may be a plate of pasta with chickpeas. *Open dinner only; closed Sun.*

Cheap

4 Moschetteri, Via S. Maria al Mare, just off Piazza Ferrari, **t** 0541 5649. The practically perfect *trattoria* in the centre, with excellent pizza and pasta, and a menu of Romagna favourites that changes every day.

Osteria de Borg, Via Forzieri 12, **t** 0541 56074. In the San Giuliano area. For a change from seafood and pizza, try this: the imaginative menu may include a variety of soups, *tortellini* stuffed with carrot or *strozzapreti* with broccoli and spicy sausage. *Open eves only, and lunch on Sun and hols; closed Mon, half of Jan and half of July.*

Entertainment and Nightlife

Music, Theatre and Cinema

The tourist office publishes *Instantaneo*, a listings guide with detailed information on what's on in the area.

Throughout the summer season **art exhibitions** cater for rainy days.

The city of Fellini, with its fourteen cinemas, also hosts a fairly continual series of **film events** – themed festivals, cartoon seasons and open-air extravaganzas – centred on the semi-official **Rimini Film Festival** in September.

In late summer and autumn Rimini stages the **Sagra Musicale Malatestiana,** a festival of classical music, **t** 0541 26239. The nearby town of Santarcangelo holds an annual **theatre festival** in July, packed with dynamic, innovative work (**t** 0541 626 185).

Clubs and Discos

Rimini and its perhaps even more in-vogue neighbour Riccione make up the undisputed clubland capital of Italy, a magnet for ravers from all over Italy and abroad. On summer weekends crowds descend from all the cities within a 200km radius, and on mornings-after the road back to Bologna is often scattered with the battered cars of partygoers who didn't make it home.

For listings and information on clubs, one-nighters and anything else coming up, check *Il Resto del Carlino* and the magazine *Chiamami Città*, or search for posters.

The main place for cruising the clubs is along the seafront, from about 10pm onwards, though there's also another little knot of activity in Rimini away from the beach in Covignano. If you get fed up with walking, a night bus runs along the whole length of the seafront between Riccione and Bellaria, and to Covignano.

Pascià, Via Sardegna 30, Riccione. One of the Riviera's best-established clubs; a large, stylish venue offering a bouncy mix of house, techno and Euro-dance.

Paradiso, Via Covignano 260. The most fashionable club of them all, with a regular diet of Euro-dance but also special events every week involving visiting DJs, performances, and the gamut of musical styles – for an astronomical entrance fee.

Bandiera Gialla, Via Antiche Fonti Romane 76. Also in Covignano, an open-air rave, which is held every weekend in summer.

1462 Pope Pius II accorded him a unique honour – a canonization to Hell. The Pope, who was behind most of the accusations, can be excused a little exaggeration. He wanted Sigismondo's land, and resorted to invoking supernatural aid when he couldn't beat him at war. Modern historians give Sigismondo better reviews, finding him on the whole no more pagan and perverse than the average Renaissance duke, and less so than many popes. The family had ruled at Rimini since the 1300s – ironically it was a pope who first put them in business. Early dukes, like Malatesta

'Guastafamiglia' ('Destroyer of Families'), were hard men, and good role models for Sigismondo, but they succeeded for a time in spreading their rule as far as Cesena and Fano. By Sigismondo's time, money and allies were suddenly lacking, and the family was deposed by the unspeakable Alexander VI in 1500.

The shortage of funds (along with Sigismondo's excommunication) was also responsible for the abandonment in 1461 of Sigismondo's personal monument, the eclectic and thoroughly mysterious work that has come to be known as the Malatesta Temple. Whatever Sigismondo's personal habits, he was a learned man and a good judge of art. To transform this unfinished 13th-century Franciscan church into his temple he called in Leon Battista Alberti to redesign the exterior and Agostino di Duccio for the reliefs inside.

Scholars have been puzzling for centuries over Sigismondo's intentions. Although the temple has been Rimini's cathedral since 1809 it is hardly a Christian building, full of undecipherable sculptural allegories with everywhere the entwined monograms of Sigismondo and his wife Isotta degli Atti; in part it seems a tribute to this famous lady, who is buried here along with her husband. Court scholar Roberto Volturio wrote that the entire temple was full of symbols that would proclaim the doctrines of arcane philosophy to the learned, while remaining hidden to vulgar folk. Sadly, that includes all of us; whatever secret neo-Platonic philosophy was current at Sigismondo's court is probably lost forever.

Alberti's unfinished exterior, grafting Roman arcades and pilasters on to the plain Franciscan building, grievously feels the lack of the planned cupola that might have tied it all together. Alberti's intentions can be seen in a medal minted at the beginning of its construction: a second-storey arch was to have been built over the portal; the gable-like pediment around it would have been rounded, and the entire work dominated by a great dome, as wide as the building itself and more than doubling its height. The big arches on the sides were meant to hold sarcophagi of Rimini's notable men; only a few were ever used. Inside these arches, four pairs of chapels hold the **sculptural reliefs** made by Agostino – among the greatest works of the Renaissance. These low reliefs, on blue backgrounds like a della Robbia cameo, depict angels and child musicians, the Arts and Sciences, St Michael, putti, Sigismondo himself and the Triumph of Scipio. Some of the best are allegorical panels of the planets and signs of the zodiac; note especially the enchanting Moon, Cynthia in her silver car, and a scene of 15th-century Rimini beneath the claws of the Crab.

Among the other works in the Temple are a fresco by Piero della Francesca of Sigismondo and his patron, St Sigismund of Burgundy, and a painted crucifix by Giotto. The tombs of Sigismondo and Isotta, with their strange device (the omnipresent monograms S and I together like a dollar sign) and elephants (the Malatesta heraldic symbol) are also fine works.

Old Rimini was the home town of the late Federico Fellini, and you may recognize some of the street scenes from *Amarcord* (the streets were actually reconstructed in Cinecittà for the film). Some ruins survive as reminders of Roman *Arminium*, a thriving Adriatic port and a rival to Classe: the foundation of an amphitheatre near the southern walls, and the **Arco di Augusto** in the southern gate near the post office.

This arch marked the meeting of the Via Aemilia and the Via Flaminia. The Roman high street, the *cardo*, is now Corso di Augusto; from here it passes through central Piazza Tre Martiri – which retains arcades in the shop fronts from the days when it was the Roman forum – and continues on to the north gate and the five-arched **Bridge of Tiberius** (AD 21), badly patched up after damage in the Greek-Gothic wars.

A few streets further over the bridge, the church of San Giuliano contains a painting of that saint's martyrdom, Paolo Veronese's last work. From here towards the sea, along the riverbank, stretches Rimini's colourful fishing port. Back at the centre, a lovely marble fountain of 1543 and a glowering statue of Pope Paul V grace **Piazza Cavour**, site of the Wednesday and Saturday morning markets. The **Palazzo del'Arengo** on the piazza has been Rimini's town hall since 1207; it is joined by an arch to the 1300s **Palazzo del Podestà,** and faces the bulky castle of the Malatesta, the **Rocca Sigismondo**, over the piazza; you can see how it originally looked in Piero's painting in the Tempio. The *rocca* did time as a prison until 1964, sat empty for years and is now an exhibiton space. Not many of the works of the trecento 'school of Rimini' can still be seen in the city, but some of the best are in **Sant'Agostino**, on Via Cairoli just off Piazza Cavour. An old Jesuit monastery on Piazza Ferrara houses the **Museo della Città** (*open Tues–Sat 8.30–12.30 and 5–7, Sun 4–7; closed Mon; adm*), home to Roman mosaics, two Guercinos and paintings by Ghirlandaio and Giovanni Bellini.

More Beaches

Holiday madness continues through the string of resorts south of Rimini. **Riccione, Misano Adriatico**, **Cattòlica** and **Gabicce Mare** are all huge places, and in the summer

Some Beach Statistics

Rimini is not the place for those who want to be alone.

tourist brochure

The subject makes Rimini's holiday barons and the hotel consortium mildly uneasy. 'There's room for everybody,' they say, and in a way they're right. The resort has 15km of broad beaches, and about 1600 hotels with some 55,000 rooms. At the usual resort ratio, that means about 85,000 beds. It could be a problem in the really busy season. If all the beds are full – plus another 25,000 day-trippers, campers and holiday apartment tenants – that makes 110,000 souls, or 7,333 per kilometre of beach front. There are plenty of other things to do in Rimini, luckily; with only 5½inches of shore per behind, if everyone hit the water at the same time the results could be catastrophic.

This really need never happen. Many of these people at any given time will be at Rimini's 751 bars, 343 restaurants, 70 dance halls and discos, 49 cinemas, 14 miniature golf courses, seven luna parks (fun fairs) and three bowling alleys, or at one of the many sailing and wind-surfing schools, or one of three dolphin shows. If all else fails to amuse you, there is Fiabilandia, an amusement park with a genuine King Kong, or the long water-slides to be found at Riccione.

they can be as crowded and intense as Rimini itself. None of them has any particular charm, and it's hard to tell one from another – they're really more or less suburban extensions of Rimini; Riccione has the aura of fashion, if you want to keep up with the Italians. The Adriatic Riviera begins to fade when the wide beaches of the Romagna give way to the more rugged coast of the Marche, but soon picks up again when the hills recede once more at Pesaro and beyond. The only real curiosity is **San Giovanni in Marignano**, just inland from Cattòlica; the villagers here have been known as the *Mangiatedeschi* ('German-eaters') since 539, when two women living in these parts lured in and wolfed down 17 Goths.

San Marino

As a perfect counterpart to the sand-strewn fun fair of Rimini, just 23km inland you may visit the world's only sovereign and independent roadside attraction. Before Rimini became the Italian Miami Beach, the 26,000 citizens of San Marino had to make a living peddling postage stamps. Now, with their medieval streets crowded with day-trippers, the San Marinesi have been unable to resist the temptation to order some bright medieval costumes, polish up their picturesque mountain villages, and open up some souvenir stands and 'duty free' shops.

Their famous stamps, though nothing like the engraved numbers of 50 years ago, are still prized by collectors, and recently the country has begun to mint its own coins again after a lapse of 39 years; nevertheless the citizens of San Marino, who may just have the highest average income in Europe, still make their living almost entirely from tourism.

Getting Around

There are frequent buses to San Marino from Rimini's train station with Bonelli (t 0541 372 432) or Benedettini (t 0549 903 854).

Tourist Information

San Marino town: Contrado Omagnano 20, t/f 0549 882 412, and in the villages.

Where to Stay and Eat

San Marino ✉ 47031

Italian currency is valid everywhere, but make sure you don't get too many San Marino coins in change; they are only good for souvenirs once you get back to Italy.
★★★★**Titano**, Contrada del Collegio 21, t 0549 991 006, f 0549 991 375 (*moderate*). On San Marino's citadel, in the middle of the old town, is the a restored century-old building where half the rooms have great views over the countryside.
★★★**La Rocca**, Not far away, on Salita alla Rocca, t 0549 991 166 (*cheap*). Ten rooms, a pool, and balconies with a view.
Buca San Francesco, t 0549 991 462 (*moderate*). The best restaurant in the centre, and a very pretty place it is, can be found at Piazzetta Placito Feretrano, snuggling up to the Hotel Titano; it has nothing out of the ordinary, but its soups, *tortellini* and *scallopine alla sanmarinese* are good.
Locanda dell'Artista, Via del Dragone 18, t 0549 996 024 (*moderate*). At Località Montegiardino. You can dine on the traditional dishes of the little republic, including some vegetarian ones, accompanied by home-baked bread and sweets; good *menu degustazione* available. *Open evenings only, closed Mon, Nov.*

The World's Smallest Republic

Also the oldest republic. According to legend San Marino was founded as a Christian settlement on the slopes of Monte Titano by a stonecutter named Marinus, fleeing from the persecutions of Diocletian in the early 4th century. 'Overlooked', as the San Marinesi charmingly put it, by the empire and various states that followed it, the little community had the peace and quiet to evolve its medieval democratic institutions; its constitution in its present form dates from 1243 when the first pair of 'consuls' was elected by a popular assembly. The consuls are now called Captains Regent, but little else has changed in 700 years.

Twice, in 1503 and 1739, the Republic was invaded by papal forces, and independence was preserved only by a little good luck. Napoleon, passing through in 1797, found San Marino amusing and half-seriously offered to enlarge its boundaries, a proposal that was politely declined. It offered shelter to Garibaldi, his wife Anita and 1,500 of his followers, fleeing Rome after the fall of the republic of 1849 with an Austrian army in hot pursuit; Garibaldi dissolved his army in the night and made a run for the coast at Cesenatico before dawn the next morning. Since then, the republic has been an island of peace, taking in thousands of refugees in the Second World War.

Entering San Marino from Rimini at the hamlet called **Dogana** (though there are no border formalities now), you pass through a string of villages along a ferociously built-up main road through a green and pretty countryside. San Marino, no midget like the Vatican City, is all of 12km long at its widest extent. At the foot of Monte Titano, rising dramatically above the plain, is **Borgomaggiore**, the largest town, with a cablecar up to the capital and citadel of the republic, also called **San Marino**. This is a steep medieval hill town carefully preserved in aspic, with wonderful views over Rimini and the coast. Not everything is as old as it looks; the Palazzo del Governo, full of Ruritanian guardsmen, is a reconstruction of 1894, with a recent restoration by Gae Aulenti. Here the Grand Council meets and the Captains Regent have their offices. A cheesy batch of private museums have been conjured up to extract lire from tourists – Medieval Criminals, Torture, Reptiles, Curiosities and Waxworks – but the best thing to do is walk through Monte Titano's forests to the three (rebuilt) medieval tower fortresses on the three peaks that give San Marino its famous silhouette; famous to philatelists anyhow, and long the symbol of the republic.

Around San Marino

Two other mountain towns near San Marino are most easily visited from Rimini: **Verucchio** is a pleasant medieval village that retains some of its gates and churches, as well as a 10th-century fortress that became the stronghold of the tyrants of Rimini, the Rocca Malatesta. There is a small Museo Archeologico at the lower end of town, with unusual ceramics from the 1400 BC Villanova culture.

San Leo, on the western side of San Marino (actually in the Marche), was according to legend founded by a companion of Marinus, but lost its independence long ago. The rough-walled, 9th-century church called the Pieve is worth a look, but San Leo's real attraction is the castle (*open 9–7; adm*), built for the Montefeltro dukes in the 15th century. Like their palace at Urbino, this fortress is a perfect representative building of the Renaissance: balanced, finely proportioned in its lines, a building of intelligence and style – impregnably hung on a breathtakingly sheer cliff. Once this mountain held a temple of Jupiter; as Mons Feretrius (referring to Jove's lightning) it gave its name to the Montefeltro family. A later fortress on this site was briefly 'capital of Italy' in the 960s, during the reign of King Berengar II. Now there is a small picture gallery in the castle and the dismal cell where the popes kept one of their most famous prisoners, Count Cagliostro, until he went raving mad and died.

Montefiore Conca in the Valconca has another Rocca Malatestiana, this one impressive in its sobriety, with sheer naked walls built in the form of a single massive tower in the early 14th century; Bellini used it in at least two of his backgrounds. Then there's **Montegridolfo**, a handsome medieval fortified village right on the border with the Marche that has been perfectly restored after years of total abandonment, and **Mondaino**, a picturesque medieval burg wrapped in its walls with a pretty semicircular piazza in the centre.

The Marches

15

The Marches

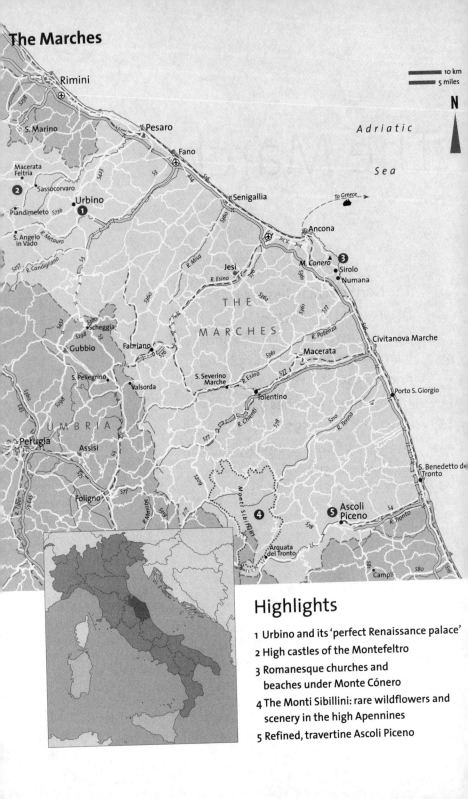

10 km
5 miles

N

Rimini

S. Marino

Pesaro

Fano

Adriatic

Sea

Macerata
Feltria

Sassocorvaro

2

Urbino

1

Piandimeleto

S73b

S. Angelo
in Vado

R. Metauro

R. Candigliano

Senigallia

To Greece →

Ancona

M. Conero

3

Sirolo

Numana

Jesi

R. Misa

R. Esino

T H E

M A R C H E S

Scheggia

Gubbio

Fabriano

S. Pellegrino

Valsorda

S. Severino
Marche

R. Esino

Macerata

Civitanova Marche

R. Potenza

Porto S. Giorgio

Perugia

Assisi

Tolentino

R. Chienti

R. Tenna

S. Benedetto del
Tronto

UMBRIA

Foligno

R. Menocchia

Monti Sibillini

4

5

Ascoli
Piceno

R. Tronto

Arquata
del Tronto

Campli

Highlights

1 Urbino and its 'perfect Renaissance palace'

2 High castles of the Montefeltro

3 Romanesque churches and
  beaches under Monte Cónero

4 The Monti Sibillini: rare wildflowers and
  scenery in the high Apennines

5 Refined, travertine Ascoli Piceno

Meglio un morto in casa che un marchigiano fuori della porta.
'Better a corpse in the house than a man from the Marches at the door.'

old Italian saying

Now what could the inhabitants of this placid little region have done to earn such opprobrium from their countrymen? They aren't so bad, really; the saying comes from the old days when many of the Marchigiani served across the Papal States as the popes' tax collectors. Since then, their neighbours have more often ignored than insulted this obscure patch of territory along the Adriatic. A *march*, or *mark*, in the Middle Ages meant a border province of the Holy Roman Empire, usually an unsettled frontier held by one of the Emperor's fighting barons. With no better name than that, one might expect this Italian region to be somewhat lacking in personality. In fact, this has always been the odd bit of central Italy. In ancient times too it was a border zone, shared by Umbrii, Gauls, Sabines and the Piceni. Today, the Marchigiani still have a little identity problem, but it doesn't keep them awake at night. Their land, tucked between the Apennines and the sea, is one of the greenest, prettiest and most civilized corners of Italy, with two lovely Renaissance art towns in Urbino and Ascoli Piceno, lots of beaches, and scores of fine old rosy-brick towns in the valleys that lead up to the impressive snowy peaks of the Sibilline Mountains.

The Northern Marches

Pésaro and Urbino

Just across the border from Emilia-Romagna, the impressive 11th–14th century **Rocca di Gradara** (*t 0541 964 181; open Mon 8.30–1.30, Tues–Sun 8.30–6.50; adm*) marks the entrance to the Marches. Tradition says this was the scene of the story of Francesca da Rimini and Paolo Malatesta, the tragic lovers consigned to hell by the heartless Dante in the fifth canto of the *Inferno* – a story exploited to the hilt, as it's within easy tour bus distance of Rimini. Beyond, the road soon arrives at provincial capital Pésaro.

Pésaro

Under the Byzantines, the five big ports of the central Adriatic – Rimini, Fano, Senigállia, Ancona and Pésaro – were known as the Pentapolis. Pésaro is the nicest, with a handsome little historic centre. The Sforzas of Milan ruled Pésaro until they sold it to the Della Rovere family of Julius II in 1512, two years after completing the crenellated **Palazzo Ducale** in Piazza del Popolo. In the Sforza years Pésaro rivalled Faenza as a producer of ceramics; see examples in the nearby **Museo Civico**, Piazza Toschi Mosca (*t 0721 387 523 or 387 541; opening hours as for Rossini's birthplace*), alongside majolica from Urbino, Deruta and Gubbio. There are also a few good pictures – and one very great one, a *Coronation of the Virgin* (1474), by Giovanni Bellini. The **Museo Archeologico Oliveriano** at Via Mazza 97 (*t 0721 33344; open Sept–June Mon–Sat 9–12; July and Aug, Mon–Sat 4–7*) displays remains left by the Romans and some of the peoples they quashed (Umbrii, Gauls, Sabines, Piceni and the rest).

Getting Around

Pésaro's railway station (all trains stop) is on the southern edge of town on Viale Roma, about ½km from the centre. At least 10 buses a day go to **Urbino**, some via Fano and (usually) Fermignano. There are several companies, all of which leave from or stop at Pésaro station; SAPUM buses (**t** 0721 371 318) are most frequent. In Urbino, the bus depot is Piazzale Mercatale, at the town's southern gate, with connections to most of the inland villages and towns in Pésaro province; all arrivals and departures are listed on a board under the loggia in Piazza della Repubblica.

Tourist Information

Pésaro: Viale Trieste 164, **t** 0721 69341, **f** 0721 30462. Via Rossini 61, **t** 0721 359 501, **f** 0721 339 30; also freephone (from within Italy) **t** 800 563 800.

Urbino: Piazza Rinascimento 1, **t** 0722 2613 **f** 0722 2441.

Where to Stay and Eat

Pésaro ✉ 61100

At first sight Pésaro looks a refined, perhaps exclusive resort; it comes as a pleasant surprise to find that prices aren't over the top.
★★★★**Vittoria**, Piazzale della Libertà 2, **t** 0721 34343, **f** 0721 65204 (*expensive*). At the top of the list comes one of the 'Hundred Historic Hotels of Italy' a renovated century-old *belle époque* villa at the centre of the beach strip; rooms are furnished with period beds, mirrors and wardrobes; there's also a pool and a billiards room.
★★★★**Villa Serena**, Via San Nicola 6, **t** 0721 55211, **f** 0721 55927 (*expensive*). Just south of Pésaro, occupies a 17th-century palace with fireplaces and antique furniture in every room, in a serene scenic park. *Closed two weeks in Jan.*
★★★★**Savoy**, Viale Repubblica 22, **t** 0721 67440, **f** 0721 64429 (*moderate*). A modern hotel, run by the same team as the Vittoria, set in an attractive shady place with a pool.
Beyond that, Pésaro's speciality is the modern, understated three-star hotel. It's difficult to recommend one over the other. There is also a selection of one- and two-star places along the beach and side streets.
★★★**Principe**, Viale Trieste 180, **t** 0721 30222, **f** 0721 31636 (*cheap*). Stands out for its excellent, popular restaurant **Teresa** (*moderate, see* below). *Closed Dec–Mar.*
The local cuisine is fishy, and includes delectables such as *ravioli* with sole fillets, *garagoli in aorchetta* (shellfish tossed with olive oil, garlic, rosemary, and wild fennel), stuffed cuttlefish and red mullet with *prosciutto*.
Alceo, Via Panoramica Ardizio 101, **t** 0721 51360 (*very expensive*). Come here for fresh fish dishes, home-made pasta and desserts, a friendly atmosphere and tables outside with sea views. *Closed Sun eve and Mon.*
Lo Scudiero, Via Baldassini 2, **t** 0721 64107 (*expensive*). Occupies the cellar of a 17th-century palace. Specialities include imaginative dishes with seafood and pasta – *ravioli* with sole, or *tagliatelle marine*; they also do a good roast lamb. *Closed Sun and July.*

Pésaro is also proud to have given the world composer Gioacchino Rossini, in 1792; you can see mementos of the *maestro* in his **Casa Natale** at Via Rossini 34 (**t** *0721 387 357, open Sept–June Thurs–Sun 9.30–12.30 and 4–7, Tues and Wed 9.30–12.30; July and Aug, Tues and Thurs 9.30–12.30 and 5–11, Wed and Fri–Sun 9.30–12.30 and 5–8*); see his piano and manuscripts at the **conservatory** he founded, in Piazza Olivieri; or take in an opera at Pésaro's grand, five-tiered **Teatro Rossini,** during the festival in late summer.

It's a lovely town to walk through, both its older quarters and arcaded streets and the new streets by the beach, full of trees and villas from the 19th century in the Liberty style, including the small but outrageous **Villino Ruggieri**, its cornice supported by terracotta lobsters, designed by Giovanni Brega in 1907. Pésaro's castle, the **Rocca Costanza,** was built in 1478 by Laurana, the designer of the palace at Urbino.

Teresa, Viale Trieste 180, t 0721 30222, f 0721 31636 (*moderate*). The fine restaurant of the Principe Hotel, with enticing dishes such as a *risotto* made with wild herbs picked locally and fried *calamari* with sage.

Antica Osteria La Guercia, Via Baviera 33, right on the corner of the Piazza del Popolo, t 0721 33463 (*cheap*). The oldest in town, serving all the classics, including homemade *strozzapreti*, 'priest-chokers'. *Closed Sun.*

Il Cantuccio di Leo, Via Perfetti 18, t 0721 68088 (*cheap*). An *enoteca* in the centre, with all kinds of dishes to go with its wines, such as boar terrines, cheeses (including French ones), pasta and meat courses; it stays open until 2am. *Closed Tues and July.*

La Tana del Lupo, in Montefabbri, by Colbordolo t 0721 495721 (*cheap*). Makes a good lunch stop about midway along the road from Pésaro to Urbino. *Closed June–Sept.*

Urbino ✉ 61029

The few hotels in Urbino can be extremely crowded in the summer, and even spring, so book ahead. Much of the civilized air of Duke Federico's time seems to have survived into our own – you may end up staying longer than you planned.

****Bonconte, Via delle Mura 28, t 0722 2463, f 0722 4782 (*expensive*). Sitting on the walls of the city, this is the most luxurious place in town short of the palace itself. Lovely views.

***Raffaello, Via S. Margherita 40, t 0722 4784, f 0722 328 540 (*expensive*). Nicely furnished rooms in an 18th-century house, on a quiet lane just above Raphael's birthplace.

***Italia, Corso Garibaldi 32, t 0722 2701, f 0722 322 664 (*moderate*). Good and central, one block from the Ducal Palace.

**San Giovanni, Via Barocci 13, t 0722 2827 (*moderate*). In an old *palazzo* with a good restaurant. *Closed Jan.*

***Tortorina, northeast of the centre at Via Tortorina 4, t 0722 3081, f 0722 308 372 (*moderate*). Has a large panoramic terrace and rooms furnished with antiques.

Locanda La Bromolona, 10km down the Fossombrone road, at Canavàccio, t/f 0722 53501 (*cheap*). Rooms in a pretty setting, in a former church.

*Pensione Fosca, Via Raffaello 67, t 0722 2542 (*cheap*). If you're looking to economize, this is the only option central Urbino has to offer, but there are several student and religious institutions in town that have space in the summer: ask at the tourist office.

Taverna degli Artisti, Via Bramante 52, t 0722 2676 (*moderate*). Arrive early, or book first to get a table here. It serves great food (including *pizza*) at excellent prices, until 2am most evenings. *Closed Tues in winter.*

Vecchia Urbino, also in the historic centre at Via Vasari 3/5, t 0722 4447 (*moderate*). An elegant option which will treat you to a feast in the autumn-winter *tartufi* and *porcini* season *Closed Tues in winter.*

L'Angolo Divino, Via Sant'Andrea 14 (off Via Cesare Battisti), t 0722 327559 (*cheap*). Occupies a pretty room in an old palace and specializes in old Urbino specialities – pasta with chickpeas, bacon, lamb or bread-crumbs, and tasty *secondi* from the grill; some vegetarian dishes. *Closed Sun eve and Mon lunch.*

Urbino

From Pésaro – and almost nowhere else – it is easy to reach the isolated mountain town of Urbino. With its celebrated **Palazzo Ducale,** and the memory of the refined Duke Federico da Montefeltro who built it, Urbino is one of the monuments of the Italian Renaissance. Today its boosters go perhaps too far – 'the ideal city of the Renaissance' and 'most beautiful palace in the world', with a lack of modesty that wasn't at all Federico's style. Even so, Urbino does represent more clearly than any Italian town a certain facet of the Renaissance: elegance, learning and intelligent patronage combined in a small place. Urbino's golden age may not have lasted long but, as an example of what a community can be, it still exerts a certain fascination.

The Court of Montefeltro

Beginning in 1234, Urbino's fortunes were attached to those of the house of Montefeltro, mountain warlords from around San Leo who gradually extended their influence in the northern Marches. Most of them were *condottieri* working throughout Italy, serving various masters. In 1443, Oddantonio da Montefeltro earned the title of duke for his services, and was then assassinated. His half-brother and successor, Federico (reigned 1444–82), was the most successful of all the family, a crafty and respected warrior who earned the money for his famous palace serving the cause of Alfonso of Naples and the Pope.

In later years, with more of a chance to stay at home, Federico became one of the quattrocento's most celebrated patrons of art and literature, as well as a slow but close student of the classics and the new humanities; he learned Greek and Latin, and the library he assembled was one of the best in Europe. Federico ruled Urbino paternally and well, always liberal to those of his subjects in need, peeering into every detail of his little state's economy and social life, and educating the sons of the poor. It is also said that he banished gambling and cursing, and made the people of Urbino exert themselves mightily to keep the place clean. His admirable wife, Battista Sforza, was a duchess beloved by her subjects, and a lady capable of delivering an impromptu speech in impeccable Latin; both were immortalized in Piero della Francesco's warts-and-all portraits – now in the Uffizi.

Their son, Guidobaldo I (1472–1508), was as enlightened a ruler as his father, married to the cultivated Elisabetta Gonzaga, and maintaining a court idealized as the height of civilized existence in Baldassare Castiglione's *The Courtier* (1528), one of the most widely read books of the century. He was also clever enough to survive and prevail after an occupation of Urbino by Cesare Borgia's Papal army in 1497; however when he died without an heir, the duchy fell to a Della Rovere nephew and relative of Pope Julius II. Urbino was willed to the papacy in 1626, and declined rapidly.

Urbino had a moment of high drama in 1944. Many of the works of art of Central Italy had been brought there for safekeeping near the end of the war. During the retreat in August, a German commander planted enough explosives under the town walls to blow the whole place to kingdom-come. Only a small number went off, and the rest were defused by the British after the liberation – a job that took a week.

The Palazzo Ducale

Open Tues–Sun 8.30–7, Mon 8.30–2; visits every 15mins in winter; adm; t 0722 2760.

So many architects helped Federico build his dream house, it is difficult to divide the credit. Alberti may have been an original adviser; the Dalmatian Luciano Laurana generally gets credit for most of the work and the elegant arcaded courtyard; the region's favourite architect, Francesco di Giorgio Martini, may have designed its two internal squares, while the finest part of it, the twin-turreted façade, is by Ambrogio Barocchi. That Italian schoolchildren all know this to be 'the most beautiful palace in the world' is an interesting reflection both on the Italians and on the quattrocento. Federico's palace is not finished, not symmetrical, and not really even very grand; its aesthetic is utterly foreign to the tastes of the centuries that followed.

For all that, it is a great building, and a test of one's faith in the genuine Renaissance – the 15th-century high noon of life and art, as opposed to the cinquecento of Spaniardism and neurotic excess. Many critics have regarded it as the culmination of Renaissance architecture, not yet entirely enslaved to perspectivism or imitation of the ancients, but a creation of freedom and delight. The palace was comfortable for the Montefeltro to live in, and an exquisite decoration for the city of Urbino.

The palace façade, overlooking the hills on the edge of town, consists of three levels of balconies between two slender towers; the decorative trim is done in a fine Dalmatian limestone that eventually hardens to look like marble. To enter the palace today, you'll need to go round the back through the Cortile d'Onore, a prototype for so many other courtyards around the western Mediterranean.

Inside, much of the palace is occupied by the **Galleria Nazionale delle Marche**, a splendid collection whose finest works were originally the property of Duke Federico. Piero della Francesca's amazing *Flagellation* is perhaps the best-known work in Urbino, an endlessly disturbing image that has troubled art scholars for centuries. Standing before a pavilion of fantasy classical architecture, three gentlemen in contemporary dress hold a serious discussion, indifferent to the scourging of Christ going on behind them – a bloodless scourging, for that matter. Piero, one of the luminaries of Federico's court, had already written one of the great Renaissance treatises on theoretical perspective; a complex system of foreshortening here is the major feature of the work. The combination of a surreal, dream-like scene and a drily scientific visual presentation gives the painting its enigmatic quality – as critics have often noted, this is one of the places where art crosses the line into sorcery. The same room contains Piero's *Madonna di Senigallia*, another superb work; the Virgin looks as if she just stepped into a grey room, holding her baby; everyday things sit on the shelves, and even the two angels look like a pair of homeowners – yet the domestic scene is rendered timeless, meditative and almost hypnotic through Piero's sorcery. Almost as strange a display of perspectivist wizardry is the *Ideal City*, often attributed to Laurana. The scene is a broad, paved square, lined with buildings in the new style, dominated by a large circular temple in the centre. Disturbingly, there are no people present – no living things at all in this display of vanishing point virtuosity.

Not to be outdone by Piero, Paolo Uccello offers a similarly mysterious *Miracle of the Profaned Host* (*under restoration at the time of writing*), while Piero's student Luca Signorelli is represented by two dark and inspired paintings, the *Crucifixion* and *Pentecost*. Other works not to miss include a *Crucifixion* by Antonio Alberti de Ferrara, taking care to show off contemporary fashions, in armour as well as court dress; the *Annunciation* of Vicenzo Pagani (and a pagan-looking work it is, too); *La Muta*, a lovely portrait of a lady by Raphael, and his *St Catherine of Alexandria*, a recent acquisition; also fine works by Luca della Robbia, Giovanni Santi (Raphael's dad), Carlo Crivelli, Verrocchio and the Venetian Alvise Vivarini. The Spanish artist Pedro Berruguete contributes the other famous *Portrait of Duke Federico*: the tough old warrior, with his broken nose, symbolically still wears his armour as he pores over a heavy book, with his little son Guidobaldo at his knee; note the badge of the Order of the Garter, conferred on Federico by King Edward IV of England.

Some of the surviving interior decoration of the palace is wonderful too – carved mantelpieces and window frames, intarsia doors, cornices and stuccoes, carved and painted ceilings, all bearing the monogram FE DUX and family emblems. Best of all is the intimate intarsia **Studiolo of Duke Federico**, which looks as if the scholarly *condottiere* might wander in at any moment. The inlaid wood designs are by Botticelli, Bramante and Francesco di Giorgio Martini, and they portray the 'Life of a Scholar' with mesmerizing *trompe-l'œil* effects. The paintings above, representing philosophers and illustrious men, are by Berruguete and Giusto di Gand, although only half of the 28 are original – the rest are in the Louvre. Reached by a spiral staircase inside one of the façade's towers are the **Cappella del Perdono,** with an ornate ceiling of hundreds of angel heads in stucco, and an equally fancy chamber called the **Tempietto delle Muse.** A *Last Supper* by Titian hangs in the duchess's bedroom, while the huge throne room, where Federico liked to entertain on a grand scale, has seven tapestries on the *Acts of the Apostles* from Raphael's cartoons.

The palace's upper floor, the **Appartamento Roveresco**, was closed after the 1997 earthquake; if it's open, look for rooms of 16th- and 17th-century paintings, and many portraits of the poor Italians dressed in black like their Spanish overlords. The palace's basement contains the laundry, kitchens, ice rooms, storage, the 'duchess's bath' and plumbing, with grafitti scrawled here and there on the walls.

The Town and Walls

Urbino is above all a university town, and, despite its small size, is a lively place full of students. Though its streets and roads are often steep, Urbino and its surrounding hills make an enchanting spot for walks. Adjacent to the ducal palace, in long Piazza Rinascimentale, the **cathedral** was rebuilt as a dull neoclassical church after an earthquake in 1789 caused its dome to collapse. Its collection of detached trecento frescoes and religious artefacts are in the **Museo Albani** (*t 0722 2892; open daily 9–12 and 3–6, in winter by request*). The oldest thing in the piazza is the little Egyptian **obelisk** from 580 BC, in front of the original Montefeltro palace, now Palazzo dell'Università, and the handsome 1451 portal of Gothic San Domenico. On Via Barocci, off Via Mazzini, the street that leads up from Urbino's main gate, the little 14th-century **Oratorio di San Giovanni Battista** (*t 0347 671 1181; open Mon–Sat 10–12 and 3–5, Sun 10–12.30; am only in winter; closed Feb*) has strikingly colourful frescoes of the *Crucifixion*, the *Madonna*, and the *Life of John the Baptist* by the brothers Iacopo and Lorenzo Salimbeni (1416), artists from San Severino Marche, near Macerata, who show a distinctive approach to early-Renaissance painting, still heavily under the influence of Giotto. On the same street, the **Oratorio di San Giuseppe** has an exquisite stucco *presepio* (crib) by a 16th-century artist from Urbino, Federico Brandani (*same opening hours*).

Urbino's most famous son, though, was Raphael (Raffaello Sanzio), born here in 1483. Now a museum, the **Casa di Raffaello** (*t 0722 320 105; open Mar–Oct Mon–Sat 9–1 and 3–7, Sun and hols 10–1; Nov–Feb Mon–Sat 9–2, Sun and hols 10–1; adm*) has

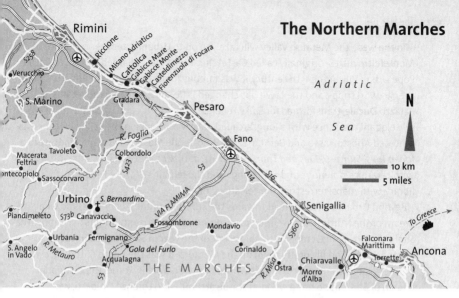

little to see – a *Madonna* by the artist as a child, and works by his father, Giovanni Santi, who taught Raphael the basics of painting and humanist thought.

All of Urbino's 16th-century walls are intact, and the garden enclosed by one of the corner bastions, the **Fortezza Albornoz,** has a fine view of the palace and town. A pleasant half-hour walk from the west end of town (2½km) will take you to the pretty church of **San Bernardino degli Zoccolanti** by Francesco di Giorgio Martini (1491); inside are the starkly impressive black marble tombs of the Montefeltro Dukes.

Towns and Villages Around Urbino

Urbino can be used as a base for excursions to the towns and villages in the rolling hills and mountains of the northern Marches – towns as serene and lovely as those in Tuscany, though much less known. Some of the most enchanting landscapes lie in the ancient fief of the Montefeltro; the rolling hills are studded with remarkable bare rocky crags, each crowned by a castle from the days when the dukes of Urbino and the Malatesta of Rimini clobbered each other for control of the turf. It's a lovely region, just being discovered by the outside world (Umberto Eco has a house here). **Fermignano**, where Bramante may have been born in 1444 (that honour is also claimed by Urbánia), is one of the most conveniently located, about 9km south of Urbino. At its centre, under a graceful medieval tower and bridge, there is a little waterfall on the Metauro River. From Fermignano, you can follow the Metauro Valley east through a rocky ravine called the **Gola del Furlo**. The Romans, under Vespasian, dug the tunnel to reach **Fossombrone**, then known as *Forum Sempronii*, after the reformer Sempronius Gracchus. Scenographically built on tiers under a Montefeltro palace, Fossombrone is full of tattered palaces and churches, but with nary a tourist in sight. Its **Palazzo Ducale** is seat of the **Museo Archeologico** (*t 0722 723 238; open June–Sept Tues–Sun 10–12 and 4–7; Oct–May open weekends 3–6.30; adm*), with some good Renaissance pavements and ceilings, and paintings and etchings by Dürer, Rembrandt and Tiepolo.

To the west, the Metauro Valley will take you on to **Urbánia**, another residence of the Montefeltro dukes; originally called Castel Durante, it was renamed in 1636 to flatter Pope Urban VIII. In the 15th century, it was famous for its majolica, manufactured in over 30 workshops, and the town has changed little since. Urbánia too retains a **Palazzo Ducale**, transformed for Duke Federico from a 13th-century castle into a properly elegant residence with a long, arcaded gallery overlooking the valley. In its heyday it hosted Ariosto, Tasso and Bembo; today it hosts the **Museo Civico** and **Pinacoteca** (*open Tues–Sun 3–6, Tues and Thurs also 10–12; at other times, call t 0722 313 109; adm*) with ceramics, drawings and engravings and the remains of Duke Federico's famous library, with maps, terrestrial and celestial globes.

Beyond Urbánia all roads lead towards the summits of the Apennines, and villagers dream of the truffles, just like their counterparts across the mountains in Umbria. The *Sagra del Tartufo* in October is the big event of the year in **Sant'Angelo in Vado**, another exceptionally pretty town on the Metauro; it was the home of the Zuccari brothers, late-Renaissance painters whose best works are in Rome. The octagonal church of San Filippo has a wooden statue attributed to Lorenzo Ghiberti, who wandered the Marches until the great Florentine baptistry door contest changed his life. From here the road begins the climb over the mountains to Arezzo and Perugia.

To the north **Piandimeleto**, **Sassocorvaro** and **Tavoleto** are three villages built around genteel Renaissance castle-palaces; Sassocorvaro's striking 15th-century **Rocca Ubaldinesca** (*guided tours only; t 0722 76177 to reserve tour in English; open daily Oct–Mar 9.30–12.30 and 2.30–6; daily April–Sept 9.30–12.30 and 3–7; adm*) is an unusual round citadel, built by Francesco di Giorgio Martini. A narrow mountain road runs north via Pennabilli to **Sant'Agata Féltria,** protected by the **Rocca Fregoso**, another fantastical castle balancing precariously on its rock. Inside (*t 0541 929 111; open daily 10–1 and 3–7; longer hours in summer; adm*) there's a collection of Renaissance frescoes. Sant'Agata really comes into its own in the autumn, when it holds a white truffle market on four consecutive Sundays, beginning with the second Sunday in October. For **San Leo**, in the northernmost corner of the Marches, *see* p.571.

Back on the Coast: Pésaro to Ancona

South of Pésaro, the string of Adriatic resorts continues through Fano and Senigállia, which are fine old towns, both members of the Pentapolis.

Fano

Older even than the Romans, Fano takes its name – *Fanum Fortunae* – from a famous temple of the goddess Fortuna. Under Roman rule it became the most important of the Marches' coastal cities, the terminus of the Via Flaminia from Rome; it still looks uncannily like the perfect provincial Roman town. Today, in the central Piazza XX Settembre, a replica Fortuna smiles on Fano from the 16th-century **Fontana della Fortuna.** Behind it, the Palazzo della Ragione (1299) is an austere Romanesque Gothic hall, linked by an arch with the **Palazzo Malatestiano** (*t 0721 828 362; open Tues–Sat 9.30–12.30 and 4–7, Sun 8.30–12.30; closed Mon; adm*), a palace built in the 1420s, when

Tourist Information

Fano: Viale Cesare Battisti 10, **t** 0721 803 534, **f** 0721 824 292.

Senigállia: Piazza Morandi 2, **t** 071 792 2725, **f** 071792 4930.

Where To Stay and Eat

There aren't any special choices in Fano or Senigállia – standard beach hotels, all less than 30 years old. Fano, however, offers the cheapest, tastiest seafood in the Marches.

Fano ✉ 61032

******Augustus**, Via Puccini 2, **t** 0721 809 781, **f** 0721 825 517 (*moderate*). A central, family-run hotel, which recently had a face-lift from head to toe. *Closed Mon.*

*****Angela**, Viale Adriatico 13, **t** 0721 801 239, **f** 0721 803 102 (*moderate*). Another reasonable option.

*****Astoria**, Viale Cairoli 86, **t/f** 0721 803 474 (*moderate*). A pleasant hotel on the best part of the beach. *Open Easter–Oct.*

****Mare**, Viale C. Colombo 20, **t/f** 0721 805 667 (*cheap*). If you're feeling nostalgic for the *pensioni* of 20 years ago, try this place off the beach, where mamma Anna cooks some of the best and most affordable seafood in Fano. **Restaurant** (*cheap*) *closed Sun eve.*

Ristorantino Da Giulio, Viale Adriatico 100, **t** 0721 805 680 (*expensive*). Another reliable favourite, serving extra fresh seafood, *marchigiano*-style: try the *fusilli con le canocchie* (a local kind of shrimp). *Closed Tues.*

Pesce Azzurro, near the port at Viale Adriatico 48, **t** 0721 803 165 (*cheap*). Unique in Italy, this was founded a decade ago by the local fisherman's cooperative, designed to promote the glories of 'blue fish' – not one specific variety, but a variety of sardines, anchovies, mackerel and other small fish, all delicious! The degradation of the Adriatic makes them harder to find with each passing year, but at this self-service restaurant, you can try them in three cheap courses, with the local white wine, Bianchello del Metauro, to wash them down. *Closed Mon, and from Oct–Mar.*

Senigállia ✉ 60019

******Duchi della Rovere**, Via Corridoni 3, **t** 071 792 7623, **f** 071 792 7784 (*expensive*). You can spoil yourself at this stylish hotel, located by the park a couple of blocks in from the beach.

*****Cristallo**, right by the rotunda at Lungomare Alighieri 2, **t** 071 792 5767, **f** 071 792 5768 (*moderate*). A typical resort hotel with lots of balconies and a roof terrace. *Open June–Sept.*

*****La Vela**, Piazzale N. Bixio 35, **t** 071 792 7444, **f** 071 792 7445 (*moderate*). A nice place near the port with a garden; it's also the furthest hotel from the railway line.

Madonnina del Pescatore, Lungomare Italia 11, 7km south in Marzocca, **t** 071 698 267 (*very expensive*). Always packed for its brilliant and creative seafood dishes, and some of the best desserts in all the Marches. Reserve. *Closed Mon, two weeks mid-Jan, Easter week and one week Sept.*

Riccardone's, Via Rieti 69, **t** 071 64762 (*expensive*). An excellent restaurant with tables out on the garden terrace and dishes made from the freshest ingredients; try their squid with artichokes or a mixed seafood grill. *Closed Tues Sept–June, open daily July–Aug.*

Osteria del Tempo Perso, Via Mastai 53, **t** 071 60345 (*moderate*). Offers a change from all the seafood, with a number of vegetarian dishes that change with the season, right in the *centro storico. Closed Thurs.*

Fano was ruled by the tyrants of Rimini. It has a lovely courtyard with crenellations, mullioned windows and a portico; the elegant loggia on the right, attributed to Iacopo Sansovino, was added in 1544. The picture gallery stars works by Michele Giambono and Guercino – and the real Fortuna. The church of **Santa Maria Nuova**, two blocks south on Via dei Pili, is decorated with stuccoes and altarpieces by Perugino and Giovanni Santi, one with a small predella panel attributed to Santi's young son Raphael. From Roman times, Fano preserves a stately gate built in the year AD 2, the **Arco di Augusto**. The church of San Michele has a relief carved on its façade showing how the arch looked before having its block knocked off with artillery in 1463. The eventually successful besieger was none other than Duke Federico of Urbino, working at that time for the pope; the defender was Sigismondo Malatesta of Rimini. The portico of San Francesco's ruined basilica holds the **Arche Malatestiane**, the Renaissance tomb of Pandolfo III Malatesta (1460) attributed to Alberti. Fano's Lido, modern and overbuilt, is one of the nicer resorts on the Adriatic; its long broad beach continues down the coast for miles, through the resort suburbs of Torrette and Marotta, and there's room for all, sprawling all the way to Senigállia.

Senigállia

Senigállia, next down the coast, was best known for its duty free port, the site of an important trade fair that attracted some 500 ships from the 12th up to the 18th century. Besides its long 'velvet beach', one of the nicest on the Adriatic, its main landmark is an elegant though serviceable fortress, the **Rocca Roveresca** (*t 071 63258; open daily 8.30–7.30; adm*), built for Duke Federico's son-in-law in 1480.

Inland: the Valle dell'Esino

The mountain valleys, stretching in parallel down to the sea, neatly divide the Marches' geography. South of the Metauro, the Esino is the next important valley, most easily reached from Falconara, south of Senigállia. The first town is Jesi (Roman *Aesis*), set on a narrow ridge between crumbling, picturesque Renaissance walls with houses built on and over their tops.

In 1194, **Jesi** was the birthplace (in a tent, in the piazza) of none other than Emperor Frederick II *Stupor Mundis*. Constance de Hauteville, at the age of 40 and after nine years of marriage to Emperor Henry VI of Hohenstaufen, was on her way home to Sicily on 26 December 1194, when she was assailed by labour pains. She pitched her tent and invited the town's matrons and 19 churchmen to witness the birth and testify to the legitimacy of her son. Near the adjacent **Palazzo del Comune** there's the engraved text of a letter from Frederick to Jesi confirming the town's privileges. In the next square, the 16th-century **Palazzo Ricci** has an odd waffle-iron façade like the Gesù Nuovo in Naples. Jesi's real treasure, however, is the lavishly stuccoed rococo gallery and a set of paintings by Lorenzo Lotto, including the strange, beautifully lit *Annunciation* (1526) in the **Pinacoteca Comunale** (*t 0731 538 343; open Tues–Sat 10–7, Sun 10–1 and 5–8; adm*), located in the Palazzo Pianetti on Via XX Settembre. Outside the walls, the church of San Marco (*to visit, ring the bell of the Clarisse's convent to the right of the church*) has some exceptional 14th-century Giottesque frescoes.

Beyond Jesi, the Valle dell'Esino is squeezed into another limestone gorge, the **Gola di Rossa**; a road off to the right leads to the village of **Genga** and the **Grotte di Frasassi** (*t 0732 97211; open Nov–Feb Mon–Fri 11-3, Sat 11–4.30, Sun and holidays 9.30–6; Mar–July and Sept daily 9.30–6; Aug daily 8–6.30; July 20–Aug 25 also open nightly 8pm–10.30pm; closed Dec 4, Dec 25, Jan 1 and Jan 10–30; tours last 70mins; adm exp*). The caves are the largest karstic complex discovered in Italy, extending over 18km; the tour takes in the first mile. The massive **Grotta Grande del Vento** 'the Cave of the Winds' is a spectacular display of glistening pastel stalactites reflected in calcareous pools. Uphill from Genga station the **Grotta del Santuario** (*open daily dawn–sunset*) is named for its octagonal domed church by Valadier (1828) with a Canova *Madonna*. Nearby is the 10th-century church of **San Vittore delle Chiese.** A rather difficult road winds 17km up to the lovely medieval village of **Arcévia**, the impregnable 'Pearl of the Mountains' perched on its crag, with a fortified gate, Palazzo Comunale and nine towers. The church of San Medardo (*currently closed for renovation*) has a *Baptism of Christ* by Luca Signorelli.

Fabriano, further up the Esino valley near the border with Umbria and a stop on the Rome-Ancona railway, was famous in Renaissance times for paper-making; the water-mark (*filigrana*) was invented here, and Fabriano – typical of the tenacity of craftwork in many Italian towns – still makes its living from the stuff, using modern methods as well as artisan techniques. The most important use for speciality paper is, of course, banknotes; besides supplying the Italian treasury, Fabriano paper changes hands each day from Kashmir to the Congo. On the edge of the *centro storico*, the convent of San Domenico houses the **Museo della Carta e della Filigrana** (*t 0732 22334; open Mon–Sat 10–6, Sun 10–12 and 2–7; adm*) to tell you how they did and do do it. The museum also has the key for the church of San Domenico (*closed for restoration*), with frescoes from the 1300s, most notably those in the Chapel of Sant'Orsola.

The centre of town is a beautiful stage set, the arcaded **Piazza del Comune**, with a crenellated Palazzo del Podestà (1250), a Palazzo Comunale and Fontana Sturinalto (1281–1351), strangely reminiscent of the ones in Perugia. Fabriano was the home of a school of painting that produced one of Italy's most influential International Gothic artists, Gentile da Fabriano (c. 1370–1427), master of the famous *Adoration of the Magi* in the Uffizi. Works by the school can be seen in the **Pinacoteca Civica** (*due to open soon after restoration*), along with a good collection of Renaissance works.

For a real detour off the beaten track, press on south to **Matélica,** another fine Marches town with a pretty main square; a civic palace, the Palazzo Pretorio, with Roman ruins inside and a clock tower from 1270 (with later touches); and a fine picture gallery, the **Museo Piersanti**, at Via Umberto I 11 (*t 0737 84445; open Easter–Oct Tues–Sun 10–12 and 5–7; Nov–Easter Sat and Sun only 10–12 and 4–6; adm*) with an exceptional *Crucifixion* by Antonio da Fabriano (1452). **Cerreto d'Esi**, nearby, has the remains of a Byzantine gate and a leaning tower, built in the time of Justinian.

Ancona

Filthy hole: like rotten Cabbage. Thrice swindled.
James Joyce

Just before the city, the mountains once more reach the sea, giving the mid-Adriatic's biggest port a splendid setting, a crescent-shaped harbour under the steep promontory of Monte Guasco; here colonists from Syracuse founded the city in the

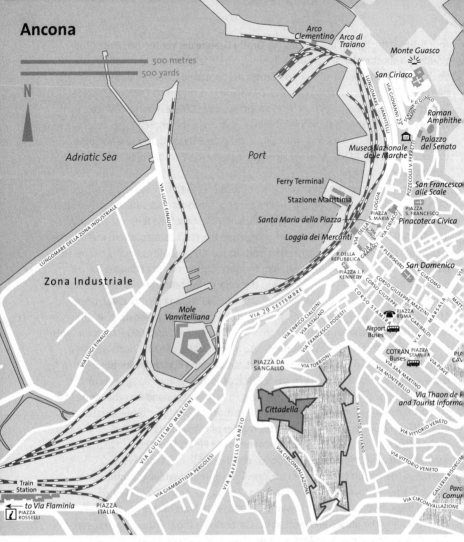

Ancona

500 metres
500 yards

N

Adriatic Sea

Port

Arco Clementino

Arco di Traiano

Monte Guasco

San Ciriaco

LUNGOMARE VANVITELLI

VIA GIOVANNI 23

SCALONE D. GUASCO

V. DELLA FERRETTI

Roman Amphithe

Palazzo del Senato

Museo Nazionale delle Marche

PIZZECOLLI V FERRETTI

San Francesco alle Scale

Ferry Terminal

Stazione Marittima

Santa Maria della Piazza

Loggia dei Mercanti

VIA LUIGI EINAUDI

LUNGOMARE DELLA ZONA INDUSTRIALE

Zona Industriale

Mole Vanvitelliana

VIA LUIGI EINAUDI

VIA 29 SETTEMBRE

VIA ENRICO CIALDINI

VIA ASTAGNO

VIA FRANCESCO PODESTI

PIAZZA DA SANGALLO

VIA TORRIONI

Cittadella

VIA GUGLIELMO MARCONI

VIA GIAMBATTISTA PERGOLESI

VIA RAFFAELLO SANZIO

VIA SANTO STEFANO

VIA CIRCONVALLAZIONE

Train Station

to Via Flaminia

PIAZZA ROSSELLI

PIAZZA ITALIA

LOGGIA

PIAZZA S. MARIA

VIA DELLA LOGGIA

VIA GRAMSCI

VIA S. MARIA

PIAZZA S. FRANCESCO

Pinacoteca Civica

P. DELLA REPUBBLICA

P. PLEBISCITO

San Domenico

V. GIACOMO

PIAZZA J. F. KENNEDY

CORSO GIUSEPPE MAZZINI

CORSO GIUSEPPE

CORSO STAMIRA

PIAZZA ROMA

Airport Buses

COTRAN Buses

PIAZZA STAMIRA

PIAZZA GARIBALDI

MARSALA

VIA PIAVE

VIA SAN MARTINO

VIA MONTEBELLO

Via Thaon de R and Tourist Informa

VIA VITTORIO VENETO

VIA VITTORIO VENETO

GALLERIA RISORGIM

VIA CIRCONVALLAZIONE

Parc Comu

5th century BC. It was the furthest north the ancient Greeks ever went in the Adriatic, and the colony was never a great success until it was built up by Roman emperors, notably Trajan, who hired Apollodoro of Damascus to lay out the port and town. Ancona later become the leading city of the Byzantine Pentapolis, and was given to the Church by Charlemagne. It recovered from the bad centuries to make a living trading with Dalmatia and the east – and battling with Venice on the seas, and the emperors, as well as the lords of Jesi, Rimini, and Macerata, on land. In 1532, Medici pope Clement VII reasserted the authority of the Church, moving in a papal army and constructing a citadel to house them.

The 20th century was murderous to Ancona. The Austrians bombarded it in 1915, an earthquake damaged it in 1930, and the British and Americans bombed it again in 1944. Then came a major flood, a serious earthquake in 1972, and a landslide that caused the abandonment of parts of the old town. For all its troubles, Ancona has come up smiling. The port is prospering, and even though most of the population now lives in newer districts to the south and west, the city is devoting its attention to the restoration of the historic centre.

Around the Port

It's surprising anything is left at all, but most of Ancona's monuments have survived the recent misfortunes, even if many are a little the worse for wear. The business centre has gravitated a few streets inland, around broad Piazza Cavour; from there Corso Garibaldi leads down to the sea. At its western end, the long curve of the port is anchored by the **Mole Vanvitelliana,** a pentagonal building that resembles a fortress, but really served as Ancona's *lazaretto* or quarantine station. At the other end the tall, graceful **Arco di Traiano** was built in AD 115, in honour of Ancona's imperial benefactor; even though the sculptural reliefs have disappeared, it is one of the better preserved Roman arches in Italy. Nearby, Pope Clement XII imitated Roman glory by having an arch put up to himself; the **Arco Clementino,** like the *lazaretto*, was the work of Vanvitelli, the court architect of the Bourbons at Naples, best known for his palace at Caserta. The elegant 15th-century Venetian Gothic **Loggia dei Mercanti,** the merchants' exchange, is the best souvenir of Ancona's heyday as a free maritime city.

To see the oldest quarters of Ancona you'll have to climb a little, starting up Via Gramsci and passing under the Renaissance decorative arch of the **Piazza del Governo**. Off in a little square to the left, **Santa Maria della Piazza** has a fine late-Romanesque façade, with figures of musicians, soldiers and odd animals carved by a 'Master Philippus'. Another two cross-streets up take you to **San Francesco alle Scale**, with another Gothic portal, and a late-Renaissance palace that houses the **Pinacoteca Civica** (*t 071 222 5045; open Tues–Sat 9–7, Mon 9–1, Sun 3–7; adm*). It contains a master-piece by the eccentric but endearing Carlo Crivelli, tidiest of all Renaissance painters – a *Madonna col Bambino*, complete with Crivelli's trademark apples and cucumbers hanging overhead. There is also a good *Madonna* by Lotto, formerly in the Santa Maria church, and yet another by Titian, floating smugly on a cloud.

On Monte Guasco

Further up, the street changes its name to Via del Guasco, and bits of decorative brickwork from Roman Ancona's theatre peek out in between and under the build-ings. This was the area hardest hit by the earthquake and landslide, and only in 1988 did the **Museo Nazionale delle Marche** re-open, in the ripe interiors of a 16th-century palace in Via Feretti 6 (*t 071 202 602; open daily except Mon 8.30–7.30; adm*). It has an exceptionally rich archaeological collection, including some exceptional Greek vases , beautiful Etruscan bronzes, gold and amber from Gaulish and Piceni tombs, and extensive Roman finds. Also damaged in 1972 was the 13th-century **Palazzo del Senato**, around the corner, Ancona's capital when it was a self-governing *comune*.

Ancona's pink and white **Cattedrale di San Ciriaco** crowns Monte Guasco, the ancient Greek acropolis, a site that in antiquity held a famous temple of Venus.

Getting Around

By Air

Ancona's Raffaello Sanzio **airport** is 10km north at Falconara, **t** 071 28271 or **t** 071 282 7233 and has daily flights from Rome, Milan, London and Munich, as well as several flights a week from Bucharest and Moscow. The terminal for airport buses is on Piazza Cavour.

By Rail

Ancona lies at the intersection of two major railway lines – the **Adriatic coast route** and the **Ancona–Rome** line, with no long waits for trains in either direction.

The station is west of the port on Piazza Roselli (take bus no. 1 or 3 to or from Piazza Repubblica near the port). A few trains continue to Ancona Marittima station on the port.

By Bus

RENI **buses** to the Cónero Riviera via Camerano depart from Piazza Cavour in the centre, **t** 071 804 6430. For towns in the province (Jesi, Recanati, Osimo, Castelfidardo, Loreto, Senigallia, and in the summer, Portonovo) CONERO buses all leave from Piazza Cavour, **t** 071 919 8623 or **t** 071 280 2092; many buses also stop at the railway station.

By Sea

There are plenty of **ferries**, ready to bustle you off to Greece, Albania, Croatia, and Turkey. If you're heading to Greece and coming from Rome or anywhere north, taking the ferry from here is a moderately better bet than making the long train trip down to Brindisi, Bari or Otranto. Fares are only slightly higher, and in both cases it will be an overnight trip. Book well in advance through a tourist office or travel agent for summer crossings.

Ferry lines to Greece include: **Minoan Lines**, Via Astagno 1, **t** 071 201 708, **f** 071 201 933; **Anek Lines**, Via Cialdini 57, **t** 071 202 223, **f** 071 56752; **Strintzis Lines**, Corso Garibaldi 28, **t** 071 207 0874, **f** 071 207 1068; **Superfast**, Via XXIX Settembre 2/0, **t** 071 200 817, **f** 071 202 219; and **Marlines** (also to Turkey), Via XXIX Settembre 6/b, **t** 071 207 3662, **f** 071 54268.

Tourist Information

Via Thaon de Revel 4, **t** 071 358 991, **f** 071 358 0592.
Branch offices are in the railway station and in the port, **t** 071 201 183.

Where to Stay and Eat

Ancona ✉ 60100

Goethe spent a night or two here, but unless you're coming or going you may like a quieter base in the Cónero.

★★★★Grand Hotel Palace, Lungomare Vanvitelli 24, **t** 071 201 813, **f** 071 207 4832 (*expensive*). The finest hotel in the city is by the port near Trajan's Arch. Comfortable and small, in a 17th-century palace, it has a roof garden with magnificent views over the bustling port.

★★★★Grand Hotel Passetto, Via Thaon de Revel 1, **t** 071 31307, **f** 071 32856 (*expensive*). Central, with a pool in summer.

★★★Fortuna, Piazza Rosselli 15, **t** 071 42663, **f** 071 42662 (*moderate*). The nicest near the station, this is convenient and comfortable if you're coming and going.

★★Viale, Viale della Vittoria 23, **t** 071 201 861, **f** 207 1166 (*moderate*). For a little tranquillity and lower prices, try Viale, located nearly a kilometre out of the centre.

★★Gino, Via Flaminia 4, **t** 071 42996, **f** 071 42179 (*cheap*). Has a restaurant that may not look like much but serves excellent fresh seafood (restaurant *moderate*). *Closed Sun.*

★★Dorico, Via Flaminia 8, **t/f** 071 42761 (*cheap*). By the station, this has simple rooms, with or without bath.

The dish to try in Ancona is *stoccafisso all'anconetana*, dried cod exquisitely prepared in a casserole with tomatoes, potatoes and marjoram. Nearly every port city in Italy developed a taste for dried cod in the Middle Ages, when barrel-loads from England and the Baltic passed through in exchange for wine; in Ancona it's preferred even to the day's catch from the Adriatic. Another local speciality to sample is *brodetto*, a tasty fish soup. Like any self-respecting port, Ancona has dozens of *trattorie* where you can put away some less grandiose marine delights at inconceivably low prices.

Passetto, Piazzale IV Novembre, **t** 071 33214 (*expensive*). An excellent seafood place with a seaside terrace, offering a *menu degustazione*, or a less pricey set menu featuring meat dishes, both including wine. *Closed Sun eve, Mon, and last two weeks in Aug.*

Moretta, Piazza Plebiscito 52, **t** 071 202 317 (*expensive*). This handsome 19th-century building has long been a favourite with the townspeople for its excellent *stoccafisso all'anconetana* and *spaghetti agli scampi*. *Closed Sun.*

Corte, Via della Loggia 5, **t** 071 200 806 (*expensive*). Set in an elegant 18th-century palace near the port, this has a very pretty summer garden, and excellent gourmet dishes, with fish and other dishes as well. *Closed Sun and Jan.*

Da Carloni, Via Flaminia 247, out of Ancona to the north at Torrette, **t** 071 888 239 (*moderate*). Another hot spot for its seafood, with reasonable prices, but the restaurant sits right on the tracks and rattles your mussels when trains pass. *Closed Mon.*

Osteria del Pozzo, Via Bonda 2, **t** 071 207 3996 (*cheap*). Right at the centre of the port; try the mixed fry. *Closed Sun and Aug.*

La Cantinetta, Via Gramsci, **t** 071 201 107 (*cheap*). Just around the corner, this offers a foretaste of Greece if you're hopping on a ferry, complete with Greek seamen fingering worry beads. It is one of the most popular places in town, though certainly not for its décor; it's famed for its *stoccafisso*, served every Friday, its nightly fish fry, traditional *vincigrassi* and oddly enough, lemon sorbet. *Closed Sun.*

Portonovo ✉ 60020

★★★★Fortino Napoleonico, **t** 071 801 450, **f** 071 801 454 (*very expensive*). As its name implies, this award-winning hotel incorporates part of a fortress built during the Napoleonic Wars; it's set apart, quiet and modern, and has its own beach and a pool; big spenders book the 'Josephine suite' – but honeymooners beware. It is also one of the finest places to dine in the Marches, there are two beautiful dining rooms and immaculate

service; be sure to notice the painting at the entrance, depicting the manager, staff and guests decked out in Napoleonic costume – the big black dog in the picture is the one that comes out to greet you. Eight superb courses include stuffed olives and scampi, sole stuffed with spinach, cream and smoked salmon, shrimps with fennel and orange, *gnocchi* with caviar, and more.

★★★★Emilia, Via Poggio 149a, **t** 071 801145, **f** 071 801 330 (*very expensive*). Offers similar luxuries in a lovely setting nearby. The owners invite artists to stay free in exchange for a painting and the place is covered with pictures, including one by Graham Sutherland.

★★★Internazionale, Via Portonovo 149, **t** 071 801 001, **f** 071 801 082 (*moderate*). A sturdy stone building in the trees, with ravishing views above the bay, its own beach and a good restaurant.

Il Laghetto, near Portonovo's little lake, **t** 071 801 183 (*moderate*). A great little place to feast on fish and *frutti di mare*, prepared in some unusual ways. *Closed Mon and mid-Jan–mid-Mar.*

Sirolo ✉ 60020

★★★Monte Cónero, built around the Badia di San Pietro, **t** 071 933 0592, **f** 071 933 0365 (*expensive*). A great get-away-from-it-all place, enjoying a quiet, sublime setting near the very top of the headland, with a pool and restaurant (*moderate*). *Closed mid-Nov–mid Mar.*

Numana ✉ 60026

★★★Gigli Eden, Via Morelli 11, **t** 071 933 0652, **f** 071 933 0930 (*moderate*). Numana has some pretty dismal spots thrown up in the recent building boom, but there are one or two worth knowing. This is at the pricier end of this range, but it's worth the bill, having nice rooms with a view, two pools, and acres of ground with plenty of trees. There's a secluded private beach, but it's a bit of a climb to get back from it.

★★Teresa a Mare, Via del Golfo 26, **t/f** 071 933 0623 (*moderate*). An alternative. *Open May–Sept.*

To reach it, either climb the long garden stairway, the Scalone Nappi, or catch the no.11 bus from Piazza Cavour. Unusually for a church this far north, the 11th-century cathedral shows a strong influence from the Puglian Romanesque, and but for the long, rounded transepts the building would not look out of place in any of the cathedral towns around Bari.

The fancy Gothic porch is by Margaritone d'Arezzo – Big Daisy's only known foray into architecture – and the sculpted portals and detached campanile were both added about 1200. The marble columns inside came originally from the Temple of Venus, some crowned with Byzantine capitals. The cathedral is dedicated to St Cyriacus, the converted Jew who revealed the whereabouts of the True Cross to St Helen and, in a clever piece of 4th-century propaganda, was said to have been martyred by the virtuous but non-Christian Emperor Julian the Apostate.

The Cónero Riviera

The same arm of the Apennines that stretches down to shelter Ancona's port also creates a short but uniquely beautiful stretch of Adriatic coast. South of Ancona, the cliffs of Monte Cónero (572m) plunge steeply into the sea, forcing the railway and coastal highway to bend inland, and isolating a number of beautiful beaches and coves only a few kilometres from the centre of Ancona; it's now a national park.

The little resort town of **Portonovo**, on the northern slopes of Cónero, can be reached by bus from Ancona in half an hour. Tucked under the cliffs, it's the most beautiful place for a swim in these parts, with a clean pebble beach, and a lovely church of the 1030s in the same style as Ancona cathedral. **Santa Maria di Portonovo**, with the same blind arcading around the roofline and a distinctive cupola in the centre, is one of the better Romanesque churches in the north; Dante mentions it – 'the House of Our Lady on the Adriatic coast' – in the 21st canto of *Paradiso*.

The southern end of Cónero is marked by the often very crowded but attractive resorts of **Sirolo** and **Numana**. Both have beaches nearby, but the best in the area are in places that can only be reached by small boat, like the **Due Sorelle**, or the stretch of jagged white cliffs called the **Sassi Bianchi**.

The Southern Marches

Down the Coast

After Monte Cónero, the Adriatic won't show you another stretch of beautiful coastline until you reach the dramatic Gargano Peninsula in Puglia. All through the southern Marches the seaside is dotted with humble but growing resort towns, all pleasant enough but nothing special: **Porto Recanati, Civitanova Marche, Porto Sant'Elpidio, Porto San Giorgio** and **Pedaso**. If you're looking for a chance to dip inland, the best places to visit would be the pilgrimage shrine of Loreto – home of the Holy House – or the fine old town of Fermo, 6km west of Porto San Giorgio.

Sweet Music: Castelfidardo and Ósimo

Many of the inland towns of this area can provide object lessons in the growth and strength of the 'new model' small-scale economy. Fermo, for example, and the villages around it produce a quarter of all the shoes made in Italy. South of Ancona, dishevelled **Castelfidardo** lives almost entirely on the manufacture of accordions. This most catholic of instruments was invented here in the 1870s, so they say, and there is a **Museo Internazionale della Fisarmonica** on Via Mordini (*t 071 7808 288; open daily 9.30–12 and 3–7*) to fill in any gaps in your accordion knowledge. Venerable **Ósimo**, 3km up the road, is more up-to-date; it makes most of Italy's electric guitars and keyboards. Its neighbours aren't impressed; they call people from Ósimo '*senza teste*' because of the 12 headless Roman statues in the **Palazzo Comunale**. Upstairs, ask to visit the mayor's office to see the beautiful, retro (for 1464) golden polyptych by the

Getting Around

There are frequent **trains** along the coast between Ancona and Pescara. Loreto is also on this line – the station is outside the town, but there is a regular connecting bus. There is also a line that cuts inland from Civitanova Marche to Macerata, and meets the Ancona-Rome line near Fabriano. COTRAN **buses** from Ancona have frequent services to Loreto and Recanati by way of Ósimo and Castelfidardo; CONTRAM buses run down the coast linking Porto Recanati to Loreto, Recanati and Macerata, and there's a bus a day linking Loreto to Camerino, Tolentino and Sarnano. Three buses from Fermo run down the coast to Porta d'Ascoli, then head inland to Ascoli Piceno and Rome (call t 0734 228 767 in Fermo, t 0734 678 555 in Porto San Giorgio).

Tourist Information

Loreto: Via Solari 3, t 071 970 276,
f 071 970 020.
Fermo: Piazza del Popolo 6, t 0734 228 738,
f 0734 228 325.

Where To Stay and Eat

Loreto ✉ 60025

The best places are outside the centre.
★★★★**Villa Tetlameya**, Via Villa Costantina 187, Loreto Archi, t 071 978 863, f 071 976 639 (*expensive*). An elegant 19th-century villa which has the most comfortable rooms and one of the best restaurants in the area.

★★★**Blu Hotel**, Via Villa Constantina 89, t 071 978 501, f 071 978 501 (*cheap*). Nearby, with simple but pleasant rooms. *Closed over Christmas.*
★★★**Vecchia Fattoria**, Via Manzoni 19, t 071 978 976, f 071 978 962 (*moderate*). The local favourite for weddings and banquets.

In the centre of town hotels are invariably clean, quiet and respectable, with a crucifix above every bed. A good many of them are run by religious orders – Ursulines, Franciscan Sisters, the Holy Family Institute of Piedmont – accommodation for pilgrims.
★★★**Casa del Clero Madonna di Loreto**, Via Asdrubali 104, t 071 970 298, f 071 750 0532 (*cheap*). A typical example, with 32 rooms, all with bath.
★★**Centrale**, Via Solari 7, t 071 970 173, f 071 750 219 (*cheap*). A more secular atmosphere, slightly cheaper. *Closed Jan.*
Andreina, Via Buffolareccia 14, t 071 970 124 (*cheap*). This has been here for donkey's years, serving wonderful grilled meats and *marchigiano* specialities. *Closed Tues.*

Fermo ✉ 63023

★★★**Astoria**, Viale Veneto 8, t 0734 228 601, f 0734 228 602 (*moderate*). Modern; the most comfortable choice in the centre, with a restaurant.
★★★**Casina delle Rose**, way up on Piazzale Girfalco 16, t 0734 224 636, f 0734 228 932 (*moderate*). An older, slightly cheaper hotel, facing the cathedral and town park and the grand views; also has a restaurant. Both the hotel restaurants are OK – a rarity in central Fermo, although there are several pizzerias.

Vivarini brothers of Venice. At the highest point in town, the 13th-century Romanesque-Gothic **cathedral** of San Leopardo has quirky medieval monsters and snakes around its doors and rose window, and in the crypt, a 4th-century Luni marble sarcophagus; the 12th-century baptistry has a fantastic 1629 bronze font and ceiling.

Loreto

The inventor of the accordion, the story goes, got his inspiration when an Austrian pilgrim on his way to Loreto left behind a button-box concertina as a gift after lodging for the night. The town puts up billboards all over Italy inviting us to visit, but few foreigners apart from the devout ever take the hint. That is a pity, for, like Urbino, Loreto is a small but concentrated dose of fine art from the Renaissance. Its story is a mystery of the faith. During the 1200s, the Church found itself threatened on all sides by heretical movements and free-thinkers. The popes responded in various subtle ways to assimilate and control them; creating the Franciscan movement was one approach, encouraging the cult of the Virgin Mary another. Conveniently, a legend of a miracle in the Marches gained currency. Mary's house in Nazareth was transported by a band of angels to a hill in Istria on 10 May 1291, then flew off again on 9 December 1294, this time landing in these laurel woods (*loreti*) south of Ancona. Supposedly the house had bestirred itself in protest over Muslim reoccupation of the Holy Land; the popes were thumping the tub for a new Crusade, and Loreto was just coincidentally located on the route to the Crusader ports on the Adriatic. Recent research has indicated that the Holy House did indeed come from Nazareth, but it seems that angels had little to do with its removal: it was in fact a dowry given by the Nikeforos Angelo, king of Epirus, to his daughter on her wedding to Philip of Taranto. When the Crusaders lost Palestine in 1291, Nikeforos had the house dismantled and took the stones with him, they ended up at Loreto.

The Santuario della Santa Casa

t 071 970 104; basilica open daily 6am–7pm (8pm in summer); Santa Casa 12.30–2.30.

Beginning in 1468, the simple church originally built to house the Santa Casa was reconstructed and embellished in a massive building programme that took well over a century to complete. Corso Boccalini, lined with the inevitable souvenir stands, leads from the town centre up to the Sanctuary, which suddenly materializes in all its glory when you enter the enclosed **Piazza della Madonna**, with the church, a great fountain by Carlo Maderno (one of the architects of St Peter's in Rome), the Palazzo Apostolico and an elegant loggia by Bramante enclosing the square. The piazza is often filled up with the 'white train' loads of sick people, in the hopes that Loreto's Madonna may succeed where modern medicine has fallen short.

The sanctuary's understated façade is typical early Roman Baroque, if a little ahead of its time (1587); no one is sure to whom to ascribe it, since so many architects had a hand in the work. Giuliano da Sangallo built the cupola (a copy of Brunelleschi's dome in Florence), Bramante did the side chapels, and Sansovino and Sangallo the Younger also contributed. One of the best features is the circle of radiating brick apses on the east end, turreted like a Renaissance castle. The only unfortunate element in the ensemble is the ungainly neoclassical campanile, topped with a bronze-plated garlic bulb, designed by Vanvitelli in the 1750s. Don't blame the architect: it had to be squat and strong to hold the 15-ton bell, which makes itself heard once it gets going.

Chapels line the walls inside, embellished by the faithful from nations around the world, including a recent ones from the United States (with an aeroplane). The English chapel holds a memory of the lyric poet Richard Crashaw, a refugee from Protestant intolerance. A good deal of Loreto's art was swiped by Napoleon; but the two sacristies on the right aisle have fine frescoes by Luca Signorelli and Melozzo da Forli. Under the dome you'll see the object of the pilgrims' attention; the Santa Casa, a simple brick room with traces of medieval frescoes, contains the venerated black

Madonna of Loreto, sculpted out of cedar in 1921; the original was destroyed in a fire. The house was sheathed in marble by Bramante to become one of the largest and most expensive sculptural ensembles ever – the better to make the flying house stay put. Its decoration includes reliefs by Sangallo and others, showing scenes from the *Life of Mary*. The upper floor of the Apostolic palace houses what the crooks missed in the **Museo-Pinacoteca** (*t 071 977 759; open April–Oct daily 9–1 and 4–7; Nov–Mar 10–1 and 3–6; adm*), especially the excellent, dramatic late paintings by Lorenzo Lotto.

Fermo

The Sabine town of *Firmum*, later a close ally of Rome, has gained importance and lost it several times; during the 10th century it was the capital of a duchy that included all the southern Marches. Fermo's handsome, brick-arcaded **Piazza del Popolo** has always been its drawing room. From 1398 to 1826 it was also the seat of its university, whose building, the Baroque **Palazzo degli Studi,** is still there at the end of the square, holding the university's superb library. Another corner of the piazza is closed by the 15th-century **Palazzo Comunale**, adorned with a bronze statue of Pope Sixtus V – by a 16th-century sculptor with a great name, Accursio Baldi – inviting you in to the art collection of the **Pinacoteca Civica** (*t 0734 84327; open Oct–May Tues–Sun 9.30–1 and 3.30–7; June–Sept Tues–Sun 10–1 and 3–7; also July–Aug Thurs 3pm–11pm*). Works include a very moving and intense *Nativity* by a young Rubens; local records recall a Fermo priest commissioning it in 1608 for the grand sum of 1700 *scudi*.

A singular relic of Roman times can be visited under the Via degli Aceti: the **Piscina Epuratoria** (*same hours as the Pinacoteca; adm*), an enormous underground reservoir built in AD 41–61 to hold and clarify rain and spring-water. Behind the Palazzo Comunale, Via Perpenti leads down to the Gothic church of **San Francesco,** with 15th-century frescoes and a tomb by Andrea Sansovino.

The Pocket Province of Macerata

You won't find a more out-of-the-way corner in central Italy. This hilly enclave lacks great attractions, but the towns that remain to Macerata put up a good front, with stout medieval walls or a gay Romanesque tower to lure you in for a short stop. Many of its villages and towns also have fine works of art in their little museums.

Macerata, Recanati and Tolentino

Macerata is a pleasant medieval-looking town of 43,000 people. About one-sixth of them can fit into the town's major landmark, a huge colonnaded hemicycle and outdoor theatre called the **Arena Sferisterio**, built in the 1820s by local subscription for a game similar to Basque pelota, *pallone a bracciale,* that required a long wall on one side. The builders of the Sferisterio endowed it with excellent acoustics, making for one of the grandest settings for opera south of Verona; the **Macerata Opera Festival** (*t 0733 230 735, f 0733 261570; box office at Piazza Mazzini 10*), from mid-July to mid-August, is a popular summer music event. Nearly as many people could fit into Macerata's central Piazza della Libertà, decorated with Macerata's proudest

Getting Around

Macerata's **train** station is down in the suburbs and is linked to Piazza della Libertà by city buses no. 2, 2a or 6. **Buses** to the province leave from the Giardini Diaz, down west from the centre, off Viale Puccinotti.

Tourist Information

Macerata: Piazza della Libertà 12, t 0733 234 807, f 0733 266 631.
Recanati: Piazza G. Leopardi, t/f 071 981471.
Tolentino: Piazza Libertà 18, t 0733 972 937.
Camerino: Piazza Cavour 2, t 0737 632 534.

Where To Stay and Eat

Macerata ✉ 62100

****Claudiani, Via Ulissi 8, t 0733 261 400, f 0733 261 380 (*moderate*). A new, modern hotel inside the walls of an old palace in the historic centre, with four-star comforts.
***Da Rosa, Via Armaroli 94, t/f 0733 232 670 (*moderate*). A pleasant enough place, in the centre very near Piazza della Libertà, and on the same street as a good *trattoria* with the same name (Via Armaroli 17, t 0733 260 124; *moderate*), with a menu that changes daily. *Restaurant closed Sun and over Christmas.*
**Arena, Vicolo Sferisterio 16, t 0733 230 931, f 0733 236 059 (*cheap*). Small but good, right next to the Sferisterio.

Macerata is the place to try *vincisgrassi*, a kind of *lasagne* with a rich sauce of chicken livers, gizzards and brains, mushrooms, ground meat and wine, topped with béchamel sauce. Before you get out your Latin dictionary, know that the name comes from the Austrian General Windischgrätz (from the Napoleonic Wars) who must have liked it a lot.
Da Secondo, Via Pescheria Vecchia, t 0733 260 912 (*moderate*). Macerata's best restaurant is in the centre, where besides *vincisgrassi* you can order the famous *fritto misto* of lamb and vegetables; there are lovely views too, and a terrace. Reserve, as it's always crowded. *Closed Mon, and part of Aug.*
Osteria dei Fiori, Via Lauro Rossi 61, t 0733 260 142 (*moderate*). Here between the Sferisterio and Piazza della Libertà is another good, busy choice, with its own version of *vincisgrassi*, or stuffed deboned pigeon, *fritto misto* and other hearty favourites. *Closed Sun and mid Aug–mid Sept.*

Tolentino ✉ 62029

****Hotel 77, just outside the centre on Viale B. Buozzi 90, t 0733 967 400, f 0733 960 147 (*moderate*). Stay here very cosily.
**Milano, Via Roma 13, t 0733 973 014, f 0733 973 077 (*cheap*). An older, more modest choice, in the centre.
Re Gioacchino, Contrada Cisterna 55, t 0733 969 347 (*cheap*). Hidden down in Tolentino's industry and urban sprawl, the town's best restaurant occupies an 18th-century villa named for Napoleon's general Joachim Murat; good classics, washed down with pitchers of Verdicchio. The owner has recently fixed up six small but comfortable bedrooms upstairs, many with frescoed ceilings. *Restaurant closed Mon.*

Camerino ✉ 62032

***I Duchi, Via V. Favorino 72, t/f 0737 630 440 (*cheap*). The best option here is this modern, family-run place in the *centro storico*.
**Roma, Piazza Garibaldi 6, t 0737 632 592, f 0737 630 125 (*cheap*). Simple, central, and cheaper (some rooms without bath).
Osteria dell'Arte, Via Arco della Luna 7, t 0737 633 558, (*moderate*). This was recently renovated, but it's one of the oldest restaurants in town, with an unusual array of pasta (with wild fennel, or in a pigeon-based ragù) and good rabbit and trout. *Closed Fri and two weeks in Jan.*

monuments: a Tuscan **Loggia dei Mercanti** (1505), built by Papal Legate Alessandro Farnese, the future Pope Paul III; the 17th-century **Palazzo del Comune** with an atrium decorated with statues and inscriptions from *Helvia Ricinia*; and an elegant 18th-century **Teatro Rossi**, designed by the great Bibbiena family of theatre designers.

On Piazza Vittorio Veneto, the **Museo Civico e Pinacoteca** (*t 0733 256 361; open 9–1 and 4–7, closed Sun pm and Mon am*) has a *Madonna* by Crivelli (no cucumbers, but a lovely work just the same), and works by Sassoferrato and Parmigiano. If you're fond of Christmas cribs, Macerata has a **Museo Tipologico del Presepio**, at Via Maffeo Pantaleoni 4, near the Sferisterio (*open by request, t 0733 234 035*), with 4,000 figures from the 17th century to now. There's an excellent collection of modern Italian painters and sculptors (Manzu, De Chirico, Carrá, Messina, de Pises, Morandi, Balla) in the **Palazzo Ricci Gallery**, Via D. Ricci 1 (*t 0733 261 484; open Tues and Thurs 4–6, Sat 10–12*). Two kilometres outside the Porta Picena, Macerata has a domed Renaissance church in the form of a Greek cross, **Santa Maria delle Vergini** (1582), with a rich stucco interior, a fine *Nativity* by Tintoretto (1587), and a stuffed crocodile.

Recanati, between Macerata and Loreto, was the birthplace of Italy's greatest modern poet, Giacomo Leopardi (1798–1837) and the town has made a discreet cottage industry out of this melancholy soul. His family, still residing in the **Palazzo Leopardi** in Piazzale Sabato del Villaggio, permits visits to the library where young Giacomo spent much of his dismal stifled childhood (*t 071 757 3380; open daily 9.30–12.30 and 2.30–5.30; in summer daily 9–7; adm*). Really keen fans can study the poet's death mask and first editions in the neighbouring **Biblioteca del Centro Nazionale di Studi Leopardiani** (*t 071 757 0604; open Mon–Fri 9–12 and 4–7, Sat 9–12, closed Sun; adm free*). Below, the gardens take in the view of the never-ending panorama of hills of Leopardi's famous poem, the *Colle dell'Infinito*. The Cappuccin church by the palace contains the unusual *Our Lady of the Salad*. Relics of another favourite son, tenor Beniamino Gigli, fill the town's **Pinacoteca** (*t 071 757 0410; open daily except Mon, April–Sept 10–1, 4–7; Oct–Mar 10–1, 3–6; adm*); other highlights are works by Lorenzo Lotto, including what may be the silliest ever *Annunciation* (1528).

South of Macerata, the valley of the Chienti carries you deeper into the province, towards the Monti Sibillini. At Corridonia, 4km south, there is an interesting 7th-century Byzantine church, **San Claudio al Chienti,** built over the ruins of an ancient Roman villa, with a pair of round campanili.The **Pinacoteca** (*open on request; contact the parish, t 0733 431 832*), has another remarkable *Madonna* by Carlo Crivelli, enclosed in a wreath of angels. Ten kilometres east of Corridonia, Monte San Giusto's church of **Santa Maria Telusiano** has a dramatic *Crucifixion* by Lorenzo Lotto (1531).

Tolentino, further up the valley of the Chienti on the SS77, is one of the larger hill-towns in the Marches, prosperous and modern on the outside and not much to look at until you reach the walled medieval centre and its **Santuario di San Nicola** (*t 0733 969 996; open 7–12 and 3–7*). San Nicola da Tolentino (1245–1305) was a miracle-working Augustan preacher – whose special concern was souls in Purgatory. Stop by to see the impressive **portal** (1430s), designed by the Florentine Nanni di Bartolo, set in a restrained Baroque façade. An artist known only as the 'Maestro di Tolentino' left a beautiful series of Giottesque frescoes in the **Cappellone**: richly coloured, intense, inspired work that bears comparison with the best trecento painting in Tuscany. Around the attractive cloister, wreathed in wisteria, are a series of **museums** (*open daily 8.30–12 and 3–7*) with silverwork, ceramics, a giant presepio and a fascinating collection of ex-votos testifying to San Nicola's spiritual prowess. Tolentino's **Piazza della Libertà** (decorated with a fine assortment of palaces), has a fascinating clock tower that will tell you the phases of the moon, the canonical hour and the day.

Camerino and the Monti Sibillini

Camerino, up-river on its ridge, passed the time during the Middle Ages in endless fighting with arch-enemy Fabriano just to the north. Home to a small university since the 1300s, Camerino has two picture galleries, the **Museo Diocesano** (*t 0737 630 444; closed for restoration until late 2001*) and the **Museo Civico** (*t 0737 402 310; open Nov–Mar Tues–Sun 10–1 and 3–6; April–Oct Tues–Sun 10–1 and 4–7*); the best works are by local quattrocento painter Girolamo di Giovanni. In the main piazza, Da Varano's elegant Renaissance **Palazzo Ducale** has an Urbino-style courtyard and several frescoed halls (now a law faculty). Beyond Camerino narrow mountain roads lead over the Apennines to Foligno and Spoleto in Umbria. The **Alte Valli del Fiastrone,** the mountainous region to the south, are peppered with castles, towers and fortresses; the most striking is the ruined white castle east of Camerino, the **Rocca di Varano,** from the 1200s; 3km away, there's a lovely, isolated duecento church, **San Giusto.**

Further south, the mountains grow higher, reaching a climax in the dark, dramatic legendary range of the **Monti Sibillini,** the most striking mountains in the Apennines, the habitat of wolves and scores of rare wildflowers and orchids, all now protected in a national park. No one is quite sure how the 'Mountains of the Sibyls' got their name; ancient writers record no such oracular priestesses in these parts. Italy, though, is full of stories about them, and supposedly these mountains gave birth to the legend of Wagner's *Tannhäuser.* The Sibillini's highest peak is **Monte Vettore** (2476m); its uncanny Lago di Pilato is associated with Pontius Pilate, who is thought to have thrown himself into its waters to drown in remorse

Arquata del Tronto is a lovely village under a 13th-century Rocca, a *comune* that borders on four regions: the Marches, Umbria, Lazio and Abruzzo. In one of its *frazioni*, Capodacqua, there is a little octagonal church, Madonna del Sole, attributed to Cola dell'Amatrice, who may also have painted the frescoes within. Just beyond Arquata you have a choice of two roads: you can take a slow but often spectacular, twisting road over the 1,500m pass, the **Forca Canapine**, and continue through the spectacular mountain meadow called the Piano Grande, or take the dull new tunnel into Umbria.

Ascoli Piceno

Urbino, at the northern end of the Marches, and Ascoli at the southern, compete for your attention as almost polar opposites. Urbino gets most of the praise, and partisans of Ascoli may find that somewhat unfair. Unlike the northern town, led by its enlightened, aesthetic dukes, Ascoli with its long heritage as a free *comune* has always had to do for itself. The difference shows; Ascoli is a beautiful city, but beautiful in a gritty, workaday manner like Florence. It has taken some hard knocks in its 2,500 years, which have helped make it a city of character.

History

Ascoli, as its name implies, had its beginnings with the Piceni, and it probably served as the centre of their confederation, united under the sign of their totem woodpecker.

To the Romans, *Asculum Picenum* was an early ally after its conquest in 286 BC, but later it proved a major headache. *Asculum* fought Rome in the Samnite Wars, and actually initiated the pan-Italian revolt of the Social Wars.

The Romans took the city in 89 BC and razed it to the ground for good measure, soon afterwards refounding it with a colony of veterans. The street plan of Ascoli today has hardly changed since then; it is one of the most perfect examples in Italy of a rectilinear Roman *castrum*. In the Dark Ages, Ascoli's naturally defensible position between the steep ravines helped avert trouble. Its citizens, too, showed admirable determination, defeating Odoacer's Goths on one occasion, and the Byzantines and Saracens on several others. Despite periods under the rule of others – Lombards, Franks, Normans and various feudal lords – Ascoli emerged by the 1100s as a strong free *comune*. Reminders of this most glorious period of the city's history are everywhere, in the 13th-century Palazzo del Popolo, the clutch of tall, noble towers like those of San Gimignano, and in Ascoli's famous festival, the Quintana, a jousting contest that takes place the first weekend in August, the rules of which were laid down in the statutes of 1378. Ascoli lost its freedom immediately, and its prosperity gradually, with the coming of papal rule in the 15th century, only recovering some of its wealth and importance in the last 100 years.

Piazza del Popolo

Like Rome, Ascoli is built of travertine. Also like Rome, it has more traffic than it can handle, and consequently the first impression will be of a grey, sooty town that shows its age. It's more wonder, then, that the central **Piazza del Popolo** can be so nonchalantly, so effortlessly, one of the most beautiful squares in all Italy. This is no grand architectural ensemble, not monumental, not even symmetrical. But the travertine paving shines almost like marble; the low arcades that surround it give the square architectural unity, and a setting for two fine buildings bearing statues of popes who keep an eye on all the bustling action in the square. The first, the 13th-century **Palazzo dei Capitani del Popolo**, was begun in the 1200s and redone in the late 16th century, after its papal governor set it on fire to discomfit his enemies. It has a façade by Ascoli's best-known architect and artist, Cola dell'Amatrice and a statue of Paul III over its huge portal. At the narrow end of the piazza, the church of **San Francesco** (1260) turns its back on the square – not really an insult, since the apse and transepts are the best part of the building, a classic, austere ascent of Gothic bays and towers under a low dome added in the late 15th century. Over the south door is a statue of Pope Julius II. The façade, around the corner, isn't much to look at; a strange, flat square of travertine decorated with a tiny plain rose window. It does have a good sculpted portal, guarded by a pair of sarcastic-looking lions. Inside, there are only grand and simple Gothic vaults to look at. The southern end of the façade adjoins the **Loggia dei Mercanti**, built by the Wool Corporation – a typical medieval-style manufacturers' guild – in the early 1500s. On the northern side, one of two Franciscan cloisters has become Ascoli's busy and colourful market.

Via del Trivio, in front of San Francesco, is the centre of activity in Ascoli; follow it northwards to Ascoli's oldest and prettiest neighbourhoods, on the cliffs above the

Getting Around

Ascoli is not the easiest place to reach. The only **train** service is a dead-end branch off the Adriatic coastline, from San Benedetto del Tronto. The station (several trains a day), is on Viale Marconi in the new town. **Buses**, for Fermo, Ancona and Rome, leave from Viale Alcide de Gasperi behind the cathedral; all information on both can be obtained from the Brunozzi Travel Agency on Corso Trento e Trieste, near Piazza del Popolo, t 0736 262 128.

Tourist Information

Piazza del Popolo 1, t 0736 253 045, f 0736 252 391.

Where to Stay and Eat

Ascoli Piceno ✉ 63100

One of Ascoli's attractions, of course, is that it is largely undiscovered, but that also means choices for accommodation are few.

******Gioli**, Via Alcide De Gasperi 14, t/f 0736 255 550 (*moderate*). A thoroughly pleasant hotel near the cathedral, with a small garden.

******Marche**, Viale Kennedy 34, t 0736 45575, f 0736 342 812 (*moderate*). Modern and comfortable; about a mile to the east.

*****Pennile**, Via Spalvieri, t 0736 41645, f 0736 342 755 (*moderate*). Another modern place, in the same area, but quiet and set in the pines.

****Pavoni**, Via Navicella 135, t 0736 343 683 (*cheap*). Ten simple rooms in the centre.

Cantina dell'Arte, Rua della Lupa 8, t 0736 251 135 (*cheap*). Here in an old palace in the centre near the post office, you can find a handful of rooms, and fine abundant servings of local specialities, grilled meats and pitchers of wine in the restaurant (*cheap*).

To most Italians Ascoli means one thing, *olive ascolane*. Stuffed, breaded and fried, the olives are wonderful, but one of the most tedious dishes imaginable to prepare; you won't find them often outside Ascoli.

Tornasacco, Piazza del Popolo 36, off Piazza Arringo, t 0736 254 151 (*cheap*). More olives and many other specialities *all'ascolana* await you here, alongside *tagliatelle* with lamb sauce, very good local cheeses and charcuterie. *Closed Fri and part of July.*

Gallo d'Oro, Corso Vittorio Emanuele 13, t 0736 253 520 (*cheap*). The 'Golden Cockerel' has been doing business for 30 years, and still offers good food (fresh seafood on Wednesay and Friday), three dining rooms, and a good tourist menu. *Closed Sun.*

C'era Una Volta, Via Piagge 336, 6km south of Ascoli on the Colle San Marco road, t 0736 261 780 (*cheap*). The speciality is hearty soups, stuffed *gnocchi*, and olives fried with lamb. *Closed Tues.*

Cefelò, t 0736 254 525 (*cheap*). Also worth trying, with *olive ascolane* and succulent meats from the grill. *Closed Tues and Sept.*

Gastronomia Enoteca Migliori, Piazza Arringo 2. One of the best places to sample the famous olives.

River Tronto, where you'll find most of the city's surviving towers. Ascoli has as many of these medieval family-fortresses as San Gimignano in Tuscany, but they are not as well known; the tallest is the **Torre degli Ercolani** on Via Soderini. Piazza Ventidio Basso, the medieval commercial centre, has two good churches. One is 11th-century **SS Vincenzo ed Anastasio**, with an unfinished Renaissance façade divided into 64 squares that once framed frescoes, and some Romanesque carvings around the portal; there is a miraculous well in the crypt that used to cure leprosy, until the waters were diverted. The second is gloomy Gothic 13th-century **San Pietro Martire**, with a portal from 1523 by Cola d'Amatrice.

From here, picturesque Via di Solestà, lined with tower houses, leads to the northern tip of Ascoli; a doughty single-arched Roman bridge, the 1st-century **Ponte di Solestà**, still carries traffic across to the northern suburbs without a creak or a groan. If you cross it, and walk along the river bank to the east, you will see signs for the church of **Sant'Emidio alle Grotte,** on the street of the same name, an elegant 1623 Baroque façade that closes off the front of a cave; here St Emidio, Ascoli's patron, was martyred, and the site became the city's earliest place of Christian worship.

All around the northern edge of Ascoli, the lovely valley of the Tronto makes a perfect picnic spot. Parts of Ascoli's walls show the characteristic diamond-shaped Roman brickwork (*opus reticulatum*). At the western entrance to the town, the **Porta Gemina,** a little Roman gate of the first century AD, survives, spanning the Via Salaria. Finally there's San Gregorio Magno, built over a Roman temple of Vesta, with two columns and more *opus reticulatum*.

Piazza Arringo

Ascoli's oldest square, monumental Piazza Arringo, is held down by the cathedral, dedicated to Sant'Emidio, a 12th-century building similar to San Francesco, but with a new façade from the 1530s, also by Cola dell'Amatrice. In a chapel on the south side you can see the inevitable cucumber in the beautiful and recently restored polyptych by Carlo Crivelli, one of his masterpieces; in the crypt, there's a curious Gothic tomb of a knight; another curious tomb, left of the altar shows the deceased leaning forwards on his books, as if lazily attending Mass. The **Museo Diocesano** (*t 0736 252 883; open Tues–Sun 10–1 and 3.30–7.30; adm*), in the adjacent bishop's palace, has two rare statues in travertine, of Adam and Eve (1300) from a pulpit; works by Cola dell'Amatrice (whose style changed tremendously after he went to Rome to see the Raphaels); and a Carlo Crivelli (three apples). The 10th-century octagonal **baptistry,** to the side of the cathedral, stands resolutely in the middle of one of Ascoli's busiest streets. Facing the cathedral, behind the fierce dragons and seahorses in the twin Renaissance fountains, is the **Palazzo Arringo,** the 13th-century town hall hidden behind an imposing Baroque façade in the 17th-century. It holds the **Pinacoteca Civica** (*t 0736 298 213; open Mon–Sat 9–1 and 3–7, Sun and holidays 9–12.30 and 4–7; adm*), with more paintings by Cola dell'Amatrice and other local artists, as well as Simone de Magistris, Titian, Guido Reni, Van Dyck, and of course Crivelli, as well as collections of ceramics and musical instruments, and a superb 13th-century English-made cope that Pope Nicolas IV (a native of Ascoli) donated to the cathedral in 1288.

Across the square, in Palazzo Panichi (Panicky Palace), the **Museo Archeologico** (*t 0736 253 562; open daily 8.30–7; adm*) has some good bronzes of the ancient Piceni, and some of the stones they hurled at the Romans, carefully engraved with curses; there is also a plan of the city in Roman times. A walk through the streets north of Piazza Arringo will take you past some of the palaces of medieval Ascoli, with many curious carvings and morally uplifting inscriptions on the old houses; one, the **Palazzo Bonaparte** on Via Bonaparte, was built by a prominent family of the 1500s that local legend claims as the ancestors of the famous Bonapartes; Napoleon himself said he didn't know if it were true or not. The 16th-century **Palazzo Malaspina** at Corso Mazzini 224 is one of the fancier buildings, and now houses a museum of contemporary art (*t 0736 248 633; open Tues–Sun 9–1 and 4–7; adm*).

Abruzzo and Molise

16

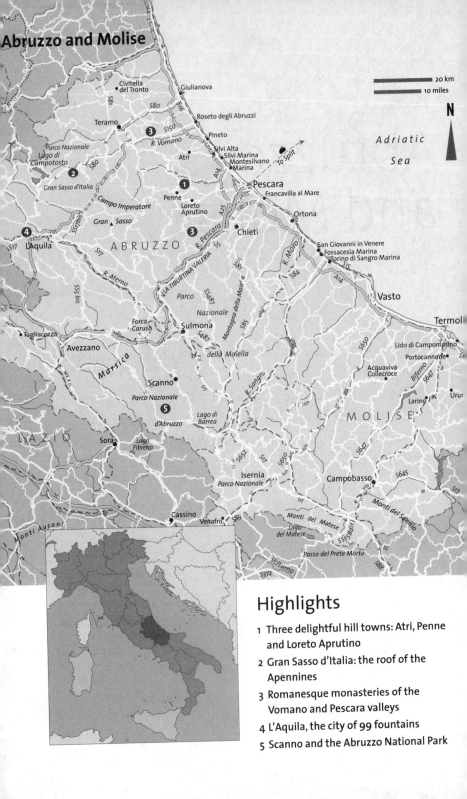

Abruzzo and Molise

Civitella del Tronto
Giulianova
S80
S16
S81
Teramo
S150
Roseto degli Abruzzi
R. Vomano
Pineto
Silvi Alta
Atri
Silvi Marina
Montesilvano Marina
To Split

Parco Nazionale Lago di Campotosto
S80
Gran Sasso d'Italia
Campo Imperatore
Pescara
Penne
Francavilla al Mare
Gran Sasso
Loreto Aprutino
Ortona
SS17bis
R. Pescara
ABRUZZO
Chieti
S5
San Giovanni in Venere
Fossacesia Marina
Torino di Sangro Marina
L'Aquila
S17
R. Aterno
VIA TIBURTINA VALERIA
Parco
S81
S4
SS5 bis
Montagna della Maie a
R. Moro
S84
A14
A25
Vasto
Termol
Nazionale
S487
Forca Caruso
Sulmona
della Maiella
S85
Tagliacozzo
Avezzano
S487
R. Sangro
Lido di Campomarino
Portocannone
Acquaviva Collecroce
Biferno
S647
S650
Marsica
S17
Urur
Scanno
Larino
Parco Nazionale
S5
MOLISE
d'Abruzzo
Lago di Barrea
LAZIO
Sora
Lago Fibreno
S647
Campobasso
S645
S17
Isernia
Parco Nazionale
S652
S17
S650
Monti del Sannio
S17
Cassino
Venafro
S85
Monti del Matese
Lago del Matese
S652 Sdinii
Passo del Prete Morto
S88
Monti Ausoni
S372
R. Volturno

Adriatic Sea

N

20 km
10 miles

Highlights

1 Three delightful hill towns: Atri, Penne and Loreto Aprutino
2 Gran Sasso d'Italia: the roof of the Apennines
3 Romanesque monasteries of the Vomano and Pescara valleys
4 L'Aquila, the city of 99 fountains
5 Scanno and the Abruzzo National Park

In Italy's long and narrow peninsula, dense with ruins, cities and art, packed with *autostrade*, pizzerias and sultry sunglassed signorinas, Abruzzo and Molise come as a breath of fresh air. Sparsely populated and marginal to the great affairs of state, these two regions stand out for their majestic natural beauty; vast tracts of unspoiled wilderness encompass the highest peaks of the Apennines, the habitat of Italy's unique species of bear. With its four national or regional parks, three of them recently established, Abruzzo has fully one-third of its land reserved for nature: the most, the Abruzzesi claim, of any region in Europe.

Because of the harsh and rugged terrain, with only small pockets suitable for agriculture, the region's economy has traditionally been pastoral, but with an emphasis on crafts: ceramics; wood, gold and iron-work; weaving and lace-making. And though many Abruzzo towns wear the proud badge of modernity, the Abruzzese have little care to compete with Milan and Rome – instead, like Candide, they tend their own garden. Yet from this mountain-bound land of country tradition came two of Italy's most urbane, sophisticated and passionate poets, Ovid and Gabriele d'Annunzio, and its greatest modern philosopher, Benedetto Croce. It is also the region most enthusiastic about rugby: L'Aquila has been Italy's national champion several times.

History

In prehistoric times the coast of **Abruzzo** formed part of a little-known Bronze Age culture, the Middle Adriatic, that produced the enigmatic *Warrior* in Chieti's archaeology museum (*see* p.608). Culture was less advanced up in the hills, but the different Italic tribes who gathered here – the Praetutii, the Vestini, the Paeligni and others, of whom almost nothing is known beyond their names – formed a formidable challenge to Roman expansion before being overwhelmed by the legions in the Social Wars of 91–82 BC.

After the fall of Rome, the Lombards ruled what is now the Abruzzo as part of their Duchy of Spoleto, while Molise went to the Duchy of Benevento. The Normans under King William I of Sicily picked up the region from the English Pope Adrian IV, and Emperor Frederick II – who inherited the Norman possessions in Italy – made the Abruzzo an independent province. Frederick had grand plans for the region, but they died with him as the Abruzzo was swallowed up by the Angevins, then kings of Naples. Like Umbria, Lazio and most of the Marche, Abruzzo and Molise then began to stagnate – the only difference being that these regions stagnated under the kings of Naples, rather than under the popes. It was the Bourbons who divided the Abruzzo into four territories – Abruzzo Citeriore, Ulteriore Primo, Ulteriore Secondo and Molise – which is why you'll often see the region's name in the plural (the Abruzzi). But if Abruzzo was neglected and sucked dry by the Neapolitans, its lot under the kings of Italy was scarcely any better, and thousands of people migrated to North America, Britain and other parts of Europe – among them the father of Dante Gabriel Rossetti and the ancestors of Madonna. Only since the Second World War, with the small boom of its compact seaside resorts, the development of small-scale industries and the building of new roads by the Cassa per il Mezzogiorno, and the growing interest in the unsullied charms of its landscape, has the tide of emigration been stemmed.

Food and Wine

Abruzzo pasta and saffron are sold all over Italy, but the great local speciality is *maccheroni alla chitarra*, square spaghetti named after the ingenious implement that is used to cut it: a wooden frame with metal strings called a guitar, which you can buy in most markets. Inland Abruzzo is mountainous, and well-suited to sheep-rearing; lamb dishes (especially grilled or roasted) are popular here, along with pork, rabbit and game dishes. The local variant of *pecorino* cheese, made from sheep's milk, is often served with pasta, while another favourite, *scamorza* (a bit like *mozzarella*) often apppears grilled as a main course. Like all coastal areas of Italy, the coastal areas of Abruzzo have their own favourite fish stews, and a squid speciality – squid stuffed with anchovies, breadcrumbs and garlic.

The food of the Molise uses many of the same basic ingredients as Abruzzo cooking, except that here you're likely come across more tripe and offal, and virtually everything tends to be flavoured with little hot red peppers, called *diavolini* ('little devils') by the Molisani – they are increasingly popular in the Abruzzo too; serious heat, long relegated to home cooking, is making a comeback in restaurants. The hand-made pasta here is *cavatelli*, shaped like tiny shells and usually dressed with a lamb sauce. Montepulciano d'Abruzzo is the best-known wine of the area. It's a smooth, dry red which, like many Italian wines, is best drunk within three years.

Belted with mountains, **Molise** is an atavistic and introspective backwoods, designated its own region not so much for historical as for cultural reasons. This rather charming patch of the Abruzzi that got away has its own customs and dialect – a direct result of its impossible geography and the large settlements established there in the 15th and 16th centuries by Slavs and Albanians. Molise is one of the last regions in Italy where women still don their traditional costumes to please themselves and not the shutter-happy hordes.

Down the Coast: from Giulianova to Térmoli

Small inexpensive seaside resorts jam-packed with Italian families in the summer, and some beautiful works of art and churches of the Romanesque era, are the main attractions along the Adriatic Coast and its hinterland. If you're not into Italian-style seaside holidays – where you pay for a beach chair, umbrella and changing facilities in neat little rows, in order to have the privilege of watching everyone else do the same thing – you may have difficulty finding stretches of beach where you can just sit on the sand under the pines.

Giulianova, Roseto and the Lower Vomano Valley

Between the Marche and Pescara, the Adriatic is lined with the same kind of small Italian family resorts found south of Ancona; places like Alba Adriatica, Giulianova, Roseto degli Abruzzi, Silvi and Pineto all offer big beaches, modern hotels, amusement arcades and playgrounds. The most interesting of these is **Giulianova**, with its medieval old town set back behind the beachfront sprawl. Within the old walls stands the town's best monument, the Romanesque **Santa Maria a Mare**, with unusual bas-reliefs on its façade (*normally closed to the public, but you may be able to make an appointment with Don Ennio to visit, t 085 800 7044*), and the Renaissance cathedral. The SS80 turns inland here for Téramo (*see p.611*).

Roseto degli Abruzzi, another resort out of the same mould, lies near the mouth of the Vomano, one of the principal rivers coming down from the Gran Sasso, and has fine views up the valley to the naked limestone peaks of the Corno Grande. From Roseto you can head up the valley (on the SS150) to see two Romanesque gems. One is the 11th-century **San Clemente a Guardia Vomano**, near Notaresco (*currently closed for restoration, but may be visited by calling Signore Fausto d'Alessandro, t 085 898 128*), whose builders made good use of Roman ruins, fitting them together like a jigsaw. The church houses an unusual and lovely 12th-century *ciborium*. The other is the abbey of **Santa Maria di Propezzano**, near Morro d'Oro (*to visit contact Signora Pompeo, owner of the bar next to the church, t 085 895 8318*), where the Abruzzese fondness for simple forms has created a handsome asymmetrical façade and a charming two-storey cloister. The interior is embellished with 12th- and 13th-century frescoes, the cloister with scenes by the 17th-century Polish artist Sebastiano Majewski. A side road to the north leads to Canzano, famous for turkey in aspic, *tacchino alla canzanese*.

Atri and Penne

Pineto, another little resort with a pretty pine-lined beach, has for its landmark the **Torre di Cerrano**, built by Charles V against the Ottoman threat and now a merchant marine research station. Pineto is a starting point for visiting **Atri** (10km inland), a lovely natural balcony 8km from the sea and 1,400 feet above it by car or ARPA bus (*15 times a day on the Pescara–Pineto route; no bus on Sundays*). Atri stands on the site of the ancient Sabine city and Roman colony of *Hatriaticum*, founded under the sign of the woodpecker, the bird of Mars. Atri disputes with Adria in the Veneto the honour of having lent its name to the Adriatic Sea, a controversy that raged among ancient scholars like Pliny, Livy and Strabo; Atri tried to boost its claim by engraving the fact on its singular coins – the heaviest ever minted in western Europe, guaranteed to put a hole in the pocket of any toga.

The Roman sites in the town include the remains of ancient baths, in the crypt of Atri's majestic 13th-century **cathedral**. This building has an austerely elegant square façade and matching campanile, and in the choir there are excellent quattrocento frescoes by Andrea de Litio, the Piero della Francesca of the Abruzzo, who gave his scenes of *The Life of the Virgin* surreal landscapes of knobbly hills and imaginary towers. In the **cathedral museum** (*t 085 879 8140; open June–Sept daily 10–12 and 4–8, Oct Thurs–Tues 10–12 and 3–5; adm*) there are ivories, polyptychs and statues, majolica by Grue of Castelli (*see p.614*), and mosaics and fragments from the 9th-century church that preceded the cathedral. During the Middle Ages and Renaissance, Atri was controlled by the Acquaviva dukes, whose frowning 14th-century **Palazzo Ducale**

Getting Around

Pescara's airport, **t** 085 432 421, has daily **flights** to and from Milan-Linate (Air One, **t** 085 432 4225).

In summer, **boats** and hydrofoils link Ortona to Vasto, and Vasto to Térmoli, the Tremiti Islands and Rodi Garganico in Puglia. Térmoli is the main port for the Tremiti (*see* Puglia, p.991), with **hydrofoils** and motorboats daily.

Services by **train** and **bus** along the coast are good. There is a direct rail line from Rome to Chieti and Pescara, via Sulmona, and between Bologna and Lecce, the length of the coast. ARPA (**t** 06 442 33928), the Abruzzo bus company, connects Chieti with Pescara (three times a day).

Tourist Information

Loreto Aprutino: Via dei Normanni 8, **t** 085 829 0484.
Montesilvano: Via Romagna 6, **t** 085 449 2796, freephone from within Italy **t** 800 656 256.
Pescara: Via Nicola Fabrizi 171, **t** 085 4290 0212.
Chieti: Palazzo INAIL, Via B. Spaventa 29, **t** 0871 63640.
Ortona: Piazza della Repubblica 9, **t** 085 906 3841.
Vasto: Piazza del Popolo 18, **t** 0873 367 312.
Térmoli: Piazza Bega, **t** 0875 706 754.

Where to Stay and Eat

Most of the hotels in the region date from the past couple of decades. Some prices have rocketed recently, but they are a bargain compared with the rest of Italy.

Giulianova ✉ 64022

★★★★Grand Hotel Don Juan, Lungomare Zara 97, **t** 085 800 8341, **f** 085 800 4805 (*very expensive*). The smartest hotel on this stretch of coast. Located on its own beach, it has a pool, tennis courts and a garden. *Closed Oct–mid-May.*
★★★Promenade, Lungomare Zara 119, **t** 085 800 3338, **f** 085 800 5983 (*moderate*). Smaller, with similar amenities but not so much style. *Closed Oct–mid-May.*
Beccaceci, Via Zola 28, **t** 085 800 3550 (*expensive*). The Abruzzo's most celebrated seafood restaurant; serves its own long-established seafood and pasta inventions – try the *linguine alla giuliese* or the squid stuffed with prawns. *Closed Sun eve, Mon and 27 Dec–10 Jan.*
Osteria della Stracciavocc', Via Trieste 124, **t** 085 800 5326 (*moderate*). Traditional cuisine. Serves outstanding pasta and seafood. *Closed Mon.*

Pescara ✉ 65100

Pescara has by far the most hotels and restaurants on the coast, but tranquillity is a rare commodity in the summer, and full board is usually required in July and August.
★★★★Carlton, Viale Riviera 35, **t** 085 373 125, **f** 085 421 3922 (*expensive*). The top hotel, a very comfortable resort palace on the sea, with a private beach that almost absorbs the racket.
★★★Bellariva, Viale Riviera 213, **t/f** 085 471 2641 (*moderate*). Unpretentious, and a good, friendly place to stay for families.
★★★Salus, Lungomare Matteotti 13/1, **t** 085 374 196, **f** 085 374 103 (*moderate*). Good standard rooms and a private beach.
Guerino, Viale della Riviera 4, **t** 085 421 2065 (*expensive*). Elegant, with a seafront terrace, this is the city's best seafood restaurant: the tasty Adriatic speciality of fillets of John Dory (*pesce San Pietro*) with *prosciutto* go down especially well. *Closed Tues and 22 Dec–5 Jan.*
Duilio, Via Regina Margherita 11, **t** 085 378 278 (*moderate*). Features seafood in nearly all its delicately prepared dishes. *Closed Sun evenings, Mon and Aug.*

(now the town hall and post office) contains a cheerful courtyard. The outskirts of Atri boast some strange geology: once-inhabited caves, eroded rock formations – *calanchi* – and 'Dantesque pits'.

The pale pink town of **Penne**, further south, was an important town of the Vestini, and today preserves a rare if eclectic urban harmony, its narrow winding streets

La Terrazza Verde, Largo Madonna 6, **t** 085 413 239 (*moderate*). One restaurant that doesn't serve fish at all. In a panoramic setting with a beautiful garden terrace high up in the hills, it serves delicious *gnocchi* and duck, a popular dish in Abruzzo, prepared in various ways. *Closed Wed and 10 days in July.*

Trattoria Roma, Via Trento 86, **t** 085 295 374 (*cheap*). Tucked away. A good place to find hearty Abruzzese cooking. It's very popular with locals, and the menu changes daily – there's always at least one good fish choice. *Closed Sun and one week in July.*

Montesilvano Marina ✉ 65016

★★★★**Serena Majestic,** Viale Kennedy 12, **t** 085 83699, **f** 085 836 9859 (*moderate*). Large, modern and comfortable; on the beach, with gardens, tennis courts and two pools.

★★★**Piccolo Mondo,** Via Marinelli 86, **t** 085 445 2647, **f** 08 445 2186 (*cheap*). Recently renovated, this is one of the best-value hotels on the coast, with just 20 rooms, a roof terrace and a garden. A good choice for a family holiday. *Full board only July–Aug.*

Chieti ✉ 66100

Venturini, Via De Lollis 10, **t** 0871 330 663 (*moderate*). For a fairly priced, fairly cooked meal, try this local institution, whose speciality is mushroom *risotto* with *mozzarella. Closed Tues.*

Nonna Elisa, Località Brecciarola, Via Peropoli 267 (near the freeway exit), **t** 0871 684 152 (*moderate*). Offers a delicious, strictly Abruzzese experience. *Closed Mon, one week in July and first week of Oct.*

Guardiagrele

Villa Maiella, Via Sette Dolori 30, **t** 0871 809 362 (*moderate*). One of the most popular restaurants in the area, with an imaginative menu based on traditional recipes, careful, enthusiastic service and excellent wine. *Closed Mon and two weeks in July.*

Lanciano

La Ruota, Via Per Fossacesia 62 (400 metres from town centre), **t** 0872 44590 (*expensive*). Very popular with the locals, it serves lovely seafood and a few meat dishes. *Closed Sun and two weeks in July.*

Vasto

All'Hostaria del Pavone, Via Barbarotta 15, **t** 0873 60227 (*moderate*). Vasto is a bit of a gastronomic capital on the coast, and here you can taste a wonderful *brodetto* – the local fish soup that has nourished generations of sailors – as well as many other fish specialities. *Closed 10 Jan–10 Feb and Tues from Oct–May.*

Térmoli ✉ 86039

★★★★**Corona,** Corso M. Milano 2/a, **t/f** 0875 84043 (*moderate*). A medium-sized traditional hotel in the centre of town. The Liberty-style dining room serves good food. *Closed Sun.*

★★★**Cian,** Lungomare Colombo 136, **t** 0875 704 436 (*cheap*). Its eight rooms are a good budget choice, on a rock above the coast, with lovely views. Decent fish restaurant. *Hotel open June-Aug only. Restaurant open off-season too, but closed Mon and Nov.*

Z'Bass, Via Oberdan 8, **t** 0875 706703 (*expensive*). A tempting fish menu and a lively atmosphere. Outdoor dining in summer. *Closed Mon from Oct–May.*

Da Noi Tre, Via Ruffini 47, **t** 0875 703 639 (*cheap*). Modest, serves good fish. *Open daily in summer; in winter closed Mon.*

Torre Saracena, 3km north of the centre, on the SS16 Adriatica Highway.**t** 0875 703 318 (*moderate*). In an ancient Saracen watchtower on the beach, it features the freshest of fish – practically hauled out of the sea as you watch – prepared in some surprising ways. It also serves a moderate priced set menu including wine. *Closed Mon and Nov.*

dotted with Renaissance mansions. Its sights include the ancient crypt of the cathedral, itself destroyed in the Second World War and rebuilt; the crypt now houses the **Museo Civico** (*open daily 10–1, 4–7; adm*), with some eccentric, fascinating medieval sculpture. **Santa Maria in Colleromano** (*ring the bell if closed; church museum open Sun 9–12*), a 15-minute walk from the centre, with good 14th–15th-century statues.

South of Pineto, the SS16bis heads inland from Montesilvano Marina, a satellite resort of Silvi, towards another clutch of interesting villages. In **Loreto Aprutino**, the church of **Santa Maria in Piano** (*open daily in summer 9–7; winter 9–4*) contains 14th–15th-century frescoes – the *Life of St Thomas Aquinas* and the spectacular *'Particular Judgement'* – portraying Heaven's elect marching to the pearly gates on a bridge the width of a hair. Loreto also has the **Museo Civico della Civiltà Contadina**, a collection of tools, traditional craft work and rather naïve tableaux of peasant life; the **Museodelle ceramiche**, displaying local ceramics; and a new **archaeological museum** (*t 0339 441 1319 for the three museums; all open Sat–Sun 10.30–12.30 and 3.30–6-30; combined adm*). In nearby Moscufo, a village devoted to the mandolin (nearly everyone who can plays one) **Santa Maria del Lago** merits a visit for its unique 12th-century pulpit adorned with painted reliefs.

Pescara

Pescara wears many hats: it is simultaneously Abruzzo's biggest resort, most pros-perous town, a fishing port and provincial capital. In ancient times its port was shared by several Italic tribes and later by the Romans, who made it the terminus of the Via Valeria–Via Tiburtina (the modern SS5). In 1864 Gabriele D'Annunzio was born here, the son of a local merchant; partly due to his influence, Mussolini poured lots of money into what had become a sleepy fishing village, and a new city was born. D'Annunzio's birthplace, or **Casa Natale** (*Corso Manthonè 101, t 085 60391; open daily 9–1.30; adm*), has a charming little courtyard. Pescara has an outdoor theatre built in D'Annunzio's honour, which is the venue for a jazz festival in the first half of July. The **Museo delle Genti d'Abruzzo** (*Via delle Caserme 22, t 085 451 0026; open Mon–Sat 9–1, Mon, Wed and Fri also 2.30–5; adm*), a comprehensive,up-to-date collection, is dedi-cated to everyday life and popular traditions in the Abruzzo over the centuries.

Pescara's golden egg, though, is its 16km-long **sandy beach**, almost solid with hotels, cafés and fish restaurants between the Pescara River and Montesilvano; whatever old buildings it had were decimated in the fierce fighting that took place along the coast in the Second World War. Still, this is no Rimini; families bake together in the day, and stroll about eating ice-cream in the evening. If you need excitement, there are riding stables, go-karts, tennis courts and, for some real thrills, the Fish Museum (*closed indefinitely for restoration*), in Pescara's bustling **fish market** on Lungofiume Paolucci.

Chieti

For something a bit weightier than gills and beachballs, head up to **Chieti**, about 13km up the Pescara River. Another provincial capital, Chieti was the Roman *Theate Marrucinorum*, a name that its bishop, Pietro Carafa, made use of when founding the Theatine Order in 1524. Bishop Carafa went on to become Paul IV, the most vicious and intolerant of popes, but it's no reflection on Chieti; Carafa was a Neapolitan.

The **Museo Nazionale Archeologico di Antichità** (*open daily 9–7; adm*), in the Villa Comunale, is Chieti's star attraction, and one of the region's most important museums: the chief repository of pre-Roman and Roman artworks unearthed in the

Abruzzo, including the shapely 6th-century BC **Warrior of Capestrano**, dressed like a Mexican bandit and accompanied by an inscription in the language of the Middle Adriatic Bronze Age culture. There is a room of other items found in Bronze Age tombs, and rooms containing Hellenistic and Roman sculptures, tombs, portraits, coins, jewellery and votive offerings, many discovered in *Alba Fucens*, in the Parco Nazionale d'Abruzzo, and *Amiternum*, near L'Aquila. The documentation of material from Abruzzo's many Upper Palaeolithic caves is displayed with ancient ceramics and artefacts from Italic necropolises.

Out of doors, Chieti retains a dramatic 12-14th century Gothic **cathedral**, begun by Charles of Anjou, and a couple of traces of *Theate Marrucinorum* – the remains of three little temples on Via Spaventa, near the post office – while in the eastern residential quarters stand the **Terme Romane** or baths (*t 0871 331 668; currently closed for restoration; to visit ask the staff at the Museo Archeologico*), of which a mighty cistern is the most impressive feature. Best of all are the lovely views, stretching from the sea to the Gran Sasso and Maiella Mountains.

The Via Valeria: Chieti to Pópoli

Inland from Chieti, the old Roman Via Valeria–Via Tiburtina accompanies the A25 up the Pescara Valley. There is certainly no shortage of Romanesque churches along the way. In the 10th and 11th centuries there was plenty of empty land in these parts for hard-working Benedictines to put to use. The Lombard dukes were favourable, and this valley developed one of the biggest concentrations of monasteries in Italy, mostly founded from the great Benedictine mother house of Montecassino.

At Manoppello Scalo you'll see a steep, prominent hill overlooking the river that once bore a sanctuary and altar (*ara*) to *Dea Bona*, the 'Good Goddess'. In its place stands the delightful 13th-century **Santa Maria Arabona**, a Cistercian Gothic church (founded from Fossanova in Lazio) that owes much of its charm to the big glass wall that now closes off the unfinished nave. Up the hill in **Manoppello** town, you can see something you can't see anywhere else – the face of Jesus. Manoppello's holy icon, the *Volto Santo*, mysteriously appeared here about 1600, about the same time that one of the greatest relics of St Peter's in Rome dropped out of sight: the veil of Veronica, on which the image of Jesus was impressed when he stopped to wipe his face on it during the carryng of the cross. Large numbers of pilgrims come to see it, at the impressive **Santuario del Volto Santo** on the heights overlooking the village.

Beyond Manoppello, on the tortuous SS539 that skirts the northern edge of the Montagna della Maiella, stands perhaps the finest of all the Benedictine churches in the Abruzzo, in one of the loveliest settings. **San Liberatore in Maiella**, on a height above the village of Serramonesca (*open usual church hours, and the monks give guided tours at 9.30, 11, 4 and 5.30; Sun at 9.30 and 12.15*). The church, begun in 1080, shows influences from both Puglia and Lombardy; inside is a n excellent carved pulpit and pavement, and fragments of frescoes that include a portrait of Charlemagne.

Near the village of **Torre de' Passeri**, more Romanesque awaits at **San Clemente in Casauria**, founded by Emperor Louis II (Charlemagne's great-grandson) in 871. The Cistercians took over and rebuilt the church in the 12th century, endowing it with a magnificent three-arched porch and intricately carved capitals, and a stunning portal with reliefs that form a fitting frame for the ornate bronze doors. The same sculptors may also have carved the baldaquin and pulpit in the Romanesque interior. Louis II's original crypt was preserved in the reconstruction of the church, and is reached by steps from the aisles.

Ortona and Lanciano

Back on the coast, south of Pescara, beyond the pleasant resort of Francavilla al Mare, lies Abruzzo's largest port, **Ortona**. Over the years Ortona has taken more than its share of damage from earthquakes and warfare, particularly in the autumn of 1943, when the Germans were well entrenched along a line north of the River Sangro, and thousands of lives were lost in the six-week Battle of the Sangro and Moro rivers before the Germans were routed. There are two large **British military cemeteries** in the vicinity, one near the River Moro, about 3km south of Ortona, and the other just south of Torino di Sangro Marina, between Ortona and Vasto.

From Ortona you can take a narrow-gauge local train for an inland loop (although admittedly the bus is much faster), seeing Guardiagrele and Lanciano on the way. The sweet hill town of **Guardiagrele** was a famous goldsmiths' centre in the Renaissance, the birthplace of the renowned Nicola da Guardiagrele in the 15th century; he made the silver crucifix in the treasury of **Santa Maria Maggiore** (*t 0871 82117 or 0348 414 5800; open mid-July–Aug daily 10–12.30 and 4–7.30; other times call ahead*). This church has a huge exterior fresco of St Christopher by Andrea de Litio, which was believed to bring good luck to any traveller who saw it.

Lanciano, a medieval market town that once attracted merchants from all over the Mediterranean to its wool and cloth fairs, retains fine grey stone monuments from its golden days such as the **cathedral**, built atop a Roman bridge. Pilgrims have long come to nearby **San Francesco** for its relics of an 8th-century miracle – some drops of blood and a little piece of human heart: according to legend the bread and wine of the Mass really did transubstantiate into flesh and blood for a sceptical monk (they say that Jesus' blood type was AB).

In the north end of town is **Porta San Biagio**, the only medieval gate to survive. In the medieval quarter called Cittanova is **Santa Maria Maggiore**, a fine French Gothic church that holds another work of Nicola da Guardiagrele. Above Cittanova is the 11th-century fortress of the **Torri Montanare**, which has great views of the hills and mountains further inland. Lanciano is also the starting point for one of the most spectacular drives in the Abruzzo – the SS84 to Roccaraso, near the Parco Nazionale d'Abruzzo.

San Giovanni in Venere and Vasto

Back on the coast, above the railway station of the small resort of Fossacesia Marina, stands one of Abruzzo's most remarkable monuments – **San Giovanni in Venere** (*t 0872 60132; open daily 8am–8pm*). 'Venere' refers to Venus, over whose temple this church was erected: temples to the love goddess were often placed in similar spots, perched high above the sea. Begun as early as the 8th century, the church was rebuilt in 1015 and converted into a Cistercian abbey in 1165. There are several Puglian-Sicilian touches in the church, perhaps introduced by Frederick II's architects – in the decoration of the narrow windows, the robust figures of the bas-reliefs, and the design of the magnificent marble **Portale della Luna**, the 'Portal of the Moon' (1230). Be sure to walk around the church to see the beautiful apses. Inside, the ceiling is supported by cruciform piers, and there are some old, if not very interesting, frescoes dating back to the 12th century. The large crypt, entered from the aisles, contains ancient columns from the temple of Venus and 12th-century frescoes of a Madonna with St Nicholas and St Michael, resplendent in fine Byzantine court dress.

Further south is **Vasto**, one of the most attractive towns on the Adriatic and the home of Gabriele Rossetti, poet and father of Dante Gabriel and Christina Rossetti. Vasto stands on a low natural terrace above its beach and port, the former attracting large numbers of French as well as Italian tourists. Its narrow streets end at the weathered but distinctive 13th-century castle, with a cylindrical tower. Vasto is proud of its painter, Filippo Palizzi (1818–99), whose works can be seen in the church of **San Pietro**, and in the local **Museo Civico** (*open Tues–Sun 9.30–12.30 and 4.30–8.30; adm*).

Térmoli

Crossing over the River Trigno, you enter Molise, which is, in the main, even more rural and unspoiled than Abruzzo, although this may not be immediately apparent from the busy beaches along the coast. Térmoli gets top billing here, a bright little fishing town with a long sandy beach, palms and oleanders. The diva of the old town, or at least the part that survived a Turkish raid in 1566, is the exotic 13th-century **cathedral**, its façade undulating with blind Puglian-style arcades; inside is a marble floor of strange mythological beasts.

Térmoli also boasts a **castle** and walls from the same period, both built by the Emperor Frederick II. After enjoying the view from the castle there's nothing more demanding to do than relax on the beach and try to decide which seafood restaurant to try in the evening. Térmoli is also a summer ferry port for the Tremiti Islands (*see* pp.991–2). If Termoli's too crowded, there's another modest resort down the coast, Campomarino. A little further south, and the road enters Puglia (*see* p.979).

Téramo

From Giulianova the SS80 heads 20km inland to **Téramo**, midway between the coast and the Gran Sasso. Originally a Roman city, Téramo knew its happiest days in the 14th century under the Angevins, and even though it wears mostly 20th-century fashions today, it preserves several fine monuments. The **cathedral** stands out with its remarkable Cosmati-decorated portal and Romanesque saints; around them a miscellany of lions, collected from here and there, lend feline elegance to the façade, which is as simple, square and ungabled as any in Abruzzo. The cathedral's Ghibelline crenellations recall the days when Téramo was the fief of its bishop, who still possesses the title 'Prince of Téramo', although he no longer makes much use of a special papal dispensation from more rough-and-ready days that allows him to wear armour under his robes and keep his sword handy by the altar. The campanile is from the 15th century. Inside there is a silver altar frontal with 30 biblical scenes, a masterpiece by Nicola da Guardiagrele (1448) who also made the silver statues of Mary and Gabriel by the door. The 15th-century polyptych is by the Venetian Jacobello del Fiore.

Near the cathedral lie the ruins of the **Teatro Romano** and, a short distance further on, the original cathedral, **Santa Maria Aprutiensis** (6th–12th-century) – its name recalling the Italic tribe of the Praetutii who gave their name to *Aprutium* (and hence to Abruzzo). Santa Maria (also called Sant'Anna), built of bits of Roman columns and other ancient fragments, is Téramo's attic of odds and ends – Lombard carvings, a 6th-century *triforium* and ancient angelic frescoes.

In the Franciscan convent of **Madonna delle Grazie** (*open Tues–Sun 10–12 and 3–5; longer afternoon hours in summer*), to the east by Piazza della Libertà, is a painted wooden statue of the Madonna and Child by one of the Abruzzo's best sculptors, Silvestro dell'Aquila (15th century). More quattrocento Abruzzese art is on display in the **Pinacoteca** on Viale Bovio, while the **Museo Archeologico** on Via Delfico displays local finds (*t 0861 250 873; both museums open Tues–Sun 9–1 and 3–7; combined ticket for the two museums and convent sold at the Museo Archeologico; adm*).

Around Téramo

Heading north from Téramo towards Ascoli Piceno on the SS81, the road passes **Campli**, just to the east, a small town with several Romanesque and Gothic monuments. The rather formidable **Palazzo del Comune** was built in the 14th century but much altered in 1520. The Romanesque church of **San Francesco** is a fine embodiment of the Abruzzese ideal that less is more; inside are some 14th-century frescoes. Its former convent now houses a **Museo Archeologico** (*t 0861 569 158; open daily 9–8;*

Getting Around

Téramo is fairly easily reached by **train**, on a spur from the coastal line at Giulianova. ARPA **buses** (**t** 0861 245 857) on both the *autostrada* and local roads also quickly link Téramo to the coast, to Ascoli Piceno and to L'Aquila.

Tourist Information

Via Carducci 17, **t** 0861 244 222 (*open Mon–Sat 9–1 and Mon–Fri 3.30–6*).

Where to Stay and Eat

Téramo ✉ 64100
****Sporting**, Via De Gasperi 41, **t** 0861 412 661, **f** 0861 210 285 (*moderate*). Téramo's

most attractive hotel because of its garden, although it's on the outskirts of town.
***Castello**, Via del Castello 62, **t/f** 0861 247 582 (*cheap*). Basic but adequate, with seven rooms, some without private bathroom.
Il Duomo, Via Stazio 9, **t** 0861 242 991 (*moderate*). Serves up local specialities throughout the year: *maccheroni alla chitarra*, and meat dishes, including grilled kid. *Closed Sun eve, Mon, second and third week of Aug and two weeks in Jan.*
Osteria al Bottaccio, Via Piano d'Accio 10 (off the Giulianova road), **t** 0861 558 335 (*cheap*). Strictly local cuisine in an informal atmosphere. *Closed Sun, two weeks in Jan and three weeks in Aug.*
Sotto le Stelle, Via dei Mille 59, **t** 0861 247 126. (*cheap*). Another informal local hangout. *Closed Sun and two weeks in Jan.*

The *Virtù* of Téramo

Téramo has its own culinary speciality called *virtù* that's customarily cooked on the first of May. Judging from its ingredients, it began as a way of using up winter stocks and adding the first of the new season's goodies – traditionally local women each contributed an ingredient. It's a cross between a soup and a stew – a type of minestrone, in fact – based on a stock to which are added twelve different kinds of dried peas, beans and lentils, along with celery, sausage and different bits and pieces of pig, such as trotters and ears, all well-salted and seasoned with herbs.

adm), containing artefacts from the 6th–3rd-century BC Italic necropolis at Campovalano, a kilometre away. Nearby there's the abbey and church of **San Pietro**, founded in the 8th century and rebuilt in the 13th; the frescoed figures on the piers inside were designed to be part of the congregation (*to visit both the necropolis and San Pietro, call Signore Pietro d'Amalio, the owner of the Alimentari store in Campovalano's main square, t 0861 56306, during shop hours*).

A few kilometres north of Campli rises the superbly positioned Renaissance town of **Civitella del Tronto**, crowned by an impregnable castle that the Bourbons managed to hold right to the bitter end in 1861. First built around the year 1000, it has half a kilometre of travertine walled terrace, lending it its distinctive crew-cut skyline.

The Gran Sasso: 'The Big Rock of Italy'

The Gran Sasso offers Alpine grandeur only an hour by motorway from Rome, and as such is an immensely popular ski and hiking resort. There are plans to designate it a nature park, but, until then, environmentalists and developers will continue to disagree on its future.

Approaching the Gran Sasso from the East, and Castelli

South of Téramo the SS150 divides into two arms embracing the **Gran Sasso**: the main road that joins up with the SS80 from Téramo and continues up the narrow upper **Val di Vomano** to the north – the most scenic road in the region (*see* p.615) – and another that follows the higher **Valle di Mavone** to the south. The latter (SS491) is an excellent approach to the mountains, with the highest peak of the Apennines, the Corno Grande (9551ft) looming ahead. Several curiosities along the SS491 offer tempting detours – near Castel Castagna there's **Santa Maria di Ronzano** (*t 0861 697 250, opening hours irregular; call the Comune di Castel Castagna, mornings only*) a three-nave church embellished with frescoes dated 1181, among the finest examples of Lombard art in Central Italy. Between Montorio al Vomano and Isola del Gran Sasso you can take in the village of **Tossìcia**, with a pretty medieval nucleus lying between two mountain streams; the tiny church of **Sant'Antonio Abate** has a grand 1471 Renaissance portal by the Venetian Antonio Lombardo.

The scenery is stunning as the road reaches **Isola del Gran Sasso**, a fine stone village and a good base for hikes up to the Campo Imperatore (*see* pp.615–616); it has

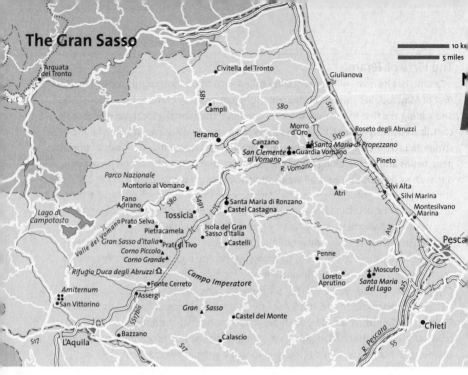

The Gran Sasso

another Romanesque church, **San Giovanni ad Insulam**, as well as a more recent shrine to the modern patron saint of Abruzzo-Molise, San Gabriele dell'Addolorata, a young Franciscan monk from Assisi who died in the monastery here in 1862. His relics draw pilgrims by the bus-load – processed through a huge, disconcerting steel-and-concrete basilica designed in shopping mall modern.

To the southeast of Isola, dramatically positioned at the foot of the great wall of Monte Camica, is **Castelli**, another good mountain base. Castelli is the great centre in the Abruzzo for ceramics, an industry that achieved art and glory in the 17th-century workshops of the Grue and Gentili families. The ceramic tradition is still continued in various workshops in the town and in the August ceramics fair, where part of the fun is tossing reject plates over the river. Castelli's **Chiesa Madre** contains a majolica *pala* by Francesco Grue, as well as 12th-century wooden statues.

More of the Grues' work (as well as that of other local craftsmen) may be seen in the **Museo della Ceramica Abruzzese** (*t 0861 979 398; open Oct–May Tues–Sun 9–1; June–Sept Tues–Sun 10–1 and 3–7; adm*). The museum also serves as a tourist office, which organizes guided tours around Castelli.

Most splendiferous of all, however, is the rural church of **San Donato**, which Carlo Levi rightfully dubbed 'The Sistine Chapel of Italian Majolica', for its ceiling (visible from the outside through a grate) of a thousand ceramic tiles – the only ceiling like it in Italy, an impressive 360 square feet covered with a colourful patchwork of different folk motifs – plenty of rabbits, skulls, portraits, notices of various kinds, geometric patterns and so on (1615–17). Also on the outskirts is the derelict Romanesque church of **San Salvatore**, with a charming medieval pulpit.

The Upper Vomano Valley: Téramo to L'Aquila

At **Montorio al Vomano** the SS150 joins the main SS80, the scenic road which, like the more efficent but less panoramic *autostrada*, links Téramo with L'Aquila. Montorio, topped by its grand but never-completed Spanish castle, has an eclectic church, the **Collegiata di San Rocco**, with a façade that has been added to whenever funds were handy; within, the carved wooden Baroque altar and tapestries are the main attraction.

Further up the valley the twin, blunt, snow-shrouded peaks of the **Due Corni del Gran Sasso** look over the shoulder of **Fano Adriano**, an old town and now a small winter and summer resort, with skiing and hiking at Pratoselva. The village's name means 'Hadrian's Temple', although none of this remains; the 12th-century **San Pietro** is modern Fano's finest church, with a Renaissance façade from 1550.

Pietracamela, even higher up in the lap of the Gran Sasso (3,296ft), is a base for hikes over the **Sella dei Due Corni** to the Campo Imperatore, and for skiing at the Gran Sasso's biggest resort, **Prati di Tivo**, a fine lofty meadow of beech forests.

The SS80 towards L'Aquila continues past the Lago di Campotosto, and then winds around the western flank of the Gran Sasso. About 10km before L'Aquila it comes to **Amiternum**, the ruins of a Sabine city mentioned in Virgil's *Aeneid*. Later a Roman colony, it was the birthplace of the poet Sallust. A small theatre, amphitheatre, houses with mosaics and frescoes, and other relics, were brought to light in 1978 (*open daily; can be seen well from outside when closed*). Nearby, medieval **San Vittorino** has, under the 12th–16th-century church of **San Michele** (*call Don Sigismondo, t 0862 461 695, to schedule a visit*), something out of the ordinary for this part of the world: catacombs, although, unlike the great ones in Rome, these ones have been embellished with 15th-century frescoes. A procession is held through them on the last Sunday in May.

Tourist Information

Centro Turistico del Gran Sasso: Corso Vittorio Emanuele 49, L'Aquila, t 0862 22146. A helpful travel agency with information on outdoor activities in the region's mountains.

Club Alpino Italiano Vicolo Fassa 34 (near Piazza Duomo), L'Aquila, t 0862 24342 (*open Mon–Sat 6pm–8pm*). Provides useful maps and hiking information.

Where to Stay and Eat

The Gran Sasso ✉ 67100

★★★★Hotel Campo Imperatore, t 0862 400 000, f 0862 606 688 (*moderate*). Mussolini's least favourite hotel (*see p.616*), at the top of the cablecar route, is very comfortable – no reason to escape, however dramatically.

★★La Villetta, by the lower funicular station at Fonte Cerreto, t 0862 606 171, f 0862 606 674 (*moderate*). Another hotel that was used to hold Mussolini in 1943. A pretty, friendly hotel that makes a good base for visiting the mountains.

★★★★Miramonti, up in Prati di Tivo, t 0861 959 621, f 0861 959 647 (*moderate*). A comfortable, modern resort hotel with a garden, pool and tennis courts. *Closed Oct.*

Il Mandrone, Frazione San Pietro, Isola del Gran Sasso d'Italia (about 20km north of Campo Imperatore), t 0861 976 152 (*cheap*). Prepares genuine mountain cuisine, including *strongole alla barcarola* – a home-made pasta dressed with 20 different wild herbs from the Gran Sasso – soups, lamb and *ricotta*-based specialities. *Closed Tues and Wed, 10 days Nov–Dec and 10 days Jan–Feb. Open daily in Aug.*

Mussolini's Least Favourite Hotel

Near the upper funicular station stands the **Albergo di Campo Imperatore**, which once sheltered a real would-be emperor. After the ad hoc Italian government of Marshal Badoglio had deposed Mussolini and begun to seek peace with the Allies in 1943, there remained the delicate question of what to do with the former Duce. After being shuttled off to a Tyrrhenian island, he was brought to this hotel, at the time inaccessible by road, which set the stage for the SS Commando Otto Skorzeny's daring rescue on 12 September 1943. German paratroopers slipped in and out by flying in a Fieseler Storch – an aeroplane the size of the average bedroom – into which Skorzeny somehow managed to squeeze the portly Mussolini before escaping. Hitler then set up a new headquarters for his associate on Lake Garda, the capital of the ill-fated Italian Social Republic. This episode fooled the Allies, and has fooled historians for decades. Only recently has it been established that Skorzeny's exploit was all a publicity stunt, part of Hitler's campaign to glorify the SS at the expense of the regular German army, which was getting beaten on all fronts, and whose political loyalty was already suspect.

Many of the trails through the Gran Sasso begin at the hotel, including one up past the Duca degli Abruzzi refuge to the **Corno Grande** (9551ft), a spectacular eight-hour walk. There are also three ski lifts in the Campo Imperatore, and four nearby at **Monte Cristo**. South of L'Aquila there is more good skiing as well as bobsledding at **Campo Felice**, above the pretty village of **Rocca di Cambio**, the highest in Abruzzo at 4700ft.

Approaches from L'Aquila and the West

If you're coming from L'Aquila, catch bus 6 or 6/d from Via Castello to the *funivia* at **Fonte Cerreto**, near Assergi, the village at the mouth of the Gran Sasso Tunnel (it's a 2km walk from the bus stop to the funicular, which usually closes in spring for maintenance, so call in advance for details, *t 0862 22147*). Alternatively, if you have a car and the roads are clear, drive up the SS17bis by way of **Bazzano** – site of an interesting 12th-century church, **Santa Giusta**. Both the funicular and the road will take you to the **Campo Imperatore** (6,973ft), a beautiful, gentle upland basin, filled with flowers in the late spring and ski bunnies in the winter.

L'Aquila

L'Aquila, the regional capital, is an intriguing town in its own right, as well as making an ideal base for travelling around the rest of the Abruzzo. The name means 'the eagle', the symbol of empire, and it's not surprising to learn that the city was founded by Emperor Frederick II in 1240 as a bulwark against the popes.

L'Aquila is one of the few cities in Italy of any importance not to have ancient precedents: instead, to populate his new town, Frederick relocated the inhabitants of surrounding castles and hamlets – 99 of them in all, according to tradition – who each built their own church in the new town. But what made L'Aquila's fortune was its loyalty to Queen Giovanna II in 1423, when the city was besieged for over a year by the Aragonese. The queen thanked the city for its steadfastness by granting it privileges that helped it to become, for several centuries, the second city in the Kingdom of Naples, a wool and livestock market town and a producer of silk and saffron. It attracted Adamo di Rottweil, a student of Gutenberg, who founded a printing press here in 1482, one of the first in Italy.

L'Aquila's good fortune made it cocky, and in 1529 it rose up against its rulers in Naples. The Spanish viceroy quickly put an end to its pretensions and punished the Aquilani by forcing them to pay for a huge new citadel to discourage any further revolts. Much of what the Spaniards didn't destroy in their reprisal fell in the earthquake of 1703.

And yet, despite its vicissitudes, L'Aquila has managed to keep a considerable portion of its labyrinthine old quarter, its walls and even some of its exceptional 13th-century monuments.

Tourist Information

Via XX Settembre 8, t 0862 22306 (*open Mon–Sat 8–2 and 3–7*).

Getting Around

Trains connect L'Aquila (with no great hurry or frequency) to Rieti in Lazio and Terni in Umbria, as well as to Pescara by way of Sulmona, the main junction for rail routes in the central Abruzzo.

L'Aquila is also less than two hours from Rome by ARPA **bus** (Rome, t 06 442 33928, L'Aquila, t 0862 412 808, Pescara, t 085 421 5099, Téramo, t 0861 245 857), with 18 departures a day (11 on Sundays) from outside Stazione Tiburtina; in Rome you must buy tickets before boarding at Via Teodorico 28 (open Mon–Sat 5.30am–9.30pm, Sun 6.30am–10.15pm).

Where to Stay and Eat

L'Aquila ✉ 67100

As elsewhere in the Abruzzo, prices are notably low compared to the Italian norm. The region's eating establishments are more original than its hotels, especially if you come at the beginning of May when the locals are cooking up pots of *virtù*, Téramo's unique speciality (*see* p.613).

*****Castello**, Piazza Battaglione Alpini, t 0862 419 147, f 0862 419 140 (*moderate*). A classy hotel opposite the castle.

*****Duomo**, Via Dragonetti 6, t 0862 410 893, f 862 413 058 (*moderate*). A 17th-century palace off Piazza Duomo, with 28 rooms, some with a view of the square.

*****Duca degli Abruzzi**, Viale Papa Giovanni XXIII 10, t 0862 28341, f 0862 61588 (*moderate*). Comfortable rooms.

***Orazi**, Via Roma 175, t 0862 412 889 (*cheap*). Not so central, but its 10 rooms – without bathrooms – are good value.

Antiche Mura, Via XXV Aprile 2, t 0862 62422 (*moderate*). Specializes in traditional Abruzzese cuisine: homely soups, homemade pasta dishes, rabbit with peppers and saffron. Don't miss the *ferratelle*, a strictly local waffle dessert. *Closed Sun*.

L'Antico Borgo, Piazza San Vito 1, t 0862 22005 (*cheap*). A restaurant offering delicious vegetarian *ravioli* and, in season, 'truffled' treats. *Closed Tues Oct–May; open daily in summer*.

La Cantina del Boss, Via Castello 3, t 0862 413 393 (*cheap*). A great place to stop for a quick snack of stuffed pizza or *frittata*, in one of the region's most done-up cellars. *Closed Sat lunch, all day Sun and July 15–Aug 15*.

Elodia, at Camarda on the SS17bis (10km north of L'Aquila), t 0862 606 024 (*cheap*). Well worth the drive for a taste of Abruzzese cuisine at its best. *Closed Sun eve, all day Mon and two weeks in July*.

A 99-headed Fountain

L'Aquila's famous **Fontana delle 99 Cannelle**, built in 1272, stands in a pink-and-white chequered courtyard in a corner of the walls near the **Porta Rivera**, not far from the railway station on the western side of the old city. The fountain's water flows through the mouths of 93 mouldering grotesque heads (and six unadorned spouts), each representing one of the hamlets that were brought together to form the city of L'Aquila. The fountain has three sides (the one to the left is a more recent addition, built in the 16th century). While you're there, try to figure out how the two sundials work on the façade of the little church opposite.

From the fountain, Via San Jacopo ascends to join Via XX Settembre, the main entry-point into the city if you're approaching from Rome. If you follow Via XX Settembre straight into a small piazza laid out as a park, turn right at the next street and then left onto the Viale di Collemaggio you will reach L'Aquila's greatest Romanesque church, **Santa Maria di Collemaggio**, founded in 1270 by the hermit Pietro Morrone. The church has one of the most sumptuous and attractive façades of any in Abruzzo, its three rounded portals decorated with spiral mouldings and niches for saints, who have mostly vanished. Above the portals runs a pretty ribbon frieze, and above that are three rose windows of different patterns, the centre one a masterpiece of the stonecarver's art.

The elegant interior has been stripped of its centuries' accumulation of art and debris, leaving the fancy Renaissance **tomb of Celestine V** as its chief decoration. Pietro Morrone was an utterly holy man but rather naïve and, in 1294, to his surprise, he was crowned pope here by cardinals who hoped to use him as their instrument. After a few months it became evident that the new Pope Celestine V wasn't quite turning out as expected and he was subtly 'encouraged' in Naples' Egg Castle (*see* p.911) to resign St Peter's throne – the only pope ever to do so voluntarily. Soon after his death, however, one of his successors canonized him, and here he rests as St Peter Celestine. He gained an additional somewhat humiliating claim to fame in 1988 when his relics were stolen and held to ransom, only to be returned without further ado when it became clear to the body snatchers that no one thought Celestine was worth the asking price. A privilege Celestine V granted the church during his brief office is a Holy Door, an uncommon feature, which is opened annually on 28 August for the faithful to pass through and receive the still-distributed papal indulgence.

Around Piazza Duomo

From Via XX Settembre and the park, Corso Federico II leads into **Piazza Duomo**, L'Aquila's main market square ever since 1304 when Charles of Anjou granted the town the right to hold one here; you'll find produce and handicrafts on sale daily from dawn to 1pm. Frequently shattered by earthquakes, the Duomo itself is dressed in a dull neoclassical façade, a wallflower next to the piazza's 18th-century Baroque **Santuario del Suffragio**, with opulent curves and a death's head above the entrance. The neighbourhood around Piazza del Duomo is one of L'Aquila's most attractive. On Via Santa Giusta, the 13th-century church of **Santa Giusta** has a good portal and rose window embellished with 12 droll figures, while all around it the streets are full of

Baroque palaces. On Via Sassa, the church of **San Giuseppe** (*usually closed to the public*) contains a 15th-century equestrian tomb by Ludovico d'Alemagna, while **Palazzo Franchi**, at No.56, contains a lovely Renaissance courtyard with a double *loggia*. From Piazza Duomo, Corso Vittorio Emanuele leads to the **Quattro Cantoni**, the 'Four Corners', the city's main crossroads. To the left, on Corso Umberto, lies Piazza del Palazzo, the *palazzo* in question being the **Palazzo di Giustizia**, from where Margherita of Austria, a daughter of Charles V born on the wrong side of the blanket, ruled as Governess of Abruzzo. The bell in the palace's tower sounds 99 strokes every day at dusk.

San Bernardino

On the other side of the Quattro Cantoni, Via San Bernardino leads to the masterpiece of Abruzzese Renaissance, the church of San Bernardino. The great revivalist preacher, San Bernardino da Siena, spent several years in the Franciscan convent in L'Aquila before he died, whereupon one of his disciples, St John of Capestrano, founded this church as his memorial. Work began in 1452, but the perfectly balanced, elegant façade was only finished by Cola dell'Amatrice in 1542. It is best seen from the bottom of the stair in front of the church; we are in Abruzzo, so the roof is gable-less. The 1703 earthquake smashed the vast interior, which was rebuilt in flagrant Baroque; the magnificent gilt wood ceiling, incorporating San Bernardino's IHS monogram, is by Ferdinando Mosca. San Bernardino's mausoleum and the tomb of Maria Pereira are both works by Silvestro dell'Aquila, a pupil of Donatello. The second chapel on the right contains a *pala* by Andrea della Robbia, grandson of the more famous Luca.

The Castello and Museo Nazionale d'Abruzzo

To the north the Corso Vittorio Emanuele runs out into the shady Parco del Castello and, above it, the grand, moated **castello**. Built in 1535 by Pier Luigi Escribà, it is a showpiece of military architecture unwillingly financed by the citizens of L'Aquila, with a grand doorway, crowned by Charles V's two-headed eagle.

The castle contains the **Museo Nazionale d'Abruzzo** (*t 0862 6331; open Tues–Sun 9–8; adm*), the region's finest, with a well-arranged collection of art salvaged from abandoned local churches and archaeological treasures. The biggest exhibit is on the ground floor, to the right of the entrance: the *Elephas Meridionalis*, a reconstructed prehistoric pachyderm, discovered near L'Aquila in 1954. Here too are Roman portraits, statues, tombs, tympanums, reliefs, tools and so on.

On the first floor the medieval section has a vast collection of religious art: superb polychrome wooden statues, including a *St Sebastian* and a *Madonna and Child* by Silvestro dell'Aquila and a fine 15th-century panel painting of St John of Capestrano. Other fine triptychs show a Sienese-Umbrian influence. On the next floor you'll find works by Andrea Vaccaro, Calabrian painter Mattia Preti and Abruzzese artists like Pompeo Cesari. The third and final floor contains 20th-century works, mainly by local artists. Concerts are held regularly in the castle's auditorium.

From L'Aquila to Pópoli

The SS17 runs southeast from L'Aquila along the southern flanks of the Gran Sasso, passing quiet villages like **Calascio**, with its impressive ruined citadel 4920ft up, or **Castel del Monte**, further up still, with an interesting medieval core. On the other side of the SS17, **Fossa** has 12th-century frescoes of the *Day of Judgement* in its church of **Santa Maria ad Cryptas** (*irregular opening hours*) that are said to have inspired Dante.

Tiny **Bominaco** (near Caporciano) is the site of the most celebrated monuments in this corner of Abruzzo, two churches that belonged to a fortified **Benedictine Abbey** (*call the custodian, Signor Cassiani, t 0862 93604, to arrange a visit*). The monastery dates from some shadowy three-digit year; **San Pellegrino** is said to have been founded by Charlemagne, though it was rebuilt in 1263. The interior, rectangular with an ogival vault, is covered with the colourful, stylized frescoes of the period: a pictorial calendar of the months and major feast days, scenes from the New Testament, saints and geometrical patterns. The sanctuary is set apart by a marble transenna carved with a griffon with a cup, and another with a fearsome dragon – not your ordinary church fare. The saint is buried under the sanctuary and it is said that you can hear his heart beating through a hole by the altar. **Santa Maria Assunta** has none of the ancient strangeness of San Pellegrino, but is a 12th-century gem, beautifully endowed with carved doors, windows, capitals and a pulpit.

Just to the west of Bominaco are the caves of the **Grotte di Stiffe** (*t 0862 86142; 50-min guided tours daily 10–1 and 3–6; adm exp, includes visit to speleological museum in town; call ahead to arrange a tour in English*), where half a mile of illuminated walkway takes you along an underground river beneath eerie stalactites.

From Navelli the road makes a dramatic writhing descent to Pópoli (*see below*), on the Via Valeria and the Rome–Pescara *autostrada*, or you can turn eastwards to **Capestrano**, birthplace of San Bernardino's saintly follower, St John of Capestrano (1386–1456). The swallows come back here, too, if not on the same tight schedule as their Californian cousins, who famously return each year to the Spanish mission of San Juan Capestrano on the so-called 'missions road' between LA and San Francisco – giving rise to the expression 'as sure as the swallows returning to Capestrano'.

Pópoli stands at the confluence of the Aterno and the Sagittario, where they meet to form the River Pescara. The town's largest church, Romanesque **San Francesco**, is topped with statues and pierced by an unusual rose window. The 14th-century **Taverna Ducale**, decorated with escutcheons, was not where Pópoli's Cantelmi dukes drank, but where they stored the tithes from their subjects. It has survived in better shape than their castle which looms over Pópoli.

Corfinio, to the west, was called Pentima until Mussolini gave it back its ancient name – for here stood the Paeligni capital *Corfinium*, famous in history as the united headquarters of the Italic tribes in the Social Wars of the 1st century BC. They renamed the city *Italica*, the first instance in history that the name signified a union of the peninsula's peoples, hoping it would soon take over from Rome as capital. Now even its ruins are meagre: there's a small **archaeology museum** in the convent of Sant'Alessandro (*for admission, ask at the church*).

Southern Abruzzo and the National Park

For many people the highlight of the region is the **Parco Nazionale d'Abruzzo**, the second largest national park in Italy and of special interest for its rare fauna and flora. For mountain-lovers there's also the **Montagna della Maiella**, a range nearly as impressive as the Gran Sasso and considerably less touristy. Man-made sights include *Alba Fucens*, Abruzzo's best archaeological site, and intriguing old towns like **Sulmona**, **Scanno**, **Pescocostanzo** and **Tagliacozzo**.

The Marsica

The region southwest of Pópoli, towards the Lazio border, is known as the **Marsica**, after its ancient inhabitants, the Marsi. The 'people of Mars' were among the most determined foes of Rome in ancient times, and they took a prominent part in the Social War in 90BC. They also had such a talent for medicine, using the local herbs, that the Romans accused them of witchcraft. Their snake goddess Angizia seems to still haunt the region today, most famously at the annual 'Procession of the Serpents' in **Cocullo**, where floats, townspeople and children parade covered in writhing snakes.

Celano, just off the A25 motorway, is an unexpectedly charming hill town spread out beneath the skirts of its four-square **Piccolomini Castle**, now home to the excellent **Museo Nazionale dela Marsica** (*open daily in winter 9–1.30, Sat and Sun 9–8; in summer daily 9–8, and some Saturdays until midnight; adm*). Here the attractions are not from the ancient Marsicans, but a wealth of medieval art, ranging from the eccentric to the downright strange: a Byzantine triptych covered in tiny pearls, a relief of a whale, and the church doors from San Pietro, with a series of mystical images thought to represent the 'triumph of the spiritual over the material'. Celano was the birthplace of the Blessed Tommaso da Celano, St Francis's his first biographer; he also composed the *Dies Irae*, the eerie medieval hymn of the dead most often heard now in the finale of Berlioz's *Symphonie Fantastique*. Nearby you can visit the **Gole di Celano**, a stunningly steep and narrow gorge, or head north on the SS5bis towards L'Aquila, by way of the mountain resort towns of **Ovindoli** and **Rocca di Cambio**.

Avezzano and *Alba Fucens*

Marsica's modern capital, **Avezzano**, has little to commend it, having been toppled by an earthquake in 1915 and bombed in the Second World War. Its one monument, the **Castello Orsini**, has a portal with a relief celebrating the victory of Lepanto over the Turks in 1571. In the **Palazzo Comunale** there's a small **museum** of inscriptions and architectural fragments from the cities of the Marsica (*t 0863 43251; closed indefinitely for restoration*). Avezzano is a departure point for the Parco Nazionale d'Abruzzo.

If the ancient Marsi were to return to their homeland today, they would be amazed to find their lake – once the largest in Central Italy – replaced by the fertile basin called the **Piana del Fucino**. But they would also tell you that their *Lacus Fucinus* had been a bit of a mess, with an inadequate outlet, and prone to flooding. To drain it, Emperor Claudius ordered what became the greatest underground engineering work of antiquity (AD 54): a 6km-long tunnel intended to spill the lake's waters into the

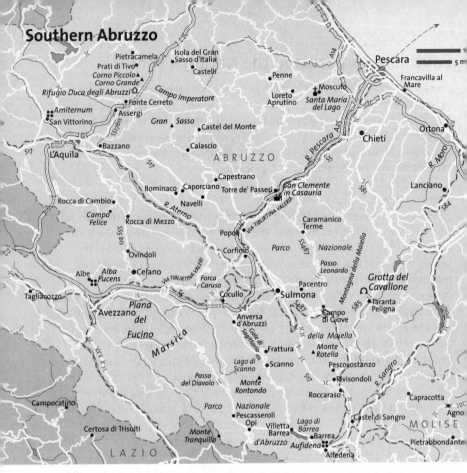

Southern Abruzzo

River Liri. However, for all the amazing skill that went into the work, the tunnel didn't work very well and was eventually blocked up. In 1240 Frederick II tried to have it unblocked, but failed, and only in 1875 did British, Italian, French and Swiss engineers finally drain the lake, reclaiming thousands of hectares. Now it's one of the most surreal landscapes in Italy, a 50-square mile expanse of geometrically straight canals and roads, numbered like the streets in an American city. Over it all loom the radio dishes of Italy's biggest space research installation, the **Centro Telespaziale**.

Of all the ancient cities of the Marsi, the only one to leave behind many traces is **Alba Fucens** (*open daily 8am until dusk*), near modern Albe, completely rebuilt after the 1915 earthquake (8km from Avezzano, and linked by ARPA bus, *t 0863 26561*). *Alba* was founded as a Roman colony in 300 BC to keep an eye on the area's tribes – hence the mighty walls. Ancient *Alba* occupies three hills, and its ruins intermingle with the ruins of medieval Alba. Much has been excavated, including the amphitheatre, the forum, the basilica, the weedy theatre, the baths and a section of the original Via Valeria. Near the amphitheatre is the well-preserved Romanesque church of **San Pietro** (*if no one's there, ask about the key at the bar near the entrance*), adorned with Cosmati work. The church was originally a temple of Diana, which the Romans once used as a prison – prisoners' graffiti can still be read on the walls.

Getting Around

As a major **rail** junction, and with bus services to most of the area, Sulmona is the best base for exploring; but bus and train connections are infrequent, so you have to be well-organized.

Buses run fairly frequently from L'Aquila to Avezzano, and from there to Pescasséroli, the administrative centre of the Abruzzo National Park. There's a direct early morning ARPA bus to Pescasséroli from Rome, which returns to Rome in the evening (mid-June–mid-Sept).

Spectacular **roads** include the SS5bis from L'Aquila to Celano, SS84 from Lanciano to Roccaraso, and SS83 from Pescina, near Celano, through the National Park.

Tourist Information

Tagliacozzo: Via Vittorio Veneto 6, t 0863 610 318.
Sulmona: Corso Ovidio 208, t 0864 53276.
Scanno: Piazza Santa Maria della Valle 12, t 0864 74317.
Roccaraso: Via Claudio Mori 1, t 0864 62210 (*open daily 9–1 and 4.30–6.30*).
National Park Visitors' Centre: Via Consultore 1, t 0863 91955 (*open daily 9–12 and 3–7*).

Where to Stay and Eat

Most hotels here only open in the summer and winter. Avezzano has the largest choice, many of them along the SS5.

Avezzano ✉ 67051

Dei Marsi, Via Cavour 79/b, t 0863 4601, f 0863 460 0100 (*moderate*). The best-value hotel in Avezzano, with modern, comfortable bedrooms and cosy common spaces.

Vecchi Sapori, Via Montello 3, t 0863 416 626 (*cheap*). A good, fairly priced restaurant with local specialities, including particularly fine pasta and lamb dishes, and fish on Tuesday and Friday.

Tagliacozzo ✉ 67069

★★★**Miramonti**, Via Variante 87, t 0863 6581, f 0863 6582 (*cheap*). Twenty-one comfortable rooms and a garden.

Sulmona ✉ 67039

★★★**Europa Park**, on SS17 (off Bivio Badia), just north of town, t 0864 251 260, f 0864 251 317 (*moderate*). Sulmona's largest and most comfortable hotel, with a bar and a good restaurant.

★**Italia**, Piazza San Tommaso 3, t/f 0864 52308 (*cheap*). Atmospheric and comfortable.

Italia, Piazza XX Settembre 22, t 0864 33070 (*moderate*). Restaurant of the same name. Prepares winning variations on traditional local cuisine: home-made pasta and lamb with rosemary. *Closed Mon.*

Clemente, Vico della Quercia 5, t 0864 52284 (*cheap*). Serves up home-made sausages and delicious local dishes: fresh pasta with lamb sauce, saffron or wild mushrooms, roast kid, and good desserts. *Closed Thurs, Christmas period and 10 days in July.*

Roccaraso ✉ 67037

★★★**Excelsior**, Via Roma 28, t/f 0864 602 351 (*moderate*). One of the classier hotels in the area. *Open mid-Dec–mid-Jan and April–Aug.*

Scanno ✉ 67038

★★★**Del Lago**, Viale del Lago 202, t 0864 74343, f 0864 74343 (*moderate*). A small, tranquil hotel with a garden in a lovely setting on the lake. *Open mid-Dec–mid-Jan and Mar–Oct.*

★★★**Margherita**, Via D. Tanturri 100, t 0864 74353 (*cheap*). Scanno hotels tend to be slightly more expensive than the surrounding area, but this one is good value.

Gli Archetti, Via Silla 8, t 0864 74645 (*moderate*). Offers refined old elegance, and dishes made from home-grown ingredients; try the grilled lamb with pears. *Closed Tues from Oct to May.*

Pescasséroli ✉ 67032

★★★★**Grand Hotel del Parco**, t 0863 912 745, f 0863 912 749 (*expensive*). The grandest hotel in the area, with a beautiful setting, a garden and a pool in summer. *Open Christmas–Easter and June–Sept.*

★★★**Il Pinguino**, Via Collacchi 2, t 0863 912 580, f 0863 910 449 (*moderate*). Another good choice in the national park, with rooms that are far too snug for a real penguin. *Full or half board only July–Aug.*

Tagliacozzo

To the west of Albe, **Tagliacozzo** is a pretty, ancient town on the slopes of Monte Bove, less than two hours by train from Rome on the Rome–Pescara route. Named after Thalia, the muse of theatre, it is known for the battle that took place on 12 August 1268, which ended the reign of the Swabians and heirs of Frederick II –. as described by Dante. The site is marked by the ruined church of **Santa Maria della Vittoria**, at **Scurcola Marsicana**, east of Tagliacozzo. In the town itself, the church of **San Francesco**, with a fine rose window and portal, contains the relics of Tommaso da Celano. Tagliacozzo's secular architecture is more interesting than its churches: the 14th-century **Palazzo Ducale** (*under restoration*), a grand building on a grand piazza, has a *loggia* on the first floor sheltering fine but damaged frescoes by Lorenzo da Viterbo. The quarter around the genteel old **Piazza dell'Obelisco**, with its Renaissance obelisk, has picturesque houses and peeling palaces from the 14th and 15th centuries.

Sulmona

South of the Via Valeria, **Sulmona**, in a green basin surrounded by mountains, was the capital of another obscure Italic tribe, the Paeligni, but is best remembered as the birthplace of Ovid (43 BC–AD 17), who is commemorated with a large 20th-century statue in Piazza XX Settembre. Much later Sulmona was made capital of the province created by Frederick II. It became a minor centre of learning and religion, home of the Celestine Order's main abbey, and of Pietro Angeleri, who lived in the hermitage of Monte Morrone before being brought down to L'Aquila and crowned Pope Celestine V (*see p.618*). In the early Renaissance its craftsmen were celebrated for their gold-work, although they have since learned a sweeter skill – what the Italians call *confetti*.

The main street, Corso Ovidio, holds Sulmona's loveliest monument, the church and palace of **Santa Maria Annunziata**, a Gothic and Renaissance ensemble begun in 1320. The three portals on the **palace** façade were done at different periods, but the result is as harmoniously sweet as confetti: the left one is finely carved florid Gothic, crowned by a statue of St Michael, while the middle portal is pure symmetrical Renaissance; the plain portal on the right was built last, in 1522. Doctors of the Church and saints stand sentry along the façade, above them runs an intricate ribbon frieze, and above that are three lacy Gothic windows. The palace's two small **museums** (*open Tues–Sun 9–1, Sat–Sun also 4–6.30*) contain traditional Abruzzese costumes, work of the

Confetti Nuts

To Italians *confetti* means the sweets covered in sugar of all kinds of colours that are given out to guests at a wedding. They have been a speciality of the Abrruzzo since the Middle Ages and, although the original *confetti* were sugared almonds, today they come in a variety of fillings that include chocolate or hazelnuts. The capital of *confetti* is Sulmona, where any number of shops in the historic centre sell confectionery made up to look like flowers or ornate gold and silver ornaments, and have lavish window displays to match. William di Carlo, which has its factory show-room near the station, reckons it is the oldest *confetti*-manufacturer in the town.

goldsmiths of Renaissance Sulmona, and sculpture and paintings from the 16th–18th centuries. The Baroque **church** façade was rebuilt after the 1703 earthquake, yet still complements the adjacent palace, where concerts are held in summer. Running through the centre of Sulmona is an unusual Gothic **aqueduct** (1256); it can be seen in huge Piazza Garibaldi, site of the 1474 **Fontana del Vecchio**, named after the jovial old man on top. Over the road stands the carved Romanesque portal of **San Francesco delle Scarpe** ('with shoes' because these Franciscans wore shoes instead of sandals); the rest tumbled an earthquake. Outside town, 5km towards Monte Morrone, are Roman ruins (a mosaic pavement), part of a **Temple of Hercules**, that locals refer to as 'Ovid's villa', though connections with the poet have been disproved.

Around Sulmona

There are picturesque hill towns near Sulmona, like **Pacentro**, 9km to the east, its lanes winding around the battlemented towers of the ruined **Castello Cantelmo**. Beyond Pacentro the SS487 heads seriously up into the rugged Maiella Mountains, and a few winding kilometres east, near Passo San Leonardo, reaches a T-junction where you can turn north to **Caramanico Terme** (a hill town spa) and the Via Valeria, or south past the **Campo di Giove**, a winter sports centre with a cablecar up the slopes of the Round Table (7,885ft), towards the dramatic SS84 and the Sangro Valley.

Pescocostanzo, Rivisondoli and Roccaraso (stops on the Sulmona–Isernia railway) are well-endowed with sports facilities. Charming **Pescocostanzo** once owed allegiance to Vittoria Colonna, poet and friend of Michelangelo, and made lace before it became a ski resort; its lovely **Collegiata di Santa Maria del Colle** (*open daily for services only*), has excellent wood carvings, dating back to the 11th century.

On the SS84 between Roccaraso and Lanciano (accessible by bus from either end), is **Taranta Peligna**, which has a new cablecar that rises up to what must be the most spectacular cave in Central Italy, the **Grotta del Cavallone** (4,674ft) (*open April–Sept; guided visits 1½ hrs; contact the Roccaraso tourist office; cablecar and adm exp*), used as a setting in D'Annunzio's play *La Figlia di Jorio*. The cave's name, the 'Big Horse', comes from the profile carved by nature on the wall at the grandiose entrance of the grotto: other rooms are adorned with stone flowers or lace, alabaster streaks that remind Italians of ham (in the 'Sala del Prosciutto') and fairies, while the 'Sala del Pantheon' is full of curious stalagmite monsters and deities.

Scanno

From Cocullo or Anversa degli Abruzzi, just west of Sulmona, the SS479 ascends the **Valle del Sagittario**, passing through the steep **Gole del Sagittario** and along the Lago di Scanno. High above the lake, **Scanno** is one of the most popular destinations in the Abruzzo, a picturesque place that fascinated 18th-century travellers who wondered at its customs and costumes, more reminiscent of Asia Minor than Italy. Even today the women of Scanno sometimes wear their traditional dress, with their turban-like head-dresses; the best time to see the costumes is on 14 August, when the folkloric Matrimonio di Scanno is celebrated. For magnificent views of the sunset, drive up the zigzagging road from here to Frattura, or take the chairlift up to **Monte Rotondo**.

Parco Nazionale d'Abruzzo

West of Cocullo is the SS83 for the **Parco Nazionale d'Abruzzo**. Founded in 1923 and enlarged in 1976, the national park covers 400 square kilometres of some of the loveliest scenery in the Apennines a paradise of flowery meadows and forests of beech, pine oak, ash, maple and yew, the last home of *ursus arctos marsicanus*, the brown Abruzzo bear, and the Abruzzo chamois; here too are Apennine lynxes, boars, wolves, badgers, red squirrels, eagles, falcons, woodpeckers, owls and many unusual species of songbirds, all protected by law from the enthusiastic Italian hunter.

After passing through the beautiful **Passo del Diavolo** ('Devil's Pass'), the road reaches the largest village in the park, **Pescasséroli**, birthplace of Benedetto Croce (1866–1952), the greatest Italian philosopher of the past two centuries.

The **national park visitors' centre** has trail maps and information on flora and fauna; also visit the small **museum** (*Viale Santa Lucia; open daily 10–1 and 3–7; adm*). A pleasant excursion from here even for non-committed hikers is the two-hour walk up to the **Valico di Monte Tranquillo**. In mid-summer and in winter you can also ride Pescasséroli's cablecar up to the summit of **Monte Vitelle**. Further south are **Opi** and **Barrea**, near the **Lago di Barrea** and the **Camosciara**, where the graceful chamois live.

Just outside the park the fine scenery continues around **Alfedena**, built on the site of the Samnite town of *Aufidena* – across the river you can see the ancient walls and necropolis. A 3km track also leads up from here to the lake of **Montagna Spaccata**.

Molise

Isolated, mountainous and even more sparsely populated than Abruzzo, **Molise** is one of the least-known regions of Italy. It belonged to the tenacious Samnites of old, and Italians still sometimes call it *Sanno*; at some point in the murky early Middle Ages it became the county of Molise and then, like the other Abruzzi, it was joined to the Kingdom of Naples. In the 14th and 15th centuries Slav and Albanian refugees from the Turkish invasion found homes here; their languages contributed to the great variety of regional dialects; there are still villages unable to understand one another today. Although an improved network of roads has ended most of Molise's isolation, the rugged, mountainous terrain makes the going slow no matter how you travel. But it's just as well, for it is a region to drink in slowly, to sip instead of gulp down. This is very much backwoods Italy; the biggest events in the region are village rodeos, and the most famous attractions are ancient remains. However, unlike so much of Italy, the constant glare of flashbulbs has not made Molise fade into a picture of itself; you will not recognize much, if any, of it. In its freshness, it is one of Italy's last frontiers.

Isernia

Heading down the SS17 from Sulmona and Castel di Sangro, you enter the dismal little capital of **Isernia**. This was the Samnite town of *Aesernium*, where the Italic tribes either first united against Rome, or fled after the Romans captured their capital

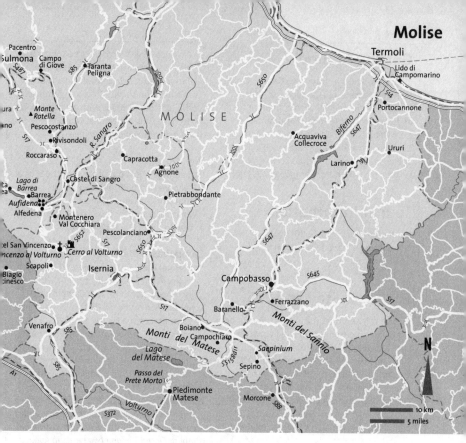

of *Corfinium* in the Social Wars – at any rate Isernia modestly puts forth a claim of being 'the first capital of Italy', although even that boast pales before the fame of its onions (fêted every 28–29 June) and its lace. Isernia has been severely damaged by earthquakes – the last of them in 1984 – and was badly bombed in 1943, so there is little to see of its old town other than the 14th-century **Fontana Fraterna**, which has somehow survived. It was built using Roman masonry and bears the inscription AE PONT – which led to a popular belief that *Aesernium* gave the world Pontius Pilate.

Today the town's main attraction is much much older – a Palaeolithic village that was uncovered in 1979. At one million years old this is the most ancient evidence of human life yet found in Europe. No human remains were found, but there are relics such as weapons, fireplaces and face paint, and plenty of remains of elephant, deer, rhinoceros, bison, bear and hippopotamus ancestors. They are well presented in the **Museo Nazionale Santa Maria delle Monache** (*Corso Marcello 48, t 0865 415 179; open daily 8.30am–7.30pm; adm*). Excavations are still under way at the site itself, which can also be visited (*t 0865 413 526; open Mon–Fri from 9am to sunset*).

North of Isernia

The *comuni* in the high altitudes north of Isernia have been compared to the isolated villages of Tibet, each perched on its lonely hilltop. Highest in all the Apennines at 4,661ft is **Capracotta**, a village immersed in mountain pastures, often

Getting Around

Isernia is linked by **train** with Naples, Rome, Sulmona, Pescara and Campobasso; other trains pass through Benevento, then continue on to the coast at Termoli, via Larino. **Buses** – from Naples, Rome, Cassino and Vasto to Campobasso and Isernia – are much quicker, and less aggravating. The **bus** service for villages, from Isernia or Campobasso, is fair.

Tourist Information

Isernia: Via Farinacci 9, **t** 0865 3992.
Campobasso: Piazza della Vittoria 14, **t** 0874 415 662.

Where to Stay and Eat

The few hotels that grace Molise tend to be either new and sterile, or old and down-at-heel. At table, the Molisani are a solidly old-fashioned and spicy crew, favouring dishes like stuffed lamb heads (*testine d'agnello*), kid tripe, a hillbilly pizza topped with greens and boiled pork (*pizza con le foglie*), smelly mountain cheese and *polenta* with red beans, olive oil, hot peppers and garlic (*polenta maritata*).

Isernia ✉ 86170

★★★**La Tequila**, Via G. Tedeschi 85, **t/f** 0865 412 345 (*moderate*). Just outside the centre in the new San Lazzaro neighbourhood.
Taverna Maresca, Corso Marcelli 186, **t** 0865 3976 (*cheap*). A fine old restaurant in the old quarter. *Closed Sun, two weeks in Aug, one week at Christmas, and Easter Monday.*

Capracotta ✉ 86082

★**Montecampo**, Contrada Santa Lucia, **t** 0865 949 128 (*cheap*). Up in the mountains and out of the way; a basic but pleasant 13-room hotel with a restaurant.

Agnone ✉ 86061

★★★**Sammartino**, Largo P. Micca 44, **t/f** 0865 78239 (*cheap*). A comfortable hotel with an excellent restaurant (*moderate*), **t** 0865 77577, where you can dine on first-rate grilled meat, including Molise's succulent baby lamb.

Da Casciano, Viale Marconi 29, **t** 0865 77511 (*moderate*). You can taste a rare dish, the lamb *sotto la coppa* (cooked under the ashes), and finish with the unforgettable *ostie*, local pastry made with walnuts, chocolate, honey and wine must. *Closed in Nov and Tues; open daily in summer.*

Venafro

Il Quadrifoglio, just out of town on the SS85 at Madonnella, **t** 0865 909 886 (*cheap*). Surprisingly, has the freshest of seafood – Venafro is a stop for the seafood trucks from the Adriatic to Rome. *Open daily.*

Campobasso ✉ 86100

★★★★**Hotel Roxy**, Piazza Savoia 7, **t/f** 0874 411 541 (*moderate*). Plush and modern, with a discotheque for those wild Campobassani nights. *Disco closed July-Sept.*
★★★**Skanderbeg**, Via Novelli 3, **t** 0874 413 341, **f** 0874 416 340 (*moderate*). Modern comforts with touches of Molise tradition.
★★**Tricolore**, Via San Giovanni in Golfo 112, **t** 0874 63190 (*cheap*). A small family-run hotel in one of the prettier parts of town.
Aciniello, Via Torino 4, **t** 0874 94001 (*cheap*). Simple but genuine in its atmosphere and cuisine, offering dishes like *pizza rustica* and rabbit. *Closed Sun and two weeks in Aug.*
Vecchia Trattoria da Tonino, Corso Vittorio Emanuele II 8, **t** 0874 415 200 (*moderate*). More refined and less strictly local; the wine list includes some of the finest Molise labels. *Closed Sun–Mon and last week of July.*
Da Emilio, Piazza Spenzieri 18, **t** 0874 416 576 (*moderate*). One of the best restaurants in the region, in Ferrazzano. You can dine on meals with a delightful Emilia-Romagna touch out on the terrace. *Closed Tues, last two weeks of Jan and first two weeks of July.*

Larino

★★★**Campitelli Uno**, Via Mazzini 9 (near the amphitheatre), **t** 0874 822 666, **f** 0874 822 339 (*cheap*). There's not much choice in Larino: the 'Uno' is modern and functional, with a good restaurant, **t** 0874 822 339. *Hotel open June-Sept; restaurant daily all year.*
★★★**Campitelli Due**, Via San Benedetto 1, **t** 0874 823 541, **f** 0874 822 339 (*moderate*). The 'Due' has better service. *Open all year.*

buried under banks of snow in winter; residents sometimes have to use their upper-floor windows as doors – a fitting place for the first Italian ski club, founded in 1914.

Nearby **Agnone**, the 'Athens of the Samnites', has been known for the past thousand years for its bells. One factory, the **Marinelli Pontifical Foundry**, still survives – the oldest in Italy, supplier to the Vatican. Bells are cast according to the ancient formula; while the molten bronze is being poured into the mould a priest is on hand to chant the medieval litanies that guarantee a clear-toned bell. You can see the foundry at work and visit its small museum at Via d'Onofrio 14 (*t 0865 78235; guided tours of the foundry in Italian Mon-Sat at midday and 4pm, Sun by appointment only; adm*). Besides bells, Agnone is known for its coppersmiths, whose workshops line the main streets of town; also be sure to note the Romanesque portal on the **cathedral**.

South of Agnone, **Pietrabbondante** has some of the most extensive **Samnite ruins** (*t 0865 76130; open Mon–Tues 8am–sunset, Wed–Sun 8–1; adm*) unearthed. The site was a religious sanctuary and includes a Greek theatre and a couple of temples, built in the 2nd century BC. The ruins are in a green field filled with flowers. **Pescolanciano**, on the way back towards Isernia, is dominated by its picturesque **Castello d'Alessandro**, founded in the 13th century and topped in later years by a pretty arcade.

West of Isernia

Spaghetti Western fans in Molise in mid-August can whoop it up at an Italian 'rodeo' at **Montenero Val Cocchiara**, northwest of Isernia; as usual in Italy, food is as much of an attraction as the events, and in this case it's barbecues. In the pre-cowboy days of the Lombards, the Benedictines built the abbey of **San Vincenzo al Volturno** to the south near **Castel San Vincenzo**. Often altered, damaged and rebuilt, the abbey was last restored in the 1950s; the **Crypt of San Lorenzo** managed to escape the assorted disasters and preserves 11th-century frescoes. The complex is now run by American cloistered nuns (*you can visit the church from 7.30am–dusk, and the crypt by appointment; t 0328 342 2393 or t 0865 955 246*).

The most impressive castle in Molise, **Cerro al Volturno** (*interior closed to the public*) was built by the same Benedictines in the 10th century, but was rebuilt at the end of the 15th century. Appearing to grow organically out of a massive rock, the castle is inaccessible except by a narrow path; in the 1920s the supporting cement bulwarks on the hill were added, all impressive enough to star on a L200 stamp. There aren't many souvenirs to buy in Cerro, but further south, in **Scapoli**, you can visit the *zampogna* (bagpipe) market in the last week of July, and choose your goat-bellied instrument from among the olive- and cherry-wood models on display. The bagpipe has a long (and still living) tradition among the shepherds of the Molise; they still take them down to play in the streets of Rome and Naples for Christmas. The market also features pipes from Scotland, Sardinia, Hungary and other regions and countries. Alternatively, you can explore the world of bagpipes inside the **Museo della Zampogna** on the edge of town (*t 0865 954 002; open Tues-Sun 9.45–1 and 3.40–7*).

On the road south towards Campania, **Venafro** was made famous by Horace for its olive oil. A little run down, it is one of the most interesting towns in Molise. Cyclopean walls run along the road into town, and in the Middle Ages the Roman amphitheatre was turned into an oval piazza and the arcades into the front doors of the houses. Portable remains of Roman *Venafrum* are now in the **Museo Archeologico** (*t 0865 900 742; open daily 8.15–7.40; adm*) in the former convent of Santa Chiara. The **Annunziata** church, has preserved its Romanesque interior, and contains 15th-century English alabasters. Venafro's **castle** (14th–16th-centuries) – empty inside but with a fabulous view of the town below – and the 15th-century fortified ducal **Palazzo Caracciolo** are under restoration, but the castle is open to visitors in the morning *(Tues–Fri)*.

The Matese

South of Isernia and Campobasso is a curve of snow-swept peaks and forests called the **Matese**, of which the southern half lies in Campania. Few Italians, much less foreigners, penetrate its quiet villages, where women in traditional dress sit out in the streets over their round *tomboli* making delicate lace. The lakes of the Matese are full of waterfowl, its streams brim with fish, and its forests are home to wildcats, wolves and other creatures seldom seen in Italy; its glens produce *funghi porcini* by the ton.

The scenery is spectacular, especially around the largest of the lakes, the **Lago del Matese**, with its resort of **Piedimonte Matese**, both in Campania. The road back to Molise (SS158dir) runs through the **Passo del Prete Morto** ('Dead Priest Pass'). The northern slopes of the Matese are equally lovely, with a quality of light that gives **Campochiaro** its name. This medieval village retains its walls and tower, and a huge Samnite temple complex has been unearthed nearby. Just to the west is the lofty little town of **Boiano**, the former Samnite stronghold of *Bovianum*. The upper part of town, called Cività, retains Megalithic-era walls and the ruins of a Lombard castle. The views are great – fabulous if you're up to a stiff two-hour climb to the summit of **Monte la Gallinola** (6,307ft) – on a clear day you can see as far as the Bay of Naples.

Saepinum

In 295 BC the Samnite city of *Saipins* was laid waste by the Romans. The inhabitants were either killed or taken into slavery, and Saipins was rebuilt as a Roman colony called *Saepinum*. As a quiet provincial town it managed to avoid most of history until the 9th century, when the Saracens destroyed it. Later in the Middle Ages, when times were surer, the site was resettled, two miles uphill from the ruins – now modern **Sepino** – and old *Saepinum* was slowly covered by the dust of the ages and quarried here and there for its stone. Dilettantes began excavating the ancient town in the 18th century, and nowadays groups of archaeologists come to uncover more of it every summer. A bus runs from Campobasso to Sepino roughly every two hours, but be warned that only one bus a day stops at the *area archeologica*, and it's a 2.5km walk back to modern Sepino to catch the return bus to Campobasso *(t 0874 790 848)*.

The charm of *Saepinum* comes partly from its remote and lovely setting in the Matese, making it one of the most evocative Roman sites in all Italy – the best example of a small provincial city. In *Saepinum* there is very little marble, no plush villas as in Pompeii and Herculaneum, but neither are there any modern intrusions beyond a few farmhouses, making use of a column here, an architrave there; it is an ancient Anytown in the empire, in its layout and amenities a miniature version of nearly every colony founded by Rome.

The defensive walls encompassing *Saepinum*, built in diamond-patterned *opus reticulatum*, are more than 1km long and defended by 27 bastions – the best preserved of which, more than 35ft high, stands near the theatre. Four gates lead into the central axis of the city. From the car park at **Porta di Terravecchia** you pass through the walls on the *cardus maximus*. This street retains its original paving stones as you approach the central crossroads with the *decumanus*, the main street. Here you'll find the forum and civic buildings. The slender Ionic columns on one corner belonged to the *basilica*, the main meeting place and law courts of a Roman city, with its podium for orators and lawyers. Just off it is an octagonal *atrium*, surrounded by the foundations of shop counters – *Saepinum's* central market. Across from the *forum* itself on the *decumanus* are, first, on the corner, the *comitium* (elections office), the *curia* (town hall), a temple, believed to have been dedicated to the cult of an emperor, the *terme* (baths) and the well-preserved Griffon fountain.

The *decumanus* continues past a house called the **Casa dell'Impluvio Sannitico** – its atrium containing a fountain and Samnite-style *impluvium* (container to collect rain water) with an inscription in Oscan, the pre-Roman language of the region – to the **Porta di Benevento**, marked by a figure of Mars. Beyond the gate stands a funeral monument, with its inscriptions lauding the virtues of the deceased Caius Ennius Marso, one of the town's leading citizens.

In the opposite direction the *decumanus* passes through *Saepinum's* main commercial district, lined with shops, taverns and private residences. It ends at the most complete gate, the impressive **Porta Boiano**, with steps to the top for an excellent view of the excavations. Figures of prisoners (or slaves?) stand on plinths on either side, and its inscription informs us that the Emperor Tiberius and his brother Drusus paid for the walls. Beyond this gate is a monumental **mausoleum of Numisio Ligure**. Along the walls are the remains of a private bath complex; beyond is the well-preserved **theatre** (*open daily 8am to sunset*), with a crescent of medieval farmhouses that were built into the upper *cavea*; in its heyday the theatre seated 3,000 spectators. The stage is now occupied by another farmhouse, which contains an interesting **museum** (*currently closed for restoration, call Isernia tourist office t 0865 3992*).

Campobasso

The capital of the County of Molise, **Campobasso** was once best known for its engraved cutlery – its knives, scissors and razors are still highly regarded – but is now better known as the site of the National School for Carabinieri and for its June procession, the *Sagra dei Misteri di Corpus Domini*. In the 17th century Campobasso's old Corpus Domini processions were banned by the bishop for making spectators laugh; and they stayed banned until 1740, when a local sculptor named Di Zinno came up with the idea of building metal contraptions to support real people in the soaring

Baroque postures of the angels and saints he carved for churches. The bishop accepted these as serious augmenters of the faith, and indeed they are, for it seems as if faith alone is holding up the bevy of six-year-old angels and saints suspended on the 13 floats or 'Mysteries' that are solemnly paraded through the streets to the accompaniment of the local bands. A long-planned **museum of Samnite antiquities** (*Via Chiarizia 12, t 0874 412 265; open daily 9–7*) has finally opened and is well worth a look. The older, upper part of town has a couple of Romanesque churches, **San Giorgio** and **San Leonardo**, and the **Castello Monforte** (now a weather station) on top.

From Campobasso buses head out to scenic villages nearby, like **Ferrazzano**, with a castle and belvedere, and **Baranello**, an ancient town, the heir of the Samnite *Vairanum*. Baranello has a little **Museo Civico** (*open Mon–Sat 8–2; call office of comune,t 0874 460 406, to arrange visit*) containing Samnite artefacts, 18th-century Neapolitan kitsch paintings and other *objets d'art*. Nearby, on the River Biferno, you can watch a water wheel grind the grains that go into Molise's folksy cuisine.

Larino

Between Campobasso and Térmoli on the coast, the small town of Larino – the Samnite *Larinum* – is prettily located amid hills of olive groves. The most important monument here, the **cathedral**, was built in 1319 and embellished with an ornate portal in its Puglian-style façade; the nearby **church of San Francesco** has some good 18th-century frescoes. Near the cathedral take a look inside the **museum of Palazzo Comunale** (*open Mon–Fri 9–1*), three rooms which house beautiful Roman polychrome mosaics from the 2nd and 3rd century AD. A larger collection of art and artefacts is waiting to be put on display in Villa Zappone.

Meanwhile the *Ara Frentana*, a cylindrical Roman altar, is visible by the road leading to the train station. This was once the centre of the ancient Samnite town; its ruined amphitheatre hosts concerts, plays and other events in summer. Between 25 May and 27 May, Larino holds a religious festival, the *Festa di San Pardo*, with a procession of 150 finely decorated ox carts. On the evening of the 25th the carts go from the cathedral to a Palaeo-Christian basilica dedicated to the three martyrs Primiano, Siriano and Cassio, to bring the statue of Primiano back to the cathedral for a late-night mass. The spectacle is at its best during the two-kilometre return trip, as the carts are escorted by thousands of people bearing blazing torches.

Albanian and Slavic Villages

In the district around Larino there are several diehard communities of Albanians and Slavs, who still maintain their language, traditions and festivals. **Ururi**, west of Larino, is an Albanian town, as is **Portocannone**, which conserves in its Romanesque church an icon of the Madonna of Constantinople, brought over by settlers. The most interesting of the Slavic villages is **Acquaviva Collecroce**, where a dialect called 'Stokavo' is spoken. In the campanile of the church of **Santa Maria Esther** there is a medieval curiosity: a stone carved with the palindromic magic square with a bastard-Latin inscription, an ancient charm.

Tuscany

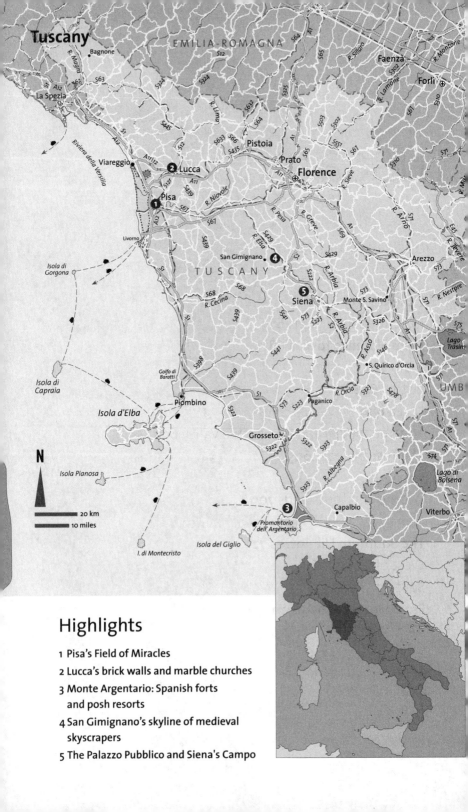

Tuscany

EMILIA-ROMAGNA

Bagnone

La Spezia

Riviera della Versilia

Viareggio

2 Lucca

1 Pisa

Livorno

Isola di
Gorgona

TUSCANY

San Gimignano **4**

Faenza

Forlì

Pistoia

Prato

Florence

Siena **5**

Monte S. Savino

Arezzo

Isola di
Capraia

Golfo di
Baratti

Piombino

Isola d'Elba

N

Isola Pianosa

20 km

10 miles

Grosseto

Paganico

S. Quirico d'Orcia

Lago
Trasim

UMB

Lago di
Bolsena

3

Promontorio
dell'Argentario

Capalbio

Viterbo

Isola del Giglio

I. di Montecristo

Highlights

1 Pisa's Field of Miracles
2 Lucca's brick walls and marble churches
3 Monte Argentario: Spanish forts
  and posh resorts
4 San Gimignano's skyline of medieval
  skyscrapers
5 The Palazzo Pubblico and Siena's Campo

No region could be more essentially Italian. Its Renaissance culture and art became the whole of Italy's, and its dialect, as refined by Dante, cast a hundred other dialects into the shadows to become the Italian language. Nevertheless, Tuscany seems to stand a bit aloof from the rest of the nation; it keeps its own counsel, never changes its ways, and faces the world with a Mona Lisa smile that has proved irresistible to northerners since the days of Shelley and Browning.

Today Britons, Dutchmen, Germans and Americans jostle each year for the privilege of paying a few million lire for a month in a classic Tuscan farmhouse, with a view over a charmed, civilized landscape of cypresses and parasol pines, orderly rows of vines and olives, and a chapel on the hill with a quattrocento fresco. In Florence and the other cities, they stand in queues like refugees, waiting to enter the churches and museums that are the shrines of Tuscan art.

For a province that has contributed so much to western civilization since the Middle Ages, Tuscany's career remains slightly mysterious. Some have attempted to credit its cultural prominence to an inheritance from the ancient Etruscans, but most of modern Tuscany was never more than provincial throughout Etruscan and Roman times. Out of the Dark Ages, inexplicably, new centres of learning and art appeared, first in Pisa and Florence, and then in a dozen other towns, inaugurating a cultural Renaissance that really began as early as the 1100s.

As abruptly as it began, this brilliant age was extinguished in the 16th century, but it left behind a new province of Europe, finished, solid and well formed. Tuscany can be excused a little complacency. Though prosperous and enlightened, fully a part of modern Italy today, the region for centuries has seemed perfectly content to let the currents of culture and innovation flow elsewhere. There's no sense in painting when anything new would have to hang next to Da Vincis and Botticellis, no incentive to build in a city full of churches and palaces by the medieval masters. After the wave of bad taste that brought the Renaissance to a close, Tuscany was shamed into an introspection and cultural conservatism of almost Chinese proportions.

Of course these centuries, during which Tuscany has quietly cultivated its own garden, have not been without some advantages. Its cities and their art treasures have been preserved with loving care. So has the countryside; if anything the last few hundred years have emphasized the frugal, hard-working side of the Tuscan character, the side that longs for the rural life, counts its pennies, and finds tripe with chickpeas a perfectly satisfying repast. All this at times makes a striking contrast with the motorways, the new industry around the cities, and the hordes of tourists descending on Florence, Pisa and Siena.

Florence

Venice, they say, moves one to dream a bit; Rome to contemplate the endless panorama of popes and Caesars; Naples convinces you that all is vanity. Florence (Firenze) on the other hand, a town long famed for good common sense and healthy scepticism, is different: it will not tempt you to easy conclusions – it is as romantic as a reference library. Florence, they say, moves one to *argue*.

So let's begin. Most writers have always assumed a certain point of view. You may think Florence is a museum city, they'll tell you, but you'll be wrong. Florence on the contrary is a thriving, progressive town that refuses to live in the past, insisting on earning its own way in the 20th century. Once it made Galileo's telescope, and today it still exports precision optical instruments. In the 1400s, it led Europe in fashion as well as art; today its busy seamstresses on back streets do much of the work for the designers in Milan. This argument is nice, but unfortunately untrue; despite its noise, ice cream, light industry and horrendous traffic, Florence is a museum city, and if you don't care to look at pictures, you'd do better just to stay on the train. But what a museum city it is! Florence's collections easily surpass those of any other Italian city, and just from the odd bits in the back rooms its curators are able to mount a score of blockbuster special exhibitions each year. Most impressive of all is the fact that nearly all the art in them was made by the Florentines themselves, testimony to the city's position during two centuries as the great innovator of Western culture.

History

The Etruscans, who founded Florence perhaps as early as 1000 BC, were typically coy about providing any further details; the city's early history remains a puzzle. Like so many cities, however, Florence seems to begin with a bridge. Dante and many other writers commonly invoke the *marzocco*, the battered ancient icon that sat in the middle of the Ponte Vecchio and any number of bridges that preceded it until a flood swept it away in the 14th century. Often pictured as a lion (like the replacement for the original made by Donatello, now on display in the Bargello Museum), the *marzocco* may really have been a cult image of the god Mars. Nothing could be more fitting, for in the centuries of its greatness Florence was a town full of trouble.

The city's apprenticeship in strife came during the Italian wars of the 4th–2nd centuries BC, when Rome was consolidating its hold on the peninsula. Florence seems to have chosen the wrong side. Sulla razed it to the ground during the Social Wars, and the town struggled back only gradually. Julius Caesar helped by planting a colony of veterans here in 59 BC. Roman Florence prospered, trading in the whole Empire. Its street plan survives in the neat rectangle of streets at the city's core. The town had an impressive forum right in the middle, at what is now Piazza della Repubblica.

If almost nothing remains from Roman times, it is only because Florence has been continuously occupied ever since, its centre constantly replanned and rebuilt. There were some hard times, especially during the Greek–Gothic wars of the 6th century and the Lombard occupation, but the city regained importance in the time of Charlemagne, becoming for a while the seat of the 'march' of Tuscany. Here, in what must have been one of the most fascinating eras of the city's history, once again we are left without much information. Florence, for whatever reason, was one of the first inland cities to regain its balance after the fall of the Empire. During the Dark Ages the city was already beginning to develop the free institutions of the later republic, and establishing the trading connections that were later to make it the merchant capital of Europe. About 1115, on the death of the famous Countess Matilda of Tuscany, Florence became a self-governing *comune*.

The Florentine Republic

From the beginning, circumstances forced the city into an aggressive posture against enemies within and outside its walls. Florence waged constant war against the extortionist petty nobles of the hinterlands, razing their castles and forcing them to live in the city. As an important Guelph stronghold, Florence constantly got itself into trouble with the emperors, as well as with Ghibelline Pisa, Pistoia, and Siena, towns that were to become its sworn enemies. In its darkest hour, after the crushing defeat at Montaperti in 1260, the Sienese almost succeeded in convincing their allies to bury Florence. A good sack would have been fun; Florence by the mid-13th century was possibly the richest banking and trading centre anywhere, and its gold florin had become a recognized currency across Europe.

In truth, Florence had no need of outside enemies. All through its history, the city did its level best to destroy itself. Guelph fought Ghibelline with impressive rancour, and when there were no Ghibellines left the Guelphs split into factions called the Blacks and Whites and began murdering each other. In a different dimension, the city found different causes of civil strife in the class struggles between the *popolo grosso* – the 'fat commons' or wealthy merchant class – and the members of the poorer guilds. Playing one side against the other was the newly urbanized nobility. They brought their gangster habits to town with them, turning Florence into a forest of tall brick tower-fortresses and carrying on bloody feuds in the streets that the city officials were helpless to stop. No historian has ever been able to explain how medieval Florence avoided committing suicide altogether. But despite all the troubles, this was the era of Dante (d. 1321, in political exile in Ravenna) and Giotto (d. 1337), the beginning of Florence's cultural golden age. Banking and the manufacture of wool (the leading commodity in the pre-industrial economy) were booming, and the florins kept rolling in no matter which faction was on top.

In 1282, and again in 1293, Florence tried to clean up its violent and corrupt government by a series of reforms; the Ordinamenti della Giustizia finally excluded the nobles from politics. It didn't work for long. Political strife continued through the 14th century, along with eternal wars with Lucca, Pisa and Siena, and novel catastrophes. In 1339 Edward III of England repudiated his enormous foreign debt and Florence's two largest banks, the Bardi and Peruzzi, went bust. Plagues and famines dominated the 1340s; the plague of 1348, the Black Death, killed three-fifths of the population (and provided the frame story for Boccaccio's *Decameron*). The nobles and merchants took advantage of the situation to establish tight boss rule. Their Guelph Party building is on Via Porta Rossa, where the spoils were divided – the original Tammany Hall. A genuine revolution in 1378 among the *ciompi*, the wool trade proletariat, might have succeeded if its leaders had been half as devious and ruthless as their opponents.

Florence's continuing good luck again saw it through, however, and prosperity gradually returned after 1400. In 1406 Pisa was finally conquered, giving Florence a sea port. Florentine armies bested the Visconti of Milan twice, and once (1410) even occupied Rome. At the dawn of the Renaissance not only Florence's artists, scholars and scientists were making innovations – the city government in the 1420s and '30s invented the progressive income tax and the national debt.

The Rise of the Medici

Although they are said to have begun as pharmacists (*medici*), by 1400 the House of Medici was the biggest merchant concern in Florence. With the resources of the Medici Bank behind him, Cosimo de' Medici installed himself as the city's political godfather, coercing or buying off the various interests and factions. In 1469 his grandson Lorenzo inherited the job, presiding over the greatest days of the Renaissance and a sustained stretch of peace and prosperity. Opposition, squashed originally by Cosimo, stayed squashed under Lorenzo. His military campaigns proved successful on the whole, and his impressive propaganda machine gave him an exaggerated reputation as a philosopher-king and patron of the arts. Lorenzo almost ruined the Medici Bank through neglect, but then made up his losses from public funds. His personal tastes in art seem to have been limited to knick-knacks, big jewels and antique bronzes, but his real hobby was nepotism. His son Giovanni, later to be made Pope Leo X at the age of 38, became a cardinal at 14.

Two years after Lorenzo's death, the wealthy classes of Florence finally succeeded in ending Medici rule when they exiled Lorenzo's weak son and successor, Piero, in 1494. The republic was restored, but soon came under the influence of a remarkable Dominican demagogue, Girolamo Savonarola. Thundering out a fierce fundamentalist line, his preaching resulted in the famous 1497 'Bonfire of Vanities' on the Piazza della Signoria, when the people collected their paintings, fancy clothes, carnival masks and books and put them to the flame (a Venetian merchant offered instead to buy the whole lot from them, but the Florentines hurriedly sketched a portrait of him too, and threw it on the pyre). But Savonarola was more than a ridiculous prude. His idealistic republicanism resulted in some real democratic reforms for the new government, and his emphasis on morals provided a much needed purgative after the reigning depravity of the previous 200 years. The friar reserved his strongest blasts, however, for the corruption of the Church; not a bad idea in the time of Alexander VI, the Borgia pope. When Savonarola's opponents, the Arrabbiati ('Infuriated'), beat his supporters, the Piagnoni ('snivellers'), in the 1498 elections, the way was clear for Alexander to order the friar's execution. Savonarola burned on 22 May 1498, on the same spot where the 'Bonfire of Vanities' had been held, and his ashes were thrown in the Arno.

The Medici returned in 1512, thanks to Pope Julius II and his Spanish troops. The Spaniards' exemplary sack of Prato, with remarkable atrocities, was intended as a lesson to the Florentines. It had the desired effect, and Lorenzo's nephew Giuliano de' Medici was able to re-enter the city. When Giuliano was elected Pope Clement VII in 1523 he attempted to continue running the city at a distance, but yet another Medici expulsion would take place after his humiliation in the sack of Rome in 1527, followed by the founding of the last Florentine republic.

By now Florentine politics had become a death struggle between an entire city and a single family; in the end the Medici would prove to have the stronger will. The last republic lived nervously in an atmosphere of revolutionary apocalypse; meanwhile Clement intrigued with the Spaniards for his return. An imperial army arrived in 1530 to besiege the city and, despite heroic, last-ditch resistance, Florence had to capitulate when its commander sold out to the Pope and turned his guns on the city itself. In 1532 the Medici broke the terms of the surrender agreement by abolishing all self-government, obtaining the title of Grand Dukes of Tuscany from Emperor Charles V.

To all intents and purposes Florentine history ends here. Cosimo I Medici (d. 1574) ruled over a state that declined rapidly into a provincial backwater. When the last Medici, fat Gian Gastone, died in 1737, the powers of Europe gave the duchy to the House of Lorraine. With the rest of Tuscany, Florence was annexed to Piedmont-Sardinia in 1859, and from 1865 to 1870 it served as the capital of united Italy.

Today, despite repeated attempts to diversify the local economy through the creation of new industrial areas on the outskirts, Florence largely lives on the sheer weight of its past creativity. It suffered badly in the Second World War, when the retreating German army blew up all the bridges over the Arno except the Ponte Vecchio, and destroyed many medieval buildings along the river's edge. Still worse damage was caused by the great floods of November 1966, which left several dead and many buildings and artworks in need of restoration work that is still continuing today. The most recent damage to be inflicted on the city came in May 1993, when a bomb – planted by the Mafia – exploded near the Uffizi, killing the family of a caretaker, destroying a Renaissance library and substantially damaging parts of the Uffizi itself, particularly the Vasari corridor. The perpetrators were tried in 1998 and 14 life sentences were given, including the conviction of Toto Riina, the 'Boss of Bosses'.

Florentine Art

Under the assault of historians and critics over the last two centuries 'Renaissance' has become such a vague and controversial word as to be nearly useless. Nevertheless, however you choose to interpret this rebirth of the arts, and whatever dates you assign it, Florence inescapably takes the credit for initiating it. This is no small claim. Combining art, science and humanist scholarship into a visual revolution that often seemed pure sorcery to their contemporaries, a handful of Florentine geniuses taught the Western eye a new way of seeing. Perspective seems a simple enough trick to us now, but its discovery determined everything that followed, not only in art but in science and philosophy as well.

Florence in its centuries of brilliance accomplished more than any city, ever – far more than Athens in its classical age. The city's talents showed early, with the construction of the famous Baptistry, perhaps as early as 700. From the start Florence showed a remarkable adherence to the traditions of antiquity. New directions in architecture – the Romanesque after the year 1000 – had little effect; what passed for it in Florence was a unique style, evolved by a self-confident city that probably believed it was accurately restoring the grand manner of the Roman world. This new architecture (see the Baptistry, San Miniato, Santa Maria Novella), based on elegantly simple geometry with richly inlaid marble façades and pavements, was utterly unlike even the creations of nearby Pisa and Siena, and began a continuity of style that would reach its climax with the work of **Brunelleschi** and **Alberti** in the 15th century.

Likewise in painting and sculpture, Florentines made an early departure from Byzantine-influenced forms, and avoided the International Gothic style that thrived so well in Siena. Vasari's famous *Lives of the Artists* (1547) lays down the canon of Florentine artists, the foundation of all subsequent art criticism. It begins with **Cimabue** (*c.* 1240–1302), who according to Vasari first began to draw away from Byzantine stylization towards a more 'natural' way of painting. Cimabue found his greatest pupil **Giotto** (1266–1337) as a young shepherd boy, chalk-sketching sheep on a piece of slate. Brought to Florence, Giotto soon eclipsed his master's fame (artistic celebrity being another recent Florentine invention) and achieved the greatest advances on the road to the new painting, a plain, idiosyncratic approach that avoided Gothic prettiness while exploring new ideas in composition and expressing psychological depth in his subjects. Even more importantly Giotto, through his intuitive grasp of perspective, was able to go further than any previous artist in representing his subjects as actual figures in space. In a sense Giotto invented space; it was this, despite his often awkward and graceless draughtsmanship, that so astounded his contemporaries.

Vasari, for reasons of his own, neglected the artists of the Florentine trecento, and many critics have tended to follow slavishly – a great affront to the master artist and architect **Andrea Orcagna** (d. 1368; works include the Loggia dei Lanzi and the Orsanmichele tabernacle) and others including **Taddeo** and **Agnolo Gaddi** (d. 1366 and 1396) whose frescoes can be compared to Giotto's at Santa Croce.

The Quattrocento

The next turn in the story, what scholars self-assuredly used to call the 'Early Renaissance', comes with the careers of two geniuses who happened to be good friends. **Donatello** (1386–1466), the greatest sculptor since the ancient Greeks, inspired a new generation of not only sculptors but also painters to explore new horizons in portraiture and three-dimensional representation. **Brunelleschi** (1377–1446), neglecting his considerable talents in sculpture for architecture and science, not only built the majestic cathedral dome, but threw the Pandora's box of perspective wide open by mathematically codifying the principles of foreshortening.

The new science of painting occasioned an explosion of talent unequalled before or since, as a score of masters, most of them Florentine by birth, each followed the dictates of his own genius to create a range of themes and styles hardly believable for one single city in a few short decades of its life. To mention only the most prominent: **Lorenzo Ghiberti** (d. 1455), famous for the bronze doors of the Baptistry; **Masaccio** (d. 1428), the eccentric prodigy much copied by later artists, best represented by his naturalistic frescoes in Santa Maria del Carmine and Santa Maria Novella; **Domenico Ghirlandaio** (d. 1494), Michelangelo's teacher and another master of detailed frescoes; **Fra Angelico** (d. 1455), the most spiritual, and most visionary of them all, the painter of the Annunciation at San Marco; **Paolo Uccello** (d. 1475), one of the most provocative of all artists, who according to Vasari drove himself bats with too-long contemplation of perspective and the newly discovered vacuum of empty space; **Benozzo Gozzoli** (d. 1497), a happier soul, best known for the springtime *Procession of the Magi* in the Medici Palace; **Luca Della Robbia** (d. 1482), greatest of a family of sculptors, famous for the cantoria of the Cathedral Museum and exquisite blue and white terracottas all over Tuscany; **Antonio Pollaiuolo** (d. 1498), an engraver and sculptor with a nervously perfect line; **Fra Filippo Lippi** (d. 1469), who ran off with a brown-eyed nun to produce **Filippino Lippi** (d. 1504) – both of them exceptional painters and sticklers for detail; and finally **Sandro Botticelli** (d. 1510); Botticelli's progress from his astounding early mythological pictures to conventional holy pictures, done after he fell under the sway of Savonarola, marks first failure of nerve in the Florentine imagination.

Leonardo, Michelangelo and the Cinquecento

With equal self-assurance the critics used to refer to the early 1500s as the beginning of the 'High Renaissance'. **Leonardo da Vinci**, perhaps the incarnation of Florentine achievement in both painting and scientific speculation, lived until 1519, but spent much of his time in Milan and France. **Michelangelo Buonarroti** (d. 1564) liked to identify himself with Florentine republicanism, but finally abandoned the city during the siege of 1530 (even though he was a member of the committee overseeing Florence's defence). His departure left Florence with no important artists except the surpassingly strange **Jacopo Pontormo** (d. 1556) and **Rosso Fiorentino** (d. 1540). These two, along with Michelangelo, were key figures in the bold, neurotic, avant-garde art that has come to be known as Mannerism. This first conscious 'movement' in Western art can be seen as a last fling amid the growing intellectual and spiritual exhaustion of 1530s Florence, conquered once and for all by the Medici. The Mannerists' calculated exoticism and exaggerated, tortured poses, together with the brooding self-absorption of Michelangelo and many others, are the prelude to Florentine art's remarkably abrupt downturn into decadence, and prophesy its final extinction.

There was another strain to Mannerism in Florence, following the cold classicism of Raphael of Urbino, less disturbed, less intense and challenging than Michelangelo or Pontormo. With artists like **Agnolo Bronzino** (d. 1572), the sculptor **Bartolomeo Ammannati** (d. 1592), **Andrea del Sarto** (d. 1531), and **Giorgio Vasari** himself (d. 1574), Florentine art loses all imaginative and intellectual content, becoming a virtuoso style of interior decoration adaptable to saccharine holy pictures, portraits of dukes, or absurd mythological fountains and ballroom ceilings. In the cinquecento, with plenty of money to spend and a long Medici tradition of patronage to uphold, this tendency got out of hand. Under the reign of Cosimo I, indefatigable collector of *pietra dura* tables, gold gimcracks, and exotic stuffed animals, Florence gave birth to kitsch.

In the cinquecento, Florence taught vulgarity to the Romans, degeneracy to the Venetians, and preciosity to the French – oddly enough having as great an influence in its age of decay as in its age of greatness. The cute, well-educated Florentine pranced across Europe, finding himself praised as the paragon of culture and refinement. Even in England – though that honest nation soon found him out:

A little Apish hatte, couched fast to the Pate, like an Oyster,
French Camarick Ruffes, deepe with a witnesse, starched to the purpose,
Delicate in speach, queynte in arraye: conceited in all poyntes:
In Courtly guyles, a passing singular odde man...
Mirror of Tuscanism, Gabriel Harvey, 1580

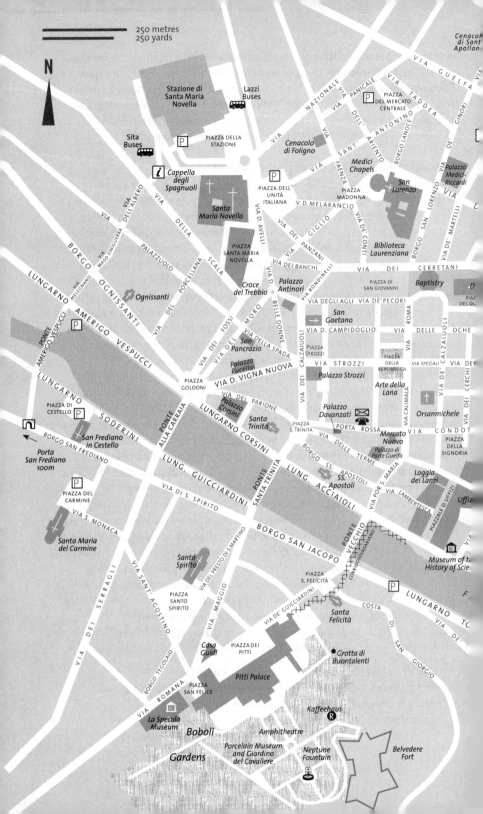

It's almost disconcerting to learn that Florence gave us not only much of the best of our civilization, but even a lot of the worst. Somehow the later world of powdered wigs and chubby winged putti is unthinkable without 1500s Florence. Then again, so is all the last 500 years of art unthinkable without Florence, not to mention modern medicine (the anatomical studies of the artists set it on its way) or technology (the endless speculations and gadgets of Leonardo) or political science (from Machiavelli). The Florentines of course found the time to invent opera too, and give music a poke into the modern world. And without that discovery of the painters, so simple though so hard for us in the 20th century to comprehend – the invention of space – Newton, Copernicus, Descartes and all who followed would never have discovered anything.

But Florence soon tired of the whole business. The city withdrew into itself, made a modest living, polished its manners and its conceit, and generally avoided trouble. Not a peep has been heard out of it since 1600.

Around the City

Florence Highlights

If you wanted to see everything worth seeing, it would take at least three weeks and cost a small fortune in admission charges. For an abbreviated tour, be sure to see the **cathedral**, **baptistry** and **cathedral museum**, and Florence's two great museums, the **Uffizi** and the **Bargello**, leaving time for a walk around the Ponte Vecchio and a stop at Orsanmichele. Around the edges of the old centre, the churches of **Santa Croce, Santa Maria Novella, Santa Maria del Carmine** and the monastery of **San Marco** contain some of the best of Florentine painting. Finally, try to make it up to **San Miniato**, for the beautiful medieval church and the view over the city. With more time, consider the florid 16th-century art in the **Palazzo Vecchio** and **Pitti Palace**, Gozzoli's frescoes in the **Palazzo Medici-Riccardi**, the **Archaeology Museum** and **Museum of Science**, and Brunelleschi's **Santo Spirito**. And for devotees of the Michelangelo cult, there's the real David in the **Accademia**, the **Medici Chapels** at San Lorenzo and the **Casa Buonarroti**.

Piazza del Duomo: The Baptistry

To begin to understand what magic made the Renaissance first bloom by the Arno, look here; this ancient, mysterious building is the egg from which Florence's golden age was hatched. By the quattrocento, Florentines firmly believed their baptistry was originally a Roman temple to Mars, a touchstone linking them to a legendary past. Scholarship sets its date of construction between the 6th and 9th centuries, in the darkest Dark Ages, which makes it even more remarkable; it may as well have dropped from heaven. Its distinctive dark green and white marble facing, the tidily classical pattern of arches and rectangles that deceived Brunelleschi and Alberti, was probably added around the 11th century. The masters who built it remain unknown, but their strikingly original exercise in geometry provided the model for all of Florence's great church façades. When it was new, there was nothing remotely like it in Europe; to visitors from outside the city it must have seemed almost miraculous.

Getting There

Florence is the central transport node for Tuscany and harder to avoid than to reach.

By Air

Florence's Vespucci airport was lengthened in 1996, and it now bustles with more international traffic than Pisa. It is 6km out at Peretola, t 055 373 498, flight information t 055 306 1700 (recorded message), and is connected to the city by a regular bus service to Santa Maria Novella Station (15mins). A taxi ride to the centre will cost about L30,000 plus relevant surcharges (baggage and so on).

If you need to get to Florence from Pisa airport, take the special train service to Santa Maria Novella, which takes one hour and leaves every hour or so.

By Train

The central station (Stazione Centrale) is **Santa Maria Novella**, call t 8488 88088 for information, *www.fs-on-line.com*. Many long-distance trains arriving at night use **Campo di Marte** station, bus nos. 12 or 91.

By Bus

It's possible to reach nearly every city, town and village in Tuscany from Florence, which is wonderfully convenient – once you know which of several bus companies to patronize. The tourist office has a full list of destinations, but here are some of the most popular:
SITA: (near station, Via S. Caterina da Siena 15, t 800 373 760 daily, Sat and Sun until 1pm): towns in the Val d'Elsa, Chianti, Val di Pesa, Mugello and Casentino; Arezzo, Bibbiena, Castelfiorentino, Certaldo, Consuma, Figline Valdarno, Firenzuola, Marina di Grosseto, Montevarchi, Poggibonsi (for Volterra and San Gimignano), Pontassieve, Poppi, Pratovecchio, Scarperia, Siena, Stia, Vallombrosa.
LAZZI: (Piazza Stazione 47r, t 055 351 061 Mon–Fri): along the Arno to the coast, including Calenzano, Cerreto Guidi, Empoli, Forte dei Marmi, Livorno, Lucca, Marina di Carrara, Marina di Massa, Montecatini Terme, Montelupo, Montevarchi, Pescia, Pisa, Pistoia, Pontedera, Prato, Signa, Tirrenia, Torre del Lago, Viareggio.

CAP: (Via Nazionale 13, t 055 214 637): Borgo S. Lorenzo, Impruneta, Incisa Valdarno, Montepiano, Prato.
COPIT: (Piazza S. Maria Novella, t 0573 21170): Abetone, Cerreto Guidi, Pistoia, Poggio a Caiano, Vinci.
RAMA: (Lazzi Station, t 055 215 155): Grosseto.

By Car

All roads into the city meet up with an inner ring of roads, the *Viali*, which goes around the historic centre, much of which is closed to traffic. There are large car parks all around the *Viali*, particularly around the **Fortezza da Basso** and **Piazza Libertà** at the 'Parterre', which are quite expensive though still not as much as the ones that are actually within the centre itself.

Getting Around

Florence is now one of the best Italian cities to get around; best, because nearly everything you'll want to see is within easy walking distance and large areas in the centre are pedestrian zones; there are no hills to climb, and it's hard to lose your way for very long.

Just to make life difficult, Florence has two sets of **address numbers** on every street – red ones for business, blue or black for residences; your hotel might be either one. However, recent years have seen some improvement in the signage department: every major piazza, landmark or monument now has a plaque fitted outside offering relevant background information, and helpful maps have been posted in strategic positions around the city.

By Bus

City buses (ATAF; *www.ataf.net*) can whizz or inch you across Florence, and are an excellent means of reaching sights on the periphery. Most lines begin at Santa Maria Novella station, and pass by Piazza del Duomo or Piazza San Marco. ATAF supply an excellent and comprehensive booklet, including a clear map, with details of all bus routes. These are available at the information/ticket booth at the station, tourist offices, some bars, and at ATAF's central office in Piazza della Stazione, t 055 565 0222. Ticket prices: L1,500 for 60

mins, L2,500 for 3 hours, L6,000 for 24 hours.
Useful buses for visitors include.

no.7: Station–Duomo–San Domenico–Fiesole

no.10: Station–Duomo–S. Marco–Ponte a
Mensola–Settignano

no.13: Station–Ponte Rosso–Parterre (car
park)–Piazza Libertà–Viale Mazzini– Campo
di Marte–Piazzale Michelangelo–Porta
Romana

no.37: Station–Ponte alla Carraia–Porta
Romana–Certosa del Galluzzo

As part of the campaign against city smog,
a fleet of Lilliputian electric buses, routes A, B
and D, have recently been introduced. These
mainly serve the centre, often taking
circuitous routes 'round the houses', and are a
good way of seeing some of the sights if
you've had enough walking. Details of routes
can be found on the ATAF maps.

By Taxi

Taxis in Florence don't cruise; you'll find
them in ranks at the station and in the *piazze*,
or else ring for a radio taxi: **t** 055 4798 or 4390.

Bicycle, Scooter and Car Hire

Hiring a bike can save you tramping time
and angst, but watch out for cars and
pedestrians. You can hire a motorbike at:

Alinari, Via Guelfa 85r, **t** 055 280 500 or Via dei
Bardi 35, **t** 055 234 6436.

Motorent, Via S. Zanobi 9r, **t** 055 490 113.

Florence by Bike, Via S. Zanobi 120/122r,
t 055 488 992.

Promoturist, Via Baccio Bandinelli 43, **t** 055 701
863. For mountain bikes only.

Between 8am and 7.30pm, you can now take
advantage of one of the (almost) free bicycles
supplied by the *comune* of Florence. There are
various pick-up points around town, the most
central being the Fortezza, the Parterre (for
the car parks), Piazza Strozzi, Piazza Stazione,
Piazza San Marco, the central market and
Porta Romana. They cost L1,000 for the day.

Tourist Information

Florence

The main **tourist office** is a bit out of the
way, near Piazza Beccaria on Via Manzoni 16,
t 055 23320 (*open Mon–Sat, 8–6*). There are

other offices at Via Cavour 1r, **t** 055 290 832
(*open Mon–Sat 8.15–7.15, and Sun in summer*),
Borgo Santa Croce 29r, **t** 055 234 0444, **f** 055
226 4524 (*open winter daily 9am–2pm;
summer Mon–Sat 8.15–7.15, Sun 8.30–1.30*) and
in Piazza Stazione, **t** 055 212 245, **f** 055 238 1226,
turismo3@comune.fi.it (*open Mon–Sat 8.30–7,
Sun 8.30–1.30*).

There are two **guides for the disabled**, both
of which can be picked up at the tourist office.
The more comprehensive is only in Italian, but
it covers access to sites in great detail and has
a good map. The other offers a basic
translation into English. During the summer,
look out for the temporary mobile 'Tourist
Help Points' set up in the centre of town.

Fiesole

Via Portigiani 3, **t** 055 598 720, **t** 055 597 8373,
f 055 598 822 (*open all year Mon–Sat
8.30–7.30, Sun 10–7*).

APT tourist service:
www.firenze.turismo.toscana.it.

Shopping

Fashion

Although central Florence sometimes seems
like one solid boutique, the city is no longer
the queen of Italian fashion. But the big
fashion names of the 1960s and 70s, and the
chain stores of the 1980s, are well represented
in smart **Via Tornabuoni**, **Via Calzaiuoli** and in
the streets around the Duomo.

Jewellery

The jewellery shops that line the **Ponte
Vecchio** are forced into competition by their
location, and you can get good prices for
Florentine brushed gold, cameos and antique
jewellery (much of it made in Arezzo these
days). They're not here just to exploit tourists –
they've been on the bridge for over 300 years.

Leather

It is worth looking around **Via della Vigna
Nuova** and **Via del Parione** for leather goods.

Marbled Paper

Florence is one of the few places in the
world to make marbled paper, an art brought

over from the Orient by Venice in the 12th century. Each sheet is hand-dipped in a bath of colours to create a delicate, lightly coloured clouded design; no two sheets are alike. Marbled-paper-covered stationery items or just sheets of marbled paper are available at:

Giulio Giannini e Figlio, Piazza Pitti 37r. The oldest manufacturer in Florence.

Il Papiro: three shops at: Via Cavour 55r; Piazza del Duomo 24r; Lungarno Acciaiuoli 42r.

La Bottega Artigiana del Libro, Lungarno Corsini 40r.

Il Torchio, Via de' Bardi 17. Here the workbench is in the shop so you can see the artisans in action. These shops also carry Florentine paper with its colourful Gothic patterns.

Markets

For bargains and surprises, try Florence's famous and boisterous street markets, usually open every day. The big **San Lorenzo market**, which has spread all over the neighbourhood around San Lorenzo church, is where ordinary Florentines probably buy most of their clothes. In this little bit of Naples transplanted to Tuscany, the range of choice is equal to three department stores; you'll see plenty of fake designer labels, and even some real ones.

Further west in Santa Croce, in the **Piazza dei Ciompi**, the *mercato delle pulci* (flea market) carries on daily, with a wide array of desirable junk, beneath Vasari's Fish Loggia; the shopkeepers, being Florentines, are a little smug and not inclined to bargain. More serious **antiques shops** tend to cluster in the streets between Via Tornabuoni and the Ognissanti, and on Via Maggio.

The **Mercato Nuovo**, or *Mercato del Porcellino*, right in the centre of town, still performs its age-old function of selling Florentine straw goods – hats and bags. There is a bustling **food market** at Sant'Ambrogio.

Where to Stay

Florence ✉ 50100

Florence has some exceptionally lovely hotels, and not all of them at grand ducal prices, although base rates are the highest in Tuscany. As in any city, the higher cost of living means you won't find much accommodation in the *cheap* price bracket. In fact, you should count on having to pay around 25 per cent more for a room here than you would anywhere else. Historic old palace-hotels are the rule rather than the exception; those listed below are some of the more atmospheric and charming, but to be honest, few are secrets, so reserve as far in advance as possible. Also note that nearly every hotel in Florence with a restaurant will require half-board, and many will also try to lay down a heavy breakfast charge as well.

There are almost 400 hotels in Florence but not enough for anyone who arrives in July and August without a reservation. But don't despair; there are several agencies that can help you find a room in nearly any price range for a small commission. If you're arriving by car or train, the most useful will be ITA.

ITA: in Santa Maria Novella station, **t** 055 282 893, *open 9–9, in winter until 8*; or in the AGIP service station at Peretola, to the west of Florence on A11, **t** 055 421 1800. Between March and November there's an office in the Chianti-Est service plaza on the A1, **t** 055 621 349. Bookings cannot be made over the telephone.

Florence Promhotels: Viale A. Volta 72, **t** 055 570 481, **f** 055 587 189. Free booking service.

For **agriturismo** or farmhouse accommodation in the countryside (self-catering or otherwise), contact: Agriturist Toscana, Piazza S. Firenze 3, **t/f** 055 287 838; or Turismo Verde Toscana, Via Verdi 5, **t** 055 234 4925.

Luxury

*****Excelsior, Piazza Ognissanti 3, **t** 055 2715, **f** 055 210 278, *www. starwood.com*. In the city the luxury leader is former Florentine address of Napoleon's sister Caroline. Lots of marble, neoclassically plush, lush and green with plants, immaculately staffed, with decadently luxurious bedrooms, many of which have river views (for a price).

****Helvetia & Bristol, Via dei Pescioni 2, **t** 055 287 814, **f** 055 281 336, *www.charming-hotels.it*. If you prefer luxury on a smaller scale, this has 52 exquisitely furnished bedrooms, each one different, all with rich fabrics adorning windows, walls and beds; Stravinsky, D'Annunzio, Bertrand Russell and Pirandello stayed here; added pluses are the restaurant (one of the finest in town) and the delightful winter garden.

***** **Regency**, Piazza d'Azeglio 3, t 055 245 247, f 055 234 6735, *www.regency-hotel.com*. In Florence's plane-tree-shaded 'London Square', there's a smaller gem, charming and intimate with only 33 rooms; between the two wings there's an elegant town garden. The public rooms are panelled, and the fare in the dining room superb.

**** **The Savoy**, Piazza Repubblica 7, t 055 283 313, f 055 284 840, *www.rfhotels.com*. The old, crumbling Savoy reopened in spring 2000 under the Forte Group, now striking a minimalist tone with décor in shades of cream, beige and grey; it has a bar and restaurant on the piazza.

**** **Lungarno**, Borgo San Jacopo 14, t 055 27261, f 055 268 437. A discreet hotel enjoying a marvellous location on the river, only two minutes' walk from the Ponte Vecchio. The ground floor sitting/breakfast room and bar, and the new restaurant, which specializes in fish, take full advantage of this with picture windows looking on to the water. The building is modern, but incorporates a medieval tower, and has just been refurbished; the small-ish bedrooms are decorated in smart blue and cream and the best have balconies with 'The View'. Book way ahead if you want one of these.

Very Expensive

*** **Hermitage**, Vicolo Marzio 1, t 055 287 216, f 055 212 208. You have to look hard to find this little hotel tucked away behind the Ponte Vecchio on the north side of the river. It is built upside down; the lift takes you to the fifth floor with its ravishing roof garden, reception and elegant blue and yellow sitting room. The bedrooms below are on the small side, but charmingly furnished with antiques and tasteful fabrics. Some have river views.

**** **Villa Belvedere**, Via Benedetto Castelli 3, t 055 222 501, f 055 223 163. Not one of the more interesting buildings to be found in this part of peripheral Florence (a kilometre above Porta Romana), but a very pleasant alternative to central accommodation all the same, with a beautiful garden, a nice pool and good views. Rooms are modern

and comfortable with lots of wood and plenty of space. For trips into town, you can catch a nearby bus. Light meals are served in the restaurant.

*** **Beacci Tornabuoni**, Via Tornabuoni 3, t 055 212 645, f 055 283 594. Another excellent small hotel which puts you in the centre of fashionable Florence, on the top three floors of an elegant Renaissance palace. The rooms are comfortable, and you can sit over your drink on the panoramic roof terrace.

Expensive

*** **Mario's**, Via Faenza 89, t 055 216 801, f 055 212 039. A haven in a street with more than its fair share of hotels, many of them of dubious quality. Convenient for the station and a block or two from the central market, the atmosphere is friendly and the décor rustic Florentine. A generous breakfast is served and guests are pampered with fresh flowers and fruit on arrival. If you don't want to sleep with your windows closed, ask for a room at the back; the street can be noisy.

*** **Silla**, Via dei Renai 5, t 055 234 2888, f 055 234 1437. Ten minutes' walk east of the Ponte Vecchio on the south bank of the river, this manages to be central, yet in a quiet and relatively green neighbourhood. The old-fashioned *pensione* is on the first floor of a 16th-century *palazzo* and the spacious breakfast terrace has great views over the Arno and beyond.

** **Casci**, Via Cavour 13, t 055 211 686, f 055 239 6461. The Lombardis, owners of this 15th-century *palazzo* (once home to Rossini), run a relaxed and cheerful ship. The reception area is full of helpful information, the breakfast room has a frescoed ceiling while the recently refurbished bedrooms are bright and modern. The choice few look on to a garden at the back.

*** **Classic Hotel**, Viale Machiavelli 25, t 055 229 351, f 055 229 353. A good alternative in a very pleasant location just above Porta Romana on the way to Piazzale Michelangelo, a five-minute walk to a bus stop for downtown. The pink-washed villa stands in a shady garden (a welcome respite from the heat of the city), and breakfast is served in the conservatory in summer.

Moderate

★★Belletini, Via de' Conti 7, **t** 055 213 561, **f** 055 283 551. A friendly place near the Medici chapels, decorated in traditional Florentine style; a couple of rooms have stunning views of the nearby domes. Good breakfast.

★Sorelle Bandini, Piazza Santo Spirito 9, **t** 055 215 308, **f** 055 282 761. Remains popular, in spite of its state of disrepair and relatively high prices. This is partly due to the romantic loggia along one side of the fourth-storey hotel, but also to its location on fascinating Piazza Santo Spirito, bustling by day and lively (and noisy) at night. Expect uncomfortable beds, cavernous rooms, heavy Florentine furniture and a certain shabby charm.

★★Il Granduca, Via Pier Capponi 13, **t** 055 572 230, **f** 055 579 252. Between Piazza Donatello and Piazza della Libertà is one of the nicest hotels in this category, with a garden, not all rooms are en suite.

★Firenze, Piazza dei Donati 4, **t** 055 268 301, **f** 055 212 370. Newly renovated in an excellent location, between Piazza Signoria and the Duomo; the rather unimaginative rooms now all have bathrooms.

★★Residence Johanna Cinque Giornate, Via Cinque Gionate 12, **t** 055 473 377 **f** 055 481 896. Good value for money in a city where bargains are few and far between, located some way from the centre (near the Fortezza da Basso). The villa stands in its own garden and there are six comfortable rooms, each equipped with a breakfast tray and kettle, as well as a sitting room with plenty of reading material. Guests are left to themselves, but other facilities are of a three-star standard.

Cheap

★Scoti, Via Tournabuoni 7, **t/f** 055 292 128. A simple, cheap *pensione* with a surprisingly upmarket address, ideal if you would rather splurge on the wonderful clothes in the surrounding shops than your hotel. It has basic, large rooms of up to four beds and no private bathrooms, but bags of atmosphere, starting with the floor-to-ceiling frescoes in the sitting room.

★Orchidea, Borgo degli Albizi 11, **t/f** 055 248 0346. Run by an Anglo-Italian family in a 12th-century building where Dante's in-laws once lived. One of the seven cheerful rooms offered has a private shower, and the best look on to a garden at the back.

Azzi, Via Faenza 56, **t/f** 055 213 806. This friendly, clean, simple *pensione* is near the market, and has the added bonus of a terrace for summer.

Fiesole ✉ 50014

Many frequent visitors to Florence wouldn't stay anywhere else: it's cooler, quieter, and at night the city far below twinkles as if made of fairy lights.

★★★★★Villa San Michele, Via Doccia 4, **t** 055 5678 200, **f** 055 678 250, *www.orient-expresshotels.com* (luxury). Built as a monastery in the 14th century, this is the superb choice if money is no object, set in a breathtaking location just below Fiesole with a façade and loggia reputedly designed by Michelangelo himself. After bomb damage in the Second World War, it was carefully reconstructed to create one of the most beautiful hotels in Italy, set in a lovely Tuscan garden, complete with a pool. Each of its 29 rooms is richly and elegantly furnished and air-conditioned; the more plush suites have jacuzzis. The food is delicious, and the reasons to go down to Florence begin to seem insignificant; a stay here is complete in itself. Paradise, however, comes at a price.

★★★Villa Fiesole, Via Beato Angelico 35, **t** 055 597 252, **f** 055 599 133 (*very expensive*). This new hotel was once part of the San Michele convent, and shares part of its driveway with the hotel of the same name. The smart, neoclassical-style interiors are variations on a fresh blue and yellow colour scheme. Light meals are served in a sunny dining room or on the adjacent terrace, and there is a pool. The whole is wheelchair-accessible. The facilities (and prices) here are decidedly four-star.

★★★Pensione Bencistà, Via Benedetto di Maiano 4, **t/f** 055 59163, *bencista@vol.it* (*expensive*). Another former monastery with views from its flower-decked terrace which are every bit as good as those at Villa San Michele, and the welcome will be more friendly. Bedrooms, each one different from the next, are all comfortably furnished with solid antique pieces. Half-board is obligatory here, but prices are reasonable.

Le Cannelle, Via Gramsci 52, t 055 597 8336, f 055 597 8292, info@lecannelle.com (*expensive*). A new, friendly B&B run by two sisters on the main street. Rooms are comfortably rustic and there is a pretty breakfast room.

*Villa Sorriso, Via Gramsci 21, t 055 59027, f 055 597 8075 (*cheap*). An unpretentious, comfortable hotel in the centre of Fiesole, with a terrace overlooking Florence.

Eating Out

Like any sophisticated city with lots of visitors, Florence has plenty of fine restaurants; even in the cheaper places standards are high, and if you don't care for anything fancier, there will be lots of good red Chianti to wash down your meal. By popular demand, the city centre is full of *tavole calde*, pizzerias and snack bars, where you can grab a sandwich or a salad instead of a full sit-down meal (one of the best pizza-by-the-slice places is just across from the Medici Chapels).

Note that many of the best places are likely to close for all or part of August; you would also be wise to call ahead and reserve, even a day or two in advance.

Florence's Most Ephemeral Art

Florentine food is on the whole extremely simple, with the emphasis on the individual flavours and fresh ingredients. A typical *primo* could be *pappardelle*, a type of wide *tagliatelle* egg-pasta, served usually with a meat sauce, or game such as wild boar, rabbit and duck. Soups are also popular: try the *ribollita*, a thick, hearty soup unique to the region, made with yesterday's bread, beans, black cabbage and other vegetables; or *pappa al pomodoro*, another bread-based soup flavoured with tomatoes, basil and sludgy local olive oil.

The most famous main course in Florence is the *bistecca alla fiorentina*, a thick steak on the bone, cut from loin of beef and cooked on charcoal simply seasoned with salt and pepper. As for vegetables, you could try *piselli alla fiorentina*, peas cooked with oil, parsley and diced bacon; or *tortino di carciofi*, a delicious omelette with fried artichokes;

fagioli all' uccelletto, cannellini beans stewed with tomatoes, garlic and sage; and *spinaci saltati* – fresh spinach sauteed with garlic and olive oil. Florentine desserts tend to be sweet and fattening: *bomboloni alla crema* are vanilla-filled doughnuts and *le fritelle di San Giuseppe* are bits of deep-fried batter covered in sugar. If you prefer cheese, try the sturdy *pecorino toscano*. For better or worse, real Florentine soul food rarely turns up on many restaurant menus, and unless you make an effort you'll never learn what a Florentine cook can do with cockscombs, intestines, calves' feet and tripe.

Very Expensive

Enoteca Pinchiorri, Via Ghibellina 87, near the Casa Buonarroti, t 055 242 777. One of the finest gourmet restaurants in Italy, boasting two Michelin stars. The owners inherited the wine shop and converted it into a beautiful restaurant, with meals served in a garden court in the summer; the cellars contain some 80,000 bottles of the best Italy and France have to offer. The cooking, a mixture of *nouvelle cuisine* and traditional Tuscan recipes, wins prizes every year. Italians tend to complain about the minute portions, but prices are reckoned to be L200,000 excluding wine. *Closed Sun, Mon and Wed lunch.*

Cibreo, Via dei Macci 118r, t 055 234 1100. One of the most Florentine of Florentine restaurants overlooks the market of Sant'Ambrogio. The décor is simple – food is the main concern, and all of it is market-fresh. You can go native and order tripe *antipasto*, cockscombs and kidneys, or play it safe with prosciutto from the Casentino, a fragrant soup of tomatoes, mussels and bell-pepper, leg of lamb stuffed with artichokes, topped off with a delicious lemon *crostata*, cheesecake, or a chocolate cake to answer chocaholics' dreams. *Closed Sun and Mon; Easter; mid-July–mid-Sept.*

Don Chisciotte, Via C. Ridolfi 4r, t 055 475 430. A small place between the Fortezza Basso and Piazza dell'Indipendenza, serving inventive Italian food with a particular emphasis on fish and vegetables. Be tempted by baked baby squid, delicate warm vegetable and fish salad, or green tagliatelle with scampi and courgettes. *Closed Sun and Mon lunch.*

Expensive

Buca Lapi, Via del Trebbio 1r, t 055 213 768. Located since 1800 in the old wine cellar of the lovely Palazzo Antinori, serving traditional favourites, from *pappardelle al cinghiale* (wide pasta with boar) and a *bistecca fiorentina con fagioli* that is hard to beat, downed with many different Tuscan wines. *Closed Sun and Mon lunch.*

Beccofino, Piazza degli Scarlatti, t 055 290 076. On the river under the British Institute, you could almost be in London or New York once inside this new, trendy restaurant, but the food is decidedly Italian. Dishes are enhanced by a creative touch and are elegantly presented. Both fish and meat dishes are excellent and change with the seasons: octopus salad, pasta flavoured with *zucchini* and saffron, sea bass on a bed of truffle-flavoured mash, steak fillet with caramelized shallots, and a fabulous *bistecca alla Fiorentina*. You can also eat a light meal in the wine bar where prices are considerably lower. *Closed Mon.*

Caffè Concerto, Lungarno C. Colombo 7, t 055 677 377. This has a lovely setting on the north bank of the Arno east of the city centre, and a warm wood and glass interior with lots of greenery. Creative cuisine, where hearty portions of traditional ingredients are given a new twist. *Closed Sun and 3 weeks in Aug.*

Moderate

Il Latini, Via dei Palchetti 6r (by Palazzo Rucellai), t 055 210 916. Something of an institution in Florence, crowded (be prepared to queue; they don't accept bookings) and noisy but fun, where you eat huge portions of Florentine classics at long tables. The *primi* aren't great; so go for the *bistecca* or, more unusual, the *gran pezzo* – a vast rib-roast of beef. The house wine is good; try a *riserva. Closed Mon and all of Aug.*

Baldovino, Via Giuseppe 22r (Piazza S. Croce), t 055 241 773. An excellent trattoria/pizzeria run by a young Scotsman, where you can eat anything from a big salad, filled focaccia or pizza (from a wood-burning oven) to a full menu of pasta, fish and steaks from the Val di Chiana. *Closed Mon.*

Alla Vecchia Bettola, Viale Ariosto 32–34r, t 055 224 158. A noisy trattoria, west of the Carmine, with great food; the menu changes daily, but you can nearly always find their classic *tagliolini con funghi porcini.* The grilled meats are tasty and succulent, and the ice-cream comes from Vivoli. *Closed Sun and Mon.*

Sostanza, Via della Porcellana 25r, t 055 212 691. Just west of Santa Maria Novella is one of the last authentic Florentine trattorias, a good place to eat *bistecca.* One of their most famous dishes is the simple, but delectable *petto di pollo al burro*, chicken breast sauteed in butter. *Closed Sat and Sun.*

Cheap

Aquacotta, Via dei Pilastri 51r, t 055 242 907. This restaurant, north of Piazza S. Ambrogio, is named for the simple but delicious bread soup, one of the specialities; you could follow that by deep-fried rabbit accompanied by crisply fried courgette flowers. *Closed Tues eve and Wed.*

La Casalinga, Via Michelozzi 9r, t 055 218 624. A family-run trattoria, also near Piazza Santo Spirito, and always busy, not surprising given the quality of the simple home cooking and the low prices. The *ribollita* is excellent. *Closed Sun.*

Trattoria Cibreo, Via de' Macci 122r, t 055 234 1100. A little annexe to smart Cibreo (*see above*), this is one of the best deals in town; the food is the same (excluding the odd more extravagant dish), but served in a rustic setting on cheaper porcelain; and your bill will be a third of that of those dining next door. *Closed Sun and Mon.*

Trattoria del Carmine, Piazza del Carmine 185, t 055 218 601. A traditional, bustling trattoria in the San Frediano district, often full. The long menu includes such staples as *ribollita, pasta e fagioli* and roast pork, but also features seasonal dishes such as *risotto* with asparagus or mushrooms, pasta with wild boar sauce and *osso buco. Closed Sun.*

Santa Lucia, Via Ponte alle Mosse 102r, t 055 353 255. North of the Cascine there is a genuine Neapolitan *pizzeria*, a noisy, steamy and unromantic place, with possibly the best pizza in Florence, topped with the sweetest tomatoes and the creamiest *mozzarella di buffala. Closed Wed.*

Specifically **vegetarian** restaurants include:
Ruth's, Via Farini 2a, **t** 055 248 0888. A new, bright and modern kosher vegetarian restaurant next to the synagogue, serving fish and Middle Eastern dishes. Try a *brick,* a savoury pastry, filled with fish, potatoes or cheese that tastes better than it sounds. *Closed Fri dinner and Sat lunch.*

Centro Vegetariano Fiorentino, Via delle Ruote 30r, **t** 055 475 030. Located west of San Marco; self-service with excellent fresh food including a wide choice of soups, salads and more substantial dishes. *Closed Sun lunch and Mon.*

Cafés and *Gelaterie*

Gilli, Piazza della Repubblica 13–14r. Many of Florence's grand old cafés were born in the last century, though this one, the oldest, dates back to 1733, when the Mercato Vecchio still occupied this area; its two panelled back rooms are especially pleasant in the winter.

Rivoire, Piazza della Signoria 5r. The most elegant and classy watering hole, with a marble-detailed interior as lovely as the piazza itself.

Dolci e Dolcezze, Piazza Cesare Beccaria 8r, **t** 055 234 5458. East of Sant' Ambrogio market, this has the most delicious cakes, pastries and marmalades in the city – the *crostate, torte* and *bavarese* are expensive but worth every lira. *Closed Mon.*

Hemingway, near Piazza Carmine, **t** 055 284 781 (*booking advised*). A lovely café which, as well as cocktails, serves interesting light meals and an excellent brunch on Sundays. The owner is a chocaholic, so the handmade chocs and puddings are a dream. Try the *sette veli* chocolate cake. *Open weekdays 4.30–late, Sun 11–8.*

Caffè Ricchi, Piazza Santo Spirito. A local institution. It has just undergone a major refit, but continues to serve excellent and good-value light lunches and wonderful ice-cream. The outside tables enjoy the benefit of one of the most beautiful piazzas in Florence.

Vivoli, Via Isola delle Stinche 7r, between the Bargello and S. Croce. Florence lays some claim to being the ice-cream capital of the world, a reputation that owes much to the decadently delicious confections and rich *semifreddi* served here. *Closed Mon.*

Baby Yoghurt, Via Michelozzo 13r. This frozen yoghurt claims to be healthy, though it tastes so creamy that it's hard to believe. Apparently, the secret lies in whipping the yoghurt for hours, before serving it topped with fresh fruit, hot chocolate or nuts.

Gelateria de' Ciompi, Via dell'Agnolo 121r. This traditional Florentine ice-cream parlour, tucked around the corner from Santa Croce, prides itself on its authentic home-made recipes, some of which are over 50 years old.

Entertainment and Nightlife

Nightlife with Great Aunt Florence is still awaiting its Renaissance; according to the Florentines she's conservative, somewhat deaf and retires early – 1am is late in this city. However, there are plenty of people who wish it weren't so, and slowly, slowly, Florence by night is beginning to mean more than the old *passeggiata* over the Ponte Vecchio and an ice-cream, and perhaps a late trip up to Fiesole to contemplate the lights.

Look for listings of concerts and events in Florence's daily, *La Nazione.* The tourist office's free *Florence Today* contains bilingual monthly information and a calendar, as does a booklet called *Florence Concierge Information,* available in hotels and tourist offices. **Box office,** Via Alamanni 39, **t** 055 210 804, is a central ticket agency for all major events in Tuscany and beyond, including classical, rock and jazz.

Performance Arts and Music

The opera and ballet season runs from September to Christmas and concerts from January to April at the **Teatro Comunale,** and the **Maggio Musicale** festival, which features all three, from mid-April until the end of June. There is usually more opera in July.

Classical concerts are held mainly at the **Teatro Comunale,** Corso Italia 16, **t** 055 211 158; **Teatro della Pergola,** Via della Pergola 12–32, t 055 247 9651; and **Teatro Verdi**, Via Ghibellina 99–101, t 055 212 320. Many smaller events take place year-round in churches, cloisters and villas, with plenty of outdoor concerts in summer. Look out for posters: they are not always well publicized.

Rock and jazz concerts are held year round. One of the best venues for live music is **Auditorium Flog**, Via M. Mercati 24b, t 055 490 437. Look out for the Musica dei Popoli festival in November. In the summer, there are lots of rock and jazz venues all over the city, many of them free, for when Florence moves outdoors to cool off.

Cinemas

Summer is a great time to catch the latest films. English-language films are shown throughout the summer on two evenings a week at the Odeon in Piazza Strozzi and open-air screens are erected in several venues in Florence with two different films in Italian every evening from mid-June until mid-September. Details appear in the local newspapers.

Cinemas showing original language (usually English) films include **Odeon**, Via Sassetti 1, t 055 214 068, and **Fulgor**, Via Masi Finiguerra, t 055 238 1881 (English on Thurs).

Wine Bars

Florence is full of wine bars, from new-generation places to simple 'holes in the wall'.
Vini, Via dei Cimatori 38r. One of the last of its kind in Florence, where you can join the locals standing on the street, glass and *crostino* in hand. *Closed Sun.*
Le Volpi e L'Uva, Piazza dei Rossi. Just south of the Ponte Vecchio, where the knowledge-able and helpful owners specialize in relatively unknown labels, and snacks include a marvellous selection of French and Italian cheeses.
Fuori Porta, San Niccolo. Possibly the most famous of all, where there are some 600 labels on the wine list and dozens of whiskeys and grappas. Among the snacks and hot dishes on offer, try one of the *crostoni*, a huge slab of local bread topped with something delicious and heated under the grill. *Closed Sun.*

Clubs and Discos

Many clubs have themed evenings; keep an eye out for posters or handouts or buy the listings magazine *Firenze Spettacolo*. Places are somewhat seasonal as well.
Universale, Via Pisana 77r. A vast ex-cinema, newly opened with designer décor, a restaurant, several bars and a pizzeria, all accompanied by live music and a giant cinema screen. Fast becoming the hottest hang-out in town, these are chic, sleek surroundings for a sleek and chic crowd. *Open 7pm–2am, closed Mon.*
Central Park, Parco delle Cascine. In summer, possibly the trendiest place in Florence, full of serious clubbers dancing to live music on three dance floors.
Full-Up, Via della Vigna Nuova 25r. Mirrored walls, disco lighting, and dated music. *Closed Sun and Mon and June–Sept.*
Mago Merlino, Via dei Pilastri 31r. A relaxed tearoom/bar with live music, theatre, shows and games.
Du Monde, Via San Niccolò 103r. A cocktail bar offering food, drink and music for the elegant Florentine until 5 in the morning.
Jazz Café, Via Nuova de' Caccini 3. A pleasant but smoky atmosphere with live jazz on Friday and Saturday nights, and a free jam session on Tuesdays. *Closed Sun and Mon.*
Riflessi d'Epoca, Via dei Renai 13r. Live jazz most nights in a smoky ambience. It stays open later than the average club (that's to say after 1am).
Maracanà, Via Faenza 4. Try this for live samba, mambo and bossanova.
The Mood, Corso dei Tintori 4. A young and energetic underground venue with a good mix of music. *Closed Mon.*
Tabasco, Piazza Santa Cecilia 3r. Italy's first gay bar, opened in the 1970s.
Piccolo Café, Borgo Santa Croce 23r. A tiny, friendly, arty gay bar. *Open daily from 5pm.*
Space Electronic, Via Palazzuolo 37, t 055 293 082. A high-tech noise box. *Open daily.*
Andromeda, Via dei Climatori 13, t 055 292 002. Particularly popular with young foreigners. *Closed Sun.*
Jackie O, Via Erta Canina 24. An old favourite for the 30ish crowd, which includes a piano bar. *Closed Mon, Tues, Wed.*

Every 21 March, New Year's Day on the old Florentine calendar, all the children that had been born over the last 12 months would be brought here for a great communal baptism, a habit that helped make the baptistry not merely a religious monument but a civic symbol, in fact the oldest and fondest symbol of the republic. As such the Florentines never tired of embellishing it. Under the octagonal cupola, the glittering 13th- and 14th-century gold-ground mosaics show a strong Byzantine influence, though some (*The Life of St John the Baptist*) may be the work of Cimabue. The equally beautiful mosaics over the altar and in the vault are the earliest, signed by a monk named Iacopo in the first decades of the 13th century.

To match the mosaics there is a beautiful inlaid marble floor decorated with the signs of the zodiac. Even more than the exterior, the patterned green and white marble of the interior walls is remarkable, combining influences from the ancient world and modern inspiration for something entirely new. It isn't cluttered inside; only a 13th-century Pisan-style baptismal font and the tomb of anti-pope John XXIII, by Donatello and Michelozzo, stand out.

Art historians used to date the coming of the 'Renaissance' to 1401, with the famous competition for the baptistry's **bronze doors**, when Lorenzo Ghiberti defeated Brunelleschi and others for the commission. The south door had already been completed by Andrea Pisano, with scenes from the life of John the Baptist in Gothic quatrefoil frames, and in his north door Ghiberti attempted no new departures. After 1425, however, he began the great east doors (the ones with tourists piled up in front) which were to occupy much of his time for the next 27 years. These are the doors Michelangelo is said to have called 'worthy to be the Gates of Paradise', and undoubt-edly they made a tremendous impression on all the artists of the quattrocento, using the same advances in composition and perspective and the same wealth of detail as the painters. The doors (they're actually copies – some of the original panels, restored after flood damage, are on display in the Museo dell' Opera del Duomo) have been cleaned recently, and stand in gleaming contrast to the others.

The Old Testament scenes begin with the creation of Adam and Eve in the upper left corner, finishing with Solomon and Sheba in the Temple on the lower right-hand panel. On the frames, busts of contemporary Florentine artists peer out from tiny circles. It is a typical exhibition of Florentine pride that Ghiberti should put his friends among the prophets and sibyls that adorn the rest of the frames. Near the centre, the balding figure with arched eyebrows is Ghiberti himself.

The Duomo

For all its prosperity Florence was one of the last cities to plan a great cathedral. Work began in the 1290s, with the sculptor Arnolfo di Cambio in charge, and the Florentines from the beginning attempted to make up for their delay with audacity and size. Arnolfo laid the foundations for an octagonal crossing 146ft in diameter, then died before working out a way to cover it, leaving future architects with the job of designing the biggest dome in the world. Surprisingly the Duomo shows little interest in contemporary innovations and styles; a visitor from France or England in the 1400s would certainly have found it drab and architecturally primitive. Visitors today often do not know what to think; they circle confusedly around its grimy, ponderous bulk (this is one of very few cathedrals in Italy that you can walk around completely). Instead of the striped bravura of Siena or the elegant colonnades of Pisa they behold an eccentric pattern of marble rectangles and flowers – like Victorian wallpaper or, as one critic better expressed it, a 'cathedral wearing pyjamas'.

The west front cannot be blamed on Arnolfo; his original design, only one-quarter completed, was taken down in the late 16th century in a Medici rebuilding programme that never got off the ground. The Duomo turned a blank face to the world until 1888, when the present neo-Gothic extravaganza was added. After this façade the austerity of the interior is almost startling. There is plenty of room; contemporary writers mention 10,000 souls packed inside to hear the brimstone and hell-fire sermons of Savonarola. Even so the Duomo hardly seems a religious building – more of a *Florentine* building, with simple arches and the counterpoint of grey stone and white plaster, full of old familiar Florentine things. Near the entrance there are busts of Brunelleschi and Giotto along the right side. For building the great dome Brunelleschi was accorded a great honour – he is the only Florentine to be buried in the cathedral.

On the left wall you will see the two most conspicuous monuments to private individuals ever commissioned by the Florentine republic. The older one, on the right, is to Sir John Hawkwood, the famous English *condottiere* whose name the Italians mangled to Giovanni Acuto, a legendary commander who served Florence for many years. All along he had the promise of the Florentines to build him an equestrian monument after his death; it was a typical Florentine trick to cheat a dead man – but still they hired the greatest master of perspective, Paolo Uccello, to make a picture that looked like a statue. Twenty years later they pulled the same trick again, commissioning another great illusionist, Andrea del Castagno, to paint the non-existent equestrian statue of another *condottiere* named Nicolò da Tolentino.

A little further down, near the entrance to the dome, Florence commemorates its own secular scripture with a fresco of Dante by Michelino, a vision of the poet and his *Paradiso* outside the walls of Florence. Two singular icons of Florence's fascination with science stand at opposite ends of the building: behind the west front a bizarre clock, also painted by Uccello, and in the pavement of the left apse a gnomon fixed by the astronomer Toscanelli in 1475. A beam of sunlight strikes it every year on the summer solstice.

There is surprisingly little religious art – most of it has been carted off to the Museo dell'Opera del Duomo (*see* below). Luca della Robbia contributed terracotta lunettes above the doors to the sacristies; the scene of the Resurrection over the north sacristy is one of his earliest and best works. He also did the bronze doors beneath it, with tiny portraits on the handles of Lorenzo il Magnifico and his brother Giuliano de' Medici, targets of the Pazzi conspiracy in 1478. In this ill-fated attempt to dispose of the Medici Giuliano was stabbed during Mass, but Lorenzo managed to escape, taking refuge in this sacristy. In the middle apse there is a beautiful bronze urn by Ghiberti containing relics of the Florentine St Zenobius. The only really conventional religious decorations are the frescoes in the dome, high overhead, mostly the work of Vasari.

Brunelleschi's Dome

Open Mon–Fri 8.30–7, Sat 8.30–5.40; closed Sun; adm.

Losing the competition for the baptistry doors was a bitter disappointment to Brunelleschi but a good piece of luck for Florence. His reaction was typically Florentine: not content with being the second-best sculptor, he began to devote all his talents to a field where he thought no one could beat him. He launched himself into an intense study of architecture and engineering, visiting Rome and probably Ravenna to snatch secrets from the ancients. When proposals were solicited for the cathedral's dome he was ready with a brilliant *tour de force*. Not only would he build the biggest dome of that era, and the most beautiful, but he would do it without any need for expensive supports while work was in progress, making use of a cantilevered system of bricks that could support itself while it ascended. Even today architects marvel at Brunelleschi's systematic way of tackling the job. Problems with weather and air pressure were foreseen and managed; hooks were inserted to hold up scaffolding for future cleaning or repairs.

Not only had Brunelleschi recaptured the technique of the ancients, he had surpassed them, with a system simpler and better than that of the Pantheon or Hagia Sophia. To the Florentines it must have come as a revelation; the most logical way of covering the space turned out to be a work of perfect beauty. Brunelleschi, in building his dome, put a crown on the achievements of Florence – after 500 years it is still the city's pride and its symbol. To climb it, take the door on the left aisle near the Dante fresco; the complex network of stairs and walks between the inner and outer domes provides a thorough lesson on how Brunelleschi did it, and the views from the top are priceless.

Giotto's Campanile

Open daily 8.30–7.30; adm.

There's no doubt: the dome steals the show on Piazza del Duomo, putting one of Italy's most beautiful bell towers in the shade both figuratively and literally. The dome's great size – 366ft to the gold ball atop the lantern – makes the campanile look small, though 280ft is not exactly tiny. Giotto was made director of the cathedral works in 1334, and his basic design was completed after his death (1337) by Andrea Pisano and Francesco Talenti. It is difficult to say whether they were entirely faithful to the plan. Giotto was an artist, not an engineer; after he died his successors realized the thing was about to topple, a problem they overcame by doubling the thickness of the walls.

Besides its lovely form, the campanile's major fame rests with Pisano and Talenti's sculptural relief – a veritable encyclopaedia of the medieval world-view with prophets, saints and sibyls, allegories of the planets, virtues and sacraments, the liberal arts and industries (the artist's craft is fittingly symbolized by a figure of Daedalus). All these are copies; the originals can be seen in the cathedral museum (*see* below). If after climbing the dome you can take another 400 steps or so, the terrace on top offers a slightly different view of Florence.

Some lesser-known monuments line the southern edge of the Piazza del Duomo. The 14th century **Loggia del Bigallo** was built for one of Florence's great charitable confraternities, the Misericordia. It originally served as a lost and found office, although instead of umbrellas it dealt in children; if unclaimed after three days they were sent to foster homes. A little way to the east, **Dante's Seat** is the ancient stone bench where, according to local legend, the poet would take the air, observing his fellow citizens and the building of the Duomo.

Museo dell'Opera del Duomo

Open Mon–Sat 9–6.30, Sun 8.30–2; adm. Please note that at the time of writing not all works are yet in their permanent positions, so some of the details below may change.

The Cathedral Museum (Piazza del Duomo 9, near the central apse) is one of Florence's finest, and houses both relics from the actual construction of the cathedral and the masterpieces that once adorned it. It reopened in early 2000 after major restructuring to improve the layout and make it more visitor-friendly: there is now full disabled access, better information, a more logical layout, in a more or less chronological order, and greatly increased floor space. There are long-term plans to incorporate two neighbouring buildings into the museum, doubling its size.

Arnolfo di Cambio's sculpture from the original façade is here, along with drawings that show how it would have looked. There are a dozen big models of proposed reconstructions from the 1580s in various hack Mannerist styles – the façade could have been much, much worse. Florentines were never enthusiastic about the worship of relics, and long ago they shipped San Girolamo's jawbone, John the Baptist's index finger and St Philip's arm across the street to this museum.

In the 1980s Michelangelo's last *Pietà* joined the company, a strange, unfinished work that so exasperated the artist that he finally took a hammer to it, breaking Christ's left arm and leg. The tall, hooded figure supporting Christ – Nicodemus – dominates the composition; according to Vasari its face is that of Michelangelo himself. The finished, polished sections of the work, Mary Magdalen and part of the body of Jesus, are not Michelangelo's work at all, but that of a student, who also did his best to patch the arm.

In the 1430s Donatello and Luca della Robbia were commissioned to create a matching pair of *cantorie*, marble choir balconies. Both works, in exquisite low relief, rank among the Renaissance's greatest productions: Donatello's features dancing *putti* in a setting of quattrocento decorative motifs, and della Robbia's a delightful horde of children dancing, singing and playing instruments, a truly angelic choir. From the campanile, besides the reliefs of Pisano, there are some fine Old Testament figures by Donatello, as well as his gruesome wood statue of Mary Magdalen, something the Florentines no longer wished to see in their baptistry.

The new part contains fascinating relics of the Duomo's past: brick moulds, tools, and a block and tackle from the original construction; models of the dome, and even Brunelleschi's death mask.

Orsanmichele

Florence likes things neat and in their place. To balance Piazza del Duomo, the religious centre, there is Piazza della Signoria, the civic centre, with an equally formidable array of architecture and art, directly to the south at the other end of Via dei Calzaiuoli, long the city's main artery. On your way there, through the crowds navigating past the Via's fashionable jewellery shops and knick-knack sellers, you pass the unusual church of Orsanmichele.

This stately square building, built up to the street, is easy to miss; it doesn't look anything like a church, and in fact began its life as a grain market, with an open loggia at street level and emergency storehouses above where grain was kept against a siege. The loggia was originally used by the city's powerful guilds, the *Arti*, as a trade and meeting hall. In 1380, when the market relocated, Simone Talenti was hired to close in the arches of the loggia and make the 'Oratory of St Michael' (as the building was familiarly known because of the ancient chapel that had preceded it) into a church, although throughout the following century it continued to be closely associated with the guilds, the leaders of each of which strove to outdo the other by commissioning sculptures from the finest artists of the day.

All around the exterior the guilds erected statues of their patron saints: a remarkable collection, including Donatello's famed *St George* (now a copy; the original is in the Bargello) and *St Mark*, a work much admired by Michelangelo. *Saints Stephen* and *Matthew* are by Ghiberti. *Doubting Thomas* is by Verrocchio. The dim interior (*open Mon–Fri 9–12 and 4–6, Sat and Sun 9–1 and 4–6; closed first and last Mon of month*), full of stained glass and painted vaults, is ornate and cosy, with more of the air of a guildhall than a church. It makes a picturebook medieval setting for the wonderful **tabernacle**, a free-standing chapel with fine reliefs and sculpted angels by Andrea Orcagna (1350), precious stones and metalwork (every guild contributed something if it could), and a *Madonna* by Bernardo Daddi.

Piazza della Signoria

Now that the city has finally chased the cars out of this big medieval piazza it serves as a great corral for tourists, endlessly snapping pictures of the Palazzo Vecchio. In the old days it would be full of Florentines, the stage set for the tempestuous life of their republic. The public assemblies met here, and at times of danger the bells would ring and the piazza quickly fill with citizen militia, assembling under the banners of their quarters and guilds. Savonarola held his Bonfire of Vanities here, and only a few years later the disenchanted Florentines ignited their Bonfire of Savonarola on the same spot (you can see a painting of the event at San Marco). Today the piazza is still the favoured spot for political rallies.

The three graceful arches of the **Loggia dei Lanzi**, next to the Palazzo Vecchio, were the reviewing stand for city officials during assemblies and celebrations. Florentines often call it the *Loggia dell'Orcagna*, after the architect who designed it in the 1370s. In its simple classicism the Loggia anticipates the architecture of Brunelleschi and all those who came after him. The city has made it an outdoor sculpture gallery, with some of the best-known works in Florence: Cellini's triumphant Perseus (*under* *restoration*) and Giambologna's *Rape of the Sabines*, his bronze equestrian statue of Cosimo – standing imperiously at the centre of the piazza – as well as some of his other works, and a chorus of Roman-era Vestal Virgins.

All the statues in the piazza are dear to the Florentines for one reason or another. Some are fine works of art; others have only historical associations. Michelangelo's *David*, a copy of which stands in front of the Palazzo near the spot the artist intended for it, was meant as a symbol of republican virtue and Florentine excellence. At the opposite extreme, Florentines are taught almost from birth to ridicule the **Neptune Fountain**, a pompous monstrosity with a giant marble figure of the god. The sculptor, Ammannati, thought he would upstage Michelangelo, though the result is derisively known as *Il Biancone* ('Big Whitey'). Bandinelli's statue of *Hercules and Cacus* is almost as big and just as awful; Cellini called it a 'sack of melons'.

Palazzo Vecchio

Open in summer Tues, Wed and Sat 9–7, Mon and Fri 9–11, Thurs and Sun 9–2; in winter Fri–Wed 9–7, Thurs 9–2; adm.

Florence's republican government was never perfect. In the better times chronic factionalism was barely kept in check, usually by the utter destruction or exile of one side or the other. Typically, however, the Florentines managed to give their aspirations a perfect symbol. The proud republic would accept nothing less than the most imposing 'Palazzo del Popolo' (as it was originally called) and Arnolfo di Cambio was able to give it to them. Even though the 308ft tower was for a long time Florence's tallest, Arnolfo avoided the sort of theatrical façade he was planning for the Duomo. The **Palazzo Vecchio** is part council hall, part fortress and part prison, and looks to fit all three roles well. Its rugged façade, copied in so many Florentine palaces, is not quite as frank and plain as it looks; all its proportions are based on the Golden Section of the ancient Greeks, rediscovered by medieval mathematicians. You may also accuse it of politically playing both sides – with square Guelph crenellations on the cornice and the swallowtail Ghibelline style on the tower.

The palace is often called the Palazzo della Signoria, the name it had under the rule of the Medici. After the final consolidation of their new government, the Duchy of Tuscany, the Medici turned the Palazzo Vecchio upside down. The house where Guelphs and Ghibellines once brawled in the council hall, and where lions were kept in the basement as a totem animal for the state, now became a florid Mannerist bower fit for a duke. Cosimo de' Medici's pet architect, Giorgio Vasari, oversaw the work in the 1550s and 1560s. Though the Medici did not reside there for long, the Palazzo was always used for state functions.

Today the Palazzo has somewhat recovered its old purpose. It serves as Florence's city hall, and the council holds its meetings in the **Salone dei Cinquecento**, built by the republic in 1495. At that time Leonardo da Vinci and Michelangelo were commissioned to fresco the two longer sides, a contest of talents that everyone in Florence looked forward to. For a number of reasons it never came off; only a small part of Leonardo's fresco was ever completed, and Vasari painted over it 60 years later.

Even the designs for both men's concepts have been lost. Michelangelo's statue of Victory, originally intended for the tomb of Pope Julius II in Rome, was installed here by Vasari in the 1560s.

Despite the Palazzo's functional role as a base for the city administration, nearly all of the more historic rooms are open to the public, so you can look round the ferociously over-decorated **Cortile**, or courtyard, redone by Vasari. Inside, upstairs on the first floor, there is the fascinating **Studiolo di Francesco I**, a little retreat created for Duke Cosimo's son, who liked to dabble in poisons, where Vasari and his assistants painted a vast allegory of mythology, science and alchemy; more Vasari in the Chambers of Leo X and Clement VII (including a famous scene of the 1527 siege); and even more Vasari in the Quartiere degli Elementi upstairs. Rooms with frescoes glorifying the Medici go on and on, but try not to miss the rooms of Eleanor of Toledo (Cosimo I's consort) done by Bronzino, or the **Sala dei Gigli**, with a fine ceiling by the da Maiano brothers and *Judith and Holofernes* by Donatello.

Museo Nazionale de Bargello

Open 8.30–1.50; closed alternate Sun and Mon; adm.

For centuries this medieval fortress-palace on the Via del Proconsolo, behind the Palazzo Vecchio, served as Florence's prison; today the inmates are men of marble – Italy's finest collection of sculpture, a fitting complement to the paintings in the Uffizi. When it was begun, about 1250, the Bargello was the Palazzo del Popolo, though by 1271 it was home to the foreign *podestà* installed by Charles of Anjou. When the Republic was reconstructed under the *Ordinamenti*, the decision was made to erect a bigger and grander seat of government – the Palazzo Vecchio. Just as that structure served as the model for so many Florentine palaces, so the Bargello was the model for the Palazzo, a rugged, austere work with a solid air of civic virtue about it. The Medici made a jail of it, but a thorough – and perhaps somewhat imaginative – restoration of the interior in the 19th century got it ready for its current job of housing the **Museo Nazionale**.

After the plain façade the delightful arcaded courtyard comes as a surprise, full of interesting architectural fragments, plaques and coats of arms in a wild vocabulary of symbols. In the ground-floor galleries there are some early works of Michelangelo, including the Bacchus, and also Giambologna's *Mercury* – a work so popular it has entered everyone's consciousness as the way Mercury should look. There are also a number of works by Cellini, including his preliminary model for *Perseus* and his bust of *Cosimo I*. Upstairs, passing through the **Loggia**, now converted into an 'aviary' for Giambologna's charming bronze birds, you come to the **Salone del Consiglio**. This 14th-century hall contains many of the greatest works of Donatello: the fascinatingly androgynous *David*, the *St George* from Orsanmichele and the enigmatic Cupid or *Amor Atys*. These three alone make up a powerful case for considering Donatello the greatest of Renaissance sculptors. The alert watchfulness of *St George* created new possibilities in expressing movement, emotion and depth of character in stone, a revolution in art that was obvious even to Donatello's contemporaries. The *David*, obviously from a different planet from Michelangelo's *David*, explores depths of the

Florentine psyche the Florentines probably didn't know they had. The same could be said of the dangerous-looking little boy Cupid. No one knows for whom Donatello made it, or who it is really meant to represent. With its poppies, serpents and winged sandals, it could easily be the ancient idol people in the 18th century mistook it for. Like Botticelli's mythological paintings it reflects the artistic and intellectual undercurrents of the quattrocento, full of pagan philosophy and eroticism, a possibility rooted out in the terror of the Counter-Reformation and quite forgotten soon after.

Among the other artists represented in the hall are Luca della Robbia, Verrocchio, Bernini, Michelozzo and di Duccio. The two bronze panels made by Brunelleschi and Ghiberti for the baptistry doors competition are preserved here; judge for yourself which is the better. Above, on the second floor, the collection continues with works mainly by Antonio Pollaiuolo and Verrocchio.

The Bargello also houses an important collection of the decorative arts – rooms full of pretty bric-a-brac such as combs, mirrors, jewel caskets, reliquaries, Turkish helmets, vases and silks, wax anatomical figures and majolica from Urbino. Some of the most beautiful pieces are in a collection of medieval French ivory – intricately carved scenes like the *Assault on the Castle of Love* and other medieval fancies. The Bargello's **chapel** has frescoes by an unknown follower of Giotto.

Dante's Florence

Dante would contemplate his Beatrice, the story goes, at Mass in the **Badia Fiorentina** (*entrance on Via Dante Alighieri; open Mon only 3–6, or during Mass, held Mon–Sat 6.15pm, Sun 11am*), a Benedictine church on Via del Proconsolo across from the Bargello, with a lovely Gothic spire to grace this corner of the Florentine skyline. The church has undergone many rebuildings since Willa, widow of a Margrave of Tuscany, began it in around 990, but there is still a monument to Ugo, the 'Good Margrave' mentioned in Dante, and a painting of the *Madonna Appearing to St Bernard* by Filippino Lippi.

Between the Badia and Via dei Calzaiuoli, a little corner of medieval Florence has survived the changes of centuries. In these quiet, narrow streets you can visit the **Casa di Dante** (*open winter Mon and Wed–Sat 10–4, Sun 10–2; summer Wed–Mon 9–6; closed Tues; adm*), which was actually built in 1911 over the ruins of an amputated tower house, although scholars all agree that the Alighieri lived somewhere in the vicinity. Nearby, the stoutly medieval *Torre del Castagna* is the last extant part of the original Palazzo del Popolo, predecessor to the Bargello and Palazzo Vecchio. After giving up on Beatrice, Dante married his second choice, Gemma Donati, in the **Santa Margherita** church on the same block. Another church nearby, **San Martino del Vescovo**, has a fine set of frescoes from the workshop of Ghirlandaio – worth a look inside if it's open.

Florence As It Was

If, tramping the long and tired streets of this city, you still haven't discovered the Florence you came to find, stop in at the **Museo di Firenze Com'Era** (Museum of Florence As It Was), Via dell'Oriuolo 24 (*open Fri–Wed 9–2; closed Thurs; adm*), north of the Bargello and not far from the Duomo. In the first room, almost covering the entire wall, is the *Pianta della Catena*, most famous and most beautiful of the early views of Florence. Made in 1490 by an unknown artist (the handsome fellow pictured in the lower right-hand corner), it is really a copy of the original, lost during the Second World War in a Berlin museum. This fascinating painting captures Florence at the height of the Renaissance. Not much has changed; the great churches are without their façades, the Uffizi and Medici chapels have not yet appeared, and the Medici and Pitti palaces are shown without their later extensions.

This museum is not large – it has only a number of plans and maps, as well as a collection of watercolours of Florence's sights from the last century. One surprising fact that becomes clear from a visit here is that today's fussy and staid Florentines are much less interested in Renaissance Florence than in the city of their grandparents. For some further evidence check around the corner on Via Sant'Egidio, where remodelling has uncovered posters from 1925 announcing plans for paying the war debt and a forthcoming visit of the Folies Bergère. The Florentines have restored them and put them under glass.

The Uffizi Gallery

Queues are very common in the summer; try to arrive early. Open summer Tues–Fri 8.30–9, Sat 8.30–midnight, Sun 8.30–8; winter Tues–Sun 8.30–6.50; adm exp. You can now pre-book by phone, t 055 294 883.

Poor Giorgio Vasari. His roosterish boastfulness and conviction that his was the best of all possible artistic worlds, set next to his very modest talents, have made him almost a comic figure in some art criticism. Even the Florentines don't like him. But on one of the rare occasions when he tried his hand as an architect he gave Florence something to be proud of. The Uffizi ('offices') were meant as Cosimo's secretariat, incorporating the old mint and archive buildings, with plenty of room for the bureaucrats needed to run the efficient, modern state Cosimo was building. The matched pair of arcaded buildings with restrained, elegant façades conceals a revolutionary but little-known innovation. Iron reinforcements inside the façades make the huge amount of window area possible, and keep the building stable on the soft ground below; it was a trick that would almost be forgotten until the building of the Crystal Palace and the first American skyscrapers. The Uffizi is also a noteworthy piece of Renaissance urban design, an intelligent conception that unites the Piazza della Signoria with the Arno.

The Uffizi has undergone major **reorganization** in the last couple of years. Some of this involved the restoration of remaining damage after the bomb (all but a very few paintings are now back on display), but improvements have also been made on a practical level. The most significant changes involve the ground floor, where major restoration has resulted in a vastly improved space; there are now three entrances (for individuals, groups and pre-paid tickets), bookshops, cloakrooms, video and computer facilities and information desks. If you are particularly keen on seeing a certain painting, note that rooms may be temporarily closed when you visit; this seems to depend on staff availability. There is a list of closures at the ticket counters.

Almost from the start the Medici began to store their huge art collections in parts of the Uffizi. The last of the Medici, Duchess Anna Maria Lodovica, willed the entire hoard to the people of Florence in 1737. Give yourself a day or two to spend on the most important picture gallery in Italy, and come early in the day, especially in summer, when queues sometimes stretch around the arcades and beyond by 11am.

The size of the collection in the Uffizi is not overwhelming, but every work is choice. All the Florentine masters are represented, and the Medici even deigned to purchase a few foreigners. Here is a brief list of the works most worth seeing: Room 2 has some fine trecento works by **Duccio di Buoninsegna** and **Cimabue**. If you can't make it to Siena this trip, be sure to see the works of that city's school, especially the **Lorenzetti brothers** and **Simone Martini**.

From the early quattrocento Florentine painters there is **Uccello's** *Battle of San Romano*; even with only one third of the original present this is one of the most provocative of all paintings, a surreal vision of war with pink, white and blue toy horses. **Piero della Francesca** contributes a *Portrait of Federico da Montefeltro* with his famous nose (*see* Urbino, p.577–81); **Filippo Lippi** is also here. **Botticelli** gets one big room to himself, in which are displayed his uncanny, erotic masterpieces including *The Birth of Venus*, *Primavera* and *Pallas and the Centaur* (another subtle allegory of the Medici triumph – the rings on Athena's gown were a family symbol), as well as some of his religious paintings and the disturbing *Calumny*, an introduction to the dark side of the quattrocento psyche.

Be sure to visit Room 15 and **Leonardo's** *Annunciation*, an intellectual revelation that is one of the foremost achievements of Florentine art. Nearby is a formidable sea monster in **Piero di Cosimo's** *Perseus and Andromeda*. In the Tribuna, a gaudy chamber designed by Bernardo Buontalenti, the Medici kept a valuable collection of Hellenistic and Roman sculpture, as well as portraits of *Cosimo* and *Eleanor of Toledo* by **Bronzino**. There's a surprising amount of German and Flemish painting, including **Dürer's** *Adoration of the Magi* and *Adam and Eve*, both looking as much like Italian painting as he could make them – and **Cranach's** *Portraits of Luther and Melanchthon*, spying on the Catholics. Venetians aren't as well represented, but there is the *Judgement of Solomon* by **Giorgione** and a *Sacred Allegory* by **Giovanni Bellini**.

Michelangelo always maintained that sculpture and fresco were the only arts fit for a man; oil painting he disdained, and just coincidentally he wasn't very good at it. The *Doni Tondi* here is the only canvas he ever finished. Next come some portraits by **Raphael, Rosso Fiorentino** and **Pontormo**; and the brightly coloured paintings of **Andrea del Sarto**. **Titian's** overdressed Spaniards and well-upholstered girls get a room to themselves. The collections continue through painters of the 17th and 18th centuries – works of **Rembrandt** (two self-portraits), **Rubens, Van Dyck**, even **Goya**; the one exceptional picture here is the *Boy Playing at Cards* by **Chardin**.

In 1565 Francesco I commissioned Vasari to link the Palazzo Vecchio and the Uffizi to the Pitti Palace across the river, so he could pass through without rubbing elbows with his subjects. After 400 years, Florence just wouldn't look right without this covered passageway, the **Corridoio Vasariano**, leapfrogging around the back of the Uffizi, then over the top of the Ponte Vecchio, through the rooftops on the other side and into the Pitti. The corridor contains a unique collection of artists' self-portraits, by Vasari himself, Velasquez, Rembrandt, Hogarth and many French artists. (*Only open at certain times of year; check with tourist office and book a visit early if possible.*)

Given the amount that Florence and the rest of Tuscany contributed to the birth of science it is only fitting to have the **Museo di Storia della Scienza** (Museum of the History of Science) in the heart of the city, just behind the Uffizi on Via Castellani (*open summer Mon and Wed–Fri 9.30–5, Tues and Sat 9.30–1; closed Sun; winter Mon and Wed–Sat 9.30–5, Tues 9.30–1, also 2nd Sun of month only 10–1; adm exp*). Even in the dark centuries Florence never abandoned its scientific interests; the collection began with an institute founded by the Medici in the 1730s, the Accademia del Cimento, whose motto was 'Try and try again'. Pride of place goes to Galileo's instruments, including his first telescope, in addition to a large number of astrolabes, early microscopes, models of the planets, and armillary spheres, many of which are beautiful works of art in their own right. The last rooms contain wax anatomical models, a 15th-century Medici fetish.

Ponte Vecchio and Ponte S. Trinità

No one knows how long the Arno has been spanned at this point. The present bridge, built in 1345, replaced a wooden construction from the 970s, which in turn was the successor to a span that may have gone back to the Romans. Like medieval bridges in London and many other European cities, the new 14th-century bridge had shops and houses built all along it. By the 16th century it had become the street of the butchers; after Vasari built Cosimo's secret passage over the top the duke evicted the butchers (he didn't like the pong) and gave their places to the goldsmiths. They have kept their spot ever since, and hordes of shoppers from around the world descend on it each year to scrutinize the Florentine talent for jewellery. This is the most prestigious shopping location in Florence, and the jewellers are happy to stay – they could not be deterred even by the 1966 flood, when a fortune in gold was washed down the Arno.

In the summer of 1944 the river briefly became a German defensive line during the slow painful retreat across central Italy. Before they left Florence the Germans blew up every one of the city's bridges, saving only the Ponte Vecchio. Somehow the city managed to talk them out of it, and instead buildings on both sides were destroyed and the rubble piled up to block the approaches. Florence's most beautiful span, the **Ponte Santa Trinità**, had to go, however. The Florentines like their city just as it is, and immediately after the war they set about replacing the bridges exactly as they were. In the case of Santa Trinità it was quite a task. Old quarries had to be reopened to duplicate the stone, and old methods used to cut it (modern power saws would have done it too cleanly). The graceful curve of the three arches was a problem; they cannot be constructed geometrically and considerable speculation went on over how the architect (Ammannati, in 1567) had done it. Finally, remembering that Michelangelo had advised Ammannati on the project, someone discovered that the same form of arch could be seen on the decoration of Michelangelo's Medici Chapels, constructed most likely not by mathematics and common engineering, but by pure artistic imagination. Fortune lent a hand in the reconstruction; of the original statues of the *Four Seasons*, almost all the pieces were fished out of the Arno and reconstructed. Spring's head was missing, however, and controversy raged for a decade over whether to replace it or leave it as it was, until some divers found it, completely by accident, in 1961.

Around Piazza della Repubblica

On the map it is easy to pick out the small rectangle of narrow, straight streets at the heart of Florence; these remain unchanged from the little *castrum* of Roman days. At its centre the old forum deteriorated through the Dark Ages into a shabby market square, surrounded by the Jewish ghetto. So it remained until Florence, in a fit of post-Risorgimento ambition, decided to make it a symbol of the city's reawakening. The square was given a new design and a thorough facelift, and a grand arch was built, with a big inscription: THE ANCIENT CITY CENTRE RESTORED TO NEW LIFE FROM THE SQUALOR OF CENTURIES. Unfortunately the results were the same as in the new façade for the Duomo; Piazza della Repubblica is one of the ghastliest squares in Italy. Just the same, it is a popular place with tourists and natives alike, full of cafés with outside tables, and something of an oasis among the severe, unwelcoming streets of old Florence.

Those streets are worth walking. Dreary as they look at first sight, they are part of the soul of Florence. Also they are full of surprises; walk down Calimala, an important shopping street south of the Piazza, and you will encounter the **Arte della Lana**, behind Orsanmichele and connected to it by an overhead passageway. The 'Wool Corporation', richest of the guilds save that of the bankers, was really a sort of manufacturers' cooperative; its headquarters, built in 1308, was restored in 1905 in a delightful William Morris style of medieval picturesque. Nearby, further towards the river, is one of Florence's oldest marketplaces, covered by a beautiful loggia built in the 1500s. The **Mercato Nuovo**, where vendors hawk purses, toys and every sort of trinket, was in medieval times a merchants' exchange; it was also the place where the *carroccio*, the decorated wagon that served as a rallying point for the citizen armies during battles, was kept in time of peace. Florentines often call this the *Loggia del Porcellino*, after the drooling bronze boar put up as a decoration in 1612, a copy of a Greek sculpture in the Uffizi (it was replaced by another copy in 1999).

Between Via delle Terme and Via Porta Rossa the 14th-century **Palazzo Davanzati** recreates the atmosphere of a wealthy merchant's house of the 15th century as the **Museo della Casa Fiorentina Antica** (*closed for restoration; exhibition on ground floor open 8.30–1.50; closed alternate Sun and Mon*). Some of the furnishings are from a century or two later, but the late-medieval atmosphere is present and, if historically accurate, a tribute to the taste of the honest burghers of the time. Some of Florence's most typical old town houses lie between here and the river. Off Via Pellicceria, behind the Mercato Nuovo, is the 14th-century Guelph Party Building, often the real seat of power in the city, built with money confiscated from exiled Ghibellines.

Closer to the Arno stands **SS. Apostoli** (11th century), with a tabernacle by Andrea della Robbia; in the narrow streets around it you'll find the Piazzetta del Limbo, where unbaptized babies were buried in the Middle Ages. Further along the river, Gothic **Santa Trinità** has a dull façade added in the 1590s. One of the chapels has colourful frescoes by Lorenzo Monaco, who also did the altarpiece; another, the Sassetti Chapel, was decorated by Ghirlandaio. Ostensibly a series on the life of St Francis, scholars always comment on the frescos as a document of Florence's social history. All the Medici, Sassetti and their friends are present in finely detailed portraits, subtly arranged to show the city's new hierarchy of political and economic power.

For more Ghirlandaio continue on to the 13th-century **Ognissanti** (All Saints' Church), with another heavy façade added later. The man who named a continent, Amerigo Vespucci, is buried by the second altar on the right. Botticelli and Ghirlandaio both contributed versions of St Jerome for the cloister (*open daily 8–12 and 4–7*), and the latter's *Cenacolo* in the refectory (*open Mon, Tues and Sat 9–12*) is one of his better known works, a Last Supper that is more a garden party, with lemon trees and exotic birds, as well as a sulky Judas, third from the right.

Conspicuous Consumption *alla Fiorentina*

The streets west of Piazza della Repubblica have always been the choicest district of Florence. Via Tornabuoni, the fanciest shopping street, is as well-known in fashion as Via Montenapoleone in Milan or Via dei Condotti in Rome. In the 15th century this was the area most of the new merchant élite chose for their palaces. Today's bankers build great skyscrapers for the firm and settle for modest mansions themselves; in medieval Florence, things were reversed. The bankers and wool tycoons really owned their businesses, and in absolute terms probably had more money than anyone had ever had before. While their places of business were usually quite simple, for themselves they built imposing city palaces; all in the same conservative style, and competing with each other in size like a Millionaire's Row of Victorian-era America.

The style, derived from the Palazzo Vecchio, began at the **Palazzo Rucellai** on Via della Vigna Nuova, a building designed by Alberti in 1446 for a prominent manufacturer and patron of learning. Much has been made of this building as a turning point in architecture; its real innovation is a consistent and skilful use of the classical 'orders', the system of proportion learned from Vitruvius. Of the other palaces in the neighbourhood north of Piazza S. Trinità, two stand out – the 1465 **Palazzo Antinori**, at the northern end of Tornabuoni, and the **Palazzo Strozzi**, two streets south. The Strozzi is the daddy of them all, the accustomed design blown up to heroic proportions; though three storeys like the rest, here each floor is as tall as three or four normal ones. Filippo Strozzi, head of a family of bankers who often felt strong enough to challenge the leadership of the Medici, built it in 1489 at the height of the clan's fortunes. Fifty years later his grandchildren were all exiles, bankers and advisers to the king of France. Both the Antinori and Strozzi palaces were the work of Benedetto da Maiano; the Strozzi often hosts art exhibitions.

Santa Maria Novella

Santa Maria Novella, begun by the Dominicans in 1246, was always associated with the great families; in the 1600s the wealthy families of the neighbourhood would

Santa Maria Novella

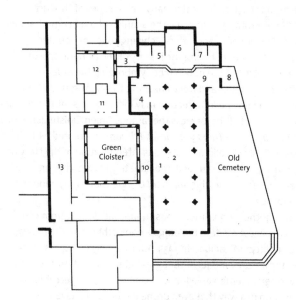

1 Masaccio's *Trinity*
2 Brunelleschi's Pulpit
3 Cappèlla Strozzi
4 Sacristy
5 Cappella Gondi
6 Sanctuary
7 Filippo Strozzi Chapel
8 Rucellai Chapel
9 Gothic Tombs
10 *Universal Deluge*
11 Spanish Chapel
12 Chiostrino dei Morte
13 Refectory

hold an annual carriage race around the two fat obelisks in the piazza. Between them they bestowed so much money to embellish it that by the 1500s the church became a museum, with important works of many late-medieval and Renaissance artists.

The brilliant black and white patterned façade, still the finest in Florence, shows the continuity of the city's style from medieval times. The lower half is part of the original work, finished before 1360, but the rest had to wait for one of the Rucellai family to commission Alberti to finish the job. It's his best work in Florence, a synthesis of classical architecture and medieval Florentine tradition, with volutes and arabesques that seem already to prefigure the Baroque. An odd touch is the image of the sun at the apex, the only image or symbol of any kind in Alberti's plan. Lower down, Cosimo I added the two unusual sundials over the left- and right-hand arches.

Inside, above the portal, is a *Nativity* by Botticelli. From there, proceeding clockwise around the church: a pulpit with reliefs by Brunelleschi; Masaccio's *Trinità* fresco, one of the earliest works with the temerity to depict God the Father; and a *Resurrection* by Vasari. In the left transept, the Gondi Chapel has Brunelleschi's only wood sculpture, a crucifix – Vasari tells how he made it to show Donatello a Christ with proper dignity, as his friend's crucifix (now in Santa Croce) made the Redeemer 'look like a peasant'. A great series of frescoes of the *Lives of St John and the Virgin* by Ghirlandaio surrounds the main altar. All his students helped him complete it – little Michelangelo included. Some equally fine frescoes by Filippino Lippi adorn the Filippo Strozzi Chapel in the right transept, where Strozzi is buried; the architect who designed his palace, Da Maiano, also carved his tomb.

There's little of interest in the right-hand chapels, but just outside the left transept are some of the best parts of this surprisingly large monastic complex. Another Strozzi Chapel, this one from the 1360s, has a fine early fresco series of the *Last Judgement* by Nardo di Cione, brother of Orcagna. The Spanish Chapel, commissioned by Cosimo I's Spanish wife Eleanor of Toledo, offers a chilling touch of Counter-Reformation with a series of frescoes detailing the history of the Dominicans: the *domini canes* ('dogs of the Lord') sit at the pope's feet, symbolizing the order that ran the Inquisition and sniffed out heretics and freethinkers. In the background an interesting view of the Duomo as a fairly pink confection may in fact represent the original plans of Arnolfo di Cambio. Best of all, however, is the famous **Green Cloister** (*entrance just to the left of the church; open Sat–Thurs 9–2; closed Fri; adm*), decorated with the most important frescoes by Paolo Uccello, a mysterious interpretation of the story of Noah that has stoked controversy for centuries. Unfortunately the frescoes are much deteriorated, but the best preserved one, the *Universal Deluge*, is uncanny enough to haunt your imagination for years.

Just behind Santa Maria another large, amorphous square will detract from your appreciation of one of Italy's finest modern buildings – none other than the railway station, designed by the architect Michelucci in 1935. Adorned only by a glass block canopy at the entrance (and an early model of that great Italian invention, the digital clock), the station is nevertheless remarkable for its clean lines and impeccable practicality; form following function in a way that even Brunelleschi would have appreciated.

San Lorenzo and the Medici Chapels

Around the railway station beats the true heart of tourist Florence, dozens of streets around the Via Nazionale packed with hotels, restaurants and bars. There's an almost Neapolitan air about the boisterous street market that surrounds the **Mercato Centrale**, built in the 1890s to replace the old market evicted from the Piazza della Repubblica, and known locally as 'Shanghai'. The market *bancarelle* extend all the way to **San Lorenzo**, a church always associated with the Medici, and a shrine to the art of Brunelleschi and Michelangelo. Brunelleschi built it in the 1420s; Michelangelo designed a façade that was never realized, leaving the odd-shaped church as charming as a huge dreadnought docked in the piazza.

The interior, however, is essential Brunelleschi, a contemplative repetition of arches and columns in grey and white, while nothing else in Florence prepares you for the two pulpits in the nave, the last violent, near-impressionistic works of Donatello. Off the left transept, the **Old Sacristy** is a beautiful vaulted chamber with calmer sculptural decoration by Donatello.

Outside the church, a separate entrance on Piazza Madonna degli Aldobrandini leads to the famous **Medici Chapels** (*open Mon–Sat 8.30–5, Sun 8.30–1.50; closed alternate Sun and Mon; adm exp*) and their celebrated sculptures by Michelangelo. First, however, you will have to pass through the Prince's Chapel, under a huge eight-sided dome that dwarfs the rest of San Lorenzo, begun in 1604 following a design by a dilettante architect member of the Medici family. Several of the Medici dukes are buried in this dreary, trashy rotunda, the true monument of the ducal period and a sobering demonstration of just how soon Florence's great age of art declined into provincialism and preciosity. It certainly cost enough – the entire lower walls and floor are done in *pietra dura* with rich marbles from around the world, a job still not completed.

From here a corridor to the left leads to the **New Sacristy**, designed by Michelangelo in a severe style to match the Old Sacristy on the other side. The two tombs, of Giuliano Medici, Duke of Nemours, and Lorenzo, Duke of Urbino, the ruler to whom Machiavelli dedicated *The Prince*, are decorated with an allegorical sculptural scheme that has caused much discussion over the centuries. Giuliano is portrayed as a soldier representing the Active Life, with figures representing Day and Night reclining on his sarcophagus below. Lorenzo, as the Contemplative Life, sits and contemplates, over-looking figures of Dawn and Dusk (true to life in one respect; the passive Lorenzo was a disappointment to Machiavelli and everyone else). The male figures, at least, are among Michelangelo's triumphs. The women, Dawn and Night, come off less well. Michelangelo never had much use for the ladies – he wouldn't even use female models – and, whatever role they played in his personal mythology, he portrays them here as imperfect men, male forms with flabbier musculature and breasts stuck on like superfluous appendages.

In front of San Lorenzo a separate entrance leads to the **Biblioteca Laurenziana** (*open Mon, Fri and Sat 9–1.45, Tues–Thurs 8–5*), designed for the Medici by Michelangelo and built by Ammannati, an important landmark in architecture: it was Michelangelo's first commission (along with the Medici Chapels), and one of the first steps on the slippery slope to Mannerism.

Palazzo Medici Riccardi

San Lorenzo became the Medici's church because it stood just round the corner from the family palace – a huge, stately building on Via Cavour constructed by Alberti and Michelozzo about the same time as the Palazzo Rucellai. The family's coat-of-arms, which you've probably already noticed everywhere in Florence, is prominently displayed in the corners. The seven, sometimes six, red boluses probably come from the family's origin as pharmacists (*medici*), and opponents called them 'the pills'. Medici supporters, however, made them their battle cry in street battles: 'Balls! Balls!'. The main reason for visiting is one of Florence's hidden delights: the **chapel** (*open Thurs–Tues 9–7, closed Wed; adm; only a few people allowed in at a time; in summer reserve on t 055 276 0340*), with extravagantly colourful frescoes by Benozzo Gozzoli. The *Procession of the Magi* is hardly a religious painting, a merry scene full of portraits of the Medici and others among the crowd following the Three Kings. The artist included himself, with his name on his hat. In the foreground of one of the panels, note the black man carrying a bow. Blacks (also Turks, Circassians, Tartars and other non-Europeans) were common enough in Renaissance Florence. Though originally brought as slaves, by the 1400s not all were still servants. Contemporary writers mention them as artisans, fencing masters, soldiers and, in one famous case, as an archery instructor, who may be the man pictured here. For an extraordinary contrast pop into the **gallery** with its 17th-century ceiling by Neapolitan Luca Giordano, showing the last, unspeakable Medici floating around in marshmallow clouds.

San Marco

*Convent open Mon–Fri and Sun 8.15–1.50, Sat 8.15–6.50; closed
1st and 3rd Sun of month and 2nd and 4th Mon of month; adm.
Church open 7–12 and 4–7 daily.*

Despite all the others who contributed to this Dominican monastery and church, it has always been best known for the work of its most famous resident. Fra Angelico lived here from 1436 until his death in 1455, spending the time turning Michelozzo's simple **cloister** into a complete exposition of his own deep faith, expressed in bright playroom colours and angelic pastels. Fra Angelico painted the frescoes in the corners of the cloister, and on the first floor there is a small museum of his work, collected from various Florentine churches, as well as a number of early 15th-century portraits by Fra Bartolomeo, capturing some of the most sincere spirituality of that age. The *Last Supper* in the refectory is by Ghirlandaio.

Other Fra Angelico works include the series of the *Life of Christ*, telling the story sweetly and succinctly, and a serenely confident Last Judgement in which the saved are well-dressed Italians, holding hands. They keep their clothes in heaven, while the bad (mostly princes and prelates) are stripped to receive their interesting tortures.

Right at the top of the stairs to the monk's dormitory, your eyes meet the Angelic Friar's masterpiece, a miraculous *Annunciation* that offers an intriguing comparison to Leonardo's *Annunciation* in the Uffizi. The subject was a favourite with Florentine artists, not only because it was a severe test – expressing a divine revelation with a composition of strict economy – but because the Annunciation, falling near the spring equinox, was New Year's Day for Florence until the Medici adopted the Pope's calendar in the 17th century.

In each of the monks' cells Fra Angelico and students painted the Crucifixion, all the same but for some slight differences in pose; walking down the corridor and glancing in the cells successively gives the impression of a cartoon. One of the cells belonged to Savonarola, who was the prior here during his period of dominance in Florence; it has simple furniture of the period and a portrait of Savonarola by Fra Bartolomeo. Michelozzo's Library, off the main corridor, is as light and airy as the cloisters below; in it is displayed a collection of choir books, including one illuminated by Fra Angelico.

If you liked Andrea del Castagno's work in the Uffizi, just around the corner from San Marco is a work many consider to be his best, the *Last Supper*, in the convent of **Sant'Apollonia**, Via XXVII Aprile 1 (*open daily 8.30–1.50; closed alternate Sun and Mon*).

Piazza Santissima Annunziata

This square, the only Renaissance attempt at a unified ensemble in Florence, is surrounded by arcades on three sides. The earliest of its buildings, one of Brunelleschi's most famous works, is also a monument to Renaissance Italy's long, hard and ultimately unsuccessful struggle towards some kind of social consciousness. Even in the best times Florence's poor were treated like dirt; if any enlightened soul had been so bold as to propose even a modern conservative 'trickle down' theory to the Medici and the banking élite, their first thought would have been how to stop the leaks. Babies, at least, had it a little better. The **Spedale degli Innocenti** (*open Thurs–Tues 8.30–2; adm*), built in the 1420s, was Florence's foundling hospital, and still functions as an orphanage today. Brunelleschi's beautiful arcade, decorated with the famous tondi of infants in swaddling clothes by Luca della Robbia, was one of the early classicizing experiments in architecture. There's a small picture gallery containing Ghirlandaio's *Adoration of the Magi* and several other works.

To complement Brunelleschi's arches the old church of **Santissima Annunziata** was rebuilt, and Michelozzo gave it a broad arcaded portico facing the street. Behind the portico the architect added the *Chiostrino dei Voti*, a porch decorated with a collection of early 16th-century frescoes, including two by Andrea del Sarto. The best of these, faded as it is, is a finely detailed *Nativity* by Alessio Baldovinetti, one of the quattro-cento's under-appreciated masters. It is the gaudiest church in Florence; its gilded elliptical dome, its unusual polygonal tribune around the sanctuary, and megatons of *pietra dura* have helped it become the city's high-society parish, where even funerals are major social events. The **Tempietta**, the candlelit chapel in the rear, also by Michelozzo, shelters a miraculous painting of *The Annunciation*.

The Accademia

Open Tues–Sun 8.15–6.50; closed Mon; adm exp.

It may not be Florence's most interesting museum, but in summer the queues at the Accademia, just off the Piazza Santissima Annunziata, are often as long as those at the Uffizi. What people are most anxious to get a look at is of course Michelangelo's *David*. The artist completed it for the city in 1504, when he was 29, and it was this work that established the overwhelming reputation he had in his own time. Just over a hundred years ago Florence decided to take this precocious symbol of republican liberty in out of the rain. Looking entirely contented with his own perfection, he stands in a classical exedra built just for him (behind protective glass). As the political symbol the republic commissioned he may be excessive – the irony of a David the size of Goliath is disconcerting – but as a symbol of the artistic and intel-lectual aspirations of the Renaissance he is unsurpassed. Other Michelangelos include the famous *non finiti*: the *Prisoners* and *St Matthew*, tortured forms still waiting for Michelangelo to come back and finish liberating them from the stone.

There is plenty of indifferent painting in the Accademia, but persevere for such works as the *Deposition from the Cross* by Perugino, the sweet and small *Madonna del Mare* by Botticelli; and *Thebaid* by a follower of Ucello. Some of the best works are in a room of lesser-known masters of the quattrocento, especially Mariotto di Cristoforo and the 'Maestro del Casione Adimare', the latter known only for the painted chest displayed here, a delightful scene of a marriage in Florence in the 1450s that has been reproduced in half the books ever written about the Renaissance. There is also a collection of musical instruments.

Museo Archeologico

Via della Colonna 36; open Mon 2–7, Tues and Thurs 8.30–7,
Wed and Fri–Sun 8.30–2; adm.

One of the most devious tricks of the Florentine museum torture is to keep your interest by changing the subject; just when you can't take another transcendent Renaissance painting, they politely offer a chance to see the greatest collection of Etruscan art in Tuscany. Nor is that all; the Egyptian collection in the Archaeological Museum is also exceptional. Again, the Medici are responsible; the museum began with purchases by Cosimo and Lorenzo il Magnifico. The Etruscans fill room after room, but the star attractions are two exquisite bronzes: the *Arringatore*, or Orator, a civic-minded and civilized-looking gentleman whom the inscription tells us was named Aurus Metellus; and the *Chimera*, a remarkable beast with the three heads of a lion, goat and snake. This 5th-century BC Etruscan work, dug up near Arezzo in 1555 and immediately snatched by the Medici, had a great influence on Mannerist artists.

Greek art is also represented; Etruscan and Roman noble families were wont to buy up all they could afford. There is an excellent *kouros*, a young man in the archaic style from 6th-century BC Sicily, an almost complete ancient chariot, some good vases, and an unusual recent find: a 4th-century BC silver urn called the *Baratti Amphora*, made in Antioch and covered with scores of small medallions showing mythological figures. Scholars believe that the images and their arrangement may encode an entire system of belief, the secret teaching of one of the mystic-philosophical cults common in Hellenistic times, and they hope some day to decipher it.

Santa Croce

Santa Maria Novella was the Dominicans' church, and so naturally the Franciscans had to have one just as big and grand. The original church, said to have been founded by St Francis himself, went by the board in Florence's colossal building programme of the 1290s. Arnolfo di Cambio planned its successor, largely completed by the 1450s, but a job of 'restoration' by Vasari in the 1560s ruined much of the original interior. The façade, in the accustomed Florentine black and white marble, nevertheless has something of the Victorian Gothic about it – just as it should, since it was only added in the 1850s, a gift from Sir Francis Sloane.

No one has yet succeeded in doing anything with the vast, hideous piazza in front of it. However, it has become the venue every June for *Calcio in Costume*, a ball game similar to rugby, believed to be descended from a Roman sport that has its origins in the exercises of the citizen militias of the Florentine Republic. It's good fun to watch the usually immaculate Florentines in their Renaissance duds mixing it up in the dirt.

The interior is a different story; like Santa Maria Novella it is a museum in itself. Starting clockwise from the left side: near the door is the **tomb of Galileo**, whose remains were moved here only after the Church grudgingly consented to allow him a Christian burial in 1737. For a while it was the custom to bury great Italians here, as a sort of Tuscan Westminster Abbey, and you'll see plenty of tombs along both sides, mostly of thoroughly forgotten men of the 19th century. Two chapels down, the

Santa Croce

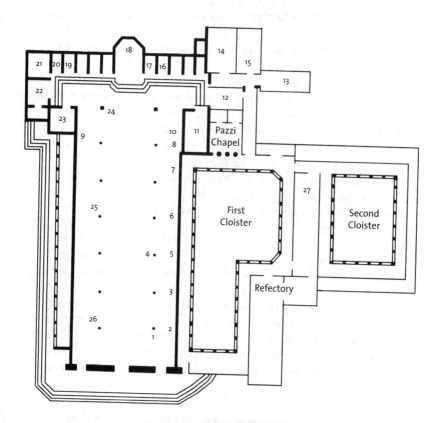

1 Madonna del Latte
2 Tomb of Michaelangelo
3 Monument to Dante
4 Benedetto da Maiano's Pulpit
5 Vittorio Alfieri's Tomb
6 Tomb of Machiavelli
7 Donatello's *Annuniciation*
8 Tomb of Leonardo Bruni
9 Tomb of Carlo Malaspini
10 Tomb of Rossini
11 Castellani Chapel
12 Baroncelli Chapel
13 Medici Chapel
14 Sacristy

15 Rinnuccini Chapel
16 Peruzzi Chapel
17 Bardi Chapel
18 Sanctuary
19 Bardi di Libertà Chapel
20 Bardi di Vernio Chapel
21 Niccolini Chapel
22 Bardi Chapel
23 Salviati Chapel
24 Monument to Alberti
25 Tomb of Lorenzo Ghiberti
26 Galileo's Tomb
27 Museo dell'Opera di S. Croce

Monument to Carlo Marsuppini is a mine of good quattrocento sculpture, mostly by Verrocchio and Desiderio da Settignano. Look in the Bardi Chapel in the left transept for the *Crucifix* by Donatello (the one Brunelleschi said looked like a peasant). Many of the small vaulted chapels that flank the high altar contain important late (1330s) works by Giotto, his assistants and his followers. In the second **Bardi Chapel** is a series of frescoes on the *Life of St Francis* that can be compared with the more famous frescoes of his life at Assisi.

The **Peruzzi Chapel** frescoes detail the *Lives of St John the Evangelist and St John the Baptist*. These works had a tremendous influence on all the later Florentine artists, but by the 18th century they were considered eyesores and whitewashed for 150 years – hence their fragmentary state. Two of Giotto's immediate artistic heirs, the Gaddi, also contributed much to Santa Croce. Agnolo Gaddi did the stained glass around the high altar, as well as the fascinating series of frescoes on the *Legend of the Cross* – how Seth received a branch from St Michael and planted it over Adam's grave, how the tree that grew from it was shaped into a beam for a bridge, then buried by Solomon when his guest the Queen of Sheba prophesied that it would some day bring about the end of the Jews. The beam was dug up and shaped into Christ's Cross, later found by St Helena, Constantine's mother, and then stolen by a Persian king and eventually recovered by the Emperor Heraclius. In the **sacristy**, off to the right, there are more fine frescoes by Agnolo Gaddi's father Taddeo, and yet more Gaddis in the Castellani Chapel (Agnolo) and Baroncelli Chapel (Taddeo).

Back down the right side of the church, Donatello's **Tabernacle** has a beautiful relief of the *Annunciation*. Then some more **tombs**: Rossini, Machiavelli, Michelangelo and Dante (not actually buried here). Michelangelo's is the work of Vasari, who thought himself just the fellow for the job. Vasari's vandalism ruined most of the chapels on this side, once embellished with frescoes by Orcagna and other trecento painters.

The Pazzi Chapel

Open Thurs–Tues 10–6, later opening hours in summer; closed Wed; adm.

One of Santa Croce's chapels is well worth its entrance fee. Brunelleschi saved some of his best work for small places. Without knowing the architect and something about the austere religious tendencies of the Florentines the Pazzi Chapel is inexplicable: a Protestant reformation in architecture unlike anything ever built before. The 'vocabulary' is essential Brunelleschi: simple pilasters, arches and rosettes in grey stone and white plaster.

The only decoration is a set of modest terracotta Apostles by Luca della Robbia, coloured roundels of the Evangelists by Donatello, and a small stained-glass window by Alessio Baldovinetti. Even so, this is enough. The contemplative repetition of elements makes for an aesthetic that posed a direct challenge to the international Gothic of the time.

Across the broad cloister, the monks' refectory and several adjoining rooms now house the **Museo dell'Opera di Santa Croce**, with more works by della Robbia, bits from a large fresco by Orcagna wrecked by Vasari's remodelling, one of Donatello's statues from Orsanmichele – the gilded bronze *St Louis of Toulouse* – and a famous, mournful *Crucifix* by Cimabue, one of the early landmarks of Florentine painting, which sadly it was only possible to partially restore after damage in the 1966 flood.

Around Santa Croce

The east end of Florence, a rambling district packed with artisans and small manufacturers, was the artists' quarter in Renaissance times. Close to the river, it suffered grievously in the 1966 floods and to some extent has never quite recovered. Few things around this district are very old, but just west of Piazza Santa Croce you will see a series of streets – Via Bentacorti, Via Torta and Piazza Peruzzi – making an almost complete ellipse. These mark the course of the inner arcade of Roman Florence's amphitheatre; some stones can still be seen among the foundations of the old palaces. To the south, on Via dei Benci near the Arno, is a collection that Herbert Horne (1844–1916), an English art historian and Florentinophile bequeathed to Italy as the **Museo Horne** (*open Mon–Sat 9–1; closed Sun and hols; adm*), with odds and ends, ceramics, and works by Giotto, Gozzoli and Desiderio da Settignano.

Michelangelo never actually lived in the **Casa Buonarroti**, Via Ghibellina 70 (*open Wed–Mon 9.30–2; adm exp*). The artist's fascination with real estate has given critics since Vasari something to gossip about; he picked this property up for some of his relatives, and later generations made it into a Michelangelo museum. Besides some drawings and models, the collection contains some of the artist's early works, the *Battle of the Centaurs* and a beautiful bas-relief called the *Madonna of the Stairs*. From here, three blocks north along Via Buonarroti will take you to the city's most colourful corner, Sant'Ambrogio market and the *mercatino* in **Piazza dei Ciompi**. This is Florence's famous flea market, where dozens of vendors wait to sell you endearing junk in all shapes and sizes behind the typically Florentine 'Fish Loggia', designed by Vasari and moved here when the old market in Piazza della Repubblica was demolished. Just to the east is the church of **Sant'Ambrogio**, which has been thoroughly Baroqued inside, but you can seek out good frescoes by Orcagna and Baldovinetti.

Across the Arno: the Palazzo Pitti

Once across the Ponte Vecchio a different Florence reveals itself: greener, quieter and less burdened with traffic. The **Oltrarno** is not a large district. A chain of hills squeezes it against the river, and their summits afford the best views over the city. Across the bridge, the Medici's catwalk passes almost over the top of **Santa Felicità**, best known as a monument to the quirky Mannerist painter Jacopo Pontormo. This artist, a recluse who lived atop a tower he built for himself, often pulling up the ladder to keep his friends at bay, frequently got himself into trouble with his neighbours for keeping the place full of dead animals and even human bodies, from which he studied form and anatomy. His work in Santa Felicità includes his acknowledged masterpiece, the *Deposition*, with its luminous, distorted figures and exaggerated expressions, as well as frescoes of the Annunciation and the Evangelists.

As the Medici consolidated their power in Florence, they made a point of buying up all the important properties of their former rivals, especially their proud family palaces. The most spectacular example of this ducal eminent domain was the acquisition by Cosimo I of the **Pitti Palace**, built in 1457 by a powerful banker named Luca Pitti. The palace and its extensive grounds, now the Boboli Gardens, were purchased by Cosimo in the 1540s; he and his wife, Eleanor of Toledo, liked it much better than the medieval Palazzo Vecchio, and soon moved in for good. The palace remained the residence of the Medici, and later the House of Lorraine, until 1868. The original building, said to have been designed by Brunelleschi, was only as wide as the seven central windows of the façade.

Succeeding generations found it too small for their burgeoning collections of bric-a-brac, and added several stages of symmetrical additions, resulting in a long bulky profile resembling some sort of Stalinist ministry. Piazza Pitti was a prized address in the old days – the greatest of all Florence fans, the Brownings, lived across from the palace, and so for a time did Dostoevsky.

There are eight separate **museums** in the Pitti, including collections dedicated to clothes, ceramics, carriages and paintings (by the likes of Titian, Raphael and Botticelli) – a tribute to Medici acquisitiveness in the centuries of decadence, a period from which, in the words of Mary McCarthy, 'flowed a torrent of bad taste that has not yet dried up...if there had been Toby jugs and Swiss weather clocks available, the Grand Dukes would certainly have collected them.' For the diligent visitor who wants to see everything, the Pitti is pitiless; it is impossible to see all in one day.

Boboli Gardens

Open daily 9–one hour before sunset; adm.

It is the loveliest park in the centre of Florence, the only park in the centre of Florence, and if you're visiting in the summer, the sooner you become acquainted with it the better. The Boboli is the only escape from the sun, humidity and crowds of July and August. Cosimo I began the planning and landscaping in the 1550s. The tone for what was to be the first Mannerist park was set early on by the incredible **Grotta del Buontalenti** (*currently under restoration; work is likely to continue for some time*), near the entrance behind the Pitti Palace. This artificial grotto is sheer madness, Gaudiesque dripping stone with peculiar creatures seeming to grow out of it. Inside are fantastic painted landscapes, surrounded by leopards, bears, satyrs and others harder to define.

There's a **museum of porcelain** (*open daily 9–1.30*), in a little palace called the Casino del Cavaliere, and the groves and walks of the Boboli are haunted by platoons of statuary, some Roman and some absurd Mannerist work, like the fat baby Bacchus riding a turtle. There's a genuine obelisk, in the centre of a miniature Roman circus, and a fountain from the Baths of Caracalla. Some of the best parts of the gardens are the furthest away: shady paths and flower beds towards the south, near Florence's southern gate, the Porta Romana.

Santo Spirito and Santa Maria del Carmine

The centre of the Oltrarno district, Piazza Santo Spirito usually has a small market going under the plane trees, as well as restaurants and a quiet café or two. The church, **Santo Spirito**, boasts a severe 18th-century façade that conceals one of

Brunelleschi's triumphs: a characteristic, contemplative interior of grey and white surrounded by ranks of semi-circular chapels. Even though later architects tinkered grievously with the plan after Brunelleschi's death, many consider this to be one of his best churches. Among the paintings in the chapels are works by Filippino Lippi (south transept, a *Madonna and Child*) and Orcagna (a fresco of the Crucifixion, in the refectory of the adjacent monastery).

With its walls of rough stone – the projected façade was never completed – **Santa Maria del Carmine** looks more like a country farmhouse than a church. Most of it was destroyed in a fire and reconstructed in the 1700s, but the **Brancacci Chapel** (*open 10–5, Sun and hols 1–5, closed Tues; adm; only 30 people admitted at a time, for 15 minutes*), another of the landmarks of Florentine art, somehow survived, and has been restored. Three artists worked on the chapel frescoes: Masolino, beginning in 1424, his pupil Masaccio, working alone from 1428, and Filippino Lippi, who completed the work in the 1480s. Scholars never tire of disputing the attributions of the various scenes, especially those that could be either Masolino's or Masaccio's. It doesn't matter; 'Little Tom' and 'Shabby Tom' both contributed greatly to the visual revolution of quattrocento painting. Both were revolutionary in their understanding of light and space, though art historians these days make more of a fuss over the precocious, eccentric Shabby Tom, who died at the age of 27 shortly after his work here. Some of the scenes – the *Expulsion of Adam and Eve*, the *Tribute Money*, and scenes from the life of St Peter – are among Masaccio's masterpieces. Almost every artist of the later 1400s and 1500s came here to do sketches and study how Shabby Tom did it; some of Michelangelo's sketches after Masaccio still survive.

A City With a View: The Forte di Belvedere

For the best views over Florence, and the best chance to get away from the city's dust and noise, you can climb up to the heights around Oltrarno. It's a pleasant walk whether you do it the short way, up Costa San Giorgio and through the old city walls, or the longer route towards Piazzale Michelangelo. This leads through an interesting, little-known corner of the city around Via dei Bardi and Via San Niccolò, two fine old streets with a scattering of Renaissance *palazzi*, and good frescoes by Alessandro Baldovinetti in the church of **San Niccolò sopr'Arno**.

At the top of a winding road and a long set of steps, Piazzale Michelangelo is a popular lookout point adorned with yet another full-size copy of the *David*. Beneath it, Via del Belvedere leads up between the walls and some country villas to the **Belvedere Fort** (*currently closed for what looks to be a long and indefinite bout of restoration*), from 1590, dominating the city's defences along the southern heights. This fort and adjacent walls replaced the earlier ones (those Michelangelo helped design) that survived the siege of 1529. The view alone makes the climb worthwhile.

San Miniato

Despite the fact that the lovely Romanesque façade of this church can be glimpsed from almost anywhere in Florence, few visitors are ever moved to see it up close. As a result, you may have one of Florence's finest churches all to yourself. Built in 1015 over an earlier church, on the spot where the head of obscure St Minias bounced after the Romans decapitated him, the exterior echoes the black-and-white geometric style of the Baptistry. Despite its distance from the city centre this has always been a church dear to the hearts of the Florentines. At the top of the façade you'll notice the gold eagle symbol of the Calimala, the medieval cloth merchants' guild. These rich businessmen had the church in their care, and over the centuries they bestowed on it many lovely things. The playful patterns are continued inside, framing a richly coloured 13th-century mosaic of Christ Pantocrator in the apse. Be sure to see the wonderful marble floor, inlaid with signs of the zodiac and fantastical animals; also the **Cappella del Crocifisso**, a joint effort by Michelozzo and Luca della Robbia. The fine pulpit and choir screen date from the early 1200s, and the Chapel of the Cardinal of Portugal contains work by Baldovinetti (who also restored the apse mosaic), Della Robbia, the Pollaiuoli and Rossellino.

Fiesole

No ordinary suburb, **Fiesole** can claim to be the mother city of Florence itself. In fact the town is of Etruscan origin, the northernmost member of the federation of city-states called the Dodecapolis. *Faesulae* dwindled in the heyday of Roman Florence, but in the Dark Ages its secure hilltop site ensured its survival. When times became a little bit safer its families began moving back down to the Arno to rebuild Florence. For centuries, Fiesole has played the role of Florence's aristocratic suburb; its cool breezes and belvedere views make it the perfect retreat from the torrid Florentine summers.

There's no escaping the tourists, however; we foreigners have been tramping up and down Fiesole's hill since the days of Shelley. They're used to us by now, and a day trip here is for many visitors an obligatory part of a stay in Florence. The no.7 city bus from the Piazza della Stazione will have you there in less than half an hour, stopping in Piazza Mino da Fiesole, the town centre.

Mino da Fiesole is a favourite son, a quattrocento sculptor whose best work can be seen in the early 11th-century **Duomo** on the piazza; the tomb of Bishop Salutati off the right aisle contains his altarpiece with the Madonna and saints. Behind the cathedral on Via Dupré is the **Museo Bandini** (*open summer daily 10–7, winter Wed–Mon 10–5, closed Tues in winter; adm*), a must for anybody who loves the iridescent Della Robbia terracottas on Tuscany's churches and would like a chance to see some up close. The museum has an entire roomful, along with a collection of 14th- and 15th-century Tuscan paintings.

Not much is left of Etruscan or Roman Fiesole, but you can visit the small **Teatro Romano** (*open in summer Wed–Mon 9.30–7; in winter Wed–Mon 9.30–5; closed Tues; adm*), excavated in 1911 and often used for plays and concerts in the summer; the archaeological area, on the hillside near the Bandini Museum on Via Partigiani, also includes scanty remains of baths and temples, and a small museum (*same hours*).

Perhaps the best sights Fiesole has to offer, though, are the perfect views over Florence and the surrounding area from old streets like Via Francesco on the edge of town. Walks around the outskirts reveal some lovely countryside and a few surprises:

the **church of San Domenico** at San Domenico di Fiesole, a couple of kilometres from town, has three paintings by Fra Angelico, who lived for a while in the adjoining monastery. Nearby on Via di Badia, the **Badia Fiesolana** (*open only Sun am*), Fiesole's original cathedral, has an unfinished 11th-century geometric façade like that of San Miniato or Santa Maria Novella, and an interior in the manner of Brunelleschi.

Florentine Excursions

The countryside around Fiesole presents a civilized landscape of villas and gardens, cypresses and parasol pines. Outside **Settignano** you'll pass the Villa Poggio Gherardo, which Florentines claim was the rendezvous for the genteel storytellers of the *Decameron*, and also the church of **San Martino a Mensola**, with some parts as old as the 9th century, and paintings by Agnolo and Taddeo Gaddi inside. Settignano (bus no.10 from the station or Piazza San Marco) has fine views over Florence and its valley.

South of Florence is one of the typically grand fortress-monasteries of the Carthusian order, begun in the 1340s. The **Certosa di Galluzzo** (*open Tues–Sun 9–12 and 3–6, closed Mon; bus nos.36 or 37 from the station*), near the SS2 highway to Siena, contains works by the della Robbias and Pontormo. A few monks look after the place, and they keep up the tradition of cooking up bottles of potent chartreuse; they will be glad to sell you one in their old pharmacy.

Like their Bourbon cousins in France, the Medici dukes liked to pass the time by building new palaces for themselves. In their case, however, the reason was less self-exaltation than pure and simple speculation; the Medici always thought generations ahead. As a result the countryside around Florence is littered with Medici villas, most privately owned but some open to the public. **Villa la Petraia** (*open 8.15–6, later in summer; closed 2nd and 4th Mon of the month; adm*), in the northern suburbs near the Via Gramsci, has beautiful gardens and a fountain statue of Venus of Giambologna.

More lovely gardens, typical of late-Renaissance landscaping, can also be seen in the same area, the suburb of Castello, at the **Villa di Castello**. Here the attraction is a fascinating example of the Medici's penchant for the offbeat and excessive, an artificial cavern called the Grotta degli Animali, filled by Ammannati and Giambologna with statues of every animal and fish known to man, along with mosaics made of seashells. Kitsch, perhaps, but a truly great example of kitsch in the best Medici tradition. (*Garden open 8.15–6, later in summer; closed 2nd and 3rd Mon of month; adm.*)

Perhaps the best know of all the Medici villas is the **Villa Careggi**, (*open Mon–Fri 9–6, Sat 9–12, but you can stroll through the grounds for free*), a villa that began as a fortified farmhouse and was enlarged for Cosimo Il Vecchio by Michelozzo in 1434. In the 1460s the villa at Careggi became synonoymous with the birth of humanism. The greatest Latin and Greek scholars of the day, Ficino, Poliziano, Pico della Mirandola and Argyropoulos, would meet here with Lorenzo Il Magnifico and hold philosophical discussions in imitation of the Platonic symposium, calling their society the Platonic Academy and inspiring the early works of Botticelli with their ideas. When Lorenzo felt his end was near he had himself carried out to the villa to die.

The Wine of the Iron Baron

Wine has been produced in the hills south of Florence since the cows came home, but what we know as Chianti was born in the 19th century, of a husband's jealousy. The 'Iron Baron' Bettino Ricasoli was extremely wealthy but not very good-looking. After serving as the second prime minister of unified Italy, he married and took his lovely bride to a ball in Florence. A young man asked her to dance. The Baron at once ordered her into their carriage and drove straight to the ancient family seat in Brolio in the Monti dei Chianti – an isolated castle that the poor woman would rarely leave for the rest of her life. To pass the time the Baron experimented in his vineyards, and over the years evolved a joyful, pleasing blend of Sangiovese and Caniolo grapes, with a touch of Malvasia. At the same time the famous dark green flask clad in straw (the *strapeso*) was invented. The Baron's Chianti and its distinctive bottle took the Paris Exposition of 1878 by storm. As imitators flooded the market, the boundaries of Chianti Classico were drawn in 1924, and the black cockerel, symbol of the Lega dei Chianti in 1385, was made its trademark, distinguishing it from Tuscany's six other Chianti-growing districts.

If you take the Via Chiantigiana (SS222) between Florence and Siena you'll find many vineyards to explore and wine-tastings to enjoy, especially at Greve, midway down the SS222, or at the Castello di Brolio itself, 10km south of Gaiole on the N484 (*open daily 9–12 and 3–sunset*).

Impruneta, the gateway to Chianti from Florence, prefers making bricks and terracotta to growing grapes, but it's worth a stop for the **Collegiato**, with beautiful works by Michelozzo and Andrea della Robbia in two of its chapels.

Up in the mountains to the east, San Polo is famous for the cultivation of irises. **Greve**, the unofficial capital of the Chianti, has an unusual arcaded triangular piazza, and attracts big crowds for the Chianti Classico Market Show in September.

North of Florence

The lush green valley of the **Mugello** and the hills around it border four different provinces; it's a little-known corner of Tuscany, even though its villages get their share of summer foreigners in holiday homes. **Vicchio**, a humble town, was the birthplace of Fra Angelico, and Giotto came from nearby Vespignano. To the west, past Borgo San Lorenzo, **San Piero a Sieve** sits beneath the huge, mouldering pentagonal San Martino fortress, built by Buontalenti for the Medici; the village church has a lovely baptismal font by Luca della Robbia. Michelozzo designed another Medici villa, a pretty building on the site of an earlier fortress at nearby **Caffagiolo** (1451).

Up in the mountains to the north, **Scarperia**'s interesting Palazzo Pretoria was a governors' palace built by the Florentines in the early 14th century, its façade covered with the coats of arms of all the town's many governors. The church of the **Madonna dei Terremoti** (Our Lady of the Earthquakes) has frescoes attributed to Filippo Lippi. **Firenzuola**, with its narrow, arcaded streets, is a lovely town – a good place to stop if you need a break on your way to Bologna.

From Florence to Pisa

There are two routes to choose from, whether you're going by train or car. Surprisingly, the valley of the Arno is the less populated and less busy route, and always has been. Trade and traffic prefer to follow a northern route through the large towns of Prato, Pistoia and Lucca.

Empoli and the Arno Valley

Montelupo, with a castle overlooking the Arno, is a pretty town given to the manufacture of delicately painted ceramics, famous throughout Tuscany. Further down the valley comes **Empoli**, known for its Collegiata on the central Piazza Farinata degli Uberti, with a green and white geometrical façade in the best medieval Florentine style. The adjacent Collegiata Museum (*open Tues–Sun 9–12 and 4–7; adm*) contains a famous *Pietà* fresco by Masolino, a pair of saints by Pontormo, and works by Botticini, Rossellino and della Robbia.

There are a pair of possible detours from Empoli: south to **Castelfiorentino** up in the hills, with its crumbling castle and a Pinacoteca (*currently closed for restoration*), with some excellent trecento paintings; or north to **Vinci**, a village in a lovely quattrocento landscape, where fans of Leonardo can visit his birthplace, and lovers of gadgets can have a good time with the intricate models of the master's inventions in the Museo Leonardiano (*open daily 9.30–7; winter 9.30–6; adm*) – the bicycle, tank and helicopter, and dozens of other things he left detailed plans for in his notebooks. The museum is housed in the 13th-century Guidi Castle, which also has a small art collection. Closer to the main Pisa and Livorno road, **San Miniato**, home of the national kite-flying festival (first Sunday after Easter), is a fine town set in some of the fairest Tuscan countryside. It has a good picture gallery, in the Museo Diocesano (*open summer Tues–Sun 9–12 and 3–5; closed Mon; winter Sat and Sun only 9–12 and 2.30–5; adm*).

Prato

Living in Florence's shadow for a thousand years has not dampened Prato's spirit as much as you would expect. A town of almost 150,000, with a textile industry that was important in Europe for 600 years, Prato could certainly express some weariness at having seen its wealth and talent constantly drained off to glorify its imperious neighbour. Twice Florence conquered the city, and on one occasion the Florentines simply bought it. Twice, in 1470 and 1512, the Pratese rebelled, but were crushed each time. The gruesome sack of the city in 1514, an atrocity with which the Spaniards and the Medici Pope Leo X meant to intimidate all Italy, quietened Prato down considerably. Now, almost 500 years later, Prato's industries are thriving once more, and the town makes a point of showing that it, too, has some culture.

Coming in by rail (the station, with its park and bridges over the Bisenzio, makes a blissful introduction to the city), one of the first things you'll see is a great puffy sculpture by Henry Moore in a roundabout.

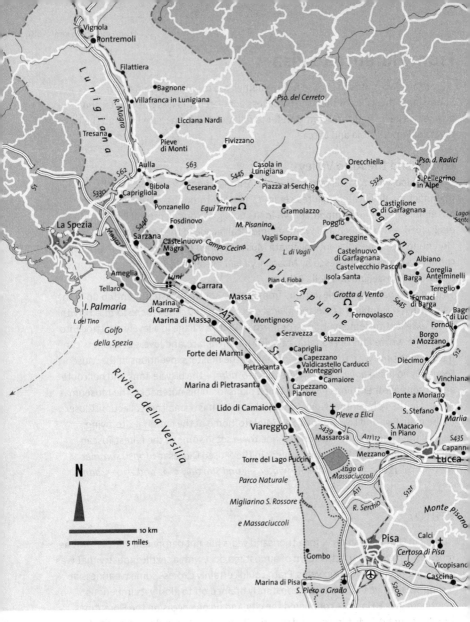

Santa Maria delle Carceri

Entering old Prato by Viale Piave, the defiantly swallowtail crenellations of the **Castello dell'Imperatore** mark a strange Ghibelline interlude in Prato's history. Frederick II built it in 1237, his only such castle in northern Italy. Its clean lines must have seemed very sharp and modern in the 13th century, but the castle's location inside the walls hints that the purpose was less to protect Prato from the Florentines than to protect imperial officials from the Pratese. There isn't much inside, but the city often uses it for special exhibitions.

Florence to Pisa and the Apuan Alps

EMILIA-ROMAGNA

Pavullo nel Frignano
S12
Montecreto
Sestola
Monte Cimone
iumalbo
Abetone
e Potenze
Cutigliano
Doganaccia
tesi
Vico
Gavinana
S. Marcello Pistoiese
Lucchio
Maresca
ciano
Controne
Pitecchio
Pontepetri
Castelvecchio
S633
S66
Castagno
Massa e Cozzile
Serravalle Pistoiese
Pescia
Montecatini Terme
Buggiano
Monsummano Terme
ontecarlo
Ponte Buggianese
Montevettolini
Altopascio
Padule di Fucecchio
Lamporecchi
Carmignano
M. Albano
Vinci
Villa d'Artimino
Anchiano
TUSCANY
Cerreto Guidi
Fucecchio
R. Niovole
R. Arno
Empoli
Ponte a Elsa
dera
Montopoli in Val d'A.
S. Miniato
S61

Vergato

S. Benedetto

S325
Pian d. Voglio
Pietramala
Castiglione dei Pepoli
Porretta Terme
Roncobilaccio
Firenzuola
Montepiano
Pso. della Futa
S632
S. Quirico
Vernio
Montecarelli
Pracchia
S64
Cantagallo
Barberino di Mugello
Sta. Agata
S503
Bosco ai Frati
Scarperia
Vaiano
Collebarucci
S. Piero a Sieve
S502
Cafaggiolo
R. Bisenzio
Monti d. Calvana
Trebbio
Borgo S. Lorenzo
Vicchio
Pistoia
Ponte Nuovo
Figline
Montemurlo
A1
Vaglia
S65
Serravalle Pistoiese
S435
Padule di Fucecchio
R. Ombrone
Prato
Bivigliano
M. Senario
A11
Pratolino
R. Magione
Sesto Fiorentino
Rufina
Poggio a Caiano
Campi Bisenzio
Florence
Fiesole
Settignano
Pontassieve
Signa
S326
Pelago
Lastra a Signa
Scandicci
Arcetri
Bagno a Ripoli
Galluzzo Certosa
Poggio Imperiale
S. Donato in Collina
Rignano sull'Arno
Chiesanuova
Grassina
Tavarnuzze
Sanmezzano
R. Pesa
Cerbaia
Impruneta
R. Sieve
S. Andrea in Percussina
R. Greve
Strada in Chianti
S. Polo in Chianti
S. Casciano in Val di Pesa
Incisa in Val d'A.

Behind the castle stands the unfinished black and white marble façade of **Santa Maria delle Carceri**, begun in 1485 by Giuliano de Sangallo. Brunelleschian architecture was always a fragile blossom, as shown clearly by the failure of this sole serious attempt to transplant it outside of Florence. It was an audacious enterprise: Sangallo, a furiously diligent student of Vitruvius and Alberti, attempted a building based entirely on philosophical principles. Order, simplicity and correct proportion, as in Brunelleschi's churches, were to be manifest, with no frills allowed. Sangallo, the favourite of Lorenzo il Magnifico, unfortunately proved a better theorist than

Getting Around

The fastest **train** line between Florence and Pisa is via Empoli, but there is also a frequent service through Prato, Pistoia and Lucca and then to Pisa or Viareggio. Prato has two train stations, the main Stazione Centrale, and the Stazione Porta al Serraglio, closer to the centre (not all trains stop here). Buses from Prato depart from Piazza Cardi, north of the Duomo, or the Stazione Centrale. In Pistoia the railway station, with connections to Florence, Pisa and occasionally Bologna, is on the southern edge of town, two blocks from the town walls on Via XX Settembre.

Most **buses** to other Tuscan cities leave Pistoia from Piazza San Francesco, at the west end of town, inside the walls off Corso Gramsci. Cars are banned from most of the centre of Pistoia (in theory anyway), but there's plenty of parking around the Fortezza di Santa Barbara.

Tourist Information

Prato: Piazza Santa Maria delle Carceri 15, t 0574 24112.

Shopping

Prato still makes its living from fine fabrics and clothing, and people from all over Tuscany come to visit the **factory outlets** where these are available at discount prices. One of the specialities is **cashmere**, produced in numerous spots.

Where to Stay

Prato ✉ 50047

Prato's hotels are mostly of the business variety, but can be a good bet in the summer when Florence is packed to the gills.

★★★Villa Santa Cristina, Via Poggio Secco 58, t 0574 595 951, f 0574 572 623 (*expensive*). A relaxing spot with a garden, pool and most other comforts, over the river in the hills to the east.

★★★San Marco, Piazza San Marco 48, t 0574 21321, f 0574 22378 (*moderate*). A pleasant place between the Stazione Centrale and the Castello, convenient if you're arriving in Prato by train.

★★Villa Rucellai, Via di Canneto 16km northeast of town, t 0574 460 392 (*moderate*). A delightful bed and breakfast in a Renaissance villa with formal gardens and pool. It's also excellent value.

★★Toscana, Piazza Ciardi 3, t 0574 28096, f 0574 25163 (*moderate*). Cheaper than the alternatives, on a quiet square on the far side of the Stazione Porta al Serraglio. Some rooms have air-conditioning.

Eating Out

One reason for staying in Prato is the food, especially if you like fish.

Osvaldo Baroncelli, Via Fra Bartolomeo 13, t 0574 23810 (*very expensive*). A small, unpretentious establishment opposite the Metastasio theatre, with an innovative chef who turns out dishes like tagliatelle with artichokes, veal *scaloppine* with truffles, duck stuffed with its own kidney or stuffed celery (a favourite Pratese dish), as well as more traditional Tuscan favourites. *Closed Sat lunch and Sun.*

Il Pirana, Via Valentini 110 (south of Viale Vittorio Veneto, the main street between the central station and Piazza San Marco), t 0574 25746 (*expensive*). Maintains a justified reputation for some of the best seafood in inland Tuscany; try the scampi. *Closed Sat lunch and Sun.*

Hotel Flora, Via Cairoli, t 0574 33521 (*moderate*). Vegetarians will want to make a bee-line for the lovely roof garden at this hotel in the centre, serving unusual salads, pâtés, quiches and organic wines, and with an excellent value set menu. *Closed lunch and all day Sun.*

La Vecchia Cucina di Soldano, Via Pomeri 23, t 0574 34665 (*cheap*). A very gratifying *trattoria* for something less elaborate, with a menu cooked and served by the Mattei family that's full of *ribollita* and *pasta e fagioli*, stuffed celery and all the other old-fashioned soups and stews, including the house speciality, a hearty beef and onion stew known as *francesina. Closed Sun.*

architect; Santa Maria came out tedious and clumsy. The interior is better than the outside, a plain Greek cross very much in the Brunelleschi manner with a frieze and tondos by Andrea della Robbia. The name of the church – *carceri* means prisons – refers to a miracle, a speaking image of the Virgin painted on a nearby prison wall, that led to the building of the church.

The Duomo

North of the church, Via Pugliesi and Via Garibaldi pass several medieval towers on their way to the Piazza del Duomo. Prato's **Cathedral of St Stephen**, in flagrant green and white stripes like the Duomo at Siena, was begun in the 13th century and finished in bits and pieces over the next 200 years. Its best features are an exotic, almost Moorish-looking campanile, an Andrea della Robbia lunette of the Madonna with St Stephen over the door, a big clock that makes you smile when you notice it sitting where the rose window ought to be, and above all the **Pulpit of the Sacred Girdle** (*Pulpito del Sacro Cingolo*), a perfectly felicitous ornament, something beautiful and special that the Pratese can look at every day when they walk through the piazza. Michelozzo designed it (1428) and Donatello added the delightful reliefs of dancing children, along the lines of his *cantoria* in the cathedral museum in Florence. Mary's girdle came to Prato during the First Crusade; the outdoor pulpit was built so that it could be displayed to the people, five times a year on major church holidays.

In the cathedral, the prime attraction is in the choir: two series of lucent, precise **frescoes** by Filippo Lippi illustrating the stories of St Stephen and John the Baptist (the nun who would later run off with Lippi is said to have been the model for Salome). A separate entrance on the side of the building leads to the **Museo dell'Opera del Duomo** (*open Mon and Wed–Sat 9.30–12.30 and 3–6.30, Sun 9.30–12.30; adm*), where you can see the original Donatello reliefs from the pulpit – copies had to be made to face the weather outside – in addition to works by Filippino Lippi, an early painting by Uccello and a sophisticated *Madonna* by the quattrocento 'Master of the Nativity of Castello'. Outside the museum, stop for a look at the Romanesque cloister, done in patterns of the same green and white stone as the exterior.

More Museums

On the sleepy streets of old Prato you'll find only a few reminders of the city's businesslike past. **Piazza del Mercatale**, by the river, is an attractive, huge, very Tuscan square, full of peeling yellow paint and flowers. Near the centre of town, on Via Rinaldesca, you'll pass the house of Renaissance Prato's most flamboyant tycoon, Francesco di Marco Datini. If there were an accountants' hall of fame, Datini would surely be one of the stars. He helped invent that dismal science, and also gets credit, according to the Pratese, for the 'invention of the promissory note'. Datini put his talents to good use, piling up an indecent fortune, fooling in politics, and dropping huge sums for charity. His **Palazzo Datini** (*c.* 1350) shows bits of the frescoes that once covered the entire façade – scenes from his own life.

Two streets to the north, the rugged, four-square **Palazzo Pretorio** was Prato's seat of government in the days of independence, and now serves as home to the **Galleria**

Comunale, a rich collection containing works by the Lippis, Bernardo Daddi and many lesser-known Renaissance artists (*currently closed*). Also on Piazza del Comune, Prato celebrates its medieval and modern textile industry in the **Museo del Tessuto** (*open daily Mon and Wed–Fri 10.30–6.30, Sat 10.30–2.30; adm*), with a unique collection of fabrics and looms dating back to the 5th century AD. The museum is only here temporarily; there are plans to expand it eventually into a new home in one of the city's old textile mills outside the walls. From there, Via C. Guasti takes you four blocks to the big 13th-century church of **San Domenico**. Its cloister houses a museum of **mural painting** (*open Mon and Wed–Sat 10–1 and 3.30–7, Sun 10–1 only; adm*), a small collection of frescoes taken from local churches and *palazzi*.

Pistoia

Many have found it a gloomy town. Pistoia does seem to get more than its share of fog and clouds, and laughter in its plain, narrow streets seems a bit out of place. Pistoia has been around since it was *Pistoria* in Roman times, and it has usually been bad luck for somebody. The Catiline conspiracy, the famous attempted coup against the Roman Republic in 62 BC, ended when the legions tracked down the escaped Catiline and his henchmen near Pistoia. In the Middle Ages, Pistoia had a dark reputation among its neighbours for violence and treachery. The Black versus White Guelph struggles that obsessed Florence for so long actually began here. Dante, himself a victim of that feud, never let a chance go by in the *Divine Comedy* to curse and condemn the fateful city. In 1329 Florence captured Pistoia once and for all. The city carried on, living well off its old speciality, iron-working. True to its reputation, Pistoia supplied the warriors and conspirators of Europe with fine daggers. Later, keeping up with technology, the city gave its name to that new invention, the pistol.

Today Pistoia, the centre of a plain full of gardens, is better known for its flowers. Its people laugh at their odd history; bring it up and they'll be ready to blame it all on those obnoxious Florentines. Pistoia's somnolence over the last 600 years has left it with an historic centre almost entirely intact, many fine buildings, and a wealth of art.

Piazza del Duomo

Old Pistoia is almost perfectly diamond-shaped, surrounded by 16th-century walls with the old moats preserved on the northern and eastern sides. Right in the middle you'll find the L-shaped **Piazza del Duomo**, an excellent example of medieval urban design. The façade of the **Duomo**, with its Pisan arcades and stripes over a Florentine tympanum by Andrea della Robbia, makes an uneasy balance between the two architectural traditions. The tall, impressive campanile tips the balance towards Pisa, with a touch of the exotic in its Moorish-inspired arches. Inside, the real attraction is the enormous **altar of St James**, about a ton of solid silver, begun in 1287 and added to over the next two centuries.

Directly across from the cathedral is the striped, octagonal **baptistry** dating from 1350 (*open Tues–Sat 9.30–12.30 and 3–6; Sun 9.30–12.30; closed Mon*), credited to

Tourist Information

Pistoia: Piazza Duomo, in the bishop's palace, t 0573 21622.
Montecatini Terme: Viale Verdi 66,
t 0572 772 244.

Where to Stay and Eat

Pistoia ✉ 51110

Pistoia is used to lodging and feeding more business than pleasure travellers; it might be better to make this city a day trip, or stay in nearby Montecatini Terme. There are a couple of options a few kilometres outside town.
★★★Il Convento, Via S. Quirico 33, 5 km east at Pontenuovo, t 0573 452 651, f 0573 453 578 (*moderate*). A former convent, preserving its exterior if not all of its interior. The setting is quiet, with views over Pistoia; there's a pool and one of the city's better restaurants.
Villa Vannini, about 6km north of town, t 0573 42031, f 0573 26331 (*moderate*). Even more rural is this delightful villa set among fir trees; there are wonderful hill walks on the doorstep, elegant, comfortable, excellent-value rooms, and a good restaurant.
★★★Leon Bianco, Via Panciatichi 2, t 0573 26675, f 0573 26704 (*moderate*). In Pistoia, comfortable, with views over the campanile, t 0573 23141, f 0573 21660 (*moderate*). The closest thing to cheap accomodation, near Piazza del Duomo, but it's a bit woebegone.
★★Firenze, Via Curtatone e Montanara 42,
Pistoia is knownfor its lack of restaurants. In the city there are simple *trattorie* and *pizzerie*.
Valle del Vincio, Via Vignano 1, t 0573 477 012 (*moderate*). Near the zoo; serves traditional dishes and lots of mushrooms.

Other dining worthies are out of town.
Rafanelli, Via Sant'Agostino 47, Sant'Agostino, t 0573 532 046 (*moderate*). Tuscan home cooking, including *maccheroni* with duck, game dishes and lamb, served in a pretty country villa. *Closed Sun eve, Mon and Aug.*
Locanda degli Elfi, Via della Chiesa 3, Località San Felice, t 0573 416 770 (*expensive–moderate*). A beautiful 18th-century villa, offering fish and local dishes. *Closed Tues.*

Montecatini Terme ✉ 51016

★★★★★Grand Hotel & La Pace, Corso Roma 12, t 0572 75801, f0572 78451 (*very expensive*). Renowned throughout Europe for genuine *belle époque* charm, this has similarly impressive luxuries; the restaurant is unquestionably elegant, but expensive. *Open April–Oct.*
★★★★★Grand Hotel Bellavista, Viale Fedeli 2, t 0572 78122, f 0572 73352 (*expensive*). Among the grandest, offering indoor pool, luxurious rooms, sauna, health club, and an infinite number of opportunities for self-indulgence. *Open April–Nov.*
★★★Corallo, Viale Cavallotti 116, t 0572 78288, f 0572 79512 (*moderate*). Small but refined, with a pool and garden, on a quiet side street near the park. *Open all year.*
★Belsoggiorno, Viale Cavallotti 131, up in Montecatini Alto, t 0572 78859 (*cheap*). Rooms overlook the garden. *Open April–Oct.*

Most guests dine in their hotels, but there are places worth making an effort to find.
Enoteca da Giovanni, Via Garibaldi 25, t 0572 71695 (*expensive*). Break loose at least once for the imaginative fare at this unique and much-honoured place, where game dishes – hare, venison, wild duck – turn into impeccably *haute cuisine* in the hands of a master chef. *Closed Mon.*
Cucina da Giovanni, Via Garibaldi. Next door to the *enoteca*, offering simple fare at more modest prices (try the *antipasti* and fabulous *maccheroncini* with duck sauce).

Andrea Pisano – one of the outstanding Gothic buildings of Tuscany, with a fine sculptural trim on the exterior and a conical dome under the roof. The 12th-century Palazzo dei Vescovi contains Etruscan and Roman finds in an **archaeological itinerary**, and the old cathedral is now included in the **Museo San Zeno**, with paintings and a reliquary by Ghiberti (*guided tours of both offered Tues, Thurs and Fri 10–1 and 3–5; joint adm*).

On the façade of the **Palazzo Comunale**, a head in black marble is set into the wall, the face of a Moorish king captured on a freebooting expedition to Mallorca. Besides the mayor, it houses the **Museo Civico**, which provides you with an introduction to the often weird 13th- and 14th-century 'Pistoian School' and much else; don't miss the hallucinatory battle scenes by Francesco Graziani.

From behind the cathedral, Via F. Pacini takes you north to another Pistoian surprise, the refined, arcaded façade of the **Ospedale del Ceppo**, done in the manner of the famous Ospedale degli Innocenti in Florence. As in Florence, the della Robbias were called upon to provide the decoration, but besides the simple terracotta medallions there is a unique terracotta frieze across the entire façade – in resplendent Renaissance Technicolor. The frieze, by Giovanni della Robbia and later artists in the 1510s and 1580s, portrays the works of the hospital and allegorical virtues. A little way to the west, the 12th-century **Sant'Andrea** (*open daily 8–12.30 and 3.30–6*) contains a real treasure, an exquisite pulpit by Giovanni Pisano, lifted on columns over figures of the four Evangelists and surrounded with reliefs full of intricately carved figures, a fitting introduction to the more famous works of the Pisano family in Pisa.

Two other churches on the northern side of Pistoia are worth a look. **San Francesco al Prato**, on the piazza of the same name, has an exceptional collection of 14th-century frescoes, and the **Madonna dell'Umiltà**, on the central Via della Madonna, is a curious, octagonal High Renaissance building. In the 1560s Giorgio Vasari was called upon to complete this long-unfinished church; he added a dome so heavy that the church has been threatening to collapse ever since.

More Stripes

From Piazza del Duomo, one block south and another east will put you in Piazza San Leone; the stubby tower here once belonged to perhaps the rottenest of all the Pistoians, a 13th-century noble thug and sworn enemy of the Church named Vanni Fucci; Dante found him in one of the lower circles of Hell, cursing and making obscene gestures up at God. **San Giovanni Fuoricivitas**, just around the corner of Via Cavour, must surely win a prize for being the stripiest church in Christendom. Turning its side to the street, and bristling with lozenge windows and blind arches, the 12th-century work looks more Pisan than anything you'll see in Pisa. Inside (if it's open) there is another fine pulpit, by a pupil of Pisano, and a della Robbia plaque of the *Visitation*.

San Domenico, nearby on Corso Silvano, is less flamboyant on the outside, but the church and adjacent convent have some good frescoes, as does the **Cappella del Tau** (*open Mon–Sat 9–2*) across the street. Some of the pictures here, scenes from the story of Adam and Eve, are little-known works by Masolino.

There is another good Gothic façade on **San Paulo**, a block to the east. The best stripes of all, however, may be on the zebras in the **Pistoia Zoo** (*open April–Sept 9–7; Oct–Mar 9–5; adm exp*), 4km northwest of town on Via Pieve a Calle. Italians don't usually care for zoos (though the Medici always kept big menageries) and this one may be the best in the country, even though it's only 20 years old.

Montecatini Terme

Only 15km west of Pistoia, this is perhaps Italy's best-known thermal spa, a party centre for crowned heads and their sycophants in the 1890s and popular ever since.

The waters, good for just about anything according to Montecatini's boasters, are the town's sole reason for being. To please its elevated clientele, Montecatini in the 19th century built itself into quite an elegant place, with a large park at the centre and imposing establishments such as the Versailles-like **Tettuccio**, where string quartets once serenaded those who came to take the waters.

Many of the other establishments are almost as good and, even if you prefer stronger stuff than mineral water for your cures, you can come for the florid 1890s architecture and genteel atmosphere. The other favourite recreation of Montecatini visitors is taking the **cable car** up to the pretty village of Montecatini Alto.

Further west towards Lucca, **Pescia** is another garden centre, with a famous whole-sale flower market. The church of San Francesco there has a painting of St Francis done shortly after his death – believed to be an accurate portrayal by an artist who knew him. In **Collodi** you'll see a park with a monument to Pinocchio; his creator, Carlo Collodi, took his pen name from his family's native town.

Lucca

The famous walls – 'much like the walls of Berwick-on-Tweed', the Lucchese for some reason like to say – do not seem very formidable, more like a garden wall than something that would keep the Florentines at bay. Behind them you can see only pine trees and neat stucco buildings with the inevitable green shutters. The walls and the surrounding areas, once the outworks of the fortifications, are now full of lawns and trees, making a sort of green belt for the little city. The Lucchese ride their bikes and walk their dogs around the ramparts, and often stop to admire the view.

Lucca at first glance may seem too bijou and tidy to be true. It is a dream city – not like Venice, but in a quiet, very domestic sort of way. After its long and brave history it has certainly earned the right to a little quiet. The annual hordes of Tuscan tourists leave Lucca alone for the most part, though there seems to be a small number of discreet visitors who come back every year. They don't spread the word, apparently trying to keep one of Italy's most beautiful cities to themselves.

Lucca's rigid grid of streets betrays its Roman origins. The town survived continuously through the bad centuries, and emerged in the age of the *comuni* as one of the leading trading towns of Tuscany, specializing in the production of silk. In the early 1300s, perhaps the height of the city's wealth and power, a remarkable adventurer named Castruccio Castracani appeared in the spotlight. Castracani, who for years had lived in exile – part of it in England – returned in 1314 when Pisan and Ghibelline troops captured Lucca. Within a year he had chased the Pisans out and seized power for himself, and by 1325 he had built for Lucca a little empire that included both Pisa and Pistoia. After routing the Florentines at Altopascio in that year he was making plans to snatch Florence too, but died of malaria just before the siege was to begin – another example of Florentine good luck. Internal bickering between the powerful families put an end to Lucca's glory days almost immediately, and the city barely escaped being gobbled up by one or other of its neighbours. As a competently

Getting There and Around

The **train** station (**t** 0583 467 013) is just south of the walls on Piazza Ricasoli, with lots of trains on the Pisa–Florence line. **Buses** leave from Piazzale G. Verdi, just inside the walls at the western end of the city: LAZZI buses run to Florence, Pistoia, Pisa, Prato or Viareggio, and CLAP buses to towns in Lucca province, including the upper Serchio Valley in the Apuan Alps (**t** 166 845 010). Get around Lucca itself like a Lucchese by hiring a **bicycle** from the tourist office in Piazzale Verdi and from Barbetti, Via Anfiteatro 23 (**t** 0583 954 444).

Tourist Information

Lucca: Vecchia Porta San Donato, in Piazzale Verdi, **t** 0583 419 689.

Where to Stay

Lucca and Around ✉ 55100

Lucca can be less than charm city if you arrive without booking ahead; there simply aren't enough rooms (especially inexpensive ones) to meet demand, and the Lucchesi aren't in any hurry to do anything about it.

★★★★★**Principessa Elisa**, Via SS del Brennero, Massa Pisana, **t** 0583 379 737, **f** 0583 379 019, (*luxury*). Outside the city, you can bed down in Castruccio Castracani's own palace, built for the great Lucchese warlord in 1321. Often rebuilt since, it currently wears the façade of a stately rococo mansion, surrounded by acres of 18th-century gardens and a pool. *Open Mar–Nov.*

★★★**Universo**, Piazza Puccini, **t** 0583 493 678, **f** 0583 954 854 (*moderate*). Inside the walls, you cannot do better than this slightly frayed, green-shuttered and thoroughly delightful hotel, right in the centre; Ruskin and nearly everyone else who followed him to Lucca slept here.

★★**Ilaria**, Via del Fosso 20, **t** 0583 47558 (*cheap*). Fourteen sparkling rooms on Lucca's canal.

★★**Diana** Via del Molinetto 11, **t** 0583 492 202, **f** 0583 47795 (*cheap*). Near the cathedral, friendly and well-run, with the nicest cheaper rooms in Tuscany, some with bath.

Eating Out

Il Giglio, Piazza del Giglio, **t** 0583 494 058 (*expensive*). Lucca's best seafood, in the Hotel Universo. River trout is a speciality, or rabbit with *polenta. Closed Tues eve and Wed.*

Il Buca di Sant'Antonio, Via della Cervia 3, **t** 0583 55881 (*moderate*). Has been an inn since 1782, offering old recipes like smoked herring and kid on a spit, and newer dishes like *ravioli* with *ricotta* and sage. *Closed Sun eve and Mon.*

Vecchia Trattoria Buralli, Via San Giorgio. For a simple lunch, head around the corner from Sant'Agostino church for Lucchese home cooking – a good bargain buffet, or pay a bit more for house specialities like the beef with rocket.

Canuleia, Via Canuleia 14, **t** 0583 467 470 (*moderate*). Near the amphitheatre in a medieval workshop, serving local food with some surprises and vegetarian dishes. *Closed Sat and Sun.*

Buatino, Via Borgo Giannotti 508, **t** 0583 343 207 (*cheap*). Supplies excellent meals in lively surroundings: *zuppa di farro* (spelt – an ancient grain often used in Tuscan cuisine and rarely found elsewhere), delicious roast pork, salt cod with leeks, and so on.

Lucca's table service will be especially memorable if you have the horsepower to reach its immediate surroundings.

Solferino, 6km west of Lucca in San Macario in Piano on the Viareggio road, **t** 0583 59118 (*expensive*). Duck with truffles, wild boar and grilled seafood are a few of the treats on the extensive menu at this restaurant, which has been run by the same family for four generations, and famous throughout Tuscany for almost as long. Simple Tuscan country specialities are in evidence, but this is one place where you might want to splurge. *Closed Wed, and Thurs lunch.*

La Mora, Via Sesto di Moriano 104, **t** 0583 406 402 (*expensive*). Another good choice, north of town in Ponte a Moriano, located in an old posthouse with four cosy rooms inside and dining under the pergola in summer; according to season, you can choose delicious ravioli with asparagus or truffles, or gourmet roast lamb.

functioning republic Lucca used tact and tenacity to survive even after the arrival of the Spaniards. After the Treaty of Cateau-Cambresis Lucca amazingly found itself standing together with Venice as the only truly independent Italian states. Like Venice the city was an island of relative tolerance and enlightenment during the Counter-Reformation, and it shared Venice's fate in 1805 when Napoleon arrived, and ordered its political extinction.

The Walls

Lucca's walls owe their considerable charm to Renaissance advances in military technology. The city began them in 1500, urged to the effort by the beginning of the Wars of Italy. The councillors wanted fortifications entirely up to date, to counter new advances in artillery, and their (unknown) architects gave them the state of the art, a model for the new style of fortification that would soon be transforming the cities of Europe. Being Renaissance Tuscans, they also made them a little more elegant than perhaps was necessary. The walls were never severely tested. Today, with the outer ravelins, fosses and salients cleared away (such earthworks usually took up as much space as the city itself), Lucca's walls are just for decoration, with a double row of shady trees planted on top to make an elevated garden boulevard that extends clear around the city. St Peter's Gate, near the station, still has its portcullis, and Lucca's proud motto LIBERTAS is inscribed over the entrance.

San Martino

Lucca's **Duomo**, perhaps the outstanding work of the Pisan style outside Pisa itself, was begun in the 11th century and only completed in the 15th. A porch with three arches, each a different size, makes the façade somewhat unusual. Above is a typical Pisan design of three levels of colonnades, and behind the arches are exquisite 12th- and 13th-century reliefs and sculpture – the best work Lucca has to offer. See especially the *Adoration of the Magi* by Nicola Pisano (*currently under restoration*), and a host of fantastical animals and hunting scenes, the 12 months and their occupations, even *Roland at Roncevalles*, all by unknown masters.

Inside, a large marble tabernacle in the left aisle contains the *Volto Santo* ('Holy Image'), a painted wooden crucifix brought from Byzantium to Italy in 782 during the Iconoclast movement. According to legend, the crucifix was carved by Nicodemus, and accurately represents the face of Jesus. The image takes part in a candlelight procession each 13 September. A door from the right aisle leads to the sacristy, where you can see Lucca's real icon, Jacopo della Quercia's remarkable **tomb of Ilaria del Carretto** (1408), a tranquil effigy complete with family dog.

Next to the cathedral is the **Museo della Cattedrale** (*open April–Oct daily 10–6; Nov–Mar Mon–Fri 10–2 and Sat–Sun 10–5; adm*), with a second work by della Quercia, *St John the Evangelist*, as well as other treasures from the cathedral and the adjoining church of San Giovanni.

From the cathedral, in a quiet corner of town near the southern wall, Via Duomo takes you to twin piazzas full of trees, the focus of Lucca's evening *passeggiata*, **Piazza del Giglio** and **Piazza Napoleone**. After Napoleon seized Lucca, he gave it to his sister

Elisa Baciocchi. This queen for a day occupied the old seat of the republican council on Piazza Napoleone and, after Waterloo, when Lucca was given to a branch of the Bourbons, the 16th-century building became the **Palazzo Ducale**, the name it still has.

San Michele in Foro

Many people mistake this church, set on a piazza right in the centre of Lucca, for the cathedral. Built about the same time, and with a similar Pisan façade, it is almost as impressive. The name comes from its location on what was Roman Lucca's forum. The ambitious façade rises high above the level of the roof, like the false fronts on buildings in Wild West towns of the 1880s. Every column in the Pisan arcading is different; some doubled, some twisted like corkscrews, others inlaid with mosaic Cosmati work, or carved into medieval monsters. The graceful, rectangular campanile is Lucca's tallest and best.

West of San Michele, in a neighbourhood perfumed by the big tobacco factory near Porta Vittorio Emanuele, the 17th-century Palazzo Mansi contains the **Pinacoteca Nazionale** (*open Tues–Sat 9–7, Sun 9–2; adm*), with mostly 16th–17th-century paintings, works by Bronzino, Pontormo and Veronese. East of the church, **Via Fillungo** and its surrounding streets make up Lucca's busy shopping area, a tidy nest of straight and narrow alleys where the contented cheerfulness that distinguishes Lucca from many of its neighbouring cities seems somehow magnified. Near Via Fillungo's northern end, the 12th-century church of **San Frediano** stands out, thanks to the big mosaic panel on its façade, showing Christ and the Apostles in an elegant, flowing style. Inside is a beautiful covered baptismal font and a terracotta of the *Annunciation* by Andrea della Robbia.

Across Via Fillungo, narrow arches lead to the **Anfiteatro Romano**. Not a stone of it remains – the marble was probably carted off for San Michele and the cathedral – but Lucca is a city that changes so gradually and organically that the outline of the amphitheatre was perfectly preserved. Where the grandstands were, you now see a complete ellipse of medieval houses, with a piazza where the gladiators once slugged it out. Down Via S. Andrea you'll pass a number of resolutely medieval palaces, including that of the Guinigi family; long the leading power-brokers of Lucca, the Guinigi once even went so far as to imitate the Visconti and Medici and seize power for themselves from 1400 to 1430. Their stronghold, the **Torre Guinigi** (*open summer 9–7.30; winter 10–4.30; summer 9–7.30; adm*), next to their palace, is one of Lucca's landmarks, the best example of the odd Italian fancy of towers with big trees growing out of the top. One of the most elaborate of the medieval family fortresses, it's well worth the climb up for the view over the city and the Apuan Alps.

Continuing eastwards you pass the Via del Fosso; the canal running down the middle was the moat (*fosso*) of Lucca's oldest fortifications. Another Guinigi house, a suburban villa before the extension of the walls, contains the **Museo Guinigi** (*open Tues–Sat 9–7, Sun 9–2; adm*), with a good selection of painting and sculpture from this side of Tuscany. Sculptures from the 9th to the 15th century show the logical development of the Pisan-Luccan style, along with some original columns from the façade of San Michele, and an inspired *Annunciation* and other works by a sculptor named

Matteo Civitoli, who deserves to be better known. Lucchese Renaissance painting, with a fond reluctance to give up the Middle Ages, is also well represented.

North of the city there are two showy but refined 16th-century villas, both with extensive 'English' gardens: **Villa Mansi** at Segromigno (*open summer 10–12.30 and 3–7, winter 10–12.30 and 3–5; adm*); and the **Villa Pecci-Blunt ex-Villa Reale**, nearby at Marlia, the country home of Elisa Bonaparte Baciocchi during her reign. Only the park and the Giardino Orsetti are open, but they are lovely (*guided tours by appt, t 0368 30108, March–Nov Tues–Sun at 10, 11, 3, 4, 5 and 6; Dec–Feb, call in advance; adm*).

The Apuan Alps and the Serchio Valley

All across northern Tuscany the mountains have never been far away. In the region's northwest corner they stretch to the very edge of the sea itself. These are no piddling foothills: two peaks within 45km of Lucca are 6,56oft high. Not many tourists find their way up the Serchio – it may be the only corner of Tuscany that hasn't been overrun. But if you simply can't look at another cathedral or picture gallery, and would like a spell in some striking yet civilized mountain scenery, this is the place.

Lucca to Bagni di Lucca

North of Lucca you quickly arrive at **Diécimo** – a name that has survived from Roman times – ten Roman miles from the city. Its fine Renaissance campanile stands out starkly among the surrounding hills. Next, **Borgo a Mozzano** is famous for its beautiful little hog-back bridge, the Ponte Maddalena, with arches in five different sizes, and a legend attached to it of how the devil built it in one night. The credit really goes to Countess Matilda of Tuscany who, besides the bridge, endowed the villages around Borgo with a set of solid Romanesque churches.

A little further up river beyond the turn, still on the SS12, **Bagni di Lucca** has an interesting 19th-century suspension bridge (1840) hung on iron chains, the Ponte alle Catene. Bagni is a town worth visiting: a spa that enjoyed a brief spell of high society's favour in the 19th century and was then quietly forgotten. It has elegant old establishments to take the waters (one like a miniature Roman pantheon), a pretty site along the river, charming villas and gardens, and even a Victorian-Gothic-Alhambresque Anglican church; among the many English visitors in the old days were Shelley, Byron and Browning. Bagni's casino (1837) invented roulette to clean them out. Up in the mountains above Bagni, **San Cassiano** has a picturesque medieval bridge and a little-known 13th-century Pisan-style church, with a delicate carved façade. From Bagni, you have a choice of continuing along the SS12 towards **Abetone**, Tuscany's only big ski resort, under Monte Cimone (the highest peak in the area), or else turning back to head up the Serchio, into the Garfagnana region.

The Garfagnana and the Lunigiana

Barga, the main town along the Serchio Valley, is a little mountain *comune* that managed to keep its independence until 1341. It has an unusual 13th-century

Getting Around

Buses run to most destinations in the valley from Lucca, but some services are slow.

Tourist Information

Bagni di Lucca: Viale Umberto I, 139, t 0583 809 911 (summer only).
Barga: Piazza Angelio, t 0583 723 499.
Fivizzano: Via Roma, t 0585 92017.
Pontrémoli: Piazza della Reppublica, t 0187 833 701.

Where to Stay and Eat

Bagni di Lucca or Barga are pleasant places to stay a few days to recharge your batteries.

Bagni di Lucca ✉ 55022

Bagni di Lucca is wonderfully genteel, with a score of quiet, modest Victorian hotels.

★★★Bridge, Piazza Ponte a Serraglio 5a, t/f 0583 805324 (*cheap*). In medieval Bagni.
★★★Silvania, Lugliano, Villa di Bagni, t 0583 805 363, f 0583 867 754 (*cheap*). Very tranquil, nice rooms, in this pretty suburb a couple of kilometres up the river.
★Roma, Via Umberto I 110, t/f 0583 87278 (*cheap*). Toscanini stayed here, a small place with a shady little garden at the back, also in Villa di Bagni.
Da Vinicio, Via del Casino, t 0583 87250 (*moderate*). A chaotic and popular *pizzeria* a block west of Bagni's bridge, also with good roast pigeon and seafood.
Circolo dei Forestieri, Loc.Ville, t 0583 86038 (*moderate*). Slightly smarter, where you can eat *filetto al pepe verde* and *crespelle ai funghi. Closed Mon.*

Barga ✉ 55051

★★★★Il Ciocco in Castelvecchio, 6km north at Pascoli, t 0583 7191, f 0583 723 197 (*expensive*). A huge resort hotel with the full works, including tennis.
★★★Villa Libano, Via del Sasso 6, t 0583 723 774, f 0583 724 185 (*cheap*). A lovely place in a courtyard, next to Barga's city park; there's a restaurant with tables out in the garden.
Terrazza, 5km north at Albiano, t 0583 766 155 (*cheap*). Again, the best restaurant is out of town, featuring the specialities of the region. *Closed Wed.*

Fivizzano ✉ 54013

★★Il Giardinetto, Via Roma 151, t 0585 92060 (*Hotel cheap, restaurant moderate*). A delightful place to sleep and eat overlooking Piazza Medicea. Rooms are comfortable, and as the name implies, there's a little garden to lounge in. The *antipasti* are especially tempting, as well as the pasta and game, and a flan with spinach and cheese, made from a Renaissance recipe. *Closed Oct.*

Pontrémoli ✉ 54027

Pontrémoli is rich in good restaurants, and has two smart hotels.

★★★Golf Hotel, Via Pineta, t 0187 831 573, f 0187 831 591 (*moderate*). New to the scene, outside town in a pine wood, offering 90 very comfortable rooms, all with bath.
★★★Hotel Napoleon, Piazza Italia 2b, t/f 0187 830 544 (*moderate*). Modern rooms.
Da Bussé, Piazza del Duomo 31, t 0187 831 371 (*moderate*). An age-old restaurant featuring Pontrémoli's special *pasta testaroli*, roast meats, stuffed vegetables and other local dishes. *Open for lunch only Mon–Thurs, lunch and dinner Sat–Sun, closed Fri.*

cathedral, begun in the year 1000 and set high on a terrace, with an almost plain, squarish façade that makes it look more like a medieval Palazzo del Popolo. Be sure to step in and see the 13th-century pulpit, by a Como sculptor named Guido Bigarelli. The pillars that support it, resting on a pair of lions devouring some poor fellows, are in the Pisan style, but the reliefs around the pulpit itself are unique, startling naïve-sophisticated versions of familiar scriptural scenes.

From Barga you can detour 17km to the **Grotta del Vento** (*open daily all year; guided tours of one hour at 10, 11, 12, 2, 3, 4, 5 and 6pm, 3-hour tours for real cave fiends at 10 and 2pm; at certain times of year only part of the cave is visited; adm exp; for* *information call t 0583 722 024*), up in the mountains, a long cavern hung with fat stalactites and set in a barren, eerie landscape of eroded limestone. Try to visit in the morning when it's less crowded.

The castle at **Castelnuovo Garfagnana**, further up the valley, properly decorative in the best 14th-century manner, was once commanded by the poet Ariosto, then in the service of the Estes of Ferrara. Further north, past **Piazza al Serchio**, the road leaves the Serchio behind and crosses over a pass into a region called the **Lunigiana**, the mountain hinterlands of the long-disappeared Roman port town of Luni. This rugged territory covered with chestnut forests has often given its governors fits; at the turn of the century it was a stronghold of rural anarchy, and in 1944 the partisans made it one of the bigger free zones in the north. It must always have been like this, for these mountains are jammed full of castles: **Monti, Fivizzano, Bagnone** and **Fosidinovo** have the best ones, and on the back roads of the region you'll find a number of tiny mountain lakes and Romanesque country churches. This hidden corner conceals a genuine prehistoric mystery.

Up in **Pontrémoli**, the northernmost town in Tuscany, the stout grey 14th-century Castello del Piagnaro has been restored as a museum (*open Tues–Sun 9–12 and 3–6; adm*) to hold over a score of large, carved 'statue-steles' of an unknown culture that flourished in Lunigiana about 2000–100 BC. The steles, sort of menhirs with personality, include some shaped into stylized warriors with daggers or axes; others are women with little knobby breasts. Dozens have been discovered in the Lunigiana, all in isolated areas. Similar things turn up in southern Corsica and in Languedoc. Interestingly, the records say Christianity only began to make headway here after 700 AD. Most of the steles at Pontrémoli have their heads knocked off, a sure sign that the Pope's missionaries were here.

The Tuscan Coast

The ancient Etruscans weren't shy; these early free traders happily accepted goods, art and ideas from all over the Mediterranean world. For the last thousand years, however, for all its accomplishments, modern Tuscany has been a moody, introspective region, and usually a little dismissive towards what goes on in the rest of the world. The Tuscan coastline somehow reflects this: there is one big port, and a few little resorts, but on the whole Tuscany turns a blank face to the sea.

Carrara and Massa

Carrara, of course, owes its living and its fame to the marble masses of the Apuan Alps that surround it. Carrara marble has added the lustre to ancient Rome, Renaissance Rome and art museums and banks the world over. The town is still busy, with scores of marble sawmills and 'artistic workshops' turning out everything from sculptures for new churches to reproductions of famous statues. Some Carraran marble went into the city's distinctive **cathedral**, with a tall bell tower and an exquisite 14th-century rose window. The quarries in the surrounding hills are an

Getting Around

The main Rome–Genoa **rail** line runs a few kilometres inland all along the coast, making transport easy. **Buses** to smaller destinations run from Massa or Viareggio.

Tourist Information

Marina di Carrara: Viale Galileo Galilei, t 0585 632 519.

Marina di Massa: Viale Vespucci 24, t 0585 240 063, f 0585 869 015, *www.bicnet.it/aptms.*

Viareggio: Viale Carducci 10, t 0584 962 233, f 0585 47336, *aptversilia@caen.it.* In summer there is also an office in the train station.

Torre del Lago: Viale Kennedy 1, t 0584 359 893.

Where to Stay

Carrara ✉ 54033

★★★Michelangelo, Corso F. Rosselli 3, t 0585 777 161, f 0585 74545 (*moderate*). Considered the best hotel, with modern rooms.

Forte dei Marmi ✉ 55042

★★★★Raffaeli Park, Via Mazzini 37, t 0584 787 294, f 0585 787 418, *rafaelli@versilia. toscana.it* (*very expensive*). Has a stretch of private beach and a pool, as does the more modest Villa Angela next door.

★★★Raffaeli Villa Angela, Via Mazzini 64, t 0585 787 472, f 0585 787 115 (*expensive*). The Park's less expensive companion.

Viareggio ✉ 55049

★★★Grand Hotel Excelsior, Viale Carducci 88, t 0584 50726, f 0584 50729 (*very expensive*). If you're Viareggio-bound, why not try out a Chini-Belluomini confection? This is one of their most extravagant ventures, built in 1923. The original décor of the public rooms is well preserved. *Open April–Oct.*

★★★Grand Hotel & Royal, Viale Carducci 44, t 0584 45151, f 0584 31438 (*expensive*). Built by Belluomini alone in a neo-Renaissance eclectic style, with an impressive lobby and an indoor pool. *Open April–Oct.*

There are scores of *cheap* hotels along the beach front – you'll have no problems finding a room, but you won't find anything special.

★Da Antonio, Via Puccini 260, t/f 0584 341 053. One of several cheap places in Torre del Lago.

Eating Out

Carrara

There are quite a few good restaurants outside town, if you're lucky you may find a bottle of Candia, the white wine eked from Carrara's mountain terraces.

Da Venanzio, among the quarries in Colonnata, t 0585 758 062 (*expensive*). Here you can try the local speciality, *lardo* – a delicately-flavoured pork fat lard preserved in salt and rosemary in large marble vats – or crêpes, delicious *tortelli*, pigeon in balsamic vinegar or even roast beef. *Closed Thurs, and Sun eve.*

Roma, Piazza Battisti, t 0585 70632 (*moderate*). In the centre, it won't disappoint; a favourite for simple Tuscan cooking. *Closed Sat.*

Forte dei Marmi

La Barca, Viale Italico 3, t 0585 89323 (*expensive*). A good seafood restaurant, with traditional Italian dishes. *Closed Tues.*

Viareggio

Viareggio has a disproportionate number of good restaurants.

L'Oca Bianca, on Via Coppino 409, t 0584 388 477 (*expensive*). Head of the list, south of the centre by the port; sample Mediterranean lobster (*aragosta*), all kinds of fish and other gourmet concoctions, elaborately prepared and served. Try the *menu degustazione* (*very expensive*). *Closed Tues.*

Giorgio, Via IV Novembre, t 0584 44493 (*moderate*). A lively, welcoming place to go for seafood, also showcasing local artists' work. *Closed Wed.*

Il Porto, Via Coppino 319, t 0584 392 144 (*moderate*). Famous for its *antipasti* and pasta dishes (with clams, mixed seafood and crab). It's very popular, so be sure to book ahead. *Closed Wed.*

Osteria Numero Uno, Via Pisano 140, south of the harbour, t 0584 388 967 (*cheap*). Thanks to this place, you won't have to break the bank seeking out seafood. *Closed Wed.*

unforgettable sight; usually they extend almost to the peaks, a shining white scar on the mountains with a narrow access road zigzagging perpendicularly to the top. This part of the Apuan Alps is haunted by Michelangelo, in old clothes and smelly goatskin boots, taking his horse into the most inaccessible corners to discover new veins of perfect white stone. Michelangelo loved spending time here with his rock, and he claimed with his usual modesty to have 'introduced the art of quarrying' into the area. Carrara's quarries are in little danger of running out; you wonder if they're joking when they mention that there are only a few cubic kilometres of good stone left.

Massa, the small city to the south that shares the honour of provincial capital with Carrara, was the seat of a duchy during the Renaissance; the only things in town to see are their 17th-century Palazzo Cybo-Malaspina, with a beautiful ornate courtyard, and an 11th-century castle (*parts closed for restoration*) with Renaissance additions. Pietrasanta, an attractive town about 10km further south, has a Renaissance cathedral and many marble works. The villages inland from Carrara, Massa and **Pietrasanta** have some of the best scenery in the Apuan Alps; mountain hiking is popular here, and there are a number of marked trails to follow.

Viareggio

From the Ligurian border almost as far as the mouth of the Arno, the coast is dotted with small resorts. **Forte dei Marmi**, built under a fortress of the Tuscan grand dukes, is the most interesting, a once-posh resort that had its moment of fashion in the 1860s. The others, very popular with people from Milan and other big Italian cities, are as polluted as the Riviera to the north, but less so than the beaches around the Arno and Livorno. In the summer, all are very crowded. **Viareggio**, the largest of them, is a town that goes back to Roman times. On top of tourism it tries to make an honest living for itself from fishing and a dockyard. Everyone in Italy knows Viareggio for its big carnival, with a parade of grandiose floats. Though it only began in the 1890s, it rivals Venice and Rome as the most popular place to be around Shrove Tuesday. The 1890s bequeathed to Viareggio a number of Art Nouveau hotels and beachfront pavilions. These, plus the two shore promenades and the large pine groves that surround the town, make it one of the more pleasant resorts on the Tyrrhenian Sea.

A few kilometres to the south, **Torre del Lago Puccini** is a beauty spot built around a small lake, and you can visit the Villa Puccini, the home where the composer (of whom they're so fond that they renamed the town) wrote most of his operas, now the **Museo Pucciniano** (*open winter Tues–Sun 10–12.30 and 2.30–5.30; summer Tues–Sun 10–12 and 3–6.30; closed Mon; adm*). Every summer there's also a small-scale Festival Pucciniano, with opera performances in an open-air theatre which is built out on to the lake – the stage is actually on the water.

Pisa

Unless you spend all your time around the raucous narrow streets around the market and the university, Pisa may strike you as an uncannily quiet, almost empty place. But this is no museum city; Pisa has a hundred thousand reasonably active and noisy people who do not choose just to live in the past. Still, the city itself seems somehow too big for them. There are no ruins, but definitely an air of unfulfilled ambitions, of a past greatness nipped in the bud.

Change the scene to about 1100, when, according to the chroniclers, Pisa, the 'city of marvels', the 'city of ten thousand towers', had a population of some 300,000. If you believe those numbers we have some fine stories about Prester John and the Sultans of Cathay to tell you, too – but the medieval writers are to be excused for their extravagance. Excepting Venice, of course, nothing like this enormous, exotically cosmopolitan city had been seen in Christian Europe since the fall of Rome. Its merchants made themselves at home in every corner of the Mediterranean, bringing back new ideas and new styles in art in addition to their fat bags of profit. Pisa in the early Middle Ages made good use of these cultural exchanges, contributing as much as any city to the rebirth of western culture.

History

In the Middle Ages Pisa liked to claim that it began as a Greek city, founded by colonists from Elis. Most historians, however, won't give them credit for anything earlier than about 100 BC, when a Roman veterans' colony was settled here. Records on what followed are scarce, but Pisa, like Amalfi and Venice, must have had an early start building a navy and establishing trade connections. By the 11th century, the effort had blossomed into opulence; Pisa had built itself a small empire, including Corsica, Sardinia and for a while the Balearics. About 1060 work was begun on the great cathedral complex and other buildings, inaugurating the Pisan Romanesque.

The First Crusade, when Pisa's archbishop led the entire fleet in support of the Christian knights, was an economic windfall for the city, but when the Pisans weren't battling the Muslims of Spain and Africa they were learning from them. Influences from Andalucian mosques turn up in most Pisan Romanesque work, and a steady exchange of ideas brought much of medieval Arab science and philosophy into Europe through Pisa's port. The influence of Pisan architecture, the highest development of the Romanesque in Italy, spread from Sardinia to Puglia; in addition, when Gothic arrived in Italy Pisa was among the few cities to take it seriously. In science, Pisa contributed a great though somewhat shadowy figure, the mathematician Niccolò Fibonacci, who either rediscovered the principle of the Golden Section or learned it from the Arabs, and also introduced Arabic numerals to Europe. Pisa's scholarly tradition over the centuries was crowned in the 1600s by its most famous son, Galileo Galilei.

Pisa was always a Ghibelline city, the greatest ally of the Emperors in Tuscany if only for expediency's sake. When a real threat came, however, it was not from Florence or any of the other Tuscan cities, but the rising mercantile port of Genoa. After years of constant struggle, the Genoese devastated the Pisan navy at the Battle of Meloria (an islet off Livorno) in 1284. It meant the end of Pisan supremacy, and all chance of recovery was quashed by an even more implacable enemy: the Arno. Pisa's port was gradually silting up, and when the cost of dredging became greater than the traffic could bear, the city's fate was sealed. The Visconti of Milan seized the economically

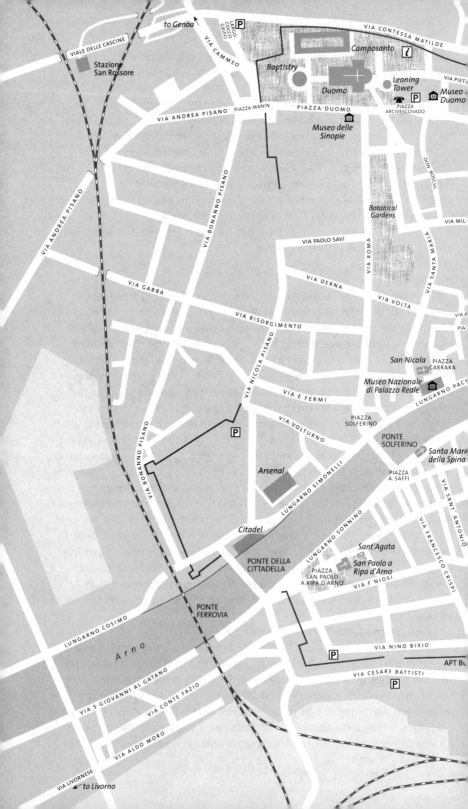

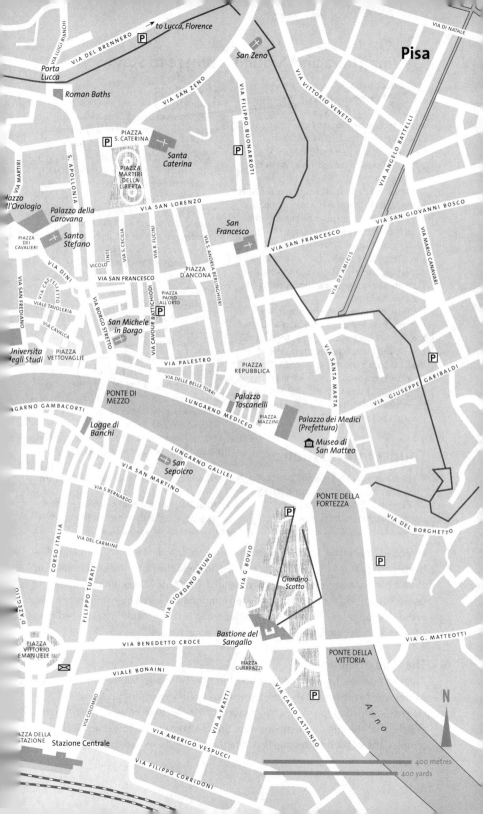

Getting There and Around

Pisa's **Galileo Galilei airport** (**t** 050 500 707) is the second busiest airport in the region (after Florence). It has its own railway station with direct connections to Florence and other cities; most trains also stop at Stazione Centrale, about a 10-minute journey. The airport is linked to the centre of Pisa by city bus no.3 too.

Pisa's **Stazione Centrale** is south of the Arno, on Piazza della Stazione (for information, call **t** 147 888 088). It is about a 20-minute walk from the centre; alternatively, take city bus no.1 from outside the station, which will take you directly to the Field of Miracles and the city centre. Some coastal lines also stop at Stazione San Rossore, near the cathedral and the Leaning Tower.

All intercity **buses** leave from near Piazza Vittorio Emanuele II, the roundabout north of the Stazione Centrale: APT buses for Volterra, Livorno and the coastal resorts (to the left on Via Nino Bixio, **t** 050 505 511); and LAZZI to Florence, Lucca and La Spezia (on Via d'Azeglio, **t** 050 42688). Many long-distance and local buses also stop at Piazza Manin, just outside the walls by the Leaning Tower.

Tourist Information

Via Cammeo, near the Leaning Tower, **t** 050 560 464. Includes hotel booking service.
Via Benedetto Croce 26, **t** 050 40096.
Just outside the central station, **t** 050 42291.

Where to Stay

Pisa ✉ 56100

Capital of day-trippers, Pisa isn't known for fine hotels, but there's usually enough room for the visitors who elect to stay overnight.

★★★★**Grand Hotel Duomo**, Via S. Maria 94, **t** 050 561 894, **f** 050 560 418. The best, very close to the Campo dei Miracoli, is this modern though richly appointed luxury hotel with a roof garden.

★★★**Royal Victoria**, Lungarno Pacinotti, **t** 050 940 111, **f** 050 940 180. A tasteful and modern establishment; its best features are rooms overlooking the Arno.

★★★**Terminus e Plaza**, Via Colombo 45, **t/f** 050 500 303 (*moderate*). One of the many middle-range hotels near the train station.

★★★**Verdi**, Piazza Repubblica 5, **t** 050 598 947, **f** 050 598 944 (*moderate*). Another good choice in this price range, located in a well-restored historic palace in the centre.

Inexpensive places are spread throughout town and often full of students; it's always best to call first, or else go up to the Campo dei Miracoli and try one of the following, all relatively convivial places within a few blocks of the cathedral:

★★**Di Stefano**, Via Sant'Apollonia 35, **t** 050 553 559, **f** 050 556 038. Central, recently upgraded to two stars.

★**Gronchi**, in Piazza Arcivesovado 1, **t** 050 561 823. The nicest of this group.

★**Giardino**, Piazza Manin, **t** 050 562 101, **f** 050 831 0392. Just outside the walls.

enfeebled city in 1396, and nine years later Florence snatched it from them. Excepting the period 1494–1505, when the city rebelled and kept the Florentines out despite an almost constant siege, Pisa's history was ended. The Medici dukes did the city one big favour, supporting the university and even removing Florence's own university to Pisa. In the last 500 years of Pisa's long, pleasant twilight, this institution has helped the city stay alive and vital, and in touch with the modern world.

The Field of Miracles

Almost from the time of its conception, this title, *Campo dei Miracoli*, was the nickname given to medieval Italy's most ambitious building programme. As with Florence's cathedral, too many changes were made over two centuries of work to tell exactly what the original intentions were. But of all the unique things about this complex, the location strikes one first. Whether their reasons had to do with

Eating Out

In Pisa you will find this difficult on a Sunday night. At other times, walks on the wild side of the Tuscan kitchen seem more common than in other towns – eels and squid, *baccalà*, tripe, wild mushrooms, 'twice-boiled soup' and dishes that waiters cannot explain.

Expensive

Ristoro dei Vecchi Macelli, Via Volturno 49, **t** 050 20424. A gourmet stronghold on the north bank of the Arno, near Ponte Solferino, with highly imaginative dishes based on coastal Tuscan traditions. *Closed Wed and Sun lunch.*

Re di Puglia, Via Aurelia Sud 7, Loc. Mortellini, **t** 050 960 157. Occupying a converted farmhouse, a kilometre from the Pisa Sud *autostrada* exit, this primarily uses produce fresh from the farm. Tuck into home-made pasta with mutton, rabbit or goat, and followed by meat cooked on the huge grill. *Dinner only, also lunch on Sun. Closed Mon and Tues.*

Moderate

Cagliostro, Via del Castelletto 26/30, **t** 050 575 413. It's hard to believe that you are in Italy at this extraordinary restaurant/*caffè*/*enoteca*/art gallery/night club and general trendy hang-out; the cooking is 'Tuscan Creative' with other dishes thrown in from around Italy. Lunch is a more modest (and cheaper) affair. *Closed Tues.*

Da Bruno, Via Luigi Bianchi 12, **t** 050 560 818. Outside the walls, a few blocks east of the Campo dei Miracoli, is another place to try out how well you like simple Pisan cooking – things like *polenta* with mushrooms and *baccalà* (dried cod). *Closed Mon eve and Tues.*

Pisa is well endowed with unpretentious *trattorie*, many located around the university.

Osteria dei Cavalieri, Via San Frediano 16, **t** 050 580 858. Seafood, vegetarian and meat fixed-price menus, and good game dishes such as rabbit with thyme. *Closed Sun.*

Osteria La Grotta, Via San Francesco 103, **t** 050 578 105. A cosy place with a simulated grotto and comforting food; traditional dishes, imaginatively prepared and without pretensions. Meat-lovers should do well here; try the *Gran Padellata del Maremmano*, a rich stew of three meats cooked with spicy sausage and vegetables. *Closed Sun.*

Il Nuraghe, Via Mazzini 58, **t** 050 443 68. Offers specialities such as *ricotta ravioli* and snails. The chef is Sardinian, so Tuscan and Sarde specialities rub shoulders. *Closed Mon.*

Lo Schiaccianoci, Via Vespucci 104, east of the station, **t** 050 21024. Seafood delicacies hold pride of place. *Closed Sun.*

Cheap

Numero Undici, Via Cavalca 11, **t** 050 54429 (*cheap*). A diminutive *trattoria* with no frills; you order from the counter, and take your plate to the table. Prices are rock bottom and the limited menu delicious. *Closed Sat lunch and Sun.*

---

aesthetics or land values – probably a little of both – the Pisans built their cathedral on a broad expanse of green lawn at the northern edge of town, just inside the walls. The cathedral was begun in 1063, the famous Leaning Tower and the baptistry in the mid-12th century, at the height of Pisa's fortunes, and the Campo Santo in 1278.

If you plan to visit all three monuments and the museums here, it's worth getting the joint ticket, the *biglietto cumulativo*, rather than paying for each separately.

The Baptistry

Open daily summer 8–7.40; spring and autumn 9–5.40; winter 9–4.40.

The biggest of its kind in Italy; those of many other cities would fit neatly inside it. The original architect, with the felicitous name of Master Diotisalvi ('God save you') saw the lower half of the building done in the typical stripes-and-arcades Pisan style.

A second colonnade was meant to go over the first, but as the Genoese gradually muscled Pisa out of its trade routes, funds ran short. In the 1260s Nicola and Giovanni Pisano redesigned and completed the upper half in a harmonious Gothic crown of gables and pinnacles. The Pisanos also added the dome over the original prismatic dome of Diotisalvi, still visible from the inside. Both of these domes were impressive achievements for their time – among the largest attempted in the Middle Ages. Inside, the austerity of the simple, striped walls and heavy columns of grey Elban granite is broken by two superb works of art. The great **baptismal font** was the work of Guido Bigarelli, the 13th-century Como sculptor who made the crazy pulpit in Barga. There is little figurative sculpture on it, but the 16 large marble panels are finely carved in floral and geometrical patterns of inlaid stones, a northern variation on the Cosmati work of medieval Rome and Campania. Nicolà Pisano's **pulpit**, made about 1260, was one of the first of that family's masterpieces, and established the form for their later pulpits, the columns resting on fierce lions, the relief panels crowded with intricately carved figures in impassioned New Testament episodes. The baptistry is famous for its uncanny acoustics; if you have the place to yourself, try singing a few notes from the centre of the floor. If there's a crowd, the guards will be just waiting for someone to bribe them to do it.

The Cathedral

Open April–Oct Mon–Sat 10–7.40, Sun 1–7.40; winter Mon–Sat 10–12.45, Sun 3–4.45; often closed to tourists for most of the day.

One of the first and finest works of the Pisan Romanesque, the cathedral façade, with four levels of colonnades, came out a little more ornate than Buscheto, the architect, planned back in 1063. These columns, with the similar colonnades around the apse and the Gothic frills later added around the unique elliptical dome, are the only showy features on the calm, restrained exterior. On the south transept, the late 12th-century **Porte San Ranieri** has a fine pair of bronze doors by Bonanno, one of the architects of the Leaning Tower. The biblical scenes are enacted under real palms and acacias; naturally, the well-travelled Pisans would have known what they looked like.

In the interior little of the original art survived a fire in 1595. The roof went, as well as the Cosmati pavement, of which a few spots still remain. But some fine work survives: the great mosaic of Christ Pantocrator in the apse is a work of Cimabue. The **pulpit**, done about 1300 by Giovanni Pisano, is the acknowledged masterpiece of that family. The men of 1595 used the fire as an opportunity to get rid of this nasty old medieval relic, and the greatest achievement of Pisan sculpture sat disassembled in crates, quite forgotten until this century. Pisano's pulpit is startling, mixing classical and Christian elements with a fluency never seen before his time. St Michael, as a *tela-mone*, shares the honour of supporting the pulpit with Hercules and the Fates, while prophets, saints and sibyls look on from their appointed places. The relief panels, jammed with expressive faces, diffuse an electric immediacy equal to the best work of the Renaissance. Notice particularly the *Nativity*, the *Massacre of the Innocents*, the *Flight into Egypt* and the *Last Judgement*.

The Leaning Tower

Due to reopen to the public in autumn 2001. Thirty people to be admitted every 30 minutes, tickets by advance boooking only. Call the tourist office or check the website, www.torre.duomo.pisa.it, for the latest details.

Most likely, the stories claiming the tilt was accidental were pure fabrications, desperate tales woven by the Pisans to account for what, before mass tourism, must have seemed a great civic embarrassment. The argument isn't very convincing. That the tower would start to lean when only 328ft tall seems hard to believe; half the weight would still be in the foundations. Even less credible would be that they doggedly kept building it after the lean commenced. The architects who measured the stones in the last century to get to the bottom of the mystery concluded that the tower's odd state was absolutely intentional. Trying to tell that to someone from Pisa, however, will be received as if you had suggested lunacy is a problem in his family.

The leaning campanile is hardly the only strange thing in the Field of Miracles. The more time you spend here, the more you will notice: little monster-griffins, dragons and such, peeking out of every corner of the oldest sculptural work, skilfully hidden where you have to look twice to see them; or the big bronze griffin sitting on a column atop of the apse (a copy), the Muslim arabesques in the Campo Santo, or the perfect classical Corinthian capitals in the cathedral nave, next to the pagan images on the pulpit. The elliptical cathedral dome, in its time the only one in Europe, shows that the Pisans not only had audacity but the mathematical skills to back it up. You may have noticed that the baptistry too is leaning – about 5ft in the opposite direction. And the cathedral façade leans outwards about an inch and a half, hard to notice but disconcerting if you see it from the right angle. So much in the Field of Miracles gives evidence of a very sophisticated, strangely modern taste for the outlandish, it may have been that the medieval master masons in charge here simply thought that plain perpendicular buildings were becoming just a little trite.

Whatever, the campanile is a beautiful building and something unique in the world – also a very expensive bit of whimsy, with some 190 marble and granite columns. At the moment, 16½ft off perpendicular, it's also proving expensive to the local and national governments as they try to shore up the lurching tower – $80 million since 1990, when rescue operations began. The first phase was completed a few years back, when counter-weights (800 tonnes of lead ingots) were stacked at the base of the tower's leaning side, stopping the tilt. The next stage is trickier: replacing the lead ingots with an underground support, laying a ring of cement around the foundations, and anchoring it to ten steel cables attached to the bedrock 164ft underground. But digging under the 14,000-tonne tower is perilous; in September 1995, while workers were freezing the ground to mute vibrations, to their horror the tower heaved a groan and tipped another tenth of an inch.

To prevent similar scares, in 1998 the tower was given a rather unsightly girdle of plastic-coated steel braces, attached by a pair of 72ft steel cables to a counterweight system hidden among the buildings on the north end of the Campo dei Miracoli, capable of increasing the tension to 100 tonnes if the tower starts to sag again during digging. The present project involves removing soil from under the north, east and west sides of the tower from a depth of about six metres below ground level, thereby decreasing the difference in depth between the north and south side. This seems to be working; the tower is not only stable but has actually righted itself by a fraction of an inch so far. Work should be completed by June 2001, and if all has gone according to plan, it will have lost 10 per cent of its present lean (about 18 inches) and be back to the angle it had 200 years ago. Struts will be sunk into the ground to block this position.

The Campo Santo and the Museums

Open summer 8–7.40; spring and autumn 9–5.40; winter 9–4.40; adm.

If one more marvel in the Campo dei Miracoli is not excessive, there is a remarkable cloister-cemetery, a rectangle of gleaming white marble, unadorned save for the blind arcading around the façade and the beautiful Gothic tabernacle of the enthroned Virgin Mary over the entrance. With its uncluttered, simple lines, the Campo Santo seems more like a work of our own century than of the 14th. The cemetery began, according to legend, when the battling Archbishop Lanfranc, who led the Pisan fleet into the Crusades, came back with boatloads of soil from the Holy Land, in which the prominent citizens of the town could be given extra-blessed burials. The building around the site was built about a century later, in the 1270s. Over the centuries an exceptional hoard of painting and sculpture accumulated here. Much of this went up in flames on a terrible night in July 1944, when an Allied incendiary bomb hit the roof and set it on fire. Many priceless works of art were destroyed and others, including most of the frescoes, damaged beyond hope of ever being perfectly restored.

The biggest loss, perhaps, was the set of frescoes by Benozzo Gozzoli – the *Tower of Babel, Solomon and Sheba, Life of Moses*, the *Grape Harvest* and others; in their original state they must have been as fresh and colourful as his famous frescoes in Florence's Medici Palace. Even better known, and somewhat better preserved, are two 14th-century frescoes of the *Triumph of Death* and the *Last Judgement* by an unknown artist (perhaps Andrea Orcagna of Florence) whose failure to leave his name unfortunately put him down to posterity as the 'Master of the Triumph of Death'. In this memento of the century of plagues and trouble, the damned are variously cooked, wrapped up in snakes, poked, disembowelled, banged up and chewed on; still, they are some of the best paintings of the trecento, and somehow seem less gruesome and paranoid than similar works of centuries to come (though good enough to have inspired that pop classic, Lizst's *Totentanz*).

Another curiosity is the **Theological Cosmography** of Piero di Puccio (*currently under restoration, call Donati Luce, t 050 560 547, for information*), a diagram of the 22 spheres of the planets and stars, angels, archangels, thrones and dominations, cherubim and seraphim, and so on; in the centre, the small circle trisected by a T-shape was a common medieval map pattern for the known earth. The three sides represent Asia, Europe and Africa, and the three lines the Mediterranean, the Black Sea and the Nile. Among the sculptures in the Campo Santo, there are sarcophagi and

Roman bath tubs, and in the gallery of pre-war photographs of the lost frescoes, a famous Hellenistic marble vase with bas-reliefs.

The collection of the **Museo del Duomo** (*same hours; adm*) is exhibited in the chapter house, in the southeast corner of the Campo dei Miracoli, near the Leaning Tower. The first rooms contain the oldest works, including two strange Islamic pieces, the strange 11th-century **griffin** originally on the top of the cathedral, believed to have first come from Egypt, and a bronze basin. Most of the statues by the Pisanos exhibited here were brought in from the elements only when they were so worn and bleached as to be barely recognizable, and resemble a convention of mummies. However, in Room 5 there is Giovanni Pisano's superb *Madonna del Colloquio*, one of the finest of the family's sculptures, and in Room 10 his lovely ivory *Madonna and Child*. The museum continues upstairs with intarsia, Roman and Etruscan odds and ends, some rare illuminated scrolls, and the Pisan Cross, carried by the Pisan soldiers on the First Crusade.

Many of the damaged frescoes from the Campo Santo were moved to the **Museo delle Sinopie** (*same hours; adm exp*), across the piazza from the cathedral, after the war, along with the *sinopie* discovered underneath when they were removed from the walls. Many of these simple sketches are works of art in their own right, and together with drawings and photos made before the bombing they help to give an idea of how the frescoes once looked.

North Pisa

With the cathedral off on the edge of town, Pisa has no real centre. Still, the Pisans are very conscious of the division made by the Arno; every year on 27 June the two sides fight it out on the Ponte di Mezzo in the *Gioco del Ponte*, a sort of medieval tug-of-war where the opponents try to push a big decorated cart over each other. From the Field of Miracles, Via Cardinale Maffi leads east to some ruins of **Roman baths** near the Lucca gate; two interesting churches in the neighbourhood are **San Zeno**, in a corner of the walls, with some parts as old as the 5th century; and **Santa Caterina**, a Dominican church with a beautiful, typically Pisan façade. Inside there is an *Annunciation* and a sculpted tomb by Nino Pisano, as well as a large painting from the 1340s of the *Apotheosis of St Thomas Aquinas*, with Plato and Aristotle in attendance and defeated infidel philosopher Averroes below.

There is a long street that begins near the Campo dei Miracoli as Via Carducci and changes its name along its route, becoming the old, arcaded **Borgo Largo** and **Borgo Stretto**. This is Pisa's traditional main artery, the most fashionable shopping street and the centre for the evening *passeggiata*. The twisting alleys of the lively market area are just off to the west, along with the **University**, still one of Italy's most important, and the **Piazza dei Cavalieri**. In 1562 Duke Cosimo I started what was probably the last crusading order of knights, the Cavalieri di Santo Stefano. The crusading urge had ended long before, but the Duke found this a useful tool for indulging the anachronistic fantasies of the Tuscan nobility – most of them newly titled bankers – and for licensing out freebooting expeditions against the Turks. Cosimo had Vasari build the **Palazzo della Carovana** for the order, conveniently demolishing the old Palazzo del Popolo, the symbol of Pisa's lost independence. Vasari gave the Palazzo an outlandishly ornate sgraffito façade; the building now holds a college of the university. Next to it, the **Palazzo dell'Orologio** was built around the 'Hunger Tower' (left of the big clock), famous from Dante's story in the *Inferno* of Ugolino della Gherardesca, the Pisan commander who was walled in here with his two young sons after his fickle city suspected him of intriguing with the Genoese.

Santo Stefano, the order's church, is also by Vasari, though the façade is by a young dilettante of the Medici family; inside are some long, fantastical war pennants that the order's pirates captured from the Muslims in North Africa.

Museo di San Matteo

Open Tues–Sat 9–7, Sun 9–2; adm.

Much of the best Pisan art from the Middle Ages and Renaissance has been collected here, in an old convent that also once served as a prison. Most came from Pisan churches, so there is a predominance of straightforward religious subjects. The Pisano family is, of course, well represented, including one magically beautiful *Madonna* in medieval Pisan dress, a wooden sculpture by Andrea Pisano. Besides the Pisan statues, reliefs, ivory work and sarcophagi, there are paintings by such artists as Masaccio (*St Paul*), Fra Angelico, Ghirlandaio, Simone Martini, Gozzoli and Brueghel.

South of the Arno

Pisa's stretch of Arno is an exercise in Tuscan gravity, two mirror-image lines of blank-faced yellow and tan buildings all the same height. Only one landmark breaks the monotony, but it is something special. Near the Solferino Bridge, **Santa Maria della Spina** sits on the bank like a precious, tiny Gothic jewel box. Though one of the few outstanding achievements of Italian Gothic, originally it wasn't Gothic at all. Partially rebuilt in 1323, its new architect – perhaps one of the Pisanos – turned it into an extravaganza of pointy gables and blooming pinnacles. All of the sculptural work is first class, especially the figures of Christ and the Apostles in the 13 niches facing the streets. The chapel takes its name from a thorn of Christ's crown of thorns, a relic brought back from the Crusades.

Not far to the west, near the walls where the famous 'Golden Gate' – Pisa's door to the sea – once stood, remains of the old Citadel and Arsenal are still visible across the river. On the southern side, **San Paolo a Ripa del Arno** has an interesting 12th-century façade similar to that of the cathedral. San Paolo stands in a small park, and it is believed to have been built over the site of Pisa's original cathedral: perhaps building cathedrals in open fields was an old custom. Behind it, the unusual and very small 12th-century chapel of **Sant'Agata** has eight sides and an eight-sided prismatic roof. A similar building can be seen at the other end of south Pisa, the octagonal **San Sepolcro** off Lungarno Galilei, built originally for the Knights Templar.

Around Pisa

Just outside Pisa there are good Romanesque Pisan churches in the villages of Calci, Vicopisano and San Casciano. **The Certosa di Pisa** (*guided tours May–Oct 9–6;*

Nov–April 9–4; closed Mon), a typically lavish 18th-century charterhouse, has a prominent site north of the Arno and a huge low building in some sort of 1920s Spanish-Californian exhibition style. West of the city at **Gombo** is a small beach where in 1822 Percy Shelley was brought ashore after being drowned, in the company of a British lieutenant, when a storm struck their small boat on the way to Livorno. His body was burned here too, as Trelawney, Leigh Hunt and Byron looked on.

Livorno and the Islands

Livorno

A few kilometres out to sea beyond Livorno's harbour, a medieval stone tower marks the tiny islet of Meloria, the place where the Genoese navy put an end to Pisa's importance as a Mediterranean power in 1284. And when the silting up of its river harbour put an end to Pisa as a great port, fate had this spot in mind to replace her. Livorno was founded in 1571 by Cosimo de Medici; over the next 200 years, while nearly all the rest of peninsular Italy was in economic decline, Livorno thrived as the nation's third port, after Genoa and Naples. It was an interesting town: after Duke Ferdinand decreed religious liberty for it, persecuted Jews, Greeks, English Catholics and even Spanish Moors settled here, along with political refugees from all over Europe. From the beginning there was a strong connection with England: an English engineer, son of the Duke of Leicester, designed the port, and trade connections were strong. Englishmen became so familiar with Livorno in the 17th century that they bestowed on it the bizarre anglicization of Leghorn.

Livorno, though the home town of the artist Modigliani, hasn't much to show for its 400 years, but its modern, ambitious outlook has earned it an important role in sea container traffic and a position as Tuscany's second city. There isn't much to see, but the city has plenty of ferries you can leap on to get to Mediterranean islands, and a reputation for seafood that is wholly deserved

While you're waiting at the port, have a look at Livorno's landmark, the **monument to Ferdinand I**, better known as the 'Quattro Mori' for the four bronze Moors in chains around the pedestal, exceptional sculptures by a 17th-century artist named Pietro Tacca (four Moors' heads are the symbol of Sardinia).

The best part of Livorno is the 'Venice' neighbourhood near the port, sliced through by small canals. Otherwise the city wears a strangely blank look, pure north-Tuscan taciturnity undiluted by medieval or Renaissance charm. It's pleasant enough, and the people are on the whole good cheerful communists, but even when the streets are crowded Livorno can seem like a city seen in a dream.

The Tuscan Archipelago

Mostly this means Elba, one of Italy's number one holiday playgrounds, though there are also six smaller islands, tracing a broad arc along the coast from Livorno to Orbetello. Some of them might also be desirable holiday destinations, but for the Italian government's bad habit of using them as prisons.

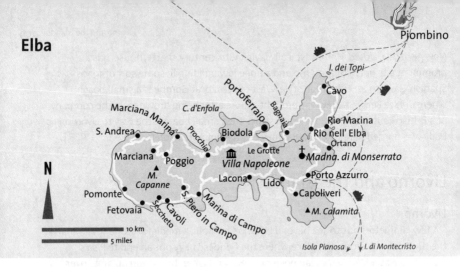

Elba

Elba, reached by ferry from Piombino or Livorno, attracts over two million visitors each year, to unspectacular, family-style holidays on its miles of beaches. The scenery, reminiscent of nearby Corsica, is often impressive; pink granite, green *macchia* and forests, and a severely mountainous coast. In ancient times Elba was best known for its iron ore, and more recently for the brief sojourn of Napoleon (1814–15). Everyone visits his thoroughly depressing palace in the otherwise lovely island capital of **Portoferraio**. Other sights are few, but you can enjoy the mountains and beaches and wash down a fish dinner with Elban *Aleatico* or *Moscato*, two of Tuscany's best wines.

As for the other islands, from north to south: **Gorgona** once had villas of wealthy Romans but now is just a gloomy prison. The larger **Capraia**, once a penal colony, has more Roman ruins, cliffs, and five hotels. Below Elba come **Pianosa**, another prison (and rather improbable setting for the US base in *Catch 22*); **Montecristo**, a beautiful, uninhabited nature reserve, accessible only for day trips from Elba; and **Giglio**, the only real resort island, which boasts superb scenery and bird life, several hotels, three little villages, one of them medieval – Giglio Castello – and fine small beaches. Finally, there's **Giannutri**, a pretty, tiny island without roads, just big enough to hold some villas and one holiday village.

Gorgona and Capraia can be reached by a regular ferry service from Livorno and Elba; Giglio and Giannutri from Porto Santo Stefano, near Orbetello.

South of Livorno

The rugged coast south of Livorno is dotted with small beaches that can be tremendously crowded all through the summer: around **Castiglioncello**, a pretty spot when things are slow, then Rosignano Solvay, Marina di Cecina, San Vincenzo, Follonica and Punta Ala, all along the coastal plain. There are Etruscan tombs, not especially interesting, at **Populonia**, one of the big Etruscan cities of which few traces remain. It stands on a mountainous promontory, at the other end of which is **Piombino**, a town full of steel works that is also the most convenient ferry port for Elba.

Grosseto, today a fair-sized provincial capital, has no ancient memories – of course it doesn't, having been underwater until late-Roman times. Grosseto does have Medici

Getting Around

Livorno's **train** station, with plenty of trains to Pisa, Florence and any point along the Tyrrhenian coast, is on the edge of the city, but there are regular **city buses** from there to the port and Piazza Grande in the centre. **Buses** for all villages in Livorno province (the strip of coast down as far as Follonica) leave from Piazza Grande. LAZZI buses for Florence depart from Scali A. Saffi, on the Fosse Reale, just off Piazza Cavour.

Ferries go from Livorno to the islands of Elba, Gorgona and Capraia (Toremar, usually at least twice daily, **t** 0586 896 113), to Bastia in Corsica (Corsica Ferries, **t** 0586 881 380, Corsica Marittima, **t** 0586 210 507) and to Olbia in Sardinia (Sarda Navigazione, **t** 0586 409 925, Moby Lines, **t** 0586 826 847). All offices are in the Stazione Marittima in the port. Ferries to Elba are heavily booked up in mid-summer and it can be easier to get the boat from Piombino, closer to Elba (*see* opposite).

Tourist Information

Livorno: Piazza Cavour 6, **t** 0586 898 111; port-side offices at Porto Mediceo and Terminal Calata Carrara (summer only).
Elba: Grattacielo building, Calata Italia 26, Portoferraio, across from the ferry dock, **t** 0565 914 671/2.
Grosseto: Via Fucini 43c, **t** 0564 414 303, near the station.
Porto Santo Stefano: Corso Umberto 55, **t** 0564 814 208.

Where to Stay

Livorno ✉ 57100
***Gran Duca**, Piazza Micheli 16, **t** 0586 891 024, **f** 0586 891 153 (*expensive*). Livorno's most interesting hotel, where some of the rooms look out over the Quattro Mori and the busy port; though modern inside, the Gran Duca is built into a surviving section of the walls right on the piazza at the entrance to the harbour area.

As it's a port town, there's an abundance of less expensive hotels. Many, though none especially distinguished, can be found across the wide piazza from the train station. Dozens more crowd the centre around the port and Via Grande; Corso Mazzini, a few blocks south of the Fosso Reale, has some nice ones.
Hotel Marina, Corso Mazzini 148, **t 0586 834 278, **f** 0586 834 135 (*cheap*). Old-fashioned, and rather nice.
*Europa, a block off Via Grande at Via dell'Angiolo 23, **t** 0586 888 581 (*cheap*). Clean, remodelled rooms, right in the centre.

Elba ✉ 57037
With more than 150 hotels around the island, Elba has something for everyone. But beware: Elba is a big package-tour destination, and despite its scores of lodgings you'll need to book ahead to avoid disappointment.
L'Ape Elbana, Salità de' Medici 2, **t/f 0565 914 245 (*moderate*). In Portoferraio, an interesting possibility is the 'Elban Bee', the oldest hotel on the island; it entertained Napoleon's guests.
****Villa Ottone, at Ottone, **t** 0565 933 042 (*expensive*). A little more up-to-date, in a 19th-century villa right on the beach, with a shady garden. *Open all year*.
La Conchiglia, Cavoli, **t 0565 987 010 (*moderate*). Small, on Elba's best beach.
Andreina, at La Cala, **t 0565 908 150 (*cheap*). Blissfully out to the way, west of Marciana Marina, with reasonable rooms.

Orbetello ✉ 58035
*Piccolo Parigi, Corso Italia 169, **t** 0564 867 233 (*cheap*). A delightful, very friendly and very Mediterranean establishment in the middle of town, ideal if you're travelling on a budget and just want to pass through for a look at the Argentario.

Porto Ercole ✉ 58018
****Torre di Calapiccola, **t** 0564 825 133, **f** 0564 825 235 (*expensive*). An out-of-town apartment complex in a great setting, with a beach and plenty of activities, or equal doses of peace and quiet if that's what you're looking for, hidden away on the western tip of the peninsula.

Porto Santo Stefano ✉ 58019
***Filippo II, **t** 0564 811 611. The best in town, close to the beaches at Poggio Calvella.

***La Caletta**, Via Civinni 10, **t** 0564 812 939, **f** 0564 817 506 (*moderate*). Pleasant rooms overlooking the sea.

Alfiero, Via Cuniberti 12, **t 0564 814 067 (*moderate*). A simple, less expensive hotel at the centre of the action around the harbour.

Eating Out

Livorno
The main purpose of a trip to Livorno is to eat seafood. The Livornese have their own ways of preparing it – much copied up and down the Tuscan coast – with the bonus that restaurants are easier on your pocket than elsewhere. Lobster, grilled fish and pasta with seafood figure on all the local menus, as does the Livornese dish, *cacciucco*, the famous fish stew that is Livorno's masterpiece. After a rich meal try a *bomba livornese:* this is the local answer to Irish coffee and is made with equal quantities of piping hot coffee and rum.

La Chiave, Scali della Cantine 52, **t** 0586 888 609 (*expensive*). Considered by many to be the best restaurant in Livorno, this of course specializes in seafood; the menu changes often but be sure to try one of the seafood pasta *primi*, such as the *tagliolini* with octopus. *Eves only.*

L'Antico Moro, Via Bertelloni 59, **t** 0586 884 659 (*moderate*). A local seafood favourite since the 1920s, on a narrow street near the city market. *Closed Wed.*

Cantina Nardi, Via L. Cambini 6, **t** 0586 808 006 (*moderate*). This wine bar is a pleasant surprise at lunchtime when a few tables are laid and excellent food is served. You can eat surrounded by hundreds of wine bottles – who could want better company? *Closed eves and Sun.*

Some of the best restaurants are to the south in the seaside suburb of Ardenza.

Da Oscar, Via Franchini 76, **t** 0586 501 258 (*moderate*). A favourite for decades, with a good selection of wines to accompany linguini and clams, excellent *risotti* and grilled *triglie* and *orate*. *Closed Mon.*

Trattoria Galileo, Via della Campana 22, **t** 0586 889 009. A popular spot in the centre, north of Piazza Repubblica, with seafood featuring prominently among other dishes.

Elba
In the long list of restaurants on the island, few really stand out. What does stand out are Elba's DOC wines; both *Elba rosso* and *Elba bianco* can hold their own with any in Tuscany.

La Ferrigna, Piazza della Repubblica 22, Portoferraio, **t** 0565 914 129 (*expensive*). One of the most popular places in Portoferraio, offering extravagant seafood *antipasti*, stuffed roast fish, and an Elban version of *Livornese cacciucco*; there are tables on the convivial piazza. *Closed Tues.*

Ristorante Boris, Loc. Valdana, Portoferraio, **t** 0565 940 018 (*moderate*). Not much fancy seafood beyond the *spaghetti vongole*, but the cooking is special. *Closed Tues in winter.*

Orbetello
Osteria del Lupacante, Corso Italia 103, **t** 0564 867 618 (*moderate*). Here you'll find dishes using the freshest fish, from salad of octopus and potato to spaghetti with sea urchin or *zucchini* flowers stuffed with baby squid. *Closed Tues in winter.*

Porto Ercole
Gambero Rosso, Lungomare Andrea Doria, **t** 0564 832 650 (*expensive*). Fancy seafood, like spaghetti with lobster sauce, at fancy prices, or *zuppa di pesce* on weekends.

La Grotta del Pescatore, Via delle Fonti, **t** 0564 835 265 (*cheap*). A cheaper alternative, where you can try a bowl of steaming *zuppa di scampi con patate*, more stew than soup

Porto Santo Stefano
Some of the places here are almost too swanky to be in such a little resort town.

Dal Greco, Via del Molo 1, **t** 0564 814 885 (*expensive*). Pricey, but worth it, an elegant place on the yacht harbour. *Terrina di pesce* with vegetables is the star dish. *Closed Tues.*

Orlando, Via Breschi 3, **t** 0564 812 788 (*moderate*). Popular and lively, one of the few genuine places left in town, specializing in grilled fish. *Closed Thurs in winter.*

Il Delfino, Piazzale Facchinetti, **t** 0564 818 394 (*expensive for full dinner, but it's also a pizzeria*). On the other harbour, with semi-outdoor dining; pleasant, but a little close to traffic. They pride themselves on inventive seafood concoctions. *Closed Thurs.*

fortifications and a small archaeological museum (*call* **t** *0564 417 629, for hours and information*). Its plain, now reclaimed from swamps and made into rich farmland, marks the beginning of the **Maremma**, a low-lying region that extends almost as far as Rome. Once one of the centres of Etruscan civilization, malaria and Roman misrule led to its almost complete abandonment. For centuries the Maremma remained a ghostly, disease-ridden marsh, though modern drainage and reclamation projects much like those in the Pontine Marshes to the south have made good farmland of it once more. Parts have been maintained in their original state as a nature park – including the **Monti dell'Uccellina**, a range of ragged hills set among parasol pine forests on the coast south of Grosseto. This is a favourite rest stop for migratory birds going to and from Africa – hence the name (*uccello* is Italian for 'bird'). Nine walks have been laid out, and there are tours in English in summer (*call the visitors' centre at Alberese,* **t** *0564 407 098; open 8–one hour before sunset; adm*). There are no roads, but you can explore the coast by boat from **Talamone**, a fishing port at its southern tip.

Near the end of Tuscany's coast is a geographical curiosity, **Monte Argentario**. Once, perhaps thousands of years ago, Argentario was an island, the member of the Tuscan archipelago closest to the shore. It gradually became joined to the mainland by two narrow sand bars, now solid and covered with trees. There's a story that sailors gave the Argentario its name in classical times, noticing the flashes of silver from the olive leaves that still cover the mountain slopes. The placid lagoons between the sand bars make up another renowned nature and bird reserve, and those who are prepared to walk out along the southernmost strip are also rewarded by the discovery of remarkably unspoilt beaches. **Orbetello**, on the central strip, was once a fashionable resort, though today this charming town must make way for trendy **Porto Ercole** and **Porto Santo Stefano**, two pretty fishing villages that in summer are a bit overburdened with Florentines and Romans on holiday.

Siena

Understanding Florence, Siena's arch-enemy and artistic rival over the centuries, requires some work – a few bulky tomes of history and art criticism for starters, and an effort of the imagination beyond that. For Siena, on the other hand, you need only come to the city and look around. Draped on its hills, Siena reveals itself as a flamboyant ensemble of medieval buildings in honest brown (*siena*-coloured) brick; on the lower slopes, gardens and olive groves fill almost half the space within the old city wall, and above it all Tuscany's tallest tower and its gayest, most dazzling cathedral compete like beauties at the fair. Medieval Siena created beauty almost effortlessly, and its fierce civic pride tolerated nothing less than the building of a city that in itself is a single great work of art.

History

A Roman foundation, Siena emerged in the age of the *comuni* as one of the leading powers of central Italy, achieving its total independence in 1125. Like Florence, Siena

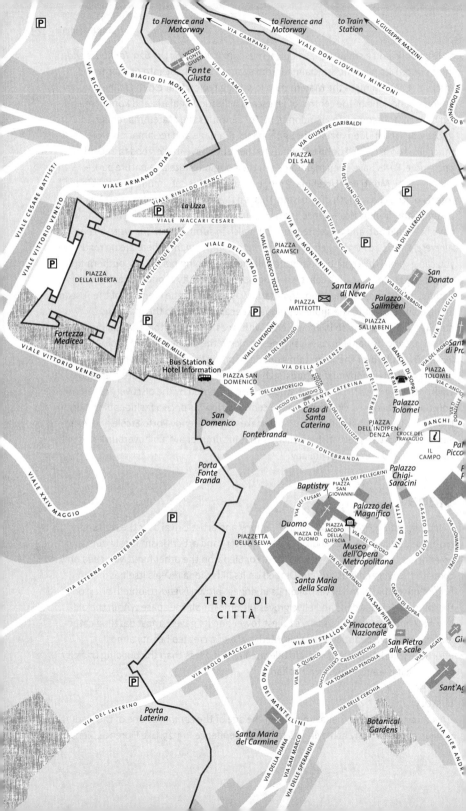

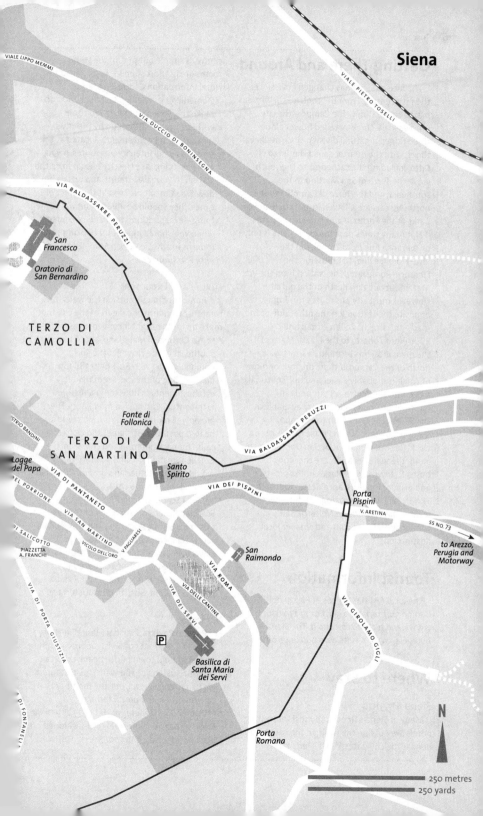

Siena

VIALE LIPPO MEMMI

VIA DUCCIO DI BONINSEGNA

VIALE PIETRO TOSELLI

VIA BALDASSARRE PERUZZI

San Francesco

Oratorio di San Bernardino

TERZO DI CAMOLLIA

Fonte di Follonica

'STRIO BANDINI

TERZO DI SAN MARTINO

Logge del Papa

VIA DI PANTANETO

DEL PORRIONE

Santo Spirito

VIA DEI PISPINI

VIA BALDASSARRE PERUZZI

Porta Pispini

V. ARETINA

SS NO. 73

to Arezzo, Perugia and Motorway

VIA SAN MARTINO

DI SALICOTTO

VICOLO DELL'ORO

V. PAGLIARESI

San Raimondo

VIA ROMA

PIAZZETTA A. FRANCHI

VIA DELLE CANTINE

VIA DEI SERVI

VIA GIROLAMO GIGLI

VIA DI PORTA GIUSTIZIA

P

Basilica di Santa Maria dei Servi

DI FONTANELLI

Porta Romana

N

250 metres

250 yards

Getting There and Around

The face of Siena has changed little since the 14th century. From the centre – the famous piazza called simply the **Campo** – the city unfolds like a three-petalled flower along three ridges, a natural division since medieval times, with the quarter called the **Terzo di Città**, including the cathedral, to the south-west; the **Terzo di San Martino** to the southeast; and the **Terzo di Camollia** to the north. No cars are allowed in, but there are **car parks** at the Fortezza and outside the gates.

Not many **trains** pass through; Siena is only on a branch line from Empoli (on the Pisa–Florence line) to Chiusi (on the Florence–Rome line). The station is on the Via Mazzini, about 2km north of the old city. However, most city **bus** routes run from opposite the station (on the other side of the road – the stop has a large map and information board) to the Piazza Matteotti, the main local bus terminus a short walk north of the Campo. If there are four or more of you it is probably easier and quicker to take a **taxi** into the centre. All bus and rail information and rail tickets are available at the SETI agency, no.56 on the Campo.

A short distance from Piazza Matteotti, on the little square in front of San Domenico and along the Viale dei Mille, are the stops for **buses** to towns and villages in the province and also for long-distance destinations. The TRA-IN (sic) line, **t** 0577 204 245, has several buses a day to Florence, Volterra, San Gimignano, Montalcino and smaller local destinations.

Tourist Information

The local APT has offices at Piazza del Campo 56, **t** 0577 280 551, **f** 0577 270 676, *www.siena.turismo.toscana.it*. The Siena hoteliers' co-op has its own bookings office.

Where to Stay

Siena ✉ 53100

Many of Siena's finest and most interesting hotels are outside the walls, in the countryside or near the city gates. What's left, in the centre, is simple but fine. In the summer, rooms are in short supply – book ahead.

Hotel Information Centre, Piazza San Domenico, **t** 0577 288 084, **f** 0577 280 290. Make this your first stop if you come without a reservation. Run by the city's innkeepers, it's conveniently located at the terminus of all intercity bus routes. If you arrive by train, take the city bus up from the station to Piazza Matteotti, and walk a block down Via Curtatone. Even at the worst of times, they should be able to find you something – except during the Palio, of course, when you should make your booking several months in advance. *Open Mon–Sat 9–7, until 8 in summer.*

Luxury and Expensive

A number of hotels outside the walls have a rural Tuscan charm and views of the city that make up for the slight inconvenience.

★★★★La Certosa di Maggiano, about 1km southeast of the city, near the Porta Romana, **t** 0577 288 180, **f** 0577 288 189 (*luxury*). One of the most remarkable establishments in Italy, set in a restored 14th-century Carthusian monastery. There are only 18 rooms; the luxuries include a heated pool, a quiet chapel and cloister, a salon for backgammon and chess, an excellent restaurant, and a library that would be an antiquarian's dream. Of course, all this doesn't come cheap.

★★★★Villa Scacciapensieri, Strada Scacciapensieri 10, 3km north of the city, **t** 0577 41441, **f** 0577 270 854 (*expensive*). As a second choice, marvel at glorious sunset views over Siena. This is a quiet country house divided into 28 spacious rooms; besides the view, it features a pool and a good restaurant with an outdoor terrace.

Moderate

★★★Palazzo Ravizza, Pian dei Mantellini, **t** 0577 280 462, **f** 0577 221 597. Thirty rooms within an elegant old town house near the Porta Laterina, just inside the walls; the restaurant isn't anything special, but the rooms are cosy and there is a pretty terrace.

★★★Duomo, Via Stalloreggi 38, **t** 0577 289 088, **f** 0577 43043. A comfortably old-fashioned place south of the Duomo.

**Canon d'Oro, Via Montanini 28, t 0577 44321, f 0577 280 868. Located near the bus station, this is both well-run and a good bargain.
***Garden, Via Custoza 2, t 0577 47056, f 0577 46050. Boasts a swimming-pool.

Cheap

Inexpensive places can be hard to find – especially before term time when they're full of students looking for a permanent place.
**Piccolo Hotel Etruria, Via delle Donzelle 3, t 0577 283 685, f 0577 288 461. You won't do better in location or amenities than the friendly, newly remodelled Etruria, off Via Banchi di Sotto near the Campo.
**Il Giardino, Via Baldassare Peruzzi 35, t 0577 285 290, f 0577 221 197. Near the Porta Pispini, with good views and a swimming-pool, and comes highly recommended in readers' letters.
*Tre Donzelle, Via delle Donzelle, t 0577 280 358. Also good, but it has a midnight curfew.

Eating Out

Sitting between three of Italy's greatest wine-producing areas, the Chianti, the Brunello of Montalcino and the Vino Nobile of Montepulciano, there is always something distinguished to wash down the simple dishes of the Sienese table. This city's real speciality is sweets; many visitors find they have no room for lunch or dinner after repeated visits to the pastry shops for slices of *panforte*, a heavy but indecently tasty cake laced with fruits, nuts, orange peel and secret Sienese ingredients, or *panpepato*, similar, but containing pepper.

Siena being a university town, snacks and fast food of all kinds are common; a *cioccina* is Siena's special variation on pizza; *pici* (thick south Tuscan spaghetti) with a sauce prepared from ground fresh pork, *pancetta*, sausages and chicken breasts, added to tomatoes cooked with Brunello wine, is the city's favourite pasta dish.

Expensive

Da Enzo, Via Camollia 49, t 0577 281 277. A traditional restaurant; the menu is long and varied with plenty of choice between fish and meat. The classic spaghetti with baby

clams (*vongole*) is good, and there is a roast fish of the day. *Closed Mon*.
Al Marsili, Via del Castoro 3, t 0577 47154. Just off the Piazza del Duomo is another of Siena's best offerings, in a singularly elegant setting – not very traditional, with dishes like gnocchi in duck sauce. *Closed Mon*.

Moderate

Osteria Le Logge, Via del Porrione 33, just off the Campo, t 0577 48013. If you've survived the wine and the pastry shops, you'll appreciate the succulent *risotti* and pasta dishes here, with exotic second courses like stuffed guinea-fowl (*faraona*) and a fine wine list. *Closed Sun*.
Tullio ai Tre Cristi, Vicolo Provenzano, t 0577 280 608. Established here since about 1830 and perhaps the most authentic of Sienese restaurants, the menu includes *ribollita*, tripe with sausages, and roast boar from the Maremma. The *pici* is home-made. There are outside tables in the summer. *Closed Mon*.
Osteria Castelvecchio, Via Castelvecchio 65, t 0577 49586. An unusually creative menu with lots of vegetarian options, located in a former stables near the Duomo. *Closed Tues*.
Osteria Il Ghibellino, Via del Pellegrino 26, t 0577 270 737. Readers' compliments abound for this place: good food, a good bargain, and a convenient location for lunch between the Duomo and the Campo; seafood Thurs and Fri. *Closed Mon*.

Cheap

Less expensive places are often a little further from the Campo.
Ristorante-Pizzeria, Via dei Fusari, hidden around the corner from Santa Maria della Scala. A good, informal no-name restaurant, perfect for lunch after slogging through the Duomo. There's an excellent value set price for a full dinner with a wide choice of dishes, and pizza even in the afternoons, but get there early; it usually fills up fast.
Il Cavallino Bianco, Via di Città 20, t 0577 44258. Serves regional food. Its main bonus is that it is open until late. *Closed Tues*.
Osteria La Chiaccera, Costa di Sant' Antonio 4, t 0577 280 631. A small, packed rustic eatery near the Casa di S. Caterina, serving *pici*, tripe, kidneys and other local specialities.

lived on wool and banking; the clothing industry was never very large, but the bankers managed to make themselves indispensable to kings and princes all over Europe.

Ghibelline by convenience, Siena found itself almost constantly at war with Guelph Florence. The greatest moment in its history came in 1260, when news arrived of a huge army raised by Florence and other Tuscan cities coming to demand Siena's surrender. The city militias – reinforced by about 5,000 Florentine political exiles – marched out and met the Florentines at Monteaperti, beating them so badly that Florence was entirely at their mercy; only the attitude of the Florentine exiles prevented the Sienese from razing Florence to the ground, a famous story told by Dante in the *Inferno*. Nevertheless, as Florence's military and economic equal, Siena enjoyed a golden age that ended in 1348, when the Black Death carried off a third of the population. Political infighting as violent as Florence's, together with a steady decline of its banking business, made recovery impossible, but with difficulty Siena held on to its independence. Only once, in 1399, when Gian Galeazzo Visconti of Milan occupied the city, did it lose its liberty, but Visconti rule lasted only until 1404.

In art, if the quattrocento was the high noon of Florence's Renaissance, the 13th and 14th centuries belonged to Siena. With palaces, churches and public buildings far grander than those of Florence at this time, Siena also led in painting. Giorgio Vasari, because he was a Florentine, gave all the credit for advances in painting to Cimabue and Giotto, but Sienese artists such as Duccio di Buoninsegna, Simone Martini, Matteo di Giovanni, and Pietro and Ambrogio Lorenzetti often surpassed their Florentine counterparts in many ways – less innovative, perhaps, but they brought the 'International Gothic' style of art to its highest form in Italy. Even as its economic decline continued, Siena remained an important artistic centre.

Throughout the 15th century factionalism kept Siena paralysed. Like Florence, the city eventually found some peace with the accession of a powerful political boss, Pandolfo Petrucci, called 'il Magnifico' like Lorenzo de' Medici. He and his successors ruled the city from 1487 to 1524. By that time Siena was only a pawn in Italian politics. In a nine years' war, starting with a popular revolt against Charles V's garrison in the city in 1552, combined Florentine and Spanish forces conquered the republic, eventually starving the city into submission in a protracted siege.

With its independence lost and its economy irrevocably ruined, Siena withdrew into itself. For centuries there was to be no recovery, little art or scholarship, and no movements towards reform. This does much to explain why medieval and Renaissance Siena is so well preserved today – for better or worse, nothing at all happened to change it. It was not until the 1830s that Siena was rediscovered, with the help of *literati* like the Brownings, who spent several summers here, and later that truly Gothic American, Henry James. The Sienese were not far behind in rediscovering it themselves. The old civic pride that had lain dormant for centuries yawned and stretched like Sleeping Beauty and went diligently back to work.

Before the century was out, everything that could still be salvaged of the city's ancient glory was refurbished and restored. More than ever fascinated by its own image and eccentricities, and more than ever without any kind of an economic base, Siena was ready for its present career as a cultural attraction, a tourist town.

The Campo and the Corsa del Palio

It is hard to imagine a lovelier square, or one more beloved by the people who live and work around it. Laid out on the site of the Roman forum of *Sena Julia*, the original settlement here, the unique, semicircular Campo was paved in brick in the 1340s. Today, lined with pavement cafés all along its steep northern arc, it is still the centre of everything.

Twice each year, on 2 July and 16 August, Siena puts on the noisiest medieval blowout in Italy, the horse race around the Campo called the **Palio**. Though its origins go back to the days of the *comune*, the Palio in its present form began in the 1600s; riders from 10 of the city's 17 quarters (each *contrada* known by its totem animal: elephant, snail, unicorn, giraffe, owl, caterpillar, and so on) career recklessly around the edge of the piazza while thousands jam the centre and any available open space to watch. The riders mean business; losers have a year of insults and rotten tomatoes to look forward to in their home district.

With no rules (not even against bribery!), they crowd and push frantically. Especially at the two right angles they must navigate, the sight of not only jockeys but horses flying through the air is not uncommon. Often less then half actually finish. The post-Palio carousing, while not up to medieval standards, is still impressive; in the winning *contrada* the parties go on for days. Siena's tranquil beauty today conceals its true character. In addition to the Palio, there was once also a festival called *Gioca del Pugno* – a general fistfight in the Campo with 300 on each side.

On the curved north end of the Campo, the **Fonte Gaia** is a large rectangular fountain decorated with mythological reliefs by Jacopo della Quercia (all copies; the badly eroded originals are in the Palazzo Publico). In the 14th century the Sienese dug up a beautiful Greek statue of Venus by Lysippus and built a pedestal for her atop the fountain. After the plague, the priests succeeded in convincing the people that the pagan statue had called down God's wrath. The statue was smashed to bits, and a band of Sienese dressed as peasants smuggled the pieces over the border with Florence and buried them, to transfer the bad luck to their enemies.

Palazzo Pubblico

This is the civic pride of Siena expressed in brick and marble, a huge building that still serves as the seat of the city council, as well as being the repository of much of the best Sienese art. Above it rises the tallest secular tower of medieval Italy, the graceful, needle-like construction that Henry James called Siena's 'Declaration of Independence'. The **Torre di Mangia** (*see* below) takes its odd name from a legendary glutton (and relative of the artist Duccio) whose job it was to ring the bell – there's a little statue of him in one of the courtyards. At the foot of the tower, the equally graceful marble loggia leads to the **Cappella di Piazza**, built to give thanks for Siena's deliverance from the Black Death.

Most of the Palazzo was built in the early 14th century. At the top you'll notice the familiar Christian symbol of the letters IHS inside a radiant sun. This was the mark of the 14th-century religious reformer San Bernardino, who often preached before huge crowds in the Campo. San Bernardino wanted to persuade the constantly warring nobles to replace their own heraldic devices with this holy sign – without much success. Around the façade are other devices from Siena's history: the city's black and white coat of arms, the wolf (according to legend Siena was founded by a son of Remus), and the balls of the Medici dukes. Inside, the ground floor is all city offices, and you'll need to climb the long stairs to see the rooms open to the public (*open Nov–mid-March 10–6.30; mid-March–Oct 10–7; Jul–Aug 10am–11pm; adm*).

Among the old municipal chambers are the **Sala di Risorgimento**, with florid late-19th-century frescoes of Garibaldi and Vittorio Emanuele II in action, and an 'allegory of Italian liberty'; a **Sala de Concistoro** (Council Room), with Gobelin tapestries and figures of political virtue from antiquity by an interesting 15th-century Sienese painter named Beccafumi; and more of the same – classical gods, Caesar, Pompey and Judas Maccabaeus – around the pretty **chapel**, frescoed with a giant St Christopher (before setting out on a journey it was good luck to glimpse this saint, and in Italy and Spain he is often painted as large as possible so no one could miss him).

The **Sala del Mappamondo**, named after a lost cosmographical fresco, has a number of 13th-century frescoes, including the famous scene of the resolute *condottiere* Guidoriccio da Fogliano, off to besiege a castle. It has traditionally been attributed to Simone Martini (*c.* 1330), the greatest of Sienese fresco artists, though the attribution has recently been called into question. Unquestionably his is the fabulous *Maestà* in the same room, a dignified Madonna surrounded by saints, believed to be his earliest work (1315). The Palazzo's greatest treasure, however, is the unique series of frescoes by Ambrogio Lorenzetti in the **Sala della Pace**, the *Effects of Good and Bad Government*. Here medieval allegory is applied to politics; two rival princes sit in state, one with Justice, Wisdom and Compassion for his counsellors, the other with such characters as Pride, Wrath and Avarice. On the long walls of the chamber two mirror-image cities are portrayed, the well-governed one (with Siena's cathedral discreetly painted in) is clean, orderly and happy, with smiling shopkeepers who look to be making nice profits; the other – urban blight, crime, oppression, corruption, housing problems and slipshod municipal services, the very picture of a 14th-century South Bronx.

For views over Siena you may climb more stairs up to the **Loggia**, where the original reliefs from the Fonte Gaia are kept – or more stairs than you have ever seen, up the 328ft Torre di Mangia (*open Nov–mid-March daily 10–4; mid-March–Oct daily 10–7; Jul–Aug daily 10am–11pm; adm*), for a view that is definitely worth the slight risk of cardiac arrest and the long queues (only 20 people are allowed in at a time).

Behind the Palazzo, steps lead down to the **Piazza del Mercato**, Siena's cheerful marketplace. At the opposite end of the Campo, narrow stairs under arches lead up to the **Croce del Travaglio**, the meeting place for the main streets from the three corners of the city. Here stands the 15th-century arcade known as the **Loggia della Mercanzia**, where guilds transacted business and Italy's most respected commercial tribunal once sat in judgement.

Terzo di Città and the Cathedral

From Via di Città, winding behind the Campo, a narrow street off to the right called Via dei Pellegrini leads to what seems at first to be a huge striped bastion in the wall.

Siena's glorious **cathedral** sits atop the highest point in the city. The apse spills down the slope, its crypt at the street level of the rest of the city. Perhaps to save space and money, the architects tucked their **baptistry** (*open summer daily 9–7.30, Oct daily 9–6, winter daily 10–1 and 2.30–5; adm*) under here. It contains some of the best art in Siena, though dim and hard to see even when the lighting machine is working. The baptismal font, one of Siena's crown jewels, has relief panels by Donatello (*Herod's Banquet*), Ghiberti (*Baptism of Christ*) and Jacopo della Quercia (*Birth of John the Baptist*). Donatello also contributed the six bronze angels and some of the other statuary. Across the street from the baptistry, the **Palazzo del Magnifico** was home to Siena's 15th-century power brokers, the Petrucci.

A flight of steps leads up to the Piazza del Duomo, but at the top you must first pass through a portal in a huge, free-standing wall of striped marble arches. Siena's cathedral, 289ft long, might have seemed big enough, but the news that Florence was beginning a bigger one came as an insult to the city's pride. In 1339 the Council adopted an incredible plan to rebuild the cathedral; the old one was to be preserved as a transept, and a new nave, almost double the length of the old one, would be built out from the southern end. Had it ever been completed, it would have surpassed even St Peter's in Rome, the biggest in the world. Only nine years later, however, the Black Death struck, and Siena soon found itself without the means to continue. The northern wall and façade still stand, their arches bricked in and incorporated into other buildings. What was to be a cathedral nave is now a piazza, and a symbol for the end of a city's ambitions.

Even after all the other grand Tuscan cathedrals, Siena's comes as a revelation. It may not be a transcendent expression of faith, and it may not be an important landmark in architecture, but it certainly is one of the most delightful ornaments in Christendom. One suspects even sober-minded art critics are tempted to buy one of the illuminated plastic models in the souvenir shops, to take home and put on top of their television sets. The tall campanile stands striped like an ice-cream parfait – stripes darker and bolder than in Pisa or Lucca. The façade, even more confectionery-like, was largely the work of Giovanni Pisano, who added many of the statues of saints, prophets and pagan philosophers on the three great portals. The upper half was completed later, in the 1390s, and the glittering mosaics in the gables were added by artists from Venice only in the 19th century.

Inside, one hardly knows where to look first. Above the striped columns and walls the ornate Gothic vaulting is painted as a blue firmament with golden stars and angels – note the long rows of finely detailed heads of saints, running all along the nave. The most spectacular feature, however, is under your feet. Beginning in the 1360s, and continuing over the next two centuries, Siena's finest artists were commissioned to create inlaid marble scenes for the **pavement**, nearly an acre of them covering the entire cathedral floor. The subjects are fascinating. Entering from the west door, for example, you see a portrait of Hermes Trismegistus, the legendary patron of alchemists whose 'works', brought from Byzantium, caused such a stir in medieval Europe. Further down come the 10 Sibyls of antiquity, and a few images straight out of a deck of tarot cards: snakes and newts, a wheel of fortune, Socrates and Crates, and other symbols too arcane to think about. Many of the best have become somewhat fragile, and are now covered up for most of the year.

The **stained glass**, some of it from designs by Duccio, is also not to be missed, along with a **pulpit** by Nicola Pisano, with reliefs of philosophers and allegories of the Liberal Arts. Also, in the left aisle, there is the **Altare Piccolomini**, with some early work by Michelangelo (the statues of four saints on the lower level), and in the transept on the same side of the church there are two beautiful Renaissance sculptural ensembles, that of Bishop Giovanni Pecci, by Donatello, and another, of a cardinal, by Tino di Camaino.

The Piccolomini family, prominent in Siena for centuries, eventually attained European renown. Some were famous generals for the emperor in the Thirty Years' War (Schiller wrote a trilogy of plays about them), and during the Renaissance two of them made it to the Vatican – Popes Pius II and Pius III. The latter, in 1495, created the **Biblioteca Piccolomini** (*open daily 10–1 and 2.30–5; summer daily 9–7.30; adm*), just off the left aisle of the cathedral, to hold the library of the former, who was his uncle. Pius II, Aeneas Silvius Piccolomini, was a genuine Renaissance man: a poet, diplomat, historian, antiquarian, religious reformer and great geographer; Columbus studied his works closely.

Pius III hired Pinturicchio to cover the library walls with frescoes of his famous uncle's life. We see Aeneas Silvius in the courts of James II of Scotland and Emperor Frederick III, proclaiming a crusade and canonizing Catherine of Siena, among others. Pinturicchio's frescoes are spectacularly colourful, incorporating dozens of careful portraits of the famous and not-so-famous of the age, with loving attention to current court fashions in dress and coiffure. No better image of *la dolce vita* at the height of the Renaissance could be imagined. Aeneas Silvius' books have been carted off somewhere, but one of his favourite things still holds pride of place in the centre of the library: a beautiful marble vase with the Three Graces, a Roman copy of a work by Praxiteles that was studied closely by a good number of Renaissance artists.

Museo dell'Opera Metropolitana

Open 16 Mar–30 Sept daily 9–7.30, Oct–15 Mar daily 9–1.30; adm.

For a close-up look at the façade of the cathedral, the only place to go is the cathedral museum, also known as the Museo Metropolitana, where most of the original sculptural work has been preserved. Some of these rank among the best Italian Gothic and Renaissance sculpture, especially statues of saints by Nicola Pisano and Jacopo della Quercia, remarkable for their kinetic possibilities – they seem ready to hop down from their pedestals and start declaiming if they suspect for a minute you've been skipping Sunday Mass. Besides them, there are some original bits of the cathedral's pavement that had to be replaced, as well as some leftover pinnacles and other architectural details.

Upstairs, the collection of Sienese paintings includes Duccio di Buoninsegna's masterpiece, the former cathedral altarpiece called the *Maestà*, with an enthroned Virgin on one side and scenes from the Passion on the other. Duccio's animated composition and expressive faces here clearly surpass the work of his more celebrated contemporary, Giotto. The cathedral treasure contains lavish golden monstrances and reliquaries, and in one corner a simple, exquisite bouquet of gold flowers – the kind of gift popes would send along with their ambassadors in the 13th and 14th centuries. Part of the museum is built into the unfinished 14th-century cathedral. From the top floor you can climb up to the **Facciatone** ('big façade') for a view over the cathedral and the city.

Ospedale di Santa Maria della Scala

Open Mar–Oct daily 10–6, Nov–Feb daily 10.30–4.30; adm.

The neighbourhood around the cathedral is Rhinoceros country. To be specific, you're in the neighbourhood of the *Selva* (forest); that beast is its symbol. Opposite the old cathedral façade one entire side of the piazza is occupied by the great **Ospedale di Santa Maria della Scala**, believed to have been founded in the 9th century and for centuries one of the largest and finest hospitals in the world. Slowly the hospital functions have been moved out (one of the last patients to die here was Italo Calvino), and now they're converting it into a museum, dedicated to all the arts and the city's history, destined to be one of the largest in the world. Don't ask when it will be finished; as a cantiere *didattico*, part of the point is that the process of museum building itself is part of the attraction. For now, go inside to see the **Sala dei Pellegrini**, with 15th-century frescoes of everyday hospital activities (Santa Maria was the seat of many revolutionary advances, such as doctors washing their hands, back in the 1300s). Some other original features of the hospital include the **Cappella del Sacro Chiodo**, with damaged frescoes by Vecchietta, the elaborate **Cappella SS Annunziata**, and the thoroughly spooky **Cappella di Santa Caterina**, which begins with a leering skull and ends with an altarpiece by Taddeo di Bartolo. Old views and relics of the hospital are displayed in many of the long hallways; in some of the oldest, you can see how the façade was originally covered with frescoes (by Pietro and Ambrogio Lorenzeti), a colourful counterpoint to the cathedral façade across the way. Another part of the complex now houses the **Museo Archeologico** (*open Mon–Sat 9–2, Sun 9–1; closed 1st and 3rd Sun of month; adm free*) with an Etruscan and Roman collection.

If you take the little stairs just west of the cathedral you'll find yourself in the **Piazza della Selva**, where a bronze rhinoceros commemorates some past Palio victory. South of the cathedral on Via San Pietro, Siena's **Pinacoteca** (*open Mon 8.30–1.30, Tues–Sat 9–7, Sun 8–1; adm*) occupies the restored 14th-century Palazzo Buonsignori, and has an excellent collection of Sienese art from its beginnings to the 17th century. The earliest works, on the top floor, include fine pieces by Guido di Siena, often called the founder of Sienese painting, and his followers. Most were brought here from churches around the city. As always, the works of Pietro and Ambrogio Lorenzetti stand out, for their dramatic faces and poses, and for their original approach to colour.

On the other floors, Madonnas and saints line up in room after room. Very few are without interest, though; the serious spirituality of all its painters, paradoxically expressed in rich settings and gorgeous colours, is a constant feature of the Siena school. Something else readily apparent is Sienese civic pride: almost all the painters have a fondness for painting their town in the background, even in a Nativity. Among later Sienese painters, Beccafumi is well represented, along with Il Sodoma, who initiated the Mannerist tradition in Siena, as well as acquiring his name from a still-popular vice. More Sodoma (an *Epiphany*) and some other fine paintings can sometimes be seen in the Piccolomini Chapel of **Sant'Agostino**, a 13th-century church two blocks south of the Pinacoteca, on Via della Cerchia.

Terzo di San Martino

Beginning again at the Loggia della Mercanzia, Via Banchi di Sotto leads down into the southeast 'third' of Siena, through the quarters of the Unicorn and the Elephant. Just off the Campo, the 1460 **Palazzo Piccolomini** (*currently closed for restoration, t 0577 280 551*) has for centuries been the home of Siena's archives. The surprise attraction here is old Siena's **account books**. From the 1200s it became a tradition to have the city's best artists paint the covers – fascinating scenes of such prosaic subjects as medieval citizens coming to pay their tax, city workers receiving their pay, and honest monks tables trying to make the figures square.

Another elegant loggia, the **Loggia del Papa** built by Aeneas Silvius (Pius II), stands on the next small piazza on the Banchi di Sotto. In the narrow lanes leading down to the Piazza del Mercato there is yet another Palio victory statuette – an elephant, for the Torre district – in the pretty little Piazzetta Franchi on Via Salicotto. The **Basilica Servi di Maria** is this *terzo's* biggest church, with good frescoes in the right transept by Pietro Lorenzetti.

Terzo di Camollia

The biggest and busiest of the *terzi*, this one runs northwards along Via Banchi di Sopra, Siena's fashionable shopping street and for centuries the town's main drag, where the entire population appears to make an evening *passeggiata* down to the Campo and back. Along it there are some of the palaces of the great medieval banking families. **Palazzo Tolomei** (1200–50) is the oldest, but much larger is the **Palazzo Salimbeni**, around a small piazza of the same name further up the street. The latter is the head office of Siena's bank, the Monte dei Paschi di Siena, founded in 1472. At the bottom of the hill behind it is the large church of **San Francesco**, with more frescoes by the Lorenzettis.

The quarter of the Goose, west of Banchi di Sopra, is a warren of narrow streets associated with the tortured life of St Catherine of Siena, co-patron of Italy and one of medieval Italy's great mystics and religious reformers. Caterina Benincasa, born in 1347, the 24th of 25 children in a poor family, began having visions at an early age and, like St Francis, she received the stigmata.

Besides her devotional writings, for which she was recently proclaimed a Doctor of the Church, she kept a busy interest in the affairs of her day; as a woman she was able constantly to insult the popes over the crooked Church they ran without coming to any harm. The **Santuario e Casa di Santa Caterina** (*open winter daily 9–12.30 and*

3.30–6; summer daily 9–12.30 and 2.30–6) still stands, on Costa Sant'Antonio just below San Domenico, and has been restored as a shrine and museum.

San Domenico itself, a lofty 13th-century church at the end of Viale Curtatone, has St Catherine's head in a golden reliquary, along with wonderfully hysterical frescoes of her life by the aforementioned Sodoma. San Domenico may seem a plain church from the outside, but you'll have a good view of its Sienese Gothic subtleties from below, at the **Fonte Branda**, a medieval fountain that was once the city's only source of water.

On the western edge of the city, the triumphant Duke Cosimo I of Florence built a fortress in 1560 to keep watch over the conquered city. The **Fortezza Medicea**, however, has nothing threatening about it; this most genteel of fortifications seems less a military work than a nobleman's villa and garden. The Sienese, who have long memories, have turned the grounds into a park called Piazza della Libertà.

Sienese Pastimes

If you have more time to spend in Siena, there are plenty of ways to do it enjoyably. Just walking around the city is a treat. Nearly any old church you find open will be worth a look inside; more than most cities, Siena has preserved its medieval interiors and their art intact. South of the cathedral, you can take a walk in the country without leaving town, in the valleys between the *terzi*. Most of the medieval walls, and eight of the gates, survive.

If you want to learn more about the *contrade* and the Palio, each of the 17 local neighbourhood organizations (which are really legally chartered communities, a fascinating survival of the 'tribes' into which Roman and pre-Roman cities were organized) maintains its own museum. They are happy to show you around with some advance warning; the tourist office can give you a list of addresses and phone numbers, and will sometimes arrange visits for you.

Just outside the city, with fine views over Siena and its countryside, the monastery of **L'Osservanza** was founded by San Bernardino in the 1420s. Severely damaged in 1944, the church and cloister have been lovingly restored according to the original plans; there are works inside by Sano di Pietro and other Sienese painters, as well as Andrea della Robbia.

The Southern Hill Towns

Southern Tuscany may not be exactly what you think. There will still be plenty of typical, carefully tended Tuscan farmland, arranged as if by an artist with every garden, orchard, wood and vineyard in its proper place, but among the variety of land-scapes in this small corner of Italy you will find marshland and rugged hills, and even lonely, deserted corners like the half-eroded heaths the Tuscans call the *Crete*. Some of the hill towns in this region go back to the Etruscans, and many can show you fine buildings and works of art from the age of the *comuni* or the Renaissance. Any number of them would make memorable day trips from Siena on the way to Rome or further down the coast.

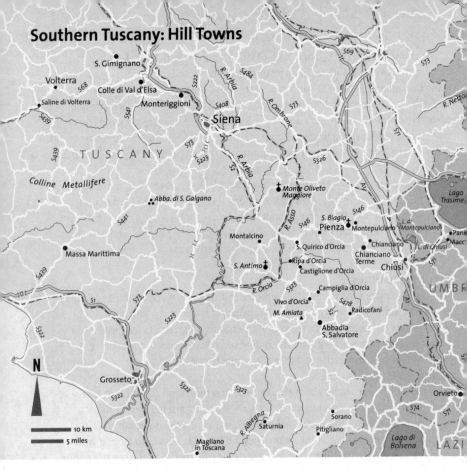

Southern Tuscany: Hill Towns

West of Siena

Colle di Val d'Elsa

This lovely village, set along a steep ridge, makes a perfect introduction to the hill towns. Though it only has around 16,000 people, Colle di Val d'Elsa boasts a wall with a grand Renaissance gate by Giuliano da Sangallo on the Volterra road, a 16th-century **cathedral** and three museums, the best of which is the **Museo d'Arte Sacra** (*open Oct–Mar Tues–Fri 3.30–5.30, Sat, Sun and hols 10–12 and 3.30–5.30; April–Sept Tues–Fri 4–6, Sat 10–12 and 3.30–6.30, Sun 10–12 and 4.30–7.30; adm*) in the old episcopal palace, with a few Sienese and Florentine paintings in addition to the frescoes commissioned by some jolly 14th-century bishop – not martyrs, but scenes of the hunt and from the Crusades, believed to be the work of Ambrogio Lorenzetti.

The Collegiani will never allow the world to forget that their town was the birthplace of Arnolfo di Cambio, the architect who built Florence's Palazzo Vecchio and began its cathedral; his house is marked with a plaque. On the way to the town from Siena, the road passes **Monteriggioni**, an old Sienese castle with huge towers mentioned by Dante, and **Abbadia a Isola** up in the hills, with frescoes from the 1400s.

San Gimignano

In many of the smaller towns of Italy you can sense a false start, a free, self-reliant *comune* of the Middle Ages that could build a wall and defend itself, yet eventually found itself lacking either the money or the will to turn itself into a Florence or a Siena. When they ceased to grow, many crystallized into their medieval form and never changed. None did this more completely than San Gimignano. Approaching the town the startling skyline can be seen poking out from the surrounding hills from miles away: a dozen, lofty square towers, some over 148ft tall, haphazardly arranged like the boxy skyscrapers of a Dallas or Calgary. The main museums and attractions of San Gimignano offer a *biglietto cumulativo* giving admission to all of them.

The Palazzo del Popolo

Unlike its 20th-century imitators, San Gimignano is an utterly charming town. Since the Middle Ages its population has dwindled to less than 8,000, and those who are left are kept busy feeding day-trippers from Florence. Its medieval beauty and serenity have made San Gimignano perhaps the trendiest tourist destination in Tuscany (seven hotels, all three-star) but it wears its strange fate well.

The usual entrance is the southern **Porta San Giovanni**, at Piazza Martiri di Montemaggio, where you can park your car. Going up through the walls into the old town, Via San Giovanni leads you past another ancient gate, the Arco dei Bacci, to the church of San Giovanni, a Pisan-style building constructed for the Knights Templar, and then to the triangular Piazza della Cisterna, with the town's well and a few of its medieval towers. If you can imagine it, San Gimignano in the 13th century was said to have had 76 of these family fortresses. Pisa's and Florence's numbered in the hundreds. Most cities eventually made regulations against them, or demolished them. For whatever reason, San Gimignano was a special case; even in the 1400s it was known as the 'city of towers'.

By city ordinance none could be taller than the 167ft **Torre della Rognosa**, part of the **Palazzo del Podestà** on the adjacent Piazza del Duomo. This was a Ghibelline tower; Frederick II built it and the Palazzo as the seat of the imperial officials. Civic pride, however, dictated an even taller one be built for the **Palazzo del Popolo**, designed perhaps by Arnolfo di Cambio in about 1300.

The tower remains San Gimignano's tallest at 177ft, and the only one you may climb; the Palazzo also has a beautiful, rustic-looking courtyard with bits of frescoes surviving around its walls, and upstairs the **Museo Civico** (*open Nov–Feb 10.30–4.50, March–Oct 9.30–7.30, closed Fri; adm; same hours for tower*), with an *Annunciation* by Filippo Lippi and other works by Florentine and Sienese artists.

Other rooms of the *palazzo* have interesting frescoes, including the Sala di Dante, an audience hall so called because Dante once spoke here, as a Florentine ambassador attempting to talk the citizens into joining the Guelph League. Dante wasn't the only Florentine to pay a call; in the quattrocento San Gimignano seems to have been almost a kind of resort for the big city; besides the artists who left behind so many fine works, Savonarola, Machiavelli and others all spent time here.

Getting Around

Buses run to most villages in the region from Piazza San Domenico in Siena (*see* p.716). To get to San Gimignano it's possible to take a train to Poggibonsi (on the Empoli–Siena line) and then a bus from there, but it can be quicker just to take a bus direct from Siena.

There is no rail service to Volterra, but an infrequent branch line service runs from Cecina on the coast to Saline di Volterra, 10km away. However, there are frequent bus services to Florence, Pisa, Siena and Massa Marittima, all from Piazza XX Settembre in Volterra.

Parking is difficult in most of these towns, but, as in San Gimignano, there are usually car parks on the perimeter roads around the *centro storico*, and it's best to walk from there.

Tourist Information

San Gimignano: Piazza del Duomo 1, **t** 0577 940 008, **f** 0577 940 903, www.sangimignano.com.
Volterra: Palazzo dei Priori, Via Turazza 2, **t/f** 0588 86150.

Where to Stay and Eat

San Gimignano ✉ 53037

In summer, you may want a hand finding a place. Try the **Hotel Association**, just inside the gate on Via S. Giovanni, **t/f** 0577 940 809. All the hotels in San Gimignano are in the moderate range or higher, but the vacuum of low-cost accommodation has been filled by a score of San Gimignese who rent out rooms, usually for about L40–50,000.

***Leon Bianco**, **t** 0577 941 294, **f** 0577 942 123 (*moderate*). An excellent hotel, on the Piazza della Cisterna, with modern rooms.

***La Cisterna**, **t** 0577 940 328, **f** 0577 942 080 (*moderate*). If the Leon Bianco is full, readers have also highly recommended this hotel, located in the same square.

Antico Pozzo, Via San Matteo 87, **t** 0577 942 014, **f** 0577 942 117 (*moderate*). Try this for a stylish, not too expensive alternative, situated right next to the main square. The building dates from the 1500s – several of the rooms have delicately frescoed ceilings.

***Le Renaie**, Loc. Pancole, about 7km towards Certaldo, **t** 0577 955 044, **f** 0577 955 126 (*moderate*). If you prefer the tranquillity of this very lovely patch of Tuscan countryside, here north of town is an attractive modern building, with a garden and pool.

With all the visitors it entertains, it should come as no surprise that San Gimignano is full of good restaurants.

Dorando, Vicolo del Oro 2, **t** 0577 941 862 (*expensive*). An option for the adventurous, where the chef attempts to recreate authentic Etruscan cuisine – *cibreo* (a chicken liver pâté so rich Catherine de' Medici nearly died from a surfeit of it), *pici* served with mint-leaf pesto, crème caramel flavoured with coriander, and things stranger still. Readers have written to us with high praise of this place. *Closed Mon*.

Le Terrazze, in Hotel La Cisterna, **t** 0577 940 328 (*moderate*). One of the most popular places, as much for its panoramic views as for the cuisine. The *medaglione al vin santo* is a surprise treat, or else the *osso buco 'alla Toscana'*, following old house specialities like *zuppa sangimignese* and *pappardelle alla lepre* (wide noodles with hare sauce). *Closed afternoons Tues and Wed*.

Il Pino, Via San Matteo 102, **t** 0577 940 415 (*moderate*). Another possibility, at the opposite end of town; the main attraction is the inviting *antipasti*. It can be pricey, however, if you indulge in the dishes with

The Collegiata

This is the name of San Gimignano's biggest church (1466–70), plain on the outside but a delightful, smaller version of Siena's cathedral within: the same striped arches, starry vaults, and a superb collection of frescoes on its walls, including a *Crucifixion* by Barna di Siena full of angels, devils, evil Romans and fainting women, among other New and Old Testament scenes, and a *Last Judgement* by Taddeo di Bartolo.

truffles that are Il Pino's pride. *Closed Thurs.* The family also offers cheap double rooms without bath, to balance your truffle bill.

Osteria delle Catene, Via Mainardi 18, **t** 0577 941 966. Has good regional food at a moderate price; try their *ribollita alla sangimignese*. *Closed Wed.*

Volterra ✉ 56048

Volterra does not see as many tourists as San Gimignano, but is nevertheless just as expensive – at least, inexpensive rooms are just as hard to find.

****San Lino, Via San Lino 26, near Porta San Francesco, **t** 0588 85250, **f** 0588 80620 (*expensive*). Tastefully remodelled rooms in an old cloister; the only place with parking.

***Villa Nencini, Borgo S. Stefano, **t** 0588 86386, **f** 0588 80601 (*moderate; some cheaper without bath*). A 16th-century house with lovely views, just north of the centre.

***Nazionale, Via dei Marchesi 11, **t** 0588 86284, **f** 0588 84097 (*moderate*). A pleasant old hotel within the walls.

Many restaurants in Volterra specialize in roast boar and the like, good medieval cuisine entirely in-keeping with the spirit of the place.

Il Sacco Fiorentino (the name refers to Lorenzo de' Medici's massacre of the citizens of Volterra in 1472), Piazza XX Settembre 18, **t** 0588 88537 (*expensive*). Combines a vast assortment of *crostini*, wonderful *gnocchi* with baby vegetables, penne with Tuscan cheeses, roast pork with black olives, rabbit cooked in garlic and Vin Santo and lamb with mint and sultanas in an imaginative menu which changes with the seasons.

Il Porcellino, Vicolo delle Prigioni 18, **t** 0588 86392 (*moderate*). The menu combines seafood and familiar Tuscan favourites with local treats like roast pigeon and boar with olives; a good bargain. *Closed Oct–Mar.*

Tre Scimmie ('three monkeys'), Via dei Sarti, **t** 0588 86047 (*moderate*). Not too many tourists make it to this small, delightful bar. *Closed Mon.*

Sant' Elisa, about 3km away on the SS68, **t** 0588 80034, **f** 0588 87284 (*cheap*). One of the restaurants most popular with the Volterrans, outside town: the country setting is plain, but the simple, home-cooked food is superb; lots of game – *pappardelle* with wild boar or deer sauce, wild boar stew with black olives. *Closed Mon.*

Massa ✉ 58024

Massa is becoming increasingly popular, and the town's capacity of 38 rooms is often stretched to the limit.

Duca del Mare, Via D. Alighieri 1/2, **t 0566 902 284, **f** 0566 901 905 (*cheap*). One of the three hotels, just below the town centre on the Via Massetana, in a lovely setting with a garden and views over the countryside (Massa lies on a rather steep hill); it's set in a modern building with a simple *trattoria*.

Girifalco, Via Massentana, **t 0566 902 177 (*cheap*). Nearly impossible to tell apart from Duca del Mare – both charge about the same price, offer the same amenities and the same views.

Da Bracali, Località Ghirlanda, **t** 0566 902 318 (*very expensive*). Offers haute cuisine variations on the local cooking and a formidable wine list, in a very elegant setting. *Closed Tues.*

Taverna del Vecchio Borgo, **t** 0566 903 950 (*moderate*). For something more ambitious, just down the street and highly recommended, not only for its food – game dishes including pheasant, boar and venison – but for its extensive list of grappas. *Closed Sun eve and Mon.*

Pizzeria Le Mure, Via Norma Parenti (behind the Duomo). Good pizza, or an inexpensive

A ticket from the Museo Civico will get you into the **Capella di Santa Fina** (*open April–Sept Mon–Fri 9.30–7.30, Sat 9.30–5, Sun 1–5; Nov–Jan and March Mon–Sat 9.30–5, Sun 1–5; Feb Mon–Sat 9.45–12 and 3.15–4.30, Sun 3.15–4.30; adm*), with an introduction to what is surely the most moronic saint story in all Italy. There are many competitors for this honour, but consider little Fina going to the well for water, and accepting an orange from a young swain. When she returned home, her mother told her how wicked she was to take it, and the poor girl became so mortified over her great sin that she lay down on the table and prayed for forgiveness without ceasing for five years. After this, St Anthony appeared to call her soul to heaven, and the table burst into bloom with violets. Domenico Ghirlandaio got the commission to paint all this; he pocketed the money and did a splendid job, with sweet faces and springtime colours. Note San Gimignano's famous towers in the background.

In a courtyard to the left of the Collegiata, the **baptistry** has another work of Ghirlandaio, an *Annunciation*. The **Museo d'Arte Sacra** and **Museo Etrusco** (*open April–Oct 9.30–7.30; Nov–20 Jan and March 9.30–5; closed 20 Jan–end Feb; adm*) occupy two sides of the courtyard – one with more 13th–15th-century sculpture, painting and illuminated choir books, and the other with finds from Etruscan tombs excavated in the area.

Behind the Collegiata, you can walk around the half-ruined fortress, the **Rocca**, or else continue north to Piazza Sant'Agostino and the church of **Sant'Agostino**, famous for a series of frescoes by Benozzo Gozzoli on the life of St Augustine. The merriest of all Renaissance painters has a good time with this one, as in the charming panel where the master of grammar comes to drag sullen little Augustine off to school.

Volterra

Volterra has a talent for making visitors a bit uneasy. Its situation, among bleak, windy hills, could be the scene for some medieval Tuscan *Wuthering Heights*. The city itself seems taciturn and grey, brooding on its ancient memories. *Velathri* was a powerful city, the northwestern corner of the Etruscan Dodecapolis. Its 5.5km circuit of walls encloses an area three times the size of the present town.

Volterra's periphery is as interesting as the town itself; besides the **Etruscan walls**, traceable for most of their length, there are the *balze*, the barren, eroded ravines that probably began as Etruscan mining cuts. They have already swallowed up medieval churches and exposed some ancient ruins, and they are still growing. It was this erosion that led to the discovery of the Etruscan necropoli around Volterra.

Not many substantial ruins have survived, but you can see the remains of a **Roman theatre** and **baths** just outside the northern wall by the Porta Fiorentina, and also some ruins in the 'archaeological park' near the **Fortezza Medicea**, a big castle built in the 1470s on what was the Etruscan acropolis. Just to the north of the fortress, the **Museo Etrusco Guarnacci**, Via Don Minzoni (*open 16 Mar–30 Oct daily 9–7; rest of the year daily 9–2; adm exp; joint ticket with the other museums*) has a huge collection of funerary urns found in the *balze* tombs since the 1700s. Most of them, with the familiar reclining figures of the deceased on top, are carved with battle scenes or images from Greek mythology.

Volterra's most conspicuous ancient relic, however, is the **Etruscan arch** in the southern wall, over Via Porta all'Arco. Much rebuilt in Roman times, the gate has three black stone protuberances, once probably images of the Etruscan versions of Jupiter, Juno and Minerva, now completely worn away. Near the other end of Via Porta all'Arco, Piazza dei Priori is the medieval centre, with the 1208 **Palazzo dei Priori**, the oldest town hall in Tuscany.

The imperial **Palazzo Pretorio** is nearly as old. Around the corner on Via Sarti, the **Pinacoteca Comunale** (*open 16 Mar–30 Oct daily 9–7, Nov–15 Mar 9–2; adm exp; you can get a joint ticket covering Volterra's other museums*) has a small collection of very fine 15th-century paintings, including a great *Annunciation* by Luca Signorelli, though the prize of the collection is the precise, intense and unforgettable *Deposition* (1521) by Rosso Fiorentino, a seminal work on the threshold between the late Renaissance and early Mannerism.

Behind Piazza dei Priori is the 15th-century **cathedral**, standing behind a large octagonal baptistry from the 1280s. Inside the Duomo, in a chapel off the left aisle, is a fresco of the Three Kings by Gozzoli and a tabernacle over the high altar by Mino da Fiesole. In the **Museo d'Arte Sacra** (*open 16 Mar–Oct daily 9–1 and 3–6; Nov–15 Mar daily 9–1 only; adm exp*), you can see a della Robbia bust of Volterra's patron, San Lino (Linus), successor to Peter as bishop of Rome – the first pope.

Etruscan and Roman Volterra made its living by mining; one of the most important resources was alabaster, still one of the mainstays of the local economy. Volterra is full of workshops where artists turn this luminous stone into vases and figurines – some of the work is very good. You can seek out the shops yourself (they are everywhere; just look for the coating of fine white dust on the buildings) or stop at the artists' co-operative on Via Turazza.

Massa Marittima and San Galgano

South of Volterra, along the SS439, you'll pass over one of the loneliest and least-known corners of Italy. The **Colline Metallifere**, as the name implies, have been attractive to miners (and nobody else) since Etruscan times. The iron the Etruscans found here and on the nearby island of Elba made them rich; today the ore is mostly worked out, but there is still plenty of borax and other minerals. After the pass called **Ala dei Diavoli**, the 'Devil's wing', you can detour west on to the SS398 to see the real kingdom of borax at **Lago Boracifero**, near Monterotondo Marittimo. It's a bizarre landscape, and it smells bad too; miniature geysers and steamy pits bubble up boric salts amid grey and yellow slag piles. Lately it's been looking even stranger. In places the ground has become covered with webs of steampipes, ever since the *comune* discovered its geothermal resources could power everything in town almost for free.

Across the metal hills, **Massa Marittima** is the unlikely setting for one of Tuscany's finest cathedrals, a big 13th-century Pisan Romanesque building set on a stepped pedestal at the end of a broad piazza. There is a beautiful altarpiece in one of the chapels, a *Madonna della Grazie* attributed to Duccio; the tomb of San Cerbone, Massa's patron, is down in the crypt, with 14th-century reliefs of the saint's life.

Massa has three museums: the well-organized but not especially interesting **Museo Archeologico** and the small **Pinacoteca** are both situated in the 1230 Palazzo del Podestà (*open Oct–March Tues–Sun 10–12.30 and 3–5; Apr–Sept Tues–Sun 10–12.30 and 3.30–7; closed Mon; adm*). The art gallery has another notable *Maestà*, by another of the Lorenzetti family, Ambrogio.

Finally, no visit to Massa would be complete without a trip to a mining museum. Mining, after all, is what Massa is all about. The **Museo di Arte e di Storia della**

The Sword in the Stone

On some of the altarpieces in churches and museums in Siena you may have noticed the odd figure of a saint in what appears to be a scene from the *Morte d'Arthur*. This is San Galgano, a dissolute young soldier who received a vision of St Michael and thrust his sword into a stone, leaving his old ways to become a holy hermit. As Michael directed, after Galgano's death a circular chapel was built around the sword.

This is the **Cappella di Montesiepi**, on a hill above San Galgano abbey, and here you will find the sword still in its stone, sticking up from the pavement in the centre of the chapel. Whatever role this legend had in someone's religious secret agenda, like all the sites associated with St Michael it is exceedingly strange, a relic from the great age of western mysticism. There are some frescoes by Ambrogio Lorenzetti on the saint's life, but note also the strange shallow dome, done in 22 concentric stripes of brick and stone and probably representing the heavenly spheres of the medieval cosmology, as in the famous fresco in Pisa's Campo Santo.

Miniera on Piazza Matteotti (*closed for restoration, t 0566 902 289 for info*) has only a small collection, but there's another one, the **Museo della Miniera** on Via Corridoni (*open for guided tours only, which leave regularly: in summer between 10.15 and 5.45; in winter between 10.15 and 4.15; closed Mon; call t 0566 902 289 for times; adm*). The entrance of this one leads down into nearly a half-mile of old mine tunnels, with exhibits to show how the job was done from medieval days to the present.

If you take the SS441/SS73 road between Massa Marittima and Siena be sure not to miss the ruined abbey of **San Galgano** (*open daily 8–12 and 2–sunset*), about halfway in between, near the village of Monticiano. A Cistercian community from France – settled here in the 1100s, and work commenced in 1218 on what must have been the grandest purely French Gothic building in Italy.

The monastery was dissolved in the 1600s, and since then the roof and the marble façade have gone, leaving as romantic a ruin as you could ask for: beautiful pointed arches and stone columns, with grass for a pavement and the sky for a roof. Parts of the vaulting remain and, besides the romanticism, San Galgano affords a rare opportunity to look at the bare structure of a Gothic building; it will increase your appreciation of the 13th century.

South of Siena

Monte Oliveto Maggiore and Montalcino

As the SS2 rolls towards Rome it passes through another empty region of chalk hills and cliffs called the *crete*; like the *balze* of Volterra, these are uncanny monuments to the power of erosion, often appearing in the backgrounds of 14th- and 15th-century Sienese and Florentine paintings. East of the highway, **Asciano** is a medieval walled village with a small collection of Sienese artists in its Museo d'Arte Sacra (*open by appt only, t 0577 718 207*), next to the Collegiata church.

Some 9km to the south, the **Monte Oliveto Maggiore** monastery complex (*open daily 9.15–12 and 3.15–5; until 5.45 in summer*) was founded by Giovanni Tolomei, a member of one of Siena's leading families who abandoned banking and civic strife for the life of a hermit. With such backing it comes as no surprise that Monte Oliveto became one of the most elegant retreats in Tuscany. A few fortunate monks – artisans who specialize in the restoration of old books – still keep the place going. Set in a striking grove of cypresses, something of an oasis among the bare chalk hills, the monastery has a lovely fortress-gate decorated with della Robbia terracottas, a simple, exceptionally well-proportioned early 15th-century church, and a library with some skilful wooden intarsia pictures by Giovanni da Verona.

The real prize, though, is the **great cloister**, with a cycle of 36 frescoes (*currently undergoing a much-needed restoration*) from the life of St Benedict, whose monastic rule Giovanni Tolomei and his new Olivetan order were attempting to restore in all its purity. Nine are by Luca Signorelli; they show the artist's usual perfection of line and characteristic colouring. The rest are the work of Sodoma, seemingly attempting to work in the style of Signorelli, but with a Mannerist tendency to more excited poses and expressions, extravagant architectural backgrounds, and the inclusion of his badger and other pets in the scenes.

South of the monastery, **Montalcino**, an easy day trip from Siena by bus, has a strong castle, the Rocca (*open summer Tues–Sun 9–8, winter Tues–Sun 9–6, closed Mon; free, but adm to go up on the walls*), that was the last word in 14th-century military architecture. It defended the town well. After the siege of Siena in 1552, a party of bitter-enders escaped here to found the 'Republic of Siena at Montalcino' – perhaps the first ever republican government-in-exile. With the help of the Rocca they held out for several years against the minions of Spain and the Medici, one of the last strongholds of Italian liberty.

Today the town is better known for its red wines, the dark, pungent Brunello and the slightly less prestigious but also very good Rosso di Montalcino, some of Tuscany's best. There is a good collection of Sienese painting in Montalcino, in the **Museo Civico e Diocesano** (*open Jan–Mar Tues–Sun 10–1 and 2–4, April–Dec 10–6; closed Mon; adm*), in Piazza Cavour.

Just south of the town another abandoned monastery, the 12th-century **Abbazia di Sant'Antimo** (*open Mon–Sat 10–12.30 and 3–6.30, Sun 9–10.30 and 3–6*). It has left behind an especially beautiful Romanesque church, with a luminous interior partially done in alabaster. Another good Romanesque church, from the 1080s, can be seen in the nearby village of **San Quirico**, back on the main road.

Pienza

Italians like to carry on, more perhaps than is necessary, about Pienza, a small town in the sheep country east of Montalcino that became one of the most characteristic early-Renaissance experiments in architecture and design. Before 1460 it was just the humble little village of Corsignano, but in that year Pope Pius II (Aeneas Sylvius Piccolomini) decreed that the town of his birth was to be glorified into a city of art, which he modestly renamed after himself.

Getting Around

There are regular **buses** from Siena to most destinations in the area. The only town directly accessible by **train** is Chiusi, on the Florence–Rome line, which also has good bus connections to Chianciano and Montepulciano. There is a railway station called Montepulciano, but it is 10km northeast of the town, and only very local trains stop.

Tourist Information

Montalcino: Costa del Municipio 8, t/f 0577 849 331.

Pienza: Pro Loco, Piazza Pio II, t 0578 749 071. Offers occasional guided tours of town.

Montepulciano: Via Gracciano del Corso 59a, off Piazza Grande, t 0578 757 341.

Chianciano: Piazza Italia 67, t 0578 63167.

Chiusi: Pro Loco, Via Porsenna 67, t 0578 227 667.

Abbadia San Salvatore: Via Adua 25, t 0577 775 811, *info@amiata.turismo.toscana.it* .

Where to Stay and Eat

Almost every town in this southern hill country has rooms to rent: ask around. Chianciano Terme has a number of fairly stuffy spa hotels.

Montalcino ✉ 53024

★★★**Al Brunello**, Loc. Bellaria, t 0577 849 304, f 0577 849 430 (*expensive*). Set in an attractive garden setting.

★★★**Dei Capitani**, Via Lapini 6, t/f 0577 847 227 (*moderate*). An old *palazzo* in the centre with wonderful views, plus a small pool.

★★**Giardino**, Via Cavour 4, t 0577 848 257 (*cheap*). Handily positioned right by the bus stop. Not all roooms have own bathroom.

Cucina di Edgardo, Via S. Saloni 9, t 0577 848 232 (*expensive*). Some of the best and most creative *cucina nuova* this side of Siena. Montalcino's famous honey laces the desserts. Be sure to reserve.

Il Pozzo, Piazza del Pozzo, Loc. S. Angelo in Colle, t 0577 844 015 (*moderate*). Worth the detour for a cheap, full-blown traditional meal. *Closed Tues.*

Pienza ✉ 53026

★★★**Il Chiostro**, Corso Il Rossellino 26, t 0578 748 400, f 0578 748 440 (*expensive*). As the name implies, this is an old cloister, in the centre just off Piazza Pio II; modernized rooms have been stylishly restored with all the amenities, and beautiful gardens fit for a pope.

★★★**Corsignano**, Via della Madonnina 9, t 0578 748 501, f 0578 748 166 (*moderate*). Modern and comfortable – fit for a pope.

The new city got off to a flying start with Pius' commissioning of Bernardo Rossellino to design a cathedral and palace around a central piazza.

The **cathedral** has a simple three-arched entrance, decorated only with the Piccolomini arms and the keys of St Peter; ironically the best features are pure Gothic in inspiration, high pointed vaulting and some pretty traceried windows. They chose a bad spot for it; the cathedral has been settling and threatening to collapse since it was built, and occasionally sulphur fumes seep out of the floor. Around the cathedral square (Piazza Pio II), Rossellino's **Palazzo Piccolomini** (*open winter Tues–Sun 10–12.30 and 4–7; summer Tues–Sun 10–12.30 and 3–6; closed Mon; adm*) is nearly a copy of Alberti's design for the Rucellai Palace in Florence, which Rossellino helped build. The best part is around the back, a three-storey loggia and a garden.

The Piccolomini had large estates around Pienza; Aeneas Silvius was born here only because the family had temporarily exiled itself from Siena, after a revolt that excluded nobles from public office. Several other palaces went up in the wake of the Piccolomini, including the Palazzo dei Canonici; most of its contents are displayed in

Ristorante del Falco, Piazza Dante 3, t 0578 748
551 (*cheap*). Offering a fair number of
spartan rooms for rent, near the bus stop.
Closed Fri.

Il Prato, Viale S. Caterina 1/3, t 0578 749 924
(*moderate*). The best place to stop for a bite
is across the piazza; there are tables outside
in the little garden and a huge menu of
simple local dishes, featuring home-made
pici (thick spaghetti), *crespelle* filled with
ricotta and other delights. *Closed Wed.*

Montepulciano ✉ 53045
Montepulciano puts out the welcome mat
at a few very amiable hotels.

★★★Marzocco, Via G. Savonarola 18, t 0578 757
262, f 0578 757 530 (*moderate*). An airy,
tranquil family-run establishment next to, of
course, the *Marzocco* itself, just inside the
main gate.

★★★Borghetto, Borgo Buio t 0578 757 535
(*moderate*). Just around the corner, with
pleasant rooms, some of which have great
views over the edge of the town.

Il Riccio, Via Talosa 21, t/f 0578 757 713 (*cheap*).
Simple and very central, with a nice open
rooftop-terrace.

If you can't find a room in town, there are
millions of them a few miles south in the spa
town of Chianciano Terme, and there are some
in Sant'Albano, 3km from Montepulciano.

For lunch or dinner there are a couple of
choices on the Corso in town; otherwise there
are good places a little way out of town.

La Grotta, t 0578 757 607 (*expensive*). Right
next to the dramatic San Biagio, serving
traditional Tuscan dishes with a creative
twist: smoked goose breast, *pici* with duck
sauce, pigeon stuffed with truffles, duck
breast with juniper berries and orange peel.
Closed Wed.

Osteria dell'Aquacheta, Via del Teatro, about
halfway up the Corso (*moderate*). Here, for
very little, you can have a tasty light lunch –
crostate or *bruschetto* and a pasta dish.

Montefollonico ✉ 53040
La Chiusa, Via Madonnina, Montefollonico,
t 0578 669 668 (*very expensive*). Located in
an old *frantoio* or olive press, in the lovely
village of Montefollonico, with panoramic
views back towards Montepulciano. (Sadly
the press was closed after a recent and
particularly virulent frost killed off most of
the olive trees in the area.) La Chiusa has
been acclaimed as the best restaurant in
southern Tuscany, and though its reputation
has wobbled in recent years you're
guaranteed at the very least an incredible
seven-course *menu degustazione* and an
exhaustive wine list. Above the restaurant
itself are some very luxurious suites and
rooms. *Closed Tues.*

the new **Museo Diocesano**, Corso Rossellini (*open winter Sat and Sun 10–1 and 3–6;
summer Wed–Mon 10–1 and 2.30–6.30; closed Tues*), which also contains an important
collection of paintings, sculptures and tapestries. Pienza never fulfilled the ambitions
of its founder; today it is just another Tuscan village known for its piazza and also for
its *cacio*: the self-proclaimed 'Capital of Sheep Cheese' has been making it since the
days of the Etruscans.

Montepulciano

Inhabitants of this town, the Roman *Mons Politianus*, are called *Poliziani*, and that is
the name by which we know its most famous son. Angelo Ambrogini, as Poliziano,
was a favourite at the court of Lorenzo the Magnificent and one of the greatest classical scholars of his day, as well as a playwright and poet (Botticelli's mythological
paintings may have been inspired by his *Stanze per la Giostra*).

Like Pienza, Montepulciano has its share of Renaissance monuments, most notably
Antonio da Sangallo's church of **San Biagio** (1518), 1km south of the town. This superb

though unfinished building captures some of the highest aspirations of Renaissance architecture. The graceful loggia of the adjacent **Canonica** (parish house), also by Sangallo, makes a fitting architectural complement.

In the town, the also unfinished **Duomo** has a beautiful altarpiece by Taddeo di Bartolo, and other works by Florentine and Sienese artists. The two cities fought over Montepulciano for centuries. Florence finally prevailed in both politics and art; the **Palazzo Comunale** (begun *c.* 1360), facing the Duomo, is a smaller copy of Florence's Palazzo Vecchio, with a façade by the Florentine Michelozzo, who also contributed a fine Renaissance façade for **Sant'Agostino** on Via Sangallo.

In the 16th century the town became something like Florence's southern outpost, and was equipped by the city's favoured architects, Sangallo the Younger and Vignola, with a set of walls, public buildings and *palazzi*. Today they exude a rather faded grandeur, and seem quite out of proportion for a small town. There are plenty of good palaces, several by Sangallo, along the main street, the Corso. Note his **Palazzo Bucelli** at No.73, with a foundation made entirely of carved Etruscan burial urns, filled with cement and stacked like bricks. Montepulciano is also much visited today for its powerful red wine, *Vino Nobile di Montepulciano*, which is on sale at any number of *enoteche* run by the producers themselves all around the town.

South of Montepulciano, **Chianciano Terme** is a large, bright and busy spa, whose motto *Chianciano – fegato sano* ('Chianciano for a healthy liver') draws in many an imbibing Tuscan for an annual flush. It's not only the perfect cure for too much *Vino Nobile*, but usually has overnight accommodation in a pinch.

Chiusi

If anyone ever read you Lord Macaulay's rouser *Horatio at the Bridge* when you were a child, you will remember the fateful name Lars Porsena of Clusium, leading the Etruscan confederation to besiege Rome in the brave days of old. Thanks to Horatio, of course, Rome survived and made a name for itself; you can come here to see what happened to Clusium – or *Camars* as the Etruscans actually called it.

Modern Chiusi isn't much, but it has a market on Mondays and a first-class archaeological museum, the **Museo Nazionale Etrusco** (*open Mon–Fri 9–2, Sat and Sun 9–1; adm*), with lots of burial urns – many decorated with scenes from Homer – and examples of the black pottery called *bucchero* that was an Etruscan speciality. Several tombs can be visited off the road to Chianciano Terme (ask the museum guards); the **Tombe delle Scimmie**, which has some wall paintings, is the most interesting.

From Chiusi, the SS478 will take you back southwestwards to the southern end of Siena province, passing **Radicófani**, a startling sight with its tall castle perched atop a weirdly eroded barren hill. Further south comes the region of **Monte Amiata**, Tuscany's highest peak (5,649ft), with Europe's second largest mercury mine; Amiata is an extinct volcano, and full of unusual minerals. There is a small ski resort at **Abbadia San Salvatore**, as well as the remains of a 12th-century Cistercian abbey that was the predecessor to San Galgano.

The southernmost corner of Tuscany is a strange and empty quarter, thriving in the days of the Etruscans but at no time since. Ruins of Etruscan tombs and walls can be seen at **Saturnia** and **Pitigliano** (*open Sun 10–1, with a tour that takes in other Jewish relics of the town*); the synagogue in Pitigliano is also worth a visit. **Sorano**, north of Pitigliano, is the natural conclusion to this somewhat disturbing region; it is almost a ghost town, most of it abandoned after landslides in the 1920s.

From Florence to Arezzo

Like all the northern part of Arezzo province, the routes along the Arno are lined with typically Tuscan small towns that managed not to be left behind in the Middle Ages. On the contrary, it is a highly industrialized region; lignite and felt hats are important, but new factories and power lines seem to be going up all the time. At **Incisa Val d'Arno** the cliffs close in towards the river; from here you have the choice of the fast route, the A1 *autostrada* direct to Arezzo, or dallying through the pretty villages in the hills above either bank of the Arno along the SS69.

San Giovanni Valdarno, the birthplace of Masaccio and a long-time Florentine fortress on the border with hostile Arezzo, is the largest and perhaps most interesting town in this area, with its arcaded piazza around the Palazzo Comunale, a building thought to be the work of Florence's Arnolfo di Cambio. The loggias that surround it are covered with the coats of arms of its Florentine governors. In the museum adjacent to the 15th-century **Basilica di Santa Maria delle Grazie** (*open Tues–Fri 11–1 and 3–5; Sat 11–1 and 3–6; Sun 3–6; closed Mon; adm*) there is a priceless *Annunciation* by Fra Angelico, an early work that seems like a study for his famous Annunciation at San Marco in Florence.

In **Montevarchi**, there is a little museum where you can see a mastodon skeleton, a relic of the area's prehistory. **Terranuova Bracciolini** is an old Aretine fortress town, its walls still standing. In the hills north of the Arno, **Loro Ciuffenna** and **Castiglion Fibocchi** are two more typical, pretty towns where little has changed – save the industry around the outskirts – since the 16th century. **Grópina**, near Loro Ciuffena, has a Romanesque church with a truly bizarre relic of the Dark Ages: a stone pulpit carved with wolves, eagles and unusual patterns; it may be from the time of the Lombards or even earlier.

Arezzo

Compared with the other cities of Tuscany, Arezzo looks a little down-at-heel and rustic, as if the art and sophistication of the Renaissance had somehow passed it by. The medieval air is part of its charm, and easily explainable: Arezzo lost its prosperity along with its independence when Florence annexed it in 1384. The lack of fine buildings, however, conceals a mildly glorious past. Arezzo was one of the richest cities of the Etruscan Dodecapolis; the famous bronze chimera in the Florence archaeology museum was found here. The long list of famous Aretini begins in Roman times with Maecenas, the fabulously wealthy friend of Augustus and patron of Horace and Virgil. In the Middle Ages, Arezzo was a typical free *comune*, a rival to Florence and a city of

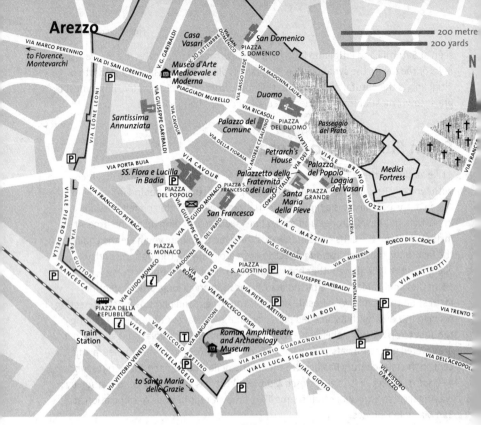

great cultural distinction. Guido d'Arezzo, the inventor of musical notation and the scale, was born here, as was Petrarch. Later came Giorgio Vasari and Pietro Aretino, the uninhibited writer and poet whose celebrated poison pen allowed him to make a fortune by *not* writing about contemporary princes and popes – the most genteel extortionist of all time. In the game of Tuscan power politics Arezzo was at its strongest in the early 14th century, under the rule of a remarkable series of warrior-bishops, of whom the best remembered is the fierce Guido Tarlati (d. 1327).

Today Arezzo is a very prosperous place. It should be, having perhaps the biggest jewellery industry in Europe, with hundreds of firms stamping out chains and rings, and bank vaults full of gold ingots. The old centre, however, hasn't really shared in this prosperity. Most people have moved out, and more and more shop fronts are given over to the city's other industry – antiques. Arezzo has become a curiosity shop, especially during the **antiques fairs**, held on the first Sunday of every month in Piazza Grande. It has also found a new role as a film set, providing a picturesque setting for Roberto Benigni's *La Vita e Bella* (*Life is Beautiful*).

The Piazza Grande

The medieval-looking houses around **Piazza Grande** make a perfect setting for Arezzo's annual medieval festival, the *Giostra del Saracino*, in early September, where the colourful old costumes are dusted off and the town sports tilt at a wooden figure called the 'King of the Indies'. The antiques fairs are also held here. Giorgio Vasari built the long **Loggia** in the manner of an ancient Greek stoa, and contributed the clock tower to the **Palazzo della Fraternità dei Laici**, an odd building, half-Gothic and half by Bernardo Rossellino. If you thought this was the town hall, you've been fooled. The *palazzo* is really the home of a lay brotherhood founded in the 1200s, and Arezzo's old

Getting There and Around

From Florence, Perugia and Cortona, the **train** is the easiest way to reach Arezzo; the station is at the southern end of town, where Via Guido Monaco crosses Viale Piero della Francesca and the old city walls. Many smaller towns, such as San Giovanni Valdarno, Poppi, Bibbiena, Sansepolcro and Castiglion Fiorentino can also be easily reached by train.

Buses for Cortona and other towns in Arezzo province, as well as for Siena, leave from the bus station, directly opposite the railway station on Viale Piero della Francesca, **t** 0575 22663. Schedules are posted for all lines.

Tourist Information

Piazza della Repubblica, in front of the train station, **t** 0575 377 678, **f** 0575 20839. Piazza Risorgimento 116, **t** 0575 239 523; *info@arezzo.turismo.toscana.it*

Where to Stay and Eat

Arezzo ✉ 52100

No hotels in Arezzo really stand out; unlike some of Tuscany's art cities, the forces of tourism have yet to convert old villas into modern accommodation. What the city does have is clean, comfortable, and up-to-date – but there's nothing to tempt you into lingering once you've seen your Pieros.

*****Minerva**, Via Fiorentina 4, **t** 0575 370 390, **f** 0575 302 415 (*moderate*). This may be the most convenient if you're travelling by car; it's a few blocks west of the city walls, with pleasant rooms. It also has an excellent, unpretentious restaurant (*moderate*).

In town, most rooms are close to the station.

*****Continentale**, Piazza Guido Monaco 7, **t** 0575 20251, **f** 0575 350 485 (*moderate*). A fine, older hotel; you can contemplate the

towers and red rooftops of town from the roof terrace. The hotel restaurant (*expensive*) serves *zuppa del Tarlati* – chicken soup prepared according to a 12th-century recipe – as well as tender turkey breast with truffles. *Closed Mon.*

****Truciolini**, Via Pacinotti 6, **t** 0575 984 104, **f** 0575 984 137 (*moderate*). Less expensive.

***Toscana**, Via Pirennio 56, **t** 0575 21692 (*cheap*). Budget hotels do exist, though not near the *centro storico*. 'Tuscany' offers clean, simple rooms near Porta San Lorentino.

***Chimera**, Via V. Veneto 46, **t** 0575 902 494 (*cheap*). Basic but clean, also in the environs of Porta San Lorentino.

Buca di San Francesco, Via S. Francesco 1, **t** 0575 23271 (*expensive*). Right opposite Piero's frescoes, this long-established restaurant is favoured by tourists – but don't let that discourage you; unusually for a tourist haunt, the Buca has an honest-to-goodness medieval atmosphere and tasty Tuscan cooking to match – adapted a little for the tastes of the uninitiated. *Closed Mon eve and Tues, also July.*

Il Saraceno, Via Mazzini 6, **t** 0575 27644. For an inexpensive meal, the place to go is Via Mazzini, just off the Corso, where this restaurant offers *pici* and *polenta*, and game dishes in season including stewed boar and rabbit. *Closed Wed.*

Antica Osteria Agania, Via Mazzini 10, **t** 0575 295 381. A slightly cheaper option with more conventional solid home cooking, just down the street.

Osteria La Capannaccia, Loc. Campriano 51c, **t** 0575 361 759 (*moderate*). For a meal in the country, this is one of the best restaurants around Arezzo; the specialities are those of the Aretine countryside – simple dishes like *minestra di pane* (bread soup), roast meats and wines from the Colli Aretini – and the price is equally unpretentious too. *Closed Sun eve and Mon.*

Palazzo del Popolo exists only in ruins, behind Vasari's Loggia on Via dei Pileati. Like Pisa's, it was destroyed by the Florentines after they captured the city.

Also on Via dei Pileati, the **Casa di Petrarca** (*open Mon–Fri 10–12 and 3–5, Sat 10–12, closed Sun*) is a replacement for the original, destroyed during the Second World War; it stands near the 14th-century **Palazzo Pretorio**, decked with the coats of arms of imperial and Florentine governors. One block south you'll see the singular façade of Arezzo's finest church, **Santa Maria della Pieve**. This church turns its back on Piazza Grande, showing only a graceful arched apse. In the front (*covered for restoration at time of writing*), a distinctive irregular campanile and four levels of columns make a unique mountaineer's version of the Pisan-Luccan Romanesque style, done in rough-hewn stone with hardly any two columns or capitals alike. Under the arch at the front portal, note the interesting early medieval reliefs of the 12 months: April with its flowers, February with its pruning hook, and the pagan two-headed god Janus for January. The interior is dim and stark, but there is a good altarpiece by Pietro Lorenzetti, with a Madonna and saints modelling Tuscan fashions of the 14th century.

The Cathedral and Art Museum

Narrow streets from Piazza Grande lead up to the **Passeggio del Prato**, a big, English-style park with lawns and monuments. All of Arezzo slopes gradually upwards from the railway station, ending abruptly here; from the cliffs on the edge of the Prato there is a memorable view over the mountains, extending towards Florence and Urbino. Overlooking the park is a half-ruined Medici fortress of the 16th century; at the other end, you'll see the back of the **cathedral** with a lovely Gothic belltower (19th century). This Duomo, built in bits and pieces over the centuries, is worth a look inside for the 16th-century stained glass windows, done by a French master named Guillaume de Marcillat, whose work resembles illuminated frescoes by a Gozzoli or Luca Signorelli. In the north aisle the 1327 **tomb of Bishop Guido Tarlati** is a fascinating early predecessor of the heroic sculptural tombs of the Renaissance, perhaps designed by Giotto; 16 relief panels tell the story of his life, his battles and his good works – all under a big Ghibelline eagle, like a party badge. The Duomo also has terra-cottas by Andrea della Robbia and a fresco by Piero della Francesca.

From here Via Ricasoli leads west towards the **Museo d'Arte Medieovale e Moderna** (*open Mon–Sat 9–7, Sun 9–1; adm*), where you can get to know some good local artists not often seen elsewhere, such as Spinello Aretino, his son, Parri di Spinello and Bartolomeo della Gatta. Renaissance ceramics from Urbino, Deruta and Montelupo are also well represented. Around the corner on Via XX Settembre you can swallow a heavy load of Mannerist excess at the **Casa di Vasari** (*open Mon and Wed–Sat 9–7, Sun 9–12.30; closed Tues; adm*). In the frescoes for his own house the indefatigable Vasari and his workshop went far beyond anything they ever did for Duke Cosimo.

San Francesco

For many, the real allure of Arezzo is behind the doors of this dowdy, barnlike, typically Franciscan church (*visits to see the newly restored frescoes by appointment only; call the tourist office or see the website at* www.pierodellafrancesca.it *for details*).

Beginning in 1452, Piero della Francesca created here one of the greatest of all Renaissance fresco cycles, the *Legend of the Cross*. As with Giotto's cycle at Santa Croce in Florence, the story is taken from Jacopo da Voragine's *Golden Legend*. Newly restored, the work shows Piero's use of glowing colours and complex perspectives, especially in such virtuoso achievements, still novel in his day, as grimly lifelike portrayals of battles and night scenes. Even Vasari was impressed, though the best compliment he can manage in the *Lives of the Artists* is that Piero's drawing of horses was 'almost too excellent for those times'.

Out on the southern edge of Arezzo, near the station on Via Margaritone, are the remains of a **Roman amphitheatre**, made into a quiet park. A former monastery, built on a curve over the amphitheatre's foundations, has been restored to house the **Museo Archeologico** (*open Mon–Sat 9–2, Sun 9–1; closed second and third Sun of the month; adm*). Not much has survived from the thriving Etruscan and Roman city of *Arretium*, but there are some mosaics and sarcophagi, Greek vases and Etruscan funerary urns. Finally, you can take a 15-minute walk from Via Mecanate out through Arezzo's southern suburbs to see a simple but exceptionally pretty Renaissance church. **Santa Maria delle Grazie**, built by Benedetto di Maiano in 1444, has a Florentine-style loggia for a porch in front, and a della Robbia tabernacle.

Around Arezzo

North of Arezzo: the Casentino and the Valtiberina

If you are going to or coming from Florence by car, the SS70 and SS7171 make an attractive alternative route to the *autostrada* up the Arno Valley. This route follows the Arno too, but up to its source and then over the Consuma pass to Florence. It traverses the region called the **Casentino**, a hard-working, backwoods corner of Tuscany full of grapes, olives, small family businesses, chestnut groves, cattle and monasteries.

Starting from Arezzo the first important town is **Bibbiena**, a typical hill town from which you can make a detour to **Chiusi della Verna**, up in a range of hills that bravely calls itself the 'Alpe di Catenaia'. St Francis lived here for many years, as a hermit on the wooded slopes of Monte Penna, and it was here in 1224 that he received the stigmata, an event recorded in the frescoes of the basilica at Assisi and scores of other churches around Italy. **La Verna**, an unusual rocky outcrop 3km above Chiusi della Verna, was the site of his hermitage; a Franciscan sanctuary still occupies the rock. They are always happy to receive visitors; in the Chiesa Maggiore and two smaller chapels you can see one of the largest collections of Andrea della Robbia terracottas – some of his best work, including a brilliant *Annunciation*. From the monastery it is an easy walk through pine groves up to the summit of Monte Penna.

North of Bibbiena the valley road divides. The SS71 northeastwards will take you to another famous monastic retreat, **Camaldoli**, set in thick forests over 3,608ft up the mountains, the home of an order founded by San Romualdo in the early 11th century. The monks still live in separate cottages, sworn to complete isolation. The narrower SS70 carries on up the Arno Valley. **Poppi**, 8km up from Bibbiena, is the real attraction

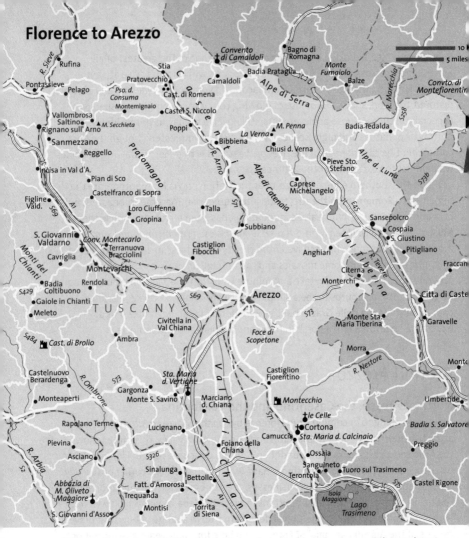

Florence to Arezzo

of this route: a beautiful little town of arcaded streets and squares with a stalwart, erect Palazzo Pretorio modelled after the Palazzo Vecchio in Florence.

From Bibbiena the road past Chiusi della Verna leads east over the mountains to the next valley, that of the Tiber. Both the Tiber and Arno are near their sources here, and in places they flow less than 15km apart. A few bumpy kilometres south of Chiusi della Verna, **Caprese Michelangelo** does not let any opportunity go by to remind you of its famous son. Besides changing its name, the hamlet has restored the artist's purported birthplace, the old town hall where his father was a Florentine governor. Now a museum, the Casa del Podestà (*open summer Mon–Fri 9.30–6.30, Sat–Sun 9.30–7.30; winter Mon–Fri 10–5, Sat–Sun 10–6*), it has full-size reproductions of Michelangelo's works, memorabilia, and dubious tributes from modern sculptors.

Further down the Tiber Valley **Sansepolcro**, similarly, lives on as a shrine to *its* favourite son, Piero della Francesca, with two of his most famous paintings in the town hall's Museo Civico (*open daily 9.30–1 and 2.30–6; until 7.30 in summer; adm exp;*

the building suffered some damage in the 1997 earthquake, but most rooms are still open). The Resurrection, an intense, almost eerie depiction of the triumphant Christ rising over his tomb and the sleeping soldiers guarding it, shares pride of place with the *Misericordia Polyptych*, a gold-ground altarpiece dominated by a giant-sized Madonna, sheltering under her cloak members of the confraternity who commissioned the picture.

Other works present are from Luca Signorelli, Pontormo and Matteo di Giovanni; more Renaissance painting, by both Sienese and Florentine artists, can be seen in Sansepolcro's Romanesque **cathedral**. For yet another Piero della Francesca, stop at the cemetery chapel on the SS221 just west of **Monterchi**, south of Sansepolcro near the border with Umbria: his *Madonna del Parto*, a rare portrayal of a weary, pregnant Virgin, is a popular icon for expectant mothers, and the drive there is spectacular, especially when the sunflowers are in bloom.

South of Arezzo: the Valdichiana

Much of this area is a broad plain called the Valdichiana, all swamps and lakes before a 19th-century reclamation plan, and now full of prosperous farms. On both sides you'll find some of the most beautiful villages in this part of Tuscany – none with much history of its own, but comfortable, essentially Tuscan towns worth a stop and a walk around if you're on your way to Rome or Perugia. **Monte San Savino**, the home town of the architect Sansovino, is one of these; he designed the market loggia and other buildings around the town. Nearby **Lucignano** will literally run you in circles – the village has a unique plan of concentric ellipses, with four picturesque piazzas in the centre. The Palazzo Comunale, now the Museo Civico, has a number of interesting frescoes to see.

Just as distinctive is **Marciano della Chiana**, an old fortress town of gates and towers. Across the Valdichiana, **Castiglion Fiorentino** was known as Castiglion Aretino until the Florentines snatched it in 1384. It, too, has a museum in its Palazzo Comunale, with 15th- and 16th-century art, and some good frescoes in the Collegiata church. The town takes its name from the big castle of **Montecchio** on the opposite hill, a landmark visible all over the Valdichiana, now abandoned. For a while in the 1400s it was the stronghold of the *condottiere* Sir John Hawkwood, he of the famous 'monument' in Florence cathedral.

Cortona

Cortona may not be entirely undiscovered, but it is still one of the real jewels among the hill towns. Set among terraced slopes covered with olives and vines, almost a kilometre above sea level, it's a web of crooked streets that climb precipitously to the old fortress – even halfway up, if there's a space between the houses, you will be able to see Lake Trasimeno below. Cortona was an Etruscan city, one of the Dodecapolis, and ragged, monolithic Etruscan stonework can still be seen at the foundations of its wall. As a medieval *comune*, it held its own against Siena, Arezzo and Perugia until 1490, when mercenary King Ladislas of Naples captured the city and sold it at a good price to the Florentines.

Tourist Information

Bibbiena: Via Berni 25, t 0575 593 098.
Sansepolcro: Piazza Garibaldi 2,
t/f 0575 740 536.
Cortona: Via Nazionale 42, t 0575 630 353.

Where to Stay and Eat

Sansepolcro ✉ 52037

★★★★La Balestra, Via del Montefeltro 29,
t 0575 735 151, f 0575 740 370 (*moderate*).
'The Crossbow' has modern, comfortable
rooms. It also has a good restaurant
(*moderate*), with delicious home-made
pasta; for seconds try the lamb chops with
courgette flowers.
★★★Fiorentino, Via L. Pacioli 60, t 0575 740 350,
f 0575 740 370 (*cheap*). Situated near the
main gate, this has been the town inn since
the 1820s; rooms provide the basics.. The
restaurant (*moderate*) is Sansepolcro's best;
it's a good place to try Italian onion soup;
other local specialities are especially well
prepared, and there's a wide assortment of
local cheese. *Closed Fri.*
Paola e Marco Mercati dell'Oroscopo, Località
Pieve Vecchia, Piazza Togliatti 66, t 0575 734
875 (*expensive*). An unusual place mixing
traditional with more creative cooking, such
as flamed king prawns in garlic sauce and a
chocolate tart with *zabaglione* and
mascarpone. *Dinner only, closed Sun.* There's
also a small hotel (*cheap*) with 12 rooms.

Caprese Michelangelo ✉ 52033

★★★Il Faggeto, t 0575 793 925 (*moderate*). Up in
the Alpe Faggeto, above Caprese
Michelangelo, is a pleasant little mountain
hotel and restaurant (*moderate*), in a lovely
forested landscape. The hotel has simple
rooms; its restaurant, the **Fonte Galletta**,
uses fresh local ingredients – chestnuts, wild
mushrooms, truffles, game and mountain
hams – to create delicious dishes. The pasta
is excellent, as are the homemade
semifreddi. Open daily Jul–Aug.

Monte San Savino ✉ 52048

★★★★Castello dei Gargonza, an entire walled
village 8km from Monte San Savino, just off
the SS73, t 0575 847 021, f 0575 847 054 (*very
expensive*). The top place in the Valdichiana,
at least for peace and quiet and medieval
atmosphere, with 20 rooms in restored
houses, a pool and forests all around; the
restaurant (*moderate*), serving local specialities accompanied by a choice wine list, is
also popular. *Closed Tues.*

As in Arezzo, Florentine rule meant a long decline for Cortona, and consequently
much that is genuinely medieval has survived. Some old streets, like Via del Gesù,
have brick or stuccoed houses with the upper floors propped out over the street on
timbers – the very picture of an old Italian town from any quattrocento painting.
Cortona also retains one superb medieval square, the **Piazza della Repubblica**, an
asymmetrical masterpiece of urban design in a very small space. The building with
the clock is the 13th-century **Palazzo Comunale**.

Directly behind it, facing the adjacent Piazza Signorelli, the Palazzo Pretorio houses
the fascinating **Museo dell'Accademia Etrusca** (*open Tues–Sun 10–7; closed Mon; adm*).
Not everything here is Etruscan, and the fine Greek vases and Egyptian artefacts
testify to the city's wealth and trade contacts long ago. Among the Etruscan art the
star exhibit is an odd bronze lamp that looks for all the world like an Aztec calendar
stone. There are paintings, too, by Lorenzetti of Siena, Pinturicchio and Luca Signorelli,
born in Cortona.

Behind the museum, yet another tiny piazza leads to the **Duomo**, rebuilt to an
uninteresting design in the 1560s. The **Museo Diocesano** (*open April–Sept Tues–Sun
9.30–1 and 3.30–7; Oct–Mar Tues–Sun 10–1 and 3–5; closed Mon; adm*), however, has

***Sangallo**, Piazza Vittorio Veneto 16, t 0575 810 049, f 0575 810 220 (*moderate*). A fine provincial hotel with all you need in the centre of town. No restaurant.

Cortona ✉ 52044

In Cortona, available lodgings have yet to catch up with demand, especially since the town is the site of both a language school and a University of Georgia art programme, operative beween June and October.

****Il Falconiere**, 3km away at San Martino a Bocena, t 0575 612 679, f 0575 612 927. The local luxury choice is outside the centre; refined, frescoed and furnished with antiques and canopied beds, it also has a pool and a first class restaurant (*expensive*) serving delicious meat and fish dishes. *Closed Wed in winter.*

***Oasi Neumann**, Via Contesse 1, t 0575 630 354, f 0575 630 354 (*moderate*). One of the nicest places to stay, with rooms in a fine old mansion, lovely gardens and a very warm welcome. *Open April–Oct.*

***San Michele**, Via Guelfa 15, t 0575 604 348, f 0575 630 147 (*moderate*). Occupies a Renaissance palace, and has most mod cons.

***San Luca**, Piazza Garibaldi 2, t 0575 630 460, f 0575 630 105 (*moderate*). Simple but comfortable; with many of the rooms enjoying wonderful views out over the surrounding countryside.

*****Athens**, Via S. Antonio, t 0575 630 508. Named after Athens, Georgia, not Greece, this is a good budget choice high up in the old town, with spacious rooms in an older building. *Open June–Nov.*

Cortona's restaurants are not fancy, but make a point of using local ingredients – home-made pasta, *salumeria* and beefsteaks from the Valdichiana, *porcini* mushrooms and truffles in season from the wooded hillsides, and the local white wines, called *bianchi vergini* (the white virgins).

Tonino, Piazza Garibaldi, t 0575 630 500 (*expensive*). Cortona's most elegant restaurant, with wonderful hot and cold *antipasti*, followed by traditional pasta dishes and the Valdichiana's tender beef. *Closed Mon eve and Tues.*

Osteria del Teatro, Via Maffei 5, t 0575 630 556. For half as many lire, this little place will fill you up with seasonal treats; in summer don't miss their *ravioli* with pumpkin flowers. *Closed Wed.*

La Grotta, Piazzetta Baldelli 3, t 0575 630 271 (*expensive*). Hidden away off the main square is a friendly but intimate restaurant that the Cortonese would like to keep a secret. *Closed Tues.*

excellent paintings, including an *Annunciation* by Beato Angelico, who spent 10 years in Cortona, as well as a famous *Deposition* and other works by Luca Signorelli: also some Duccio di Buoninsegna and Pietro Lorenzetti, and a Roman sarcophagus with reliefs of the Battle of Lapiths and Centaurs that was closely studied by, and served as inspiration for, Donatello and Brunelleschi.

Up and Down Cortona

If you have the urge to do some climbing you can visit **San Francesco** (1245), where both Luca Signorelli and Brother Elias, St Francis' businesslike successor, are buried. From here carry on up to the medieval neighbourhood around **San Nicolò**. This handsome little Romanesque church, built by an anachronistic architect in the 1440s, was the seat of San Bernardino da Siena's Company of St Nicholas, for whom Luca Signorelli painted a magnificent standard of the *Deposition* still hanging by the altar.

The town's four gates are set at the four points of the compass. The northern **Porte Colonia** has an Etruscan-Roman arch; the southern, on Via Nazionale, has a little terrace with the best view over Lake Trasimeno. Climb higher, to an area within the walls devoted to olives and vegetable gardens, and there will be even better views from the 19th-century **Basilica Santa Margherita.** The original church was built by Santa Margherita (1247–97) a beautiful farmer's daughter and mistress of a young nobleman; upon his sudden death she got religion, became a Franciscan tertiary and founded a convent and hospital where she cared for the sick. Her remains are in a silver urn on the altar. The overgrown **Medici Fortress** at the top of Cortona's hill, built on the site of the ancient Etruscan acropolis, is a great place for a picnic.

Outside Cortona, down on the plain near the city's modern suburb of Camucia, be sure to stop to see **Santa Maria del Calcinaio** (1485), with elegant Renaissance symmetry by Giorgio Martini, on a simple central plan with an octagonal drum and dome. The stained glass is by Guillaume de Marcillat, who worked at Arezzo cathedral. Unfortunately it's rarely open; ask at the tourist office. Nearby there are some Etruscan tombs: the intriguingly named, circular **Tanella of Pythagoras** and the **Tanella Angori**.

Umbria

18

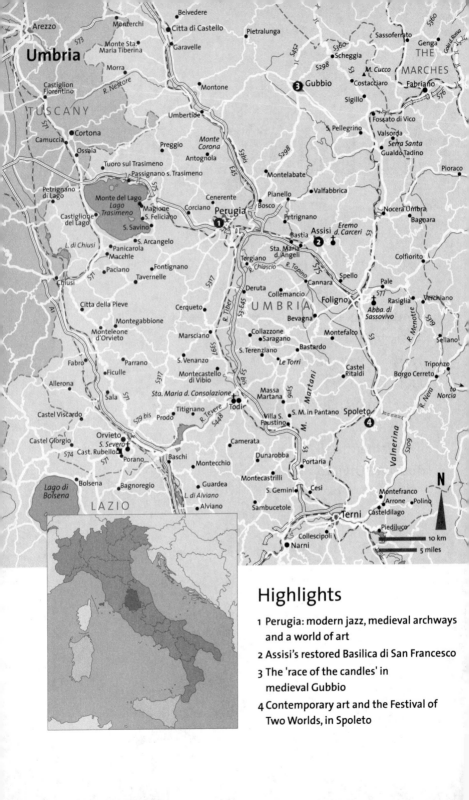

Highlights

1 Perugia: modern jazz, medieval archways and a world of art
2 Assisi's restored Basilica di San Francesco
3 The 'race of the candles' in medieval Gubbio
4 Contemporary art and the Festival of Two Worlds, in Spoleto

The Umbrians tell it this way: in the centre of the world there is a sea, in the centre of the sea lies a peninsula, in the centre of the peninsula there is a region, in the centre of the region there is a town, in the centre of the town there is a bar, in the centre of the bar stands a billiard table, in the centre of the billiard table there are four markers, and in the centre of these markers lies the centre of all creation.

The town is Foligno, and the Umbrians, as unabashedly parochial as only Italians can be, are only partly in jest. Their rural little city-region, the 'Green Heart of Italy', is also her introspective soul, scarcely touched by the onrush of contemporary events. There are exceptions; in September 1997, fate unkindly sent an earthquake centred on – of all places – the very centre of the universe, Foligno. The damage to the famous Basilica of St Francis in Assisi, now largely repaired, captured most of the world's attention, but towns and villages across the region suffered greatly, and in many places you'll find the Umbrians are still calmly and determinedly putting the pieces back together just the way they were.

Outside of earthquakes, Umbria is rarely in the news; it bowed out of time long ago, a medieval backwater that stagnated for centuries under papal rule. As Americans say of North Carolina, it is 'a vale of humility between two mountains of conceit', and Tuscany and Rome are veritable Everests of conceit, casting long shadows even back in the days of the Umbrii, an Italic tribe that gave the region its name. The Umbrii were best known for their pacifism in a bossy peninsula. Rather than fight the Etruscans, they assimilated their ways, and used their alphabet whenever they had something to say (which, as far as anybody knows, was only once). Later, in the Etruscan twilight, the Umbrii were one of the few tribes passive (or smart) enough to accept the Romans without spilling buckets of blood.

Mild-tempered, isolated from outside influences – Umbria is the only Italian region that neither touches the sea nor shares a frontier with another country – the Umbrians tend to be complacent in their cocoon and conservative in their ways, refusing even to improve the recipe for the medieval paving stones they call bread. But for many this basic lack of interest in the outside world, combined with Umbria's gentle beauty, makes the region an ideal retreat for the spirit. St Francis of Assisi's doctrine of mystical love for all creation seems to come out of the soft bluish-green hills of Umbria, which has proved a fertile land for saints, producing a bumper crop – not only St Francis and St Clare, but also St Benedict, the founder of monasticism, St Rita, the saint of impossibilities, and St Valentine, the patron of lovers. Umbrians visit their relics the way we would call on a fond uncle or aunt.

Umbria is lush and green, even in the middle of its blistering summer. Its medieval towns, hilltop tiaras of pinkish-grey stone, are evocative and lovely, and their churches and museums contain artworks that rival those of big sister Tuscany. But perhaps the greatest gift Umbria has to offer to the modern visitor is its stillness. You can see it in the soulful, introspective works of the Umbrian school of painting, in early Peruginos and gilded Pinturicchios – but especially in the paintings of Piero della Francesca, born on the Tuscan-Umbrian frontier, whose figures, having achieved mathematical perfection, are beyond all time. 'Umbria,' as the friendly nun said on the bus, 'speaks in silences.'

Lake Trasimeno

Approaching Umbria from Tuscany, this section begins where that one left off, near the banks of Lake Trasimeno, easily reached by train from Cortona. The fourth-largest lake in Italy after Lombardy's big three, Trasimeno has a subtle charm: sleepy, placid and shallow, kissed by gently rolling hills covered with olives and vineyards. Special flat-bottomed boats skim over its waters, fishing for eels; the lake is doing its darnedest to become a peat bog. Of late, the villages around Trasimeno have become popular with English expatriates, searching for new pastures away from the crowded hillsides of Chiantishire.

The Lake Towns

In 217 BC the peace of Trasimeno's north shore at **Tuoro** was shattered when Hannibal ambushed the pursuing Romans, a battle that ended with the dismal destruction of two legions of the SPQR. It is said that 15,000 legionaries perished – their rivers of blood are commemorated in the name of the hamlet **Sanguineto**, and their whitened bones in **Ossaia** (from *ossa*, bones). After its defeat at Trasimeno the Roman military machine grimly threw even more legions to their death against

Getting Around

Besides the FS state **railways**, Umbria has its own private line, the FCU (*Ferrovia Centrale Umbria*). This humblest of railroads runs from Sansepolcro in Tuscany to Città di Castello, Umbertide, Perugia, Todi and Terni. The main FS Rome–Ancona line reaches Terni, Spoleto and Foligno; at Foligno you can change trains for the branch line to Perugia. From Terni trains head south for Rieti and L'Aquila in Abruzzo. Trains between Rome and Florence stop at Orte (where you can change for Terni), Orvieto and Terontola (junction for Perugia).

Towns not reached by train, like Gubbio, are served by **buses**, though services aren't frequent, especially at weekends. This is one region where you should seriously consider hiring a **car**.

Train travel to Lake Trasimeno and the lake towns can be awkward: Castiglione del Lago is a stop on the Florence–Rome line, but only on slower trains. Most do stop at Terontola, the junction for Perugia, Tuoro and Passignano; from Siena change at Chiusi for Castiglione or Città della Pieve. Perugia is the main **bus** terminus for the area. Connections from Cortona and Siena are less frequent. A fairly frequent bus service runs round the north shore (Tuoro–Passignano–Magione–San Feliciano–San Savino–Perugia) and around the southern shore (Perugia–Magione–S. Arcangelo–Panicarola–Macchie–Castiglione del Lago). Tourist offices have timetables.

On the lake itself a regular **boat** service links Castiglione, Tuoro and Passignano with each other and with Isola Maggiore. Connections are frequent in summer, but there are only one or two boats a day in winter. For sailing times, contact t 075 827 157.

Tourist Information

Castiglione del Lago: Piazza Mazzini 10, t 075 965 8210, www.comune.passignano-sul-trasimeno.perugia.it
Passignano sul Trasimeno: Via Roma 25, t 075 965 2484.

Where to Stay and Eat

Medieval Perugians were so fond of fish from Trasimeno that Nicola Pisano sculpted some on his famous fountain in front of the cathedral in their city. Today the catch isn't big enough to send far outside the lake area, but you can try some at the little restaurants around the lake, most of them unpretentious.

Hannibal at Cannae, before giving the Carthaginians the run of the peninsula, defeating them by refusing to fight.

Passignano sul Trasimeno, nearby, the lake's busiest resort, enjoys a favoured location on its own promontory and walled old quarter. From here a road ascends to **Castel Rigone**, a restful little town with a fine Renaissance church called the Tricine.

On the west bank of Trasimeno, **Castiglione del Lago**, with its picturesque promontory, is the biggest town on the lake, with a castle and beaches. Boats sail from here or Passignano to pretty **Isola Maggiore**, of fishermen and lace-making womenfolk. In 1211, while visiting the island, St Francis threw back a pike a fisherman had given him, only to be followed across the lake by his grateful 'brother fish' until the saint blessed him – events commemorated in the island church of San Michele. A pretty path encircles the island, a good spot for a picnic.

Castiglione is also a good base for visiting Etruscan Chiusi in Tuscany and **Città della Pieve**, the latter the home town of Pietro Vannucci (1446–1523), better known as *Il Perugino*. He left several works in his home town: a lovely fresco of *The Adoration of the Magi* in Santa Maria dei Bianchi (*open June–Sept daily 10.30–12.30 and 4–7; Oct–May Fri–Sun 10–12.30 and 3.30–6*) and some paintings in the Duomo (*open daily 9.30–5*). Perugino is a disturbing character, and you will find his art sometimes

Passignano sul Trasimeno ✉ 06065

★★★**Villa Paradiso**, Via Fratelli Rosselli 5, t 075 829 191, f 075 828 118 (*moderate*). A large but comfortable hotel with a rustic feel and a swimming pool.

★★★**Lido**, Via Roma 1, t 075 827 219, f 075 827 251 (*moderate*). Right on the water and a little cheaper, with well-equipped rooms, and a garden to sit and watch the ferries sailing to and fro. *Open April–Nov.*

★**Del Pescatore**, Via San Bernadino 5, t 075 829 6063, f 075 829 201 (*moderate*). Basic rooms are also available here, but the main business at the 'Fisherman's' is food, especially lake fish, served in the attractive *trattoria. Closed Tues.*

Fischio del Merlo, Via A. Gramsci 14, t 075 829 283. Similar fare is on offer here. *Closed Tues.*

Castiglione del Lago ✉ 06061

★★★**Duca della Corgna**, Via Buozzi 143, t 075 953 238, f 075 965 2446 (*moderate*). Comfortable and relaxing, in a quiet wooded setting. The restaurant only opens in the summer months.

★★★**Trasimeno**, Via Roma 174, t 075 965 2494, f 075 952 5258 (*moderate*). Has a pool to make up for the lake's indifferent waters. *Open July and Aug only.*

L'Acquario, Via Vittorio Emanuele 69, t 075 965 2463 (*moderate*). A reliable option in the historic centre serving delicately smoked eel fillets, *risotto* of lake fish, or carp wrapped in *porchetta* (a typical Trasimeno dish). *Closed Wed, and Tues in winter.*

Isola Maggiore

★★**Da Sauro**, Via Guglielmi, t 075 826 168, f 075 825 130 (*moderate*). This is perhaps the most unusual place to stay in the area – it's certainly the best place in Umbria to get away from it all. Gracious and uncomplicated with just 12 rooms, it's the only hotel on the island. It has a brilliant restaurant, naturally specializing in fish from the lake: eels, carp and more, along with traditional Umbrian dishes. Altogether excellent value.

Città della Pieve ✉ 06062

★★**Vanucci**, Via Icilio Vanni 1, t 0578 299572, f 0578 298063 (*moderate*). There's nothing fancy in Città della Pieve; this is adequate for a night or two.

Da Bruno, Via Pietro Vannucci 90, t 0578 298 108 (*moderate*). Fine, unpretentious fare.

Trattoria Serenella, Via Fiorenzuola 28, t 0578 299 683 (*moderate*). Similar offerings.

beautiful, but perhaps more often unsatisfying. Although a forerunner of the High Renaissance, the teacher of Raphael and a master of technique, Perugino was the most bitter of Renaissance artists. Born into a desperately poor family, he became a miser, riding from job to job with saddlebags full of money. Midpoint in his career he became an atheist; even so, he cranked out two more decades of richly rewarded but vacuous religious scenes before dying, stubbornly unconfessed on his deathbed (extremely rare in the 16th century), rejecting any future with the sweet-faced angels he depicted for others.

Perugia

What a town for assassinations!
H.V. Morton

Balanced on a commanding hill high above the Tiber, Perugia is a fascinating medieval acrobat adroitly able to juggle several roles at the same time: those of an ancient hill town, a magnificent *città d'arte*, and a slick, cosmopolitan modern city, famous for its two universities and its chocolates. It is a fit capital for Umbria, with splendid monuments from the Etruscan era to the late Renaissance, artistically stacked side by side; its gallery contains the region's finest paintings, but in its medieval alleyways cats sleep undisturbed.

History

An ancient Umbrian centre, conquered or assimilated by the Etruscans relatively late (around 500 BC), *Peiresa* grew to become one of the 12 cities of the Etruscan Federation, and was peacefully integrated into the Roman world in 310 BC. It had the misfortune to be the refuge of Mark Antony's brother in one of the civil wars, and was subsequently besieged and accidently burned to the ground by one of its own residents when it finally surrendered to Augustus' forces. Augustus had the city rebuilt and renamed *Augusta Perusia*.

Early in the Middle Ages Perugia became an autonomous and rather rascally city that liked nothing better than a punch-up with its neighbours. Strife, external and internal, was to be a constant until the 19th century, and if the city was well fortified against assaults, the towers and palaces of its citizens were equally well fortified against one another. The most prominent family from the 13th century on, the Baglioni, were prevented from taking power by their chief rivals, the Oddi. Their feud was interrupted by the *condottiere* Braccio Fortebraccio ('Arm Strongarm', the Popeye of his day; his escutcheon shows spinach sprouting in a helmet), who took the city in 1414 with the pope's army, and ruled it well.

After Fortebraccio's enforced peace, the Oddi and Baglioni were at it again. Even in the murderous Renaissance the Baglioni were notorious for their audacious liquidations of Oddi and rivals within their own family. One Baglioni gangster even tried to assassinate Pope Julius II when he came to visit Perugia, a failed attempt regretted by Machiavelli because it would have made the family immortal – for its

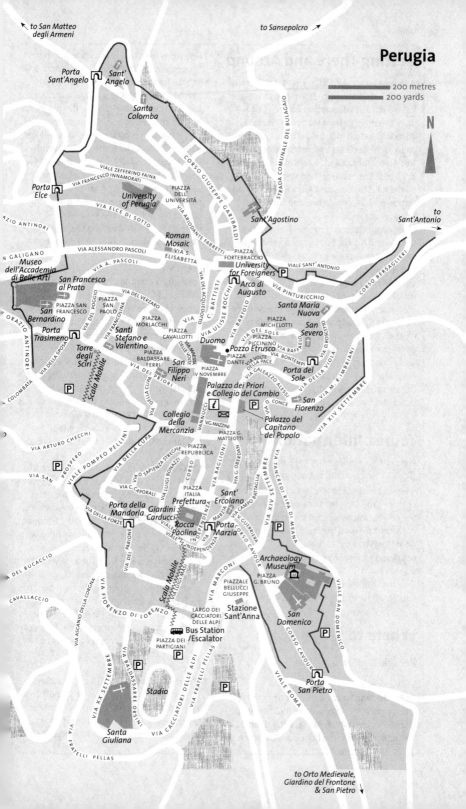

Getting There and Around

Perugia has an **airport**, 12km east of the city, but it has flights only to Milan and in summer to Sardinia. For information, call **t** 075 692 9447. The main FS **train** station in Piazza Vittorio Veneto is 3km below the city centre and has connections to Terontola (for Lake Trasimeno, Arezzo and Florence) and Foligno (for Assisi, Spoleto, Terni and Rome). Halfway up the hill, Stazione Sant'Anna is the FCU rail station for Todi, Umbertide and Sansepolcro, **t** 075 575 401.

The provincial **bus** terminus has services to Gubbio and Norcia, **t** 075 573 1707, and other destinations in the region, as well as Rome and Florence (**t** 075 500 9641) and Siena (**t** 075 500 4888). It's in Piazza dei Partigiani, linked to Piazza Italia by escalators (*scala mobile*) that are among the most scenographic anywhere.

If you're **driving**, parking can be a headache: most of the city is closed to traffic, and garages and car parks charge by the hour. You'll find them in Piazza Italia, Piazza Piccinino, and at Piazza Pellini, Mercato Coperto and Piazza Partigiani, all connected to the centre by elevator or escalator.

Tourist Information

Piazza IV Novembre, **t** 075 573 6458, **f** 075 573 9386, or Via Mazzini 21, **t** 075 5723 3327.

Check out the web site *www.umbria2000.it*, or there's the **Digiplan** computer, which (on the rare occasions when it's working) is always right. Look for it on the *scala mobile*, just up from the Piazza dei Partigiani; it will print out details on almost any hotel, restaurant or sight in town.

Churches: Unless otherwise stated, churches in Perugia are open 8–12 and 4–sunset.

Where to Stay

Perugia ✉ 06100

Very Expensive

★★★★★Brufani, Piazza Italia 12, **t** 075 573 2541, **f** 075 572 0210. A renovated, traditional 19th-century hotel which has recently doubled in size to provide some 80 rooms. There are fine views over the countryside, luxurious fittings and an attractive central courtyard.

★★★★★Le Tre Vaselle, Via Garibaldi 48, **t** 075 988 0447, **f** 075 988 0214, *www.3vaselle.it*. Between Perugia and Deruta, this luxurious hotel is situated in an old *palazzo* and adjoining houses on the edge of the village, surrounded by Lungarotti vineyards and olive groves. It has a baby-sitting service, a swimming pool, whirlpool, sauna, fitness suite – the works. It is often used for conferences, but these are run in a separate part of the building. The expensive restaurant is ranked among the top in Umbria, but standards are not consistent.

Expensive

★★★★Perugia Plaza, Via Palermo 88, **t** 075 34643, **f** 075 30863. A prestigious hotel set in greenery at the foot of the city. It is big and comfortable, with a pool and sauna, and an excellent restaurant, the **Fortebraccio**, with reasonable fixed-price menus. *Closed Mon.*

★★★★La Rosetta, Piazza Italia 19, **t/f** 075 572 0841. Another older hotel, deservedly popular, with a variety of rooms from different periods and remodellings. It boasts a celebrated restaurant, and dining in the garden in summer; the rooms, either modern or furnished with antiques, are cosy and quiet.

★★★★Giò Arte e Vini, Via Ruggero d'Andreotto 19, **t/f** 075 573 1100. It's well worth the short drive to experience this memorable hotel, dedicated to the noble art of wine-drinking. Each room is furnished with rustic Umbrian furniture, including a display case filled with bottles of wine. Guests are encouraged to taste them and buy from the amply stocked cellars on departure – a pleasantly sophisticated variation on the mini-bar. The restaurant is another treat: every evening, the *sommelier* chooses three different wines and, for a surprisingly modest fee, diners can quaff to their heart's content.

Moderate

★★★Fortuna, Via Bonazzi 19, **t** 075 572 2845, **f** 075 573 5040. A good location just off Corso Vannucci, with more comfort than charm.

★★Aurora, Viale Indipendenza 21, **t/f** 075 572 4819. Conveniently situated a minute's walk from Piazza Italia, on the main road up from the station. Rooms are rather spartan, but comfortable enough for a short stay, and service is friendly.

Cheap

*Etruria, Via della Luna 21, **t** 075 572 3730. A simple place just off Corso Vannucci, although only a few rooms are en suite.

The following are similar – basic but clean and comfortable – and central:

*Piccolo, Via Bonazzi 25, **t** 075 572 2987.

*Paola, Via della Canapina 5, **t** 075 572 3816.

Eating Out

Some of Perugia's best restaurants are in the hotels listed above, in particular the **Perugia Plaza**, **La Rosetta**, and **Giò Arte e Vini**.

Expensive–Moderate

Osteria del Bartolo, Via Bartolo 30, **t** 075 573 1561. Offering a taste of old Umbria, with inventive and beautifully prepared dishes created from ancient recipes you won't find cooked anywhere else. *Closed Sun.*

Aladino, Via delle Prome 11 (the extension of Via del Sole), **t** 075 572 0938. One of the most popular restaurants in the city, just north of the Duomo, specializing in sunny Sardinian and more fresh Mediterranean dishes to go with its selection of fine wines. *Eves only, closed Mon.*

Falchetto, Via Bartolo 20, **t** 075 573 1775. Also near the cathedral, this reeks of medieval atmosphere and serves good filling Umbrian mountain specialities – *salumeria, crostini* (pâté on toast), *tagliatelle* with truffles, *pasta e fagioli* (pasta with beans), grilled lamb and trout, all well prepared and followed by delicious desserts. *Closed Mon.*

Ubu Re, Via Baldeschi 17, **t** 075 573 5461. Alternatively, head for this quattrocento *palazzo* in the same quarter. The chef here has a lighter touch, but also offers good variations on the usual hearty Umbrian theme, including an excellent *coscio di agnello alle olive* (leg, or more specifically thigh, of lamb cooked with olives) and a well-stocked wine cellar. *Eves only, closed Mon, and part of July and Aug.*

Il Cantinone, Via Ritorto 6, **t** 075 573 4430. Just to the left of the cathedral, most of the offerings here are simple: *spaghetti all' amatriciana*, beans and sausage, also *filetto tartufato* – fillet of steak smothered with a black truffle sauce. *Closed Tues.*

La Bocca Mia, Via Rocchi 36, **t** 075 572 3873. Some of the best seafood in town is served here, near the Etruscan Arch. 'My Mouth' also has a good reputation for desserts, which are not usually an Umbrian strong point. *Closed Sun.*

Cheap

Paiolo, Via Augusta 11, **t** 075 572 5611. Good value meals, as well as delicious pizzas, in a Renaissance *palazzo. Closed Wed, and part of Aug.*

Osteria Il Gufo, Via della Viola 18 (by San Fiorenzo), **t** 075 573 4126. Seasonal dishes with flair, and if you watch the prices you can dine very well very cheaply. *Eves only, closed Sun and Mon.*

Cambio, Corso Vannucci 29, **t** 075 572 4165. Serves reasonable meals and simple lunches. *Closed Wed.*

Ceccarani, Piazza Matteotti 16. If you want to make a picnic, this is the place to come for Perugia's best bread, baked in some 30 different ways – some of them, to the vast relief of visiting foreigners unaccustomed to the traditional Umbrian saltless variety, even made with salt.

Sandri, Corso Vannucci. One of the prettiest pastry shops in Italy, with a frescoed ceiling and divinely artistic confections; their window has even more colours than the Pinacoteca across the street.

Entertainment

The principal Perugian occupation is the evening *passeggiata* down Corso Vannucci, with a stop for a bite or a drink at the Bar Ferrari, perhaps, before hanging out in Piazza IV Novembre.

Other activities include July's **Umbria Jazz** festival, which has drawn lights like Wynton Marsalis to Perugia's stadium. In September the **Sacra Musicale Umbra** features sacred music in Perugia's churches.

iniquity. But the Baglioni had more immediate concerns than fame; as the Renaissance papacy became powerful, the popes' legates were eroding their old privileges. When Pope Paul III raised the price of salt in 1540, it was the excuse Perugia needed to revolt in what is known as the Salt War. While the city vainly awaited aid from Florence, the papal army captured it. To add still more salt to the wound, Paul III used the Baglioni palaces as the foundation for his fortress, the Rocca Paolina.

As a protest, to this day, Perugians, and indeed all Umbrians, eat bread made without salt (they often swear it tastes better!). From then on, until the Risorgimento, Perugia, like the rest of Umbria, was firmly held in the unnourishing bosom of the Papal States, states that were, as Goethe remarked, kept 'alive only because the earth refuses to swallow them'.

Up to Piazza Italia

Most people ascend into Perugia from the west on Via XX Settembre. Between the FS and Sant'Anna stations, Largo Cacciatori delle Alpi gives on to Piazza dei Partigiani, from where elevators ascend to the Piazza Italia, fully inside the city. On the way you can stroll through a surreal, shadowy medieval quarter – all located underground. These streets were vaulted over to support the **Rocca Paolina**, the popes' fortress, designed after the Salt War by Sangallo, and a much-hated symbol of papal authority that was joyfully ripped apart in 1860 when Perugia joined the new Italian Kingdom.

Only a bulwark remains of the handsome but useless structure, pierced by the beautiful Etruscan gate called the **Porta Marzia**, dating from the 3rd century BC; Sangallo liked it enough to take it apart and reconstruct it. Porta Marzia leads into **Via Baglioni Sotterranea** (*open daily 8–7*), the main underground street. By literally burying the Baglioni palaces, Pope Paul III effectively put a halt to that murderous family's influence; today, this silent, sunless land of good medieval brick is their memorial.

On top of the Baglioni palaces lie the **Giardini Carducci**, a terraced public garden with a view of the Umbrian countryside. Next to the gardens stand the dignified public buildings and hotels of **Piazza Italia** that replaced the Rocca Paolina; the proud griffon, emblazoned on the **Prefettura**, is the symbol of both the old and new *comune*.

Corso Vannucci

Two of Perugia's principal streets radiate from Piazza Italia: Via Baglioni and pedestrian-only **Corso Vannucci**, a splendid curve lined with the fortified palaces of Perugia's no-account nobility. Their forbidding residences are now elegant cafés and shops; their street has been renamed after Perugino (Pietro Vannucci) who in 1499 was commissioned to fresco the hall and chapel of the **Collegio del Cambio**, or Bankers' Guild (*open 1 Mar–31 Oct and 20 Dec–6 Jan, Mon–Sat 9–12.30 and 2.30–5.30, Sun 9–12.30; 1 Nov–19 Dec and 7 Jan–28 Feb, Tues–Sat 8–2, Sun 9–12.30; Nov–Feb closed Mon; adm*). The hall is adorned with fashionably clothed allegorical figures. Perugino painted a self-portrait in the middle of the left wall, and his pupil, Raphael, then a mere pup of 17, painted the figure of Fortitude. The same ticket is good for the **Collegio della Mercanzia**, decorated with almost Moorish style 15th-century carvings and inlays, located at the far end of the Palazzo dei Priori.

Palazzo dei Priori

Next to the Collegio del Cambio, this huge, magnificent complex, crowned with toothsome crenellations and pierced by narrow mullioned windows, has been the civic centre of Perugia since 1297. The façade on the Corso Vannucci was added in 1443, and wears a lovely portal; enter here for the lift to the third-floor **Galleria Nazionale dell'Umbria**, the finest and largest ensemble of Umbrian paintings, with many Florentines to keep them company (*open daily 9–7, closed 1st Mon of month; adm exp*).

The pious Umbrians never painted anything secular, and the gallery's Madonnas and saints may give you holy vertigo after a while. If you feel it coming on, save your eyes for the masterpieces: Fra Angelico's triptych of the *Dominicans* and *Madonna With Angels and Saints*; and Piero della Francesca's *Sant'Antonio* polyptych. In the *Annunciation* at the top, Piero creates an eerie stillness with his mathematical purity – on either side of the angel and Virgin rows of arches recede into a blank wall. Giovanni Boccati's *Madonna dell'Orchestra* is a lovely, musical work.

There are paintings by Perugino and Pinturicchio, who both worked on the *Miracles of San Bernardino of Siena*. At his best Perugino eschews drama and tension, preferring simplicity, gentle lines and static compositions often filled with a 'sweetness' that Raphael mastered, and which gives sugar-shock to people who cut their teeth on Michelangelo.

The second Perugian native, Pinturicchio (Bernardino di Betto; 1454–1513), was called the 'rich painter', for his use of gold and gorgeous colours. Although Pinturicchio refused to participate in the High Renaissance, his most interesting works here are his small experiments in perspective. Near the end of the gallery are some good 16th-century views of Perugia, bristling with now mostly vanished towers; other city scenes, by Bonfigli, are in the chapel.

At the end there's a surprise: an interesting collection of 19th-century views of the city by a local artist, Giuseppe Rossi, showing the Rocca Paolina and the old market square, along with some of the 19th-century engineers' plans for shoring up Perugia and keeping it from sliding into the valley.

Piazza Quattro Novembre

Harmonious Corso Vannucci ends with melodic rapture in this lovely square, a fine example of the subtle art of medieval town planning. Built long ago over a 1st-century AD Roman reservoir, the sloping piazza is adorned with the most beautiful Gothic fountain in Italy, the circular **Fontana Maggiore**, designed by Fra Bevignate in 1280, with bas-relief panels executed by Nicola and Giovanni Pisano. The 48 panels on the lower basin show the scenes of the months, sciences, Aesop's fables and Roman history; the upper basin has 24 saints; on the topmost basin pose three water-nymphs. Facing the fountain is the 13th-century façade of the Palazzo dei Priori, with stairs leading up to its main door.

Above the portal are Perugia's original griffon (perhaps crafted from an Etruscan creature) and the lion of the Guelph party; the scrap iron dangling beneath it is said to be chains and bolts from the gates of Siena, captured after a famous victory at Torrita in 1358 (this isn't true – the real war trophies, whatever they were, disappeared two centuries ago; these chains simply held them up). The door below leads to the **Sala dei Notari**, a monumental vaulted council hall covered with fine 13th-century frescoes by an anonymous painter (*open Tues–Sun 9–1 and 3–7*).

Across the piazza stands the Gothic 15th-century **cathedral of San Lorenzo**, its best exterior feature the **Loggia di Braccio Fortebraccio**, added by the *condottiere* in 1423. The stylized bronze pope in front is Julius III: the pulpit behind him was constructed for charismatic San Bernardino of Siena to preach to the crowd in the piazza. The sombre interior contains the 'wedding ring' of the Virgin, which the Perugini pinched from Chiusi. The onyx stone ring, size XXXL, is kept in a reliquary with 15 locks (in case the Chiusini try to steal it back) in the **Cappella del Santo Anello**, and displayed only on 30 July. On the same side of the church look for the bas-reliefs by Agostino di Duccio. The other thing to look out for is Luca Signorelli's luminous and recently restored *Pala di Sant'Onofrio* (1484), one of his earliest and best works, showing the Madonna enthroned with saints and a pot-bellied angel tuning a lute, in the Cappella del Sacramento. Much of the cathedral's other art is in the **Museo dell'Opera** (*closed for restoration*).

Oratorio di San Bernardino

Flanking the Palazzo dei Priori, medieval Via dei Priori leads down past Perugia's tallest surviving tower-fortress, the 13th-century **Torre degli Sciri** (many fell victim to the city's internal warfare), and an Etruscan arch remodelled as the medieval **Porta Trasimena**. Turn at the Renaissance church of **Madonna della Luce** for Piazza San Francesco. Perugia was never a lucky city for St Francis: as a young rake he spent a year in prison after a Perugian raid on Assisi, and became ill (events that led to his conversion); and his 13th-century church, **San Francesco al Prato**, with its lovely Cosmatesque work, was partly ruined in a landslide in 1737. Next to it, however, stands a Renaissance gem, the **Oratorio di San Bernardino** (1461), its façade rich with colourful marbles and Agostino di Duccio's exquisite bas-reliefs. They are in the same almost Art Deco spirit as his more famous ones in Rimini, with especially good angels that wouldn't look out of place in the Rockefeller Center. If it's open, go in to see the 3rd-century AD sarcophagus used as the altar and Benedetto Bonfigli's gonfalon, depicting the Madonna sheltering Perugia from the plague (1464), from the church of San Francesco. An alternative route back to Piazza IV Novembre, by Via del Poggio, Via Tartuga and Via Aquilone, will take you past the beautiful **Teatro Morlacchi**, designed in 1788 by Alessio Lerenzini. After Piazza Cavallotti you can walk through a medieval architectural triumph of interwoven arches and asymmetrical vaults, **Via Maestà delle Volte**.

North Perugia

From Piazza Dante, next to the cathedral, Via del Sole leads up to the fine old **Piazza Michelotti**, the highest point in the city, with good views. Just below the piazza, Via dell'Aquila descends to **San Severo** (*open daily April–Sept 10–1.30 and 2.30–6.30, Oct–Mar 10.30–1.30 and 2.30–4.30; adm*), an ancient church Baroqued in the 18th century, but preserving intact a Renaissance chapel containing Raphael's first important commission, a fresco of the *Holy Trinity* painted in 1505.

Via Ulisse Rocchi, also beginning in Piazza Dante, heads down to what has become Perugia's symbol, the **Arco di Augusto**, a magnificent gate built over a span of 2,000 years – the lowest section by the Etruscans and the upper part by the Romans after the siege by Augustus (whose new name for the city, *Augusta Perusia*, is still legible over the arch), while on top of all is a pretty loggia added in the 16th century.

Beyond the gate lies Piazza Fortebraccio and the 18th-century Palazzo Gallenga Stuart, home of the **University for Foreigners** (Università Italiana per Stranieri), founded in 1921 as a centre for studies in Italian language and culture. Behind the university, steps lead down to Via Sant'Elisabetta and the Istituto di Chimica, built around a beautiful 2nd-century AD **Roman mosaic** portraying the myth of Orpheus (*open Mon–Fri 8–8, Sat 8–1; closed public hols*). To the north, in a former Olivetan monastery, is the main **University of Perugia**, founded in 1307.

At the northernmost edge of Perugia (take Via Garibaldi or Via Z. Faina) stands a tower built by Fortebraccio and a remarkable, 5th-century round church, **Sant'Angelo**, dedicated to St Michael and standing on the site of an ancient temple, of which 24 columns were re-used in the church. Another church at the other end of Via Garibaldi, **Sant'Agostino**, contains lovely inlaid choir stalls by Baccio d'Agnolo and frescoes from the 14th–16th centuries.

South Perugia

Perugia's second main street, Via Baglioni, widens below Piazza IV Novembre to form Piazza Matteotti, built over the Etruscan walls and lined with early Renaissance palaces. From here, Via Oberdan descends to Perugia's oddest church, **Sant'Ercolano** (1326), a tall octagon with a railway station clock and lace curtains in the upstairs window. The Porta Marzia (*see p.756*) is nearby, while Corso Cavour descends to Piazza G. Bruno and huge **San Domenico**, founded in 1305 and rebuilt in 1632, with an immense 15th-century stained-glass window, the beautiful 14th-century **tomb of Pope Benedict XI** and terracottas by Agostino di Duccio.

San Domenico's monastery contains the excellent **Museo Archeologico Nazionale dell'Umbria** (*open Mon–Sat 9–7, Sun 9–1; adm*), with material from prehistoric and Etruscan Umbria, especially the Iron Age settlement at Belverde sul Monte Cetona. Much comes from Etruscan cemeteries – a lovely 3rd-century BC incised bronze mirror, gold filigree jewellery, sarcophagi, a stone slab – the famous *Cippus Perusinus* – with one of the longest Etruscan inscriptions found, funerary urns, vases (one showing a hero who looks just like a dentist about to examine a monster's teeth), bronzes, armour, and a *kottabos*, thought to have been used in Etruscan party games. The Romans contribute busts, statues and tombs.

Further down, Corso Cavour passes through **Porta San Pietro**, a 15th-century gate by Agostino di Duccio, then, as Borgo XX Giugno, continues to **San Pietro** (*interior closed 12–3*) – begun by the monks of Montecassino in 926 and remodelled since, but main-taining its ancient basilican form in the interior. It has a colourful ceiling and works by Perugino (in the nave and sacristy), beautiful inlaid choir stalls and stone pulpits; an inlaid door leads out to a terrace with a stunning view towards Assisi. Across the street you can take a breather in the 18th-century **Giardini del Frontone**.

Around Perugia

Near Ponte San Giovanni, west of Perugia, signs lead to its finest Etruscan tomb, the 2nd-century BC **Ipogeo dei Volumni**, in a modern yellow shelter (*open Mon–Sat 9.30–12.30 and 3–5, Sun 9.30–12.30; July and Aug 9.30–12.30 and 4.30–6.30; adm; 5 people at a time, for 5 mins each*). The hypogeum is shaped like an Etruscan house, with an underground atrium (under a high gabled roof). The main room holds the travertine urns containing the ashes of four generations of the family. The oldest one, that of Arnth, is a typical Etruscan tomb with a representation of the deceased on the lid; that of his 1st-century AD descendant, Publius Voluminius, demonstrates a rapid Romanization, decorated with unusual stucco high-reliefs.

Deruta

About 10km south of Perugia, Deruta is Umbria's most famous ceramics centre, having produced its colourful majolica since the Middle Ages. Shops in the streets are adorned with contemporary examples of the art, while pieces from the past may be seen in the **Pinacoteca Comunale** and **Museo delle Ceramica** (*open April–June daily 10.30–1 and 3–6; July–Sept daily 10–1 and 3.30–7; Oct–Mar Wed–Mon 10.30–1 and 2.30–5, closed Tues; adm*), along with detached frescoes from local churches.

Assisi

Rome may be the Eternal City, capital of an empire and Whore of Babylon; Florence the birthplace of the Renaissance, of modern Western culture and the Italian language; and Foligno's billiard table the centre of the cosmos; but Assisi is the gentle soul of Italy, imbued with the spirit of the country's patron saint, known affectionately as *Il Poverello*, the Little Poor One. The importance of St Francis (1182–1226) in the history of Christianity cannot be overestimated; he was the first to crack the strict hierarchy of the established Church, a democrat who preached a natural, everyday religion of love, and who had a simple, humble faith without dogma that had such a deep, mass appeal that the Church quickly institutionalized his teachings. Francis's own life, as an imitation of Christ, became part of the new iconography of the great religious revival he initiated.

Born to a wealthy cloth merchant named Pietro Bernardone, he was baptized Giovanni, but always called Francesco by his Francophile father. Francis grew up speaking Provençal, the language of his Occitan mother, and spent a merry, wild youth as a troubadour. He was captured in Assisi's war against Perugia, and spent a year in prison reflecting on the vanity of the world. When released, he gave everything he owned to the poor, tended lepers and preached his message of poverty, humility and joy, attracting a band of followers. Although Francis refused to take priestly orders, he received authorization for his community from Innocent III in 1209.

Francis spent much of his career preaching and wandering, travelling through Spain to Morocco, accompanying the Crusaders to Egypt and the Holy Land. His songs and canticles, drawing on his troubadour days, were among the first vernacular verses composed in Italy, and the foundation for a 13th-century literary movement, of which the most famous work was the *Fioretti*, 'The Little Flowers', believed to be in part written by Francis himself. In 1221 the Franciscan Rule of poverty, chastity and obedience was sanctioned by Honorius III. Francis subsequently received the stigmata, and died two years later.

More than any other saint, Francis crosses ecumenical boundaries; in 1987, when Pope John Paul II invited representatives of all the world's religions to pray together, he chose Assisi as the host city. But Assisi is not only Italy's greatest pilgrimage shrine after Rome, it's a beautiful medieval town as well, built high on a spur of Monte Subasio, overlooking the velvet green Umbrian countryside.

Don't become too distracted by the crowds or souvenir shops peddling toy monks, child-size crossbows and other baubles (no Italian shrine would seem right without them); but for a taste of Assisi as Francesco and Chiara (*see* p.767) would recognize it still, stroll through the city's steep, dimly lit lanes at midnight, when all is silent and still. There are two periods when Assisi is anything but silent or still: Easter week, when its processions and mystery plays bring thousands of people to the city; and the *Calendimaggio* (first ten days in May), a medieval celebration that commemorates Francis's troubadour past with songs, dances, torchlit processions and competitions between Upper and Lower Assisi.

Tragically, as everyone knows, an earthquake in September 1997 brought the roof of the basilica down, killing two friars and two journalists who were examining the damage caused by the first shock of the day. The upper church reopened in November 1999 after extensive restoration and structural reinforcements. The two arches that collapsed have been repaired, but are blank. Sixteen technicians are still working on the incredibly painstaking task of piecing the frescoes back together; much of what they are working with is little more than fine rubble. However, the other frescoes in the nave were virtually unscathed and the façade has been beautifully restored. The *palazzi* on the east side of Piazza del Comune were all badly damaged, as were many other buildings around the town, but the scaffolding is off and most have reopened.

The Basilica di San Francesco

Open daily summer 6.30am–7pm, winter 6.30am–6pm.
No shorts or bare shoulders.

Before Francis died he asked to be buried with the criminals on 'Infernal Hill' outside the city walls. His lieutenant, Brother Elias, was not about to go against his wishes, but he waited until Francis was canonized in April 1228, and the next day began work on an ambitious two-storey basilica on the hill, now re-christened the Hill of Paradise. Not all of the order agreed that such a project was fitting for a holy man wedded to poverty, but brother Elias and Pope Gregory IX, who laid the cornerstone, won the day, creating not only the chief Franciscan memorial, but a rare work of art as well.

The two churches that make up the basilica are believed to have been designed by Brother Elias himself, who created here what was to become a model for numerous other Franciscan churches, especially in the simple lines of the Gothic upper church.

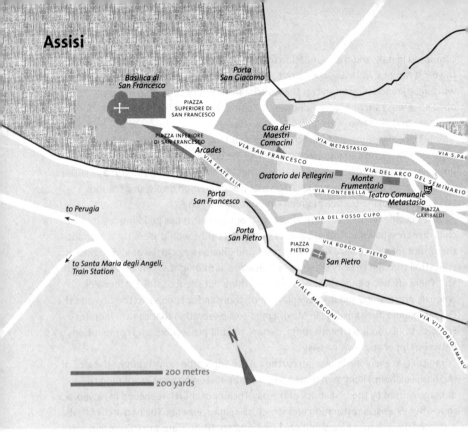

The Lower Church

The lower church most resembles a crypt with its low dark vaults, although once your eyes adjust to the dim light you can see that they are covered with beautiful frescoes by the masters of the 13th and 14th centuries (bring plenty of coins to illuminate them). The first chapel to the left of the frescoed nave contains magnificent frescoes on the *Life of St Martin* by Simone Martini, painted around 1322, while the third chapel on the right contains frescoes on the *Life of Mary Magdalen*, attributed to Giotto (1314). The frescoes attributed in Assisi to Giotto (from *c.* 1295), constitute one of the longest-raging controversies in art history. The Italian faction is convinced that the frescoes in the lower and upper churches are the climax of Giotto's early career, while most foreign scholars believe Giotto didn't paint them at all. In any case, Martini's 'International Gothic style' poses a serious artistic challenge to the great precursor of the Renaissance.

Giotto is also credited with the four beautiful allegorical frescoes over the high altar: *Poverty*, *Chastity*, *Obedience* and the *Glory of St Francis*. In the left transept are fine works by Pietro Lorenzetti of Siena, among the best in the basilica, especially the lovely *Madonna della Tramontana*, with *St Francis and St John*, a *Crucifixion* and a *Descent from the Cross*. In the right transept is Cimabue's *Madonna and Saints*, with a famous portrait of St Francis (1280), believed to be an accurate likeness; a female saint nearby, by Simone Martini, is believed to be St Clare.

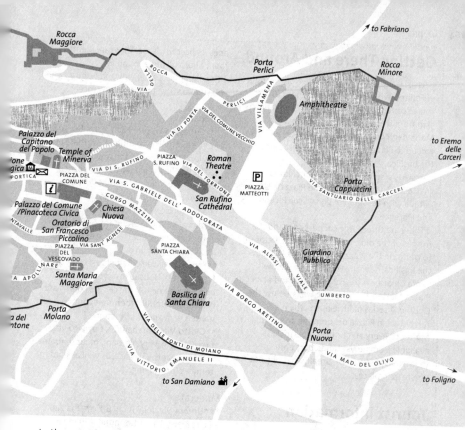

In the **crypt** lie the tombs of Francis and four of his closest followers, discovered in 1818 having been secretly sealed off in the 15th century to protect them from Assisi's devious, relic-snatching enemy, Perugia. From the transepts stairs lead up to a terrace and the **Museo-Tesoro della Basilica** (*open April–Oct daily 9.30–12 and 2–6; Nov–Mar closed Sun; adm*) containing whatever wasn't pillaged over the centuries – a beautiful Venetian cross, a French ivory Madonna from the 13th century, a Flemish tapestry of St Francis, and more, including the contents of the former 'secret sacristy': Pope Honorius III's Bull approving the Order's Rule (1223), the saint's tunic, cowl, girdle and sandals, an ivory horn given to Francis by the Sultan of Egypt which he would blow to assemble his followers, the Laud to the Creator and Benediction of Brother Leone on parchment, in the saint's own hand, and a chalice and paten used by Francis and his Franciscan followers.

The Upper Church

In comparison with the lower church, the upper church, facing its emerald-green lawn, is strikingly bright and airy, and dazzles with its colour. It contains two major series of medieval frescoes; the earthquake left them cracked and broken in places, but more or less intact. The lower set on the *Life of St Francis* is by Giotto or his school, and the upper, with Old and New Testament scenes, is attributed to Pietro Cavallini. What makes most Italian scholars attribute the St Francis frescoes to Giotto is the

Getting There and Around

Assisi is a 30-minute **train** ride from Perugia or Foligno, where you'll have to change if you've come from Rome or Terni. The station is 5km from the centre, in the suburb of Santa Maria degli Angeli; connecting buses will take you up to Piazzale Unità d'Italia, just below the basilica.

Assisi is also linked by **bus** from Piazza Matteotti, Largo Properzio and Piazzale Unità d'Italia with Perugia, Foligno, Ascoli Piceno and Florence.

There are three large **car parks** around the fringes of the old city, most of which is closed to traffic: in the Piazzale Unità d'Italia, below the basilica; near the Porta Nuova, below Santa Chiara, off the Foligno road; and at Piazza Matteotti, within the walls, below the Duomo. A series of little buses, the A and B, run between Piazza del Comune and Piazza Matteotti every 20 minutes or so (tickets available from news stands, bars and tobacconists); Assisi isn't really that big, but it's steep in places.

Tourist Information

Piazza del Comune 12, **t** 075 812 534, **t** 075 812 450, **f** 075 813 727, *www.umbria2000.it*. There's also a seasonal office (*Easter–Oct*) at Largo Properzio.
Hotel booking service: Via Cristofani, **t** 075 816 566, **f** 075 812 315, *caa@krenet.it*.
Churches: Unless otherwise stated, churches are open daily 7–12 and 2–sunset.

It's worth bearing in mind that in the wake of the 1997 earthquake many of Assisi's buildings are in an ever-changing state of disrepair and/or restoration; while most sites have been restored and reopened – many in time for the 2000 jubilee – others may have closed or reopened since the time of writing; call the tourist office for the latest details.

Where to Stay

Assisi ✉ 06081

Tourists have been coming to Assisi for longer than any other town in Umbria, and it does its best to please. There are plenty of rooms, but still not enough for Calendimaggio, Easter, July and August, when you should strive to book in advance.

Expensive
★★★★**Subasio**, Via Frate Elia 2, **t** 075 812 206, **f** 075 816 691. The traditional, formal Subasio has long been Assisi's top hotel, and is linked to the Basilica of St Francis by a portico. Many of the rooms have views over the famous mystical countryside from vine-shaded terraces, and it has an attractive medieval-vaulted restaurant. St Francis never slept here, but the King of Belgium and Charlie Chaplin did.
★★★**Fontebella**, Via Fontebella 25, **t** 075 812 883, **f** 075 812 941. Housed in a 17th-century *palazzo* a bit nearer the centre. Rooms are comfortable, public rooms elegant and its garden is an added attraction.
★★★**Giotto**, Via Fontebella 41, **t** 075 812 209, **f** 075 816 479. Very pleasant, modern rooms located near the basilica, as well as garden terraces for relaxing.

Moderate
★★★**Umbra**, Via degli Archi 6, **t** 075 812 240, **f** 075 81365. This little, family-run inn is a real charmer, at the end of a narrow alley near Piazza del Comune; it's quiet, sunny and friendly with a little walled garden in front. Rooms can be a bit small but are tranquil, and many have balconies overlooking the countryside (some are *expensive*). Their restaurant is one of Assisi's most attractive, featuring variations on the best of regional cuisine such as *risotto* with white truffles from Gubbio and a cellar full of excellent wine; in good weather meals are served in the garden.
★★★**Hotel dei Priori**, Corso Mazzini 15, **t** 075 812 237, **f** 075 816 804 (some rooms *expensive*). Housed in a gracious 18th-century *palazzo*, well restored and conveniently just off the main piazza.
★★★**Hermitage**, Via G. Degli Aromatari 1, **t** 075 812 764, **f** 075 816 691. Comfortable and reasonably priced, in a good central position just a short walk from the basilica.
★★**Ideale per Turisti**, Piazza Matteotti 1, **t** 075 813 570, **f** 075 813 020. The name says it all –

it really *is* 'Ideal for Tourists' – a fine, small hotel with a garden and views, near the amphitheatre.

Il Palazzo, Via San Francesco 8, **t 075 816 841, **f** 075 812 370, *hotel.ilpalazzo@edisons.it*. Occupies a 13th-century building right in the centre, halfway between San Francesco and Piazza del Comune. Its 12 rooms are simply but tastefully furnished with antiques.

Country House, S. Pietro Campagna 168, **t/f 075 816 363. Nearly 1km away and a bit hard to find – a 10min walk to the west gate of Assisi – is this old stone building, in a pretty country setting. It has lovely rooms, furnished with items from the owner's antiques shop on the ground floor. There's no restaurant, but the *signora* prepares a substantial, reasonably priced evening meal for guests in her kitchen; ask her about it in the morning before you go out.

Cheap

*Anfiteatro Romano, Via Anfiteatro 4, **t** 075 813 025, **f** 075 815 110. A good quiet choice near Piazza Matteotti, with only seven rooms, some with private bath.

Pallotta, Via S. Rufina 4, **t/f 075 812 307. A few simple rooms attached to a good, traditional eatery.

If everything is full, try the large pilgrimage houses in Santa Maria degli Angeli; but be prepared to be on best behaviour: unmarried couples may be separated, and some of the dormitories have curfews too.

Cenacolo Francescano, Via Piazza d'Italia 70, **t 075 804 1083, **f** 075 804 0552. One of the best, with 130 basic rooms, all with private bath, a short walk from the train station.

Della Pace, at Via di Valecchie 177, **t/f** 075 816 767. A new dormitory, located 1km out of Porta San Pietro.

Alternatively, go to the tourist office for a list of smaller religious houses and rooms in private houses, of which there are dozens, catering to pilgrims but happy to house tourists too.

Sant'Antonio's Guest House, Via G. Alessi 10, **t** 075 812 542, **f** 075 813 723. One of the nicest, run by American sisters, offering pleasant rooms in a 12th-century villa. Guests can also have a good cheap lunch here, but no dinner; beware the early curfew.

Eating Out

Moderate

Buca di San Francesco, Via Brizi 1, **t** 075 812 204. Besides the Umbra, mentioned above, Assisi has this well-known restaurant, below street level in a cavernous medieval cellar. Try the delicious *cannelloni*, home-made pasta with meat and *porcini* mushrooms, pigeon cooked Assisi-style, or *filet al Rubesco* (fillet of steak cooked in red Umbrian wine), accompanied by good wines from Umbria and other regions. *Closed Mon, Jan, Feb and most of July.*

Il Medio Evo, Via dell'Arco dei Priori 4, **t** 075 813 068. Another venerable choice with an elegant medieval atmosphere and delicious *antipasti* with Umbrian *prosciutto*, pasta with truffles in season, and *faraone all'uva* (guinea fowl cooked with grapes). *Closed Wed, Sun eve, most of Jan and the middle two weeks of July.*

San Francesco, Via S. Francesco 52, **t** 075 812 329. Defying the old Italian rule that places with views serve food for dogs, with a verandah beautifully overlooking the basilica: here good Umbrian cuisine combines with an *enoteca* wine list. *Closed Wed and some of Aug.*

Cheap

Piazzetta dell'Erba, Via S. Gabriele dell'Addolorata 15b, **t** 075 815 352. Near the Temple of Minerva, featuring delicious daily specials at kind prices. *Closed Mon.*

La Stalla, Via Eremo delle Carceri, at Fontemaggio, **t** 075 812 317. A typical country *trattoria*, converted from an old barn, making a lovely stop on the road up to the breathtaking sanctuary of Eremo delle Carceri. Good hearty fare is served at very reasonable prices, washed down with flagons of local wine. *Closed Mon.*

Don't neglect one of the rich strudels or chocolate and nut breads in the speciality bakery in Piazza del Comune, near the Temple of Minerva, or at **La Bottega del Pasticcera**, Via Portica 9 – especially good for sustenance as you follow the pilgrim routes up and down windy streets, lanes and alleyways around the old town.

artist's mastery of composition; Giotto amazed his contemporaries by his ability to illustrate the physical and spiritual essentials of a scene with simplicity and drama, cutting directly to the core. The scenes begin with the young *St Francis Honoured by a Simple Man*, who lays down his cloak and foretells his destiny; he returns his clothes to his father, who in his anger and disappointment has to be restrained; Pope Innocent III has a dream of Francis supporting the falling Lateran; the demons are expelled from Arezzo by Brother Sylvester; Francis meets the Sultan of Egypt, and creates the first Christmas crib, or *presepio*, at Greccio; he preaches to the attentive birds, then to Pope Honorius III; he appears in two places at the same time, and, next, receives the stigmata from a six-winged Christ. He dies, bewailed by the Poor Clares, and is canonized.

The transepts were painted in 1277 by Giotto's master, Cimabue, though these works had deteriorated into mere shadows of their former selves even before the earthquake turned them to crumbs; what can be salvaged will, and by hook or by crook some kind of Cimabue clones will eventually refill the rebuilt transepts, good enough to give most of us non-experts a feeling for what was lost, perhaps even of the great *Crucifixion*. Behind the basilica, propped up on huge arches, the enormous convent is now used as a missionary college.

To the Piazza del Comune

From the basilica, Via San Francesco leads up past many fine medieval houses to the centre of Assisi. On the way there are several buildings of note: No.14, the Mason's Guild or **Casa dei Maestri Comacini** (since most of those who built the basilica came from Como); at No.11, the pretty, frescoed **Oratorio dei Pellegrini**, a 15th-century gem surviving from a hospice built for pilgrims; and at No.3, the **Monte Frumentario**, a 13th-century hospital, converted into a granary. Next to it is a 16th-century fountain, still bearing the warning that the penalty for washing clothes here is one *scudo* and confiscation of the laundry. Near the entrance to the piazza is the **Collezione Archeologica** (*open April–Sept Tues–Sun 10–1 and 3–7; Oct–Mar 10–1 and 2–5; closed Mon; adm*), located in the crypt of a now-vanished church, with a small collection of Etruscan urns. A passageway from the museum leads into the ancient **Roman forum**, which lies directly under the piazza above. Here you can see bases of statues, a platform that may have been an altar, an inscription to the Dioscuri, steps to the temple of Minerva, and remains of a fountain.

The long, attractive **Piazza del Comune** was built up after the barbarians destroyed the forum. It has always been the main axis of Assisi, and is embellished with the 13th-century buildings of the old *comune* (the **Torre del Popolo**, the **Palazzo del Comune** and the **Palazzo del Capitano del Popolo**), and what at first looks like a decrepit bank building, but is in reality a Roman **Temple of Minerva**, its Corinthian columns and travertine steps incorporated into the church of Santa Maria. When Herr 'anti-Middle Ages' Goethe came to Assisi it was to see this façade – and nothing else. To the left of the Palazzo, the **Chiesa Nuova** was built by Philip III of Spain on property owned by St Francis' father. In an adjacent alley, the **Oratorio di San Francesco Piccolino** (of 'little baby St Francis') is believed to mark the saint's birthplace.

Upper Assisi: the Cathedral and the Castle

From the piazza, Via San Rufino leads up to the **Cattedrale di San Rufino**, with its huge campanile and beautiful Romanesque façade, designed by Giovanni da Gubbio in 1140 and adorned with three fine rose windows and the kind of robust medieval carvings of animals and saints that Goethe disdained. The interior was redone in the 16th century and is of little interest, but if it is open you can see the porphyry font where Saints Francis and Clare were baptized, as well as Emperor Frederick II, who was born in Jesi in the Marches. It is an amazing coincidence that the two leading figures of the 13th century should have been baptized in the same place; the holy water must have had a special essence in it, as both Francis and Frederick were profoundly influenced by the East and were among the very first poets to write in vernacular Italian, rather than Latin.

From the cathedral a stepped lane leads up to the **Rocca Maggiore** (*open 10–sunset; adm*), Assisi's well-preserved castle, built in 1174 and used by Corrado di Lutzen (who cared for the little orphan Emperor Frederick II), then afterwards destroyed and rebuilt on several occasions. It offers excellent views of Assisi and the countryside. From the Rocca you can visit more of Roman *Asisium* – the remains of the **amphitheatre** in the public gardens, and the **theatre** in Via del Torrione. The **Porta Perlici** near the amphitheatre dates from 1199, and there are some well-preserved 13th-century houses on Via del Comune Vecchio.

Basilica di Santa Chiara

Chiara Offreduccio (St Clare, 1194–1253) ran away from her wealthy and noble family at 17 to become a disciple of St Francis, and later head of the Franciscan Order for women, the Poor Clares. Gentle, humble and well-loved, she once had a vision of a Christmas service in the Basilica of St Francis while at the monastery of San Damiano, over a kilometre away, a feat that led Pope Pius XII in 1958 to declare her the patron saint of television. Her **basilica**, built in 1265, below Piazza del Comune (by way of Corso Mazzini), is a pink and white striped beauty with a lovely rose window, made memorable by the huge flying buttresses that support its outward side, masterpieces of medieval abstract art. The basilica was built on the site of old San Giorgio, where Francis attended school and where his body lay for two years before being moved to his own basilica on the other side of town.

The basilica was badly damaged by the earthquake, but the exterior is restored and the interior is due to reopen in the summer of 2001. The interior was decorated with fine frescoes by followers of Giotto, although many are now in fragments. The chapel on the right contains the famous *San Damiano Crucifix* that spoke to St Francis, commanding him to 'rebuild my church', while the adjacent chapel of the Holy Sacrament has fine Sienese frescoes; these two chapels were part of San Giorgio. By the altar, the portrait of St Clare, with scenes from her life, is by the Byzantine-ish 13th-century Maestro di Santa Chiara, while St Clare's body, darkened with age, lies like Sleeping Beauty in a crystal coffin in the neo-Gothic crypt.

From Santa Chiara, Via Sant'Agnese leads to the very simple church of **Santa Maria Maggiore**, built in 1163 on the site of a Temple of Apollo, traces of which are still visible in the crypt. Near here was discovered the **house of Sextus Propertius**, the Roman poet of love (46 BC–AD 14), complete with wall paintings, which may open to the public some fine day. Between here and the Piazzale Unità d'Italia, stroll along Via Cristofani and Via Fontebella, the latter adorned with wrought-iron dragons and another old fountain.

On the Outskirts of Assisi

The seminal events of Francis' life all took place in the countryside around Assisi. From Santa Chiara a gentle 2km walk leads down to **San Damiano** (*open summer daily 10–12.30 and 2–6; winter until 4.30*), a small, simple, asymmetrical church, where Francis heard the voice of the crucifix that changed his life and composed his masterful *Canticle of All Things Created*. He brought Clare here to live with her sisters in frugal contemplation.

Another Franciscan shrine, the peaceful **Eremo delle Carceri** (*open 6.30am–5pm, summer until 7.30pm*), lies along the scenic road up Monte Subasio, a pleasant walk or drive 4km east of Assisi. This was Francis' forest hermitage, where he would walk through the woods, and where he preached to the birds from a simple stone altar; here you can see his humble bed hollowed from the rock. The handful of Franciscans here live a traditional Franciscan existence, off the alms they receive.

Santa Maria degli Angeli, near the railway station, is a large unwieldy nutshell of a basilica built in 1569 to protect a sacred kernel – the tiny Porziuncola, an ancient chapel belonging to the Benedictines in the 6th century, where angels were wont to appear. The chapel was given by the Benedictines to St Francis in return for a yearly basket of carp from the Tescio river, still faithfully paid by the Franciscans, and St Francis founded his first friary here, the remains of which have been partially excavated under the high altar. Here St Clare took her vows of poverty as the spiritual daughter of Francis; here Francis died, 'naked on the bare earth', in the infirmary, now the **Cappella del Transito**, with a statue of St Francis by Andrea della Robbia.

The garden contains the roses that St Francis threw himself on while wrestling with temptation, staining their leaves red with blood, only to find that they lost their thorns on contact with his body. Still thornless, they bloom every May. Francis' cave has been covered with the frescoed Cappella del Roseto, and there's an old pharmacy and **museum** (*open Easter–Oct daily 9–12 and 2.30–4.30*), with a portrait of St Francis by an unknown 13th-century master, another sometimes attributed to Cimabue and a *Crucifix* by Giunta Pisano.

The big feast day in the basilica, the *Festa del Perdono*, was initiated by Francis after he had a vision of Christ at the Porziuncola, who asked what would be most helpful for the soul. Francis asked for forgiveness for any who crossed the threshold; and indulgences are still given out every 1st and 2nd August.

Towns Around Assisi: Bettona and Spello

There are a couple of pretty towns easily reached from Assisi. **Bettona**, a small hill town to the southwest, still retains a considerable portion of its Etruscan walls, and in

Where to Stay and Eat

Bettona ✉ 06084

Hotel S. Andrea, Via Caterina 2, **t** 075 987 114, **f** 075 986 9130 (*expensive–moderate*). A brand new offering to the hotel scene, adding a totally unexpected corner of contemporary style to sleepy Bettona. Situated in an old stone building which has been in turn a hospital, an *oratorio* and a *frantoio* – an oil press – the 19 rooms are beautifully furnished in simple good taste. There is a good restaurant, **Opera Prima** (*moderate*), which serves Umbrian dishes with the odd twist.

Spello ✉ 06038

****Palazzo Bocci, Via Cavour 17, **t** 0742 301 021, **f** 0742 301 464, *bocci@abitarelastoria.it* (*moderate*). Occupies an elegant, frescoed 17th-century building with beautiful rooms and a hanging garden; dining is *bello* and mellow in Spello under the vaulted ceiling at the hotel's restaurant **Il Molino**, **t** 0742 651 305, just opposite, in Piazza Matteotti – try the home-made pasta or traditional, utterly tender Umbrian meats cooked over the flames with a few glasses of Spello's own wines. *Closed Tues.*

***La Bastiglia, Via dei Molini, **t** 0742 651 277, **f** 0742 301 159 (*expensive–moderate*). Located in a charmingly restored mill, this stands out for its pleasant rooms, beautiful terrace, views and good restaurant.

***Altavilla, Via Mancinelli 2, **t** 0742 301 515, **f** 0742 651 258 (*moderate*). A pleasant terrace and 24 well-furnished rooms run by the Prioetti family.

Il Cacciatore, Via Giulia 42, **t 0742 651 141, **f** 0742 301 603 (*moderate*). Staying here saves you a walk to its very popular restaurant, with beautifully prepared home-made pasta and other dishes at decent prices. *Closed Mon.*

La Cantina, Via Cavour 2, **t** 0742 651 775 (*moderate*). The seasonal menu might feature *oca al sagrantino e castagne* (goose braised with chestnuts in Sagrantino wine), or *agnello al limone* (lamb cooked with lemon) or, in summer, lighter dishes such as fresh grilled trout. *Closed Wed.*

its stern Palazzo del Podestà a small **Museo Civico** (*open Mar–Oct daily 10.30–1 and 2–6, until later in July and Aug; Nov–Feb Tues–Sun 10.30–1 and 2.30–5, closed Mon; adm*), with two minor Peruginos, as well as works by Dono Doni and Andrea della Robbia. There is a small archaeological museum containing local finds (Etruscan onwards) in the same building (*currently closed*).

Rosy-tinted **Spello**, an outstanding medieval hill town towards Foligno, was the Roman *Hispellum* and still retains its republican-era main gate, the **Porta Consolare**. But Spello's special claims to fame are its frescoes by Pinturicchio (1501) in the Cappella Baglioni in the Romanesque church of **Santa Maria Maggiore** (*open daily summer 8.30–12.30 and 3–7, winter 8.30–12.30 and 3–6*), painted with the same brilliant palette that he used in Siena's Piccolomini Library; the *Annunciation* is especially lovely. Even the floor, made of Deruta majolica tiles, is bright and colourful. Pinturicchio also painted the altarpiece in **Sant'Andrea** (*open 3–6 and sometimes 8–12.30, depending on the priest*), up the street, a church that's also famous for its 13th-century Umbrian crucifix. Further up, there are excellent views from the **belvedere**, near the scant remains of the Roman acropolis and the medieval castle. Around Spello you'll find two other Roman gates in the walls: the **Porta Urbica**and the **Porta Venere**, a beautiful, almost perfectly preserved monumental gate from the time of Augustus, flanked by a pair of tall cylindrical towers, a relic even more remarkable than the famous Arco di Augusto in Perugia.

North of Perugia

The two main attractions north of Perugia are artsy Città di Castello and medieval Gubbio, the former linked by train with Perugia, the latter by bus. There is little worth stopping for in between – typical rural Umbrian countryside, low hills, tobacco fields and flocks of sheep.

Città di Castello

An ancient Umbrian town on the upper Tiber, Città di Castello is now one of Italy's major tobacco towns, though one that preserves its civic monuments from the 1300s (the **Palazzo del Podestà** and **Palazzo Comunale**, with a lofty vaulted hall). The part-Romanesque, part-Renaissance **Duomo** has a tilted Ravenna-style campanile, a Rosso Fiorentino, a 6th-century treasury and a lovely 12th-century silver altarpiece in its **museum** (*open Tues–Sun April–Sept 10–1 and 3–6, Oct–Mar 10.30–1 and 3–5.30; closed Mon; adm*). Another church, **San Domenico**, has ruined frescoes and a copy of Raphael's *Crucifixion* (the original is now in the National Gallery, London).

Città di Castello's best pictures, however, are in the **Pinacoteca** of the Palazzo Vitelli, Via della Cannoniera 22, a harmonious Renaissance palace by the younger Antonio da Sangallo, with exterior graffiti by Vasari. The gallery includes fine Renaissance works, with civic standards by Luca Signorelli and Raphael, Ghirlandaio, the della Robbia family and Ghiberti. The **Collezione Burri** (*open Mar–Oct Tues–Sat 9–12.30 and 2.30–6, Sun 9–1; Nov–Feb Tues–Sat 10.30–12.30 and 2.30–4.30; closed Mon; adm*), in the Palazzo Albizzini, has paintings by local 20th century painter Alberto Burri.

Gubbio

It's hard to think of any other Italian town as resolutely medieval as good grey Gubbio, the sombre stone 'City of Silence', with its orderly Roman street plan draped over the steep, lower slopes of Monte Ingino. As one of Umbria's most visited hill towns, its dark magic has become grist for the tourist mill, but you'd have to be very particular to think Gubbio is spoiled. Like many other towns in the area, it is a ceramics centre, inheriting the tradition if not the secrets of the 16th-century Mastro Giorgio, who discovered a beautiful ruby lustre to add to his majolica. Mastro Giorgio's secret died with him, but Gubbio's potters still make fine ware, black like that of the Etruscans, or in lovely muted colours.

Gubbio was an important town of the ancient Umbrii, known as *Eugubium*. Long an independent *comune*, it was plagued in the Middle Ages by wolves, one of which in particular terrorized the populace. St Francis heard of it and, ignoring the towns-people's pleas for his safety, went out and had a word with it, brought it to the town, and made a public agreement that in exchange for regular meals it would stop preying on Gubbio, an agreement sealed with a shake of the paw. The wolf kept its part of the bargain, and is immortalized in a bas-relief over the door of a little church in Via Mastro Giorgio. Gubbio was captured by Urbino in 1384, and from that time on its fortunes followed those of the Marches. It has retained two exceedingly medieval

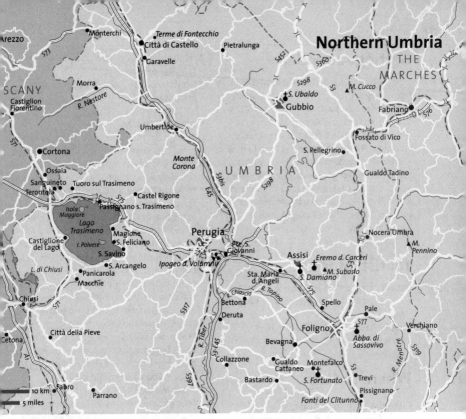

festivals, however, which fill the solemn streets with colour and exuberance, most tumultuously the festival of the *Ceri* on 15 May in honour of San Ubaldo, Gubbio's patron, who persuaded Frederick Barbarossa not to attack the town in 1155; the *festa* itself is first documented a couple of years later, although it may have borrowed something from a lost pagan rite. The *ceri* (or 'candles') are tall, wooden, phallic towers, each topped by a wax saint representing a clan – San Ubaldo, San Giorgio and Sant'Antonio Abate. The *ceri* are baptized with a jug of water, and then carried on supports by teams of 10 men. The climax of the day comes when the teams race pell-mell through the crowds up to the mountaintop church of San Ubaldo, a steep race that San Ubaldo invariably wins. On the last Sunday in May, crossbowmen from Sansepolcro come to compete in the *Palio dei Balestrieri*, a contest dating back to 1461.

Some of Gubbio's churches remain closed since the earthquake, though damage was relatively minor compared to the one in 1982, which left 1,500 people homeless.

Gubbio, from the Bottom Up

Approaching Gubbio from the west, the first thing you see is the large, well-preserved 1st-century AD **Roman theatre**, used these days for summer performances of classical plays and Shakespeare. Lower Gubbio proper is entered by way of green **Piazza dei Quaranta Martiri**, named in memory of the 40 citizens executed on this spot by the Nazis in reprisals for partisan activities in the vicinity. To the right, the church of **San Francesco** has a fine triple apse and some good, though damaged,

Getting Around

Città di Castello is on the FCU local **rail** line from Perugia. There are no trains to Gubbio, but some 10 **buses** a day along the beautiful SS298 from Perugia, stopping at the Piazza Quaranta Martiri in Gubbio, where schedules are posted. There are also buses from here to Fossato di Vico, 20km south, the closest train station on the Foligno–Ancona line to Rome, and to Città di Castello, Arezzo, Florence and Rome. There is a **bus and train information office** in Gubbio: Via della Repubblica 13, t 075 922 0066.

Tourist Information

Città di Castello: Via Sant'Antonio 1, t 075 855 4817, f 075 855 2100, or Piazza Fanti, t 075 855 4922, f 075 855 2100.
Gubbio: Piazza Oderisi, t 075 922 0693, f 075 927 3409.

Where to Stay

Città di Castello ✉ 06012

★★★★**Tiferno**, Piazza R. Sanzio 13, t 075 855 0331, f 075 852 1196 (*expensive*). The best place to stay and dine in central Città di Castello, a 17th-century palace with good comfortable rooms and one of the best restaurants in the area, with dishes like *ravioli* with shrimp in orange sauce, or pigeon with white grapes – not perhaps for everyone.
★★★**Hotel delle Terme**, at Fontecchio, t 075 852 0614, f 075 855 7236 (*cheap*). A large hotel and a pleasant place to stay, even if you don't take advantage of the thermal treatments on offer and make do with the fine open-air pool.
There are other cheaper choices in the town itself; all good, clean, if uninspiring hotels.

★★**Europa**, Via V.E. Orlando 2, t 075 855 0551, f 075 852 0765.
★★**Umbria**, Via dei Galanti, t 075 855 4925, f 075 852 0911.

Gubbio ✉ 06024

Though not yet in the same league as Assisi, Gubbio gets its fair share of visitors. Reservations are essential in July and August; to avoid disappointment.
★★★★**Relais Ducale**, Via Galeotti, t 075 922 0157, f 075 922 0159 (*expensive*). Recently opened in the heart of medieval Gubbio, occupying three historic buildings, linked by a lift. All are sumptuously furnished with antiques.
★★★★**Park Hotel ai Cappuccini**, Via Tifernate, t 075 9234, f 075 922 0323 (*expensive*). A beautifully restored, award-winning Franciscan monastery, 3km out of town, set in its own grounds with a cloister and chapel, a pool and sauna inside.
★★★**Bosone**, Via XX Settembre 22, t 075 922 0688, f 075 922 0552 (*moderate*). Located in a picturesque old *palazzo* just off Piazza Grande. Rooms are comfortable.
★★★**San Marco**, Via Perugina 5, t 075 922 0234, f 075 927 3716 (*moderate*). Modern comforts in a former convent, with a pretty garden terrace. All rooms have bath.
★★★**Gattapone**, Via G. Ansidei 6, t 075 927 2489, f 075 927 1269 (*moderate*). Another pleasant locale in the medieval centre, which has just been given a facelift.
★★★**Beniamino Ubaldi**, Via Perugina 74, t 075 927 7773, f 075 927 6604 (*moderate*). Recently upscaled, this occupies a seminarians' college just outside the walls; and yes, it has a bar (and restaurant, too).
★★**Dei Consoli**, Via dei Consoli 59, t 075 927 3335 (*cheap*). Small and simple, excellently located near Piazza Grande. It has a good restaurant in a medieval cellar, with tasty *spiedini* (meat on a spit).

frescoes, especially the 15th-century series on the Madonna in the left apse by Gubbio's own Ottaviano Nelli. Lining the other side of the piazza is the **Loggia deiTiratoio**, or Weavers' Loggia, a 14th-century arcade under which newly woven textiles could be stretched to shrink evenly – one of the few such loggias to survive.

From the piazza, picturesque medieval lanes line the banks of the rushing Camignano. Many of the houses and modest *palazzi* date back to the 13th century,

*Galletti, Via Ambrogio Piccardi 1, overlooking the river, **t** 075 927 7753 (*cheap*). Simple rooms, some with bath. The restaurant, which serves roast duck and lamb, has outdoor tables in a pretty setting.

Eating Out

Città di Castello

Città di Castello is one place in Umbria where you can find good bread, especially the *pane nociato*, with walnuts.

Il Bersaglio, Via V.E. Orlando 14, **t** 075 855 5534 (*moderate*). Just outside the city walls, offering a wealth of pasta dishes, well-prepared meat and game and especially good truffles and wild mushrooms, many of them gathered by the restaurant owner himself, Luigi Manfroni; try the local Colli Altotiberini wines. *Closed Wed.*

Amici Miei, Via del Monte 2, **t** 075 855 9904 (*cheap*). Incredible value for wonderful home cooking using fresh, seasonal ingredients: *strangozzi* with goose sauce, calves' kidneys, roast lamb and duck. *Closed Wed.*

SS Adriatica, Fraccano, on the SS257, **t** 075 855 3870. A 10km drive to this village east of Città di Castello will take you to a small restaurant of the kind fast disappearing from Italy: choose from a limited but excellent menu of the day – usually a good pasta dish followed by meat grilled over the fire in front of you – and have a pleasant surprise when it comes to the bill.

Gubbio

Gubbio has no good wines, but there are local herbal poisons like Amaro Iguvium and Liquore Ingeno to top off a meal.

Taverna del Lupo, Via Ansidei 21a, **t** 075 927 4368 (*expensive*). With a name recalling the legend of St Francis, in an atmospheric

medieval setting, this serves excellent, traditional fare such as boar sausage, game in the autumn, and *risotto ai tartufi* (Gubbio, like Piedmont, is a land of white truffles, which are even more expensive than the black truffles of the Valnerina in southern Umbria), as well as delicious pasta dishes like lasagne with *prosciutto* and truffles and *frico*, a local speciality of mixed meats with cress. *Closed Mon.*

Fornace di Mastro Giorgio, Via della Fornace di Mastro Giorgio, **t** 075 922 1836 (*expensive*). Another local classic in the workshop where the master ceramicist once created his famous ruby glaze. Happily, the new management seems determined to continue the fine work of their predecessors, including some of Umbria's more esoteric specialities on their unusual menu. *Closed Tues.*

Funivia, on Monte Ingino, **t** 075 922 1259 (*moderate*). On a clear day, this provides an exceptional dining experience, offering fabulous views as well as delicious pasta with truffles or *porcini* mushrooms, and tasty *secondi* like grilled lamb or stuffed pigeon. Good desserts and local wines. *Closed Wed.*

La Balestra, Via della Repubblica 41, **t** 075 927 3810 (*moderate*). Features unusual *antipasti* (*aringa*), dishes like *fondutina con tartufo*, home-made pasta and a good selection of meats. *Closed Tues.*

S. Francesco e il Lupo, Via Cairoli 24, **t** 075 927 2344 (*moderate*). Local products, *porcini* mushrooms, and truffles are on offer, or you can just order pizza. *Closed Tues.*

Bargello, Via dei Consoli 37, Largo Bargello, **t** 075 927 3724 (*moderate*). Also offers pizza as well as *polenta* (quite popular in this corner of Umbria), *agnolotti*, *agnello scotta-dito* ('burn-your-fingers lamb') and other grilled meats. *Closed Mon.*

here and there adorned with carved doors or windows, or an extra door called the *Porta del Morto*, used solely to remove the dead. The main street, Via dei Consoli, passes by one of Gubbio's finest buildings, the 14th-century **bargello**, the police station and governor's office; its fountain used to be Gubbio's main water source. Further up, the street widens to form magnificent **Piazza della Signoria**, its belvedere hovering over a steep drop and a stunning view of the town below.

The king of the piazza is the beautiful **Palazzo dei Consoli**, a lofty, graceful 14th-century town hall attributed to Gubbio's best architect, Gattapone. Supported on the hill by a mighty substructure of arches, the *palazzo* is graced with an elegant loggia, a slender campanile, Guelph crenellations, and asymmetrically arranged windows and arches. Inside are two museums: the **Museo Archeologico**, with an Etruscan and Roman collection, and the **Museo Civico** (*both museums open April–Sept daily 10–1 and 3–6; Oct–Mar daily 10–1 and 2–5; closed 14–15 May, 25 Dec and 1 Jan; adm*), with archaeological odds and ends and a unique treasure, the bronze Eugubian Tablets, discovered in the 15th century near the Roman theatre. These are the only extant records ever found in the Umbrian language, five written in Etruscan characters, the other two in Latin letters – they concern priestly rites and auguries. A stiff climb up the stairs leads to the gallery, with some of Gubbio's ceramics and a collection of art spanning the centuries. Most memorable, however, is the grand view from the loggia.

Further up stands Gubbio's simple **Duomo**, built in the 13th century and most notable for the pattern of its stone vaulting and its 12th-century stained-glass windows. Local talent is well represented in the side chapels, and in the presbytery there's a *Nativity* attributed to Pinturicchio's talented student Eusebio di San Giorgio. The high altar is a Roman sarcophagus. Opposite, the **Palazzo Ducale** (*open Mon–Sat 9–7, Sun and hols 9–1; closed 1st Mon of month; adm*) was designed for Federico da Montefeltro by Luciano Laurana, as a more compact version of the ducal palace in Urbino. The courtyard is well worth a look.

From the Duomo you can make the stiff climb up Monte Ingino to the sanctuary of **San Ubaldo**, but it's much easier to take the funicular (*open winter 10–1 and 2.30–5; summer 8.30–7.30*) up from the Porta Romana on the southeast side of town. In San Ubaldo you can examine the three *ceri*, and see that it's no wonder that the Gubbites need a considerable amount of Dutch courage to run up the mountain lugging these towers on their shoulders. There's a café where you can while away the afternoon, or you can walk further up for even more spectacular views from the **Rocca** (2,913ft).

Two churches near Porta Romana and the lower funicular station contain some of the finest works by Gubbio's Ottaviano Nelli. In **Santa Maria Nuova** is the lovely and joyous *Madonna del Belvedere*, Nelli's masterpiece, from 1403 (*to visit, enquire at Palazzo Ducale, t 075 927 5872*). The 13th-century **Sant'Agostino**, just outside the gate, has some fine frescoes by Nelli and his students in the apse.

Via Flaminia: Gualdo Tadino to Spoleto

Whether you're travelling by car, bus or train, the eastern Umbrian towns along the ancient Via Flaminia (SS3) offer both lovely scenery and monuments, including some unexpected artistic treasures. Admittedly most people don't know about Foligno's cosmic billiard table, but many have heard of Spoleto's renowned **Two Worlds Festival**, the concept of which has given birth to a twin Spoleto festival in Charleston, North Carolina. Spoleto is also one of Umbria's loveliest hill towns, while Nocera Umbra, Trevi, Montefalco and Clitunno are small but worthy destinations in between.

Gualdo Tadino and Nocera Umbra

Gualdo Tadino is a lofty little town where the Byzantine eunuch general Narses defeated the Goths in 552, a battle essential in preserving the Marches for the Eastern Church. It has a handful of good paintings in its **Pinacoteca**, housed in the church of San Francesco; some are by 15th-century native Matteo da Gualdo. From Gualdo the road descends the Valle del Topino (Little Mouse Valley) to **Nocera Umbra**, famous for its sparkling mineral water. It was at the epicentre of the 1997–8 earthquakes, and it's still a mess – virtually a ghost town. The *centro storico* is cordoned off with access only during the day. Inside the barrier, every other building seems to be propped up with heavy scaffolding or steel girders. Some 6,000 people, as well as offices and banks, have been accommodated in containers and prefab housing. The surrounding hills are dotted with cranes and abandoned buildings. Reconstruction is slow.

Foligno

Foligno is an ancient and important town, the Roman *Fulginia*, and it was one of the earliest printing centres in Italy, producing the first book in Italian (Dante's *Divina Commedia*) in 1470. But the 20th century was rough on Foligno – it was bombed to smithereens in the war, although some of the old quarter survived, especially the central Piazza della Repubblica. This in turn was walloped in Sepember 1997 when Foligno, the centre of the cosmos, became the epicentre of the quake.

The 14th-century Palazzo dei Signori, the Trinci, is now a **Pinacoteca** (*open Tues–Sun 10–7; adm*); in the chapel you can see more works by Gubbio's Ottaviano Nelli. The nearby **Duomo** has retained an impressive south front of 1201, which rates as one of the most unorthodox in Italy: among the zodiac, monsters and medieval bestiary is a portrait of Emperor Frederick II, arch enemy of the popes, and even a little Islamic star and crescent. The oldest thing in Foligno is the Romanesque **Santa Maria Infraportas**, with 12th-century frescoes in the Byzantine style.

More interesting than Foligno itself are the sites that surround it, all linked to the city by bus, with the exception of the 13th-century **Abbazia di Sassovivo** (*under restoration, but it is possible to visit by arrangement, t 0742 350 473*) an hour's walk to the east, with its serene cloister. This area was hit especially hard by the quake: while collapsed buildings have been cleared, scaffolding and cranes are still everywhere. Southwest lie three charming hill towns: **Bevagna**, with two Romanesque churches, San Silvestro (*open 9.30–12 and 3–7*) and San Michele Arcangelo (*closed*); tiny medieval **Gualdo Cattaneo** and the old town of **Montefalco**, called the 'Balcony Rail (*Ringhiera*) of Umbria' because of its lofty, commanding position. The pride of Montefalco is its rich 15th-century fresco cycle on the *Life of St Francis* by Benozzo Gozzoli, painted in the apse of the church-museum of **San Francesco** (*open 10.30–1 and 2–6*). Above the church the attractive, round **Piazza della Repubblica** affords excellent views of the countryside, especially from the tower of the Palazzo Comunale. Most of Montefalco's other churches contain good frescoes as well, especially **Sant'Agostino**, near the frescoed main gate **Porta Sant'Agostino**, and **San Fortunato**, beyond the Porta Spoleto, which boasts a few Gozzolis of its own.

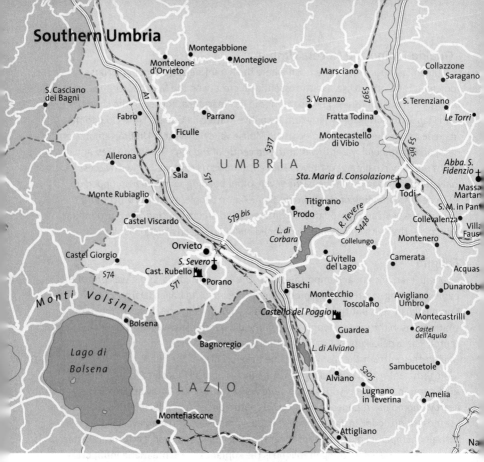

Trevi, just on the eastern side of the main road, is another charming hill town, wrapped in olive groves that produce Umbria's rich green oil (buses link the train station with the town up above). Its name, like that of the famous fountain in Rome, derived from *Tre Via*, or Three Roads. Its tight, narrow streets contain some good medieval buildings while just south is the 15th-century church of **Madonna delle Lacrime**, sheltering a good *Adoration of the Magi* by a sceptical 76-year-old Perugino. In town, the Palazzo Lucarini now hosts the **Trevi Flash Art Museum** (*open Wed–Sun 10–1 and 3–6, for exhibitions only – call t 0742 381 818 for details; adm*), a joint endeavour of *Flash Art* magazine and the *comune*, offering a permanent collection of contemporary Umbrian, Italian and foreign artists, as well as changing exhibitions. The convent of the church of San Francesco is the new home of the **Museo Civico** (*open April, May and Sept Tues–Sun 10.30–1 and 2–6; June and July Tues–Sun 10.30–1 and 3.30–7; Aug Tues–Sun 10–1 and 3–7.30; Oct–Mar Fri–Sun only 10–1 and 2.30–5; closed Mon; adm*) and its paintings: a *Madonna* by Pinturicchio (a copy of the one in London's National Gallery), a *Deposition* by the school of Sodoma, and a fine *Incoronazione di Maria* by Spagna.

Further south, just off the Via Flaminia, the **Fonti di Clitunno** (*open 9–12 and 2–dusk*), ancient *Clitumnus*, is famous for its snow-cold clear spring and pool. The ancient

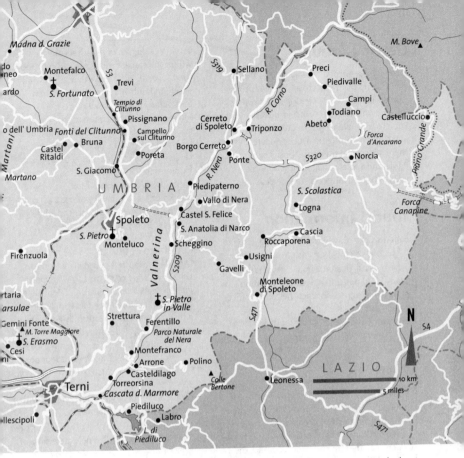

Romans built villas on the surrounding hillside, and bred pure white oxen on its dark green banks. The Roman villas and temples that once stood here are long gone, but bits of them were reassembled in a mysterious little building called the **Tempietto del Clitunno** (*open summer Tues–Sun 9–8; winter Tues–Sun 9–2; closed Mon*). Two centuries ago, this was believed to be a pagan temple converted to Christian use; Goethe dissented, believing it to be an original Christian work. For once this most misinformed of all geniuses got it right. The most recent studies put the Tempietto somewhere in the 6th century, or even as late as the 8th, making this obscure, lovely building in a way the last work of classical antiquity, Christian enough, but an architectural throwback to a world that was already lost.

Spoleto

Set among thickly wooded hills, ancient Spoleto is one of the most attractive towns in Italy, one that provides, in its numerous well-preserved monuments, a nearly complete history of the peninsula. At night, when its chief landmarks are illuminated and the city lights twinkle, it becomes a magical place, a setting fit for the dynamic

Getting Around

The Rome–Ancona **railway** follows the Via Flaminia up from Spoleto all the way up to Gualdo Tadino, before veering east towards Jesi and Ancona. There are also **buses** linking Spoleto to Gualdo Perugia, Città di Castello and Gubbio. During the Due Mondi festival, there are special trains and buses between Rome and Spoleto to accommodate the crowds of festival-goers from the capital.

Tourist Information

Foligno: Corso Cavour 126, t 0742 354 459/349 854, f 0742 340 545, *www.umbria2000.it*.

As in Assisi, the earthquake devastation left many buildings unstable and restoration may still be in progress; contact the tourist office to find out the latest details.

Spoleto: Piazza della Libertà 7, t 0743 220 311, f 0743 46241.

Festivals

Spoleto's Festival of Two Worlds: *held over 3 weeks between mid-June and mid-July.* Italy's leading arts festival, dreamed up 50 years ago by Giancarlo Menotti; a veritable feast of music, theatre and dance. Contact the Associazione Festival dei Due Mondi, Piazza del Duomo, t 0743 45028, f 0743 220 321, *www.spoletofestival.net* for information, programmes and tickets.

Where to Stay and Eat

Foligno ✉ 06034

★★★Villa Roncalli, just south of the centre on Viale Roma 25, t 0742 391 091, f 0742 391 001 (*moderate*). A fashionable 17th-century villa hotel with a shady garden and pool and the city's finest restaurant (*expensive*) serving Umbrian dishes with a gourmet flair. *Closed Mon and 2 weeks in Aug.*

★★Belvedere, Via Ottaviani 19, t 0742 353 990, f 0742 356 243 (*moderate*). Near the station, family-run with pleasant rooms.

Osteria del Teatro, Via Petrucci 8, t 0742 350 745 (*expensive*). A delightful restaurant with

vaulted ceiling, theatre posters and a garden where you can eat courgette fritters, deep-fried sage, *ravioli* filled with pumpkin and excellent lamb and beef (the *tagliata* is particularly good). *Closed Wed.*

Da Remo, Via Filzi 10, t 0742 340 522 (*moderate*). A Liberty-style villa which has been a classic for the past four generations, serving *strangozzi* (fat spaghetti) and roast kid simmered in Montefalco's Sagrantino wine. *Closed Sun eve and Mon.*

Bacco Felice, Via Garibaldi 73, t 0742 341 019. A cosy place where wine lovers can while away an evening over bottles and cheeses.

Montefalco ✉ 06036

★★★★Villa Pambuffetti, Via della Vittoria 20, t 0742 378 823, f 0742 379 245, *villabianca@ interbusiness.it* (*expensive*). A delightful 19th-century villa owned by a local noble family who now run it as a beautifully kept inn, with 15 rooms, all decorated differently, some with family antiques. The villa is in a lovely park with huge trees and an outdoor pool.

★★Ringhiera Umbra, Corso G. Mameli, t/f 0742 379 166 (*cheap*). A cheaper but comfortable choice just under Piazza del Comune, with a good restaurant (*moderate*).

Montefalco is perhaps best known for its red wines, *Sagrantino* – with a delicate aroma of blackberries – and *Rosso di Montefalco*.

Coccorone, off the central square at Vicolo Fabbri, t 0742 379 535 (*cheap*). An elegant, understated place with tempting crêpes and *tagliatelle al tartufo* as a starter and *faraona ai salmi* (braised woodcock) and grilled pigeon as main dishes. *Closed Wed.*

Il Falisco, Via XX Settembre 14, t 0742 379 185 (*cheap*). Offers local specialities such as *filetto al sagrantino*, beef fillet cooked in Sagrantino wine. *Closed Mon.*

Trevi ✉ 06039

★★Del Pescatore, Via Chiesa Tonda 50, t/f 0742 381 711 (*cheap*). A good peaceful *pensione*, with nine pleasant rooms, near a babbling brook. Downstairs, the excellent **Taverna del Pescatore**, t 0742 780 920 (*moderate*), is run by another branch of the same family, with an imaginative menu based on meat or fish, both very good value and beautifully prepared. *Closed Wed.*

**Il Terziere, Via Salerno 1, t 0742 78359 (*moderate*). Good views and dinners .

Clitunno ✉ 06042

Clitunno is a quiet alternative to Spoleto if you've come for the festival.

***Il Vecchio Molino, Via del Tempio 34, Località Pissignano, t 0743 521 122, f 0743 275 097 (*expensive*). It may be close to the road, but don't be put off: once inside the 'Old Mill' the sounds are of gurgling water; two streams run through the garden.

**Fontanelle, Via d'Elci 1, t 0743 521 091, f 0743 275 052 (*moderate*). A hotel and restaurant surrounded by refreshing greenery. The restaurant serves Umbrian specialities like country *prosciutto*, *strangozzi* , and platters of tender lamb, chicken and pigeon.

**Ravale, Via Virgilio, Fonti del Clitunno, t 0743 521 320 (*moderate*). Simple rooms, and a modest *ristorante-pizzeria* (*also moderate*).

Spoleto ✉ 06049

During the festival accommodation is tight in Spoleto and the area from Foligno to Terni, so reserve months in advance. The tourist office in Spoleto has a list of private rooms to rent, but again, book ahead.

****Gattapone, Via del Ponte 6, t 0743 223 447, f 0743 223 448 (*expensive*). In a stone house, clinging to the slope near the Rocca and the Ponte delle Torri, with fabulous views; even during the festival rush this 'bijou' hotel remains serene.

****Albornoz Palace, Viale Matteotti, t 0743 221 221, f 0743 221 600, *info@albornoz-palace.com* (*expensive*). Refined and stylish, with a pool, just outside the historic centre, near Piazza della Libertà.

****Dei Duchi, Viale Matteotti 4, t 0743 44541, f 0743 44543 (*expensive*). An attractive modern hotel, popular with performers.

***Charleston, Piazza Collicola 10, t 0743 220 052, f 0743 221 244 (*moderate*). In a pretty 17th-century *palazzo*, with 18 comfortably furnished rooms in the *centro storico*.

***Clarici, Piazza della Vittoria 32, t 0743 223 311, f 0743 222 010 (*moderate*). More modern, in the lower part of town, but still decorated with taste and style.

**Dell'Angelo, Via Arco di Druso 25, t/f 0743 222 385 (*cheap*). Central, seven double rooms.

**Il Panciolle, Via Duomo 4, t 0743 45677 (*cheap*). Worth bearing in mind for its good restaurant (*moderate*) where meat is grilled over an open fire. *Closed Wed.*

La Macchia, Loc. Licina 11, t/f 0743 49059 (*cheap*). A quiet hotel just north of the town centre off the Via Flaminia. . The style is modern, but the furniture in the 12 bedrooms is made by local craftsmen. The restaurant specializes in the local *cucina spoletana*, and there's a nice garden.

Tartufo, Piazza Garibaldi 24, t 0743 40236 (*expensive*). The black diamonds of the Valnerina (*tartufi*) appear in various forms with pasta or eggs; other dishes include grilled lamb, kid and veal. Prices depend on indulgence. *Closed Sun eve and Mon.*

Apollinare, Via S. Agata 14, t 0743 223 256 (*expensive*). These romantic dining rooms are housed in a 12th-century Franciscan convent, with a few rooms too; its former occupants wouldn't recognize the elaborate concoctions that emerge from the kitchen. *Closed Tues.*

Pentagramma, Via Martani 4, t 0743 223 141 (*moderate*). A warm and welcoming place near Piazza della Libertà in a former stable, and a favourite festival rendezvous. It is owned by the daughter of Arturo Toscanini, and serves local dishes: *garbanzo* soup, *strangozzi di Spoleto* (pasta with olive oil, garlic, tomato and basil), truffles, lamb and trout. *Closed Mon and part of July and Aug.*

Trattoria Pecchiarda, Vicolo San Giovanni, t 0743 221 009 (*moderate*). Tucked off Via Porta Fuga, this place serves delicous dishes prepared with olive oil from the owner's grove, served with his own white or red Colli Spoletini wine. *Closed Thurs exc in summer.*

Monteluco ✉ 06049

***Paradiso, t 0743 223 427, f 0743 223 082 (*moderate*). A garden, great views, and peace and quiet.

***Michelanglo, t 0743 47890, f 0743 40289 (*moderate*). Large rooms and very friendly staff, near the top of town. *Open April–Oct.*

**Ferretti, t 0743 49849, f 0743 222 344 (*cheap; rooms with bath may be moderate*). A *pensione* with plenty of charm; some rooms have balconies looking out on to the pretty tree-shaded piazza.

Festival dei Due Mondi (Two Worlds Festival), founded by composer Gian Carlo Menotti and the late Thomas Schippers in 1958, and now Italy's most important performing arts festival. The annual influx of international culture has left a mark on this once drowsy hill town: monuments have been restored, art galleries and trendy shops line the medieval streets, and prices, during the three weeks of the festival (some time between mid-June and mid-July) get knocked way out of line.

Ancient Umbrian *Spoletium* was settled by the Romans in 242 BC, a few decades before an over-confident Hannibal came knocking at the gates, expecting an easy victory after his rout at Lake Trasimeno. But *Spoletium* held firm and repulsed him, and Hannibal, who intended to move on to Rome from there, took his elephants to graze in the Marches instead. The Goths under Totila wrecked the city, while the Lombards, slowly piecing it back together, made it a powerful duchy, so powerful that in 890 Duke Guido III made an armed play for the imperial crown against the heirs of Charlemagne; later the duchy became a fief of Countess Matilda of Tuscany, the Guelphiest of Guelphs, and in the 13th century it was incorporated into the Papal States. In 1499 it was ruled by Lucrezia Borgia, a 19-year-old recently married to the second of her three husbands by her intriguing father. By all accounts Lucrezia did well, but was sent off two years later to marry Alfonso d'Este of Ferrara.

If you arrive in Spoleto by train you are greeted, not by an Umbrian hill town, but by a huge iron sculpture by Alexander Calder, a relic of the 1962 festival now used to shade a taxi stand. Buses every 10 minutes link the station to central **Piazza della Libertà**, with the tourist office and the nearby **Roman theatre**, some 380ft in diameter, built in the 1st century AD and restored for festival performances. The stage structure was removed in the Middle Ages and replaced by the pleasant Convent of Sant'Agata, which now houses Spoleto's **archaeological museum** (*theatre and museum open daily 9–7; closed 1 Dec, 1 Jan and 1 May; adm*), with inscriptions and architectural fragments, and busts of Julius Caesar, Augustus and other distinguished Romans. More Roman memories are nearby, beyond the Piazza Fontana: the **Arco di Druso**, built in the year AD 23 to celebrate a victory over the barbarians. This once marked the entrance to the Roman forum, now Piazza del Mercato, but before you get there take the steps down to the 12th-century **Crypt of San Isacco**, with its curiously primitive frescoes. The church above, **Sant'Ansano**, was built into a Roman temple, remains of which may be seen near the altar. In Piazza del Mercato the landmark is an 18th-century fountain by Carlo Fiaschetti.

The next square, pretty Piazza Municipio, contains a **Roman house** believed to have once been the address of Emperor Vespasian's mother, with an atrium, bedrooms and baths, some with surviving mosaics. The house can be visited, as can the **Pinacoteca** in the nearby Palazzo Comunale (*open Tues–Sun 10–1 and 3–6; adm*), with works by native son Giovanni di Pietro (known as Lo Spagna), L'Alunno and other Umbriani.

The Rocca and Ponte delle Torri

From the Piazza del Municipio, Via Saffi climbs up to the Piazza Campello, with a 17th-century fountain called the **Mascherone** after its grotesque face. Above this looms the **Rocca**, the impressive six-towered castle built by Gattapone for the 14th-century papal legate, Cardinal Albornoz. It is built of third-hand stone, first used in the Roman amphitheatre and later cannibalized by the Goth supremo Totila for his own fortress.

The Rocca was a popular papal resort frequented by Julius II, accompanied on occasion by Michelangelo who loved the peace of the surrounding hills. Until 1983 it was used as a prison; now that its long restoration is nearing completion, there are plans to install a museum dedicated to the Duchy of Spoleto, a lab for the restoration of books and art, an exhibition and conference area and an open-air theatre.

For now, the best thing to do is stroll along the garden walk that encircles the Rocca, with great views of Spoleto below. The **Porta della Rocca** leads down to Master Gattapone's masterpiece, and one of the great engineering works of the trecento, the **Ponte delle Torri**, a bridge and aqueduct of 10 towering arches linking Spoleto with the slopes of Monteluco, spanning a 260ft ravine and the Tessino river far below. Gattapone built the bridge on a Roman foundation; it leads to the towers that gave it its name, and to the road for San Pietro and San Francesco (*see* below).

Sant'Eufemia and the Duomo

Below the Rocca on Via Saffi stands the pure and lovely 12th-century **Sant'Eufemia** (*open 8–12.30 and 2.30–6; in summer till 8*), with a dignified façade and beautiful Romanesque interior of ancient capitals and columns, a *matroneum* (women's gallery) and picturesque vaults. Next door is the dramatic **Via dell'Arringo**, a grand stairway descending to **Piazza del Duomo**, which must have been what sold Menotti on Spoleto when he travelled about, seeking a venue for the Two Worlds Festival: it doubles perfectly as an outdoor auditorium for concerts, with the cathedral and Umbrian hills as a backdrop. Thomas Schippers, co-founder of the festival, was so fond of the concerts and piazza that he asked to be buried here when he died, in 1977.

The elegant **Duomo** (*open Mar–Oct daily 7.30–12.30 and 3–6; Nov–Feb daily 7.30–12.30 and 3–5*) was consecrated in 1198 by the most powerful of medieval popes, Innocent III, having been rebuilt after Emperor Frederick Barbarossa – the greatest of papal enemies – had razed its predecessor. It has several unusual features: four rose windows and four circular emblems of the Evangelists of varying sizes, like buttons, adorn its horizontally divided façade, surrounding a gold-ground Byzantine-style mosaic of 1207. Its campanile is built out of Roman odds and ends, and very un-Italian flying buttresses help to hold it up.

Although the interior was unfortunately re-done in the 17th century, it contains several treasures, most piously the 12th century *Santissimo Icone*, with a picture of the Madonna, brought to Spoleto from Constantinople. Pinturicchio painted the frescoes in the first chapel, the Eroli, and the apse contains lovely frescoes on the *Life of the Virgin* by Fra Filippo Lippi, who portrayed himself among the mourners in the scene of the Virgin's death. The fun-loving monk from Florence died in Spoleto while working on the project, and it was finished by his chief helper, Fra Diamanti; when Lorenzo de' Medici asked that Lippi's body be returned to Florence, the Spoletini refused, and Lorenzo had to be content with ordering a fine Florentine tomb for him, now in the right transept.

Lower Spoleto

On the opposite side of town (Via del Duomo to Via Filitteria) there's another grand theatre, the **Teatro Nuovo**, used both for the festival and for the even older September Festival of Experimental Opera. Nearby, the colourful church of **San Domenico** was built in the 1200s, and contains some interesting if fragmentary frescoes. From San Domenico walk down to the tall-towered 13th-century **Porta Fuga**, and then along Via Cecili, where you can take in an excellent stretch of Spoleto's **walls**, an intriguing record of the town's history, beginning at their 6th-century BC 'Cyclopean' base of huge polygonal rough blocks built by the ancient Umbrii, and going all the way up to the 15th-century additions on the top.

The street ends at Piazza Cairoli; from here Via dell'Anfiteatro descends past the ruined **amphitheatre**, now part of a barracks, to Piazza Garibaldi, with the fine 12th-century church of **San Gregorio** and the Roman **Ponte Sanguinario** ('bloody bridge'), supposedly named after the Christians martyred in the amphitheatre. From the bridge, signs point the way to the cemetery church of **San Salvatore**, a 15-minute walk. Built in the 4th century, it has an unusual façade, and preserves much of its original vertical lines and simplicity despite subsequent rebuildings. The elegant, fluted Corinthian columns in the interior were incorporated from a Roman temple.

Monteluco

Beautiful, forested Monteluco is Spoleto's holy mountain, lying just to the east of town, connected by bus from the Piazza della Libertà, or by walking from the Ponte delle Torri. If you're walking, take the right-hand fork for the Romanesque church of **San Pietro**, only a few minutes away, with a romp of a façade dating back to the dukes of Spoleto. If you've visited the medieval cathedrals of the north you'll recognize the animals, real and imaginary, that the Lombards delighted in portraying: here is a fox playing dead to capture some too-curious chickens, battles with lions, oxen, eagles, a wolf in monk's clothing, and the rest.

The other (left) fork in the road demands vigorous walking through holm oak forests to reach the 12th-century church of **San Giuliano** (*key at the restaurant next door*), with a façade incorporating some 6th-century elements of its predecessor. Anchorites and hermits, refugees from the wars in the Holy Land, settled here in the 7th century; in the 13th century St Francis and San Bernardino of Siena came to meditate here, and St Francis founded the tiny monastery of **San Francesco** near Monteluco's summit, a serene spot enjoying a lovely view of the surrounding countryside. Monteluco now has more summer villas and hotels than hermitages, but it's still a cool and tranquil place to spend an afternoon, and a good place to look for accommodation.

The Valnerina

The Nera, one of the main tributaries of the Tiber, flows from the mighty Monti Sibillini along the southern edge of Umbria. Many of its sights are still Italian secrets; its black truffles, waterfalls and saints enjoy a national reputation, but the rest is touristically *terra incognita*.

Norcia and Cascia

Little Norcia gave the world St Benedict (480–543), the father of monasticism, and his twin sister St Scolastica. It has also been known at times for witches, barber surgeons (who, in the 16th century, were the only ones capable of properly castrating a boy with operatic potential), cheeses and boar hams (in Umbria, a *norcineria* is a cheese and ham shop). An ancient place, mentioned by Virgil, it looks more Spanish than Italian, and, although earthquakes have slapped it around, old Norcia survives around central Piazza San Benedetto. It has a stern statue of St Benedict for a centrepiece, the 14th-century church of **San Benedetto**, built over the late-Roman house where the famous twins were born, and the handsome **Palazzo Comunale**, with a 13th-century campanile, next door to all shops decked with bristling hams. The other side of the square is occupied by the **castle**, designed in 1554 by Vignola for Pope Julius III, now housing a modest museum of Umbrian art.

Eighteen kilometres from Norcia lies the beautiful **Piano Grande**, an unusual flat meadow measuring 16 square kilometres and surrounded by rolling hills and mountains that seem covered with huge swathes of coloured velvet in May and June. It is a rarefied landscape (used by Franco Zeffirelli in his 'Franciscan film' *Brother Sun, Sister Moon*), where herds graze and fields produce the famous minute lentils of **Castelluccio**, the old village in an upper corner of the plain. Castelluccio had 700 inhabitants in 1951, and now has around 40; winter conditions are so bad that the village is often cut off. From the summit of Monte Vettore (8,121ft), the tallest peak in the area, you can see both the Adriatic and Tyrrhenian seas on clear days. In the winter there's skiing at Forca Canapine, on the south side of Piano Grande.

Cascia, in the Corno valley south of Norcia, is an even more popular pilgrimage destination, thanks to Santa Rita, the 'Saint of Impossibilities', who was born near here in 1381, and suffered a rotten husband (hence all the tired Italian housewives you see) and a smelly wound in the middle of her forehead, but had to wait until the Fascist era to get a sanctuary.

Down the Valnerina: Crayfish and Mummies

Back in the main valley on the SS209, **Scheggino** is a small but pretty town on the Nera river, laced with tiny canals full of trout and a rare species of crayfish (*gamberettini*) imported from Turkey. It is also the fief of Italy's truffle tycoons, the Urbani family. Further down the valley a sign indicates the turn-off for the **abbey of San Pietro in Valle** (*open daily 10.30–1 and 2.30–5*), founded in the 8th century by Faroaldo II, duke of Spoleto. Set far up above the road, with views across the valley to an abandoned citadel, the church has a lovely 12th-century campanile embedded with Roman bits, and a two-storey cloister with a Roman sacrificial altar in the centre. Inside, the nave is covered with frescoes from 1190, an unusual example of the Italian response to the Byzantine style. The altar is a rare example of Lombard work, sculpted on both the front and back; one of their early saints is interred to the right in a lovely 3rd-century Roman sarcophagus. On either side of the altar are 13th-century frescoes by the school of Giotto, with a pretty Madonna. In the back the cylindrical Etruscan altar is now used for monetary rather than animal offerings. Among the stone

Getting Around

Terni and Narni are the only towns served by rail. Both are on the Rome–Ancona line, and from Terni there are also trains to Rieti and L'Aquila in Abruzzo. From Spoleto's Piazza della Repubblica **buses** depart frequently for Cascia and Norcia; others go to Scheggino, where you can catch a Terni provincial bus down the rest of the valley to Terni, Narni or Orvieto.

Tourist Information

Norcia: in the Municipio, t 0743 828 044.
Cascia: Via G. da Chiavano 2, t 0743 71401, f 0743 76630.
Terni: Viale C. Battisti 7/a, t 0744 423 047, f 0744 427 259.
Narni: Piazza dei Priori 3, t/f 0744 715 362
Amelia: Via Orvieto 1, t 0744 981 453, f 0744 981 566.

Where to Stay and Eat

Norcia ✉ 06046

★★★Nuovo Hotel Posta, Via C. Battisti 10, t/f 0743 817 434 (*moderate*). A fine establishment, with pleasant rooms. The restaurant serves the famous, hearty, robust fare of Castelluccio lentils, boar salami, *tortellini alla norcina*, lamb with truffles, topped off, if you dare, by a tumbler of Norcia's nasty grappa flavoured with black truffles.
★★★Grotta Azzurra, Via Alfieri, t 0743 816 513, f 0743 817 342 (*moderate*). Also a good stopover, but with a different approach to local culinary traditions: a lighter touch, perhaps, its mandatory truffled dishes competing with a tasty *risotto* with crayfish from the Nera, *fettuccine* with trout, or delicious grilled mushrooms. *Closed Tues.*
Dal Francese, Via Riguardati 16, t 0743 816 290 (*moderate*). The ideal place for a bumper

meal in this corner of Umbria, where the truffle is king. Try the smoked turkey and home-made salami for *antipasto*, followed by a pasta medley of *tris al tartufo, gnocchi al tartufo* or *tortellini con crema di tordi* (thrushes) *e tartufi*; for a main course choose between trout dishes, tender grilled lamb or the unusual *braciola in agrodolce con tartufi* (sweet-and-sour chop with truffles). Good wine list. *Closed Fri exc in summer.*

Cascia ✉ 06043

★★★Cursula, Via Cavour 3, t 0743 76206, f 0743 76262 (*moderate*). Cascia's top offering, owing to its extremely pleasant rooms, and good Umbrian home cooking in the restaurant (*moderate*).
★★Mini Hotel La Tavernetta, Via Palombi, t/f 0743 71387 (*cheap*). A family-run place with clean comfortable rooms and a good restaurant (*moderate*) serving well-cooked local dishes based on wild mushrooms, salami, trout and lamb. *Closed Tues.*

Scheggino ✉ 06040

★★Del Ponte, Via Borgo 15, t 0743 61253, f 0743 61131 (*cheap*). A charming little hotel right on the river Nera, offering 12 rooms with bath, and delicious meals in the restaurant (*moderate*), based on Scheggino's two specialities, crayfish and truffles. For a trip to Umbrian heaven, try the *fettuccine* with a sauce of both. *Closed Mon.*

Ferentillo ✉ 05034

★★★Fontegaia, on the SS209, towards Ferentillo in Montefranco, t 0744 388 621, f 0744 388 598 (*moderate*). Has the most pretensions in the Valnerina; rooms are very comfortable; there's a children's playground and beautiful gardens for dining al fresco; the restaurant (*moderate*) is a favourite for locals going out for a special occasion, if a bit heavy-handed with the cream sauces.

fragments arranged on the wall there's a real rarity – a bas-relief of a monk with oriental features, believed to depict one of two Syrian monks who set up a hermitage here in the 7th century. The monks' quarters have been coverted into a hotel and restaurant (**t** *0744 780 129*).

The abbey is in the *comune* of **Ferentillo**, defended by two 14th-century fortresses that rise up like matching bookends. In Precetto, the oldest section of town, the crypt

★★★**Monterivoso**, on the mummy road (*see* Santo Stefano), t/f 0744 780 725 (*moderate*). An old mill, beautifully converted into a hotel in 1997. Antique furnished rooms look out over the lawn – a pool is planned but the municipal one in Ferentillo, 3 minutes away, is especially nice; the restaurant is good, too. **Piermarini**, Via della Vittoria 53, t 0744 780 714 (*moderate*). A wonderful restaurant in which to taste local dishes, prepared as '*La Nonna*' (granny) would have prepared them. There's *coratina di agnello* (lamb's innards) with wild asparagus, homemade pasta with truffles, delicate lamb cutlets *scottadito* served with olive foccaccia, fresh-water trout and river crayfish. In autumn, mushrooms and chestnuts appear on the menu.

Arrone ✉ 05031

★★**Rossi**, on the SS209, t 0744 388 372, f 0744 388 305 (*cheap*). Sixteen modern rooms, all with bath, and one of the best restaurants in the area (*moderate*), with excellent *crostini*, spaghetti with truffles, the usual grilled meats and a variety of trout dishes, served in a pretty garden in summer. *Closed Fri*.
Rema, further up the Polino road, by the aqueduct (*cheap*). A fine little *trattoria* with an outdoor grill, and the usual Umbrian fare at old-fashioned prices; try the *ciriole* (homemade spaghetti) with mushrooms and grilled lamb *scottaditta* ('burn your fingers'). *Closed Mon*.

Terni ✉ 05100

Terni is a good base for visiting the Valnerina if you're dependent on public transport; it's also worth looking for lodgings here if Spoleto is filled up for the Two Worlds festival.
★★★★**Valentino**, Via Plinio il Giovane 3, t 0744 402 550, f 0744 403 335. If you want something central, this has comfortable modern rooms, and one of Terni's classiest restaurants, **La Fontanella**.

★★★★**Garden**, Via Bramante 6, t 0744 300 041, f 0744 300 414 (*expensive*). Terni's prettiest hotel, with plant-filled balconies, a pool and all mod-cons.
★★★**Hotel de Paris**, Viale Stazione 52, t/f 0744 58047 (*moderate*). Conveniently located by the station, has just had a complete facelift.
★★★**Casalago**, at Mazzelvettam, t 0744 368 421, f 0744 368 425 (*moderate*). A largish hotel with a garden overlooking Lake Piediluco.
Villa Graziani, 4km from the centre in Papigno, t 0744 67138 (*moderate*). An 18th-century place once graced by Byron; you can dine well and fashionably on a mix of Umbrian specialities and Italian classics. *Closed Sun eve and Mon*.
Lu Somaru, Viale Cesare Battisti 106, t 0744 300 486 (*moderate*). A popular choice on the west edge of the centre, offering Umbrian specialities, out in a garden in summer. *Closed Fri*.

Narni ✉ 05035

Most of the hotels are down by the river and station at Narni Scalo.
★★★**Dei Priori**, Vicolo del Comune 4, t 0744 726 843, f 0744 726 844 (*moderate*). The finest in the centre, in a medieval palace on a narrow lane, with comfortable rooms; its restaurant, **La Loggia**, t 0744 722 744 (*moderate*), predates the hotel and has long been on the maps of visiting gourmets, although its reputation has slipped of late. *Closed Mon*.
★★★**Il Minareto**, Via Cappuccini Nuovi 32, t 744 726 343, f 0744 726 284 (*moderate–cheap*). For a touch of the Arabian Nights, this Moorish-style villa, on the outskirts of town, has eight rooms near a tiny lake and garden.
Cavallino, Via Flaminia Romana 220, outside town towards Terni, t 0744 761 020 (*cheap*). A good old-fashioned inn, with a few inexpensive rooms and solid Umbrian cookery that has kept folk coming back for more for over 30 years. *Closed Tues, and part of July*.

of **Santo Stefano** (*open daily 10–12.30 and 2.30–5; knock on door marked 'custode' opposite church*) contains something most people don't expect to find in Umbria: **mummies**. Here you can see, accidentally preserved by the soil and ventilation, the poor mummified Chinese newlyweds who came here in the last century for a honeymoon and got cholera instead, two gruesome French prisoners who were hanged in the Napoleonic era, and a grinning pyramid of skulls; a desiccated vulture mummy points the way inside with its wing. Sad to relate, the mummies are now imprisoned in glass display cases, ruining much of their charm.

Picturesque **Arrone**, spilling over its rock, was once run by feudal lordlings, the bitter enemies of the abbots of Ferentillo. Their tower, sprouting a tree, is the local landmark. From Arrone, the road leads up to Piediluco and **Polino**, also endowed with a feudal tower and a monumental fountain; above Polino the Colle Bertone affords panoramic picnicking sites.

Cascate delle Marmore and Lake Piediluco

Between Arrone and Terni the road passes below another pretty hill townlet, **Torreorsini**, before reaching the 416ft-high, green and misty **Cascata delle Marmore**, one of Europe's tallest waterfalls – when it's running. Surprisingly, the Cascata is an artificial creation; in 271 BC Curius Dentatus, best known as the conqueror of the Sabines, first dug the channel to drain the marshlands of Rieti, diverting the Velino river into the Nera. Although the falls are usually swallowed up by hydroelectric turbines, the big waters are let down at regular – though ever-changing – times; after dark they are brilliantly illuminated (*16 Mar–30 April: Mon–Fri 12–1 and 4–5, Sat 11–1 and 4–9, Sun 10–1 and 4–9; May: Mon–Fri 12–1 and 4–5, Sat 11–1 and 4–10, Sun 10–1 and 3–10; June: Mon–Fri 4–5 and 9–10, Sat 11–1 and 3–10, Sun 10–1 and 3–10; July–Aug: 12–1, 5–6 and 9–10, Sat 11–1 and 3–10, Sun 10–1 and 3–10; Sept: 12–1, 4–5 and 9–10, Sat 11–1 and 4–9, Sun 10–1 and 3–9; Oct: Sat 11–1 and 4–8, Sun 10–1 and 3–8; Nov–15 Mar: Sun and hols only 3pm–4pm*).

There are two places from which to view the falls – from down below on the SS209, or from the belvedere on top, in the village of Marmore. A path through the woods connects the two, though it's steep, prone to be muddy, and much nicer to walk down than up (the path at the bottom begins 100 yards downstream from the falls). There are some pleasant places to swim near the bottom, but you can't use them when the falls are on – a siren goes off 15 minutes before the falls are turned on to warn swimmers not to linger. Both places are easily reached by bus from Terni, 6km away.

Above Marmore, **Lake Piediluco** zigzags in and out of the wooded hills, one of which is crowned by a 12th-century fortress. There are a couple of beaches, but unfortunately the lake is better to look at than swim in – the water is cold and dangerous. Perched high above the east shore of the lake is the pale old village of **Labro**, former nest of noblemen on the run, now almost completely taken over by Belgian expats. Just below the lake the Arrone road passes by **Villalago**, which has an outdoor theatre used during the Umbria Jazz Festival and other summertime events, and lovely gardens for picnicking.

Terni

Because doves mate on his day (or so they say), the first bishop of Terni, San Valentino, became the special patron of lovers and the greetings-card industry. Curiously, the stodgy Terni-ites themselves have only recently picked up on the notoriety of their old bishop, and at the St Valentine's Market you may even see a pink heart or two as you go to pay your respects to his headless body in the basilica. Terni has little else to offer, besides trains and buses to other places, and shots of viper juice (or *Viparo*, the local *aperitivo* that has all the qualities of flat rum and cola. As one of Italy's chief steel and armaments manufacturers – the gun that shot Kennedy was made in Terni – the city was condensed into rubble by air raids during the Second World War. It was during the original building of the steelworks that bulldozers uncovered one of the largest and richest Etruscan necropoli, although all the finds have been carted off to Rome's Villa Giulia Museum. The ancient Romans called it *Interamna Nahars* and it was traditionally considered the birthplace of the historian Tacitus, although scholars now quibble that Terni actually produced a more meagre Tacitus, Claudius Tacitus, emperor for a day. These days the city is a Cinecittà wannabe in Italian film; much of Roberto Benigni's *La Vita è Bella* was made here.

Of Roman Terni only part of the **amphitheatre** (AD 32) remains, now employed as a pensioners' *bocce* court in the city's prettiest area, off the main Corso del Popolo. Visible from the Corso and Piazza Europa, the tiny round church of **San Salvatore**, locally known as the Sun Temple, was built in the 5th century, with a nave added in the 12th. Nearby stands the **Palazzo Spada** (1546) by Antonio da Sangallo the Younger, the best of Terni's surviving palaces. Palazzo Gazzoli, on Via del Teatro Romano, houses the **Pinacoteca Comunale**, with Umbrian paintings, a *Marriage of St Catherine* by Gozzoli and, best of all, a large collection of works by Terni's own Orneore Metelli (1872–1938), a shoemaker and great naïve artist.

San Gemini Fonte, 13km north of Terni, is known for its mineral springs, located in a pretty park of old oaks. Four kilometres further on lie the evocative ruins of the Roman city of *Carsulae*, destroyed by the Goths and never rebuilt. Lying unfenced out in the open, *Carsulae* is made lovely by its pretty environs: you can stroll along the original Via Flaminia, past the ruins of a theatre, amphitheatre, a mausoleum, temples and an arch dedicated to Trajan. Further north, **Acquasparta**, within its medieval walls, has more locally famous curative waters; in the summer it hosts a German *lieder*-singing contest.

Narni

Narni, on a cliff over the Nera, is a picturesque hill town, tumbling in a jumble under its well-preserved castle, built in the 1370s by the ubiquitous Cardinal Albornoz. It was a Roman colony, and birthplace of Emperor Nerva, who lasted somewhat longer than Terni's emperor. Narni has several gems – in its **Duomo**, founded in the 12th century, there's a lovely early medieval screen of marble and Cosmati work. In the attractive 13th-century **Palazzo del Podestà** hang a Ghirlandaio, a Gozzoli, and other paintings; with the nearby **Loggia dei Priori** by Gattapone it forms a fine setting for Narni's springtime medieval pageant, the *Corso dell'Anello* – the Tournament of the Ring – in which the various quarters of the town compete in a festival traditionally held on the second Sunday in May, one of the most spectacular and evocative *feste* in Umbria.

Narni has several other interesting churches, including the pretty 12th-century **Santa Maria in Pensole** and the 15th-century **Sant'Agostino**, on the other side of town. Down by the river and Narni's train station are the romantic ruins of the **Ponte d'Augusto**, the 1st-century bridge that carried the Via Flaminia over the Nera.

Amelia

North of Narni, halfway between the Nera and the Tiber, lies the ancient agricultural town of Amelia. Both Cato and Pliny wrote that *Ameria* was centuries older than Rome, and as towering evidence of the fact stand its ancient **Pelasgian-Umbrian Walls**, dating back to the 5th century BC, built from massive polygonal blocks, 12ft thick and 25ft high. The **Duomo**, founded in 1050, with its original campanile, contains two Turkish banners captured at the Battle of Lepanto. On the first Sunday in October, wine is miraculously made to pour from Amelia's fountains.

Near the Tiber, **Lugnano in Teverina** has a 12th-century church, **Santa Maria Assunta**, a Romanesque gem with a curious porch and bas-reliefs, topped by an eagle instead of a cross; inside there's a good triptych by L'Alunno.

Penna in Teverina, near Orte, is an old fortified town with a castle much disputed by Rome's eternal Punch and Judy factions, the Colonna and Orsini families, until the Colonna simply sold it to the Orsini. Some members of the family liked the area so much that they constructed a **Palazzo Orsini** with a fine 19th-century Italian garden attached. Other relics of that century are the *Mammalocchi*, allegorical figures in travertine standing at the entrance to another estate.

Todi and Orvieto

Two of Umbria's best-known hill towns are easily accessible from Rome; Orvieto especially, with its stupendous cathedral and wine, is a popular destination for day-trippers. Todi is a bit further and a bit more sombre, more mysteriously Umbrian, a good foil to Orvieto. For a memorable dose of beauty and culture take in both towns and the lovely scenery in between, with a stop at Baschi for an amazing meal at one of the jewels in Italy's gastronomic crown.

Todi: the World's Most Liveable Town

Despite a name that suggests an Italian *Wind in the Willows*, Todi is a serious-minded place, perched atop its high and lonely hill, with more affinity to eagles than amphibians; it was the former who showed the ancient Umbrians where to plant the city they called *Tuter*, high atop what is now the Rocca. Later the Etruscans built their city lower down, around the Piazza del Popolo, and, according to legend, one day they went nasty, slaughtering their Umbrian neighbours and making the rest slaves. In Todi's plump and prosperous Middle Ages the eagle struck again, this time swooping down on Amelia and Terni (symbolized by the two eaglets on Todi's coat of arms); yet at the same time it produced one of Italy's great uncanonized saints, Jacopone dei Benedetti (1228–1306), the master of the *Laudesi* – medieval Franciscan poets – who, like St Francis, sang songs of praise to cheer the people. Jacopone, before becoming 'Christ's clown', was a wealthy lawyer, married to a noble lady. Like any true Italian he loved to see her dressed up to the nines and, although she gently protested, she let him have his way. Then came the day, at a public festival, when the platform she stood

Getting Around

Todi is linked by **bus** with Terni, Perugia and Rome, and by the FCU's little choo-choo **trains** with Perugia and Terni. Trains arrive at the Stazione Ponte Rio, **t** 075 894 2092. Orvieto is on the main railway line between Florence and Rome, and is also linked by bus with Terni. In both towns municipal buses make the trip up the hill; in Orvieto there is also a **funicular** from the station to the top of the town. Unfortunately, only one bus a day runs between Todi and Orvieto, passing through the lovely scenery above the Tiber valley.

Tourist Information

Todi: Piazza Umberto I 6, **t** 075 894 3395, **f** 075 894 2406.

Where to Stay

Todi ⊠ 06059

Relais Todini, on the road to Collevalenza di Todi, **t** 075 887521, **f** 075 887182 (*very expensive*). A 14th century *palazzo* superbly furnished with antiques, plus a heated pool, tennis, elegant restaurant, and beautiful views up to Todi. The 750-acre park is home to camels, kangaroos, zebras and penguins; there are horses or carriages to ride, and boats for puttering about on the four lakes.

****Fonte Cesia, Via L. Leoni 3, **t** 075 894 3737, **f** 075 894 4677 (*expensive*). Stylish accommodation in an 18th-century building near Piazza Jacopone in the historic centre.

San Lorenzo Tre, Via S. Lorenzo, **t** 075 894 4555 (*moderate*). In a listed *palazzo* in town, with atmospheric 19th-century furnishings.

***Villa Luisa, Via A. Cortesi 147, **t** 075 894 8571, **f** 075 894 8472 (*moderate*). A pleasant place near the centre, with a large garden.

There are no cheap hotels, but there are some *agriturismo* places nearby.

L'Arco, at Cardigliano, **t** 075 894 7534.
Poponi, Via delle Piagge 26, **t** 075 894 8233.
Castello di Porchiano, at Porchiano, **t** 075 885 3127.

Eating Out

In Todi, local specialities in the kitchen include the usual pigeon, lamb and *porchetta*, though here the homemade fat spaghetti is called *ombricelli*, served by preference *alla boscaiola* (tomatoes, piquant black olives and hot peppers); the wine to look for, dating back to the days of the Roman Republic, is the dry white Grechetto di Todi.

Umbria, Via S. Bonaventura 13, **t** 075 894 2737 (*expensive*). Head under the stone arches just off the Piazza del Popolo for fine Umbrian cuisine with an enchanting Umbrian view. Meals begin with a delicious variety of *antipasti*, followed perhaps by *spaghetti alla tudertina*. Book for a table with an unobstructed view. *Closed Tues.*

Lucaroni, Via Cortesi 57, **t** 075 894 3572 (*expensive*). More sophisticated dishes, such as a delicious *risotto* with pigeon, black truffles and port and an excellent *linguini* with crab – a refreshing change after so many Umbrian meat dishes. *Closed Tues.*

Italia, Via del Monte 27, **t** 075 894 2643 (*moderate*). Tucked away down a narrow alley off the main piazza is this unpretentious *trattoria*, with cheerful red tablecloths and a rustic feel. The kitchen offers a few specialities, notably the *capriccio*, an oven-baked pasta dish. *Closed Mon.*

Antica Hosteria de la Valle, Via Ciufelli 19, **t** 075 894 4848 (*moderate*). An atmospheric *osteria* with a creative menu. The *antipasto della casa* is recommended: cheese fondue with truffles, rustic pâté and a selection of *bruschette*. Seasonal vegetables, fruit and aromatic herbs feature strongly and result in dishes such as lamb cooked with orange. Book ahead. *Closed Mon.*

on collapsed; as she lay there, Jacopone ripped aside her garments to examine her injuries, only to discover that under her silks she wore a rough hair shirt. She died, and he became a convert – but such an eccentric one that the Franciscans at first refused him admission. In the end, however, he found his niche with the Spirituals, the most unworldly branch of the order, living in a monastery at Collazzone, near Perugia, where he is believed to have composed the famous Latin *Stabat Mater Dolorosa* and the *Stabat Mater Speciosa*.

Modern Todi is a sophisticated little place, famous for its carpentry and wood-working. In the past few years it has, believe it or not, consistently been voted the world's most liveable town by the University of Kentucky, an accolade which has brought American tycoons rushing to buy up its villas. In April Todi hosts one of Italy's major antiques fairs, and in August and September the *Mostra Nazionale dell'Artigianato*, a national crafts fair.

Tempio della Consolazione

The best way to approach Todi is from the southwest, where the road, winding its way to the clouds, passes by way of one of the most perfect of Renaissance churches, the ivory-coloured Tempio della Consolazione, designed by Cola da Caprorola in 1508, and completed 99 years later. Its serene purity of form, geometrically harmonious lines and lovely proportions are the hallmarks of Bramante, who may well have had a hand in the design. The Tempio's lonely setting lends it a special charm, best viewed from Todi's citadel. The white classical interior (*open April–Sept daily 9–1 and 2.30–6; Oct–March daily 10–12.30, Sat and Sun only also 2.30–6*), in the symmetrical form of a Greek cross, contains Baroque statues of the apostles.

Piazza del Popolo

Todi's streets all converge on its magnificent Piazza del Popolo, the centre of civic life since the days of the Etruscans. The piazza is a medieval pageant in grey stone; sternest of them all, the **Palazzo dei Priori** (1293–1337) has square battlements with a chunky tower, while the **Palazzo del Popolo** (1213), with the swallowtail crenellations, and its adjacent **Palazzo del Capitano** (1290) manage to drum up more charm, with a grand Gothic stairway and attractive mullioned windows. Up on the fourth floor there's a **Pinacoteca** that you can take in if it rains (*open 10.30–1 and 2–4.30; till 6 in the summer; closed Mon; adm*).

On the far side of the piazza the squarish **Duomo** is enthroned atop another distin-guished flight of steps. Begun in the 12th century, the façade has a fine rose window and delicately decorated portal, while the interior is embellished with good Gothic capitals and a Gothic arcade with a 14th-century altarpiece; parishioners who turned around to gossip during Mass were confronted by a not-too-terrifying 16th-century vision of the *Last Judgement*, painted by Farraù da Faenza.

Before leaving the piazza, be sure to take a look from its belvedere.

San Fortunato and the Rocca

Todi's medieval lanes invite aimless roaming, but if you're pressed for time head straight for the Franciscan church of **San Fortunato**, built in 1292 (take Via Mazzini), located in a prominent position atop a broad stairway. A bronze statue of Jacopone stands near the foot of the steps; his locally revered tomb is in San Fortunato's crypt. The church's unfinished façade has three recessed Romanesque portals, the central one especially lovely with its carvings of acanthus leaves and human figures. The airy interior contains Todi's greatest work of art, a fresco by Masolino of the *Madonna and Child*. Above San Fortunato, at the top of the town, the **Rocca** is Todi's ruined 14th-century citadel, public park and magnificent belvedere, offering an unforgettable view of the valley of the Tiber and the Tempio della Consolazione.

Orvieto

Orvieto owes much of its success to an ancient volcano. First it created the city's magnificent pedestal – a 1,066ft, sheer-cliffed mesa, straight out of the American southwest – and then it enriched the hillsides below with a special mixture of volcanic minerals that form part of the secret alchemy of Orvieto's famous white wine. Although new buildings crowd the outskirts of Orvieto's unique crag, the medieval town on top, crowned by its stupendous cathedral, looks much the same as it has for the last 500 years.

Attracted by Orvieto's incomparable natural defences, the Etruscans settled it early and named it *Velzna* (or *Volsinium* as the Romans pronounced it). It was one of the twelve cities of the Etruscan confederation, and one that fought frequently with the Romans until those upstarts laid it waste in 280 BC. The Etruscans departed in a huff and founded a new *Volsinium* on the shores of Lake Bolsena, leaving behind their old city (*Urbs Vetus*, hence 'Orvieto'). Orvieto in the Middle Ages was an important stronghold of the Papal States – important primarily for popes who could take refuge here when their polls went down with the fickle Romans.

The Duomo

Closed for visits Sun am, and between 12.45 and 2.30.
For Cappella di San Brizio, see below.

It was during one of Orvieto's papal visitations, in the 1260s (Urban IV), that the Miracle of Bolsena occurred. A Bohemian priest named Peter, passing through on his way to Rome, was asked to celebrate Mass in the town of Bolsena, just to the south. Father Peter had long been secretly sceptical about the doctrine of transubstantiation (that the Host in truth becomes the body of Christ), but during this Mass the Host itself answered his doubts by dripping blood on the altar linen. Marvelling, Peter took the linen to the pope in Orvieto, who declared it a miracle and instituted the feast of Corpus Christi. St Thomas Aquinas, also in Orvieto at the time, was instructed to compose a suitable office for the new holy day, while the pope promised Orvieto (a bit unfair to poor Bolsena!) a magnificent new cathedral to enshrine the blood-stained relic.

The cornerstone was laid in 1290 and, though begun in the Romanesque style, its plan was transformed into Gothic by master architect Lorenzo Maitani of Siena in 1310. Subsequent master architects included such luminaries as Andrea Pisano, Orcagna and Sammicheli, but even then the mighty edifice, visible for miles around, wasn't completed until the 1617.

Tourist Information

Piazza del Duomo 24, t 0763 0763 341 772,
f 0763 344 433, www.comune.orvieto.tr.it.

Where to Stay

Orvieto ✉ 05018

Orvieto's hotels have character.

****Palazzo Piccolomini**, Piazza dei Ranieri 36,
t 0763 341 743, f 0763 391 046 (*expensive*). A
superbly restored medieval palace in the
historic centre, sumptuous and luxurious
since its opening in late 1997.

****Maitani**, Via Maitani 5, t/f 0763 342 012
(*expensive*). Just opposite the cathedral,
comfortable rooms with bath.

****Villa Ciconia**, Orbetello Scalo, north on the
SS71, t 0763 305 582, f 0763 302 077 (*expensive*). A 16th-century villa, set in an oasis of
green bordered by two rivers in the ugly
sprawl of Orbetello Scalo, with well-equipped
rooms and a finely frescoed restaurant
serving equally fine food.

****Aquila Bianca**, Via Garibaldi 13, t 0763 341
246, f 0763 342 273 (*moderate*). Old-
fashioned, not luxurious, but with a good
central position, and a wine cellar for the
all-important business of tasting Orvieto.

***Virgilio**, Piazza Duomo 5/6, t 0763 341 882,
f 0763 343 797 (*moderate*). Occupies a
recently refurbished trecento building
just across from the cathedral.

***Valentino**, Via Angelo da Orvieto 32,
t/f 0763 342 464 (*moderate*). A 16th-century
house, well furbished with mod cons, as
well as a garage, near San Domenico.

Posta, Via Luca Signorelli 18, t 0763 341 909
(*cheap*). Has a a patch of garden to sit in,
right off Corso Cavour in the historic centre.

Duomo, Via di Maurizio 7, t 0763 341 887
(*cheap*). Basic rooms near the cathedral.

Eating Out

There are plenty of good restaurants in
Orvieto to suit all budgets, although the bus-
loads of day trippers from Rome have helped
to keep some mediocre and often overpriced
venues in business – choose with care. Besides
the town's famous wine, local specialities to
look for are *cinghiale in agrodolce* (sweet and
sour boar) and *gallina ubriaca* (Umbrian
'drunken chicken').

La Taverna de' Mercanti, Via Loggia dei
Mercanti 34, t 0763 393 327 (*expensive*).
Creative variations on regional *cucina* in the
stylish setting of the old cellars of the Hotel
Piccolomini. *Closed Tues.*

Le Grotte del Funaro, Via Ripa Serancia 41,
t 0763 343 276 (*moderate*). An elegant
restaurant in one of Orvieto's prettier
corners – a set of tufa caves –that serves
solid Umbrian cuisine, with especially good
pasta and mixed grilled meats, and pizza at
night. *Closed Mon, exc in July and Aug.*

Sette Consoli, Piazza Sant'Angelo, t 0763 343
911 (*moderate*). Uses the best local ingredients with imagination (*pappardelle* with
duck sauce, *gnocchi* with *zucchini* and mint)
and has a good choice of wines, with dining
outside in the summer and a good *menu
degustazione* with three wines. *Closed Wed.*

Osteria dell'Angelo, Corso Cavour 166, t 0763
341 805 (*moderate*). Local ingredients set off
with flair, with dishes such as tongue and
goose liver terrine, *ravioli* with a *pecorino*
and nettle sauce, rack of lamb roasted with
aubergine and good desserts. The wine list
is particularly good. *Closed Mon.*

Etrusca, Via Lorenzo Maitani 10, t 0763 344
016. Lovely traditional food in a cinquecento
building near the cathedral; this comes top
among the *trattorie. Closed Tues.*

La Palomba, Via Cipriano Manente 16, t 0763
343 395 (*cheap*). A family-run place popular
with the locals. *Bruschette* are generously
doused with local oil, pasta is homemade
and the price is right. *Closed Wed.*

Vissani, on the SS448 towards Civitella del
Lago, t 0744 950 206 (*very expensive*). In this
almost passionately religious inner sanctum
of *cucina altissima*, you may dip your fork
(but only if you've diligently reserved a table
in advance) into such marvels as oysters
with roast onions and thyme sauce, suckling pig with bilberries, or lobster in broccoli
leaves; each dish is accompanied by a specially prepared bread. A fabulous array of
Italian and French cheeses and exquisite
wines will help make your meal unforgettable, though so too will the bill. *Closed all
day Wed, Thurs lunch and Sun eve.*

The end result is one of Italy's greatest cathedrals, with a stunning, sumptuous façade resembling a giant triptych. This is Maitani's masterpiece, and the reason the church is called the 'Golden Lily of Cathedrals'. As you approach, you are struck first by the dazzling, Technicolor hues of its mosaics, then by the elaborate prickly spires and tracery, and then by the richness and beauty of the sculptural detail. It is said that 152 sculptors worked on the cathedral, but it was Maitani himself who contributed the best work – the remarkable design and execution of the celebrated **bas-reliefs** on the lower pilasters that recount the Christian story from the Creation to the Last Judgement, a Bible in stone that captures the essence of the stories with vivid drama and detail, Maitani's *Last Judgement*. Maitani also cast the four bronze figures of the Evangelists' symbols, all ready to step right off the façade, and sculpted the angels in the lunette over the central portal, who pay homage to a *Madonna* by Andrea Pisano (*removed for restoration*). The great rose window is by Orcagna, and the controversial bronze doors, portraying *Works of Mercy*, are by Emilio Greco, finished in 1965.

In contrast with the soaring verticality of the façade, the sides and interior are banded with horizontal zebra stripes. Inside, in the muted light filtered through alabaster windows, the stripes merge into shadows. The lack of clutter does much to reveal the cathedral's fine proportions and height. The columns of the nave support rounded arches, and above them runs a pretty clerestory. In the nave note Gentile da Fabriano's 1426 fresco of the *Madonna and Child*, near the baptismal font, and the 1579 *Pietà* by Ippolito Scalza, a native of Orvieto.

The greatest treasures, however, are in the chapels, especially the **Cappella della Madonna di San Brizio** (*open Mon–Sat 10–12.45 and 2.30–7.15, Sun and hols 2.30–5.45; buy tickets at the tourist office or souvenir shops in Piazza del Duomo; only 25 people admitted at a time*), embellished with one of the finest fresco cycles of the Renaissance. The project was begun in 1447 by Fra Angelico, with the assistance of Benozzo Gozzoli. The Angelic One finished two sections – the serene *Christ in Judgement*, with the prophets, while Gozzoli contributed the hierarchies of angels. Before he could finish, however, Fra Angelico was summoned to Rome. Orvieto then commissioned Perugino to complete the work, but he never got around to it, and finally, in 1499, the city hired Luca Signorelli, who finished the vaults according to Fra Angelico's design.

The walls, however, are Signorelli's own masterpiece; his breathtaking and awesome compositions of the *Last Judgement*, the *Preaching of the Antichrist* (a very unusual subject) and the *Resurrection of the Dead* are generally acclaimed to be the forerunners of Michelangelo's *Last Judgement* in the Sistine Chapel. Yet it is hard to say that Michelangelo surpassed them; Signorelli's remarkable foreshortening skills, draughtsmanship and ability to simplify nature and architecture into their essential geometrical forms give the frescoes tremendous power. To the left of the figure of the preaching Antichrist, Signorelli has portrayed himself and Fra Angelico, both listening solemnly, as does Dante standing amid the crowd, while in the background chaos and catastrophe are busy at work. Then the world ends, a darkened sky is shot with streaks of fire, the earth shakes, and in literal detail the dead re-emerge from the earth, skeletons pulling themselves out of the ground forming new coats of flesh.

Some are met by Charon, who rows them across to an overcrowded Renaissance Hell, to keep company with Signorelli's faithless mistress. Below the frescoes Signorelli painted medallions of the great poets and the pre-Socratic philosopher Empedocles, and some scenes from the *Divine Comedy*.

To the left, the **Cappella del Corporale** is frescoed with scenes of the *Miracle of Bolsena* by Ugolino of Siena (1360s) and the 1339 *Madonna dei Raccomandati* by Lippo Memmi. The magnificent silver and enamel *Reliquary of the Corporale* on the altar is by another Sienese, Ugolino di Vieri; the blood-stained linen cloth it holds is shown only on major religious holidays, and is taken around Orvieto in procession during the feast of Corpus Christi.

The Piazza del Duomo

The cathedral square is a fitting setting for the Golden Lily. On one side a row of old houses includes a couple of wine bars where you can try Orvieto's vintages and *salumeria*, while on top of the square clock tower a 14th-century figure named Maurizio strikes the hours. Opposite, in Palazzo Faina, is the beautifully renovated **Museo Claudio Faina e Civico** (*open Oct–Mar Tues–Sun 10–1 and 2.30–5; closed Mon; April–Sept daily 9.30–6; adm*), containing one of Italy's top private archaeological collections and Orvieto's excellent Etruscan collection, excavated from local tombs. The ground floor has the civic collection, with decorations from the Belevedere temple and the *Venus of Cannicella*; the two upper floors house the private collection. The top floor enjoys one of the best views of the cathedral.

On the south side of the cathedral the **Palazzo Papale**, or Popes' Palace, begun by Boniface VIII in 1297 and finished in the 1500s, contains the **Museo dell'Opera del Duomo** (*closed for restoration until kingdom come*), with art that once filled the cathedral – statues by grand masters such as Arnolfo di Cambio and the Pisanos, and grand statues by little-known hands, especially the colossal *Apostles*. The best work is a lovely, richly coloured polyptych by Simone Martini. The adjacent Palazzo Apostolico (1304) holds the **Museo Archaeologico Nazionale** (*open Tues–Sat 9–1.30 and 2.30–7, Sun 9–1; adm*), with another excellent collection, especially Etruscan, with two reconstructed tombs.

Smaller Churches

In contrast to its heavenly cathedral (even Pope John XXIII said that on Judgement Day the angels would bear it up to paradise), the rest of Orvieto is unpretentious and worldly, a solid, bourgeois, medieval town. On Via del Duomo stands the **Torre del Moro**, a medieval tower you can ascend, and further on the pretty 13th-century **Palazzo del Popolo**, a tufa palace with mullioned windows and arches; the little piazza in front is the site of a colourful vegetable market. From here Via della Pace leads back to the narrow church of **San Domenico**, built in 1233, just after St Dominic's canonization – the first church ever dedicated to him. The most scholarly Dominican of them all, St Thomas Aquinas, taught here at the former monastery. This claim to fame, however, did not spare the church from a savage amputation of its naves in 1934 to make room for a barracks.

From Via del Duomo, Orvieto's main drag, Corso Cavour, continues west to the city's main square, Piazza della Repubblica. On the corner the 12th-century church of **Sant'Andrea** has an extremely unusual 12-sided campanile, pierced by mullioned windows and topped by bellicose crenellations. A 6th-century church was discovered underneath Sant'Andrea and underneath it were found an Etruscan street and buildings (*the sacristan has the key to the excavations*). Sant'Andrea basks in the memory of great events that took place within its walls: here Innocent III proclaimed the Fourth Crusade, and here, in 1281, Charles of Anjou and his glittering retinue attended the coronation of Pope Martin IV.

Beyond Piazza della Repubblica lie some of Orvieto's most ancient streets, lined with tufa houses; follow them back to the northwesternmost corner of town, site of the church of **San Giovenale**, first built in 916, rebuilt in 1687 and crammed full of frescoes from the 12th–15th centuries.

Orvieto claims one other noteworthy church, **San Lorenzo de Arari**, reached by Via Maitani from the Piazza Duomo, or on Via Scalza from Corso Cavour. Built in the 14th century, San Lorenzo shelters a cylindrical Etruscan altar under its high altar, both of which are protected by a lovely 12th-century stone canopy. Byzantine-style frescoes cover the walls, with elongated figures and staring eyes; another set of frescoes depict the life of St Lawrence, who retained his sense of humour even while being literally grilled ('Turn me over, I'm done on this side,' he said).

Pozzo di San Patrizio

Orvieto's northeastern end (near the upper station of the funicular) is dominated by a **citadel** built in 1364 by the great papal legate, Cardinal Albornoz. Only the walls, a gate and a tower survive, encompassing a pretty little garden of parasol pines. There are lovely views from the ramparts, stretching from the shallow Paglia river all the way to the Tiber valley. Next to the citadel lie the foundations of an **Etruscan temple** and the **Pozzo di San Patrizio**, or St Patrick's Well (*open daily summer 10–7, winter 10–6; adm*), designed in the 1530s by Antonio da Sangallo the Younger on the orders of the calamitous Pope Clement VII. It is a unique work of engineering, meant to supply Orvieto in times of siege; to reach the spring below, Sangallo had to dig down the equivalent of seven storeys, and to haul the water to the surface he designed two spiral stairs of 248 steps, which never cross – one for the water-carriers and their donkeys going down, another for going up. Clement, having just fled the sack of Rome, was perhaps justified in the paranoia that made him desire such a monumental drinking hole, but it was never needed. The stairs are dimly lit by windows on to the central shaft, but beware if you descend; you have to get back up again. Bring a sweater, too.

Down below Orvieto's northern cliffs, along the road that leads to the railway station, there are several **Etruscan tombs**, nothing special as Etruscan tombs go, but worth a look if you don't have a chance to see any of the more elaborate models. The most impressive is the 6th-century BC **Crocifisso del Tufo** (*open daily 9 until one hour before sunset; adm*), on the SS71 north of Orvieto.

The Vine of Life

Refined over the centuries, Umbria's most famous wine is grown in 16 designated areas in the provinces of Terni and Viterbo, and consists of a careful mixture of grapes, with Tuscan Trebbiano and Verdello dominant. Light straw-coloured Orvieto DOC comes in four different varieties: dry (Orvieto *secco*), which now predominates because of the market, although you can still find the more authentic moderately dry (*abboccato*, often served with appetizers), medium sweet (*amabile*) and sweet (*dolce*), made like a sauterne from noble rot (*muffa nobile*). If made in the oldest growing zone, right near Orvieto, it's called Classico. The tourist office has a list of local vineyards which welcome visitors.

Villages Around Orvieto

Between Orvieto and Todi, **Baschi** is a harmonious hill town above the Tiber valley, near where the river widens to form the **Lago di Corbara**; the area is a popular centre for *agriturismo*, for those who dream of staying in a farmhouse amid the vineyards. **Porano**, south of Orvieto, is a pretty town with a castle, set in the rolling hills.

Walled **Ficulle**, north of Orvieto on SS71, was the birthplace of Rome's tragic hero of the Middle Ages, Cola di Rienzo, and its castle of the Marchese Antinori (*call t 0763 86051 to arrange a visit*) produces some of Orvieto's finest wine.

Lazio

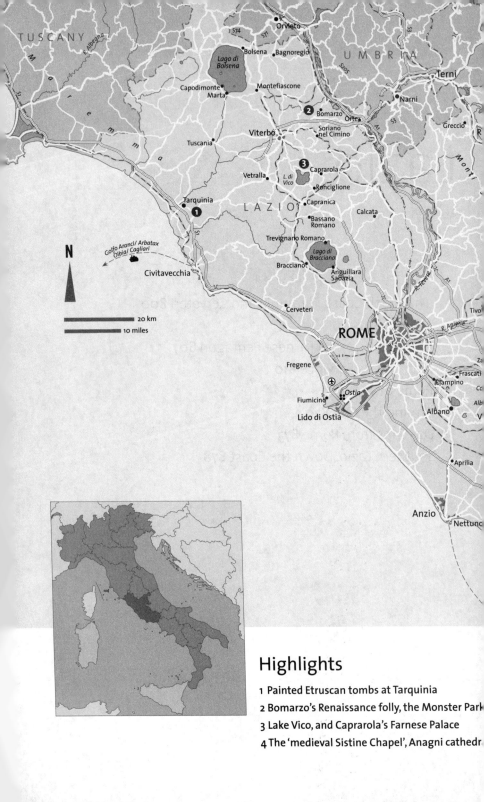

Highlights

1 Painted Etruscan tombs at Tarquinia
2 Bomarzo's Renaissance folly, the Monster Park
3 Lake Vico, and Caprarola's Farnese Palace
4 The 'medieval Sistine Chapel', Anagni cathedr

On a Saturday night variety show, the television host discusses the founding of Rome with two comedians dressed up as Romulus and Remus; turning to Remus, the sillier-looking of the pair, he asks: 'What did you ever do?' Remus gets a big laugh from the audience by proudly claiming, 'Well, I founded Lazio.'

Despite being the location of the capital city, Lazio does not get much respect from the average Italian, who thinks of it as a sort of vacuum, half swamps and half poor mountain villages that need to be crossed to get to Rome. Northerners often lump it in with Campania and Calabria as part of the backward south. To an extent it is, though great changes have come in the last 60 years with land reclamation and new industry. Lazio's problem is a simple one: Rome, that most parasitic of all cities. Before there was a Rome this was probably the wealthiest and most densely populated part of non-Greek Italy, the homeland of the Etruscans as well as the rapidly civilizing nations of Sabines, Aequi, Hernici, Volscii and the Latins themselves, from whom Lazio (*Latium*) takes its name.

After the Roman triumph the Etruscan and the Italic cities shrivelled and died; those Romans who proved such good governors elsewhere caused utter ruin to their own back yard. A revival came in the Middle Ages, when Rome was only one of a score of squabbling feudal towns, but once again, when the popes restored Rome, Lazio's fortunes declined. To finance their grandiose building projects, Renaissance popes literally taxed Lazio into extinction; whole villages and large stretches of countryside were abandoned and given over to bandits, and land drained in medieval times reverted to malarial swamps. Modern Rome, at least since Mussolini's day, has begun to mend its ways; the government still considers Lazio a development area, and pumps a lot of money into it.

The North Coast: Tarquinia and Cerveteri

It will seem hard to believe, but this bare stretch of coast north of Rome was the richest and most heavily populated part of Etruria, including the only two sites worth visiting for those not enchanted with archaeology: the museums and necropoli at Tarquinia and Cerveteri.

Tarquinia and Vulci

Beginning from the Tuscan border on the coastal highway (the Roman Via Aurelia), truly dedicated Etruscophiles may wish to detour into the hills to **Vulci**, an important town in the 9th–1st centuries BC, and a renowned bronze-working centre. There are scanty ruins of the city, a small museum in modern Vulci's 13th-century **Castello dell'Abbadia** (*t 0761 437 787*), and a large if not exciting necropolis with something like 15,000 tombs (*open April–Sept Tues–Sun 9–7, Oct–Mar Tues–Sun 9–4; adm*).

Getting Around

From Lepanto bus terminus in Rome, there are frequent COTRAL **buses** to Cerveteri and Tarquinia.

Tourist Information

Tarquinia: Piazza Cavour 1, t 0766 856 384 (*open Mon–Sat 8–2*).

Where to Stay and Eat

Tarquinia ✉ 01016
★★★San Marco, Piazza Cavour 18, t 0766 842 234, f 0766 842 306 (*moderate*). Après tombs, sleep at this well-run hotel, with a good traditional restaurant. *Closed Tues*.
Due Orfanelle, Vicolo Breve 4 (off Via di Porta Tarquinia), t 0766 856 307 (*cheap*). Dine on local dishes and especially good grilled meat. *Closed Tues*.

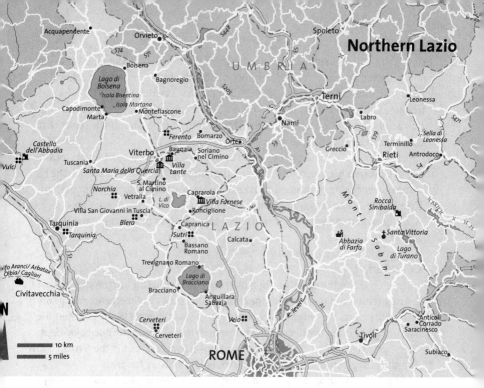

After the turn-off for Vulci, continuing southwards, the next Etruscan site is at the large, modern town of **Tarquinia**, of interest in its own right, with **Santa Maria di Castello**, a Cosmatesque 12th-century church at the top of the town, and the elegant rococo façade of the **Chiesa del Suffraggio** in the centre. Near this, in the 15th-century Palazzo Vitelleschi, many of the finest discoveries from the Etruscan city and its necropolis have been assembled for the **Museo Nazionale Tarquiniense**, on Piazza Cavour (*t 0766 856 036; museum open Tues–Sun 8.30–7.30; necropolis open Nov–Mar 8.30–4.30, April–Oct 8.30–7.30; adm for both, cheaper joint ticket available*).

Undoubtedly the stars of the collection are the famous winged horses from the 'Altar of the Queen' temple on the acropolis: beautiful beasts, but made of clay like most Etruscan temple decorations – which explains why so few have survived. Well-carved sarcophagi are present in abundance, and Greek vases by some of the greatest 6th–5th-century BC Attic painters. The Etruscans were talented at ceramics, too, as seen by the large amount of fine *bucchero* ware, their black pottery incised or painted with the usual puzzling Etruscan images. Some of the paintings from the tombs have been relocated here for their protection, including scenes of chariot-riding and athletics – almost any subject is likely to turn up on Etruscan tomb walls.

There are not enough staff to keep all the hundreds of tombs open at Tarquinia's **Monterozzi necropolis**, a 15-minute walk, starting from Via Porta Tarquinia in the town (*open Tues–Sun 9–one hour before sunset; adm*), all that remains of the city that dominated southern Etruria for centuries and enforced on Rome its early dynasty of Etruscan kings. The few you can see on any given day, however, rank among the finest products of Etruscan art. Tombs like that of 'the Lionesses', with their beautiful 'Ionic style' paintings, seem remarkably close to the art of the ancient Minoans. These paintings began to appear in the 6th century BC, and only in the tombs of the richest Etruscans; more typical of the rest is the 'Tomb of the Warrior', hung with arms and trophies – all carved from the tufa. There are more tombs in a recent, separate excavation across the road, including images of the *Vanth* and the *Caronti*, the spirits that came to carry away Etruscan souls.

Further down the coast, on the way to Cerveteri, you'll pass the not-so-old-looking city of **Civitavecchia**, a port for Rome and the gateway for ferries to Sardinia. The big fortress overlooking the harbour was designed by Michelangelo for the popes, but there's little else to detain you. Unless, that is, you feel a sudden desire to bolt for the island of *nuraghi* and *mallorredus*, in which case repair to the offices of the Tirrenia Line or the FS ferries.

Cerveteri

Cerveteri, down the coast, was originally *Caere*, the richest if not the strongest of the Etruscan cities, and the one with the closest cultural ties to Greece. According to Herodotus it was the only non-Greek city with a sanctuary at Delphi. Cerveteri, like Tarquinia, has extensive **necropolises** (*2km from town, signposted; open May–Sept Tues–Sun 8.30–sunset, Oct–April Tues–Sun 8.30–4; adm*), laid out in the form of a town. The site is large; study one of the site maps before walking too far.

The most striking section is called the Banditaccia Necropolis, where the heavy stone domes, set low to the ground, look more like bunkers than tombs. In them you see the forerunners of all the round tombs in Rome, such as the Mausolea of Augustus and Hadrian. Be sure to see the 'Tomb of the Capitals', carved from tufa to resemble the interior of an Etruscan house (the Etruscans built all their homes, public buildings and even temples out of wood, plaster and terracotta, which explains why only tombs are left).

The 'Tomb of Shields and Chairs' has unusual military decoration; another, even stranger, is covered with stone reliefs of cooking utensils and other household objects. In town, the Castello Orsini houses the **Museo Nazionale** (*t 06 994 1354; open Tues–Sun 8.30–7.30; adm*), which has finds dug out from the Banditaccia, although the best pieces are now in the Villa Giulia and Vatican Museums in Rome.

Viterbo

Ah, Viterbo. Where else can one rest in a café on Death Square, or stroll over to the Piazza of the Fallen to pay one's respects to Our Lady of the Plague? Surrounded by grey, forbidding walls and the ghastly modern districts, the city is actually rather cute at the centre, full of grand churches and palaces, and medieval streets brightened with fountains and flowers. The population seems evenly divided between teenagers on scooters, as bejewelled and trendy as their counterparts in Rome, and blasé soldiers from Italy's biggest army base. Like the rest of Lazio, Viterbo has had more than its share of troubles, most of them traceable to the proximity of Rome. That

Getting Around

Viterbo actually has three **railway stations**, all just outside the city walls. Regular **FS** trains to Orvieto and Florence stop at **Stazione Porta Fiorentina**, north of the walls on Viale Trento. Most trains for Rome leave from here too, also stopping at **Stazione Porta Romana**, on Viale Raniero Capocci, the big boulevard east of the walls. In addition there is a local line run by the Lazio transport authority **COTRAL**, which rattles along a separate route from its station next to Porta Fiorentina, via Bagnaia, Soriano nel Cimino and Civita Castellana, to Piazzale Flaminio (Roma-Nord) station in Rome.

But at the end of the day, the fastest way to reach Viterbo from Rome is by COTRAL **buses** (freephone within Italy, **t** 800 431 784), leaving roughly every thirty minutes from Stazione Saxa Rubra in Rome. More buses for Tarquinia, Bolsena, Civitavecchia and other provincial towns leave from Piazza Martiri d'Ungheria, next to Piazza dei Caduti in the town centre.

Tourist Information

Piazza San Carluccio 5, **t** 0761 304 795.

Where to Stay

Viterbo ✉ **01100**

★★★★**Terme dei Papi**, Strada Bagni 12, **t** 0761 3501, **f** 0761 352 451 (*very expensive*). A well-run spa hotel, with a naturally heated outdoor pool where swimming in January is fashionable. *Pool open Sept–June Wed–Mon 9.30–4.30; July–Aug daily 9am to dusk; free for hotel guests, otherwise L20,000 Mon-Fri, L25,000 at weekends.*

★★★**Milano Due**, Via San Luca 17, **t/f** 0761 303 367 (*moderate*). Recently redone with modern décor.

★★★**Leon d'Oro**, Via della Cava 36, **t** 0761 344 444 (*moderate*). Quiet and a little staid.

★★**Roma**, Via della Cava 26, **t** 0761 226 474, **f** 0761 305 507 (*cheap*). A cheaper option almost next door, with parking.

Eating Out

Restaurants here adhere to traditional Viterban dishes: slender fettuccine called *fieno* (hay), roast baby lamb, eels and fish from the lakes: *lattarini*, *coregone* (lake whitefish) or *persico* (perch).

Il Richiastro, Via della Marrocca 18, **t** 0761 228 009 (*moderate*). In the courtyard and cellars of a medieval palace near Piazza Dante, you can dine on smoked trout, roast lamb, *polenta* and unusual home-made desserts, all fresh according to the season, prepared with pride and care, for bargain prices. *Open Thurs–Sat and Sun lunch only; closed July and Aug.*

Scaletta, Via Marconi 45, **t** 0761 340 003 (*cheap*). Another old favourite, with traditional cooking, and pizza in the evening. *Closed Mon.*

Tre Re, Via Marcel Gattesco 3, **t** 0761 304 619 (*cheap*). North of Piazza del Plebiscito, serves excellent dinners. *Closed Thurs and two weeks in Aug.*

geographical necessity, however, also gave Viterbo its greatest period of glory. For much of the 13th century, Viterbo, and not Rome, was the seat of the popes.

History

A small city in Etruscan and Roman times, Viterbo's modern history begins with its fortification by the Lombards in the 8th century. By 1100, it was a free *comune*, one of the few cities in this part of Italy strong and energetic enough to manage it. Viterbo was usually an enemy of Rome and, when Arnold of Brescia's revolution made Pope Eugenius III a refugee in 1145, he came here. Emperor Frederick I Barbarossa soon restored the popes to Rome, but again in 1257 Martin V found Viterban hospitality gratifying when the Guelph-Ghibelline wars made Rome too hot for him. In this most confusing period of Italian history, over a dozen popes were crowned, died or at least spent time here, in short stays on their way to or from France, Tivoli – and sometimes even Rome. In 1309, when the 'Babylonian Captivity' carted the papacy off to Avignon, Viterbo could only decline, and when the popes returned, the city that had once been Rome's strongest rival found itself a mere provincial town of the Papal State.

Piazza del Plebiscito

In Viterbo's centre, two not-so-fierce-looking lions, the city's ancient symbol, gaze out over the typical pair of buildings representing the often conflicting imperial and local powers: the 13th-century **Palazzo dei Priori** (or **Palazzo Comunale**, now the town hall) and its clock tower, and **Palazzo del Podestà** of the 1460s. The politicians won't mind you looking around the former and its fine Renaissance courtyard; ask to see the **Sala Regia** (*t 0761 304 643; open daily 10–1, Mon–Fri also 3–6.30, Sat and Sun 10–1 also 3.30–7.30*), decorated with fanciful Mannerist frescoes on the history of Viterbo from Etruscan times. Across the square is the church of **Sant'Angelo**, the façade of which has for centuries incorporated a Roman sarcophagus (now replaced by a mere photograph) containing the body of a medieval lady of incomparable virtue named Galiena; accounts of her fatal charm and sad demise vary from one Viterban to another.

There are any number of directions you can take from here. Via Ascenzi, under the arch, leads to Piazza dei Caduti and the **Madonna della Peste** (*usually closed*), an octagonal Renaissance church next to the tourist office. Beyond that, by the walls, the **Rocca** was built by Cardinal Albornoz in 1354 to keep watch on the Viterbans when the pope returned to Rome. This squat palace-fortress holds the small **Museo Archeologico** (*t 0761 325 929, open daily 9–7; adm*), containing reconstructions of Etruscan houses (not tombs, for once!) and finds from the Roman theatre in Fèrento and Musarna. Two of Viterbo's 13th-century popes are buried in the church of **San Francesco**, near Porta Murata at the northern end of the walls. Nearby, off Piazza Verdi, the late 19th-century church of **Santa Rosa** houses the considerable remains of Viterbo's 13th-century patroness, too holy to decompose and usually on display for all to see. Santa Rosa's preaching helped the Viterbans defy a siege by the heretical Emperor Frederick II in 1243 and, to commemorate her, each year on 3 September the men of the town carry a 99ft illuminated wooden steeple called the *macchina* – which is always in danger of toppling – through the streets, surmounted by an image of Rosa. Money permitting, local artists create a new *macchina* every five years (the startlingly modernistic 1993 model was an aesthetic success, but for the present one they've gone back to the neo-Baroque).

East from Piazza del Plebiscito, Via Cavour takes you past the **Casa Poscia**, a rare 13th-century house on a stairway to the left of the **Fontana Grande**, the best of Viterbo's many fountains. Via Garibaldi leads on further east to the Roman Gate and **San Sisto**, a church in parts as old as the 9th century, with an altar made of ancient sculptural fragments. Outside the walls and across Viale Capocci, 13th-century **Santa Maria della Verità** was vandalized by 18th-century redecorators; the plaster frosting is gone now, but only fragments have survived of the Renaissance frescoes by Melozzo da Forlì. The **Cappella Mazzatosta**, behind an iron grille, has the best painting Viterbo can offer: frescoes of the *Marriage of the Virgin* by Renaissance artist Lorenzo da Viterbo (1469), strongly influenced by Piero della Francesca. The adjacent cloisters house the **Museo Civico** (*t 0761 325 462; open Tues–Sun 9–7, in winter only until 6; adm*) with an archaeological section and a good picture gallery. The most fascinating items on display, however, are the fake ancient monuments created in the 15th century by a mad monk who called himself Annius of Viterbo. They were meant to support the equally fantastical histories Annius wrote to boost his home town – how Viterbo was founded by Hercules and refounded by Noah, and enjoyed a visit from the Egyptian god Osiris when it was the 'capital of the Etruscans.'

San Pellegrino and the Palazzo Papale

From Piazza del Plebiscito the best route of all is down Via San Lorenzo into the heart of Viterbo's oldest quarter. Three streets down and off to the left, **Santa Maria Nuova** is the best-preserved of the city's medieval churches. An ancient image of Jupiter is set into the portal, and St Thomas Aquinas once preached from the small outdoor pulpit in the corner. On the other side of Via San Lorenzo, Viterbo's old market square faces the 11th-century church of the **Gesù**, a medieval tower-fortress, one of several left in the city, and a *palazzo* that long ago was the town hall. To the south, trailing down from the aforementioned **Piazza della Morte** – ironically one of the lovelier squares in Viterbo – the San Pellegrino quarter hangs its web of alleys, arches and stairs along Via San Pellegrino with a romantic and thoroughly medieval air, though in fact few of the buildings are quite that old. The **Museo della Macchina di Santa Rosa**, Via San Pellegrino 60 (*t 0761 345 157; open Oct–Mar Fri–Sun 10–1 and 4–8, April–Sept Wed–Sun 10–1 and 4–8*) chronicles Viterbo's famous *festa*.

In the opposite direction from San Pellegrino, a bridge on Roman and Etruscan foundations – the **Ponte del Duomo** – carries over to Piazza San Lorenzo and the **Palazzo Papale**, begun in 1266. This squarish, battlemented building, very much in the style of a medieval city hall, is a finer building than the pope's present address in Rome, though admittedly much smaller. On the best part, the open Gothic loggia, you will see lions (for Viterbo) interspersed with the striped coat of arms of the French pope Clement V, who completed the building. Three popes were elected at conclaves in the palace's Great Hall.

Popes and cardinals did not always have an easy time in Viterbo. When Clement IV died – two weeks after he arrived – arguments between the French and Italian cardinals led to a two-year deadlock. Eventually the exasperated people of Viterbo tried to speed up the conclave by locking them in the palace and tearing off the roof; somehow the prelates got around this by making tents in the Great Hall. Finally the Viterbans decided to starve them out, and before long the Church was blessed with the undistinguished compromise choice of Gregory X. He had the roof fixed, but should have repaired the floor as well, since it collapsed six years later, killing his successor, John XXI. He is buried next door in the plain Romanesque **cathedral**.

Around Viterbo: Hot Mud and Tombs

West of the city, some of the Etruscans' and Romans' favourite thermal springs still do whatever it is they do that makes Italians so happy. At the ancient **Springs of**

Bullicame you can stop by the roadside for a dip in a sulphurous pool, check into a hotel spa, have an aerosol inhalation to help your sinuses, and an icing of hot mineral mud to calm your nerves.

Further west, **Tuscània** stands alone at the centre of one of the emptiest, eeriest corners of Italy, a region of low green hills where you will find Etruscan ruins, old castles and religious shrines, but no people. Tuscània was a leading Etruscan city around the 4th century BC and regained its importance for a short while in the early Middle Ages. Today the city has nearly recovered from a bad earthquake in 1971, and its lovely medieval centre has a fine ensemble of buildings around **Piazza Basile**, including a fountain that has been flowing since Etruscan times (though this incarnation of the **Fontane delle Sette Canelle** is 13th-century). Etruscan sarcophagi are on display at the **Museo Nazionale Archeologico** (*t 0761 436 209; open Tues–Sun 8.30–7.30*) in the former Santa Maria del Riposo convent. The real attraction in Tuscania is two unique early churches on the hill above the town: **San Pietro** and **Santa Maria Maggiore** (*both open daily 9–1; in summer also 3–7; in winter also 2–5*), both begun in the 8th century, with additions in the 11th and 12th centuries. Besides their carved altars, pulpits and painting from the 8th–14th centuries, both have unusual sculpted façades – San Pietro's especially, with colourful Cosmati work, fragments of ancient sculpture and outlandish grotesques. Perhaps some of the churches of Rome looked like this before their Renaissance and Baroque rebuildings. Santa Maria Maggiore has a wonderful medieval *Last Judgement* frescoed inside.

Another road east from Viterbo – this one an 8km dead end – leads to the site of **Fèrento**, a rival city that Viterbo destroyed in the Middle Ages. Little is left, really, save a very well-preserved **Teatro Romano**, where concerts are sometimes held in the summer (*open Tues–Sun 9–1.30; longer hours in summer*). East of Viterbo, the road for Orte enters the old suburb of La Quercia, passing in front of a landmark of Renaissance architecture: **Santa Maria della Quercia**, built in the late 1470s. The distinctive 1509 façade has a carved oak tree (*quercia*) and lions, and lunettes by Andrea della Robbia over the doors. Inside, the beautiful marble tabernacle contains a miraculous painting of the Virgin, and there is also a fine Gothic cloister; ask the custodian to let you into the fascinating **Museo degli Ex-Voto**, filled with plaques painted over the centuries with scenes of the Madonna's miracles. **Bagnaia**, 6km east, was an old hill village expanded by wealthy Viterban bishops into a summer resort. In the 1570s Cardinal de Gambara commissioned Vignola to create **Villa Lante** (*t 0761 288 008; gardens open Tues–Sun 9–one hour before sunset; guided tours every half-hour; adm*), with one of the most striking of all Renaissance palace complexes: two villas share a large park and classic geometric Italian garden, full of groves and statuary; water rises from a number of fountains then cascades back down decorative stairs and terraces aligned on a long axis towards the incredible Grand Fountain, embellished with stone ships and giant Moors. De Gambara was a relative of the Farnese, and Villa Lante was his attempt to upstage their flashy palace at Caprarola; note the carved reliefs of prawns (*gamberi*), the ubiquitous family symbol.

This road continues into the beech forests of the Cimino Hills, meeting **Soriano nel Cimino**, with a medieval castle and an extinct volcano, Monte Cimino, for a neighbour.

South of Viterbo, if you're heading for Lake Vico (*see* p.808), you'll pass through the lovely town of **San Martino al Cimino**, built around a fine 13th-century French Gothic Cistercian abbey; the town itself is an unusual example of Baroque planning, full of trees and half-surrounded by a single curving lane of terraced houses.

The Monster Park at Bomarzo

Some of the same sculptors who worked on St Peter's in Rome made this shabby little nightmare, hidden away in the Lazio hills. The two works seem somehow related, opposite sides of the coin that may help in explaining the tragic, neurotic atmosphere of late 16th-century Italy. One of the Orsini, that ancient and powerful Roman family, commissioned this collection of huge, strange sculptures; he called it his *Sacro Bosco* – Sacred Wood – and in its present state it is impossible to tell whether it was the complex allegory it pretends to be, or just a joke.

The **Parco dei Mostri** (*t 0761 924 029; open daily 8–sunset; adm exp*) – one of the most popular sights in Lazio – lies just outside Bomarzo, one of the most woebegone little towns in this part of Italy. The setting adds to its charm, as does the habit of the present owners of running it like an Alabama roadside attraction, complete with bars, a restaurant and a playground with a small-scale football field for the kids. Near the entrance you come upon the impressive though dilapidated Tempietto, a domed temple of unknown purpose attributed to Vignola. From there you wander the ill-kept grounds, encountering at every turn colossal monuments and eroded illegible inscriptions: a 20ft-tall screaming face, where you can walk inside the mouth, under an inscription that reads 'every thought flees', and find a small table and benches, apparently waiting for a dinner party; a life-size elephant, perhaps one of Hannibal's, crushing a terrified Roman soldier in its trunk; a giant wrestler, in the act of ripping a defeated opponent in two from the legs; and a leaning tower, just for fun. In every corner decayed Madonnas, mermaids, sphinxes, nymphs and harpies wait to spook you. All are done in a distorted, almost primitive style. The Monster Park will make you feel like an archaeologist, discovering some peculiar lost civilization. Perhaps the Italians understand it too well; it may be the only important monument of the 16th century that neither the government nor anyone else is interested in preserving.

Three Lakes, and a Farnese Pentagon

All of the lakes of northern Lazio are volcanic craters; long ago they must have been like the famous Phlegraean Fields outside Naples. They are also the most appealing features in the Lazio landscape: not exactly off the main tourist track, but for swimming they are often more pleasant than the coastal beach resorts near Rome.

Lake Bolsena

Pristine, lovely and full of fish, Bolsena is the largest and northernmost of the three lakes. **Bolsena** town, at the northern end, was Etruscan *Velzna*, founded by refugees after the Romans destroyed the original Velzna (Orvieto, in nearby Umbria), in 264 BC. In the centre are narrow beaches and resort hotels, and behind them the 15th-century

---

Est! Est!! Est!!!

In the year 1111, a German abbot, Giovanni Defuc, and his servant Martin were on their way to Rome for the coronation of Emperor Henry V. The good abbot liked his wine, and Martin's job was to keep ahead of him and act as a roving *sommelier*, testing the plonk in each cellar; if it was good, he would write *Est* ('there is') on the door; if it was exceptional, Martin would write *Est, Est*. When he tried the muscatel at Montefiascone, he was overwhelmed. *Est! Est!! Est!!!* he wrote. His master agreed, and after the coronation he and Martin returned and drank until Defuc dropped dead, leaving Martin to wite his epitaph *'per il troppo Est qui morì il mio signore'* –my master died of excess here – which still graces his tomb in the church of San Flaviano.

---

church of **Santa Cristina**, with a holy grotto and catacombs underneath. It's a stiff climb under medieval arches up to the **Castello Monaldeschi** (*t 0761 798 630; open all year Tues–Fri 10–1; April–Sept Sat–Sun also 4–8; Oct–Mar Sat–Sun also 3–6; adm*) with a good archaeological collection. Just above the castle, excavations of the ruins of old Velzna are currently underway (*open Tues–Sun 9–1.30*) Boat tours (*t 0761 798 033 for information*) are available from Bolsena to the lake's two islands: the pretty rock of **Martana**, with steep granite cliffs and woods above, and **Isola Bisentina**. This was a favoured retreat of the Farnese in the 1500s, when the family was just beginning its spectacular career. They commissioned Antonio da Sangallo the Younger to build them a palace and a large domed church, **SS. Giacomo e Cristoforo**, now in decay. The island's hill also has a string of Calvary Chapels. At the southern end of the lake, **Capodimonte** on its small promontory offers more beaches and boat excursions.

Towns around Lake Bolsena include **Acquapendente**, at the northern extremity of Lazio, with an ancient crypt under its cathedral, built as a copy of the Holy Sepulchre in Jerusalem, and a nature reserve on nearby Monte Rufeno. **Bagnoregio**, east of Bolsena town, is worth a visit for the bizarre ghost town of **Città di Bagnoregio**, a 1km walk over a pedestrian bridge from the town. Set in a weirdly eroded landscape, Città goes back to the Etruscans, and its walls retain one of the few surviving Etruscan gates. It was gradually abandoned after an 18th-century earthquake made it nearly inaccessible; a few adventurous folk are fixing up some of the houses now.

Montefiascone, just south of the lake, has been famous for its wine since a medieval German bishop did himself in by drinking too much of it. His tomb is in the 12th-century church of **San Flaviano**. Montefiascone makes a good living from its wine, and the embroidered legend that goes with it (*see* above)

Lake Vico and Caprarola

The smallest and perhaps loveliest of the lakes, Vico is ringed by rugged hills. Unspoiled marshes line some of its shore – now a wildlife reserve – and its ancient crater has a younger volcano (also extinct) poking up inside it: **Monte Venere**. Just over the hills from the lake, don't pass up a chance to see one of Italy's most arrogantly ambitious late-Renaissance palaces, the **Villa Farnese**, in Caprarola (*t 0761 646 052; villa open Tues–Sun 8.30–6.45; visits to the gardens start at 10, 11, 12, 2 and 3, and in May–Aug also 4 and 5; adm*).

When Alessandro Farnese, member of an obscure Lazio noble family, set his sister Giulia up as mistress to Pope Alexander VI, his fortune was made; Alessandro later became Pope Paul III, a great pope who called the Council of Trent, rebuilt Rome, and kept Michelangelo busy – also a rotten pope, who oppressed his people, reinvigorated the Inquisition, and became the most successful grafter in papal history. Before long the Farnese family ruled Parma, Piacenza and most of northern Lazio. With the fantastic wealth Alessandro accumulated, his grandson, also named Alessandro, built this family headquarters. Vignola, the family architect, turned the entire town of Caprarola into a setting for the palace, ploughing a new avenue through the town as an axis that led to a grand stairway, then a set of gardens (now disappeared), and then another stairway up to the huge pentagonal villa, built over the massive foundations of an earlier, uncompleted fortress.

The palace is empty today; the Farnese lost everything in later papal intrigues, and someone, some time, probably had to sell the furniture. Nevertheless it is still an impressive place; the tour includes Vignola's elegant courtyard, a room with uncanny acoustic tricks that the guides love to demonstrate, frescoes of the *Labours of Hercules*, another with a wonderful ceiling painted with the figures of the constellations, and Vignola's decorative masterpiece – an incredible **spiral staircase** of stone columns and frescoes. The best part, however, is the 'secret garden', a park full of azaleas and rhododendrons leading up to a sculpture garden of grotesques and fantastical *telemones* that recall the Bomarzo Monster Park (there is a connection, as one of the Orsini was Alessandro Farnese's secretary), and finally a delightful, smaller villa, the **Palazzina del Piacere**. The hills between Lake Vico and the coast conceal no less than 12 minor Etruscan sites; all you'll see of these vanished cities, however, are the usual rock-cut tombs, some with temple-like carved façades, as at **Blera** and **Norchia**. Also at Norchia is a strange avenue stretching over 1,200ft cut deeply into the easily worked tufa.

Sutri and Città Castellana

Between Lakes Vico and Bracciano, **Sutri** is famously old, perhaps as old as 1000 BC, a strategic spot for the Etruscans and again in the Middle Ages, when it was rebuilt on

Getting Around

Bracciano town is on the FS **rail** line between Rome and Viterbo, but the way to get to the lakes is by COTRAL **buses**. There are frequent services from Lepanto and Agnanina termini in Rome to Bracciano and Vico respectively, and from Viterbo to Lake Bolsena.

Where to Stay and Eat

★★★**Bella Venere**, Località Scardenato, Caprarola, **t** 0761 612 342, **f** 0761 612 344

(*moderate*). A gem of a small hotel on Lake Vico with gardens, a beach, tennis courts and a large restaurant (*cheap*). *Closed Nov.*

★★★**Sans Soucis sul Lago**, Via dei Noccioleti 18, **t** 0761 612 052, **f** 0761 612 053 (*cheap*). Also on Vico, at Punta del Lago near the road to Ronciglione, with a beach and garden, and views over the lake.

Gino al Miralago, Lungolago Marconi 58, **t** 0761 870 910 (*cheap*). A lovely waterfront *trattoria* in Marta, on the south side of Lake Bolsena. *Closed Tues.*

a safer height and became a proper hill town. Remains of the ancient town can be seen in the **Parco Archeologico Preistorico-Paesaggistico** (*open summer 9–1 and 3–8; winter 9–5; adm*), including tombs, an amphitheatre carved out of the tufa that may date back to the Etruscans, and a cave church that was once a temple of Mithras.

Città Castellana, in the hills to the east, was the home of the Faliscans, a small people related to the Latins who were conquered by Rome in 395 BC. People around here still call themselves *Falisci*, and the faces on the street do often bear striking resemblances to the ancient portrait busts in the **Museo Archeologico dell'Agro Falisco** (*open daily except Mon, in winter 9–2 and 3–4; in summer until 5 or later, if they feel like it*) housed in one of the most elegant of all Renaissance fortresses, the **Rocca** built by Giuliano and Antonio da Sangallo for the popes. This lovely and distinguished town, where few tourists ever seem to penetrate, has another attraction, a **cathedral** with a gorgeous, completely preserved Cosmati façade (1210), all glittering gold mosaic work and reliefs. The Faliscan lands lie in the shadow of **Monte Soratte** (Mount Soracte), a landmark peak that was a holy site for pagans and Christians (the 5th century chapel at its summit was reconstructed from a temple of Apollo), and a favourite subject for Romantic-era painters. South of Città, **Calcata** is central Italy's improbable New Age village, colonized by artists and alternative folk.

Lake Bracciano

This broad sheet of water is one of Rome's most popular swimming holes, and yet remains remarkably clean and beautiful. There is little of monumental interest around the lake – but a good view of it can be gained from the grim 1470s castle of the Orsini family, the **Castello Orsini-Odescalchi** (*t 06 9980 4348; open all year Tues–Sun 10–12; April–Sept also 3–6.30; Oct–Mar also 3–5; adm exp*), in the town of Bracciano. Boats run from there around the lake in summer. The two pretty lakeside villages of Trevignano and Anguillara have medieval centres and many places to eat.

Rieti and its Province

This comes as something of a digression, but this strip of land reaching over the Apennines to touch the borders of the Marche is also a part of Lazio. Before the Roman conquest in 290 BC it was the land of the Sabines, sometime allies but often fierce enemies of Rome. The Romans pushed their Via Salaria through here on its way to the Adriatic, generally following the route of the modern SS4 to Ascoli Piceno, and made it an important staging post.

Lazio's Least-known Towns

Rieti, the capital, has a 12th-century cathedral and a small picture collection in its Museo Civico (*t 0746 287 456; open Tues–Sat 8.30–1.30 and 3–7, Sun 11–1 and 4.30–6.30; adm*), and about a kilometre of well-preserved and very medieval-looking walls. The territory around it, once swamps, was drained by the Romans when they built the Marmore Falls in Terni; now it's a fertile plain with views of some of the highest peaks of the Apennines – the Gran Sasso is just over the border in Abruzzo (*see p.613*).

Getting Around

Rieti is on the **rail** line between Terni and L'Aquila, but service is infrequent. There are several **buses** each day to Rome (from Stazione Tiburtina), Terni and L'Aquila.

Tourist Information

Rieti: Piazza Vittorio Emanuele II,
 t 0746 203 330.
Terminillo: Via dei Villini 33, Pian de' Valli,
 t 0746 261 121.

Where to Stay and Eat

Rieti ✉ **02100**
★★★★Quattro Stagioni, Piazza C. Battisti 14, t 0746 271 071, f 0746 271 090 (*moderate*). An elegant, comfortable hotel.
Il Grottino, Piazza C. Battisti 4, t 0746 497 683 (*cheap*). Close to the Four Seasons, serves good, traditional meals. (*Closed Tues*).
Bistrot, Piazza San Rufo 25, t 0746 498 798 (*cheap*). A more adventurous menu draws local foodies to this family-run eatery. Reserve. *Closed Sun, and Mon lunch.*

There is plenty of lovely scenery and good walking country in the province, most of it in rather remote areas. South of Rieti there are the hills around the artificial lakes of **Salto** and **Turano**; on the way to the latter you will see an impressive medieval castle, the Rocca Sinibalda. North of Rieti, **Monte Terminillo** has a modest ski resort on the slopes of its 6,993ft peak; in summer the road around it makes a panoramic drive to **Leonessa**, an attractive medieval town that is one of the quietest, most out-of-the-way places in Italy. St Francis spent much time in these mountains; among the humble sanctuaries where he preached, **Greccio**, on its lovely mountaintop site west of Rieti, is said to be where the saint made the first Christmas crib; the event is celebrated with a real-life nativity scene on 24 and 26 December and 6 January.

Rome

To know what Rome is, visit the little church of San Clemente, unobtrusively hidden away on the back streets behind the Colosseum. The Baroque façade conceals a 12th-century basilica with a beautiful marble choir screen 600 years older. In 1857 a cardinal from Boston discovered the original church of 313, one of the first great Christian basilicas, just underneath. And beneath *that* are two buildings and a Temple of Mithras from the time of Augustus; from it you can walk out into a Roman alley that looks exactly as it did 2,000 years ago, now some 28ft below ground level. There are commemorative plaques in San Clemente, placed there by a Medici duke, a bishop of New York, and the last chairman of the Bulgarian Communist Party.

You are not going to get to the bottom of this city, whether your stay is for three days or a month. With its legions of headless statues, acres of paintings, 913 churches and megatons of artistic sediment, this metropolis of aching feet will wear down even the most resolute of travellers (and travel writers). The name Rome passed out of the plane of reality into legend some 2,200 years ago, when princes as far away as China first began to hear of the faraway city and its invincible armies. At the same time the Romans were cooking up a personified goddess, the Divine Rome, and beginning the strange myth of their destiny to conquer and pacify the world, a myth that would still haunt Europe a thousand years later.

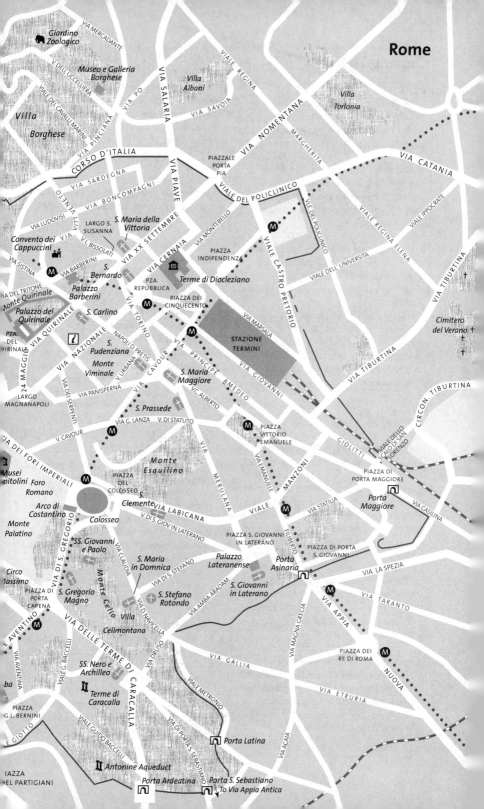

Getting There

By Air

The main airport, **Leonardo da Vinci**, is usually referred to as **Fiumicino** (**t** 06 65951). Taking a **taxi** from there into Rome should cost about L70,000, including airport and luggage supplements. There are two **rail** links from the airport to the city: to Stazioni Trastevere, Ostiense, Tuscolana and Tiburtina (*every 20mins; L7,500*) and a direct service to Stazione Termini, Rome's main rail station (*hourly; L15,000*).

Between 10.20pm and 7am, COTRAL **buses** run from outside the Arrivals hall to Stazione Ostiense, near ⓂPiramide (*hourly; L6,000*). The train takes about 30mins from Fiumicino to Tiburtina; the bus takes at least 50mins.

A secondary airport, **Ciampino** (**t** 06 794 941) is the base for a few passenger and charter flights. A COTRAL **bus** runs from here to the Anagnina stop at the southern end of the **metro** A line, from where it's about 20mins to Stazione Termini (*daily 6.15am–10.20pm*).

By Rail

Almost all long-distance trains arrive at and depart from the huge, chaotic but efficient **Stazione Termini**. The information and ticket windows are often terribly crowded, so allow plenty of time. There is a taxi stand in front, along with city buses to most points in Rome, and the main metro station is underneath.

There are plenty of other stations: **Tiburtina** (ⓂTiburtina), on the eastern edge of town, and **Ostiense** (ⓂPiramide), south of the Monte Aventino, serve some long-distance north–south lines.

During the night (*12 midnight–5am*), Stazione Termini is shut and trains stop at the other stations. A few trains to Tuscany and Umbria start from **Ostiense** and stop at **Trastevere**, on Viale Trastevere.

The Lazio transport authority, COTRAL, also operates its own little rail network: the Roma-Nord line to **Viterbo**, from their own station on Piazzale Flaminio, north of Piazza del Popolo, and a line to **Ostia** and the Lido, from Porta San Paolo (next to the main Stazione Ostiense FS) and ⓂMagliana (Line B).

By Bus

COTRAL buses serve almost every town in Lazio. They leave from different locations around the edge of Rome, depending on the destination: buses heading north-northwest leave from Saxa Rubra (on the Roma-Nord rail line) and Lepanto (ⓂLepanto); for the south, southwest and east, buses leave from ⓂAnagnina, ⓂEUR Fermi and ⓂTiburtina. For details (in Italian) about schedules and fares, call freephone, **t** 167 431 784 (*Mon–Fri 9–1 and 2–5*). Many different companies offer long-distance bus services to and from Rome; check with the tourist office.

By Road

All the *autostrade* converging on Rome run into the giant ring road, the *Grande Raccordo Anulare* or *GRA*. From there, good routes into the city are the Via Aurelia (SS1) from the west, the local SS201 *autostrada* from the airport in the southwest, and the A24 from the east. Rome is, as it has been for 2,000 years, the hub of a network of ancient routes serving every direction, now transmogrified into state roads (SS) but retaining their old names; they still provide the most direct means of escape.

Getting Around

Looking at the map, Rome seems to be made for getting around on foot. This may be so in the *centro storico* around Piazza Navona, but elsewhere it's deceptive – city blocks in the newer areas are huge, and it will always take you longer than you think to walk anywhere. The hills, the outsize scale and the traffic also make Rome a tiring place, but there is some pleasant strolling to be had in the old districts west of the Corso, around the Isola Tiberina, in old Trastevere and around the Monte Celio.

By Metro

Rome's underground system is not particularly convenient, as it seems to avoid the historic parts of the city; imagine trying to dig any sort of hole in Rome, with legions of archaeologists ready to pounce. The two lines, A and B, cross at Stazione Termini and will take you to the Colosseum, around the Monte Aventino, to Piazza di Spagna, San Giovanni in

Laterano, San Paolo Fuori le Mura (Outside the Walls), Piazza del Popolo, or within eight blocks of St Peter's. Single tickets (L1,500), also good for city buses – valid for 75mins from obliteration in the turnstile – are available from machines in metro stations and tobacconists, bars and kiosks.

By Bus and Tram

Buses are by far the best way to get around. Pick up a map of the bus routes from the **ATAC** (city bus company) booth outside Stazione Termini. Bus tickets (L1,500) are good for travel on any ATAC city bus or tram and one metro ride – within 75mins of the first use of the ticket – which must be stamped in the machines in the back entrance of buses or trams. There are also special-price full-day tickets (which include the metro too), as well as weekly and monthly passes available from tobacconists. Most routes run frequently, and are often crowded.

Some Useful Bus Routes

19 (tram) Piazza Risorgimento (near the Vatican)–Viale delle Milizie–Villa Borghese–Viale Regina Margherita–Porta Maggiore–San Lorenzo and Via Prenestina.

23 Musei Vaticani–Castel Sant'Angelo–Tiber banks–Porta San Paolo–S. Paolo.

30 (tram) Villa Borghese–Viale Regina Margherita–San Lorenzo–S. Giovanni in Laterano– Colosseum–Viale Aventino–Porta San Paolo (a fun trip, taking in many sights).

36 Termini–Via Nomentana (Sant'Agnese).

46 Piazza Venezia–Corso Vittorio Emanuele–Vatican.

56 Largo Argentina–Via del Corso–Via del Tritone–Via Vittorio Veneto.

64 Termini–Via Nazionale–Corso Vittorio Emanuele–Vatican (the main bus route from the centro storico to the Vatican).

115 Termini–Via Nazionale–Via del Tritone–Via del Corso–Piazza Venezia–Largo Argentina–Mausoleo di Augusto (a circular minibus, weekdays 8am–9pm).

116 Via Veneto–Piazza Barberini–Via del Tritone–Piazza del Parlamento–Corso Rinascimento–Corso Vittorio Emanuele–Campo de' Fiori–Piazza Farnese–Via Giulia (a circular minibus, weekdays 8am–9pm, Sat 8am–midnight).

117 Piazza di Spagna–Via del Babuino–Piazza del Popolo–Via del Corso–Piazza Venezia–Via dei Fori Imperiali (a circular minibus).

218 S. Giovanni in Laterano–Porta San Sebastiano–Via Appia Antica–Via Ardeatina (passing the catacombs and tombs).

By Taxi

Official taxis (painted yellow or white) are in plentiful supply, and easier to get at a rank in one of the main piazzas than to flag down. They are quite expensive, with surcharges for luggage, on Sundays and after 10.30 pm. Fares and charges are clearly explained in English inside every taxi. Don't expect to find one when it's raining.

To phone for a taxi, call **t** 06 3570, or **t** 06 4994; you don't pay extra for calling a cab, but expect to pay for the time it takes for it to reach you.

By Car

Absolutely not recommended! Rome isn't as chaotic as Naples, but nearly so. Parking is expensive and difficult to find; many areas in the centre are closed to traffic (and the signs for them are hard to spot) and riddled with narrow, one-way streets. Rome and its cars are mortal enemies; sooner or later one or the other will have to succumb.

Tourist Information

The main office at Via Parigi 5, **t** 06 4889 9253, three blocks north of Stazione Termini, just behind the Terme di Diocleziano, is currently closed for renovations.

The city runs a tourist information hotline with English-speaking operators (**t** 06 3600 4399), and has a website (www.romturismo. com), which provides updated information in English on sites and events.

There are also tourist information kiosks (all open 9–6) on the corner of Via del Corso and Via Condotti; next to Castel Sant'Angelo; halfway down Via dei Fori Imperiali; just off Piazza Navona; in front of the Palazzo delle Esposizioni, on Via Nazionale; beside Santa Maria Maggiore and beside San Giovanni in Laterano; and at Stazione Termini (open 8am–9pm) and at Fiumicino airport.

The **Hotel Reservation Service, t** 06 699 1000 (*open daily 7am–10pm*) offers commission-free reservations at hundreds of hotels.

Enjoy Rome, Via Varese 39, **t** 06 445 1843, also near Stazione Termini, is an efficient privately run English-speaking information service which organizes inexpensive walking tours. Two weeklies available from news-stands, *Romac'e'* (with a short English section at the back) and *Time Out* (in Italian), are the best sources of information on what's on in Rome in the arts, culture and entertainment.

The **main post office** is at Piazza San Silvestro, **t** 06 6771.

Shopping

Rome isn't as exciting for big-game shoppers as Milan, though when it comes to clothing you will find all the major designers and labels well represented. There is no shortage of shops selling **antiques**, a great number of them clustered together between the Tiber and Piazza Navona; look especially off Via Monserrato, Via dei Coronari and Via dell'Anima. For **old prints**, generally inexpensive, try Casali, Piazza Rotonda 81/a; Alinari, Via Alibert 16/a is a good address for artistic **black and white pictures** of old Rome. L'Art Nouveau, Via dei Coronari 221, offers just what its name implies. **Antiques** also show up in the celebrated Sunday morning **flea market** at Porta Portese, as well as anything else you can imagine, all lumped together in often surreal displays (*open just after dawn–around 12 noon*). Beware the pickpockets.

The most **fashionable shopping** is on the streets between Piazza di Spagna and the Corso. Some special items: Massoni, Largo Goldoni 48, near Via Condotti, much frequented by film stars, sells some of Rome's finest **jewellery**; for **menswear**, Testa, Via Borgognona 13, and Via Frattina 42, or Valentino Uomo, Via Condotti 13, or for **custom tailoring**, Battistoni, Via Condotti 61/a. For **women's clothes** try the outlets of the big designers in the same area: Missoni, Via del Babuino 96; Giorgio Armani, Via Condotti 77; and Via del Babuino 102; Mila Schöen, Via Condotti 51; or the Rome-based Fendi, Via Borgognona 8, 10, 12 and 39. For **leather**, the

Gucci outlet is at Via Condotti 8, and do not miss Fausto Santini, Via Frattina 120. **Discounted designer fashion** may be had at Il Discount dell'Alta Moda, Via Gesù e Maria 16/a; for **high-fashion shoes**, try Barrilà, Via Condotti 29, and Via del Babuino 33; and for **Borsalino hats**, Troncarelli, Via della Cuccagna 15, near Piazza Navona.

For a special bottle of **wine**, try Enoteca Costantini, Piazza Cavour 16, for a wide selection. If you wish to stock up on Italian **coffee**, Tazza d'Oro, Via degli Orfani 84, has special bags of the city's best, the 'Aroma di Roma'. If you need a good **book**, try the Anglo-American Book Co., Via della Vite 57, the Lion Bookshop, Via dei Greci 36, or the Economy Book Center, Via Torino 136, near Via Nazionale.

For an amazing selection of **fancy kitchen gear**, there's C.U.C.I.N.A., Via del Babuino 118/a, while for serious, **professional pans, pots and tools** head to Zucchi, Via Sant'Antonio all'Esquilino 15, near Santa Maria Maggiore. Try Image, Via della Scrofa 67, for **alternative posters, postcards and photographs**; and De Ritis, Via de' Cestari 1, for the latest **ecclesiastical fashions**, along with madonnas, crucifixes and chalices.

Sports and Activities

Rome's main public **swimming pool** is the Piscina delle Rose, Viale America 20, in EUR, **t** 06 592 6717 (Ⓜ EUR Fermi) (*open June 15–Sept daily 9–7*). There is also an attractive private pool at the Centro Sportivo Italiano, Lungotevere Flaminio 55, about half a mile north of Piazza del Popolo, **t** 06 323 4732 (*open in summer*).

Rome's two first-division **football** clubs, AS Roma and Lazio, both play on Saturday or Sunday afternoon at the Stadio Olimpico, Via del Foro Italico (Ⓜ Linea A to Ottaviano, then bus no.32) during the season (*Sept–May*). Tickets for Lazio start at L28,000; contact Lazio Point, Via Farini 34, **t** 06 482 6688; or Orbis.

Where to Stay

Rome ✉ 00100

For a city that has been entertaining visitors for the last 2,000 years, Rome has not acquired any special flair for accommodating them. Perhaps it is just the uninterrupted flow of the curious and faithful that keeps prices higher and service and quality lower than elsewhere in Italy. From *belle époque* palaces on Via Veneto to grimy hovels on the wrong side of Stazione Termini, there will always be somewhere for you to come home to after a hard day's sightseeing, although places with a history, a view or quiet gardens are rare. Exceptions exist, but this is probably not the place to make the big splurge. Check into some comfortable spot in the area that suits your fancy, and save your big hotel money for Venice or the Amalfi Coast. In the 1890s, when the Stazione Termini district was the choicest part of Rome, the streets around the station spawned hundreds of hotels, some quite elegant. Today much of the city's accommodation is still here. Unfortunately it has gone the way of all such 19th-century toadstool neighbourhoods: overbuilt, dingy and down-at-heel, not at all the place to savour Rome. It's also inconvenient for most of the sights.

Luxury

★★★★★**Hassler-Villa Medici**, Piazza Trinità dei Monti 6, **t** 06 699 340, **f** 06 678 9991. One of Rome's best hotels, with a fine location at the top of the Spanish Steps and wonderful views over the city for those who book far enough in advance. Around for over a century, it has regained its position as the élite hotel of Rome, with a beautiful court-yard, deferential service and large wood-panelled rooms.

★★★★★**Excelsior**, Via V. Veneto 125, **t** 06 47081, **f** 06 482 6205. Also located in a choice area, though lacking the aura it had in the 1950s. The reception areas have thicker carpets, bigger chandeliers and more gilded plaster than anywhere in Italy, and most of the rooms are just as good – don't let them give you a modernized one. There are saunas, a famous bar and as much personal attention as you could ask for.

★★★★**D'Inghilterra**, Via Bocca di Leone 14, **t** 06 699 811, **f** 06 6992 2243. Another favourite near Piazza di Spagna. Parts of this building date from the 15th century, when it served as a prince's guest house; in its career as a hotel, since 1850, it has played host to most

of the literati and artists of Europe and America.

★★★★**Forum**, Via Tor de' Conti 25, **t** 06 679 2446, **f** 06 678 6479. The only fancy establishment near the ancient Forum; it's somewhat worn, but has unbeatable views from the roof terrace.

★★★★**Columbus**, Via della Conciliazione 33, **t** 06 686 5435, **f** 06 686 4874. Staid but reliable with nice rooms, some with views over St Peter's; prices are a bit high.

Very Expensive

★★★★**Cardinal**, Via Giulia 62, **t** 06 6880 2719, **f** 06 678 6376. In the heart of the *centro storico*; perhaps the best place to experience Renaissance Rome – in a building attributed to Bramante and completely restored, without spoiling the atmosphere.

★★★**Carriage**, Via delle Carrozze 36, **t** 06 699 0124, **f** 06 678 8279. Almost at the foot of the Spanish Steps; sleepy but well-run.

★★★**Fontana**, Piazza di Trevi 96, **t** 06 678 6113, **f** 06 679 0024. This would be a good hotel anywhere; and it also happens to be right across the street from the Trevi Fountain – something to look at out of your window that will guarantee sweet dreams, even if you don't wake up next to Anita Ekberg.

★★★**Gregoriana**, Via Gregoriana 18, **t** 06 679 4269, **f** 06 678 4258. Close to the Spanish Steps but reasonably priced; small, tasteful and gratifyingly friendly, with a devoted regular clientele – there are only 19 rooms, so book early.

★★★★**La Residenza**, Via Emilia 22, **t** 06 488 0789, **f** 06 485 721. Near the Via Veneto; stands out as a very pleasant base, with beautifully appointed rooms in an old town house, and some luxuries more common to the most expensive hotels.

★★★**Teatro di Pompeo**, Largo del Pallaro 8, **t** 06 6830 0170, **f** 06 6880 5531. A small hotel built on Teatro di Pompeo by Campo de' Fiori, perfect for peace and quiet.

★★★**Villa Florence**, Via Nomentana 28, **t** 06 440 3036, **f** 06 440 2709. Near the Porta Pia; a very well-run and friendly hotel in a refurbished 19th-century villa with a garden.

★★★**Villa del Parco**, Via Nomentana 110, **t** 06 4423 7773, **f** 06 4423 7572. Similar, but slightly more expensive.

***Hotel Sant'Anselmo**, Piazza Sant'
Anselmo 2, t 06 574 3547, f 06 578 3604. Up
on the Monte Aventino, a very peaceful hotel
with a garden and comfortable rooms.
***Villa San Pio**, Via Sant'Anselmo 19, t 06 578
3214, f 06 574 112. Run by the same
management, and just as peaceful.

Expensive
**Campo de' Fiori, Via del Biscione 6,
t 06 6880 6865, f 06 687 6003. Small
comfortable rooms and a roof terrace
overlooking Campo de' Fiori.
**Margutta, Via Laurina 34, t 06 322 3674,
f 06 320 0395. In a quiet street off Via del
Babuino, with simple accommodation.
**Sole, Via del Biscione 76, t 06 6880 6873,
f 06 689 3787. A large old hotel with lots of
character, just off the Campo de' Fiori
market square.
**Primavera, Via San Pantaleo 3, t 06 6880
3109, f 06 686 9265. A slightly cheaper hotel
just west of Piazza Navona.

Moderate
**Abruzzi, Piazza della Rotonda 69, t 06 679
2021. Has views over the Pantheon, but none
of the rooms have private bath.
*Campo Marzio, Piazza Campo Marzio 7,
t/f 06 6880 1486. Just north of the
Pantheon; no rooms have private baths.
*San Paolo, Via Panisperna 95, t 06 474 5213,
f 06 474 5218. In a good location in the Monti
neighbourhood between Via dei Fori
Imperiali and Stazione Termini; has simple
rooms with or without private baths.
The area around Termini offers a wide choice
of inexpensive hotels, ranging from plain,
family-run establishments – often quite
comfortable and friendly – to bizarre dives
with exposed plumbing.
*Katty, Via Palestro 35, t/f 06 444 1216. Simple
and clean, on a street on the east side of the
station which has several cheap hotels.

Eating Out

Unlike many other Italians, the Romans
aren't afraid to try something new. Chinese
restaurants have appeared in droves, not to
mention Arab, Korean and macrobiotic places.

This should not be taken as a reflection on
local cooking. Rome attracts talented chefs
from all over Italy, and every region is
represented by a restaurant somewhere in
town, giving a microcosm of Italian cuisine
you'll find nowhere else.

The grand old tradition of Roman cooking
has specialities such as *saltimbocca* (literally
'jump in the mouth'), paper-thin slices of veal
cooked with *prosciutto*, *stracciatella* (a soup
with eggs, parmesan cheese and parsley), fried
artichokes called *carciofi alla giudia* and veal
involtini. In the less expensive places you are
likely to encounter such favourites as *baccalà*
(salt cod), *bucatini all'amatriciana* (in a tomato
and bacon sauce) or *alla carbonara* (with egg
and bacon), tripe and *gnocchi*. Unless you ask
for something different, the wine will
probably come from the Castelli Romani –
light, fruity whites, of which the best come
from Frascati and Velletri.

Though you can drop as much as L170,000
(without wine) if you follow the politicians
and the TV crowd, prices generally manage to
keep close to the Italian average – Rome is
much more reasonable than Milan. Watch out
for tourist traps – places near a major sight
with a 'tourist menu', for example. Rome also
has some expensive joints that could best be
described as parodies of old, famous
establishments; they advertise heavily and
aren't hard to smell out. Hotel restaurants,
those in the de luxe class, can often be quite
good but ridiculously expensive.

Very Expensive
La Pergola dell'Hotel Hilton, Via Cadlolo 4,
t 06 3509 2211. Perched high above the city,
this is currently Rome's most celebrated
restaurant for *alta cucina* served in elegant
surroundings with all of Rome at your feet.
Reserve well ahead. *Open for dinner only;
closed Sun, Mon and Jan.*
La Rosetta, Via della Rosetta 8, near the
Pantheon, t 06 686 1002. Rome's best fish-
only restaurant; even if you aren't dining,
step in to admire the heap of shiny fish,
oysters and sea-urchins arranged on the
marble slab in the hall. Reserve well ahead.
Closed Sun and Aug.
Piperno, Via Monte de' Cenci 9, t 06 6880
6629. There is no better place to try *carciofi*

alla giudia than right on the edge of the old ghetto at Rome's most famous purveyor of Roman-Jewish cooking – simple dishes on the whole, but prepared and served with refinement. *Closed Sun eve and Mon.*

Across the river, Trastevere, with its attractive piazzas and tables outside, has long been a popular corner of the city for dining. Many of its restaurants specialize in fish:

Alberto Ciarla, Piazza San Cosimato 40, **t** 06 581 8668. South of Santa Maria in Trastevere; the French-trained owner, proud enough to put his name on the sign, sees to it that everything is delicately and perfectly done, and graciously served: oysters, seafood *ravioli* and quite a few adventurous styles of *pesce crudo* (raw fish) are among the most asked for. *Dinner only; closed Sun.*

Sabatini, Piazza Santa Maria in Trastevere 13, **t** 06 581 2026. Not far away, this place has been a Roman institution for many a year, as much for the cuisine (again, lots of seafood) as for the tables outside, which face the piazza and its church. *Closed Tues in winter, Wed in summer, and two weeks in Aug.*

Vecchia Roma, Piazza Campitelli 18, **t** 06 686 4604. Good food, an imaginative seasonal menu and a quiet setting with outdoor tables; close to Piazza Venezia. *Closed Wed.*

Checchino dal 1887, Via di Monte Testaccio 30, **t** 06 574 6318. If you find yourself anywhere around Porta San Paolo and the Testaccio district at dinnertime, don't pass up a chance to dine at the acknowledged temple of old Roman cooking, which has been owned by the same family for 107 years – the longest known in Rome. Both the fancy and humble sides of Roman food are well represented, with plenty of the powerful offal dishes that Romans have been eating since ancient times – look out for brains (*cervello*) and tripe (*trippa*). The setting is unique – on the edge of Monte Testaccio, with one of Rome's best cellars excavated underneath the hill. *Closed Sun eve, Mon and Aug.*

Antico Arco, Piazzale Aurelio 7, **t** 06 581 5274. Well worth the climb up the Monte Gianicolo; this is a reliable, informal restaurant for no-nonsense creative Italian cuisine. Reserve. *Closed Sun, Aug, and open only for dinner.*

Expensive

Dal Toscano, Via Germanico 58, **t** 06 397 25717. Perhaps your best option in the tourist-trap Vatican area: family-run and very popular with Roman families, offering well-prepared Tuscan specialities like *pici* (rough, fresh spaghetti rolled by hand) in game sauce, and *fiorentina* steak – and home-made desserts. Reserve. *Closed Mon.*

Papà Baccus, Via Toscana 33, **t** 06 4274 2808. Another Tuscan place off the Via Veneto, also family-run but slightly fancier and more expensive. Remarkably good *prosciutto*, delicious potato *ravioli* and, in winter, baked fish with artichokes, along with regional soups and *fiorentina*. Reserve. *Closed Sat lunch, Sun, and two weeks in Aug.*

Myosotis, Vicolo della Vaccarella 3, **t** 06 686 5554. A great family-run restaurant with an ample menu of traditional and creative meat and fish dishes. Near the Pantheon. *Closed Sun and Aug.*

Nino, Via Borgognona 11, **t** 06 678 6752. The Piazza di Spagna area is not as promising for restaurants, but there are a few, of which this is perhaps the best. A flask full of cannellini beans simmers in the window, the signpost for true, well-prepared Tuscan cuisine. *Closed Sun.*

Al Presidente, Via in Arcione 95, **t** 06 679 7342. A few steps from the Trevi Fountain, this is a safe option offering fish in all styles. *Closed Tues and Wed lunch, four weeks between Jan and Feb, and two weeks in Aug.*

Dal Bolognese, Piazza del Popolo 1, **t** 06 361 11426. With tables outside on the grand piazza and a view of the Pincio, this is the place to go to sample Emilian specialities – don't miss the tortellini or any other fresh pasta dish, and finish with *fruttini*, a selection of real fruit shells each filled with its own sorbet flavour. *Closed Mon and Aug.*

Paris, Piazza San Calisto 7/a, **t** 06 581 5378. Just beyond Piazza Santa Maria in Trastevere; serves classic Roman-Jewish cuisine; particularly good is the *minestra di arzilla* (skate soup). *Closed Sun eve and Mon.*

The quarters just outside the Aurelian wall and north and east of the Villa Borghese are more good places to look for restaurants:

Le Coppedè, Via Taro 28/a, between Via Nomentana and Villa Ada, **t** 06 841 1772.

A neighbourhood restaurant totally devoted to Pugliese cuisine, which is lighter than typical Roman fare.

Moderate

Less expensive places are not hard to find in the *centro storico*, although chances to eat anything more refined than hearty Roman cuisine are low.

L'Eau Vive, Via Monterone 85, **t** 06 6880 1095. An exception to the above: only in Rome would you find a good French restaurant run by a Catholic lay missionary society – *sole meunière* and onion soup in the well-scrubbed and righteous atmosphere not far from the Pantheon. A nourishing meal at a modest price, served with serenity, will have you joining in a prayer to the Virgin before dessert; the fixed lunch menu is a great bargain. *Closed Sun and Aug*.

Roman Lounge de l'Hotel d'Inghilterra, Via Bocca di Leone 14, **t** 06 699 81500. Another exception: an elegant retreat in the heart of the shopping district at the foot of the Spanish Steps, which at lunchtime offers an interesting cheap *piatto unico* (one-dish menu); if you like their style you can return for a very expensive dinner.

Grappolo d'Oro, Piazza della Cancelleria 80, **t** 06 686 4118. Near Campo de' Fiori; offers exceptionally good value traditional Roman cooking. (*Closed Sun*).

Il Collegio, Via Pie' di Marmo 36, **t** 06 679 2570. Not far from the Pantheon; has tables outside and a few Roman first courses along with more imaginative dishes and a good chocolate soufflé. *Closed Sat lunch and Sun*.

Armando al Pantheon, Salita de' Crescenzi 31, **t** 06 6880 3034. Nearby, an authentic Roman *trattoria* famous for *spaghetti cacio e pepe* (with pecorino cheese and black pepper) or *all'amatriciana*, *saltimbocca*, and a delicious *ricotta* tart. *Closed Sat eve, Sun, and Aug*.

Da Lucia, Vicolo del Mattonato, **t** 06 580 3601. Situated two streets north of Piazza Santa Maria in Trastevere, this small family *trattoria* offers local cooking in a typical setting. *Closed Mon and Aug*.

Antico Falcone, Via Trionfale 60, **t** 06 3974 3385. If you are near the Vatican, an area of forgettable tourist restaurants, venture a little way north to this simple place housed in what's left of a 15th-century farmhouse, for tasty *rigatoni alla nasona* (pasta with melted cheese and tomato sauce), *melanzane* (aubergines) *alla parmigiana* and *carciofi alla giudia* when the artichokes are in season. *Closed Tues*.

Gino in Vicolo Rosini, Vicolo Rosini 4, off Piazza del Parlamento, **t** 06 687 3434. An excellent budget *trattoria* in the centre, near the parliament, often crammed with civil servants and the occasional deputy. *Closed Sun and Aug*.

If the thought of a full meal sandwiched between Roman antiquities and Baroque treasures seems a bit much, consider lunch in a wine bar, which offer good selections of cured meat and cheese, soups, salads and occasional quiches and flans, and desserts (usually) made in-house. Choose from about 20 wines *in mescita* (by the glass) and hundreds by the bottle:

Semidivino, Via Alessandria 230, **t** 06 4425 0795. A classy and intimate wine bar – also good for a first-rate meal based on excellent salads, an interesting selection of cheese and pork-cured meat and comforting soups. *Closed Sat lunch, Sun, and Aug*.

Trimani Winebar, Via Cernaia 37/b, near Stazione Termini, **t** 06 446 9630 *Closed Sun and Aug*.

La Bottega del Vino di Anacleto Bleve, Via Santa Maria del Pianto 9/11, in the Ghetto, **t** 06 686 5970. *Closed Sun and Aug, open for lunch only Mon, Tues and Sat, open for dinner too Wed–Fri*.

Cavour 313, Via Cavour 313, **t** 06 678 5496 *Closed Sun in summer, Sat eve in winter*.

Among the vast array of unexciting restaurants that cram the streets around Termini there are also several African places:

Africa, Via Gaeta 46, **t** 06 494 1077. An Ethiopian/Eritrean restaurant that offers spicy meals at very low prices. *Open for breakfast; closed Mon*.

Also try the student area of San Lorenzo, east of the station, where there is a much better assortment of *trattorie*:

Tram Tram, Via dei Reti 44, **t** 06 490 416. Crowded and trendy. *Closed Mon*.

Pizzerie

Roman pizza is crisp and thin, although the softer, thicker Neapolitan-style pizza has recently won a fat slice of the market. Most *pizzerie* have tables outside and are open only for dinner, often until 2am.

Da Baffetto, Via del Governo Vecchio 11, **t** 06 686 1617. A beloved institution not far from Piazza Navona.

Ivo, Via San Francesco a Ripa 158, in Trastevere, **t** 06 581 7082. Large and crowded, on the other side of the river. *Closed Tues.*

Formula 1, Via degli Equi 13. As racy as its name. *Closed Sun; open eves only.*

Panattoni, Viale Trastevere 53, **t** 06 580 0919. Perhaps the best place to see *pizzaioli* at work. Known by locals as the *obitorio* (mortuary) because of its marble-topped tables and bare walls. *Closed Wed.*

Dar Poeta, Vicolo del Bologna 45, **t** 06 588 0516. More on the verge of Neapolitan pizza, and perhaps the only one in town with a pizza dessert, *calzone di ricotta* (filled with *ricotta* and chocolate) and a non-smoking room. *Closed Mon.*

Al Forno della Soffitta, Via dei Villini 1/e, off the Via Nomentana, **t** 06 440 4642. For strictly authentic Neapolitan pizza, head to this pricey *pizzeria*, where they also have delicious pastry delivered daily from Naples. *Closed Sun and Aug.*

Entertainment and Nightlife

The best entertainment in Rome is often in the passing cosmopolitan spectacle of its streets; as nightlife goes, it can be a real snoozer compared with other European cities, though if you don't expect too much you'll have a good time.

Like all Italians, many Romans have most of their fun with their families and a close-knit circle of friends, and teenagers will spend hours simply hanging out in or outside bars, before heading off to a club or back home.

If you're determined, however, the back streets around the Piazza Navona or Campo de' Fiori swarm with people in the evenings, and these are the places to come to plan your night ahead, as leaflets and free tickets are always being handed out. Often these are to new places that have opened, offering a long-awaited alternative to the ultra-chic posturing in the 'in' spots of the hour.

Another source is *Romac'e'* (from newsstands), with comprehensive listings and a small section in English, or the weekly *Time Out*, with listings and articles (in Italian).

Rome can be uncomfortably sticky in August, but, unlike in Milan, there's plenty going on. The *Estate Romana* (Roman Summer) is a three-month long festival of outdoor events, music, theatre and film (shown on outdoor screens around the city), and most museums run longer hours. Ask at the tourist office for information, check *Romac'e'*, and keep an eye out for posters.

A far older Roman party is the traditional **Festa de' Noantri** in Trastevere (16–31 July), where you may well find a gust of old Roman spontaneity along with music from all across the spectrum, acrobats, dancing and stall upon stall extending down Viale Trastevere and into the quarter's piazzas.

Opera, Classical Music, Theatre and Film

If you want to go to any events or concerts in Rome, try to get tickets as soon as possible to avoid disappointment. **Orbis**, Piazza Esquilino 37, **t** 06 474 4776, is a reliable agency for concert, opera and theatre tickets (*open Mon–Sat 9.30–1 and 4–7.30*).

From November until May you can take in a performance at the **Teatro dell'Opera di Roma**, Via Firenze 72 (box office, **t** 06 4816 0255, information, **t** 06 481 601).

Other concerts are performed at and by the **Accademia Nazionale di Santa Cecilia**, in the auditorium on Via della Conciliazione 4 (box office, **t** 06 6880 1044, information, **t** 06 361 1064), and by the **Accademia Filarmonica** at the **Teatro Olimpico**, Piazza Gentile da Fabriano 17 (box office, **t** 06 323 4936, information, **t** 06 323 4890).

Medieval, Baroque, chamber and choral music are frequently performed at the **Oratorio del Gonfalone**, Via del Gonfalone 32/a, **t** 06 687 5952.

Traditionally during the summer there has been a range of special seasons, although of late Rome has become noticeably sluggish in organizing programmes. Evening concerts are held outside in the **Teatro di Marcello, t** 06 481 4800, or **t** 06 780 4314 (*mid-June–Sept*), and concerts are performed by the Accademia di Santa Cecilia and visiting international orchestras at **Villa Giulia** (*July*).

The opera moves outside in the summer – in the **Terme di Caracalla** up until a few years ago, when it was feared that the site was being damaged. Every year there is talk of a return to the glorious baths, but for now the **Villa Borghese** and the **soccer stadium** serve as alternative venues.

Alternatively, you may want to do as the Romans do and head out to Umbria for the **Spoleto Festival** or the **Umbria Jazz** festival (*see* **Umbria** for both), or fight it out for a ticket to one of the big-name rock concerts at Stadio Flaminio or Palaeur (EUR's Palazzo dello Sport), neither of which wins any blue ribbons.

Despite the Italian tendency to dub all foreign films, you can find films in *versione originale* at the **Alcazar**, Via Cardinal Merry del Val 14, **t** 06 588 0099 (*Mon*); **Nuovo Sacher**, Largo Ascianghi 1, **t** 06 581 8116 (*Mon and Tues*); Quirinetta, Via Minghetti 4, **t** 06 679 0012; and **Pasquino**, on Piazza Sant'Egidio, near Santa Maria in Trastevere, **t** 06 5833 3310 (*daily*).

Cafés and Bars

When you're tired of window-shopping you can rest your legs at Rome's oldest café (1760), the **Antico Caffè Greco**, Via Condotti 86, and sit where Keats and Casanova sipped their java – an institution that offers the cheapest chance for a 20-minute dose of *ancien régime* luxury in Rome.

Another of the city's grand cafés is the **Caffè Rosati**, in Piazza del Popolo, an elegant place founded in 1922, and popular with the Roman intelligentsia, no doubt attracted by its extravagant ice-creams.

Other cafés can be dignified, historic or crazily expensive – for example, the 150-year-old **Babington's Tea Rooms**, on Piazza di Spagna, for scones and tea or a full lunch in the proper Victorian atmosphere. At trendy **Sant'Eustachio**, Piazza Sant'Eustachio, near Piazza Navona, home of Rome's most famous coffee, tell them to mind the sugar.

Another kind of Roman bar is represented by the ultra-hip and overpriced **Bar della Pace**, Via della Pace 3, frequented by celebrities and a

place for serious posing. A funky and friendly atmosphere can be found most evenings at **La Vineria**, Campo de' Fiori 15, a relaxed traditional wine bar/shop with tables outside.

It's not hard to find *gelato* on every corner in Rome, but hold out for the best the city has to offer, at the celebrated **Il Gelato di San Crispino**, Via della Panetteria 42, near the Trevi Fountain.

Another novelty are sweets from **Il Forno del Ghetto** (*closed Sat*), the Jewish bakery at the west end of Via del Portico d'Ottavia (note the incredible building it's in – a recycled ancient structure covered in reliefs and inscriptions).

Rock, Jazz and Clubs

Rome has a select band of clubs with live music – *Romac'e'* will have details of current programmes at the following venues. All are what Italians call *di tendenza*, meaning they keep up with current UK and US trends.

Il Locale; Vicolo del Fico 3, **t** 06 687 9075, a club that features hip and trendy Italian bands.

Big Mama, Vicolo San Francesco a Ripa 18, in Trastevere, **t** 06 581 2551, one of the main **rock** venues.

Alpheus, Via del Commercio, 36/38, in Ostiense, **t** 06 574 7826, a **blues** club.

Caffè Latino, Via di Monte Testaccio 96, **t** 06 5728 8556, a mostly dance-club with live latin music – well off the usual tourist circuit in a 'groovy' zone.

Alexanderplatz, Via Ostia 9, in Prati, **t** 06 3974 2171, a suave jazz venue.

New Mississippi Jazz Club, Borgo Angelico 18/a, near San Pietro, **t** 06 6880 6348, may be a little less suave but features foreign as well as Italian performers.

Alien, Via Velletri 13, near Piazza Fiume, **t** 06 841 2212, Alpheus, Via del Commercio 36/38, off Via Ostiense, **t** 06 574 7826 is an established venue for serious **dancing** .

Gilda, Via Mario de' Fiori 97, close to the Spanish Steps, **t** 06 678 4838 is less juvenile, catering to Roman yuppies (jacket required).

Most indoor clubs and music venues close down completely in late July and August. This is the time, though, when **beach discos** along the coast at Ostia, Fregene and points further afield are hugely popular – and great fun, compared to the stuffy winter venues.

In our prosaic times, though, you may find it requires a considerable effort of the imagination to break through to the past Romes of the Caesars and popes. They exist, but first you will need to peel away the increasingly thick veneer of the 'Third Rome', the burgeoning, thoroughly up-to-date creation of post-Reunification Italy. Ancient Rome at the height of its glory had perhaps a million and a half people; today there are four million, and at any given time at least half of them will be pushing their way into the Metro train while you are trying to get off. The popes, for all their centuries of experience in spectacle and ceremony, cannot often steal the show in this new Rome, and have to share the stage with a deplorable overabundance of preposterous politicians, with *Cinecittà* and the rest of the cultural apparatus of a great nation, and of course with the tourists, who sometimes put on the best show in town. The old guard *Romani*, now a minority in a city swollen with new arrivals, bewail the loss of Rome's slow and easy pace, its vintage brand of *dolce vita* that once impressed other Italians, let alone foreigners. Lots of money, lots of traffic and an endless caravan of tour buses have a way of compromising even the most beautiful cities. Don't concern yourself; the present is only one snapshot from a 2,600-year history, and no one has ever left Rome disappointed.

History

The beginnings are obscure enough. Historians believe the settlement of the Tiber Valley began some time around 1000 BC, when an outbreak of volcanic eruptions in the Alban Hills to the south forced the Latin tribes down into the lowlands. Beyond that there are few clues for the archaeologists to follow. But remembering that every ancient legend conceals a kernel of truth – perhaps more poetic than scientific – it would be best to follow the accounts of Virgil, the poet of the Empire, and Livy, the great 1st-century chronicler and mythographer. When Virgil wrote, in the reign of Augustus, Greek culture was an irresistible force in all the recently civilized lands of the Mediterranean. For Rome, Virgil concocted the story of Aeneas, fleeing from Troy after the Homeric sack and finding his way to Latium. Descent from the Trojans, however specious, connected Rome to the Greek world and made it seem less of an upstart. As Virgil tells it, Aeneas' son Ascanius founded *Alba Longa*, a city that by the 800s was leader of the Latin Confederation. Livy takes up the tale with Numitor, a descendant of Ascanius and rightful king of Alba Longa, tossed off the throne by his usurping brother Amulius. In order that Numitor should have no heirs, Amulius forced Numitor's daughter Rhea Silvia into service as a Vestal Virgin. Here Rome's destiny begins, with an appearance in the Vestals' chambers of the god Mars, staying just long enough to leave Rhea Silvia pregnant with the precocious twins Romulus and Remus.

When Amulius found out he of course packed them away in a little boat, which the gods directed up the Tiber to a spot near today's Piazza Bocca della Verità. The famous she-wolf looked after the babies, until they were found by a shepherd, who brought them up. When Mars revealed to the grown twins their origin, they returned to Alba Longa to sort out Amulius, and then returned (in 753 BC, traditionally) to found the city the gods had ordained. Romulus soon found himself constrained to kill Remus, who would not believe the auguries that declared his brother should be king, and thus set the pattern for the bloody millennium of Rome's history to come. The legends portray early Rome as a glorified pirates' camp, and the historians are only too glad to agree. Finding themselves short of women, the Romans stole some from the Sabines. Not especially interested in farming or learning a trade, they adopted the hobby of subjugating their neighbours and soon polished it to an art.

Seven Kings of Rome

Romulus was the first, followed by Numa Pompilius, who laid down the forms for Rome's cults and priesthoods, its auguries and College of Vestals. Tullius Hostilius, the next, made Rome ruler of all Latium, and Ancus Martius founded the port of Ostia. The next king, Tarquinius Priscus, was an Etruscan, and probably gained his throne thanks to a conquest by one of the Etruscan city-states. Tarquin made a city of Rome, building the first real temples, the *Cloaca Maxima* or Great Drain, and the first *Circus Maximus*. His successor, Servius Tullius, restored Latin rule, inaugurated the division between patricians (the senatorial class) and plebeians, and built a great wall to keep the Etruscans out. It apparently did not work, for as next king we find the Etruscan Tarquinius Superbus (about 534 BC), another great builder. His misfortune was to have a hot-headed son like Tarquinius Sextus, who imposed himself on a noble and virtuous Roman maiden named Lucretia (of Shakespeare's *Rape of Lucrece*). She committed public suicide; the enraged Roman patricians, under the leadership of Lucius Junius Brutus, chased out proud Tarquin and the Etruscan dynasty forever. The republic was established that day, with Brutus as first consul, or chief magistrate.

The Invincible Republic

Taking an oath never to allow another king in Rome, the patricians designed a novel form of government, a republic (*res publica* – public thing) governed by the two consuls elected by the Senate, the assembly of the patricians themselves; later innovations in the Roman constitution would include a tribune, an official with inviolable powers elected by the Plebeians to protect their interests. The two classes fought like cats and dogs at home but combined with impressive resolve in their foreign wars. Etruscans, Aequi, Hernici, Volscii, Samnites and Sabines – all powerful nations – were defeated by Rome's citizen armies. Some of Livy's best stories come from this period, such as the taking of Rome by marauding Gauls in 390 BC, when the cackling of geese awakened the Romans and saved the citadel on the Capitoline Hill.

By 270 BC Rome had eliminated all its rivals to become master of Italy. It had taken about 200 years, and in the next 200 Roman rule would be established from Spain to Egypt. The first stage had proved more difficult. In Rome's final victory over the other Italians the city digested its rivals: whole cities and tribes simply disappeared, their peoples joining the mushrooming population of Rome. After 270 it was much the same story, but on a wider scale. In the three Punic Wars against Carthage (264–146 BC) Rome gained almost the whole of the western Mediterranean; Greece, North Africa and Asia Minor were absorbed in small bites over the next 100 years. Rome's history was now the history of the western world.

Imperial Rome

The old pirates' nest had never really changed its ways. Rome, like old Assyria, makes a fine example of that species of carnivore that can only live by continuous conquest. When the Romans took Greece they first met Culture, and it had the effect on them that puberty has on little boys. After some bizarre behaviour, evidenced in the continuous civil wars (Sulla, Marius, Pompey, Julius Caesar), the Romans began tarting up their city in the worst way, vacuuming all the gold, paintings, statues, cooks, poets and architects out of the civilized East. Beginning perhaps with Pompey, every contender for control of the now constitutionally deranged republic added some great work to the city centre: Pompey's theatre, the Julian Basilica, and something from almost every emperor up to Constantine. Julius Caesar and Augustus were perhaps Rome's greatest benefactors, initiating every sort of progressive legislation, turning dirt lanes into paved streets and erecting new forums, temples and the vast network of aqueducts. In their time Rome's population probably reached the million mark, surpassing Antioch and Alexandria as the largest city in the western world.

It was Augustus who effectively ended the Republic in 27 BC, by establishing his personal rule and reducing the old constitution to formalities. During the imperial era that followed his reign, Rome's position as administrative and judicial centre of the empire kept it growing, drawing in a new cosmopolitan population of provincials from Britain to Mesopotamia. The city became the unquestioned capital of banking and finance – and religion; Rome's policy was always to induct everyone's local god as an honorary Roman, and every important cult image and relic was abducted to the Capitoline Temple. The emperor himself was *Pontifex Maximus*, head priest of Rome, whose title derives from the early Roman veneration of bridges (*pontifex* means keeper of bridges). St Peter, of course, arrived, and was duly martyred in AD 67. His successor, Linus, became the first pope – or *pontiff* – first in the long line of hierophants who would inherit Rome's long-standing religious tradition.

For all its glitter, Rome was still the complete predator, producing nothing and consuming everything. No one with any spare *denarii* would be foolish enough to go into business with them, when the only real money was to be made from government, speculation or property. At times almost half the population of Roman citizens (as opposed to slaves) was on the public dole. Naturally, when things went sour they really went sour. Uncertain times made Aurelian give Rome a real defensive wall in AD 275. By AD 330 the necessity of staying near the armies at the front led the western emperors to spend most of their time at army headquarters in Milan. Rome became a bloated backwater, and after three sackings (Alaric the Goth in 410, Gaiseric the Vandal in 455 and Odoacer the Goth in 476), there was no reason to stay. The sources disagree: perhaps as many as 100,000 inhabitants were left by the year 500, perhaps as few as 10,000.

Rome in the Shadows

Contrary to what most people think, Rome did not ever quite go down the drain in the Dark Ages. Its lowest point in prestige undoubtedly came in the 14th century, when the popes were at Avignon. The number of important churches built in the

Dark Ages (most, unfortunately, baroqued later) and the mosaics that embellished them, equal in number if not in quality to those of Ravenna, testify to the city's importance. There was certainly enough to attract a few more sacks (Goths and Greeks in the 6th-century wars, Saracens from Africa in 746).

As in many other western cities, but on a larger scale, the bishops of Rome – the popes – picked up some of the pieces when civil administration disintegrated and extended their power to temporal offices. Chroniclers report fights between them and the local barons, self-proclaimed heirs of the Roman Senate, as early as 741. It must have been a fascinating place, much too big for its population though still, thanks to the popes, thinking of itself as the centre of the western world. The forum was abandoned, as were the gigantic baths, rendered useless as the aqueducts decayed. Almost all of the temples and basilicas survived, converted to Christian churches. Hadrian's massive tomb on the banks of the Tiber was converted into a fortress, the Castel Sant'Angelo, an impregnable haven for popes in times of trouble.

The popes deserve credit for keeping Rome alive, but the tithe money trickling in from across Europe confirmed the city in its parasitical behaviour. With two outrageous forgeries, the 'Donation of Constantine' and the 'Donation of Pepin', the popes staked their claim to temporal power in Italy. Charlemagne visited the city after driving the Lombards out in 800; during a prayer vigil in St Peter's on Christmas Eve, Pope Leo III sneaked up behind the Frankish king and set an imperial crown on his head. The surprise coronation, which the outraged Charlemagne could not or would not undo, established the precedent of Holy Roman Emperors having to cross over the Alps to receive their crown from the pope; for centuries to come Rome was able to keep its hand in the political struggles of all Europe.

Arnold of Brescia and Cola di Rienzo

Not that Rome ever spoke with one voice; over the next 500 years it was only the idea of Rome, as the spiritual centre of the universal Christian community, that kept the actual city of Rome from disappearing altogether. Down to some 20–30,000 people in this era, Rome evolved a sort of stable anarchy, in which the major contenders for power were the popes and noble families. First among the latter were the Orsini and the Colonna, racketeer clans who built fortresses for themselves among the ruins and fought like gangs in 1920s Chicago. Very often outsiders would get into the game. A remarkable woman of obscure birth named Theodora took the Castel Sant'Angelo in the 880s; with the title of Senatrix she and her daughter Marozia ruled Rome for decades. Various German emperors seized the city, but were never able to hold it. In the 10th century, things got even more complicated as the Roman people began to assert themselves. Caught between the people and the barons, nine of the 24 popes in that century managed to get themselves murdered. The 1140s was a characteristic period of this convoluted history. A Jewish family, the Pierleoni, held power, and a Jewish antipope sat enthroned in St Peter's. Mighty Rome occupied itself with a series of wars against its neighbouring village of Tivoli, and usually lost. A sincere monkish reformer appeared, the Christian and democrat Arnold of Brescia; he recreated the Senate and almost succeeded in establishing Rome as a free *comune*, but in 1155 he fell into the hands of the German emperor Frederick Barbarossa, who sold him to the English pope (Adrian IV) for hanging.

Too many centuries of this made Rome uncomfortable for the popes, who frequently removed themselves to Viterbo. The final indignity came when, under French pressure, the papacy decamped entirely to Avignon in 1309. Pulling strings from a distance, the popes only made life more complicated. Into the vacuum they created stepped one of the noblest Romans of them all, later to be the subject of Wagner's first opera. Cola di Rienzo was the son of an innkeeper, but he had a good enough education to read the Latin inscriptions that lay on ruins all around him, and Livy, Cicero and Tacitus wherever he could find them. Obsessed with re-establishing Roman glory, he talked at the bewildered inhabitants until they caught the fever too. With Rienzo as Tribune of the People, the Roman Republic was reborn in 1347.

Power does corrupt, however, in Rome more than any spot on the globe, and an increasingly fat and ridiculous Rienzo was hustled out of Rome by the united nobles before the year was out. His return to power, in 1354, ended with his murder by a mob after only two months. Rome was now at its lowest ebb, with only some 15,000 people, and prosperity and influence were not to be completely restored until the reign of Pope Nicholas V after 1447.

The New Rome

The old papacy, before Avignon, had largely been a tool of the Roman nobles; periods when it was able to achieve real independence were the exception rather than the rule. In the more settled conditions of the 15th century, a new papacy emerged, richer and more sophisticated. Political power, as a guarantee of stability, was its goal, and a series of talented Renaissance popes saw their best hopes for achieving this by rebuilding Rome. By the 1500s this process was in full swing. Under Julius II (1503–13) the papal domains for the first time were run like a modern state; Julius also laid plans for the rebuilding of St Peter's, beginning the great building programme that transformed the city. New streets were laid out, especially Via Giulia and the grand avenues radiating from Piazza del Popolo; Julius' architect, Bramante, knocked down medieval Rome with gay abandon; Raphael nicknamed him 'Ruinante'.

Over the next two centuries the work continued at a frenetic pace. Besides St Peter's, hundreds of churches were either built or rebuilt, and cardinals and noble families lined the streets with new palaces, imposing if not always beautiful. A new departure in urban design was developed in the 1580s, under Sixtus V, recreating some of the monumentality of ancient Rome. Piazzas linked by a network of straight boulevards were cleared in front of the major religious sites, each with its own Egyptian obelisk.

The New Rome, symbol of the Counter-Reformation and the majesty of the popes, was, however, bought at a terrible price. Besides the destruction of Bramante, buildings that had survived substantially intact for 1,500 years were cannibalized for their marble; the popes wantonly destroyed more of ancient Rome than Goths or Saracens had ever managed. To pay for their programme, they taxed the economy of the Papal States out of existence. Areas of Lazio turned into wastelands as exasperated farmers simply abandoned them; the other cities of Lazio and Umbria were set back centuries in their development. The New Rome was proving as voracious a predator as the old. Worst of all, the new papacy in the 16th century instituted terror as an instrument of public policy. In the course of the previous century the last vestiges of Roman liberty had been gradually extinguished.

The popes tried to extend their power by playing a game of high-stakes diplomacy between Emperor Charles V of Spain and King Francis I of France, but reaped a bitter harvest in the 1527 sack of Rome. An out-of-control imperial army occupied the city for almost a year, causing tremendous destruction, while the disastrous Pope Clement VII looked on helplessly from the Castel Sant'Angelo.

Afterwards the popes were happy to become part of the Imperial-Spanish system. Political repression was fiercer than anywhere else in Italy; the Inquisition was refounded in 1542 by Paul III, and book burnings, torture of freethinkers and executions became even more common than in Spain itself.

The End of Papal Rule

By about 1610 there was no Roman foolish enough to get burned at the stake; at the same time workmen were adding the last stones to the cupola of St Peter's. It was the end of an era, but the building continued. A thick accretion of Baroque, like coral, collected over Rome. Bernini did his Piazza Navona fountain in 1650, and the Colonnade for St Peter's 15 years later. The political importance of the popes, however, disappeared with surprising finality. As Joseph Stalin was later to note, the popes had plenty of Bulls, but few army divisions, and they drifted into irrelevance in the power politics of modern Europe during the Thirty Years War.

Rome was left to enjoy a decadent but pleasant twilight. A brief interruption came when revolutionaries in 1798 again proclaimed the Roman Republic, and a French army sent the pope packing. Rome later became part of Napoleon's empire, but papal rule was restored in 1815. Another republic appeared in 1848, on the crest of that romantic year's revolutionary wave, but this time a French army besieged the city and had the pope propped back on his throne by July 1849. Garibaldi, the republic's military commander, barely escaped with his life.

For twenty years Napoleon III maintained a garrison in Rome to look after the pope, and consequently Rome became the last part of Italy to join the new Italian kingdom. After the French defeat in the war of 1870, Italian troops blew a hole in the old Aurelian wall near the Porta Pia and marched in. Pius IX, who ironically had decreed papal infallibility just the year before, locked himself in the Vatican and pouted; the popes were to be 'prisoners' until Mussolini's Concordat of 1929, by which they agreed to recognize the Italian state.

As capital of the new state, Rome underwent another building boom. New streets like Via Vittorio Veneto and Via Nazionale made circulation easier; villas and gardens disappeared under blocks of speculative building (everything around Stazione Termini, for example); long-needed projects like the Tiber embankments were built; and the new kingdom strove to impress the world with gigantic, absurd public buildings and monuments, such as the Altar of the Nation and the Finance Ministry on Via XX Settembre, as big as two Colosseums. Growth has been steady; from some 200,000 people in 1879, Rome has since increased twentyfold.

The Twentieth Century

In 1922 the city was the objective of Mussolini's 'March on Rome', when the Fascist leader used his blackshirt squads to demand, and win, complete power in the Italian government, though he himself famously made the journey into town by train, and in his best suit. Mussolini was one more figure who wanted to create a 'New Roman Empire' for Italy. For twenty years Piazza Venezia was the chosen theatre for his oratorical performances.

'Il Duce' also had big ideas for the city itself: it was under Fascism that many of the relics of ancient Rome were first opened up as public monuments in order to remind Italians of their heritage, and Via dei Fori Imperiali was driven past the Forum, destroying some of the archaeological sites in the process.

Mussolini's greatest legacy was the EUR suburb, the projected site of a world exhibition for 1942, and a showcase of his preferred Fascist-classical architecture. At the end of the war it was only half built, but the Italians, not wishing to waste anything, decided to finish the project, and it now houses a few of Rome's museums and sports venues.

Since the war Rome has continued to grow fat as the capital of the often ramshackle, notoriously corrupt political system thrown up by the Italian Republic, and the headquarters of the smug *classe politica* that ran it. Rome has been accused by Lombard regionalists of drawing off wealth from the productive areas of Italy in much the same way that it once demanded to be fed by the Empire; nevertheless, Romans have joined in Italy's 'moral revolution' of the last few years, abusing the old-style political bosses, despite the fact that a great many in this city of civil servants themselves benefited from the system.

Today's visitors to the city enjoy the benefits of substantial improvements made for the Holy Year 2000 – known to Italian Catholics as the *giubileo*, or jubilee – including over 700 public works projects (restorations, refurbished museums, upgraded transportation and additional car parks, some of them notoriously dug into Romes omnipresent archaeological remains). Among the highlights for those who have not been to Rome for a few years are the Domus Aurea Musei Capitolini, the façade of Saint Peter's, the Vittoriano monument on Piazza Venezia, and Trajan's markets.

Around the City

Piazza Venezia

This traffic-crazed, thoroughly awful piazza may be a poor introduction to Rome, but it makes a good place to start, with the ruins of old Rome on one side and the boutiques and bureaucracies of the new city on the other. The piazza takes its name from the **Palazzo Venezia**, built for the Venetian Cardinal Pietro Barbo (later Pope Paul II) in 1455, but long the embassy of the Venetian Republic. Mussolini made it his

residence, leaving a light on all night to make the Italians think he was working. His famous balcony, from which he would declaim to the 'oceanic' crowds in the square (renamed the Forum of the Fascist Empire in those days) still holds its prominent place, a bad memory for the Italians. Nowadays the *palazzo* holds a **museum** of

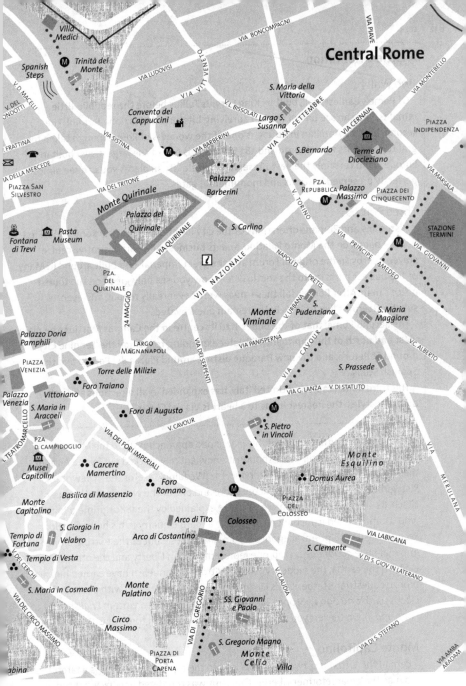

Central Rome

Villa Medici

Trinità del Monte

Spanish Steps

S. Maria della Vittoria

Convento dei Cappuccini

Largo S. Susanna

S. Bernardo

Terme di Diocleziano

PIAZZA INDIPENDENZA

Palazzo Barberini

PZA. REPUBBLICA

Palazzo Massimo

PIAZZA DEI CINQUECENTO

Monte Quirinale

Palazzo del Quirinale

S. Carlino

STAZIONE TERMINI

Fontana di Trevi

Pasta Museum

PIAZZA SAN SILVESTRO

PZA. DEL QUIRINALE

VIA NAZIONALE

Monte Viminale

S. Pudenziana

S. Maria Maggiore

Palazzo Doria Pamphili

Largo Magnanapoli

S. Prassede

PIAZZA VENEZIA

Torre delle Milizie

Foro Traiano

Palazzo Venezia

Vittoriano

S. Maria in Aracoeli

Foro di Augusto

S. Pietro in Vincoli

Monte Esquilino

Domus Aurea

Musei Capitolini

Carcere Mamertino

Foro Romano

PIAZZA DEL COLOSSEO

Monte Capitolino

Basilica di Massenzio

Arco di Tito

Colosseo

S. Clemente

Tempio di Fortuna

S. Giorgio in Velabro

Arco di Costantino

VIA LABICANA

S. Maria in Cosmedin

Tempio di Vesta

Monte Palatino

SS. Giovanni e Paolo

Circo Massimo

S. Gregorio Magno

Monte Celio

PIAZZA DI PORTA CAPENA

Villa

Renaissance and Baroque decorative arts (*t 06 679 8869; open Tues–Sun 9–6; adm exp*). The palace complex was built around the ancient church of **San Marco**, with a 9th-century mosaic in the apse. Parts of the building are as old as AD 400, and the façade is by the Renaissance architect Benedetto di Maiano.

A Little Orientation

Two Walls

Of Rome's earliest wall, built by King Servius Tullius before the republic, little remains; you can see one of the last surviving bits outside Stazione Termini. The second, built by Aurelian in AD 275, is one of the wonders of Rome, though taken for granted. With its 19km length and 383 towers, it is one of the largest ever built in Europe – and certainly the best-preserved of antiquity. In places you can see almost perfectly preserved bastions and monumental gates.

Three Romes

Historians and Romans often think of the city in this way. Classical Rome – the First Rome – began on the Monte Palatino, and its business and administrative centre stayed nearby, in the original Forum and the great Imperial Fora built around it. Many of the busiest parts lay to the south, where now you see only green on the tourist office's map. After Rome's fall these areas were never really rebuilt, and even substantial ruins like Trajan's Baths remain unexcavated.

The Second Rome, that of the popes, had its centre in the Campus Martius, the plain west and north of the Capitoline Hill, later expanding to include the 'Leonine City' around St Peter's, and the new Baroque district around Piazza del Popolo and the Spanish Steps.

The Third Rome, capital of United Italy, has expanded in all directions and many different styles; the nearest it has to a heart is Via del Corso.

Long ago the southern edge of this piazza had approaches up to the Monte Capitolino. The hill is still there, though it's now entirely blocked out by the **Altar of the Nation** (also known as the *Vittoriano*, the 'Wedding Cake' or the 'Typewriter'), Risorgimento Italy's own self-inflicted satire and one of the world's apotheoses of kitsch. Its size and its solid marble walls are explained by the 1880s prime minister who commissioned it; he happened to have a marble quarry in his home district. Recounting its sculptural allegories would take pages – but of the two big bronze imperial-style *quadrigae* on top, one represents Italian Liberty and the other Italian Unity. In the centre, the modest virtues of Vittorio Emanuele II have earned him a 38ft bronze equestrian statue. Italy's Unknown Soldier sleeps below with a round-the-clock guard (*t 06 699 1718; open Tues–Sun 10.30–4.30; guided visits in English at 10.30, noon and 3*). On the left you can see the republican Roman tomb of C. Publius Bibulus.

Monte Capitolino

Behind the *Vittoriano*, two stairways lead to the top of the hill. This is a fateful spot; in 121 BC the great reformer Tiberius Gracchus was murdered here by what today would be called a 'right-wing death squad'. Almost a millennium and a half later Cola di Rienzo was trying to escape Rome in disguise when an enraged mob recognized him by the rings on his fingers and tore him to pieces. Rienzo built the left-hand staircase, and was the first to climb it. It leads to **Santa Maria in Aracoeli**, begun in the 7th

Seven Hills

Originally they were much higher; centuries of building, rebuilding and river flooding have made the ground level in the valleys much higher, and emperors and popes shaved bits off their tops in building programmes. The **Monte Capitolino**, smallest but most important, now has Rome's City Hall, the Campidoglio, roughly on the site of ancient Rome's greatest temple, that of Jupiter Greatest and Best. The **Palatino**, adjacent to it, was originally the most fashionable district, and got entirely covered by the palaces of the emperors. The plebeian **Aventino** lies to the south of it, across the Circus Maximus. Between the Colosseum and the Stazione Termini, the **Esquilino**, the **Viminale** and the **Quirinale** stand in a row. The Quirinale was long the residence of the popes, and later of the Italian kings. Finally, there is the **Monte Celio** south of the Colosseum, now an oasis of parkland and ancient churches.

Rome has other hills not included in the canonical seven: **Monte Vaticano**, from which the Vatican takes its name, **Monte Pincio**, including the Villa Borghese, and the **Gianicolo**, the long ridge above Trastevere the ancients called the Janiculum.

Fourteen Regions

Ancient Rome had neither street lights nor street signs; modern Rome has plenty of both. Being Rome, of course the street signs are of marble. In the corner, you will notice a small number in Roman numerals; this refers to the *rione*, or ward. In the Middle Ages, there were 14 of these, descendants of the 14 *regii* of the ancient city; even after the fall of Rome they maintained their organization.

century over the temple of Juno Moneta – the ancient Roman Mint was adjacent to it. The Aracoeli, which in Rienzo's time served as a council hall for the Romans, is one of the most revered of churches; legend has it that one of the Sibyls of Tivoli prophesied the coming of Jesus and told Augustus to build a temple here to the 'first born of God'. Inside you can seek out frescoes by Pinturicchio (*San Bernardino of Siena*) and Gozzoli (*San Antonio of Padua*), and a tombstone by Donatello, near the entrance.

The second stairway takes you to the real heart of Rome, Michelangelo's **Piazza del Campidoglio**, passing a rather flattering statue of Rienzo set on a bronze pedestal. Bordering the piazza, a formidable cast of statues includes the Dioscuri, who come from Pompey's Theatre, and Marforio (in the Musei Capitolini courtyard), a river god once employed as a 'talking statue', decorated with graffiti and placards commenting on current events of the day.

The great 2nd-century AD bronze equestrian statue of the benign and philosophical emperor **Marcus Aurelius**, which stood on the plinth in the middle of the piazza from the 16th century until 1981, has been fully restored and regilded and is now in the Musei Capitolini. Fortunately enough, since it was an old Roman saying that the world would end when all the gold flaked off. The Christians of old only refrained from melting him down for cash because they believed he was not Marcus Aurelius, but Constantine. A faithful copy now stands in the piazza.

Passing the Time of Day in Ancient Rome

Recreating some of the atmosphere of the old days is not hard: a score of books have been written on the subject, of which one of the best is *Daily Life in Ancient Rome* by Jerome Carcopino. Roman poets such as Horace, Martial and especially Juvenal also have plenty to say about it. Life in Rome at the height of empire was an imperial pain: ridiculously high rents, high taxes, street crime, noise around the clock and neighbours from Baetica or Rhaetia with peculiar habits – but naturally everyone in the empire dreamed of some day moving there. The most significant difference between the way they lived then and our times was the sharp contrast between the quality of life in public versus private places. The average Roman citizen, usually unemployed or underemployed, could loll about magnificent baths and forums all day; only with reluctance did he drag himself home to his nasty, cramped fourth-floor flat at night.

Public Rome

The Roman *forum*, developed from the Greek *agora*, took the form of an open space surrounded by temples, basilicas and colonnades. In the centre, the original Roman Forum and the Fora of Augustus and Trajan made up a single vast complex, the public stage of Roman life. A typical Roman citizen would be there in the morning, to transact business, meet friends, watch the cosmopolitan crowd go by, or indulge in the favourite pastime of watching court proceedings in the basilica. Often they would have their own actions running; the Romans were easily the most litigious nation in all history. Surrounding the *fora* would be the market-places, some of them imposing buildings like the Market of Trajan (in its time not unlike today's covered market in Istanbul).

For all their skill at plumbing, the Romans never managed to bring running water into their flats. The baths, therefore, were a daily spot on any respectable Roman's agenda. He could have stayed all day, for these great establishments were a stage for public life, and cheap and accessible even to the poorest man. Every neighbourhood had some, and, counting the ones built by the emperors, they covered almost 10 per cent of Rome. The biggest ones, with bathing halls bigger than St Peter's, also included parks, museums, libraries, lunch counters and, of course *palaestrae* – athletic grounds for the Romans' favourite games. No civilization, perhaps, ever conceived a more useful way for its citizens to spend their leisure time. There were other places to pursue the classical *dolce vita* – the emperors' extensive gardens (usually open to

The Musei Capitolini

Open Tues–Sun 9.30–7; until 11pm on Saturday; adm.

Michelangelo's original plans may have been adapted and tinkered with by later architects, but nevertheless his plan for the Campidoglio has come out as one of the triumphs of Renaissance design. The centrepiece, the **Palazzo Senatorio**, Rome's city hall, with its distinctive stairway and bell tower, is built over the ruins of the Roman *tabularium*, the state archive. At the base of the stair note the statue of Minerva, in

the public), the temples, which in an irreligious age were really glorified art museums, and the taverns – one on every block, usually with upstairs and gambling in the back room. Romans were terrible gamblers; even the virtuous Augustus would regularly present his children, slaves and dinner guests with bags of *sestertii* to wager against him. Finally there were the races and games in the Colosseum or the Circus Maximus, all of them extraordinarily brutal and bloody, which occupied an average of around 90–100 days a year. These were free, though you needed a ticket just to remind you of the imperial largesse that made it all possible. You also needed a toga, unless you were in the plebeian cheap seats, for these were among this informal city's few dress-up occasions.

Private Rome

Over 90 per cent of Romans lived in flats, in pretty but generally poorly built *insulae* up to 10 storeys in height. From the outside they looked much the same as some of the older Roman apartment blocks today, only with more imaginative façades of brick, stucco and patterned timbers. Many had balconies, and every part of these balconies and windows that received any sun would be full of climbing vines and flowers. Unfortunately most of the streets were less than 12ft across.

Rich and poor Romans lived mixed together in every *regio*: the very rich in walled houses (like those at Pompeii), set perhaps next to a four-storey block with wine and oil shops, taverns and ironmongers on the ground floor, middle-class bureaucrats and clients of the rich on the first (with perhaps three or four slaves), and the very poor above them. These had the furthest to climb, and were doomed in case of fire or collapse. Both were constant worries. Crassus, who ruled Rome in the first Triumvirate with Caesar and Pompey, got his start as a weasling building contractor, following the fire squads.

People who lived in flats did not use them much for entertaining, or even for cooking. They had paid water-carriers, but no heating except braziers, no glass windows and little furniture. The shops that filled the ground floors of most buildings always spilled out into the narrow streets, joining the market barrows and the grammar school classes, which rented space under shop awnings or in porticoes – learning to live with distractions was a part of any Roman's education. Traffic problems were probably Rome's biggest headache after the 2nd century BC; Julius Caesar decreed an end to chariots and carriages (the rich had to get by with slave-borne litters) and banished wagons during daylight hours.

her aspect as the allegorical goddess Roma. Flanking it, Michelangelo redesigned the façade of the **Palazzo dei Conservatori** (on the right), and projected the matching building across the square, the **Palazzo Nuovo**, built in the early 18th century. Together they make up the recently restored Capitoline Museums. Founded by Pope Clement XII in 1734, the oldest true museum in the world, the Capitolini display both the heights and depths of ancient society and culture. For the heights there are the reliefs from the triumphal arch of Marcus Aurelius – scenes of the emperor's clemency and piety, and his triumphal receptions in Rome. Marcus always looks a little worried, perhaps thinking of his good-for-nothing son Commodus, and the empire he would inherit, sinking into corruption and excess. What was to come is well illustrated by the degenerate art of the 4th century, like the colossal bronze head, hand and foot of Constantine, parts of a colossal statue in the Basilica of Maxentius (in the courtyard).

In between these extremes come roomfuls of statuary, including the *Capitoline She-Wolf*, the very symbol of Rome (note that the suckling twins were added to the Etruscan bronze she-wolf in the Renaissance); statues of most of the emperors, busts of Homer, Sophocles and Pythagoras; the voluptuous *Capitoline Venus*; a big baby Hercules (who may have inspired Donatello's famous *Amor* in Florence); and the *Muse Polyhymnia*, one of the most delightful statues of antiquity. Later works include lots of papal paraphernalia, a statue of Charles of Anjou by Arnolfo di Cambio and – in a small **Pinacoteca** in the Palazzo dei Conservatori – some dignified Velázquez gentlemen, looking scornfully at the other paintings, and two major works by Caravaggio, the *Fortune Teller* and *John the Baptist*. There are also some lovely 18th-century porcelains – orchestras of monkeys in powdered wigs, and such like.

The best overview of the Roman Forum is to be had from behind Palazzo Senatorio. From there a stairway leads down from the left side to Via dei Fori Imperiali and the entrance to the Forum. On the way, beneath the church of San Giuseppe Falegnami, you can visit the **Carcere Mamertino** (*open April–Sept daily 9–12.30 and 2.30–6; Oct–Mar daily 9–12 and 2–5*), the small calaboose used by the ancient Romans for their most important prisoners – the Catiline conspirators, Vercingetorix (the Gaulish chief captured by Caesar), and finally St Peter. The southern end of the Capitol, one of the quietest corners of Rome, was the site of the temple of Jupiter Optimus Maximus (Greatest and Best), built originally by the Etruscan kings. At the time it was the largest in Italy, testimony to Rome's importance as far back as 450 BC. Along the southern edge of the hill, the cliffs you see are the somewhat reduced remains of the **Tarpeian Rock**, from which traitors and other malefactors were thrown in Rome's early days.

Along the Tiber

The early emperors did their best to import classical Greek drama to Rome, and for a while, with the poets of the Latin New Comedy, it seemed the Romans would carry on the tradition. Great theatres were built like the **Teatro di Marcello**, begun by Caesar and completed by Augustus. By the second century AD, however, theatre had already begun to degenerate into music hall, lewd performances with naked actresses and grisly murders (condemned prisoners were sometimes butchered on stage), and shows by celebrity actors. Marcellus' theatre survived into the Middle Ages, when the Orsini family converted it into their palace-fortress, the strongest after the Castel Sant'Angelo. You can still see the tall arches of the circumference surmounted by the rough medieval walls.

The streets to the west contain a mix of some of Rome's oldest houses with new buildings; the latter have replaced the old walled **ghetto**. There has been a sizeable Jewish community in Rome since the 2nd century BC; after conquering the Jews at the end of the 1st century AD, Pompey and Titus brought them to Rome as slaves. They helped finance the career of Julius Caesar, who would prove to be their greatest bene-factor. For centuries they lived quite happily near this bend in the river, until Paul IV took time off from burning books and heretics to wall them into the tiny ghetto in 1555, he forced them to wear orange hats and attend Mass on Sunday, and limited them to the rag and old iron trades. Tearing down the ghetto walls was one of the first acts of the Italian kingdom after the entry into Rome in 1870. The eclectic **synagogue** was built in 1904; there are guided tours, and a museum of the **Jewish Community** (*open Mon–Thurs 9.30–2 and 3–5, Fri 9.30–2, Sun 9.30–12; adm*).

Opposite the synagogue, the **Isola Tiberina** is joined to both sides of the river by surviving ancient bridges. In imperial times the island was sacred to Aesculapius, god of healing; a legend records how some serpents brought from the god's shrine in Greece escaped and swam to the spot, choosing the site by divine guidance. Now, as in ancient times, most of the lovely island is taken up by a hospital, the Ospedale Fatebenefratelli ('do-good brothers'); in place of the Temple of Aesculapius, there is also the church of **San Bartolomeo**, most recently rebuilt in the 1690s.

The **Velabrum,** in the earliest days of Rome, was a cattle market (interestingly, in the Middle Ages, the Roman Forum itself was used for the same purpose). In this area, east of the Isola Tiberina, is **San Giorgio in Velabro**, in parts as old as the 7th century; there is a Cosmatesque altar, and there are early Christian fragments on the left wall. The lovely portico has been completely restored after a Mafia bombing in 1993. Of the two ancient arches outside, the **Arco degli Argentari** was erected by the money-changers in honour of Septimius Severus. The larger, the unfinished, four-sided *Janus Quadrifons,* dates from the time of Constantine.

Piazza Bocca della Verità

Tourists almost always overlook this beautiful corner along the Tiber, but here you can see two well-preserved Roman temples. Both go under false names: the round **Temple of Vesta**, used as an Armenian church in the Middle Ages, and the **Temple of Fortuna Virilis** – it now seems almost certain that they were actually dedicated to Hercules Victor and Portunus (the god of harbours) respectively. Some bits of an exotic Roman cornice are built into the brick building opposite, part of the **House of the Crescenzi**, a powerful family in the 9th century, descended from Theodora Senatrix. Look over the side of the Tiber embankment here and you can see the outlet of the **Cloaca Maxima**, the sewer begun by King Tarquin. Big enough to drive two carriages through, it is still in use today.

Just upstream, past the Ponte Palatino, a single arch decorated with dragons is all that remains of the *Pons Aemilius*. Originally built in the 2nd century BC, it collapsed twice and was last restored in 1575 by Gregory XIII, only to fall down again 20 years later. Now it is known as the 'broken bridge', or **Ponte Rotto**.

Across from the temples, the handsome medieval church with the lofty campanile is **Santa Maria in Cosmedin**, built over an altar of Hercules in the 6th century and given to Byzantine Greeks escaping from the Iconoclast emperors in the 8th. The name (like 'cosmetic') means 'decorated', but little of the original art has survived;

most of what you see is from the 12th century, including some fine Cosmatesque work inside. In the portico, an ancient, ghostly image in stone built into the walls has come down in legend as the **Bocca della Verità** – the Mouth of Truth. Medieval Romans would swear oaths and close business deals here; if you tell a lie with your hand in the image's mouth he will most assuredly bite your fingers off. Try it.

The Heart of Ancient Rome

In the 1930s Mussolini built a grand boulevard between the Vittoriano and the Colosseum to ease traffic congestion and show off the ancient sites. He called it the Via del Impero, coinciding with his aspirations of returning Rome to greatness through a new empire in Africa. After Mussolini's demise the road was re-christened **Via dei Fori Imperiali**, after the Imperial Fora which it partly covers. The **Imperial Fora** of Augustus, Nerva and Trajan were built to relieve congestion in the original Roman Forum. **Trajan's Forum** (the Foro di Traiano), built with the spoils of his conquest of Dacia (modern Romania) was perhaps the grandest architectural and planning conception ever built in Rome, a broad square surrounded by colonnades, with a huge basilica flanked by two libraries and a covered market outside (the world's first shopping mall). A large part of **Trajan's Markets** (the Mercati di Traiano) still stands, with entrances on Via IV Novembre and down the stairs just to the side of Trajan's Column (*open Tues–Sun 9–one hour before sunset; adm; t 06 679 0048*). Behind it, you can see Rome's own leaning tower, the 12th-century **Torre delle Milizie**. All that remains of Trajan's great square is the paving and its centrepiece, **Trajan's Column** (the Colonna Traiana). The spiralling bands of reliefs, illustrating the Dacian Wars, reach to the top, some 96ft high. They rank with the greatest works of Roman art; plaster casts are on display at eye level in the Museo della Civiltà Romana. Behind the column, **Santa Maria di Loreto** is a somewhat garish High Renaissance bauble, built by Bramante and Antonio da Sangallo the Younger. The Romans liked the church so much that in the 1730s they built another one just like it next door, the **Santissimo Nome di Maria**. Scanty remains of **Caesar's Forum** (the Foro di Cesare) and **Augustus' Forum** (the Foro di Augusto) can be seen along the boulevard to the south.

The Roman Forum

For a place that was the centre of the Mediterranean world, there is little to see; centuries of use as a quarry have seen to that. The word *forum* originally meant 'outside' (like the Italian *fuori*), a market-place outside the original Rome that became the centre of both government and business as the city expanded. The entrances are on Via dei Fori Imperiali at Via Cavour, and at the end of the ramp that approaches the Forum from the Colosseum side (*open daily 9–one hour before sunset; t 06 3996 7700*). The **Via Sacra**, ancient Rome's most important street, runs the length of the Forum. At the end of it beneath Capitolini Hill you will be facing the **Arch of Septimius Severus** (AD 203), with reliefs of some rather trivial victories over the Arabs and Parthians; conservative Romans of the time must have strongly resented this upstart African emperor planting his monument in such an important spot. The arch also commemorated Septimius' two sons, Geta and Caracalla; when the nasty

Caracalla did his brother in, he had his name effaced from it. In front of it, the **Lapis Niger**, a mysterious stone with an underground chamber beneath it, is the legendary tomb of Romulus (*closed to the public*). The inscription down below – a threat against the profaning of this sacred spot – is one of the oldest ever found in the Latin language. The famous Golden Milestone also stood here, the '*umbilicus*' of Rome and the point from which all distances in the Empire were measured. To the right is the **Curia** (the Senate House), heavily restored after centuries' use as a church (the good Baroque church behind it is **SS. Luca e Martina**, built by Pietro da Cortona in the 1660s). To the left of the arch the remains of a raised stone area were the **Rostra**, the speakers' platforms under the republic, decorated with ships' prows (*rostra*) taken in a sea battle in about 320 BC. Of the great temples on the Capitol slope only a few columns remain; from left to right, the **Temple of Saturn**, which served as Rome's treasury, the **Temple of Vespasian** (three standing columns) and the **Temple of Concord**, built by Tiberius to honour the peace – so to speak – that the emperors had enforced between patricians and plebeians.

In front of the *rostra*, in the open area once decorated with statues and monuments, the simple standing **column** was placed in honour of Nikephoros Phocas, Byzantine Emperor in AD 608 – the last monument ever erected in the Forum; the Romans had to steal the column from a ruined building. Just behind it a small pool once marked the spot of one of ancient Rome's favourite legends. In 362 BC, according to Livy, an abyss suddenly opened across the Forum, and the sibyls predicted that it would not close unless the 'things that Rome held most precious' were thrown in. A consul, Marcus Curtius, took this as meaning a Roman citizen and soldier. He leapt in fully armed, horse and all, and the crack closed over him.

This section of the Forum was bordered by two imposing buildings, the **Basilica Aemilia** to the north and the **Basilica Julia** to the south, the latter built by Caesar with the spoils of the Gallic Wars. The **Temple of Caesar** closes the east end, built by Augustus as a visual symbol of the new imperial mythology.

The adjacent **Temple of the Dioscuri** makes a good example of how temples were used in ancient times. This one was a meeting hall for men of the equestrian class (the knights, though they were really more likely to be businessmen); they had safe-deposit boxes in the basement, where the standard weights and measures of the empire were kept. Between them, the round pedestal was the foundation of the small **Temple of Vesta**, where the sacred hearth-fire was kept burning by the Vestal Virgins; ruins of their extensive apartments can be seen next door.

Two more Christian churches stand in this part of the Forum. **SS. Cosma e Damiano** was built on to the **Temple of Antoninus Pius and Faustina** in the 6th century; most of the columns survive, with a fine sculptural frieze of griffons on top. **Santa Francesca Romana** is built over a corner of Rome's largest temple, that of **Venus and Rome**. Built by Hadrian, this was a curious, double-ended shrine to the state cult, one side devoted to the Goddess Roma and the other to Venus – in the imperial mythology she was the ancestress of the Caesars.

The church entrance is outside the Forum, but the adjoining convent, inside the monumental area, houses the **Antiquarium Forense**, a tired collection of Iron-Age

Rome 300 AD

*before names of sights
indicates significant
remains.

modern streets and
squares are shaded in to
help orientation.

Campus Martius
1 Stadium of Domitian
2 Baths of Nero
3 *Temple of Hadrian
4 Domitian's Odeon
5 Stagnum Agrippae
6 *Pantheon
7 Baths of Agrippa
8 S{ae} pta Julia
9 Temple of Isis
10 Porticus Divorum
11 Portico of Vipsania
12 Pompey's Theatre

13 *Republican Temples
   (Largo Argentina)
14 Portico of Minucia
15 Theatre of Balbus
16 Porticus Philippi
17 *Portico of Octavia
18 Circus Flaminius
19 *Temple of Apollo
20 Temple of Bellona
21 *Temple of Marcellus
22 *Temple of Hope (S. Nicolo)
23 Forum Holitorium
24 Temple of Aesculapius
25 Warehouses

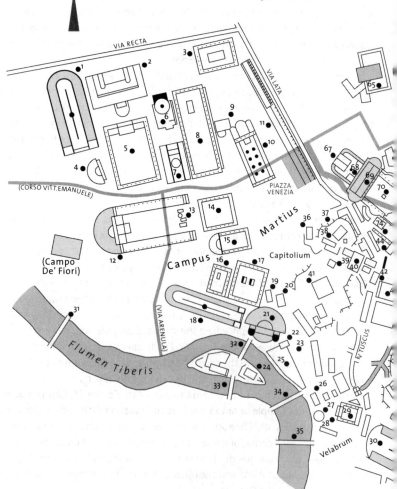

Velabrum and Tiber Island

26 *Temple of Portumnus
27 *Temple of Hercules Victor
28 Forum Boarium
29 Statio Annonae/ Altar of
   Hercules
30 Circus Maximus
31 Bridge of Valentinian
32 *Pons Cestius
33 *Pons Fabricius
34 * Pons Aemillius
35 Pons Probus

Capitol

36 *Insula (Apartment House)
37 Arx (Citadel)
38 Temple of Juno Moneta
39 Asylum - Temple of Veiovis
40 *Tabularium
41 Temple of Jupiter

Forum

42 *Temple of Saturn
43 *Arch of Septimius Severus
44 *Curia
45 Basilica Aemilia
46 Basilica Julia
47 *Temple of the Dioscuri
48 *House of the Vestal Virgins
49 *Basilica of Maxentius
50 *Arch of Titus
51 *Temple of Venus and Rome
52 Temple of Elagabalus
53 Nero's Colossus
54 *Arch of Constantine
55 *Colosseum

Palatine

56 *Palace of Tiberius
57 Temple of Cybele
58 *House of Augustus
59 *Staduim
60 Septizonium

Caelian and Quirinal

61 Temple of Claudius
62 *Ludus Magnus
63 Baths of Titus
64 Baths of Trajan
65 Temple of Serapis
66 Baths of Constantine

Imperial Fora

67 Temple of Trajan
68 *Trajan's Column
69 Basilica Ulpia
70 Forum of Trajan
71 *Trajan's Market
72 *Forum of Augustus
73 *Forum of Nerva - Temple of
   Minerva
74 Temple of Venus Genetrix
75 Forum of Caeser
76 Forum of Vespasian

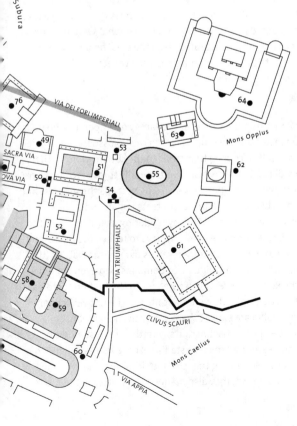

burial urns and other paraphernalia from the Forum excavations. Between the two churches the mastodontic **Basilica of Maxentius**, finished by Constantine, remains the largest ruin of the Forum, its clumsy arches providing an illustration of the ungainly but technically sophisticated 4th century.

Near the exit, the **Arch of Titus** commemorates the victories of Titus and his father Vespasian over the rebellious Jews (AD 60–80), one of the fiercest struggles Rome ever had to fight. The reliefs show the booty being carted through Rome in the triumphal parade – including the famous seven-branched golden candlestick from the holy of holies in the Temple at Jerusalem.

South of the arch a path leads up to the **Monte Palatino** (*t 06 3996 7700; open daily 9–one hour before sunset; adm; a L30,000 cumulative ticket, valid 5 days, is available, including the Palatino, Colosseum, Cripta Balbi, Palazzo Massimo, Palazzo Altemps, Terme di Diocleziano, and Baths of Caracalla; it can be acquired at any of these sites*). Here, overlooking the little corner of the world that gave our language words like *senate, committee, rostrum, republic, plebiscite* and *magistrate*, you can leave democracy behind and visit the etymological birthplace of *palace*. The ruins of the imperial *Palatium* once covered the entire hill. As with the Forum, almost all the stone has been cannibalized, and there's little to see of what was once a complex half a mile long, to which a dozen of the emperors contributed.

There are good views across the Circus Maximus from just above what was once the portico from which the emperor could watch the races. Don't miss the chance to take a stroll through the gardens planted by the Farnese family over what were the imperial servants' quarters – one of the most peaceful spots in the city. The one modern building on the Palatino houses the *Antiquarium*, a good little collection of relics found within a stone's throw of the building.

The Colosseum

Its real name was the Flavian Amphitheatre, after the family of emperors who built it, beginning with Vespasian in AD 72; Colosseum refers to the Colossus, a huge gilded statue of Nero (erected by himself, of course) that stood in the square in front. There doesn't seem to be much evidence that Christians were literally thrown to lions here – there were other places for that – but what did go on was perhaps the grossest and best-organized perversity in all history. Gladiatorial contests began under the republic, designed to make Romans better soldiers by rendering them indifferent to the sight of death. Later emperors introduced new displays to relieve the monotony – men versus animals, lions versus elephants, women versus dwarfs, sea-battles (the arena could be flooded), public torture of condemned criminals, and even genuine athletics, a Greek import the Romans never much cared for. In the first hundred days of the Colosseum's opening, 5,000 animals were slaughtered. The native elephant and lion of North Africa and Arabia are extinct thanks to such shenanigans.

However hideous its purpose, the Colosseum ranks with the greatest works of Roman architecture and engineering; all modern stadiums have its basic plan. One surprising feature was a removable awning that covered the stands. Sailors from Cape Misenum were kept to operate it; they also manned the galleys in the mock sea-battles. Originally there were statues in every arch and a ring of bronze shields around the cornice. The concrete stands have eroded away, showing the brick structure underneath. Renaissance and Baroque popes hauled away half the travertine exterior – enough to build the Palazzo Venezia, the Palazzo Barberini, a few other palaces and bridges and part of St Peter's. Almost all of the construction work under Vespasian and Titus was performed by Jewish slaves, brought here for the purpose after the suppression of their revolt (*open daily 9–one hour before sunset; adm; audioguide in English L7,000*).

Just outside the Colosseum, the **Arch of Constantine** marks the end of the ancient Triumphal Way (now Via di San Gregorio) where victorious emperors and their troops would parade their captives and booty. The arch, with a coy inscription mentioning Constantine's 'divine inspiration' (the Romans weren't sure whether it was yet respectable to mention Christianity), is covered with reliefs stolen from older arches and public buildings – a sad commentary on the state of art in Constantine's day.

Domus Aurea and the Monte Esquilino

When Nero decided he needed a new palace, money was no object. Taking advantage of the great fire of AD 64 (which he apparently did *not* start), he had a huge section of Rome (temporarily renamed Neropolis) cleared to make a rural estate in the middle of town. The **Golden House** was probably the most sumptuous palace ever built in Rome, decorated in an age when Roman art was at its height, but Nero never lived to see it finished – he committed suicide during an army coup by Spanish legions. When the dust settled the new emperor Vespasian realized that this flagrant symbol of imperial decadence had to go. He demolished it, and Titus and Trajan later erected great bath complexes on its foundations; Nero's gardens and fishponds became the site of the Colosseum. In the 1500s some beautifully decorated rooms of the Domus Aurea were discovered underground, saved for use as the basement of Titus' baths. Raphael and other artists studied them closely and incorporated some of the spirit of the fresco decoration into the grand manner of the High Renaissance (our word 'grotesque', originally referring to the leering faces and floral designs of this time, comes from the finds in this 'grotto'). The Domus Aurea is now open for guided visits by reservation only (*call t 06 3974 9907; tours are Wed–Mon 9–8; audioguide in English L12,000. Bring a sweater as the underground rooms can be chilly*).

The **Monte Esquilino** is better known today as the Colle Oppio. Much of it is covered with parks; besides the Domus Aurea there are very substantial ruins of the **Terme di Traiano**, still unexcavated. On the northern slope of the hill, **San Pietro in Vincoli** takes its name from relics supposed to be the chains Peter was locked in before Nero had him crucified. They are kept over the main altar, though the real attraction of this church for non-Catholics is the famous, ill-fated **tomb of Julius II** which tortured Michelangelo for so many years. Of the original project, planned as a sort of tabernacle with 40 individual statues, the artist completed, as well as the statues of Leah and Rachel, the powerful figure of *Moses*, the closest anyone has come to capturing prophetic vision in stone, even if he bears a striking resemblance to Charlton Heston. All the other statues on the tomb are the work of Michelangelo's students.

San Clemente

This church, a little way to the east of the Colosseum on Via San Giovanni in Laterano, is one of the more fascinating remnants of Rome's many-layered history. One of the first substantial building projects of the Christians in Rome, the original basilica of c. 375 burned along with the rest of the quarter during a sacking by the Normans in 1084. It was rebuilt soon afterwards with a new Cosmatesque pavement, and the 6th-century choir screen – a rare example of sculpture from that ungifted time – saved from the original church. The 12th-century mosaic in the apse represents the *Triumph of the Cross*, and the chapel at the entrance contains a beautiful series of quattrocento frescoes by Masolino. From a vestibule, nuns sell tickets to the **Lower Church** (*open daily 9–12.30 and 3–6; adm*). This is the lower half of the original San Clemente, and there are remarkable, though deteriorated, frescoes from the 900s and the 12th century. A plaque from Bulgaria commemorates SS. Cyril and Methodius, who went from this church to spread the Gospel among the Slavs; they translated the Bible into Old Slavonic, and invented the first Slavic alphabet (Cyrillic) to do it.

From here, steps lead down to the lowest stratum, 1st and 2nd century AD buildings divided by an alley; this includes the **Mithraeum**, the best-preserved temple of its kind after the one in Capua. The larger, neighbouring building was filled with rubble to serve as a foundation for the basilica, and the apse was later added over the Mithraeum. Father Mulhooly of Boston started excavating in the 1860s, and later excavations have revealed a Mithraic antechamber with a fine stuccoed ceiling, a Mithraic school with an early fresco, and the temple proper, a small cavern-like hall with benches for the initiates to share a ritual supper.

Mithraism was a mystery religion, full of secrets closely held by the initiates (all male, and largely soldiers) and it is difficult to say what else went on down here. Two altars were found, each with the usual image of the Persian-import god Mithras despatching a white bull, including a snake, a scorpion and a crow, and astrological symbolism. Underneath all this, there is yet a fourth building level, some foundations from the republican era. At the end of the 1st-century building you can look down into an ancient sewer or underground stream, one of a thousand entrances to the surreal sub-Roma of endless subterranean caves, buildings, rivers and lakes, mostly unexplored and unexplorable. A century ago a schoolboy fell in the water here; they found him, barely alive, in open country several kilometres from the city.

Corso Vittorio Emanuele

This street, chopped through the medieval centre in the 1880s, still hasn't quite been assimilated into its surroundings; nevertheless, this ragged, smoky traffic tunnel will come in handy when you find yourself lost in the tortuous, meandering streets of Rome's oldest quarter. Starting west from Piazza Venezia, the church of the **Gesù** (1568–84) was a landmark for a new era and the new aesthetic of cinquecento Rome. The transitional, pre-Baroque fashion was often referred to as the 'Jesuit style', and here in the Jesuits' head church architects Vignola and della Porta laid down Baroque's first law: an intimation of paradise through decorative excess. It hasn't aged well, though at the time it must have seemed to most Romans a perfect marriage of Renaissance art and a reformed, revitalized faith. St Ignatius is buried in the left transept right under the altar, Spanish-style; the globe incorporated in the sculpted Trinity overhead is the biggest piece of lapis lazuli in the world.

Further west the street opens into a ghastly square called Largo Argentina. Remains of several republican-era temples, unearthed far below ground level, occupy the centre. Next comes another grand Baroque church, **Sant'Andrea della Valle**, with the city's second-tallest dome. Maderno, one of the architects of St Peter's, did most of the work. The curving façade across the street belongs to **Palazzo Massimo alle Colonne**, the masterpiece of the Renaissance architect Baldassare Peruzzi; he transplanted something of the Florentine style of monumental palaces, adding some light-hearted proto-Baroque decoration. If you can, have a look at the adjacent church of **S. Pantaleo de Parione** (*rarely open*), with its outlandish sculptural frieze of shields, trays and popes' hats piled like a rubbish heap. The Palazzo Braschi next door houses the small **Museo di Roma** (*promised opening June 2001*).

Right across the street is one of the earliest and best of the palaces on Corso Vittorio Emanuele, the delicate **Piccola Farnesina** by Antonio da Sangallo the Younger. It houses another little museum, a collection of ancient sculpture called the **Museo Barracco** (*t 06 6880 6848; open Tues–Sun 9–7; adm*). A third museum – not a well-known one – is just around the corner from Sant'Andrea: the **Burcardo Theatre Museum**, Via Sudario 44 (*open Mon, Wed, Fri 9.30–1.30; Tues, Thurs 9.30–4*) is a collection of fascinating old relics from the Roman theatrical tradition.

The biggest palace on the street, attributed to Bramante, is the **Palazzo della Cancelleria**, once the seat of the papal municipal government. St Philip Neri, the gifted, irascible holy man who is patron saint of Rome, built the **Chiesa Nuova** near the western end of the Corso (1584). Philip was quite a character, with something of the Zen Buddhist in him. He forbade his followers any sort of philosophical speculation, but made them sing and recite poetry; two of his favourite pastimes were insulting popes and embarrassing initiates – making them walk through Rome with a foxtail sewn to the back of their coat to learn humility. As was common in those times, sincere faith and humility were eventually translated into flagrant Baroque. The Chiesa Nuova is one of the larger and fancier of the species. Its altarpiece is a *Madonna with Angels* by Rubens. Even more flagrant, outside the church you can see the curved arch-Baroque façade of the **Oratorio dei Filippini** by Borromini. The form of music called the *oratorio* takes its name from this chapel, a tribute to St Philip's role in promoting sacred music.

Campo de' Fiori

Few cities can put on such a variety of faces to beguile the visitor; depending on where you spend your time in Rome, you may come away with the impression of a city that is one great Baroque stage set, a city of grimy early 1900s *palazzi* and bad traffic, or a city full of nothing but ruins and parks. Around **Campo de' Fiori,** one of the spots dearest to the hearts of Romans themselves, you may think yourself in the middle of some scruffy south Italian village. Rome's market square, disorderly, cramped and chaotic, is easily the liveliest corner of the city, full of market barrows, buskers, teenage Bohemians and the folkloresque types who have lived here all their lives – the least decorous and worst-dressed crowd in Rome. The best time to see the square is during the morning market (*Mon–Sat 8–1*) or at night along with adjacent Piazza Farnese. During papal rule the old square was also used for executions – most notoriously the burning of Giordano Bruno in 1600. This well-travelled philosopher was the first to take Copernican astronomy to its logical extremes – an infinite universe with no centre, no room for Heaven, and nothing eternal but change. The Church had few enemies more dangerous. Italy never forgot him; the statue of Bruno in Campo de' Fiori went up only a few years after the end of papal rule.

Just east of the square, the heap of buildings around Piazzetta di Grottapinta is built over the *cavea* of the **Teatro di Pompeo**, ancient Rome's biggest. This complex included a *curia*, where Julius Caesar was assassinated in 44 BC. Walk south from Campo de' Fiori and you will be thrown back from cosy medievalism into the heart of the High Renaissance with the **Palazzo Farnese**, one of the definitive works of that Olympian style. The younger Sangallo began it in 1514, and Michelangelo contributed to the façades and interiors. The building now serves as the French Embassy.

Most of the palaces that fill up this neighbourhood have one thing in common – they were made possible by someone's accession to the papacy, the biggest jackpot available to any aspiring Italian family. Built on the pennies of the faithful, they provide the most outrageous illustration of Church corruption at the dawn of the Reformation. Alessandro Farnese, who as Pope Paul III was a clever and effective pope – though perhaps the greatest nepotist ever to decorate St Peter's throne (*see* Caprarola, pp.808–809) – managed to build the Palazzo Farnese 20 years before his election, with the income from his 16 absentee bishoprics.

Palazzo Spada, just to the east on Via Capo di Ferro 13, was the home of a mere cardinal, but its florid stucco façade (1540) almost upstages the Farnese. Inside, the **Galleria Spada** (*t 06 6880 9814; open Tues–Sat 9–7, Sun 9–6; adm*) is one of Rome's great collections of 16th- and 17th-century painting. Guido Reni, Guercino and other favourites of the age are well represented. Don't miss the courtyard, which has decoration similar to the façade; look through a glass window, through the library, to one of Rome's little Baroque treasures: the recently restored *trompe l'œil corridor*, designed by Borromini to appear four times its actual length (the statue at the end of the path is actually less than a yard in height). To the south, close to the Tiber, **Via Giulia** was laid out by Pope Julius II: a pretty street lined with churches and *palazzi* from his time. Many artists (successful ones) have lived here, including Raphael.

Piazza Navona

In 1477 the area now covered by one of Rome's most beautiful piazzas was a field full of huts and vineyards, tucked inside the imposing ruins of the Stadium of Domitian. A redevelopment of the area covered the long grandstands with new houses, but the decoration had to wait for the Age of Baroque. In 1644, the Pamphili family won the papal sweepstakes with the election of Innocent X. Innocent, a great grafter and such a villainous pope that when he died no one – not even his newly wealthy relatives – would pay for a proper burial, built the ornate **Palazzo Pamphili** (now the Brazilian

Embassy) and hired Borromini to complete the gaudy church of **Sant'Agnese in Agone**, begun by Carlo and Girolamo Rainaldi.

Borromini's arch-rival, Bernini, got the commission for the piazza's famous fountains; the Romans still tell stories of how the two artists carried on. Borromini started a rumour that the tall obelisk atop the central **Fontana dei Fiumi** was about to topple; when the alarmed papal commissioners arrived to confront Bernini with the news, he tied a piece of twine around it, secured the other end to a lamppost, and laughed all the way home. The fountain is Bernini's masterpiece, Baroque at its flashiest and most lovable. Among the travertine grottoes and fantastical flora and fauna under the obelisk, the four colossal figures represent the Ganges, Danube, Rio de la Plata and Nile (with the veiled head because its source was unknown). Bernini also designed the smaller **Fontana del Moro**, at the southern end. The third fountain, that of Neptune, was an empty basin until the nineteenth century, when the statues by Giacomo della Porta were added to make the square seem more symmetrical. Off the southern end of the piazza, at the back of Palazzo Braschi, **Pasquino** is the original Roman 'talking statue', embellished with placards and graffiti ('pasquinades') since the 1500s – one of his favourite subjects in those days was the insatiability of families like the Farnese; serious religious issues were too hot to touch, even for a statue.

Piazza Navona seems mildly schizoid these days, unable to become entirely part of high-fashion, tourist-itinerary Rome, yet no longer as comfortable and unpretentious as the rest of the neighbourhood. One symptom will be readily apparent should you step into any of the old cosy-looking cafés and restaurants around the piazza: they're as expensive as in any part of Rome. The best time to come to Piazza Navona is at night when the fountain is illuminated – or, if you can, for the noisy, traditional toy fair of the **Befana**, set up between just before Christmas and Epiphany. **Palazzo Altemps**, on Piazza Sant'Apollinare, now contains part of the excellent **Museo Nazionale Romano** (*open Tues–Sun 9–7.45; adm*); recently restored, it contains mainly Roman sculpture, grouped according to the private collections in which they were once held – highlights are the Ludovisi throne and a statue of Aries finished by Bernini. Some of the churches in the neighbourhood are worth a look, such as **Santa Maria della Pace** (*closed for restoration*), with Raphael's series of *Sibyls and Prophets* on the vaulting and a cloister by Bramante. **San Luigi dei Francesi** (*open daily 7.30–12.30 and 3.30–6.30; closed Thurs pm*), the French church in Rome, contains the great *Life of St Matthew* by Caravaggio in a chapel on the left aisle. Towards the Pantheon, **Sant'Ivo alla Sapienza** once served the English community in Rome. Borromini built them one of his most singular buildings (1660), with its dome and spiralling cupola (*open Sun 10–12*).

The Pantheon

When we consider the fate of so many other great buildings of ancient Rome we begin to understand what a slim chance it was that allowed this one to come down to us. The first Pantheon was built in 27 BC by Agrippa, Emperor Augustus' son-in-law and right-hand man, but was destroyed by fire and replaced by the present temple in AD 119–128 by the Emperor Hadrian, though curiously retaining Agrippa's original inscription on the pediment. Its history has been precarious ever since. In AD 609 the empty Pantheon was consecrated to Christianity as 'St Mary of the Martyrs'.

Becoming a church is probably what saved it, though the Byzantines hauled away the gilded bronze roof tiles soon after, and for a while in the Middle Ages the portico saw use as a fish market. The Pantheon's greatest enemy was Gian Lorenzo Bernini, who not only 'improved' it with a pair of Baroque belfries over the porch (demolished in 1887), but had Pope Urban VIII take down the bronze covering inside the dome to melt down for his baldaquin in St Peter's. Supposedly there was enough left over to make the pope 60 cannons. (Urban was of the Barberini family, and Pasquino's comment about this act was, 'What the barbarians didn't do, the Barberini did.')

You may notice the building seems perilously unsound. There is no way a simple vertical wall can support such a heavy, shallow dome (steep domes push downwards, shallow ones outwards). Obviously the walls will tumble at any moment. That is a little joke the Roman architects are playing, for here they are showing off as shamelessly as in the Colosseum, or the aqueduct with four storeys of arches that used to run *up* to the Monte Palatino. The wall that looks so fragile is really 23ft thick and the dome on top isn't a dome at all; the real hemispherical dome lies underneath, resting easily on the walls inside. The ridges you see on the upper dome are courses of cantilevered bricks, effectively almost weightless. The real surprise, however, lies behind the enormous original bronze doors, an interior of precious marbles and finely sculpted details, the grandest and best-preserved building to have survived from the ancient world (*open Mon–Sat 9.30–7.30, Sun 9–6*). The movie directors who made all those Roman epics certainly took many of their settings from this High Imperial creation, just as architects from the early Middle Ages onwards have tried to equal it.

Brunelleschi learned enough from it to build his dome in Florence, and a visit here will show you at a glance what Michelangelo and his contemporaries were trying so hard to outdo. The coffered dome, the biggest cast concrete construction ever made before the 20th century, is the crowning audacity, even without its bronze plate. At 141ft in diameter it is probably the widest in the world (a little-known fact – but St Peter's dome is 6ft less, though much taller). Standing in the centre and looking at the clouds through the 28ft *oculus*, the hole at the top, is an odd sensation.

Inside, the niches around the perimeter held statues of the Pantheon's 12 gods, plus those of Augustus and Hadrian; in the centre, illuminated by a direct sunbeam at midsummer noon, stood Jove. All these are gone, of course, and the interior decoration is limited to an *Annunciation*, attributed to Melozzo da Forlì, and the tombs of eminent Italians such as Raphael and Kings Vittorio Emanuele II and Umberto I. The Pantheon simply stands open, with no admission charges, probably fulfilling the same purpose as in Hadrian's day – no purpose at all, save that of an unequalled monument to art and the builder's skill.

Just behind the Pantheon the big church of **Santa Maria sopra Minerva** is interesting for being one of the few medieval churches of Rome (*c.* 1280) to escape the Baroque treatment; its Gothic was preserved in restoration work in the 1840s. Two Medici popes, Leo X and Clement VII, are buried here, as is Fra Angelico. Santa Maria's Florentine connection began with the Dominican monks who designed it; they also did Florence's Santa Maria Novella. A work of Michelangelo, *Christ with the Cross*, can be seen near the high altar; the Carafa Chapel off the right aisle, where you can pay your respects to Pope Paul IV, has a series of frescoes (1489) on the *Life of St Thomas* by Filippino Lippi, his best work outside Florence.

Via del Corso

The Campus Martius, the open plain between Rome's hills and the Tiber, was the training ground for soldiers in the early days of the republic. Eventually the city swallowed it up and the old path towards the Via Flaminia became an important thoroughfare, *Via Lata* (Broad Street). Not entirely by coincidence, the popes of the 14th and 15th centuries laid out a new boulevard almost in the same place. **Via del Corso**, or simply the Corso, has been the main axis of Roman society ever since. Goethe left a fascinating account of the Carnival festivities of Rome's benignly decadent 18th century, climaxing in the horse races that gave the street its name. Much of its length is taken up by the overdone palaces of the age, such as the Palazzo Doria (1780), where the **Galleria Doria Pamphili** (*t 06 679 7323; open Fri–Wed 10–5; visits to the apartments on the half-hour between 10.30 and 12.30; adm exp*), still owned by the Pamphili, has a fine painting collection – with Velázquez's *Portrait of Innocent X*, Caravaggio's *Flight into Egypt*, and works by Rubens, Titian, Brueghel and more. Guided tours of the apartments (in English by request) give an idea of the lifestyle a family expected when one of their members hit the papal jackpot.

Continuing northwards, the palaces have come down in the world somewhat, tired-looking blocks that now house banks and offices. Look on the side-streets for some hidden attractions: **Sant'Ignazio**, on Via del Seminario, is another Jesuit church with spectacular *trompe l'œil* frescoes on the ceiling; a block north, columns of the ancient **Temple of Hadrian** are incorporated into the north side of the city's tiny Stock Exchange. **Piazza Colonna** takes its name from the column of Marcus Aurelius, whose military victories are remembered in a column (just like those of Trajan); atop stands a statue of St Paul. The obelisk in adjacent Piazza di Montecitorio once marked the hours on a gigantic sundial in Emperor Augustus' garden; **Palazzo Montecitorio**, begun by Bernini, now houses the Italian Chamber of Deputies.

A little way east of Piazza Colonna is the **Fontana di Trevi**, into which you can throw your coins to guarantee your return trip to Rome. The fountain, completed in 1762, was originally planned to commemorate the restoration of Agrippa's aqueduct by Nicholas V in 1453. The source was called the 'Virgin Water' after Virgo, a young girl who had shown thirsty Roman soldiers the hidden spring. It makes a grand sight, enough to make you want to come back – not many fountains have an entire palace for a stage backdrop. The big fellow in the centre is Oceanus, drawn by horses and tritons through cascades of travertine and blue water. Across from the fountain, little **SS. Vincenzo and Anastasio** has the distinction of caring for the pickled hearts and entrails of dozens of popes; an odd custom. They're kept down in the crypt. Just a short walk from the Trevi Fountain is the **Museo Delle Paste Alimentari**, on Piazza Scanderbeg 117 (*t 06 699 1119; open daily 9.30–5.30; adm exp*), where a small, modern display traces the history of Italy's most famous food.

Further north, the Corso reaches close to the Tiber and the dilapidated and overgrown **Mausoleo di Augusto**, a cylinder of shabby brick once covered in marble and golden statues. All the Julian emperors except Nero were interred here, in the middle of what were Augustus' enormous gardens. After the centuries had despoiled the tomb of its riches the Colonna family turned the hulk into a fortress. Further indignities were in store. Until 1823, when the pope forbade them, bullfights were popular in Rome, and a Spanish entrepreneur found the circular enclosure perfect for the *toreros*. After that the tomb was used as a circus, before Mussolini, wishing to afford the founders of Imperial Rome due respect (and perhaps intending to be buried there himself), declared it a national monument and had trees planted around it. Even so, no one seems to know what to do with it; it sits locked and empty.

Across the street, Augustus' **Ara Pacis** (Altar of Peace) has had a better fate. Bits and pieces of the beautiful sculpted reliefs, dug up in 1937, were joined with casts of others from museums around Europe to recreate the small building almost in its entirety. One of antiquity's noblest (and least pretentious) conceptions now sits under a glass pavilion; among the mythological reliefs, note the side facing the river, with the emperor and his family dedicating a sacrifice (*closed for restoration*).

Piazza di Spagna

The shuffling crowds of tourists who congregate here at all hours of the day are not a recent phenomenon; this supremely sophisticated piazza has been a favourite with foreigners ever since it was laid out in the early 16th century. The Spaniards came first, as their embassy to the popes was established here in 1646, giving the square and the steps their name. Later, the English Romantic poets made it their headquarters in Italy; typical mementos – locks of hair, fond remembrances, death masks – are awaiting your inspired contemplation at the **Keats-Shelley Memorial House** at No.26 (*t 06 678 4235; open Mon–Fri 9–6; Sat 11–6; adm*). Almost every artist, writer or musician of the last century spent some time here, but today the piazza often finds itself bursting at the seams with wayward youth from all over the world, caught between the charms of Rome's firts McDonald's and the fancy shops of Via Condotti.

All these visitors need somewhere to sit, and the popes obliged them in 1725 with the construction of the **Spanish Steps** (Scalinata di Trinità dei Monti), an exceptionally beautiful and exceptionally Baroque ornament. The youths who loll about here are taking the place of the hopeful artists' models of the more picturesque centuries, who once crowded the steps, striking poses of antique heroes and Madonnas, waiting for some easy money. At the top of the stairs the simple but equally effective church of **Trinità dei Monti** by Carlo Maderno (early 16th century) was paid for by the King of France. At the southern end of Piazza di Spagna, a Borromini palace housed the papal office called the *Propaganda Fide*, whose job was just what the name implies. The column in front (1857) celebrates the proclamation of the Dogma of the Immaculate Conception. Via del Babuino, a street named after a siren on a fountain so ugly that Romans called her the 'baboon', connects Piazza di Spagna with Piazza del Popolo. Besides its very impressive antique shops, the street carries on the English connection, with All Saints' Church, a sleepy neo-pub and an English bookshop just off it.

Piazza del Popolo

If you have a choice how you enter Rome, this is the way to do it, through the gate in the old Aurelian wall and into one of the most successful of all Roman piazzas, copied on a smaller scale all over Italy. No city has a better introduction, and the three diverging boulevards direct you with thoughtful efficiency towards your destination. Valadier, the popes' architect after the Napoleonic occupation, gave the piazza the form it has today, but the big obelisk of Pharaoh Ramses II, punctuating the view down the boulevards, arrived in the 1580s. It is 3,200 years old but, like all obelisks, it looks mysteriously brand-new; Augustus brought it to Rome from Heliopolis and planted it in the Circus Maximus; it was transferred here by Pope Sixtus V. The two domed churches designed by Rainaldi, set like book-ends at the entrance to the three boulevards, are from the 1670s, part of the original plan for the piazza to which Bernini and Fontana may have contributed.

Nero's ashes were interred in a mausoleum here, at the foot of the Monte Pincio. The site was planted with walnut trees and soon everyone in Rome knew that Nero's ghost haunted the grove, sending out demons – in the forms of flocks of ravens that nested there – to perform deeds of evil. In about 1100 Pope Paschal II destroyed the grove and scattered the ashes; to complete the exorcism he built a church on the site, **Santa Maria del Popolo**. Rebuilt in the 1470s, it contains some of the best painting in Rome: Caravaggio's stunning *Crucifixion of St Peter* and *Conversion of St Paul* (in the left transept), and frescoes by Pinturicchio near the altar. Raphael designed the Chigi Chapel, off the left aisle, including its mosaics.

Villa Borghese

From Piazza del Popolo a winding ramp leads up to Rome's great complex of parks. Just by coincidence this was mostly parkland in ancient times. The **Monte Pincio** once formed part of Augustus' imperial gardens, and the adjacent **Villa Medici** occupies the site of the Villa of Lucullus, the 2nd-century BC philosopher and general who conquered northern Anatolia and first brought cherries to Europe. Now the home of the French Academy, the Villa Medici was a posh jail of sorts for Galileo during his Inquisitorial trials. The Pincio, redesigned by Valadier as a lovely formal garden, offers rare views over Rome. It is separated from the **Villa Borghese** proper by the Aurelian wall and the modern sunken roadway that borders it; its name, Viale del Muro Torto (crooked wall), refers to a section that collapsed in the 6th century and was left as it was because it was believed to be protected by St Peter.

Exploring the vast spaces of Villa Borghese, you will come across charming vales, woods and a pond (rowing boats for rent), an imitation Roman temple or two, rococo avenues where the bewigged dandies and powdered tarts of the 1700s came to promenade, bits of ancient aqueduct and a dated and dingy **zoo** (*t 06 360 8211; open daily 9.39–5; adm exp*). On the northern edge of the park is a ponderous boulevard called **Viale delle Belle Arti**, where academies have been set up by foreign governments to stimulate cultural exchange. The **Galleria Nazionale d'Arte Moderna** (*t 06 322 981; open Tues–Fri 8.30–7.30, weekends 9–7; adm exp*) makes its home here in one of Rome's most inexcusable buildings (1913), but the collection includes some great works of Modigliani and the futurists, as well as a fair sampling of 19th- and 20th-century artists from the rest of Europe.

From there, gingerly skirting the Romanian Academy, you come to the **Museo Nazionale di Villa Giulia** (*t 06 321 7224; open Tues–Sun 8.30–7.30; adm*). If you cannot make it to Tarquinia, this is the place to get to know the Etruscans. Some of their best art has been collected here; laboriously reconstructed terracotta façades give you an idea of how an Etruscan temple looked. As usual, the compelling attraction is the Etruscans' effortless, endearing talent for portraiture: expressive faces can be seen in terracotta ex-votos (some of children), sarcophagi and even architectural decoration. Serious art is often more stylized; fine examples are the charming couple on the *Sarcophago dei Sposi* from Cerveteri, and the roof statues from the Temple of Portonaccio at Veii – these by Vulca, the only Etruscan artist whose name has survived along with his work. The museum building and its courts and gardens are attractions in themselves; Julius III had Vignola and Ammannati build this quirky Mannerist villa in 1553, and Vasari and Michelangelo may also have helped.

The fantastic trove of ancient relics and late-Renaissance and Baroque painting and sculpture – including masterpieces by Bernini and Caravaggio – at the **Museo e Galleria Borghese** (*t 06 328 101, tickets by reservation; open Mon–Sat 9–5, Sun 9–1; adm exp; some tickets available same day at the museum box office*) is testimony to the legendary greed and avarice of Cardinal Scipione Borghese, nephew of Pope Paul IV. He amassed, by any means available, one of the great private collections of the 17th century and built a magnificently decorated palace on the family's property to hold it all. The display is all the more impressive because a descendant of the Cardinal 'sold' many pieces to his brother-in-law, Napoleon Bonaparte, who put them in the Louvre.

The **Museo Borghese** (ground floor) offers an intriguing mix of great art and Roman preciosity. Often the two go hand-in-hand, as with the sensuously charged show-pieces of Bernini: *Apollo and Daphne*, *The Rape of Proserpina* and especially his *David*, which the artist modestly chiselled in his own image. Canova, the hot item among sculptors in Napoleon's day, contributes a titillatingly languorous statue of Pauline Borghese (Napoleon's sister) as the *Conquering Venus*. Even the ancient world is recruited to the the fun, with such works as the famous Hellenistic *Sleeping Hermaphrodite*. Also downstairs are several Caravaggios, including the *Madonna of the Palafrenieri*, *David with the Head of Goliath* and *St Jerome*.

No less impressive are the paintings in the **gallery** upstairs, representing many of the finest 16th- and 17th-century painters: Titian's *Sacred and Profane Love*, *St Sebastian* and *Christ Scourged*, two Bernini self-portraits, Raphael's *Deposition*, Correggio's *Danae* and Rubens' *Deposition*.

Via Veneto and the Quirinale

This chain of gardens was once much bigger, but at the end of the last century many of the old villas were lost to the inevitable expansion of the city. Perhaps the greatest loss was the Villa Ludovisi, praised by many as the most beautiful of all Rome's parks. Now the choice 'Ludovisi' quarter, it has given the city one of its most famous streets, Via Veneto, the long winding boulevard of grand hotels, cafés and boutiques that stretches down from Villa Borghese to Piazza Barberini. A promenade for the smart set in the 1950s, it wears something of the forlorn air of a jilted beau now that fashion has moved on.

Pull yourself away from the passing show on the boulevard to take in the unique spectacle provided by the **Convento dei Cappuccini** at the southern end of the street, just up from Piazza Barberini (*entrance halfway up the stairs of Santa Maria della Concezione; open Fri–Wed 9–12 and 3–6; adm*). Unique, that is, outside Palermo, for, much like the Capuchin convent there, the Roman brethren have created a loving tribute to our friend Death. In the cellars 4,000 dead monks team up for a *Danse Macabre* of bones and grinning skulls, carefully arranged by serious-minded Capuchins long ago to remind us of something we know only too well.

On the other side of Piazza Barberini, up a gloomy Baroque avenue called Via delle Quattro Fontane, you'll find the **Palazzo Barberini**, one of the showier palaces in Rome, decorated everywhere with the bees from the family arms. Maderno, Borromini and Bernini all worked on it, with financing made possible by the election of a Barberini as Pope Urban VIII in 1623. Currently it houses the **Galleria Nazionale di Arte Antica** (*t 06 481 4591; open Tues–Sun 9–7.30; adm exp*) – a misleading title, since this is a gallery devoted to Italian works of the 12th–18th centuries. Often the original decoration steals the show from the pictures: Bernini's Great Hall, for example, with a ceiling fresco by Pietro da Cortona, the *Triumph of Divine Providence*, or the ceiling in Room 7, with a fresco by Andrea Sacchi where the enthroned Virgin looking down on the round earth seems like a Baroque attempt to create a new Catholic astronomy. Works present include a Bernini self-portrait, Raphael's famous portrait of his beloved mistress *La Fornarina*, the 'baker's girl', more portraits by the Genoese artist Baciccio, lots of Caravaggios, Lippi's *Madonna* and two rather sedate pictures by El Greco. A large section of 15th-century artists not from Tuscany proves that not all the action was happening in Florence.

San Carlino (*currently closed for restoration*), on the corner of Via delle Quattro Fontane and Via Quirinale, is one of Borromini's best works – and his first one (1638), a purposely eccentric little flight of fancy built exactly the size of one of the four massive pillars that hold up the dome in St Peter's. Follow **Via Quirinale** and you'll reach the summit of that hill, covered with villas and gardens in ancient times, and abandoned in the Middle Ages. Then even the name Quirinale had been forgotten, and the Romans called the place 'Montecavallo' after the two big horses' heads projecting above the ground. During the reign of Sixtus V they were excavated to reveal monumental Roman statues of the **Dioscuri** (Castor and Pollux), probably copied from Phidias or Praxiteles.

Together with a huge basin found in the Forum, they make a centrepiece for Piazza del Quirinale. Behind it, stretching for half a kilometre drearily along the street is the **Palazzo del Quirinale** (*t 06 46991; open 8.30–12.30; adm exp; changing of the guard Mon–Sat at 3, Sun at 4*), built in 1574 to symbolize the political domination of the popes, later occupied by the kings of Italy, and now the official residence of the country's president.

Around Stazione Termini: Terme di Diocleziano and the Museo Nazionale Romano

Rome's great big station takes its name from the nearby **Terme di Diocleziano**, just on the other side of Piazza dei Cinquecento. Until the popes dismantled it for building stone this was by far Rome's biggest ruin; its outer wall followed the present-day lines of Via XX Settembre, Via Volturno and Piazza dei Cinquecento, and the big semi-circular **Piazza della Repubblica**, with its mouldering, grandiose 1890s *palazzi* and huge fountain, occupies the site of the baths' exercise ground, or *palaestra*. Altogether the complex covered some 11 hectares.

Michelangelo, not on one of his better days, converted a section of the lofty, vaulted central bathhouse into the church of **Santa Maria degli Angeli**, conserving some of the building's original form, and adding a broad new cloister. The cloister, garden and adjacent building (*open Tues–Sun 9–7.45; adm*) now house a small display of epigraphs and inscriptions on marble and terracotta fragments, lapidaries and sarcophagi from the **Museo Nazionale Romano**, the greatest Italian collection of Roman antiquities after the museum in Naples – recently relocated to five different sites, after spending much of the last century in storage. The most impressive part of the museum is the recently restored **Palazzo Massimo alle Terme** (*t 06 491 5576; open Tues–Sun 9–7.45; adm exp*) opposite the station, with astonishingly vivid frescoes and mosaics that once decorated villas in Rome and its suburbs, as well as fine Roman statuary, coins and gold jewellery. The nearby **Aula Ottagona**, on the corner of Via Parigi and Giuseppe Romita (*open Mon–Sat 9–2, Sun 9–1*) displays the musuem's remarkable bronze statues, which once decorated the baths. **Palazzo Altemps**, near Piazza Navona (*see p.847*), houses the museum's sculptures, while the **Crypta Balbi,** on Via dell Botteghe Oscure, near Largo Argentina (*open Tues–Sun 9–7.45; adm*), a 1st-century family crypt, is its newest addition.

Back at the Terme, a block north of the baths, Piazza San Bernardo has two interesting churches: **San Bernardo**, built out of a circular library that once occupied a corner of the baths' walls, and **Santa Maria della Vittoria**, home to one of the essential works of Baroque sculpture, the disconcertingly erotic *St Teresa in Ecstasy* by Bernini (in a chapel off the left aisle).

The Patriarchal Basilicas: Santa Maria Maggiore

Besides St Peter's there are three Patriarchal Basilicas, ancient and revered churches under the care of the pope that have always been a part of the Roman Pilgrimage. Santa Maria Maggiore, San Paolo Fuori le Mura and San Giovanni in Laterano are all on the edges of the city, away from the political and commercial centre; by the Middle Ages they stood in open countryside, and only recently has the city grown outwards to swallow them once more.

Santa Maria Maggiore (*open daily 7–7*), on Monte Esquilino, was probably begun about 352, when a rich Christian saw a vision of the Virgin directing him to build a church; Pope Liberius had received the same vision at the same time, and the two supposedly found the site marked out for them by a miraculous August snowfall. The church took its current form in the 1740s, with a perfectly elegant façade by Fernando

Santa Maria Maggiore

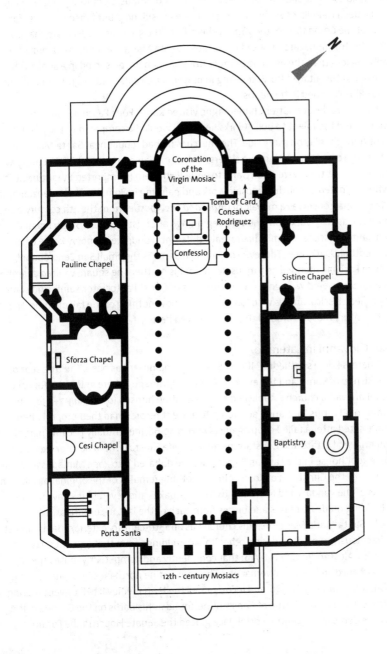

N

Coronation
of the
Virgin Mosiac

Tomb of Card.
Consalvo
Rodriguez

Confessio

Pauline Chapel

Sistine Chapel

Sforza Chapel

Cesi Chapel

Baptistry

Porta Santa

12th - century Mosiacs

Fuga and an equally impressive rear elevation by other architects; the obelisk behind it came from the Mausoleum of Augustus. Above everything rises the tallest and fairest **campanile** in Rome, an incongruous survival from the 1380s. Inside, the most conspicuous feature is the coffered ceiling by Giuliano da Sangallo, gilded with the first gold brought back from the New World by Columbus, a gift from King Ferdinand and Queen Isabella of Spain. In the apse there are splendid but faded mosaics from 1295 of the *Coronation of the Virgin*; others, from the 5th century, decorate the nave and the 'triumphal arch' in front of the apse. Santa Maria Maggiore has a prize relic – nothing less than the genuine manger from Bethlehem, preserved in a sunken shrine in front of the altar; in front, kneeling in prayer, is a colossal, rather grotesque statue of Pope Pius IV added in the 1880s.

In 822, two decades after Charlemagne visited Rome, Pope Paschal I found the money and the talent to build works he hoped would be compared to the magnificent ruins that lay on every side. The churches he had rebuilt near Santa Maria Maggiore commemorating two sisters, early Christian martyrs of the 1st century, were not large, but they were a start, and to embellish them he imported Byzantine artists who originated a rebirth of mosaic work and painting in Rome. **Santa Pudenziana**, on Via Urbana, conserves a mosaic of *Christ and the Apostles* from the 4th century, a thoroughly classical work from the very beginnings of Christian art. At **Santa Prassede**, on Via Santa Prassede, the mosaics reveal a different world; the shadowy Rome of the not-entirely Dark Ages. The jewel of Santa Prassede is the small **San Zeno Chapel**, which Paschal intended as a mausoleum for his mother. The square vaulted chamber is entirely covered with gold-ground mosaics of Christ Pantocrator, saints and some dignified classical angels who look as if they know nothing of the fall of Rome. The 9th-century mosaics around the altar are even better, if less golden.

San Giovanni in Laterano

Where is Rome's cathedral? It isn't St Peter's, and never has been. The true seat of the Bishop of Rome, and the end of a Roman Pilgrimage, is here in the shadow of the Aurelian wall, a church established by Constantine himself (*open daily 7–7.30*). The family of Plautius Lateranus, according to ancient records, had their property here confiscated after a failed coup against Nero in AD 66. It eventually became part of the imperial real estate and Constantine and his wife Fausta (whom he later executed) once kept house in the Lateran Palace. Later he donated it to Pope Miltiades as a cult centre for the Christians of Rome. Almost nothing remains of the original basilica; the sacks of the Vandals and Normans, two earthquakes and several fires have resulted in a building made up of bits and pieces from each of the last 16 centuries.

Like Santa Maria Maggiore, this church has an 18th-century exterior that is almost miraculously good, considering other Italian buildings from that age, with a west front by Alessandro Galilei (1736) that confidently and competently reuses the High Renaissance architectural vernacular. The equally fine north façade is older, done by Domenico Fontana in 1586, and incorporates the twin medieval bell tower. Entering at the west you pass a statue of Constantine, found at his baths on the Quirinale; the bronze doors in the central portal once graced the Senate House in the Forum.

Inside, the nave is dominated by giant statues of the Apostles (c. 1720), glaring down like Roman emperors of old. There is some carefree and glorious Baroque work in the side chapels – also remains of a fresco by Giotto, behind the first column on the right. Near the apse, decorated with 13th-century mosaics (of a reindeer worshipping the cross, an odd conceit probably adapted from older mosaics in Ravenna), the Papal Altar supposedly contains the heads of Peter and Paul. Below floor level is the tomb of Pope Martin V; pilgrims drop flowers and coins on him for good luck.

Rome in the later Middle Ages had evolved an architectural style entirely its own, uninterested in Gothic or reviving classicism, or, for that matter, in anything else that was going on in the rest of Italy. Sadly, almost all of it disappeared in the Renaissance and Baroque rebuildings. The towers of Santa Maria in Cosmedin and Santa Maria Maggiore are good examples of it, as well as the expressive mosaics of Pietro Cavallini and his school and the intricate, geometrical Cosmatesque pavements in this church and so many others. Perhaps the most striking survival of this lost chapter in art is the Lateran **cloister** (*t 06 6989 6433; open daily 9–6, until 5 in winter; adm*), with its pairs of spiral columns and 13th-century Cosmatesque mosaics; it completely upstages everything else in the church. All around the cloister walls, fragments from the basilica's earlier incarnations have been assembled, a hoard of broken things that includes an interesting tomb of a 13th-century bishop, the work of Arnolfo di Cambio.

The **Lateran Baptistry** (*open daily 8–12.30 and 4–6.30*) is no ordinary baptistry – nothing less than the first one in Christendom, converted from an older temple by Constantine; its octagonal form has been copied in other baptistries all over Italy. Inside there are unusual pairs of bronze doors on either side: one from 1196 with scenes of how the Lateran basilica appeared at that time, and the other from the Baths of Caracalla, 'singing' doors that make a low, harmonic sound when you open them slowly. Built around the baptistry are three venerable chapels with more mosaics from the early Middle Ages. The entrance to the baptistry is in Piazza San Giovanni in Laterano, behind the **Lateran Palace**, rebuilt in 1588 over the original building that had served as home for the popes from the 4th to the 14th centuries.

Across the piazza, which has the obligatory obelisk at its centre, you will see the **Scala Santa** (*open daily 6.30–12 and 3–6.30*), supposedly the stairs of Pilate's palace in Jerusalem, ascended by Christ on his way to Judgement and brought to Rome by Constantine's mother, St Helena. The more serious pilgrims ascend them on their knees. The Chapel of San Lorenzo at the top, a part of the medieval Papal Palace, contains two miraculous portraits of Jesus, painted by angels. While you're here, you have a good opportunity to explore the Aurelian Wall. The stretch of it behind the Lateran Palace looks much as it did originally, and the nearby **Porta Asinara** (next to Porta San Giovanni) is one of the best-preserved monumental ancient gateways.

Monte Celio

South of the Colosseum you can see nothing but trees, but on every inch of this vast tract of parkland, ancient neighbourhoods wait just a few feet beneath the surface. Modern Rome never expanded in this direction, and almost the whole of it has been preserved as open space. It's a fascinating place to walk around, if you can avoid the traffic thundering down the big boulevards towards the southern suburbs. The Monte Celio is only a small part of it, but it is one of the least known and most delightful corners of Rome. Have a picnic in the **Villa Celimontana** behind Piazza della Navicella and you may have squirrels for company.

Some of Rome's most ancient churches repose in quiet settings here, all worth a look inside if they are open: **Santo Stefano Rotondo** (*closed Sun and Mon morning*), the oldest circular church in Italy, was built around 470 over the ruins of a market-place of Nero's time; across the street more mosaics from the age of Paschal I (c. 820) can be seen in **Santa Maria in Dominica**, standing in **Piazza della Navicella**, with a fountain made in the form of an ancient Roman ship. Take the narrow road (just down hill from the church) that cuts down into the hill to **SS. Giovanni e Paolo**, built in the 4th century in the top floor of three Roman houses, which could be visited were they not closed for restoration. Down the western slope you reach **San Gregorio Magno**, begun by Pope Gregory the Great in 590. St Augustine lived here before being sent by Gregory to convert the Angles and Saxons of Britain. Adjacent to the church are several chapels with remarkable frescoes by Guido Reni, Domenichino and Pomarancio (*t 06 700 8227; open Tues–Sun 9–12; adm*).

Circus Maximus and Terme di Caracalla

Piazza Porta Capena, at the foot of the Monte Celio, has an odd decoration, an obelisk erected by Mussolini to commemorate his conquest of Ethiopia – he stole it from the Ethiopian city of Axum, although at long last it is scheduled to be returned to its rightful owner. The piazza itself is a vortex of Mussolinian pretensions; the dictator built himself a new Triumphal Way (now Via San Gregorio) along the route of the original one, to celebrate his piddling triumphs in Roman imperial style. An enormous building that was to house the Ministry of Africa to administer Mussolini's colonies found a more agreeable use after the war – as home of the United Nations Food and Agricultural Organisation (FAO). To the west, a broad green lawn is all that's left of the **Circus Maximus**. Archaeologists have estimated that as many as 300,000 Romans could squeeze in here and place their bets on the chariot races. Founded by King Tarquin and completed by Trajan, the stadium proved too convenient a quarry; but the banked, horseshoe-shaped depression still follows the grandstands' line.

The **Terme di Caracalla** (AD 206–220), in a large park south of Porta Capena, rank with those of Diocletian as the largest and most lavish baths (*t 06 975 8626; open Tues–Sun 9–1hr before sunset, Mon 9–2; adm*). Roughly 1,000ft square, with libraries and exercise courts, the baths probably boasted more gold, marble and art than any building complex in Rome; here the Farnese family dug up such masterpieces as the *Hercules* and the *Farnese Bull*, now in the Naples Museum. In the 1700s these baths were one of the obligatory sights of the Grand Tour; their lofty, broken arches and vaults appealed to the Romantic love of ruins like no others. Much of the central building survives, with its hot and cold rooms, great hall and swimming pool, all decorated with mosaics. A large tunnel connects the baths with the area around Palazzo Venezia, a mile away; its purpose was to transport the vast amounts of wood needed to keep the baths hot. Mussolini initiated the custom (discontinued due to the frailty of the ruins) of holding summer operas here; he liked to drive his roadster through the tunnel and pop out dramatically on stage at the start of the festivities.

Behind the baths a stretch of the **Antonine Aqueduct** that supplied it can still be seen. On the other side, facing Via Terme di Caracalla, **SS. Nereo e Achilleo** (*open daily 10–12 and 4–6; ring for custodian*) has more mosaics from the time of Leo III (c. 800), a Cosmatesque floor and choir and some gruesome 16th-century frescoes of the martydoms of the saints.

The Via Appia Antica: Rome's Catacombs

Rome's 'Queen of Roads', the path of trade and conquest to Campania, Brindisi and the East, was begun in 312 BC by Consul Appius Claudius. Like most of the consular roads outside Rome, over the centuries it became lined with cemeteries and the elaborate mausolea of the wealthy: ancient Roman practice, inherited from the Etruscans, prohibited any burials within the *pomerium*, the sacred ground of the city itself. Later the early Christians built extensive catacombs here – the word itself comes from the location, *ad catacumbas*, referring to the dip in the Via Appia near the suburban Circus of Maxentius. The Via Appia Antica (as distinct from the Via Appia Nuova) makes a pleasant excursion outside the city, especially on Sundays when it is closed to traffic.

The road passes under the Aurelian wall at **Porta San Sebastiano**, one of the best-preserved of the old gates. It houses the **museum of the walls** (*open Tues–Sat 9–7, Sun 9–5; adm*), admission to which also gives you access to a well-preserved section of the 4th-century wall alongside it. Continuing along the road, after about 500 metres, with some ruins of tombs along the way, there is the famous church of **Domine Quo Vadis**, on the spot where Peter, fleeing from the dangers of Rome, met Christ coming the other way. 'Where goest thou, Lord?' Peter asked. 'I am going to be crucified once more,' was the reply. As the vision departed the shamed Apostle turned back, to face his own crucifixion in Rome.

Another kilometre or so takes you to the **Catacombe di San Callisto**, off on a side road to the right (*t 06 5130 1560; open daily 8.30–12 and 2–5; closed Wed and Feb; guided tours only; adm*). Here the biggest attraction is the 'Crypt of the Popes', burial places of 3rd- and 4th-century pontiffs with well-executed frescoes and inscriptions. A word about catacombs: popular romance notwithstanding, these were never places of refuge from persecution, but simply burial grounds. The word 'catacombs' was only used after the 5th century; before that the Christians called them 'cemeteries'. The burrowing instinct is harder to explain. Few other places have ancient catacombs (Naples, Syracuse, Malta and the Greek island of Milos are among them). One of the requirements seems to be tufa, or some other stone that can be easily excavated. Even so, the work involved was tremendous, and inexplicable by necessity. Christians were still digging them after they had become a power in Rome, in Constantine's time. No one knows for certain what sort of funeral rites were celebrated in them, just as no one knows much about any of the prayers or rituals of the early Christians; we can only suspect that a Christian of the 4th century and one of the 16th would have had considerable difficulty recognizing each other as brothers in the faith.

Most catacombs began small, as private family cemeteries; over generations some grew into enormous termitariums extending for miles. Inside, most of the tombs you see will be simple *loculi*, walled-up niches with only a symbol or short inscription. Others, especially the tombs of popes or the wealthy, may have paintings of scriptural scenes, usually very poor work that reflects more on the dire state of the late Roman imagination than on the Christians.

You can detour from here another 500 metres west to the **Catacombe di Santa Domitilla** on Via delle Sette Chiese 282 (*t 06 511 0342; open daily 8.30–12 and 2.30–5; closed Tues and Jan; guided tours only; adm*). Domitilla was a member of a senatorial family and, interestingly, the catacombs seem to incorporate parts of earlier pagan *hypogea*, including a cemetery of the Imperial Flavian family; the paintings include an unusual *Last Supper*, portraying a young and beardless Jesus and Apostles in Roman dress. There is an adjacent basilica, built about the tombs of SS. Nereus and Achilleus, on Via delle Sette Chiese. Not far away on Via Ardeatina 174 is a monument to martyrs of a very different sort, the **Mausoleum of the Fosse Ardeatine** (*open Mon–Fri 8.15–6.45, weekends 8.15–3.30*), dedicated to the 335 Romans massacred by the Nazis on this spot in 1944 in retaliation for a partisan attack.

Back on the Via Appia Antica, there are several catacombs near the corner of Via Appia Pignatelli, including a Jewish one (*closed*); the largest are the **Catacombe di San Sebastiano** (*t 06 788 7035; open Mon–Sat 8.30–12 and 2.30–5; guided tours only; adm*). This complex, too, began as a pagan cemetery and has intriguing paintings and incised symbols throughout. The place had some special significance for the early Christians, and it has been conjectured that Peter and Paul were originally buried here, before their removal to the basilicas in Constantine's time.

Further south, by now in fairly open country, there are the ruins of the **Circus of Maxentius** (*t 06 780 1324; open Oct–Mar, Tues–Sun, 9–5; April–Oct, Tues–Sun, 9–7; adm*), built in the early 4th century, and then the imposing, cylindrical **tomb of Cecilia Metella** (*t 06 481 5576; open Tues–Sun 9–one hour before sunset; adm*), from the time of Augustus. In the Middle Ages the Caetani family turned the tomb into a family fortress, guarding the road to the south; at other times, before and since, it was a famous rendezvous for *banditti*. The road continues, flanked by tombs and parasol pines, with stretches of the original paving, for 16km beyond the walls of Rome.

Monte Aventino

Every now and then, when left-wing parties walk out of negotiations, Italian news-papers call it an 'Aventine Secession', a reference to events in Rome 2,500 years ago. Under the republic, the Monte Aventino was the most solidly plebeian quarter of the city. On several occasions, when legislation proposed by the senate and consuls threatened the rights or interests of the people, they retired *en masse* to the Aventino and stayed there until the plan was dropped. Rome's unionists are probably unaware that their ancestors had the honour of inventing the general strike.

The Aventino had another distinction in those times. In its uninhabited regions – the steep, cave-ridden slopes towards the south – Greek immigrants and returning soldiers introduced the midnight rituals of Dionysus and Bacchus. Though secret, such goings-on soon came to the attention of the senate, which rightly saw the orgies as a danger to the state and banned them in 146 BC. They must not have died out completely, however, and in the Middle Ages the Aventino had a reputation as a haunt of witches. The early Christian community also prospered here, and their churches are the oldest relics on the Aventino today.

Coming up from the Circus Maximus along Via Santa Sabina, **Santa Sabina** is a simple, rare example of a 5th-century basilica, with an atrium at its entrance like a Roman secular basilica, and an original door of cypress carved with scriptural scenes. This has been the head church of the Dominicans ever since a 13th-century pope gave it to St Dominic. Both Santa Sabina and the church of **Sant'Alessio**, down the street, have good Cosmatesque cloisters.

At the end of this street, one of the oddities only Rome can offer stands on its quiet square, oblivious of the centuries: the **Priorato dei Cavalieri di Malta**, a fancy rococo complex designed by Giambattista Piranesi. The Knights of Malta – or more properly, the Knights Hospitallers of St John – no longer wait here for the popes to unleash them against Saracen and Turk. Mostly this social club for nobles bestirs itself to assist hospitals, its original job during the Crusades. The order's ambassadors to Italy and the Vatican still live here. You can't go inside, but the gate is the most visited in Rome for the intriguing view from the keyhole, a clear view across town to St Peter's.

Elsewhere on the Aventino, **Santa Prisca** has beginnings typical of an early Roman church; its crypt, the original church, was allegedly converted from the house of the martyr Prisca, host to St Peter; the Apostle must have often presided over Mass here. **San Saba**, on Via San Saba, was founded in the 7th century by monks fleeing the Arabs in Jordan and Syria, with a 1205 rebuilding, including some Cosmatesque details, a superb mosaic floor and a crypt with 7th–11th-century frescoes.

Monte Testaccio and Rome's Pyramid

Porta San Paolo stands in one of the best-preserved sections of the Aurelian wall. The gate itself looks just as it did 1,700 years ago, when it was the Porta Ostiense; it changed its name after Paul passed through it on the way to his execution. Near the gate is something unique: the 92ft **Pyramid of Caius Cestius** (AD 12), a strange self-tribute for a Roman; at least Cestius, who had served in Egypt, paid for his own grandiose tomb himself.

Behind it, inside the walls, the lovely **Cimitero Protestante** (*open daily 8–dusk*) is a popular point of Romantic pilgrimage. The graves of Shelley and Keats are there, more recently joined by 400 British soldiers who died during the march on Rome in 1944.

Just to the west is the youngest of Rome's hills, **Monte Testaccio**, made up almost entirely of pot-shards. In ancient times, wine, oil, olives, and nearly everything else was shipped in big *amphorae*; here, in what was Rome's port warehouse district, all the broken, discarded ones accumulated in one place. The hill, now grassed over, is 115ft at its highest point – there is a big cross on top – and it covers a large area. The vast cellars the Romans left beneath it are now used as workshops, wine cellars and nightclubs that make Testaccio a swinging area after dark.

San Paolo Fuori le Mura (Outside the Walls)

Paul was beheaded near the Ostia road; according to an old legend, the head bounced three times, and at each place where it hit a fountain sprung up. The Abbazia delle Tre Fontane, near EUR, occupies the site today. Later, Constantine built a basilica alongside the road as a fitting resting place for the saint. Of the patriarchal basilicas this one has had the worst luck. Today it sits in the middle of factories, gasworks and concrete flats.

Once St Paul's was the grandest of them all; 9th-century chroniclers speak of the separate walled city of 'Giovannipolis' that had grown up around it, connected to the Aurelian wall by a 1½km-long colonnade built by Pope John VIII in the 870s. The Norman sack of 1084, a few good earthquakes, and finally a catastrophic fire in 1823 wiped Giovannipolis off the map, and left us with a St Paul's that for the most part is barely more than a century old. Still, the façade of golden mosaics and sturdy Corinthian columns is pleasant to look at, and some older features survive – the 11th-century door made in Constantinople, a Gothic baldaquin over Paul's tomb by Arnolfo di Cambio, a beautiful 13th-century Cosmatesque cloister (almost a double of the one in the Lateran), and 5th-century mosaics over the 'Triumphal Arch' in front of the apse, the restored remains of the original mosaics from the façade, contributed by Empress Galla Placidia. Art Deco is not what you would expect from those times, but Americans at least will have a hard time believing these mosaics were not done by President Roosevelt's WPA. The apse itself has some more conventional mosaics from the 13th-century Roman school, and the nave is lined with the portraits of all 263 popes. According to one Roman legend, when the remaining eight spaces are filled, the world will end.

EUR

By the late 1930s Mussolini was proud enough of his accomplishments to plan a world fair. Its theme was to be the Progress of Civilization, measured no doubt from the invention of the wheel up to the invention of the Corporate State. A vast area south of Rome was cleared and transformed into a grid of wide boulevards broken by parks and lagoons. Huge Mussolini-style pavilions were begun, and a design was accepted for an aluminium arch – forerunner of the famous one in St Louis but many times bigger – that would overarch the entire fairground. War intervening, the arch never appeared, and the Esposizione Universale di Roma never came off.

After 1945 the Italians tried to make the best of it, turning EUR into a model satellite city and trade centre, on the lines of La Défense in Paris. The result will derange your senses as much as it does the average Roman's: a chilly nightmare of modernism with Boulevards of Humanism, Electronics and Social Security.

Still, for those who can appreciate the well-landscaped macabre, EUR can be fun. Some of the older corners reveal giant Fascist mosaics of heroic miners, soldiers, assembly-line workers and mothers, and at the end of the Boulevard of Civilization and Labour you can have a look at the modest masterpiece of Mussolini architecture – a small, elegantly proportioned **Palazzo della Civiltà del Lavoro**, nicknamed the

Square Colosseum. Liberal, post-war Italy has rarely, if ever, been able to conceive anything with such a sure sense of design and a feeling for history.

EUR is also home to a few good museums. The **Museo della Civiltà Romana**, Piazza G. Agnelli 10 (*t 06 532 6041; open Tues–Sat 9–7, Sun 9–1; adm*), a collection of antiquities and exhibits including a huge scale-model of ancient Rome with every building present, is a great place to seed your imagination with visions of the old city's splendour. Others in the area include a **museum of prehistory and ethnography**, nearby in Piazza Marconi 14 (*t 06 549 921; open Tues–Sat 9–8, Sun 9–1; adm*), covering civilizations before classical Rome, and a **museum of the late-Middle Ages**, on Viale Lincoln 3 (*open Tues–Sat 9–5, Sun 9–1; t 06 5422 8199; adm*).

Trastevere

So often just being on the wrong side of the river encourages a city district to cultivate its differences and its eccentricities. Trastevere isn't really a Left Bank – more of a pocket-sized Brooklyn, and as in Brooklyn those differences and eccentricities turn out to be the old habits of the whole city, preserved in an out-of-the-way corner.

The people of Trastevere are more Roman than the Romans. Indeed, they claim to be the real descendants of the Romans of old; one story traces their ancestry back to the sailors who worked the great awning at the Colosseum. Such places have a hard time surviving these days, especially when they are as trendy as Trastevere is right now. But even though such things as Trastevere's famous school of dialect poets may be mostly a memory, the quarter remains the liveliest and most entertaining in Rome. The young crowd that Trastevere attracts now provides much of the local colour, their colourful trendy clothes somehow a perfect match for the medieval alleys.

Just over Ponte Garibaldi is Piazza Sonnino, with the **Torre degli Anguillara**, an uncommon survival of the defence towers that once loomed over medieval Rome, and the 12th-century church of **San Crisogono**, with mosaics by Pietro Cavallini (master of the Roman 13th-century school) built over the remains of an earlier church. Near the bridge, the dapper statue in the top hat is Giuseppe Gioacchino Belli, one of Trastevere's 19th-century dialect poets.

Turn left on to one of the narrow streets off Viale di Trastevere and make your way to the church of **Santa Cecilia in Trastevere**, founded over the house of the 2nd-century martyr whom centuries of hagiography have turned into one of the most agreeable of saints, the inventor of the organ and patroness of music. Cecilia was disinterred in 1599, and her body was found entirely uncorrupted. Clement VIII commissioned Maderno to sculpt an exact copy from sketches made before her body dissolved into thin air; this charming work can be seen near the altar, beneath an altarpiece by Giulio Romano. Nearby is a tabernacle by Arnolfo di Cambio similar to the one in St Paul's; the apse has 9th-century mosaics. The church also has other treasures: Renaissance tombs, including one of a 14th-century cardinal from Hertford; frescoes by the school of Pinturicchio in a chapel on the right, and a crypt built in the underlying Roman constructions, thought to be Cecilia's home. Up in the singing gallery (*open Tues and Fri 10.30–11.30; adm*) are the remains of the original church wall decoration – a wonderful fresco of the *Last Judgement* by Cavallini.

Across Viale di Trastevere – an intrusive modern boulevard that slices the district in two – lies the heart of old Trastevere, around **Piazza Santa Maria in Trastevere** and its church. Most of this building dates from the 1140s, though the original church, begun perhaps in 222, may be the first anywhere dedicated to the Virgin Mary. The medieval building is a treasure-house of Roman mosaics, starting with the frieze with the Virgin breast-feeding Christ flanked by ten female figures on the façade, and continuing with the remarkable series from the *Life of Mary* by Cavallini in the apse, a bit of the early Renaissance 100 years ahead of schedule (*c.* 1290). Above them are earlier, glittering mosaics from the 1140s. The piazza, and the streets around it, have been for decades one of the most popular spots in Rome for restaurants; tables are spread out wherever there's room, and there will always be a crowd in the evening.

Two Roads to St Peter's

One is broad and straight, the route of the many; the other is tortuous and narrow, and after it but few inquire. **Via della Lungara**, the route of the slothful from Trastevere, takes you past **Villa Farnesina** (*open Mon–Sat 9–1; adm*), an early 1500s palace built for the Chigi family. Inside are some of the best frescoes in Rome: the *Galatea* by Raphael and the *Cupid and Psyche Gallery*, designed by Raphael and carried out by his pupils; a prospect of the constellations and a room of false perspectives by Baldassare Peruzzi, who also designed the building; and works of Sodoma. Across the street, the **Palazzo Corsini** (*t 06 6880 2323; open Tues–Sat 9–7, Sun 9–1; adm*) contains an exceptional collection of 16th- and 17th-century art, including works by Caravaggio, Van Dyck, Guido Reni, Salvatore Rosa and many others – it's out of the way, but this may be the best of all Rome's many small state picture galleries.

The other road may be more difficult to find, but repays the effort with lovely gardens and views over Rome from the Gianicolo, the ancient *Janiculum*. First find Via Garibaldi, in the back streets behind Ponte Sisto, and it will carry you up to the Renaissance church of **San Pietro in Montorio**, once erroneously believed to be the spot of St Peter's crucifixion. A popular church for weddings, it has fine paintings in the shallow chapels, including a marvellous *Flagellation* by Sebastiano del Piombo – but the real draw here is Bramante's famed **Tempietto** in the adjacent courtyard.

In so many Renaissance paintings – Perugino's *Donation of the Keys* in the Sistine Chapel or Raphael's *Betrothal of the Virgin* in Milan – the characters in the foreground take second place in interest to an ethereal, round temple centred at the perspectival vanishing point. These constructions, seemingly built not of vulgar stone but of pure intelligence and light, could stand as a symbol for the aspirations of the Renaissance. Bramante was the first actually to try to build one; his perfect little Tempietto (1502), the first building to re-use the ancient Doric order in all of its proportions, probably inspired Raphael's painting two years later.

Via Garibaldi continues up the Janiculum to the gushing Acqua Paola Fountain, where you should turn right along the Passeggiata del Gianicolo. The Garibaldi Monument stands at the summit, overlooking the Botanical Gardens and the rest of Rome. At the other end of the hill, going towards the Vatican, the road curves downwards, passing the Renaissance church of **Sant'Onofrio** (*open daily 9–1*), with frescoes by Peruzzi in the apse. After descending the *passeggiata*, cross the modern Piazza della Rovere into the Borgo district. On your right is the hospital of Santo Spirito and the church of **Santo Spirito in Sassia**. This name may ring a bell for antiquarians. 'Sassia' refers to the Saxons of England, who upon their conversion became among the most devoted servants of the Church. English princes founded this hospital in the 8th century – astounding when you think about it. The Angles and Saxons who settled in Rome made up almost a small village unto themselves at this bend of the Tiber, and their 'burgh' gave its name to the neighbourhood called the Borgo today.

Castel Sant'Angelo

t 06 681 9111; open Tues–Sun 9–8; adm exp; audioguide in English; guided visits in English of the passetto *(covered passageway) and* prigioni *(prison cells) are arranged in the bookshop. Call ahead to check tour times, which vary.*

Though intended as a resting place for a most serene emperor, this building has seen more blood, treachery and turmoil than any in Rome. Hadrian designed his own mausoleum three years before his death in AD 138, on an eccentric plan consisting of a huge marble cylinder surmounted by a conical hill planted with cypresses. The marble, the obelisks and the gold and bronze decorations did not survive the 5th-century sacks, but in about 590, during a plague, Pope Gregory the Great saw a vision of St Michael over the mausoleum, ostensibly announcing its end, but perhaps also mentioning discreetly that here, if anyone cared to use it, was the most valuable fortress in Europe.

There would be no papacy, perhaps, without this castle – at least not in its present form. Hadrian's cylinder is high, steep and almost solid – impregnable even after the invention of artillery. With rebellions of some sort occurring on average every two years before 1400 the popes often had recourse to this place of safety. It last saw action in the sack of 1527, when the miserable Clement VII withstood a siege of several months while his city went up in flames. The popes also used Castel Sant'Angelo as a prison; famous inmates included Giordano Bruno, Benvenuto Cellini and Beatrice Cenci (better known to the English than the Italians, thanks to Shelley's verse drama). Tosca tosses herself off the top at the end of Puccini's opera.

Inside, the recently restored spiral ramp leads up to the **Papal Apartments**, decorated as lavishly by 16th-century artists as anything in the Vatican. The **Sala Paolina** has frescoes by Perin del Vaga of events in the history of Rome, and the **Sala di Apollo** is frescoed with grotesques attempting to reproduce the wall decorations of Nero's Golden House. Above everything, a mighty statue of Michael commemorates Gregory's vision.

As interesting for its structure as anything on display inside, Castel Sant'Angelo makes a great place to rest after the Vatican. The views from the roof are some of the best in Rome, and there's a café on the 4th floor. The three central arches of the **Ponte Sant'Angelo** were built by Hadrian, although the statues of angels added in 1688 steal the show; at once dubbed Bernini's Breezy Maniacs, they battle a never-ending Baroque hurricane to display the symbols of Christ's Passion.

Vatican City

St Peter's

Along Borgo Sant'Angelo, leading towards the Vatican, you can see the famous **covered passageway** (*passetto*), used by the popes since 1277 to escape to the castle when things became dangerous. The customary route, however, leads up **Via della Conciliazione**, a broad boulevard drilled by Mussolini through the tangled web of medieval streets. Critics have said it spoils the surprise, but no arrangement of streets and buildings could really prepare you for Bernini's Brobdingnagian **Piazza San Pietro**. Someone has calculated there is room for about 300,000 people in the piazza, with no crowding. Few have ever noticed Bernini's joke on antiquity; the open space almost exactly matches the dimensions of the Colosseum. Bernini's **Colonnade** (1656), with 284 massive columns and statues of 140 saints, stretches around it like 'the arms of the Church embracing the world' – perhaps the biggest cliché in Christendom by now, but exactly what Bernini had in mind. Stand on either of the two dark stones at the foci of the elliptical piazza and you will see Bernini's forest of columns resolve into neat rows, a subtly impressive optical effect like the hole in the top of the Pantheon.

Flanked by two fountains, the work of Maderno and Fontana, the Vatican **obelisk** seems nothing special as obelisks go, but is actually one of the most fantastical relics in all Rome. This obelisk comes from Heliopolis, founded as a capital and cult centre by Akhnaton, the half-legendary Pharaoh who, according to Freud, founded the first monotheistic religion, influencing Moses and onwards. Caligula brought it to Rome in AD 37 to decorate the now-disappeared Circus Vaticanus (later known as the Circus of Nero) where it would have seen Peter's martyrdom. In the Middle Ages it was placed to the side of the basilica, but Sixtus V moved it to where it now stands in 1586.

It may be irreverent to say so, but the original St Peter's, begun over the Apostle's tomb by Constantine in 324, may well have been a more interesting building: a richly decorated basilica full of gold and mosaics with a vast porch of marble and bronze in front and a lofty campanile, topped by the famous golden cockerel that everyone believed would some day crow to announce the end of the world. This St Peter's, where Charlemagne and Frederick II received their imperial crowns, was falling to pieces by the 1400s, conveniently in time for the popes of the Renaissance to plan a replacement. In about 1450 Nicholas V conceived an almost Neronian building programme for the Vatican, ten times as large as anything his ancestors could have contemplated. It was not until the time of Julius II, however, that Bramante was commissioned to demolish the old church and begin the new. His original plan called for a great dome over a centralized Greek cross. Michelangelo, who took over the work in 1546, basically agreed, and if he had had his way St Peter's might have become the crowning achievement of Renaissance art that everyone hoped it would be.

Unfortunately over the 120 years of construction too many popes and too many artists got their hand in – Rossellino, Giuliano da Sangallo, Raphael, Antonio da Sangallo, Vignola, Ligorio, della Porta, Fontana, Bernini and Maderno all contributed something to the hotchpotch we see today. The most substantial tinkering came in the early 17th century, when a committee of cardinals decided that a Latin cross was

Vatican Practicalities

The entrance to the **Vatican Museums** is on Viale Vaticano, to the north of Piazza San Pietro. The museums are open Nov–Feb Mon–Sat 8.45–1.45 (last admission 12.45); the rest of the year Mon–Sat 8.45–4.45 (last admission 3.45); adm exp; closed Sun, except the last Sun of each month and religious holidays, when they are open 8.45–1.45 (last admission 12.45); free.

St Peter's is open April–Sept daily 7–7; Oct–Mar daily 7–6; the basilica is closed when there are official ceremonies in the piazza, although visitors are allowed during mass. The dress code – no shorts, short skirts or sleeveless dresses – is strictly controlled by the papal gendarmes.

The Vatican Information Office, t 06 6988 4466, in Piazza San Pietro is very helpful. Open daily 8–7.

There are **Vatican post offices** on the opposite side of the square – with a much more reliable and faster postal service than the Italian one – and inside the Vatican Museums for distinctive postcards home.

The information office arranges 2hr-long morning tours of the **Vatican Gardens**, easily Rome's most beautiful park, with a remarkable Renaissance jewel of a villa inside: the **Casino of Pius IV** (1558–62) by Pietro Ligorio and Peruzzi. Tours May–Sept Mon–Tues and Thurs–Sat; Oct–April Sat only; adm exp; reserve a few days in advance with the information office.

Underneath the crypt of St Peter's, archaeologists in the 1940s discovered a perfectly preserved **street of Roman tombs** with many beautiful paintings. Open Mon–Sat 9–5; adm exp; t 06 6988 5318; tours can be arranged through the **Ufficio degli Scavi**, just to the left of St Peter's; in the summer book early as fragile conditions permit only 15 people at a time.

The rest of the Vatican is strictly off limits, patrolled by Swiss Guards, still recruited from the three Catholic Swiss cantons.

Michelangelo also designed the **wall** that since 1929 has marked the Vatican boundaries. Behind it are things most of us will never see: several small old churches, a printing press, the headquarters of *L'Osservatore Romano* and Vatican Radio (run, of course, by the Jesuits), a motor garage, a 'Palazzo di Giustizia' and even a big shop – everything the world's smallest nation could ever need. Modern popes, in glaring contrast to their predecessors, do not take up much space.

The current Papal Apartments are in a corner of the Vatican Palace overlooking Piazza San Pietro; John Paul II usually appears to say a few amplified words from his window at noon on Sundays.

For tickets to the Wednesday morning **papal audience**, held at 11am in the piazza from (May–Sept) or in the Nervi Auditorium (Oct–April), apply in advance at the **Papal Prefecture** – through the bronze door in the right-hand colonnade of Piazza San Pietro

The prefecture is open Mon–Sat 9–1.30, t 06 6988 3114, f 06 6988 5863; collect tickets Mon–Sat 3–8 at the Portone del Bronzo on Piazza San Pietro.

desired, resulting in the huge extension of the nave that blocks the view of Michelangelo's dome from the piazza. Baroque architects, mistaking size and virtuosity for art, found perfect patrons in the Baroque popes, obsessed by the power and majesty of the papacy. Passing though Maderno's gigantic façade seems like entering a Grand Central Station full of stone saints and angels, keeping an eye on the clocks overhead as they wait for trains to Paradise. All along the nave, markers showing the length of other proud cathedrals prove how each fails to measure up to the Biggest Church in the World. This being Rome, not even the markers are honest – Milan's cathedral is actually 63ft longer.

The best is on the right: Michelangelo's *Pietà*, now restored and kept behind glass to protect it from madmen. Sculpted when he was 25, it helped make Michelangelo's reputation. Its smooth and elegant figures, with the realities of death and grief sublimated on to some ethereal plane known only to saints and artists, were a turning point in religious art. From here the unreal art of the religious Baroque was the logical next step. Michelangelo carved his name in small letters on the band around the Virgin's garment after overhearing a group of tourists from Milan who thought the *Pietà* the work of a fellow Milanese. Not much else in St Peter's stands out. In its vast spaces scores of popes and saints are commemorated in assembly-line Baroque; the paintings over the altars have been replaced by mosaic copies. The famous bronze statute of St Peter, its foot worn away by the touch of millions of pilgrims, is by the right front pier. Stealing the show, as he knew it would, is Bernini's great, garish **baldacchino** over the high altar, cast out of bronze looted from the Pantheon roof.

Many visitors head straight for Michelangelo's **dome** (*open May–Sept daily 8–6; Oct–April daily 8–5; adm*). To be in the middle of such a spectacular construction is worth the climb itself. You can walk out on to the roof for a view over Rome, but even more startling is the chance to look down from the interior balcony over the vast church 250ft below. In the **treasury** (*open April–Sept daily 9–6; Oct–Mar daily 9–5; adm*), built in the 18th century, there are a number of treasures – those that the Saracens, the imperial soldiers of 1527, and Napoleon couldn't steal. The bronze cockerel from the old St Peter's is kept here, along with relics, Baroque extravaganzas and a gown that belonged to Charlemagne.

Do not pass up a descent to the **Sacred Grottoes** (*same hours as Basilica*), the foundation of the earlier St Peter's converted into a crypt. Dozens of popes are buried here, along with distinguished friends of the Church like Queen Christina of Sweden and James III, the Stuart pretender. Perhaps the greatest work of art here is the bronze tomb of Sixtus IV, a definitive Renaissance confection by a Pollaiuolo, though the most visited is the simple monument to John XXIII.

The Musei Vaticani (Vatican Museums)

The admission may be the most expensive in Italy, but for that you get 10 museums in one, with the Sistine Chapel and the Raphael rooms thrown in free. Altogether almost 7km of exhibits fill the halls of the Vatican Palace, and unfortunately for you there isn't much dull museum clutter that can be passed over lightly. Seeing this infinite, exasperating hoard properly would be the work of a lifetime. On the bright side, the pope sees to it that his museum is managed more intelligently and thoughtfully than anything run by the Italian state. A choice of colour-coded itineraries, which you may follow according to the amount of time you have to spend, will get you through the labyrinth in two or four hours.

Near the entrance, the first big challenge is the large **Museo Egizio** – one of Europe's best Egyptian collections – and then some rooms of antiquities from the Holy Land and Syria, before the **Museo Chiaramonti**, full of Roman statuary (including famous busts of Caesar, Mark Antony and Augustus) and inscriptions. The **Museo Pio Clementino** contains some of the best-known statues of antiquity: the dramatic *Laocoön*, dug up in Nero's Golden House, and the *Apollo Belvedere*. No other ancient works recovered during the Renaissance had a greater influence on sculptors than these two. A 'room of animals' captures the more fanciful side of antiquity, and the

The Vatican Museums

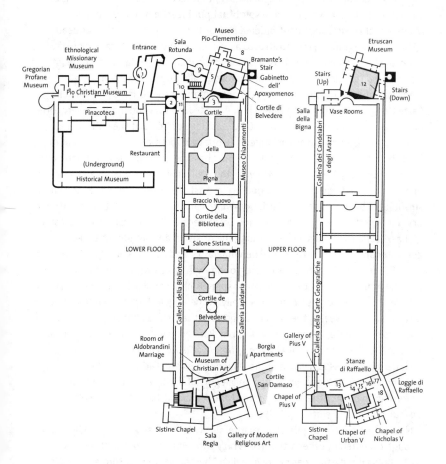

LOWER FLOOR

UPPER FLOOR

1 Spiral	10 Hall of the Greek Cross
2 Quattro Cancelli	11 Museum of Pagan Antiquities
3 La Pigna	12 Rooms of Greek Originals
4 Egyptian Museum	13 Hall of Immaculate Conception
5 Animal Room	14 Stanza dell'Incendio
6 Gallery of Statues	15 Stanza della Segnatura
7 Mask Room	16 Stanza di Eliodoro
8 Gallery of Busts	17 Sala di Constantino
9 Hall of the Muses	18 Sala dei Chiaro Scuri

2nd-century 'Baroque' tendency in Roman art comes out clearly in a giant group called 'The Nile', complete with sphinxes and crocodiles – it came from a Roman temple of Isis. The bronze papal fig-leaves that protect the modesty of the nudes are a good joke at first – it was the same spirit that put breeches on the saints in Michelangelo's *Last Judgement*, ordered by Pius IV once Michelangelo was dead.

The best things in the **Museo Etrusco** are Greek, a truly excellent collection of vases imported by discriminating Etruscan nobles that includes the famous picture of *Oedipus and the Sphinx*. Beyond that, there is a hall hung with beautiful high-medieval tapestries from Tournai (15th century), and the long, long **Galleria delle Carte Geografiche**, lined with carefully painted town views and maps of every corner of Italy; note the long scene of the 1566 Great Siege of Malta at the entrance.

Anywhere else, with no Michelangelos to offer competition, Raphael's celebrated frescoes in the **Stanza della Segnatura** would have been the prime destination on anyone's itinerary. The *School of Athens* is too well known to require an introduction, but here is a guide to some of the figures: on Aristotle's side, Archimedes and Euclid surrounded by their disciples (Euclid, drawing plane figures on a slate, is a portrait of Bramante); off to the right, Ptolemy and Zoroaster hold the terrestrial and celestial globes. Raphael includes himself among the Aristotelians, standing between Zoroaster and the painter Sodoma. Behind Plato stand Socrates and Alcibiades, and to the left, Zeno and Epicurus. In the foreground, Pythagoras writes while Empedocles and the Arab Averroes look on. Diogenes sprawls philosophically on the steps, while isolated near the front is Heraclitus – really Michelangelo; Raphael put him in at the last minute after seeing the work in progress in the Sistine Chapel.

Across from this apotheosis of philosophy, Raphael painted a Triumph of Theology to keep the clerics happy, the *Dispute of the Holy Sacrament*. The other frescoes include the Parnassus, a vision of the ancient Greek and Latin poets, the *Miracle of Bolsena*, the *Expulsion of Heliodorus*, an allegory of the triumphs of the Counter-Reformation papacy, the *Meeting of Leo I and Attila* and, best of all, the solemn, spectacularly lit *Liberation of St Peter*.

Nearby, there is the **Loggia** of Bramante, also with decoration designed by Raphael, though executed by other artists (*visits only with written permission*), and the chapel of **Nicholas V**, with frescoes by Fra Angelico. The **Appartamento Borgia**, a luxurious suite built for Pope Alexander VI, have walls decorated by Pinturicchio. These run into the **Opere d'Arte Religiosa Moderna**, a game attempt by the Vatican to prove that such a thing really exists.

The Sistine Chapel (Cappella Sistina)

To the sophisticated Sixtus IV, building this ungainly barn of a chapel may have seemed a mistake in the first place. When the pushy, despotic Julius II sent Michelangelo up, against his will, to paint the vast ceiling, it might have turned out to be a project as hopeless as the tomb Julius had already commissioned. Michelangelo spent four years of his life (1508–12) on the Sistine Ceiling. No one can say what drove him to turn his surly patron's whim into a masterpiece: the fear of wasting those years, the challenge of an impossible task, or maybe just to spite Julius – he exasperated the pope by making him wait, and refused all demands that he hire assistants to expedite the work.

Everywhere on the Sistine Ceiling you will note the austere blankness of the backgrounds. Michelangelo always eschewed stage props; one of the tenets of his art was that complex ideas could be expressed in the portrayal of the human body alone. With sculpture, that takes time. Perhaps the inspiration that kept Michelangelo on the ceiling so long was the chance of distilling out of the Book of Genesis and his own genius an entirely new vocabulary of images, Christian and intellectual. Like most Renaissance patrons, Julius asked for nothing more than virtuoso interior decoration. What he got was the Old Testament of the deepest recesses of the imagination.

The fascination of the Sistine Ceiling, and the equally compelling **Last Judgement** on the rear wall, done much later (1534–41), is that while we may recognize the individual figures we still have not captured their secret meanings. Hordes of tourists stare up at the heroic Adam, the mysterious *ignudi* in the corners, the Russian masseuse sibyls with their longshoremen's arms, the six-toed prophets, the strange vision of Noah's deluge. They wonder what they're looking at, a question that would take years of inspired wondering to answer. Mostly they direct their attention to the all-too-famous scene of the Creation, with perhaps the only representation of God the Father ever painted that escapes being merely ridiculous. One might suspect that the figure is really some ageing Florentine artist, and that Michelangelo only forgot to paint the brush in his hand. The restoration of the ceiling and *Last Judgement*, paid for by a Japanese television network, have accurately revealed Michelangelo's true colours – jarring, surprise colours that no interior decorator would ever choose, plenty of sea-green, with splashes of yellow and purple and dramatic shadows. No new paint was applied, only solvents to clear off the grime. Most visitors overlook the earlier frescoes on the lower walls, great works of art that would have made the Sistine Chapel famous by themselves: scenes from the *Exodus* by Botticelli, Perugino's *Donation of the Keys*, and Signorelli's *Moses Consigning his Staff to Joshua*.

More Miles in the Big Museum

There's still the **Vatican Library** to go, with its seemingly endless halls and precious manuscripts tucked neatly away in cabinets. The brightly painted rooms contain thousands of reliquaries and monstrances, medieval ivories, gold-glass medallions from the catacombs, every sort of globe, orrery and astronomical instrument. If you survive this, the next hurdle is the new and beautifully laid out **Museo Gregoriano**, with a hoard of classical statuary, mosaics and inscriptions collected by Pope Gregory XVI. Then comes a museum of **carriages** (*closed for restoration*), the **Museo Pio-Cristiano** of early-Christian art and, finally, one of the most interesting of all, though no one has time for it: the museum of **ethnology**, with wonderful art from every continent, brought home to Italy by missionaries over the centuries.

By itself the Vatican **Pinacoteca** would be by far the finest picture gallery in Rome, a representative sampling of Renaissance art from its beginnings, with some fine works of Giotto (*Il Redentore and the Martyrdoms of Peter and Paul*) and contemporary Sienese painters, as well as Gentile da Fabriano, Sano di Pietro and Filippo Lippi.

Don't overlook the tiny but electrically surreal masterpiece of Fra Angelico, the *Story of St Nicolas at Bari*, or the *Angelic Musicians* of Melozzo da Forlì, set next to Melozzo's famous painting of Platina being nominated by Sixtus IV to head the Vatican Library – a rare snapshot of Renaissance humanism. Venetian artists are not well represented, but there is a *Pietà* by Bellini and a *Madonna* by the fastidious Carlo Crivelli. Perhaps the best-known paintings are the *Transfiguration of Christ*, Raphael's last work, and the *St Jerome* of Da Vinci.

Peripheral Attractions

There are plenty of interesting things on Rome's outskirts – here is a brief overview, clockwise around Rome from the north. By the Tiber, the **Foro Italico** was Mussolini's most blatant monument to himself: he left his mark everywhere, on a giant obelisk, in the paving stones and around the grandiose **Marble Stadium**, chiselled too deep ever to be eroded. The sports complex hosted the 1960 Olympics. Across the Tiber, on Via Salaria, **Villa Ada** was once the hunting reserve of Vittorio Emanuele III; it's now a huge city park. The **Catacombe di Priscilla**, Via Salaria 430, are well worth the nun-led tour of the 2nd-century frescoes and the tombs of many early popes and martyrs (*t 06 8620 6272; open Tues–Sun 8.30–12 and 2.30–5; April–Sept 5.30; closed Aug; adm*).

Via XX Settembre, the big road out from Monte Quirinale, passes the Aurelian Wall at **Porta Pia**, redesigned by Michelangelo. Here it becomes Via Nomentana, a boulevard lined with villas not yet swallowed up by creeping urbanization. A kilometre east, stop at the charming complex of **Sant'Agnese Fuori le Mura** (Outside the Walls) (*open Mon 9–12, Tues–Sat 9–12 and 4–6, Sun 4–6*), including a 4th-century church with an early mosaic of St Agnes in the apse, and 15 ancient marble columns. Along the stairway down to the church, early Christian reliefs and inscriptions are displayed; inside the church is the entrance to the small, aristocratic **catacombs** (3rd-century), absorbing parts of earlier pagan catacombs (*t 06 861 0840; guided tours arranged Wed–Sun during church hours; adm*).

Around the back, through gardens where neighbourhood children play, stands one of Rome's least known but most remarkable churches. **Santa Costanza** was built as a mausoleum for Constantia, Emperor Constantine's daughter. In this domed, circular building – one of the finest late-Roman works – you can see the great religious turning point of the 4th century come alive; among the exquisite mosaics are scenes of a grape harvest, and motifs familiar to any ancient devotee of Dionysus or Bacchus. In the two side chapels are later mosaics of Christ and the Apostles.

At the end of Viale Regina Elena, behind the university, **San Lorenzo** is one of Rome's seven pilgrimage churches. The original building, begun under Constantine, was reconstructed in the early 13th century and contains fine Cosmati family work around the altar. From here you can re-enter the city through the impressive **Porta Maggiore**, built under Emperor Claudius; the walls here carry an aqueduct on top. You can also see the **Temple of Minerva** nearby, on Via Giolitti, a round brick ruin from the 3rd century AD, and **Santa Croce in Gerusalemme**, another of the seven churches, founded by Constantine but now thoroughly baroqued.

Almost directly under the train tracks, the **Underground Basilica**, only unearthed in 1916, was built underground for a secret, possibly illegal religious sect in the 1st century AD. Scholars haven't guessed what the cult's beliefs were from its strange stucco reliefs, but venture to call it 'neo-Pythagorian' (*contact the Soprintendenza Archeologica di Roma, Piazza Santa Maria Nova 53, t 06 699 0110, to visit*).

Day Trips from Rome

Ostia, the Port of Empire

According to the archaeologists, Rome's port was founded in the 4th century BC, 400 years after Rome itself. But in the centuries of conquest Ostia grew into a major city in its own right, with a population of c. 100,000 and nearly 2km of *horrea* (warehouses) near the mouth of the Tiber. In the 4th century, when the trade flow slowed, and even the grain supply from Africa was diverted to Constantinople, Ostia lost its *raison d'être*. Malaria thrived, and by AD 800 the site was abandoned. Old Father Tiber obliged the future by covering Ostia in sand and mud. Mussolini shovelled it out in the 1930s, recovering an ancient attraction often overlooked. It's easy to reach by train: get off at the Ostia Antica stop (*site open daily 9–one hour before sunset; adm*).

As in Pompeii, you can imagine life in a big ancient city; the temples, baths, frescoed houses, barracks and warehouses are amazingly intact. Ostia's **Forum**, with its columns of temples, is set around a little hill wistfully called the 'Capitol'. The small **theatre** has an interesting **Mithraeum**, like the one under San Clemente in Rome; there's a police station (*Caserma dei Vigili*) and the oldest **synagogue** in Italy. One vast square, the 'Piazzale delle Corporazione', preserves mosaics symbolizing the trades. A floor mosaic in **Fortunatus's Tavern** boasts an early specimen of advertising: 'Fortunatus says: if you're thirsty, have a bowl of wine.' Near the ruins, spare a few minutes for the sleepy hamlet of **Ostia Antica**, also called the 'Borgo', founded as a fortress town in 830 by Pope Gregory IV; it wasn't enough to keep the Saracens out when they sacked Rome 19 years later. There is a small Renaissance church dedicated to **Sant'Aurea** (a 3rd-century Ostian martyr), and the elegant **castello**, erected in 1483 by Julius II (still only a cardinal), to keep out the Turks.

Tivoli and the Villa Adriana

Ancient *Tibur*, set in a cliff with a beautiful view over the Roman Campagna, became a sort of garden suburb for the senatorial class in the early days of Empire. But a place with a view is also easily defensible, and by the early Middle Ages, despite all the dirty work of Goths and Huns, Tibur had changed its name to Tivoli and transformed itself from posh resort to feisty, independent hill town. Once, in its struggles with Rome, it even defeated its neighbour and captured a pope. Wealth returned in the Renaissance in the form of cardinals; one, Ippolito d'Este, son of Duke Ercole I of Ferrara, created perhaps the most fantastically worldly villa and gardens Italy has ever seen.

That is no small statement, but the **Villa d'Este** (*t 0774 312 070; open Tues–Sun 9–one and a half hours before sunset; adm; some days the fountains are not running – check*

Getting Around

There are frequent **trains** to Ostia and Ostia Lido on the overground COTRAL line from ⓜMagliana (Line B) in Rome. The best way to get to Tivoli and Villa Adriana is by COTRAL **bus**, from Ponte Mammolo terminal. For the Castelli Romani, there are frequent COTRAL **buses** from Anagnina, at the end of Metro Line A (a 20min ride from the centre of town).

There is a frequent COTRAL **bus** service from Rome to Subiaco (departures from Stazione Ponte Mammolo Metro Line B) as well as to Palestrina (from Stazione Anagnina at the end of Metro Line A) and to the Castelli Romani (also from Anagnina).

Tourist Information

Tivoli: Largo Garibaldi, t 0774 334 522.
Subiaco: Via Cadorna 59, t 0774 822 013.
Frascati: Piazza Marconi, t 06 942 0331.

Where to Stay and Eat

Ostia Antica

Al Monumento, Piazza Umberto I 8, t 06 565 0021 (*cheap*). Try the grilled fish for lunch. Near the castle. *Closed Mon and the last two weeks of Aug.*

Tivoli ✉ 00019

★★★Padovano, Via Tiburtina 130, Tiburtina, t 0774 530 807, f 0774 531 382 (*moderate*). A good place to stay, and a bargain.
Sibilla, Via della Sibilla 50, t 0774 335 281 (*moderate*). Famous above all for its location, incorporating the famous 'Temple of the Sibyls' in its building. The place lives off tourists, but the food is still good and the price is right. *Closed Mon.*

Frascati

Zarazà, Via Regina Margherita 45, t 06 942 2053 (*moderate*). One of the places that make Frascati a good place to eat: a restaurant with a picturesque panorama, local cooking and good Frascati wine. *May–Sept closed Mon, Oct–April closed Sun–Mon.*

Nemi ✉ 00040

★★★Culla del Lago, Via Spiaggia del Lago 38, t 06 9366 8231 (*moderate*). If you have a car, the area around Nemi is a nice place to stay: try the 'Cradle of the Lake' just outside Nemi in Castel Gandolfo, by the Lago di Albano.
Da Baffone, Via dei Laghi km 15, t 06 963 3892 (*moderate*). Serves dishes with wild mushrooms, as well as good roast meats and exceptional house wine. *Closed Mon.*

at the Tivoli tourist office) still has the charm to attract hordes of day-trippers year-round. The villa itself, designed by Pietro Ligorio and decorated with Mannerist frescoes, is upstaged by the gardens, set on a series of terraces on the slopes. Among palms and cypresses, flowers and lawns, every turn exposes a confectionery fountain: Bernini's 'Fountain of Glass', the 'Grotto of Diana', the 'Fountain of Dragons' – along with artificial waterfalls and pools. The cardinal's water organ and mechanical birds don't work, but you won't regret you came.

Tivoli has a gaudy 17th-century **cathedral** and a Romanesque church, **San Silvestro**, with early medieval frescoes, which you will pass on the way to another Renaissance cardinal's fantasy, the **Villa Gregoriana** (*open daily 9–one hour before sunset; adm*). Built in a natural chasm, the shady paths and gardens are irresistible to visitors, who trip gaily down to the bottom – then realize they face quite a climb back to ground level. It's worth the trip, if you're up to it, for the spectacular natural waterfall on the River Aniene, and a smaller, artificial one designed by Bernini.

On the edge of the abyss, you'll notice two small, remarkably well-preserved Roman temples, one circular and the other rectangular, called the **Temples of the Sibyl** and **Vesta**. There was indeed a college of sibyls in Tibur, as at Cumae near Naples, and they may possibly have kept one of these temples. Wherever, the presence of these oracular ladies, cousins to the oracle at Delphi, show the influence of Greek thought and religion in Latium from the earliest times.

Just outside the town (CAT bus no.4 from Largo Garibaldi), signs direct you to **Hadrian's Villa**, the grandest palace complex ever built in Italy (*t 0774 530 203; open daily Oct–April 9–5; May–Sept 9–8, last entry 1½ hours before closing; adm exp*). To get an idea of the scale on which a 2nd-century emperor could indulge his fantasies, stop at the model of the villa near the entrance. All marble and travertine, and the same size as the ancient centre of Rome, Hadrian's dream house shows the excess that even an intelligent and useful emperor was capable of, and had features that would surprise even Californians – like a heated beach with steam pipes under the sand.

Hadrian was an architect, whose design credits include the Pantheon; he travelled widely through the empire gathering inspiration for his villa, creating reproductions of the Canopic Temple of Alexandria, the Platonic Academy and Stoa Poikile of Athens, set among huge baths, libraries, a Praetorian barracks, temples, theatres and a little palace on an island in an artificial lagoon, that may have been his own private retreat. Many of the best statues in the Vatican and other museums were found here.

Subiaco and Palestrina

To see any of the hill towns to the east and south, you'll need a car. Quite a few interesting little villages have managed so far to escape modern tourism: lovely **Anticoli Corrado** on its steep cliff, and **Saracinesco**, founded on a nearly inaccessible crag by Saracen raiders in the 9th century; the present townspeople are their direct descendants. Few towns can claim as glorious a past as **Subiaco**, where St Benedict retired in the late 5th century to write his *Rule* and set Christian monasticism on its way. All through the dark centuries his monasteries (originally Subiaco had twelve) provided a haven for learning and piety, and as late as the 1460s the first printed books in Italy were made here by two monks from Germany.

Today the oldest buildings are in the **convent of Santa Scolastica** (*t 0774 85525; open daily 9–12.30 and 3.30–7*), named after Benedict's twin sister, with cloisters from the 6th and 11th centuries, and a medieval church decorated by the Cosmati. Beyond this, in a dramatic setting above a river gorge (a 2.5 km walk from the town), the **monastery of San Benedetto** (*t 0774 85039; open daily 9–12.30 and 3–6*) has a treasure of late-medieval and Sienese quattrocento frescoes (including a rare life portrait of St Francis of Assisi), in a mazelike complex of chapels, passages and steps cut into the rock; at the bottom is the cave called the *Sacro Speco*, where Benedict lived as a hermit for three years. Nearby, in the gorge of the Aniene, there is a little lake with a waterfall, which may have been constructed by Nero, who had a villa at Subiaco.

South of Tivoli, **Zagarolo** is a town of Baroque churches, a medieval citadel and one thoroughly strange Baroque gate, perhaps the work of Vignola. Nearby **Palestrina**, the ancient *Praeneste*, occupies the site of the greatest Hellenistic temple in Italy, the Sanctuary of Fortuna Primigenia. Originally home to an oracle of the Latin tribes, this complex, built on a series of mountain-side terraces, was as large as the town built on top. Part of the highest terrace was employed as a foundation for the 17th-century

Colonna-Barberini Palace, which now houses the **Museo Nazionale Archeologico Prenestino** (*t 06 953 8100; open daily 9–one hour before sunset; adm*); here the star attraction is a mosaic with scenes of Egypt, showing the flooding of the Nile. The ruins of the oracle chamber can be seen on the museum's grounds. On the way down to the town centre, you can seek out some unusual relics: ruins of a temple of Serapis, a treasury, and the cathedral, built over what was probably a temple of Jupiter.

The Castelli Romani

Before there was a Rome these towns around the Alban Hills were the strongest members of the Latin Confederation. Since being pounded into submission some 2,200 years ago, their role has been reduced to that of providing the capital with wine, flowers and a place to spend summer weekends. The countryside is beautiful, though the Castelli are nearly surrounded by the Roman suburbs. **Frascati**, the nearest and most popular of the Castelli, was a medieval replacement for the ancient Latin city of Tusculum, destroyed in 1191. Frascati took some hard knocks in the Second World War, but is still lovely, with winding alleys and a great view of the countryside. The elegant park in the grounds of the 17th-century **Villa Aldobrandini** (*open Mon–Fri 9–1, 3–6, winter until 5*) has famous views over Rome. Nearby **Grottaferrata** was built around the 11th-century abbey, founded by Saints Nilus and Bartholomew and still in the care of Greek Catholic monks; its **Basilica di Santa Maria** combines Byzantine mosaics with Italian medieval frescoes; one chapel was painted by Domenichino, and outside is a fine columned campanile from the 1200s (*t 06 945 9309; abbey open daily 8.30–12 and 4.30–6*). **Marino**, like Frascati, is famed for its wine; the town fountains flow with it during the grape festival on the first Sunday of October. From here the Via dei Laghi passes **Lago di Albano** on the way to Velletri and the south. After the lake there is a turn-off to **Rocca di Papa**, a dramatically sited town with a medieval citadel called the *Quartiere dei Bavaresi* after Emperor Ludwig's Bavarian troops stationed here in the 1320s. From the town you can drive up to the highest of the Alban Hills, **Monte Cavo** (3,228ft), passing a spot where Hannibal camped during the Punic Wars.

From Rome the Via Appia Antica passes the other side of Lago Albano in a dead straight line as far as **Castel Gandolfo**, the Vatican enclave where popes take their summer holidays. After that comes **Albano Laziale**, named for the ancient Alba Longa, mother city of Rome. Septimus Severus built a huge army base for the 2nd legion here, and its relics can be seen all over town: bits and snatches of the past abound, including a 3rd-century cistern – still in use – and the principal gate, rediscovered in 1944 when the houses that covered it were bombed. The town's two central churches were both originally part of a vast bath complex: **San Pietro**, with a fine Romanesque campanile, and **Santa Maria della Rotonda**, a remarkable miniature Pantheon that was a *nymphaeum*, and still has some mosaics of sea-monsters and a relief of Mithras. Albano's museum, on Viale Risorgimento, stands near another strange relic, the so-called 'Tomb of the Horatii and Curiatii', built in an Etruscan style.

From Albano the Appian Way (SS7) continues south for **Ariccia**. Anyone familiar with Sir James Frazier's *The Golden Bough* (the foundation work of modern anthropology) will remember the priest of Diana who ruled the Ariccian Grove, the 'King of the

Wood', and how as late as Roman times any man who cared to could cut some mistletoe from one of the sacred oaks, kill the king and take his place. There are still oak groves around Ariccia, and 'Diana's Mirror', the beautiful **Lake Nemi**, is still an enchanted spot, a deep blue oval surrounded by wooded hills and villas. The town of Nemi itself, a pretty place known for violets and *fragoline* (tiny strawberries), is also worth a detour. Beyond Nemi, **Velletri** is the last of the Castelli, with a Baroque cathedral and an odd, 149ft striped tower of 1353 called the Torre del Trivio.

The Monti Lepini: Cori, Ninfa and Sermoneta

In the Middle Ages, the Monti Lepini was the closest people could live to the malaria-ridden coast; now the charming old hill towns are well off the beaten track. **Cori**, like Rome and so many other Latin towns, likes to trace its founding to Trojan refugees. It may well be 3,000 years old; that, at least, is the date archaeologists assign to its 'cyclopean' walls, built of huge, neatly fitted polygonal stones, still visible in many places. There are also many Roman ruins, including an intact bridge and the Temple of Hercules (really of Jupiter), a small Doric building complete but for its roof.

Nearby **Ninfa** (*t 0773 695 404; open April–first Sun of Nov, first Sat and Sun of each month; from April–June also the third Sun of each month; adm exp; call to be sure it's open*) was once a powerful city, one that witnessed the election of two popes. Now it is called the 'medieval Pompeii'. Like many others, this city belonged to the Caetani, one of the most powerful of the great Roman families. After one family faction seized it from another and sacked it in 1382, Ninfa dwindled. Malaria set in and the area was abandoned by the 17th century. In the 1920s, Caetani descendants began turning the site of the city into what has become a stunning botanical garden, where ruins of the medieval monuments survive in a setting of small streams and lakes, overgrown with wildflowers and trees. It is now run by a foundation with the help of the WWF.

Norma, built on a steep, curving cliff, seems a city hanging in the air. Nearby are more cyclopean walls around the ruins of **Norba**, once capital of Rome's bitter enemies, the Volscians. It was besieged and destroyed by the legions during the Social Wars in 89 BC, never to be rebuilt – though it's reconstructed in a **Museo Virtuale**.

Many of the medieval refugees from Ninfa went just up the hill to **Sermoneta**, a lovely and dignified hill village that gives you two good reasons for a detour: a fascinating castle tour at the **Castello Caetani**, complete with a Renaissance ghost, and one of the most transcendant Madonnas you'll ever see, by the cheerful Florentine Benozzo Gozzoli, in the 12th-century **Collegiata di Santa Maria**.

At the eastern end of the Monti Lepini, **Priverno** was another capital of the Volscians, and home to the warrior maiden Camilla who led them (at least in the pages of the *Aeneid*) against the Trojans. Now it has an excellent archaeology museum, a wealth of little churches with medieval frescoes (you'll have to find a key), and ruins of its ancestor, ancient *Privernum*, down on the plain amid fields of Priverno's famous artichokes.

For the fact that Priverno has a Gothic cathedral, thank the French Cistercian architects from nearby **Fossanova** and its 12th-century abbey (*t 0773 930 961; open*

Mon–Sat 7–12 and 3–4). The Cistercians, masters at reclaiming swamplands, got these from the pope in 1130 and soon started work on this austere but graceful Gothic pile for their headquarters. The Italians never were much interested in the style, of course, and Fossanova survives along with several other churches in southern Lazio, all built or inspired by the Cistercians, as rare examples on this side of the Alps. The church, of cathedral proportions, is a fine, sedate Burgundian Gothic work with a beautiful rose window. Not much is left inside, except the stately rows of piers and pointed arches. Fossanova was a great centre of learning in its day (St Thomas Aquinas spent time here), but after the 1400s both wealth and talent deserted it. After centuries of decadence, it was expropriated in 1873, and its treasures dispersed. Up in the Monti Ausoni above Fossanova, **Sonnino** was bandit country even a century ago; the village commemorates its badmen in a *Museo dei Briganti*.

Southern Lazio: Down the Coast

The Pontine Marshes

...nowhere else has the creative power of Fascism left a deeper
mark. The immense works can be summed up in the lapidary
phrase of Il Duce:'You redeem the land, you found some cities.'
from a 1939 Italian guidebook

You wouldn't have been travelling this way 60 years ago, when the broad plain of the Pontine Marshes was the biggest no-man's-land in Italy, wracked by malaria and healthy only for the water-buffalo. Under the Romans, canals were dug to reclaim the swamps, but they became blocked up in the Dark Ages. Once again during the 13th century some of the marshes were drained, but a few centuries of papal rule had the area back to its pristine soggy emptiness when Mussolini decided to make it one of the showpieces of his regime.

Today, except for the small corner preserved as a park and wildlife refuge, the Pontine Marshes no longer exist, and brand-new towns like Aprilia, Pomezia, Pontinia and Sabaudia sit amid miles of prosperous farms as curious monuments to the brighter side of fascism. So does **Latina**, largest of the Pontine towns and Italy's youngest provincial capital, founded in 1932, a bright and busy place built on a radial plan with plenty of trees and chunky Mussolini *palazzi* – all generally tasteful, save only perhaps the block of government offices laid out in the shape of a giant M.

Down the Coast: Anzio, Monte Circeo and Terracina

If you drive along the coast you'll pass plenty of beaches, including those of the small resort of **Anzio**, ancient *Antium*, popular with the Romans. This Volscian town, from which Coriolanus made his rebellion against Rome, later became the home of one of Augustus's imperial palaces; ruins include that of a theatre. Later holidaymakers included a pope or two, and the Roman families that left a host of Liberty-style villas a century ago. Anzio really became popular in January 1944, when

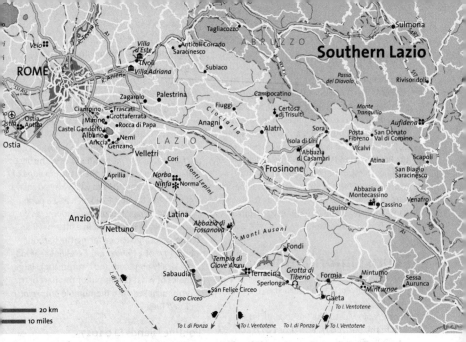

the British and US forces found its beaches an ideal spot for a landing; that bloody but successful end-run forced the Germans to abandon their Gustav Line and opened the way for the liberation of Rome. Large military cemeteries surround the town.

Between Anzio and Cape Circeo the coast is a solid stretch of beaches and dunes. **Monte Circeo**, at the end, was an island in ancient times, one of many candidates for Homer's Isle of Circe from the *Odyssey*. **San Felice Circeo,** offers boat trips to the rock. Since 1934 much of this area has been included in the **Parco Nazionale del Circeo**, an unspoiled expanse of watery landscape. Migratory birds of all kinds stop here, and besides a wealth of wild flowers and primeval forests you may see woodpeckers, peregrine falcons and herons – and maybe that overdressed sea bird, the *Cavaliere d'Italia*.

Being Italy, the next compelling sight is never far; here, the Cooperativa *La Mela Cotogna (based in Sabaudia at Via Carlo Alberto 104,* **t** *0773 511 206),* organizes guided visits to the villa of **Emperor Domitian**, reachable by boat across the lake of Sabaudia, in the National Park. **Sabaudia** itself is another of Mussolini's Art Deco new towns (1933), and probably the most successful of them; as a publicity stunt, the Duce collared every loose labourer in Italy and got the town built in 253 days.

Further down the coast the Ausonian Mountains crowd the sea at **Terracina**, once the Volscian port of *Anxur*, later a major node on the Appian Way and the biggest port between Rome and Naples. Now it's a busy, attractive town scattered with ruins. The best are high up in the **Capitolium**: three Etruscan-style temples of the 1st century BC – like the gate at Albano Laziale discovered when the buildings on top were destroyed in 1944. The hotchpotch **cathedral** started its career as a temple to Augustus and deified Rome; in places you can still see the ancient columns through the walls. There is an exotic 13th century campanile, and mosaics and Cosmati work inside.

Down in the modern town, built around the harbour and an 18th-century ship canal built by the popes, there are ruins of a bath complex and an amphitheatre. **Terracina**

Getting Around

The Rome–Naples **rail** line runs parallel to the coast. For Terracina and Sabaudia, get off at Priverno; for Sperlonga, at Fondi; for Gaeta, at Formia, and take local buses. There are also regular COTRAL **buses**, departures from Roma EUR Fermi. Formia is the year-round port for the **Pontine Islands**, with daily **ferry** departures. In the summer you can also catch a **hydrofoil** and ferry from Anzio or Terracina; in winter there's a ferry from Terracina (daily 8am) and a regular hydrofoil service from Anzio (Sat, Sun and Mon).

Tourist Information

Latina: Via Duca del Mare 19, t 0773 695 404.
San Felice Circeo: Piazza Lanzuisi,
t 0773 547 770.
Ponza: Molo Musco, the Pro Loco, just uphill from the port, t 0771 80031, or t 0771 809 866. Useful for ferry/hydrofoil information.

Where to Stay and Eat

Sperlonga ✉ 04029

★★★La Playa, outside town in Via C. Colombo at Località Fiorelle, t 0771 549 496, f 0771 548 106 (*expensive*). Sperlonga has some nice spots around its beaches, and this is a fine modern example, with pool and a bit of beach. *Closed Jan–Mar.*
★★★Parkhotel Fiorelle, t 0771 549 246 (*moderate*). Very close, slightly cheaper.
La Bisaccia, Via Romita 25, t 0771 54576 (*moderate*). There are plenty of relatively inexpensive fish restaurants by the sea; this is a charming little place in town, serving only fish and pasta dishes. *Closed Tues and Nov.*

Gaeta ✉ 04024

★★★Summit, near Gaeta, on the coastal Via Flacca km 23, t/f 0771 741 741 (*very expensive–moderate*). A fine modern resort hotel in a good location, if a bit large. *Open March–Oct.*

Masaniello, Piazza Commestibili 6, t 0771 462 296 (*moderate*). Perhaps Gaeta's oldest restaurant, although the succulent fish specialities are prepared in a style that's more typical of Campania than Lazio.

Formia ✉ 04023

★★★★Grande Albergo Miramare, Via Appia 44, t/f 0771 320 047 (*moderate*). One of the best places on the coast: on the southern edge of the town, a beautiful old villa with extensive gardens on the shore, a beach and a pool, and modernized but pleasant rooms, as well as an elegant restaurant in a little pavilion.
Zì Anna, on Largo Paone facing the harbour, t 0771 771 063 (*moderate*). Excellent seafood, classically prepared, and a surprisingly large choice of what comes out of this part of the Tyrrhenian Sea. Also memorable *primi piatti*. *Closed Tues.*

Pontine Islands ✉ 04027

★★★La Torre dei Borboni, Via Madonna 1, t 0771 80135, f 0771 809 884 (*very expensive–moderate*). The most picturesque place to stay on Ponza, with a third of its rooms and apartments in an 18th-century castle with wonderful views and a private beach. Prices double in high season. *Closed mid-Oct–May.*
★★★Gennarino a Mare, t 0771 80071, f 0771 80140 (*very expensive–moderate*). Near Ponza's central beach, which has a good restaurant (*cheap*), with a few tables on a floating platform. Again, prices double in summer. *Closed Thurs out of season.*
Da Luisa, Via Chiaia di Luna, t 0771 80128 (*moderate*). A cheaper alternative.

Otherwise there are several places where you can rent a simple room quite cheaply.
La Lanterna, Corso Carlo Pisacane (*cheap*). A family-run place for a home-style meal.

A wonderful Neapolitan pastry-shop on the main drag sells delicious *sfogliatelle ricce* (warm, crisp pastry filled with a *ricotta*-based cream, spices and candied orange peel) and *torta caprese* (chocolate and almond cake).

is a resort with an enormous beach west of the centre along Lungomare Circeo. At the eastern entrance to town, Trajan cut a passage through the mountains, the 'Pisco Montano', to allow the Via Appia to continue along the coast. In Roman times, every

sailor on the Tyrrhenian knew the landmark **Temple of Giove Anxur**, high up on
Monte Sant'Angelo above the city; take the Strada Panoramica up to the top; the
temple's mighty stone platform survives, with views for miles along the coast.

From Terracina you can detour to **Fondi**, an old town on the plain surrounded by
lakes, orchards and vegetable gardens. Fondi has stuck to its rectilinear Roman street
plan without change; through the centuries it added a cathedral full of curiosities,
and a bluff and businesslike 14th-century castle that contains a small museum.

Sperlonga and Gaeta

Continuing towards Naples, **Sperlonga** is one of the most pleasant small resorts on
the central Tyrrhenian coast, with a picturesque, whitewashed medieval quarter on
its steep promontory and miles of fine beaches to either side. About 3km beyond it
lies the sea cave called the **Grotto of Tiberius** (*site and museum open daily 9–7; winter
9–4; adm*), once fitted out as a pleasure dome for the hedonistic emperor (read the
decadent details in Suetonius's tell-all *Lives of the Caesars*). Outrageous sculpture has
been found here, smashed to pieces and now reconstructed; the best bits are two
enormous compositions representing scenes from the *Odyssey*. Entrance to the site is
through the museum that has been built to house them.

At the end of this scenic stretch of coast, **Gaeta** stands behind its medieval walls on
a narrow peninsula, the grandest sight between Monte Argentario and the Bay of
Naples. In the early Middle Ages, this town was an important Mediterranean trading
centre, a rival to Amalfi and Pisa. Its naturally defensible site made it a valued stronghold for centuries after; it was briefly the last redoubt of the House of Bourbon in 1861
when the King of Naples and his palace guard withstood a siege from the army of the
new Italy, hoping for help from France that never came. Now, Gaeta gracefully juggles
its two modern roles: a romantic, evocative resort, and a US naval base.

The town has a quiet medieval atmosphere, with a 13th-century castle and
crumbling old streets and alleys around the harbour. The much rebuilt **cathedral** has
a spectacular 185ft **campanile** begun in the 11th century; its coloured tiles and interlaced arches betray the influence of the minarets of Spain and North Africa. The hill
above Gaeta, **Monte Orlando**, is now a park and closed to traffic, but you can take a
shuttle bus up to the top for the views and the rich and well-preserved tomb of a
Roman general named Munatius Planctus, the founder of Lyon, France.

The resort strip spreads around the gulf to Gaeta's sister city **Formia**, the major port
for ferries to the Pontine Islands, which enjoyed a blessed past as one of the gilded
resorts of Imperial Rome, like Capri or Baiae. Mark Antony's men caught up with the
virtuous but capitally tedious orator Cicero here, after the assassination of Caesar,
and knifed him in the baths of his villa. Little of ancient Formia survived through the
Dark Ages, and the little city that replaced it suffered grievously in 1944; there are still
plenty of Roman ruins, including the so-called 'Tomb of Cicero'. Today Formia is
entirely new, a happy and growing place that seems to have a bright future.

Before Campania, the last town along the coast is **Minturno**, a medieval
replacement for ancient *Minturnae*, the ruins of which, closer to the coast, include a
restored theatre, bits of temples and an aqueduct.

Ponza and the Pontine Islands

An ancient volcano gave birth to the five small islands of the Pontine archipelago, and to it they owe much of their charm and eccentricities. Two are inhabited: **Ponza**, the larger and more visited, is stunningly beautiful and shaped like a crescent moon. The curve of its fishing harbour, with its oddly shaped sea rocks, arches and coves, shelters a charming pastel-tinted town and small tower. On the other side of the island, but within walking distance, is the island's famous 'moonlit' beach, the **Chiaia di Luna**, a crescent-shaped beach beneath the steep pale cliffs. Wandering (or, far better, sailing) along its long, jagged shores, you'll discover such wonders as a volcanically created swimming pool and the glaringly white Infernal Cove, both near **Le Forna** (the only other real settlement on Ponza). Hire a boat at Ponza town or Santa Maria to visit the **Grotte di Pilato**, three grottoes connnected by tunnels dug in Republican times as part of a luxury villa, and used to store live fish for its kitchens.

The other inhabited island, tiny **Ventotene**, is a table of reddish tufa sitting on the surface of the sea; Augustus' daughter Julia found it the perfect place to build a grand villa to receive her many lovers far from the wagging tongues of Rome – although her scandalous behaviour eventually caught up with her and Ventotene became her rock of exile instead of a bower of bliss – a few bits still remain beyond the rocky beach of Cala Rossano. Later Julians found it a usefully isolated place to do their dirty work, too; Caligula's mother starved herself to death here, and Nero had his young, unwanted wife Octavia murdered in her bath; the meagre ruins of her villa stand evocative and lonely on windswept Punta Eolo. The town of **Porto Ventotene** is piled over the old Porto Romano, carved out of tufa. There is a small museum in the Municipio (*t 0771 80108; open mornings Mon–Sat*), displaying items found in Julia's villa. You can stroll around the island in less than an hour, past little fields of lentils. Here and there you will find little paths winding towards the sea, the cliffs and beaches.

The Ciociaria: Anagni and Ferentino

If you're in a hurry to get to Naples from Rome the quickest route is the *Autostrada del Sole*, following the route of the Roman Via Casilina behind the coastal mountains. After Velletri, in the Castelli Romani, however, there are still detours to delay you. This humble corner of Lazio is known as the **Ciociaria**, after the *ciocie*, or bark sandals, worn by the countrymen not so long ago when this was one of the backwaters of Italy.

Anagni, small as it is, held centre stage in European politics several times in the Middle Ages. Four 14th-century popes were born here, and others made it their summer home. Greatest among them was Boniface VIII, a nasty intriguer from the Caetani family who loudly proclaimed the temporal supremacy of the popes long after anyone took the idea seriously. Captured in Anagni by his Roman enemy Sciarra Colonna, who was working for the King of France, Boniface received a resounding slap in the face that put a temporary end to papal dreams of world domination.

Parts of the **Palazzo di Bonifacio VIII** can still be seen (*t 0775 727 053; open daily 9–12.30 and 3–6; adm*), along with the stout and squarish **cathedral**, one of the finest in central Italy, sharing a little of the genius of the Tuscan and Puglian churches of the same period. Outside, it is 11th-century Romanesque; a rebuilding in the 1300s left it tentatively Gothic within. There is a Cosmatesque pavement and a wonderful 13th-century stone baldaquin over the altar, but the real attraction is the 'Medieval Sistine Chapel', the **Crypt of San Magno** (*open daily 9–1, Sun 9–11.30, also Mon–Sat in winter 3–6, in summer 4–7; adm*), entirely covered in blue and gold Byzantine-style frescoes from the 12th and 13th centuries that are among the best of their kind in Italy. The subject matter ranges from the life of San Magno (who, unfortunately, seems to have never really existed) to the story of the Ark of the Covenant, along with the entire Apocalypse, and a fascinating medieval cosmography, with the zodiac, celestial spheres and four elements. Underneath is one of the most richly detailed Cosmati pavements anywhere, signed by Master Cosma himself.

Up in the mountains above Anagni, **Fiuggi** has been a popular spa for centuries; Michelangelo came here to take the waters after the strain of working on the Sistine Chapel, and the 1900s left the town an ensemble of ornate hotels, tree-lined boulevards and a casino. East of Anagni, the attractive hill town of **Ferentino** sits inside a complete circuit of pre-Roman cyclopean walls. Its landmark church is the refined French Gothic **Santa Maria Maggiore**, built by the Cistercians. Up on the old acropolis is a handsome **cathedral** with a complete set of Cosmatesque furnishings paid for by Innocent III, the most powerful of medieval popes, who spent much time in Ferentino. Further up is a row of huge masonry arches that were once a Roman **covered market**.

Alatri and Arpino

Alatri, 2,400 years ago, was one of the main cities of the Hernici, an Italic tribe that differed from its neighbours by being a firm ally of Rome, a wise policy that spared Alatri the destruction that befell many of the other ancient cities of Lazio.

Consequently Alatri remains the best example we have of a pre-Roman Italian town, with almost a complete circuit of cyclopean walls from about the 6th century BC. Besides these, there is another set of walls at the top of Alatri's hill marking the boundaries of the acropolis, where today the **cathedral** and the Bishop's Palace stand over the temples of the long-forgotten Hernici. In the lower town, Santa Maria Maggiore contains some fine medieval polychromed woodcarving, and a Byzantine icon called the Madonna of Constantinople. Just outside the town there is an early Carthusian monastery, the **Certosa di Trisulti** (*t 0775 47024; open Mon–Sat 9.30–12 and 3–5.30, Sun 3–5.30 only; longer afternoon hours in summer*), with buildings as old as 1210 and a perfectly preserved 18th-century pharmacy – this part of Lazio has been famed for medicinal herbs since ancient times, and you can learn more about them here, as well as in the **botanical garden** run by the WWF outside town.

Along the old Via Casilina, little **Frosinone** serves as provincial capital for the Ciociaria, and the centre for all bus lines in the region. A side road from here (SS214) will take you on a delightful detour to the **Abbey of Casamari** (*open daily 9–12 and 3–6*), a little-known 13th-century French Cistercian complex with a church much like the one at Fossanova, and then to **Isola del Liri**, a town with a dramatic waterfall in the middle, which hosts a blues festival each July. Further down the Via Casilina, **Aquino** is the elegant home town of Cicero and of the stupefyingly mediocre painter called the Cavaliere d'Arpino, who painted the dome of St Peter's in Rome. The town has Roman-era ruins, including a small decorative arch, and two museums: one dedicated to lutes and mandolins, for which Arpino was once famous, and the other to the works of the sculptor Umberto Mastroianni – uncle of the actor Marcello, who was born in a village nearby.

For something out of the way, venture up into the highest corner of Lazio, the Valley of the Comino on the borders of the Abruzzo National Park. In this mountainous region there are beautiful **lakes** at Posta Fibreno and Biagio Saracinesco, and ruins of a 12th-century castle at **Vicalvi**. **Atina** is the most important town, and has been since the days of the Samnites; relics from its past are preserved in the Municipal Museum.

Montecassino

If divine guidance led St Benedict from Subiaco to found a monastery here, as the legend states, perhaps God just wasn't thinking clearly that day. Montecassino may be the most famous monastery in Italy, and it certainly owns the most dramatic site, high on a mountaintop over the Garigliano Valley, but the location has caused the honest monks nothing but trouble over the centuries. They were essential in keeping alive the traditions of letters and scholarship in the Dark Ages – all the more remarkable when you consider that Montecassino has been utterly destroyed five times.

Benedict came in 529, but the Lombards wrecked the place only 60 years later. The Saracens and the Normans repeated the scene in the 9th and 11th centuries, and an earthquake finished off what must have been one of Italy's treasures of medieval architecture in 1348. Each time the place has been rebuilt, but the reason why Montecassino attracts so much strife was demonstrated again during the Italian Campaign of 1944. The rock happens to be the most strategically important spot in central Italy, the key to either Rome or Naples, depending on which way your army is walking. In 1944 the Germans made it the western bastion of their Gustav Line and it held up the Allied advance for four months. Enough bombs were dropped to destroy the monastery and flatten the forests around it, without seriously disconcerting the defenders. The polyglot Allied forces of New Zealanders, Indians, Moroccans, Canadians and Free French made unsuccessful attacks between January and May. It was the Poles who finally beat their way in, losing over 1,000 men on the way up; their cemetery can be seen near the hill. Rebuilding began almost immediately after the war. The Renaissance basilica and cloisters have been faithfully reconstructed, along with the 'Loggia del Paradiso' and its famous views, though the only surviving art is a set of remarkable mosaics in the crypt, made by German monks in 1913; a small museum holds shattered fragments of the rest. (*t 0776 311 529; open daily April–Oct 8.30–12 and 3.30–6, Nov–Mar 8.30–12 and 3.30–5*). On the way back down the mountain to Cassino town (which was also levelled in the fighting and completely rebuilt) you'll pass the site of Roman Cassino, with an archaeological museum and ruins that include a barbaric-looking amphitheatre in *opus reticulatum* (*open daily until one hour before sunset; adm*).

Campania

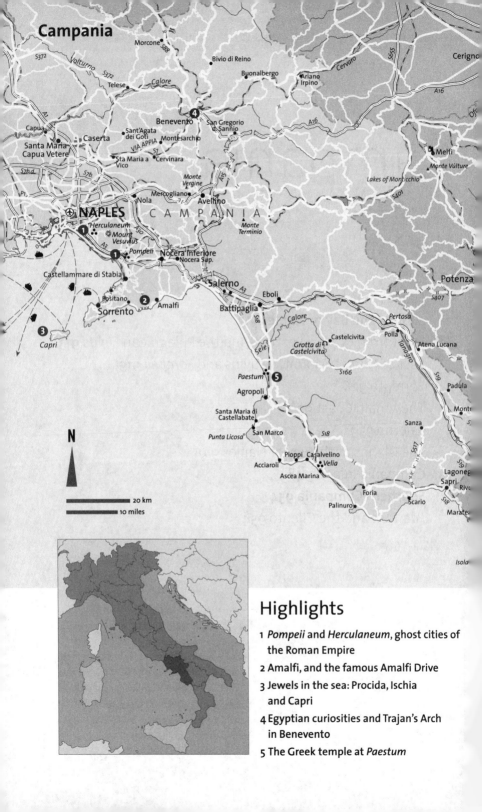

Campania

Highlights

1 *Pompeii* and *Herculaneum*, ghost cities of the Roman Empire

2 Amalfi, and the famous Amalfi Drive

3 Jewels in the sea: Procida, Ischia and Capri

4 Egyptian curiosities and Trajan's Arch in Benevento

5 The Greek temple at *Paestum*

The *Feste* of Campania

In Campania any excuse will do for throwing a party and the region plays host to some of Italy's most spectacular and colourful traditional festivals or *feste*. Most of the festivities are linked to religious events and feast days, and the Madonna features prominently, often decked out garishly with bright fairy-lights and gaudy flowers and hauled through the streets atop tiny Fiats hastily covered with red velvet (with peepholes for the driver), or on platforms stoically borne by the village's fittest and strongest young men. But many of the celebrations also have a strong pagan flavour, especially those linked to the land and the harvest, and some of the feast-day paraphernalia is unmistakably phallic (spot the towers and obelisks).

Whatever the occasion, a village *festa* is a chance to see local traditions and ancient rites in full swing. This being Campania, where eating is in itself a second religion, a visit to a *festa* will invariably involve consuming vast quantities of food, often superbly cooked in makeshift kitchens organized by the local women, and served for knock-down prices. The following are some of the best *feste* to look out for, but keep a watch for others by checking billboards in the piazzas of towns and villages.

La Sagra dei Gigli (the lily festival), at Nola, 27 June. The whole town commemorates the return of 5th-century bishop St Paulinus after his long imprisonment in Africa. The original Nolesi welcomed him home with bunches of lilies. Today, the townspeople recall this by hauling 80ft-tall wooden 'lilies' through the streets.

Festa di Sant'Anna, around Ischia, 26 July. A dazzling torchlight procession of hundreds of boats, transformed into floats, to honour the island's patron saint.

Festa dell'Obelisco di Paglia (feast of the straw obelisk), at Fontanarosa, near Avellino, 14 August. A harvest thanksgiving ritual, with a giant 100ft-high spire of plaited straw, around which villagers dance and sing.

La Sagra del Grano (the wheat festival), at Foglianise, near Benevento, 14 August. A striking display of allegorical floats depicting famous churches and monuments, all of them made out of straw and corn-stalks.

Festa dell'Assunta (feast of the Assumption), at Positano, 15 August. An ancient celebration in honour of the Virgin, which also recreates the landing – and the defeat – of the hated Saracens. Local townspeople dress up in costumes and stage a parade of decorated boats, before the grand finale: a dramatic firework display over the sea. In neighbouring Montepertuso there is another attractive *festa* two weeks later, the **Sagra del Fagiolo** or feast of the bean.

Festa di San Gennaro, in Naples, 19 September. This major event commemorates Naples' patron saint, with a service held in the cathedral to witness the miracle of the liquefaction of his blood (*see* p.907). Afterwards, relieved citizens (the miracle always works) take to the streets to watch the silver statue of the saint being paraded through the streets. Needless to say, no one goes to work that day.

Festa dell'Immacolata (feast of the Immaculate Conception), at Torre del Greco, December. More than 100 local men carry a huge triumphal float, topped by the Madonna, through the streets, to commemorate the town's lucky escape from the 1861 eruption of Vesuvius.

The Italian south – the Mezzogiorno, the Noonday – is one of the extremities of Europe, poised in a calm sea between the Balkans and the Sahara. The contrasts within the south are greater than in the other two-thirds of Italy; from the dreamy coastline of Amalfi and Positano it is only an afternoon's drive to the grimmest deforested wastelands of the Basilicata. Some sections of the south are prosperous and forward-looking, and not too distant from their northern counterparts, while others lag astonishingly behind, despite all the efforts of the government and the Cassa per il Mezzogiorno. Some areas are surprising, others surprisingly empty.

In Roman times, to distinguish the *Campania* around Naples from parts further north (the present Roman *Campagna*), the southern section acquired the name of *Campania Felix* – and a happy land it was, the richest and most civilized province in Italy, with a mix of Greek and Etruscan culture superimposed on the native Samnites and Ausones, not to mention the merry Oscans and their perfumed city of Capua. Campania's charm, then as now, starts with one of the most captivating stretches of coastline in Italy – the Amalfi Coast – followed by Capri and Ischia, Sorrento, Vesuvius, the Phlegraean Fields around Pozzuoli, and the beautiful but lesser-known Cilento Coast at the southern tip of the region. Roman emperors and senators spent as much time here as business would allow, and even today it is said that the dream of every Italian is to have a villa at Capri or Sorrento overlooking the sea.

In the middle of all this, of course, sprawls Italy's third-largest city, Naples – a place that may well be either your favourite or least favourite Italian city – or both at the same time. Campania shares fully in all the complexes and problems of the Italian south as a whole. It has large new industries, ambitious planning schemes to attract more, and substantial difficulties with pollution, poverty, soaring unemployment, corruption and crime. Though the potential certainly exists, there is a long way to go before the region can reclaim the position it had in the days of the Caesars.

Naples

*The most loathsome nest of human caterpillars I was ever
forced to stay in – a hell with all the devils imbecile in it.*

John Ruskin

For many, Naples is the homeland of a particular Italian fantasy, the last bastion of singing waiters and red-checked tablecloths, operatic passion and colourful poverty, balanced precariously between Love's own coastline and the menace of Vesuvius. But mention Naples or the Neapolitans to any modern, respectable north Italian, and as they gesticulate and roll their eyes you will get lesson in the dynamics of Italy's 'Problem of the South'. Many Italians cannot accept that such an outlandish place can be in the same country as them, a sentiment that probably contains as much envy as contempt. Naples, the city that has given the world Enrico Caruso, Sophia Loren, pizza and syphilis (the disease appeared here in 1495, and was immediately blamed on the French garrison), may also be the first city to make social disorder into an art form.

Degradation, Italian-style

On Naples' Piazza Garibaldi you can buy a boiled pig's organ on a stick, served with a slice of lemon, and watch eight-year-old *scugnizzi* – street children – puff on contraband Marlboros while casually tossing firecrackers into traffic. Fireworks, along with slamming doors, impromptu arias, screams, ambulance sirens and howling cats, are an essential part of the Neapolitan ambience. This anarchic symphony is harder to catch these days, unfortunately, drowned as it is under the roar of Italy's worst traffic. In central Naples, three-quarters of a million rude drivers chase each other around a street plan that hasn't changed much since Roman times. Meanwhile, the nation's worst air pollution keeps the hospitals full – in spite of occasional half-hearted attempts to solve the problem by only allowing drivers to use their cars on alternate days – and every few weeks an old lady on a back street burns to a crisp while the firemen, just down the block, gamely push illegally parked cars out of their way.

Another chronic problem is housing, enough of a nightmare even before the earthquake of 1980; on the outskirts of the city, you may see Napoletani living in stolen ship cargo containers, with windows cut in the sides, in shacks made of sheet metal and old doors, or in abandoned buses. In the city centre, thousands of earthquake refugees are still camping in hotels. One bizarre side-effect of this housing shortage – found all over Italy, but particularly visible here – is the 'quivering car' phenomenon. You'll see them everywhere, especially up on Posillipo hill, cars parked nose to tail, their windows blacked out with newspaper, turned into temporary bedrooms by courting couples, or even married couples who have no privacy at home. A cruel prank of Neapolitan kids is to sneak up on the cars and set fire to the newspaper.

Reform has been the buzz word in recent years but the city still has to deal with the spectre of the Camorra, a loose term for the crime syndicates that keep Naples as securely strung up as any mountain village in Sicily. Crime is so well organized here, to give one example, that seagoing smugglers have formed a trade union to protect their interests against the police.

In the 18th century, when the city and its spectacular setting were a highlight of the Grand Tour, the saying was 'See Naples and die...'. Nowadays you usually can't see much of anything through the smog, but you'll probably survive if you're careful crossing streets. Don't let Naples' current degradation spoil your visit, though; you haven't seen Italy – no, you haven't seen the Mediterranean – until you have spent some time in this fascinating metropolis. The only thing subtle about Naples is its charm, and the city may win your heart at the same time as it deranges your senses.

On the Other Hand...

If Naples immediately repels you, however, it means you are probably a sticky sort, and will miss all the fun. The city has an incomparable setting, and much of it is still admittedly beautiful, but its real attraction is a priceless insight into humanity, at the hands of a population of 2.2 million dangerous anarchists. The Napoletani may be numbered among the few peoples of Europe who truly realize they are alive, and try to enjoy it as best they can. Their history being what it is, this manifests itself in diverse ways.

Naples

VIA PIETRO CASTELLINO

VIA SIMONE MARTINI

V. M. D. VITO PISCICELLI

V. G. B. RUOPPOLO

VIA. GIACINTO GIGANTE

VIA MATTEO RENATO IMBRIANI

VIA SALVATORE ROS

PZA MEDAGLIE D'ORO

SANTA CROCE

VIA G.

VIALE MICHELANGELO

VIA ACITILLO

VIA LUCA GIORDANO

PZA VANVITELLI

SCARLATTI

VIA A.

VIA FRANCESCO CILEA

VIA ANIELLO FALCONE

VIA DOMENICO CIMAROSA

Montesanto Funicular

VIA TITO ANGELINI

CORSO

VITTORIO

EMANUELE

Castel Sant'Elmo

Certosa di San Martino

Funicolare Centrale

QUAR
SPAG

Villa Floridiana

Funicolare di Chiaia

VIA ANIELLO FALCONE

VIA

VIA TORQUATO

TASSO

CORSO

VITTORIO

EMANUELE

VIA DI PARCO MARGERITA

PZA AMEDEO

VIA DEI MILLE

VIA MICHELANGELO SCHIPA

VIA FRANCESCO CRISPI

Museo principe de Aragona Pignatelli

PZA DEI MARTIRI

RIVIERA DI CHIAIA

Villa Comunale

PZA VITTORIA

VIA PIEDIGROTTA

PZA DELLA REPUBLICA

VIA FRANCESCO CARACCIOLO

VIA GIORDANO BRUNO

VALLE ANTONIO GRAMSCI

VIA FRANCESCO CARACCIOLO

Tomba de Virgilio

PZA SANNAZZARO

Funicolare di Pesillipo

MERGELLINA

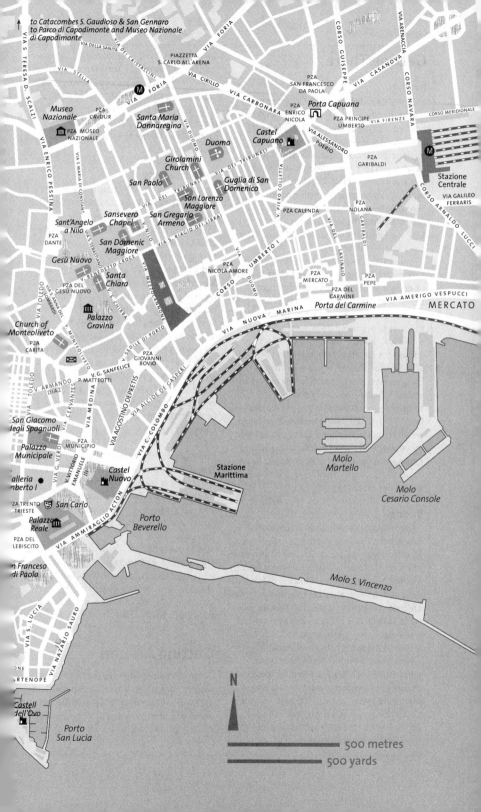

Getting There

By Air

Naples' **Capodichino airport** is on the north side of the city, relatively close to the centre. It has frequent direct services to and from all major Italian destinations and to many foreign cities, including London (several flights daily). For airport information, call **t** 081 789 6111. From 6am to midnight there is a **bus service** every 50 minutes (a **blue bus** run by Sepsa), between the airport and Piazza Municipio near the ferry harbour. For the Stazione Centrale there is the half-hourly **city bus** (no.14) which does not run as late. The journey takes 20–45 mins, depending on the time of day. As on all city buses, tickets should be bought at a news-stand or ticket booth before boarding. Lastly, Curreri (**t** 081 801 5420) runs four **daily buses** (at 9am, 2, 4.30 and 7pm) to Sorrento departing from the stop outside the Arrivals hall (on the right).

If you opt for a **taxi**, remember that on top of the fare on the meter you will officially be charged extra supplements for the airport trip and for luggage – plus, very possibly, additional unexplained 'extras' as well (*see* below). If in doubt, ask to see the list of prices, which should be displayed in the cab, or try to agree on the fare to your destination before getting into the cab. If traffic is not too heavy – and this is a big if – the fare to the centre should not exceed L35,000.

By Sea

Naples' port has more **ship** and **hydrofoil** connections than anywhere else in the Mediterranean, so you can choose to arrive by sea from – or flee to – a wide variety of places, among them the islands in the Bay of Naples, Sicily and the Aeolian Islands. Generally, ferries are cheaper than hydrofoils, but take roughly twice as long. One of the best sea excursions is the **night ferry** to the Aeolian Islands, which arrives as the sun is rising over Vulcano.

Ferries and hydrofoils leave from three different points in Naples, but most longer-distance ferries operate from the **Stazione Marittima**, in the centre of the port near the Castel Nuovo. Consult the individual companies for timetables, otherwise look in the daily newspaper *Il Mattino* or in *Qui Napoli*. The main companies operating from Stazione Marittima are **Tirrenia**, **t** 081 720 1111, for Palermo and Cagliari; and **Siremar**, **t** 081 580 0340, for the Aeolian Islands and **Milazzo** in Sicily. In addition, one company, **SNAV**, **t** 081 761 23 48, operates a daily long-distance hydrofoil service from **Mergellina quay** to the Aeolian Islands.

By Rail and Bus

Most visitors arrive by **train** at the modern **Stazione Centrale** on Piazza Garibaldi, which is also a junction for city buses and the local Circumvesuviana railway. Trains along the coast towards Rome or Reggio di Calabria pass through every half-hour on average.

In addition, many trains also stop at **Napoli Mergellina** and **Napoli Campi Flegrei**, on the western side of the city, and at some other local stations. There are also good rail connections from Naples to Palermo (4–8 hours, depending on the train) via Messina.

As well as the state FS lines, there are three local railway lines serving the Bay of Naples area. One, the **Ferrovia Circumvesuviana**, **t** 081 772 2444, runs trains to Herculaneum, Pompeii and Sorrento from the Stazione Centrale and from the **Stazione Circumvesuviana** in Corso Garibaldi.

Another separate line, the **Ferrovia Cumana**, **t** 081 551 3328, runs regular trains to the Campi Flegrei area, including Pozzuoli and Baia, from the station at Piazza Montesanto.

A third line, the **Ferrovia Circumflegrea**, also **t** 081 551 3328, runs from the same station at Piazza Montesanto to points west, including Licola and Cuma.

Most **bus** services to destinations within the province and the Campania region operate from Piazza Garibaldi, in front of the FS Stazione Centrale. An exception is the bus service to Salerno along the coast, which runs from Via Pisanelli, near Piazza Municipio.

Getting Around

Transport around the city is a fascinating subject. Such is the state of most **public transport** and so impenetrable is the **traffic** that **walking** is often by far the most practical way of getting anywhere, apart from up to the heights by the *funiculari*. **Orientation** is a little difficult. If you arrive by sea – the only proper way to do it – you'll get a good idea of the layout. Naples' dominant landmarks, visible from almost anywhere in town, are Castel Sant'Elmo and the huge, fortress-like monastery of San Martino. They are neighbours on the steep hill that slopes down to the sea near the port, neatly dividing the city into its old and new quarters.

Modern Naples is on the western side, the pleasant districts of Mergellina, Vomero and Fuorigrotta, to which middle-class Napoletani escape from the city centre at the end of each day, on their creaking old funicular railways. To the east, towards Vesuvius, lies the centre, along Via Toledo, and beyond it the oldest neighbourhoods, tall tenements jammed into a grid of narrow streets, reaching a climax in the oriental bazaar atmosphere around the Piazza Mercato and Piazza Garibaldi.

By Bus

Given the problems involved in using cars and even taxis in Naples, visitors often find themselves left with the buses, which is small cheer, since the city has the worst bus system in Italy. Buses will be slow and indecently crowded and there are no schedules, no maps, and no sources of accurate information. The confusion is compounded by the recent division of services run by the old bus company Atam under its successor ANM and other smaller companies. Most bus lines start at either Piazza Garibaldi or Piazza del Plebiscito. Some that might be useful are: no. 2, from Piazza Garibaldi to Corso Umberto and Piazza Municipio; no. 3, from Piazza Municipio to Riviera di Chiaia and Mergellina; no. 110 or no.127, from Piazza Garibaldi to Piazza Cavour and Capodimonte, no. 152, from Piazza Garibaldi to Pozzuoli.

The relatively new **Artebus** service runs through the most interesting areas of town and can be used for short hops between sights. It departs from Mergellina and must be arranged through your hotel (*Fri–Sun; free*).

One benefit of reforms aimed at cleaning up the city's image and attracting tourists is the introduction of the new-style '**Giranapoli**' ('Around Naples') bus tickets. There are two types, one lasting 90 minutes for L1,500, and a day ticket for L4,500. If you plan on staying in Naples for more than 9 days, invest in a monthly pass (L45,000). All tickets enable you to travel on all buses, the funiculars and the Metropolitana throughout the city.

By Metro and *Funicolare*

Naples also has a sort of underground. The **Metropolitana FS**, a single line from Gianturco to Pozzuoli, is really a part of the state railway, and uses the same underground tracks as the long-distance trains. The FS runs it as anarchically as the buses, but it will be helpful for reaching the station (Piazza Garibaldi), the archaeological museum, points in Vomero and Fuorigrotta, and Solafatara. As on the buses, few people ever buy tickets.

A much more agreeable way to travel, though you can't go very far, is on the three *funicolari*, or inclined railways, up to Vomero. The longest – one of the longest in the world, in fact – is the **Funicolare Centrale**, which leaves from Via Toledo, just behind the Galleria, and heads up to Via Cimarosa. The **Funicolare di Chiaia** also ends nearby in the same street, having started from Piazza Amedeo in Chiaia. Finally, the **Funicolare di Montesanto** travels up to Via Morghen from Montesanto Station, the start of the suburban Circumflegrea and Cumana rail lines. All three *funicolari* bring you out near the San Martino Museum and the Castel Sant'Elmo. All run daily until about 10pm.

By Taxi

Neapolitan taxi drivers are uniformly dishonest. Also, the traffic is frequently so thick that relatively short journeys can take so long (and cost so much) that they're really not worth it. If you want to take a taxi to a specific destination, always try to agree on the fare in advance, whether there is a meter or not. There are plenty of taxi ranks or you can call **t** 081 556 4444.

By Car

The first thing to get straight is simply – *leave your car elsewhere*. Cars disappear in Naples with alarming frequency, and foreign number plates are especially prized. When it comes to driving, there are no rules, except to get there first, and fatalities are common.

Tourist Information

Azienda Autonoma di Soggiorno on Piazza del Gesù Nuovo, t 081 552 3328 or t 081 551 2701, in the old town (*open Mon–Sat 9–8, Sun and hols 9–3*), a well-run, friendly information booth. The main office is in the Royal Palace, t 081 252 5711, f 081 418 619.

EPT, Piazza dei Martiri 58, t 081 405 311. The provincial tourist office, which provides information about excursions outside the city. The EPT has another office at the Stazione Centrale, t 081 268 779, which may be some help in finding a hotel. Two others are to be found at the airport, t 081 780 5761, and the Stazione Mergellina, t 081 761 2102.

Qui Napoli, an excellent free monthly handbook available at tourist offices and some hotels, carries useful information, timetables, listings and calendars of events. The EPT produce good maps of the city centre and the bay itself (both free).

AAST at Piazza del Gesù Nuovo provides information on accompanied walks, set up by Naples in an attempt to draw visitors into the old city. Points of interest along them stay open longer hours.

Laes (Libera Associazione Escursionisti Sottosuolo, t 081 400 256). Operates guided tours on a fascinating trip around subterranean Naples, starting from Piazza Trieste e Trento (next to Piazza del Plebiscito) (*weekends at 10am*).

Internet access at reasonable prices can be found at Clicnet, Via Toledo 393, t 081 552 9370 (*open daily 9.30–9.30*).

Shopping

Surprisingly, no one ever thinks of Naples as a shopping destination; this is a mistake, as there are as many pretty things to be bought here as anywhere else, and usually at lower prices. The back streets around Spaccanapoli and other old sections are still full of **artisan workshops** of all kinds. The Royal Factory at Capodimonte, founded by the Bourbons, still makes what may be the most beautiful **porcelain and ceramic figures** in Europe, sold at the fancier shops in the city centre. Another old Neapolitan tradition is making **cameos** from seashells; you'll see them everywhere –

the shops outside the Certosa di San Martino have a good selection at relatively low prices.

Via San Biagio dei Librai, in the middle of the Spaccanapoli, is, as its name implies, a street of **booksellers** – some of the best old-book-dealers in Italy – but the street is also full of odder surprises for shoppers as well. Many of the religious goods shops have good works in **terracotta**; the Doll Hospital at No.81, t 081 203 067, is one of Naples' most charming shops.

In the back streets near the Archaeological Museum, there are **antique and junk shops** that won't overcharge you unless you let them. The swankiest antique shops tend to be along Via Merelli off Piazza dei Martiri. The city also has an immense twice-monthly **antiques market**, the Fiera dell'Antiquariato, held on alternate Saturday and Sunday mornings in the gardens of the Villa Comunale.

You can buy old **prints** of Naples and beyond at Bowinkel, Piazza dei Martiri 24, t 081 764 4344, and once-in-a-lifetime **souvenirs** at the 150-year-old Fonderia Chiurazzi, Via Ponti Rossi 271, t 081 751 2685, which makes artistic bronzes, specializing in reproductions of works in the Museo Archeologico. If you pay billions of lire, they'll do them life-size, or even bigger.

For **clothes and shoes** the best area is again off Piazza dei Martiri, in particular along the flashy Via Chiaia. You can find its other end to the right of the central Piazza del Plebiscito.

Last of all do not miss the *bancarelle* and open **street markets** around Piazza Garibaldi. The daily catch of **fish**, live squid and octopus is a must, just to the right off Corso Garibaldi. Here you can also find **fruit** stalls that sell huge lemons from the Sorrentine peninsula.

Where to Stay

Naples ✉ 80100

Naples can present real problems for the casual traveller who arrives expecting to pick up a reasonably priced room without difficulty, a situation that only gets worse as Naples becomes more popular. There are options at either extreme of the price range but few choices in between. The best area to stay is down on the waterfront where you have easy access to shopping, museums and restaurants. It's less claustrophobic too. The area around the station offers thousands of cheap rooms, but many of them are real dives. Sticking to those selected here you shouldn't go too wrong and at least you'll be safe.

Very Expensive

Naples has fewer than its share of top-quality hotels; the Germans blew up a few before their retreat in 1944. Two of the best are in a row along Via Partenope, overlooking the Castel dell'Ovo, where the views over the bay compensate for the traffic noise below. ****Excelsior**, Via Partenope 48, t 081 764 0111, f 081 764 9743, *info@excelsior.it*. Visiting sheikhs, kings and rock stars favour this, Naples' finest hotel, with its beautiful suites and a tradition of perfect service since 1909. You pay for space – elegant lounges, a rooftop restaurant, rooms with large beds and antique furniture. It's a place for those who think the hotel is the most important part of a holiday. It faces Vesuvius. ****Vesuvio**, Via Partenope 45, t 081 764 0044, f 081 764 4483, *info@vesuvio.it*. In spite of its name, this grandiose hotel lacks the head-on view of Vesuvius, but otherwise provides the same stuff as the Excelsior. It has a lovely roof garden for dining, important since none of the rooms has a balcony.

Expensive

****Miramare**, Via Sauro 24, t 081 764 7589, f 081 764 0775, *info@hotelmiramare.com*. A gem; the manager Enzo Rosalino exudes the kind of old-world charm more often found outside cities. There are personal touches in each of the 30 rooms and the atmosphere is cosy and intimate. Some rooms are too small but the old lift and the lavish breakfast laid out on the rooftop (hung with hammocks) more than make up. Rooms not facing the sea are quieter. ****Paradiso**, Via Catullo 11, t 081 761 4161, f 081 761 3449. A very good bet, with stunning views over the bay – make sure you book a sea-facing room. ****Parker's**, Corso Vittorio Emanuele 135, t 081 761 2474, f 081 663 527, *ghparker@tin.it*. Further inland (near the Corso V. E. stop on the Cumana line) this delightful hotel is Naples' oldest. The airy rooms have ample charm, with plenty of polished wood,

chandeliers and comfortable furniture. Choose a sea-facing room with a balcony for the palm-fronted vista of Vesuvius and distant Capri. The view is even more spectacular from the award-winning restaurant on the terraced roof.

Moderate

****Cavour**, Piazza Garibaldi 32, t 081 283 122, f 081 287 488. Near the Stazione Centrale, this is a well-run, decent hotel in a desperate area. Book the top-floor suites, which enjoy terraces, views over Vesuvius and a respite from the bustle below. Rooms are nicely decorated in Liberty style. Bathrooms are good in an area where plumbing hasn't been overhauled since the Greeks. The restaurant gets two Michelin *fourchettes*. ***Ausonia**, Via Caracciolo 11, t/f 081 682 278. This is a clean, comfortable *pensione* with 20 rooms and nautical-style decoration. The owner is kind and cheerful. Located within a *palazzo*, looking on to an interior courtyard, this is a quiet option in the Mergellina area.

Cheap

***Fontane al Mare**, Via N. Tommaseo 14, t 081 764 3470. Naples has a dearth of reasonable cheap hotels, so it is definitely worth booking in advance for a room at this hotel. There are only 21 rooms located on the last two floors of an old *palazzo* next to the Chiaia gardens. To take the lift, you will need to bring L200 coins. Ask for rooms without a bathroom since they enjoy the sea view and are better value. It's well known and popular with the local *carabinieri* college. ***Zara**, Via Firenze 81, t 081 287 125. With only 10 rooms, two with baths, this is, sadly, one of the best Naples can do in this category. **Fiore**, Via Milano 109, t 081 553 8798. This Polish-Italian *pensione* – once rumoured to have Naples' fattest cat, now replaced by Lily the dog – is barely acceptable, but good for the area (bring L50 coins for the lift).

Eating Out

Neapolitans spend as much time worrying about what's for dinner as any people in the world, but like most other Italians they have a perfectly healthy attitude towards the subject. Neapolitan cuisine is simple – one of the most celebrated dishes is *spaghetti alle vongole* – and even in more pretentious places you will find favourites of the Neapolitan *cucina povera*, like *pasta e fagioli*. There are very few bad restaurants in the city, but an infinity of tiny, family-run *trattorie* or *pizzerie*; you will depart from most of them satisfied.

For famous Neapolitan pizza, look for the genuine Neapolitan pizza oven, a built-in, bell-shaped affair made of stone with a broad, clean tile floor; the fire (for which only certain kinds of wood will do) is at the back, nice and close to the pizza, not hidden underneath.

Watch out for house wines; in cheaper places this is likely to be Gragnano from nearby Monte Faito – rough stuff. On the other hand you can find some real surprises from Campania; a dry white called Greco di Tufo, and Taurasi, a distinguished red – as well as Falerno, descendant of the ancient Falernian that Latin poets never tired of praising. Some restaurants in Naples are the cheapest in all Italy; others can be alarmingly expensive, especially if you order fish.

Expensive

La Cantinella, Via Nazario Sauro 23, t 081 464 8684. Near the Castel dell'Ovo on the esplanade, this is believed by many to be Naples' finest – also the place to be seen for the Parthenopeans, still with a telephone on each table despite the invention of mobiles. Their *linguine Santa Lucia*, made with home-made pasta, octopus, squid, prawns, clams and fresh baby tomatoes, takes some beating. The *risotto* is also excellent. It's not cheap, but you can easily spend more nearby. The atmosphere is smart but relaxed and the service welcoming and friendly.

La Bersagliera, Borgo Marinara 10, t 081 764 6016. In an excellent location beneath the Castel dell'Ovo, this large 1900s restaurant cuts an elegant image. The fish is delicious and the wine is good too, especially the white Fiano de Avellino. *Closed Tues.*

La Sacrestia, Via Orazio 116, t 081 761 1051. Run for generations by the Ponsiglione family, this restaurant is a temple of Neapolitan gastronomy; it's superby sited too, over-looking the bay from the Mergellina heights.

Try the *risotto* with newborn squid (*risotto con neonati di seppietta*). *Closed Mon.*

Giuseppone a Mare, Via Ferdinando Russo 13, t 081 575 6002. Overlooking Cape Posillipo since 1889, this is one of Naples' most celebrated institutions, especially popular for weddings and celebrations. The fish is excellent, the setting memorable, and you won't forget the bill either. *Closed Mon.*

Don Salvatore, Via Mergellina 5, t 081 681 817. This restaurant has been around for more than 40 years on the Mergellina esplanade, during which time it has built up a well-deserved reputation for turning out fine Neapolitan dishes, accompanied by some of the area's best wines. There are set menus for those who want an introduction to Naples' best, and pizza for those who want to keep the bill down. *Closed Wed.*

Mimì alla Ferrovia, Via Alfonso d'Aragona 19, t 081 553 8525. This comes as a nice surprise in the area at the end of Piazza Garibaldi, and is popular with the local media posse. Again, you'll find no new-fangled concoctions, just honest dishes based on fresh ingredients and recipes handed down for generations. The speciality is *pasta e ceci*, a khaki-green soup of flat pasta and chickpeas best savoured with eyes closed. Ignore the brusque service and concentrate on the seafood and divine *mozzarella*. *Closed Sun.*

Moderate

La Cantina di Triunfo, Riviera di Chiaia 64, t 081 668 101. This small restaurant on the north side of Piazza della Repubblica offers Neapolitan *cucina povera* raised to an art form: wintry soups of chestnuts and lentils, or lighter versions of broad beans and fresh peas in spring, *polpette di baccalà* – balls of minced salt-cod, fried or served in a fresh tomato sauce – and mouth-watering pasta dishes that change with the season. Desserts are as good as the rest. The *crostata d'arance e mandorle* (orange and almond tart) is excellent. The wine list is exceptional too, and many of the 80 grappas are home-made. Book, as space is limited. *Closed Sun.*

Taverna e Zi Carmela, Via Niccolò Tommaseo 11/12, t 081 764 3581. Track down this restaurant on the esplanade of Via Partenope beyond the Castel dell'Ovo but before the Villa Communale. Aunt Carmela runs a busy, well-kept ship, with her own cooking; other members of the family wait at table. Seafood is a speciality *Closed Sun.*

O Sole Mio, Via Tommaso Campanella 7, **t** 081 761 2323. Run by a fisherman's family near the Mergellina; go straight for the seafood, in all its many forms, though you will also find meat on the menu. Try the tasty *cassuola di pesce* (fish casserole) but tuck your napkin into your collar, Neapolitan-style, before you start. *Closed Tues.*

Cheap

Da Pasqualino, Piazza Sannazzaro 78/9, **t** 081 681 524. At this long-established *pizzeria* near the Mergellina quay you can get two pizzas and lots of easy-drinking local wine. If the tables in the piazza are full, head upstairs past frantic cooks furiously shovelling pizzas and deep-frying *crochette* – potato croquettes with *mozzarella* cheese.

Da Michele, Via Sersale 1, **t** 081 553 9204. This is the place to go for a quick snack. Neapolitans cluster outside it and it might be the only place you'll ever see them queueing, with their little tickets, to get their massive pizzas. The pizzas only come in two models: *margherita* and *marinara*.

Pizzeria Port'Alba, Via Port'Alba 18, **t** 081 459 713. Founded in 1830, this little place in the historic centre does excellent pizzas for both lunch and dinner. You can also get full dinners, including the house speciality, *linguine al cartoccio* – seafood pasta made into a foil parcel and baked in the oven – for a reasonable sum (it's vast, so go easy on the *antipasti*). You can choose either to sit outside under the Port'Alba itself or inside, in which case the upstairs area is more snug.

Lombardi a Santa Chiara, Via Benedetto Croce 59, **t** 081 552 0780. Slightly more upmarket, but only slightly, this busy restaurant just off Piazza del Gesù Nuovo offers memorable *antipasti* of fried courgettes, baby *mozzarella* and artichokes, before you ever get to eat your pizza, wonderfully cooked in the classic wood oven. If you can't stomach another pizza the *bucatini al pomodoro* is a simple treat. Noisy but friendly, this place fills up quickly, so book ahead or be prepared to wait. *Closed Sun.*

Brandi, Salita Sant'Anna di Palazzo 1/2, **t** 081 416 928. This pretty, lively *pizzeria* claims to have invented the *margherita*, Naples' most famous pizza, with *mozzarella*, tomatoes and fresh basil, in honour of the 19th-century queen whose favourite dish it apparently was. She would pick up pizza on the way back from balls, to eat cold in the morning. They have two floors and a small terrace. The seafood pizza is topped with octopus cooked with their ink sacs intact.

Da Pietro, Via Luculliana 27. There are a handful of tables here and no menu, but despite this it occupies a million-dollar position down on the Borgo Marina next to the Castel dell'Ovo; you can enjoy tasty seafood dishes (but little else) at reasonable prices while you relax next door to far more prestigious establishments.

Trattoria Nennella, Vico Lungo Teatro Nuovo 103–105. You'll find this amazing bargain in the Quartieri Spagnuoli. It offers a taste of true Neapolitan food and spirit in a simple setting (paper cups and tablecloths and photocopied hand-written menus); while Signora Nennella plots your meal in the kitchen, her son runs the show. Don't be surprised to see men in suits having their lunch break – local businessmen discovered it long ago. You are likely to be the only foreigner. *Open weekdays lunch only.*

Cafés and *Gelaterie*

As well as the inventors of the pizza, Neapolitans are, it is generally recognized, Italy's most dedicated and punctilious coffee consumers, and the city accordingly has its crop of elegant, ornate (now often faded) 19th-century *gran caffè*, mostly not too far from the Galleria and the Piazza del Plebiscito.

The best location is occupied by **Gambrinus**, Piazza Trieste e Trento, **t** 081 417 582, overlooking the Teatro San Carlo and Piazza Plebiscito, but as you would expect it's not cheap. Other fine places to take coffee can be found along the waterfront, particularly out towards Mergellina; look out for **Ciro**, generally considered the best. Naples also, naturally, produces some great ice-cream and pastries. *Gelaterie* can be found all over town, but **Scimmia**, Piazza della Carità 4, just off the Via Toledo not far from Spaccanapoli, has long been regarded as one of the city's best. For an ice-cream with a view **Bilancione**, Via Posillipo, will supply both. For *sfogliatelle*, **Scaturchio**, Piazza San Domenico Maggiore, is acclaimed as the *pasticceria* of Naples.

Entertainment and Nightlife

For concerts, shows, and other cultural events – Naples always has plenty – you'll find the best information on programmes and times in the newspaper *Il Mattino*, or in the free monthly guide *Qui Napoli*.

Opera, Classical Music and Theatre

For opera-lovers one of the ultimate experiences is a night at the **San Carlo** (box office t 081 797 2111), but tickets are extremely hard to come by, and very pricey. Hotels may be able to get them most easily. Otherwise you must go to the box office in person. If you do manage to get a ticket, be sure to dress up.

You may have more luck catching a **concert** at the Auditorium RAI-TV, Via Guglielmo Marconi (Fuorigrotta), t 081 725 1111; at the Conservatorio San Pietro a Maiella, Via San Pietro a Maiella, t 081 564 4411; or at the Associazione Alessandro Scarlatti, Piazza dei Martiri 58, t 081 409 494, which holds concerts for jazz, chamber music and a bit of everything else.

Check with the tourist office or in *Qui Napoli* for programmes, and don't forget that many, often free, concerts are staged in the city's churches. Look out for street billboards with details of coming events. You may be able to get tickets for major events at the **ticket offices** in the Box Office, Galleria Umberto I 15–16, t 081 551 9188 and Concerteria, Via Schipa 23, t 081 761 1221.

Unless your Italian is fluent, **theatre** will probably be a frustrating experience, and if you go for one of the superbly executed **dialect plays**, you may not understand a word. If that's not enough to put you off, the best theatres to try are the Politeama, Via Monte di Dio, t 081 764 5016; the Cilea, Via S. Domenico, t 081 714 3110; the Bracco, Via Tarsia 40, t 081 564 5323; and the Sannazaro, Via Chiaia 157, t 081 411 723.

Clubs, Bars and Discos

Neapolitans are night-owls, probably thanks to their Spanish heritage, and many, especially in summer, don't even think about going out to dinner until 10pm. That doesn't leave too much time for partying, once the 2–3 hour ritual of eating is over, but there are some reasonable clubs and late-night bars (as well as some terrible ones). The thing to remember is that some areas are best left alone after midnight, most notably the Piazza Garibaldi area near the station, and the so-called *quartiere*, the narrow side streets that run off the Via Toledo. And if the vampish hookers at every street corner after dark take your fancy, remember to take a second look – those girls could well be boys. Naples is famous even in drag-obsessed Italy for its transvestites, and some of them are positively remarkable. A list of clubs can be found in *Qui Napoli*.

La Mela, Via dei Mille 41, t 081 413 881. Good reports from the young and beautiful crowd.

Madison Street, Via Sgambati 47, t 081 546 6566. Naples' biggest disco, with theme nights and an affluent young crowd.

My Way, Via Cappella Vecchia 30/c, t 081 764 4735. Another popular nightspot, where Neapolitans have danced into the small hours for as long as anyone can remember.

Velvet, Via Cisterna dell'Olio, in the centre. An alternative disco with a rougher edge.

Otto Jazz Club, Piazzetta Cariati 32, t 081 552 4373. Jazz which looks for inspiration as much to the famous Neapolitan folk songs as to New Orleans. It serves light meals, and has a list of 200 cocktails. Don't take too much cash with you, as this very pleasant club is in a pretty hard area – it's best to get a taxi home. *Open Thurs–Sun.*

Virgilio Sporting Club, Via Tito Lucrezio Caro 6, t 081 769 5261, up on Posillipo Hill. A more tranquil nightclub, in its own park, with tables outside. *Open Fri–Sun midnight–4am.*

The **bars** of Via Paladino are where it all happens (*movida*, Napoli-style). Piazza Bellini, especially in summer, is where the young and trendy come to see and be seen; it is also one of the few piazzas in Naples whose cafés have outside tables. Try to get a table at **Intra Moenia**, the literary café-cum-publishing house, t 081 200 720, to see a different side of Naples.

The Napoletani do not stand in lines, or fill out forms, or stop for traffic signals; they will talk your ears off, run you over in their ancient Fiats, criticize the way you dress, whisper alarming propositions, give you sweets, try to pick your pockets with engaging artlessness, offer surprising kindnesses, and with a reassuring smile they will always, always give you the wrong directions. In an official capacity, they will either break the rules for you or invent new ones; in shops and restaurants, they will either charge you too much or too little. The former is much more common, though whichever it is, they will undoubtedly do it with a flourish.

If the accounts of long-ago travellers are to be believed, Naples has always been like this. Too much sunshine, and living under such a large and ill-mannered volcano, must contribute much to the effect. It would be somewhat harder to explain some of Naples' ancient distinctions. First and foremost, Naples is Italy's city of philosophers. Her greatest, Giambattista Vico, was a Neapolitan, and others, such as St Thomas Aquinas and Benedetto Croce, spent much of their time here.

Naples can also claim to be first in music. Among native composers are Gesualdo, Scarlatti and Leoncavallo, and Neapolitans claim their conservatory is the oldest in Europe. Even today, members of the opera company at San Carlo look down on their colleagues at Milan's La Scala as a band of promising upstarts who could stand to take their jobs a little more seriously. Neapolitan popular song, expressive and intense, is an unchained Italian stereotype; the Napoletani maintain its traditions as jealously as they do their impenetrable dialect – flavoured with Arabic and Spanish galore – one of the most widely spoken and robust in modern Italy.

History

Naples' rise to become the metropolis of Campania was largely the result of the lucky elimination of her rivals over the centuries. Capua, *Cumae* and Benevento rose and fell, and *Pompeii* and *Herculaneum* disappeared under volcanic ash, but fortune has always seemed to protect Naples from the really big disasters. As a Greek colony founded by *Cumae* in 750 BC, the city began with the name *Neapolis* (new city), and prospered moderately throughout the periods of Greek, Samnite and Roman rule. Belisarius, Justinian's famous general, seized the region for Byzantium in AD 536, after invasions of the Goths and Vandals, but a duke of Naples declared the city independent in 763, acknowledging only the authority of the pope.

The chronicles are understandably slim for this period; early medieval Naples offers us more fairy-tales than facts. Many of its early legends deal with none other than the poet Virgil; somehow, folklore in the Dark Ages transformed the greatest Latin poet into Master Virgil, a mighty magician who was given credit for many of the unexplainable engineering feats of the ancient Romans. Naples claimed him for its founder, and its legends told of how he built the Castel dell'Ovo, balancing it on an egg at the bottom of the harbour. Master Virgil also built a talking statue that warned the city of enemies, earthquakes or plagues, and medieval chroniclers mention the bronze horses and bronze fly he built over two of the city's gates, still to be seen then, and said to be magical charms on which the city's fortunes depended.

Naples lost its independence to the Normans in 1139, later passing under the rule of the Hohenstaufen emperors along with the rest of southern Italy. Charles of Anjou took over in 1266, and lopped off the head of the last Hohenstaufen, Conradin, in what is now Naples' Piazza del Mercato. Under the Angevins, Naples for the first time assumed the status of a capital. The Angevin kings of Naples, however, did little to develop their new realm, expending most of their energy in futile attempts to recapture Sicily, lost to them after the Sicilian Vespers revolution of 1282. After their line expired in 1435, with the death of Giovanni II, the kingdom fell to Alfonso V of Aragon – a fateful event, marking Spain's first foothold on the Italian mainland.

Habsburgs and Bourbons

Aragonese rule seemed promising at first, under the enlightened Alfonso. Later, though, it became clear that the Spaniards were mainly interested in milking Italy for taxes with which to finance further conquests. The city itself, as the seat of the viceregal court, prospered greatly; by 1600 its population of 280,000 made it the largest city on the Mediterranean. The long period of Spanish control did much to give Naples its distinct character, especially during the 17th and 18th centuries, when the city participated almost joyfully in the decadence and decay of the Spanish Empire. This period saw the construction of the scores of frilly, gloomy Baroque churches – now half-abandoned, with bushes growing out of the cornices – that add so much to the Neapolitan scene. In manners especially, the imperial Spanish influence was felt. 'Nothing', in the words of one observer, 'is cheaper here than human life.'

In 1707, during the War of the Spanish Succession, Naples passed under the rule of Archduke Charles of Austria. Prince Charles of Bourbon, however, snatched it away from him in 1734, and mouldering, picturesque Naples for the next century and a half made the perfect backdrop for the rococo shenanigans of the new Bourbon kingdom. The new rulers were little improvement over the Spaniards, but immigrants from all over the south poured into the city, chasing the thousands of ducats dropped by a free-spending court. Naples became the most densely populated city in Europe (a distinction it still holds today); crime and epidemics became widespread.

Nevertheless, this was the Naples that attracted 18th- and 19th-century aesthetes doing the Grand Tour. Goethe flirted with *contessas* here, while English poets flirted with dread diseases and Lord Nelson made eyes at Lady Hamilton. The Neapolitans are frank about it: Naples owed its prominence on the tour less to Vesuvius and the ruins of *Pompeii* than to good old-fashioned sex – Naples at the time was the easiest place in Europe to find some, and everyone knew it, saving Goethe and the rest the trouble of ever mentioning the subject in their travel accounts and letters home.

Garibaldi's army entered Naples in February 1861. As the new Italy's biggest basket case, the city has since received considerable assistance with its planning and social problems – though unfortunately not nearly enough to make up for the centuries of neglect. The Second World War didn't help: for four days in late September 1944 the city staged a heroic though unsuccessful revolt against the Germans; even more damage was done by Allied bombing; and the retreating Nazis rounded off the destruction by destroying the city's port and utilities as they left.

While the post-war period saw considerable rebuilding, it also brought new calamities. Illegal and speculative building projects grabbed most of the already-crowded city's open space (you'll notice the almost total absence of parks), and turned the fringe areas and much of the once-beautiful Bay of Naples shore into a nightmare of human detritus, one of the eeriest industrial wastelands of Europe.

In the political turmoil that took over Italy at the beginning of the 1990s, with the collapse of the old parties, Naples became one of the major bases of support for the neo-Fascist MSI party – yet another twist to the city's history. It has, however, marked up one genuine accomplishment in the books in the last few years, though not one that will have much effect on the most serious problems – the Centro Direzionale, a huge modernistic development on the lines of a Neapolitan Manhattan built over the wastelands around Corso Malta, north of the Central Station. In spite of a few hiccups, most notably when the new palace of justice was mysteriously burnt to the ground (no prizes for guessing by whom), the project is currently nearing completion, its aim being to provide a new centre for the regional economy.

Antonio Bassolino, the communist anti-Mafia mayor who in 1994 narrowly beat Alessandra Mussolini, Benito's granddaughter and Sophia Loren's niece, was over-whelmingly re-elected for a second term in 1997. In his first term, the worst of the ghettos around the port went, tourist trails across Spaccanapoli were encouraged, and churches and sites long closed were reopened. Most spectacularly of all, the Piazza del Plebiscito, for a long time choked by traffic and fated to remain the city's car park, was emptied and cleaned up. But the excitement has fizzled out – Camorra families are still bombing each other right in the middle of town and Bassolino has lost his halo – although in 2000 he was elected Presidente della Regione. He is accused of addressing only the outer layer of Naples' problems rather than tackling major issues and of anointing his successor before his term ended.

At the moment there seems to be a realization that Naples has reached a point of no return. It has to clean itself up or perish; discussions of the city's problems in the press are often conducted in apocalyptic tones. Leave some room for exaggeration – the Napoletani probably couldn't enjoy life without a permanent state of crisis.

The City

Piazza del Plebiscito

After years as a car park this immense and elegant square, the centre of modern Naples, has been rescued and restored to the city. Children now come here to kick a football under the eyes of adoring parents. The recent shows staged here by the city for the benefit of national television have even forced some northern Italians to revise their opinions of Naples and admit that it may not be all that bad after all.

The huge domed church, embracing the piazza in its curving colonnades as does St Peter's in Rome, is **San Francesco di Paola**. King Ferdinand IV, after the British restored him to power in 1815, made a vow to construct it; the great dome and classical portico were modelled after the Pantheon in Rome. There's little to see in the austere interior, and no one with an understanding of Naples will be surprised to find the colonnades given over to light manufacturing and warehouse space.

Across the square rises the equally imposing bulk of the **Palazzo Reale** (Royal Palace) (*t 081 794 4021, open weekdays and holidays 9–8, Sat 9–12; adm*), begun by the Spanish viceroys in 1600, expanded by the Bourbons and finished by the kings of Italy. Umberto I, a good friend of the Neapolitans, added the eight giant figures on the façade, representing the Naples' eight ruling houses. It seems the 19th-century sculptors had trouble taking some of them seriously; note the preposterous figures of Charles of Anjou, whom the Neapolitans never liked, and Vittorio Emanuele II, the latter probably an accurate portrayal. There are Ruritanian stone sentry boxes and stone peacocks in the courtyard to recall the Bourbons, and a number of rooms inside that can be visited – the ones that escaped the bombings in the Second World War, including a suitably grand staircase, a theatre, and several chambers in 18th-century style. The theatre saw the premières of many of the works of Alessandro Scarlatti. The rear of the palace, now the home of Naples' important **Biblioteca Nazionale**, faces a pretty, little-visited garden across from the Castel Nuovo.

The Bourbons were great opera buffs, and they built Italy's largest opera house, the **San Carlo**, right next to their palace. Begun in 1737, making it older than La Scala, the theatre was sumptuously restored after a fire in 1816, when Naples was the capital of opera; so important was the theatre to the people of Naples that King Ferdinand made sure the workmen got the job done in record time – 300 days. Today the San Carlo is still among the most prestigious opera houses in the world (the Neapolitans of course would place it first), and its productions are certainly among the most polished and professional, and occasionally among the most adventurous – each season at least one lesser-known Neapolitan opera is performed. Tickets are as expensive as anywhere (they can cost up to L500,000 on an opening night). Brief tours of the theatre are possible for much less (*t 081 797 2111 for information*).

Opposite the San Carlo is the grandest interior of Southern Italy, the **Galleria Umberto I**. This glass-roofed arcade, one of the largest in the world, was begun in 1887, nine years after the Galleria Vittorio Emanuele in Milan. The arcade is cross-shaped, with a mosaic of the zodiac on the floor at the centre; its arching dome is 184ft tall; surprisingly, the Neapolitans do not seem to like it anything like as much as they once did; even at high noon, you are likely to find its vast spaces deserted but for a few small clouds of forceful, grey-suited men arguing politics around the entrances.

Castel Nuovo

City administration offices open Mon–Fri 8–1; museums open Mon–Fri 9–7 and Sat 9–1.30; t 081 795 2003; adm.

The port of Naples has been protected by this odd, beautiful castle, looming over the harbour behind the Palazzo Reale and San Carlo, for some 700 years now. Charles of Anjou built it in 1279; many Napoletani still call it by the curious name of Maschio Angioino (Angevin Boy/Keep). Most of what you see today, however, including the eccentric, ponderous round towers, is the work of Guillermo Sagrera, the great Catalan architect who built the famous Exchange in Palma de Mallorca.

Between two of the entrance towers, the conquering Aragonese hired the finest sculptors from all over Italy to build Alfonso's Triumphal Arch, a unique masterpiece of Renaissance sculpture and design inspired by the ancient Roman triumphal arches. The symbolism, as in the Roman arches, may be a little confusing. The figure at the top is Saint Michael; below him are a pair of sea gods, and further down, allegorical virtues and relief panels portraying Alfonso's victories and wise governance.

Inside, the castle currently houses parts of the Naples city administration. If you come during office hours, someone will probably show you the **Sala dei Baroni**, where the city council meets; it has a cupola with an unusual Moorish vaulting, an eight-pointed star made of interlocking arches. King Ferrante used this as his dining hall, and it takes its name from the evening when he invited a score of the kingdom's leading barons to a ball, and then arrested the lot. There are also two **museums**: one, housed in the Gothic Cappella Palatina, next to the council hall, contains some lovely 14th- and 15th-century frescoes; the other, in the south wing, has paintings, and an extensive collection of silver and bronzes, from the 15th century to the present day.

Via Toledo

From the landward side of Piazza del Plebiscito and the palace, Naples' most imposing street, the Via Toledo, runs northwards past the Galleria to Piazza Carità where it becomes Via Roma. Its name commemorates its builder, Don Pedro de Toledo, the Spanish viceroy at the beginning of the 16th century, and a great benefactor of Naples. Stendhal, in 1817, rightly called this 'the most populous and gayest street in the world', and it is still the city's main business and shopping street, leading up to Capodimonte and the northern suburbs. Don Pedro's elegant Renaissance tomb, among others, can be seen in the little church of **San Giacomo degli Spagnuoli**, now swallowed up by the 19th-century **Palazzo Municipale** complex, originally home to the Bourbon royal bureaucracy.

Going north along Via Toledo, any street on your left can be the entrance to the dense, crumbling, slightly sinister inner sanctum of the Neapolitan soul, the vast slum called the **Quartieri Spagnuoli**. It can be a fascinating place to walk around, in daytime at least. Lately though, thanks to battling factions of the Camorra, the Quartieri have achieved even more than their accustomed share of notoriety; for a while the hoods were bumping each other off at a rate of one a week. Though the Quartieri cover almost all the area sloping up to San Martino and Vomero, the most populous and colourful part is that immediately adjoining Via Toledo, a grid of narrow streets laid out by Don Pedro de Toledo and now called the Tavoliere, or chessboard.

To the right of Via Toledo, the confusion of Naples' half-crumbling, half-modern business centre conceals a few buildings worth a look. The **Palazzo Gravina**, on Via Monteoliveto, is a fine palace in the northern Renaissance style, built between 1513 and 1549. It now houses Naples University's Faculty of Architecture. Almost directly across the street, the **church of Monteoliveto** (*open Tues–Sat 8.30–12.30*) is a little treasure house of late Renaissance sculpture and painting, with tombs and altars in the chapels by southern artists like Giovanni da Nola and Antonio Rosellino, as well as some frescoes by Vasari.

Spaccanapoli

This street's familiar name means 'Split-Naples', and that is exactly what it has done for the last 2,600 years. On the map it changes its name with alarming frequency – Via Benedetto Croce and Via San Biagio dei Librai are two of the most prominent – but in Roman times you would have found it by asking for the *decumanus inferior*, the name for the second east–west street in any planned Roman city. No large city in all the lands conquered by Rome has maintained its ancient street plan as completely as Naples (the Greeks laid out these streets, of course, but the Romans learned their planning from them). It is easier to imagine the atmosphere of a big ancient city here than in Rome itself, or even in *Pompeii*. The narrow, straight streets and tall *insulae* cannot have changed much; only the forum and temples are missing.

This is the heart of old Naples – and what a street it is, lined with grocery barrows and scholarly bookshops, shops that sell old violins, plaster saints, pizza or used clothes pegs. Drama is supplied by the arch-Neapolitan characters who live here, haunting the street-corners and entertaining wan hopes of dodging the manic motorists; the colour comes from the district's laundry – down any of the long alleys of impossibly tall tenements you may see as many as a hundred full clothes-lines, swelling bravely in the breeze and hoping for a glint of southern sun.

It has always been a poor neighbourhood, though even now it is not a desperate one. As always, its people live much of their life on the streets, carrying out whatever is their business from makeshift benches on the kerbs. Visitors will probably find that claustrophobia is right around the corner, but anyone born and raised here would never feel at home anywhere else.

Santa Chiara and the Gesù Nuovo

Your introduction here, off Via Toledo, is the cramped, disorderly, most characteristic of Neapolitan squares: **Piazza del Gesù Nuovo**, decorated by the gaudiest and most random of Neapolitan decorations, the **Guglia della Immacolata**. A *guglia* (pinnacle), in Naples, is a kind of rococo obelisk, dripping with frills, saints and putti.

The unsightly, unfinished façade behind the Guglia, covered with pyramidal extrusions in dark basalt, belongs to the **church of Gesù Nuovo**. As strange as it is, the façade, originally part of a late 15th-century palace, has become one of the landmarks of Naples. The interior is typically lavish Neapolitan Baroque, gloriously overdone in acres of coloured marbles and frescoes, some by Solimena. One of his best works (dated 1725) is here above the main door inside, depicting three angels driving the Syrian minister Eliodorus out of the Temple of Jerusalem.

Santa Chiara, across the piazza, dates from the early 14th century, though it once had a Baroque interior as good as the Gesù. Allied bombers remodelled it to suit modern tastes in 1943, and only a few of the original Angevin tombs have survived. To get some idea of what the interior must have been like, stop in and see the recently restored **Majolica Cloister**, nothing less than the loveliest and most peaceful spot in Naples – especially in contrast to the neighbourhood outside. The cloister can be visited as part of the new **Complesso di Santa Chiara** (*t 081 797 1256, open Mon–Sat 9.30–1 and 3.30–5.30, Sun and hols 9.30–1; adm*), which includes a museum housing the church treasures, marbles and an area of Roman-period archaeological excavations. So much in Naples shows the Spanish influence – like the use of the title 'Don', now largely limited to Camorra bosses – and here someone in the 1740s transplanted the Andalucian love of pictures done in painted *azulejo* tiles, turning a simple monkish cloister into a fairyland of gaily coloured arbours, benches and columns, shaded by the only trees in the whole district.

Recently, during the restoration of a vestibule off the cloister, it was discovered that underneath the indifferent 17th-century frescoes (reached via the back of the church) there were some earlier, highly original paintings of the Last Judgement. They have since been uncovered and restored, revealing an inspired 16th-century vision of the event in a style utterly unlike the slick virtuosity of the time, with plenty of novel tortures for the damned, and angels welcoming cute naked nuns among the elect.

The Cappella Sansevero

A few streets further down Via Benedetto Croce is tiny Piazza San Domenico, which has monuments from Naples' three most creative periods. **San Domenico Maggiore** built between 1283 and 1324, was the Dominican church. St Thomas Aquinas lived in the adjacent monastery. Later this became the favourite church of the Spanish, and it contains some interesting Renaissance funerary monuments; a better one, though, is across the piazza in the church of **Sant'Angelo a Nilo** (*closed for restoration*) – the tomb of Cardinal Brancaccio, designed by Michelozzo, with a relief of the Assumption of the Virgin by Donatello (the two artists had collaborated on the baptistry in Siena).

The second Baroque pinnacle decorates the Piazza, the **Guglia di San Domenico**, begun after a plague in 1650. But best of all, just around the corner on Via F. de Sanctis, you can inspect Neapolitan rococo at its very queerest in the **Sansevero Chapel** (*open Mon–Sat 10–8, Sun and hols 10–1.30, closed Tues; adm*). Prince Raimondo di Sangro (b. 1701), responsible for the final form of this, his family's private chapel, was a strange bird, a sort of aristocratic dilettante mystic. Supposedly there is a grand allegorical scheme behind the arrangement of the sculptures and frescoes he commissioned, but a work like this, only 200 years old, seems as foreign to our sensibilities and understanding as some Mayan temple. The sculptures, by little-known Neapolitan artists like Giuseppe Sammartino and Antonio Corradini, are inscrutable allegories in themselves, executed with showy virtuosity. Francesco Queirolo's *Il Disinganno* (disillusion) is an extreme case – one of the few to carve a fishing-net, or the pages of a book, out of marble. Sammartino's *Cristo Velato* displays a remarkable illusion of figures under transparent veils. There are a dozen or so of these large sculptural groups, all under a crazy heavenly vortex in the ceiling fresco, by Francesco Mario Russo. Down in the crypt are two complete human cardiovascular systems, removed and preserved by Prince Raimondo in the course of his alchemical experiments.

Near San Domenico, a block south of the Spacca, is Naples' university, one of Europe's oldest and most distinguished. The Emperor Frederick II founded it in 1224, as a 'Ghibelline' university to counter the pope's 'Guelph' university at Bologna, as well as to provide scholars and trained officials for the new state he was trying to build. It still occupies its ancient, woefully overcrowded quarters around Via Mezzocannone.

Around the Piazza del Duomo

Continuing down the Spaccanapoli (here Via San Biagio dei Librai), just around the corner on Via San Gregorio is the **San Gregorio Armeno church**, with another gaudy Baroque interior. If the gilding and the painting by Luca Giordano of the Arrival of Saint Basilio are not your cup of tea, try the cloister (*open daily 9.30–12.30*). This is another oasis of tranquillity and a step back to the 16th century. Since the 1500s the cloister has served the convent of Benedictine nuns. At the centre of the cloister there is a fountain sculpted in 1733 depicting Christ meeting the Samaritan woman. On the way out, note the revolving drums for communicating with the outside world pre-1922, when the monastic order was totally closed off from the profane. A caustic note by the nuns on one of them dismisses the popular misconception that they were for abandoned newborn babies. In December, this street and others around it become Naples' famous **Christmas Market**, where everyone comes to buy figurines of the Holy Family, the Three Kings and all the other accessories required for their Christmas *presepi*, or manger scenes, one of the most devotedly followed of local traditions. For several weeks, hundreds of stands fill up the neighbourhood's narrow streets.

A little further north up Via San Gregorio is **San Lorenzo Maggiore** (late 13th century), one of Naples' finest medieval churches; Petrarch lived for a while in the adjacent monastery. In addition, recent excavations have uncovered extensive **Greek and Roman remains** on the site. Entering via the cloister, where the base of a Roman *macellum* (market place) is being excavated, head down the stairs at the back to see this fascinating piece of subterranean Naples. **San Paolo**, across the street, isn't much to see now but, before an earthquake wrecked it in the 17th century, its façade was the portico of an ancient Roman temple to Castor and Pollux. Andrea Palladio studied it closely, and it provided inspiration for his classical villas and churches in the Veneto.

After Spaccanapoli, **Via dei Tribunali** (the *decumanus maximus*) is the busiest street of old Naples, and has been for a long time. The arcades that line the street in places, a sort of continuous covered market, are a thousand years old or more. Here, at the otherwise unremarkable **Girolamini Church** (*open daily 9.30–1*), you may see the modest tomb of Naples's greatest philosopher, Giambattista Vico.

Northwest of the Girolamini, around **Via Anticaglia**, you'll find a few crooked streets, the only ones in old Naples that do not stick to the rectilinear Roman plan. These follow the outline of the **Roman Theatre**, much of which still survives, hidden among the tenements. A few arches are all that is visible from the street.

The Cathedral of San Gennaro

The wide Via del Duomo is a breath of fresh air in this crowded district – exactly what the city intended when they ploughed it through Old Naples after the cholera epidemic of 1884. The Duomo itself is another fine medieval building (*interior under restoration*), though it is hidden behind an awful pseudo-Gothic façade pasted on in 1905. The best things are inside: the Renaissance **Cappella Minùtolo**, the tomb of Charles of Anjou and the **Cappella San Gennaro**, glittering with the gold and silver of the cathedral treasure, and with frescoes by Domenichino and Lanfranco, the latter's a swirling *Paradiso* in the dome (1643). The **Basilica Santa Restituta**, a sizeable church in its own right, is tacked on to the side of the cathedral. Its columns are thought to be from the temple of Apollo that once occupied the site. Begun in AD 324, though often rebuilt, this is the oldest building in Naples. The ceiling frescoes are by Luca Giordano.

Just off the basilica, the 5th-century baptistry contains a good Byzantine-style mosaic by the 14th-century artist Lello di Roma; the baptismal font itself probably comes from an ancient temple of Dionysus. From Santa Restituta's chapel you can access a collection of archaeological remains dating from the Greeks to the Middle Ages (*open daily 9–12 and 4.30–7, Sun and hols 9–12; adm*). The last and most elaborate of the *guglie*, the **Guglia San Gennaro**, designed by Cosimo Fanzago, can be seen just outside the south transept.

You can also visit the **Crypt of San Gennaro**, patron of Naples, with elaborate marble decoration from the Renaissance, and the tomb of Pope Innocent IV. Whoever is really buried here, San Gennaro (Januarius) is a rather doubtful character; most likely he is a Christian assimilation of the Roman god Janus. The saint's head is kept upstairs in the chapel named after him, along with two phials of his blood that miraculously liquefy and 'boil' three times each year – the first Sunday in May, 19 September and 16 December – to prove that San Gennaro is still looking out for the Napoletani. The only time the miracle has ever failed, during the Napoleonic occupation, the people of the city became enormously excited and seemed ready to revolt. At this the French commander, a true son of the Enlightenment, announced that San Gennaro had 10 minutes to come through – or else he'd shoot the Archbishop. Somehow, just in time, the miracle occurred.

On a small piazza a block north of the Duomo, **Santa Maria Donnaregina** offers more overdone Baroque, but off to the side of this 17th-century work is the smaller, original church, built in 1307 by Queen Maria of Hungary (Charles of Anjou's wife, her title reflecting a claim to the throne). Her elaborate tomb, and some frescoes from the first half of the 12th century, are the sights of the church. South of the cathedral in the Via del Duomo is the **Filangieri Museum** (*closed for restoration*) housed in the 15th-century Palazzo Cuomo, with a small collection of china, armour and curiosities.

Piazza Garibaldi

In Italian, the word for a market stall is *bancarella*. In Naples they are as much a part of life today as they were in the Middle Ages; the city has as many of them as all the rest of Italy put together. The greatest concentration can be found in the **Forcella market district**, in the narrow streets east off the Via del Duomo, selling everything from stereos to light bulbs. According to government economists, at least one-third of Naples' economy is black, or at least grey: either outright illegal, or not paying taxes or subject to any regulation. Bootleg cassette tapes are one example; Naples is one of the world leaders in this thriving industry, and you'll have your choice of thousands of titles along these streets, though ask to hear your tape before you part with any money. Hundreds of tired-looking people sit in front of little tables, selling contraband American cigarettes. This is one of the easiest means for Naples' poor to make a living, and it is all controlled by the Camorra. You will see plenty of designer labels on the *bancarelle* – if they're real, don't ask where they came from.

Piazza Mercato, one of the nodes of the Neapolitan bazaar, has been a market square perhaps since Roman times. In the old days this was always the site of major executions, most notably that of 16-year-old Conradin, last of the Hohenstaufens and rightful heir to the throne of the Kingdom of Sicily, by Charles of Anjou in 1268, an act that shocked all Europe. Charles ordered him buried underneath the Piazza – he couldn't be laid in consecrated ground since he had just been excommunicated for political reasons by Charles's ally the pope. In 1647 Masaniello's Revolt started here during the festival of Our Lady of Mount Carmel; Masaniello (Tommaso Aniello), a young fisherman of Amalfi, had been chosen by his fellow conspirators to step up in the middle of the ceremonies and proclaim to the people and the viceroy that the new tax the viceroy had introduced 'no longer existed'. As the plotters had hoped, a spontaneous rising followed, and for a week Masaniello ruled Naples while the frightened viceroy hid in Castel Sant'Elmo. In Naples such risings can burn out as quickly as a match; the viceroy's spies first secretly drugged Masaniello, so that he appeared drunk or mad to the people, and then they murdered him and sent his head to the viceroy. That was the end for Naples, but the incident touched off a wave of revolts across the south that took the Spaniards three years to stamp out.

The Porta Capuana

Northwest of the Piazza Garibaldi some of Naples' shabbiest streets lead to the Piazza Enrico de Nicola, once the city's main gate. The Porta Capuana, built in 1484, seems a smaller version of the Castel Nuovo's triumphal arch, crowded in by the same squat round towers. The **Castel Capuano**, next to it, began its life in the 13th century as a castle-residence for the Hohenstaufen kings. Since then it has been reshaped so many times that it no longer looks like a castle; for four centuries it has served as Naples' law courts. If anything makes wandering into this unlikely district worthwhile it is **Santa Caterina a Formiella**, facing the Porta Capuana, a church by the obscure architect Romolo Balsimelli that is one of the masterpieces of 16th-century Italian architecture. Completed in 1593, the church's bulky, squarish form was a Renaissance eccentricity, but a stepping-stone towards the Baroque. Despite long neglect during which its dome tilted at a more precarious angle each year, the church has reopened to the public and projects are under way to conserve its interior.

Museo Archeologico Nazionale

Open Wed–Mon 9am–7.30pm; adm.

Back on the western side of the old city, Via Toledo, after passing Spaccanapoli and changing its name to Via Roma, continues northwards through the **Piazza Dante**, one of the most delightful and animated corners of the city. Beyond this, as Via Enrico Pessina, in an area of oversized tenements and busy streets, it opens to display the crumbling red *palazzo* that contains the National Archaeological Museum.

Naples has the most important collection of Roman-era art and antiquities in the world, due partly to Vesuvius, for burying *Pompeii* and *Herculaneum*, and partly to the sharp eyes and deep pockets of the Farnese family – many of the best works here come from the collection they built up over 300 years. Unfortunately, the place is run by Neapolitans; at any given time, half of the collections will be closed for 'restorations' that never seem to happen, and what they condescend to let you see may well be the worst-exhibited and worst-labelled major museum in Europe.

On the **first floor**, room after room is filled with ancient sculpture. Many of the pieces on view are the best existing Roman-era copies of lost Greek statues, including some by Phidias and Praxiteles; some are masterpieces in their own right, such as the huge, dramatic ensemble called the Farnese Bull, the Tyrannicides (with other statues' heads stuck on them), and the truly heroic Farnese Hercules that once decorated the Baths of Caracalla. Several provocative Aphrodites compete for your attention, along with a platoon of formidable Athenas, the famous Doryphorus (spear-bearer), and enough Greek and Roman busts to populate a Colosseum.

Upstairs, most of the rooms are given over to finds from *Pompeii*. The collection of Roman mosaics, mostly from *Pompeii* and *Herculaneum*, is one of the two best anywhere (the other is in Antalya, Turkey); the insight it provides into the life and thought of the ancients is priceless. One feature it betrays clearly is a certain fond silliness – plenty of chickens, ducks and grinning cats, the famous *Cave Canem* (Beware of the Dog) mosaic from the front of a house, comic scenes from the theatre, and one especially wonderful panel of crocodiles and hippopotami along the Nile. Some of the mosaics are very consciously 'art', including one showing a detailed scene of the Battle of Issus, where Alexander the Great defeated the Persian king, and another with a view of the Academy of Athens that includes a portrait of Plato.

Besides the mosaics, nowhere in the world will you find a larger collection of Roman mural painting, much of it fascinatingly modern in theme and execution. Many of the walls of Pompeiian villas were decorated with architectural fantasias that seem strangely like those of the Renaissance. Other works show an almost Baroque lack of respect for the gods – the *Wedding of Zeus and Hera*. Scholars in fact do denote a period of 'Roman Baroque', beginning about the 2nd century. From it come paintings graced by genuine winged *putti*, called *amoretti* in Roman days. Among the most famous pictures are *The Astragal Players* – young girls shooting craps – and the beautiful *Portrait of an Unknown Woman*, a thoughtful lady holding her pen to her lips who has become one of the best-known images from Roman art. A recent addition is a section devoted entirely to the Temple of Isis at *Pompeii*. Five rooms display sculptures, frescoes and paintings from the temple, discovered in 1765. Other attractions include collections of jewellery, coins, gladiators' armour, the famous *sezione pornografica* – the porn section (*closed for years and unlikely to reopen soon*) – Greek vases, bronzes and a detailed scale model of all excavations at *Pompeii* up to the 1840s. The Egyptian collection is not large, but it is fun, with a dog-headed Anubis in a Roman toga, some ancient feet under glass, and a mummified crocodile.

Capodimonte

North of the museum, the neighbourhoods along Via Toledo – briefly named Via Santa Teresa degli Scalzi – begin to lose some of their Neapolitan intensity as they climb to the suburban heights. On the way, after changing its name once again to

Corso Amedeo di Savoia, the street passes an area full of cemeteries in Roman times. Three Christian underground burial vaults have been discovered here, with an extraordinary total area of over 100,000 square metres, only a small part of which has been completely explored.

Two may be visited: the **Catacombe di San Gennaro**, reached through the courtyard of the Basilica dell'Incoronata a Capodimonte – look for the yellow signs (*tours daily at 9.30, 10.15, 11.00 and 11.45; adm*), is the more interesting, with extensive early Christian mosaics and frescoes, some as early as the 2nd century. The **Catacombe di San Gaudioso** (*tours daily at 9.45 and 11.45; adm*), which include the 5th-century tomb of the saint of the same name, a martyred African bishop, were discovered under the Baroque church of Santa Maria della Sanità, on Via Sanità ('sanity street').

The **Parco di Capodimonte**, a well-kept and exotically tropical park, began as a hunting preserve of the Bourbons in the 18th century. Charles III built a Royal Palace here in 1738 that now houses Naples' picture gallery, the **Museo Nazionale di Capodimonte** (*open Tues–Sun 8.30–7.30; adm*). The collection is the best in the south of Italy, and especially rich in works of the late Renaissance. Some of the works you shouldn't miss are: an *Annunciation* by Filippino Lippi; a Botticelli *Madonna*; the mystical portrait of the mathematician Fra Luca Pacioli by an unknown *quattrocento* artist; two wry homilies by the elder Brueghel, *The Misanthrope* and *The Blind*; works by Masaccio and Mantegna, and a hilarious picture of *St Peter Martyr* by Lotto, showing that famous anti-Semitic rabble-rouser conversing nonchalantly with the Virgin Mary – with a hatchet sticking out of his head. Five big, beautifully restored Caravaggios take up one room; others are devoted to important works by Titian.

One entire wing of the museum is filled with delightfully frivolous 18th-century **porcelain figurines**; the Bourbons maintained a royal factory for making such things at Capodimonte, which is still in operation today. In another hall, there are scores of 19th-century watercolour scenes of Naples and the Campanian countryside (the best of them by Giacinto Gigante). Here, for the first time, you will see the Naples that so struck the 18th-century travellers. Not much has changed, really; if only all the traffic could magically disappear, it would be almost the same spectacular city today.

The museum's collections are mostly up on the second floor; the first, the old *piano nobile* (royal apartments), is still much the way the Bourbons left it. Persevere through the score of overdecorated chambers; the **Salotto di Porcellana**, a little room entirely lined with Capodimonte porcelain, makes the whole thing worthwhile.

The Certosa di San Martino

Up on the highest point overlooking Naples, the 17th-century **Castel Sant'Elmo** (*open Tues–Sun 8.30–7.30; adm, last tickets 6.30*) is an impressive enough Baroque fortification, partly built of the tufa rock on which it stands (the city now uses it to park the cars the police tow away). Next to it, hogging the best view in Naples, the Carthusians built their original, modest monastery of San Martino, some time in the early 14th century. Two centuries later, like most Carthusian branch offices, they were rolling embarrassingly in lucre; building the poshest monastery in all Italy was the only thing to do. The rebuilt **Certosa** (charterhouse) is only marginally smaller than

Fort St Elmo. Built on the slope of the mountain, it is supported by a gargantuan platform, visible for miles out to sea and containing enough stone to construct a small pyramid.

Nobody knows exactly what is in the **Museo Nazionale di San Martino** (*open weekdays and Sun 8.30–7.30, Sat 9–11, closed Mon; adm*), which now occupies the monastery. Intended as a museum specifically of Naples, its history, art and traditions, San Martino suffers from the same mismanagement as the archaeological museum; only parts are ever open. The Certosa's famous **Chiostro Grande**, at the time of writing, has become a wilderness of weeds and scaffolding. But none of this should discourage you from taking the long ride up the **Montesanto Funicular**. The views and architecture are marvellous, and at least they always keep the collection of *presepi* (Christmas cribs) open – what the Neapolitans come here to see.

Upon entering the monastery complex, the first attraction is the **church**, another of the glories of Neapolitan Baroque, with an excess of lovely coloured inlaid marble to complement the overabundance of painting. The work over the altar, the *Descent from the Cross*, is one of the finest of José Ribera. This tormented artist, often called *Lo Spagnuolo* in Italy, has paintings all over Naples. His popularity does not owe everything to his artistic talent; apparently he formed a cartel with two local artists and cornered the market by hiring a gang of thugs to harry other painters out of town.

Even in its present state, the Chiostro Grande – the grand cloister – is a masterpiece of Baroque, elegantly proportioned and gloriously original in its decoration. Also, thanks to a sculptural scheme by a pious, mad artist named Cosimo Fanzago, it is the creepiest cloister east of Seville. Fanzago (who was also one of the architects of San Martino) gives us eight figures of saints that seem more like vampires in priestly robes and mitres, a perfect background for his little enclosed garden, its wall topped with rows of gleaming marble skulls.

Most of the San Martino museum's publicly visible collections are in the halls surrounding the cloister – costume, painting, ship models and every sort of curiosity; at the corners are belvederes from which to look over Naples (outside the complex, a series of lovely terraced gardens offer a similar view). The *presepi* take up a few large rooms near the entrance.

West of the Piazza del Plebiscito

The hill called **Pizzofalcone** rises directly behind the Piazza del Plebiscito; around it was the site of *Parthenope*, the Greek town that antedated *Neapolis* and was eventually swallowed up by it (though Neapolitans still like to refer to themselves as Parthenopeans). *Parthenope* had a little harbour, formed by an island that is now almost completely covered by the ancient, strangely-shaped fortress of the **Castel dell'Ovo** – the one Master Virgil is said to have built balanced on an egg, hence the name. Most of it was really built by Frederick II, and expanded by the Angevins.

It is closed to the public, but the Egg Castle has been the scene of many unusual events in Italian history. Long before there was a castle, the island may have been part of the original Greek settlement of Parthenope. Later it contained the villa of the Roman general and philosopher Lucullus, victor over Mithridates in the Pontic Wars;

Lucullus curried favour with the people by opening his sumptuous gardens, and his famous library, to the public. In the 5th century AD the villa became a home in exile for Romulus Augustulus, last of the western Roman emperors. The Goths spared him only because of his youth and simple-mindedness, and pensioned him off here.

Modern Naples: the Villa Comunale

Once past the Egg Castle, a handsome sweep of coastline opens up the districts of **Chiaia** and **Mergellina**, the most pleasant parts of the new city. Here the long, pretty **Villa Comunale**, central Naples' only park, follows the shore. In it, there is an **Aquarium** (*t 081 583 3263, open winter Tues–Sat 9–5, Sun 9–2; summer Tues–Sat 9–6, Sun 10–6; adm*), built by the German naturalist Dr Anton Dohrn in the 1870s. All the varieties of fish, octopuses and other marine delicacies here are from the bay; depending on the hour, you will either find them fascinating or appetizing. When the Allied armies marched into town in 1943, the Neapolitans put on a party for the officers. There being nothing decent to eat anywhere in Naples, they cleaned out the aquarium and managed an all-seafood menu. General Mark Clark, the commander, is said to have got the prize specimen, a baby manatee, though how they prepared it is not recorded.

Ask to see the murals and you will be led upstairs to see Dohrn (a colleague of Charles Darwin) and buddies depicted by the German artist Hans von Marees. The wall opposite shows boys frolicking naked under the orange groves. Recently restored after the 1980 earthquake, the murals are an insight into the secret life of aquariums.

Behind the park, on the Riviera di Chiaia, the **Museo Principe di Aragona Pignatelli Cortes** (*open Tues–Sun 8.30–7.30; adm*) will show you more of the same kind of decorative porcelain as at Capodimonte, along with a score of 18th- and 19th-century noble carriages, furniture and art. If you're not tired of little smiling figurines, you can plunge deeper into Chiaia to see the greatest collection of all at the **Museo Duca di Martina** (*open Tues–Sun 8.30–7.30; adm*), also known as the Museo Nazionale della Ceramica – known to Neapolitans as the **Villa Floridiana**, after the 18th-century estate it occupies, with one of the loveliest gardens in Naples and one of Italy's great hoards of bric-a-brac. The museum is on Via Cimarosa, near the Funicolare di Chiaia.

Mergellina

Beginning a few streets beyond the western end of the Villa Comunale, Mergellina is one of the brightest and most popular quarters of Naples, a good place for dinner or a *passeggiata* around the busy Piazza Sannazzaro. Its centre is the **Marina**, where there are hydrofoils to Sorrento and the islands in the summer months, and excursion boats which do daily tours of the shore between the Egg Castle and Punto Posillipo.

From the harbour, Mergellina rises up the surrounding hills; there is a funicular up to the top (every 15 minutes). On the hillside, between the railway bridge and the tunnel that leads under the hill to Fuorigrotta, there is a Roman funerary monument that tradition holds to be the **Tomb of Virgil** (*open Tues–Sun 9–1*). The poet died in Brindisi in 19 BC on his way back from a trip to Greece. *Neapolis* was a city dear to him – he wrote most of the Aeneid here – and Virgil was brought here for burial, though ancient authors attest that the tomb was closer to the aquarium.

Just below it lies the entrance to a little-known wonder of the ancient world. The **Crypta Neapolitana** (*closed, and sadly not due to reopen in the foreseeable future*) is a 1,988ft road tunnel built during the reign of Augustus, to connect *Neapolis* with Pozzuoli and Baiae, the longest such work the Romans ever attempted.

Around the Bay of Naples

Naples' hinterlands share fully in the peculiarities and sharp contrasts of the big city. Creation left nothing half-done or poorly done; against any other part of the monotonous Italian coastline, the Campanian shore seems almost indecently blessed, possessing the kind of irresistibly distracting beauty that seduces history off the path of duty and virtue. Today, for all the troubles that come seeping out of Naples, this coast is still one of the capitals of Mediterranean languor.

In Roman days, it was nothing less than the California of the ancient world: fantastically prosperous, lined with glittering resort towns and as favoured by artists and poets as it was by rich patricians. Like California, though, the perfume was mixed with a little whiff of insecurity. Vesuvius would be enough, but even outside of the regular eruptions and earthquakes, the region is Vulcan's own curiosity shop. West of Naples especially, there are eternally rising and sinking landscapes, sulphurous pools, thermal springs and even a baby volcano – altogether, one of the most unstable corners of the broad earth's crust.

West from Naples:
Pozzuoli and the Phlegraean Fields

The coastal road leaving the city, with views of Vesuvius all through the suburb of Posillipo, passes the tiny **island of Nisida**; this was a favoured spot in ancient times, and legend has it that Brutus and Cassius planned Caesar's murder here in the villa of one of their fellow conspirators. Naples' suburbs continue through **Agnano**, a town of hot springs set around a mile-wide extinct crater, and stretch as far as Pozzuoli.

Pozzuoli, Sophia Loren's home town, is a modest city, with only its ruins to remind it of the time when Roman *Puteoli*, and not Naples, was the metropolis of the bay. The **Amphitheatre** (*open daily 9am–one hour before sunset; adm*), on Via Domiziana, near the station, was the third-largest in the Roman world (after Rome and Capua), with 60 gates for letting the beasts in. Pozzuoli's other main ruin is an embarrassment to the town; for centuries people here were showing off the ancient *Serapeum* – temple to the popular Egyptian god Serapis – until some killjoy archaeologist proved the thing to be an unusually lavish *macellum*, or market. Only the foundations remain, now forming the centrepiece of the Piazza Serapide, near Pozzuoli's small harbour.

For all ancient Puteoli's size and wealth, little else remains. There is a reason: *Bradyseism*, a rare seismic phenomenon that afflicts this town and parts of the bay. It manifests itself in the form of 'slow' earthquakes. The level of the land has fallen

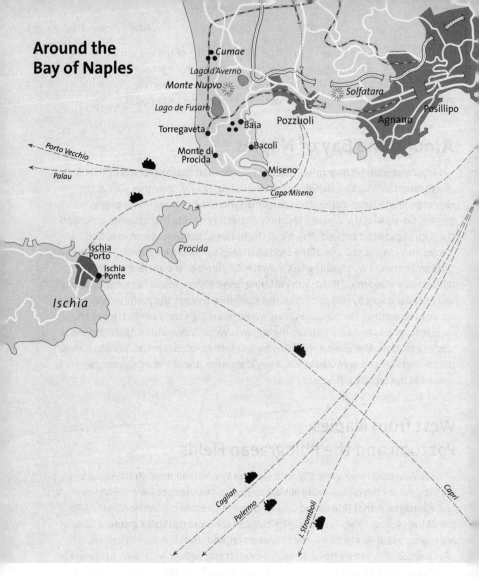

Around the Bay of Naples

Cumae
Lago d'Averno
Monte Nuovo
Solfatara
Lago de Fusaro
Posillipo
Torregaveta
Baia
Pozzuoli
Agnano
Monte di Procida
Bacoli
Porto Vecchio
Miseno
Palau
Capo Miseno
Ischia Porto
Procida
Ischia Ponte
Ischia
Caglian
Palermo
I. Stromboli
Capri

nearly 20ft since Roman times, and began rising again in the 15th century. Most recently falling, all of *Puteoli* that hasn't been shaken to pieces over the centuries is now underwater. Roman docks can still sometimes be seen beneath the surface.

Solfatara

What's troubling Pozzuoli can be seen more clearly just outside the town at Solfatara, the storm centre of what the Greeks called the **Phlegraean** (fiery) **Fields**, (the Campi Flegrei). To the Romans, it was the *Forum Vulcani*, and a major attraction of the Campanian coast. It hasn't changed much since. Solfatara (*open daily 8.30–7; adm*) is another crater of a collapsed volcano, but one that just can't be still; sulphur gas vents, bubbling mud pits and whistling superheated steam fumaroles decorate

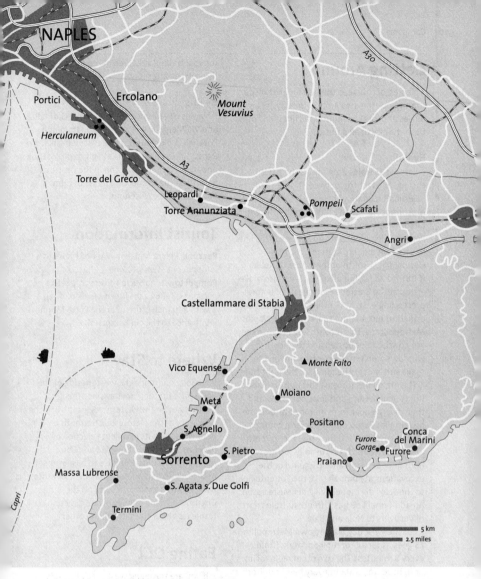

the eerie landscape. Dangerous spots are fenced off, and guides are sometimes available to lead you around. Their favourite trick is to hold a smoking torch to one of the fumaroles – making a dozen others nearby go off at the same time. The effect is produced by the steam condensing around smoke particles. Solfatara is perfectly safe, even though the ground underneath feels hot and sounds strangely hollow. It is; scientists keep a close watch on the huge plug of cooled lava that underlies the whole of the area about Pozzuoli, and they say the pressure on it from below is one-third as much as it was under Vesuvius in AD 79.

We promised you a baby volcano, and you'll see it near the coast west of Pozzuoli. **Monte Nuovo** has been quiet for some time (inexplicably passing up the opportunity

Getting Around

Naples, of course, is the hub for all transport throughout the area around the bay; buses, ferries and local commuter rail lines lead out from the city to all points.

By Rail

Regular **FS trains** aren't much help here, except for a fast trip between Naples and Salerno. Fortunately there are local lines. The most important is the refreshingly efficient **Circumvesuviana**, the best way to reach Pompeii, Herculaneum and Sorrento. This line has its own modern station, on Corso Garibaldi just south of the Piazza Garibaldi (t 081 772 2444), but all of its trains also make a stop at the Stazione Centrale itself before proceeding east. At Centrale their station is underground, sharing space with the Naples Metropolitana; this is confusing because there are no schedules posted and the ticket windows aren't marked – ask someone to make sure you are heading for the right train. The main lines run east through **Ercolano** (for Herculaneum) and Torre del Greco, and then diverge near Torre Annunziata, one line heading for Sarno, out in the farm country east of Vesuvius, and the other for Sorrento. Circumvesuviana trains usually run every half-hour between 5am and 10.45pm. For the excavations at **Pompeii** take the Sorrento line to the Scavi di Pompeii/Villa dei Misteri stop. An additional line has infrequent trains north of Vesuvius to Nola and Baia.

For the west bay, Naples' own **Metropolitana FS** goes as far as Pozzuoli-Solfatara (trains every 8 minutes). The two other regional lines both have trains about every half-hour from Piazza Montesanto Station, near the Piazza Dante. The **Ferrovia Cumana** (t 081 551 3328) runs along the shore, through Fuorigrotta, Bagnoli, Pozzuoli and Baia to Torregáveta (trains every 10 minutes).

The remarkable **Circumflegrea** (also t 081 551 3328), easily the most macabre railway in the western world, also finishes at Torregáveta, after passing through plenty of places you won't want to visit (trains every 20 minutes) but usually goes only as far as Licola. For the stop at the archaeological site of Cumae it runs six trains daily, three in the morning and three in the afternoon.

By Bus

Naples **city bus** no.152, from Piazza Garibaldi and Via Mergellina, travels to Solfatara and Pozzuoli. A **blue bus** run by Sepsa departs from Piazza Garibaldi and calls at Solfatara, Pozzuoli and Baia. From the bus stop in the centre of Baia, there are connecting buses to Cumae, Bacoli and Cape Misenum.

Tourist Information

Pozzuoli: Piazza Matteoti 1/A, t 081 526 6639 (*open June–Sept 9–2 and 4–8*).
Pompei town: Via Sacra 1, 80045, t 081 850 7255, f 081 863 2401 (*open Mon–Sat 9–3*), with a branch office near the Porta Marina entrance to the old Pompeii site.

Where to Stay

Nobody has made the **western** side of the bay a base for their holiday since the 4th century AD. On the **eastern** side of the bay, the proximity of the picturesque **Sorrentine peninsula**, with its excellent selection of hotels between Vico Equense and Sorrento, means you would be unwise to base yourself in the built-up semi-industrial area. **Sorrento** itself is only 40 minutes away on the Circumvesuviana railway in one direction, **Naples** is about the same in the other.

Eating Out

If you are travelling west specially to visit the classical sites you may prefer to grab a sandwich; the mini-market in **Solfatara** is a good place to pick up a *panino* for a picnic on the acropolis at Cuma (modern Cumae). At **Baia** there is a mini-market opposite the station. If you're in need of a proper sit-down, there are a few good places to have lunch.

Pozzuoli

Il Tempio, Via Serapide 13, t 081 866 517 (*moderate*). The harbour area of modern

Pozzuoli is not particularly scenic, but if you are fresh off the ferry from the islands of Ischia and Procida, or visiting the amphitheatre and Serapeum, there are two recommendations. Overlooking the ruined temple in Pozzuoli's main square, this restaurant is justly famous for its *antipasti*. Leave all the decision-making to the waiter and he will happily bring you plate after plate of mostly fish-based dishes – including octopus, fried squid, baby red mullet, clams and giant prawns – until you tell him to stop. Many people call it a day after this, and few ever get beyond the *primi*. *Closed Wed.*

La Granzeola, Via Cupa Fasane, t 081 524 3430 (*expensive*). On the way out of Pozzuoli along the coastal road, owner-chef Carmine Russo turns fish bought directly off the local boats into a dazzling array of unusual and tasty dishes. Try the *rigatoni con ragù di cozze* – short tubes of pasta with a mussel sauce. *Closed Sun.*

Baia to Cuma

L'Altro Cucchiaro, Via Lucullo 13, t 081 868 7196 (*expensive*). You can dine here on divine concoctions of seafood and pasta, as well as superb fish. The restaurant is just opposite Baia's railway station and is perfectly placed to restore your energies for a visit to the archaeological park. *Closed Sun evenings, Mon and three weeks in Aug.*

Villa Chiara, Via Torre di Cappella 10, t 081 868 7139 (*moderate*). One of several decent seafood places between Cuma and Fusaro.

Giardino degli Aranci, Via Cuma 75, t 081 854 3120 (*moderate*). If you are hungry after visiting the archaeological site at Cuma, this fish restaurant is a safe bet.

Torregáveta

Al Pontile, Via Spiaggia Torregáveta, t 081 868 9180 (*cheap*). Restaurants in shabbyish Torregáveta are cheaper than in the towns inside the bay; this restaurant has full dinners for reasonable prices.

Ercolano

The only on-site facilities at Herculaneum are toilets. There are a couple of options for a quick snack or a sit-down meal in the vicinity.

Bar degli Amorini. Opposite the entrance to the ruins, the bar has a deceptively small front, but upstairs there is a reasonable dining area, good for a snack or pizza.

Cagnano, Via Roma 17 (*cheap*). If you have any energy left after tramping around Herculaneum, this very simple *trattoria* is a short walk up the hill from the ruins , and serves huge bowlfuls of pasta, including a memorable *spaghetti alle vongole*.

Pompei

If you are spending the whole day in **ancient Pompeii** (which is only too easy) there is a restaurant on the site just beyond the ancient forum area through the Arch of Tiberius. The food from the self-service is nothing special; if you wish to escape the crowds opt for the waiter service and sit out under the colonnade adjoining the ancient baths.

Otherwise, restaurants in **modern Pompei** have a captive market in visitors to the ruins, and tourists are easy targets. You can choose for yourself among the ubiquitous multilingual menus, or try one of the following if you're in the mood for a treat:

Zi Caterina, Via Roma 20, t 081 850 7447 (*moderate*). With live lobsters in the tank and other noteworthy seafood dishes, this is also a good place to try *Lacrima Cristi* wine from the nearby slopes of Vesuvius. *Closed Tues evening.*

Al Gamberone, Via Piave 36, t 081 863 8322 (*moderate*). Close to Pompei's main church, you can feast here on prawns doused in cognac and other good fish dishes. In summer you can dine outside under the lemons and oranges. If you don't want fish there is an array of other dishes including a good *cannelloni*. *Closed Fri.*

Anfiteatro, Via Plinio 9, t 081 863 1245. Here the seafood is more modest – it's one of the few places in Pompei you'll see *baccalà* (salt cod) on the menu, along with truly good *spaghetti alle vongole*. It is immediately outside the exit of the excavations, next to the amphitheatre. *Closed Fri.*

In the harbour at **Castellamare di Stabia**, the sprawl of sheds is much favoured by locals who come to dine *al fresco* in the hot summer evenings.

to celebrate its 450th birthday, on 29 September 1988). The same earthquake in 1538 that wrecked much of Pozzuoli gave birth to this little cone. It's only about 460ft tall, and an easy climb up to the crater (you can have a picnic inside it).

Capo Miseno

Baia, the next town along the coast, was nothing less than the greatest pleasure dome of classical antiquity. Anybody who was anybody in the Roman world had a villa here, with a view of the sea, beach access, and a few hundred slaves to dust the statues and clean up after the orgies. You'll find little hint of that today: Goths, malaria and earthquakes have done a thorough job of wrecking the place. Most of ancient Baia is now underwater, a victim of the same *bradyseism* that afflicts Pozzuoli. In summer, a glass-bottomed boat departs from Baia harbour to see this Roman Atlantis (*t 081 526 57 80; tours depart Sat 12 and 4, Sun 10.30, 12 and 4; they last 70 mins*). On land the humble remains of the imperial villa can be visited at the **Parco Archeologico** (*open daily 9–one hour before sunset; adm*).

At Baia, the coast curves southwards towards Bacoli and **Capo Miseno** (Cape Misenum), a beautiful spot that for centuries was the greatest naval base of the Roman Empire, home to 10,000 sailors. As at Baia, foundations, columns and cornices are everywhere, though nothing of real interest has survived. Nearby **Lake Miseno**, also called the 'Dead Sea', was once a part of the base, joined to the sea by a canal.

Two other lakes, both created as a by-product of volcanic action, lie north of Capo Miseno; one, the **Lago di Fusaro,** is a large, shallow oyster farm, cut off from the sea by a sand bar near the woebegone fishing village of **Torregáveta**, the terminus of the Circumflegrea and Cumana railways. The decaying rococo palace on an island is the casino, built in 1782 by the Bourbon kings' favourite architect, Luigi Vanvitelli. **Lago d'Averno** – Lake Avernus – may ring a bell: it's the mouth of Hell, according to the ancient Greeks, who believed any passing bird would be suffocated by the infernal fumes rising from it. Cornelius Agrippa didn't have much respect for mythology, and he turned the lake into a part of the naval base by cutting another canal.

Cumae

As the story has it, King Tarquin of Rome came here, to the most venerable and respected oracle in all the western Mediterranean, with the intention of purchasing nine prophetic books from the Cumaean Sibyl. Unwisely, he said they were too dear, whereupon the Sibyl threw three of the books into the fire and offered him the remaining six at the same price. Again he complained, and the Sibyl put three more in the flames; finally Tarquin gave up, and took the last three at the original price. It was a good bargain. The Sibylline Books guided Rome's destiny until they too were burned up in the great fire of 82 BC.

Cumae had other distinctions too. As one of the first Greek foundations in Italy the city was the mother colony for Naples and many other cities of Magna Graecia. In 421 BC *Cumae* lost its independence to the Samnites, and declined steadily from then on; Arab raiders, who did so much damage everywhere else around Campania, finally wiped the city off the map in the 9th century AD. They did a good job of it, and there is little to see at the site (*open daily 9–one hour before sunset; adm*), only foundations of a few temples on the high **acropolis**, worth the climb for the views around Capo Miseno. One of the ruins was a famous Temple of Apollo, rebuilt by Augustus in thanks to the god after his victory at Actium. Just below the summit, you may visit the **Cave of the Cumaean Sibyl** itself, discovered by accident in 1932. This was the setting of Aeneas' famous encounter with the Sibyl who leads him into the underworld, described in Book 6 of Virgil's *Aeneid*. It is a place of mystery, a long series of strange, trapezoidal galleries cut out of solid rock – impressive enough, even stripped of the sumptuous decoration they must once have had (all ancient oracles were marvellously profitable). Nobody has a clear idea how old it is; by classical times, it had taken the form of an oracle quite like the one at Delphi. At the far end of the cave a plain alcove with two benches marks the spot where the Sibyls would inhale fumes over the sacred tripod, chew laurel leaves and go into their trance.

East of Naples: Mount Vesuvius and *Pompeii*

Despite its fearsome reputation, and its formidable appearance looming over Naples, **Mount Vesuvius** is a midget as volcanoes go – only 4,202ft. No one even suspected it was a volcano, in fact, until it surprised the people of *Pompeii*, *Herculaneum*, and *Stabiae* on 24 August AD 79.

That titanic eruption did not include much lava, but it buried *Herculaneum* under mud and the other two cities under cinders and ash, while coating most of Italy with a thin layer of dust. Over a hundred eruptions since have destroyed various towns and villages, some more than once. But, like at Mount Etna in Sicily, people just can't stay away from Vesuvius' slopes. Volcanic soil grows grapes and olives in abundance, though the novelty of it often makes the Italians exaggerate their quality. The AD 79 explosion hasn't been equalled since; it blew the top of the mountain clean off, leaving two peaks, with the main fissure in between. The lower one is called Monte Somma, or *nasone* ('big nose') by the Neapolitans; the higher peak is Vesuvius proper.

Vesuvius was last heard from in 1944. The final eruption left the lava flows you'll see on the upper slopes; it also sealed the main fissure, putting an end to the permanent plume of smoke that was a familiar landmark. You can bet the scientists are watching Vesuvius, however, despite its long hiatus: if it erupted now, it would be a catastrophe – the area around the volcano is one of the most densely populated in all Italy.

To visit the main crater, between the two peaks (*open daily 9–5; adm*), take the Vesuvius bus from the Circumvesuviana stop in Ercolano; then you have a stiff half-hour climb up the ash path. Dismiss all hopes of an easy ascent to the top singing '*Funiculi, funicula*' from the legendary Thomas Cook cable railway, long since defunct. The white scar up the side of the crater – left by a second funicular which was due to replace the 1970s' chairlift – continues a running saga. Work halted after argument for control over it between the two *comuni* of Torre del Greco and Ercolano. While they argued, the money 'disappeared'. Now the environmentalists have got a headache campaigning for colouring the concrete back Vesuvius style.

Herculaneum

Open daily Mar–Sept 8.30–7.30, Oct–Feb 8.30–5; last tickets 1½hrs earlier; adm.

Naples' discouraging industrial sprawl spreads eastwards as far as Torre del Greco; the drab suburb of Ercolano is a part of it, built over the mass of rock that imprisons ancient *Herculaneum*, a smaller and less famous sight than *Pompeii* but just as much worth visiting. Some people like it better than its more famous sister site.

Unlike *Pompeii*, an important commercial centre, *Herculaneum* seems to have been a wealthy resort, only about one-third the size. Also, Vesuvius destroyed them in different ways. *Pompeii* was buried under layers of ash, while *Herculaneum*, much closer to the volcano, drowned under a sea of mud. Over time the mud hardened to a soft stone, preserving the city and nearly everything in it as a sort of fossil – furniture, clothing and even some of the goods in the shops have survived.

Like *Pompeii*, *Herculaneum* was discovered by accident. In the early 1700s, an Austrian officer named Prince Elbeuf had a well dug here, and not too far down, the workmen struck a stone pavement – the stage of the city's theatre. The Bourbon government began some old-fashioned destructive excavation, but serious archaeo-logical work began only under Mussolini. Only about eight blocks of shops and villas, some quite fashionable, have been excavated. The rest is covered not only by tens of metres of rock, but also by a dense modern neighbourhood; bringing more of *Herculaneum* to light is a fantastically slow and expensive operation, but new digs are still going on. At any given time, most of the buildings will be locked, but the guards wandering about have all the keys and will show you almost any of them upon request (they are not supposed to accept tips, but they often seem to expect them).

Many of the most interesting houses can be found along **Cardo IV**, the street in the centre of the excavated area. On the corner of the *Decumanus Inferior*, the **House of the Wooden Partition** is a fine example of the façade of a Roman house: inside there is an amazingly preserved wooden screen used for separating the *tablinum* – the master's study – from the *atrium*. Next door, the **Trellis House** was a modest dwelling, with a built-in workshop. The **House of the Mosaic Atrium**, down the street, is another luxurious villa built with a sea view from the bedrooms upstairs. On the other side of the *decumanus*, Cardo IV passes the **Samnite House** (so named because of its early-style *atrium*), and further up a column with police notices painted on it stands near the **House of the Neptune**, with a lovely mythological mosaic in the atrium.

The **Suburban Baths**, near the entrance to the site, are probably the best-preserved baths of antiquity, with stucco reliefs depicting warriors, and a central furnace that is perfectly intact. Other buildings worth a visit are the **House of the Deer,** with its infamous statue of a drunken Hercules relieving himself picturesquely; the well-preserved **Baths**; and the *Palaestra*, or gym, with its unusual serpent fountain and rather elegant, cross-shaped swimming pool.

Beyond Ercolano, the coastal road carries on through modern housing blocks built to rehouse the homeless after the 1980 earthquake. The men of **Torre del Greco** have long been famous for gathering and working coral, a business threatened by pollution: much of the coral is now imported from Asia, though still worked locally.

The Roman Villa at Oplontis

Torre Annunziata, the next town, is another sorry place with a serious drug problem – but renowned for its pasta production. The Roman villa here, known as the **Villa Poppaea** at Oplontis, Via Sepolcri (*open daily 9–one hour before sunset; adm*) is worth a detour. If you are arriving on the Circumvesuviana, exit the station, walk downhill over the crossroads, and head for the open area on the left opposite the military zone.

Two-thirds of the villa have been fully excavated, revealing an extremely opulent pad with its own private bath complex, servants' quarters, monumental reception rooms and ornamental pool. There are beautiful wall paintings depicting scenes of monumental halls hung with military arms, a magnificent tripod set between a receding colonnade, bowls of figs and fresh fruit, vignettes of pastoral idylls including one with Hercules under a tree with the apples of the Hesperides. The part of the villa near the road is dominated by the great *atrium* hall and the family quarters. Outside the latrines, partitioned for each sex, it may have been one of the slaves who left his name, scrawled in Greek, 'Remember Beryllos'.

An amphora marked with the name Poppaea has given rise to the suggestion that the villa may have belonged to the wealthy Roman family, the *gens* Poppaea, who also owned the House of Menander at *Pompeii*. The most infamous member of this family was Sabina Poppaea, who used her fabulous charms to captivate the emperor Nero, leaving her second husband Otho – another future emperor – who was rapidly dispatched to Lusitania. Spurred on by her, Nero killed off his mother Agrippina and his first wife Octavia. Nero eventually killed Poppaea by mistake in a fit of rage in AD 65, viciously kicking her in the abdomen while she was pregnant.

Pompeii

Open Mar–Sept 8–6 and Oct–Feb 8.30–3.30; adm.

Herculaneum may have been better preserved, but to see an entire ancient city come to life, the only place on earth you can go is this magic time capsule, left to us by the good graces of Mount Vesuvius. *Pompeii* is no mere ruin; walking down the old Roman high street, you can peek into the shops, read the graffiti on the walls, then wander off down the back streets to explore the homes of the inhabitants and appraise their taste in painting – they won't mind a bit if you do. Almost everything we know for sure concerning the daily life of the ancients was learned here, and the huge mass of artefacts and art dug up over 200 years is still helping scholars to re-evaluate the Roman world.

Though a fair-sized city by Roman standards, with a population of some 20,000, *Pompeii* was probably only the third or fourth city of Campania, a trading and manufacturing centre of no special distinction. Founded perhaps in the 7th century BC, the city came under the Roman sphere of influence around 200; by the fateful year of AD 79 it was still a cosmopolitan place, culturally more Greek than Roman. Vesuvius' rumblings, and the tall, sinister-looking cloud that began to form above it, gave those Pompeiians with any presence of mind a chance to leave. Only about 10 per cent of the population was foolish enough to stay behind and perish.

Roman Frescoes

Not surprisingly, *Pompeii* and *Herculaneum* have been of prime importance in the study of Roman painting. It is impossible to know how much of this art was borrowed from the Greeks or the Etruscans, although by the time of Augustus it appears that Rome and Campania were in the vanguard. New fashions set in the palaces of the Palatine Hill were quickly copied in the villas of the Roman California. Or perhaps it was vice versa.

Wealthy Romans tended to regard their homes as domestic shrines rather than a place to kick off their *caligae* and relax after a hard day at the forum (the public baths served that role – the ancient Italians behaved much like the modern ones, who do everything in groups of ten and can't bear being alone); at home they used as many mosaics and wall paintings as they could afford to lend the place the necessary dignity. In *Pompeii* and *Herculaneum*, four styles of painting have been defined by art historians, although as you roam the ruins you'll find that they often overlap.

Style I (2nd century BC) was heavily influenced by Hellenistic models, especially from Alexandria: walls are divided into three sections, often by bands of stucco, with a cornice and frieze along the top and square panels (*dados*) on the bottom, while the middle sections are skilfully painted to resemble rich marble slabs. The prediliction for deep colours, combined with the lack of windows, often makes these small rooms seem somewhat claustrophobic to us (*see* the Samnite House, *Herculaneum*).

Later Romans must have felt the same lack of air and space for, in about 90 BC, they moved on to the 'architectonic' **Style II**. Columns and architraves were painted around the edges of the wall, an architectural screen designed to provide an illusion of depth and space on the large central panels. At first the centres were more pseudo-marble, but landscapes and mythological scenes soon became more popular.

After the city was buried under the stones and ash of the eruption the upper floors still stuck out; these were looted, and gradually cleared by farmers, and eventually the city was forgotten altogether. Engineers found it while digging an aqueduct in 1600, and the first excavations began in 1748 – a four-star attraction for northern Europeans on the Grand Tour. The early digs were far from scientific; archaeologists today sniff that they did more damage than Vesuvius. Resurrected *Pompeii* has had other problems: theft of artworks, a good dose of bombs in the Second World War, and most recently the earthquake of 1980. The damage from that is still being repaired today, though almost all the buildings are once more open to visitors.

There are two ways to see *Pompeii*; spend two or three hours on the main sights, or devote the day to scrutinizing details, for a total immersion in the ancient world you won't find anywhere else (the detailed guidebooks sold in the stands outside will help you with this). Your ticket (hang on to it) also entitles you to entrance to the Villa of the Mysteries (*see* p.925). This is located five minutes' walk up the Viale Villa dei Misteri, to the left on exiting the Circumvesuviana. This is best left to the end of your sightseeing (*site open daily Mar–Sept 8–6, Oct–Feb 8.30–3.30; adm*).

The Villa of the Mysteries near *Pompeii* is a prime example; it is also one of the oldest to have portraits of real people, or at least local character types.

Vitruvius, the celebrated writer on architecture, sternly disapproved of **Style III**, which abandoned the pretence and architectural dissimulation in favour of more playful compositions in perspective, still always done with a strict regard for symmetry. A favourite motif was patterns of foliage, fountains and candelabras, decorated with delicate, imaginative figures; these would be called 'grotesques' in the Renaissance, when Raphael and his friends rediscovered some in a Roman 'grotto' that was really a part of Nero's Golden House. The middle panels are often done in solid colours, with small scenes at the centre to resemble framed paintings. In *Pompeii* examples include the Houses of Lucretius Fronto and the Priest Amandus, the latter done by a remarkable artist who comes close to scientific perspective, albeit with several vanishing points.

The last fashion to hit *Pompeii* before Vesuvius did, **Style IV**, combines the architectural elements of Style II and the framed picture effects of Style III, but with a much greater degree of elaboration and decoration. Additional small scenes are placed on the sides – among the subjects covered are landscapes, still lifes, genre scenes from everyday life and architectural *trompe l'œil* windows done with a much more refined use of perspective (*see* the House of the Vettii). Sometimes an entire stage would be painted, with the curtain pulled aside to show a scene from a play; borders are decorated with garlands of flowers, leering satyrs, grotesques and frolicking Cupids (Italians call these *amoretti*, or 'little loves'). Humorous vignettes of the gods and incidents from Virgil's *Aeneid* were popular, along with images of *Pompeii*'s divine patroness, Venus. She also inspired the subject matter of the frescoes you have to bribe the guards to see.

Pompeii isn't quite a perfect time capsule; a little background will help to complete the picture. The site today is all too serene, with a small-town air; in fact almost every building was two or three storeys high, and most streets of a Roman town were market-places – rather like modern Naples. As long as daylight lasted, *Pompeii* would have been crowded with improvised *bancarelle*; any wagon-driver who wished to pass would need all manner of creative cursing. At least the streets are well-paved – better than Rome itself in fact; Campania's cities, the richest in western Europe, could well afford such luxuries. All the pavements were much smoother and more even than you see them now. The purpose of the flat stones laid across the streets should not be hard to guess. They were places to cross when it rained – streets here were also drains – and the slots in them allowed wagon wheels to pass through.

The shops, open to the street in the day, would be sealed up behind shutters at night, just as they are in the old parts of Mediterranean cities today. Houses, on the other hand, turned a blank wall to the street; they got all their light and air from skylights in the *atrium*, the roofed court around which the rooms were arranged.

Later, fancier villas have a second, open court directly behind the first, designed after the Greek *peristyle*. As in Rome, no part of town was necessarily the fashionable district; elegant villas would be found anywhere, often between two simple workmen's flats. And don't take the street names too seriously. They were bestowed by the archaeologists, often, as with the Via di Mercurio (Mercury Street), after mythological subjects depicted on the street fountains.

Around the Forum

Past the throng of hawkers and refreshment stands, the main entrance to the site takes you through the walls at the **Porta Marina**. Just inside the gate, the **Antiquarium** displays some of the artworks that haven't been spirited off to the museum in Naples, as well as some truly gruesome casts of fossilized victims of the eruption, caught in their death poses.

Two blocks beyond the Antiquarium and you're in the **Forum**, oriented towards a view of Vesuvius. Unfortunately this is the worst-preserved part of town. Here you can see the tribune from which orators addressed public meetings, and the pedestals that held statues of heroes and civic benefactors, as well as the once-imposing **Basilica** (law courts), temples to Apollo and Jupiter, and, among other buildings, a public latrine and a **Macellum**, or market, decorated with frescoes.

Down Mercury Street

Heading for *Pompeii*'s old East End, there are several interesting houses along the Via di Mercurio, and the **Temple of Fortuna Augusta** on the corner of Via di Nola. The real attractions in this part of town, though, are a few lavish villas off on the side streets: the enormous **House of Pansa**; the **House of the Faun**, with the oldest-known welcome mat (set in the pavement, really); and the wonderful **House of the Vettii**, owned by a pair of wealthy brothers who were oil and wine merchants.

Here are several rooms of excellent, well-preserved paintings of mythological scenes, as well as the famous **picture of Priapus**. This over-endowed sport, in legend the son of Venus and Adonis, and a couple of wall paintings along the lines of the Kama Sutra, has managed to make *Pompeii* something more than a respectable tourist trap. There are quite a few paintings of Priapus showing it off in the houses of *Pompeii*, besides the phallic images that adorn bakers' ovens, wine shops and almost every other establishment in town. The Pompeiians would be terribly embarrassed, however, if they knew what you were thinking. They were a libidinous lot, like anyone else fortunate enough to live on the Campanian coast during recorded history, but the omnipresent phalluses were never meant as decoration. Almost always they are found close to the entrances, where their job was to ward off the evil eye. This use of phallic symbols against evil probably dates from the earliest times in southern Italy; the horn-shaped amulets that millions of people wear around their necks today are their direct descendants. Even so, not long ago women visiting *Pompeii* were not allowed to set eyes on the various erotic images around the site, and were obliged by the guides to wait chastely outside while their male companions went in for a peek.

The nearby Via di Nola, one of *Pompeii*'s main streets, leads to the north. It passes the **Central Baths**, a construction that was not yet completed when Vesuvius went off, and the **House of Marcus Fronto**, with more good paintings and a reconstructed roof.

The 'New Excavations'

Beginning in 1911, the archaeologists cleared a vast area of western *Pompeii*, around what was probably the most important thoroughfare of the city, now called the Via dell'Abbondanza. Three blocks west of the Forum, this street leads to the Via dei Teatri and the **Triangular Forum**, bordering the southern walls. Two **theatres** here are worth a visit, a large open one seating 5,000, and a smaller, covered one for concerts. The big quadrangle, originally a lobby for the theatres, seems to have been converted at one point into a gladiators' barracks. This is only one of the disconcerting things you will find on the streets of *Pompeii*. The ruined temple in the Triangular Forum was already long ruined in AD 79, and scholars who study the art of the city find the last (fourth) period betrays a growing lack of skill and coarseness of spirit – it seems 1st-century *Pompeii* had its share of urban problems and cultural malaise.

The Via dell'Abbondanza

Next to the theatres, a small **Temple of Isis** testifies to the religious diversity of *Pompeii*; elsewhere around town there is graffiti satirizing that new and troublesome cult, the Christians. Three blocks north, there is a stretch of Via dell'Abbondanza that is one of the most fascinating corners of *Pompeii*. Among its shops are a smith's, a grocer's, a weaver's, a laundry and a typical Roman tavern with its modest walk-up brothel. The most common are those with built-in tubs facing the street – shops that sold wine, and oil for cooking and for lamps. Notices painted on the walls announce coming games at the amphitheatre, or recommend candidates for public office.

Some of the best-decorated villas in this neighbourhood are to be found along the side streets: the **House of Loreius**, the **House of Amandus**, and an odd underground chamber called the **Cryptoporticus**. *Pompeii*'s two most impressive structures occupy a corner just within the walls: the **Palaestra**, a big colonnaded exercise yard, and the **Amphitheatre**, the best-preserved in Italy, with seating for about 20,000. Tacitus records that a fight broke out here between the Pompeiians and rival supporters from Nocera in a match staged in AD 59. Nero exiled those responsible for the games and forbade further spectacles for ten years.

Not all of *Pompeii*'s attractions are within the walls. If you have the time, it would be worth visiting the tombs around the **Via delle Tombe**. The Romans buried their dead outside their cities, the manner of burial depending on wealth and status. Here you can see impressive funerary monuments to local dignitaries and their families.

Finally, the famous **Villa dei Misteri**, a surburban villa located close to the same road out of *Pompeii*, is thought to have been used as a place of initiation in the forbidden Bacchic (or Dionysiac) Mysteries, one of the cults most feared by the Roman Senate, and later by the emperors. Scenes from the myth of Dionysus and of the rituals themselves are painted on the walls.

Modern Pompei

The town of Pompei (the modern town has one 'i'), an important pilgrimage centre, is also worth a visit, if nothing else for a look at the wonderfully overdone church, dedicated to the **Madonna di Pompei** (*open daily 6–2 and 3–6.30*). For a good view over the town and the excavations take the lift up the tower (*open daily 9–1 and 3–5; adm*). The Madonna of the church holds a special place in the affections of Neapolitan women. You'll probably see them, busily saying their rosaries, asking for the Madonna's intercession to help sort out their problems. If they have bare feet, this is not poverty, but devotion – usually the fulfilment of a personal pledge to the Madonna in thanks for a favour received. Neapolitans who ask for the Madonna's help often promise to walk there barefoot from Naples (26km) if their prayers are answered. It is only justice that Pompei should play host to the **Vesuvian Museum** on Via Colle San Bartolomeo (*open Mon–Sat 8–2; closed Sun*), a couple of minutes' walk from Piazza B. Longo in front of the church. This has more than enough to satisfy most basic volcano questions: prints of the volcano erupting, exhibits on the materials produced in eruptions and much more that is explosive.

On leaving Pompei the road leads to the beginning of the Sorrentine peninsula. At the foot of the peninsula lies **Castellammare di Stabia**, which little suggests the beauty further on. Roman *Stabiae* was the port of *Pompeii*, and the other big town destroyed by Vesuvius. Most famously it was where Pliny the Elder, who was in command of the fleet at *Misenum* during the AD 79 eruption, met his death as he tried to bring help to those fleeing the catastrophe. The description of the eruption and these events are recorded for posterity in his nephew's letter to Tacitus. Here, beneath a 12th-century Hohenstaufen **castle**, are the modern shipyards of the Italian navy. From Castellammare, you can take a short ride in the cable car (*open April–Oct*) up to **Monte Faito**, a broad, heavily forested mountain that may well be the last really tranquil spot on the bay – though a few hotels have already appeared – and a pleasant place for walks.

Sorrento

After Pompei, the coastline swings outwards to meet Capri. At first, there is little intimation that you are entering one of the most beautiful corners of all Italy. The first clue comes when the busy coast road begins to climb into a corniche at **Vico Equense**, a pretty village that is fast becoming a small resort, absorbing some of the overflow from Sorrento; there is a nice beach under the cliffs at the back of the town.

Sorrento began its career as a resort in the early 19th century, when Naples began to grow too piquant for English tastes. The English, especially, have never forsaken it; Sorrento's secret is a certain perfect cosiness, comfortable like a favourite cardigan. Visitors get the sense that nothing distressing is going to happen – and nothing ever does. It helps that Sorrento is a lovely, civilized old town. Not many resorts can trace their ancestry back to the Etruscans, or claim a native son like the poet Torquato Tasso. (Today, the Sorrentines are more proud of a songwriter named De Curtio, whose *Come Back to Sorrento*, they claim, ranks with *O Sole Mio*.)

Sorrento doesn't flagrantly chase after your money, unlike other places in Italy, and it lacks the garishness of, say, Rimini. But Sorrento's one big drawback is its lack of a

Getting Around

One line of the Circumvesuviana (*see* p.916) goes to Sorrento, where its terminal is two streets east of Piazza Tasso. Trains usually run every half-hour between 5am and 10.45pm. On a *direttissima*, of which there are several daily, the Naples–Sorrento trip takes 1 hour 10 minutes; locals are much slower. There is an **airport** bus to Sorrento three times a day.

Sorrento is also well connected in summer by **ferries** and **hydrofoils** which ply from the Marina Piccola to Capri, Amalfi, Positano and Naples during daylight hours. In winter only reduced services to Capri and Naples operate. **Caremar**, t 081 807 3077, f 081 807 2479, run five ferries daily to Capri and back, which take 45 minutes. **Linea Jet**, t 081 878 1861, run hydrofoils to Capri eight times a day, taking 20 minutes. **Alilauro**, t 081 878 1430, run 17 daily hydrofoil crossings to Capri. They also offer a fast alternative to the Circumvesuviana to Naples, a hydrofoil which takes 30 minutes. These run to both Molo Beverello near the Castel Nuovo and to the berths at Mergellina. The same company operates four services daily to Positano, which continue to Amalfi, and a single daily service from Sorrento to Ischia leaving at 9.30 and returning at 5.20.

Tourist Information

Sorrento: Via L. de Maio 35, 80067, t 081 807 4033, f 081 877 3397. Very helpful for rooms (*open 8.45–7.15; closed Sun and hols*).
Vico Equense: Via S. Ciro 16, 80069, t 081 879 8826, f 081 879 9351.

Where to Stay

Sorrento ✉ 80067

Sorrento isn't the status resort it once was, but it still seems to have more four-star places than anywhere in Italy; most of them are good bargains too, compared to their equivalents further north.

Very Expensive–Expensive

★★★★Excelsior Vittoria, Piazza T. Tasso 34, t 081 807 1044, f 081 877 1206, *exvitt@exvitt.it*. For a plunge into a Grand Tour atmosphere, this is the place to stay. Built at the turn of the century and owned by the same family for four generations, it's set in its own plush park complete with orange and olive groves, overlooking the sea. Wagner, Dumas, Nietzsche, Princess Margaret, Sophia Loren and Luciano Pavarotti have all stopped by here for a night or two.
★★★★Imperial Tramontano, t 081 878 2588, f 081 807 2344, *imperial@tramontano.com*. In a central location, set in incredible tropical gardens on Via Vittorio Veneto, this is one of the places long favoured by British travellers, as is evident from the club-like décor. There is a lift down to the private beach and, if you can't make it that far, there is also a pool.
★★★★Bellevue-Syrene, Piazza della Vittoria 5, t 081 878 1024, f 081 878 3963. Another villa-hotel near the Tramontana. This one has lush gardens and beautifully restored rooms as well as a lift to the beach. The cliff-top colonnade is a lovely spot for a drink even if you are not staying. Don't be put off by the pompous staff.

Moderate

★★La Tonnarella, Via Capo 31, t 081 878 1153, f 081 878 2169. In an attractive villa with some of the best views in Sorrento, with a pleasant private beach, and a good restaurant to boot, this hotel is a real bargain. Book early.
★★★Minerva, Via Capo 30, t 081 878 1011, f 081 878 1949. On the road east out of Sorrento, with 50 nice rooms, some with stunning views over the sea. *Closed Nov–Mar.*

decent beach – though at the fancier hotels you may enjoy taking a lift down to the sea. There are also several *stabilimenti* – piers jutting out into the sea, which are kitted out with loungers and beach umbrellas, which you pay a hire charge to use.

Sorrento was never a large town, though in the Middle Ages it was for a while an important trading post. The Sorrentini still recall with pride that their fleet once beat

Vico Equense ✉ 80069

Loreley et Londres, Via Califano 2, **t** 081 807
3187 (*moderate*). A *pensione* with lovely sea
views. The friendly staff make up for the
slightly drab décor, and the sea terrace
provides the most romantic sunsets in town.
In summer you have to stay half board to
get a room with a sea view, but there's also a
lift down to a private sea-bathing platform.
Closed mid-Nov–mid-Mar.

★★★★**Capo La Gala, t** 081 801 5758, **f** 081 879
874 (*cheap*). In Vico Equense the best places
to stay are outside the town centre. This is a
beautiful modern resort hotel, on the beach
at nearby Scrajo (where there are heathily
pungent sulphur springs). Every room has a
terrace on the beach. *Closed Nov–Mar.*

★**City,** Corso d'Italia 221, **t/f** 081 877 2210
(*cheap*). This is one of the nicest of several
simple hotels around the town centre. It is
close to everything but not too noisy.

Eating Out

Very Expensive–Expensive

Da Pappone, t 081 808 1209. This elegant
restaurant at Nerano, on the road from
Sorrento to Massa Lubrense, specializes in
fish fresh out of the sea, and elaborate (but
pricey!) *antipasto* surprises.

Caruso, Piazza Tasso, **t** 081 807 3156. The menu
here is vast and inventive, from a fine,
transclucent *carpaccio di manzo* with celery
and Parmesan to a rich *spigoletta salmonata
con pistacchi*. It all comes with sleek service
and an extensive wine list. The wintry
atmosphere and lack of outside tables
doesn't deter customers – booking for
dinner is essential. Try to leave room for the
dessert trolley. *Closed Mon from Oct to April.*

Don Alfonso, Piazza Sant'Agata, **t** 081 878
0026, **f** 081 533 0226, in Sant'Agata Sui Due
Golfi. A three-Michelin-starred restaurant

that some food critics reckon to be the best
in southern Italy. Food here is an art form,
beautifully cooked and presented on fine
china with wine served in crystal glasses. It's
run by husband-and-wife team Alfonso and
Livia Laccarino. Nine kilometres outside
Sorrento, the trip is well worth it; if you can't
make it home, book a room. *Closed Sun eve
Sept–May and Mon all year.*

Moderate–Cheap

O'Parrucchiano, Corso Italia 71, **t** 081 878 1321. If
setting is what you're after, this is the place.
Choose from a modest menu and dine
among a riot of tropical greenery, either in
the greenhouse or beneath the pergolas.

La Lanterna, Via S. Cesareo 23–25, **t** 081 878
1355. This is right in the thick of it all in
Sorrento, with outside tables. It has friendly
and efficient service and, most important,
impeccable *risotto alla pescatore*. *Closed Jan,
Feb, and Mon except July–Aug.*

Da Gigino, Via Degli Archi 15, **t** 081 878 1927. A
bustling family *trattoria* serving pizza and
pasta alongside sophisticated dishes such as
salmone e pesce spada affumicato con rucola
(smoked salmon and swordfish with rocket).

Trattoria da Emilia, Via Marina Grande 62,
t 081 807 2720. Come here for one of the
best deals in town and lots of cheery bustle.
Another family-run *trattoria*, with tables on
a terrace overlooking the sea, and a great-
value menu based on fresh local ingredients
and classic Sorrento recipes. *Closed Tues.*

Panetteria-Pizzeria Franco, Corso Italia 265,
t 081 877 2066. A great place for a take-away
or a very cheap meal. Sit at one of the long
wooden tables beneath the hams to watch
your pizza prepared. Popular with locals.

Maria Grazia, Via Marina del Cantone 65,
Nerano, **t** 081 808 1011. This restaurant's
namesake is renowned for her melt-in-the-
mouth *spaghetti con le zucchine*. People
come from all over the coast to savour it.

Amalfi's fleet in a sea battle (even though it was in 897). Today the population is only
15,000, although this figure is inflated daily in the summer months by the scores of
coaches and cruise ships disgorging British and American passengers. Sorrento comes
alive at dusk for the *passeggiata*, which goes on till late in the evening. Half the shop
windows seem to be displaying *intarsia* – surprisingly fine pictures done in inlaid

woods, a local craft for centuries. Look out too for the laboratories, open to the street, producing perfume and *limoncello*, the distinctive lemon liqueur made from the lemons grown throughout the peninsula.

Around Sorrento, as far as the mountains permit, stretches one of the great garden spots of Campania, a lush plain full of vines and lemon groves. From the town, to the west you can follow the winding path to the Bagni Regina Giovanna, a natural triangular seapool where you can see the scanty ruins of the Roman Villa di Pollio. You can also take the short trip to **Massa Lubrense**, an uncrowded fishing village with more fine views. Campanella Point, opposite the rugged outline of Capri, takes its name from the big bell that was hung here and rung to warn the towns around the bay when pirates were sighted.

The Amalfi Coast

When confronted with what is generally acclaimed to be the most beautiful stretch of scenery in the entire Mediterranean, the honest writer is at a loss. Few who have been there would argue the point, but describing it properly is another matter. Along this coast, where one mountain after another plunges sheer into the sea, there is a string of towns that not long ago were accessible only by boat. Today, a spectacular corniche road of 'a thousand bends' covers the route; necessity makes it so narrow that every encounter with an oncoming vehicle is an adventure, but everyone except the driver will have the treat of a lifetime. Nature here has created an amazing vertical landscape, a mix of sharp crags and deep green forests; in doing so she inspired the Italians to add three of their most beautiful towns.

This coast has always attracted foreigners, but only relatively recently has it become a major resort area. Places like Positano have become reserves for the wealthy, where swarms of day trippers are likely to descend at any moment. Rumour has it that the boutiques here are so fashionable that the Romans come to Positano to shop for their summer wardrobe. But tourism will never spoil this area; all the engineers in Italy couldn't widen the Amalfi road, and the impossible terrain leaves no room at all for new development.

Positano

To complement the vertical landscape, here is Italy's most nearly vertical town. Positano spills down from the corniche like a waterfall of pink, cream and yellow villas. The day-trippers may walk down to the sea; only the alpinists among them make it back up (fortunately, there is a regular bus service along the one main street). After the Second World War, Positano became a well-known hideaway for artists and writers – many of them American, following John Steinbeck's lead – and fashion was not slow to follow. Now, even though infested with coach parties, Positano reverts to the Positanesi in the off-season, and quietens down considerably. When you get to the bottom, there is a pebbly, grey beach and the town's **church**, decorated with a pretty tiled dome like so many others along this coast.

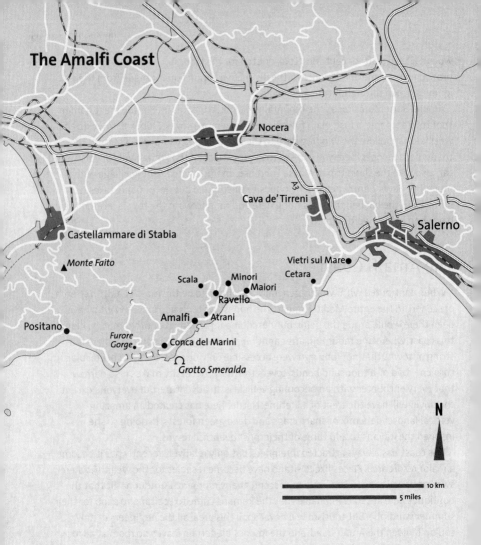

The Amalfi Coast

Nocera

Cava de' Tirreni

Salerno

Castellammare di Stabia

▲ Monte Faito

Vietri sul Mare

Cetara

Scala · Minori · Maiori

Ravello

Amalfi · Atrani

Positano

Furore Gorge

Conca del Marini

Grotto Smeralda

N

10 km

5 miles

If you have time, take a trip further up to **Montepertuso**, a village perched 3km above Positano, which takes its name (meaning 'hole in the mountain') from an old legend – the devil challenged the Virgin Mary to blow a hole in the mountain, saying the winner could have control of the village. The devil tried, but failed miserably, while the Virgin coolly walked through the mountainside, leaving a hole still visible today.

The next town east along the Drive from Positano, **Praiano**, could be Positano's little sister: with a similar beach and church, but not quite as scenic and perpendicular, and not quite as beleaguered by tourism. Her natural attractions, however, leave her ripe for creeping exploitation. After Praiano, look out for the most impressive natural feature along the Drive, the steep, impenetrable **Furore Gorge**. On either side are tiny isolated villages along the shore, with beaches – if only you could get to them. Further

Getting There and Around

The **express bus** from Naples to Salerno, which usually runs every half-hour, leaves Naples from the **SITA** office on Via Pisanelli, just off the Piazza Municipio, **t** 081 552 2176, and arrives in Salerno at the terminal at Corso Garibaldi 117, **t** 089 226 604.

SITA also runs the buses from Salerno for the **Amalfi coast**, with regular departures for **Sorrento** (in front of the Circumvesuviana station), or stopping short at Amalfi, Ravello or other towns en route; they are so frequent that it is easy to see all the main coast towns on a day-trip, hopping from one to the next. Buses are definitely the best way to do it; driving yourself can be a very hair-raising experience when it's busy.

Tourist Information

Positano: Via Saracino 4, **t** 089 875 067, **f** 089 875 760.
Amalfi: Corso Roma 19, **t** 089 871 107, **f** 089 872 619.
Ravello: Piazza Duomo, **t** 089 857 096, **f** 089 857 977.
Maiori: Corso Regina, **t** 089 877 452, **f** 089 853 672.
Salerno: Piazza V. Veneto (outside the railway station), **t/f** 089 231 432. A very helpful office. Its list of hotels throughout the province (including the Amalfi coast) is excellent.

Where to Stay

Positano ✉ 84017

With Positano's high-fashion status come some of the highest hotel prices in Italy. With a car, you can expand your horizons to include some of the more secluded spots along the coast. Tourism has yet to infiltrate the heart of Praiano and if you climb up behind the road, you will find a sleepy fishing village, undisturbed by the whirr of cameras or the rumble of coaches. Still, there is some pleasant accommodation running along the coast, much of it just outside the village at Vettica Maggiore – a little way back towards Positano along the Amalfi drive.

Luxury

*****San Pietro**, Via Laurito 2, **t** 089 875 455, **f** 089 811 449. If you're feeling self-indulgent – and very rich – you may care to stay at a place many believe to be the finest resort hotel in the country. It lies 1½km outside Positano en route to Amalfi. The entrance is hidden behind an old chapel, with only a discreet sign to alert you to the intimate paradise which spills down the cliff face beneath you. It's all part of the management's plan to maintain the privacy and tranquillity of its celebrity clientele. Amid the richly coloured gardens, 58 individual rooms are immaculately maintained, each offering a private terrace and spectacular views round every corner – even when you're soaking in a hot tub. It also offers a private beach and its own excursion boat.

*****Le Sirenuse**, Via Cristoforo Colombo 30, **t** 089 875 066, **f** 089 811 798, *info@sirenuse. it*. The former home of a noble Neapolitan family to whom it still belongs, it became a hotel in 1951 and takes its name from the islands of the Sirens which it overlooks. It'a all done with style, down to the swimming pool with its mosaic tiles. Cool and sophisticated, close to the shops and restaurants.

Very Expensive–Expensive

****Palazzo Murat**, Via dei Mulini 23, **t** 089 875 177, **f** 089 811 419, *hpm@starnet.it*. In the heart of Positano, this 18th-century *palazzo* once belonged to Napoleon's brother-in-law Joachim Murat, briefly King of Naples. It has plenty of old-world charm, with a courtyard shaded by lofty palm trees, where classical concerts are staged in summer. An elegant hotel with oodles of atmosphere.

****Covo dei Saraceni**, Via Regina Giovanna 5, **t** 089 875 400, **f** 089 875 878, *covo@starnet. it*. This is a comfortable hotel in one of the best locations in town, at the bottom of the hill on the edge of the harbour, with views up through town and out to sea. The rooms are simple and spacious, and furnished with antique furniture. Relax, and let the sound of the sea lull you to sleep at night.

Moderate

***Casa Albertina**, Via Tavolozza 3, **t** 089 875 143, **f** 089 811 540, *info@casalbertina.it*. On a more modest level, this hotel is furnished in a lovely understated manner, the better to accentuate the views over Positano and the sea. It's a family-run place a few minutes from the beach, with a nice restaurant on the rooftop terrace; in the busy season its quietness can be an advantage. Be aware that half board is compulsory in the high season. *Closed Nov–Mar.*

***Tramonto d'Oro**, Via Capriglione 119, t 089 874 955, f 089 874 670. This is an exceptional bargain offering a pool, beach access and great views. Staff are friendly and helpful and the rooms are decorated with attractive tiling and bright materials. The high number of regular customers speaks for itself.

Cheap

A few very cheap *pensioni* can also be found along Via Fornillo and on the other streets leading down to the beach. In Praiano, too, there are some cheaper old *pensioni* by the port, usually full to bursting in summer.

California, Via Cristoforo Colombo 141, t 089 875 382, f 089 812 154, *albergo.california@hpe.it*. This is one of the best bargains in Positano, with 15 very pleasant rooms and a lovely terrace for breakfast and other meals. Set slightly back from the sea, it is still well located, and charmingly run.

***Le Terrazze**, t 089 831 290. Look out for this clean and reliable option, run by the Tramonto d'Oro and right on the sea.

Amalfi ✉ 84011

Unlike Positano, Amalfi has been a resort for a long time, and some of its older establishments are among the most distinctive on the Mediterranean coast.

Very Expensive

*****Santa Caterina**, Via Nazionale 9, t 089 871 012, f 089 871 351. Just outside Amalfi, this converted villa has perhaps the loveliest gardens of all. It sits on a cliff-top providing sea views from most rooms. Its staff are courteous, its atmosphere cool and elegant.

Expensive

****Luna**, Via P.Comite 33, t 089 871 002, f 089 871 333. St Francis himself is said to have founded the Luna, though the lifts and Hollywood-style pool are a little more recent. This former monastery, above the drive on Amalfi's eastern edge, was already a hotel in the waning days of the Grand Tour – Wagner stayed here while searching for his Garden of Klingsor, and they can show you the room where Ibsen wrote *A Doll's House*. Among other famous guests, the owners claim the Luna to have been a favourite of both Mussolini and Otto von Bismarck. Deftly modernized, it provides comfortable rooms and attentive service.

****Cappuccini Convento**, Via Annunziatella 46, t 089 871 877, f 089 871 886, *cappuccini@amalfinet.it*. This old monastery (not a convent!) is your best bet if you want to get away from it all. It was built by Emperor Frederick II on a mountainside over the town in the 12th century. Today there is an ancient lift running down through the cliffs to the beach. The cells converted into hotel rooms are dark and unsophisticated, in keeping with the closed monastic order that once prevailed here. In the heart of it all is a chapel and cloister; they seem to ensure a spiritual hush. Set high above the tourist-infested streets, its colonnade bedecked with flowers offers Amalfi's best views.

Moderate

Lidomare, Largo Duchi Piccolomini 9, t 089 871 332, f 089 871 394, *lidomare@amalficoast.it*. A pleasant hotel in Piazza dei Dogi, not far from the cathedral but away from the crowds. Bright and airy rooms, a dim but cosy breakfast area and very obliging staff.

Sole, Largo della Zecca 2, t 089 871 147, f 089 871 926. Further along the Corso Roma, this cheaper option is located in a quiet piazza, behind the beach front. It's clean and airy, but there are only 15 rooms so you'll need to book in advance.

Cheap

Sant'Andrea, Via Santolo Camera 1, t 089 871 145. This tiny and elaborately furnished hotel is one of a fair collection of cheap places with good views of the cathedral. Expect an effusive welcome from your obliging hostess.

Ravello ✉ 84010

Ravello also has its share of dream hotels, offering no beaches, but unforgettable gardens and views down over the coast. In the shadow of Amalfi and Ravello, the two pleasant lidos of Minori and Maiori may seem dull, but they can be useful bases, especially if hotels in the better-known resorts are full.

Luxury

*****Palumbo**, Via S. Giovanni del Toro 28, t 089 857 244, f 089 858 133, *palumbo@amalfinet.it*. This is one of Ravello's finest, with an incredible guest book full of the names of the famous over the last century and a half. The entrance opens on to an elegant Arab-style courtyard which only hints at the 11 rooms, each individually decorated with antiques. The restaurant is highly renowned, and the excellent Episcopio wine really is house wine – made on the premises. It's certainly élitist and your absolute privacy is guaranteed – but if you are searching for a taste of the real Italy, the smart, international atmosphere might just disappoint. There is also a simpler *dipendenza* (cheaper) with six rooms.

Very Expensive

***Villa Cimbrone**, Via Santa Chiara 26, t 089 857 459, f 089 857 777, *villacimbrone@amalfinet.it*. With the lushest gardens on the coast, this is a very special place to stay. It's another elegant old villa, once the property of an English duke, set in its own parkland perched dizzyingly high on the cliffs. The 10 rooms are beautifully decorated (half with sea views) and the view from the terrace where breakfast is served is a feast of its own. There are drawbacks, such as the lack of a restaurant and the 10-minute walk to get there, but it has a swimming pool.

Expensive

****Caruso Belvedere**, Via S. Giovanni del Toro 2, t 089 857 111, f 089 857 372. This hotel was once popular with the Bloomsbury set and with Greta Garbo (she had room 21). Behind its sun-bleached façade, it encapsulates the quiet elegance of the old patrician villa it once was – even the laundry room holds a fading fresco. The present owner's grandfather, a cousin of the famous Neapolitan tenor Enrico Caruso, opened it as a hotel 100 years ago. In the beautifully laid out gardens, there is a belvedere over the sea and mountains, and the well-tended vegetable garden and vineyard on another level provide fresh produce and the hotel's own wine. Guests are encouraged to take half board, which is no real hardship since the food is superb, and meals are taken on one of the loveliest terraces in Ravello.

****Villa Maria**, Via Santa Chiara 2, t 089 857 255, f 089 857 071. A light, airy charm prevails in this gracious villa. It is one of the prettiest hotels, and perhaps the most welcoming place to stay in Ravello. First choice among such leading lights as Tim Robbins and Susan Sarandon, as well as the disgraced Andreotti (whose visit is barely acknowledged), it is made all the more attractive by the helpful and friendly owner, Vincenzo Palumbo, known to everyone as *il professore* or 'Prof'. The vast suite has one of the most breathtaking terraces in Ravello and there is a beautiful eating area in the garden, sheltered by vines and graced with yet another astonishing view. Even if you don't stay here, it's worth coming to eat. The restaurant recently won an award in the highly reputed Italian '*gambero rosso*' (red shrimp) scheme, and is known throughout the region.

Moderate

***Hotel Giordano**, Via Trinità 14, t 089 857 255, f 089 857 071, *giordano@amalfinet.it*. Under the same ownership as the Villa Maria, and only a few minutes' walk away, this modern hotel has a heated outdoor swimming pool. A comfortable alternative, it is reasonably priced and well stocked with useful information on the area. Villa Maria guests have equal access to the facilities.

****Cetus**, t/f 089 261388. Heading out to Salerno, you'll find this hotel in the tiny resort of Cetara, which is based around a fine sandy bay and ancient village. The hotel clings precariously to the cliffs between the devilish drive and the deep blue sea. Attractively redecorated with a hint of Art Deco, its isolated position and undisturbed bay make the Cetus a rising star among hotels on this coastline, its only disadvantage being the long journeys when travelling back and forth along the often packed Amalfi Drive. *Closed Nov–Mar.*

Cheap

★★Villa Amore, Via dei Fusco, t/f 089 857 135. For a five-star view at a third of the price in Ravello, why not check into this delightful small hotel? It has 12 clean simple rooms, and a lovely terrace where you can take cappuccino with the canaries. It retains a warm, homely atmosphere not common to most of the larger hotels in this area.

Villa Giuseppina, Via Toricella, t/f 089 857 106. This hotel in unspoilt Scala is another gem, offering comfort and charm at affordable prices. Good food and great views from the swimming pool make this a tranquil spot to while away those hazy days of summer.

Margherita, Via Toricella, t/f 089 857 106. An older-style hotel attached to Villa Giuseppina and sharing its facilities. You can enjoy some lovely walks down to Amalfi. Just be sure to catch the bus back.

★★Vittoria, Via F. Cerasuoli 4, t 089 877 652. One of several *pensioni* near the beach in Maiori that offer some of the most convenient budget accommodation on the Amalfi coast. Clean but unglamorous, it will suit anyone hoping to explore the coast without paying the price of its celebrity.

Eating Out

Positano

In the high season at least, most of the resort hotels along the coast will expect you to take half board, which means having either lunch or dinner in their restaurant; that's not always bad – some of the hotels have gourmet restaurants and are often good value. There are equally good places elsewhere to enjoy – if you can escape! Like many of the restaurants on the Costiera, a good number of Positano's eateries close from November till Easter.

Expensive

La Cambusa, Spiaggia Grande, t 089 875 432. In a lovely position with a terrace looking out on to the beach, this is a Positano favourite. The chef serves excellently cooked fresh fish and seafood in more ways than you can think of. A house speciality is *penne con gamberetti, rucola e pomodoro* (pasta with prawns, rocket and fresh tomatoes).

Buca Di Bacco, Via Rampa Teglia 8, t 089 875 699. Across the road from La Cambusa, this is another Positano institution and the place to stop off for a drink on the way back from the beach. The fish is always well-cooked here, and you'd be crazy to go for anything else. It also has a few rooms.

Chez Black, Via Brigantino 19, t 089 875 036. Right on the beach in Positano – and at the centre of the action in summer – this is a slick and sophisticated joint run by local entrepreneur Salvatore Russo. As with all the restaurants along the Spiaggia Grande, it's not what you eat, but who sees you, that matters. Those privileged enough to be seated in a director's chair, close to the water's edge, will know they have arrived. Good Neapolitan favourites like *spaghetti alle vongole* are done well here too; try a banana split with *liquore Strega* for dessert.

Moderate

O'Caporale, Via Regina Giovanna 12, t 089 811 188. Just off the beach, this restaurant offers simple and well-cooked seafood. The succulent swordfish and *zuppa di pesce* come particularly recommended.

Lo Guarracino, Via Positanesi d'America 12, t 089 875 794. Situated in one of Positano's loveliest spots, on a terrace perched over the sea, the restaurant is reached by a short walk along the cliff path towards Fornillo beach. The *pizzeria-cum-trattoria* is pleasantly informal after trendy Spiaggia Grande, and a favourite with the Positanesi. The atmostphere is very friendly.

Grottino Azzurro, Via Chiesa Nuova, t 089 875 466. This is a family-run *trattoria* further uptown, where the *signora* comes to the table to advise you on the catch of the day, and how best you should sample it.

Da Laurito, t 089 875 022. In summer, for a memorable experience, watch out for the little boats marked 'Da Laurito' leaving the jetty at Positano beach. This is a free ferry service to a delightful *trattoria* around the next bay, set on a small beach, with makeshift tables laid out under a straw canopy. Specialities are good old-fashioned recipes such as *totani con patate* (squid cooked with potatoes in an oil and garlic sauce), all washed down with white wine spiked with fresh peaches. At the end of your meal, they'll ferry you back again as part of the service. *Meals served 1–4pm only.*

Petit Ristorante, Via Praia 15, **t** 089 874 706. Just east of Praiano, a sharp turn down to the beach brings you to a restaurant tucked away in a tiny bay at the foot of Il Furore. This is an informal place with tempting smells to beckon the hungry bather to eat at tables outside, surrounded by gaily painted fishing boats, choosing from simple dishes such as fresh grilled fish and salad. *Closed Oct–Easter.*

Cheap

Genuinely cheap places are hard to find; there are some *pizzerie* around Via Fornillo.

Taverna del Leone, Via Laurito 43, **t** 089 875 474. If you have a car, try this busy *pizzeria* just outside Positano towards Amalfi. It's usually bustling with young Positanesi, who come to eat tasty nosh and flirt in relaxed surroundings at lowish prices. The adjoining restaurant is more formal, but popular too.

S. Gennaro da Vittorio, Via S. Gennaro 99, **t** 089 874 293. Near Praiano's western end, this restaurant serves up huge platefuls of *antipasti* and typical dishes. A great place if you're on a budget or just very hungry. The the meal ends with a glass of *limoncello* (bittersweet lemon liqueur) on the house.

Il Ritrovo, Via Monte 53, **t** 089 875 453. A pretty *trattoria* at Montepertuso, above Positano, with tomatoes strung from the beams and good local dishes including, a rarity in these parts, grilled meats. A rustic experience for anyone wishing to escape the crowds.

Amalfi

Amalfi has several fine restaurants, including those in the luxury hotels. But for a sense of this exuberant little city, try one of the many attractive restaurants listed below. Amalfi lacks Positano's pretensions, but what you lose in finery, you make up for in the fundamentals – good, honest grub!

Expensive

Da Gemma, Via Fra Gerardo Sasso 9, **t** 089 871 345. Established in 1872, this is one of Amalfi's oldest restaurants, with a terrace for outdoor dining and an excellent fish menu. Their *zuppa di pesce* is a wonderfully rich mixture of all sorts of different fish and seafood, although it's pricey. Leave room for the *melanzane al cioccolato* (grilled aubergines in chocolate sauce), an unexpected, heavenly combination. *Closed Wed.*

La Caravella, Via Matteo Camera 12, **t** 089 871 029. Near the tunnel by the beach, this is a busy restaurant which serves generous helpings of homemade pasta, including delicious *ravioli* stuffed with seafood, and a good range of homemade desserts – the *tiramisù* is a treat. There is an index to help you find your way round the vast wine list; around the corner is the restaurant's wine cellar housing over 1,000 wines. *Closed Tues.*

Antico Hostaria Bacco, Via G. B. Lama 9, Furore, **t** 089 830 360, **f** 089 830 352. Up in the hills on the road to Agerola, this is a wonderful detour for drivers; the drive is spectacular. The Ferraioli family serve delicious seafood *antipasti* and pasta – *ferrazzuoli* with sword fish and rocket – and, for dessert, their own *melanzane al cioccolato* (*see* above). They also offer the local white wine – Costa d'Amalfi Furore. There are a few charming rooms (*moderate*), with views to the sea.

Moderate

Lo Smeraldino, Piazzale dei Protontini 1, **t** 089 871 070. Make your way towards the far end of the port for this restaurant on the water's edge. You'll be offered the area's speciality, *scialatielli ai frutti di mare* – fresh pasta with mixed seafood – and a range of good *secondi*, most notably an excellent *fritto misto*. Good food and bustling waiters are the order of the day in this popular eatery. *Closed Wed.*

La Taverna del Duca, Largo Spirito Santo 26, **t** 089 872 755. Heading up the main street towards the Valley of the Mills, you could do worse than stop here. Tables lie scattered around a small piazza and diners eat off hand-painted plates. A relaxing midday stop, offering pizza, pasta and traditional Amalfi cooking. *Closed Thurs.*

Cheap

Tarì, Via P. Capuano, **t** 089 871 832. A pretty, welcoming *trattoria* north of the cathedral with traditional checked tablecloths and service with a smile. Its cool, cavernous surroundings beckon in the hot and weary traveller and there are no unpleasant surprises with the bill. *Closed Tues.*

Il Mulino, Via delle Cartiere 36, **t** 089 872 273. This is the place to come if you want a really cheap meal away from the bustle of day-trippers. Keep heading north up the hillside and you won't miss it. *Closed Mon.*

Da Baracca, Piazza dei Dogi, **t** 089 871 285. This place is everything an Italian *trattoria* should be. Tables and chairs spill out on to a tranquil piazza just west of the cathedral, where diners are shielded from the midday sun by a shady awning and leafy plants. Friendly waiters proffer snacks and plates of steaming pasta – and there are no hidden costs to leave you with a sour taste.

San Giuseppe, Via Ruggiero II 4, **t** 089 872 640. The pizza at this family-run hostelry is sublime – it should be: the owner is a baker. Homely bowls of pasta are also available, brought to you by a trio of portly brothers, and consumed amid the noise of television and shrieking children. *Closed Thurs.*

Ravello

Unusually, most of the best dining in Ravello is in the hotels; non-residents are welcome at any of them, either for lunch or dinner.

Moderate

Cumpà Cosimo, Via Roma 44–46, **t** 089 857 156. By comparison to its hotels, most of Ravello's restaurants pale into insignificance. One exception is Cumpà Cosimo, where owner-cook Signora Netta Bottone is always happy to advise diners on her latest concoctions and try out her schoolbook English. She's something of an earth mother, and swears by the fresh produce grown on the family farm in Scala. Framed recommendations, lovingly cut from both national and international papers, line the walls enthusing over recipes handed down by Grandma and the warm, homely atmosphere of this traditional restaurant.

A holiday high spot, where any meal feels like a family affair.

Vittoria, Via dei Rufolo 3, **t** 089 857 947. This large *trattoria* just off the main piazza serves good food at reasonable prices – a rarity in Ravello. The servings are generous. Head to the back of the restaurant for tables laid out on the shady patio.

Zi'Ntonio, **t** 089 857 118. If you make the trip up to Scala, alongside Ravello, look out for this restaurant, which serves well-cooked local dishes on a beautiful covered terrace. *Closed Tues.*

Mammato, Via Arsenale 6, **t** 089 877 036. You'll get good fresh fish at this glass-fronted restaurant in Maiori. Overlooking the sea, Mammato is a popular and relaxed venue for beach bums and locals alike. *Closed Wed.*

Torre Normanna, Via D. Taiani, **t** 089 877 03. As you leave Maiori, you'll see this Saracen tower jutting into the sea. It's only worth stopping at if you can eat on the outside terrace (*summer only*) The setting is accompanied by very good food.

Cheap

Il Giardinello, Corso V. Emanuele 17 **t** 089 877 050. Pass under the leafy archway of this pretty, floral establishment on a side street in sleepy Minori, and you find yourself in an elegant restaurant humming with appreciative diners. The menu is varied and interesting, with plenty of fish, but also pasta and the house speciality – pizza for four! *Closed Wed.*

Ristorante La Locanda, Corso Umberto 1, **t** 089 761 070. Even if Vietri sul Mare. is not on the agenda, this restaurant is one delightful reason for stopping there. Despite the electronic doorbell, the atmosphere is mellow and welcoming. Guests eat upstairs in a stone-walled dining room that flickers with candlelight, so it's probably more suited to dinner *à deux* than a rowdy party. The food is inventive and plentiful, served on the hand-painted plates which have made the town famous. Finishing touches, rarely found in an area now consumed by tourism, make this a truly memorable experience – and if you're smitten, you might even take home some original pottery of your own. *Closed Mon.*

down the road you'll notice the lift leading down to the **Grotta Smeralda** (*open April–Oct daily 9–5; Nov–Mar daily 10–6; adm*). The strange emerald-green light that is diffused throughout this sea-level cavern gives it its name. Beyond this, **Conca dei Marini** is another vertical village, with a beach and a Norman lookout tower to climb.

Amalfi

Sometimes history seems to be kidding us. Can it be true, can this minuscule village once have had a population of 80,000? There is no room among these jagged rocks for even a fraction of that – but then we remember that in Campania anything is possible, and we read how most of the old town simply slid into the sea during a storm and an earthquake in 1343. Until that moment, Amalfi was a glorious place, the first Italian city to regain its balance after the Dark Ages, the first to recreate its civic pride and its mercantile daring, showing the way to Venice, Pisa and Genoa, though she kept few of the prizes for herself.

It is only natural that the Amalfitani would try to embroider their history a bit to match such an exquisite setting. Legends tell of a nymph named Amalphi who haunted this shore and became the lover of Hercules. As for their city's founding, they'll tell you about a party of Roman noblemen, fleeing the barbarians after the fall of the Empire, who found the site a safe haven to carry on the old Roman spirit and culture. Amalfi first appears in the 6th century; by the 9th it had achieved its independence from the dukes of Naples and was probably the most important trading port of southern Italy, with a large colony of merchants at Constantinople and connections with all the Muslim lands. All this came at a time for which historical records are scarce, but Amalfi's merchant adventurers must have had as romantically exciting a time as those of Venice. The city's luck turned sour in the 1130s, with a brief occupation by the Normans, and two terrible sackings at the hands of its arch-enemy, Pisa, which finally broke Amalfi's power forever.

The disaster of 1343 ensured that Amalfi's decline would be complete, but what's left of the place today – with its 5,000 or so people – is beautiful almost to excess. Over the little square around the harbour, a conspicuous inscription brags: 'Judgement Day, for the Amalfitani who go to heaven, will be a day like any other day.' The square is called **Piazza Flavio Gioia**, after Amalfi's most famous merchant adventurer; he's probably another fictitious character – more Amalfitano embroidery – but they claim he invented the compass in the 12th century.

From here, an arch under the buildings leads to the centre of the town, the **Piazza del Duomo**, with a long flight of steps up to the lovely **cathedral** (9th–12th centuries). Not even in Sicily was the Arab-Norman style ever carried to such a flight of fancy as in this delicate façade, with four levels of interlaced arches in stripes of different-coloured stone (much restored a century ago). The lace-like open arches on the porch are unique in Italy, though common enough in Muslim Spain, one of the countries with which Amalfi had regular trade relations. The cathedral's greatest treasure is its set of bronze doors, cast with portraits of Christ, Mary, St Peter and Amalfi's patron, St Andrew; the first of such bronze doors in Italy, they were made in Constantinople in 1066 by an artist named Simon of Syria (he signed them), commissioned by the leader of the Amalfitan colony there. The cathedral's interior, unfortunately, was restored in the 18th-century Baroque alla Napoletana, with plenty of frills in inlaid coloured marble. Down in the crypt you can see more coloured marble work and frescoes, a gift of Philip II of Spain, and also the head of St Andrew; this relic was a part of Amalfi's share of the loot in the sack of Constantinople in 1204.

One of the oldest parts of the cathedral to survive is the **Chiostro del Paradiso** (*open daily 9–9 in summer, till 5 in winter; adm*), a whitewashed quadrangle of interlaced arches with a decidedly African air (*under restoration*). To the side of the cloister is the **Basilica del Crocifisso**, the original cathedral, where amid the surviving frescoes many of the bits and pieces of old Amalfi that have endured its calamities have been assembled: there are classical sarcophagi, medieval sculptures and coats of arms. Best of all are the fragments of Cosmatesque work, brightly coloured geometric mosaics that once were parts of pulpits and pillars, a speciality of this part of Campania. Don't miss the lovely 16th-century *Madonna col Bambino* by the stairs down to the Crypt.

From the centre of Amalfi, you can walk in a few minutes out to the northern edge of the city, the narrow 'Valley of the Mills', set along a stream between steep cliffs; some of the mills that made medieval Amalfi famous for paper-making are still in operation, and there is a small **Paper Museum** (*open 9–1, closed Mon and Fri; adm*) in the town. You can also watch paper being made and buy paper products at **Armatruda**, Via Fiume, t 089 871 315, in central Amalfi, near the museum.

Villages Inland: Ravello and Scala

As important as it was in its day, the Amalfitan Republic never grew very big. At its greatest extent, it could only claim a small part of this coast, including these two towns up in the mountains; like Amalfi they were once much larger and more prosperous. **Ravello** is another beauty, a balcony overlooking the Amalfi coast and a treasure house of exotic medieval art and tropical botany. The sinuous climb can be made by bus or car, but be aware that parking here is a nightmare. Ravello seems to have been a resort even in Roman times; numerous remains of villas have been found. As the second city of the Amalfitan Republic, medieval Ravello had a population of 30,000 (at least that's what they claim); now it provides an example of that typically Italian phenomenon – a village of 2,000 with a first-rate cathedral.

Ravello's chief glories are two wonderful gardens. The **Villa Cimbrone** (*open daily 9–8; adm*) was laid out by Lord Grimthorpe, the Englishman who designed Big Ben. The view over the Amalfi coast is now owned by the Swiss Vuillemier family who also run the Hotel Palumbo and it is, without doubt, one of the most beautiful properties in all Italy. The **Villa Rùfolo** (*open daily 9–8 ; adm*), as Wagner fans will be interested to know, is none other than Klingsor's magic garden. Wagner says so in a note scribbled in the villa's guest book. He came here looking for the proper setting in which to imagine the worldly, Faustian enchanter of Parsifal, and thus his imagination was fired. The villa itself is a remarkable 11th-century pleasure palace, a temporary abode of Charles of Anjou, various Norman kings and Adrian IV, the only English pope (1154–9), who came here when fleeing a rebellion in Rome. Even in its half-ruined state, it is worth a visit; inside there is a small collection of architectural fragments, including a Moorish cloister and two crumbling towers, one of which can still be climbed. The garden, with more fine views, is a semi-tropical paradise; in summer it reverberates with 'sounds and sweet airs' as the setting for open-air concerts.

The **cathedral** is named after Ravello's patron, San Pantaleone, an obscure early martyr; they have a phial of his blood in one of the side chapels, and it 'boils' like the blood of San Gennaro in Naples whenever the saint is in the mood. Lately he hasn't been, which worries the Ravellans. The cathedral has two particular treasures: a pair of bronze doors by Barisano of Trani (1179), inspired by the Greek ones at Amalfi, and an exquisite pair of marble ambones, or pulpits, that rank among the outstanding examples of 12th–13th-century sculptural and mosaic work; the more elaborate one, its columns resting on six curious lions, dates from 1272. You can see similar decorative work at the churches of **Santa Maria a Gradello** and **San Giovanni del Toro**. From Ravello, it's only a lovely 1½km walk to **Scala**, smallest and oldest of the Amalfitan towns, with an interesting old **cathedral**.

Between Amalfi and Ravello, before reaching the turn-off inland, the Amalfi Drive passes through **Atrani**, an old village whose church has another tiled dome, and yet another set of bronze doors from Constantinople. Beyond the Ravello turn, next along the way towards Salerno, come **Minori** and **Maiori**. Minori is a typical Costiera hill-town which, despite encroaching tourism, maintains considerable charm. Its bigger sister is somewhat less enticing, mainly due to a major flood in 1954 which washed away most of the seafront; today most of the buildings and hotels along the shore are depressingly modern. **Erchie**, a tiny hamlet on the shore far below the road, seems a lovely spot – if you can figure out a way to get down to it. Then, near the end of the Dʄrive, the real world comes back into view as the busy port of Salerno stretches before you. Here you find the tiny resort of **Cetara**, with a fine beach behind a newly constructed fishing port, and, just before Salerno, **Vietri sul Mare**, another steep and pretty town, famous throughout Italy for its beautiful majolica ware. There are ceramics shops everywhere, where you can watch craftsmen hand-painting jugs, vases and tiles, and pick up souvenirs at good prices.

Salerno

Anywhere else in the south of Italy, a city like Salerno would be an attraction in itself; here it gets lost among the wonders of the Campanian coast – the big town at the end of the Amalfi Drive – and few people stop for more than a brief visit. Still, Salerno has its modest charms: for one, it's clean and orderly, which should endear it to people who hate Naples. Its setting under a backdrop of mountains is memorable. The Italian highway engineers, have brought a highway to Salerno on a chain of viaducts, one lofty span after another, an unusual and pleasing ornament for the city; at night the road lights hang on the slopes like strings of fairy lights.

Salerno's ancient distinction was its medical school, the oldest and finest of medieval Europe. Traditionally founded by the legendary 'Four Doctors' – an Italian, a Greek, a Jew and an Arab – the school was of the greatest importance in the

Where to Stay

Salerno ✉ 84100

Salerno's hotels are modest and utilitarian in general. However, if you just want to stay a couple of nights, the hotels and restaurants should satisfy the needs of most explorers.

Moderate

****Jolly Hotel delle Palme, Lungomare Trieste 1, t 089 225 222, f 089 237 571. A pleasant and reliable option, good value for money, in a good position on the seafront.

***Plaza, Piazza Vittorio Veneto 42, t 089 224 477, f 089 237 311. Across from the station, offering modern and comfortable rooms; more than acceptable for an overnight stay.

***Montestella, Corso Vittorio Emanuele 156, t 089 225 122, f 089 229 167. Another decent hotel close to the railway station.

***Fiorenza, Via Trento 145, t/f 089 338 800. This clean and well-run hotel has 30 rooms and is convenient for the beach.

Cheap

**Salerno, Via G. Vicinanza 42, t 089 224 211, f 089 224 432. Simple and comfortable; one of several cheaper hotels on or around the Corso Vittorio Emanuele.

Eating Out

Expensive

Nicola dei Principati, Corso Garibaldi 201, t 089 225 435. Situated in the old centre of Salerno, this restaurant serves mainly fish dishes, including an excellent *linguine con astice* (long pasta with lobster).

Il Timone, Via Generale Clark 29, t 089 335 111. Head for the Mercatello district several miles to the east of the town centre. The speciality here is *tubetti alla pescatrice* (little pasta tubes served with a delicious fisherwoman's sauce). *Closed Mon and Sun evenings.*

Alla Brace, Lungomare Trieste 11–13, t 089 225 159. As well as the usual fish dishes, there is a host of delicious local specialities such as stuffed peppers, *ravioli* filled with *ricotta*, and an unusual potato soufflé. There is also a wide range of homemade desserts.

Moderate

Vicolo della Neve, Vicolo della Neve 24, t 089 225 705. Right in the *centro storico*, this is one of the liveliest restaurants in town. It is decorated with wall paintings by some of the many artists who have established it as their local. The chef turns out good Campanian favourites such as *melanzane alla parmigiana*, aubergines cooked in layers with *mozzarella*, parmesan, tomato and basil, and the classic *pasta e fagioli*. Excellent pizza, too. *Open eves only; closed Wed.*

Al Cenacolo, Piazza Alfano I, t 089 228 818. At the foot of the cathedral, this place serves excellent seafood; it's recommended by the locals. *Closed Mon and Sun evening.*

Cheap

Da Sasa, Via Degli Orti 9, t 089 220 330. A good cheap *trattoria*, with traditional cooking.

Ristorante Pinocchio, Lungomare Trieste 56–58, t 089 229 964. For good pizza and seafood, this place is also great value. Head here to dine shoulder to shoulder with the Salernitani. *Closed Fri.*

Pantaleone, Via dei Mercanti 75, t 089 227 7825. The oldest – and still the best – pastry shop in town.

transmission of Greek and Muslim science into Europe. Most of us, however, may recall Salerno better as the site of the Allied invasion in September 1943.

Salerno's port is on the outskirts of town, and the shore all through the city centre is graced with a pretty park, the **Lungomare Trieste**. Parallel with it, and two streets back, the Corso Vittorio Emanuele leads into the old town. Here it changes its name to Via dei Mercanti, the most colourful of Salerno's old streets. The **cathedral**, a block to the north on Via del Duomo, is set with its façade behind a courtyard (*currently under restoration*), with a fountain at the centre, and a detached campanile – as if it were not a church at all, but a mosque. The Corinthian columns around it come from the ancient city of *Paestum*, not far down the coast. The cathedral's treasures include a pair of bronze doors from Constantinople, and another pair of Cosmatesque pulpits, though a surprise comes with the overwhelming mosaic floor, a 1,968 square foot expanse of marble and polychrome tiles of Byzantine inspiration. Many of the best original details are preserved in the adjacent **Museo del Duomo** (*open daily 9–6*).

From Salerno you can make an easy excursion up into the mountain town of **Cava de' Tirreni**. Near it is the little-visited Benedictine monastery called **La Trinità di Cava** – which has preserved a wealth of frescoes, stone-carving and Cosmati work.

The Islands of the Bay of Naples

Without a doubt, the islands in the Bay of Naples – Capri, Ischia, and to a far lesser extent Procida – are the holiday queens of the Italian islands. Every schoolchild has heard of Capri, the notorious playground of Emperor Tiberius and Norman Douglas' 'gentlemanly freaks'. Despite their location, the three islands have very different geological origins. Ischia and Procida are a part of the enormous submerged volcano of Campano, which stretches from Ventotene in the Pontine Islands to Strómboli and the Aeolian Islands. In not too ancient times, the two islands were connected and, if the Greek geographer Strabo is to be believed, also to the Phlegraean Fields on the mainland. Phlegraean means 'fiery' in Greek, and Strabo records how, during an eruption of the now dormant volcano Epomeo on Ischia, an earthquake split Ischia–Procida from the mainland, then, in another upheaval, jolted the once united island in twain. In this same geological cataclysm, Capri broke off from the Sorrentine peninsula, a blow that shattered its coasts to form the island's famous cliffs.

Capri

Capri is pure enchantment, a delicious garden of Eden with over 800 species of flowers and plants cascading over a sheer chunk of limestone, which has been eroded into fantastic forms, most famously the **Grotta Azzurra** – its shimmering, iridescent blueness is caused by the reflection of light on the water in the morning. In summer (*1 June–30 Sept*), boats for the Blue Grotto leave at 9am – when the sea is calm. The entrance to the cave is quite low, and if there's any swell on the sea at all someone is sure to get a nasty knock on the head. The sea excursion around the island is a rare experience, but again possible only in good weather. Besides visiting other caverns, such as the **Grotta Bianca** and the **Grotta Verde** (the White Cave and the Green Cave), it provides breathtaking views of the cliffs and Capri's uncanny rock formations.

Flower-bedecked Capri town is a charming white village packed with jewellery shops and designer boutiques. The town is the base for several walks, each more splendid than the last – aim for the famous **Faraglioni**, three towering limestone pinnacles in the sea. From Via Tragara a stairway descends to the point and the **Porto di Tragara**, where you can take a swim. Nearby is the **Tragara Terrace**, with views over monolithic **Pizzolungo** and the **Arco Naturale**, where dark pines – as everywhere on

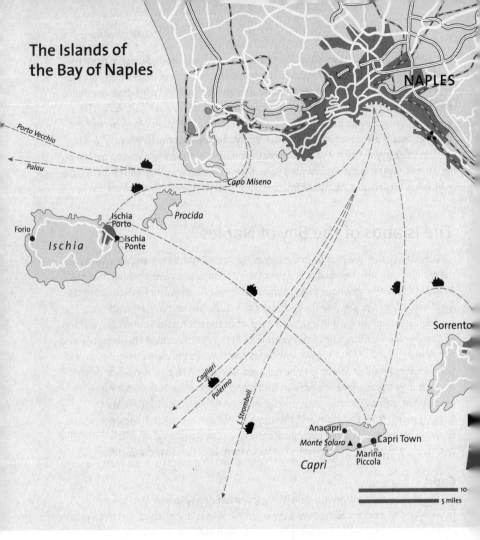

The Islands of the Bay of Naples

NAPLES

Porto Vecchio

Palau

Capo Miseno

Ischia Porto

Procida

Forio

Ischia

Ischia Ponte

Sorrento

Cagliari

Palermo

I. Stromboli

Anacapri

Monte Solaro ▲

Capri Town

Marina Piccola

Capri

10

5 miles

Capri – cling to every tiny ledge. Or head for **La Certosa,** a charming golden-hued 14th-century Carthusian charterhouse built over one of Tiberius' villas and topped by a 17th-century Baroque tower. A few minutes away are the **Gardens of Augustus,** founded by Caesar himself. A wide variety of trees and plants grow on the fertile terraces and belvederes overlooking one of the most striking views in the world.

A narrow road – Via Krupp (*currently closed for reinforcement work*) – takes you down the cliffs in a hundred hairpin bends to the **Marina Piccola.** There is a bus, fortunately, that makes the steep climb back up the cliffs to Capri town. A longer walk takes you to the **Villa Jovis** (*open 9–one hour before sunset; adm*), Tiberius' pleasure palace, and the infamous **Salto di Tiberio,** always pointed out as the precipice from which the emperor hurled his victims.

More striking views may be had from Capri's more laid-back second town, **Anacapri,** up on the island's top shelf. There are regular buses connecting it to **Marina Grande** and Capri town, and a chairlift that goes up even further to the summit of **Monte Solaro**, for a fabulous view of the island and the whole of the Bay of Naples.

Ischia

Green, mountainous and volcanic, Ischia comes a close second to Capri in the beauty and fashion pageant, blessed with something its more famous sister totally lacks: beautiful beaches. On one – Maronti – the island's volcanic origins are more than evident. The hot mineral springs that gush all year round have attracted cure-seekers since Roman times, and are still recommended today for people suffering from rheumatism, arthritis, neuralgia and obesity. Because many of the springs are radioactive, a doctor's permission is often required before you take a soak (there are physicians on the island who specialize in prescribing such treatments, and they charge a pretty penny). The hottest spring on the island is Terme Rita, at Casamicciola, which belches from the earth at around 180°F.

Ischia Porto and adjacent **Ischia Ponte** are lively and very fashionable, the former boasting the curative radioactive hotsprings, the second the storybook **Castello d'Ischia**, the fortress islet where Michelangelo's great friend the poet Vittoria Colonna spent so many years. Also called the Castello Aragonese, the islet can be visited, with its narrow streets and 500-year-old houses; the views from the walls are superb. More wonderful views await from the summit of the extinct volcano, **Montagnone** (836ft), stretching over the Phlegraean Fields on the mainland, Ischia's little sister island Procida, and the rest of Ischia as well.

Procida

Lovely, uncomplicated and tiny, Procida is in many ways the archetypal image of all that an 'Italian island' evokes in any holiday dreamer's mind, scented by groves that produce the finest lemons in Italy (the *granita* served in almost every local bar is a treat) and embellished with colourful houses as original as they are beautiful. Procida has been the setting for two famous love stories, and most recently for the Oscar-wining film *Il Postino*. Its main port, overlooked by the ancient village of **Corricella**, is a pastel fantasy with the undulating rhythm of a hundred arches. Steep stone stair-ways cascade down among the arches; from the little port they're like a hundred watchful eyes, scanning the sea for the fishermen's return.

Perched up on the promontory overhead, the **Terra Murata** (298ft, Procida's highest point) is the old walled town, where you can visit the 16th-century **Castello d'Aragona** and the church of **San Michele Arcangelo**, which, despite its exotic, almost Saracen appearance from a distance, wears a simple unadorned façade, rebuilt after the various pirates' depredations. The domes are untiled – Procida receives so little rain that tiles aren't strictly necessary, or at least worth the cost.

Beyond this minimal urban centre, Procida is an enchanting Ruritania of lemon groves and crumbling old villas, rural beauty spots, shaded walkways and narrow roads, old farmhouses and crumbling small *palazzi* – you can walk around it in a day, or take the bus to the south end, where **Chiaiolella**, a small fishing port, has a long stretch of sand facing the tiny wooded **islet of Vivara** – reached via a pedestrian-only

Getting to the Islands

In summer, there are as many as six **ferries** and 20 **hydrofoils** a day from **Naples** to **Capri**, and as many to **Ischia**. There are also regular departures to **Procida**. In addition, there are frequent ferries and hydrofoils daily from **Sorrento** to Capri, from **Pozzuoli** to Procida and between the islands of Ischia and Procida. All are very short rides.

Local and longer-distance ferries and hydrofoils from **Naples** leave from three different points along the harbour – **Molo Beverello** and the **Stazione Marittima**, both in the centre of the port, and **Mergellina**, further to the west. Be sure to check you know the right dock for your ticket and destination. Listed here are the principal ferry and hydrofoil operators; check with them for timetables, or look in the daily newspaper *Il Mattino*.

From Molo Beverello:

Caremar (ferries and hydrofoils), t 081 551 3882, for Capri, Ischia and Procida.

Navigazione Libera del Golfo (hydrofoils), t 081 552 7209, for Capri.

Linee Lauro (ferries and hydrofoils), t 081 551 3352, for Ischia.

Alilauro (hydrofoils), t 081 552 2838, for Sorrento and Capri.

From the Stazione Marittima:

Tirrenia (ferries), t 081 720 1111, for Palermo (Sicily) and Cagliari (Sardinia).

Siremar (ferries), t 081 720 1595, for the Aeolian Islands and Milazzo.

Ustica Lines (hydrofoils), t 081 761 2565, for the Egadi Islands and Trapani in Sicily.

From Mergellina (hydrofoils only):

Alilauro, t 081 761 1004, for Ischia and Positano.

SNAV, t 081 761 2348, for Capri, Ischia (Casamicciola), Procida and the Aeolian Islands.

In addition, from **Salerno** there is a boat called the *Faraglione* that offers a different way of seeing the Amalfi coast, a daily ferry that hugs the shore to Capri, stopping at **Amalfi** and **Positano** along the way. It leaves Salerno at 7.30 each morning from **Molo Manfredi**, at the western end of town.

This service does not run between 15 October and 6 January.

Getting Around

Capri

Arriving in Marina Grande, you can ascend to either Capri or Anacapri by **bus** (daily 8am–10pm every 15 mins, 10pm–midnight every half-hour). There is also a **funicular** that runs up to Capri town (summer daily 6.30am–12.30am every 15 mins; Oct–April daily until 9pm).

The **chairlift** from Anacapri to Monte Solaro (*a 12-minute ride*) runs continuously (summer 9.30–sunset; Nov–Feb 10.30–3; closed Tues). **Buses** run from Capri town to Anacapri, Marina Piccola and Damecuta.

There are also buses from Anacapri to the Grotta Azzurra, Faro and Marina Piccola. Daily tours of Capri by **motor launch** leave from Marina Grande (June–Sept; first tour 9am).

Otherwise you can **walk** to most places; the beautiful trails across the island are major attractions. Pack a mac, as it can rain.

Ischia

Ischia is considerably larger than Capri, large enough to be divided into six self-contained communities. **Buses** (and **taxis**) to the various towns on the island depart from the square next to Santa Maria di Portosalvo in Ischia Porto, near the beginning of the SS270, which circles the island. An entire circuit of the island takes about two and a half hours.

If you're planning a day trip round the island, your best bet is to buy a **ticket** valid for 24hrs, otherwise a standard ticket (valid for 1hr) is about half the price. A weekly bus pass is also good value. It might be helpful to know that buses marked CD run clockwise, while those marked CS run anti-clockwise. You may prefer to rent a *motorino* (moped) as traffic is less threatening than on the mainland (L30–40,000 per day).

Procida

There are frequent **ferry** and **hydrofoil** services from both Naples and Ischia to Procida. The harbour itself is tiny, and if you want to explore further afield, jump on one of the colourful **buggies** that serve as taxis.

Alternatively, there is a **bus service** about every half-hour between the harbour and the other end of the island at Chiaiolella, stopping at more or less every point in between.

Tourist Information

Capri Town: Piazza Umberto 1, **t** 081 837 0686.
Marina Grande (Capri): at Banchina del Porto, **t** 081 837 0634. For accommodation.
Anacapri (Capri): Via G. Orlandi 59/a, **t** 089 837 1524.
Ischia Porto (Ischia): Via Jasolino, **t** 081 507 4211, near the ferry landing.
Centro Servizi Turisitici (Ischia): Via Jasolino 72, **t** 081 98 061. Well stocked with leaflets.
Marina Grande (Procida): Via Roma 92, **t** 081 810 1968, **f** 081 981 904 (*open summer 9–1 and 3.30–7.30, winter 9–1*), beside the ticket office near the ferry departure point.

Where to Stay

Capri ✉ 80073

Not surprisingly, hotel prices on Capri are well above average for the surrounding area on-shore, and rooms for the summer months are often booked up months in advance.

Luxury

★★★★★**Grand Hotel Quisisana**, Via Camerelle 2, **t** 081 837 0788, **f** 081 837 6080, *info@quisi. com*. If money is no object, this luxurious palace of a hotel is the place to stay in Capri town.Originally a sanatorium built by an Englishman, George Clark, it's set in its own grounds. With acres of white tiled floors, white sofas and lamps borne by carved ebony figures, it is not merely the luxury but the sheer size that impresses (especially on an island where space is at a premium).

Very Expensive

★★★★**La Scalinatella**, Via Tragara 8, **t** 081 837 0633, **f** 081 837 8291. For more luxury, but with the focus on privacy, this is a jewel of a hotel, with 31 beautifully decorated rooms and stunning views. There is a pool and

good restaurant but there are no large public areas; no tour groups.
★★★★**Hotel Punta Tragara**, Via Tragara 57, **t** 081 837 0844, **f** 081 837 7790, *hotel.tragara@ capri.it*. Outside Capri town at Punta Tragara, this de luxe resort hotel offers a pool and more in a building designed by Le Corbusier. The architect's distinctive modern style and the predominance of strong reds, oranges and dark wood fittings come at a price but the views from the rooms are spectacular.

Expensive

★★★★**La Palma**, Via V. Emanuele 39, **t** 081 837 0133, **f** 081 837 6966, *palma@caprinet.it*. Good value by Capri standards, set in its own gardens in Capri town, with majolica-tiled floors in the rooms and a pleasant airy feel. Established as a hotel in 1822, it's older than the Quisisana; the staff are charming and the whole atmosphere more comfortable than many of the more expensive hotels.
★★★★**Villa Brunella**, Via Tragara 24, **t** 081 837 0122, **f** 081 837 0430, *villabrunella@capri.it*. Further up on the way to the panoramic Punta Tragara, this is a pretty hotel with rooms on terraces that overlook Monte Solaro. There is a pool. The emphasis is on villa-style accommodation and privacy, suiting anybody who has come here looking for a retreat.

Moderate

★★★**Floridiana**, Via Campo di Teste, **t** 081 837 0166, **f** 081 837 0434. Situated in Capri town with fine panoramas of the sea. A little outside the limelight, but the management are upgrading many of its rooms in open and unashamed pursuit of another star from the tourist board. Until prices go up this is reasonable value. Single travellers do not pay outrageous supplements – merely half the cost of a double room. *Open all year.*
★★**Villa Krupp**, Viale Matteotti 12, **t** 081 837 0362, **f** 081 837 6489. One of the most historic of the lower-priced hotels in Capri. Situated above the path up to the Gardens of Augustus, the hotel has enviable views, and a welcoming ambience. Trotsky stayed here and even left a typical Russian samovar behind. Book ahead.

Cheap

★Stella Maris, Via Roma 10–19, t 081 837 0452, f 081 837 8662. Clean, well-run and central, this is a cosy family-run affair. Here for generations, the family is intensely proud of its hospitality, so you will not want for towels and personal touches. Most rooms look down to the Marina Grande below, and over to distant Ischia.

★La Tosca, Via D. Birago, t/f 081 837 0989. Still in Capri town, overlooking the other coast, this is a hotel with clean tiled rooms and high ceilings. Ask for a room with a view.

Ischia Porto ✉ 80077

★★★★Excelsior Belvedere, Via E. Gianturco 1, t 081 991 522, f 081 984 100 (*expensive*). Situated down a side street off Corso Vittoria Colonna, this is the finest hotel in Ischia Porto, with a fine pool and garden. A stylish choice. *Closed Nov–Mar.*

★★★★Mare Blu, Via Pontano 40, t 081 982 555, f 081 982 938 (*expensive*). For a few less *lire*, you can indulge in a spot of luxury at this sleek hotel, in a charming position on the waterfront, just a short walk from the centre of town. There's a private beach belonging to the hotel just over the road, two pools and a memorable view of the Aragonese castle. *Closed Nov–Mar.*

★★★★Villa Rosa, Via G. Gante 13, just off Via Roma, t 081 991 316, f 081 992 425 (*moderate*). An elegant hotel screened from the outside world by a leafy forecourt. Leave behind the heat and bustle of the streets for this cool inner sanctum, tastefully furnished with a minimum of fuss and surprisingly well-priced for a hotel of such finesse. Small pool and garden. *Closed Nov–Mar.*

Ischia Ponte ✉ 80077

★★★Monastero, Castello Aragonese 39, t 081 992 435 (*cheap*). This is one of the least expensive places to stay in Ischia Ponte. Situated within the Castello Aragonese itself, there are 14 clean and simple rooms, housed in the former monks' cells. It's a bit of a climb, but the view is unforgettable.

Ischia, Lacco Ameno ✉ 80076

★★★★★Grand Albergo Mezza Torre, Via Mezza Torre, t 081 986 111, f 081 986 015, *info@*

mezzatorre.it (*very expensive*). Through a terracotta archway and down a long road, just off the SS270 outside Lacco Ameno, this is an elegant choice with a very different style. Housed in a 16th-century tower, its 60 rooms share the grounds of a small castle that belonged to the film director Luchino Visconti. After some controversy, it is now being restored. It cannot be beaten for old-fashioned luxury and a distinctive country-house atmosphere, with a pool just above the beach.

Procida ✉ 80079

There are very few places to stay on Procida. However, it's an ideal spot for relaxing in the sunshine away from the crowds, simpler than either of its neighbours. There are enough ferries not to feel isolated, but your evenings will be quiet. The nightlife popular on the other islands has yet to catch on here.

★★★Crescenzo, Via Marina Chiaiolella 33, t 081 896 7255, f 081 810 1260 (*cheap*). Right on the harbour front in Chiaiolella, and a short walk from the beach, this hotel is a landmark in Procida. Its rooms are simply but pleasantly furnished, and the restaurant, which serves local specialities and pizza in the evening, is worth a try even if you are not staying here. Most rooms come with showers and the roof terrace offers a great view.

★★Riviera, Via Giovanni da Procida 36, t 081 896 7197 (*cheap*). This pretty hotel is on the main bus route through the centre of the island, and about 10 minutes walk outside Chiaiolella. There are 23 rooms in a relaxed and sunny environment, with very friendly, chatty owners.

Eating Out

Capri

Expensive

La Capannina, Via delle Botteghe 12–14, t 081 837 0732. Set in a secluded garden in Capri town, this has long been Capri's best restaurant, with delicately prepared shellfish, pasta and fish, and good desserts.

I Faraglioni, Via Camerelle 75, t 081 837 0320. Serves delectable house specialities like *crêpes al formaggio*, thin pancakes filled with cheese, and *risotto ai frutti di mare*.

Moderate

Da Paolino, Via Palazzo a Mare 11, **t** 081 837 6102. Look out for this restaurant on the way down from Capri town to Marina Grande. Eat in an arbour of lemon trees, tasting dishes mainly inspired by the fruit.

Da Gemma, Via Madre Serafina 6, **t** 081 837 0461, **f** 081 837 8947. An island institution up the stairs past the cathedral and down the tunnel to the right in Capri town. As nice in winter as it is in summer, it's a welcoming *trattoria*, walls decked with ceramic plates. Superbly cooked local dishes include a fine *risotto alla pescatore* and a delicious *mozzarella* grilled on a lemon leaf.

Da Gelsomina la Migliara, Via La Migliara 72, **t** 081 837 1499. In Anacapri, about a half-hour's walk out of the village from the Piazzetta, this *trattoria* offers home-made wine to go with its home-cooked island specialities, including mushrooms gathered on Monte Solaro.

Ischia Porto

On Ischia, fish inevitably features prominently on the menu, and has inspired a fine selection of imaginative local dishes.

You will also find meat, and specifically rabbit. For some reason, Ischia is fairly hopping with rabbits, and the locals have dreamed up endless ways of eating them – in stews, roast, or even with pasta.

Gennaro, Via Porto 66, **t** 081 991 125, **f** 081 983 636 (*expensive*). Serves superb giant prawns and many other delicious Ischian specialities. Gennaro Rumore is a charismatic and convivial host and probably the best-known restaurateur on the island. He has entertained the likes of Tom Cruise, Nicole Kidman and Andrew Lloyd Webber, who gave him a superb write-up in the British press. The food is a perfectionist's dream, carefully prepared and guaranteed to leave your tastebuds tingling.

Da Cocò, Piazzale Aragonese, **t** 081 981 823 (*moderate*). Just before you reach the causeway on the seafront you can enjoy traditional food in unpretentious surroundings at this relaxed eatery run by

Salvatore di Meglio, a retired fisherman who claims to be 'in love with the sea'. It comes highy recommended by the locals who cram into the noisy and friendly dining area.

Zi Nannina a Mare, Via Cristoforo Colombo, **t** 081 991 350 (*moderate*). A delightful family-run *trattoria* with an outdoor terrace offering traditional, well-cooked specialities of the region, based on either fish or meat.

Il Damiano, Via della Vigna, on the SS270, **t** 081 983 093 (*expensive*). Leaving Ischia Porto and heading out towards Casamicciola, check out this restaurant, which has superb views over the sea, plus beautifully cooked seafood and fish dishes – best of all the *linguine all'aragosta* (pasta with a lobster sauce). *Open eves only.*

Ischia Ponte

Giardini Eden, Via Nuova Cartaromana 68, **t** 081 985 015 (*expensive*). On the sea, this is the best place for views and seafood. You're guaranteed to dine on the freshest fish, since it's as good as plucked out of the water in front of you. If you don't fancy the steep descent from the road, the restaurant offers a free taxi-boat service (*eves only*) from the Via Pontana. It's surrounded by thermal pools, which you can try out at a price.

Ciro e Caterina, Via Luigi Mazzella 80, **t** 081 99 31 22 (*cheap*). At this restaurant not far from the castle tables spill out beneath a palm tree. Try the rich and tasty *gnocchi* dish and look out for the very helpful, mildly eccentric owner.

Ischia, Lacco Ameno

Al Delfino, Corso A. Rizzoli 116, **t** 081 900 252 (*moderate*). Head here for a delicious meal right on the harbour front. Steaming plates ae carried from the kitchen across the street to the clientele in the glass-fronted restaurant; try the *spaghetti alle vongole*.

Procida

La Medusa, Via Roma 116, **t** 081 896 7481 (*moderate*). This is one of several good restaurants along the port at Marina Grande. Try the house speciality, a *spaghetti ai ricci di mare* (spaghetti with sea urchins). To accompany it, try the excellent local wine – literally 'on tap'.

bridge, where the birds are protected these days but the rabbits are fair game. The areas around **Centane**, especially Punta Solchiaro, are especially pretty, with views over the entire east coast of the island from the belvedere.

Campania Inland

There's more to the region than just the Bay of Naples. However, the coast and its endless attractions draw off most of the tourists, and it's a rare soul indeed who ever makes it up to old Capua, or the excellent little city of Benevento.

Capua

This is a double city, consisting of the modern town, founded in the 9th century, and the ancient one, once the second city of Italy, but deserted in the Dark Ages and now modestly reborn as **Santa Maria Capua Vetere**. Capua can trace its founding to the Oscans, blithe folk of ancient Italy who introduced farce to the theatre, and gave us the word *obscene*. The Oscan farces, banned by all decent Roman emperors, created the prototypes of the *commedia dell'arte* stock characters – which should give you an idea of the spirit of old Capua, a city best known for beautiful women and perfume, and as renowned for loose morals in its day as Sybaris. All but the jealous Roman historians liked to give Capua credit for defeating Hannibal. The Capuans had always hated those dreary dour Romans, and they eagerly took the Carthaginians' part. Hannibal's men enjoyed Capuan hospitality in the winter of 216 BC; they came out in the spring so dreamy-eyed and dissipated that they never beat the Romans again.

Of course there was hell to pay when the Romans came back, but Capua survived, and even flourished for several centuries more as the greatest city of the region. Finally, though, some even worse enemies than the Romans arrived – the Arabs, who utterly destroyed the city in about AD 830. The survivors refounded Capua on a new site, a few kilometres to the north. At Santa Maria Capua Vetere, you can see the remains of the second-largest **amphitheatre** in Italy (*open summer 9–6; winter 9–4; adm*) – largest of all before Rome built its Colosseum. A short walk away you'll find something much more interesting – perhaps the best example of a ***mithraeum*** discovered anywhere in the Mediterranean (*open 9–4.30; closed Mon*). The cult of the god Mithras, imported from Persia by the legionaries, was for a while the most wide-spread of the cults that tried to fill the religious vacuum of the imperial centuries. Some scholars see in it much in common with Christianity, but the resemblance isn't obvious; Mithraism was an archaic, visceral cult, with mystery initiations and bull's blood. Though it originally took hold in the army, and always remained a men-only affair, as late as the 3rd century AD it still claimed more adherents than Christianity. The upper classes were never too impressed with it; which is why it lost out to the Christians, and why such well-executed frescoes as these are rare. The *mithraeum* is an underground hall used in the initiations and dominated by a large scene of Mithras, a typical Mediterranean solar hero, slaying a white bull with a serpent under its feet; the fresco representing the moon on the opposite wall is less well-preserved.

The new **Archaeological Museum of Ancient Capua**, Via Roberto D'Angio (*open 9–7; closed Mon*) provides a convenient introduction to the site, complementing the more important Museo Campano at new Capua. Also around Santa Maria, there is a crumbling triumphal arch, and some elaborate Roman tombs, off the road to Caserta.

The new Capua has all the most interesting finds from the old one at the **Museo Provinciale Campano**, Via Principi Longobardi 1/3 (*open Tues–Sat 9–1.30, Sun 9–1; adm*) though most people will probably make do with the new museum at Santa Maria Capua Vetere. Just north of the town, on the slopes of Mount Tifata, a site once occupied by a temple of Diana now contains the 11th-century basilica of **Sant'Angelo in Formis**. The 12th-century frescoes here are some of the best in the south, oddly archaic figures that would seem much more at home in Constantinople than in Italy. And, more than mere artistry, there is an intense spiritual vision about these paintings – note especially the unearthly, unforgettable face of the enthroned St Michael above the portal. North of Capua, near the border with Lazio, the last town in Campania along the Via Appia is **Sessa Aurunca**, with a Roman bridge and some other scanty ruins, as well as a 12th-century cathedral, interesting for its surviving ancient and medieval sections.

Caserta

In one shot, you can see the biggest palace in Italy, and also the most wearisome; both distinctions belong uncontestably to the **Reggia**, or Royal Palace, built here by the Bourbon King of Naples, Charles III (*Royal Apartments open Tues–Sat 9–2, Sun and hols 9am–10pm; adm*). His architect, Luigi Vanvitelli, spared no expense; like the Spanish Bourbons, those of Naples were envious of Versailles, and wanted to show the Louis back home that they, too, deserved a little respect.

The Reggia, begun in 1752, has some 1,200 rooms, not much compared to the 2,800 of the Bourbon palace in Madrid, but larger than its Spanish cousin just the same (it's also larger than Versailles); the façade is 804ft across. Inside, as in Madrid, everything is tasteful, ornate and soberingly expensive; the only good touches from Vanvitelli's heavy hand are the elegant grand staircases.

The **park** (*open Tues–Sun 9–one hour before sunset; adm*) makes the trip worthwhile, an amazingly long axis of pools and cascades climbing up to the famous **Diana fountain**, with a lifelike sculptural group of the goddess and her attendants catching Actaeon in the act. There is an **English garden**, the sort fashionable in the 18th century. Take a picnic.

The village of **San Leucio**, 3km north of Caserta, was founded by the Bourbon kings as a paternalistic utopian experiment – and for the manufacture of silk. Ferdinand IV, for most of his life, personally saw to every detail of its operation, even christening the children of the workers. The successor of his Real Fabbrica is still a silk centre. Some 9km to the east there is the half-deserted town of **Casertavecchia**. The building of the Reggia drew most of the population down to modern Caserta, but the old town still has the 12th-century **cathedral** (*open 3–4*) with an octagonal *ciborium* (a cylindrical or prismatic dome) that is one of the glories of Arab-Norman architecture.

Getting Around

The interior of Campania makes up a rather large piece of territory – the three main towns are all provincial capitals. None is on the main railway lines, however, and you will have to scrutinize the schedules in Naples carefully to find your way around. For **Capua** take the Piedimonte Matese train from Naples to Santa Maria Capua Vetere. Trains to **Caserta** are rather more frequent and very convenient for the Royal Palace – the Reggia – which is just in front of it. Remote **Benevento** is not well connected with any of Italy's main transport systems. It is on the Naples–Foggia railway line, but be careful about Naples–Benevento trains, as some are run by a private railway, and you will need to find out which – ask at the information booth in the station – to buy the right ticket. The private line is faster.

Buses for Caserta, Capua, Avellino and Benevento leave Naples from Piazza Garibaldi, in front of the Stazione Centrale. The CTP (Consorzio Trasporti Pubblici), **t** 081 700 1111, runs regular buses to **Caserta** (1hr) stopping at the station. From here you can also take buses to Santa Maria Capua Vetere. Benevento is most easily reached by bus. The Consorzio Trasporti Irpini, **t** 081 553 4677, has regular services to **Avellino** (50min) and **Benevento** (1½hrs) from Piazza Garibaldi in Naples. In Benevento, buses to Naples and a variety of other places (including one daily to Rome) leave from Piazza Pacca. There are several companies; check at the EPT for schedules.

Tourist Information

Caserta: in the Royal Palace, **t** 0823 322 170.
Benevento: Via Nicola Sala 31, **t** 0824 319 911, **f** 081 24 312 309, information office: in Palazzo Bosco, Piazza Roma 11, **t** 0824 319 938, info@eptbenevento.it.
Avellino: Via Due Principati 5, 83100, **t** 0825 74695.

Where to Stay and Eat

Neither Capua nor Caserta makes a very attractive base for an overnight stay. The environs of Caserta, though, do have some good restaurants. Benevento sees few tourists and accommodation is therefore limited. This is one of the reasons why it is even more attractive to those chancing upon it. There are several good restaurants and prices, in general, are markedly lower than the well-visited coast and Naples. It is an ideal base for making forays into inland Campania, as well as Caserta and Capua.

Dining in Benevento can be interesting; it's another world from the Campanian coast, with seafood replaced on the menu by rabbit, duck, lamb and veal. Samnium makes some good but little-known wines; ask for a bottle of stout-hearted Solopaca red with the repast.

Around Caserta

Ritrovo dei Patriarchi, Via Conte Landolfo 14, Località Sommana, **t** 0823 371 510 (*moderate*). At this restaurant outside

The Duchy of Benevento

Ever since the Middle Ages, the land around Caserta and Capua has been called the Terra del Lavoro – cultivated land, a broad garden plain that is one of the most fertile corners of Italy. Today its lush landscapes have suffered from creeping industrialization, though it's to the south, between Caserta and Naples, that the worst depredations can be seen. The Napoletani call the towns around Afragola, Acerra and Secondigliano the 'Triangle of Death' – a wasteland of shanties and power lines, ruled by the Camorra, that has Italy's worst unemployment, and its worst social problems.

Go east instead, up into the foothills of the Apennines towards Benevento, yet another small city that has often played a big role in Italian history. On an old tower in the centre of town, the city fathers have put up maps of southern Italy, showing the boundaries of the two important states of which Benevento was capital. At first, as *Malies* or *Maloenton*, it was the main town of the Samnites, warlike mountain people

Casertavecchia you'll find game in abundance, including pheasant, venison, partridge and wild boar, depending on the time of year. There are also good hearty soups and vegetable dishes. *Closed Thurs.*

Rocca di Sant'Andrea, Via Torre 8, t 0823 371 140 *(moderate)*. This restaurant in the centre of Casertavecchia offers delicious pasta dishes and a variety of *secondi*, many of which are based on meat grilled on the open fire in front of you. There is also a good choice of homemade desserts. *Closed Mon.*

La Castellana, Via Torre 4, t 0823 371 230 *(cheap)*. When available, you can feast on wild boar or venison at this *trattoria* near Rocca di Sant'Andrea. There is also an innovative selection of soup and pasta *primi*. *Closed Thurs.*

Benevento ✉ 82100

****Gran Hotel Italiano**, Viale Principe di Napoli 137, t 0824 24111, f 0824 21758 *(moderate)*. Located just a block from the Stazione Centrale, this is the best the city can offer – seventies architecture and décor except for two amazing original prints by Piranesi. Nevertheless, the infectious enthusiasm of the owner, Signor Italiano, the hotel's decent standards and its very helpful staff, all at provincial prices, make this good value. The 20-minute walk into the historic centre is its principal drawback.

Ristorante Teatro Gastronomico, Via Traiano-Palazzo L. Andreotti, t 0824 54605 *(moderate)*. This fun restaurant in the piazza in front of Trajan's Arch serves up a truly gastronomic menu of local specialities under a barrel vault painted with *trompe l'œil* architectural backdrops lined with real balconies.

Trattoria Nunzia, Via Annunziata 152, t 0824 29431 *(moderate)*. Set in the pretty medieval area, and now in its third generation, this place will surprise you with specialities like *cavatielli fagioli e cozze* (delicious home-made pasta with beans and mussels) and the near perfect English of Signora Nunzia's son. If you're too full to face the walk back to your hotel, they might even offer you a lift.

★★Della Corte, Piazza Piano di Corte, t 0824 54819 *(cheap)*. It's hard to beat this *pensione* both for charm and for its location right in the heart of the historic quarter. The rooms are clean and quiet and the place and proprietor have character. The hotel only has seven rooms and as yet remains fairly undiscovered. Finding the hotel by car, if you have one, can be quite a feat. Head for Corso Garibaldi, then ask.

Pizzeria Rodolfo, Via Meo Martini *(cheap)*. Many consider Rudolph's to be the best *pizzeria* in Benevento.

Pizzeria Romana. If you are basing yourself in Benevento to explore inland Campania, this stand-up *tavola calda* on the corner of Corso Dante and Corso Vittorio Emanuele, a block west of the cathedral, provides an excellent selection of very affordable delicacies for perfect picnics in the gardens of the Reggia at Caserta and other sites.

who resisted Roman imperialism for so long. The Romans later made a big city of it, an important stop along the Appian Way. They Latinized the name to *Maleventum* – ill wind – but after a lucky defeat of Pyrrhus of Epirus here in 275 BC they thought it might just be a *Beneventum* after all. In AD 571, the city was captured by the blood-thirsty Lombards, becoming their southern capital. After the Lombards of the north fell to Charlemagne, the Duchy of Benevento carried on as an independent state; at its greatest extent, under relatively enlightened princes like Arechi II (c. 800), it ruled almost all of southern Italy. The Normans put an end to it in the 1060s.

Coming to Benevento in the winter, you're bound to think the Romans were crazy to change the name. When the Salernitani are ready to hit the beaches, the Beneventani are still shivering on street corners in fur caps, victims of the worst weather in southern Italy. It is claimed this makes them more serious and introspective than people on the coast – certainly it seems a thousand miles away. Benevento has often been shaken by earthquakes, and the city took plenty of hard shots during the battles of 1943, but there are still attractions to make a stop worthwhile.

Benevento's **cathedral** is in the lower town, the part that suffered most from bombings. The cathedral itself was a near total loss; only its odd 13th-century façade remains, built of bits of Roman buildings – reliefs, friezes and pillars – arranged every which way. In the old streets behind it, you can see a dismally-kept **Roman theatre** (*open daily 9am–one hour before sunset; adm*) – not an amphitheatre, but a place for classical drama, something rare this far north. By the time the Romans conquered them, the culture of the Samnites was almost completely Hellenized. This theatre, built under Hadrian, originally seated 20,000; it is still used now. All through this quarter, the **Triggio**, you will see bits of Roman brick and medieval masonry in the walls of houses. There is half a Roman bridge (the Ponte Leproso – leper's bridge) over the river Sabato, ruins of baths, remains of a triumphal arch, and gates and fortification walls built by the Lombards. On Via Posillipo, a Baroque monument houses the *Bue Apis*, a sacred Egyptian bull sculpture found in Benevento's Temple of Isis.

Trajan's Arch

Some people claim Benevento's triumphal arch to be better than Rome's; built in AD 117, it is a serious piece of work – over 50ft of expensive Parian marble from Greece – and better preserved than the ones in the capital. It marks the spot where the Appian Way entered *Beneventum* (now Via Traiana on the edge of the old town); the carved reliefs on both faces record significant events in the emperor's career.

Trajan (AD 98–117), the conqueror of Dacia (modern-day Romania) and Mesopotamia, ranks among the greatest of the emperors, and a little commemoration would not seem out of hand; nevertheless cynics will enjoy the transparent and sometimes heavy-handed political propaganda of ornaments like this. In one of the panels, Trajan (the handsome fellow with the curly beard) is shown distributing gifts to children; in another he presides over the *institutio alimentaria* – the dole. Most of the scenes are about victories: Trajan announcing military reforms, Trajan celebrating a triumph, Jove handing Trajan one of his thunderbolts, and finally the Apotheosis, where the late emperor is received among the gods while the goddess Roma escorts Hadrian to coronation as his divinely ordained successor.

The Museo Sannio

Corso Garibaldi is Benevento's main street, just south of Trajan's Arch. Near its eastern end stands the city's oldest church, **Santa Sofia**, built in the late 8th century. It is unusual for its plan – an irregular six-pointed star – and was built for the Lombard Prince Arechi II by an architect grounded in the mystic geometry of the early Middle Ages. The vaulting is supported by recycled Roman columns; other columns have been hollowed out for use as holy water fonts. The church cloister (*under restoration*) contains one of the south's more interesting provincial museums, the randomly open **Museo Sannio** (*in theory open 9–1; closed Mon*). Sannio refers to Samnium, as Benevento's province is still officially called. The 12th-century cloister has a variety of strange twisted columns under pulvins carved with even stranger scenes: monster-

Some Samnite Curiosities

Two rooms in the Museo Sannio are filled with objects from the Temple of Isis. Anyone who has read Apuleius' *The Golden Ass* will remember just how important the cult of the transcendent goddess Isis was throughout the Roman world. This Egyptian import certainly seems to have found a home in Beneventum; nowhere in Europe has so much fine Egyptian statuary been retrieved. The temple had imperial backing. One of the statues is of the founder, Emperor Domitian himself, in Egyptian dress. Other works portray priestesses, sacred boats and sphinxes, another Apis bull, and a porphyry '*cista mistica*', carved with a snake. The image of Isis is also there, formidably impressive, even without a head.

Somehow this leads naturally to Benevento's more famous piece of exotica – the witches. In the days of the Lombards, women by the hundreds would dance around a sacred walnut tree on the banks of the River Sabato ('sabbath'). Even after the official conversion to Christianity in 663, the older religion persisted, and Benevento is full of every sort of 'witch' story as a result. The best piece of modern sculpture in the Museo Sannio is a representation of the witches' dance. Of course the city has found ways to put the legend to use. In any bar in Italy, you can pick up a bottle of 'liquore Strega' (*strega* means witch) and read on the label the proud device: 'Made next to the train station in Benevento, Italy'.

hunting, dancing, fantastical animals, bunnies and a camel or two. The best things are in the archaeological section: classic Campanian copies of Greek vases – ceramics production was the engine that drove *Campania Felix*'s economy in its glory days.

Over the road is the little-known **Hortus Conclusus**, a small enclosed garden. The dedicatory **obelisk** from the Isis temple stands in front of the town hall. The Corso takes you to the **Rocca de' Rettori**, a fortress built by the popes in the 14th century; for centuries Benevento was a papal enclave surrounded by the Kingdom of Naples. The fortress is now a part of the museum. Behind it is a lovely park, the **Villa Comunale**.

Samnium

Samnium is one of Italy's smallest provinces, but there are a few towns and villages of interest; the countryside, full of oak and walnut forests, is often reminiscent of a corner of Umbria. **Morcone**, to the north, has a memorable setting, draped on the curving slope of a hill like a Roman theatre. **Telese**, to the west on the road towards Lazio, lies near a small but pretty lake, with a popular spa. The ruins of the Samnite-Roman town of *Telesia* are remarkable for their perfectly octagonal walls, with gates at the cardinal points. Further north you'll find **S. Lorenzello** – famous for its ceramics and for being transformed into an antiques market every last weekend of the month.

Best of all is the town of **Sant'Agata dei Goti**, north of the Via Appia between Benevento and Caserta, with its long line of buildings like a man-made cliff over-hanging a little ravine. Sant'Agata takes its name from the Goths who founded it in the 6th century; it was badly damaged in the 1980 earthquake, and its *castello* and the 12th-century church of Santa Menna are still undergoing restoration.

Southern Campania

Continuing this broad arc around Naples, there are few attractions south and east of Benevento, but some attractive mountain scenery in the region of **Irpinia** – most of the province of Avellino. In places, the mountains bear fine forests of chestnuts and oaks, and plantations of hazelnut trees; other parts are grim and bare, testimony to the 19th-century deforestation that ruined so much of southern Italy. Irpinia was also the region worst affected by the 1980 earthquake. The provincial capital of **Avellino**, important in Norman times, has been wrecked so many times by earthquakes and invaders that little remains. In the centre, though, the 17th-century Palazzo della Dogana still retains its façade of ancient statues and its original clock tower.

The main highway south from Caserta, around the back of Vesuvius, isn't much more promising. Nola, the main town here, began as another Oscan foundation. It had a famous early bishop, St Paulinus, a friend of St Augustine and also said to be the inventor of the bell (bells are *campane* in Italian, from their Campanian origin). To celebrate the anniversary of St Paulinus' return from imprisonment by the Vandals, every 27 June the people of **Nola** put on one of the south's more spectacular festivals, the 'lily festival'. Further south, in the hills above **Nocera Inferiore**, the ancient hamlet of **Nocera Superiore** has kept intact its 4th-century church, an unusual round building with a cupola that may have been converted from a pagan sanctuary.

Paestum and the Cilento

Paestum: A Lost City

Site open daily 9–one hour before sunset; closed first and third Mon of month for restoration work; museum open Tues–Sun 9–2 only; adm.

The coastal route begins in a fertile plain that meets the Cilento near the ruins of *Paestum*, site of the only well-preserved Greek temples north of Sicily – and of another key Mediterranean player: the anopheles mosquito. The mosquito in fact gets the credit for preserving *Paestum*'s ruins so well. By the 9th century, this once-great city was breathing its last, a victim of economic decline and Arab raiders. As its people abandoned it for safer settlements in the hills, *Paestum* was swallowed up by thick subtropical forests; when the people left, malarial mosquitoes took over. By the Middle Ages, the site of *Paestum* was uninhabitable and the city's very existence was forgotten. After being hidden away, like the Mayan temples in the Mexican jungle, for almost a thousand years, the city was rediscovered in the 18th century; a crew of Charles III's road builders stumbled on to the huge temples in the midst of the forest.

Originally *Poseidonia*, the city was founded in the 7th century BC by the Sybarites, as a station on the important trade route up Italy's west coast. The Romans took over in 273 BC, and the name became Latinized to *Paestum*. Famous for its roses, it prospered until the end of the Roman era. Today the forests have been cleared, and the ruins of the city stand in the open. Not only the celebrated temples have survived; much of the 5km circuit of walls still stands, along with some of the towers and gates.

Most of *Paestum's* important buildings were grouped along an axis between the **Porta Aurea** and the **Porta Giustizia**, with the forum at its centre. The two grand temples (both wrapped in scaffolding) are at the southern end, two Doric edifices in the finest classical style known as the **Basilica** and the **Temple of Neptune** – the names are early archaeologists' guesses.

The Neptune temple, the best preserved, was built about 450 BC. It is 200ft long, and the whole structure survives except the roof and the internal walls. It may have been dedicated to Apollo, like a similar temple at Tarentum, but Hera and Zeus are also possible contenders. The Basilica was divided to house two cults, connected with Hera, the tutelary goddess of the city. It is a century older, and a little smaller. Missing its Doric frieze and pediment the first archaeologists did not recognize the building for a temple – hence the name Basilica.

The aesthetic may not be quite what you would expect – the dimensions are squat and strong rather than tall and graceful. Still, this is the classic austerity of Greek architecture at its best and there is more to it than meets the eye: if you look closely along the rows of columns, or the lines of the base, you may notice that nothing in either of them is perfectly straight; the edges bulge outwards, as they do in the Parthenon and every other Greek building – this is an architectural trick called *entasis*, which creates an optical illusion, making the lines seem straight at a distance.

Based on a simple system of perfect proportion, temples like this are the most sober and serious buildings in western architecture. With some imagination you can picture them in their original beauty, covered in a sort of enamel made of gleaming ground marble, setting off the brilliant colours of the polychromed sculptural reliefs on the pediments and frieze.

To the north, around the broad **Forum** – really a simple rectangular space in the manner of a Greek *agora* – are the remains of an ampitheatre, a round *bouleterion*, or council house, and other buildings. Still further north is the third and smallest of the surviving temples, the **Temple of Ceres**.

Paestum's **museum** holds most of the sculptural fragments and finds from the town. Some of the best reliefs are not from *Paestum* at all, but from the recently discovered **Sanctuary of Hera**, at the mouth of the River Sele. This temple, mentioned by many ancient writers, is said to have been founded by Jason and the Argonauts. From tombs excavated just outside the city come examples of Greek fresco painting – the only ones in existence. Look out for the most famous fresco, *The Diver*, which you will have seen reproduced innumerable times elsewhere. The Greeks took painting as seriously as they did sculpture, but surviving examples are rare. While you are exploring *Paestum*, keep an eye out for the famous roses (*bifera rosaria Paestum*). More than one 19th-century traveller claimed to have found them growing wild.

The Cilento Coast

For many, part of *Paestum's* attraction will be the fine, long beaches that line this part of the coast. Further south, the shore becomes jagged and mountainous, passing groves of pines alternating with rugged cliffs and pocket-sized beaches. Most of the villages along it have become quiet, cosy resorts that cater mostly to Italians. **Agropoli**

Getting Around

Paestum has a **station** on the main railway line between Naples and Reggio di Calabria, but only local trains stop there. More conveniently, there are frequent **buses** from the Piazza Concordia in Salerno (on the shore, by the Porto Turistico). They are run by several companies; some follow the coast route, while others go through Battipaglia. Some of these continue on to various resort towns on the Cilento coast.

All the **Cilento towns** are connected by **bus** to Salerno's Piazza Concordia; there is a bewildering list of companies, towns and schedules, but fortunately the EPT in Salerno publishes a full list of them in the front of their annual hotel book. The **railway** line only touches the Cilento coast at two points – Ascea and Pisciotta – and, as at Paestum, not too many trains stop.

Tourist Information

Paestum: in Piazza V. Veneto, t 089 231432, close by the main station, for transport and hotels in Paestum and the Cilento.
AAST: in the central Piazza Amendola, 84100, t 089 224 744, f 089 752 839; information

office, Via Magna Grecia 155 (near the archaeological zone), t 0828 811 016, f 0828 722 322, *www.fromitaly.it/Paestum*.
Palinuro: Piazza Virgilio, t 0974 938 144.

Where to Stay and Eat

Most people think of Paestum as a day trip, but there are enough hotels around the site, and on the nearby beaches, to make an overnight stay possible – and convenient. Some of the best accommodation is at Laura beach, about 5km north of Paestum.

Hotels on the Cilento are on the whole modern and unremarkable, though there are some exceptions. Most of the restaurants are in the hotels, and in summer the chances are you'll be stuck on full, or at least half, board. There is consolation in the fact that such arrangements are often an excellent deal.

If you are travelling through Battipaglia make sure you stop at one of the shops selling the locally produced *mozzarella di bufala*. Bite into it on the spot – you'll never taste anything like it anywhere else.

Paestum ✉ 84063

****Le Palme**, Via Sterpinia 33, t 0828 851 025, f 0828 851 507 (*moderate*). Set back from

comes first, then **Santa Maria di Castellabate**, **San Marco** and **Punta Licosa**, on the western point of the Cilento, named after the siren Leucosia – legend has it that she threw herself into the sea after failing to entice Ulysses on to the rocks. From here, you can take a boat out to the unidentified ancient ruins on the uninhabited islet of Licosa. Further down the coast, **Acciaroli** and **Pioppi** are among the nicer resorts.

Further south still, inland from Ascea Marina, you can visit the ruins of another Greek city, *Velia*. Don't expect anything spectacular of the order of *Paestum* – *Velia* disappeared gradually, and most of its remains were carried off for building stone long ago. *Elea*, as it was known then, was a colony of the Ionian city of Phocaea, and a sister city of another important Phocaean foundation – Marseille, in France. *Elea*'s name lives on in philosophy; the Elean school produced some of the most brilliant minds of the ancient world: logical grinds like Parmenides, who proposed the first theory of atoms, and wiseacres like Zeno with his pesky paradoxes. Fortifications survive, including one well-preserved gate – the Porta Rosa – and just enough of the *agora*, baths and streets to enable us to guess at how the city may have looked.

Both **Ascea Marina** and its neighbouring *località* of **Casalvelino** have pretty beaches, but the best ones of all, perhaps, can be found in the rugged terrain around **Palinuro**.

Laura beach in Paestum, this is a popular hotel with its own private beach a short walk away.

★★★Laura, Via Marittima, **t/f** 0828 851 068, (*moderate*). This good family hotel, just north of Le Palme, is pretty and relaxed, with helpful management. It too has its own private beach, and 13 rooms.

Nettuno, t 0828 811 028 (*moderate*). In the archaeological zone itself, under the city walls near Porta Giustizia, the excellent Nettuno has been a family-run restaurant specialising in seafood for over 70 years.

Museo, t 0828 811 135 (*moderate*). Also in the archaeological zone, next door to the museum, this seafood restaurant is excellent value, with an informal dining room and outdoor terrace.

Bar Anna, t 0828 811 196 (*moderate*). If you are just seeking a snack close to the museum, then this bar run by the kindly Signora Pia offers a good selection of cold *antipasti*, as well as the local buffalo *mozzarella* in a tomato salad (*insalata alla caprese*). *Closed Mon in winter.*

Palinuro ✉ 84064

Towards the southern end of the Cilento coast, Ascea has a small collection of hotels around its marina, but Palinuro has developed into a fully fledged holiday town.

★★★★King's Residence, Via Piano Faracchio, **t** 0974 931 324, **f** 0974 931 418 (*expensive*). This hotel outside Palinuro is in a stunning setting, perched high in a crow's nest position high on the cliffs and overlooking the Buondormire ('sleep well') bay. Every room comes with a terrace or balcony. A pathway runs down to the pretty little private beach, kitted out with a small bar for drinks and light meals. *Closed Nov–Feb.*

Da Carmelo, t 0974 931 138 (*moderate*). Just outside Palinuro, 1km along the road towards Camerota, this is a lively *trattoria* where guests dine well on dishes prepared according to old traditional recipes. Seafood comes highly recommended by the throng of participating locals, and it is worth going out of your way just to savour the excellent *antipasti*. Self-catering apartments are also available above the restaurant.

Taverna del Porto (*cheap*). Down by the harbour in Palinuro, this two-tiered bar and restaurant serves lunch at tables a stone's throw from the water's edge – making it ideal for a post-swim light lunch – and dinner in the more formal upper level.

This town, which has a small **museum** of archaeological finds, takes its name from Aeneas' pilot Palinurus, who is supposedly buried here – Virgil made the whole story up for the *Aeneid*, but that hasn't stopped it from sticking fast in local legend. Beyond Palinuro, the sandy coast curves back north into the Gulf of Policastro; here two more pleasant beach villages, **Scario** and **Sapri**, mark the southern boundary of Campania.

The Inland Route: Around the Cilento

South from Salerno, the *autostrada* skirts the back of the Cilento down to Calabria. Christ may have stopped at **Eboli**, but there's no reason why you should – and that goes for **Battipaglia** and **Polla** too. The delights of this region are subterranean, two first-rate caves on opposite slopes of the Monti Alburni. **Pertosa** (*open April–Sept daily 8–7; Oct–Mar 9–4; adm*), near the highway, is the better choice, with guided tours by boat and on foot; the pot-holers (spelunkers) suspect it is connected to the other one, at **Castelcivita**, near the village of **Controne**, which is part of the **National Park of Cilento**, a conservation project established locally to attract tourists.

At **Teggiano** there is a 13th-century castle and cathedral, as well as a little museum. **Padula**, just off the highway, is the unlikely location of the **Certosa di San Lorenzo**, after San Martino in Naples probably the biggest and richest monastery in the south. The Certosa has been closed for over a century, but in its heyday it would have held hundreds of Carthusians, in a complex laid out in the form of a gridiron (recalling the martyrdom of St Lawrence, the same plan used in El Escorial in Spain, also dedicated to the saint). Though it was expanded and rebuilt over 400 years, the best parts are Baroque: an enormous, elegant cloister, some wonderfully garish frescoes and lavish stucco figures in and around the chapel, and eccentric but well-executed decorative details throughout. There is a small **archaeological museum**.

Calabria and the Basilicata

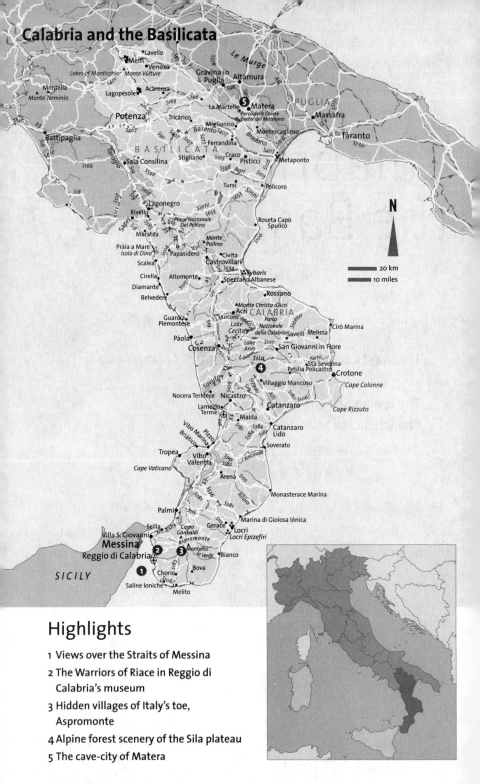

Calabria and the Basilicata

Highlights

1 Views over the Straits of Messina
2 The Warriors of Riace in Reggio di Calabria's museum
3 Hidden villages of Italy's toe, Aspromonte
4 Alpine forest scenery of the Sila plateau
5 The cave-city of Matera

Italy may be a country unusually blessed by fortune, but her favours are by no means evenly spread. To balance regions like the Veneto or Campania with their manifold delights, nature has given Italy its own empty quarter, the adjacent regions of Calabria and the Basilicata.

Calabria is the toe of the Italian boot, a gnarled, knobbly toe, amply endowed with corns and bunions and pointed accusingly at neighbouring Sicily. Almost all of it is ruggedly mountainous, leaving just enough room at the edges for the longest, broadest, emptiest beaches in Italy. It can claim three natural attractions: a scenic western coast, the forested highland regions of Aspromonte at the toe, and the Sila, in the centre. Most man-made attractions have been shaken to bits by Calabria's eternal plague of earthquakes, and there are plenty of ruins and ghost towns.

The **Basilicata**, still better known to many people under its old name of *Lucania*, takes on all comers for the title of Italy's most obscure region. It offers plenty of lonely, wild-west landscapes and two increasingly popular destinations, the resort of Maratea and the strange city of Matera, where people used to live in caves.

Magna Graecia

It was not always this way. Starting in about 750 BC, the Greeks extensively colonized southern Italy. *Rhegium*, today's Reggio di Calabria, came first, followed in short order by *Sybaris, Croton* and *Locris*, among others. These towns, happily situated along the major trade route of the Mediterranean, rapidly became as cultured as those of Greece itself – and far wealthier. It was a brilliant hour, and a brief one. After a time, blessed with a lack of external enemies, the cities of 'greater Greece' took to fighting among themselves in a series of ghastly, cruel wars over the most trivial of causes, often resulting in the total destruction of a city and the massacre of its inhabitants. Weakened by their own barbarous behaviour, the Greek cities then became pawns between Rome and Carthage in the Punic Wars; the victorious Romans took a terrible vengeance on those such as *Taras* (Táranto, in modern Puglia) that supported the wrong side. Roman rule meant a slow decline for the survivors, and by the 6th century the beautiful cities of Magna Graecia had been abandoned to the malarial mosquitoes.

Don't, however, come to Calabria looking for classical ruins. The great museum at Reggio gives a hint of what these cities were, but at the sites themselves almost nothing remains. Golden *Sybaris* has only just been found by the archaeologists, and only at *Metapontum* will you see so much as a few standing columns. Some may call the emptiness a monument to Greek hubris, or perhaps somehow these cities were doomed from the start. Considering Magna Graecia can be profoundly disconcerting; even in the ancient Mediterranean it is strange and rare for so many big cities to disappear so completely.

Nor has this corner of Italy been any more hospitable to civilization in the centuries since. Calabria in particular has suffered more at the hands of history than any region deserves. Since the Romans and the malaria mosquito put an end to the brilliant, short-lived civilization of Magna Graecia, Calabria has endured one wrenching earthquake after another, not to mention Arab raiders and Norman bully-boys, Spaniards and Bourbons, the most vicious of feudal landlords and the most backward and ignorant of monks and priests. By the 18th century, all these elements had combined to effect one of the most complete social breakdowns ever seen in modern Europe. Calabria staggered into anarchy, its mountains given over to bands of cut-throats while the country people endured almost subhuman poverty and oppression. Not surprisingly, everyone who was able chose to emigrate; today there are several times as many Calabresi living in the Americas as in Calabria itself.

A New Land

While famine, disease and misgovernment were putting an end to old Calabria, natural disasters like the terrible earthquake of 1783, and the even worse one in 1908 that destroyed the city of Reggio, were erasing the last traces of it. Calabria's stage was cleared for a modest rebirth, and the opportunity for it came after the Second World War, when Mr Rockefeller's DDT made the coasts habitable for the first time in over a millennium. Within a few years, government land reform improved the lives of thousands in both regions, and the Cassa per il Mezzogiorno's roads and industrial projects set out to pull their economies into the 20th century.

Today, despite the many problems that remain, it's possible to see the beginnings of an entirely new Calabria. A thousand years or more ago, the Calabrians deserted their once-great port cities for wretched though defensible villages in the mountains. Now they are finally moving back, and everywhere around Calabria's long and fertile coasts you will see new towns and cities; some, like Locri or Metaponto, are built over the ruins of the Greek cities that are their direct ancestors.

Most of this new Calabria isn't much to look at yet; the bigger towns, in fact, can be determinedly ugly (like Crotone). Calabria these days, for all its history, has an unmistakable frontier air about it. The people are simple, suspicious and a little rough. Unlike other Italians, they seem to have lots of children; they work hard, fix their own cars and tractors, and lay their concrete everywhere. So far, the changes have amounted to such a humble revolution that few people have even noticed, and the emigration rate remains enormous. But both these regions are, if anything, lands of survivors, and by now they may be taking their first steps on the road to reclaiming their ancient prosperity and distinction.

The West Coast: Maratea to Reggio di Calabria

Just south of Campania's Cilento peninsula, a little corner of the Basilicata stretches out to touch the Tyrrhenian Sea. The scenery here differs little from the steep cliffs and green slopes of the Cilento; after Sapri, the SS18 becomes a spectacular and rugged corniche road, passing over cliffs covered with scrubby *macchia*, and soft grey beaches on hidden coves – not so hidden any more, since a few hotels have been springing up on them, as at Acquafredda, just over the border.

Getting Around

Two major rail lines pass through these regions: the Rome–Naples–Villa San Giovanni/Reggio di Calabria route along the west coast (15 trains a day), and the branch that runs from Battipaglia in Campania through Potenza and Metaponto on its way to Táranto (6 trains a day). A third line follows the long shore of the Ionian Sea from Reggio to Táranto. Reggio di Calabria has two railway stations: the Stazione Marittima, from which crossings are made to Messina in Sicily, and the Stazione Centrale; if you're making a quick stop for the museum, the Marittima is closer.

Rail connections to anywhere in the **interior** are chancy at best: a few trains go through to Cosenza, but you'll usually have to change at Paola or Sibari. There are also regular buses from Paola to Cosenza. At Catanzaro it's the same; most trains stop only at Catanzaro Lido, 9km away (though there is a regular local bus to the city centre). In Cosenza buses leave from Piazza L. Fera, at the northern end of Corso Mazzini, for Catanzaro (several daily) and points around the province, including towns in the Sila.

A pleasant way to see the **Sila** itself is on the old private FCL narrow-gauge railway that runs three trains each day between Cosenza and San Giovanni in Fiore. The FCL station in Cosenza is hard to find as it's behind the now disused FS station in the town. Near the tip of Calabria there is another attractive local rail line, around the Tropea peninsula between Pizzo and Rosarno.

Matera is served only by another FCL private rail line, which runs 12 trains a day from Bari in Puglia – in fact, a day trip from Bari, only 46km, may be a convenient way to see Matera. The station there is on Via Nazionale on the western edge of town. There is also a very slow FCL line between Potenza and Bari, via Altamura. FCL and other companies also operate daily bus services from Matera's Piazza Matteotti to Ferrandina, Potenza, Naples and Metaponto.

Airports in Calabria are at Lamezia-Terme (the main regional airport) on the Plain of Santa Eufemia near the SS280 Catanzaro turn-off from the SS18, which has scheduled flights to most of the major Italian cities, and at Reggio di Calabria, just south of the city, with regular services only to Rome and Milan.

Car and passenger **ferries** to Sicily leave from Villa San Giovanni – the quickest route, with the most frequent services – and Reggio di Calabria. There are three companies: the FS, t 0965 758 241, Caronte, t 0965 756 725, and Tourist Ferry, t 0965 751 413. Don't worry; the service is very frequent, and whenever you arrive you'll be directed to whichever ferry is leaving next.

Tourist Information

Maratea: (AAST), Piazza del Gesù 32, t 0973 877 455.
Cosenza: Corso Mazzini 92, t 0984 27485.
Vibo Valentia: Galleria Vecchio, t 0963 42008.
Villa San Giovanni: in the Piazza Stazione, t 0965 751 160.
Reggio di Calabria: Via Roma 3, t 0965 892 512, f 0965 890 947; Via Tripepi 72, t 0965 898 496/7, f 0965 898 497; other offices are at the Stazione Centrale and the airport;
Gambarie: Piazzale Mangiaruca, t 0965 743 295.

Where to Stay and Eat

Seldom in Calabria or the Basilicata will you see a hotel older than the 1960s – a comment both on how much the regions have changed since the Second World War, and how little they had ever had to do with tourism beforehand. In the 1960s there were thoughts of a tourist boom – Calabria as the new Riviera – but problems with bureaucracy, bad planning and a lack of good sites for hotels has prevented this from taking off as expected. Still, you will find acceptable hotels almost everywhere; if you are just passing through,

Maratea and the Coast

The centre of the Basilicata's coast is **Maratea**, a pretty hill village of tiny alleys and steps, with more modern additions tucked between the cliffs by the sea far below it.

there are plenty of options along the SS18. If you have a car the best deals are often in the family-run *Aziende Agrituristiche*, where you'll taste the famed southern Italian hospitality and probably the best food in the region.

Maratea ✉ 85046

*****Santavenere**, Via Santavenere, t 0973 876 910, f 0973 877 654 (*luxury*). Maratea has become a mature enough resort to have some excellent accommodation. At the top of the tree is this elegant hotel, 1½km north of Porto di Maratea at Fiumicello-Santa Venere. A modern building, furnished with unusual elegance, in a fine setting on cliffs above the sea, it has a private beach and a pool. It also has an excellent restaurant.

****Villa del Mare**, t 0973 878 007, f 0973 878 102, *villadelmare@tiscalinet.it* (*moderate*). Just off the SS18, up on the cliffs, with a lift down to its private beach, this is one of the best of the less expensive choices up the coast from Maratea at Acquafredda.

***Villa degli Aranci**, Via Profiti 7, t/f 0973 876 344 (*moderate*). A good cheaper hotel near the Santavenere at Maratea-Fiumicello.

Za Mariuccia, Via Grotte 2, t 0973 876 163 (*expensive*). A good but pricey seafood *trattoria* in Maratea Porto, with tables overlooking the sea. The extensive menu includes excellent *risotto* and pasta dishes that use scampi, lobster and the very best of whatever Maratea's fishermen have come up with on that particular day. *Closed Fri.*

Rovita, Via Rovita 13, t 0973 876 588 (*expensive*). Another of Maratea's treasures, in the historic centre. Here excellent fish is matched with equally good pasta and meat dishes, all making the most of local Basilicata produce – rocket, aubergines and so on. *Open Sept–April; closed Tues.*

La Torre, t 0973 876 227. The most popular *trattoria* in the historic centre, on the main piazza. You'll need to arrive early if you want to claim one of the tables outside.

Caffè e Dolcezze, Piazza Raglia 19. This tiny café is a great place to stop for a coffee in the old town. There's only one table inside, and it's surrounded by are a series of glass-fronted drawers packed with all kinds of colourful sweets, liquorice and candied fruits.

Práia a Mare ✉ 87028

Calabria, Via Roma 58, t 0985 72350 (*cheap*) A simple place near the sea with its own stretch of beach. Práia makes a good place to look for a cheap room, as there are at least ten other places just like this one.

Vecchio Frantoio, Corso da Viscigliosa (*cheap*). Serves a wide selection of fresh grilled fish and seafood served with *porcini* mushrooms or rocket.

Cosenza ✉ 87100

Unfortunately there are no hotels in the old citadel. Until they appear, the following are the best Cosenza can offer:

****Royal**, Via Molinella 24/e, t 0984 412 165, f 0984 412 461 (*moderate*). Comfortable, reasonably priced and the smartest in town.

***Centrale**, Via dei Tigrai, t 0984 73681 (*moderate*). Another well-run place in the new town to consider staying.

*Bruno**, Corso Mazzini 27, t 0984 73889 (*cheap*). The best budget option, very basic, but only a short walk from the centre.

L'Arco Vecchio, Piazza Archi di Ciaccio 21, t 0984 72564 (*moderate*). An eatery in the heart of the old quarter, with a sophisticated feel.

Da Giocondo, Via Piave t 0984 28910 (*cheap*). Does nicely for a good meal in an informal and busy atmosphere, in the new town.

Bella Calabria, t 0984 793 531 (*cheap*). Waiters in tuxedos lend a smart feel to this place, where you eat *al fresco* at the foot of the cathedral in Piazza Duomo.

Artcafé, Piazza Duomo, t 0984 32682. After dinner in the old town stroll across the square for a drink and jazz. *Closed Mon.*

The Sila ✉ 87100

***Grande Albergo Parco della Fate**, t 0984 922 057, f 0984 701 272 (*moderate*). In alpine

Maratea has in the last few years become quite sophisticated and expensive, though the atmosphere is still pretty laid-back. Besides some of the best coastal scenery in the deep south, you can enjoy relatively uncrowded beaches and modest hotels at Acquafredda, Maratea Marina (where trains on the main Rome–Reggio rail line stop),

forests at Villaggio Mancuso, this hotel allows you to see the Sila in style.

***San Francesco Terme**, Località Bagni, t 0984 953 068, f 0984 953 251 (*moderate*). Situated near Spezzano Albanese, this hotel mainly caters to the spa customers.

***Dino's**, Viale della Repubblica 166, t 0984 992 090, f 0984 992 370, *dino@fitad.it* (*cheap*). San Giovanni in Fiore makes another possible base for visiting the Sila; just outside the town in Pirainella, this hotel is comfortable enough for a stop-over. Dino's also has the best restaurant in the area, specializing in roast kid and trout, and other delights of the uplands (and it's a good bargain too).

Elsewhere around the Sila, there is very modest accommodation available at Bocchigliero and Longobucco, to the north near the Sila Greca. Around the Albanian villages, accommodation is mostly in Spezzano Albanese.

***Due Torri**, t 0984 953 613, on the SS19. (*cheap*) The cheap and cheerful option near Spezzano Albanese.

Alternatively, you could find a good base for visiting the Sila at Tiriolo, on its southern end not far from Catanzaro

Vibo Valentia ✉ 89900

**Miramonti, Via F. Protetti, t 0963 41053 (*moderate*). A simple, honest hotel typical of Vibo Valentia.

**Terrazzino, t 0963 571 091 (*cheap*). A very basic *pensione* at Bivona on the coast near the castle.

L'Approdo, Via Roma 22, t 0963 572 640 (*moderate*). In Vibo Marina, this locally celebrated seafood establishment is the best restaurant in the area. Elaborate *frutti di mare*, *antipasti*, grilled fish and swordfish *involtini* invite a worthwhile splurge.

Pizzo ✉ 88026

***Murat**, Piazza della Repubblica 41, t 0963 534 201, f 0963 534 469 (*moderate*). A rare old-fashioned establishment in the very

heart of the old village that offers a very pleasant place to stay.

Casa Janca, Riviera Prangi, Località Marinella, t 0963 534 890 (*moderate*). The real reason to stop is this *agriturismo*, a country house quirkily decorated by Rita Callipo. In summer you'll have to take full board; you'll be grateful as people flock from Catanzaro for glorious Calabrian cooking (*cheap*).

Tropea/Cape Vaticano ✉ 88038

The best places to stay are around Tropea and nearby Parghelia – there are scores of new resort hotels in all price ranges around Tropea itself, as well as at Parghelia and Zambrone to the east, where the beaches are.

*****Baia Paraelios**, t 0963 600 300, f 0963 600 074 (*very expensive*). Set on one of the prettiest parts of the coast, Baia Paraelios is a group of well-furnished cottages set on a terraced hill overlooking a beautiful beach. Like many places along this coast you must reserve some time ahead (*open May–Sept*).

Da Isabella, t 0963 392 891/0333 524 5467 (*cheap*). This pretty villa, set in its own lush garden, is run by friendy Isabella Tomaschek, who speaks some English. The atmosphere is intimate, the rooms are cosy and you can start your day with an English breakfast – unusual among the region's *cucina povera*. You'll find it up the hillside in Zambrone, off the coastal road towards Tropea.

Vittoria, t 0963 81358, (*moderate*). A bit out of the way, but one of the best seafood restaurants with outdoor dining in the area.

Al Centro Storico, Via Pietro Vanea, (*moderate*). This seafood restaurant in Tropea has outside tables on a little square.

Terra di Dentro, Via Roma. The best in Calabrian specialities to take home, from fine wines to hot peppers and *'nduja*, the spicy hard salami that is an essential component of Calabrian soul food.

Scilla ✉ 89058

***Del Pino**, Località Melia, t 0965 755 126, f 0965 755 154 (*moderate*). Up in the hills

and several other points along the coast. The town itself lies under what must be the queerest hilltop Jesus in Italy; all marble, and 66ft tall. Designed by Bruno Innocenti in 1963 at the start of Maratea's push to become a resort, from a distance it looks more like a perfume bottle with wings.

above the village, this is a fancy option for the area, with a pool.

★★Sirene, Via Nazionale 57, t 0965 754 019 (*cheap*). The only hotel in Scilla itself. It has simple, inexpensive rooms and a great position just off the beach. Book in advance.

Alla Pescatora, Marina di Scilla, t 0965 754 147 (*moderate*). Right on the beach, this place offers *al fresco* dining and a great octopus *antipasto* among other seafood specialities. *Open April–Sept only; closed Wed.*

Il Castello di Alta Fiumana, Località S. Trada, t 0965 759 804, f 0965 759 566 (*moderate*). Another good eating option in Villa S. Giovanni-Cannitello. The restaurant sits on a hill and has great views over the straits.

Pizzeria S. Francesco, Via Cristoforo Colombo 29 (*cheap*). Head here for generous pizzas on the seafront. The owner seems keen to polish up her excellent English by helping you in any way she can.

Reggio di Calabria ✉ 89100

★★★★Miramare, Via Fata Morgana 1, t 0965 812 444, f 0965 812 450, *miramare@reggiocalabriahotels.it* (*expensive*). A characterful hotel on the seafront offering comfort alongside a certain old-world charm.

★★Lido, Via III Settembre 6, t 0965 25001, f 0965 899 393 (*moderate*). A modest well-positioned hotel, a short walk from the Museo Nazionale and the beach.

★★Eremo, Via Eremo Botte 12, t 0965 22433 (*cheap*). The pleasant, plant-filled Eremo is one of the few hotels in the vicinity that has access for wheelchairs. Its only drawback is its position up the hill.

★★★Diana, Via Vitrioli 12, t 0965 891 522. A funky but friendly hotel just off Corso Garibaldi in a mouldering *palazzo*.

★★Il Ducale, Corso Vittorio Emanuele III 13, t 0965 891 520 (*moderate*). An attractive restaurant in the centre of town, beside the Museo Nazionale. Many of the dishes on the menu are unavailable, and the food may not quite live up to its elegance, but, given Reggio's shortage of restaurants, it's fine.

Bracieria, Via Tripepi 81–83, t 0965 29361 (*moderate*). A wide variety of local dishes are served at this warm, cosily furnished restaurant, on a parallel to Corso Garibaldi in the centre. Highly recommended by locals.

Il Mio Ristorante, Via Provinciale 41, t 0965 682 654 (*moderate*). The place to come for something a bit more elegant, just outside town in Gallina. It has beautiful views of the straits and serves up first-class swordfish, *aragoste* and good desserts. *Closed Mon.*

Villeggiante, Via Condera Vallone Mariannazzo 31, t 0965 25021 (*cheap*). Traditional Calabrian cuisine is served at this large and popular restaurant, up the hill towards Chiesa Eremo, with views over the straits.

Aspromonte ✉ 89050

★★★Centrale, Piazza Mangeruca 22, Gambarie, t 0965 743 133, f 0965 743 141 (*cheap*). Gambarie has almost all of the hotels on Aspromonte, and there isn't a lot of difference between them. The 'Central' is large and adequate, if a bit characterless.

Ristorante Nunziatina, Sant'Alessio di Aspromonte, t 0965 741 006 (*cheap*). This place on the road up to Gambarie is typical of the informal outdoor restaurants that open in summer throughout the region; a few tables under the trees, and good simple cooking for next to nothing. It's a local favourite and a stronghold of mountain cooking, with homemade Calabrian pastries for dessert.

Villa Rosa, t 0965 740 500, (*moderate*). A wonderful place, with outdoor dining on a panoramic terrace covered with flowers, and delicious dishes served by cheery staff; try the pasta with *porcini* mushrooms, or something from the sizzling barbecue. It's on the road to Gambarie just beyond Santo Stefano. Ring Rosa in advance.

Sapori di Calabria, t 0965 743 168. A very friendly delicatessen on Gambarie's main square where you can buy gift-wrapped *porcini* mushrooms, or order a delicious chunky sandwich for a picnic.

Some 10 kilometres further down the coast and you're in Calabria, on the outskirts of another resort on a less dramatic stretch of coast: **Práia a Mare**, where there is a 14th-century castle. From the beach you can rent a boat to visit the 'Blue Grotto' on the **Isola di Dino**, an uninhabited islet just off the shore. Further south along the road is the now pretty much overdeveloped **Scalea,** and beyond it **Diamante,** a picturesque village of narrow streets, stacked on a rock above the sea. **Páola,** where the road from Cosenza meets the coast, is a larger, somewhat dishevelled resort, a fitting introduc-tion to the towns of the 'Calabrian Riviera' to the south. Above it stands the 15th-century **Santuario di San Francesco di Pola,** dedicated to the town's most famous son, Calabria's patron saint – not the same Francis as the Saint of Assisi – and the object of pilgrimages from all over southern Italy.

Cosenza

So far, there hasn't been much reason to leave the coast. **Cosenza** may not be a stellar attraction, but as cities go it's the best Calabria can do. One of Calabria's chief towns throughout most of recorded history, it began as the capital of the Bruttians, the aboriginal nation from whom today's Calabrians are descended. Medieval Cosenza was busy: the Arabs took it twice, Norman freebooters fought over it, and at least one king of France passed through on his way to the Crusades.

The **River Busento** divides Cosenza neatly between the flat modern town and the old citadel on the hill. The river is famous, if only because buried somewhere beneath it is no less a personage than Alaric the Goth. Alaric – no drooling barbarian, but just another scheming Roman general with a Teutonic accent – came to Cosenza in 410, fresh from his sack of Rome and on his way to conquer Africa. He died of a fever here, and his men temporarily diverted the Busento and buried him under it, probably along with a fair share of the Roman loot. Archaeologists are still looking for it.

For all its history, Cosenza has little to show; even in Calabria, no place is more prone to earthquakes – four big ones in the last 200 years, with added destruction by Allied bombers in 1943. The **cathedral,** a simple Gothic structure, has survived the latest earthquakes, although it didn't back in 1184 – what we see now was rebuilt under the reign of Frederick II on the ruins of the original 7th-century basilica. Inside lie buried one of Frederick's sons and Isabella of Aragon. Its best bits have been moved to the cloister of the church of **San Francesco d'Assisi,** down the hill on Via San Francesco. It contains two real treasures: a little-known masterpiece of medieval art, a Byzantine-style crucifix in gold and enamel, made in Sicily in the 12th century and given by Frederick himself on the occasion of the cathedral's consecration in 1222; and the shiny 13th-century Byzantine icon of the Madonna del Pilerio, believed to have saved the city from the bubonic plague of 1576 and thus made patron of Cosenza. A few blocks south of the cathedral, on Piazza XV Marzo, there is a small **Museo Civico** (*open Mon and Thurs 9–1.30 and 3.30–6.30; Tues, Wed and Fri 9–1.30; adm*), with paintings and archaeological finds, and from there you can also climb up to the **castle** over-looking the city (*open daily July and Aug 8–midnight, Sept–June 8–8*). Originally built by the Normans, it was modified by Frederick II, the Aragonese and the Angevins. The medieval 'reception room' has capitals with floral motifs carved in pink sandstone.

The Sila

Cosenza is the best base from which to see this region, a lovely, peaceful plateau between mountains that offers an unusual experience of Alpine scenery near the southern tip of Italy. Much of the Sila is still covered with trees – beeches, oaks and pines. In summer you can find wild strawberries, and in winter – well, maybe – wolves. Some of Italy's last specimens make their stand in the Sila's wilder corners. Artificial lakes, built since the war as part of Calabria's hydroelectric schemes, add to the scenery, notably **Lake Arvo** and **Lake Cecita**, between Cosenza and the town of San Giovanni in Fiore. The Sila is the best place in Calabria for motoring or hiking, and maps and information are available from the Cosenza tourist office. Most likely you will see only the largest and prettiest section, the **Sila Grande**, in the middle, though more adventurous souls can press on to the barely accessible **Sila Greca**, to the north, or south to the **Sila Piccola**, around the little mountain resort of **Villaggio Mancuso**.

On the eastern flank of the Sila Piccola, not far from **Crotone**, is the interesting little town of **Santa Severina**, with a Norman castle and a cathedral with a Byzantine baptistry. Despite the name, the Sila Greca is in fact inhabited by Albanians of the Greek Orthodox faith. They came to Calabria and Sicily as refugees from the Turks in the 15th century, and today constitute one of Italy's largest ethnic minorities. Albanians can be found all over Calabria, especially here and in the north around Castrovillari; you'll know you've stumbled on one of their villages if you see a Byzantine-domed church or a statue of Skanderbeg, the Albanian national hero.

South of Cosenza

Back towards the coast south of Cosenza, and just a few kilometres from the main road up in the hills, is the town of **Nocera Terinese**, famous for only one thing – its festival every Easter, when processions of flagellants go around the town, fervently beating themselves into a bloody mess with thorn bushes, in one of the local events that is most regularly deployed to demonstrate Calabria's distance from the modern world. Further south again, the road descends to the plain of Santa Eufemia, one of the new agricultural areas reclaimed from the mosquito. The town of **Maida**, site of one of the first French defeats during the Napoleonic Wars, gave its name to London's Maida Vale. **Pizzo** also has its Napoleonic association. The great cavalry commander, Marshal Murat, whom Bonaparte had made King of Naples, tried after Waterloo to regain his throne by beginning a new revolution in Calabria. When his boat landed here in 1815, the crowd almost tore him to pieces. The Bourbons executed him a few days later in the castle, built in the 1480s by Ferdinand of Aragon.

The best part of Calabria's coast begins near Capo Vaticano. **Vibo Valentia**, a new provincial capital, has views overlooking the coast, a 12th-century castle, remains of the fortifications of the ancient Greek city of *Hipponion*, and a number of over-wrought Baroque churches. Finds from the excavations of Hipponion are on view in the museum in the castle (*open daily 9–7; adm*). South of Vibo the main road cuts inland, but the railway and some back roads head around Cape Vaticano; this is a district of fashionable, pretty beach resorts, and difficult mountains. **Tropea** is a lovely town along the coast; next to it, on a rocky peninsula that was once an island, you can climb up to the romantically ruined Benedictine monastery of Santa Maria dell'Isola. The town offers some spectacular views, taking in on a clear day the island volcano of Strómboli and Sicily's northern coast.

Further south, the towns along the coast are more accessible, and some of them have grown into fair-sized holiday spots. Outside Palmi there is a museum and cultural complex, the **Casa di Cultura Leonida Repaci**, that, among other collections, houses the best folk museum in Calabria, and a modern art gallery with works by De Chirico and other 20th-century Italian painters (*open Mon–Wed 8–2 and 3–6, Tues, Thurs and Fri 8–2*).

Scilla, at the entrance to the Straits of Messina, marks the spot where the mythological Scylla, daughter of Hecates, changed into a dog-like sea monster, seized some of Odysseus' crewmen near the end of the *Odyssey*. In classical times Scylla meant the dangerous rocks of the Calabrian side of the straits, a counterpart to the whirlpool Charybdis towards the Sicilian shore. So many earthquakes have rearranged the topography since then that nothing remains of either. Still, the narrow straits are one of the most dramatic sights in Italy, with Messina and the Monte Peloritani visible over in Sicily, neatly balancing Reggio and the jumbled peaks of Aspromonte in Calabria.

Reggio di Calabria

The last big earthquake came in 1908, when over 100,000 people died here and in Messina across the straits. Both these cities have a remarkable will to survive, considering all the havoc earthquakes have played on them in the last 2,000 years. Perhaps the setting is irresistible. Fortune has favoured them unequally in the rebuilding; though both are about the same size, Messina has made of itself a slick, almost beautiful town, while Reggio has chosen to remain swaddled in Calabrian humility. Its plain grid of dusty streets and low buildings was laid out only after the earthquake of 1783, when the destruction was even greater than in 1908 and the city had to be rebuilt from scratch.

The Allies also did a pretty thorough job of bombing Reggio in the Second World War; after all that, it's not surprising that there is little left to see of the city that began its life as Greek *Rhegium* in the 8th century BC. Some bits of Greek wall and Roman baths, and some once-grand 19th-century buildings along the waterfront promenade, are almost the only things in the city older than 1908.

Part of Reggio's shabbiness is without question due to the corrosive social effect of the local Calabrese mafia, known in dialect as the *'ndrangheta*, which continues to have a hold here stronger even than those that its wealthier partners in crime, the Sicilian Mafia and the Neapolitan Camorra, exert over their own respective backyards.

In recent years, however, thought and effort has gone into the development of the city centre, most noticeable on the seafront, where a wide and elegant promenade is under construction. The city's main attraction is undoubtedly its **Museo Nazionale della Magna Graecia** (*open daily 9–8; in summer until 11pm on Sat; closed first and third Mon of the month; adm*), which houses the finest collection of Greek art between Naples and Sicily. Besides the Warriors of Riace, some of the best things in the collection are the terracotta **ex voto plaques**, recovered from the temples of

The Warriors of Riace

Reggio's museum, directly north of the city centre on Corso Garibaldi, is a classic of Mussolini architecture built in chunky travertine. Containing a hoard as precious as anything in Greece itself, the museum would make a trip to Reggio worthwhile just for the Warriors of Riace, two bronze masterpieces that rank among the greatest productions of antiquity to have come down to us. If you haven't heard of them, it is because they were only found in 1972, by divers exploring an ancient shipwreck off Riace on Calabria's Ionic coast. They are normally kept down in the basement in a room of their own, next to a big exhibition detailing the tremendously complex original restoration job done in the seventies. These fellows, both about six-foot-seven and quite indecently virile, may perhaps have come from a temple at Delphi; no one really knows why they were being shipped to Magna Graecia. One of them has been attributed to the great sculptor Phidias.

The Warriors share the basement with a few other rare works of Greek sculpture, notably the unidentified, 5th-century BC subject called 'the Philosopher', as well as anchors and ship fittings, and *amphorae* that once held wine or oil – all recovered from the shipwreck, from mud well over a metre deep. The divers are convinced that the dangerous waters around Calabria may hold dozens of such treasures, so some more artefacts may have found their way to the museum by the time you arrive.

Magna Graecia. Most of these offerings show goddesses in the magical archaic Greek style – usually Persephone – who had influence over death – being abducted by Hades, receiving propitiatory gifts, or accepting souls into the underworld. Chickens are a recurring motif, not too surprisingly, since to the ancient Greeks a soul rises out of its burial urn the same way a chicken hatches from an egg.

Other works help complete the picture of life and art in Magna Graecia: Greek painted ceramics from Locris and from Attica, fragments of architectural decoration from various temples – some still with bits of their original paint, records of city finances on bronze tablets, coins, some treasure recovered from tombs, and a rare early Hellenistic mosaic of a dragon, actually made in Calabria. The museum also has a collection of paintings, including two works by Antonello da Messina.

Aspromonte

All around the toe of Italy, from Palmi as far as Locri, the interior of the peninsula seems utterly impenetrable, a wall of rough peaks looming over the narrow coastal plain. In fact all of the toe is really one great round massif, called Aspromonte. The tortuous mountain roads allow few easy opportunities for climbing inland, but from the north end of Reggio a 30km route, the SS184, will take you up to **Gambarie**, with pine forests and views over the straits and Sicily. In winter Gambarie is Calabria's unlikely ski resort, with just enough snow to get by in an average year; in summer it's a good starting-off point for walkers.

Aspromonte, with its 22 summits and its Greek-speaking villages, was the haunt of the chivalrous 19th-century bandit Musolino, a sort of Calabrian Robin Hood still remembered in these parts. His well-tended grave is in the cemetery in his birthplace, **Santo Stefano**, just below Gambarie. Scholars who have studied the Greeks here speculate that they may be descendants of the original Greek population of Magna Graecia, holding on to their cultural identity thanks only to the barely accessible locations of their mountain villages.

On the coastal plain, snow is hardly ever seen. This is one of Italy's gardens, a panorama of lemon and orange groves. Two more exotic crops have also given fame to the region: jasmine, which grows so well nowhere else in Italy; and bergamot, a small, hard, green orange, discovered only some 200 years ago. Now it is an indispensable ingredient in the making of the finest perfumes (and also the stuff used to flavour Earl Grey tea). If it is a clear day, the straits around Reggio can treat you to some of the grandest views in the south; much of the Sicilian coast is visible, and perhaps even Mount Etna will peek out from behind its entourage of clouds.

If you are especially lucky, you may be treated to an appearance of the famous **Fata Morgana**, the mirages of islands or many-towered cities that often appear over the straits. The name comes from the enchantress Morgan le Fay. Arthurian romance came to southern Italy with the Normans, and rooted itself deeply in these parts; old Sicilian legends have a lot to say about King Arthur. In one of the tales, Arthur sleeps and awaits his return not up in chilly England, but deep in the smoky bowels of Etna. Roger de Hauteville himself, a close relation of William the Conqueror, is said to have seen the Fata Morgana, and his learned men interpreted the vision as a divine invitation to invade Sicily. Roger demurred, thinking it would be better to wait and take Sicily on his own than do it with the aid of sorcery.

The Ionian Sea

Italy's Longest Beach

From Reggio as far as Táranto, the coasts of Calabria and later the Basilicata are one long beach – about 500km of it, broken in only a few places by mountains or patches of industry. All along this route, the pattern will be the same: sleepy new concrete settlements on the shore, within sight of their mother towns, just a few kilometres further up in the mountains. In summer, you will see great rivers, like the Amendola, filled not with water but with pebbles; the terrible deforestation of Calabria in the 19th century (committed mostly by northern Europeans with the assistance of corrupt Italian governments) denuded much of the interior, and made its rivers raging torrents in the spring. Recent governments have worked sincerely to reforest vast tracts, especially on Aspromonte, but wherever you see bare rock on the mountains, there is land that can never be redeemed.

Many of the new villages and towns on the bottom of the toe have become little resorts – two *pensioni* and a *pizzeria*, on average; none is worth special mention, but you'll never have trouble finding clean water and a kilometre or so of empty (and usually trash-strewn) beach. About 3km south of **Locri** there are fragmentary ruins of the Greek city *Epizefiri (open 9–one hour before sunset; closed first and third Mon of*

Tourist Information

Locri: Pro Loco, Corso da Merici, t 0964 21910.
Crotone: Via Torino 148, t 0962 23185.
Catanzaro: Galleria Mancuso, t 0961 741 764.
Metaponto Lido: Viale delle Sirene, t 0835 741 933. One of the coastal resorts that open local information desks in the summer.

Where to Stay and Eat

Marina di Gioiosa Iónica ✉ 89046

★★★San Giorgio, Via I Maggio 3, t/f 0964 415 064 (*cheap*). None of the various tiny lidos on Calabria's Ionian shore is particularly inviting for more than a short stopover, but this is one of the more pleasant spots, just north of Locri. The hotel has a nice garden, beach and pool.

Gerace ✉ 89048

La Casa di Gianna, Via Paolo Frascà 4, t 0964 355 024, f 0964 355 081, *casadigianna@yahoo.it* (*expensive*). Someone with a 16th-century villa to spare has recently taken the initiative to convert it into a luxurious ten-roomed hotel. Hidden down a narrow medieval street, the building is centred round an atrium, which bathes the upper floors in light. The bedrooms are tasteful, while the restaurant downstairs is cool and elegant. This is one place along the Ionian coast where you can sleep and eat in style.

A Squella, t 0964 356 086 (*cheap*). Just at the entrance of the town on the Locri road, this little *trattoria* serves good pizza as well as a full menu with traditional favourites like bean and chicory casserole and pasta with chick peas and hot peppers. *Open for lunch only out of season.*

Stilo ✉ 89900

★★San Giorgio, Via Citarelli 8, t/f 0964 775 047 (*moderate*). There is just one hotel in Stilo, but one with an unusual degree of character: the San Giorgio occupies a former cardinal's palace and is furnished partly in period style, with a pool and a terrace with panoramic views. Full board obligatory in August. *Open April–Oct.*

La Vecchia Miniera, t 0964 731 869 (*moderate*). Just outside Bivongi, near the Cascate del Marmárico. Try the mountain trout or pasta with stewed kid sauce. Also organizes tours of the falls and other sites. *Closed Mon.*

Catanzaro ✉ 88100

★★★Grand Hotel, Piazza Matteotti, t 0961 701 256, f 0961 741 621 (*moderate*). This modern and attractive place in the centre of town is one of a few simple hotels in Catanzaro.

★★Belvedere, Via Italia 33, t 0961 720 591 (*cheap*). Still comfortable, and cheaper.

Due Romani, Via Murano, off the coastal SS106, t 0961 32097 (*moderate*). Down in Catanzaro Lido, stop for dinner at the 'Two Romans'. It specializes in seafood, including

month), a few bits of wall and bases of temples. Most of the art excavated from Locri has been taken to the Reggio museum and further afield (including perhaps, the famous Ludovisi throne in Rome, which has been called a fake). Enough was left behind in Locri to make the Antiquarium near the sea worth a visit (*open daily 9–8; adm*). When pirates and malaria forced the Locrians to abandon their city in the 8th century, they fled to the nearby mountains and founded **Gerace**. Though the population of its melancholy medieval centre today is only about 300, Gerace was an important centre in the Middle Ages; it has Calabria's biggest cathedral, an 11th-century Norman Romanesque work supported by columns from the ruins of Locri.

Roccella Iónica is an up-and-coming little town. Its hilltop setting and half-ruined castle provide one of the few breaks in the monotony of beach along the coast road. Up in the hills above Monasterace Marina, the Greek village of **Stilo** is famous for its 10th-century Byzantine church, La Cattólica, with five small domes and remains of medieval frescoes. Further north, there is little to detain you along the shore of the

the best and most copious *griglia mista* the authors have ever had in Italy.

La Corteccia, Via Indipendenza 30, t 0961 746 130 (*moderate*). There's little choice and little seafood in Catanzaro itself, but this is as good a place as any to fill up on traditional cuisine at reasonable prices.

Wine Shop, Vicolo San Rocchello (*cheap*). This wine shop (with no name) is another, more rough-and-ready, place to sample some powerful local specialities.

*Coniglio d'Oro, Località Vaccariti, Tiriolo (on the main street north of the centre) t 0961 991 056. This welcoming, small family-run place is the least expensive of three good hotels in Tiriolo, a pretty village on the southern end of the Sila, once famed for the costumes of its women (you still may see one). It offers a nice alternative to staying in nearby Catanzaro, and it also makes a good base for exploring the interior. The 'Golden Rabbit' also has a good and very reasonable *pizzeria-ristorante*.

Crotone ✉ 88900

On the whole, dining along this stretch of coast is simple – a little seafood shack that is only open in the summer, or a small, lively *pizzeria* with a sunny little terrace.

Da Annibale, Via Duomo 35 (in Le Castella on Capo Rizzuto, south of Crotone), t 0962 795 004 (*moderate*). One of the few places on the Ionian coast where you can have an elaborate meal. Try the swordfish *involtini*.

Il Girrarosto, Via Vittorio Veneto 30, t 0962 22043 (*moderate*). A very good restaurant in the centre of Crotone. The cook specializes in roast lamb and kid, but also really knows what to do with swordfish and other seafood. The terrace is a bonus, too.

Da Peppino, Piazza Umberto (*cheap*). This bustling *trattoria* is a simple option, serving pizza and seafood at its tables on a leafy piazza near the cathedral.

Policoro and Metaponto ✉ 75025

Along the Basilicata's short stretch of Ionian coast, Policoro makes the most convenient place to stop over.

****Degli Argonauti, Marina di Pisticci, t 0835 470 242, f 0835 470 240 (*very expensive*). A haven for swimming enthusiasts, this plush hotel is centred round its own lagoon-like swimming pool. At an astounding 6,000 square metres, it guarantees you'll have plenty of room to splash around in. But this is no stop-over; in the summer a week's stay and full board are minimum requirements. This requirement may be lifted at the very beginning and end of the season.

***Callà, Corso Pandosia 1, t 0835 972 129 (*cheap*). One of a number of decent middle-range hotels in Policoro.

***Kennedy, Viale Jonio 1, t/f 0835 741 960, (*cheap*). A bargain on the beach at Metaponto Lido.

Ragno Verde, Via Colombo 13, t 0835 971 736. A good family *trattoria* in Policoro. *Closed Sun.*

Gulf of Squillace as far as **Catanzaro**, the Calabrian capital. Really an overgrown mountaintop village that has straggled gradually down to the sea since the war, it is a piquant little city, the kind of place where the young men call you *capo* or *cavaliere* and ask for a light while they give you the once-over. The city park, the Villa Trieste, has nice views, and there is a recently opened museum of carriages at Località Siano, in the north of the town (*open Mon–Fri 8.30–12 and 4–6; adm*), but little else to see.

Crotone: The City of Pythagoras

Heading into the gulf of Táranto, the ghost cities of Magna Graecia make the only distractions along a lonely coast. **Crotone**, the Greek *Croton*, is no ghostly ruin, but a dismal middle-sized industrial city. The old Croton was often the most powerful of the Greek cities in Calabria, though it was more famous in the ancient world as the adopted home of the philosopher Pythagoras. With his scientific discoveries, mathematical mysticism and belief in the transmigration of souls, Pythagoras cast a spell over the Greek world, and particularly over Magna Graecia. He was hardly a disinterested scholar in an ivory tower; around the middle of the 6th century BC he seems to have led, or merely inspired, a mystic-aristocratic government in Croton based on his teachings. When a democratic revolution threw him out, he took refuge in Metapontum. Croton had a reputation, too, for other things: its medical school, the success of its athletes at the Olympic games, and especially its aggressive and unyielding attitude towards its neighbours. From all this, nothing is left but the **Museo Archeologico** on Via Risorgimento (*open daily 9–8; closed first and third Mon of the month*), with a large collection of terracotta ex votos like those at Reggio. On a promontory south of Crotone, a single standing column from a temple of Hera makes a romantic ruin on **Capo Colonne.**

Some 8okm north, you can dip easily into the mountains at **Rossano**, one of the better-kept hilltowns. The town's particular treasure, originally in the cathedral, is a beautiful 6th-century manuscript called the *Purple Codex*, believed to be the oldest illuminated gospel anywhere, made in Syria and almost certainly brought here by eastern monks fleeing their Muslim invaders. It can now be seen in the **Museo Diocesano**, next to the cathedral (*open Tues–Sat 9.30–12 and 4–6, Sun 10–12 and 4.30–6; closes at 8 in summer*).

Past Rossano, the mountains recede into the **plain of Sybaris**, named after the Greek city so renowned for luxurious decadence that even today it is echoed in the word 'sybarite'. The misfortune of *Sybaris* was to have jealous Croton for a neighbour. Croton besieged Sybaris and took it in 510 BC. After razing the city to the ground, the Crotonites diverted the River Crati over the ruins so that it could never be rebuilt. They did such a good job, in fact, that until a few years ago modern archaeologists could not even find the site; some scholars became convinced the whole story of Sybaris was just a myth. Now that they've found it, excavations are feverishly under way, and it is hoped that the richest city of Magna Graecia may yield the archaeologists something worth the trouble it has caused them. Above Sybaris proper, levels of excavation reveal ruins of *Thurii*, an Athenian colony and base in the Peloponnesian Wars, and a Roman town above that called *Copia*. You can now wander round the excavation site (*open daily 9–one hour before sunset*), but only with a guide, or visit the new **museum** (*open daily 9–8; adm*), a kilometre further north. Sybaris stands at the mouth of the Crati, which is now a wildlife preserve for a small colony of that increasingly rare species, the Mediterranean seal.

Policoro and *Metapontum*

Nearing the northern boundaries of Calabria, there are castles frowning down over the sea at Roseto and Rocca Imperiale (*open summer only*), the latter built by Frederick II. The Basilicata's share of the Ionian coast offers little change from Calabria. Two areas have been excavated, showing a long, tidy grid of streets with foundations of houses but, so far, no important temples. The new town of Policoro stands near the ancient city of *Eraclea*, and its **Museo Nazionale della Siritide** (*open daily 9–7; Oct–Mar 9–6; adm*) has a good collection of Greek vases and terracottas. North of Policoro, *Metapontum* was another rich city. It based its prosperity on growing and shipping wheat; today its famous silver coins, always decorated with an ear of wheat, are especially prized by collectors. It has more ruins to show than any of the other Calabrian sites, but do not expect anything like Paestum or Pompeii. On the banks of the Bradano, facing the coastal SS106, stands the Temple of Hera that used to be called the *Tavole Palatine* by locals – the Round Table of King Arthur. Fifteen columns remain.

The Basilicata Inland

Matera and its Province

The interior of the Basilicata has never been one of the more welcoming regions of Italy. Divided about equally between mountains and rolling hills, the isolation of this land has usually kept it far from the major events of Italian history. The territory may be familiar if you have read Carlo Levi's *Christ Stopped at Eboli*, a novel written when the Basilicata was a national scandal, the poorest and most backward corner of all Italy – and the writer had been sent into internal exile there by the Fascists. None of the famous 18th- and 19th-century travellers ever penetrated deeply into the region, and even today it is a part of the country few foreigners ever visit.

Not that they have been overlooking anything. Of all the Basilicata's towns, the only one that offers a real reason for stopping is Matera, a lively provincial capital of some 55,000 people that has become famous as a kind of freak show attraction. Until recently, the city had a certain notoriety as the most desperately poor provincial capital in Italy – and the scene of Carlo Levi's chilling book.

Matera has been an inhabited town since before recorded history in these parts began, and for centuries, probably millennia, its people built cave-homes and cave-churches in the easily worked tufa stone. Times are better now, but Matera has chosen to preserve rather than obliterate its terrible past by turning its poorest sections, the **Sassi**, into a sort of open-air museum – one that has made UNESCO's list of World Heritage Sites. Sassi are the cave neighbourhoods that line the two ravines between which Matera is built. Visitors as recently as 40 years ago reported people living in their cave homes in almost inconceivable poverty, sharing space with pigs and chickens, their children imploring outsiders not for money, but for quinine.

Most of the buildings (and all of the caves) in the Sassi are abandoned today – you may think it somewhat macabre, visiting the scenes of past misery, but the Sassi are indeed fascinating in their own way. Don't be surprised to see a tour group of bewildered foreigners being dragged through the cave neighbourhoods' steps and winding lanes. There are two Sassi, the wealthier **Sasso Barisano** north of the town centre, and the poorer **Sasso Caveoso** to the east. If you visit, before long a child or old man of the neighbourhood will come up and approach you with the offer of guide service – worth the trouble and slight expense if you have the time and find the Sassi interesting. They know where the old churches with the Byzantine frescoes are (some as old as the 9th century), and, if you can pick out enough of their southern dialect, they have plenty of stories to tell. Local guides are also probably a better option than the

Tourist Information

Matera: Via Viti de Marco 9, **t** 0835 333 541. You can also find out about this surprisingly switched-on city from MATERANET (*www.hsh.it*).

Potenza: Via Cavour 15, **t** 0971 411 839, **f** 0971 36196, and Via Alianelli 4, **t** 0971 21812.

Venosa: Via F. Frusci 7, off Piazza Municipo, **t** 0972 36542.

Where to Stay and Eat

This is an isolated region, and Matera and Potenza are the only places really equipped for visitors; with the exception of Venosa, expect only simple accommodation everywhere else.

Matera ✉ 75100

★★★**Hotel Sassi,** Via San Giovanni Vecchio 89, **t** 0835 331 009, **f** 0835 333 733 (*moderate*). This is *the* place to stay in Matera, right in the heart of the Sasso Barisano. A restructured 18th-century complex, each one of the 15 rooms is differently shaped to respect the original layout, and they all come with balconies overlooking the Sassi. Simple but very tasteful décor and friendly and efficient service.

★★★**Italia,** Via Ridola 5, **t** 0835 333 561, **f** 0835 330 087 (*moderate*). A pleasant enough hotel; some of its rooms have good views over the Sassi.

★**Roma,** Via Roma 62, **t** 0835 333 912 (*cheap*). This clean, spartan *pensione*, with shared bathrooms, is Matera's only budget choice.

Il Castello, Via Castello 1, **t** 0835 333 752 (*moderate*). One of several good restaurants in Matera. They serve an interesting *orecchiette* with mushrooms and sausage, as well as good fish and meat. *Closed Wed.*

Basilico, Via San Francesco 33, **t** 0835 336 540 (*moderate*). It looks a bit out of place in Matera with its hypermodern pastel décor and *cuisine soignée*, but in fact most people come here for really good pizza at reasonable prices. *Closed Fri.*

Il Terrazzino, Vico S. Giuseppe 7, **t** 0835 332 503 (*moderate*). Come here for a wide choice of simple but piquant Basilicatan dishes, and a terrace overlooking the Sassi. You'll find it just off Piazza Vittorio Veneto. *Closed Tues.*

Lucana, Via Lucana 48, **t** 0835 336 117 (*moderate*). A popular *trattoria* serving a variety of local favourites. Order the truly special *antipasti della casa*, which is a delectable meal in itself.

Del Corso, Via Luigi La Vista 12, **t** 0835 332 892 (*cheap*). For a pittance, you can gorge yourself here in the company of discerning locals. *Closed Sun.*

Potenza ✉ 85100

This is the kind of place where you will share a quiet hotel with a small group of government inspectors and travelling *salami* salesmen. They're all on expense accounts, so there are no bargains.

★★**Miramonti,** Via Caserma Lucana 30, **t** 0971 22987/**f** 0971 411 623 (*cheap*). If you do find yourself spending a night in Potenza, you could try this straightforward hotel.

maps and itineraries you can pick up from the tourist office. Alternatively the very good Tour Service Matera on the main Piazza Vittorio Veneto 42 (**t** 0835 334 633), offers a wide range of tailor-made guided tours.

Not all of Matera's sights are in the Sassi; there's also a 13th-century **cathedral**, a fine Romanesque building with some richly decorated side chapels; the churches of **San Francesco** and **San Giovanni Battista**, both with good façades, a 15th-century castle, the gloomy **Castello Tramontano** above the city; an eccentric 18th-century church called the **Purgatorio** with a leering skull over the main portal; and a first-class local archaeological museum, the **Museo Ridola** (*open daily 9–7; adm*), housed in the Baroque former convent of Santa Chiara.

The dry, austere countryside around Matera is full of tufa quarries, caves and churches. Across the Gravina ravine from the Sasso Caveoso (the one south of the

Taverna Oraziana, Via O. Flacco 2, t 0971 21851 (*expensive*). This is Potenza's one exceptionally good restaurant. Console yourself here with fine fresh pasta and local produce, which are used to recreate traditional old local recipes. *Closed Fri and Aug.*

Fuori le Mura, Via 4 Novembre 34, t 0971 25409 (*moderate*). Alternatively, try this singular, employee-owned restaurant renowned locally for its enormous choice of *antipasto* treats and good roast pork and lamb. *Closed Mon.*

Falcon Castel t 0971 86239 (*cheap*). In Lagopesole, this *trattoria* just below the castle will surprise you with a hearty meal of local specialities.

★★★Degli Ulivi, t/f 0835 757 020 (*moderate*). In Ferrandina, 25km south of Matera, there is only one tiny *locanda*; however, this hotel outside the town itself on the SS407 makes a comfortable stopover if you are passing through on the way to Táranto.

★★Margariello, Corso Umberto 55, t 0835 561 225 (*cheap*). In Stigliano, where no one ever goes, you can sample the modest charms of the Margariello for a rock-bottom price. Shared bathrooms.

Melfi ✉ 85025

★★★Due Pini, t 0972 21031, f 0972 21608 (*moderate*). Outside town at the railway station, this is yet another place for travelling salesmen, convenient for an overnighter.

Vaddone, Corso da Sant'Abruzzese, t 0972 24323 (*moderate*). This family-run restaurant offers good regional cuisine washed down with local Aglianico and Vúlture wines. *Closed Sun evenings and Mon.*

Il Tratturo Regio, Contrada del Casonetto, t/f 0972 239 295 or t/f 0972 24120 (*cheap*). If you have a car, you can do much better staying in this *Azienda Agrituristica* – quite well signposted. The young Imbriani family will welcome you with their enthusiastic energy and feed you with their freshly made *ricotta* and *mamma's* best home-cooking. They speak excellent English, and you may well be tempted to stay longer than you planned.

Il Pescatore, Monticchio Laghi, t 0972 731 036 (*moderate*). If you're visiting the Lakes of Monticchio to the south of Melfi, you'd do well to avoid the snack bars and track down this restaurant, on the road round the smaller of the two lakes.

Venosa ✉ 85029

★★★Orazio, Corso Vittorio Emanuele II 142, t 0972 31135, f 0972 35081 (*cheap*). A night at this beautifully restored *palazzo* is a real bargain – rooms are fully equipped, there's a communal terrace on the first floor with lovely views over the valley, and downstairs there's a lounge area where you can watch TV or read the verses of local poet Horace. If you can secure a room here, a couple of nights in Venosa is an attractive option.

Il Grifo, Via delle Fornci, t 0972 35188 (*cheap*). This busy restaurant beside the castle comes recommended. Try out the *lagane*, a delicious kind of local pasta.

cathedral), the cliffs called the **Murgia Timone** hold some more interesting cave churches, some with elaborate fronts, even domes, cut out of the tufa, and medieval frescoes. You'll need a map and some help from the provincial tourist office, or else a guide, to find them. Among the most interesting are those of **Santa Maria della Palomba**, **La Vaglia**, the **Madonna delle Tre Porte** and **Santa Barbara**.

In the remote south of Matera province, the two otherwise unremarkable villages of **Tursi** and **Stigliano** have exceptional churches. Tursi boasts the sanctuary of **Santa Maria d'Anglona,** out in the country on the road to Policoro, and in Stigliano, the 17th-century **church of San Antonio** has an odd waffle-iron rococo façade even better than the one on the Gesù Nuovo in Naples. South of Stigliano, the wild countryside around **Aliano** offers some of the more outlandish scenery in southern Italy. Deforestation and consequent erosion have turned parts of it into a lunar landscape, exposing weirdly twisted rock formations called *calanchi*. **Aliano** itself is the village where Carlo Levi actually stayed during the time he describes in *Christ Stopped at Eboli*. The house in which he lived is at the bottom of the village, and now houses a **museum** (*open Mon–Sat 10.30–12.30 and 5–7, Sun 9.30–12.30*), dedicated to the writer and to local folklore, customs and traditional life.

Monte Vúlture and the Castles of Emperor Frederick

The Western Basilicata is a province to itself, with a capital at **Potenza**, a plain modern hilltop city regularly rattled to pieces by earthquakes. The northern end of the province, astride the important routes between Naples and Puglia, was a very busy place in the Middle Ages, full of castles and fought over by Normans, Angevins and Holy Roman Emperors. Frederick II, in particular, haunted these bleak hills; he spent three months here, just before moving on to Puglia, where he died of dysentery. But his son Manfred and Elena of Epirus spent their honeymoon here – at the well-preserved castle of **Lagopésole**, halfway between Potenza and Melfi. Earlier in his reign, the great Hohenstaufen had spent some time at the **castle at Melfi**, a fortress that two centuries before had been the de Hautevilles' first Italian headquarters, where Robert Guiscard was crowned Duke of Puglia and Calabria. The castle (*interior under restoration*) is well up to cinematic standards – none of Frederick's geomantical mysticism here; unlike Castel del Monte, this one was built strictly for defence. Little remains of the original furnishings, but there is a small **archaeological museum** (*open Tues–Sat 9–2, Sun 9–1; adm*). Melfi itself is a sleepy town, with little but the castle and its 11th-century cathedral to remind it of times when it often occupied the centre stage of European politics.

Looking out from Melfi's castle, the horizon to the south is dominated by the ragged, faintly menacing outline of **Monte Vúlture**, a long-extinct volcano with a forest where once it had a smoking crater. Around the back side of the mountain, the Basilicata keeps one of its few beauty spots, the little **Lakes of Monticchio**, with lovely woods and a funicular to the top of the mountain. Out east from Melfi, there is another old castle at **Venosa**, an important town in Roman times and the birthplace of the poet Horace. Just outside the town, on the road to Puglia, you can visit what has survived of one of the most ambitious church building projects ever undertaken in the south. The Benedictine **Abbazia della Trinità** (*open daily April–Sept 9–7, rest of the year 9–one hour before sunset*), begun in the 1050s, was never completed, but it became the resting place of four of the five famous Norman brothers: William, Drogo, Robert (Guiscard) and Humphrey de Hauteville. Their tombs are in the older, completed church, along with some very fine surviving frescoes and carved capitals; among the heaps of stones tumbled about you may notice some Hebrew inscriptions; ancient and medieval Venosa both had important Jewish communities, and some Jewish catacombs have been discovered along with Christian ones on the hill east of the abbey.

Puglia

22

Puglia

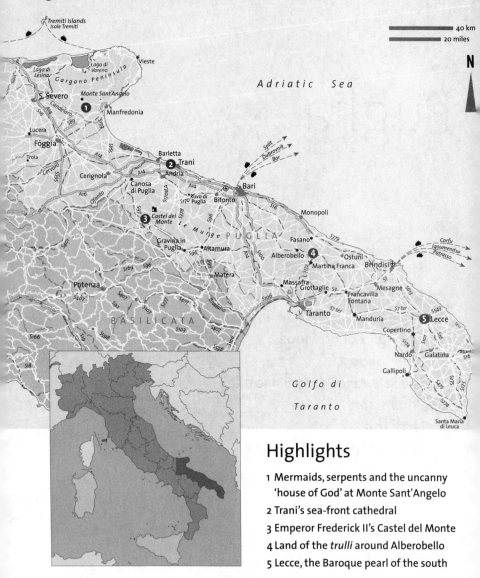

Highlights

1 Mermaids, serpents and the uncanny 'house of God' at Monte Sant'Angelo
2 Trani's sea-front cathedral
3 Emperor Frederick II's Castel del Monte
4 Land of the *trulli* around Alberobello
5 Lecce, the Baroque pearl of the south

In many ways this region will be the biggest surprise of Italy's south. From the forests and shining limestone cliffs of the beautiful Gargano Peninsula in the north, through the long plain of the *Tavoliere* to the southernmost tip of Italy's heel, Puglia offers the most variety of any of the southern regions, not only in nature, but in its towns and in its art: in Puglia you can see Byzantine art around Táranto, a score or so of Europe's finest Romanesque cathedrals, Santa Claus' tomb, the end of the Appian Way, the loveliest Baroque city in the Mediterranean, and a town of buildings with roofs shaped like oilcans.

Ancient Puglia was home to a number of quiet, modestly cultured and prosperous nations, notably the Daunii around Fóggia and the Messapians in the south. Under Roman rule it was a quiet and predominantly agricultural province, Rome's gateway to the east, and one of the parts of Italy most heavily influenced by the proximity of Greek culture. In the Middle Ages, Puglia was the home of a unique culture influenced by Normans, Arabs and Greeks. In a brief but intense period of prosperity, helped along greatly by the Crusades, Puglia's cities were fully equal in wealth and artistic talent to those of the north.

Puglia's greatest artistic productions are the medieval cathedrals and churches of Trani, Bari, Ruvo, Altamura, Molfetta, Bisceglie, Bitonto and Barletta, all close together in Bari province. The fascinating Castel del Monte, west of Bari, and the great castle at Lucera, are only two of the important sites associated with the reign of the *Stupor Mundis* – 'wonder of the world' Emperor Frederick II.

To get to know Puglia better, keep an eye open for some of the less important sights – pre-classical ruins, dolmens, relics of Greek Italy, religious centres, and especially the unique rural civilization of the *trulli* country. Puglia is not often spectacular, but the depth and meaning of its culture will come as a surprise; it is one of the regions most worth knowing.

Food and Wine in Puglia

La cucina pugliese makes use of all the natural resources at its disposal. Bari is particularly famous for fish, while Táranto has excellent mussels, mostly from the Mare Grande – and here called *mitili*, instead of *cozze* as they are in the rest of Italy. They feature prominently on the menus of virtually all Táranto's restaurants. In the hill towns of the interior, however, fish is a rarity and is replaced by meat – especially pork, rabbit and lamb. The 'national' dish of Puglia is *fave e cicoria*, a delicious purée of dry broad beans served with sautéed wild chicory.

The local olive oil is dark and strong, closer to that of Greece than the lighter oils of Tuscany and Umbria; the olives too are smaller and fuller flavoured, coming from trees whose roots have to dig deep into the soil to reach water.

As in most of southern Italy, sheep make up a great part of the livestock, and the region's sheep's cheeses include the local styles of *pecorino* and *ricotta* – look out for the unusually strongly flavoured *ricotta forte*. It goes particularly well in sauces with the local pasta – *orecchiette*, 'little ears' – formed by shaping the uncooked pasta with the thumb. Another cheese speciality is *burrata*, a tear-shaped *mozzarella* shell filled with a heart of shredded *mozzarella* and cream. Puglia grows some of the best almonds in the world – used in the preparation of delicious cookies and desserts.

Pugliese wine, like the cuisine, tends to be strong and full-bodied, and has had a high reputation since Roman times. Today there are about 24 different wines produced in Puglia, including whites, reds, rosés, sparkling wines and the particularly sweet Muscat. Two that are worth looking out for are the powerful red, *Cacc'emmitte*, from Fóggia province, and the comparatively light, delicate dry white from Locorotondo.

Fóggia and its *Tavoliere*

Fóggia

Fóggia, after Bari and Táranto the third city of Puglia, was once Frederick's capital, where between campaigns he enjoyed quiet moments with his English wife, his harem, his falcons and his Muslim sorcerers. It must have been quite a place, but old Fóggia has since been obliterated by two of the usual southern plagues: earthquakes have levelled it on several occasions, and the French sacked it in 1528. Allied bombers finished off the remains, and the Fóggia you see today is a newborn – homely and

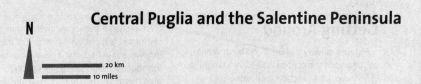

Central Puglia and the Salentine Peninsula

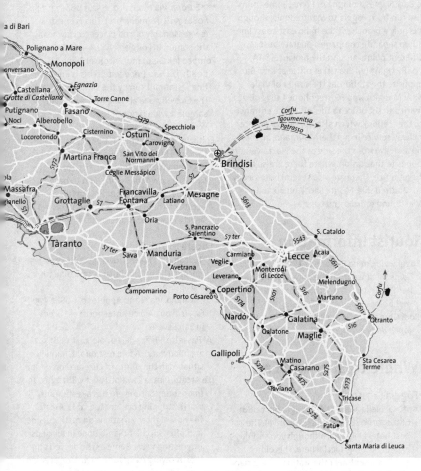

awkward, but still somehow endearing. Its citizens haven't forgotten Frederick, but these days they seem more proud of a composer of operas named **Umberto Giordano**, born here in 1867. The municipal theatre is named after him, and there is a big statue of him in the Piazza Giordano in the city centre, among a wonderfully eccentric set of more statues representing characters from his works. Giordano's big hit was *Andrea Chenier*; another of his works, with the intriguing title of *Fedora*, is claimed as the only opera that calls for bicycles on stage. You'll be able to see one or the other during Fóggia's autumn opera season. There's a little left of old Fóggia to see: a charming **cathedral** divided neatly in half, like a layer cake, 12th-century

Getting Around

Fóggia's **railway** station is on Piazza Veneto, at the end of the central Viale XXIV Maggio. It is an important junction for north–south trains – you often have to change there – and there will usually not be a long wait for trains to Bari, Naples, Bologna or Rome. Some trains also run from Fóggia to Manfredonia, though it is only a branch off the main east-coast line.

Two separate companies operate **buses** to different points around the province: **SITA**, t 0881 773 117 (with a ticket office at Kiwi Bar opposite the station, at the corner of Viale XXIV Maggio), and **FG**, freephone t 167 296 247 (with a ticket office to the left of the entrance to the station), which also operates a private railway service in northern Gargano; all the buses leave from the side of the Piazza Veneto opposite the station, where there is also a bus ticket office. There are also several buses a day to Manfredonia, Monte Sant'Angelo and Vieste, and to Troia and Lucera.

Tourist Information

Fóggia: Via Emilio Perrone 17, t 0881 723 141. Some distance from the railway station and hard to find, on the second floor of an apartment block (*open Mon–Fri 9–12.30*).
Rodi Garganico: Piazza Rovelli t 0884 965 576 (*open daily 8–2 and 4–10*).

Where to Stay and Eat

Fóggia ✉ 71100

★★★★Cicolella, Viale XXIV Maggio 60, t 0881 688 890, f 0881 678 984 (*expensive*). The best hotel in Fóggia, although you should expect nothing special here. This old establishment near the station is Victorian on the outside, but remodelled within; the restaurant (*expensive*) is also one of the best in town, a rare find, and a good place to introduce yourself to Puglian specialities like *orecchiette*. The fish here is fresh and very good, and the roast lamb also comes highly recommended. *Restaurant closed weekends*.
★★★Europa, Via Monfalcone 52, t 0881 721 743, f 0881 771 492 (*moderate*). This is one of a few reasonably priced places to stay near the station in Fóggia.
Pompeo (ex Giordano), Vicolo al Piano 14, t 0881 724 640 (*moderate*). This is another fine restaurant run by the same family as the Cicolella (*see above*), where you can sample a wide range of local and seasonal specialities. *Closed two weeks in Aug*.
Epitazio, Via Manzone 54, t 0881 770 356 (*cheap*). This wonderful, anachronistically good and friendly *trattoria*, also run by the Cicolella's owners – who seem to have a monopoly on eating out in Fóggia – has an excellent-value fixed price menu. Traditional, hearty local food is on offer.

Lucera ✉ 71036

★★Balconata, Viale Ferrovia 15, t 0881 546 725 (*cheap*). The only hotel in Lucera; fine for a stop-over.
★★★Milano, Via Teano Appulo 10, t 0882 375 643 (*cheap*). A nice hotel north of Lucera in San Severo.
Al Passetto, Piazza del Popolo 24, t 0881 542 213 (*moderate*). A fine restaurant, handily situated in the centre of Lucera. *Closed Mon*.
Le Arcate, Piazza Cavalotti 29, t 0882 226 025 (*moderate*). San Severo has a restaurant worth stopping over for too: at Le Arcate they use lighter variations on rustic cuisine, and offer succulent lamb done in all kinds of interesting ways. Some of the desserts are worth saving room for. *Closed Mon evenings*.

Romanesque on the bottom and Baroque on top. The early medieval door on the north side was only rediscovered during the Second World War, when bombs knocked down the adjacent building that was hiding it. A few twisting streets to the north, on Piazza Nigri, is Fóggia's **Museo Civico** (*open daily 9–1, also Tues, Thurs and Fri 5–7*), with a collection devoted to archaeological finds. The scientific section has been relocated to the **Museo di Storia Naturale**, Via Bellavia (*open Mon–Sat 9–1, Mon and Fri also 4.30–7; adm*). The single portal with an inscription incorporated into one side of the building is the last surviving remnant of Frederick's palace. Near the museum, on Piazza Sant'Egidio, the **Chiesa della Croce** (1693–1742) is one of Puglia's more unusual churches: an elegant Baroque gate leads to a long avenue, which passes under five domed chapels that represent stages in the passion of Christ before arriving at the church itself.

Lucera and Troia

Why does Lucera have a cathedral from the 14th century, while almost all the other Puglian towns built theirs back in the 12th century or earlier? Well, there's a story. In the 1230s Emperor Frederick II was hard pressed. Excommunicated by his devious rival, Pope Gregory IX, and at war with all the Guelph towns of Italy, Frederick needed some allies he could trust. At the same time he had a problem with brigandage in some of the predominantly Muslim mountain areas of Sicily. His solution: induce 20,000 Sicilian Arabs to move to Puglia, with land grants and promises of imperial employment and favours.

The almost abandoned town of *Luceria*, once an important Roman colony, was the spot chosen, and before anybody knew it Frederick had conjured up an entirely Muslim metropolis 290km from Rome. The Emperor felt right at home in Lucera and the new city became one of his favourite residences; later it would be the last stronghold of his son, Manfred, in the dark days that followed Frederick's death. Charles of Anjou took the city in 1267; attempts at forced Christianization, and the introduction of settlers from Provence, caused revolts among the people, which the Angevins finally settled in 1300 by butchering the lot.

Little remains of Muslim Lucera, or even of the Lucera of the French; most of the Provençals could not take the summer heat, though some of their descendants still live in the hills to the south. Charles II began the simple, Gothic **cathedral** of 1300 directly after the massacre of the Saracens. Other monuments include the church of **San Francesco**, a typical barn-like Franciscan church built from recycled Roman ruins, as well as parts of a gate and an amphitheatre from Roman Luceria on the edge of town. Smaller fragments reside at the **Museo Civico** (*open Tues–Sat 9–1 and 4–7, Sun 9–1; adm*), just behind the cathedral. Frederick's **castle**, 2km north of the centre – follow the signs (*open daily 9–1; summer also 4–7*), one of the largest ever built in Italy, was begun in 1233, the same year as the importation of the Saracens. It is still an impressive sight, with its score of towers and walls nearly a kilometre in circumference, set on a hill looking out over Lucera and the Fóggia plain. Only ruins are left of Frederick's palace inside.

South and west of Fóggia, in the foothills of the Apennines bordering the Molise and the Basilicata, you might consider a side trip to Troia. Its famous **cathedral** is one of the oldest and most spectacular of its kind in Puglia, and an excellent introduction to the glories of the Puglian Romanesque. Troia, once the Roman town of *Aecae*, was refounded in 1017, and prospered from the start. Popes held two small church councils here in the 11th and 12th centuries; and the cathedral was begun in 1093, though not finished until the time of Frederick. Much of the inspiration for the Puglian style came from Pisa, and the Pisan trademark – blind arcades decorated with circle and diamond shapes – is in evidence here, and also the most beautiful rose window in Italy, a unique, Arab-inspired fantasy from Frederick's time; the circle is divided into 11 sections, each with carved stone lattice-work in a different geometric design. Inside it is strangely and intentionally asymmetrical, with everything on the right side just slightly out of alignment.

Two more places of interest are **Bovino**, a resolutely medieval-looking village with a 13th-century cathedral and some Roman remains, and **Ascoli Satriano**, where a very well-preserved triple-arched Roman bridge still spans the River Carapelle (*call t 0885 796 450 to arrange a visit*). You can also make a detour to see substantial remains of the abandoned Roman town of *Herdonio*, near **Ordona**.

The Gargano Peninsula

It looks a little out of place, being the only stretch of scenic coast between Venice and the tip of Calabria. The 'spur' of the Italian boot is, in fact, a lost chip of the former Yugoslavia, left behind when two geological plates separated to form the Adriatic, several million years ago. For a long time, before silt washed down by the rivers gradually joined it to the mainland, the Gargano was an island. It might as well have remained so, for the Gargano is as different from the adjacent lands in attitude as it is in its landscape.

Manfredonia

If you are coming from the north, you will enter the Gargano by way of Lesina and the Gargano's two lakes: the **Lago di Lesina** and the **Lago di Varano**, two large lagoons cut off from the sea by broad sand spits. From Fóggia, the logical base for attacking the Gargano would be Manfredonia, a dusty port town with a beach and a pretty centre at the southern end of the peninsula. This town was founded by Frederick's son Manfred, and it prospered well enough until Dragut's Turkish pirates sacked and razed it in 1620 (a local girl ended up the favoured wife of the sultan). Of old Manfredonia, all that is left is Manfred's castle, rebuilt by Charles of Anjou; it now contains a small **archaeological museum** (*open daily 8.30–1.30 and 3.30–7.30; closed first and last Mon of the month; adm*). The town also has a brash 17th-century **cathedral**.

Along the Fóggia road, about 2km south of the centre of Manfredonia, you can see the ruins of *Sipontum*, a Roman town that was finally abandoned to the malaria mosquitoes when Manfred moved the population to his healthier new city. The more recent town of **Siponto**, next to it, is now a popular beach resort.

As evidence of how important Sipontum was in the early Middle Ages, there is the impressive 11th-century church of **Santa Maria di Siponto**, in the same style of decoration as the cathedral at Troia, only built on a square, Byzantine-Greek plan. It is built over a much earlier underground Christian building, from around the 5th century. Another 11th-century church, very similar to Santa Maria di Siponto, survives another 9km up the road – **San Leonardo**, an even better work, with finely sculpted portals and a small dome.

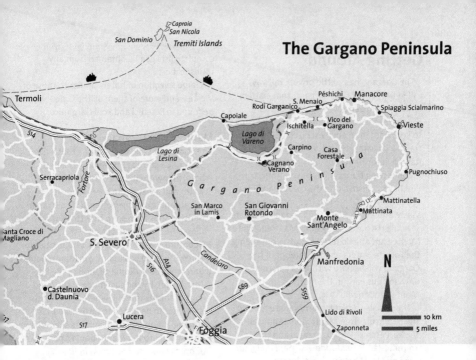

Monte Sant'Angelo

The tourists who come to the Gargano for the beaches probably never notice, but this peninsula is holy ground, and has been perhaps since the time of the ancient Daunians. Sanctuaries, ancient and modern, are scattered all over it; there are many stories of the apparitions of saints and angels, and even 25 years ago a holy man who received the stigmata lived at San Giovanni Rotondo.

The centre of all this, for the last thousand years at least, has been **Monte Sant'Angelo**, one of the most important pilgrimage towns in Italy. Before Christianity, the cavern now dedicated to Saint Michael was the site of a dream oracle; a 5th-century bishop of Sipontum had a vision of the archangel, who left his red cloak as a token and commanded the sanctuary be converted to Christian worship. Early on, the new Monte Sant'Angelo was attracting pilgrims from all over Europe – continuing a tradition that had begun long before the site was Christianized. Among the pilgrims were the first Normans, in the 9th century. They returned home with tales of a rich and fascinatingly civilized Puglia – a place they suspected just might be a pushover for mounted, heavily armoured knights. The first Norman adventurers were not slow in taking up the challenge. All the other sites dedicated to St Michael around the coasts of Europe – including of course Mont St-Michel in Normandy – are the spiritual descendants of this one, founded as the cult of St Michael spread across Christendom in the early Middle Ages. That Monte Sant'Angelo is a special place becomes evident even before you arrive. The trip up from Manfredonia passes through an uncanny landscape: chalky cliffs dotted with caves, ancient agricultural terraces, and a strange clarity in the light and air. After much twisting and grinding of gears, you arrive at a quiet, whitewashed city, a maze of steps and tunnels.

Getting Around

The Gargano has a little **private railway**, called the Ferrovia del Gargano, that clatters amiably from San Severo, 30km north of Fóggia, up the western edge of the peninsula to Rodi Garganico and Péschici (about six trains a day; freephone **t** 167 296 247 within Italy for information).

Connecting **buses** will take you from Péschici to Vieste along the coast road (SP52). Buses (run by FG) are less frequent between Vieste and Manfredonia and Fóggia. There are several **SITA** buses a day from Manfredonia to Monte Sant'Angelo (**t** 0881 773 117), but seeing the Foresta Umbra and the interior of the Gargano will be hard without a car; there is only one bus early in the morning, from Monte Sant'Angelo.

There is also a regular **ferry** service around the peninsula from Manfredonia that calls at Vieste, Péschici, Rodi Garganico and the Tremiti Islands (*mid-June–mid-Sept daily; early June and late Sept four times weekly; April–May twice weekly*); the rest of the year, the islands are reachable only from Termoli and Manfredonia.

Tourist Information

Manfredonia: Corso Manfredi 26, **t** 0884 581 998 (*open Mon–Sat 8.30–1.30*).
Vieste: Corso Fazzini 8, **t** 0884 707 495 (*open Mon–Fri 8–2, Tues and Thurs also 4–7*), and in Piazza Kennedy, **t** 0884 708 806 (*often open longer hours and at weekends*).

Where to Stay and Eat

The Gargano has a large number of *aziende agrituristiche* – some of which are simple bed-and-breakfast places in the country, others offering delicious home-cooked meals at very reasonable prices. Whichever, if you are travelling by car they make a good and inexpensive alternative to staying in hotels;

complete lists can be obtained from any tourist office.

A large selection of hotels similar to those of Vieste – and more of them all the time – will be found in Péschici and Rodi Garganico.

Manfredonia ✉ 71043

★★★★Gargano, Viale Beccarini 2, **t** 0884 587 621, **f** 0884 586 021 (*moderate*). The best hotel in town, with a pool filled with sea water and a view from every room. Its restaurant (*expensive*) offers a whole range of fish dishes from soup to *fritto misto*. *Closed Tues and most of Nov.*
★Sipontum, Via di Vittorio 229, **t** 0884 542 916 (*cheap*). A good basic choice in Manfredonia.
Il Baracchio, Corso Roma 38, **t** 0884 583 874 (*moderate*). Try the cool modern surroundings of this restaurant, where the octopus salad has to be tasted to be believed. It's among a number of restaurants specializing in seafood around Manfredonia's port. *Closed Thurs and two weeks in July.*

Monte Sant'Angelo ✉ 71037

Al Grottino, Corso Vittorio Emanuele 179, **t** 0884 561 132. This is a place where you can get a dinner for half what it's worth – roast lamb and kid, truly elegant *antipasti*, sweets and cheeses. *Closed Mon.*
Garden Paradise, Via Basilica 51, **t** 0884 563 904 (*cheap*). Handy for lunch, with lots of pasta dishes but no fish.

Vieste ✉ 71019

The best beach hotels are slightly garish.
★★★★Pizzomunno, Lungomare Enrico Mattei, **t** 0884 708 741, **f** 0884 707 325 (*very expensive*). Less than 1km south of the town centre, this gorgeous place keeps holidaymakers busy with sailing, sports, a pool, a beautiful beach and a noisy disco. *Closed Nov–Mar.* They also have an exceptional, highly rated restaurant (*expensive*).
★★★Falcone, Lungomare Enrico Mattei 5, **t** 0884 708 251 (*moderate*). Vieste's second

The medieval centre of town, the **Junno**, is one of the most beautiful old quarters in southern Italy, a nonchalant harmony of colour and form that only a few coast towns in Puglia can achieve. Here you will find the **Santuario di San Michele** (*open Easter–Oct daily 6.30–sunset; Nov–Mar 7.30–12.30 and 2.30–5*), behind an eight-sided tower built

choice, with a private beach and most of the resort amenities at a much better rate.

★San Giorgio, Via Madonna della Libertà, **t** 0884 708 618 (*cheap*). This *pensione* in the centre of Vieste is a good budget choice. It also has a decent restaurant for guests only. Full board is mandatory during August.

★★★Gabbiano Beach, **t** 0884 706 376, **f** 0884 706 689 (*cheap*). This is one of the least expensive of a series of good hotels that can be found along the coastline around Vieste – usually in lovely spots, but convenient only if you have a car. It has its own beach, a nice swimming pool and sailing facilities. You'll find it 7km north of Vieste on the road to Péschici. *Closed Oct–Mar.*

★★Péschici, Via San Maritino 31, **t** 0884 964 195 (*cheap*). Good views, and more facilities and services than most two-star hotels. Full board is mandatory during August. *Closed in winter.*

★★★Albano, Via Scalo Marittimo 33, **t** 0884 965 138 (*moderate*). Another reasonably priced option below the historic centre of Rodi Garganico, with air-conditioning, and a good if unexciting restaurant.

★Roccamare, Via Varano, **t** 0884 965 461. This cheap and friendly hotel, perched on a cliff-face below the centre of Rodi, is quite a special place. Ask for one of the four smaller rooms that share a huge whitewashed terrace with expansive sea views.

Note that not all the good **restaurants** in Vieste are in hotels.

Vecchia Vieste, Via Mafrolla 32, **t** 0884 707 083 (*moderate*). A traditional restaurant, with friendly staff, offering seafood specialities like *involtini alla Viestiana. Closed Nov–April.*

San Michele, Viale XXXIV Maggio 72, **t** 0884 708 143 (*moderate*). Many people in Vieste think this is their finest restaurant. Come here to eat fish grilled or in soups. *Closed Mon in low season; winter closure depends on business, usually Nov–Feb.*

Box 19, Via Santa Maria di Merino 19, **t** 0884 705 229 (*moderate*). You can eat seafood or grilled meats here for similar prices to those at the San Michele. *Closed Mon in low season, and Nov.*

Dragone, Via Duomo 8. **t** 0884 701 212 (*expensive–moderate*). Set in a natural cave in the centre of the old town, this is one of Péschici's best restaurants. *Closed Tues in low season, and Nov–Mar.*

Al Castello, Piazza Castello 29, **t** 0884 964 038 (*moderate*). A hotel restaurant that serves reasonable seafood and meat dishes, with tables outdoors in the pedestrian zone of the old quarter.

Regina, Corso Madonna della Libera 46 (*cheap*). The set menu offered by this restaurant and *birreria* is Rodi Garganico's best bargain. There's plenty to choose from, including 'Regina' *penne* with mushrooms, tomatoes, *mozzarella* and *pancetta*, followed by steaming mounds of fragrant *cozze* (mussels).

Helvetia, Via Fontanella 2, **t** 0884 965 490 (*cheap*). This friendly *pizzeria*, with a terrace overlooking a small citrus grove, serves a wide range of snacks at lunchtime, including tasty *bruschette*.

Tremiti Islands ✉ 71100

★★Al Faro, **t** 0882 463 424 (*cheap*). If you want to stay over it's worth booking in advance at this eight-room *pensione* near the central square on San Domino. The rooms are rather cramped but its restaurant is excellent value for money. Half board is obligatory but that is no hardship as the restaurant offers good home-cooking influenced by the food traditions of the San Nicola monastery, all washed down with some delicious good-quality wines. *Closed Oct–Easter.*

★Gabbiano, **t** 0882 463 401 (*cheap*). A good alternative where it's also essential to book.

If you want a picnic for a day on the rocks, the grocer beside the chemist (near the main square) will wrap you up delicious slices of steaming potato pizza – surprisingly just the right thing for a day on the beach.

---

by Charles of Anjou that reproduces the proportions (on one level) and much of the decoration of Frederick's Castel del Monte. The exterior of the sanctuary seems to be a normal church, with a Gothic porch and portals (mostly built in the 19th century; see if you can guess which of the two identical portals is the original 12th-century work).

Above the doors is a Latin inscription: 'Terrible is this place; this is the house of God and the Gate of Heaven'.

Inside, instead of the expected church, there is a long series of steps leading down to the cavern, passing a beautiful pair of bronze doors made in Constantinople in 1076, perhaps by the same artists who did the ones at Amalfi cathedral. In the darkness most of the scenes are difficult to make out, but Jacob's ladder and the expulsion from Eden stand out clearly. Down in the cave it is chilly and dark; in the old days pilgrims would come down on their knees, shuffling through the puddles to kiss the image of the archangel. The grotto is laid out like a small chapel. There are plenty of bits of medieval sculptural work around, but the best is a wonderful crazy-medieval bishop's chair, from the 12th century.

The town records give us an almost endless list of celebrity pilgrims: a dozen popes, King Ferdinand of Spain, four Holy Roman Emperors, Saints Bernard, Thomas Aquinas, Catherine of Siena, and so on – even St Francis, and they can show you the mark he made on the cavern wall. Behind the altar, you can see the little well that made this a holy site in the first place. Long before there was a St Michael, indigenous religions of Europe had a great interest in springs and underground streams. Many scholars believe the idea of dragons began with a primeval fascination with buried streams and accompanying lines of telluric forces beneath the earth's surface; the sleepless 'eye' of the dragon is the fountain, where these forces come to the surface. In the icons of Monte Sant'Angelo, as well as in the endless souvenir figurines hawked outside the sanctuary, Michael is shown dispatching Lucifer in the form of a dragon.

There's more to see in Monte Sant'Angelo, and more oddities. Downhill from the sanctuary, next to the half-ruined church of San Pietro, stands the 12th-century work called the **tomb of Rotari** (*open daily 8.30–1 and 2.30–7.30; adm*). The idea that this was the tomb of 'Rotarus', a Lombard chief, stems from a misreading of one of the inscriptions. It is now believed this was intended to be a baptistry – a very large and unusual baptistry, if so; it is hard to make out the original intention, since much of it has been swallowed up into the surrounding buildings. Some of the sculpted detail is extremely odd; note the figures of a woman suckling a serpent – or dragon.

Also in the Junno district, the town has opened a small museum of the folk arts and culture of the Gargano, the **Museo Tancredi** (*open daily 8.30–7.30; adm*). On the top of the town, there is a romantically ruined Norman castle, rebuilt by the Aragonese kings, but left quite alone ever since.

San Giovanni Rotondo and Padre Pio

From the back of Monte Sant'Angelo, a narrow road leads into the heart of the Gargano, eventually branching off to the 'Forest of Shadows' (*see* below) or **San Giovanni Rotondo**, a little town on the slopes of Monte Calvo. Here, besides the strange round temple that gives the town its name (believed, like the tomb of Rotari, to have been intended as a baptistry), there is a 16th-century monastery that for over 50 years was the home of Padre Pio de Pietralcina, a simple priest who not only received the stigmata – the bleeding wounds of Christ – on his hands, feet and side, but also had the ability to appear before cardinals in Rome while his body was sleeping back in the Gargano. The Church always has its suspicions about phenomena like these, but over the last 30 years veneration of Padre Pio has spread all over the world, and San Giovanni is a major pilgrimage site. After careful 'research', Vatican experts have decreed that the devil had nothing to do with Padre Pio's miraculous healing powers and the saint was beatified in May 1999.

West of San Giovanni and also an old stop on the pilgrimage route to Monte Sant'Angelo is the town of **San Marco in Lamis**, which has similarly always been a monastic centre. The present, huge Franciscan house dates from the 16th century.

Vieste

Once past Monte Sacro, on the coast north of Monte Sant'Angelo, you are in the holiday Gargano, on an exceptionally lovely coastline of limestone cliffs, clean blue sea and good beaches decorated with old watchtowers, or stumps and columns of rock and other curious formations. Vieste, at the tip of the peninsula, is in the middle of it, a lively and beautiful white town on white cliffs, surrounded by beaches. Though managing to retain its old charm, Vieste has become the major resort of the southern Adriatic, and boutiques and restaurants crowd the town centre. On Via Duomo, near the centre of the old town, is the **Chianca Amara** or 'bitter stone', where, it is believed, 5,000 of the town's people were beheaded by the Turks when they sacked Vieste in 1554. Nearby is the 11th-century **cathedral**, with 18th-century additions, and, beyond that, another **castle** built by Frederick II, with fine views over the town, and the **Grotta Sfondata** ('bottomless lagoon'), one of a few marine grottos and lagoons accessible by boat tours from Vieste. There is also a peculiar early Christian *hypogeum* (cave for burials) on the coast, at the site of a long-disappeared town called *Merinum*.

On the Gargano's northern coast, **Péschici** and **Rodi Garganico** are two other pretty fishing villages that are now fast-developing resorts, and particularly crowded in August. Boats call at both towns for the Tremiti Islands, and from either village, or from Vieste itself, it is a relatively easy excursion by bus or car up the mountains to the **Foresta Umbra**, the 'forest of shadows', a thick, primeval forest of beeches, oaks and pines, similar to those that covered most of Puglia in the Middle Ages.

The Tremiti Islands

In winter this minuscule archipelago, 40km from the coast, has a population of about 50. August, however, finds it crawling with most of the 100,000 holiday-makers who annually spill over from the resorts of the Gargano. The islands have the same well-scoured limestone coasts as the peninsula, though there is only one beach, on the larger islands of **San Domino**.

The Tremiti islands enter the history books first as a place of exile – Augustus' daughter and Charlemagne's troublesome Italian father-in-law were both confined here – or as a monkish retreat. From the 18th century they were used as a penal colony. The only sight on the smaller island of **San Nicola** where ferries from the mainland disembark, is a huge half-ruined fortress monastery begun by Benedictines in the 11th century. Local ferries run from there to San Domino which has the only hotels. It's a beauty of an island, well-forested and surrounded with wonderful coves and lagoons set in a translucent blue-green sea. If you can avoid coming in July or Auust when hordes of day-trippers and ravenous mosquitoes sail in, the Tremitis can be a perfect spot to let your watch run down.

Down the Coast to Bari

If you take the main route, a little bit inland, you will be passing through more of the *Tavoliere*, the long, dull plain that stretches the length of Puglia. *Tavoliere* means a chessboard; 2,000 years ago, when the Romans first sent in surveyors to apportion the land among their Punic War veterans, this flat plain – the only one south of the Po – gave the methodical rectangularity of the Roman mind a chance to express itself. They turned the plain into a grid of neatly squared roads and farms; many of their arrow-straight roads survive, and the succeeding centuries have managed to throw only a few kinks into the rest. If not for the olive groves and vineyards, you might think you were in Iowa.

Barletta's Colossus

The coastal road, though just as flat, has more to see than the inland route, passing through a string of attractive medieval port towns, each with its contribution to the Puglian Romanesque in the shape of a grand old cathedral. **Barletta**, the first of them coming from the north, is the best introduction and it contains a unique and astounding sight. On Corso Vittorio Emanuele, beside the church of San Sepolcro, stands the largest surviving ancient bronze statue, locally known as the **Colosso**. To come upon this 20-foot figure in the middle of a busy city street, wearing an imperial scowl and a pose of conquest, with a cross and a sphere in his hands, is like lapsing into a dream. Scholars have debated for centuries who it might be. It's obviously a late Roman emperor, and the guesses have included Valentinian, Heraclius and Marcian; the last is most probable, and especially intriguing, since the triumphal column of Marcian (a useless emperor with no real successes to commemorate) still stands in Istanbul, and the statue of the emperor that once stood on top of it was probably carried away by the Venetians after the sack of Constantinople in 1204. A ship full of booty from that sack foundered off Barletta's coast, and the Colosso washed up on a nearby beach; the superstitious citizens let it stay there for decades before they got up enough nerve to bring it into the city. The figure is surpassingly strange, a monument to the onset of the Dark Ages; the costume the emperor wears is only a pale memory of the dress of Marcus Aurelius or Hadrian, with a pair of barbaric-looking leather boots instead of imperial buskins.

San Sepolcro, finished in the 13th century, is interesting in its own right. Above the plain French Gothic vaulting, there is an octagonal dome, recalling the Holy Sepulchre in Jerusalem. Corso Garibaldi leads from here into the heart of old Barletta and the 12th-century **cathedral**. Look on the left-hand wall, between the façade and the campanile, and you will see a cornice supported by 13 strange figures. If you are clever and have a good eye, you may make out the letters on them that make an acrostic of

Richardus Rex I – Richard the Lionheart, who contributed to the embellishment of the cathedral on his way to the Crusades.

Nearby is the 13th-century church of **Sant'Andrea**, with another fine façade, the main portal of which, from 1240, was the work of the Dalmatian sculptor Simon di Ragusa. The Third Crusade was launched from Barletta's often-rebuilt **Castello** (*open Tues–Sun 9–1 and 3–6; adm*), in a great council of Frederick and his knights. Apart from a collection of antiques, coins and armour, the castle also houses the **Pinacoteca Giuseppe de Nittis**, which has in its collection the only surviving statue of Frederick II – a little the worse for wear, poor fellow – as well as a large collection of works by the local, Impressionist-influenced painter Giuseppe de Nittis (1846–84). The admission ticket to the castle will also get you into the **Cantina della Disfida**, in Via Cialdini, where in 1503, after much drinking and brawling, 13 'Italian' knights challenged 13 French knights to a duel for control of the besieged town. The Italians won, and Barletta's siege was lifted. The historical event gets re-enacted in one of Puglia's largest pageants on the second weekend in September.

Trani

The next town along the coast, Trani is a sun- and sea-washed old port that still has a large and prosperous fishing fleet. It was an important merchant town in the early Middle Ages – it once fought a war with Venice, and its merchant captains created perhaps the first code of laws of the sea since ancient times. Trani's famous **cathedral** (*open daily 8–12.15 and 3–7*) stands in an open piazza on the edge of the sea, another excellent work of the Puglian Romanesque, and a monument to the age of the Crusades. At the centre of the façade is another pair of 12th-century bronze doors, like the ones in so many other cities of the south. These ones are special, though, since the artist who did them and several others in the town is a native, Barisano of Trani.

Inside, the most remarkable things are underground. This cathedral is in fact three buildings stacked on the same site; the lower church, called **Santa Maria della Scala**, is really the earlier, Byzantine cathedral, and below that is the **Crypt of San Leucio**, an unusual early Christian church or catacomb with solid marble columns and bits of medieval frescoes. Some of Trani's other notable buildings include the newly restored **Castello Svevo** (*open daily 8.30–7.30; adm*), another of Frederick II's symmetrical fortresses, on the seafront; the **Ognissanti** (*usually closed*), a typical church of the 12th-century Knights Templar; the **Palazzo Cacetta**, a rare (for southern Italy) example of late Gothic architecture from the 1450s; and two small churches that were once synagogues, **Santa Maria Scuolanove** and **Sant'Anna**, converted after the Spaniards expelled Trani's long-established Jewish community in the 16th century.

From Trani, **Bisceglie** is the next town, with another good Romanesque cathedral. Then comes **Molfetta**, a city with a reputation for drugs and gangsters. Molfetta has a cathedral like Trani's on the harbour's edge, the **Duomo Vecchio**. This may be the most peculiar of them all: its plan, subtly asymmetrical like that of Troia, has a wide nave covered by three domes, the central one being elliptical. The west front is almost blank, while the back side has elaborate carved decoration, and a door that leads into the apse. Molfetta also has another cathedral, the Baroque **Duomo Nuovo**, from 1785.

Getting There and Around

Two FS **railways** serve this area and, unusually for Puglia, you're more likely to find a train than a bus to many destinations. All the coastal towns from Barletta to Monópoli are on the main FS east coast route. From Barletta, there is an FS branch line to the south with infrequent services to Spinazzola and Altamura. In addition, one of the three **private regional lines** that operate from Bari, the Ferrovia Bari-Nord, t 080 521 3577, runs a very frequent service through the inland towns such as Ándria, Ruvo and Bitonto.

There are also reasonably regular **buses** along the coast road, and inland from Barletta or Bari. Unfortunately, Castel del Monte is just about the hardest place to reach in Puglia: call the castle or the tourist office in Ándria for timetables for the infrequent bus service.

Tourist Information

Barletta: Corso Garibaldi 208, t 0883 531 555 (open Mon–Fri 8–2, Tues and Thurs also 4–7).
Trani: Piazza Trieste 10, t 0883 588 830 (open Mon–Sat 8–2, Tues and Thurs also 3–6).

Ruvo di Puglia: Via Vittorio Veneto 48, t 080 361 549 (open Mon–Fri 9.30–12 and 5.30–7.30, weekends 9.30–12).
Ándria, t 0883 592 283.

Where to Stay and Eat

Hotels are sparse; each town has a restaurant.

Barletta ✉ 70051
★★★★**Artù**, Piazza Castello 67, t 0883 332 121 (moderate). Between the castle and the cathedral, this will do if you are set on staying in Barletta.
Antica Cucina, Via Milano, t 0883 521 718 (expensive). Light, tasty fish dishes and good desserts. Closed Sun evenings, Mon and July.

Trani ✉ 70059
★★★★**Régia**, Piazza Mons. Addazi 2, t 0883 584 444, f 0883 506 595 (moderate). A recently restored 18th-century palazzo opposite the cathedral, with ten comfortable rooms in a prime position. Its restaurant is good value too, with an attractive terrace. Closed Mon.
★★★★**Royal**, Via De Robertis 29, t 0883 588 777 (moderate). Quiet rooms, all renovated in the original Liberty style.

Castel del Monte

Open daily 10–1.30 and 2.30–7; adm; official guides offer good tours in Italian and English (donations are appreciated); call them in summer at the castle, t 0883 569 848, in winter at the Ándria tourist office.

In Enna, the 'navel of Sicily', Emperor Frederick built a mysterious octagonal tower at the highest point of the town. In Puglia, this most esoteric of emperors erected an equally puzzling palace. It, too, is a perfect octagon, and if you have been travelling through the region with us, you will have noticed that nearly every town has at least one eight-sided tower, bastion or campanile, and that often enough Frederick was originally behind them. Castel di Santa Maria del Monte, to give it its original title, was begun by Frederick in the 1240s on a high hill overlooking the Puglian *Tavoliere*, south of the town of Ándria.

At each of the eight corners of Castel del Monte is a slender octagonal tower. The 80ft-tall building has only two storeys; each with eight rooms, all interconnected, and each facing the octagonal courtyard. Historians have tried to pass off the castle as one of Frederick's hunting lodges. This is implausible: the rooms each have only one small window, and in spite of the wealth of sculpted stone it would have seemed more like a prison than a forest retreat – in fact the emperor's grandsons, the heirs of

Padri Bernabiti, on Piazza Tiepolo, t 0883 481 180 (*cheap*). Basic, clean rooms with great views, although the fathers will only let married couples share a room. Reserve. Closed 1–5pm; curfew 1am.

★Lucy, Piazza Pleblistico 11, t 0883 481 022 (*cheap*). Round the block from the harbour, this *pensione*, with high-ceilinged rooms, and balconies overlooking a pleasant square, is an excellent budget option.

Torrente Antico, Via Fresco 3, t 0883 487 911 (*expensive*). Serves local produce – both fish and fowl – in interesting ways, and the best local wines. *Closed Sun eve, Mon and July.*

La Nicchia, Corso Imbriani 22, t 0883 482 020 (*cheap*). Best value for shellfish. *Closed Thurs.*

Il Pozzo dei Desideri, Via Zanardelli 36, t 0883 481 902 (*cheap*). You're guaranteed a bellyful at this attractive restaurant, along one of the cobbled streets just off the harbour. You can also expect special touches such as delicious free home-baked *focaccia* bread.

There are also plenty of cute places in the harbour, but they tend to be overpriced.

Molfetta ✉ 70056

★★★Molfetta Garden, Via Provinciale per Terlizzi, t 080 334 1722 (*moderate*). A good-value, modern hotel.

Bufi, Via Vittorio Emanuele 15, t 080 397 1597 (*expensive*). Old and in many cases near-forgotten recipes presented in innovative ways. The wine-cellar is spectacular. *Closed Mon and last two weeks in Jan.*

Bistrot, Corso Dante 33, t 080 397 5812 (*moderate*). Adventurous and cheaper than Bufi; specialities include chef's *gamberi* and *spaghetti Forza Quattro*. *Closed Wed and two middle weeks of Aug.*

Ándria

La Fenice, Via Firenze 35, t 0883 550 260 (*expensive*). Excellent (if overpriced) cuisine including a choice of three tempting *menu degustazione*: fish, meat and traditional dishes. *Closed Mon.*

Gravina in Puglia

Madonna della Stella, Via Madonna della Stella, t 080 325 6383 (*moderate*). Everything is strictly local at this panoramic restaurant. *Closed Tues and Feb.*

Osteria, Piazza Pellicciari 4, t 080 326 1872 (*cheap*). This eclectic little place has a Pugliese/Emilian mix of delicious specialities like *cavatelli ai legumi* and pumpkin or walnut *ravioli*. *Closed Sun eve, Mon and last two weeks of Aug.*

---

his son Manfred, were imprisoned here for 30 years. Neither is it a fortification: there are no ramparts, no arrow slits, and not even a defensible gate. Some writers suggest that Frederick had an artistic monument in mind. The entrance to the castle, the so-called 'triumphal arch', is a work unique for the 13th century: an elegant classical portal that prefigures the Renaissance. Inside, every room was decorated with friezes, columns and reliefs in Greek marble, porphyry and precious stones. Almost all have gone, vandalized by the noblemen who owned the castle over the last five centuries. Only the delicately carved Gothic double windows survive, one to each room.

At Castel del Monte, however, it is the things you can't see that are most interesting. This is nothing less than the Great Pyramid of Italy, and the secrets Frederick built into it have for centuries attracted the attention of cranks and serious scholars alike. The guides are full of opinions; one suggests that the castle was built for meetings of a secret society, and considering the atmosphere of eclectic mysticism that surrounded the emperor and his court, this is entirely plausible. Whole books have been written about the measurements and proportions of the castle, finding endless repetitions of the Golden Section, its square and cubic roots, relations to the movements of the planets and the stars, the angles and proportions of the Pythagorean five-pointed star, and so on. A link between the castle and the ancient surveying of the Puglian plain is a fascinating possibility. Frederick's tower in Enna has been found to be the centre of an enormous rectilinear network of alignments, uniting scores of ancient temples, towers and cities in straight lines that criss-cross Sicily. That tower may have been built on the site of a forgotten holy place; the alignments and the vast geometrical temple they form probably predate the Greeks. No one has suggested that Castel del Monte replaced any ancient site, but the particular care of Puglia's ancient surveyors – and the arrangement of the region's holy places, sanctuaries and Frederick's castles – suggest that something similarly strange may be hidden here.

Around the *Tavoliere*

The nearest town to Castel del Monte is Ándria, a large and thriving market centre. Another of the cities associated with Frederick, Ándria has an inscription from the emperor on its St Andrea's Gate, honouring it for its loyalty. Two of Frederick's wives, Yolande of Jerusalem and Isabella of England, daughter of King John, are buried in the crypt of Ándria's cathedral.

Back towards the northwest, on the banks of the River Ofanto between Barletta and Canosa di Puglia (SS93), you can visit the site of the **Battle of Cannae**; here, in 216 BC, Hannibal trapped and annihilated four Roman legions in one of the most famous battles of history. Military strategists still study the Carthaginians' brilliant ambush, the last serious defeat Rome was to suffer for centuries. At the time, Hannibal and his elephants had already been in Italy for two years. Cannae was the opportunity he was waiting for, and historians are puzzled why he didn't immediately follow it up with a march on Rome – probably it was due to a lack of siege equipment. The chance was missed; Hannibal spent another eight years campaigning successfully but fruitlessly in Italy, while the Romans locked themselves up in their towns and sent their armies off to conquer Spain and North Africa. Cannae taught the Romans to be careful, and it could be said that Hannibal's victory meant the defeat not of Rome, but of Carthage.

In Roman times, **Canosa di Puglia** was one of the most important towns in the region; the reminders of its former status include three large tombs on the outskirts of town, excavated in 1843, and a collection of archaeological relics in the **Museo Civico** (*open Tues–Sun 8–2*). Canosa isn't much today, but its otherwise undistinguished five-domed cathedral has in its courtyard the **tomb of Bohemund**, a striking marble chapel with a small cupola (octagonal, of course) that holds the remains of the doughty Crusader. Bohemund was the son of Robert Guiscard; renowned for valour and chivalry, he seized the main chance when the First Crusade was being preached, and ended up Prince of Antioch. The most remarkable feature of his tomb is the pair of bronze doors, signed by an artist named Roger of Melfi. The one on the left, inscribed with geometrical arabesques, is a single slab of bronze. Inside the cathedral, notice the early medieval bishop's chair, resting on two weary-looking elephants.

Four Towns, Four More Cathedrals

In this corner of Bari province, there are altogether eight noteworthy cathedrals on a narrow strip of land only some 64km long. They are the only real monuments – nothing has been built ambitiously and well around here since the 14th century – and they stand as the best evidence of Puglia's greatest period of culture and prosperity. One of the best cathedrals in Puglia is at **Ruvo di Puglia**, an ancient settlement that was famous in classical times for pottery – reproducing Greek urns at a lower price, above all between the 5th and the 3rd centuries BC when the trade was at its height. A large collection of locally made urns, and some Greek imports, can be seen at the **Museo Jatta**, in Piazza Bovio (*open Mon–Sat 8.30–1.30, Fri and Sat also 2.30–7.30*). The **cathedral** is a tall, almost Gothic work, with a richly decorated façade incorporating a fine rose window. The little arches along the sides of the building are decorated with intricate figures of pagan gods, copied from surviving pieces of ancient Ruvo's pottery.

Bitonto, the centre of olive oil production in Puglia, has a **cathedral** which is considered by many to be the classic of Puglian Romanesque; the best features of the exterior are the side galleries and the carvings of fantastical animals and scriptural scenes over the three front portals. Inside, there is a famous pulpit of 1226 displaying a fierce-looking eagle; on one side a curious, primitive relief shows Emperor Frederick, Isabella of England, and their family.

Puglia's southern borders make up a distinct region, a slightly elevated jumble of plain and rolling hills called **Le Murge**. The most important town, **Altamura**, thriving nowadays on its well known bread which is shipped all over Italy, was founded by Frederick on the site of an abandoned ancient city. For centuries it was a town of some distinction, even having its own university. Its advanced outlook led Altamura to support the French and the short-lived Parthenopean Republic during the Napoleonic Wars. As a result, the Army of the Holy Faith, a mob led by a cardinal and egged on by monks, sacked and burned the city in 1799. The university never recovered, but Altamura still has a beautiful **cathedral**, begun by Frederick in 1232; heavy damage from an earthquake in 1316 accounts for the departures from the Puglian norm. The building retains its exceptional rose window and portal, but the twin towers above were added during the Renaissance. For some reason, in the course of doing so, they turned the cathedral backwards – the old portal and rose window were carefully taken apart, and placed where the apse used to be. The **Museo Archeologico**, Via Santeramo 88 (*open Mon–Sat 8.30–1.30 and 2.30–7.30, Sun 8.30–1.30 only*) houses one of Italy's most interesting collections, with first-rate finds related to the people of the Murge from prehistoric times to the Middle Ages.

Gravina in Puglia, on the road towards Potenza, has the fourth cathedral, but it is only a dull 15th-century replacement for the Norman original. Gravina does have other charms. The town is set above a steep ravine, lined with caves where the inhabitants took refuge from pirates and barbarians during the Dark Ages. One of the town's churches, **San Michele dei Grotti**, is a cave too (*contact the Cooperative Benedetto XIII, t 0338 567 8017, inside the cathedral, for free tours in English of San Michele and other cave-churches; donations appreciated*), with a heap of human bones believed to be those of victims of Arab pirates during the 8th century. Other churches show somewhat eccentric versions of Renaissance styles, notably the **Madonna delle Grazie**, near the railway station. On Piazza Santomasi there is a **museum** (*open Tues–Sat 9–1 and 4–7, Sun 9–1 only*), which contains a full-size reconstruction of another ancient cave church, with fragments of Byzantine frescoes.

Bari

Somehow Bari should be a more interesting place. The second city of the peninsular Mezzogiorno is a bustling town full of sailors and fishermen, and also boasts a university and a long heritage of cultural distinction. Bari nonetheless will be a disappointment if you come here expecting Mediterranean charm and medieval romance. If, on the other hand, you'd like to see a southern city that has come close to catching up with the rest of Italy economically, Bari will be just the place. Its newer districts, jammed with noisy traffic, exhibit a thoroughly northern glitter, and the good burghers who stroll down the Corso Cavour for their evening *passeggiata* are among the most overdressed in Italy. Be warned, though – and you probably will be – that the city has one of the highest street-crime rates in the country.

The Town that Stole Santa Claus

Bari can trace its history back to before the Romans, but it began to make a name for itself only in the 10th century. As an important trading city, and seat of a nominally independent Byzantine governor, Bari was sometimes a rival of Venice, though more often its ally. Robert Guiscard and his Normans, who took the city in 1071, favoured Bari and helped it become the leading town of Puglia.

Sixteen years later, in 1087, a fleet of Barese merchantmen in Antioch got word that some of their Venetian counterparts were planning a little raid on Myra, on what is now the southern coast of Turkey. Their intention was to pinch the mortal remains of St Nicholas, Myra's 4th-century bishop, canonized for his generosity and good deeds. Relic-stealing was a cultural imperative for medieval Italians, and the Baresi sneaked in by night and beat the Venetians to their prey, something that did not happen often in those days.

The Greek Christians of Myra were disgusted by the whole affair, but the Baresi had them outmatched, and so St Nicholas went west (his sarcophagus was too heavy to move, and so you can still see it today in the museum at Antalya, Turkey). Every year on 8 May the Baresi celebrate their cleverness with a procession of boats in the harbour, and an ancient icon of the saint is held up to receive the homage of the crowds on shore, recreating the scene of Nicholas' arrival 900 years ago.

To provide a fitting home for such an important saint, Bari began almost immediately to construct the **Basilica di San Nicola**, at the centre of the old town. Unfortunately, the original ambition overreached the ability of succeeding generations to finish the job. The two big towers remain unfinished and much of the decorative scheme was abandoned, giving the church a dowdy, barn-like appearance. Still, this is the first of the great Puglian churches, the place where the style was first translated from Norman French to southern Italian. Inside, the only surprise is the tomb of Bona Sforza, Queen of Poland and Duchess of Bari. The daughter of a 16th-century Duke of Milan, she inherited Bari on her mother's side and as a teenager was packed off to marry Sigismund, one of Poland's greatest kings. She survived him, and had a brief but eventful career as a dowager queen before retiring to sunny Puglia in her last years. Near the main altar, note the wonderful 11th-century bishop's throne,

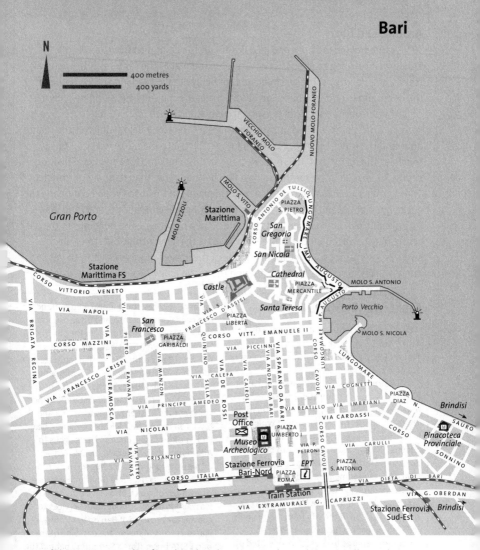

Bari

one of the greatest works of medieval sculpture in Puglia; its legs, carved into the figures of men groaning as if they were supporting some unbearable burden, must have been a good joke on any fat bishop over the centuries.

Down in the crypt, you can pay your respects to St Nicholas. There will nearly always be somebody down there, praying or conducting a service; St Nicholas' tomb has always been one of the south's most popular places of pilgrimage. Most of the visitors are local, but an Orthodox chapel has been added to house pilgrims from Greece and Russia. The church is also home to a centre for ecumenical studies, as the Baresi try to make amends after nine centuries. One of St Nicholas' tricks is to exude gallons of a brownish liquid the faithful call manna, to which all sorts of miracles are attributed; half the families in this part of Puglia have a phial of it for good luck.

Around Old Bari

The **cathedral** (*open 8.30–1 and 5–7*) is difficult to distinguish from San Nicola, although it was begun almost a century later. The plan is the same, as is the general feeling of austerity broken by small areas of richly detailed carving around some of the doors and windows. Unlike San Nicola, the cathedral still has its original beam ceiling, interrupted only by an octagonal cupola, and much more suited to its Romanesque plainness. Two unusual features are the stone baldaquin over the main altar, and the *trullo*, the large round building adjacent to the north wall that once served as the baptistry. Old Bari, as we have said, is a bit drab for a medieval historic centre. There is a reason for this, in that Bari has had more than its share of trouble. The Normans levelled it once after a revolt; a plague in the 1650s wiped out nearly the entire population; and the port area was heavily bombed in the Second World War.

As a result, old Bari in some parts has the air of a new town. The buildings in the old centre may be all rebuilt or restored, but at least the labyrinthine old street plan survives – it's famous, in fact, for being one of the easiest places in all Italy to get lost. There will be no trouble, however, finding the **castle** (*open Tues–Sun 8.30–7.30; adm*),

Getting Around

Bari itself is a compact city, and once there it doesn't take long to see the sights on foot. This isn't Naples, but the traffic and parking are predictably horrible.

Bari's **airport**, about 9km west of the city at Palese, has regular connections to Rome, Milan, Turin, Pisa and some other destinations. There is a special bus to the airport which leaves from the central train station (L5,000).

If you discover a sudden desire to bolt, there are regular **ferries** from Bari to Corfu, mainland Greece (Igoumenitsa and Patras), Albania, Croatia and Turkey. All ferries leave from the Stazione Marittima on the Mole San Vito, at the opposite end of the city from the main FS rail station (connected by bus no.20).

Car ferry services to Greece are operated by the **Ventouris line**, c/o Pan Travel, Via 24 Maggio 40, **t** 080 521 0504 (June–Sept daily; the rest of the year three times a week), and **Superfast**, **t** 080 528 2828, whose ferries are faster but slightly more expensive. **Adriatica**, Via Liside 4, **t** 080 553 1555, or Stazione Marittima, **t** 080 523 5825, runs ferries to Dubrovnik on Croatia's Dalmatian coast (Fri and Sun) and to Montenegro (Tues, Fri and Sat). **CTS**, Via Fornari 7, **t** 080 521 3244, is one of the most helpful travel agents in town.

Bari is an important junction on the main FS east-coast **railway** line, with many long-distance services; there is also a busy branch line from Bari to Táranto, and three private regional railways that run from the city. The Ferrovia Sud-Est (FSE), **t** 080 546 2111, runs a line from Bari's central FS station (on Piazza Aldo Moro) to Lecce and Táranto (competing with the FS) and towns in the *trulli* country. Nearby, the Ferrovia Bari-Nord station, **t** 080 521 3577, runs frequent trains to Andria and towns en route; while Ferrovie Calabro-Lucane (FCL), **t** 080 572 5111, on Corso Italia, goes to Altamura and to Matera in the Basilicata.

There are long-distance **bus** services from Bari to Rome, Naples and other major Italian cities, most of which also leave from the Piazza Aldo Moro, although bus services to coastal towns north of Bari operate from Piazza Eroi del Mare (on the east side of the port). SITA buses (Largo Sorrentino behind the FS train station) connect Bari with inland and southern towns, while the private rail lines' bus services (FCL and FSE) leave respectively from stations on Corso Italia and Largo Ciaia. The bright orange **city buses** run from 5.30am to 11pm (L1,000 per trip); their main terminus is Piazza Aldo Moro.

Tourist Information

Piazza Aldo Moro 32/A, **t** 080 524 2244, next to the FS station (*open Mon–Sat 8.30–1*).

just across the Piazza Odegitria from the cathedral. The Normans began it, Frederick II completed it, and later centuries added the polygonal bastions to deflect cannon-balls. Inside, some sculpted reliefs and windows survive from Frederick's time, along with bits of sculpture and architectural fragments from all over Puglia. Excavations have revealed parts of Roman Bari, which lies directly underneath.

Modern Bari

On your way to the railway station, you will cross the Corso Vittorio Emanuele – site of the city hall and Bari's famous fish market, and the boundary between the old city and the new. When Bari's fortunes began to revive, at the beginning of the 19th century, Joachim Murat's Napoleonic government laid out this broad rectilinear extension to the city. It has the plan of an old Greek or Roman town, only with wider streets, and it fits Bari well; many of the streets have a view open to the sea. Via Sparano di Bari and Corso Cavour are the choicest shopping streets. Bari's museums are in the new town. The **Pinacoteca Provinciale** (*open Mon–Sat 9.30–1 and 4–7, Sun 9.30–1; adm*) is in the Palazzo della Provincia on Lungomare Nazario Saura, and has a

Stop Over, Via Nicola 47, t 080 523 2716 (*open Mon–Fri 9.30–1 and 4.30–8*). More useful.

Where to Stay

Bari ✉ 70100

Bari is the most convenient base for the region, but beware: the city is a business centre, full of bad hotels at absurd prices.

★★★★**Villa Romanazzi Carducci**, Via Capruzzi 326, t 080 542 7400, f 080 556 0297 (*expensive*). One upmarket hotel in Bari that is not a rip-off. It has ample, comfortable rooms facing a rather spartan garden.

★★★**Grand Hotel Moderno**, Via Crisanzio 60, t 080 521 3313, f 080 521 4718 (*moderate*). At half the price of the Villa Romanazzi, you could do worse than this pleasant hotel.

★★★**Costa**, Via Crisanzio 12, t 080 521 9015, f 080 521 0006 (*moderate*). Another unremarkable but pleasant hotel.

★★**Albergo Giulia**, t 080 521 6630, f 080 521 8271 (*cheap*). In the same building as the Costa, this is one of the best cheap hotels.

Eating Out

Bari is famous for fish and, like all the smaller towns around it, still sends its own fishing fleet out each morning.

Murat de l'Hotel Palace, Via Lombardi 13, t 080 521 6551 (*expensive*). For the adventurous, this is a chance to forget about local specialities for once, and eat at a highly rated restaurant devoted to daring and innovative Italian cuisine. *Closed Sun and Aug.*

Deco' del Kursaal Santa Lucia, Largo Adua 5, t 080 524 6070 (*expensive*). A traditional, classier place near Molo San Nicola. *Closed Mon and Aug.*

Taverna Verde, t 080 554 0870 (*cheap*). A few steps down the road, at no.19, a popular place for fish and beer – a good combination if you've had enough of wine. *Closed Sun, last two weeks of Aug, and 24 Dec–6 Jan.*

Terranima, Via Putignani 213, t 080 521 9725 (*moderate*). Arguably the best *trattoria* in town, the daily menu here features few choices, but very solid dishes served in a pretty ambience. *Closed Sun and Aug.*

Al Pescatore, Via Federico II di Svevia 6, t 080 523 7039 (*moderate*). Come here for excellent fresh grilled fish served in informal surroundings. *Closed Sun.*

Da Tommaso, t 080 530 0038 (*cheap*). Another good place for fresh seafood, outside town at Palese Marina. *Closed Mon.*

Enzo e Ciro, Via Imbriani 79, t 080 554 1535 (*cheap*). The place to come if you're after a good pizza. *Closed Sun in summer.*

Getting Around

One of the best ways to see the area is on the Ferrovia Sud-Est **rail** line between Bari and Táranto or Lecce, which stops at most of the *trulli* country towns such as Putignano, Alberobello, Locorotondo and Martina Franca, where the Lecce and Táranto lines divide. The FSE also operates **bus** services to the area from Táranto and Bari.

Tourist Information

Ostuni: Corso Giuseppe Mazzini 6, t 0831 301 268, in the old town in summer (*open Mon–Fri 9–12.30 and 6–9*); Via Dottor V. Continelli 47, t 0831 303 775, in the new town the rest of the year (*open Mon–Fri 8–2 and 4–8*).

Martina Franca: Piazza Roma 35, t 080 480 5702 (*open June–Sept Mon–Sat 8.30–1 and 5–9; Oct–May Mon–Sat 8.30–1, Tues and Thurs also 5–8*).

Fasano: Piazza Ciaia, t 080 441 3086 (*open Mon–Sat 8–2 and 4–8*).

Where to Stay and Eat

All across this area there are dozens of privately owned *trulli* whose owners rent them out to visitors as part of the local *Agriturismo* programme. You can get more information from local tourist offices.

Alberobello ✉ 70011

Because the *trullo* towns are easily accessible by rail from Bari or Táranto, not many people stay over. But Alberobello's unaffected hospitality makes it one of the most pleasant bases imaginable, and there is a wide choice of both hotels and restaurants.

★★★★★Hotel dei Trulli, Via Cadore 32, t 080 432 3555, f 080 432 3560 (*expensive*). This group of *trulli*, set in a garden, comes top of the list. Each cottage has its own patio and is beautifully furnished. There is also a pool.

Il Poeta Contadino ('The Peasant Poet'), Via Indipendenza 21, t 080 432 1917 (*very expensive*). One of Puglia's finest 'creative' restaurants. The atmosphere is soothing and sophisticated, and both food and wine are among the best you'll find. *Closed Sun eves, and Mon from Sept–Jan.*

Trullo d'Oro, Via Cavallotti 27, t 080 432 1820 (*moderate*). Fancier cuisine: try the *spiedini* Puglian-style. *Closed Mon and 6 Jan–Feb.*

Cucina dei Trulli, Via Ferdinando IV 31, t 080 432 1511 (*cheap*). A family-run restaurant, which has been in business for over a century as part of the budget hotel

---

good selection of southern Italian art. The **Museo Archeologico** (*closed for restoration*) occupies a corner of Bari University's sprawling, crowded palace on the Piazza Umberto I, near the railway station. The star exhibits are classical ceramics: painted vases from Attica, including one very beautiful figure of the Birth of Helen from Leda's egg, and Puglian copies, as good as the best of the Greeks. Much of the rest of the collection is devoted to the pre-Greek Neolithic cultures of Puglia.

The *Trulli* Country

Southeast of Bari is a small but especially attractive region of little towns set amid an extraordinary, unique man-made landscape, given its character by one of the oldest forms of building in Italy still in regular use – the strange, whitewashed dome-roofed houses known as *trulli*.

Alberobello, Locorotondo and Ostuni

The **Valle d'Itria**, between the towns of Putignano and Martina Franca, is the best place for *trullo*-hunting. Alberobello, the *trullo* capital, has over a thousand of them

Lanzillotta; excellent home-cooking. *Closed Tues in winter.*

Locorotondo ✉ 70010

This village is the centre of Puglia's most famous wine region, and for dinner, a bottle of Locorotondo wine is mandatory: a pale, dry white, much more delicate than most of the strong wines of Puglia.

Casa Mia, Via Cisternino, **t** 080 431 1218 (*cheap*). They'll be glad to slip you a bottle of Locorotondo with the stuffed peppers or *coniglio al forno* at this fine establishment. It's a few miles along the road towards Ostuni. *Closed Tues.*

Centro Storico, Via Eroi di Dogali 6, **t** 080 431 5473 (*moderate*). The owner's love of food is obvious in the care taken with cooking and presentation at this small, intimate *trattoria*. *Closed Wed in winter.*

Ostuni ✉ 72017

★★Tre Torri, Corso Vittorio Emanuele 298, **t** 0831 331 114 (*cheap*). Ostuni and its stretch of coast are well equipped with hotels. This pleasant hotel is fine for a short stay.

★★★★Hotel Rosa Marina, on the SS379 north of Ostuni, **t** 0831 350 411 (*expensive*). Along the shoreline at Rosa Marina, the sharp modern design of this hotel stands out from the crowd; it's a comfortable place too, with a pool, private beach and all the amenities.

Martina Franca ✉ 74015

★★★Dell'Erba, Via dei Cedri 1, **t** 080 430 1055 (*moderate*). There are childminding facilities, a garden, and a pool here, and an excellent restaurant.

Castellana Grotte ✉ 70013

Fontanina, **t** 080 496 8010 (*moderate*). If you don't mind spending a bit more, this is another welcoming restaurant that serves generous portions of traditional food, on the Alberobello road outside town. *Closed Mon.*

Taverna degli Artisti, Via Matarrese 23, **t** 080 496 8234 (*cheap*). You might like to try the *cannelloni* or the lamb *torcini* at this friendly establishment. *Closed Sun.*

Savelletri di Fasano ✉ 72010

★★★★★Masseria San Domenico, on the Strada Litoranea, **t** 080 482 7990 (*very expensive*). Recently opened, and not far from Egnazia, this is one of the most relaxing and luxurious hotels in Puglia. The renovated buildings of an old country house set amid the olive groves look out on to a beautiful swimming pool (filled with filtered seawater) in the shape of a natural lake.

(and nearly as many craft shops) in two adjacent neighbourhoods called the Rione Monti and the Ala Piccola. Even the modern church of Sant'Antonio has been built in *trullo*-fashion. There are plenty more out in the countryside too, and particularly so around **Locorotondo**, a town on a hill with views all around the Itria valley. Locorotondo itself is a gleaming white town topped not with *trulli*, but tidy rows of distinctive gables. The street plan, from which the town takes its name, is neatly circular, built around an ancient well dedicated to St George.

The towns and villages in this district must be counted among the most beautiful in southern Italy. In each of them, white arches and steps climb the hillsides, sometimes punctuated by *trulli* and topped with surprisingly grand Baroque churches. You can spend as much time exploring these little towns as you care to. **Ostuni** is one of the loveliest, with an ornate 16th-century cathedral and a handful of other Renaissance and Baroque confections standing out among its white streets – including even a Neapolitan-style *guglia* (spire). The **Chiesa delle Monacelle** (*open daily 9–1 and 4.30–7.30; longer hours in summer; adm*) is home to Delia, the archaeological highlight of Ostuni, a well-preserved skeleton of a pregnant young woman found in a crouched position, her skull decorated with coloured beads and stones

The Love of *Trulli*

It takes you by surprise. Turning a corner of the road or passing the crest of one of the low hills of the Murge, all at once you meet a kind of landscape you have never seen before. Low stone walls neatly partition the countryside, around acres of vines propped up on arbours, covering the ground like low flat roofs. The houses are the strange part, smooth whitewashed structures in a bewildering variety of shapes and forms, each crowned with one or more tall conical stone roofs. These are the *trulli*, and when there are enough of them in one place, they make a picture that might be at home in Africa, or in a fairytale, but certainly nowhere else in Italy.

The *trulli* are still built these days; the dome is easier to raise than it looks, and the form is adaptable to everything from tool sheds to petrol stations. It is anybody's guess as to their origins; some scholars have mentioned the Saracens, others, less probably, the Mycenaean Greeks. None of the *trulli* you see today is more than a century or two old. They are exotically beautiful, but if the form has any other advantage, it would be that the domes give warmer air a chance to rise, making the houses cooler in the broiling Puglian summers. Beyond that one modest tangible contribution, there is no real reason for building *trulli* – only that they are an inseparable part of the lives of the people who live in this part of Puglia. There is no special name for the area around Alberobello where most of the *trulli* are concentrated; people simply call it the '*trulli* district'.

Trulli are built of limestone, with thick, whitewashed walls and only a few tiny windows. The domes are limestone too, a single row of narrow slates wound in a gradually decreasing spiral up to the top. Most have some sort of decoration at the point, and a few of the older ones are embellished with some traditional but obscure symbols, painted like Indian teepees.

Trulli seem only to come in one size; when a *trullo*-dweller needs more room, he simply has another unit added on. In this way, some of the fancier trullo palaces come to resemble small castles – Loire châteaux built for hobbits. Grandest of all is the one on Piazza Sacramento in Alberobello, the only specimen with a second floor; they call it the Sovrano, the Supreme *Trullo*.

before burial during what must have been a mystic, religious ceremony. The church also hosts a permanent display on prehistoric agriculture in southern Italy. The evening *passeggiata* in Ostuni goes on until well past midnight, and souvenir shops, restaurants and *pizzerie* stay open late. Ostuni also has the advantage of being near the sea, at the centre of the long strip of modest but peaceful beach resorts that line the coast between Monópoli and Bríndisi.

Martina Franca is the highest town in Puglia with a garland of Baroque monuments, including the old Palazzo Ducale and a cathedral at the top. In July and August, the town becomes an important point on the cultural map when it hosts the Valle d'Itria Festival, an international music festival that attracts major opera, classical and jazz performers from around the world (*t 080 480 5100, or information on tickets from the tourist office*).

Caves, *Laure* and a Dolmen

Nor are the attractions of this area limited to *trulli* and white towns. The people around the **Castellana Grotte** never tire of bragging that their famous grottoes are the most beautiful in Italy. They may be right: the deepest section of the grotto tour, called the **Caverna Bianca**, is a glistening wonderland hung with thousands of bright glassy stalactites *(open April–Sept daily 8.30–12 and 2.30–6; Oct–Mar daily 9–12 and 2–5; Aug also tours at 9pm; tours hourly (last about 1hr 45min); adm exp)*. Like much of Puglia, this region is what geologists call karst topography: made of easily dissolving limestone, the territory is laced with caves, accompanied by streams and rivers that disappear into the ground, only to pop back up to the surface a few miles away.

In the Middle Ages the more inviting of the caves filled up with Greek Basilian monks. Here, following their burrowing instinct just as they did in Asia Minor and elsewhere, the Greek hermits turned literally dozens of caves into hidden sanctuaries and chapels. The best are around Táranto, but there are a couple – **Grotto di San Biagio** and **Grotto di San Giovanni** – outside the town of San Vito dei Normanni, and some more along the ravines near the town of Fasano, where they are called *laure*.

Also near Fasano, just off the Ostuni road at the village of Montalbano, you can visit what may be the most impressive **dolmen** in the south. Puglia's earliest cultures were not often great builders, but they could be counted among the most sophisticated of all the Mediterranean Neolithic peoples. Much of their geometric pottery, which you can see scattered among Puglia's museums, is distinctively beautiful. This dolmen, a chamber formed by one huge slab of rock propped horizontally over two others, has acquired an odd local nickname: the **Tavole Palatine**, or Table of the Knights – the Round Table of King Arthur.

Along the coast near Fasano is the small resort of **Torre Canne**, and north of that, in an isolated setting by the sea, straddling the coastal road, the ruins of the Messapian-Roman town of **Egnazia**. The site is worth a brief visit, if only to admire the stupendous polychromatic mosaics with geometrical patterns and wild beasts, currently housed in the small museum, which also contains some Messapian arte-facts, pottery and architectural fragments *(open July–Sept daily 8.30–1 and 2.30–dusk, till 11pm on Sat; Oct–June closed Sun afternoon; adm)*.

Táranto

According to legend, Táranto was founded by *Taras*, a son of Poseidon who came riding into the harbour on the back of a dolphin. According to the historians, however, it was only a band of Spartans, shipped here in 708 BC to found a colony. They chose a good spot: probably the best harbour in Italy, and the only good one at all on the Ionian Sea. Not surprisingly, their new town of *Taras* did well. Until the Romans cut it down to size, *Taras* was the metropolis of Magna Graecia, a town feared in war but more renowned in philosophy. *Taras*, now Táranto, is still an interesting place, with an exotic old quarter, a good museum, and excellent seafood. Nevertheless, the best part of the story is all in the past.

Getting Around

There are two **railway** lines; both use the central station in Táranto, at the far west of town – between the old town and the steel mills – on Piazzale Duca d'Aosta. Regular FS trains leave for Lecce, Bríndisi, Bari and further north, as well as for the horrible endless trip around the Ionian Sea to Reggio di Calabria.

On one or another of the FS lines you can get to Massafra, Castellaneta, Grottaglie or Manduria. FSE (Ferrovie Sud-Est) local trains, which operate from one side of the station, will take you to Locorotondo, Martina Franca and Alberobello (**t** 099 470 4463).

The FSE also operates a large proportion of the province's **bus** services (**t** 099 470 4627): several a day for Alberobello, Bari or Lecce leave from Piazza Castello. FSE buses for Ostuni and Manduria leave from Via di Palma. SITA buses to Matera also leave from Piazza Castello, and there are daily buses to Naples run by Miccolis from the train station. Buses to Metaponto leave from Piazza Castello.

Tourist Information

Corso Umberto I 113, **t** 099 453 2392 (*open Mon–Fri 9–1 and 4.30–6.30, Sat 9–12*).

Where to Stay and Eat

Táranto ✉ 74100

Most of the better hotels are inconveniently located on the far eastern edge of town.

***Plaza, Via d'Aquino 46, facing Piazza Archita **t** 099 459 0775, **f** 099 459 0675 (*moderate*). One well-run spot in the centre is the Plaza. Most of the rooms have a balcony over the square.

Sorrentino, Piazza Fontana 7, **t 099 470 7456 (*cheap*). The real bargain places are scattered around the old town, and this clean and shipshape place in the picturesque environs of the fish market is one of the best.

Posillipo a Mare, Via Cariati 38, **t** 099 411 519. One of a number of popular places to eat right across the street from Táranto fish market, where you can feast on all different kinds of fruits of the sea and rub elbows with half of Táranto. *Closed Fri.*

Al Gambero, Vico del Ponte 4, **t** 099 471 1190 (*moderate*). Come here for something a little more elegant. It's just across the channel, and has earned a high reputation for its creative dishes involving nearly all the fantastic array of marine delicacies the Ionian Sea has to offer. *Closed Mon and Nov.*

Le Vecchie Cantine, Via Girasoli 23, **t** 099 777 2589 (*expensive*). This sophisticated place is one of the best, as well as one of the newest, places to eat. The menu changes on a daily basis but is always focused on fish. *Open eves only, closed Wed in winter, and Jan.*

Da Mimmo, Via Giovinazzi 18, **t** 099 459 3733 (*cheap*). Another good seafood restaurant, which features prominently the local speciality: delicious, fresh mussels, or *cozze* (also called *mitili*). Dishes available may include roast squid and *tubettini alle cozze*. *Closed Wed and two weeks in Aug.*

Ristorante-Pizzeria Mario, Via Acclaio 68, **t** 099 26008 (*cheap*). One of many good places to eat in the new city. It has very tasty seafood dinners for practically nothing.

Ristorante Basile, Via Pitagora 76, **t** 099 452 6240 (*cheap*). Across from the main city park, this is perhaps even better. Fine dinners at rock-bottom prices. *Closed Sat.*

Ceglie Messapica ✉ 72013

Tre Trulli, Via Carducci, **t 0831 377 557 (*cheap*). Not many people come to Ceglie, but if you're in the area, it makes a pleasant stopover. This simple hotel is one of a number of inexpensive options.

Messapica, Piazza del Plebescito (*cheap*). A *trattoria* serving typical home-made dishes.

La Taverna dei Dominicani, Via Dante 15, **t** 0831 384 910 (*moderate*). Sophisticated cuisine in a restored pilgrims' hostel.

Al Fornello da Ricci, Contrada Montevicoli, **t** 0831 377 104 (*expensive*). One of the finest restaurants in Puglia – an absolute must for foodies interested in Puglian cuisine. *Closed Mon eves, Tues, three weeks in Sept and 10 days in Jan.*

Castellaneta Marina ✉ 74011

****Golf Hotel, Località Riva dei Tessali, **t** 099 843 9251, **f** 099 843 9255 (*expensive*). A resort complex of cottages in a grove near the links – a genuine novelty in these parts.

History: Rotten Shellfish, Sheep with Overcoats

With its harbour, and with the help of a little Spartan know-how on the battlefield, *Taras* had little trouble acquiring both wealth and political power. By the 4th century BC, the population had reached 300,000. In its balmiest days, *Taras'* prosperity depended on an unusual variety of luxury goods. Its oysters were a highly prized delicacy, as far away as Rome. Another shellfish, the murex, provided the purple dye – really a deep scarlet – used for the robes of Roman emperors and every other style-conscious ruler across the Mediterranean. This imperial purple, the most expensive stuff of the ancient world, was obtained by allowing masses of murex to rot in the sun; an enormous heap of the shells, with perhaps the mollusc who coloured Caesar's cloak somewhere near the bottom, was mentioned by travellers only a century ago. For a similarly high price the Tarantines would have been happy to provide you with the cloth, too. Their sheep were known for the softest and best wool available, and the Tarantine shepherds actually put coats on their flocks to keep it nice.

If contemporary historians are to be believed, *Taras* managed to avoid most of the terrible inter-city conflicts of Magna Graecia simply by being much larger and more powerful than its neighbours. And it was spared civil troubles by a sound constitution, with a mix of aristocratic and democratic elements. Pythagoras spent part of his life in *Taras*, an exile from his native Croton, and he helped to set a philosophical tone for the city's affairs. The height of *Taras'* glory was perhaps the long period of rule under a Pythagorean mathematician and philosopher named Archytas (*c.* 400 BC), a paragon of wisdom and virtue in the ancient world. Plato himself came to visit Archytas, though he never mentions *Taras* in his writings.

When *Taras* and Rome went to war in 282 BC, they did so as equals. *Taras* called in Pyrrhus of Epirus as an ally, but after 10 years of inconclusive Pyrrhic victories, the Romans gained the upper hand and put an end to *Taras'* independence. Rome graciously refrained from razing the city to the ground after *Taras* helped Hannibal in the second Punic War; just the same, the Tarantines felt the iron grip of the victors, and their city quickly dwindled both in wealth and importance. Of all the Greek cities of the south, *Taras*, along with Reggio, proved to be the best survivor. Throughout the Dark Ages the city never quite disappeared, and by the time of the Crusades it was an important port once more.

The modern city, italianized to Táranto, substantially industrialized and a major base for the Italian navy, has known little of philosophers or well-dressed sheep, but still manages to send its fame around the world in other ways. The city gave its name to the country quick-dance called the *tarantella*, and also to the *tarantula*. Before you change your travel plans, there really are no large hairy poisonous spiders in Puglia, just a few innocent little brown ones. Their bite isn't much, but a little notoriety still clings to them, thanks to the religious pathology of the south Italians. Throughout antiquity and the Middle Ages various cults of dancing were current around the Mediterranean. Everything from the worship of Dionysus to the medieval Dance of Death touched this region and, when the Catholic church began to frown on such carryings on, the urge took strange forms. People bitten by spiders became convinced they would die, and that their only salvation was to dance the venom out of their system – dance until they dropped, in fact. Sometimes they would dance for four days or more, while musicians played for them and their friends sought to discover the magic colour – the 'colour' of that particular spider – that would calm the stricken dancer. *Tarantism*, as 19th-century psychologists came to call it, is rarely seen anywhere in the south these days, and for that matter neither is the *tarantella*, a popular style of music that took its name from this bit of folklore, and was first in vogue around the beginning of the 1800s.

The Città Vecchia

Perhaps unique among cities, Táranto has two 'seas' all to itself. Its harbour consists of two large lagoons, the **Mare Grande** and the **Mare Piccolo**. The city is on a narrow strip of land between them, broken into three pieces by a pair of narrow channels. Today, the westernmost section, around the railway station, is almost entirely filled up with Italy's biggest steel plant, begun as the showpiece project of the Cassa per il Mezzogiorno in the early fifties. This gargantuan complex provides an unexpected and memorable sight if you enter the city by night. Directly below the station along the Via Duca d'Aosta, a bridge takes you over to the old town, a nearly rectangular island that is only four blocks wide, but still does its best to make you lose your way. The ancient Tarantines, lacking any sort of hill, made the island their acropolis – though in those days it was still attached to the mainland. Most of the temples were here, along with a famous gold-plated bronze statue of Zeus that was the second-largest piece of sculpture in the world, surpassed only by the Colossus of Rhodes.

Today all that remains of ancient *Taras* are some columns from a **Temple of Poseidon**, which have been re-erected in the main square next to Táranto's **Castello**, built in the 1480s by King Ferdinand of Spain, and now the navy headquarters. From the square, a **swinging bridge**, something rare in Italy, connects the old town with the new. The Mare Piccolo, besides being an enormous oyster and mussel farm for the fishermen of Táranto, is also the home of one of Italy's two main naval bases. Very early in the morning, when the bridge is open, you may see big warships waiting their turn with little fishing boats to squeeze their way through the narrow channel.

Follow the fishermen home, and you'll end up in the **fish market** on Via Cariati, near the docks at the opposite end of the Città Vecchia. In sometimes slick and up-to-date Italy this is one of the places where you can most truly believe you are in the Mediterranean: a wet and mildly grubby quay awash with the sounds and smells of the sea, where tired fishermen appear each morning at dawn to have coffee, sort out the catch, and bang the life out of octopuses on the stones. Of course there are plenty of cats around; true 'aristocats' they are, the descendants of the first cats of Europe. Ancient historians record how the ancient Tarantines imported them from Egypt.

From the fish market, pick your way a short distance across the Città Vecchia to the **cathedral**, built and rebuilt in a hotchpotch of different styles, beginning in the 11th century. Most of the last, florid Baroque remodelling has been cleared away, saving only a curious coffered ceiling, with two golden statues suspended from it. Roman columns and capitals support the arches, and there is a good medieval baptismal font under a baldaquin. Some bits of mosaic survive on the floor; mosaics in the Byzantine manner were important in all Puglia's medieval churches. Táranto's **cathedral** is dedicated to St Cataldus, a Munster Irishman who did good works here on his way to the Crusades; you can see his tomb down in the crypt.

The rest of the Città Vecchia holds few surprises. The area was down at heel and half-forgotten for a long time but with Táranto's new-found prosperity the city is putting a good deal of money into housing rehabilitation and restoring old palaces and other monuments, a process that is already making a difference. As in Bari, crossing over from the sleepy old town into the hyperactive new centre is a startling contrast. Táranto has no need to envy Bari these days; its new town is bright, busy and sprawling, with as many grey-suited businessmen as blue-clad sailors.

The Museo Nazionale

Open Tues–Sat 8.30–1.30 and 2.30–7.30, Sun and Mon 8.30–1.30; temporary display open daily 8.30–7.30.

The best of Magna Graecia is on display here, at Piazza Archita (entrance at Corso Umberto I no. 41), two streets west of the swinging bridge (though at the time of writing, the collections are temporarily on display at the Palazzo Pantaleo, in the historic centre). With building activity going full blast around Táranto, new discoveries are being made all the time; already the collection rivals those of Reggio and Naples. There are some fine pieces of sculpture from temples and funeral sites, including the well-preserved 6th-century BC tomb of an athlete, a head of Aphrodite and several other works attributed to the school of Praxiteles, and also a wonderful bronze of the god Poseidon, in the angular, half-oriental Archaic style.

The museum also has what is believed to be the largest collection of Greek terracotta figures in the world. They are fascinating in their thousands, the middle-class *objets d'art* of antiquity. The older ones are more consciously religious images of Dionysus, Demeter or Persephone that served the same purpose as the icon on the wall of a modern Italian family. Later examples give every evidence of creeping secularism; the subjects range from ladies at their *toilette* to grotesque theatre masks, comic dancers to mythological figures. One figurine reproduces a statue of Nike, or Victory, erected in *Taras* after one of Pyrrhus' defeats of the Romans – moved to the Roman forum when the war went the other way.

Among the fragments from *Taras'* buildings there is an entire wall of leering Medusas, protection against the evil eye – as much a preoccupation among the ancient Greeks as it is with southern Italians today. Besides large collections of delicate jewellery and coins (many minted with the city's own symbol of *Taras* riding his dolphin), there is also an important selection of Greek ceramics. In one room, a rare evocation of Magna Graecia at play is provided by scenes on vases of Athene and contending athletes.

Towns Around Táranto

Grottaglie, just 15 minutes by train to the east of the city, is the ceramics capital of southeast Italy. The town's potters continue to produce plates, vases and pots in enormous quantities, and attract throngs of visitors on summer weekends, eager to buy their traditional, and sometimes more modern, styles. Further along the road and rail line towards Bríndisi is **Francavilla Fontana**, which takes its title of 'free town' from a favour granted by King Ferdinand IV. The town conserves several 14th–18th-century palaces, including a small one belonging to the 18th-century Bourbon kings, as a reminder of its days as a feudal stronghold. Nearby **Oria** has a similar history; Frederick II built a strong **castle** here in 1227–33 (*open daily spring/summer 9–12 and 4–6; the rest of the year daily 4–6, weekends also 9–12; adm; free guided visits in English*), with three tall round towers, which now holds a collection of antiquities and bric-a-brac. In the Middle Ages, Oria had an important Jewish community; the ghetto and its buildings are still intact.

Oria is believed to have been the capital of the ancient Messapians, a quietly civilized people who suffered many indignities at the hands of the Greek colonists, and finally succumbed to the allure of classical culture. **Ceglie Messapica**, south of Ostuni, was another of their cities, and it is here you can see the *specchie*, the Messapians' most noteworthy surviving monuments. These are tall conical stepped towers; they get their name intriguingly from the Latin *speculum* (mirror), but no one has the faintest idea whaat they are or what purpopse they served. One is in Ceglie itself, and the other two are out in the country. The most impressive, the 36ft **Specchia Miano**, is 7km down the road from Ceglie to Francavilla – turn right up the road to Masseria Bottari farm and walk through the field on the right.

Manduria was another Messapian city, mentioned in the histories as fighting continuous wars with the Greeks of *Taras*. Ruins of its fortifications can still be seen – three concentric circuits of which the outermost is 5km around – along with caves, necropolises and a famous well mentioned in Pliny's *Natural History*. To find the well, turn right in front of the church of the Capuccini, on Via Sant'Antonio. The new city has a cathedral with a beautifully carved Renaissance rose window and portals.

Massafra

West of Táranto, a very short distance back toward Le Murge and Matera, you can visit one of the most unusual cities of Puglia. Massafra, even more than Matera, was a city of troglodytes and monks. A steep ravine, the **Gravina di San Marco**, cuts the city in two. The ravine and surrounding valleys are lined with caves, and many of these were expanded into cave-chapels, or *laure*, by Greek monks in the early Middle Ages. Between the caves and the old church crypts, it has been estimated that there are over a hundred medieval frescoes in, around and under Massafra – some of considerable artistic merit. One of the best is a beautiful Byzantine Virgin called *La Vergine della Scala*, in a sanctuary of the same name – the Santuario della Scala – reached from Via del Santuario in the old town of Massafra by a long naïf-Baroque set of stairs. The Madonna is shown receiving the homage of two kneeling deer, the subject of an old legend. Adjacent to the sanctuary, some 13th-century paintings can be seen in the Cripta della Bona Nova. At the bottom of the ravine is the Farmacia del Mago Greguro, a now rather neglected complex of caves that it is believed were used by the monks to store and prepare medicinal herbs.

Other cave churches and frescoes can be seen at **Mottola, Palagianello** and **Ginosa,** built like Massafra over a ravine full of caves. **Laterza,** perched on a 650ft-deep gorge near the border with the Basilicata, has about 180 caves and *laure,* of which some 30 can be visited. **Castellaneta** also has a ravine, the steepest and wildest of them all, and some cave churches, but this town cares more to be known as the birthplace, in 1895, of Rudolph Valentino. There's a monument to him in the main square, with a life-size ceramic statue of the old matinée idol dressed as the Sheikh of Arabia.

The Salentine Peninsula

It has lovely Lecce and dowdy Bríndisi, some flat but unusual countryside, the sun-bleached and sea-washed old towns of Gallípoli and Ótranto, lots of caves and Neolithic remains. Its coastline, while not as ruggedly beautiful as that of the Gargano, does have its charms, not least of which is that it is relatively uncrowded. Not many foreign tourists make their way to this distant Land's End, although it teems with Italians in August. If you are beachcombing or backpacking, and can resist the temptation presented by the ferries to Greece, this might be a perfect place to spend a lazy week or so.

Bríndisi

The word *brindisi* in Italian means to toast. It's just a coincidence; the name comes from the original Greek colony of *Brentesion,* and it isn't likely that anyone has lately proposed any toasts to this grey and dusty port. Bríndisi today is what it was in Roman times: the gang-plank to the boat for Greece. On the Viale Regina Margherita, to the right of the port, a small piazza at the top of a formal stairway holds a magnificent **Roman column,** once topped by the statue of an emperor, that marked the end of the Appian Way.

For six centuries, all of Rome's trade with the East, all its legions heading toward new conquests, and all its trains of triumphant or beaten emperors and generals passed through *Brundisium.* From the 11th century on, the city reassumed its old role when it became one of the most important Crusader ports. A memory of this survives too; if you enter the city from the north or west, you will pass the **Tancredi Fountain,** an Arab-inspired work built by the Norman chief, Tancred. Here the Christian knights watered their horses before setting out for the Holy Land.

As a city where people have always been more concerned with coming and going than settling down, Bríndisi has not saved up a great store of monuments and art. Travel agents and shipping offices are more in evidence than anything else. If you're staying, there are a few things to look at. Alongside the 12th-century **cathedral,** rebuilt in warmed-over Baroque, there is a small exotic-looking portico with striped pointed arches; this is all that remains of the **Temple,** headquarters church of the Knights Templar, and closely related to the Temple in London. Nearby, a small collection of ancient Puglian relics has been assembled at the **Museo Archeologico** (*open daily 9–1;*

Getting Around

Bríndisi's Casale **airport** is 4km north of the city and has regular flights to Rome, Milan and Verona. There is a frequent bus service between the airport and the main FS rail station in the city centre.

Bríndisi is the most important Italian port for **ferries** to Greece, and has daily connections almost year-round to Corfu, Patras and Igoumenitsa, with several a day in the busy summer season. All ferries leave from the Stazione Marittima, in the centre of the port. The EPT office has up-to-date information on schedules and prices. That may not be much help in summer – as frequently as the boats run, it is a good idea in July and August to book a passage before you get to Bríndisi.

If you do need to buy a boat ticket here, avoid absolutely the ticket touts clustered around the train station and the Stazione Marittima; even the enormous number of agencies in Bríndisi offering ferry tickets are notoriously unreliable. It is always advisable to look around and to buy tickets from the boat companies themselves or an approved agent.

The two most established ferry companies and their main agents in Bríndisi are **Adriatica**, Stazione Marittima, **t** 0831 523 825; and **Hellenic Mediterranean**, Corso Garibaldi 8, **t** 0831 528 531.

The most reliable agents are **UTAC Viaggi**, Via Santa Lucia 11, **t** 0831 560 780, and **Grecian**

Travel, Corso Garibaldi 65, near the harbour, **t** 0831 597 884.

Between June and September ferries also operate between the little port of Ótranto and Corfu and Igoumenitsa. They are faster than many Bríndisi boats, but also more expensive.

In Bríndisi, **buses** to all provincial towns and nearby cities leave from the Viale Porta Pia; Marozzi, **t** 0831 521 684, and Miccolis, **t** 0831 560 678, operate bus services to Rome and Naples respectively, with several daily departures from Lungomare Regina Margherita, near the tourist office.

Lecce, despite its location, is well served by **rail**; the city is a terminus for long sleeper runs across Italy to Rome and Milan. All of these trains also pass through Bríndisi, and both towns have very frequent trains heading for Bari or Táranto. In addition, there is always the tired but game **FSE**, which has services from Lecce to Ótranto, Gallípoli and Nardò, as well as some to Bari and Táranto via Manduria (Lecce FSE information, **t** 0832 668 233).

In Lecce, most **buses** to towns in the Salentine, run by **STP**, **t** 0832 302 873, leave from Via Adua near the old western walls; while **FSE**, Via Torre del Parco, near Porta Napoli, **t** 0832 347 634, connects Lecce with Táranto, from where you can reach other destinations in the region.

A new company called Salento in Bus, **t** 0832 217 077, *www.salentonline.it*, has regular services between the main towns south of

April–Sept Mon–Fri also 3–6.30; Oct–Mar Tues and Thurs 3–6.30). Down Via San Giovanni, a few blocks south, another curious souvenir of the Templars has survived, the round church of **San Giovanni al Sepolcro**, built in the late 11th century, with fanciful carvings of dancers and lions on the portal. Back on the waterfront, on Viale Regina Margherita, there is a small local ferry that runs across the harbour to the 150ft **Monument to Italian Sailors**, erected by Mussolini in 1933. A lift goes up to the top, from where there are good views of the comings and goings of the port.

Santa Maria del Casale

The greatest of Bríndisi's attractions, however, lies just north of the city, near the sports complex on the way to the airport. Santa Maria del Casale (*to visit ring the bell at the gate*) is a church unlike any other in Italy; built in the 1320s, in an austere, almost modern economy of vertical lines and arches, the façade is done in two shades of sandstone, not striped as in so many other Italian churches, but shaped into a variety of simple, exquisite patterns. The interior, a simple, barn-like space, is painted

Lecce. They also lay on guided tours of the peninsula. Tickets can be bought from a newsagents, bars and tobacconists in Lecce (look out for the 'SalentoInBus' signs); buses leave from nine different stops round town.

The Via Appia (roughly following the modern SS7) reaches its end in Brindisi, as it has done for over 2,000 years. Traffic leaving the port can be very slow in summer; it's more leisurely to get away from the city on the SS16.

Tourist Information

Brindisi: Piazza Dionisio, off Lungomare Regina Margherita, t 0831 523 072 (*open Mon–Fri 7.30–2*).

Where to Stay and Eat

Brindisi✉ 72100

Brindisi 's hotel-keepers, accustomed to people staying overnight while waiting for the boat to Greece, have not been inspired to exert themselves, and there are no really outstanding places in the city. If you're waiting for a train or ferry, there are any number of *pizzerie* and *trattorie* along the Corso Umberto and Corso Garibaldi where you can find cheap, filling and quick food.

****Internazionale**, Lungomare Regina Margherita 26, t 0831 523 473 (*moderate*).

This is an older hotel, though very well kept and probably the best in Brindisi ; you're likely to encounter grandmotherly furnishings, and maybe you'll get one of the rooms with a marble fireplace. It is also worth knowing that it is extremely convenient for the ferry docks.

***Barsotti**, Via Cavour 1, t 0831 560 877 (*moderate*). A plain but acceptable place, near the train station.

Europa, Piazza Cairoli 5, t 0831 528 546, f 0831 528 547 (*cheap*). A reasonable quality hotel, centrally located on one of the two main squares between the train station and the ferry terminal.

La Lanterna, Via G. Tarantina 14, t 0831 564 026 (*expensive*). Behind the Appian Way column in Brindisi , this is certainly the city's most elegant restaurant. It manages to mix traditional and newly invented ways of cooking and presenting meat, seafood and pasta. *Closed Sun and three weeks in Aug.*

Trattoria Pantagruele, Via Salita di Ripalta 1–3, t 0831 560 605 (*moderate*). Come here for something simpler, but still good. Save room for the delicious home-made desserts. *Closed Sat lunch and Sun, and two weeks in Aug.*

Giàsotto l'Arco, Corso Vittorio Emanuele 71, t 0831 996 286 (*moderate*). An interesting, traditional restaurant at Carovigno, about 18 miles north of Brindisi . Book the table on the balcony if you can. *Closed Mon and Jan.*

with equally noteworthy frescoes in the Byzantine manner. The wall over the entrance is covered with a remarkable visionary *Last Judgement* by an artist named Rinaldo of Táranto, full of brightly coloured angels and apostles, saints and sinners; a river of fire washes the damned into the inferno while above, the fish of the sea disgorge their human prey to be judged. Many of the other frescoes, in the nave and transepts, have become badly faded, though they are still of interest.

Lecce

Unfortunately for the traveller, you will have to come a long way – to the furthest corner of Puglia – to find the most beautiful town in southern Italy. Lecce is worth the trip; its history, and its tastes, have given it a fate different from any other Italian town. FIrst and foremost, Lecce is the capital of southern Baroque – not the chilly, pompous Baroque of Rome, but a sunny, frivolous style Lecce created on its own.

Lecce started as a Messapian town, and flourished as the Roman *Lupiae*, but really came into its own during the Middle Ages, as the centre of a semi-independent county comprising most of the Salentine Peninsula. It enjoyed royal favour under the Spaniards in the 16th century. Located near the front lines of the continual wars between Habsburg and Turk, Lecce often found itself the centre of attention even though it was not a port. During the Spanish centuries, while every other southern city except the royal seat of Naples was in serious decline, 'the Athens of Puglia' was enjoying a golden age, attaining distinction in literature and the arts. Lecce also found the wealth to rebuild itself, and took the form we see today with the construction of dozens of palaces, churches and public buildings in the city's own distinctive style.

Even though Lecce was doing well under the Spaniards and Bourbons, it hardly enjoyed the privilege of being ruled by them. On the contrary, Lecce's resistance to the new order manifested itself in four serious revolts. First, in 1648, came a popular revolution coinciding with Masaniello's revolt in Naples and, like it, bloodily repressed by Spanish troops. A second rebellion, in 1734, almost succeeded; the rebels were tricked into submitting by the Bourbons, who offered them reforms that were later withdrawn. In the wake of the French revolution, another revolt occurred, and the last came in 1848; the Leccesi worked hard for the unification of Italy, and contributed both men and ideas to the fight.

Tourist Information

Lecce: Via Vittorio Emanuele II 24, t 0832 248 092 (*open Mon–Fri 9–1 and 5–7*).

Where to Stay and Eat

Lecce ✉ 73100

Lecce's hotels are like the town itself, quiet, tasteful and restrained.

*****Patria Palace Hotel**, Piazzetta Riccardi 13, t 0832 245 111, f 0832 245 002, *patria-palace@hotmail.com* (*very expensive*). This comfortable place has all the facilities; many rooms have a view of Santa Croce.

****Risorgimento**, Via Augusto Imperatore 19, t 0832 242 125, f 0832 245 571 (*moderate*). Perhaps the best value hotel in Lecce; an attractive, gracious, older establishment in the centre.

****Grand Hotel**, Viale Oronzo Quarta 28, t 0832 309 405, f 0832 309 891 (*moderate*). This hotel near the station offers a tiny bit of faded elegance at very reasonable rates.

***Cappello**, Via Montegrappa 4, t 0832 308 881, f 0832 301 535, *hcappello@tin.it* (*cheap*). One of only two choices if you want anything cheaper. You'll find it south of the town centre.

***Oasi**, Via Mangianello 3, t 0832 351 359 (*cheap*). This tiny, spartan *pensione* is the most basic accommodation you'll find anywhere in Lecce.

Gino e Gianni, Via Adriatica, t 0832 399 210 (*moderate*). Though a little bit distant from the centre, this is a popular place with a long list of seafood dishes prepared following the local traditions – although Lecce is an inland city, the sea is not far away, and many of its restaurants specialize in fish. *Closed Wed and two weeks in Aug.*

Villa Giovanni Camillo Della Monica, Via S. S. Giacomo e Filippo 40, t 0832 458 432 (*moderate*). In a renovated 16th-century *palazzo*, along the rundown Via Giacomo e Filippo, this fine restaurant in a marbled courtyard stands out as an oasis of old-world elegance; but the real treat here is the beautifully presented food. Try the luscious *entrecôte* with asparagus and Chardonnay sauce, or bream wrapped in aubergine.

Casareccia, Via Colonnello Archimede Costadura 19, t 0832 245 178 (*cheap*). A friendly and reliable *trattoria* for excellent home-cooking. *Closed Sun eves and Mon.*

Leccese Baroque

One critic has called Baroque the 'most expensive style of architecture ever invented'. Considering all the hours of skilled labour it took to carve all those curlicues and rosettes, it's hard to argue. Lecce, like southern Sicily, some parts of Spain, and Malta – all places where southern Baroque styles were well developed – was fortunate to have an inexhaustible supply of a perfect stone. Pietra di Lecce is a kind of sandstone of a warm golden hue, possessing the additional virtues of being extremely easy to carve, and becoming hard as granite after a few years in the weather. Almost all of Lecce is built of it, giving the city the appearance of one great, delicately crafted architectural ensemble.

The artists and architects who made Lecce's buildings were almost all local talent, most notably Antonio and Giuseppe Zimbalo, who between them designed many of Lecce's finest buildings in the mid-17th century, and carried the style to its wildest extremes. Leccese Baroque does not involve any new forms or structural innovations; the ground plans of the Zimbalos' buildings are more typical of late-Renaissance Italy. The difference is in the decoration, with an emphasis on vertical lines and planes of rusticated stonework, broken by patches of the most intricate and fanciful stone-carving Baroque ever knew. These churches and palaces, along with the hundreds of complementary little details that adorn almost every street – fountains, gates, balconies and monuments – combine to form an elegant and refined cityscape that paradoxically seems all gravity and restraint. Leccese Baroque owes more than a little to Spanish influences, and the city itself still has an air of Spanish reserve about it. As a king of Spain once described a similar Baroque city – Valletta, in Malta – Lecce is a 'town built for gentlemen'.

Piazza Sant'Oronzo

A Baroque city was conceived as a sort of theatre set, its squares as stages on which these decorous gentlemen could promenade. An odd chance has given Lecce's main piazza something even better – a genuine arena right in the middle. In 1901, much to the surprise of the Leccese, workmen digging the basement for a new bank building discovered a **Roman amphitheatre**, with seats for some 15,000, directly under the city centre. In the 1930s, the half that lay under the piazza was excavated; occasionally the city uses it for concerts and shows. Only the lower half of the grandstands has survived; the stones of the top levels were probably carted away for other buildings long ago, allowing the rest to become gradually buried and forgotten.

In Brindisi, by the column that marked the end of the Appian Way, you may notice the pedestal of a vanished second column. Lightning toppled that one in 1528, and the Brindisians let it lie until 1661, when the city of Lecce bought it and moved it here, attaching a copper statue of their patron, Sant'Oronzio (Orontius), the first bishop of Lecce, and supposedly a martyr during the persecutions of Nero. What appears to be a small pavilion in the middle of the square, overlooking the amphitheatre, is the **Sedile**, an elegant early masterpiece of the Leccese style (1596) that once served as the town hall. The lovely portico, now glassed in, now hosts official functions.

Santa Croce and San Matteo

North of Piazza Sant'Oronzio, the most outrageous Baroque of all awaits along Via Umberto I. **Santa Croce** was begun in 1549, but not completed until 1680, giving Lecce's Baroque berserkers a chance at the façade. The lower half of it is original, done mainly in a sober Renaissance style. The portal, however, and everything above it, is a fond fancy of Zimbalo and his colleague, Cesare Penna. Among the florid cake-icing decoration the rose window stands out, made of concentric choirs of tiny angels. Look carefully at the figures on the corbels supporting the second level: among the various cartoon monsters can be made out Romulus' and Remus' she-wolf, a few dragons, a Turk, an African, and an equally exotic German. Santa Croce's interior is one of Lecce's best, with beautiful altars in the transept chapels by Penna and Antonio Zimbalo. Giuseppe Zimbalo also designed the **Palazzo del Governo**, originally a monastery.

Behind Santa Croce, the pretty **Giardino Pubblico** and the nearby **castello**, built by Emperor Charles V, mark old Lecce's eastern edge. The castle (*currently under restoration*) will be used to host conferences and exhibitions. For an interesting walk, start from the Piazza Sant'Oronzio down Via Augusto Imperatore (Augustus was in Lecce when he got the news of Julius Caesar's assassination). This street passes another Baroque church, **Santa Chiara** (*currently under restoration*), and a Salesian convent with a skull and crossbones over the portal – the ultimate Spanish touch. Even better, in a small garden opposite the church there is the most preposterous statue of **Vittorio Emanuele** in all Italy, surpassing even the bronze colossus on the Altar of the Nation in Rome. This Vittorio is smaller, but the contrast between his ponderous moustaches and jaunty stance leaves him looking half like a pirate, half like the leader of a firemen's band.

The next Baroque church is **San Matteo** (1700), one of the last, and architecturally the most adventurous of the lot, with an elliptical nave and a complex façade that is convex on the lower level and concave above. Continue straight down Via Perroni and you will come to one of Lecce's fine Baroque town gates, the **Porta San Biagio**. To prove that this city's curiosities are not all Baroque, we can offer the neoclassical **war memorial**, across Piazza Roma near the gate, and off to its right a block of mansions, built around the turn of the century, in a style that imitates the Alhambra in Spain, complete with pointed arches, minarets and Koranic inscriptions.

Piazza del Duomo

Leaving Piazza Sant'Oronzio by Via Vittorio Emanuele, you pass the church of **Santa Irene**, a relatively modest Baroque church of the 1720s, with a splendid statue of the saint above the main portal. If you're not careful you may entirely miss the little alley off to the left that leads to the **Piazza del Duomo**, one of the finest Baroque architectural groups anywhere, all recently restored. It was the plan of the designers to keep this square cut off from the life of the city, making it a sort of tranquil stone park; the alley off Via Vittorio Emanuele is the only entrance.

The **cathedral** (1659–70) is one of the finest works of Giuseppe Zimbalo. To make the building stand out in the L-shaped medieval piazza, the architect gave it two façades: one on the west front and a second, more gloriously ornate one, facing the open end of the piazza. The angular, unusually tall campanile (240ft), with its simple lines and baby obelisks, echoes the Herreran style of Imperial Spain. If you can get in, the long climb is worth the trouble, with an exceptional view over most of the Salentine Peninsula. Adjoining the cathedral are the complementary façades of the **Palazzo Vescovile** and the **Seminario**, the latter the work of Giuseppe Cino, a pupil of Zimbalo.

Behind the cathedral, in the back streets off Via Paladini, there is a small but well-preserved **Teatro Romano** with an adjacent **museum** (*open Mon–Fri 10–1, Sat, Sun and hols 10–1 and 6–9; adm*). In the opposite direction, Via Libertini passes several good churches, including the unique **Rosario** (1691–1728), also known as **San Giovanni Battista**, the last and most unusual work of Giuseppe Zimbalo. Just beyond it, the street leaves the city through the **Porta Rudiae**, the most elaborate of the city's gates, bearing yet another statue of Sant'Oronzio. Leading away to the right from here, Via Adua follows the northwestern face of this diamond-shaped city, passing the remains of the walls Charles V rebuilt to keep out Turkish corsairs; further up, at the next gate, the **Porta di Napoli**, you don't need to read Latin to recognize another relic of Charles' in the **triumphal arch**, erected in 1548. Most destructive and least modest of monarchs, Charles erected monuments like this all around the Mediterranean, usually after unsuccessful revolts, to remind the people who was boss. This one, featuring crowned screaming eagles and a huge Spanish coat of arms, is a grim reminder of the militaristic, almost totalitarian government with which the Habsburgs tried to conquer Europe.

In a little park in front of the Porta di Napoli, there is an attractive monument to the less grisly, though thoroughly useless King Ferdinand I, called the **Obelisk**. From here, a road off to the right leads to the city cemetery, home to a tribe of contented cats who pass in and out through a quite elegant 19th-century neoclassical gate; next to it stands the church of **SS. Nicolò e Cataldo** (*open daily 9–12; also June–Aug Mon–Sat 5–7; earlier afternoon hours the rest of the year; donations wecome*), founded in 1180 by Count Tancred. The façade is typical Baroque, but if you look carefully you will notice that the portal and rose window are much older. Behind the 18th-century front hides one of the best Puglian Romanesque churches, and one of the only medieval monuments to survive in Lecce. The nave and the dome are unusually lofty; the carvings on the side portal and elsewhere are especially good, with a discipline and tidiness that is unusual for medieval sculpture (to see these, you'll have to enter the cemetery, around the left side of the church).

Museo Sigismundo Castromediano

Viale Gallípoli, at the southern end of the old town, not far from the railway station; open Mon–Fri 9–1.30 and 2.30–7.30, Sun 9–1.30; closed Sat.

The founder of this collection, now Lecce's city museum, was a duke, and also a famous local patriot who fought against the Bourbons and earned long spells in the Neapolitan dungeons. His prison memoirs shocked Europe in the 1850s and moved William Gladstone to a few rousing anti-Bourbon speeches. Duke Sigismundo would be happy if he could see his little collection, now one of the best-arranged and most modern museums in Italy – a corkscrew-shaped ramp through its middle makes it accessible to wheelchair-users, and virtually all the exhibits are clearly labelled. The most prized works are several excellent Puglian and Greek vases, found all over the Salentine Peninsula, though there is also a good collection of medieval art and architectural fragments, and a small picture gallery.

The Tip of the Salentine

Italy's furthest southeastern corner is one of the quieter parts of the country. It offers a low, rocky coastline, rather like that of the Gargano but without the mountains, a number of towns in the Leccese Baroque style, and a lonely beach or two. One of the most noticeable features of the countryside – and this is true for all of the Salentine Peninsula – is the eccentricity of the rural architecture. There are a few of the ancient predecessors to *trulli*, low-domed houses of unknown age, as well as some little houses with flat roofs curled up at the corners, some recent artistic experiments in cinder-block, and many tiny pink Baroque palaces, sitting like jewel-boxes in a prairie landscape of olive trees, tobacco and wild flowers, even in December.

Flying Saints and Greeks

The towns here show an almost African austerity, excepting perhaps **Nardò**, decorated with a lovely square called the Piazza Salandra, in which there is a *guglia* (spire) as frilly as those in Naples. Nardò's much-rebuilt 11th-century cathedral retains some medieval frescoes. Near the town walls, on Via Giuseppe Galliano, is a strange, unexplained circular temple called the Osanna, built in 1603. Among the other interesting towns and villages around Lecce are **Acaia**, with a romantically ruined Renaissance castle, Galatina with a wonderful set of Renaissance frescoes in the 1392 church of Santa Caterina, and **Calimera**, one of the centres of Puglia's tiny Greek community – oddly enough the town's name means 'good morning' in Greek. Very few people anywhere in Puglia actually still speak Greek, though their thick dialect has led many writers into thinking so; any Greeks left are more likely to be descendants of 16th-century refugees from Albania than survivors of Magna Graecia.

Nearby **Copertino**, in the early 17th century, was the home of the original flying monk. St Joseph of Copertino, a carpenter's son born in a stable, was a simple fellow, if his many biographers are to be believed, but he got himself canonized for his nearly effortless talent for levitating. Thousands saw him do it, including the Pope's emissaries, a king of Poland, and a Protestant German duke, who immediately converted. Joseph's heart is buried under the altar of the little church named after him. Copertino also has a large Angevin castle.

On the Ionian coast, **Porto Cesáreo** is a peculiar little resort, facing two islets inhabited entirely by rabbits. Further south, **Gallípoli**, like its namesake on the Hellespont, was once thought of highly by somebody; the name comes from the Greek *kalli polis*, or 'beautiful city'. The old quarter still has a Greek air about it, with houses scoured by the sea air and fishermen folding their nets in the port. The oldest part, once an

Tourist Information

Ótranto: Piazza Castello, t 0836 801 436 (open June–Sept daily 8–2 and 4–8; shorter hours the rest of the year).

Where to Stay and Eat

Gallípoli ✉ 73014

Most of the available accommodation is along the outlying beaches.

***Al Pescatore, Riviera Colombo 39, t/f 0833 263 656 (moderate). This is the place to stay in the old town. Its 16 rooms are set round a pleasant courtyard, while its seafront restaurant draws in the crowds every night.

****Costa Brada, t 0833 202 551, f 0833 202 555, costabrada@softhome.net (expensive). A fine modern resort hotel at Baia Verde, on the Via Litoranea to S. Maria di Leuca.

***Le Sirenuse, t 0833 202 536, f 0833 202 539, atcarol@tin.it (moderate). A typical white Mediterranean palace, also housing a good restaurant.

*Nardo, Via A. de' Gasperi 35, Nardo, t/f 0833 571 994 (cheap). A friendly hotel above a café with comfortable modern rooms and large balconies. If you have transport, this could be a good base for lazing on the coast or exploring further inland.

Scoglio delle Sirene, Riv. N. Sauro 83, t 0833 261 091 (moderate). A cheerful seafood trattoria overlooking the beach in the old town. This is a quiet alternative to the popular string of restaurants behind the castle, where you often have to queue for a table.

Il Capriccio, Viale Bovio 14, t 0833 261 545 (expensive). Come here to try out the local speciality, orecchiette alla Gallípolina. Like elsewhere along these coastal areas, you can choose from a great variety of seafood dishes. Closed Mon and Nov.

Rossini, Via Lamarmora 25, t 0833 573 009 (moderate). A fish restaurant with a terrace, along the coastal road towards Porto Cesáreo. Specialities include a rich risotto or gnocchi con crema di gamberetti e rucola (gnocchi with creamed shrimp and rocket).

Fico d'India (cheap). A funky roadside bar beside the crumbling Torre Uluzzi, north of Santa Caterina, which does simple food well; panini, salads, as well as a dreamy fruit salad with yoghurt, honey and cinnamon. It stays open late and is a popular venue for live 'world' music.

Ótranto ✉ 73028

***Albania, Via S. Francesco di Paola 10, t 0836 801 183 (cheap). This 10-roomed place is one of several newly opened and pleasant hotels in Ótranto.

**Miramare, Viale Lungomare 55, t 0836 801 023, f 0836 801 024 (cheap). Another newish hotel near the beaches.

Da Sergio, Corso Garibaldi 9, t 0836 801 408 (moderate). Ótranto's best restaurant, even though the eponymous Sergio prides himself on having a local clientele, and is inclined to be patronizing to foreigners. His father is a fisherman, and the restaurant has particularly good, fresh fish. Closed Wed, Jan and Feb.

---

island, is now bound to the mainland and dominated by a huge castle with squat rounded bastions parts of which back to the Byzantines. There is a Baroque cathedral that would look right at home in Lecce and a Baroque *nymphaion*, a trough-like fountain decorated with caryatids and badly faded mythological reliefs. Gallípoli has the best sort of **museum** (open April–Sept daily 9–1 and 5–7; Oct–Mar daily 9–1 and 4–6), on Via della Pace – nothing pretentious, nothing even labelled, but good fun, in a big atrium lined with dusty bookshelves and full of cutlasses, whalebones, old cannonballs, coins, amphorae, and even a crocodile skeleton.

The Salentine's southern tip, not surprisingly, is called Land's End – *Finibus Terrae*. The spot is marked by the church of **Santa Maria di Leuca**, built over the ruins of a temple of Minerva that must have been a familiar landmark to all ancient mariners. The church's altar stone fulfilled the same purpose in the original temple. As in the

Land's Ends of Celtic Europe, this corner of the Salentine has quite a few standing stones and dolmens, left from the days of the Messapians or earlier. The most important Neolithic monument is called the *Centropietre* – 'hundred stones' – near the village of **Patù**; it is a small temple of two aisles divided by columns, with flat stone slabs for a roof. Coming back up the Adriatic side towards Ótranto, the coast is lined with caves, many showing evidence of Stone Age habitation or later religious uses. The **Grotta Zinzulusa**, hung with stalactites, may be the one worth visiting. Just to the north is a thermal spa, **Santa Cesarea Terme**, built on an old neo-Moorish bath-house.

Ótranto

Readers of Gothic novels might choose to leave Ótranto out of their itineraries, but there's no reason to be afraid. Horace Walpole, when he was writing his *Castle of Ótranto*, knew nothing about the place; he merely picked the name off a map. There really is a **castle** (*open daily 8–1; also mid-June–mid-Sept 5–midnight*), built by the Aragonese in the 1490s, which in Walpole's times was probably already in ruins. It has recently been thoroughly restored and is now used as a meeting point for cultural events. Ótranto (stress on the first syllable, as for most Puglian towns) today is an austere and arch-Mediterranean town draped over bare hills, one probably most familiar to outsiders as a better option than Bríndisi for ferries to Greece.

Although originally a Messapian settlement, the city first appears in history as Greek *Hydruntion*, conquered and probably resettled by *Taras*, and its proud citizens still refer to themselves as *Idruntini*. It rivalled Bríndisi as Rome's window on the east, and reappeared in the 11th century as one of the leading Crusader ports. Ótranto's finest hour came in 1480, during Naples' wars with the Turks and their Venetian allies; according to a delicately embroidered legend, Turkish pirates sacked the city, killing some 12,000 or so, and massacred the 800 survivors when they refused, to a man, to forsake Christianity. The place hasn't been the same since; only recently, thanks to the tourist ferry business, has Ótranto begun to regain some of the importance it had in the Middle Ages.

If you're not bound for Greece, the best reason for visiting is the **cathedral**, begun in the 11th century by the Normans, and the only one in the south to have conserved an entire **medieval mosaic pavement**. The vigorous, primitive early medieval figures are the work of a priest named Pantaleone, from about 1165. Three great trees stand at the centre of his composition, supporting small encircled images that encompass all creation: scriptural scenes, animals, heroes, symbols of the months and seasons, Alexander the Great, and even King Arthur.

Historical Terms

Acroterion: decorative protrusion on the rooftop of an Etruscan, Greek or Roman temple. At the corners of the roof they are called *antefixes*.

Ambones: twin pulpits in some southern churches (singular: *ambo*), often elaborately decorated.

Atrium: entrance court of a Roman house or early church.

Badia: *abbazia*, an abbey or abbey church.

Baldacchino: baldaquin, a columned stone canopy above the altar of a church.

Basilica: a rectangular building usually divided into three aisles by rows of columns. In Rome this was the common form for law courts and other public buildings, and Roman Christians adapted it for their early churches.

Borgo: from the Saxon *burh* of Santo Spirito in Rome: a suburb.

Bucchero ware: black, delicately thin Etruscan ceramics, usually incised or painted.

Calvary chapels: a series of outdoor chapels, usually on a hillside, that commemorate the stages of the Passion of Christ.

Campanile: a bell-tower.

Campanilismo: local patriotism; the Italians' own word for their historic tendency to be more faithful to their home towns than to the abstract idea of 'Italy'.

Camposanto: a cemetery.

Cardo: transverse street of a Roman *castrum*-shaped city, perpendicular to the Decumanus Major.

Carroccio: a wagon carrying the banners of a medieval city and an altar; it served as the rallying point in battles.

Cartoon: the preliminary sketch for a fresco or tapestry.

Caryatid: supporting pillar or column carved into a standing female form; male versions are called *telamones*.

Castrum: a Roman military camp, always neatly rectangular, with straight streets and gates at the cardinal points. Later the Romans founded or refounded cities in this form, hundreds of which survive today (Lucca, Aosta, Florence, Pavia, Como, Brescia, Ascoli Piceno, Ancona are clear examples).

Cavea: the semicircle of seats in a classical theatre.

Cenacolo: fresco of the Last Supper, often on the wall of a monastery refectory.

Ciborium: a tabernacle; the word is often used for large freestanding tabernacles, or in the sense of a *baldacchino* (q.v.).

Comune: commune, or commonwealth, referring to the governments of the free cities of the Middle Ages. Today it denotes any local government, from the Comune di Roma down to the smallest village.

Condottiere: the leader of a band of mercenaries in the late Middle Ages and Renaissance.

Confraternity: a religious lay brotherhood, often serving as a neighbourhood mutual-aid and burial society, or following some specific charitable work (Michelangelo, for example, belonged to one that cared for condemned prisoners in Rome).

Cosmati work: a distinctive style of inlaid marble or enamel chips used in architectural decoration (pavements, pulpits, paschal candlesticks, etc.) in medieval southern Italy. The Cosmati family of Rome were its greatest practitioners – hence the name. *Cosmatesque* describes work in this style.

Cupola: a dome.

Cyclopean walls: fortifications built of enormous, irregularly-shaped polygonal blocks, as in the pre-Roman cities of Latium.

Decumanus: street of a Roman *castrum*-shaped city parallel to the longer axis, the central, main avenue called the Decumanus Major.

Duomo: cathedral.

Forum: the central square of a Roman town, with its most important temples and public buildings. The word means 'outside', as the original Roman Forum was outside the first city walls.

Fresco: wall painting, the most important Italian artistic medium since Etruscan times. It isn't easy to do; first the artist draws the *sinopia* (q.v.) on the wall. This is covered with plaster, but only a little at a time, as the paint must be on the plaster before it dries. Leonardo da Vinci's endless attempts to find clever short-cuts ensured that little of his work would survive.

Ghibellines: (see *Guelphs*). One of the two great medieval parties; supporters of the Holy Roman Emperors.

Gonfalon: the banner of a medieval free city; the *gonfaloniere*, or flag bearer, was often the most important public official.

Grotesques: carved or painted faces used in Etruscan and later Roman decoration; Raphael and other artists rediscovered and copied them from the 'grotto' of Nero's Golden House in Rome.

Guelphs: (see *Ghibellines*). The other great political faction of medieval Italy; supporters of the Pope.

Hypogeum: underground burial cavern, usually of pre-Christian religions.

Intarsia: work in inlaid wood or marble.

Laura: a Greek cave-chapel or monastic cell of southern Puglia, often with frescoes.

Lozenge: the diamond shape – like stripes, one of the trademarks of Pisan architecture.

Narthex: the enclosed porch of a church.

Naumachia: mock naval battles, like those staged in the Colosseum.

Opus reticulatum: Roman masonry consisting of diamond-shaped blocks.

Palazzo: not just a palace, but any large, important building (though the word comes from the Imperial *palatium* on Rome's Palatine Hill).

Palio: a banner, and the horse race in which city neighbourhoods contend for it in their annual festivals. The most famous is at Siena, but they have been revived elsewhere.

Pantocrator: Christ 'ruler of all', a common subject for apse paintings and mosaics in areas influenced by Byzantine art.

Pietra dura: rich inlay work using semi-precious stones, perfected in post-Renaissance Florence.

Pieve: a parish church, especially in the north.

Predella: smaller paintings on panels below the main subject of a painted altarpiece.

Presepio: a Christmas crib.

Pulvin: stone, often trapezoidal, that supports or replaces the capital of a column; decoratively carved examples can be seen in many medieval southern cloisters.

Putti: flocks of plaster cherubs with rosy cheeks and bums that infested much of Italy in the Baroque era.

Quadriga: chariot pulled by four horses.

Quattrocento: the 1400s – the Italian way of referring to centuries (*quattrocento, cinquecento*, etc.).

Sinopia: the layout of a fresco (q.v.) etched by the artist on the wall before the plaster is applied. Often these are works of art in their own right.

Stigmata: a miraculous simulation of the bleeding wounds of Christ, appearing in holy men like St Francis in the 12th century, and Padre Pio of Puglia in our own time.

Telamon: see *Caryatid*.

Thermae: Roman baths.

Tondo: round relief, painting or terracotta.

Transenna: marble screen separating the altar area from the rest of an early Christian church.

Travertine: hard, light-coloured stone, sometimes flecked or pitted with black, sometimes perfect. The most widely used material in ancient and modern Rome.

Triclinium: the main hall of a Roman house, used for dining and entertaining.

Triptych: a painting, especially an altarpiece, in three sections.

Trompe l'œil: art that uses perspective effects to deceive the eye – for example, to create the illusion of depth on a flat surface, or to make columns and arches painted on a wall seem real.

Tympanum: the semicircular space, often bearing a painting or relief, above the portal of a church.

Language

The fathers of modern Italian were Dante, Manzoni and television. Each did their part in creating a national language from an infinity of regional and local dialects; Dante, a Florentine, the first 'immortal' to write in the vernacular, did much to put the Tuscan dialect in the foreground of Italian literature with his *Divina Commedia* (Divine Comedy). Manzoni's revolutionary novel, *I Promessi Sposi* (The Betrothed), heightened national conscious-ness by using an everyday language all could understand in the 19th century. Television in the last few decades is performing an even more spectacular linguistic unification; although the majority of Italians still speak a dialect at home, school and at work, their TV idols insist on proper Italian.

Perhaps because they are so busy learning their own beautiful but grammatically complex language, Italians are not especially apt at learning others. English lessons, however, have been the rage for years, and at most hotels and restaurants there will be someone who speaks some English. In small towns and out of the way places, finding an Anglophone may prove more difficult. The words and phrases below should help you out in most situations, but the ideal way to come to Italy is with some Italian under your belt; your visit will be richer, and you're much more likely to make some Italian friends.

For a list of foods, see **Food and Drink**, pp.88–9.

Pronunciation

Italian words are pronounced phonetically. Every vowel and consonant (except 'h') is sounded. Consonants are the same as in English, except 'c' which, when followed by an 'e' or 'i', is pronounced like the English 'ch' (*cinque* thus becomes 'cheenquay'). Italian 'g' is also soft before 'i' or 'e' as in *gira*, pronounced 'jee-ra'. The letter 'h' is never sounded, and 'z' is pronounced like 'ts'.

The consonants 'sc' before the vowels 'i' or 'e' become like the English 'sh' as in 'sci', pronounced 'shee'; 'ch' is pronouced like a 'k' as in Chianti, kee-an-tee; 'gn' as 'ny' in English (*bagno*, pronounced 'ban-yo'); while 'gli' is pronounced like the middle of the word 'million' (Castiglione, for example, is pronounced 'Ca-steely-oh-nay').

Vowel pronunciation is: 'a' as in English father; 'e' when unstressed is pronounced like 'a' in 'fate' as in *mele*, when stressed can be the same or like the 'e' in 'pet' (*bello*); 'i' is like the 'i' in 'machine'; 'o' like 'e', has two sounds, 'o' as in 'hope' when unstressed (*tacchino*), and usually 'o' as in 'rock' when stressed (*morte*); 'u' is pronounced like the 'u' in 'June'.

The stress usually (but not always!) falls on the penultimate syllable. Accents indicate if it falls elsewhere (as in *città*) Also note that, in the big northern cities, the informal way of addressing someone as you, *tu*, is widely used; the more formal *lei* or *voi* is commonly used in provincial districts, *voi* more in the south.

Useful Words and Phrases

yes/no/maybe *si/no/forse*
I don't know *Non lo so*
I don't understand (Italian) *Non capisco (italiano)*
Does someone here speak English? *C'è qualcuno qui che parla inglese?*
Speak slowly *Parla lentamente*
Could you assist me? *Potrebbe aiutarmi?*
Help! *Aiuto!*
Please/Thank you (very much) *Per favore/(Molte) grazie*
You're welcome *Prego*
It doesn't matter *Non importa*
All right *Va bene*
Excuse me/I'm sorry *Permesso/Mi scusi/ Mi dispiace*

Be careful! *Attenzione!*
Nothing *Niente*
It is urgent! *È urgente!*
How are you? *Come sta?*
Well, and you? *Bene, e Lei?*
What is your name? *Come si chiama?*
Hello *Salve or ciao (both informal)*
Good morning *Buongiorno (formal hello)*
Good afternoon, evening *Buonasera (also formal hello)*
Good night *Buona notte*
Goodbye *ArrivederLa (formal), arrivederci, ciao (informal)*
What do you call this in Italian? *Come si chiama questo in italiano?*
What?/Who?/Where? *Che?/Chi?/Dove?*
When?/Why? *Quando?/Perché?*
How? *Come?*
How much? *Quanto?*
I am lost *Mi sono smarrito*
I am hungry/thirsty/sleepy *Ho fame/sete/sonno*
I am sorry *Mi dispiace*
I am tired *Sono stanco*
I am ill *Mi sento male*
Leave me alone *Lasciami in pace*
good/bad *buono; bravo/male; cattivo*
hot/cold *caldo/freddo*
slow/fast *lento/rapido*
up/down *su/giù*
big/small *grande/piccolo*
here/there *qui/lì*

Travel Directions

One (two) ticket(s) to Naples, please *Un biglietto (due biglietti) per Napoli, per favore*
one way *semplice/andata*
return *andata e ritorno*
first/second class *Prima/seconda classe*
I want to go to... *Desidero andare a...*
How can I get to...? *Come posso andare a...?*
Do you stop at...? *Si ferma a...?*
Where is...? *Dov'è...?*
How far is it to...? *Quanto siamo lontani da...?*
What is the name of this station? *Come si chiama questa stazione?*
When does the next ... leave? *Quando parte il prossimo...?*
From where does it leave? *Da dove parte?*
How much is the fare? *Quant'è il biglietto?*
Have a good trip *Buon viaggio!*

Shopping, Services, Sightseeing

I would like... *Vorrei...*
Where is/are... *Dov'è/Dove sono...*
How much is it? *Quanto costa questo?*
open/closed *aperto/chiuso*
cheap/expensive *a buon prezzo/caro*
bank *banca*
beach *spiaggia*
bed *letto*
church *chiesa*
entrance/exit *entrata/uscita*
hospital *ospedale*
money *soldi*
newspaper (foreign) *giornale (straniero)*
pharmacy *farmacia*
police station *commissariato*
policeman *poliziotto*
post office *ufficio postale*
sea *mare*
shop *negozio*
room *camera*
tobacco shop *tabaccaio*
WC *toilette/bagno*
men *Signori/Uomini*
women *Signore/Donne*

Days

Monday *lunedì*
Tuesday *martedì*
Wednesday *mercoledì*
Thursday *giovedì*
Friday *venerdì*
Saturday *sabato*
Sunday *domenica*
Holidays *festivi*

Transport

airport *aeroporto*
bus stop *fermata*
bus/coach *autobus/pullman*
railway station *stazione ferroviaria*
train *treno*
platform *binario*
taxi *tassì*
ticket *biglietto*
customs *dogana*
seat (reserved) *posto (prenotato)*

Numbers

one *uno/una*
two/three/four *due/tre/quattro*
five/six/seven *cinque/sei/sette*
eight/nine/ten *otto/nove/dieci*
eleven/twelve *undici/dodici*
thirteen/fourteen *tredici/quattordici*
fifteen/sixteen *quindici/sedici*
seventeen/eighteen *diciassette/diciotto*
nineteen *diciannove*
twenty *venti*
twenty-one/twenty-two *ventuno/ventidue*
thirty *trenta*
forty *quaranta*
fifty *cinquanta*
sixty *sessanta*
seventy *settanta*
eighty *ottanta*
ninety *novanta*
hundred *cento*
one hundred & one *centouno*
two hundred *duecento*
one thousand *mille*
two thousand *duemila*
million *milione*

Time

What time is it? *Che ore sono?*
day/week *giorno/settimana*
month *mese*
morning/afternoon *mattina/pomeriggio*
evening *sera*
yesterday *ieri*
today *oggi*
tomorrow *domani*
soon *fra poco*
later *dopo/più tardi*
It is too early/late *È troppo presto/tardi*

Driving

near/far *vicino/lontano*
left/right *sinistra/destra*
straight ahead *sempre diritto*
forward/backwards *avanti/indietro*
north/south *nord/sud*
east *est/oriente*
west *ovest/occidente*
crossroads *bivio*
street/road *strada/via*

square *piazza*
car hire *noleggio macchina*
motorbike/scooter *motocicletta/Vespa*
bicycle *bicicletta*
petrol/diesel *benzina/gasolio*
garage *garage*
This doesn't work *Questo non funziona*
mechanic *meccanico*
map/town plan *carta/pianta*
Where is the road to...? *Dov'è la strada per...?*
breakdown *guasto*
driving licence *patente di guida*
driver *guidatore*
speed *velocità*
danger *pericolo*
parking *parcheggio*
no parking *sosta vietata*
narrow *stretto*
bridge *ponte*
toll *pedaggio*
slow down *rallentare*

Useful Hotel Vocabulary

I'd like a double room please *Vorrei una camera doppia (matrimoniale), per favore*
I'd like a single room please *Vorrei una camera singola, per favore*
with bath, without bath *con bagno, senza bagno*
for two nights *per due notti*
We are leaving tomorrow morning *Partiamo domani mattina*
May I see the room, please? *Posso vedere la camera, per cortesia?*
Is there a room with a balcony? *C'è una camera con balcone?*
There isn't (aren't) any hot water, soap, *Manca/Mancano acqua calda, sapone,* ...light, toilet paper, towels *...luce, carta igienica, asciugamani*
May I pay by credit card? *Posso pagare con carta di credito?*
May I see another room please? *Per favore, potrei vedere un'altra camera?*
Fine, I'll take it *Bene, la prendo*
Is breakfast included? *E' compresa la prima colazione?*
What time do you serve breakfast? *A che ora è la colazione?*
How do I get to the town centre? *Come posso raggiungere il centro città?*

Further Reading

General and Travel

Barzini, Luigi, *The Italians* (Hamish Hamilton, 1964). A perhaps too clever account of the Italians by an Italian journalist living in London, but one of the classics.

Douglas, Norman, *Old Calabria* (Century, 1983). Reprint of a rascally travel classic.

Goethe, J. W., *Italian Journey* (Penguin Classics, 1982). An excellent example of a genius turned to mush by Italy; brilliant insights and big, big mistakes.

Haycraft, John, *Italian Labyrinth* (Penguin, 1987). One of the latest attempts to unravel the Italian mess.

Hutton, Edward, *Florence, Assisi, and Umbria Revisited; Venice and Venetia; Siena and Southern Tuscany; Naples and Campania Revisited and Rome* (Hollis & Carter).

Keates, Jonathan, *Italian Journeys* (Picador, 1991). An argument for re-examining the neglected charms of northern Italy.

McCarthy, Mary, *The Stones of Florence and Venice Observed* (Penguin, 1986). Brilliant evocations of Italy's two great art cities, with an understanding that makes many other works on the subject seem sluggish and pedantic; don't visit them without it.

Morris, James, *Venice* (Faber & Faber, 1960). Another classic account of 'the world's most beautiful city'.

Morton, H. V., *A Traveller in Rome and A Traveller in Southern Italy* (Methuen, 1957, 1969). Among the most readable and delightful accounts of the region in print. Morton is a sincere scholar, and a true gentleman. Also a good friend to cats.

Newby, Eric, *Love and War in the Apennines* (Picador, 1983). Newby's account of his war days, when Italian villagers hid him from the Nazis in the Appenines.

Nichols, Peter, *Italia, Italia* (Macmillan, 1973). An account of modern Italy by an old Italy hand.

History

Acton, Harold, *The Bourbons of Naples* (Methuen, 1956).

Burckhardt, Jacob, *The Civilization of the Renaissance in Italy* (Harper & Row, 1975). The classic on the subject (first published 1860), the mark agaist which scholars still level their poison arrows of revisionism.

Carcopino, Jérome, *Daily Life in Ancient Rome* (Penguin, 1981). A thorough and lively account of Rome at the height of Empire – guaranteed to evoke empathy from modern city dwellers.

Ginsborg, Paul, *A History of Contemporary Italy: Society and Politics 1943–1988* (Penguin, 1990). A good modern account of events up to the fall of Rome.

Hale, J. R. (ed.), *A Concise Encyclopaedia of the Italian Renaissance* (Thames and Hudson, 1981). An excellent reference guide, with many concise, well-written essays.

Hibbert, Christopher, *Benito Mussolini; Rise and Fall of the House of Medici and Rome* (Penguin, 1965, 1979, 1985).

Joll, James, *Gramsci* (Fontana, 1977). A look at the father of modern Italian communism, someone we all should get to know better.

Masson, Georgina, *Frederick II of Hohenstaufen* (London, 1957).

Morris, Jan, *The Venetian Empire* (Faber & Faber, 1980). A fascinating account of the Serenissima's glory days.

Norwich, John Julius, *The Normans in the South* (Thames and Hudson, 1967).

Origo, Iris, *The Merchant of Prato* (Penguin, 1963). Everyday life in medieval Tuscany with the father of modern accounting, Francesco di Marco Datini.

Procacci, Giuliano, *History of the Italian People* (Penguin, 1973). An in-depth view from the year 1000 to the present—also an introduction to the wit and subtlety of the best Italian scholarship.

Rand, Edward Kennard, *Founders of the Middle Ages* (Dover reprint, New York), a little-known but incandescently brilliant work that can explain Jerome, Augustine, Boethius and other intellectual currents of the decaying classical world.

Art and Literature

Boccaccio, Giovanni, *The Decameron* (Penguin, 1972). The ever-young classic by one of the fathers of Italian literature. Its irreverent worldliness still provides a salutary antidote to whatever dubious ideas persist in your mental baggage.

Calvino, Italo, *Invisible Cities* and *If Upon a Winter's Night a Traveller* (Picador). Provocative fantasies that could only have been written by an Italian. Even better is his recent compilation of Italian folktales, a little bit Brothers Grimm and a little bit Fellini.

Cellini, *Autobiography of Benvenuto Cellini* (Penguin, trans. by George Bull). Fun reading by a swashbuckling braggart and world-class liar.

Clark, Kenneth, *Leonardo da Vinci* (Penguin).

Dante Alighieri, *The Divine Comedy* (plenty of equally good translations). Few poems have ever had such a mythical significance for a nation. Anyone serious about understanding Italy and the Italian world view will need more than just a passing acquaintance with Dante.

Gadda, Carlo Emilio, *That Awful Mess on Via Merulana* (Quartet Books, 1980). Italy during the Fascist era.

Gilbert and Linscott, *Complete Poems and Selected Letters of Michelangelo* (Princeton Press, 1984).

Henig, Martin (ed.), *A Handbook of Roman Art* (Phaidon, 1983). Essays on all aspects of ancient Roman art.

Lawrence, D. H., *Etruscan Places* (Olive Press).

Levi, Carlo, *Christ Stopped at Eboli* (Penguin, 1982). Disturbing post-war realism.

Levy, Michael, *Early Renaissance* (Penguin, 1967) and *High Renaissance* (Penguin, 1975). Old-fashioned accounts of the period, with a breathless reverence for the 1500s – but still full of intriguing interpretations.

Murray, Linda, *The High Renaissance* and *The Late Renaissance and Mannerism* (Thames and Hudson, 1977). Excellent introduction to the period; also Peter and Linda Murray, *The Art of the Renaissance* (Thames and Hudson, 1963).

Pavese, Cesare, *The Moon and the Bonfire* (Quartet, 1979). Post-war classic.

Petrarch, Francesco, *Canzoniere and Other Works* (Oxford, 1985). The most famous poems by the 'First Modern Man'.

Vasari, Giorgio, *Lives of the Artists* (Penguin, 1985). Readable, anecdotal accounts of the Renaissance greats by the father of art history, also the first professional Philistine.

Wittkower, Rudolf, *Art and Architecture in Italy 1600–1750* (Pelican, 1986). The Bible on Baroque, erudite and full of wit.

Italy: The Ancient Cities

With Roman roads and a
composite of major cities from
500 BC to 500 AD.

N

100 km
50 miles

■ Important Greek cities c. 500
● Etruscan foundations

Augusta
Praetoria
Salassi
Comum
Tridentum
Segusio
Mediolanum
Augusta
Taurinorum
Brixia
Verona
Aquileia
Cremona
Mantua
Patavium
Tergeste
Veneti
Parma
Ligures
VIA
EMILIA
Bononia
ROMEA
Ravenna
Album
Ingaunum
Luni
Classe
VIA
AURELIA
Ariminium
Umbrii
Pisae
FAESULAE
Fanum Fortunae
VOLTERRAE
ARRETIUM
VIA
CASSIA
POPULONIA
CLUSIUM
Picentii
VETULONIA
PERUSIA
VIA
FLAMINIA
Spoletium
VOLCI
Asculum
Sabines
TARQUINIA
VEII
Alba
VIA
SALARIA
CAERE
Tibur
Fucens
Ortona
Rome
VIA
TIBURTINA
Ostia
Latini
Hernici
VIA
Sulmo
Antium
Volscia
CASALINA
Samnites
Anxur
VIA
Ausonii
Daunii
APPIA
Capua
Luceria
Sipontum
CUMAE
Beneventum
Cape Misenum
Puteoli
Venusia
PITHECUSA
Pompeii
NEAPOLIS
Salernum
VIA APPIA
Surrentum
TARENTUM
ELEA
METAPONTUM
Mess
Sal
Siculans
SYBARIS
CROTON
Bruttians
Magna
Graeci
EPIZEPHRYEAN LOCRI
RHEGIUM
SYRACUSE

Index

Main page references are in **bold**. Page references to maps are in *italics*.

Also available from Cadogan Guides...

The Italy Series

Italy
The Bay of Naples and Southern Italy
Lombardy and the Italian Lakes
Tuscany, Umbria and the Marches
Tuscany
Umbria
Northeast Italy
Italian Riviera
Bologna and Emilia Romagna
Rome and the Heart of Italy
Sardinia
Sicily
Rome, Florence, Venice
Florence, Siena, Pisa & Lucca
Rome
Venice

The France Series

France
Dordogne & the Lot
Gascony & the Pyrenees

Brittany
The Loire
The South of France
Provence
Côte d'Azur
Corsica
Paris
Short Breaks in Northern France

The Spain and Portugal Series

Spain
Andalucía
Northern Spain
Bilbao and the Basque Lands
Granada, Seville, Cordoba
Madrid, Barcelona, Seville
Madrid
Barcelona

Portugal
Portugal: The Algarve
Madeira & Porto Santo